# Nineteenth-Century Literature Criticism

# Guide to Gale Literary Criticism Series

| For criticism on | Consult these Gale series |
| --- | --- |
| Authors now living or who died after December 31, 1999 | *CONTEMPORARY LITERARY CRITICISM (CLC)* |
| Authors who died between 1900 and 1999 | *TWENTIETH-CENTURY LITERARY CRITICISM (TCLC)* |
| Authors who died between 1800 and 1899 | *NINETEENTH-CENTURY LITERATURE CRITICISM (NCLC)* |
| Authors who died between 1400 and 1799 | *LITERATURE CRITICISM FROM 1400 TO 1800 (LC)*<br><br>*SHAKESPEAREAN CRITICISM (SC)* |
| Authors who died before 1400 | *CLASSICAL AND MEDIEVAL LITERATURE CRITICISM (CMLC)* |
| Authors of books for children and young adults | *CHILDREN'S LITERATURE REVIEW (CLR)* |
| Dramatists | *DRAMA CRITICISM (DC)* |
| Poets | *POETRY CRITICISM (PC)* |
| Short story writers | *SHORT STORY CRITICISM (SSC)* |
| Literary topics and movements | *HARLEM RENAISSANCE: A GALE CRITICAL COMPANION (HR)*<br><br>*THE BEAT GENERATION: A GALE CRITICAL COMPANION (BG)* |
| Asian American writers of the last two hundred years | *ASIAN AMERICAN LITERATURE (AAL)* |
| Black writers of the past two hundred years | *BLACK LITERATURE CRITICISM (BLC)*<br><br>*BLACK LITERATURE CRITICISM SUPPLEMENT (BLCS)* |
| Hispanic writers of the late nineteenth and twentieth centuries | *HISPANIC LITERATURE CRITICISM (HLC)*<br><br>*HISPANIC LITERATURE CRITICISM SUPPLEMENT (HLCS)* |
| Native North American writers and orators of the eighteenth, nineteenth, and twentieth centuries | *NATIVE NORTH AMERICAN LITERATURE (NNAL)* |
| Major authors from the Renaissance to the present | *WORLD LITERATURE CRITICISM, 1500 TO THE PRESENT (WLC)*<br><br>*WORLD LITERATURE CRITICISM SUPPLEMENT (WLCS)* |

ISSN 0732-1864

Volume 159

# Nineteenth-Century Literature Criticism

Criticism of the
Works of Novelists, Philosophers, and Other
Creative Writers Who Died between 1800
and 1899, from the First Published Critical
Appraisals to Current Evaluations

**Jessica Bomarito**
**Russel Whitaker**
Project Editors

THOMSON
GALE

Detroit • New York • San Francisco • San Diego • New Haven, Conn. • Waterville, Maine • London • Munich

## Nineteenth-Century Literature Criticism, Vol. 159

**Project Editors**
Jessica Bomarito and Russel Whitaker

**Editorial**
Kathy D. Darrow, Jeffrey W. Hunter, Jelena O. Krstović, Michelle Lee, Rachelle Mucha, Thomas J. Schoenberg, Noah Schusterbauer, Lawrence J. Trudeau

**Data Capture**
Francis Monroe, Gwen Tucker

**Indexing Services**
Laurie Andriot

**Rights and Acquisitions**
Margaret Abendroth, Emma Hull, Jessica Schultz

**Imaging and Multimedia**
Dean Dauphinais, Robert Duncan, Leitha Etheridge-Sims, Lezlie Light, Michael Logusz, Dan Newell, Kelly A. Quin, Denay Wilding

**Composition and Electronic Capture**
Kathy Sauer

**Manufacturing**
Rhonda Dover

**Associate Product Manager**
Marc Cormier

**LIBRARY OF CONGRESS CATALOG CARD NUMBER 84-643008**

ISBN 0-7876-8643-3
ISSN 0732-1864

Printed in the United States of America
10 9 8 7 6 5 4 3 2 1

# Contents

Preface vii

Acknowledgments xi

Literary Criticism Series Advisory Board xiii

# Preface

Since its inception in 1981, *Nineteeth-Century Literature Criticism* (*NCLC*) has been a valuable resource for students and librarians seeking critical commentary on writers of this transitional period in world history. Designated an "Outstanding Reference Source" by the American Library Association with the publication of is first volume, *NCLC* has since been purchased by over 6,000 school, public, and university libraries. The series has covered more than 450 authors representing 33 nationalities and over 17,000 titles. No other reference source has surveyed the critical reaction to nineteenth-century authors and literature as thoroughly as *NCLC*.

## Scope of the Series

*NCLC* is designed to introduce students and advanced readers to the authors of the nineteenth century and to the most significant interpretations of these authors' works. The great poets, novelists, short story writers, playwrights, and philosophers of this period are frequently studied in high school and college literature courses. By organizing and reprinting commentary written on these authors, *NCLC* helps students develop valuable insight into literary history, promotes a better understanding of the texts, and sparks ideas for papers and assignments. Each entry in *NCLC* presents a comprehensive survey of an author's career or an individual work of literature and provides the user with a multiplicity of interpretations and assessments. Such variety allows students to pursue their own interests; furthermore, it fosters an awareness that literature is dynamic and responsive to many different opinions.

Every fourth volume of *NCLC* is devoted to literary topics that cannot be covered under the author approach used in the rest of the series. Such topics include literary movements, prominent themes in nineteenth-century literature, literary reaction to political and historical events, significant eras in literary history, prominent literary anniversaries, and the literatures of cultures that are often overlooked by English-speaking readers.

*NCLC* continues the survey of criticism of world literature begun by Thomson Gale's *Contemporary Literary Criticism* (*CLC*) and *Twentieth-Century Literary Criticism* (*TCLC*).

## Organization of the Book

An *NCLC* entry consists of the following elements:

- The **Author Heading** cites the name under which the author most commonly wrote, followed by birth and death dates. Also located here are any name variations under which an author wrote, including transliterated forms for authors whose native languages use nonroman alphabets. If the author wrote consistently under a pseudonym, the pseudonym will be listed in the author heading and the author's actual name given in parenthesis on the first line of the biographical and critical information. Uncertain birth or death dates are indicated by question marks. Single-work entries are preceded by a heading that consists of the most common form of the title in English translation (if applicable) and the original date of composition.

- The **Introduction** contains background information that introduces the reader to the author, work, or topic that is the subject of the entry.

- A **Portrait of the Author** is included when available.

- The list of **Principal Works** is ordered chronologically by date of first publication and lists the most important works by the author. The genre and publication date of each work is given. In the case of foreign authors whose works have been translated into English, the list will focus primarily on twentieth-century translations, selecting those works most commonly considered the best by critics. Unless otherwise indicated, dramas are dated by first performance, not first publication. Lists of **Representative Works** by different authors appear with topic entries.

- Reprinted **Criticism** is arranged chronologically in each entry to provide a useful perspective on changes in critical evaluation over time. The critic's name and the date of composition or publication of the critical work are given at the beginning of each piece of criticism. Unsigned criticism is preceded by the title of the source in which it appeared. All titles by the author featured in the text are printed in boldface type. Footnotes are reprinted at the end of each essay or excerpt. In the case of excerpted criticism, only those footnotes that pertain to the excerpted texts are included. Criticism in topic entries is arranged chronologically under a variety of subheadings to facilitate the study of different aspects of the topic.

- A complete **Bibliographical Citation** of the original essay or book precedes each piece of criticism.

- Critical essays are prefaced by brief **Annotations** explicating each piece.

- An annotated bibliography of **Further Reading** appears at the end of each entry and suggests resources for additional study. In some cases, significant essays for which the editors could not obtain reprint rights are included here. Boxed material following the further reading list provides references to other biographical and critical sources on the author in series published by Thomson Gale.

## Indexes

Each volume of *NCLC* contains a **Cumulative Author Index** listing all authors who have appeared in a wide variety of reference sources published by Thomson Gale, including *NCLC*. A complete list of these sources is found facing the first page of the Author Index. The index also includes birth and death dates and cross references between pseudonyms and actual names.

A **Cumulative Nationality Index** lists all authors featured in *NCLC* by nationality, followed by the number of the *NCLC* volume in which their entry appears.

A **Cumulative Topic Index** lists the literary themes and topics treated in the series as well as in *Classical and Medieval Literature Criticism, Literature Criticism from 1400 to 1800, Twentieth-Century Literary Criticism,* and the *Contemporary Literary Criticism* Yearbook, which was discontinued in 1998.

An alphabetical **Title Index** accompanies each volume of *NCLC*, with the exception of the Topics volumes. Listings of titles by authors covered in the given volume are followed by the author's name and the corresponding page numbers where the titles are discussed. English translations of foreign titles and variations of titles are cross-referenced to the title under which a work was originally published. Titles of novels, dramas, nonfiction books, and poetry, short story, or essay collections are printed in italics, while individual poems, short stories, and essays are printed in roman type within quotation marks.

In response to numerous suggestions from librarians, Thomson Gale also produces an annual paperbound edition of the *NCLC* cumulative title index. This annual cumulation, which alphabetically lists all titles reviewed in the series, is available to all customers. Additional copies of this index are available upon request. Librarians and patrons will welcome this separate index; it saves shelf space, is easy to use, and is recyclable upon receipt of the next edition.

## Citing *Nineteenth-Century Literature Criticism*

When citing criticism reprinted in the Literary Criticism Series, students should provide complete bibliographic information so that the cited essay can be located in the original print or electronic source. Students who quote directly from reprinted criticism may use any accepted bibliographic format, such as University of Chicago Press style or Modern Language Association style.

The examples below follow recommendations for preparing a bibliography set forth in *The Chicago Manual of Style,* 14th ed. (Chicago: The University of Chicago Press, 1993); the first example pertains to material drawn from periodicals, the second to material reprinted from books:

Guerard, Albert J. "On the Composition of Dostoevsky's *The Idiot.*" *Mosaic: A Journal for the Interdisciplinary Study of Literature* 8, no. 1 (fall 1974): 201-15. Reprinted in *Nineteenth-Century Literature Criticism.* Vol. 119, edited by Lynn M. Zott, 81-104. Detroit: Gale, 2003.

Berstein, Carol L. "Subjectivity as Critique and the Critique of Subjectivity in Keats's *Hyperion.*" In *After the Future: Postmodern Times and Places,* edited by Gary Shapiro, 41-52. Albany, N. Y.: State University of New York Press, 1990. Reprinted in *Nineteeth-Century Literature Criticism.* Vol. 121, edited by Lynn M. Zott, 155-60. Detroit: Gale, 2003.

The examples below follow recommendations for preparing a works cited list set forth in the *MLA Handbook for Writers of Research Papers,* 5th ed. (New York: The Modern Language Association of America, 1999); the first example pertains to material drawn from periodicals, the second to material reprinted from books:

Guerard, Albert J. "On the Composition of Dostoevsky's *The Idiot.*" *Mosaic: A Journal for the Interdisciplinary Study of Literature* 8. 1 (fall 1974): 201-15. Reprinted in *Nineteenth-Century Literature Criticism.* Ed. Lynn M. Zott. Vol. 119. Detroit: Gale, 2003. 81-104.

Berstein, Carol L. "Subjectivity as Critique and the Critique of Subjectivity in Keats's *Hyperion.*" *After the Future: Postmodern Times and Places.* Ed. Gary Shapiro. Albany, N. Y.: State University of New York Press, 1990. 41-52. Reprinted in *Nineteeth-Century Literature Criticism.* Ed. Lynn M. Zott. Vol. 121. Detroit: Gale, 2003. 155-60.

## Suggestions are Welcome

Readers who wish to suggest new features, topics, or authors to appear in future volumes, or who have other suggestions or comments are cordially invited to call, write, or fax the Associate Product Manager:

Associate Product Manager, Literary Criticism Series
Thomson Gale
27500 Drake Road
Farmington Hills, MI 48331-3535
1-800-347-4253 (GALE)
Fax: 248-699-8054

# Acknowledgments

The editors wish to thank the copyright holders of the criticism included in this volume and the permissions managers of many book and magazine publishing companies for assisting us in securing reproduction rights. We are also grateful to the staffs of the Detroit Public Library, the Library of Congress, the University of Detroit Mercy Library, Wayne State University Purdy/Kresge Library Complex, and the University of Michigan Libraries for making their resources available to us. Following is a list of the copyright holders who have granted us permission to reproduce material in this volume of *NCLC*. Every effort has been made to trace copyright, but if omissions have been made, please let us know.

## COPYRIGHTED MATERIAL IN *NCLC*, VOLUME 159, WAS REPRODUCED FROM THE FOLLOWING PERIODICALS:

*Antioch Review,* v. 40, fall, 1982. Copyright © 1982 by the Antioch Review Inc. Reproduced by permission of the Editors.—*Clio: A Journal of Literature, History, and the Philosophy of History,* v. 17, winter, 1988 for "Ruskin and Pater—Hebrew and Hellene—Explore the Renaissance" by Wendell V. Harris. Copyright © 1988 Henry Kozicki. Reproduced by permission of the author.—*Dalhousie Review,* v. 69, fall, 1989 for "Concluding or Occluding Gestures: How Appropriate Is Pater's 'Conclusion' to *The Renaissance*?" by Lesley Higgins. Copyright © 1990. Reproduced by permission of the publisher and author.—*ELH,* v. 66, winter, 1999. Copyright © 1999 The Johns Hopkins University Press. Reproduced by permission.—*English Literature in Transition,* v. 17, November 4, 1974; v. 19, November 4, 1976. Copyright © 1974, 1976 *English Literature in Transition: 1880-1920.* Both reproduced by permission.—*Euphorion: Zeitschrift Für Literaturgeschichte,* v. 76, 1982; v. 81, 1987. Both reproduced by permission.—*European Romantic Review,* v. 11, summer, 2000 for "An Apology for the Conduct of the Gordons: *Dichtung* and *Wahrheit* in Achim von Arnim's *Mistris Lee*" by Sheila Dickson. Copyright © 2000 by Logos Press. Reproduced by permission of the author and Taylor & Francis Ltd. http//:www.tandf.co.uk/journals.—*German Quarterly,* v. 74, summer, 2001. Copyright © 2001 by the American Association of Teachers of German. Reproduced by permission.—*The Journal of Aesthetic Education,* v. 35, spring, 2001. Copyright © 2001 by the Board of Trustees of the University of Illinois. Reproduced by permission of the University of Illinois Press.—*Journal of Pre-Raphaelite Studies,* v. 2, November, 1981. Copyright © 1981 by the *Journal of Pre-Raphaelite Studies.* Reproduced by permission.—*Mississippi Quarterly: The Journal of Southern Culture,* v. XXXV, fall, 1982; v. XLI, winter, 1987-88; v. LI, fall, 1998. Copyright 1982, 1987-88, 1999 Mississippi State University. All reproduced by permission.—*Nineteenth-Century Contexts,* v. 21, 1999 for "Pater, Mill, Mansel and the Context of the Conclusion to *The Renaissance*" by J.B. Bullen. Copyright © 1999 OPA (Overseas Publishers Association) N.V. Reproduced by permission of the author and Taylor & Francis Ltd. http//:www.tandf.co.uk/journals.—*Nineteenth-Century Prose,* v. 31, spring, 2004. Reproduced by permission.—*Seminar: A Journal of Germanic Studies,* v. XIII, February 1, 1977; v. XV, September, 1979. Copyright © The Canadian Association of University Teachers of German, 1977, 1979. Both reproduced by permission.—*Southern Literary Journal,* v. XXXIII, spring, 2001. Copyright © 2001 by the University of North Carolina Press. Used by permission.—*Studies in American Humor,* n.s. 4, winter, 1985-86. Copyright © 1985-86 American Humor Studies Association. Reproduced by permission.—*Studies in English Literature: 1500-1900,* v. XII, autumn, 1972. Copyright © 1972 The Johns Hopkins University Press. Reproduced by permission.—*Studies in Romanticism,* v. 17, spring, 1978. Copyright 1978 by the Trustees of Boston University. Reproduced by permission.—*Style,* v. 30, spring, 1996. Copyright © *Style,* 1996. All rights reserved. Reproduced by permission of the publisher.—*University of Hartford Studies in Literature,* v. 16, 1984. Copyright © 1984 by the University of Hartford. Reproduced by permission.—*The Victorian Newsletter,* spring, 1975 for "Pater's Conception of the Renaissance: From Sources to Personal Ideal" by Billie Andrew Inman; fall, 1985 for "Pater's Temporizing: The 'Conclusion' to the *Renaissance*" by Ross Borden. Both reproduced by permission of the publisher and the author.

## COPYRIGHTED MATERIAL IN *NCLC*, VOLUME 159, WAS REPRODUCED FROM THE FOLLOWING BOOKS:

Brown, Carolyn S. From *The Tall Tale in American Folklore and Literature.* The University of Tennessee Press, 1987. Copyright © 1987 by The University of Tennessee Press. Reproduced by permission of The University of Tennessee Press.—Burwick, Roswitha, and Frederick Burwick. From "*Hollin's Liebeleben*: Arnim's Transmutation of Science into Literature," in *The Third Culture: Literature and Science.* Edited by Elinor S. Shaffer. Walter de Gruyter, 1998. Copyright © 1998 by Walter de Gruyter & Co. Reproduced by permission.—Fletcher, Ian. From *Walter Pater.* Longmans, Green &

## PHOTOGRAPHS AND ILLUSTRATIONS APPEARING IN *NCLC*, VOLUME 159, WERE RECEIVED FROM THE FOLLOWING SOURCES:

# Thomson Gale Literature Product Advisory Board

The members of the Thomson Gale Literature Product Advisory Board—reference librarians from public and academic library systems—represent a cross-section of our customer base and offer a variety of informed perspectives on both the presentation and content of our literature products. Advisory board members assess and define such quality issues as the relevance, currency, and usefulness of the author coverage, critical content, and literary topics included in our series; evaluate the layout, presentation, and general quality of our printed volumes; provide feedback on the criteria used for selecting authors and topics covered in our series; provide suggestions for potential enhancements to our series; identify any gaps in our coverage of authors or literary topics, recommending authors or topics for inclusion; analyze the appropriateness of our content and presentation for various user audiences, such as high school students, undergraduates, graduate students, librarians, and educators; and offer feedback on any proposed changes/enhancements to our series. We wish to thank the following advisors for their advice throughout the year.

# Achim von Arnim
## 1781-1831

(Born Carl Joachim Friedrich Ludwig Achim von Arnim) German fiction writer, poet, playwright, essayist, and critic.

The following entry provides critical commentary on Arnim's works from 1977 to 2004. For further information on his career, see *NCLC*, Volume 5.

## INTRODUCTION

Achim von Arnim was one of the most original writers of the German Romantic era, an innovative author and editor who strove to capture the spirit of German nationalism in his body of work. The peak of his literary career roughly coincided with the rise and fall of Napoleon Bonaparte, and his writings reflect the sense of trepidation and passion that characterized the political and social climate of that period. Arnim was a versatile talent, and over various phases of his career he poured his energy into producing fiction, poetry, journalism, plays, and essays. He also gained renown as an editor, and helped compile the influential collection of folk songs *Des Knaben Wunderhorn: alte deutsche Lieder* (1806-08). Arnim remains best known for his imaginative and comical historical novels and novellas, which brought together aspects of medieval history and literature, traditional German folklore, and dominant trends in contemporary culture, notably the burgeoning disciplines of psychology and political science. As a prose stylist, he made a vital contribution to the development of a distinctively modern German literary style. Although Arnim's reputation has been largely overshadowed by the careers of more prominent German Romantic authors such as Johann Wolfgang von Goethe, Heinrich von Kleist, and the Brothers Grimm, he remains an important figure from the literary life of the period, and recent years have witnessed renewed scholarly interest in his works.

## BIOGRAPHICAL INFORMATION

Arnim was born in Berlin on January 26, 1781, the son of a Prussian diplomat. His mother died only three weeks after his birth, leaving Arnim and his older brother in the care of their maternal grandmother. De-

scended from Prussian aristocracy, Arnim had regular encounters with Berlin nobility throughout his childhood, and during his early adult years he was a frequent visitor at courts and salons throughout Europe. An exceptional student, Arnim enrolled in the University of Halle in 1798 to study law. His real passion, however, lay in the sciences, particularly physics, chemistry, and mathematics, and as an undergraduate he published papers in the journal *Annalen der Physik*. Arnim's scientific background also informed his first novel, *Hollins Liebeleben* (1802). Arnim's literary career began in earnest in 1801, when he enrolled at the University of Göttingen. There he became acquainted with members of the older generation of Romantic authors, notably Johann Wolfgang von Goethe and August Winkelmann, who encouraged Arnim to become a writer. Perhaps more significant, during this period Arnim became friends with Clemens Brentano, another young writer who shared his interest in German folklore. The two remained friends for the rest of Arnim's life, forming the core of a group of young Romantic writers that eventually came to include Jacob and Wilhelm Grimm. In 1801 Arnim embarked on an extended tour of Europe with his older brother. Their travels through central Europe, France, and England had a powerful effect on Arnim's literary imagination and would inspire many of the historical and folk motifs that defined his mature work. Upon returning to Germany in 1802, Arnim visited Brentano in Frankfurt, where he met his friend's sister Bettina, whom he later married. From Frankfurt, Arnim traveled with Brentano throughout Germany, Italy, and France, stopping at a number of cities and towns that would later figure prominently in his fiction and poetry.

After the death of his father in 1804, Arnim returned to Berlin. Later that year Arnim and Brentano began discussing the possibility of publishing a collection of German folk songs. They devoted the next year to culling ballads and poems from various libraries, and in 1806 they published the first volume of *Des Knaben Wunderhorn.* The completion of the work took on special urgency for the young authors, particularly after Napoleon's defeat of the Prussian army at Austerlitz in December 1805. The severe political and social upheaval of the ensuing years exerted a powerful hold on Arnim's literary imagination, and he soon became deeply involved with efforts to protest the occupation government. He edited the short-lived *Zeitung für Einsiedler* (*Newspaper for Hermits*), a revolutionary and iconoclastic literary gazette that satirized both the contemporary political climate and the literary establishment. In 1810, Arnim worked with Heinrich von Kleist to edit the radical newspaper *Berliner Abendblätter,* although their efforts quickly attracted the suspicion of censors, and the newspaper ceased publication before it had an impact. During this tumultuous period Arnim met the Grimm brothers, who would be among his closest friends and unsparing critics for the remainder of his life. In 1809 Arnim published a collection of novellas, *Der Wintergarten,* which he dedicated to Bettina Brentano. The couple became engaged in 1810 and married the following year. Arnim's next book of novellas, which included the famous *Isabella von Ägypten,* appeared in 1812. A year later, following the retreat of Napoleon's armies, Arnim briefly joined the Landsturm (national guard), although he was soon barred from further military service for protesting the disbandment of his unit. In 1813, Arnim also published *Schaubühne,* a collection of patriotic plays, although his efforts to get the works produced for the theater proved disappointing, and he eventually withdrew additional volumes of plays from publication.

The final decade and a half of Arnim's life proved difficult for the struggling author. Estranged from the literary and political establishments in Berlin, he became increasingly disillusioned with his own writings. Family life also exerted a constant strain on Arnim's creative energies, and by 1817 he had retreated to the countryside to manage his family's estates, while Bettina lived with their children in Berlin. During these years, however, he produced some of his most respected works, including the first volume of the novel *Die Kronenwächter* (1817) and the novellas *Der Tolle Invalide auf dem Fort Ratonneau* (1818) and *Die Majoratsherren* (1820). In his later years Arnim became willfully detached from the mainstream, both the world of letters and Berlin society. During the last decade of his life Arnim devoted himself almost exclusively to writing political essays, although he continued to compose fiction, producing three novellas between 1821 and 1824. Arnim died of an apoplectic stroke on January 21, 1831. At the request of his wife Bettina, his unpublished manuscripts were left in the hands of Wilhelm Grimm, who eventually arranged for the publication of Arnim's complete works.

## MAJOR WORKS

Arnim's first major work, *Des Knaben Wunderhorn,* appeared in 1806. Edited in collaboration with Clemens Brentano, this collection of spiritual hymns, workingmen's ballads, and popular songs was culled from German-speaking countries throughout Europe, including those of the Hapsburg Empire and Switzerland. The mix of popular and literary qualities in the songs reflects Arnim's desire to integrate diverse motifs and themes while also reconciling high and low forms of art. At the same time, *Des Knaben Wunderhorn* represents a reaction against the extreme rationalism of French culture in favor of the forces of history, nostalgia, and common popular experience. The collection also reflects Arnim's lifelong interest in medieval narrative motifs and themes, elements that recurred in his later writings.

Arnim remains best known for his fiction. Most of his novels and novellas are rooted in German history and reflect his lifelong obsession with nationalistic ideals. In his unfinished novel *Die Kronenwächter,* Arnim explores the religious conflicts that beset the German states during the time of the Reformation. The plot of the novel revolves around two principle characters, Berthold and Anton, both of whom are preordained to become guardians of the Kronenberg Castle. Whereas Berthold is conventional and unassuming, Anton is larger-than-life, a violent, hard-drinking artist. Like all of Arnim's fiction, *Die Kronenwächter* follows an elaborate, digressive, and often convoluted story line, and it is rich with imagery from nature, folklore, and magic. At the same time, Arnim infuses his history with subtle references to the critical political issues of the Napoleonic era, lending the work contemporary relevance.

In the novella *Isabella von Ägypten,* Arnim explores the tension between fate and self-determination. Set during the early years of the reign of Charles V, *Isabella von Ägypten* incorporates elements from medieval witchcraft, astrology, and dreams to recount the story of a gypsy princess, Isabella, who liberates her people from European oppression by becoming the lover of the young Charles V, with whom she has a son. Populated with a violent mandrake, a dead bear skinner, and a golem modeled after Isabella, the story is one of Arnim's most wildly imaginative works. The novella also offers a sobering commentary on the imperial hubris of Charles, lamenting his failure to unify the German-speaking world. Like most of Arnim's fiction, *Isabella von Ägypten* freely mixes actual historical characters and events with elements of the fantastic, creating a world that was at once familiar and strange to contemporary readers.

## CRITICAL RECEPTION

Contemporaries recognized Arnim as an author of rare genius, a writer with a prodigious imagination and a distinctive prose style. Even his friends, however, found his fiction to be undisciplined, and his sprawling narratives and elaborate poetic conceits sometimes alienated both readers and critics. In general, modern criticism of Arnim's work has been scarce, although in the late twentieth century scholars began to recognize the unique value of his idiosyncratic prose style and eccentric imagination. Roland Hoermann has insisted that the chaotic nature of Arnim's work, in fact, represents a profound ambivalence within the author, a conflict between rationality and spontaneity that lies at the heart of his artistic vision. Many critics have focused on the connection between Arnim's nationalistic ideals and his literary sensibility, while other scholars, notably Sheila Dickson, have examined the scientific aspects of Arnim's writings, arguing that many of his plots and themes are rooted in his understanding of physics. In recent years Arnim's work has also invited a number of theoretical interpretations, as scholars try to decipher the symbolic meanings behind the proliferation of images in his writings.

# PRINCIPAL WORKS

*Hollins Liebeleben* (novel) 1802

*Des Knaben Wunderhorn: alte deutsche Lieder.* 3 vols. [with Clemens Brentano] (songs) 1806-08

*Der Wintergarten* (novellas) 1809

*Armuth, Reichthum, Schuld und Buße der Gräfin Dolores: Eine wahre Geschichte zur lehrreichen Unterhaltung armer Fräulein aufgeschrieben.* 2 vols. (novel) 1810

*Halle und Jerusalem: Studentenspiel und Pilgerabenteuer* (play) 1811

*Isabella von Ägypten, Kaiser Karl des Fünften erste Jugendliebe: Eine Erzählung; Melück Maria Blainville, die Hausprophetin aus Arabien: Eine Anekdote; Die drei liebreichen Schwestern und der glückliche Färber: Ein Sittengemälde; Angelika, die Genueserin, und Cosmus, der Seilspringer: Eine Novelle. Nebst einem Musikblatte* (novellas) 1812; abridged edition of *Isabella von Ägypten* published in *Fiction and Fantasy of German Romance,* 1927

*Schaubühne* (plays) 1813

*Die Kronenwächter* (unfinished novel) 1817

*Der Tolle Invalide auf dem Fort Ratonneau* (novella) 1818

*Die Majoratsherren* (novella) 1820

*Landhausleben* (short stories) 1826

*Ludwig Achim's von Arnim Sämmtliche Werke.* 22 vols. (short stories, novels, novellas, plays) 1839-57

# CRITICISM

**Helene M. Riley (essay date February 1977)**

SOURCE: Riley, Helene M. "Scientist, Sorcerer, or Servant of Humanity: The Many Faces of Faust in the Work of Achim von Arnim." *Seminar: A Journal of Germanic Studies* 13, no. 1 (February 1977): 1-12.

[*In the following essay, Riley analyzes the prevalence of supernatural and occult elements in Arnim's writings, examining in particular the author's fascination with Faustian characters and themes.*]

Like many of the German writers and philosophers of the Romantic age, Achim von Arnim showed a keen interest in the supernatural, the occult, the magical, and in those forces and phenomena which exert a decisive influence on man's existence, while defying rational comprehension and explanation.

Arnim's inquiries into the causal factors and manifestations of various physical and metaphysical powers covered a broad range of subjects. Early in his career, while he was still a student of law in Halle, he became interested in the study of natural phenomena, which preoccupied him for the first few years after his matriculation in 1798.[1] But even after his interests shifted to endeavours of a literary nature, he continued to incorporate into his writings views and conclusions which he had attained in the course of scientific research. Thus the hypothetical principle of the 'formative power' ('gestaltende Kraft'), which he had first posited in his 'Versuch einer Theorie der elektrischen Erscheinungen,' reappears in slightly varied form on the literary level as the major life-sustaining and progressive element in his characters. Similarly, his familiarity with the theories of Friedrich Hufeland, Anton Mesmer, and John Brown[2] is evident from certain behavioural aspects of literary characters such as the Marquis in Arnim's novel *Gräfin Dolores,*[3] or Berthold and Anton in *Die Kronenwächter.* Finally, Arnim's metaphysical view of life manifests itself in an ardent belief in the all-pervading divine will—a conviction which he explicitly states in his discussion of the 'Oeuvres historiques de Frédéric le Grand.'[4] Closely related to this belief is the postulate that certain individuals are chosen to carry out the divine will regardless of their human frailties and deficiencies. A predestined course of action for the main character is evident in many of Arnim's plots, most strikingly perhaps in *Isabella von Ägypten.* In the figure of Faust, with which Arnim was preoccupied to such an extent that it appears in works throughout his creative period, his views concerning the magical and supernatural find their most distinct explication. The analysis of three of these Faustian characters of Arnim's will therefore constitute the basis of this inquiry.

Arnim portrays the physical scientist, who avails himself of demonic and magical powers to achieve his aims, in the figure of the 'wondrous doctor,' to whom he devotes a chapter in the Dolores-novel. The source for this character portrayal was Arnim's meeting with Gottfried Christoph Beireis, professor of physics and medicine at the University of Helmstedt. On 30 July 1806 Arnim mentions the visit in a letter to Brentano: 'Vorgestern in Helmstädt bei Beireis; ein direkter, negativer Gegensatz zu Goethe, alles Formel.'[5] Goethe, too, received an account of this visit from Arnim: 'Die Frage ist,' writes Arnim,

> ob es gut tut, einer bösen Kraft sich zu bemächtigen, um sie dienend gut zu machen; . . . Thedel von Wallmoden in einem alten Gedichte, was ich kürzlich in Helmstädt erhalten, wußte dem Teufel ein wunderbares schwarzes Pferd, das glühende Kohlen fraß, abzudringen, mit dem er ihm nachher auf alle Art zusetzte; so könnte sich die Welt auch wohl dieses Lügengeistes bemächtigen, wenn er ihr nicht übermächtig wäre. Ist Beireis von ihm besessen, oder besitzt er ihn? Die Frage legte ich mir oft vor, wenn ich ihm in die freundlichen, unruhigen Augen sah, als er sich rühmte,

> alles zu besitzen in dem Hause, wonach sein Herz verlange, und sah ihn wie einen wahnsinnigen Geizigen Kieselsteine für Geld zählen, die öde Rumpelkammer von Haus, ein wüstes Gärtchen voll Unkraut, in dem sich ein paar magre Katzen sonnten, einen Herd, wo statt des Essens eine krumme Retorte langsam destillierte, und sah dann doch seine Menschenkenntnis . . . In sechsunddreißig Erklärungen stellt er die gesamte Welt am Schlusse seiner logischen Vorlesungen dar . . .[6]

This satanic spirit of lies, which Arnim senses in Beireis, is the pretence of knowledge and the mere appearance of excellence he encounters at the educational and political institutions of his country. In Beireis Arnim sees the personifications of that *illusion* of learning and knowledge which does not defer to the divine order of the universe. The rigidity and calculation with which the pseudo-scientist manipulates his surroundings is depicted by Arnim almost always as pernicious. In this manner the poet incorporates the Beireis-episode into his novel *Gräfin Dolores.* The home of the 'wondrous doctor' coincides in significant details with that of Beireis described above. The count, husband of the novel's heroine, encounters in it a world of pretence and illusion, in which all living creatures are mechanized. The count notes 'with disgust' the 'repugnant drilling' of the domestic animals to perform certain tricks,[7] and he observes the girl Arnika Montana and her brother speak and sing by means of an ingenious device through a glass box and the life-sized doll of a flautist, respectively. In the aftermath of his visit the count dreams that the girl had fallen prey to 'a terrible magician, who appeared to him like the doctor' (*SRE,* I, 277). The world which Arnim depicts here is one in which ingenuity devoid of divine guidance has reduced the living creatures to mere robots. It is a contrived, artificial, and terribly desolate and empty imitation of life, which the pseudo-scientist has concocted. It leads to the mortification and stagnation of the spirit and body of those who succumb to it. To Arnim the magical is pretence and illusion, and it can produce only a semblance of life, never a creature imbued with the divine spirit.

A destructive force similar to that of the wondrous doctor is portrayed by Arnim in the Marquis, the seducer of the countess Dolores: 'Der Marchese hatte sich alle Geheimnisse der Rosenkreuzer angeeignet, um sie, vermischt mit dem Mesmerschen Magnetismus als eine furchtbare Geisterhand in das Innerste der Gemüter auszustrecken' (*SRE,* I, 254).[8] That Arnim personally had occupied himself with the study of magnetism is evident from his letter to Brentano, dated 9 July 1802: 'Ich habe einmal Deine ganze Familie aus der Verbindung von Feuer und Magnetismus konstruiert,' he writes, 'und Dich auch; Bettine ist die höhere Vereinigung von beiden' (*AW,* I, 121). Nevertheless, in Arnim's works the pseudo-scientific interference in an individual's destiny by means of such irrational powers is always connected with disastrous consequences for the victim. The fate of Melück Maria Blainville[9] and her lover, whom she wishes to possess so passionately that she resorts to magical means in order to obtain his heart, is yet another example of Arnim's view of the baleful powers of the occult.

The poet's negative attitude towards the powers of illusion and magic stems from his belief in a natural, organic method of self-renewal, which is inherent in each individual. This self-regeneration, which alone can maintain permanent mental and physical health and happiness, is hindered in the development of its potential by the intervention of supernatural forces. As is evident in Arnim's review of the works of Frederick the Great, he considers the cause of the decline of the Roman empire to be the growing belief of its people that they lacked the power of self-renewal and self-enhancement (*Œuvres*, p. 335). Without such a formative force the renewal and regeneration of an age and its people are impossible, and without such regeneration hopeless stagnation and degeneration result.

The process of such a regenerative transformation is depicted in the 'miraculous cure' of Berthold and Anton by Faust in Arnim's novel **Die Kronenwächter**. Both Berthold and the child Anton are mortally ill, although they suffer from different ailments. Berthold 'fühlte sich allmählich absterbend dem Fleische,' he had become 'so ohnmächtig und siech,' and 'die Jahre brannten tief in sein trauerndes Herz, als wären's unbewußte Sünden' (*SRE*, I, 593). In order to understand the significance of this scene it is necessary to realize that Berthold's illness has a symbolical meaning. His years of infirmity, which draw on his strength like 'unconscious sins,' must be understood in a wider sense. In his function as mayor Berthold is the leading political figure in the town, and Arnim portrays in him the disease of the times from which in his view the German people suffer: war and strife, political, social, and economic upheavals, and intrigue.[10] The child Anton, on the other hand, is dying of a superabundance of strength: 'seine Augen glühen und seine feurigen Wangen glänzen, seine Worte irren und seine Arme winden sich jammervoll, er faßt an sein Haupt, es schmerzt ihm' (*SRE*, I, 608f). The two patients are exemplary cases of the asthenical and hyperesthenical conditions, which result, according to John Brown's theories, from a disproportionate reciprocal effect of external incitements and internal excitability. Brown's theses were widely disseminated during the Romantic era.[11]

The physician who is called to assist the two patients in regaining their health is Faust. He attempts to achieve a physiological *coincidentia oppositorum*, which he brings about by pseudo-scientific and quasi-magical means. He explains to Berthold that 'too strong blood' is as detrimental to human health as 'too weak' blood, inasmuch as the healthy body shows a harmony of such antithetical physiological phenomena (*SRE*, I, 607). Faust therefore offers to cure both Berthold and Anton by means of a blood transfusion, which would infuse the weak Berthold with Anton's 'young, superpowerful blood' (*SRE*, I, 607). Again it is necessary to recognize that Arnim has little interest in depicting a blood transfusion *per se*. Rather, the scene is a figurative portrayal of the concept of salvation, in which Faust plays the role of the life-restoring mediator.[12] But Faust is unable to heal Berthold in more than a physiological manner. Berthold receives a new life from Faust, but spiritual strength, such as he would need to continue the historical leadership of his forbears, the Hohenstaufen, cannot be transmitted by Faust's magical cure. The spiritual rejuvenation which the doctor cannot impart is the ingredient that Berthold senses is missing. He feels 'betrayed' by Faust, who nevertheless heals him from his physical weakness. Shortly before his death Berthold recognizes his miraculous cure as fraudulent: 'ich bin von einem Arzt, als ich sterben sollte, mit einem zweiten Leben, das er mir wunderbar schenkte, gar schrecklich betrogen' (*SRE*, I, 779), he says; and the narrator comments: 'Guter Berthold, du warst betrogen, armer Anton, dir kostet's dein junges Blut!' (*SRE*, I, 797).

An analysis of Faust as the mediator illumines the reasons for his 'successful' failure. First, he is described by Meister Sixt as the 'Doktor Faust aus Kindlingen,'[13] who has 'transfigured the entire science of medicine' (der 'die ganze Heilkunde transfiguriert' hat—*SRE*, I, 604). Faust's methods of healing are not as subtle as those of other physicians, who treat and touch the diseased parts with care. Faust's treatment is brutal: he cauterizes, cuts, and burns. He denies the body the chance to heal in a natural manner, i.e., in slow, organic regeneration; instead, his operations are radical and violent. Just as violent is his method of 'rejuvenation,' which is described to Berthold by Meister Sixt: '"Ich meine,"' says Berthold, '". . . daß ich für meine inwohnende Kraft seit den heftigen Blutstürzen zu lang gewachsen bin, nur wer mich zusammendrängen könnte, der könnte mich heilen und verjüngen."'—"Das kann Faust gewißlich", rief Sixt, "er hat mir schon so eine Geschichte erzählt, wie er die Konfiguration eines Menschen kondensiert und konzentriert habe, um ihn von dem horrorem vacui zu heilen . . .'" (*SRE*, I, 605).

All of the termini which Arnim uses to describe Faust's method contain the elements of transformation and synthesis. The passage is characterized by such verbs as to transfigure, to condense and concentrate, etc, and by the noun configuration (i.e., the structural synthesis of single elements). Evidently Faust is aware that physical health depends upon the harmonious function and correlation of the individual parts, and upon a balance of divergent physical tendencies. Faust, too, wants to achieve a synthesis of the opposing forces in the sick organism in order to bring about a condition of health, but he does it with inappropriate means. He relies entirely upon strictly artificial, pseudo-scientific methods, which leave no room for divine guidance. Both his ludicrous personal attire and the artificiality of the mechanical paraphernalia with which he works are reminiscent of the 'wondrous doctor' in the *Gräfin Dolores*: he wears red plus-fours with countless ribbons and a wreath of amulets around his hips; his fingers are covered with 'unzähligen Ringen voll Grabsteine'; 'auch einen prachtvollen, türkischen Dolch trug der feurige Drache,'[14] Arnim continues: '. . . und sein Diener stellte einen kleinen Turm voll künstlicher Scheiben, Zifferblätter in die Mitte der Stube, in welchem unzählige Räder schnurrten . . . Es war, als ob eine kleine Welt mit ihm zöge' (*SRE*, I, 606).

In accordance with his mechanized instruments is his own insensitive bedside manner. After he has addressed Berthold in Latin, has calculated his 'Konstellation an der Maschine' by Berthold's birthday, 'und den Pulsschlag nach einem Perpendikel,' he announces Berthold's imminent death: '"Die Konstellation ist zu Ende", schrie der Doktor, "es stürzt bald alles zusammen"' (*SRE*, I, 606). At the same time, however, he offers him a rejuvenation by his hand. This rejuvenation is of a technical, and not of an idealistic or spiritual nature, for Faust works with suction pumps, pressure machines, and planetary clocks. The infernal aspect of Faust, however, is most evident in his incredible arrogance and blasphemy:

> 'Die Kunst des Arztes besteht darin, im alten Menschen einen neuen zu erbauen.'—'Da soll ich also wieder zum Kinde werden!' rief Berthold.— 'Gewissermaßen', fuhr Faust fort, 'fanget Ihr ein neues Leben an . . . ; dreitausend habe ich erneut und jene Mühle, in der die Alten jung werden, von der das Volk erzählt, *die Auferstehung selbst ist nur als Nachbedeutung meiner wunderbaren Kunst zu betrachten.*'
>
> (*SRE*, I, 607, emphasis mine)

These lines must be interpreted with the fact in mind that the Romantics viewed illness as a symbolical manifestation of the destruction of the cosmic harmony in the individual, because the ailing organism separates itself from the cosmic unity, of which he is to be a reflection on the microcosmic level. The process of healing, or restoration of the harmony, therefore, is an *imitatio Christi*. In this perspective physician and priest have closely related functions, because sickness and sin contain analogous elements of the destruction of the

originally harmonious relationship between man and nature, God and the world. The healing of the sick is therefore in the Romantic view not only a physical restoration, but a return to the original childlike and innocent relationship of man to his creator. The idea that Berthold should 'become a child again,' and that he would 'begin a new life,' is likewise based on the regenerative principle of the resurrection myth. When Faust therefore exalts his art in such a manner that he views the resurrection only 'as of secondary import' to his medical successes, then he separates himself from the concept of the *imitatio* and becomes the antichrist. Berthold's healing through Faust therefore makes him 'a child again' only 'to some extent' ('gewissermaßen'). His physical rejuvenation is not matched by a spiritual recovery, and therefore he senses his healing as a betrayal by Faust. The 'successful failure' of Faust's efforts illustrates again Arnim's belief that results obtained by reliance upon the human intellect or on magical means, without deference to the divine order of nature can show only apparent success.

A Faustian character of an entirely different nature is depicted by Arnim in the play *Auch ein Faust.* Since its transcription from the original and subsequent publication by Dorothea Streller in the *Jahrbuch der Sammlung Kippenberg*,[15] this short play, which Arnim calls a comedy, has received no attention from the critics.[16] Although the exact date of its creation is not known, it almost certainly postdates 1818, the year in which Arnim's preface to Marlowe's *Faust* appeared in the German edition translated by Wilhelm Müller.[17] In this preface Arnim renders a brief, but critical survey of the various literary treatments of the Faust legend, including those of Goethe, Maler Müller, and Klinger. Friedrich Klinger's novel *Fausts Leben, Taten und Höllenfahrt* was written ca/1791, and it shows Faust as the inventor of the printing process, an idea which Arnim later transferred to his own play.[18] In his concluding remarks Arnim suggests various new possibilities of treatment for the Faust legend: 'Das Zweifelhafte menschlicher Verdienste, eben in dieser Erfindung [printing] dargestellt, überhaupt das Unverhältniss zwischen Absicht und Erfolg gäbe Stoff zu einem *neuen* Faust' (*Marlowe,* 36). The 'Verteufelung durch Kritik ist wohl noch nie in ihrem ganzen Umfange dargestellt worden,' he continues, and suggests, that a 'Faust als Schriftsteller' might be a suitable topic (*Marlowe,* 36).

Unrecognized by Streller, Arnim has incorporated a number of these elements into his comedy *Auch ein Faust,* along with several concepts which predate the genesis of the play considerably.[19] Arnim sets the introductory scene in a gaol cell, into which Faust was thrown by the pope. Faust is 'diesmal der Erfinder der Buchdruckerkunst, die ihm der Teufel lehrt, sich aber dafür die Seele erbittet. Faust ist listig, er will sich frey machen, indem er die Bibel druckt' (Streller, 156). The loss of liberty, the motif of incarceration, is found frequently in Arnim's stories. It shows certain parallels with the symbolic meaning of illness as sinfulness, inasmuch as imprisonment generally presumes an offence or public transgression of some kind. But, as Arnim elaborates in his essay 'Was soll geschehen im Glücke,'[20] 'das Unglück hat das Glück der Ueberlegung: wir können jetzt ruhig überdenken' (199), and such reflection restores man's spiritual powers. This is the case with Faust: 'Der Geyer des Bewustseyns nagt mich ewig, / Seit ich verschlossen bin in diesen Kefig' (Streller, 156) he complains, and eventually he recognizes that it was 'die Ruhmsucht' which has made him Satan's slave (Streller, 158). In Faust's ability to recognize the danger inherent in his covenant with the devil and to counteract the evil force with his own spiritual restorative powers, the principle of the 'formative power' is evident.

Arnim's question to Goethe, posed in September 1806, 'whether it is good to seize upon an evil power in order to force it to become beneficial through service,' is answered in this play ambiguously. Satan has instructed Faust in the art of printing, but Faust has not acquired the skill effortlessly. When the journeymen demand that he teach them 'die ganze Kunst in eingen Worten,' when they want 'den Zauber' only 'und keine Mühe,' Faust answers, 'was ihr da sucht das hab ich nie gefunden' (Streller, 156). Similarly to Goethe's Faust, Arnim's Faust shuns no effort in order to reach his aspirations. His continuous striving, that inherent capacity to perceive one's own actions critically and to change one's behaviour if necessary, saves Faust from Satan's grip. Nevertheless, the rejuvenation of Faust's powers of perception during the period of incarceration does not suffice for his redemption. Rather, his recognition of the omnipotence of the divinity, that force which 'alle Kräfte rings in sich verbindet' (Streller, 160), leads to Faust's remorse and consequent return to family and work.

Arnim touches not only upon the relationship between the human, magical, and divine powers and the effect of their interplay on the individual. He also attempts to show how originally benevolent human intentions can be used in a manner which is diametrically opposed to their initial purpose. This is what Arnim meant when he spoke of the 'dubiety of human accomplishments,' and of the 'incongruity between intent and success' as a possible variation on the Faust theme. Arnim depicts this polarity between intent and success in a number of figures, which pass before Faust in pairs. Both members of each pair belong to the same profession, but the individuals view their endeavours from different vantage points. Thus the 'satanic' farmer ('der teuflische Bauer')

declares: 'Ein blankes Schwerdt ist unser Pflug, / Das hauet mir schon Saat genug.' His motto is 'Wir säen nicht, wir erndten nur' (Streller, 158). 'Der irdische Bauer,' on the other hand, replies that his only son has been killed, that his crops are being destroyed before they are ripe, and that famine scourges the land (Streller, 158-9). Arnim portrays in the 'satanic' farmer the peasant who sought to improve his living conditions through open revolt and war. The small local uprisings, recorded as early as 1461, led in the sixteenth century to the Peasants' War. Thus Arnim wants to show that an originally good intention, namely the goal of the peasants to achieve better social and economic living conditions, may by its manner of execution bring untold agony and suffering to large segments of the population. The poet expresses this incongruity symbolically in the sword as the satanic farmer's plough: the object of war and destruction becomes synonymous with the tool that ordinarily provides food and sustenance for man.

Similar confrontations between 'satanic' and 'terrestrial' weavers and miners intensify the contrast between positive intent and possible negative execution. The 'satanic' weaver's product is a transparent, veil-like concoction, which corrupts the morals of those who wear it as garment, but for which he receives great monetary rewards. The solid cloth of the 'terrestrial' weaver, on the other hand, finds no buyer, and the craftsman is forced to starve. Lastly, the 'satanic' miner un-earths poisons with the aid of witches, whereas the 'terrestrial' miner produces gold for the ruling class; he himself, however, 'walks with the beggar's staff' ('Und ich geh am Bettelstab'—Streller, 159).

All of these examples of course are variations on the question of 'whether it is good to seize upon an evil power' in order to achieve beneficial results; or, in other words, whether the end justifies the means. All of the 'satanic' labourers achieve great earthly rewards, whereas the 'terrestrial' workmen reap only a meagre subsistence for their honest labours, but it is obvious that Arnim advocates the latter's conduct. His Faust, after having recognized that his own motivations, namely to achieve fame and glory, are in accord with those of the 'satanic' individuals who pass before him, is gripped by remorse and banishes the devil into the printing press. This 'banishment of Satan into the press' is a metaphorical expression for the 'bedevilment by the critics,' which Arnim himself felt keenly during his productive years, and against which he vented his feelings repeatedly in letters and essays.[21] Although the theme lacks further development in the comedy, its occurrence in conjunction with a Faust figure lends credence to the assumption, that *Auch ein Faust* was written after Arnim's preface to Marlowe's *Faust,* where the idea is first suggested.

The foregoing analysis of three of Arnim's Faustian characters allows the following conclusions. Although he was himself trained in methods of scientific research, Arnim viewed the purely rational approach to the solution of existential problems as invalid. This is evident from the portrayal of the 'wondrous doctor' in the Dolores-novel. The result of his scientific experiments and the implementation of his ingenious ideas is a total mechanization of his surroundings. Even the free movement of his domestic animals and pets is limited to his command. The resultant atmosphere is one of dehumanization and stagnation. Inasmuch as the mechanical flautist and the voice from the glass box are secretly activated and operated by the girl Arnika and her brother, the mechanized world of the doctor is furthermore unmasked as artificial, illusory, and manipulative. Arnim considers this pseudo-scientific approach to the creation of man's surroundings pernicious in its effect on the inhabitants.

The restoration of human physical and spiritual power by such pseudo-scientific means is depicted by Arnim as equally ineffectual in Berthold's 'miraculous cure' through Faust. The element of the magic and the supernatural, evident in Faust's reliance on amulets and astrological data, is an additional negative factor in the scene. The connection of the occult with Faust, who reveals his satanic nature in his blasphemous speech, illumines Arnim's intention to discredit any achievement obtained by such means. In Arnim's view the use of magic circumvents and inhibits the organic regenerative development of man both physically and spiritually. Inasmuch as Arnim contrasts the physical healing of Berthold through Faust with the spiritual rejuvenation symbolized by the resurrection myth, Faust's methods are depicted as fraudulent.

Finally, in the phantasy piece **Auch ein Faust,** Arnim seeks to portray man's inability to control the factors between intent and execution of his aspirations, and the consequent necessity of relying upon divine power and grace. Faust's 'Ruhmsucht,' a basically negative motivation, leads to his invention of the printing press and the printing of the Bible—in Arnim's view a positive accomplishment. Faust's ambition therefore makes him a servant of God and humanity. On the other hand the invention of the printing process makes possible not only the dissemination of God's word, but also the opportunity for the vocal critic to circulate his opinions. Since Arnim frequently disagreed with critical opinion concerning the merits of contemporary literature, he saw the latter effect of the 'Faustian invention' as negative in nature. Against this inherent ambiguity, which Arnim perceived in all human endeavours and accomplishments,[22] he found consolation in the belief, that 'a superior will manifests itself also on earth, against which human cunning and valour are of no avail.'[23]

## Notes

1. No good Arnim biography is available. Herbert R. Liedke's work *Literary Criticism and Romantic Theory in the Works of Achim von Arnim* (New York, 1937) does, however, contain much valuable biographical information. In the third chapter (pp. 32-55) Liedke discusses Arnim's change of interest from the field of science to that of literature. The Arnim biography by René Guignard, *Achim von Arnim 1781-1831,* Publications de la Faculté des Lettres d'Alger II, 9 (1936), contains many traditional value judgments concerning Arnim which have been disclaimed by more recent critics.

2. See Friedrich Hufeland, *Über Sympathie* (Weimar, 1811), and Friedrich Anton Mesmer, *Mesmerismus. Oder System der Wechselwirkungen, Theorie und Anwendung des thierischen Magnetismus als die allgemeine Heilkunde zur Erhaltung des Menschen,* publ. by Karl Christian Wolfart (Berlin, 1814). Both works appeared after the first edition of *Gräfin Dolores,* but these theories were already quite well known in the eighteenth century. Concerning John Brown's findings, see also Andreas Röschlaub, *Untersuchungen über Pathogenie oder Einleitung in die Heilkunde,* 3 vols. (Frankfurt, 1800-1), 375f.

3. *Armut, Reichtum, Schuld und Buße der Gräfin Dolores: Eine wahre Geschichte zur lehrreichen Unterhaltung armer Fräulein.* The first edition appeared Easter 1810 in the Realschulbuchhandlung, Berlin.

4. Arnim's essay appears in Herbert R. Liedke, 'Achim von Arnims Stellung zu Karl Ludwig von Haller und Friedrich dem Großen: Zwei unbekannte Rezensionen,' *Jahrbuch des freien dt. Hochstifts* (1963), 296-340. The reference to an all-pervading divine will appears on p. 335. Quotations from this work are cited henceforth under *Œuvres.* Translations are mine.

5. *Achim von Arnim und die ihm nahe standen,* ed. Reinhold Steig, 3 vols. (Stuttgart, 1894-1913); quotation from I, 188.

6. *Arnims Werke,* Part I, ed. Monty Jacobs (Berlin, n. d.), p. 134. Cited henceforth as *AW,* I.

7. Achim von Arnim, *Sämtliche Romane und Erzählungen,* 3 vols., ed. Walther Migge (München, 1962-5), I, 273. Cited henceforth as *SRE,* I. Translations are mine.

8. Note Migge's explanation concerning Mesmer and the Rosenkreuzer, *SRE,* I, 1066 and 1068.

9. Melück is the heroine of Arnim's story 'Melück Maria Blainville, die Hausprophetin aus Arabien.'

10. In a letter to Goethe dated 9 September 1806, Arnim exclaimed: 'Wehe der Jugend, die in diese lähmende, ungewisse Zeit fällt, wehe dem Alter, das eine bessere Zeit sah oder keine bessere' (*AW,* I, 133).

11. For an excellent discussion of the influence of contemporary medical thought upon Romantic literature consult Peter Schmidt, 'Gesundheit und Krankheit in romantischer Medizin und Erzählkunst,' *Jb. des freien dt. Hochstifts* (1966), 197-228.

12. Arnim's preoccupation with the rejuvenation myth is treated in Roland William Hoermann, 'The romantic myth of the artist's regeneration and its expression in the symbolism of Achim von Arnim's prose' (Diss. Wisconsin, 1956). Hoermann's inquiry centres on the artist as mediator figure.

13. Actually the legendary Faust practised black magic and came from Knittlingen near Pforzheim. He lived ca 1480-1539.

14. Arnim's reference to Faust as a 'fiery dragon' unmasks him as the personification of evil *per se.* Note Arnim's remarks in his essay 'Von Volksliedern': 'Es ist das Eigentümliche des Bösen wie der Krankheit: wo es erscheint, da erscheint es ganz, in ganzer Tätigkeit. Das Gute hingegen und die Gesundheit wie Sterne dunkeler Nacht wird selten sichtbar; dafür leuchtet sie ewig, während der fliegende feurige Drache in Funken zerstiebt' (*AW,* I, 72).

15. Dorothea Streller, 'Achim von Arnim und "Auch ein Faust",' *Jb. der Sammlung Kippenberg,* N. F. 1 (1963), 150-62 (cited as Streller). Translations are mine.

16. An excellent report on the most recent trends in the secondary literature concerning Arnim can be found in Volker Hoffmann, 'Die Arnim-Forschung 1945-1972,' *DVjS* [*Deutsche Vierteljahrsschrift*], Sonderheft (October 1973), 270-342. See also the first chapter of my dissertation, 'Das konfigurative Strukturprinzip in der Kurzprosa Achim von Arnims' (Diss. Rice, 1975).

17. Christoph Marlowe, *Doktor Faustus. Tragödie,* translated by Wilhelm Müller (Berlin, 1818). The references concern Arnim's preface to this edition and are cited as *Marlowe.*

18. When he mentions in the preface (p. 35) the similarity of names between Faust and the inventor of the printing process, Arnim refers to Johann Fust (ca 1400-66), who was Gutenberg's creditor. Shortly before completion of the first Gutenberg bible Fust brought suit against Gutenberg. On 6 November 1455 the court granted possession of Gutenberg's invention and materials to Fust, who immediately established a commercial printing shop with the aid of Gutenberg's former employee, Peter Schoeffer.

19. After having noted Arnim's suggestions for a new treatment of the Faust theme, Streller continues: 'Angesichts dieser bedeutsamen Vorschläge, die Arnim einem modernen Bearbeiter des Faust-Stoffes macht, nimmt sich sein eigenes Lustspiel, das "auch einen Faust" zum Gegenstand hat, recht bescheiden aus' (Streller, 151). After a very brief analysis of the comedy Streller concludes: 'In diesem bunten, traumhaften Reigen von Bildern, Gestalten und mannigfachen Rhythmen um die Figur des Faust liegt das Wesen und der Reiz des kleinen Lustspiels, das im übrigen sprachlich nicht viel zu bieten hat' (Streller, 153f).

20. Jörn Göres, '"Was soll geschehen im Glücke." Ein unveröffentlichter Aufsatz Achim von Arnims,' *Jb. d. dt. Schillergesellschaft,* 5 (1961), 196-221.

21. In his essay 'Von Volksliedern' Arnim refers to the critics as 'jenes Völkchen . . . das immer läuft und klappert, sich immer was zu sagen hat und eigentlich nie etwas sagt' (*AW,* I, 87); and in a footnote, which elaborates on his remarks concerning 'das kritische Elend, was nachahmend auch bei uns über der Poesie schwebt,' he explains: 'Zur Ehre der Deutschen kann man sagen, daß sie nicht Erfinder dieser Höllenkünste der Rezensierbuden und des kritischen Waschweibergeschwätzes sind, ungeachtet dergleichen Mode bei ihnen insonders gefaßt (*AW,* I, 87).

22. In his letter to Goethe, dated 28 May 1806, Arnim says: 'Es gibt der Widersprüche so viele . . . das Beste in der Welt bleibt immer, daß sich alles auch verkehrt anwenden läßt' (*AW,* I, 132).

23. Referring to the end of the French Revolutionary War, Arnim contends that it is 'ein Zeugniß daß ein höherer Wille auch auf Erden geschehe, gegen den menschliche List und Kühnheit vergebens anstreben . . .' (*Œuvres,* p. 335).

## Colin Butler (essay date spring 1978)

SOURCE: Butler, Colin. "Psychology and Faith in Arnim's *Der tolle Invalide.*" *Studies in Romanticism* 17, no. 2 (spring 1978): 149-62.

[*In the following essay, Butler evaluates the tension between religious belief and secular rationalism in* Der Tolle Invalide. *Butler argues that Arnim's insights into the ever-changing nature of human existence are what make the novella a decidedly modern work.*]

It seems to be generally agreed that Arnim's fiction tends to pull in more than one direction at once.[1] Brian Rowley speaks for many when he notes "an uneasy yoking of centrifugal forces" deriving from the competing claims of "the life of the spirit" and "physical reality." With a characteristically modern emphasis on the latter, Rowley contends that "Arnim is at his best in those stories in which he is able to explore the psychology of human inadequacy," and concludes: "Arnim's tragedy, we may feel, is that he was born too soon to exploit the vein of psychological analysis he had hit upon."[2] *Der tolle Invalide* is usually held to be rather more coherent than most of Arnim's work; but even in its case, Ernst Feise for one feels obliged to point out that "im Gegensatz aber zu Hoffmanns Doppelheit der zwei Welten, der nur realen und der eigentlich wahren höheren . . . haben wir bei Arnim . . . ein unvollständiges Ineinanderaufgehn der beiden Sphären. Die Oberhandlung ist im Grunde subjektiv. Sie könnte fortfallen, ohne dass die real-rationale Handlung dadurch völlig entwertet würde."[3] My first concern will be to show that *Der tolle Invalide* makes psychological sense: the percipience it demonstrates would seem to make that a worthwhile undertaking in its own right. Then I shall try briefly to relate the resultant secular interpretation to the *Novelle*'s ostensible transcendentalism in order to see in what way they may be said to fit together.

*Der tolle Invalide,* a *rite de passage,* is set in the Seven Years' War. A wounded French prisoner, Francoeur, attracts the love of an uneducated and inexperienced girl, Rosalie, and they become engaged. On learning of this, Rosalie's mother consigns her to the Devil "mit feierlicher Rede" (p. 738). Such is the virulence the mother displays as she curses Rosalie that she appears to her daughter to be transformed ("Wie verzog sich das Gesicht meiner [Rosalie's] Mutter; mir war's, als ob eine Flamme aus ihrem Halse brenne . . ." [p. 738]); and the sheer emotional shock of the moment makes Rosalie laugh in despair. This is interpreted by her mother as the Devil laughing through her, and she departs "triumphierend" (p. 738), leaving Rosalie in a swoon. The curse seems to affect Francoeur as well, for after their marriage his behaviour becomes so bizarre that, once repatriated, he is judged unfit for active service and ordered to convalesce in Marseilles (a neglected head wound is also suggested as the cause of his trouble). Rosalie, who feels herself to blame for her husband's disgrace, secretly secures from the Commandant of Marseilles Francoeur's posting to the greater privacy of Fort Ratonneau, in the Bay of Marseilles. A period of apparently tranquil family life is terminated when an unguarded remark by Basset, the Commandant's servant—who has overheard the Commandant reviewing Francoeur's case to himself and who has taken it upon himself to bring along a priest, Father Philip, to exorcize Francoeur's "devil"—causes Francoeur to decide with more or less conscious wilfulness that Rosalie has been unfaithful to him with the Commandant, to proclaim a "divorce" from her and to lock himself in the well-supplied munitions tower of the fort with the intention of waging war not on the English but on the man allegedly involved in his private dishonour. Fearing that Francoeur might blow himself and everybody else up, Rosalie seeks to save herself and the child born to her and Francoeur earlier in their marriage by taking to a small boat in which, exhausted, she falls asleep. They are saved from what would almost certainly have been a fatal collision in the dark with a larger vessel by flares sent up at just the right moment by Francoeur, who does not know where they are and in fact fails to see them, but who is combining a longstanding interest in fireworks with a general resolve not to let any ships slip through the roadstead under cover of night without paying him a toll. Rosalie returns to land with new confidence, leaves the child in the care of Father Philip, braves Francoeur's guns, and provokes an internal struggle in him which ends with his surrendering and rejoining his wife and child. Since no harm has been done, he is not court-martialed. Instead, he is adopted by the Commandant, and his family life seems set fair for the indefinite future.

It is Rosalie herself who tells the Commandant how she came to meet Francoeur and what happened afterwards, in order to persuade him that Francoeur should be treated not "nach der Strenge des Gesetzes" but "nach seinem Unglück."[4] This is not to say that she understands what has taken place. On the contrary, her narrative is a highly idiosyncratic version of events—a tale within a tale rather than an explanation—as her inexperience and religious literalism lead her to conceive them, and her acquiescence in a "solution" of Francoeur's difficulties that will inevitably lead to catastrophe indicates just how much she still has to learn. Although she insists (twice) that her love is to blame, her idiom of devils and curses is inadequate to explain why this should be; and she is overly solicitous of her husband's pride. She cannot yet see that there is a difference between pride and touchiness, or that her solicitousness is not necessarily a good thing. Nevertheless, in keeping with a well-established Romantic convention, Rosalie's folksiness does bespeak one advantage: that she is possessed of a potentially sound inner life which, once matured, will enable her to see intuitively how things really are. For the moment, however, she has to make up for her shortcomings by rationalizing as best she can—behind her husband's back.

Since Rosalie does not tell us what has happened to her father, it must be his absence as such that is important:

it has allowed her mother to dominate her completely. Her mother is clearly intended by Arnim to be seen as emotionally deficient—witness her compulsive need for distraction in the form of endless company and games of chance—and this deficiency has caused her for her own benefit to suppress Rosalie's natural evolution as a separate human being. However, Rosalie's description of herself as "träumerig" (p. 737) does suggest the beginnings of individuation even as the vagueness of the word implies that, both at the time in question and at the time of her story to the Commandant, she is unable to recognize her developing condition for what it is. Indeed, just how little of the wisdom of hindsight is yet hers is indicated by her unthinking reiteration of her mother's interpretation of the "freundliche Reden" (p. 737) of their guests as "Zudringlichkeit" (p. 737). Perhaps it was; the reader has no way of knowing. Neither, apparently, has Rosalie, which is why the possibility does not enter her mind that what was being expressed by her mother was not solicitude for her welfare but neurotic possessiveness.

The war drives her mother back upon herself ("wir lebten zu ihrem Ärger sehr einsam" [p. 737]). She reacts with the indiscriminate hatred characteristic of the person whose worst enemy is herself and forces the first explicit division between herself and her daughter by wilfully constraining what appears to be the latter's natural compassion. What then amounts to a necessary bid for independence—it is not less that for not being construed by Rosalie as such—is precipitated by Francoeur, who focuses and intensifies a number of burgeoning desires in Rosalie, one of which (there are others intermixed) is to complete herself in an adult relationship with someone other than her mother. It should be stressed that there is nothing calculated in this. Francoeur is entirely passive, the significance of which will become clear shortly; and Rosalie, on her own testimony, has simply no idea of what is happening to her ("da weiss ich nicht wie mir geschah; die Mutter war vergessen" [p. 737]). Their joint predicament is that they have been swept into a relationship requiring a wholeness neither has *at this stage*. Under normal circumstances, this would not matter too much. As things are, it is crucial.

That Rosalie goes to tend and feed Francoeur at their first encounter—that, in fact, she was burning[5] to tend and feed to a degree in excess of compassion alone even before the invitingly helpless Francoeur was wheeled prostrate into her life—indicates the sort of complication that has been set in train. Rosalie has not resolved her relationship with her mother, of whom she remains afraid, she has merely taken advantage of her mother's temporary absence to enter into an additional one ("die Mutter war vergessen . . .");[6] she eagerly as-sumes responsibility for Francoeur's material circumstances (the pattern is repeated in Marseilles); she undoubtedly falls in love with him; and, above all, she derives satisfaction from nourishing him ("welche Seligkeit, dem Notleidenden die warme Suppe zu reichen!" [pp. 737-38]). What has happened is that, owing to her upbringing, Rosalie's inner life has been so held back that the daughter, the woman, the wife, and the mother, which Arnim sees as all co-existing harmoniously in the mature of the sex, are in Rosalie's case in a state of confusion. Her legitimate need for autonomy has perforce placed her in a state of involuntary disobedience to her mother; and her overwhelming need to be a wife and mother herself has found its first overt expression in her mothering her husband-to-be.

Rosalie's insistent maternalism finds, at least initially, a willing subject in Francoeur. When—in her mother's absence—Francoeur places his ring on Rosalie's finger, he pretends to a degree of manhood which he does not yet possess. As a soldier, he has distinguished himself by obeying the orders of others, but it is as somebody wounded and incapable that Arnim introduces him into the story. His physical condition is the outward sign of a callowness that reciprocates Rosalie's present peculiarities only too well. That is to say, his personality is still sufficiently indeterminate to provide her with the means to satisfy (albeit provisionally) both her longing for a child and for a husband. Just how wanting Francoeur's personality is at this juncture becomes painfully apparent with his treatment of Rosalie's mother. It is true that, since Rosalie is not freely given, he has no option but to take her, but the legalistic defiance he resorts to in place of tactful firmness is all his own ("er hielt mich fest und sagte ihr [der Mutter]: dass wir verlobt wären, ich trüge schon seinen Ring" [p. 738]). Like Rosalie, whose "defection" he has confirmed, and her mother, who would rather have kept her daughter for herself, the immature Francoeur is at once co-author and future victim of a state of affairs which, while potentially beneficial, exceeds his immediate resources. Rosalie's mother, a prime example of the double-edged nature of "human inadequacy," provides an indication of what is to come. Incapable of the self-sufficiency she has hitherto used Rosalie to avoid, she becomes consumed by resentment and seeks by means of her curse to destroy the daughter she can neither retain by force nor release with her blessing. What is not so obvious at first glance is that this is her way of suffering; and it is perhaps even less obvious that she can only make others suffer as well if they are inwardly open to attack anyway.

For a curse, if it is to be effective, has to be acknowledged in some way, and although Rosalie is rightly indifferent to the calumnies her mother heaps upon her, she is vulnerable for two reasons: she has not grown free from her mother, but absconded; and she understands neither her old situation nor her new one, of which the old remains an active ingredient. Caught between filial and uxorial exactions she is able neither to comply with nor even adequately to discriminate; she feels in awe of her mother and beholden to her without recognizing that her mother's power is over a phase of her being that she is in the process of outgrowing. Such recognition would, of course, be an intuitive consequence of that outgrowing. And when that is eventually accomplished, the curse will have no further hold over her, and the way will be open for guilt and fear to be superseded by insight and concern.

Francoeur, too, is inwardly vulnerable. Contrary to Rosalie's belief that he is not affected by her mother's aspersions on her character, it is evident that he is unsettled to a degree (the very ridiculousness of his "divorce" later on suggests the effect of a chronic and deep-seated fear). But the timing and the violence of the whole episode are as responsible for this as what is actually said. Like Rosalie, Francoeur is in a delicate state of transition, and his first moments of love are fittingly balanced by Arnim between freshness and naïveté, as is the description of their engagement, with its little ring, its sincerity and its innocent heedlessness. The mother's drastic intervention acts upon Francoeur in a way that is diffuse and fundamental, as if his very being has been interfered with—an implication Arnim reinforces by leaving the perturbing but insufficiently explicit adverb "schlimm" (p. 738), which Rosalie uses to communicate the nature of the effect her mother's intervention has on Francoeur, unelaborated by any direct authorial comment. Ominously vague, the word persists in the mind of the reader even as the consequences of the episode it refers back to persist in the subterranean obscurity of Francoeur's psyche. It is as much his confidence in himself that is undermined as his confidence in Rosalie. This is what gives his jealousy its inane and *self*-destructive character; and why Arnim makes its eventual disappearance depend not on some forensic demonstration of innocence but on a revelatory change in his emotional economy. Francoeur's madness is the externalization of the great strain he is under as he tries to reconcile his love with apprehension, insecurity, and an oppressive sense of obligation. Moments of tenderness with (for Rosalie) a significantly not unwelcome infantile inflection ("nur mit mir war er sanft wie ein Kind" [p. 740]) are intermitted with threatening recollections of the mother whose dominance he has challenged and the black-robed priest who has married him and reminded him of his responsibilities. And when his child is born, with its requirement of a further and very special kind of love, Francoeur, predictably, becomes more unstable than ever.

It is a commonplace of psychological fiction that a *modus vivendi* that is maintained by means of suppression will eventually be destroyed from within by the pressures it generates, however promising it may appear at first sight. Although Ratonneau would seem both to the Commandant and to Rosalie the ideal place for Francoeur ("er hat da wenig Veranlassung zu Torheiten, und die er begeht, bleiben verschwiegen" [p. 741]), in fact it imitates Francoeur's marriage in that it simultaneously keeps him in a state of nonage—it is a further instance of Rosalie's presuming to know what is best for him, and she is helped in this by the paternal and well-meaning Commandant—*and* requires him to accept a degree of responsibility he cannot for the time being live up to. His oblique admission of inadequacy to the Commandant indicates that he is aware of this, but as his "Zutrauen" is met only with a benevolent but unperceptive "Vertrauen" (p. 742), he is compelled to do what he can. He seeks to control his troubled inner life by means of a resolute insistence on externals. His nervous tension finds a respectable outlet in a refurbishing of the fort ("er war hastig, aber alles zu einem festen Ziele" [p. 743]); and his relationship with Rosalie is temporarily improved by a combination of shared hard work and definite objectives ("bei dieser Tätigkeit liessen ihn seine Grillen ruhen" [p. 743]). It would seem that Francoeur has at last been able to fulfil the roles of soldier, husband, and father, and this is undoubtedly what he wants. However, his very energy indicates that his will and subconscious are not yet in complete agreement, and that he will therefore be unable to keep his idyll going indefinitely.

That the spark which causes his idyll to explode is a fallacy—Rosalie's assumed infidelity—is only appropriate, given the falseness of the idyll itself. Francoeur's fear of infidelity and belittlement is well founded, though not in the way he thinks. Owing to its unresolved stresses, his marriage, like his present military status, is only formally valid. In possession neither of himself nor of his wife, he rationalizes his situation by contending outrageous *dis*possession, casts out Rosalie and her child, and declares war on the Commandant. By this means, he gains a measure of freedom from the pressures at work within him; but it is the negative freedom of unhindered indulgence of his limitations, which is why it is expressed by an act of confinement. Literally and figuratively, Francoeur is trapped. He cannot return to the innocence of the bachelor soldier from which his own development has removed him and, unaided, he cannot take that development to its life-changing conclusion either. His involuntary mutiny against his own best interests has its counterpart in his mutiny as a soldier. Both mean death, the one metaphorically as an indicator of the quality of his life at this point, and the other as a plain matter of fact. Both are retrievable only if his progress towards manhood and responsibility, which began with his falling in love with Rosalie and which has been aborted by the attendant circumstances of that same event, may be resumed. As a psychological matter, the situation falls more within Rosalie's competence than within that of a court-martial, the proviso being that she can stop applying herself to the symptoms of Francoeur's disorder and attend to what is really wrong with him.

Arnim describes Rosalie as "verwirrt" (p. 746), and that is all to the good, for it means that it has at last been brought home to her that what she has been taking to be the right way of going about things has been fundamentally incorrect. Francoeur's "divorce" is a blessing in disguise: it compels Rosalie to become a mother in the only worthwhile sense, namely, as that of her child; and it puts Francoeur out of her immediate reach. Like her husband's immurement and her own earlier rejection by her mother (whom in his destructive resentment and underlying need of love Francoeur has come increasingly to resemble), Rosalie's boat ride appears paradoxical in that it opens the way to future harmony by means of separation. That it takes place at night is doubly apposite. It is the time of maximum obscurity; but it is also the time when the arcane processes of the subconscious come into their own.

Here as elsewhere, more than one interpretation is applicable, but in psychological terms the key to eventual resolution of the *Novelle* is a development in Rosalie of which she herself has hitherto been less than fully aware. It manifests itself while she is asleep, when her subconscious, which has been quietly evolving in its own way, has the opportunity to disclose itself in a dream. Rosalie's relations with her mother have corresponded to her growth as a person. As a child (one gathers), she was compliant, and as an immature bride, she was rebellious and fearful. But her own maternity has helped her to become more of a woman in her own right ("und mit der Qual der Geburt schien der Teufel, der mich geplagt, ganz von mir gebannt" [p. 740]), even though, not surprisingly in the circumstances, the full significance of that change has remained latent rather than patent (its placement in Rosalie's narrative is suitably *en passant*). In the boat, her mother flashes back into her mind, not now as the overwhelmingly terrifying figure she had once described as a "black bat," but as a woman and a mother herself whose general behaviour and particular anguish are, at last, becoming intelligible (it is as someone burning *inwardly* and in need of help that Rosalie sees her now; she is, literally, gaining insight into her mother's condition for the first time). Whether Rosalie would have made the all-important connection between her mother's self-consuming state and Francoeur's, had she been allowed to dream on, is an open question. In the event, the connection is practically forced upon her by the (unintentional) intervention of Francoeur himself. His "nächtliche Erleuchtung" (p. 748), an appropriately mixed symbol of animosity, distress, and essential virtue, saves Rosalie physically at the point where she is finally in a position to save him psychologically. The rightness of what she will go on to do will come from *her* rightness and will therefore not be an imposition, like her plot with the Commandant (Francoeur was right to suspect an *affaire* there; a conspiracy of good intentions, it threatened his manliness by placing at once too much and too little reliance on it and was therefore just as damaging in its way as a sexual liaison would have been). Nor can anyone else act for her. Her authority is peculiarly her own, and those who are not privy to its source—the Commandant, Basset, and Father Philip—are necessarily reduced to the role of spectator.

It is perhaps worth emphasizing here that Rosalie's response to the major events of her life is always immediate and total. Recalling what it was like to be cursed by her mother, she says: "die Welt war mir halb verschlossen, und ich gehörte mir nicht mehr ganz" (p. 738); and the possibility that Francoeur has been blown up while she is in the boat provokes the fear that she has lost "ihr halbes Leben" (p. 746). It is evident from the *Novelle* as a whole that her language does not exaggerate: the love she feels for her mother needs to be distinguished from that which she feels for her husband and child respectively, but that all three are constituent parts of her being is revealed by the thoroughgoing nature of the consequences as long as any is in any way disturbed. At the beginning of the *Novelle,* their differences in kind are blurred, but, as she matures, they gain in intensity and definition to the point where all confusion is eliminated. This means, however, that no one of them can compensate for the others. When Rosalie saves her child from the fort, her attitude is not that "at least" she has saved one of the people dear to her but that in having to separate herself from Francoeur she has incurred the net loss of part of herself ("Kind, das tue ich nur deinetwegen, mir wäre besser mit ihm zu sterben" [p. 746]). With the child but without Francoeur, she would remain incomplete. It is therefore personally necessary for her to save Francoeur if she can (and her mother, too, though in the nature of things this is a lesser imperative).

Rosalie's apparent abandonment of her child is explicable in terms of these considerations. Her maternalism has been a prominent feature of the *Novelle,* and its misapplication has helped nobody. Now that she is a little older and a lot wiser, it makes sense that she should return to Francoeur and their original bond of love—there is a natural sequence to these things that needs to be redressed retrospectively—in order to secure the foundation of their marriage, before coming back to the child which, as *theirs* now and not hers alone, represents the final stage in the evolution of their relationship so far as the *Novelle* is concerned. In terms of the plot, Rosalie has to risk death by her actions. But it is plain that at least part of Arnim's interest is less in courage under fire than in what this confrontation *in extremis* signifies psychologically. The drama of Rosalie's position lends clarity to the terms of her dilemma and absolute weight to the choice she makes; but for her actually to be killed would mean a wholly gratuitous suspension of the logic of her personal development before it has had time to work itself out. The technical problem for Arnim is to create a sense of things hanging in the balance while at the same time keeping his thumb in the scales. He solves it by making the reader fully aware of the loss Rosalie and her riven family would incur if she did *not* go through with her ordeal, and by making her safety clearly dependent not on authorial whim but pre-established appropriateness.

The love Rosalie reveals to Francoeur as she confronts him is of such a pure and undivided kind, and at the same time so convincingly human, that even if one feels that such devils as inhabit Francoeur may not in practice be exorcized in *precisely* the way of the *Novelle,* one remains persuaded that they ought to be; for the change she occasions in him by provoking his love directly is no more than the change that that selfsame love would have brought about in him anyway had its natural course not been interrupted by Rosalie's mother and further complicated by Rosalie herself. Or rather, almost no more. For what Francoeur, like Rosalie, has gained from what has happened is a knowledge of life and death such as to transform an untested adolescent passion into a vital force ("ein unendliches Gefühl meines [Francoeur's] Daseins, dessen Augenblicke mir genügen" [p. 753]). His manhood now properly established, Francoeur has no need either to exclude himself from others or to seek to dominate them (Rosalie's mother affords a comparable example of the releasing power of love). Husband, son-in-law, father, and soldier[7] are genuinely reconciled within him, as are wife, daughter, and mother in Rosalie, and it is *inter alia* this new-found compatibility of loves and obligations that permits Arnim to describe the couple as "die Wiederbeglückten, die Fluchbefreiten" (p. 754) as he brings his story to its conclusion.

In its few pages, ***Der tolle Invalide*** provides vivid and lucid insights into some of the major changes of life: growing up, falling in love, making new bonds, remaking old ones, and so forth. Unlike Rosalie, who yet provides the reader's cue, Arnim *deliberately* tells more than he explains, and thereby obliges the reader to enter into an active and interrogatory relationship with the text if he is to make anything of it: the *Novelle* relates a series of effects, and the reader has to consult and clarify

his own experience in order to identify their causes. It remains to be asked, however, what the *Novelle*'s undoubted psychological finesse has to do with its religious meaning, which, after all, is insisted on by Arnim at every turn and is evidently intended to be taken *au pied de la lettre*. That the data for a psychological interpretation are there in abundance is, I think, indisputable. But the real question the *Novelle* poses is not whether a psychological interpretation is possible but whether those same data do not compel another kind of meaning altogether.

Like most other books, ***Der tolle Invalide*** was written to be read *seriatim*: one proceeds from one piece of information to the next until at last the conclusion is reached. Only then, so Arnim's intention would seem to be, does it become possible to see that what one has been reading may be understood as the working out of an *a priori* principle of development, just as in one's own life one has to live through a succession of phases before one may see them retrospectively as parts of a definite progression.

That one realizes one's being through time and in specific circumstances in accordance with an inherent conatus is a conception that is fundamental to ***Der tolle Invalide.*** Rosalie and Francoeur are beings evolving towards a condition which, although they would be unable to account for it formally, will be "known" by them from the inside—experientially—as wholeness and which, moreover, is somehow dimly anticipated by them even before it has been fully attained. So powerful is this drive to completion that they find themselves engaged and married well before either is aware of what is really happening; but at the same time they are able to sense that they are doing the right thing, even though a combination of ignorance and adversity will make the going exceptionally difficult (and therefore, from an artistic point of view, exceptionally revealing).

From a psychological point of view, the turning point of the *Novelle* is the moment on the river when, prepared by her maternity and her changed recollection of her mother and subjected to the double shock of the "divorce" and the near-collision, Rosalie makes all the right subconscious associations and begins to perceive just what is wrong with Francoeur. It requires yet more time, and the pressure of knowing that her husband's death is inevitable unless something is done, before the complex processes that continue in Rosalie after she has left the boat reach the point of action. But when she finally declares: "Ich kenne ihn . . . ich will den Teufel beschwören in ihm, ich will ihm Frieden geben" (p. 751), one feels that she has acquired an elementally direct understanding of both herself and Francoeur which of itself is sufficient to carry the *Novelle* through to its conclusion. Given that the manner and timing of her brush with death are precisely what the *Novelle* needs to go forward, it could be argued that Arnim has resorted to a rather blatant use of coincidence to keep his story on the move; but it could also be argued that as long as his psychology remains unforced, a little nudging of reality is perhaps justifiable none the less. After all, coincidences do happen.

But to argue like that would be to argue from the very *parti pris* Arnim is concerned to question. For him, coincidence and psychologizing belong together as complementary products of an understanding of human existence that is severely limited. Such an understanding fosters the view that psychology is *no more than* the study of systems of emotional logic in beings that are tacitly assumed to be dissociated from the rest of creation; and that this "rest of creation" then only affects these beings fortuitously. It is plain that Arnim finds such an understanding unacceptable. For him, the optimal development of the psyche is not an end in itself in a largely incomprehensible universe but a means to making that universe less incomprehensible. Thus his purpose is not to cancel psychology, but to transcend it. On the face of it, this would seem an obvious enough remark, since the *Novelle*'s religious position is clear. But Arnim is less interested in making dogmatic assertions than in establishing their credibility. What remains now is to see how he sets out to achieve this.

From the point of view of the *Novelle*'s religious theme, the turning point will be seen to have been reached when Rosalie ceases to rely on herself and places her trust in God. It is not as good fortune but as an intimation of His providence that she construes the events of her boat ride; and although she is not then given a blueprint for action (she prays for one, but her prayer seems to go unanswered), she remains so confident that some kind of divine purpose is manifesting itself in her affairs that she eventually becomes ready even to divest herself of her child and offer her life as a sacrifice if that is what God's will requires of her. And though once she has achieved that readiness the actual sacrifice is not needed, the *Novelle* continues in such a way as to suggest that her faith is in nowise illusory.

It is easy to see all this as a gratuitous superimposition, a case of faith's being not far removed from simple gullibility; yet to do so is wholly to mistake what Arnim is up to. To restate an earlier point in a different way, there is for Rosalie no gap between feeling and being. Indeed, feeling is the ground of her being. Her feelings, as has been noted, have an inherent conative character; and, were she ever to hear them used of her, she would

in her own way find "complete" and "incomplete" to be meaningful descriptive terms. Arnim's proposition—a variant of the argument from design—is that the characteristics of experience Rosalie exemplifies are not adventitious but purposeful; and it is not just to an achieved state of being that he looks for supporting evidence but also to her innate drive towards that state. For the more readily experience, regardless of the will of the experiencing subject or the influence of circumstances, may be described in teleological terms, the stronger the case becomes for supposing it to be a means to enable the nature of creation (of which man is a part) to be intuited. On this view, providence is not the *ad hoc* interference of some invisible puppet master in a world that is otherwise discontinuous with its creator but the opportunity the general structure of creation supplies for its divine origin to be experienced; grace is that which enables man to take that opportunity and recognize its significance; faith is conscious commitment to that recognition; and sin is the attempt to assert one's own will in defiance of the felt bias of creation. Obviously, Rosalie's apprehension of "a meaning for existence that is already given with existence"[8] will, like Francoeur's, not take place until her drive to completion has been experienced negatively as disarray and positively as a qualitative advance towards wholeness. But once she has experienced existence as shape and direction, she will enable Arnim, through her, to make the conjectural leap from pattern to design, from psychology to theology; which, of course, will add a new dimension to her feeling that she is "nicht mehr schicksallos."

The difficulty remains, however, that what appears to be evidence of divine providence has to be seen as such by Rosalie; but what disposes her to do so are the inner modifications she is undergoing; which means that what she lives out as faith in God may therefore after all be no more than faith in herself.[9] The *Novelle* is completely ambiguous about this. Its psychology is such that each stage in the individual and common development of Rosalie and Francoeur logically creates the conditions for the next until both may be said to be in full possession of themselves and of life at its finest; and its theology is such that the more they gain possession of themselves, the more willingly they see themselves as parts of a larger whole. By leaving it to his principal characters, and particularly to Rosalie, actually to connect the two, Arnim keeps his *Novelle* free to balance secular and transcendental interpretations against each other, even though his own preference is clear enough. He manifestly aspires, in typical Romantic fashion, to a single order of validity that will comprehend all others. But because the possibility is built into the very structure of *Der tolle Invalide* that the divine, which ought to subsume the psychological, is in fact contingent on it, the *Novelle* simultaneously provides, again in typical Romantic fashion, a radical critique of that aspiration; and the act of interpretation itself becomes a part of what is presented to the reader *for* interpretation.[10]

In sum, **Der tolle Invalide** is so constructed as to appeal equally to more than one order of intelligibility. Technically, the psychological and religious themes mesh perfectly, in the sense that any given episode may be used indifferently to support either; and the equivocal nature of their interrelationship is by no means abrogated by the obviousness of Arnim's own convictions. For what the *Novelle* provides is not a got-up illustration of finished beliefs but the emergence of the possibility of faith from the character of human experience. The psychological theme of **Der tolle Invalide** articulates certain inner developments in such a way as to facilitate understanding and evaluation within a restricted conceptual framework, and its success in that regard inclines one to concur with Rowley's tentative regret that Arnim was "born too soon" to make more of an obvious talent. But by venturing into the conceptual no-man's-land where empirical verification and possibility begin to separate, Arnim anticipates another and to my mind even more important modern concern: the extrapolation of the meaning of life from the forms living takes. Of course, "modern" in this context implies less an improvement on the past than an acknowledgement that its problems remain with us. And it is not the least of the strengths of **Der tolle Invalide** that, for all its love of life[11] and its evident religious optimism, it is at the same time able to compel a clear reckoning with that unpalatable fact.

### Notes

1. Goethe, for example, remarked to Kanzler von Müller in a letter of July 8th, 1825, that Arnim "ist wie ein Fass, wo der Böttcher vergessen hat, die Reifen festzuschlagen, da läuft's denn auf allen Seiten heraus." Quoted by Ralph Tymms in "Achim von Arnim," *German Romantic Literature* (London: Methuen, 1955), p. 267. Tymms himself complains of Arnim's "frequent diffuseness and excessive attention to irrelevant detail" (p. 266).

2. Brian Rowley, "The *Novelle*," in *The Romantic Period in Germany,* ed. Siegbert Salomon Prawer (London: Weidenfeld and Nicolson, 1970), pp. 121-46. These quotations are from pp. 142 and 143. Although first published as an *Erzählung* (see Migge, p. 917), *Der tolle Invalide* has been classed as a *Novelle* since at least Wilhelm Grimm's 1839 edition of Arnim's complete works (see Wolfdietrich Rasch, "Achim von Arnims Erzählkunst," *Der Deutschunterricht,* VII, 2 [1955], 40).

3. Ernst Feise, "*Der tolle Invalide* von Achim von Arnim," *JEGP* [*Journal of English and Germanic Philology*], 53 (1954), 408.

4. Ludwig Achim von Arnim, *Der tolle Invalide auf dem Fort Ratonneau* (1818), in *Sämtliche Romane und Erzählungen,* ed. Walther Migge, II (Munich: Hanser, 1962-65), 733-55. These quotations are from p. 740; all further references to this work are cited in the text.

5. Fire and its cognates make up one of the *Novelle*'s most important leitmotifs. Cf. Feise, p. 407, and Benno von Wiese, "Achim von Arnims *Der tolle Invalide auf dem Fort Ratonneau,*" *Die deutsche Novelle* (Düsseldorf: Bagel, 1962), II, 72-73 et passim.

6. The negative side of Rosalie's behaviour is important enough for Arnim to point it up twice more. When her mother runs away, Rosalie simply feels "entfesselt von jeder Rücksicht" (p. 738); and her rejection by her friends is interpreted by her in similarly advantageous terms. Unable to define her relations with others, she is happy to have them defined for her ("So war ich nun von aller Welt ausgestossen und es tat mir wohl" etc. [p. 738]).

7. The Commandant also plays the role of father to Francoeur, and their private relationship is a male version of that of Rosalie and her mother. His declaration of war on his father is a mixture of weakness and the need for independence, and his eventual adoption is a sign of self-confident maturity ridding him of his sense of oppression.

8. John Macquarrie, *Principles of Christian Theology,* 2nd ed. (New York: Charles Scribner's Sons, 1977), p. 80. I have found this book useful in a number of respects. For a discussion of Arnim's religious beliefs in connection with his hierarchical conception of the family and the state, see Gerhard Möllers, "Wirklichkeit und Phantastik in der Erzählweise Achim von Arnims," Diss. Münster 1971, pp. 25-44.

9. That it may be possible for us to know that the way we experience is intentional from the way we experience but that we have no means apart from further appeals to experience to "verify" that possibility are considerations that have received perhaps their most comprehensive fictional treatment in the works of Franz Kafka. There is, of course, a good deal more to Kafka than to Arnim, including a much more systematic examination of the possibility (latent in Francoeur) that the crucial experience of completeness, as distinct from an un-

doubted yearning for it, may not even be available to everyone—a possibility that opens up an almost infinite range of probes and strategies in response to the question: why not? Since it never loses sight of the ambiguous status of experience as a means to truth, *Der tolle Invalide* may be seen as a prototype of Kafka's *Vexierbilder*—a profoundly inconclusive literary form in which the data of experience are given in great detail but any given construction put on those data will never entirely free itself from its opposite.

10. The question of intention arises here. A carefully placed "wohl" introduces Rosalie's boat ride (p. 748); and in addition to the psychological theme, Francoeur's head wound, by providing a purely physical "explanation" of events, further counterbalances the *Novelle*'s religious purport. But most telling is the fact that the search for the meaning of his own material was a conscious part of Arnim's compositional procedure. In a letter to Wilhelm Grimm dated December 1819, he wrote: "Wenn Du meine Pläne zu verwickelt findest, ich kanns nicht bestreiten. . . . Ich kann mich erst beruhigen, wenn ich durch die Begebenheit so weit fortgerissen bin, dass ich Gottes Barmherzigkeit anrufen möchte, um mir herauszuhelfen. Dann habe ich erst ein Gefühl, dass ich den Sinn und das Leben der Geschichte getroffen habe, und endlich findet sich doch immer ein Ausgang" (quoted in Rasch, pp. 42-43). There is, to be sure, not the same anguish to Arnim's investigation of the reliability of "Gefühl" and the shortcomings of reason as there is to, say, Kleist's (e.g., *Amphitryon*), since Arnim's religious faith gave him a fixed point Kleist never had. But the difference is one of inflection. A sense of competing possibilities is certainly common to both.

11. For a personal appreciation of Arnim's "Fülle von Leben," see Grimm's preface to volume I of his edition of Arnim's works, rpt. in *Kleinere Schriften von Wilhelm Grimm,* ed. Gustav Hinrichs (vols. I-III, Berlin: Harrwitz und Gossmann, 1881-83; vol. IV, Gütersloh: Bertelsmann, 1887), I, 311-14.

## Bruce Duncan (essay date September 1979)

SOURCE: Duncan, Bruce. "Fate and Coincidence in Arnim's *Seltsames Begegnen und Wiedersehen*." *Seminar: A Journal of Germanic Studies* 15, no. 3 (September 1979): 181-89.

[*In the following essay on Arnim's sprawling historical novella, Duncan examines contemporary critical reception of the book, noting the difficulties posed by the story's ill-defined structure and implausible plot devices. In Duncan's view the various coincidences that drive the narrative of* Seltsames Begegnen und Wiedersehen, *rather than diminishing the work's value, actually reveal the author's broader concerns with shifting qualities of temporal causality, as well as with the indeterminate and ambiguous nature of history itself.*]

*Seltsames Begegnen und Wiedersehen* seems particularly susceptible to the charge of formlessness traditionally levelled at Arnim's work.[1] Wilhelm Grimm complained of his friend's stories, 'Was mich stört, ist Deine Art, einer geschlossenen, in sich vollendeten Geschichte, wenn sie bis auf einen gewissen Punct in dieser Begränzung fortgelebt hat, verborgene Thüren von allen Seiten zu öffnen, daß sie nun in alle Welt ausgeht und oft als ein Weltereigniß endigt, so daß ein Edelstein, den ein Liebender heimlich verborgen getragen, der ihm sein Licht gewesen, und alle seine Tiefen durchleuchtet hat, zuletzt als Sonne am Himmel glänzt und stolz im Meer und nicht in jener Brust sich senkt, was uns menschlich näher gewesen.'[2]

*Seltsames Begegnen* fits this pattern well. Julie's engagement to Stauffen and her subsequent rejection of him, after she learns that he has killed her father in battle, complete a tragic love story.[3] But this is just the beginning. New characters appear, old ones reappear, and we follow both lovers for another six years, even though they fail to exchange another word. Their final meeting during the retreat from Moscow ends the tragedy. But why do we hear of Stauffen's intervening years in Spain and the reunion with his mother? And why are we introduced to Constanze's uncle, who turns out to be Stauffen's long-lost father? The unbelievable—and seemingly gratuitous—coincidences create a confusing and implausible story. Furthermore, the crypt of Julie's father and the prophecy of Stauffen's mother provide a characteristic that so infuriated both Arnim's friends and foes: the apparently anomalous injection of the supernatural into an otherwise 'realistic' story.

In looking for a unifying principle to all this, it is possible to approach *Seltsames Begegnen* as Arnim's bitter recollection of the years from 1806 to 1812. By 1818, when the novella appeared, it was evident that Prussia would continue to adhere to traditions which precluded genuine reform and that the promises of the war years would not be realized.[4] Plagued by debts and censorship, as well as by the shrillness of the 'Ultras' (cf *Metamorphosen der Gesellschaft*), Arnim could view the Restoration only with disappointment, even though he had never entertained very high hopes for Prussia's political enlightenment in the first place.[5] The bitterly comic portrayals of social disorder derive from Arnim's personal experience of Prussia's stagnation.[6] The servants, Constanze, and the police inspector might well be considered figures from the post-Napoleonic era. In contrast, the relatively sympathetic portrayal of Stauffen (like that of Francoeur) shows the complexity of Arnim's response to the French invasion. Despite his considerable national and racial prejudices,[7] Arnim sympathetically portrayed fraternization as early as 1809 in *Der Wintergarten.*

But a close reading of this novella, combined with a look at Arnim's other works, suggests that it encompasses a much wider scope than could a mere love story or *Tendenzstück.*[8] Grimm's complaint correctly describes the story's structure, albeit in negative terms. The action begins in Berlin and quickly spreads out to include Spain and Russia. Similarly, the temporal sphere expands rapidly. From the occupation of Berlin we look back to the Battle of Jena/ Auerstedt and proceed to the retreat from Moscow. Furthermore, the uncle invites us to compare the national uprisings of 1812 with the French Revolution. Julie's dead father even steps outside the temporal order altogether by recalling the myth of Barbarossa. Within Berlin itself the action extends to a variety of social groups: the lovers, the *Schwesternbund,* and the world of the servants.

Arnim connects these diverse elements by a series of miraculous coincidences. Stauffen *happens* to be quartered with the daughter of the man he killed; a twist of fate has placed him on the French side in the first place; later he *happens* to meet his mother in the ruined church. She in turn *happens* to see the letter with the handwriting that *happens* to resemble her lost husband's, etc. Almost every page offers us a coincidence of some sort. Möllers points out (pp. 124 f), 'daß Arnim mit Hilfe von *Zufällen* Situationen herbeiführt, die einen aufdeckenden Charakter haben . . . Sie dienen der Aufdeckung der wahren Beschaffenheit der Wirklichkeit, sei es nun der Bestimmung einer charakteristischen Anlage, sei es dem Prüfen der Konsequenzen einer verkürzten Theorie.'

But the device goes even further. Arnim's coincidences do more than introduce situations; each one results in ambiguities that invite the reader to speculate on the kind of causality at work here. When Stauffen tells Julie how he killed an old man in battle, his show of feeling so stirs her that they confess their love and become engaged. But when the victim turns out to be her father, tragedy begins. Constanze's letter, which leads Stauffen to despair by rejecting his attempted reconciliation, also precipitates the reunion of mother and son. Even theft has ambiguous results: if Hans had not taken the necklace, Julie would never have discovered her father's

fate; when Stauffen steals the painting of the Virgin, he both dooms himself and saves the holy picture from destruction. Dichotomies appear even in trivial occurrences: the rain that inconveniences Julie also cools her temper and even brings the police inspector into her house when she needs him. In addition to these bifurcated effects, we also encounter acts similar in nature that nevertheless yield different results: when Charlotte puts on Julie's dress, she completely disrupts the social order; Stauffen on the other hand saves himself and his mother by wearing the porter's clothes.

The characters themselves have trouble comprehending such events and often seek meanings too hurriedly. Julie's difficulty, for example, lies in her eager ascription of fate to her love for the *Rittmeister.* She contends 'daß sie erst jetzt durch die Hand des Geschicks, das ihr den Mörder ihres Vaters unter Hunderttausenden der Feinde als Bräutigam zugeführt, die Weisung erhalten habe, daß eine Liebe zu den noch unversöhnten Feinden des Vaterlandes immerdar ein Frevel bleibe' (II, 772). She, like the characters in almost all of Arnim's works, is forced to make decisions based on a world she does not understand. In Arnim's view the disruptions of his era inhibit the kind of intuitive understanding necessary to differentiate between transitory illusion and the higher world-order. Some of his figures, like Hugh Schapler in *Gräfin Dolores* or 'der glückliche Färber,' miraculously achieve happiness because, like the youngest child in a fairy tale, they unconsciously remain true to their destinies. The tragic figures at the other extreme misunderstand the signals and deviate from their proper path.[9] Julie is torn between her two 'Verbindungen,' the word Arnim uses to describe both her engagement and the *Schwesternbund* (p. 761). In her mistaken loyalty to Constanze's patriotic ideals she must deny her emotions, for Constanze 'hat Verstand, viel Verstand, aber kein gutes Herz' (p. 773). All that binds Julie to these rigid beliefs is a sense of duty, so that in her final meeting with the wounded officer she is caught between shame and compassion.[10] This does not imply, however, that Julie need simply follow the dictates of her heart and choose Stauffen. The inner turmoil caused by her engagement, even before she learns of her father's death, is all too clear. The disapproval of her 'sisters' leaves her 'in dem unleidlichsten Zustande von äußeren und innern Widersprüchen zerrissen.'[11]

To ask whether Julie should give her loyalty to Constanze or to Stauffen too narrowly defines the alternatives. In a period of crisis, of disharmony, what appears to be a choice may in fact not be one at all. Arnim complains in *Owen Tudor* 'wie doch der Mensch so gern trennen mag, was Gott zusammenfügte. Da hat er sich die Worte *antik* und *modern* erfunden, um durch die Weltgeschichte eine Brettwand zu ziehen, die ihm jede Aussicht über das Ganze raubt' (III, 74). Friedrich Wilhelm I, in *Der glückliche Färber,* 'wußte die Krise zu meistern, indem er den Wandel der Zeit nicht im Sinne eines *Entweder Oder,* sondern vielmehr in dem eines *Sowohl als Auch* begriff. Er trennte nicht radikal zwischen "Altem" und "Neuem" sondern suchte beides miteinander zu vereinigen, um so dem Anspruch seiner Zeit gerecht zu werden' (Göres, p. 115). Some figures, like Karl in *Isabella von Aegypten,* are given a clear alternative, but they fail to grasp it. Like the Foolish Virgins, they miss a unique opportunity because they are preoccupied with their own narrow concerns.[12] They sense the malaise of their times and search for solutions. But what they should seek lies outside the boundaries of their particular logic. 'Arnims Personen und Figuren leben in einem größeren Raum, als ihn die Dreidimensionalität zu fassen vermag. Eine *empirische Wirkung* kann demnach durchaus eine *irrationale Ursache* im Anschauungsraum haben' (Helmstedt, p. 130).

This is how we must understand the seemingly outrageous coincidences in *Seltsames Begegnen.* We see a single causality at work in two spheres. The rules that govern the dimly perceived higher order are not always verifiable by empirical evidence. But their validity is absolute, even when the limited perspective of a concrete historical setting makes them seem to be illogical. By the same token solutions based only on immediate concerns are illusory. In a manuscript entitled 'Ueber historische Größe'[13] Arnim says that great figures in history only appear to enjoy good luck,

> denn darin liegt eben ihr Glück, daß sie höher stehen, wo die dunklen Farben schon planetisch zu leuchten aber auch zu blenden pflegen, sie sehen da hundert Wege wo uns nur zweie scheinen, Herkules muß sehr jung oder geistesschwach gewesen seyn . . . als er so simpel stand zwischen Zweyer[;] dafür sind diese großen Menschen so ruhig wie die Flußtiefen, während die anderen lermen, fürchten[,] hoffen; während andere meinen, um groß zu seyn, um sich auszuzeichnen müße man sich in allem unterscheiden, leben sie ganz eifrig menschlich in allen übrigen Verhältnissen, wie sie göttlich leben in ihrem höheren Verhältnisse, denn der Mensch ist ein Ebenbild Gottes, wenn er ganz Mensch ist.

While Arnim certainly does not rule out fate's impingement on worldly affairs,[14] he does not see the two realms as competing forces. The question is one of perspective. Both the temporal and eternal spheres are ruled by the same laws, but Arnim's tragic figures, like Rilke's 'Lebendige,' 'machen alle den Fehler, daß sie zu stark unterscheiden' (*Duineser Elegie* I). Difficulties arise in the historical world when we base our actions on inappropriate criteria that reflect only a subset of reality. When egocentricity, misplaced loyalties, or rigid beliefs make these criteria absolute, the result is 'Zerrissenheit,' a state of disorientation and dissatisfaction. When they recognize only radical choices, these characters exclude where they should combine. As Constanze says, 'Meine politischen Sorgen hatten mich dem eigenen Hause entfremdet' (p. 776).

Julie first claims to have chosen between friend and foe and then dedicates her steadfastness to her father's memory: '"Das Andenken meines Vaters," sagte sie, "die Erinnerung seiner Grundsätze ist mir wieder kräftig durch die Seele gegangen, und ich gebe mein Wort, meine Ehre, meine Liebe zu ihm zum Pfande, daß ich mir selbst nicht wieder ungetreu werden will"' (p. 772). But her father's loyalties and principles are of another order altogether: 'nie war ein Vater der Liebe und Achtung so würdig gewesen durch Treue in seinem Wandel als Mensch, Bürger und Soldat. Ohne große Erwartungen von dem Erfolge des Krieges zu hegen, war er doch von der Rechtlichkeit desselben so durchdrungen, daß er jeden Versuch, ihm eine ehrenvolle Ruhe zu sichern, zurückwies, er hatte sein Vaterland früher als seine Tochter unter seinen Augen aufwachsen sehen, und mochte dessen Fall nicht überleben' (p. 768). Julie sees herself choosing between fixed opposites; her father displays 'Treue in seinem Wandel.' Throughout the historical changes in which he participates, his personal integrity remains intact because it is based on an unshakeable sense of continuity. Each of his particular acts underlines the universal. Absorbed in something greater than himself, he can respond to the essential nature of events. In death he prefigures a future harmony. Instead of a uniform from his own period he wears 'die Rüstung des Stammvaters unseres gutsherrlichen Geschlechts' (p. 779). The arrangement in the crypt will last until Germany's liberation, but the patriotic ideals are not adversative: we find both 'Freunde und Feinde, bleich aber unversehrt wie die Siebenschläfer in der Stunde ihres Erwachens' (p. 778). When Julie encounters this scene, she can respond only to her father's death at the hands of the enemy. She drops the lilies she has brought, and they lie 'zerstreut und entwurzelt auf dem Boden' (p. 778), in contrast to the harmony before her.

It is important to note, however, that the crypt remains a *prefiguration* of harmony: the father is 'versteinert.' The times are still marked by disorientation. Although this lack of order plays itself out as a battle between nations, its cause lies elsewhere. Napoleon, 'der Alleszerreißende' (p. 795), has not so much pitted French against German as young against old. Stauffen, we must remember, is in fact himself a German. Ambition, a desire to distinguish himself in the new order, drives him to kill his countryman. The fault lies not only with the invader. Prussia's own internal weaknesses have led it to respond inappropriately, sending old men into battle: 'ohne bösen Willen muß die Jugend in solchen Greisen die heiligsten Gefühle verletzen' (p. 759). Arnim, who supported and had a commission in the *Landsturm*,[15] obviously does not intend this reproach literally. Rather he describes a period in which the reconciliation of old and new is impossible.[16]

In the story this discontinuity is symbolized by a break between generations. Constanze, Julie, and Stauffen have all lost their parents.[17] The orphaned Julie clearly lacks adequate direction: '[Sie] fand es unleidlich, von einer Freundin gleichen Alters immer gehofmeistert zu werden' (p. 762). Stauffen's case is even more obvious; we learn 'daß der Rittmeister von Geburt ein Deutscher sei, nur durch ein Spiel des Zufalls während der Revolution aller Unterstützung seiner unbekannten Eltern beraubt, sich gezwungen gesehen, gegen seine bessere Überzeugung mit den andern in den Kampf zu ziehen . . .' (p. 763). His rootlessness causes him to act against his better judgment; were he to follow his true feelings, he would abandon the army before events trap him: 'Wie war so viel eitle Torheit in ihm untergegangen, seit er Julien liebte, nie konnte ihn wieder der Zaubernebel seines Handwerks umhüllen, seinen Soldatenrock hatte er ausgewachsen, er war ihm nach allen Seiten zu eng und zu kurz . . .' (p. 772). But before he acts on this impulse, he receives orders to go to Spain. Here his isolation in the army exerts an even more divisive effect. The originally disinterested participant becomes a passionate partisan: 'So ward auch der Rittmeister aus dem Widerwillen, den er ursprünglich gegen diesen Krieg hegte, allmählich zum wachsamsten unermüdlichsten Unterdrücker Spaniens umgebildet . . .' (p. 782).

But one more chance remains. Another coincidence temporarily extracts Stauffen from the military and leads him to his mother, Klara. The reunion seems at first a gratuitous addition to the narrative, but it is in fact consistent with the story's symbolic structure. As the theme of the white hair suggests (pp. 759, 783, 794), this encounter represents Stauffen's final opportunity to establish a harmonious relationship with his past. Klara's deafness indicates that the connection is already impaired. Nevertheless, the hope reasserts itself that he will abandon his unnatural commitment to the invader, which has already severed his relationship with Julie, and become true to his proper destiny. But, as Arnim describes it, the French habits that Stauffen has acquired die hard and he yields to the impulse to steal a picture from Klara's church. The portrait of the Madonna reminds him of Julie, but its theft, together with his re-entry into France, where he no longer belongs to his mother (p. 786), somehow represents the fatal break with his German roots. When she learns of this act, his

mother foretells his tragic end. As in so many of Arnim's works, this prophecy represents not a prediction based on evidence, but a prescience obtained through a higher reality. 'Du bist Proteus,' says Jan to Hemkengriper in *Holländische Liebhabereien*, 'du kannst weissagen; wie das Vergangene, so liegt auch das Künftige vor dir offen, Raum und Zeit schließen den Kreis deines Blickes nicht' (III, 376). Like the Delphic oracle, Arnim's prophetic figures speak the truth, even when empirical evidence appears to contradict them.[18]

Is, then, the *Rittmeister* a victim of fate, or even of the 'Willkür, die über einen Soldaten schaltet' (p. 791)? As is so frequently the case, Arnim gives two apparently conflicting answers. On the one hand he tells us that Stauffen cannot hide 'vor seinem Geschick, vor dem ewigen Strafgericht' (p. 795) and seems to imply that external occurrences have doomed the officer. The letters to Julie, for example, which might have rescued the situation, arrive too late, because Napoleon has severed all personal communication from Spain. But the causality works equally well in the other direction. External occurrences are also to be seen as manifestations of internal conditions. Napoleon's edict merely confirms an already existing state. The communication between Julie and Stauffen has already reduced itself to unread letters. Similarly, on the one hand Constanze's machinations prevent a reconciliation; on the other they represent Julie's abandonment of her true feelings. Constanze acts on delegated authority.[19] And when Julie discovers what her friend has done, she does not feel betrayed, because Constanze merely carried out her wishes. Thus from one point of view Stauffen's death is fated; from another, however, it is the ultimate expression of his 'Zerrissenheit.' He views the 'Unglückszeichen' that mark his downfall as proof of his doom. By failing to heed them as warnings he continues to reject his true destiny. Like Julie he ascribes his actions to fate and thus precludes any reconciliation. By the time Hans tries to relieve the dying Stauffen's suffering by loosening the uniform that the officer had long before 'outgrown,' it is too late. The crippled *Rittmeister* curses 'den Urheber seines Lebens, den Urquell alles Lebens' (p. 794). The break with his heritage is complete.

It is important to note that Arnim does not identify Stauffen's and Julie's proper destinies with Prussian ascendancy. The crypt holding Julie's father prefigured a kind of ecumenical harmony. Similarly, Julie and Stauffen's mother return to Spain with the stolen portrait: 'nichts war von der Kirche übrig, so wunderbar war das heilige Bild erhalten, daß eine neue unentweihte Kirche, wie ein Vorhimmel sich darüber wölbe allen Glücklichen zur Erhebung, allen Unglücklichen eine beruhigende Grabesdecke, von dem Lichte einer anderen Welt durchstrahlt' (p. 796). Prefigured harmony is the ultimate that a fragmented world can offer. The Restoration, like the Napoleonic Era before it, affords only glimpses of the higher reality with which one must reconcile one's individual development. In an age which distinguishes where it should unite, which promotes false loyalties and lifeless principles, reconciliation of an individual with his proper destiny can occur only symbolically.

**Seltsames Begegnen,** then, is not a story that loses its way. Nor does its contrived plot represent an artistic lapse. Instead, the novella presents a richly symbolic structure that reflects Arnim's complex approach to history. The story's coincidences serve an important function: the ambiguities they create invite the reader to speculate on the causal relationships at work in the historical world and thus to gain insight into the higher reality that ultimately determines our destinies.

### Notes

1. Volker Hoffmann's 'Die Arnim-Forschung 1945-1972,' *DVjS* [*Deutsche Vierteljahrsschrift*], Sonderheft (1973), pp. 270-342, and several subsequent studies have demonstrated the inappropriateness of this accusation. Cf, for example, Helene M. Kastinger Riley, 'Das konfigurative Stilprinzip in der Kurzprosa Achim von Arnims' (diss. Rice University, Houston, 1975), and Hermann F. Weiss, 'Achim von Arnims Harmonisierungsbedürfnis. Zur Thematik seiner Novellen,' *Jb. d. Görres-Ges.,* 15 (1974), 81-99.

2. Reinhold Steig, *Achim von Arnim und die ihm nahe standen* (Stuttgart/Berlin, 1894-1913), II, 188. Similarly, Steig I, 266, where Brentano objects to his friend's 'Verknüpfen.'

3. Gerhardt Möllers, 'Wirklichkeit und Phantastik in der Erzählweise Achim von Arnims. Arnims Erzählkunst als Ausdruck seiner Weltsicht' (diss. Münster, 1972), p. 118.

4. Cf Jörn Göres, 'Das Verhältnis von Historie und Poesie in der Erzählkunst Ludwig Achim von Arnims (diss. Heidelberg, 1956), pp. 24 f. Arnim was most concerned that innovations proceed from all classes working together. His opposition to Hardenberg's reforms was based on their imposition from above: cf Jürgen Knaack, *Achim von Arnim—Nicht nur Poet. Die politischen Anschauungen Arnims in ihrer Entwicklung* (Darmstadt, 1976), pp. 42 ff.

5. E.g., Steig I, 180 ff; Knaack, pp. 47 f; Göres, pp. 24 f.

6. *Arnims Sämtliche Romane und Erzählungen,* ed. Walther Migge (Munich, 1961-5), II, 918. Hereafter cited in the text by volume and page number only.

7. Note the descriptions of the 'Voltigeurs und Italiener,' II, 793. For a discussion of Arnim's anti-semitism, cf my *'Die Versöhnung in der Sommerfrische. Eine Erzählung Achim von Arnims,'* to appear in *Aurora* (1978). Perhaps Arnim's sympathetic portrayal of Stauffen was influenced in part by the stepson of his friend Reichardt, who also served as a *Rittmeister* in the French army (cf Steig II, 70).

8. The title's use of *Begegnen,* rather than the more concrete *Begegnung,* might well suggest this broader perspective.

9. Heinz Günter Helmstedt, 'Symbolik der Geschichte bei Ludwig Achim von Arnim' (diss. Göttingen, 1956), pp. 164 ff.

10. This scene, indeed the whole story, shows the inadequacy of Paul Aron's contention that 'Die Helden und Heldinnen der Novellen Arnims sind eher moralische als leidenschaftliche Naturen. Sie wissen ihre Seele höheren Idealen aufzuopfern, gehen an ihrer Leidenschaft nicht zugrunde, auch wenn ihre Liebe unglücklich ist' ('Achim von Arnim als Novellist' [diss. Frankfurt, 1925], p. 83).

11. False reconciliations (including that between Julie and Constanze [p. 772]) are parodied by the police inspector: 'ich . . . glaube die Genugtuung mit mir nehmen zu können, daß durch meine Zwischenkunft der häusliche Zwist in Frieden ausgeglichen ist. Solch eine Begutigung ist der schönste Lohn aller meiner Tätigkeit, ja wenn ich einst von hinnen scheide, werden die Leute sagen, sie haben einen guten Mann begraben' (p. 767).

12. The series of stories about old maids in *Gräfin Dolores* (I, 135 ff) recalls Christ's parable.

13. In the Goethe-Schiller Archiv in Weimar (Nr. 97, U 28). The title and date ('nach 1806') are by another hand. I am grateful to Dr. Karl-Heinz Hahn for his permission to use this material, and to the American Council of Learned Societies for the grant that enabled me to visit the archives.

14. E.g., in *Angelika, die Genueserin* (II, 680 ff). For another discussion of Arnim's ontology, cf my 'Some Correspondences between Arnim's *Majoratsherren* and Fichte's Concept of the *Ich,' Monatshefte,* 68 (1976), 51-9.

15. Cf Knaack, pp. 43 f, and Steig I, 312 ff.

16. For Arnim's views on the necessity of this reconciliation, cf '"Was soll geschehen im Glücke." Ein unveröffentlichter Aufsatz Achim von Arnims,' ed. Jörn Göres, *Jb. d. Dt. Schillerges.*, 5 (1961), 196-221.

17. This theme appears again and again in Arnim's works: an orphaned state consistently represents distorted or stagnated human development. As in the case of Brentano the theme is in part autobiographical. Arnim lost his mother at birth, and his father, for the price of 1000 *Taler,* relinquished all parental rights to the maternal grandmother. She seems to have cared for Arnim and his brother conscientiously, but without warmth, and the boy's strongest affections were reserved for his uncle, Graf von Schlitz. Since the submission of this article Helene M. Kastinger-Riley has published *Ludwig Achim von Arnims Jugend- und Reisejahre* (Bonn, 1978).

18. Cf, for example, the misleading prophecy in *Raphael und seine Nachbarinnen* (III, 252, 271, 275).

19. For a discussion of the tragic consequences implied in the delegation of responsibility, cf E. M. Wilkinson and L. A. Willoughby, 'The Blind Man and the Poet,' *German Studies Presented to W. H. Bruford* (London, 1962), pp. 29-57.

## Lawrence O. Frye (essay date 1982)

SOURCE: Frye, Lawrence O. "Mesmerism and Masks: Images of Union in Achim von Arnim's *Hollins Liebeleben* and *Die Majoratsherren*." *Euphorion: Zeitschrift Für Literaturgeschichte* 76, nos. 1-2 (1982): 82-99.

[*In the following essay, Frye investigates Arnim's use of mesmerism, an eccentric healing science popular during the Romantic period, as a narrative motif in the works* Hollins Liebeleben *and* Die Majoratsherren.]

The presence of the mesmerist presumes a sick patient, whose ill health has been caused, according to the mesmerist, by some obstacle to the natural flow of that invisible magnetic fluid which inhabits all forms of existence in our universe, from the celestial to the earthly and in animal as in mineral. When Arnim opens his *Majoratsherren* with reference to the oddities which the illustrator Chodowiecki has preserved for us, with their glimpse into the heights of spiritual clarity of those days (33),[1] he may well have the engraving from 1790 in mind in which the magnetist, in a room illu-

mined only by candlelight, passes his outstretched hand over a woman in an apparent magnetic sleep.[2] While the mesmerist went about his healing with the appropriate stroking of the subject according to the subject's magnetic flow-paths, the magnetic sleep could also produce other interesting phenomena. In such a sleep the subject might function as a medium, crossing the borders of time, space, and matter. If the spirit of earlier or coming times, or other places and other lives should then seem to speak through the subject, it would do so as through a so-called sixth sense, also variously called a clairvoyant or prophetic sense. The normal five senses are turned off to the outside sensory world: the body—whether in a magnetic (or hypnotic) sleep, a somnambulistic, or a catatonic state—is dead to the world; the conscious mind sleeps, while the unconscious wakes.

Although others have not recognized the applicability of mesmerism to the two works under discussion here, we will proceed of different mind.[3] Arnim's first work, **Hollins Liebeleben** (1802), introduces the role of the mesmerist in a relatively conventional manner as a single episode (28-33).[4] While the episode is brief, its crucial consequences carry through to the conclusion of the action. Nevertheless, it begins with the frivolity of a parlor game, thus in the theatrical spirit in which mesmerist sessions were treated by many. Hollin is mesmerist, his beloved Marie and her mother are the subjects; it is a family affair, with Marie's father and brother attending. Magnetization should provide a cure for an ailment no worse than fatigue. In the late, and more familiar *Die Majoratsherren* (1820), the magnetic relationship has left the parlor, the public and those simple gestures of the magnetizer for a relationship so private and so far off on the fringe of normal societal forms that, except for one brief and practical encounter in Esther's store and the Majoratsherr's final moments at the side of the dead Esther, the entire relationship takes place from window to window over the alley separating the two: in a form not of direct verbal but rather spiritual exchange through a kind of hypnotic trance. The main thread of the narrative is spun out of a series of four such sightings. While Esther's behavior corresponds to that of a disturbed medium, the mesmerist-doctor role of the Majoratsherr has been radically modified: he not only "reads" his subject from afar, but he too is sick and clairvoyant. The window through which he observes Esther at night is a metaphor for his psychic condition: it offers, initially, a small but clear bright spot (*helle Stelle*) for looking into her room in a manner which for him involves the "second sight" of the spiritual—or clairvoyant—eye (*hellsehen*, 38). In this context the otherwise enigmatic reference to himself as only apparently alive (39) is understandable, for as the spiritual eye gains in clarity, the physical eye dims, and with it the functioning of the whole sensory system as it relates to the external world: *Aber, wer auch bis zu der innern Welt vorgedrungen,—wenn auch noch scheinbar lebend, wie ich,—ist dennoch abgestorben bei ihrem Bestreben, ihrer Tätigkeit* (39). The reader is led likewise to believe that Esther, when she lies death-like before being strangled by Vasthi, is in a catatonic state. Even from this rather limited perspective of the *Majoratsherren* one can readily see certain polar tendencies in interplay with one another: a man and a woman who are separated from each other by boundaries in space and to normal sensory interaction, but who make a unique kind of unconscious, telepathic communication; and the one who, by conventional mesmerist expectations, should restore the other to health by virtue of his psychic contact suffers a comparable lack of vitality and effectiveness.

The mesmeric situation which Arnim establishes in both works contributes to a momentum of tragic irony. A small example suggests the possibility: a prophetic sick woman advised the Majoratsherr to come home from Paris with the promise of quietude (37); since he has experienced anything but calm (except ultimately in death), the validity of the prophetic comes into question. A central image in the work is that of the swallows nest which suddenly appears on his special window for viewing Esther. Inasmuch as the nest obstructs his clear vision of Esther, its symbolism is explicated for his own contrasting options: *Nun ihm Esther verborgen, konnte er sich an den lieben Geschöpfen, an ihrer Lust, an ihrem Fleiße nicht satt sehen, es war ihm zu Mute, als ob er sich selbst da anbaue, als hänge sein Glück davon ab, daß sie fertig würden* (44). The choice is between the domestic joy of building one's own fixed, stable nest in this world and in its time, or of letting the spirit take flight, as had the birds, into loftier and unbounded zones (*Im hohen Flug ist kein Gewinn, / Der fern aus Lüften schaut, / Und ging er auch zur Ewigkeit / Er paßt nicht in die Zeit*, 44-45). The real irony lies not so much in the opposition felt between the practical activity of building one's worldly nest and the involuntary visions of second sight, nor in the additional fact that the Majoratsherr's tragic fate seems to be sealed with the disappearance of his nest and the restoration of a clear view into Esther's room: the irony lies more in the fact that the gift of second sight, the sixth sense of the magnetic spirit, which seems to present a tragic obstacle to attaining one's earthly dreams, is the sensorium through which these dreams are most clearly envisioned. This is the more profound irony to that apparent one which has the mesmeric promise of restored health turn into the unresolvable rupture of a unified psychic and physical life. In both **Hollin** and the **Majoratsherren** magnetic contact reveals an inextricable, bond be-

tween male and female, and radiating out from that bond a kind of life-web of unification through time and space. However, the construction of this unification image with real materials is another matter. Both works, after they grant brief physical contact to their respective pairs, separate the lovers and allow no direct, conscious, verbal communication to take place until the end. But then, at reunion, communication is as from mask to mask; and union is not for living but in death.

Compared to the manner in which Arnim presents manifestations of the mesmerized subject in these works, E. T. A. Hoffmann's portrayal is both much more dramatically ambivalent and threatening. While on the one hand the liberation of the spirit from its corporeal prison and its flight to a so-called higher life is celebrated, on the other the frightening external features of the magnetic couple—electric sparks, seizures, demonic and petrifying eyes—as well as the spiritual, mental bondage in which the magnetizer can put his subject are underscored. In the latter vein one reads in *Die Automate*: *Ich sehe nun wohl, daß dem unsichtbaren Wesen, das sich uns durch den Türken auf eine geheimnisvolle Weise mitteilt, Kräfte zu Gebote stehen, die mit magischer Gewalt unsre geheimsten Gedanken beherrschen. . . .*[5] The ambiguity of such sensations and perceptions is recorded in Hoffmann's *Der Magnetiseur,* when Marie writes:

> *. . . wie er in krampfhafter Bewegung seltsame Kreise mit den Armen und Händen beschrieb. Sein Gesicht, sonst so ruhig und ernst, war zur grausigen Larve verzogen, und aus seinen glutroten Augen schlängelten sich in ekelhafter Schnelle blanke, glatte Basiliske, wie ich sie sonst in den Lilienkelchen zu erblicken wähnte. . . . er [Alban] lebt ja in meinem Innern und weiß meine geheimsten Gedanken. . . . Es ist nicht allein der Körper, den er gesund zu erhalten weiß, nein!—es ist der Geist, den er dem höhern Leben zuführt.*[6]

The mesmerist Alban intentionally moves into areas for which mesmerists had become fascinatingly notorious by the end of the eighteenth century. Theatrical scenarios with strange apparati and gestures are utilized in order to confuse and captivate. Moreover, the theoretically medical relationship of mesmerist-patient often, so one suspected, moves into an immorally manipulated erotic relationship of male-female. In the case of Alban, the erotic aspect is programmatically expanded to become the total subjugation and control—in the name of cure, in the name of love—of Marie. As Alban expounds:

> *Ist es denn nicht lächerlich zu glauben, die Natur habe uns den wunderbaren Talisman, der uns zum König der Geister macht, anvertraut, um Zahnweh oder Kopfschmerz, oder was weiß ich sonst, zu heilen?—Nein,*

*es ist die unbedingte Herrschaft über das geistige Prin-*
*zip des Lebens, die wir, immer vertrauter werdend mit*
*der gewaltigen Kraft jenes Talismans, erzwingen.[7] . . . .*
*Nur meines Blicks, meines festen Willens bedurfte es,*
*sie in den sogenannten somnambulen Zustand zu*
*versetzen, der nichts anders war, als das gänzliche*
*Hinaustreten aus sich selbst und das Leben in der*
*höheren Sphäre des Meisters. Es war mein Geist, der*
*sie dann willig aufnahm und ihr die Schwingen gab,*
*dem Kerker, mit dem sie die Menschen überbaut hatten*
*zu entschweben.[8]*

Here in Hoffmann, the mesmeric relationship alone embraces the polar forces of good and evil, of heavenly potential and diabolical intent and destructive end. In Arnim's narratives the cosmic ladder from earth to airy regions, from hell to heaven, also has its place: included within the range of mesmeric perceptions, but not as part of the mesmerist's attitude and procedure. Hoffmann also lingers with the uncanny sensations of being mesmerized and then presents the act of the subject's hidden thoughts and spirit being brought to the surface and revealed: as liberation from their corporeal and individuated confinement, and/or as possession and enslavement under the will of the mesmerist. Arnim does not sensationalize nor problematize the mesmerist's role in this fashion. The possibility of liberating the spirit from any fixed and finite form is certainly an interest which mesmerism may satisfy. But erotic or psychic domination, while it is otherwise of extensive interest to him, falls outside the domain of his magnetic encounters. In fact, the heightened spiritual sensitivity prevailing during such encounters tends to render both parties insensitive to physical stimuli for their own sake. Arnim's male figures in particular—in contrast to Hoffmann's Alban—suffer from a certain impotence of will in such situations. If one should speak of the bondage of either character in a magnetic relationship, then it is rather a Hollin or Majoratsherr who is entrapped by his images of the beloved.

In speaking of bondage and liberation, one may begin with the peculiarly personal form of the problem in Arnim, in which the direct avenue of verbal communication is interrupted. This fettering of the tongue establishes the clear task of finding some alternate form of expression for the spirit, for satisfying *die tief geheime Sehnsucht des Herzens, aus der verschlossenen Brusthöhle hinaus blicken zu können* (III,33). The quest for union of two lovers thus is coupled with the task of liberation: liberation, in the general sense, of the hidden, inner spirit and, as a specific aspect, of impeded verbalization. The other side of liberation for Arnim is the self-destructive danger of the spirit fleeing the present for some higher home—*als ob jenes Menschengeschlecht sich zu voreilig einer höheren Welt genahet habe* (III, 33).

But the question of liberation is not restricted to the inner spirit. It extends to the demand for personal rights, material and social, and to accompanying changes in social and political structures. In order to do so effectively, Arnim's view of the historical period in which the action takes place must offer a spectrum of forces and tendencies rich and diverse enough to be refracted within the characters as if their own private worlds were the sole loci of such multi-dimensionality. So one views the historical setting less straight-on than indirectly. As in the opening to *Die Majoratsherren,* we are to see not the main figures and events of the time, but rather reflections in miniature of its irregularities, peculiarities, and what the eye can only catch indirectly and with some distortion. Thus the relevance of a Chodowiecki: *Wir durchblättern eben einen älteren Kalender, dessen Kupferstiche manche Torheiten seiner Zeit abspiegeln* (III, 33). Perspective and thematics merge in a period full of secret societies, exorcists, prophets, etc. Arnim is engaged in a kind of archaeology of the covert. These texts consequently seem to link two temporally contrasting perspectives: from historicizing narrational positions which excavate shards of uncompleted and broken portraits of a time still impinging on the present; and from the individual voices which, if in vain, tried to express their unified visions of the future. The prophetic and the historical views coincide only partially; deciphering arts that they both are, they do illuminate each other.

The relationship between narrating voice and narrative is fairly clear in *Die Majoratsherren.* One narrates about a period of but days in the 1780's for the major portion of the narrative, then to spin a remaining thread, after the death of the Majoratsherr and Esther, quickly into the last years of the first decade of the new century. The moment of narration is roughly anywhere from after 1806/7 into the second decade—up to the time of actual composition at the end of the decade. The narrator stops just short of covering the author's, Arnim's, own lifetime; the personal narrational connection is also established in the opening lines with the note *daß unsre früheren Jahre ihr* [jener Zeit] *zugehörten* (33). The point of view is initially that of an antiquarian of the arcane, who, in the last few pages on the lieutenant and his lady of the court, then functions more as caricaturist of the ridiculous, until he concludes in the final paragraph with the voice of a collective memory of the more recent, lamentable past. Historically, as one knows, he dwells on a brief period preceding the French Revolution (explicitly mentioned in the first lines of the story and later envisioned in the lieutenant's collection of coats-of-arms, 41); although the piece was presumably written in the post-Napoleon years, the vantage point reached narratively in the final paragraph is the Napoleonic era of German occupation after 1806 (Kontinentalsperre). In this course of development, the imprisoned and beleaguered spirit in pre-revolutionary days (Majoratsherr and Esther) has been released in death from body and world to find its rest before the storm of war. But in the other strand of action, the demand for one's rights and the accompanying change in the social power structure (Lieutenant and Vasthi) from pre-revolutionary days has been answered with the desired turn of Fortune's wheel and material success—as well as with spiritual and political subjugation (Lieutenant and Europe). Both lines of action are moved by desires for freedom, albeit with different biases, and both are rewarded with a form of freedom, but at opposite ends from each other. Needs of the material world (portrayed as rather beastially ludicrous) are satisfied, as well as those of the spirit (signs of angels and regained paradise): but not in harmony with each other. And what either party projected for itself as a desirable future does not match what one reviews from the later historical vantage point.

Late 1801 is the time of composition of ***Hollins Liebeleben.*** The letters are not dated by years, but the epistolary narrative must run from 10 December [1800] to 28 October [1801], with the action of the appended narrative by *Frank an den Herausgeber* following quickly thereafter. (Assuming that Arnim could not record *Maria Stuart* from the June, 1800 Weimar premiere, his knowledge of it for the performance rendered in Frank's narrative came after publication in April, 1801.) Because of the epistolary form and the contemporary material in the letters and in Frank's report one gains the impression of narrations out of the present: from plentiful allusions to events from the 1790's (for example, works published by Tieck and Goethe; the life of Horace Benedikt von Saussure, who died in 1799 and whose life and works are the subject of the paper by Odoardo which is appended to the rest of the novel; politically divided duelling fraternities; and the drama by Schiller, which brings the work into 1801). Other than Goethe's analogous use of the *Hamlet* performance in *Wilhelm Meister,* Arnim's incorporation of the *Maria Stuart* performance is not only an artistic event in a work of fiction but an historical event as well for dating the moment of fictional action in non-fictional time. While the narrator (and author) in ***Die Majoratsherren*** looks back to an historical period just beyond the pale of personal memory for the bulk of his narrative, the narrators in ***Hollins Liebeleben*** (both epistolary and third-person) are immediate witnesses of the action as it either unfolds (epistolary) or as it has just unfolded (third-person narratives of Frank and, to an extra degree of remoteness, Odoardo on Saussure).

However, even in this first literary work by Arnim, matters are slightly more complex. Even in an epistolary novel, Arnim apparently wishes to achieve two basic temporal perspectives: one of simultaneity of action and narration, and another of retrospective narration of an action. The Saussure narrative, with its completely different subject matter, provides the most contrastive retrospective view of a life narrated after its completion. However, what is done here in an obviously distancing, jolting manner demanding reflection on the similarities and differences between Saussure and Hollin, is presumed of us in Frank's narrative as well. In *medias res* of Hollin's epistolary self-narration, Frank intrudes with his retrospective report. Although this may sound like Werther's editor over again, Frank's report gives intimations of death which the epistolary narrative in its hopeful exuberance did not overtly give. Moreover, although Frank is an unexpected witness to Hollin's last days, his narrative allegedly follows many years later: *Ich mußte leider gegenwärtig sein, jetzt nach Jahren erfüllt mich noch innige Wehmut* (64). The key to this internally illogical fiction of a retrospective narration from later years may lie in the comment by Frank on the following page:

> *Du wirst es schon aus den Briefen Hollins wissen, daß Marien aller Briefwechsel mit Hollin unmöglich gewesen, nicht weil es ihr Vater insbesondre gegen ihn, sondern weil er es in Rücksicht aller Männer verboten und die Mutter, welche mit allen Vorzügen und allen Fehlern der vergangenen Zeit begabt war, unerbittlich strenge über diesen Befehl wachte.*

(65)

It is not merely a matter of achieving an objective overview of a completed life but also of a whole past era—a *vergangene Zeit.* The fact that he was writing about his own age did not deter Arnim from suddenly trying to present it as an earlier time (as part II of Brentano's *Godwi* does of part I). Thus Arnim is already trying, awkwardly, to accomplish in ***Hollin*** what he does so well in such later works as ***Die Majoratsherren***: to present—through the private actions of his characters—the public life of two different and contrasting ages, the earlier one through its own eyes as well as from the vantage point of the later age; and the later is the heir, even if it be the heir in some forms of polarity, to the earlier age.

Since there are no contents yet to Frank's "later times", we cannot say what they will have brought, but, as in ***Die Majoratsherren,*** Hollin has a vision definable in terms of freedom and union. His initial sense of restriction is at once vaguely personal as well as national; it is also social and material in nature, for he does not have the status nor means, according to her parents, to court and wed Marie. By the end of the epistolary narrative the personal and material guests for freedom have been answered: *Ich fühle nicht mehr die Fesseln, welche mich niederdrückten, meine Galeerenarbeit ist geendet, süß ist die Ruhe in Deinen Armen. Kaum kann ich Worte finden, so freudig braust alles Leben in mir auf* (63). The succeeding action, which is executed through the performance of *Maria Stuart,* shifts to an ironically different view: Hollin as Mortimer decries the political bondage under the state and opts for a spiritual freedom beyond this material world in death:

> *Was willst du, feiler Sklav der Tyrannei?*
> *Ich spotte deiner, ich bin frei! . . .*
> *Maria, heil'ge bitt für mich!*
> *Und nimm mich zu dir in dein himmlisch Leben!*
>
> (74-75)

In this tragi-comedy of errors Hollin is eternally united with Marie as Maria Stuart (and only momentarily with Marie as the newly recognized mother of his child not to be born, until each dies). Worldly and heavenly forms of freedom and union—as in **Die Majoratsherren,** if not in neatly contrasting pairings—diverge from their envisioned forms, and no unity has been achieved within this vocabulary of freedom.

The attempt to intertwine various kinds of freedom—social, political, and spiritual—may seem capricious on Arnim's part, although that is what he presumes of his settings. The recurring relevance of political freedom and social change in the Arnim works can obviously be attributed to the volatile times and shifting fortunes of European politics which Arnim writes about, whether pre-Revolution, the early stages of the Napoleonic-German wars of 1800-1801, the years of Napoleonic occupation after 1806, or even the post-Napoleonic era of Restoration. To place the occult, particularly in the form of mesmerism, in the foreground of the period of unrest preceding the French Revolution has its historical as well as thematic reasons. Pre-revolutionary Paris was, to be sure, the locus of Mesmer's rise to fame (where he arrived from Vienna in February, 1778).[9] We should note an even more interesting development in mesmerism in the 1780's. While it counted greater numbers of the upper and privileged classes of the ancien régime among its followers (the cost of admission to its sessions may have contributed), in the couple of years before the Revolution it became more strongly associated with the revolutionary movement. On a less doctrinaire side, Mesmer claimed that his "humanity encompasses all ranks of society".[10] More radical splinter groups, represented by such as Nicolas Bergasse, fused the mesmerism and revolutionary movements and sought social change in the name of liberty, egalitarianism and the toppling of tyranny in every form—scientific as well as political.[11]

Healing of body and spirit, uniting of human and cosmic spirit, uniting of human with human, the liberating of the individual psyche, the liberating of the social and political self: historically, mesmerism (or "animal magnetism", as it was often called) cast visions of such extensive dimensions well into the nineteenth century.[12] It gives Arnim's characters a varied, if controversial, new field from which they might construct the stuff of their own dreams. When we consider the occasional coupling in mesmerism of egalitarianism and aristocrats of the ancien régime, we can understand the ambivalence of the Majoratsherr who is privileged to be socially useless and free to turn to higher things of the spirit, but who cannot accept an order which benefits him at others' expense; he accordingly does not make use of the home at his disposal, hands over practical matters and benefits to his cousin, and even considers earning a living for himself: *Ich sollte reich sein auf Unkosten eines Armen? Hab ich nicht manches gelernt, was mir einen Unterhalt verschaffen kann? . . . Fort mit der Sündenlast des Reichtums* (54-55). The attitude which would change the old order to which he has fallen heir has not the resources to be translated into action. What social liberation is accomplished (including the ambiguous reference to the freeing of the Jews from their Ghetto, 67), accompanies his demise, and shall we say the demise of that part of his age which he represents. Although he does not suffer from social privilege, Hollin too tries to blend visions of spiritual and social-political freedom. Exhilarated by the mesmerized Marie, he sees her as a heavenly presence reminiscent of Egmont's dream-vision of Klara—as *mit einer Heiligen-Glorie umgeben* (33). *Ich rief der deutschen Freiheit ein herzlich Lebehoch! Sie alle riefen und tranken mit. Es war mir, als wenn ich hier zuerst die Ahndung einer andern Freiheit fühlte, noch ist mir alles dunkel, aber ich sehe den leuchtenden Punkt, wohin ich eilen muß* (33). We have already witnessed Hollin die frustrated in the realization of his initial vision. What began as a unified vision ends with only its spiritual version of liberation and union for Hollin and the Majoratsherr alike. Social and political versions either dissipate or are gained by others without spiritual content. And, while the comprehensive vision began in a mesmeric context, the visionary himself ends in a comparably fluid dimension of either vision or theatrical performance.

Since there is something incomplete about the execution of the visions of the spirit, one must ask how Arnim translates them into action, into time and space. Hollin's mesmeric encounter with Marie indicates how, "as if transfigured, she expressed views which she otherwise could never have had": it must be

> *daß unser Wesen nur in gewissem Sinne auf die Grenzen des Körpers eingeschränkt sei, daß es durch die*

*ganze unendliche Kette seiner Bedingungen mit einem Körper verbunden in allen verteilt, besonders in der Luft, als der eigentlichen Werkstatt des Lebens, im schnellen Vorübergehen des befreundeten Lebens, das Verbinden des Getrennten, das Bild der Vereinigung alles Lebens erkennt.*

(32)

The revelations of dissolving forms entrance Hollin. As he hovers over the beauty of Marie: *Du kennst den eigentümlichen schauerlichen Eindruck des Zwielichts, in dem alle bestimmte Gestaltung schwindet . . .* (31). The mesmerized eye penetrates the surfaces of matter and consciousness, and thus also the divisions of time and space. As all fixed forms dissolve, one senses the union of all that is separated in life—*das Verbinden des Getrennten, das Bild der Vereinigung alles Lebens.*

A formative process is further required to communicate such revelations of the spirit. Rather than mesmerism itself being so applicable here, it is the imagination which plays a role in creating images. (The distinction avoids the contemporary accusation of some that the voice of the mesmerized patient, of the medium, was simply that of an excited imagination.)[13] Just before the mesmerism scene, Hollin feels his innermost feelings being unlocked by Marie:

*meine heimlichsten Gefühle und Wünsche eröffneten sich, alle alten Aussichten und tausend neue für mein künftiges Leben unterwarfen sich ihr, die wunderbaren Sprünge ihrer Phantasie führten ihr meine ganze Welt in kurzen Bildern vorbei, alles schien durch ihre Mühe sich zu veredeln.*

(30)

The higher world likewise takes shape in the imagination in *Die Majoratsherren*:

*und es erschien überall durch den Bau dieser Welt eine höhere, welche den Sinnen nur in der Phantasie erkenntlich wird: in der Phantasie, die zwischen beiden Welten als Vermittlerin steht, und immer neu den toten Stoff der Umhüllung zu lebender Gestaltung vergeistigt, indem sie das Höhere verkörpert.*

(63-64)

One may note that the imagination is a creative agent reliant on sense perceptions as well as the existence of a covert, higher world of the spirit. The mesmeric situation functions to release the spirit. The imagination then assumes the function of giving it form—or, from a different point of view, of ennobling, of modifying sense perceptions according to the spirit.[14] Since the imagination and art are not identical, how the imagination renders its images, how and in what form it communicates them is the question relevant to the following discussion of the literary text.

The total vision is described spatially, as one of interconnection and union, as a higher world made visible, as a living configuration. But its execution is described temporally as a concatenation of images whose significance is non-mimetic and whose progression is discontinuous, in capricious leaps. Since Arnim suggests that matter, as the object of our sense perceptions, comes to life only as it is infused with higher meaning through the imagination, such matter becomes representational: what the imagination creates, and sees, is a kind of signifying mask. The mask is meant to be neither raw life nor a higher world but rather a construct mediating between the two. It is what Arnim calls variously an image or symbol. Hollin suggests in this vein: *sei Dir mein Wort das Schönste, Heiligste Deiner Gefühle und dieses nur Symbol des Höchsten, was du ahndest, und so in unendlicher Reihe fort alles nur Symbol, Andeutung des Höhern* (40). This endless concatenation of symbols which approximates an absolute seems to be Arnim's version of the Schlegelian irony in which one must attempt to express the inexpressible, aware of the impossibility during the act itself and aware of the discrepancy between the word which expresses and what is to be expressed. One must also leap the gap between the discontinuity of the form and the higher continuity, or unity, which it signifies.

Of particular interest in Arnim is his method of presenting mimetic and non-mimetic material in sequence: of concatenating raw material and the imagination's image of that material—players and masks side-by-side. The order of sequence and the degree of congruity between mask and player become crucial. We consider some examples. The Majoratsherr visits the old lady of the court (*Hofdame*): from a combination of screeching tree-frog and suspect flowers he thinks he sees a dozen infirm diplomats taking notice; in a black poodle he sees the incarnation of the devil (53). These are simple examples of rendering the image of the imagination: first the raw material of perception and then the signifying mask of the imagination (via second sight) is given. The interpretive act is even included in the connecting verbs of believed to see and considered. The perspective is rendered here by the narrative voice and gives an effect of distance and of witnessing the poetic process at work. What the images, or masks, achieve, which the simple objects alone could not, is a scenario of the grotesque, and of an ugly and evil presence. The Majoratsherr's special gift is introduced earlier, when the collection of French coats-of-arms assumes a miniature dramatic form, in which old knights find their heraldic emblems and arms too decayed to use effectively; the dramatized mask more effectively signifies the impending revolutionary change than does the static collection (41). The omission of narrative mediation and of traces of mental or poetic translation also gives the mask (even as mental drama) a certain existential autonomy competing with that of the raw material.

The effect of autonomy of the imagination as mask, and thus the impression of realness, increases when the mask precedes the bare face. We think of the Majoratsherr's sighting of Death sitting on a carriage with Famine and Suffering between the horses (before it is corrected to a physician on call with a lean coachman, 41); or of Vasthi wearing a black raven on her head (before it is reported as a black kerchief, 46-47). A similar method is used later in a concatenated manner to produce a small segment of action: he runs downstairs and encounters a swarm of monstrous, feathered shapes, whose red noses hung over their beaks like nightcaps; he then runs up to the attic and sees holy figures sitting quietly around him (57). The raw material for this little drama—as erratic quest in a cosmic house encompassing heaven and hell—is mentioned after the holy figures: *heilige Gestalten, fromme Symbole, weiße Tauben.* His cousin completes the basic picture: doves roosting under the roof, turkeys downstairs (58). These examples all reflect on the focal point of the story-line; the discrepancy between what Esther and the Majorasherr originally were in fact and what they represent, appear to be. At the mid-point of the story we hear: *Sie haben mir in aller Kürze gesagt, ich sei nicht, was ich zu sein—scheine, und ich entgegne darauf, daß auch Sie nicht sind, was Sie scheinen* (51). What each represents is what the other is, or was—thus the formula that one is the other. If they could exchange roles, the masks would disappear. (Esther, stepdaughter of a revolting woman in a socially unacceptable milieu—for Arnim, Jewish—is really the first-born and heir to the Majoratshaus, and daughter of a beautiful woman; the Majoratsherr, first-born of that beautiful woman and heir to the Majoratshaus, is really the illegitimate son of the revolting court-lady). Representational form precedes the knowledge of the original facts. Until their discovery, the story-line is busy decoding them from the interplay of the masks; after their discovery, it is busy trying to unite the couple and, ideally, bridge the discrepancy between mask and player. One is not, however, completely able either to abandon the mask or retrieve the original reality.

With the conventional use of the concept mask, one may think of a configuration which conceals, and when one removes the mask, one discovers the "real" substance underneath: as if the mask were but surface, an esthetic construct, a fiction; and underneath, concealed, lay truth; as if the mask existed on a level of suspicious play, and underneath lay a better, serious level. The situation is not quite so neat with Arnim. The mask is indeed a construct of the imagination and of art. As such it does play with so-called reality, for it rearranges its components with the function of ordering and beautifully structuring one's world. When it comes to truth, Arnim proceeds as if such mask-structures have the potential to reveal it more effectively than one's mere sense-world, for they are the forms in which the spirit has infused and animated the sense-world. There can then be an aspect of play not only in the mask but between the mask and the bare face, as one tries to detect correspondences between the two, or as the two seek balance with each other. Just as the bare face of existence may seem dead and devoid of, or concealing, spirit, the signifying mask may obscure that face for which it is a sign. The mask then plays out a part of its conventional role, that of concealing: while revealing higher meaning, it may conceal the dumb player. Such is momentarily the case in our examples of Esther and Majoratsherr as what they seem to be, of raven before we see the kerchief, of Death riding the carriage before we see the physician.

That there are dangers to concealment under a mask, even when the mask is alive and quite amused with itself, is clearly demonstrated in **Hollin.**[15] Unlike **Die Majoratsherren,** Hollin's masquerades are intentional. The fallacy of his life lies in the intent to translate the play of masks directly into raw reality, to take the imagination not as sign system but as something livable, as what is signified. The confusion of mask with life is fatal, but it characterizes his entire story-line. He applies what he says in the midst of his travels too literally: *Ernst und unverdrossen fange ich an mein Schicksal zu bauen, alle Phantasie muß jetzt zum Leben werden, wozu sonst die volle Kraft dazu?* (42) Both introduction and final reunion with the beloved Marie occur as concealment under a mask. Having first hidden from her sight behind a bush,[16] he then (in Goslar) presents himself at her hotel door as a waiter. Not sure it is Marie who is staying in the next room, and hearing the ring of the mother for the night porter while he serenades the younger unknown beauty with his guitar, he decides on the joke to answer the summons. Hearing the complaint against his other, serenading self, he encounters the real waiter as he is closing the door. The joke has turned against him, for when he discovers that his Marie is in the room, he is in danger of compromising her honor with such an apparent nocturnal visit. The unmediated masquerade is akin to the act of a somnambulist, for it seems *als hätte ich im Schlafe mein Haus angezündet, in dem Wahne eines Lustfeuerwerks und fände mich beim Erwachen in den Flammen* (27-28).

It is appropriate to this incident that one day later the actual mesmerism session occurs, in which he justifies the dissolving of recognizable, fixed shapes in the name of visions from the unconscious. During the ensuing separation from Marie, one remarkable encounter with another woman, Hermine, is like the second act to the waiter scene. Unwitting roles again come dangerously close to determining real actions. The setting is an amusement quarter (15 June; B.s equivalent to Vauxhall): a cacophony of music, rockets, water and light show, vendors, gamblers, and theatrical performance vies with the tumult of nature's own demonstration of a thunder-lightning-rain storm. In this confusion of performances by nature and illusion, Hollin takes cover from the rain with the performer Medea on the otherwise empty stage. While she (Medea-Hermine) is in the one guise, he is taken for her expected lover—until a tree goes up in flames from a lightning strike (47-49). Even after the mistaken identity is recognized, the encounter continues as masquerade when he exchanges his wet clothes for a theatrical costume—until he rushes off this time to help save a burning house (49-50).

Hollin has a growing tendency to live out his life in literal masks as player in an esthetic performance (kept barely away from the literal and metaphorical flames of destruction). This, combined with a couple of succeeding moments of phantasizing, prepares the concluding performance of *Maria Stuart.* His next letter (10 August) describes new friends (Poleni and four daughters) and the transporting effect of their musical concert (memories of Marie, sacred realm of tones): as in the mesmerist session, a dissolving sensation is felt; now it is of his hopes. The sad verse of a folksong, rather than reality, is the source of his presentiments, by which he now identifies freedom with death (51-52). The second letter after this (5 October) adds further images from within: in a critical fever Hollin dreams of Marie, dressed in black with a regal crown, touching the forehead of his own dead body (59). Images of his own life, past and future, are regularly seen in the mind's eye as shapes only tenuously connected to reality—through Marie's hypnotic trance, in music, in a fever dream. Hollin is conditioned to enact the masks of his imagination by way of the comparably fictional enactment of a life in *Maria Stuart.*

The partial rendering of *Maria Stuart* accomplishes a number of things in *Hollin.* It constructs as continuous action and decipherable meaning what hitherto has accumulated as a concatenation of discontinuous aspects and forms—as both story-line and epistolary form. It executes the union of Marie and Hollin, desired and postponed for months, although it does so under the masks of Maria Stuart and Mortimer. It also expresses the freedom sought, although as a spiritual freedom in death, not a political freedom nor the freedom to live their lives together. These dramatic masks are a consistent form of enactment for the mesmeric images. While

both are constructs of the mind with their own autonomy, the dramatic form of performance allows physical participation, and thus the greater illusion that body and spirit are in concert.

And there comes the tragic irony. Hollin makes his role his life, and Mortimer's suicide is his own (who earlier could neither condone nor condemn suicide). Not surprisingly, while the role determines the life, the reality with which he infuses his role heightens the esthetic effect (70 ff.).[17] Mask and bare face coincide but do not harmonize. The foundation to this irony is that both Hollin's and Marie's readings of their lives in preparation for this reunion have been false: a delusion for the illusion by which they now conclude them. Misperceptions that each has been untrue in his love are corrected too late, only after the drama has been played out. One cannot say that there was no truth or validity to somnambulistic visions, or to any other mask-scene. The error lay in the manner in which correspondence was found between them and lived reality. That there *is* a correspondence between mask and lived reality is the ultimate demonstration of the *Maria Stuart* performance; but the nature of the correspondence is again askew and consequently destructive. In the end, the original mesmeric visions are not executed faithfully in the esthetic performance which seems to give them coherent life. Coherence and inspiring beauty can be misleading features, presumably, in both vision and dramatic performance; and this is borne out in part by the altered form which coherence and beauty suffer between vision and final performance. Only fulfillment in spirit is found, with nothing left for life. The misreading of life has contributed to this. One may conclude further that by taking the mask literally, by taking its representational value as material value, one has emptied it of its full spiritual potential. In this respect too, then, the concept of mask can be reduced to a conventional meaning of lifeless artifact and empty shell which only feigns the life and meaning it signifies.

The function and form of the *Maria Stuart* performance in **Hollin** are assumed in **Die Majoratsherren**—more subtly and cohesively—by the brief concluding scene casting Adam, Eve, and Angel of Death; it too has its real life counterparts visibly present and performing on their realistic level: Esther, Vasthi and Majoratsherr (62-64). As in *Maria Stuart,* the two levels, mask and reality, infuse and determine one another. This Adam-Eve scene is also the culmination and integration of earlier disjointed pieces which have gradually been falling together from sources both factual and psychic in nature. Unlike **Hollin, Die Majoratsherren** presents no literal theatrical performances or masquerades. The mind does the staging of psychic material. As indicated earlier, such moments have the effect of autonomous actions; it is thus as if both Majoratsherr and reader are witnessing an actual performance in which the likewise witnessing narrative voice complements the use of dialogue. Esther's participation, which provides the actual gestures, is transmitted via the Majoratsherr-narrative eye.[18] Psychic material and normal sensory activity are so interlocked in their rendering that transitions may go unnoticed, and one may be momentarily confused (Majoratsherr and reader alike) as to which level of reality, or of fiction, one is on.[19]

To get some picture of how the different material is assembled, we recall that there are four telepathic sessions at the window. Each is occasioned by the sound of a shot which puts Esther into her trance. It is not until just before the fourth session that Majoratsherr and reader discover that only the inner ear of Esther, and through her that of the Majoratsherr, perceives the shot which, traumatically for Esther, marked the suicide of an earlier, rather mindless suitor (59). At this moment in the first three sessions Esther speaks in different voices, gesticulates, and sometimes dances as if she is hosting an elegant social affair; the Majoratsherr, as psychic stage director, visualizes what Esther speaks and mimes. In the second (49-52) and third sessions (56-57), he is an invisible fellow actor; in the third session, the effect of theatrical performance becomes content when a masquerade ball takes place. Toward the end of his first session (42-43) he also sees the figure of his mother take a *beflügelte Lichtgestalt* with Esther's transfigured features from Esther's forehead.

Different material from outside these sessions is processed into them: after the first session, the Majoratsherr is told that the first-born steer and rams are the (useless) Majoratsherren of the Jews, and their roaring and pawing in the cemetery signifies the death of one of the clan. This piece of lore anticipates the death of Esther and hence also deciphers the allegorical figure of light already seen. A dream provides additional material from the Majoratsherr's unconscious: his hopelessly fatal love for Esther takes allegorical form when Esther appears to him as Angel of Death, in a dress with countless eyes on it and offering a goblet of death which he drinks (45). There will eventually be three Angels of Death: Esther for the Majoratsherr, and his mother as well as Vasthi for Esther (we might add a very metaphorical fourth in the lieutenant for the Majoratsherr, 60); we learn only late (59) the practical function of the Angel of Death which Vasthi fills—for purposes of removing the Jewish dead quickly, to choke them as a seal of finality. The Majoratsherr's reading provides material on Adam and Eve: according to which Eve (read Esther) usurps the position of the first woman Lilith (read Majoratsherr's mother, alias Esther's real mother), who then returns as the Angel of Death. Infor-

mation on the real identity of Esther is overheard in part on the street (49, is injected into the second trance session where it is supplemented by Esther's information on him, all of which is then edited with information from the lady of the court (alias the Majoratsherr's real mother, 53-55).

One further factor should be mentioned which, although it does not re-emerge directly in the Adam-Eve scene, plays a role in the hopelessness of the love between Esther and the Majoratsherr. The arrival of Esther's hapless, dependent fiance (55) is re-worked in the masquerade of the third trance session: he does acrobatics and tricks to earn money (57). The masquerade is meant here to assume a grotesque, repulsive form; the mask, and art, are reduced to mere entertainment for material gain. At this moment, more sharply than in ***Hollin,*** mask and art sink to forms devoid of higher, spiritual content.[20] We must believe the scene also reflects on the Majoratsherr: who wondered whether he could turn his own artistic accomplishments into bread-earning means (54-55) and, with equal hesitancy, is unable to come to Esther's rescue. While the fiance remains at the bottom, material and grotesque rung of the esthetic ladder, the Majoratsherr is at the top, most spiritual, but terrestrially useless rung.

In the fourth and final trance, the allegory of love reunites Adam and Eve in paradise. Esther and the Majoratsherr may be that couple in spirit. The terrestrial Esther, however, receives the poisonous drop from the sword, then washed in the goblet by the Angel of Death (read the Majoratsherr's would-be mother, alias Lilith, alias Esther's real mother), in dress of glittering eyes;[21] the Angel receives the winged soul of Esther, returned home. Such is the dramatic vision which follows Vasthi's real role as Angel of Death. Two types of sight, two levels of existence side by side and balancing each other, just as the Adam and Eve scene is the spiritual signifier of an otherwise dead sign in the room—an actual picture of Adam and Eve which is reported after the vision (64).[22]

On the allegorical level of second sight, there where the masks of Adam, Eve, sword-carrying Angel and winged soul perform as constructs of his psychic vision, the Majoratsherr does not appear. As always in such moments of second sight, his body, consciousness and will are turned off. He has created the performance alone. It must be said that Esther's own trance (more properly, catatonic state) ended with her death which, with Vasthi's help, immediately precedes this scene; the signal that this is purely what he sees and constructs, not a transmission of what occurs in Esther's trance, is the extinguished light (*da erlosch das Licht,* 63);[23] the winged figure of light from the first session also appeared at such a moment.

The truth of the performance which the Majoratsherr has projected into Esther's room demands his participation, for his part of the story-line is still missing. We recall that before he leaps the alley, it occurs to him that his whole scene might have relevance to this world's reality (*daß etwas Wirkliches auch für diese Welt an allem dem sein könne,* 64). He refers to Vasthi having strangled Esther. And he jumps—unconsciously (*seiner selbst unbewußt,* 64); leaping was never one of his conscious talents (42, 56). His proof of murder lies in the goblet of water, in which Esther's Angel of Death (alias her true mother) washed her sword, according to his psychic drama. He drinks and dies—by a suicide more astounding than Hollin's. Within the context of his visionary drama, Esther has now become his Angel of Death. Vasthi and the goblet of water have, however, nothing logically to do with each other. Vasthi may also be viewed as an Angel of Death, but the goblet belongs to the one in the mask of his vision. Consequently, neither the mode by which he gets to the murder site— jumping unconsciously—nor the type of proof used there belongs squarely in the conscious world of will and empirical logic. They both derive from a world of representation (*Vorstellung*—as both idea and performance). Ironically, the Majoratsherr's impulse to jump is to establish the link to the natural world. It therefore seems inappropriate to suggest that the leap is either into faith or a Fichtean leap from the natural world to that of the spirit.[24] Except for actually dying, he remains in the same representational—or spiritual— world which he was in before leaping.

Hollin lives out Mortimer's death in *Maria Stuart* partly as an amusing way to meet Marie again and partly from error of perception vis-à-vis reality. The Majoratsherr's error is not one of perception. Such is one change in approach since the early **Hollin.** But he too errs by applying the mask-shapes of his perceptions as literally true in real situations. The real situations show no enhancement from the confusion. The masks appeal to one by virtue of the structured, significant form they assume, like all systems of the imagination and art; and the effect of a higher realness may cause one to forget they are but constructs fed by two worlds. Moreover, we have seen how, as they reach their final, most structured form and pull their creator in to participate and test their realness, they present a modified reduction in the original comprehensiveness of vision. The fact that this reduction is weighted on the spiritual side to the elimination of the practical (an increasingly unaccommodating reality contributes to the selection of figures like Maria Stuart, Mortimer, Adam and Eve, who barely find relevance in the world as it is) suggests they are programmed to stand in for life, but not to benefit it directly. It also suggests that the visionary mode of mesmerism tends eventually to determine and reduce the contents in execution. So the masks assume a most spiritual form in these final scenes; elsewhere, where figures are devoid of vision and spirit (lieutenant, or Esther's helpless fiancé), the masks may be reduced to the extreme of spiritless caricatures of life.

The Majoratsherr may not really fail "to see his life and death as a dialectical process which culminates in the reconciliation of his materialistic and spiritualistic natures",[25] but he does fail to execute it. That his development need be "a process through temporal reality to spiritual transcendence" is misleading,[26] for it suggests a merely linear, one-directional development; while such a process is certainly indicated, here and elsewhere in Arnim, the changing interplay with the material world and the various stages which reconciliation has reached are of more consequence than the simple tendency alone.[27] In both **Hollin** and **Die Majoratsherren** reconciliation, the ultimate *Bild der Vereinigung, is* represented in shifting structures: as idea in the mesmerism scene in **Hollin** and piece by piece in the more sophisticated mesmeric scenes in the **Majoratsherren**; the theatrical performance of *Maria Stuart* and the psychic performance of Adam and Eve (plus leap) are the culminating forms of representing union. They are not complete however, and remain at the stage of representation. The physical participation of actor and of leaper is crucial, for it provides a point of intersection between mask and material world. That point of intersection verifies the force of the mask in life and its relevance to it; that the intersection is in death shows what need there remains to find a more conscious and complete relevance to existence as something livable. Lack of consciousness and involuntary behavior (and, it seems, insufficient direct verbal exchange) were a peculiarity of the mesmeric condition and continue to inhabit the mask forms of experience which ensue from it. Tragically here (other than, say, in **Der tolle Invalide** or **Raphael**), matter and spirit, and the various freedoms, remain unreconciled polarities: overcome to a degree *in* the masks produced by the imagination and art, but never fully liberated from the form of masks.

### Notes

1. Achim von Arnim, *Sämtliche Romane und Erzählungen,* 3 Bde., ed. Walther Migge (München: Hanser, 1962-65), III (1965). Further references in the text to *Die Majoratsherren* are to this volume.

2. Cf. Walter Artelt, *Der Mesmerismus in Berlin,* in: *Abhandlungen der Geistes- und Sozialwissenschaftlichen Klasse,* no. 6 (Akademie der Wissenschaften und der Literatur in Mainz; Wiesbaden: Steiner, 1965), 474 & illus. l.

3. Strangely, only Arnim's early scientific studies on electricity and magnetism and mesmerism's known relevance in the *Gräfin Dolores* are alluded to by Maria Tatar, *Spellbound. Studies on Mesmerism and Literature* (Princeton: Princeton University Press, 1978), 75-76. Only passing reference is made to the "psychology" of the Majoratsherr, although the link between his "hallucinations", or imagination, and the creative act is made in the illuminating essay by Heinrich Henel, *Arnim's 'Majoratsherren'*, in: *Weltbewohner und Weimaraner. Ernst Beutler zugedacht*, ed. Benno Reifenberg Emil Staiger (Zürich, 1960), 83-85. A note suggests that mesmerism can not "provide us with any explanation" in Bruce Duncan, *Some Correspondences Between Arnim's 'Majoratsherren' and Fichte's Concept of the Ich*, Monatshefte 68 (1976), 52, 59 (note 11). Only a recent paper, which I have just received, traces connections between Jung-Stilling and *Die Majoratsherren*: Gustav Beckers, *Phänomene des 'Tierischen Magnetismus' in Achim von Arnims Novelle Die Majoratsherren*, in: *Akten des VI. Internationalen Germanisten-Kongresses* (Verlag Peter Lang: Basel, 1980), 453-460.

4. Reported in Hollin's letter from the Brocken, 19-20 April: Arnim, II (1963). Further references in the text to *Hollins Liebeleben* are to this volume.

5. *Die Automate* (1814), in: *Die Serapions-Brüder*, II (1819): E. T. A. Hoffmann, *Die Serapions-Brüder* (Darmstadt: Wissenschaftliche Buchgesellschaft, 1968), 333.

6. In: *Fantasiestücke*, II (1814): E. T. A. Hoffmann, *Fantasie- und Nachtstücke* (Darmstadt: Wissenschaftliche Buchgesellschaft, 1968), 168.

7. *Fantasiestücke*, 170.

8. *Fantasiestücke*, 173. For an example of the reputed erotic manipulation of the patient, see Artelt, 404-405.

9. Robert Darnton, *Mesmerism and the End of the Enlightenment in France* (Cambridge, Harvard University Press, 1968), 48.

10. Darnton, 73.

11. Darnton, 73-125.

12. One important student of mesmerism in the more circumspect Berlin circles was Carl Alex. Ferd. Kluge, whose *Versuch einer Darstellung des animalischen Magnetismus als Heilmittel* (1811; 1815; 1819) was important for Hoffmann. I find no mention of Kluge in Tatar. Cf. also Artelt, 418.

13. See, for example, Christoph Wilhelm Hufeland's charge from 1784 (reprinted 1794): Artelt, 399. Others, including Hufeland later, found no influence of the imagination on mesmeric phenomena: cf. Artelt, 414.

14. Henel differentiates between the psychological phenomenon (hallucinations), the imagination, and the creative act only as aspects of the same thing (83-85). Arnim presents the line connecting the unconscious, the imagination, and the creative act from an intriguing perspective in *Raphael und seine Nachbarinnen*: the supposed "ape" (alias baker Bäbe) paints precisely in the style of Raphael (continuations of the Psyche-series); he executes these artistic doubles as an "Automat" following the instructions of the master while the latter is in a somnambulistic state (III, 252-253, 266-269). Here, as in our other texts: the unconscious is released through magnetization; the unconscious is source for, and assumes creative form; there is a problematic gap between source and execution (Raphael's mind and Bäbe's hand), between the unconscious and the conscious (Bäbe as "Automat" must be an unconscious vessel for Raphael's unconscious); the break in transmission, in the translation of the unconscious into artistic form becomes problematic: the subject matter of the paintings reflects this, for Bäbe's own animal identity (and imagination) emerges and thus a reduction in the spiritual quality of the transmission occurs ("das Geistige wird Schein und Täuschung", 253).

15. I discuss the dangers, as well as the constructive functions, of esthetic forms in Arnim elsewhere.

16. The bush scene, where the two do not meet, is the introduction into Hollin's hide-and-seek syndrome (21). Even before this, Hollin meets Marie's brother, Lenardo, in two forms: as sympathetic acquaintance and as anonymous duelling opponent, whom he nearly kills (16-18).

17. A typical feature in Arnim's works is that as an esthetic role and a greater degree of personal content mix, the esthetic effect is heightened and human danger increased. Cf. note 15.

18. The rendering of the lieutenant solely from a narrative point of view has a decidedly parodistic effect: his appearance, in its extremeness and incongruities, gives the impression of a mask without there being one. Grotesqueness seems to derive, as at times with the Majoratsherr, from an interplay between expected reality and mask forms deviating from it; but with the cousin we are aware that his person is one-dimensional—mask and per-

19. Henel notes that because the narrator does not [always] mediate the Majoratsherr's sightings of Esther, they may seem to be his fantasies; but he nevertheless sees what her voice animates (82). However, Henel stresses that most of what the Majoratsherr sees is based on his own thoughts (even though all of his images are stimulated by effects of other things). Henel seems to seek rational, empirical explanations for what Arnim keeps moving between the rational and the unconscious, the empirical and the spiritual—breaking down barriers between such categories.

20. The shifting effects of masks makes it questionable that Henel's application of the grotesque to the text (after Kayser) is adequate: merely differentiating between the fantastic and the satiric for Majoratsherr-Esther and lieutenant-"Hofdame", respectively (100). Cf. note 18 above.

21. It is unclear why Henel identifies the "beautiful Angel of Death" from the vision as Vasthi, thereby confusing levels of perception and action (89). He tacitly seems to correct the identification later (90-91).

22. Henel claims it is atypical that the spiritual vision (mask) precedes the real phenomenon (93; he means, presumably, the reporting sequence, since the perceptual sequence is often left undetermined). My earlier discussion showed this is not unusual, but rather an essential technique.

23. Henel writes that Adam and Eve appear to Esther (81); he cannot mean the real Esther, for she is already dead by strangulation. He clarifies this later (90-91). He also reminds us that, by the Majoratsherr's own words, one can distinguish between what is seen with "the eye of truth" and what the Majoratsherr gives shape to himself (102). How that is done is not clear, in Henel or in the text for that matter. The Majoratsherr gives us one example ("spiritless" coats-of-arms collection, 41); how this example essentially differs from others is perplexing. One can distinguish between times when Esther's trance-voice is heard and when it is not (whether seeing her with Adam-Eve, or having one's own dream): but all cases involve access to the spirit-unconscious, and all involve a formative process for rendering what is sensed.

24. On the "Sprung in den Glauben" see Henel, 91; on the Fichtean leap see Duncan, 55. There is a goblet of water in the room but the one he relates to is its mask-version from the vision, even if he dies drinking the real version. The action does find its "sinnvollen Höhepunkt" in the death scene (Henel), but the ironies of how seem most relevant.

25. Duncan, 56. Cf. Henel also (76,79).

26. Duncan, 58

27. Cf. note 15 above.

## Roland Hoermann (essay date 1984)

SOURCE: Hoermann, Roland. "Folk Culture, 'Naturposie,' and the *Wunderhorn* of Arnim and Brentano." In *Achim von Arnim,* pp. 19-43. Boston: Twayne Publishers, 1984.

[*In the following excerpt from his study of the author, Hoermann examines Arnim's interest in European folklore, both as a repository of diverse cultural traditions and as a distinctive literary form. He investigates the various influences that informed Arnim's conception of the European folk tradition, including his extensive travels throughout the continent from 1801 to 1804, as well as the pioneering work of such folklorists as Ludwig Tieck.*]

### A Vision of a Golden Age of the Arts

Arnim's extensive European travels between 1801 and 1804 had made him aware of the richness and essential unity of cultural and folk-art traditions in the two dozen disunited German states, in the Hapsburg Austrian Empire, and in Switzerland. He had witnessed firsthand British national unity in the face of English, Scottish, Welsh, and Irish diversity, and he knew that this pluralism had led to an Elizabethan golden age and to a Shakespeare. The British florescence struck Arnim as being comparable to German writing of the Reformation in its "free-wheeling" provincial naturalism and in its multiplicity of forms, styles, and themes—quite apart from that epoch's resemblance to the sociopolitical ferment and awakening national pride of Arnim's own day. Moreover, the younger Romanticists were concerned with countering the rationalistic threat of French hegemony by reemphasizing the pluralizing role of folk culture in maintaining a consciousness of historical models and national continuity.

An early influence on Arnim's and Brentano's involvement with folk culture was their association with Ludwig Tieck. While Tieck promoted the notion of bringing folk materials and chapbooks to the attention of the educated classes, the younger pair felt that these groups were too exclusively attuned to the refinements of the French neoclassical conventions for them to enjoy the rustic charms of popular poetry. Instead, the *Liederbrüder* wished to invert Tieck's formula by popularizing the loftier standards of the "high" tradition within their folk audience, thereby expanding and ennobling the latter's taste.

This mission of popular edification underlies Arnim's letter of July 9, 1802 [I:37 ff.], in which he proposes the founding of an academy for the popular arts. His plan was based on two premises: (1) that the various literary, theater, and musical or dance forms of folk art have always coexisted, their mutual reinforcement thus conforming to the basic philosophy of Romantic syncretism; and (2) that only a rapprochement between the disastrously split "high" and folk-art traditions in German lands could lead to a florescence of German culture—which would be a precondition for any national confederation.

As a first step in the citizenry's realizing its new sense of national identity, Arnim hoped to found a publishing house, while a streamlined system of musical notation was to facilitate the public's acquaintance with the simpler melodies and songs of such composers as Mozart, with an eye toward improving the taste of a maturing populace. A network of hostels throughout the German lands was to serve the newly resurrected craft of minstrelsy, whose members were to be furnished by the folk academy with better and simpler musical instruments, along with training in "street-theater." A composite German folk language should be first normalized and adapted for purposes of poetry and song and then spread throughout Europe as a new *lingua franca* of the arts and sciences. This revitalized, popular culture could qualify as "the lightning rod for the world" in short-circuiting international tensions. Art, with guild-like apprenticeship training, would be returned to the common people's lives as part of a mighty stream of art-consciousness and productivity, eliminating the separation into "high" and "low" art forms, parallel to Herder's success in banishing value judgments with respect to the international differences between folk traditions. The sensibility for monumental and profound values—surviving only in the high art of writers like Goethe and Schiller—had to be cultivated on the household level.

By way of reply, the older, more realistic and more disciplined Brentano indicated he would like to believe that Arnim's plan was meant seriously, for nothing would please him more than to dedicate his life to a common project on behalf of the renascence of poetry [I:43]. Brentano doubted, however, that Arnim's family and his social status would permit him to devote his life

to such an undertaking. He further wondered whether ancestral inertia would allow Arnim to embrace poetry beyond the safe and comfortable involvement in versifying clever rhymes of good taste. Would Arnim's private life countenance a close working relationship with someone as demanding as Clemens, or would their friendship be confined to the propriety of mere "good fellowship" [I:42]? We do not know whether Arnim ever responded to this challenge directly.

In the meantime, Arnim did try to embody some related ideas, dealing with the Romantic minstrel's mediation between his people and the divine inspiration of Poetic Fantasy, in the dithyrambic and satirical verse-novel, *Ariels Offenbarungen* (1804). This work reveals an all-inclusive, unfocused view of the minstrel's function, as betrayed by Arnim's characterization of Ariel as being ". . . neither just a dancer or poet: he practices strange arts . . ." [I:51]. In other words, this ideal minstrel was part magician, part prophet, part prankster, and part artist. Brentano's skepticism seems to have only partially dissuaded Arnim from his millennial formulation of Germany's coming renaissance in science and poetry (or, in the speculative phraseology of the older Jena school—the coming dawn of "poeticized science"). For, in a letter of April 4, 1803, from Paris, he announced to Clemens that the support of Count von Schlabrendorf for his great plan had made Arnim's "life's hope and airy mirage" seem to settle closer to earth by the height of about one mountain range [I:68]. At this point Arnim invited Brentano to join him in Paris to work toward realization of the grand scheme. Brentano did not reply for some time and then, on April 20, only to ignore the plan, to beg off from a Paris reunion, and propose instead that they author a joint publication of their own poems and songs, as a more realistic start for possible future collaboration [I:72].

### THE *WUNDERHORN* FOLK-SONG COLLECTION

According to Heinz Rölleke, the editor of the definitive *Wunderhorn* edition, Brentano had early entertained the idea of collaborating with Tieck, whose adaptations of love lyrics of the Hohenstaufen era (*Minnelieder aus dem schwäbischen Zeitalter*, 1803) had suggested to the younger poet the idea of a joint continuance of this undertaking[1]. This explains Brentano's early start in the collecting of manuscripts, which (after his overtures to Tieck had failed) were available then for *Wunderhorn* use when he joined forces with Arnim. But as early as 1802 he had been encouraging his younger Prussian friend [I:40] likewise to collect German-language editions of old songs, legends, and dramatic tales from the Middle Ages, the Reformation, and the Baroque. Later, their focus included the search for corroborating evidence that a *Volksgeist* ("Spirit of the People") operating as a unifying and creative force had in fact not only existed in Elizabethan England and the other Germanic countries of northern Europe but also in the early stages of German literary development. By February, 1805, Arnim found it necessary to reassure his partner living 150 miles to the southwest: "With respect to the book of folk songs, I thought we agreed a long time ago—I don't want to publish it without you nor with anyone other than you" [I:134]. The contrast he had experienced upon leaving the homogeneous French culture for his encounter with the land of Shakespeare and Ossian had further sensitized Arnim to the importance and natural strength of the folk component in any movement of national cultural resurgence. Initially, Brentano's large collection of legends, medieval love songs, old chronicles, and broadsides formed the core of the *Wunderhorn* project—certainly for the first volume—while Arnim concentrated on copying specimens out of old songbooks contained in the libraries of cities he visited on his many travels [I:130].

Earlier, James Macpherson, in his (counterfeited) Ossian collection, *Fragments of Ancient Poetry* (1760), had stimulated anti-Rationalist interest and the collecting zeal of pro-English writers like Johann Georg Hamann, Johann Gottfried Herder, Gottfried August Bürger, and Goethe—who were rebelling against French "pseudoclassical" culture and worshipped Shakespearean naturalism as the authentic "Germanic" medium. Three years after Herder's pioneering essay on *Ossian und die Lieder alter Völker* (*Ossian and the Songs of Ancient Peoples,* 1773) in which the term *Volkslied* appears for the first time, the poet G. A. Bürger enthusiastically called for a German "Percy" to match the feat of that English bishop who had retrieved British texts from oblivion in his famous *Reliques of Ancient English Poetry* (1765). But even the German "Storm and Stress" movement (1770-1785) had failed to produce the Percy whom Bürger had invoked.

More than anything else, Arnim would have wished to be his people's Percy, a "minstrel laureate"—a kind of itinerant folk hero in the battered green cloak he had envisioned for the figure of Grüne(n)wald in his *Wunderhorn* dedication to Goethe [XIII:1 ff.]. As late as 1811 he confided to the Grimms that he would consider it God's blessing if he were found worthy of producing a song that would grip an entire people [III:135]. Indeed, his most exuberant, life-affirming figures are always those that embody the lyric spirit of poetic fancy, whether it be the magical Ariel of the *Offenbarungen* and of the *Wintergarten* frame, the effervescent Aura in *Die Ehenschmiede,* the singer in *Fürst Ganzgott und Sänger Halbgott,* or the Grünewald-Güldenkamm minstrel in both volumes of *Die Kronenwächter.*

In a letter of February 15, 1805, addressed to Arnim in Giebichenstein, Brentano had proposed a format for their project: "to undertake a reasonably priced book of folk songs . . . It must be a delicate balance between the Romantic and the everyday mood, it must contain religious, tradesmen's, and common laborers' songs, songs of the times of day and year, and humorously frivolous songs . . . It must be so arranged that no age is excluded; in it the better folk songs could be preserved and modern ones could be composed for inclusion" [I:132]. We find, then, in the *Wunderhorn* an entire gamut of alteration and adaptation, ranging from the approximately one sixth that are genuine and unchanged folk songs to the six songs that are explicitly Arnim's and Brentano's original compositions.

The general effect of the changes was to sentimentalize or add romantic pathos. Brentano particularly enjoyed incorporating his own brand of ironic wit or "restoring" the received texts by artificially archaizing them with dialect colorations. Of the two, Brentano favored more the preservation of the original style and mood, showing his better intuitive grasp of the authentic unity and charm inherent in the primitive poetic stage these folk lyrics exemplify. Arnim, in his determination to adapt to contemporary standards of taste, was usually responsible for replacing the figures' down-to-earth motivation, the abrupt transitions, and originally laconic speech gestures with softened, unvulgarized romantic sentiments, moralistic diffuseness, or capriciousness[2]. Both editors, however, felt free to append additional stanzas to the frequently terse originals, thereby altering the denouement or superimposing a sophisticated motivation. No especial conscientiousness was shown toward accuracy of source attribution, since both appreciated the invention of witty "inside" allusions.

Although not always comfortable with Arnim's editorial arbitrariness in overseeing the publication of Volume One, Brentano was the first to urge—on the basis of the volume's enormous and unexpected success—that the pair should immediately consider sequels. In an exchange of views with Clemens relating to the publication of the second and third *Wunderhorn* volumes in 1808, Arnim justified his brand of creative modernization by citing Goethe's 1806 *Wunderhorn* support for the intermingling of old with new elements [I:235]. Thus he seems to justify Macpherson's highly successful *Ossian* hoax primarily because it was successful and did stimulate audience interest as well as engendering new creative endeavors, e.g., Sir Walter Scott's ballads and romances [I:236].

There is little doubt that Brentano's influence dominated the two sequels whose compilation—just as in the case of Volume One—required only about six weeks of joint work, this time in Kassel, with occasional advice offered by Jacob and Wilhelm Grimm. A primary cause for the lack of a more reasonable grouping of the songs in the other volumes was the long printing delay in Heidelberg, where Arnim, saddled with assimilating more and more recently arrived contributions, merely authorized the appending of such texts in the order of their arrival. When Brentano noticed from his copy of the proofs how structurally flawed the volumes were becoming, he decided to make the best of a bad situation by encouraging Arnim to juxtapose radically different kinds of verse so that no reader could assume any purposeful order of presentation [R, IX/I:22 f.]. At the end of August, 1808, and in despair at Arnim's carelessness, Brentano traveled from Kassel to the Frankfurt presses of the Heidelberg publisher to save what could still be saved, but most of the damage of gross misprinting and consequent distortion or unintelligibility had already been done. From this point on, Brentano lost all interest in the fate of the **Wunderhorn,** and Arnim on his own supervised its second edition in 1819; in the complimentary copy found in Brentano's library after his death the pages were still uncut [R, IX/I:24].

At one point, the erstwhile partners had begun collecting materials for a fourth **Wunderhorn** volume, which was to contain corrections and addenda; but their interest flagged, and it was left to Ludwig Erk to publish this material posthumously in 1854 from Arnim's manuscripts, as Volume XXI of the latter's collected works.

Beyond the two editors' general preferences and stylistic idiosyncrasies, no particular editorial criteria can be ascertained for the treatment of texts; nor can editorial responsibility for the final version of any specific text be positively fixed, although the *Kinderlieder* cycle appended to Volume Three is solely Brentano's contribution. Out of his concern for German political unity, Arnim had vetoed Brentano's Herderian idea of dividing the songs according to the clearly discernible North and South German cultural traits, for Arnim claimed that it was impossible to decide where the boundary between North and South actually was [R, IX/I:19]. Instead, the first volume appears to group its titles in terms of motif chains or topical sets, while the second and third are arranged more according to genre distinctions. Toward the end of Volume Two and in Volume Three, some vestiges remain of the original attempts at grouping into drinking songs, amorous and tailor songs, adventure songs, historical *Romanzen,* and devotional songs to Mary; but Arnim's editorial weariness in Volume Three resulted generally in Brentano's idea of geographical-cultural origin having prevailed, for Arnim evidently appended the last clusters exactly as Brentano shipped them in—and therefore as they had been collected regionally "in the field" [R, IX/I:23].

The title, **Des Knaben Wunderhorn,** has a double derivation: (1) the collection's opening song bears this name and is a free adaptation from a 1784 collection edited by one of their contributors, Anselm Elwert, whose translation of Thomas Warton's English version of a medieval Anglo-Norman romance, the "lai du corn," represents an even freer corruption of the original text about the youth and his horn; (2) reinforcing this main source is the use of "Wunder-Horn" in the 1684 title of a related work hailing from the Bremen-Oldenburg area [R, IX/I:69, 77]. The strategic dedication is to Geheimrat ("privy councillor") von Goethe and comprises little more than a lengthy anecdote from Jörg Wickram's *Rollwagenbüchlein* (*Little Post-Carriage Book,* 1555) introducing to us the figure of Grüne(n)wald the minstrel (also written "Güldenkamm" in the "Anton" novel), one of Arnim's favorite masks for the poet-singer in general and specifically for the guitar-playing Brentano and his talented voice.

As a means of becoming acquainted with the kind of finished product the **Wunderhorn** offers its readership, I have assembled a random sequence of texts—centering in various naive but elemental facets of the love theme—for closer consideration. In Volume One the following two ditties occur in the order cited, "Wenn ich ein Vöglein wär" [R, VI:217], followed directly by "An einen Boten" [R, VI:209][3]:

Wenn ich ein Vöglein wär

[Herder's *Volkslieder,* I:67]

Wenn ich ein Vöglein wär
Und auch zwei Flüglein hätt,
Flög ich zu dir;
Weils aber nicht kann sein,
Bleib ich allhier.

Bin ich gleich weit von dir,
Bin ich doch im Schlaf bei dir
Und red mit dir;
Wenn ich erwachen thu,
Bin ich allein.

Es vergeht keine Stund in der Nacht
Da mein Herze nicht erwacht
Und an dich gedenkt
Daß du mir viel tausendmal
Dein Herze geschenkt.

Were I a Little Bird

[Melodies by Reichardt, Beethoven,

Weber, Schumann, Reger]
Were I a little bird
With two small wings awhir,
I'd fly to you;

But since this cannot be,
Here's where I'll coo.

Though I am far from you,
When asleep I'm still with you
And talk to you;
But then when I wake up,
I'm all alone.

In the night not an hour passes by
When my heart doesn't wake with a sigh,
Recalling how you
Have giv'n me thousands of times
Your heart that's so true.

#### An einen Boten

[*Feiner Almanach,* II:106]
Wenn du zu mein Schätzel kommst,
Sag: ich ließ sie grüßen;
Wenn sie fraget, wie mirs geht?
Sag: auf beyden Füßen.

Wenn sie fraget: ob ich krank?
Sag: ich sey gestorben;
Wenn sie an zu weinen fangt,
Sag: ich käme morgen.

#### To a Messenger

[Melody by Max Reger]
If you should chance to meet my sweet,
Say: I give regards yet;
Should she ask you how I feel,
Say: my condition is guarded.

Should she ask if I am ill,
Say: I died of sorrow;
Should she then begin to cry,
Say: I'll come tomorrow.

The first of these songs displays the metrical and rhyme irregularities of the authentic folk song (in keeping with Herder's historical and comparatist editorial practices): the iambic stanzas show a basic three-beat rhythm, except for the third and fifth lines, which in each case have a refrain-like "stopping" function. The variation in the number of unstressed syllables (sprung rhythm) is typical for the German tradition. The second song, even with its defective rhyme in lines 1 and 3, is either a more modern song or is one step closer to literary normalization. It is standard trochaic tetrameter, with even-numbered lines closing in spondees. Although Arnim's original verse was heavily influenced by his work with the four-beat folk stanza (doggerel, or *Knittelvers*), his own poetry almost always employs iambic meter. The second of these love songs humorously reflects a less naive stereotype in that it is based on a kind of antiphonal model, whose speaker is obviously not about to languish from a broken heart.

It is unclear why the "motif-chain" or genre principle is so inconsistently maintained as an organizational feature of Volume One: for example, another love song—also utilizing the bird image (this time a falcon)—"Der Falke" [R, VI:59], was placed almost two hundred pages earlier[4]:

#### Der Falke [Der gelähmte Flug]

[mündlich]

Wär ich ein wilder Falke
Ich wollt mich schwingen auf
Und wollt mich niederlassen
Vor meines Grafen Haus.

Und wollt mit starken [*sic*] Flügel
Da schlagen an Liebchens Thür
Daß springen sollt der Riegel
Mein Liebchen trät herfür.

"Hörst du die Schlüssel klingen?
Dein Mutter ist nicht weit,
So zieh mit mir von hinnen
Wohl über die Heide breit."

Und wollt in ihrem Nacken
Die goldenen Flechten schön
Mit wilden [*sic*] Schnabel packen,
Sie tragen zu dieser Höhn.
Ja wohl zu dieser Höhen,
Hier wär ein schönes Nest.
Wie ist mir doch geschehen,
Daß ich gesetzet fest.

Ja, trüg ich sie im Fluge,
Mich schöss der Graf nicht todt,
Sein Töchterlein zum Fluche,
Das fiele sich ja todt.

So aber sind die Schwingen
Mir allesamt gelähmt,
Wie hell ich ihr auch singe,
Mein Liebchen sich doch schämt.

#### The Falcon [Lamed Flight]

[oral transmission]
If I were a wild falcon
I'd soar up in the clouds
And I would only set down
Before my liege-lord's house.

And there with wings a-beating
At sweetheart's door so fierce,
Its bolt would crack in pieces,
And then my sweet appears.

"You must have heard her keys ring,
Your mother's about to rail,
So come beyond her hearing
With me o'er hill and dale."

And from her nape so child-fine
My beak would seize her hair
Dear braided golden tie-lines,
And tow her high to my lair.

Yes, high atop that summit,
Indeed a charming nest.
Alas I still can't grasp it
That here I'm chained at rest.

Were I to tow her head, still,
Our lord would hardly shoot:
My fall and daughter's death-spill
Would damn his days forsooth.

But as my lot is other
My wings are both quite lame,
My song counts nothing with her,
For me she feels but shame.

Like "An einen Boten," this falcon *Romanze* (despite the anonymous attribution) was taken from Nicolai's folk song satire, *Ein feiner kleiner Almanach* [I:30]; but it has been considerably changed by Arnim[5]. The balladesque tone of this *Romanze,* with its conceit of the pet canary that would like to be a masterful falcon, and with the unexpected, half-humorous confessional twist at the end of the fifth and in the last stanza reflecting the poet's own persona, make this a good example of the romantic pseudo-folk-song idiom. The very obvious or clumsy rhyme identity on *todt* ("dead") in the sixth stanza (one of the authentic ones) might betray the latter's folk format, but in any case, when sung, such defective rhymes would be much less noticeable.

A universal inversion of this "impeded suitor" is the melancholic love song focusing on "the abandoned maiden," found in the second **Wunderhorn** volume of 1808 [R, VII:50]:

Lass rauschen, Lieb, lass rauschen

[mündlich]

Ich hört ein Sichlein rauschen,
Wohl rauschen durch das Korn
Ich hört ein Mägdlein klagen,
Sie hätt ihr Lieb verlorn.

Laß rauschen, Lieb, laß rauschen,
Ich acht nicht, wie es geht,
Ich thät mein Lieb vertauschen
In Veilchen und im Klee.

Du hast ein Mägdlein worben
In Veilchen und im Klee,
So steh ich hier alleine,
Thut meinem Herzen weh.

Ich hör ein Hirschlein rauschen
Wohl rauschen durch den Wald,

Ich hör mein Lieb sich klagen,
Die Lieb verrauscht so bald.

Laß rauschen, Lieb, laß rauschen
Ich weiß nicht, wie mir wird,
Die Bächlein immer rauschen,
Und keines sich verirrt.

What Rustling, Love, What Rustling?

[oral tradition]

I heard a sickle rustling,
A-rustling through the rye,
I heard a maid lamenting,
Her love had said goodbye.

What rustling, Love, what rustling?
I'd care not what comes next,
I'd fain exchange my darling
'Mongst clover and violets.

You wooed a trusting maiden
'Mongst clover and violets,
But now I stand all lonely,
My heart this sorely frets.

I hear a deer a-rustling,
A-rustling through the thicket,
I hear my love complaining
How love rushes by so quick.

What rustling, Love, what rustling?
I feel so strange this way,
The brooklets go on rustling,
And none has gone astray.

The last two strophes of the poem are original with Arnim or Brentano, according to Uhland, who reproduced the **Wunderhorn** version exactly but gave as source for the first strophe *Grasliedlein* [1535, no. 15] and for the second and third strophes W. Schmeltzel's *Quodlibet* [1544, no. 25]. This double heritage may account for the unmodulated transitions between stanzas, but folk art is replete with such leaps—and the resulting multiple resonance is something the German romanticists admired in older, rustic writing and aspired to in their own work.

Apart from the question of composite genesis and editorial intervention, a folk poem such as this with its generalized, laconic allusions may still offer difficulties of interpretation. The setting here suggests an erstwhile lover who is separated from his beloved—because he is on a journey [lines 11-12], or because his love has simply faded [line 7], or because he has forsaken her [lines 4, 15-16]. He seems to sympathize with her plight, for whenever he hears some rustling, it reminds him of her sorrow at being deprived of his love. For his part, he would gladly be rid of these love memories and his loneliness [lines 11-12]—which only obscure life's meaning [lines 18-20]—in exchange for another girl's company [line 7]. He recognizes that the world's brooklets faithfully and perpetually follow their appointed destinies; but human love seems to echo life's brevity, fickleness, and inscrutability, causing the lover to try to forget death's imminence (the rustling sickle) and life's aimlessness [lines 5-6, and "rustling" in general] by plunging into love's vacillating pleasures [lines 7-8]. This would-be hedonism could express his desire to suppress his conscience pangs, but it could also reflect the infidelity of the lover whose suffering (due to inevitable physical separation) drives him to wish it were otherwise.

In order to justify the switch in pronoun reference in the middle strophe without having to identify these verses as the swain's monologue (in which the self-accusation of lines 9-10 are set off pronominally from the self-indulgence of lines 11-12), Rölleke attributes this stanza to the abandoned girl. In so doing, he assigns the song more clearly to the classic antiphonal folk lament with its typically unmodulated transitions, generating the impression here that the respondents are "speaking past each other." If two love-lonely strangers accidentally meet here (as seems plausible also from the repetition of line 8 two lines later), then it appears that the young man seeks to "comfort" her in the second stanza by gently—and subjunctively—suggesting the replaceability of his former love at this juncture [lines 7-8]. It is not entirely clear from her response in lines 11-12, or from his in line 16, whether she succumbs to his hint, but the generally melancholy tone suggests not. The mood and the ear-catching refrain of this miniature elegy seem to have influenced a later song by Wilhelm Müller, and poems by Rückert and Eichendorff.

A variant of the abandoned-maiden theme, that of the exploited girl's revenge, is also present in this collection [R, VI:329][6]. It is interesting in part because it echoes Goethe's popular version of the well-known "Heidenröslein" theme:

### Knabe und Veilchen

[mündlich]

KNABE

> Blühe, liebes Veilchen,
> Das so lieblich roch,
> Blühe noch ein Weilchen,
> Werde schöner noch.
> Weißt du, was ich denke?
> Liebchen zum Geschenke
> Pflück ich, Veilchen, dich,
> Veilchen, freue dich!

VEILCHEN

> Brich mich stilles Veilchen,
> Bin die Liebste dein,
> Und in einem Weilchen
> Werd ich schöner seyn!
> Weißt du was ich denke?
> Wenn ich duftend schwenke
> Meinen Duft um dich:
> Knabe, liebe mich!

(Boy and the Violet

[oral transmission]

BOY

> Bloom, o little violet,
> With such a lovely smell,
> Bloom a little while yet,
> Grow more lovely still.
> Know why I'm so smart?
> As a gift for sweetheart
> I will pluck you, pet,
> Smile, o violet!

VIOLET

> Break me quiet violet,
> You I do love best,
> In a little while yet
> I'll be handsomest!
> Know why I'm so smart?
> When my perfumed art
> Wafts around you, pet:
> Dear, it's you I'll get!)

Brentano objected to Arnim's inclusion of this poem because it was written—despite the reference to "oral transmission"—by a known literary author, C. A. Overbeck, for his *Poetische Blumenlese für das Jahr 1778* (*Poetic Flower-Harvest for the Year 1778*), edited by Brentano's archenemy, Johann Heinrich Voss. Although it was considered a fashionable song at the time, Arnim decided to use only the first stanza of the original, omitting the remaining five, and adding his own second stanza in final position for the violet's response. In Arnim's own stanza, then, the violet makes the interesting transposition of consciousness, almost as though "she" were the avenging angel of the boy's conscience, when she suggests that she will become more bewitchingly beautiful after he has plucked her—which, objectively viewed, is absurd unless the flower itself symbolizes the boy's beloved—which in turn would cause other interpretive difficulties. Subjectively, however, by being "attached" as his property, the violet-girl becomes psychologically more valuable to him, can envelop him in her invisible spellbinding aroma, and thus will utilize his assured proximity to enthrall him. Her announcement to this effect therefore also functions as the subtle reflex of a threatening or ironic posture on her part, even though she professes love for him. The irony emanates primarily from the first, original stanza, where we see that the brash swain—on second thought—will pluck the violet immediately as a sacrifice to his real love [line 6], and the violet is even supposed to appreciate this "rape"! If one rejects the interpretation of the violet's ironic threat in response to the boy's discovery of erotic violence, an opposite formulation results in which the boy "chooses" (by plucking) the ethereal Virgin Mary (whose symbolic blue is represented by Arnim in Klelie's "Song of the Violets" in his *Kirchenordnung* novellette [3:121 f.]) as a sacrificial "gift" (spiritual guaranty) to his fiancée.

An ultimate variation on the abandoned-maiden theme—telling of the unmarried mother's disgrace and her too tardily commuted death sentence—is found in Volume Two of the **Wunderhorn** [R, VII:201]. This specimen is of further interest because of certain resemblances to Brentano's later balladesque novella, *Vom braven Kasperl und dem schönen Annerl* (*The Story of Honest Casper and Fair Annie*, 1817), as well as to the Gretchen complex of Goethe's *Faust* and to Schiller's ballad, "Die Kindesmörderin" (The baby-murderess, 1781):

### Weltlich Recht

[Reichardts Musikalische Zeitung, 1806, no. 10, p. 40]

Joseph, lieber Joseph, was hast du gedacht,
Daß du die schöne Nanerl ins Unglück gebracht.

Joseph, lieber Joseph, mit mir ists bald aus,
Und wird mich bald führen zu dem Schandtor hinaus.

Zu dem Schandtor hinaus auf einen grünen Platz,
Da wirst du bald sehen, was die Lieb hat gemacht.
Richter, lieber Richter, richt nur fein geschwind,
Ich will ja gern sterben, daß ich komm zu meinem
   Kind.

Joseph, lieber Joseph, reich mir deine Hand,
Ich will dir verzeihen, das ist Gott wohl bekannt.

Der Fähndrich kam geritten und schwenket seine Fahn,
"Halt still mit der schönen Nanerl, ich bringe Pardon."

Fähndrich, lieber Fähndrich, sie ist ja schon todt:
Gut Nacht, meine schöne Nanerl, deine Seel ist bei
   Gott.

### Worldly Justice
Joseph, my dear Joseph, what did you, pray, think
When you led this Annie fair right over the brink.

Joseph, my dear Joseph, my name is abased,
They will soon conduct me through the town, disgraced.

Beneath the gate of shame and to a grassy plot,
Where you're going to see what joy our love has
   wrought.

Judge, o my dear Judge, do judge me quick, not mild,
Dying is for me the only chance to see my child.

Joseph, my dear Joseph, let me have your hands,
I intend to pardon you as God commands.

The corp'ral came on horse, a flag to clear the space,
"Hands away from Annie, here is pardoning grace."

Corp'ral, my dear Corp'ral, already she's 'neath the
   sod:
Now sleep, my fairest Annie, your soul resides in
   God.

The first five couplets are spoken by the disgraced maiden and reveal the ironic pathos befitting a young mother whose baby's life has been "terminated." The next, penultimate stanza, through the corporal's breathless one-line intervention, whips up listener suspense one last time at the possibility of Nanerl's rescue and exculpation. But this hope is laconically dashed in the final couplet by the lover-accomplice's somewhat complacent revelation to the corporal that he has not ridden fast enough to save Nanerl from execution. The complexity of perspectives in this ballad, as well as the ill-adapted length of the epic hexameter line, suggest literary influences from the "Kunstpoesie" domain. But clear "folk-song" provenance from the tradition of "Naturpoesie" is also evident in frequently "sprung" rhythms due to the diachronic "warping reiteration" (*Zersingen*), which can appear aggravated in hybrid versions such as this by the synchronic abridgments of regional (or compilers') contaminations. Indeed, the formula "Joseph, lieber Joseph," together with its variants on "Richter" and "Fähndrich," sounds almost like a literary parody of the well-known Christmas folk song.

A final stage in the **Wunderhorn**'s treatment of the universal love relationship is documented by the song of farewell from the third volume [R, VIII:34]:

### Lebewohl

Morgen muß ich weg von hier
Und muß Abschied nehmen;
O du allerhöchste Zier,
Scheiden das bringt Grämen.
Da ich dich so treu geliebt
über alle Maaßen,
Soll ich dich verlassen.

Wenn zwei gute Freunde sind,
Die einander kennen,
Sonn und Mond bewegen sich,
Ehe sie sich trennen.

Noch viel größer ist der Schmerz,
Wenn ein treu verliebtes Herz
In die Fremde ziehet.

Dort auf jener grünen Au
Steht mein jung frisch Leben,
Soll ich dann mein Lebelang
In der Fremde schweben?
Hab ich dir was Leids gethan,
Bitt dich, wolls vergessen,
Denn es geht zu Ende.

Küsset dir ein Lüftelein
Wangen oder Hände,
Denke, daß es Seufzer seyn,
Die ich zu dir sende:
Tausend schick ich täglich aus,
Die da wehen um dein Haus,
Weil ich dein gedenke.

                    Farewell

                [oral tradition]
I must bid this place goodbye,
Take my leave tomorrow;
O you jewel of jewels on high,
Parting brings such sorrow.
Though I've loved you heart and soul,
More than words can argue,
I must now forsake you.

When a bond links two good friends
Who have known each other,
Sun and moon their orbits bend
Ere farewell they'll suffer.
Much more painful is the hurt
When a truly loving heart
Heads for distant places.

There upon that grassy field
Waits my fresh young life's bout,
Must I graze through all my days
In some distant hide-out?
If I've caused you hurt or pain,
Please let's do forget it,
Since our hours are numbered.

If a breeze with kisses nighs
For your cheek or hand, dear,
Know that these are just my sighs,
Which to you I'll send here:
Thousands I'll have daily moaned
Circling round your house intoned,
For I'll have your mem'ry.

The contradictory impulses behind this classic scene of farewell—the fatalistic need to depart into "die Fremde" ("alien lands," probably symbolizing here "growing up") and soulful yearning for the sweetheart and home that one is leaving behind—are typical components of German romanticism. The haphazard rhyme scheme, the asymmetrical seven-line stanza, and the uncomfort-

able line-stopping spondees of the even-numbered lines probably all mark this version as essentially an authentic folk text from the late 1600s [R, IX/3:56], although the final stanza has been altered to supply a more admirable image of the departing young man.

Following publication of the first **Wunderhorn** volume in 1806 a small but articulate and important sector of the intellectual world criticized both editors for their unscientific method of text presentation. Their own friends, the brothers Grimm, were thoroughly dismayed by the nonhistorical approach, Friedrich Schlegel lamented the editors' lack of thoroughness, and even one of their main contributors, Anselm Elwert, objected to the intrusion of songs by known authors from the sixteenth century, such as Luther, Weckherlin, and Opitz. Büsching and von der Hagen, who published their own bibliophile folksong collection in the following year, were severely critical, as was Voss, who spoke of counterfeited texts and faked attributions. Meanwhile, the first **Wunderhorn** volume sold extraordinarily well at the bookstalls, and the support of another influential friend, Joseph Görres, enhanced the collection's impact. But by far the most effective lightning rod in deflecting criticism and gaining adherents for the **Wunderhorn** enterprise was the review by Goethe in the *Jenaer Allgemeine Literaturzeitung*[7], which included the following praise:

> Actually, this little book should be available in every home where alert people live, by the window, beneath the mirror, or anywhere else where songbooks and cookbooks are usually kept. Then it could be opened at any moment of enthusiasm or vexation and always furnish something supportive or stimulating, even if one had to flip through several pages first. But most appropriate of all would be to have this volume on the piano of amateur or professional musicians, for them to either match these song texts with familiar, traditional melodies as they deserve, or to adapt them suitably to other tunes—or, God willing, to be inspired by these lyrics into composing new, impressive melodies. . . . If these songs were then to be gradually transmitted in their own stylistic and melodic idiom from ear to ear, from mouth to mouth, they would, in time, return enlivened and exalted to the populace, whence they had originally—in a sense—emerged and then we could say that the little volume had fulfilled its mission and could once more, as a written document, disappear from the scene, since it would have been assimilated into the nation's life and culture.

And Goethe's reply to the criticism of the historical, ethnological school regarding the "mutilation" of "original" texts was anticipated by the opening lines of his review, and again toward the end, where he rejected the idea of an analysis of the **Wunderhorn** texts for purposes of establishing the degree of editorial tinkering;

for ". . . who isn't aware of what trials a song must live through when it goes for a time through the people's mouths—and not only through the mouths of uneducated people! Why shouldn't that person, who is the first to write it down and place it alongside others, also have a certain right to treat the text similarly?" Thus the *Wunderhorn*'s publication elicited one of the earliest characterizations of that folk-song phenomenon known as reiterative warping or "oral-aural weathering" at the hands (and in the mouths) of a populace.

Although Arnim conceived of the compilation as ultimately a pedagogic act of sociopolitical popularization, rather than as one of bibliophile restoration, and even though the anticipated renascence of folk culture and religious consciousness did not materialize, the *Wunderhorn*'s appearance in the year of national debacle at Jena had a vibrant impact, especially—and ironically—in "high art" circles. That folk idiom which Herder in 1776 had called *Stamm und Mark der Nation* ("blood and marrow of the nation") has, in fact, been preserved, via the *Wunderhorn*'s mediation, in much of the poetry of Joseph Eichendorff, Heinrich Heine (despite his ironic rejection of romantic sentimentality), Eduard Mörike, Ludwig Uhland, Justinus Kerner, and Annette von Droste-Hülshoff. Musical settings of *Wunderhorn* texts were executed by such distinguished artists as Schumann, Brahms, Richard Strauss, and Mahler.

In the last analysis, the service which this most influential of all German folk-song collections performed for German culture was to prevent the folk-song movement from being monopolized by historical academicians and by scholarly comparativists, either of which, if given free rein at that time, might have denied the working classes and petite bourgeoisie popular access to their vanishing heritage. Arnim mirrors the closing of this era of youthful endeavor for the cultural commonweal in his nostalgic "Ariel" frame to *Der Wintergarten,* where the poet figure laments: "We had hoped for a wonderful era for Germany and worked hard for her—she was to be like a fabulous prismatic mirror in uniting the whole world. But—to make a long story short—she was like a peace dove in the storm: war broke out, and down upon us, and smashed our mirror . . ." [2:345].

### Natur- und Kunstpoesie (Folk and "High" Literature)

Arnim's chief motivation for engaging in literary journalism via his *Zeitung für Einsiedler* (1808) had also been to promote his original ideal of a new German golden age of literature based on a reborn national folk-consciousness, toward which the *Wunderhorn* achieve-

ment represented a significant first step. The failure of his little gazette to elicit from such key literary figures as Goethe and Tieck the same kind of support as was enjoyed by the *Wunderhorn* struck him with particular and personal force at this nadir of German national history. The experience of such a journalistic fiasco, so hard on the heels of the great *Wunderhorn* notoriety, characteristically did not moderate Arnim's stubborn idealism by disposing him to learn from justified criticism, as one might expect. Rather, his golden-age project now "went underground," as it were, as an historical-mythical vision of purely subjective and privately intellectual scope, thereby allowing his literary expressions of this ideal to remain indifferent to substantive criticism. As a practicing idealist and writer, Arnim found it impossible to accept the Grimms' or Görres's views of an absolute, nonrecurring phase of "golden youth" in mankind's artistic, existential—and for that matter, social—development. Undeniably there had once been an extended tribal nation-community, with a single, dignified and profound folk-consciousness that was cumulatively expressed in the art of anonymous masters, serving to reflect and produce a natural unity of epic experience; just as surely did Arnim perceive these components of a "Nationalpoesie" (also termed "Volkspoesie" or "Naturpoesie") as being ever-present as a cultural possibility.

Arnim admitted to the Grimms that the ancient poets of the people (*Volksdichter*) were a different breed from their modern equivalents [III:134 f.]. But instead of being divinely or artistically ordained, this difference, he insisted, was sociologically conditioned. Arnim perceived the individual ancient poets, whom Jacob Grimm had lumped together anonymously as part of divine revelation [III:89], as having lived in a homogeneous and simple community. Hence almost any inspired utterance could be a "universal" statement encompassing the whole of their existence, making its author almost automatically a *Volksdichter.* And cumulatively the statements of several such poets of the people could therefore easily form a more or less homogeneous literary unit, or epic cycle—such as *Das Nibelungenlied,* often cited by Jacob to bolster his own argument. But the modern poet of the people, Arnim asserted, lives in a highly differentiated society, where access to folk universality is blocked by the complexity of specialized experience, as well as by stylistic intricacies inherent in the culture's linguistic self-awareness.

The tragic fact of the matter is that both sides in this protracted dispute concerning "Natur- und Kunstpoesie" (1810-1817) felt it necessary, probably unconsciously, to repress the deeper reason why Arnim's position was untenable with regard to the infusion of upper-class values into a reborn folk culture—namely, that in order to have rebirth there must still be life. German society was already so self-consciously fragmented when the *Wunderhorn* appeared in 1806 that Arnim's grafting of a Prussian political ideal onto the medieval paragon of a unified but structured cultural community capable of generating a single folk-consciousness was in fact quixotic.

When such an artistic distortion of historically certified fact is aesthetically successful as in the case of Shakespeare's history plays, the public usually is willing to forgive, to forget, and even permanently to color the fact with fancy through the bestowal of its applause. But lacking such an artistically compelling quality, Arnim's mythicizing attempts were seen by his favorite critics, the Grimms, as a kind of parasitism, whereby an inferior talent seeks to legitimize his claim to public attention by exploiting the historical identities of figures and events already accepted or admired as being important dramatic symbols. To such historical positivists this technique represented seeking to "have one's historical cake and re-digesting it, too." They especially lamented Arnim's sacrifice of the inner truth in his deviations from history for the sake of what they frequently considered to be a sort of macaronic plot-construction lacking inner necessity, focus, and motivation. The result approached in their eyes what has come to be known as "Romantic irony"—that is, the romantic poet's negative display of an authorial will by destroying in his narrative an already-achieved conventional reality in order to invent an ultimate participatory role for his own subjectivity, thereby in effect inventing himself as well as the reader. Using historical events and personalities as "disrespectful" pretexts and foils for his own private (but published!) sport was in the Grimms' estimation embarrassingly frivolous and—in the case of a flagrantly unsuccessful work (such as *Halle und Jerusalem*)—bordered on blasphemy [III:99 f.].

By 1817, and with the publication of the "Berthold novel" as Part One of *Die Kronenwächter,* both sides had wearied of further haggling over their fundamental difference in poetic perspective and certainly despaired of ever converting their adversary. The Grimms, especially Jacob, persisted in their belief in the linear uniqueness and sacred intent behind the historical succession of literary data, correlating the epic (pre-Renaissance) phase with *Naturpoesie* and the individualistic (modern) phase with subjectively fragmented and arbitrary *Kunstpoesie.* Arnim persisted equally in his more modern cyclic conviction of the ultimate subjectivity of all experiential documentation authored by individual writers—whether part of an historically homogeneous social consciousness or part of a modern, introverted, consciousness—insisting that the generative *Naturpoesie* and formative *Kunstpoesie* are interdependent in every work of literary art. Thus, Jacob's polarization represented to Arnim a false dichotomy. In terms of cultural dynamics (as repeatedly expressed from *Ariel* through the *Wunderhorn* and **"Von Volksliedern,"** to the *Einsiedlerzeitung* and beyond), Arnim's longing was aimed at reconciling the natural craftsmanship inherent in the popular folk tradition—guided by a reintegrated aristocratic consciousness of the service ideal and its symbolism—with the uprooted, largely middle-class energies of that academic elite which, after all, had erupted in the Storm-and-Stress upsurge of aesthetic protest and radical melancholy in the 1770s. The reuniting of these two streams of *Naturpoesie* and *Kunstpoesie* had become by now the aim of Arnim's aesthetic doctrine and the hallmark of his own authorial performance.

*Notes*

1. Clemens Brentano, *Sämtliche Werke und Briefe,* ed. Jürgen Behrens et al. (Stuttgart: Kohlhammer, 1975 ff.), *Des Knaben Wunderhorn,* ed. Heinz Rölleke (Stuttgart, 1975), IX/1:18. Subsequent references to this edition appear as in-text, parenthesized citations: e.g., [R, IX/1:18].

2. That Arnim was aware of his, on occasion, almost rococo preciousness is evident from his self-parody of the poet figure in the *Romanze* "Hylas" [*Gräfin Dolores,* 1:445] who sings in all seriousness lines of, and about, rhyming compulsion.

3. "Wenn ich ein Vöglein wär'" was taken over unchanged from Herder's *Volkslieder* (2 vols., 1778/1779); likewise "An einen Boten" was accurately reprinted from Nicolai's *Ein feiner kleiner Almanach* (2 vols., 1776/1778), except that it appears on p. 206 of Nicolai's second volume instead of p. 106, as cited.

4. In the German of the *Wunderhorn* Arnim and Brentano have frequently introduced the archaic "weak" adjective declension (lines 5 and 15 of this song) to add a certain medieval flavor to a more recent text [R, IX/1:152]. A similar effect results from modern *ei* and *t* appearing quite regularly as *ey* and *th,* resp., as in *seyn* and *Thür* here; likewise *todt* for *tot.* Some of these archaic spellings, however, were simply in the process of transition between Goethe's and Arnim's generation.

5. The first and third stanzas of the original were assimilated in the *Wunderhorn* version, but the latter's remaining five stanzas offer new material (hence the euphemism of "oral transmission"). A different variant, based closely on the version in the *Bergreihen* [2:14] was discovered—probably by Brentano—in time for the editors to reprint it

unchanged in the third volume of the *Wunderhorn,* under the title of "Der Berggesell" (The Journeyman-Miner [XVII, 25 ff.]).

6. The editors of the four *Wunderhorn* volumes in Arnim's posthumous *Werke* (Rudolf Baier and Ludwig Erk) deleted and altered some of the original versions, including elimination of this song, "Blühe, liebes Veilchen," from Vol. XIII entirely.

7. Issue of January 21-22, 1806 (3:1; nos. 18/19), p. 137 f.

## Thomas P. Bonfiglio (essay date 1987)

SOURCE: Bonfiglio, Thomas P. "Electric Affinities: Arnim and Schelling's *Naturphilosophie.*" *Euphorion: Zeitschrift Für Literaturgeschichte* 81, no. 3 (1987): 217-39.

[*In the following essay, Bonfiglio examines narrative structures in Arnim's fiction. In his view the profusion of images in Arnim's work, far from causing the story to disintegrate, actually helps anchor the narrative. In essence, Arnim's extravagant use of metaphoric language serves as a cohesive force, both ideologically and on the level of storytelling.*]

From Goethe to the present, the proper reception of the works of Achim von Arnim has suffered from their illusion of dissonance. Recent criticism, however, has demonstrated structural complexity where once was seen structural confusion. This study synthesizes two trends in the post-war reception of Arnim and demonstrates, with ***Isabella von Ägypten*** as example, that a fundamental electromagnetic cosmology informs Arnim's poetics.

Wolfdietrich Rasch holds that the apparent structural incongruity is really Storm and Stress theory in narrative practice. He shows that all parts in the wandering narrative are interrelated in a "Gewebe der Kunst,"[1] and states that Arnim uses the fantastic to place an event "in ein scharfes Licht,"[2] where that event becomes "blitzartig erhellt."[3] In the oral tradition sudden illumination, while seemingly random caprice, serves to hold the attention of the physically present audience. Here volatility is ideologically generated.

Helene Riley explains Arnimian incongruity as a result of textual antitheses:

> Die Antithetik ist aber nicht das Grundprinzip, wie vielfach in der Forschung angenommen, sondern sie ist Mittel zum Zweck, das Ganze in seinen Teilen zu veranschaulichen.[4]

What appears to be incongruity is an elusive attempt to reflect the general in the particular by using antitheses. In a similar vein, Hans Meixner investigates the problem of the myriad of images in Arnim and constructs a hall-of-mirrors metaphor thereof:

> Die figurale Bedeutung der Hauptpersonen, das Exemplarische der Situationen, in die sie gestellt sind, und das Typische des Geschehens, in das sie verwoben sind, [werden] spiegel- oder gegenbildlich in anderen Personen, Situationen und Geschehniszusammenhängen wiederholt und variiert.[5]

Of note is Meixner's use of "verwoben," the loom image that will be subsequently addressed. He has also struck upon the complex fabric of interplay when he speaks of a "Lebenstotalität, [. . .] auf die das Individuelle nur verweist,"[6] as well as when he claims: "Jedes Individuelle in seiner Erscheinung [ist] nur eine Variante des Allgemeinen."[7] These essays point to a global network of antitheses that generate transitory images.

Hans Steffen's study of light symbolism provides a model for the intricacy of interplay:

> Aber es mag deutlich geworden sein, daß die Lichtzeichen wie ein Netz das Romanganze überziehen. In ihrem Strahl modellieren sich die Figuren und offenbaren die Dinge einen diesseitigen oder jenseitigen höheren Sinn. Dinge und Figuren stehen nebeneinander, gehen ineinander über und ineinander auf. So ist das Ganze durchwoben von der Symbolik des Lichtes, vielmehr, es mündet alles in sie hinein. Dinge und Figuren bespiegeln einander, im Zeichen des Lichtes scheint die Grenze zwischen Ding und Mensch aufgehoben.[8]

Steffen's idea of an interwoven net is an excellent image for configuration, and corresponds to Rasch's observations on textual interrelation and Riley's study of antitheses:

> Antithetik und Symbolik gehen ineinander über. So kommt es zum Zusammenspiel aller Figuren, die sich wie die Fäden eines bunten Teppichs knüpfen, dessen Webmuster eben diese antithetische Grundfigur ist, die in den arabeskenhaften Formen und Verästelungen immer wieder auftaucht.[9]

Reality's loom creates a network of interrelations that are based upon larger polarities. Ludwig Völker sees this as a unity of "der spannungsvollen Einheit widersprüchlicher Tendenzen,"[10] While Lawrence Frye sees "Ein eher mosaikartiges als organisches Bild der Vereinigung."[11] Frye shows that this seems to be an imperfect relation:

> As in the opening to ***Die Majoratsherren,*** we are to see not the main figures and events of the time, but rather reflections in miniature of its irregularities, pecu-

liarities, and what the eye can only catch indirectly and with some distortion. Thus the relevance of a Chodowiecki: *Wir durchblättern eben einen älteren Kalender, dessen Kupferstiche manche Torheiten seiner Zeit abspiegeln.*[12]

These are correspondences among networks of irregularities. It is necessary to isolate the constituents of these networks. Frye discusses "a spectrum of forces and tendencies rich and diverse enough to be refracted within the characters as if their own private worlds were the sole loci of such multi-dimensionality."[13] Thus there is a notion, operating in Arnim's fiction, of character as symbol, image and metaphor alluding to other networks of meaning, both at the same and at higher levels. These networks are insufficient or ironized images of totality, as Frye shows:

> This endless concatenation of symbols which approximates an absolute seems to be Arnim's version of the Schlegelian irony in which one must attempt to express the inexpressible, aware of the impossibility during the fact itself and aware of the discrepancy between the word which expresses and what is to be expressed. One must also leap the gap between the discontinuity of the form and the higher continuity, or unity which it signifies.[14]

This aberrant concatenation of symbols, which gives insight into the ideal norm, transcends time, space and causality. Peter Horst Neumann found that there is not a temporal causal sequence between motivation and action in **Isabella.** Quite often motivation is stated *"post facto."* This led Neumann to posit the structural principle of "retrospektive Motivierung."[15] This is not really a causal principle but rather a product of the webbing of multivalent multidirectional interrelated metaphors in Arnim. This has also been seen on the linguistic level by Albert Béguin, who has noted that there is a network of word-play that connects words suprasyntactically.

> Il a tenté d'en donner l'impression, en s'abandonnant lui-même à un automatisme, propre à l'écrivain: au jeu des syllabes, aux échos par lesquels les mots s'appellent et s'allient sans lien logique.[16]

Thus there is an atemporal, acausal and aspatial network at play here. What then are the forces that hold this structure together? Perhaps the key lies in the following passage from Frye:

> In both **Hollin** and the **Majoratsherren** magnetic contact reveals an inextricable bond between male and female, and radiating out from that bond a kind of life-web of unification through time and space. However, the construction of this unification image with real materials is another matter. Both works, after they grant brief physical contact to their respective pairs, separate the lovers and allow no direct, conscious, verbal communication to take place until the end.[17]

Frye has indicated that this web exists in an (ideal) magnetic field. Could it not be possible that the incalculable intersections of the web are those masks and symbols discussed so far and that the entire structure is held in place in an imaginative structure that resembles a magnetic field?

Frye states that the mask "is meant to be neither raw material nor a higher world but rather a construct mediating between the two. It is what Arnim calls variously an image or symbol."[18] Thus the image or symbol is held in place between two realities. This coincides with Claude David, who claims

> L'univers ambigu du fantastique suppose une cassure; c'est un monde que Dieu a déserté, mais sur lequel son ombre continue à peser, un monde tendu entre le ciel et l'enfer.[19]

Frye also sees the erratic in Arnim as "ein ständiges Hin und Her gegensätzlicher Anziehungskräfte."[20] It is plausible that symbols and images are the actual loci of polar harmony. In the ironized and realistic situation, however, there is an imbalance that distorts the aesthetic symmetry of the images (masks) that are held in a magnetic field. It is, however, plausible to posit an ideal symmetrical aesthetic image, a product of harmonious balance, that reality tries to copy. As the sign is a trope of the signified, the real image that is the product of imbalance would be a warped reduction of the ideal. This helps explain the genesis of the irregular images at, for instance, the opening of the **Majoratsherren.** In distorting these images the relationship of image to image(s) would also be distorted, thus creating a warped reality.

It is possible to relate the phenomenon of balance to symbol formation and to state that the symbol is a multivalent image held in place in the electromagnetic field between matter and spirit. This would advise an investigation of contemporary electromagnetic theory.

As most German intellectuals of his time, Arnim was exposed to the ideas of the philosopher F. W. Schelling, who was acquainted with both Arnim and Bettina. Certain aspects of Schelling's nature philosophy, as set down in his *Einleitung zu dem Entwurf eines Systems der Naturphilosophie* (published in 1799), serve as an excellent model for viewing Arnim's use of polarities and images. It has special import for a study of antitheses of light and gravity as well as for a study of his use of metaphor.

Schelling sees the universe as existing in a state of tension between *natura naturans* and *natura naturata,* between that which is becoming and that which has become. Matter is for Schelling not a substance but a nexus of opposing forces that combine to produce *aus flüssigem in festen Zustand freiwillig gleichsam regelmäßige Gestalten.*[21] This is a tension between fluidity and stasis or expansion and contraction. Schelling believes that these polarities, call them A and B, can combine and recombine with their synthetic products. A and B combine to produce C, which in turn can exist in tension with either A or B. The new poles of A and C now produce a new synthesis D, which in turn can recombine with either A or C. This process of recombination is called epigenesis, the geometrically progressing proliferation of opposites. Schelling describes this as *die beständige Fortdauer des Gegensatzes.*[22] This produces a universe that is constructed like a geodesic dome or structure of adjacent equilateral triangles. Each corner of each triangle is a product of opposing forces and is related, however remotely, to the universal totality. Thus Schelling says *also ist die Natur in jedem Product noch unendlich, und in jedem liegt der Keim eines Universums.*[23]. Thus the general is embodied in the particular or, more correctly, the infinite is reflected in the finite.

In order to demonstrate the idea of reflection of the whole in the part Schelling uses the following anecdote:

> *Ein Reisender nach Italien macht die Bemerkung, daß an dem großen Obelisk zu Rom die ganze Weltgeschichte sich demonstrieren läßt;—so an jedem Naturproduct. Jeder Mineralkörper ist ein Fragment der Geschichtsbücher der Erde.*[24]

This is a crystalline model of the universe in which each facet gathers the light of the whole and is indeed structurally related to the whole. The crystal is a useful metaphor here because of its illuminative and geometric properties. Each facet thereof is determined by polarization: *die Bedingung aller Gestalten ist Dualität.*[25] The nature of this polarity, in so far as it concerns the forms of matter, is electricity: *die elektrischen Erscheinungen sind das allgemeine Schema für die Construction der Materie überhaupt.*[26] Elsewhere he says: *Alles, was für uns sensibel ist [. . .] ist ohne Zweifel für uns sensibel nur durch Elektrizität, und das einzig unmittelbar Sensible möchte wohl die Elektrizität sein.*[27] These passages serve to illustrate the immense importance placed upon electricity, perhaps the greatest discovery of the eighteenth century. It is used to explain all phenomena and approaches the status of the life blood of the universe itself.

All bodies exist within the system of expansion and contraction of electrical energy. Thus Schelling asks, *Was sind denn die Körper selbst als verdichtete (gehemmte) Elektrizität?*[28] Incorporation is stasis of metamorphosis: *Organisationen [. . .] gehen durch Metamorphosen aus dem einen Element ins andere über; und was scheint das Thier, dessen Lebensfunktionen fast alle in Contraktionen bestehen, anders zu seyn als ein solcher Sprung?*[29] Schelling means that an animal is an image created by the temporary reduction and concentration of electrical energy in one place. Schelling sees this process of metamorphosis as the proper state between the poles of expansion and contraction:

> *Die Metamorphose wird nicht regellos geschehen können. Denn sie muß innerhalb des ursprünglichen Gegensatzes bleiben und ist dadurch in Grenzen eingeschlossen [. . .] Daher, wo der Gegensatz aufgehoben oder verrückt wird, die Metamorphose unregelmäßig wird.—Denn was ist auch Krankheit als Metamorphose?*[30]

Differentiation and change are the laws of existence and these laws are perceptible in every natural product. They are a sort of *Grundtypus der allen zugrunde liegt—und den sie, unter mannichfaltigen Abweichungen zwar, aber doch alle ausdrücken.*[31] A disturbance in polarity creates an aberrant change.

The fundamental polarity is that of gravity and light. Light is defined by Schelling as *jenes allgemeine Aufheben der Indifferenz*[32] that *setzt den ganzen Körper in Lichtzustand.*[33] Thus the return to metamorphosis is the reinstating of antitheses, and its product is light: *Wo daher der Gegensatz hergestellt wird, ist für uns Licht.*[34] The product of incorporation or stasis is a darkening, and its antithesis, the transition to metamorphosis, is light. Light stands in opposition to gravity: *die Aktion des Lichts muß mit der Aktion der Schwere, welche die Zentralkörper ausüben, in geheimem Zusammenhang stehen.*[35] Thus light and gravity combine to generate matter. The preponderance of gravity acts as a delimiting force; the preponderance of light indicates metamorphosis. Electricity is basically metamorphosis, and gravity is the force that makes it rest in one place. When electricity is condensed by gravity, it forms an image. The importance of this is that it implies that the ideal image (assuming that light is desirable and darkness not) is one that is in some state of flux.

When Arnim was eighteen years old, he published his ***Versuch einer Theorie der elektrischen Erscheinungen,***[36] where he employed some of Schelling's ideas in arguing for a fluid theory of electricity:

> *Hr. Schelling stellt als ausgemacht auf:*
>
> *I. daß die elektrische Materie ein zusammengesetztes Fluidum,*
>
> *II. ein Produkt der Lichtmaterie und einer anderen für jetzt noch unbekannten Materie sey, und*

*III. daß die beiden Elektrizitäten sich durch ihre ponderablen Basen reel unterscheiden, d. h. durch das quantitätische Verhältnis ihrer ponderablen Basen zum Licht.*[37]

Arnim does not adequately explain the *unbekannte Materie* in this essay, although he relates it to gravity, as is evident in the use of *ponderabel*. Arnim subsequently goes on to quote Schelling directly again:

*I. Wie eine chemische Zersetzung der Lebensluft die Phänomene des Verbrennens bewirkt, so bewirkt eine mechanische Zerlegung derselben die Phänomene der Elektrizität.*[38]

By *Lebensluft,* Arnim indicates atmosphere. The important concepts here are that electricity is a permeating and thus omnipresent fluid, and that it exists in quantitative proportion to light and gravity. Roman III above indicates a mechanics of electricity. An analysis of electric "fluid," with regard to the common designations used in mechanics, produces a Newtonian model of electricity involving polarities and vectors.

Based on this discussion of resemblances between Schelling and Arnim, it will be demonstrated that the following implicit points organize *Isabella von Aegypten*:

—Textual images are syntheses of polar forces.

—Each image embodies and reflects the totality.

—The basic poles are gravity and light.

—The ideal image mediates between matter and spirit and is both reflective and illuminative.

Each image in Arnim has two basic aspects that are interrelated. The first of these is its determination by larger polar forces; the second its relationship to other images. Each is a synthesis of antitheses and a metonymic part of a totality. A change in polarity alters the image. The result is that the new image has a different relationship to the whole.

The use of textual light imagery begins in the *Anrede an meine Zuhörer,* the preface to *Novellensammlung 1812,* which contains *Isabella.* The narrator claims that when he balances in the tension between control of and submission to poetic inspiration, his muse takes him to the *Urquell des höheren Lichtes.*[39] This sets up a dichotomy between the sphere of higher light and the sphere of phenomenal light. The former is described as

*Eben so die Theorie einer andern Welt [. . .] wie unser Licht, ohne von einer Theorie erfaßt zu werden, die Theorie aller unsrer Naturerscheinungen aufschließt.*

(449)

The higher light reveals the higher world in an automatic manner. One arrives there by heeding the voice of inspiration, and not through systematic induction. This illumination is a result of an establishment of opposition between will and inspiration. This corresponds to Schelling's maxim that light arises from the reinstatement of antitheses.

The reflection and reduction of higher light takes place in the first sentence of the story proper. Bella gazes with *glänzenden schwarzen Augen zum Schieber hinaus in den Schein des vollen Mondes.* (452) The moon is described in terms of its shine, denoting both reflection and light. Bella's gleaming black eyes indicate a reflection of the moonshine, which is in turn a reflection of sunshine. Thus there is a double reflection.

The actual source of light, the sun, is more distant in the heavens and not directly visible at this time. The moon acts as a mirror that relays this distant light. The light is again reflected in Bella's black eyes that, by virtue of their color, must absorb some light as well. It is as if the image is a product of light descending to earth, being pulled downward and darkening in the phenomenal process.

Bella cries in the moonlight for her father who has been innocently hanged on a tripod. The tripod is a manifold image of the cross, which gets reflected and trebled in this image. The tripod is *dreibeinig aber nich dreieinig.* (453) In this assonant pun all letters except the medial consonant *b* are identical. The one-to-one correspondence between the tripod and the Holy Trinity (*Dreieinigkeit*) is broken by the anomalous consonant. This is a metonymic reduction of an ideal Christian model.

The old gypsy Braka commands Bella: *nimm diesen Wein und dieses Töpfchen mit Schmorfleisch, halte ihm ein Totenmahl.* (453) This alludes to the Last Supper but the temporal sequence is reversed, taking place after the death of Bella's father Also, the Christian parallels are distorted further by the fact that Bella's father, Herzog Michael, married. The allusions to Christ are distributed among Bella, whom Braka describes as *unsre einzige Hoffnung,* (453) Michael, and the Mandrake that Bella creates. Michael is hanged with two others (an allusion to the Crucifixion) for having committed thievery: *er habe zwei Hähne gestohlen, und im Fortgehen habe ihn ihr Krähen verraten.* (455) This theft interrupts direct analogy with Christ which analogy is, however, taken up again in the betrayal and its association with cock-crowing. This alludes to the betrayal of Christ by Judas. Isabella's mission is to bear, by Charles V, a son who will lead her people back home. This also alludes to the Second Coming. The myriad of Christian images is presented in a distorted and fragmentary manner that is also anachronistic. We are dealing here with distorted images of Christian symbolism.

This illustrates the use of images as aberrant embodiments of higher, more remote entities. The sign is here a distortion of the signified. The use of Christian symbolism is an effective illustration of this distorting process because the reader is already aware of the ideal structure involved and can compare the latter to the distorted images. The reader feels as if the text were having difficulties receiving a clear picture of a transmission from above. Something is causing sporadic and distorted reception.

There is a continuous textual attempt at parallel delineation that falls short of one-to-one correspondence. The best textual example of this is the creation of the Golem Bella. She is an image of Bella, who is in turn an image of a higher entity. Golems are *Figuren aus Ton nach dem Ebenbilde eines Menschen abgedruckt.* (507) This alludes to the creation of man from clay in the image and likeness of God. The Golem-maker fashions his copies from an image of the person captured by his *Kunstspiegel*:

> *Der Kunstspiegel steckte in einem Guckkasten und die ganze Kunst war, Bella zu demselben hinzulocken.*
>
> (508)

The image of the *Guckkasten* is also revealing. It is said to show *eine Welt im Kleinen, alle Städte, alle Völker in bunten Bildern.* (508) This is a microcosm that contains a mirror, and that mirror captures an image of Bella. It is from this captured reflection that a likeness is created. This microcosm relates to the macrocosm of the real world, which, in itself, has a microcosmic relationship to a still higher macrocosm. Just as the Golem is created from an image transmitted from macrocosm to microcosm, so is Bella an image of a still higher entity.

This relationship, however, is not the perfect one-to-one correspondence of microcosm to macrocosm. The human form is not a miniature replica of God, nor is Golem a perfect miniature of Isabella.

> *Wenn es noch ein Paradies gäbe, so könnten wir so viel Menschen machen, als Erdenklöße darin lägen: da wir aber ausgetrieben aus dem Paradies, so werden unsre Menschen um so viel schlechter, als dieses Landes Leimen sich zum Leimen des Paradieses verhält!*
>
> (509)

The implicit relationship is as follows. That which humans create compares to humans, as our earth compares to the Garden of Eden. Both the Mandrake and the Golem are basic human derivatives that allude to and confuse a higher model.

The narrator characterizes Charles as confident that he can see through the *sinnetäuschende Kunst* (509) that has created Golem Bella, and tells the reader that this state of deception and ambiguity is a universal constant:

> *Auch hierin fand sich Cenrio heimlich wieder viel besser unterrichtet, ungeachtet ihm einige Dinge im Kopfe herumgingen, die er nicht bequem reimen konnte, vielleicht weil die Natur bloß Assonanzen machen wollte.*
>
> (526-527)

The narrator is operating here with the poetological distinctions among consonance, assonance, and dissonance. Consonance is pure harmony, assonance partial harmony, and dissonance the absence of harmony, or cacophony. It is said above that nature works in assonance, or in partial or distorted correspondences. The text imitates natural processes by dealing with assonances itself. These are series of distorted images of distorted images, sequences of anomalous relationships.

The Mandrake is another example of an image of an image, a derivative of a derivative. He, like Golem Bella, is a human construct. He is to humans as humans are to God. In the last reduction, however, the creative inheritance has been crippled. The Mandrake does not have the creative powers of the image that created him.

The images discussed above are aberrant reductions of higher entities. In the reduction, however, one sees structural identities with a higher model. This corresponds to Schelling's idea that the general is always, however remotely, visible in the particular.

The ideal textual figures, the gypsies, are transubstantiative and exist in flux between matter and spirit. Isabella and her gypsies are frequently associated with ghosts. They inhabit a house that is rumored to be haunted. This spectral aspect of Bella's nature is delineated in her reception by Charles. He initially thinks she is a ghost, and her presence has a transcendent effect upon him.

> *Der Erzherzog war in den bloßen Gedanken an die schöne Unbekannte, die er an dem Tage sehen sollte, so verliebt, daß es ihm wie eine Ueberfahrt auf dem langsamen Styx zu einem neuen Leben schien, wo alles freier, wunderbarer, liebreicher und schreck licher ihm erscheinen sollte.*
>
> (496)

The realm beyond the Styx is the abode of the dead, which is inhabited by the Shades, the souls of the dead. This passage indicates that transubstantiation occurs when Bella and Charles are juxtaposed, as if poles.

Bella's transforming effect is felt not only by Charles, but also by his tutor Adrian, The latter watches Bella sleep and undergoes a spiritualizing transformation:

> *Venus war jetzt Fleisch geworden, er rief sie in Horazens Verse leise an, und wer weiß wozu ihn diese läppische Schulweisheit verführt haben möchte, wenn er nicht mitten in seiner Adonisrolle seine Tonsur und sein graues Haar im Spiegel gesehen hätte. Ihm schauderte, es war ihm, als habe er einen Heiligen gesehen, der sich am Nachtmahlwein vor seinem Tode betrunken.*

(525)

The allusion to Adonis is especially interesting, as it was he who spent half his time the upper world and half in the lower world by decree of Zeus. Thus Adrian, via Bella's influence, is also on the verge of life and death, matter and spirit.

> *Befragen wir unser Herz wie wir sterben möchten: sicher wie Karl, die Geliebte unsrer Jugend als einen heiligen Engel zwischen uns und der Sonne, von der wir scheiden, weil sie uns blendet; gleichsam wie einen farbigen Vorhang, daß selbst die Schatten der blumenpflückenden und nichts fassenden Hände gefärbt erscheinen.*

(553)

Bella is a mediator between Charles and the higher light. She is also a curtain for a shadow play. It is through her that one can extrapolate to the workings of the higher world, which is immaterial, as is evident in the hands that grasp nothing. The illusion of color is gotten form the fabric itself; the higher entity is colorless. The curtain metaphor conveys the properties of woven fabric. This recurs in the ***Novellensammlung*** in the form of various tapestries and webs of interconnected metaphors.

The textual metaphors are incomplete illusions that silhouette the referent in an insufficient representation. The ideal image (e. g. Bella) is reduced, protean, and multivalent and, therefore, capable of metonymically alluding to the whole; it exists in transition from matter to spirit, from stasis to metamorphosis, while the undesirable image tends toward stasis. This image is found in the Mandrake and to some extent in Charles and Adrian. By ideal image is meant that image that most nearly approximates the concepts of matter-in-flux that Schelling describes.

Negative images are products of the preponderance of gravity and of the terrestrial. Due to their resistance to flux, they are minimally allusive. The negative demonic image is reflected textually in the image of a dog whose power is controlled by the gypsies. In this image the demonic is used in a constructive, almost sublimated

fashion. Perhaps the most interesting aspect of the demonic Simson is that he is exchanged for the materialistic Mandrake. This transfer of energy is expressed in the imagery of the text. Bella's hair aids in the transfer:

> *Und so sank ihr Haar, in dessen glatten Locken sich oft die Sterne wie im Haupthaar der Berenize gespiegelt hatten, im raschen Schnitt einer Schere wie ein schwarzer Schleier auf den Boden rings um sie her, ihren Hund Simson eine Kette daraus zu flechten, die ihm den Tod brächte*

(465)

The allusion is to the constellation Coma Berenices, or Berenice's locks of hair. She was the wife of Ptolemy III of Egypt, and she sacrificed her hair to Aphrodite. The astronomer Conon of Samos claimed it had formed a constellation. In this passage Bella's smooth, shiny black hair acts as a mirror for the stars, a collective metaphor for the higher or noumenal light. Bella is here a transmitter associated with reflection of higher light. The translucent aspect of fabric is present in the black veil metaphor, a darkening medium. Bella's hair, vehicle of mediation and reflection of higher light, is cut and used as a sort of chain with which Simson is to uproot the Mandrake. When the Mandrake is uprooted and consequently born, a hefty thunderclap slays Simson. This recalls Samson's loss of power after the cutting of his hair.

Bella sacrifices a part of her mediative abilities and uses them as a means of transforming controlled demonic energy into materialistic and capitalistic energy. This is a transformation of spirit into matter. The cutting of her hair is in itself indicative of a loss of power. Here it indicates a shift in reflective power, a new aberration. Since Bella's hair was described as a reflective medium, its alteration indicates a change in the reflected image. The thunderclap that slays Simson also strikes Bella senseless. When she awakes she sees *im ersten Morgenschimmer ihren toten Simson.* (465) This dawn of a new day and, indeed, of a new era, bears the new reflection, as is evident in the use of *Schimmer.* It is as if the explosive thunderclap had sprung the old system, and the first reflections from the rubble reveal the demon slain and the first silhouette of dawning materialism. *Ein menschenähnliches Wesen, gleichsam einen beweglichen Umriß* (468) is what Bella finds on the end of her braided hair.

The focal shift has produced a materialist demi-god in the aberrant image of Christ. His orientation is diurnal and his perceptions are literal. Charles, the Mandrake, Adrian and Golem are conspirators in contraction or stasis. They reify and concretize images and, in doing so, also despiritualize them. They focus on the image and the word as thing. They thus become matter, and their materialization absorbs light and becomes the graveness of gravity.

An incipient depolarization has effected this structural darkening. The juxtaposition of the proper poles, represented by Charles and Bella, generates illuminative transubstantiative images. That the transubstantiative image is, in fact, also illuminative relates to Schelling's theorem that light is generated by matter in flux. Bella first appears to Charles as if a lustrous tapestry: *in eine Leinewand statt des Hemdes gewickelt, die von einem goldnen Gürtel festgebunden wurde.* (461) This is the first textual use of the word *Leinewand,* which has an interesting double entendre. It is both textile fabric and text-ile of the artist, a canvas, upon which is formed a luminous image of Bella. She is like a woven image, a tapestry. This idea of lustrous artifact is also seen in the golden belt that holds the fabric, as well as in *die runden, blendenden Arme* (461) and in *die zierlichen, leisen Tritte der schimmernden Füße.* (461)

Bella has access to Charles' room through a *versteckte Tapetentüre,* (460) through which she moves freely. The literal meaning here is, of course, a wallpapered door. It figures, however, in the central allusion involving fabric and tapestry (cf. "Tapet"). She moves to Charles spatially through the veil of image. She also observes him through a *verstecktes Türloch.* (460)

Bella's movement through the textile images toward Charles is a movement from the transubstantiative to the concrete. She moves from lesser to greater definition. This corresponds to interaction between the noumenal and phenomenal spheres. This is spirit becoming matter, a displacement of forms to the phenomenal, which brings about a change in Bella. She possesses

> *dieselben geliebten Züge, aber ohne den farbigen Fruchtstaub, den das Anfassen der neugierigen Welt so leicht von dem unschuldigen Leben hinwegwischt, was uns Weintrinkern wie ein edles Faß vorkommt, das mit einer geringeren Menge unedlen Gewächses aufgefüllt worden: der Wein ist darum doch klar, edel, aber nicht mehr rein.*
>
> (536)

She has deviated from the state of immaculate conception to that of deception. The birth of the Mandrake involves Bella's lying to Braka and the death of a kitten, described as *den kleinen Mord.* (472) Bella feels *daß sie gesündigt; der Himmel ward dunkel über ihr, die Erde frostig unter ihr und die Luft unstet um sie her.* (472) These words allude to the atmosphere at the time of the Crucifixion, which has already been alluded to earlier. This involves darkening and corruption of the original ideal.

The reunion of Charles and Bella at the Kirmess is the center point of the story. Frau Nietken is immediately associated with light. The first indication of Nietken's presence is when Braka sees *die Lampe ihrer alten Diebesschwester, der Nietken.* (485) The party enters the house and is led

> *in einen Keller und durch den Keller in ein Bodenzimmer, das durch die Türe eines Nebenzimmers erleuchtet wurde.*
>
> (485)

The direction is upward to a source of higher light. This is an interesting Platonic arrangement. It reflects the situation in Plato's cave in which higher luminary sources produce imagery upon the cave wall. Here is similar effect is achieved by displacing the source of light to another room. This bears similarity to Bella's transgressing veil-like partitions in order to meet Charles. She is also to meet him in the house of Nietken. Braka leads the way

> *in dieses zweite erhellte Zimmer, wo eine dicke alte Frau, die in einem schönen, grünen, seidnen Kleide einer Platznelke glich, weil sie dasselbe hin und wieder, teils mit ihrem rotwollenen Unterrocke durchschimmern ließ.*
>
> (485)

The same Platonic paradigm that is seen in the Gypsy house now applies to Nietken herself, who stands at the center of the story and who brings about the union of Charles and Bella. Her translucent shimmering is compared to a pink carnation, which, of course, is a hybrid of white and red. The basic concept is one of translucent mediation of a removed source of higher light. This would coincide with her function as a fulfiller of the divine purpose of union between Charles and Bella.

This illustrates a metonymic relationship among paradigmatic images. The room alludes to the Platonic cave and reduces and distorts it by its transference to the image of Nietken. This is metonymic in so far as it is a distorted representation of another model. The ideal paradigm of a mask that shows a higher reality is resynthesized here in the bizarre figure of Nietken.

Nietken's room contains *die seltsamsten Vorräte von Altertümern aller Art.* (486) These are all associated with light:

> *Die Stühle zum Beispiel in der Dachkammer waren von hölzernen Mohren getragen, über jedem ein bunter Sonnenschirm [. . .] in der Mitte des Zimmers hing eine wunderliche gedrehte Messingkrone, sie hatte sonst die jüdische Synagoge zu Gent beleuchtet, jetzt steckte ein gewundenes buntes Wachslicht zu Ehren der Mutter Gottes darauf [. . .] an den Wänden hingen gewirkte Tapeten [. . .]*
>
> (486)

It is interesting to note that the crown is depicted as a source of light. The clear tonal qualities of the word *Messing*, conveyed by the velar nasal, add to the image of brightness. The use of the word *Wachslicht,* as opposed to simply *Kerze,* emphasizes an incandescent source of light. The location of the crown is elevated, indicating a source of higher light. Its use as a shrine to the Holy Mother indicates its function as an upwardly directed metaphor. This room is bathed in a variegated, almost prismatic dispersal of color.

The coincidence of the union between Charles and Bella and of the increase in variegation is most interesting. The Kirmess itself is a celebration of color. During this union there is an interesting delineation of mediating textual imagery. Bella confesses her love and tells Charles

> *wie ich mit dir gegangen, ahnte ich von allem dem nichts; und sieh, wie die Spinnweben am Baum im Mondschein sichtbar glänzen, während ich des Tau-werks des Schiffes dort im Dunkel nicht unterscheiden kann; so fühle ich höhere Wege und Ahne doch nicht. was mir in den nächsten Tagen bevorsteht.*
>
> (513)

This union also has celestial manifestations:

> *Er sagte, daß Adrian von dem Orte forteile, weil er ein wunderbares Sternzeichen entdeckt [. . .] er schwor, daß diese Nacht den wunderbarsten Sohn der Venus und des Mars gezeugt habe [. . .]*
>
> (514)

The image of the spider webs in the trees is interesting in that the usual term *Gewebe* is not present, but replaced by the uncommon *Spinnweben.* The former would have sufficed to allude to the process of weaving and to fabric in general. The latter, however, strengthens this allusion even further by foregrounding the image of spinning or weaving. This is a veil of illusion reflecting the reflected light of the moon. The masts and rigging of the ships in the distance portend a journey in a new web of reflection. If one views the web metaphor as a fabric of reality, then the passing of the ship's rigging, here related to the web, implies that a structure of reality is passing. This portends the slackening of the tensile fabric.

The congress of Charles and Bella, in that is has astrological significance, also constitutes a turning point both in story and history. The metaphor of a ship passing in the night indicates a transition to an uncertainty. The metaphoric foregrounding of the ship's *Tauwerk* and its subsequent departure indicate a transition from an old synthesis to a new one. Bella ponders the ambiguities:

> *nachdem das Geräusch seiner Abreise vorübergegangen, währenddessen Bella kaum durch die Scheiben ihm trübe nachzublicken wagte, als das Schiff im Dunkeln anfing zu schwanken, die weißen Segel sich ausbreiteten und die Ruderer endlich das Wasser anregten: "Ach," dachte sie, "die mächtige Gewalt des Tauwerks, das sich vorher unserm Blicke verbarg, tritt so schnell hervor, uns zu trennen, wird es auch eine unsichtbare Gewalt geben, die uns wieder verbindet?"*
>
> (515)

The initial perception is mediated through panes, indicating a distanced and unclear view of an image that is progressively fading. The earlier fabric of bonds is fading out of the light; the weave is changing.

This is also indicated in a transmutation in Bella. In order to evade the advances of two noblemen, she must disguise herself as a peasant. The Kirmess is still in progress, and the peasants appear *unter großen Mänteln und Larven versteckt.* (517) They are not in, but underneath cloaks and masks.[40] The uses of *Mantel* and *Larve* are ambiguous. The former also has the figurative meaning of cloak or hull. The latter, in addition to the meaning of mask, also means larva, indicating a transmutation or chrysalis. This takes place *hinter dem Schirme,* (517) again a translucent image. Bella exchanges clothes with one of the peasants and thus metamorphoses, as indicated in the textual use of *verlarvt.*

The separation of Charles and Bella is coincident with loss of mediative power. These are reflected in Bella's dream of her father. She dreams that

> *seine Beine waren aber aneinandergewachsen, und seine Hände an den Leib gelegt.*
>
> (519)

He has now adopted some of the characteristics of the Mandrake. His hands are associated with his body. His image is thus organicized and corporealized. This indicates a dominance of terrestrial orientation. This is made especially acute when delineated in the realm of dream, which is normally associated with access to the higher sphere. The loss of mediative power is also present in the narrative voice. The narrator asks, when two Bellas stand face to face, *wie läßt sich alles gegenseitige Erstaunen malen?* (520) This is accompanied by a maid who drops a lamp in astonishment. Bella, an image of the deity, and Golem, an image of Bella, face each other *gegenseitig,* as if two mirrors. The resultant usurpation of reflective or mediative power is indicated in the falling of the lamp and especially in the narrative doubt as to the ability to paint, i.e. render a synthetic image of, the occurrence. Thus the text itself reflects the loss of illuminative power.

The haunted house is now the residence of the Mandrake. Bella approaches her old house and

*verkroch sich zwischen den Säulen einer kleinen Kapelle der heiligen Mutter, die neben ihrem ehemaligen Hause ganz verlassen unerleuchtet stand.*

(531)

The shrine to the Holy Mother, a metonymic allusion to the higher order, is unilluminated. It is metonymic because it is a distorted model of a greater process, a single limited aspect trying to reflect the whole. The darkening process has spread, and it has interrupted transmission between the higher world and its metonymically distorted microcosms: Thereupon follows a celestial response to Bella in her desperation:

*Als der Mond an dem hohen, pyramidalen Kirchturm, der vor ihr wie ein Schatten stand, wie das Licht eines Leuchtturms emporstieg, und sie dachte der Pyramiden Aegyptens und ihres Volkes.*

(533)

The use of a pyramidal structure is textually consistent. It corresponds to the ship's *Tauwerk,* which is used as a metaphor for the structure of the cosmos. This is a more appropriate metaphor than the web, for the latter evokes a two-dimensional image and the former a three-dimensional one. The *Tauwerk* is a conical network that incompletely represents the cosmos, as do the cathedral tower and pyramid. An increase in gravity has altered the structure of reality; this is figuratively represented in a description of Lady Chievres, whose husband appoints the Mandrake minister of finance (*Reichsalraun* [543]). She appears

*in einem weißen Damast, auf dessen vorderer Fläche Adam und Eva unter dem Apfelbaume gewebt waren.*

(541)

The act of appointing the Mandrake to the position of minister of finance effects the completion of his development as the embodiment of materialistic spirit. It also effects the completion of a Second Fall. This is indicated in the image of Adam und Eve under the Tree of Knowledge. The use of *gewebt* corresponds to the numerous textual instances of the use of a woven fabric to denote mediation. This indicates a new synthesis. The weave has changed to form a new bond. This is the bond of exchange of capital, a new socio-economic fabric.

There is, however, a momentary breakthrough of these higher forces. Gypsies come to fetch Bella and stand beneath her window:

*Sie hatten ihre Hände und Kleider mit einer Phosophorauflösung getränkt, die in jener Zeit nur ihnen bekannt war; sie leuchteten in Dampfwolken und wo sie*

*einander berührten oder aneinander strichen, wurde dies Leuchten zu einem hellen Glanze, der einige Zeit nachwährte [. . .]*

(547)

The use of phosphorous is textually consistent. Friction causes, in a sporadic manner, an electrical discharge that fades slowly. This phenomenon, against the background of night, gives the impression of an emergence of light from background to foreground. This is a luminous penetration of a medium. It recalls the translucent shimmering of Nietken and the Platonic cave metaphor. This is another instance of the allusive network of the text. This particular phosphorescent image alters the underlying Platonic metaphor in a new way. Ideal images are not only distorted; they are made absurd, and their absurdity shows the pathology of the cosmos. Bella's countrymen, the peripatetic gypsies, have arrived. It is as if the hand of a wandering spirit had passed through the membrane of terrestrial reality to take Bella away.

There is a contrast between Bella's submission to forces greater than the self and Charles' resistance to these forces. His resistance is indicated in his opposition to the dream state, which is a state of communication with higher forces. This is evident:

*als der Erzherzog aus dem bänglichen Schlusse seines Herrschertraumes zum Lichte aufwachte, das allen Träumen mit den kecken Worten entgegenzutreten scheint: ihr seid nicht wahr, denn ihr besteht nicht vor mir!—da meinte auch er, alles Traurige, was ihn bedroht, sei ein Hirngespinst gewesen. Wer spinnt aber im Innern unsres Hirnes? Der die Sterne im Gewölbe des Himmels in Gleichheit und Abwechslung bewegt!*

(544)

This is one of the central passages of the work. It contains associative connections among dream, spirit, fabric, and higher light. The dream is a message from the higher sphere. It is a tapestry spun by a higher power. There is a connection among *Hirngespinst, spinnen* and, implicitly, *Gespenst.* The spiritual realm is a creative realm of fabrication of images. This is evident in the primary metaphor that describes the firmament as a vault within which the higher power moves luminary bodies in an alternating and balanced manner. The vault of heaven or *Gewölbe* also contains the network imagery present in the fabric metaphors, especially the *Tauwerk.* The vault is a lattice-work of support members interconnected in a geodesic fashion. This construct is also a balanced and ordered source of light.

The allusions found in the firmament image recur in the ultimate textual metaphor, the cathedral:

*Welche Einheit und Ausgleichung aller Verhältnisse, wie fest begründet alles an der Erde und doch dem Himmel eigen, zum Himmel führend, an seiner Grenze am herrlichsten und prachtvollsten geschlossen. Zum Himmel richtet die Kirche wie betende Hände, unzählige Blütenknospen und Reihen erhabener Bilder empor, alle zu dem Kreuze hinauf, das die Spitze des Baues als Schluß des göttlichen Lebens auf Erden bezeichnet, das als die höchste Pracht der Erde, die sich dadurch zu unendlichen Taten begeistert fühlt, einzig mit dem Golde glänzt, womit kein andres Bild oder Zeichen neben ihm in der ganzen heiligen Geschichte, die der Bau darstellt, sich zu schmücken wagt.*

(533)

The description of the church begins with similar images of uniformity and harmony. This image borders on heaven and constitutes the culmination of terrestrial existence. It is also the culmination of terrestrial imagery and the ideal ordering principle thereof. The image of a gothic spiral, crowned by a cross, recapitulates the earlier image of a pyramidal church tower capped by the moon. This gothic spiral receives the higher light and disperses it throughout inner space, as in the pyramid. This image also recapitulates the metaphor of the *Tauwerk*. This is evident in the lattice work of intersecting support in the gothic spiral. It also corresponds to the vault of the firmament examined above, as it is also an arched structure of intersecting beams. The relationship between the firmament and the tower is one of macrocosm to microcosm, the latter being a reduced image of the former.

Perhaps the most significant statement in this passage is that this construct represents all holy (i. e. Judeo-Christian) history. This paradigm is thus in itself the structure of reality. The relegation of such a profound and sweeping statement to a mere imbedded relative clause is in itself significant. It is as if reader were being given sporadic and instantaneous glimpses of truth. The narrator does not represent this by extended treatise, but flashes it, as if it were being reflected in a mirror, the focal point of which just happened to cross the reader's eye at that point in time. Such is the nature of derivative reality.

Illumination and flux occur when poles are juxtaposed and when a balance is established between them. The tension between poles is often textually represented via images of stretched fabric that act as metaphoric representations of the force vectors that constitute the nexus of an electromagnetic field.

*Endlich kam Braka zurück und da ihr an der Türe nicht aufgemacht worden, schlich sie in den Garten, wo sie das wunderbare Bild wie versteinert sah, den kräftigen Michael im Totenhemde mit der glänzenden silbernen Krone, über ihm das bleiche Mädchen, die schwarzen Locken über ihm hinwallend, an ihrem Kleide gehalten von dem schwarzen Hunde mit feurigen Augen.*

(456-457)

Bella is here balancing on the river bank out of which the apparition of her father has arisen. There is also tension present in the image. One imagines two opposing vectors, Bella and Simson, with Bella's dress absorbing the stress. This fabric then is taut between the polarized vectors. It is also the fabric that holds or enshrouds Bella. Capitulation to the image of her father constitutes passing from the earthly to the spiritual realm. What keeps her from self-sacrifice is the image of the dog with demonic attributes. Bella exists then in between these two realms in a sort of purgatory that corresponds to the general gypsy state of penance.

Balancing is a trait of Bella's gypsy countrymen as well *wie sie schwere Tische auf ihren Zähnen im Gleichgewichte trugen, wie sie sich springend in der Luft über schlugen oder auf den Händen gingen.* (454) Herzog Michael can carry *acht Männer auf Arm und Schultern.* (455) He is a fulcrum around which these forces pivot and through which they enter into a dependent relationship. Similarly, demonic forces and higher forces interrelate through Isabella in the image of her balancing on a river bank. These normally antipodal forces enter into a unified field and are contained via Bella. There are also germs of correspondence here with the cathedral or firmament images. The use of the word *Gleichgewicht* corresponds to the *Gleichheit* and *Ausgleichung* used in those images. There is a common equilibrium and balancing of forces involved.

The persecution of the gypsies and the subsequent execution of Herzog Michael indicate a disturbance in those fulcra that exert a harmonizing influence. There ensues in the work a displacement of the lines of tension between Bella and the demonic Simson. Bella cuts her hair and weaves it into a chain that she fastens between Simson and the Mandrake. This indicates a displacement of a pole from the former to the latter. Her shiny black hair was also a medium for reflection of celestial light, and a loss of reflective power was indicated in the cutting thereof. The medium also gets rewoven into a chain, which indicates a confining. This is also a transition from a medium of aesthetic appeal to one of little beauty. The actual uprooting of the Mandrake is a violent act. There is great tension placed upon the chain of hair, which tension is broken by the uprooting. The terrifying thunderclap that ensues evokes images of destruction. The celestial location of the explosion conveys a collapsing of the firmament structure. This collapse is coincident with the generation of the Mandrake, of whom it is said: *sein gelbfaltiges Gesicht schien entgegengesetzte Menschenalter zu vereinigen.* (471) The use of *scheinen* with *Gesicht*, the latter connoting a sur-face, indicates a new reflective medium. The use of *vereinigen* with *entgegengesetzt* indicates a polar tension. This shift in tension has effected a reformation of the fabric and resulted in a new image, for a stretching of the fabric must effect a change in its mediative properties.

A metonymic reduction of the fabric metaphor is found in the image of the spider web discussed above. The description of the web contains a synthesis of the phenomena of reflection, mediation, balance and tension. The web is apparently independent and autonomous, and it also possesses an extreme lightness in defiance of gravity. It is a self-sufficient reduction of the universal blueprint. It is also a tense medium upon which the spider walks tightrope.

A metonymic relationship occurs between the spider web and the massive *Tauwerk,* or ship's rigging, which exemplifies the function of metaphor in the text. Each intersection of lines in the *Tauwerk* is three-dimensional, as opposed to the web, which connotes a flatter or two-dimensional image. Thus each intersection relates to numerous other intersections, as in a model of a molecule. Such is the relation among metaphors in the text; they are multivalently interconnected. The Mandrake, for instance, denotes terrestriality, as he is a plant, sensuality, as the plant was considered to have aphrodisiac powers, and materialism, as the root was considered to be a means to wealth. The gypsies denote liberated wandering, occult practices, juggling and balancing, spirituality, non-materialism and folk poetry. All of these connotations are employed in the text. Indeed, the near-obsessive consistency and intricateness of metaphor demonstrates that each is chosen precisely for its multivalent properties. Bella's hair, for instance, was compared to the constellation Coma Berenices, thus to a source of higher light. It also reflects that constellation, thus being a reflective medium. Its blackness indicates absorption of light and thus distortion of the original image. Its cutting indicates a loss in illuminative power. It is woven into a chain, indicating a resynthesis, i. e. a new weave or pattern, as well as bondage. It is also used in the tension between the Mandrake and Simson, and is involved in the sacrifice of the latter and the genesis of the former. Thus the single image of Bella's hair is a radiant metaphor that expands outward in a three dimensional pattern, as in the intersections of the *Tauwerk.*

These multivalent metaphors are not sequentially arranged in a cause-and-effect pattern.[41] The work illustrates its theses not by deductive processes but via metaphors that interconnect by association. If polarities shift, then their products will be changed. If each product alludes to the whole, then there will be a new allusion; the new image is a trope of the light image that strikes it. It is *eine Welt im Kleinen.* Just as the *Guckkasten*

generated an aberrant copy of Bella, so does a tropic image distort what it reflects. This is the reason for the misunderstandings and bizarre situations among various characters in the text. Each character is also an image that is an idiosyncratic trope of the information it receives. The tropes become darker as gravity increases and lighter as polarity and electromagnetic energy increase. Thus an image is a synthesis of polar forces.

Each intersection in the webbing of the *Tauwerk* is an image that gathers ambient light and reflects other images in the structure as a whole. Each intersection is also connected, however remotely, to the whole. The ratio, however, between the whole and each image is not an analogous one, but an anomalous one. It is a metonymic correspondence of differences, distortions and aberrations.

When Golem Bella was fashioned from the *Guckkasten,* there was a discussion of an implicit ratio. The ratio was Golem: Bella = Bella: x. This indicates that there are progressive levels of reduction in image formation. A close reading of the text reveals that the *Tauwerk* is also a reduced image of a higher ideal textual metaphor. This is the gothic cathedral.

The cathedral has the attributes of a permanent and immovable image; the *Tauwerk* is relatively flexible. This indicates the discrepancy between the higher ideal structure and the compromised real structure. The permanence of the cathedral is strengthened by its association with the firmament. The cathedral exists as an image between the highest noumenal structure and the *Tauwerk.* The reader is told that there is *kein andres Bild neben ihm in der ganzen heiligen Geschichte.* (553) Thus it is the ultimate phenomenal image and the penultimate universal image.[42] When put into practice and subject to historical forces, the terrestrial image becomes warped and the correspondences to the higher image become vague. Thus we see the incomplete Christian imagery at the onset of the work. It is as if the *Tauwerk* were swaying within *dem hohen, pyramidalen Kirchturm,* (533) and dispersing the light within the pyramidal structure in a diffuse and aberrant manner.[43] Consequently, one is left with partial images of distorted Christendom. These are prismatic diffractions: the prism is also a pyramid.[44]

Figures like Bella and the gypsies sway with the shifting *Tauwerk.* They are masters of balance who possess faith and fearlessness. This enables them to perform acrobatics. It also enables Bella to take her leap of faith into the arms of her people. The shifting *Tauwerk* frightens figures like the Mandrake and Charles, who resist swaying ambiguity. This is evident in a humorous scene involving the Mandrake, who has been bound underneath an oven.

*Der Kleine, der schwebend angebunden hing und unter sich die Fliesen sah, die ein Meer mit Schiffen darstellten, glaubte in seinem Halbrausche, er fliege über dem Meere, und wollte sich damit sehen lassen. Als ihm aber die Bande gelöst wurden und er mit der Nase auf dieses Meer fiel, da glaubte er sich verloren.*

(539)

The Mandrake is transported into a state that has been associated with Bella. The use of *Schweben* has described her etherealness in several instances. The verb is also used in association with the spider. This is a very positive context in the work. When the Mandrake is placed in this situation, however, it becomes a ludicrous one. It lacks the appealing aesthetic qualities that it has when it includes Bella. It is also different in three other ways. Firstly, the Mandrake is simply hanging over the tiles. He is not really balancing there and is actually bound. This binding image relates associatively to the chain of hair by which he was born, which chain was involved with the sacrifice of mediative power. Secondly, the Mandrake takes illusion for reality. He gets lost in the particular image that confronts him and loses relation to the general structure. Illusion is not transparent to him as it is to Bella. Thirdly, and this point is connected to the second, he is afraid of drowning. His particular attention eclipses the general faith necessary to sustain his fall. It is interesting to note that once his bonds are removed, he enters into a panic. He needs to be anchored in order to feel secure. The chain is the vestigial umbilical cord of his birth.

The chain also finds expression elsewhere in the text and represents the tension of bondage and not of balance. The former affects Bella in her dealings with Charles and the Mandrake:

*Ein Schlag, mächtig wie jener, der sie auf dem Galgenberge betäubte, doch ohne jenes Schrecken, hatte ihre Erinnerung aufgeklärt, und wie das goldne Vlies an einer starken, unauflöslichen Kette um seinen Hals hing, so war sie an seinen Blicken hängengeblieben.*

(493)

This passage contains an explicit reference to the birth of the Mandrake. The thunderclap occurred when the chain of Bella's hair uprooted the Mandrake. A similar thunderclap occurs when Bella's dependency on Charles is described by analogy with a chain. The loss in reflective power that was brought about by the genesis of the Mandrake is accompanied by a loss in balancing power. Bella has now "gravitated" toward Charles. It is as if the *Tauwerk* has become bottom-heavy, the greater proximity to the earth darkening the images that are distorted by the stretched structure. Charles

*versank in einen schönen Traum; es war ihm, als sähe er mit den prachtvollen Goldketten, die ihm der Alraun gefunden, die spanischen Großen, die selbst vor dem*

*Könige mit bedecktem Haupte zu erscheinen wagten, zur Erde gedrückt; es war ihm, als könnte er viele tausend Soldaten mit diesen Ketten ziehen.*

(546)

This is the chain as agent of bondage to the material. This is evident in the phrase *zur Erde gedrückt*. It is also the agent of authoritarian oppression and of war. It is a tool of gravity and not of levity.

Proper harmony is one of a balance between metamorphosis and stasis, as has been described in the body of this study. There would be an outward progression toward synthesis that would be checked by an arresting movement toward containment and analysis. This cycle would repeat itself as if an alternating current of progressive and contractive energy. This resembles basic concepts of Romantic Irony in that the broad generalizing statement must be ironized and qualified in order to move to the next higher generalization.

The polar alternation is the ideal model. It has been demonstrated that the ideal polarity is reflected in a multitude of microcosms, each of which reflects the universal polarization in a metonymic manner. A close reading of the parallel microcosmic versions of universal polarity has demonstrated that within each polarity there is a certain tension that maintains balance, and that this creates a three-dimensional structure. This structure has its roots in the fundamentally Romantic science of Arnim, and is based on Schelling's maxim that matter is the synthetic product of light and gravity. The most brilliant and polychromatic of textual images are those resulting from an opposition of poles.

The text seems to lack any substantial argument for a dualistic world view. The sharp contrasts and near-exclusivity of the conscious level versus the inner workings of the psyche, as one sees in Tieck's *Der blonde Eckbert* or *Der Runenberg,* are not found here. Novalis' insistence upon a marriage of nocturnal dream and diurnal sobriety is also absent here. The text deals with polarity and not with dualism. This means that there is no real schism between self and nature, as everything exists in a degree of polar tension and is universally related, however remotely. Nevertheless, the self can be unaware of its universal connections and can also exist in a reduced relationship to the whole. It cannot, however, be apart from the whole. Primal polarities combine and find their loci within the individual, who is one of the multitude of intersections in the universal network. There seems to be little *Sehnsucht* here. One does not long for reunion but exists instead in union. The question really deals with the behavioral requisites for experiencing union, which hold that the self will exist in a state of grace and will communicate with the higher realm if the self establishes a polarity and balances in tension between poles.

The quality of "universal" experience in this tensile balance is, however, greatly reduced. One may be part of the whole, but not the whole itself. The particular part is, however, a microcosmic distortion and reduction of the macrocosm, but it is still connected to it. Arnimian Irony does not result from self/nature or self/non-self dualism. It is similar to Schlegelian Irony in that it demonstrates insufficiency and limit, but it differs by lacking the autonomy of mind characteristic of early Romanticism. It advocates an intuitive balancing between poles that is based on a universal electromagnetic model. This is not a sentimental state but one of cosmic participation that is not ruptured or disjointed, only indirect and reduced.

## Notes

1. Wolfdietrich Rasch, *Achim von Arnims Erzählkunst,* Deutschunterricht, 7, (1955), p. 38.

2. Rasch, p. 47.

3. Rasch, p. 47.

4. Helene Kastinger Riley, *Idee und Gestaltung: Das konfigurative Strukturprinzip bei Ludwig Achim von Arnim* (Bern: Herbert Lang, 1977), p. 43.

5. Horst Meixner, *Romantischer Figuralismus: Kritische Studien zu Romanen von Arnim, Eichendorff und Hoffmann* (Frankfurt: Athenäum, 1971), pp. 76-77.

6. Meixner, p. 77.

7. Meixner, p. 77.

8. Hans Steffen, *Lichtsymbolik und Figuration in Arnims erzählender Dichtung,* in *Die deutsche Romantik,* ed. Hans Steffen (Göttingen: Vandenhoeck und Ruprecht, 1971), p. 188.

9. Steffen, p. 196.

10. Ludwig Völker, *Naturpoesie, Phantasie, Phantastik. Ueber Achim von Arnims Erzählung Isabella von Aegypten,* in *Romantik: Ein literaturwissenschaftliches Studienbuch,* ed. Ernst Ribbat (Königstein: Athenäum, 1979), p. 131.

11. Lawrence O. Frye, *Textstruktur als Kunstauffassung: Achim von Arnim und die Aesthetik Schillers. Literaturwissenschaftliches Jahrbuch,* XXV (1984), pp. 153-154. Frye also says, in the same passage, "Das Gewicht der Mosaikstücke wird auch außerhalb des Aesthetischen oft symbolisch bewertet." Frye sees, in Arnim, a mixing of aesthetic and non-aesthetic realms.

12. Lawrence O. Frye, *Mesmerism and Masks: Images of Union in Achim von Arnim's Hollins Liebeleben and Die Majoratsherren,* Euphorion, 76 (1982), p. 86.

13. Frye, *Mesmerism,* p. 86.

14. Frye, *Mesmerism,* p. 92. Frye says, as is evident here, that balance is often spatially represented in Arnim.

15. Rasch, p. 55.

16. Albert Béguin, *L'âme romantique et le rêve* (Paris: Corti, 1939), p. 250.

17. Frye, *Mesmerism,* p. 84. Frye has shown the element of independence in ideal aesthetic balance. He sees it as "das, was sich ohne Zwang und Mühe machen läßt und von allem Druck befreit oder frei ist" (*Textstruktur,* p. 141).

18. Frye, *Mesmerism,* p. 91.

19. Claude David, *Achim von Arnim: Isabella von Aegypten. Essai sur le sens de la littérature fantastique* in *Festschrift Richard Alewyn,* ed. Herbert Singer und Benno von Wiese (Köln: Böhlau, 1967), p. 330.

20. Frye, *Textstruktur,* p. 143. Frye argues that aesthetic forms of representational activity convey a shifting balance of various polar forces.

21. F. W. J. Schelling, *Sämmtliche Werke* (Stuttgart: Cotta, 1858), III, p. 272.

22. Schelling, p. 309.

23. Schelling, p. 271.

24. Schelling, p. 291.

25. Schelling, p. 299.

26. Schelling, p. 299.

27. Schelling, p. 295.

28. Schelling, p. 319.

29. Schelling, p. 300.

30. Schelling, p. 300.

31. Schelling, p. 300.

32. Schelling, pp. 318-319.

33. Schelling, p. 319.

34. Schelling, p. 319.

35. Schelling, p. 318.

36. Achim von Arnim, *Versuch einer Theorie der elektrischen Erscheinungen* (Halle: J. J. Gebauer, 1799).

37. Achim von Arnim, *Versuch einer Theorie der elektrischen Erscheinungen,* p. 67.

38. Achim von Arnim, *Versuch einer Theorie der elektrischen Erscheinungen,* p. 68.

39. Achim von Arnim, *Sämtliche Romane und Erzählungen,* ed. Walther Migge (München: Hanser, 1965), II, p. 449. All primary quotations are taken from this edition.

40. Frye, *Textstruktur,* p. 144. This is the *Musikantenbande* that Frye sees as aiding Bella in her escape from the ineffectual realm of aesthetic "Schein." This corresponds to Frey's point that the moment of most striking aesthetic effect, here a dazzling example, is also a most dangerous and ambivalent moment. Here Frye says, "Denn das ästhetisch Auffallendste, Glänzendste und Beeindruckendste kann dem Menschen auch am gefährlichsten sein." Frye argues that the irony therein is that at this aesthetic moment one must leave the aesthetic realm in order to survive ethically, and that this escape is actually aided by consequences of the aesthetic itself.

41. Lothar Ehrlich, *Ludwig Achim von Arnim als Dramatiker: Ein Beitrag zur Geschichte des romantischen Dramas,* WZUH, 19, no. 5 (1970), p. 58. Ehrlich has noted this structural principle in his study of Arnim's dramas: "Die Szenenfolge hat keine Kausaleffekte, sondern eine additive Reihung von realtiv autonomen Szenen, die retardierend wirken und unterschiedlich plastisch gestaltet sein können." Each scene is a three-dimensional intersection of the *Tauwerk* that stands in associative and not causal relationship to other scenes.

42. Heinz Günther Hemstedt, *Symbolik der Geschichte bei Ludwig Achim von Arnim,* Diss. Göttingen 1956, p. 201. Hemstedt sees a transcendent unity in which all earthly oppositions culminate: "Die Ganzheit ist die höhere Welt [. . .], die alle irdischen Gegensätze in einer letzten metaphysischen Einheit aufhebt."

43. Hans Vilmar Geppert, *Achim von Arnims Romanfragment Die Kronenwächter* (Tübingen: Niemeyer, 1979), p. 123. Geppert holds that, in the Arnimian cosmology, terrestrial reality is a crystalline formation that scatters the light of the higher existence.

44. Ernst Schürer, *Quellen und Fluß der Geschichte: Zur Interpretation von Achim von Arnims Isabella von Aegypten,* in *Lebendige Form: Interpretationen zur deutschen Literatur. Festschrift für Heinrich Henel,* ed. J. L. Sammons und E. Schürer (München: W. Fink, 1970), p. 202. Here Schürer compares the pyramid and the *Leuchtturm.*

## Vickie L. Ziegler (essay date 1991)

SOURCE: Ziegler, Vickie L. Introduction to *Bending the Frame in the German Cyclical Narrative: Achim von Arnim's* Der Wintergarten *& E. T. A. Hoffmann's* Die Serapionbrüder, pp. 9-24. Washington, D.C.: The Catholic University of America Press, 1991.

[*In the following essay, Ziegler examines the various sources that inspired the composition of* Der Wintergarten, *among them Arnim's extensive readings of German history and folklore, as well as the "cyclical" narratives of such writers as Boccacio and Goethe. Writing shortly after the defeat of the Prussian army at the hands of Napoleon Bonaparte, a period of extreme volatility in Germany's political, cultural, and social climate, Arnim strove to create a distinctly romantic representation of Germany's illustrious past, reinterpreting various historical and literary sources into a more modern form.*]

### INTRODUCTION

Es müßte sonderbar in ihren Winter hinein blühen, wenn inhen so der sinn für das Große eines Volks aufgehen sollte und für sein Bedürfnis.

—**"Von Volksliedern,"** *1805*

Things would have to flower remarkably in their winter, if for them the sense of the greatness of a people and its needs were to open up.

—**"On Folk Songs,"** *1805*[1]

While the works of Achim von Arnim often seem like the forlorn stepchildren of German Romantic literature, even within a mistreated family, one child may suffer more from misunderstanding and neglect than the others. The condescending dismissal that ***Der Wintergarten*** has suffered is probably due in large part to the dependence of the work on sources, which is initially its most striking characteristic. With the exception of Wulf Segebrecht, most critics have not been willing to look more deeply at this narrative.[2]

***Wintergarten*** deserves a better fate than an airy dismissal as a badly seasoned rehash of older material, not only because it was important to Arnim's own development as a writer, but also because Arnim had to examine problems similar to the post-World War II German political situation. In both cases, Germans had experienced the capitulation of their country in the face of a devastating defeat as well as the total collapse and decay of value systems in the personal and political spheres. Seen as a linchpin in Arnim's early development, *Wintergarten* takes on added significance. *Wintergarten* was not simply a futile literary exercise from a man who read too much; it was Arnim's attempt to advance his own deeply held beliefs about the interdependent role of literature, political action, and religious belief.

In 1808, when Arnim began collecting materials for this cycle, he had already immersed himself for years in the study of older German literature, the first fruits of which were the *Wunderhorn*.[3] There are two main streams apparent in this pursuit: the belief, which was with him from the very first, that art is a means for all sorts and conditions of men to come together and the didactic, exemplary value of older literary works.[4]

Because of this didactic tendency, Arnim's goals differed from those of the philologically inclined literati. Johann Friedrich Voß, for example, the renowned Homer translator, blasted Arnim for the liberties taken with original texts.[5] Clemens Brentano wanted to restore an old folksong; Arnim wanted to change the points of emphasis. The purpose of this new version was to make material from the past accessible to his contemporaries so that it could have the desired exemplary effect.[6] Arnim believed that it was the mission of art to present this material in such a way that those in a different age understood it and learned the necessary lessons.[7]

Drawing the appropriate conclusion from the past to affect one's behavior in the present seemed particularly crucial to Arnim in the early years of the nineteenth century as Napoleon stormed through Europe. His concern with the fate of his countrymen was already apparent in the important essay, **"On Folk Songs,"** written in 1805. This work contains numerous passages lamenting the spiritual decline of Germany from its earlier greatness, implying the existence of a more propitious period in Germany history.[8] The belief in a Golden Age was one that Arnim had in common with other Romantics; Möllers notes that he agreed with Grimm's concept of a paradisiacal time which marked the beginning of human history, when God's will and man's were identical. Arnim's own adaptation of these ideas differed from those of other Romantics. Unlike Novalis, who projected human wishes into the past, Arnim believed in the continual presence of this primordial time in human history.[9] Another passage from the folk song essay bears this belief out: "Und als ich dieses feste

Fundament noch unter den Wellen, die alten Straßen und Plätze der versunkenen Stadt noch durchschimmern sah, . . ." ["And as I saw, still under the waves, this firm foundation, the old streets and squares of the sunken city still gleaming through the water . . ."].[10]

If the primordial time still exists buried in the events of the day, then a way must be found to bring it to view in the present. Like other Romantic writers, Arnim saw art as an intermediary between different worlds, but he connected it with other purposes. Novalis saw art as a passport to the past that never was, while E. T. A. Hoffmann used literature as a means to explore the mysterious demi-mondes of the subconscious existence. But for Arnim, art was to be the midwife to a rebirth of the best of the German spirit into a present which sorely needed it.[11]

Even in the poem **"Zueignung"** (**"Dedication"**), which appears at the very beginning of the work and which dedicates *Wintergarten* to Bettina, Arnim brought in the theme of preservation of the inspirational.[12] (Bettina Brentano, whom Arnim would later marry, was the sister of Clemens Brentano.) The setting of the poem was an orangerie in Aschaffenburg in mid-September, 1808, where Arnim and Bettina parted and where he watched the stagecoach disappear.[13] Arnim uses the real situation to introduce an artistic allegory grafted onto the orange tree, which bears blossoms and fruit at the same time.[14] Just before he introduces the picture of the gardener picking the flowers and the fruit, he says of the spirit: "Der Geist sich offenbart in Frucht und Blüte" ["The spirit reveals itself in fruit and blossom"] (125), while the fruit of the orange tree is "schöner Künste Frucht" ["The fruit of beautiful arts"] (126). The gardener lets the fruit that spills out of the rusty helmet fall, since he has an abundance, but as it falls, it hits a tambourine lying in the grass and produces music:

> Ich fand das Tamburin mit Wohlgefallen,
> Das unten lag, worauf sie (Frucht vz) tönend fiel,
> Das Schöne ist auf Erden unverloren,
> Es klingt zur rechten Zeit, den rechten Ohren.

> (126)

With joy I found the tambourine which lay below, on which the fruit fell with a ringing sound. Beauty is not lost on earth if it resounds at the proper time to the right ears.

These lines could be read as an announcement of Arnim's plans for *Der Wintergarten*: He would like to ensure both that the fruits are not lost and that the appropriate ears hear the sounds.[15] In both cases, in the orangerie and in the *Wintergarten,* the garden does serve as a sort of refuge where art may fulfill its role.

While the image of the helmet in the poem is problematical, the description of it implies a positive disposition towards it on the part of the author:

> Es war ein Helm von altem, rost'gen Eisen,
> Worin der Gärtner seine Frucht gepflückt,
> Manch schwerer Hieb ließ sich darauf noch weisen,
> Doch schwerer hat ihn schöne Frucht gedrückt;
> So mußt der Helm vor meinen Augen reißen,
> Der fest geschmiedet schien und reich beglückt:
> Der alten Waffen schwer errungner Segen,
> Und schöner Künste Frucht, läßt sich nicht hegen.
>
> (126)

It was a helmet made of rusty old iron, which the gardener used for picking fruit, many a heavy blow had left a mark which still remained, yet beautiful fruit had weighed down more heavily upon it; so before my very eyes, the helmet had to split, which seemed so strongly forged and richly graced: The hard-won blessing of the old weapon and the fruit of beautiful arts cannot be contained together.

The helmet could well be a symbol for Prussia: the battle scars, the appearance of strength and wealth, the advantages that were won with old weapons. Yet this helmet cannot hold the fruits of art, which could be a disguised call on Arnim's part for a Germany that could learn from the fruits of the spirit.

Arnim's intent to hunt for such fruits is apparent at the very beginning of **Wintergarten,** when he cites Ritter von Thurn, a figure out of French didactic narrative (127), in an idyllic and idealistic introduction, linking the records of the past with service to God and their relationship to the present.[16] This quiet prelude contrasts sharply in form and content with the reference to current events which comes immediately after the remarks of Ritter von Thurn:

> Diese guten Worte eines alten Ritters mögen in diesem verdrießlichen, immer wiederkehrenden Winter, wo allen schönen Kindern Zeit und Weile land wird, *wohl zur rechten Zeit wiederholt werden*; doch *keinem geziemen sie besser, als der nun zerstreuten, übellaunigen Wintergesellschaft,* zu deren Unterhaltung die folgenden Geschichten zusammengebracht wurden, *die sehr unzufrieden mit der ganzen Welt,* doch immer etwas Neues von ihr wünschte, endlich aber mit allem, was bloß erzählt und nicht geschehen, ganz nachsichtig, aufmunternd, wohlwollend und zufrieden schien.
>
> (127) (emphasis mine)

These good-natured words from an aged knight could certainly be repeated at an appropriate time in this vexatious winter, which keeps returning, where for all handsome children time and leisure seem long; yet for no one are they more suited than for the distracted, ill-humored winter gathering, for whose entertainment the following stories were collected, people who were very dissatisfied with the entire world yet who always wanted something new from it, who however seemed finally forbearing, well disposed, indulgent, and satisfied towards everything that was merely told and did not occur.

The stormy style of this description reflects the miserable morale of the Prussians in their winter of discontent, a situation to which Arnim alludes when he introduces the only rule for the stories, namely to make no specific references to current events, but rather to collect stories from other times and countries (132).

The majority of these inner stories deal with the manner in which the individual, faced with a personal or political crisis, behaves; it must have seemed particularly crucial to Arnim in 1808 to improve the present by analyzing the past. Prussia had capitulated to Napoleon's forces during the campaign of 1807 and lost territory west of the Elbe. Frustrated by the prostration of his country, Arnim had no ready outlet for his overwhelming desire to help. Military service as well as the bureaucracy were out of the question, the latter partly because of Arnim's ideas about a new social order.

In addition to urging the citizenry to defend their country in his short-lived periodical *Der Preuße* (*The Prussian*), Arnim also wrote political articles and essays. One of the most famous, **"Was soll geschehen im Glücke"** (**"What should happen with a fortunate turn of fate"**) contains valuable insights into Arnim's ideas about Napoleon[17] as well as thematic parallels with some of the **Wintergarten** material. The opening lines of the essay reveal Arnim's ideas about Napoleon's place in history and the formation of a new nobility through education.[18] The problem with Napoleon, as Arnim saw it, was that he had betrayed the goals of the French Revolution; however, because the uprising was a movement of the people, the death of Napoleon would not end it. Arnim's solution to the issues raised by the French Revolution was a radical one and would not have been much appreciated by the ruling classes of this time: "Das ganze Volk muß aus einem Zustande der Unterdrückung durch den Adel zum Adel erhoben werden" ["The entire nation must be elevated by the aristocracy from a condition of oppression to nobility"].[19] Behind these remarks stands Arnim's love for and almost messianic belief in the value of older literature in forming this new chivalric order.[20]

The onslaught of the current national catastrophe brought on by the French caused Arnim's earlier ideas about the didactic value of art and its connection with religion, history, and politics to express themselves in **Der Wintergarten.** The preceding discussion has shown that **Wintergarten** had to be didactic and had to depend heavily on sources for Arnim to achieve the goals most dear to him. Many of these sources were, as Göres points out,[21] not originally moral stories per se, but Arnim changed their focus in his adaptation and made them exempla for the characters in the frame. This process is at work in the story of the first evening, **"Die Liebesgeschichte des Kanzlers Schlick und der schönen Sienerin" ("The love story of Chancellor Schlick and the beautiful Sienese")**, which Arnim changed from a rollicking and bawdy Renaissance novella into a more idealized love story. In it he analyzes the importance of faithfulness and the effect of European politics on love; both of these themes relate to the situation of the lady of the country house, madly in love with a French officer.

Arnim chose the frame story genre because it offered several advantages, such as introducing material from widely different sources. Another attraction for him was that the gathering of a group of people listening to someone else provides a setting that lends itself to didactic purposes, a tendency that becomes apparent as the guests are mustered in the initial frame. The meeting of well-bred friends and strangers in an isolated house was already well known to Arnim through Boccaccio and Goethe. However, although the country houses in Boccaccio and Goethe are places of refuge either from the plague or from the French Revolution, Arnim does not intend for his Germans to enjoy the privileges of class and position; leisure and solitude available to them in this house should make it easier for them to receive the lessons of the stories, so that they, as they do at the end, can make their contributions to rebuilding German society.

The plague that threatens the *Wintergarten* guests is neither bubonic nor revolutionary, but a disease of the soul. Arnim's guests have no names, but this anonymity does not serve to flatten them out into mere stereotypes or to mint them as coinage of representative ideas. This namelessness rather serves to emphasize the connection between these people and Arnim's readers, particularly when it becomes a matter of the lessons that Arnim wants to convey. The inner stories function either as positive, negative, or analogical examples that can work directly on the guests and Arnim's readers.

The only figure who does not fit the description of the frame characters as outlined is the first one to appear, the half-allegorical, half-real Winter. We see him at the beginning and at the end as a bent, gray, aged man and, in between, as a season. Arnim's integration of Winter in these two guises into the narrative is as pervasive as the snow that Winter brings along. As Migge points out, Arnim loved to let allegorical or mythical figures assume a real shape in his stories, with enough of their transcendental nature showing to disquiet the other characters.[22] He uses this procedure with Winter; although we first see him as a freezing gray old man in need of a ride, the narrator himself seems to doubt his existence as a real person (130). Rather, he encourages the reader to believe that the character symbolizes the frozen passiveness of Prussia after the departure of the victorious French troops:

> So zog also der Winter ein, wo die Feinde ausgezogen, und meine frohen Erwartungen und Gedanken erstarrten wie der lebendige Strom, der durch die Straße floß. Alles besetzte und bewachte dieser traurige Winter mit seiner langweiligen Heerschar, selbst wo die kaufmännischen und adligen Häuser ihre hohen Stirnen, mit mancherlei Bildwerk gekrönt, erheben, hing er seinen weißen Glanzteppich auf, und selbst an dem Boden knirschten die gejagten Füße noch unwillig, daß auch der treue Boden, den selbst die Feinde mußten stehen lassen, seine Farbe angenommen.
>
> (130)[23]

Thus the winter moved in, where the enemies had evacuated, and my joyful expectations and thoughts grew stiff like the lively stream which flowed through the streets. With his tedious legion, this dismal winter occupied and guarded everything. Even where the houses of the merchants and the aristocracy raise their high foreheads, crowned with various kinds of sculpture, he hung up his glistening white carpet, and even on the ground the driven feet crunched resentfully, because the faithful earth, which even the enemies had to leave alone, had also taken on his color.

The narrator continues with this militaristic tone in the frame of the second evening, but after that, there is only one reference to winter. It comes in a comparison of avalanches with people's moods in the seventh evening, before the reappearance of Winter as the fiancé of the lady of the house in the eighth evening. When Winter returns in human form, the first signs of spring, warmth, and light, also arrive (347). This appearance of the sun parallels the inner story of Jacob Böhme and Aurora, with the emphasis on the dawning of God's revelation to him. Since it is the lady of the house who will eventually see the error in her choice of lovers, it is she who has preoccupied herself with the study of Böhme and who in some way serves as the model reader Arnim wished to have. Well educated, sensitive, and sensible, she needs only exposure and help to understand.

The central position of the lady of the house in this cycle reveals itself immediately in the narrative. After Winter is introduced, she appears in the unusual guise of a motionless statue covered with snow, who runs in alarm at the narrator's unexpected arrival. Her position and the fact that she appears blanketed in snow underscore her central role in the novella in the frame and foreshadow her engagement to Winter. Hopelessly in love with the French officer, the lady accepts Winter's suit out of resignation and despair.

The narrator entreats the inhabitants of the country house to let him in and, as he arrives on the scene of their future evenings, several elements appear in the description that are of significance to the major themes of the story. The room to which he is led has been redone in the Gothic manner (131), indicating the importance of an older period in German history, as well as the interest of the estate's owner in this time. The first object he sees upon entering the room is the painting of the French officer, standing in a place of honor with flowers before it; that, plus the sighing of a flute clock, indicate that there is a melancholy aspect surrounding the picture. The lady of the house confirms this impression in saying that her nerves are on edge because she has suffered greatly and that the snow covers many painful memories (131). Because of her misguided choice of admirers, she has no real sense of direction and purpose, since personal inclination and national loyalty do not coincide. However, she has in her personality those traits that make change possible, and she likes the older periods of German art, which pleases the narrator (131).

The succession of other guests and members of the group follows much more briskly, without the lingering attention that Arnim devotes to the lady. Her sister, an intelligent, sensible woman who has never fallen in love, spends most of her time embroidering and pouring tea.

The young invalid with a wooden leg attracts the reader's attention immediately; his character description is perhaps the most positive of any in the group.[24] The invalid, unlike the others present, has suffered in the service of his country; for this reason, Arnim assigns him a didactic role vis-à-vis the others in the group, with special attention paid to his assault on the lady's misplaced affections. This role comes quickly to the fore in the frame for the first evening, as the invalid tells the love story of the Chancellor Schlick and the beautiful Sienese, relating it to her love for the French officer. While his overriding interest lies in winning the lady for himself (and thereby for their country), he also exemplifies the sort of self-sacrificing bravery that should inspire some other members of the circle (the narrator clearly describes this function at the beginning of the fourth evening, which deals with war) (211). In the frame of the sixth evening, the envoy tries to induce the invalid to write his memoirs, ". . . Warum lassen Sie untergehen was Sie allein berichtigen können?" ["Why do you let perish what you alone could correct?"] (303) since memoirs are the most valuable kind of history.

The envoy, unemployed due to the German defeat, is the next guest to make his appearance. He remains a shadowy figure until the third evening's frame, where the reader initially sees him in an unimportant role. (The invalid and the narrator, mentally lamed by the cold, begin to dissect the personalities of the colony members in such a way that they distort reality [196].) Yet the first appearance of the envoy in center stage reveals his importance, as the narrator's preface implied that it would. The envoy makes an elegant, eloquent, and forceful speech, reflecting many of Arnim's own ideas about the connection between blood revenge and piety, the German's adulation for anything foreign, and the ensuing inability to sacrifice for the common good. Because of his experience abroad and his proximity to the government, he sees his countrymen both as individuals and as citizens of the state. The envoy performs an extremely important function in the frame, providing an intellectual counterweight to the invalid, whose longstanding passion for the lady of the house often softens his sharp mind or sinks him into the sloughs of despond. The envoy's return to the diplomatic service of his country provides an example to the other members of the circle, such as the *Geniale,* who comes with him, and the readers.

Both the invalid and the envoy have served their country in their respective spheres. For this reason, each of them operates some of the time in a different didactic role, functions that set them apart from the other frame characters. While the invalid can bring home to the hearers the real dimensions of military courage and the cruelty of war, the envoy can teach the guests about the essence of history and the value of the past for the present. Because he is an envoy, he has an important double perspective: he sees himself not only as a German among Germans, but also as an observer of Germans abroad.

Neither the actress who accompanies the envoy nor the sister of the lady of the house plays a real role in the frame. However, the last three women to appear figure in several evenings: the *Geniale* (the ingenious woman), the *Gesunde* (the healthy woman), and the *Kranke* (the sick woman). The *Geniale,* who makes her entrance by graciously pressing snowballs into the hands of her acquaintances (132), reappears in the seventh frame, *Winterlaunen* (Winter moods), which offers a light-hearted pause between the stories about Jacob Böhme and Prince Charles. The pause, **"Die drei Erznarren" ("The three notorious fools"),** is intended to drive away the depressing mood of the *Winterlaunen,* caused by the depressing situation in which they find themselves. Although many of the frames deal with the intellectual problems confronting the Prussians because of Napoleon, this one concentrates on the group's mood and emotion. No member of the company registers mood changes as quickly as the mercurial *Geniale*. Her perverse humors call forth all sorts of criticism from the others, which she takes to heart. She ends the story by going off with the envoy to help her country.

The *Gesunde* and the *Kranke* appear as a pair in the introduction and in the fifth frame. One immediately senses some of the liberated woman in the *Gesunde*, a quality reinforced during her major appearance as a sort of Amazon in the fifth frame (132, 249). Her vigor manifests itself in a kind of aggressiveness. The *Kranke*, on the other hand, participates in only passive activities. A gossip, she introduces the fifth frame **"Mistris Lee"** story, saying the English lord entertained her with it (250). The balancing of these two opposites in the fifth frame, their only major appearance, shows a certain deftness in Arnim, not only because of their opposite natures, but also because **"Mistris Lee"** has qualities in common with both of them.

As he develops the story about the lady of the house and the French officer in his description of the frame society, Arnim gives definite hints as to how he intends to apply the examples of the inner stories to the characters in the country house. Naturally, Arnim did not intend to reach only those Prussian women in love with French officers, but all those less devoted to their nation than they could be.

Arnim's choice of a cyclical frame as the vehicle to present his lessons from older literature enables him to bring his intelligent and sensitive countrymen right into the country house, where they may feel affinities with certain characters and expose themselves to the benefits of the stories as well. The conventions found in the *Decameron*—the isolated society in which each individual tells a story and the rule which forbids reference to the events of the day—these Arnim retained as had Goethe before him.[25] He kept as well something much more important from Goethe, something which characterizes the German cyclical narratives: the interaction between the inner stories and the frame. Like Arnim, Goethe depended heavily on sources for his inner stories. Unlike Arnim, the novellas that Goethe took from sources have often been exhaustively and exhaustingly analyzed, while in Arnim's case, most critics have ignored his adaptations and the reasons for them. Most of Arnim's inner stories were not originally intended to function in the specific, applied manner for which Arnim used them. He cut them loose from their literary moorings, not because he was insensitive to the artistic unity of the original, but because he saw in that original what Göres refers to as the "verdeutlichende Exempel" (elucidating model).[26]

In order to understand more fully how Arnim developed the network of relationships between the frame and the inner stories, one must examine the technical aspects of various elements of the frame and inner story as they appear in the *Wintergarten.* The frame itself was not a means to ban threatening forces from a group escaping from the current crisis.[27] While that was true in the *Decameron,* and partially true in Goethe's *Unterhaltungen* (*Conversations*), it is not the case with *Wintergarten,* though it may seem that the ban on stories of the present places it in this category. The rule serves two functions: it creates an oasis, and banishes the distracting present with its nefarious tendency to preoccupy totally the minds of the audience (132). The rule serves not to provide the opiate of oblivion, but to offer mental space for those lessons from the past helpful in coping with the present.[28] Arnim's use of the frame structure for mastery of a situation rather than for escapism has an antecedent in *Unterhaltungen*; we find a similar function in Hoffmann's *Die Serapionsbrüder,* particularly in those stories dealing with madness.

Unlike Goethe and Hoffmann, Arnim uses a first-person narrator, who has many apparent similarities with himself.[29] Like Arnim, the narrator has been on a research trip looking for old songs and he enjoys older art as much as his creator (127, 131). In his introduction to the Concordia story, he refers to his writing it down on the basis of other stories (161). The frame of the eighth evening contains the narrator's account of his own interest in Böhme and his collection of Böhme materials (348).[30] Arnim chose a first-person narrator very like himself because of his deep, personal involvement with the major themes of the work, the degree of intimacy that such a narrator brings, and the added realism in the reproduction of an oral narrative situation. In addition, the narrator, who is part of the colony, yet outside it, can stand aside and comment on events in a more impartial way than some members of the group.

In Goethe's *Unterhaltungen,* the inner stories fall into thematic groups, a convention that probably came from Boccaccio, who had a subject for each day. Since *Wintergarten* has never been taken seriously as a successor to *Unterhaltungen,* the existence of a definite thematic pattern has not received the attention it deserves.[31]

Table One shows that the most important narrators are the invalid, the envoy, and the narrator.

### TABLE ONE

| | | |
|---|---|---|
| FIRST WINTER EVENING | SCHLICK | INVALID |
| SECOND WINTER EVENING | CONCORDIA | NARRATOR |
| THIRD WINTER EVENING | ALTDEUTSCHE LANDSLEUTE | ENVOY |
| FOURTH WINTER EVENING | PHILANDER | INVALID |

| FIFTH WINTER EVENING | MISTRIS LEE | ARIEL |
| SIXTH WINTER EVENING | FROISSART | ENVOY |
| SEVENTH WINTER EVENING | SCHELMUFFSKY | *GENIALE* |
| EIGHTH WINTER EVENING | BÖHME | NARRATOR |
| | PELIA | LADY OF THE HOUSE |
| NINTH WINTER EVENING | CHARLES STUART | NARRATOR |

The invalid, the envoy, and the narrator reveal their worries about the spiritual state of the German people, concerns that appear in the frame as well as in the older exemplary material. The inner stories circle round the interrelated themes of national history, love, and the inner man.

The Schlick story portrays the hopeless conflicts engendered when adulterous love runs afoul of national and political allegiance. **"Albert und Concordia"** and **"Altdeutsche Landsleute"** (*Compatriots from an Earlier Age*) describe marital love in the context of constancy to ethical and religious norms of conduct. In each, the love story takes place against the backdrop of a political situation: in **"Albert und Concordia,"** the formation of an ideal society in the wilderness; in **"Altdeutsche Landsleute,"** against the fidelity of Germans to each other in occasionally hostile foreign courts.

The theme of war, begun in **"Altdeutsche Landsleute,"** reaches a peak in the fourth evening. Here the invalid's rules for soldiers in the frame and the Philander story from the Thirty Years' War appear, as well as the discovery of Ariel sleeping on the desecrated *Viktoria* monument. Affairs of state predominate in the Jean Froissart chronicle of the sixth evening, as they do also in the account of Charles Stuart in the ninth. However, **"Mistris Lee,"** the middle story and frame five, concentrates on right and wrong behavior, particularly in the person of Mistris Lee, the enigmatic "neue Amazone" ("new Amazon"). Negative and positive examples also appeared in the stories of the second and third evenings, but always in conjunction with general or abstract themes, such as the ideal society or the conduct of war.

The Schelmuffsky story forms a pleasant interlude before the dawning of a new day, heralded in the eighth evening, which is devoted mostly to Böhme. The inspirational quality of Böhme's life can, as Arnim presents it, herald the beginning of a new dawn for Germany; attendant on the advent of this time of light is the death of Winter, announced in the frame, a death that occurs on several levels.

### Notes

1. *Achim von Arnims Sämmtliche Werke* 6 (Berlin, 1857), p. 450.

2. Brian Rowley, "The Novelle" in *The Romantic Period in Germany,* ed. Siegbert Prawer (New York, 1970), p. 141. Most critical comments on *Der Wintergarten* have been negative in nature, as a brief and representative survey of the critical literature of the past fifty years will show. Gertrud Hausner, "Achim von Arnim und die Literatur des 17. Jahrhunderts" (Diss., Vienna, 1934), p. 44, says that *Wintergarten* merely adapts and links together older German stories. Werner Vordtriede, "Achim von Arnim," *Deutsche Dichter der Romantik,* ed. Benno von Wiese (Berlin, 1983, p. 319) is also somewhat condescending about the work. In his Princeton University dissertation of 1968, "Achim von Arnim, Writer in Transition: Themes and Techniques in Short Prose Narratives," Hermann Weiss refers to Arnim's work in *Wintergarten* as merely editorial (p. 1). A new evaluation of Arnim's work, Roland Hoermann's *Achim von Arnim* (Boston, 1984), mentions *Wintergarten* only in passing (pp. 6, 89). Much recent research about Arnim's political ideas centers on the *Wunderhorn* or other essays and stories without analyzing *Wintergarten,* but Bernhard Gajek's article, "Achim von Arnim: Romantischer Poet und preußischer Patriot (1781-1831)" in *Sammeln und Sichten: Festschrift für Oscar Fambach zum 80. Geburtstag,* ed. Joachim Krause, Norbert Oellers, and Karl Konrad Polheim (Bonn, 1983), pp. 264-82, contains much interesting material about Arnim's thoughts and plans for *Nationalerziehung.* Jürgen Knaack, in his dissertation, "Achim von Arnim—Nicht nur Poet: Die politischen Anschauungen Arnims in ihrer Entwicklung" (Hamburg, 1976) mentions *Wintergarten* only briefly, p. 28. Knaack says that Arnim chose exemplary stories from German history to avoid censorship.

Vordtriedé, "Achim von Arnim," notes that in his later works Arnim took from older sources (p. 326).

See also Bernd Fischer, *Literatur und Politik. Die 'Novellensammlung von 1812' und das 'Landhausleben' von Achim von Arnim* (Frankfurt, 1983).

The most recent and most welcome contribution to an understanding of *Wintergarten* comes from Wulf Segebrecht, in an article, "Die Thematik des Krieges in Achim von Arnims Wintergarten" in *Aurora* 45 (1985), pp. 310-16. Segebrecht was not the first to write positively about the work; in the notes to his edition of von Arnim's works, Walther Migge, in *Achim von Arnim: Sämtliche Romane und Erzählungen* 2 (Munich, 1963), p. 870, saw

Arnim's own original contribution quite clearly. All subsequent quotations from *Wintergarten* and other works by Arnim will be from this edition and will be in the text.

Research of Arnim's sources has been unsatisfactory for various reasons. Anton Reichl's catalog, "Über die Benutzung älterer deutscher Literaturwerke in Achim von Arnims 'Wintergarten,'" in *Schulprogramm Arnau* (Böhmen), 1889-90, I, II, overlooks a great deal and in addition, contains mistakes. Reichl seldom analyzes, preferring a mere register of variations. Konrad Kratzsch's work, "Untersuchungen zur Genese und Struktur der Erzählungen Ludwig Achim von Arnims" (Jena, 1968), contains some interesting observations in spite of its clumsy Marxism. In another article, "Die Vorlagen zu Achim von Arnims 'Wintergarten' aus den Beständen der Arnim Bibliothek in der Zentralbibliothek der deutschen Klassik," in *Marginalien: Blätter der Pirckheimer Gesellschaft* 29 (April 1968), pp. 29-44, Kratzsch expands the material in the above mentioned dissertation.

3. See Jörn Göres, "Das Verhältnis von Historie und Poesie in der Erzählkunst Achim von Arnims" (Diss., Heidelberg, 1956). In Arnim's preoccupation with the past, Göres sees a high degree of continuity; for him, *Wintergarten* represents part of an unbroken line in Arnim's intellectual development, a line that began with the publication of *Wunderhorn* and continued through the writing of *Die Kronenwächter* (pp. 145-46).

4. Helene M. Kastinger Riley, *Achim von Arnim* (Hamburg, 1979), p. 45. See also p. 44, where she notes that a lecture Arnim gave just after he left secondary school deals with the belief that art is part of humanity's birthright. See also Knaack. *Achim von Arnim,* pp. 24, 26.

5. See Riley, *Achim von Arnim,* pp. 52-53; Gerhard Möllers, "Wirklichkeit und Phantastik in der Erzählweise Achim von Arnims" (Diss., Münster, 1971), p. 37.

6. See Werner Hoffmann, *Clemens Brentano: Leben und Werk* (Bern, 1966), p. 230; Heinz Rölleke, "Anmerkungen zu 'Des Knaben Wunderhorn'" pp. 276-94, especially pp. 283 and 287, in *Clemens Brentano: Beiträge des Kolloquiums im Freien Deutschen Hochstift,* 1978, ed. Detlev Lüders (Tübingen, 1980). Rölleke criticizes Arnim's mixing of old and new and brings up the problems Arnim had with Brentano because of their different approaches.

7. Cited by Riley in *Ludwig Achim von Arnims Jugend- und Reisejahre* (Bonn, 1978), p. 62. For a historical account of the situation in Prussia, see Karl Otmar Freiherr von Aretin, *Vom Deutschen Reich zum Deutschen Bund,* pp. 515-672, esp. "Der Untergang des alten Preußen," pp. 599-602, in *Deutsche Geschichte, 2, Frühe Neuzeit* (Göttingen, 1985). Reinhold Steig, *Achim von Arnim und Clemens Brentano,* (Stuttgart, 1894), 1, provides much material about Arnim's anguish over Prussia's collapse. In a letter to Brentano on September 8, 1806, he wrote: "Wer des Vaterlandes Noth vergißt, den wird Gott auch vergessen in seiner Noth!" (p. 191). See also pp. 207-24, especially pp. 207-9. Here Steig describes how Arnim rode in a transport with wounded soldiers and how Arnim watched Hohenlohe's surrender in Stettin after the event. In a letter to his aunt, written on November 18, 1806, Arnim wrote: "Sie erinnern Sich vielleicht meiner ruhigen Überzeugung, die ich in Strelitz oft streitend vorgelegt, daß ohne eine innere höhere Staatsentwicklung kein glücklicher Krieg möglich sei" (p. 209). This comment of Arnim's reflects once again his conviction that the inner disposition of a people has a significant bearing on events.

8. See Arnim, *Sämmtliche Werke,* 6 (Hildesheim, 1982), pp. 452, 474.

9. Gerhard Möllers, "Wirklichkeit und Phantastik in der Erzählkunst Achim von Arnims" (Diss., Münster, 1971), pp. 32-33.

10. Arnim, *Sämmtliche Werke* 6, p. 446.

11. See Möllers, "Wirklichkeit," pp. 31-35; Knaack, *Achim von Arnim,* pp. 23-24; Göres, *Verhältnis,* pp. 17-21, on the relationship of poetry and history for Arnim.

12. Irmgard Berchtenbreiter, *Achim von Arnims Vermittlerrolle zwischen Jakob Böhme als Dichter und seiner Wintergartengesellschaft* (Munich, 1972), p. 282, says that Arnim took from the *Orangengarten,* ". . . einen Vorsatz mit, der als stilistisches Programm verstanden sein will." On p. 283, she suggests links between this poem and other parts of *Wintergarten*: "Vom 'Orangengarten' her ließe sich sagen: sie preist den alten, schöngeschmückten 'Helm' und kann nichts finden an einer zeitigen 'Frucht', wie sie der Ankömmling schätzen gelernt hat. Allerdings lebt sie in einer Epoche, die nicht die 'rechte Zeit' ist, daß das Schöne klinge. Es wird noch einen 'Winter' lang dauern, ehe ein Neues, eine 'Frucht' keimt, die der Kunst der Vergangenheit an die Seite zu setzen wäre. So ist es dann auch, als man sich

endlich-am 'Schluß'-trotzdem im Sehen zu ertüchtigen versucht, eines jener 'alten Kunstwerke', dem die 'Wintergesellschaft' ihre Aufmerksamkeit schenkt."

13. Steig, *Achim von Arnim und die ihm nahe standen* (Stuttgart and Berlin, 1913) 2, p. 192, as well as Otto Betz/Veronika Straub in *Bettina und Arnim: Briefe der Freundschaft und Liebe 1806-08*, 1, pp. 303-4, say that this parting was at Aschaffenburg in mid-September, 1808. Thomas Sternberg, *Die Lyrik Achim von Arnims* (Bonn, 1983), places the parting at Aschaffenburg in one place (p. 219) and in Augsburg at another (p. 260).

14. Sternberg, *Lyrik*, says that Arnim liked to place reality and poetry in a continuous dialogue, with poetry firmly planted in reality, while those unusual events in reality should be poeticized. He sees this process at work in the "Zueignung" poem (see pp. 219, 260, note #21). See also Berchtenbreiter, *Achim von Arnim*, pp. 282-83, who says that the poem has connections between the opening scene with the lady of the house and the final one in *Wintergarten*.

15. Sternberg, *Lyrik*, pp. 219, 116. Sternberg sees the garden as "privates Freudenreich."

16. See also Migge, p. 887. See Hermann F. Weiss's perceptive article, "Achim von Arnims Harmonisierungsbedürfnis: Zur Thematik und Technik seiner Novellen" *LWJB* [*Literaturwissenschaftliches Jahrbuch*] 15 (1974), pp. 81-99, esp. p. 95, for comments on the role of Divine Providence in Arnim's work. For an informative survey of interest in older German literature from the seventeenth to the early nineteenth century, see Gisela Brinker-Gabler, "Tiecks Bearbeitungen altdeutscher Literatur: Produktion, Konzeption, Wirkung" (Diss., Cologne, 1973), pp. 12-100, esp. 19, 25, 29, 49-50, where she deals with patriotic motivation for the study of older literature. See also Migge, *Achim von Arnim* 1, pp. 1074-78. Möllers, "Wirklichkeit," pp. 36-37, analyzes Arnim's goal of national regeneration through examples from the past.

17. In the article in which Arnim's essay is printed "'Was soll geschehen im Glücke' Ein unveröffentlicher Aufsatz Achim von Arnims" *Jahrbuch der deutschen Schiller-Gesellschaft* 5 (1961), pp. 196-221, Jörn Göres writes about Arnim's attitude toward Napoleon; see pp. 208-9.

18. Göres, "Glücke," p. 199.

19. Göres, "Glücke," p. 200.

20. See also Göres, "Glücke," p. 215.

21. Göres, *Verhältnis,* p. 63.

22. Migge, pp. 876-77.

23. Segebrecht, "Thematik des Krieges," pp. 311-12, comments on the significance of this mood and its relation to the allegory of Winter; he sees winter as an allegory not only for the postwar period, but also for the frozen social situation, which Arnim's work tries to address.

24. Ibid., p. 312, interprets the role of the *Invalide* in a manner similar to that of this study. In n. 4 on the same page, Segebrecht remarks on the frequency of appearance in Arnim's work of invalids, who symbolize for those around them the cruelty of war.

25. See Wolfdietrich Rasch, "Achim von Arnims Erzählkunst," *Der Deutschunterricht* 7 (1955), pp. 38-55, p. 42; Göres, *Verhältnis,* p. 63.

26. Göres, *Verhältnis,* p. 63.

27. Weiss, *Achim von Arnim*, p. 44, writes: ". . . earlier proponents of the frame ban the threat of tragedy from both the frame and the stories," implying that this situation obtains for *Wintergarten*.

28. Weiss's analysis in *Achim von Arnim* of the relationship of politics to *Wintergarten* seems to deal only briefly with the relationship. "The frame narrator alludes to the depressing political situation in Germany . . . , but never elaborates on it, merely informing us that the group was very dissatisfied with life" (p. 56).

29. Weiss, *Achim von Arnim*, notes that all of Arnim's cyclical narratives have first-person narrators, p. 49.

30. See Migge, p. 875. Arnim made a thorough study of Böhme and had an unfinished biographical manuscript, which was lost after an auction of Arnim's *Nachlass* (literary remains) in 1929.

31. K. Kratzsch, in his dissertation, "Untersuchungen," p. 7, notes that the order of the stories has not been examined and believes that Arnim had a plan he did not follow.

## Sara Friedrichsmeyer (essay date 1997)

SOURCE: Friedrichsmeyer, Sara. "Romantic Nationalism: Achim von Arnim's Gypsy Princess Isabella." In *Gender and Germanness: Cultural Productions of Nation*, edited by Patricia Herminghouse and Magda Mueller, pp. 51-65. Providence: Berghahn Books, 1997.

[*In the following essay, Friedrichsmeyer reviews the diverse critical responses to Arnim's novella* Isabella von Ägypten *since the time of its original publication.*

*Rather than providing an interpretation of the work within the framework of Romanticism, Friedrichsmeyer here evaluates the novella within the context of Arnim's interest in German nationalism, paying particular attention to the characters of Isabella and the gypsies. By upholding traditional values of loyalty and respect for nature, Friedrichsmeyer argues, Arnim's gypsies provide an ideal model for future citizens of a unified German state.*]

If literary historians still debate Achim von Arnim's position along the continuum from Romanticism to Realism,[1] it is not his **"Isabella of Egypt"** (**"Isabella von Ägypten"**) that has them perplexed. Published in 1812 in a collection with three other texts and dedicated to the Grimm brothers, it displays humor, some irony, and a distinctly nonrational tinge—so distinct in fact that the unwary reader is quickly disoriented. The present and past, the natural and the supernatural, the mimetic and the imaginative flow into one another free of authorial markers. "Romantic" elements—such as ghosts, the occult, the night, mistaken identity, disguises—abound along with the grotesque and the fantastic.

And then the characters: assembled in the novella along with an *Alraun,* a little mandrake root-become-man, are an old Gypsy woman who choreographs the seduction scene and who looks, quoting Heine, like "the fairest of the seven deadly sins" (95); a fat corpse clad in a bearskin who has risen from his grave in his quest for money; and a golem, a soulless figure of clay shaped like the beautiful Isabella. As Heine commented in *The Romantic School (Die romantische Schule),* this novella could teach even the French a lesson in the terrible, the uncanny, the gruesome, and the ghostly (95). Within the context of Heine's essay, these words, of course, should be understood as less than unbridled applause.[2]

The novella's structure is also typically Romantic in its assiduous avoidance of formal structuring principles, in part because von Achim refused to subject his works to conscious shaping (Hoermann 1-2). This homage to his own creative genius, however, did not serve him well. While von Arnim's friend Wilhelm Grimm had praise for **"Isabella"**—he counted it "among the most beautiful and unique" of all von Arnim's works—he also admitted to being disturbed by the author's insistence on opening hidden doors that allowed the action to escape in all directions (III: 188).[3]

Von Arnim garnered little attention as a writer until Heine hailed him a "great poet" and "one of the most original minds of the Romantic School" (90). Heine's essay—in which he also complained that von Arnim was usually "as serious as a dead German" (91-92)—

helped to awaken interest especially in **"Isabella,"** which he singled out for special praise (94). Subsequent generations of scholars have concurred with this judgment, and the novella is today discussed as belonging to the canon of the genre (Hoermann, Preface n.p.) and one of the "exemplary literary texts" of German Romanticism (Seyhan 107).[4]

Rather than examining further the novella's status within a canon or its paradigmatic Romanticism, I am interested here in von Arnim's treatment of Isabella and the Gypsies, and in how that treatment reflects von Arnim's own hopes for a German nation. On one level this is Isabella's story. And—for readers who like a Romantic story—it is quite intriguing. We meet Isabella in a haunted house in Ghent after her father has been falsely executed for stealing. Von Arnim introduces her and continues to speak of her in terms of her physical attributes and even more often of her innocence. She possesses "a beauty that unfolds more gloriously every day" (491); she is "saintly" (556) and is eulogized in her coffin as "the Pure One" (555).[5] We are also meant to be persuaded of her uniqueness. Living at a time when Gypsies could be killed on sight (455), she can emerge only after dark. Just as von Arnim thus carefully sequesters her from bourgeois society, he also separates her from the Gypsies, whom she considers "rough" (453). Treated by the Gypsies as a "higher being," she has come to think of herself as such (464).

Isabella controls the romantic plot devices and drives the action: she reads occult manuscripts, learns many secrets of the universe, and creates the miniature man, the *Alraun.* She is also the pivotal figure in the legend von Arnim retells, according to which the Gypsies have been forced to wander in a diaspora as punishment for the refusal of their ancestors to grant refuge to the Virgin Mary on her flight to Egypt.[6] In von Arnim's version the parallels to the Biblical salvation story are stressed, and Isabella's link with the Virgin Mary positions her as a mediator for her entire people (534). It is she who in a "dream of annunciation" (Hoermann 95) is told by her dead father that she will bear a son who will lead her people back to Egypt to reclaim their rightful homeland (520).[7]

The subtitle, however, points to another level for reading the story: "The First Love of Emperor Charles V" ("Kaiser Karl des Fünften erste Jugendliebe"). The Holy Roman Emperor Karl V ruled over a vast Hapsburg empire in the early sixteenth century, but not over a German nation.[8] By choosing this setting, von Arnim directs his reader's attention to the Reformation and the ensuing peasant wars that could have resulted in a move toward political unity for the German-speaking lands.

This part of the story belongs not to Isabella, but to Karl, and von Arnim tells it in high moral terms. As the novella has it, the drive to nationhood was thwarted because the emperor lacked a strong ethical dimension. He betrayed Isabella because of his inability to distinguish between spiritual love and the sensuality of the golem. And because he lacked "pious harmony" and proved so vulnerable to "contemptible greed," he was unable to inspire any movement toward national unity, the lack of which is cited as a source of great unhappiness even for the narrator's own generation (552).

Von Arnim's Karl V has found nothing to replace the lost spiritual harmony of the Middle Ages; he is materialistic, opportunistic, haughty, and given to sensuality. Isabella therefore leaves him to fulfill her own destiny; she gives birth to their son Lrak (the narrator carefully informs the reader to note the reversal of letters) on her peregrinations to Egypt. Von Arnim is little interested in the lives of the lovers after their separation, but by the end of the novella he has them dying on the same day, Isabella in Egypt and Karl in the monastery to which he has retreated after giving up his empire. And by this time, the emotional and structural emphasis of the narration has shifted to Karl. Isabella's death is related solely through his vision; its importance is measured in terms of its effect on Karl during his final earthly moments. Lying in his coffin, he glimpses a vision of an ethereal Isabella. "She waved to him and he followed her . . . and saw a bright morning light in which Isabella was showing him the way to heaven" (552). The eternal feminine has brought redemption to one more erring striver.

\* \* \*

During his European travels from 1801 to 1804,[9] von Arnim acquired the notion of distinct peoples with distinct folk traditions. Much of his early collaborative work with Brentano was consequently aimed at documenting and then propagating a specifically German tradition and national character, a "Volksgeist."[10] Many of his later works, including **"Isabella,"** maintained this concentration. His focus in **"Isabella"** on the development, or in this case nondevelopment, of the German nation has not been overlooked by critics. The *völkisch* elements of the novella were fastened on by scholars in the 1930s and early 1940s (cf. Lenz). Since then, however, and perhaps therefore, they have been rather studiously ignored.

In von Arnim's own time, friends and critics, especially those who shared his patriotic values, often directed their comments to his flagrant merging of history and fiction. In his dedication to the collection in which **"Isabella"** appeared,[11] the author alluded to his differences with the Grimm brothers:

> *In eurem* Geist hat sich die Sagenwelt
> Als ein geschloss'nes Ganze [sic] schon gesellt,
> Mein Buch dagegen glaubt, daß viele Sagen
> In unsern Zeiten erst recht wieder tagen,
> Und viele sich der Zukunft erst enthüllen,
> Nun prüfet, ob es Euch das kann erfüllen.
>
> (447)[12]

The dedication, however, did not placate Jacob Grimm. Von Arnim's willful tampering with history, he scolded after reading **"Isabella,"** could create an "untrue" reality, causing confusion and even false conceptions of the past (III: 191-94; III: 99-100).[13] This topic continued to be a focus of von Arnim's correspondence with the Grimms over many years. In a manifesto of sorts written during their discussion of **Die Kronenwächter** (**The Crown Guardians**), von Arnim maintained that his friends' convictions concerning history and poetry contradicted his own in a most dramatic way. The impetus for writing, he claimed, "whether provided by 'real' history . . . or by one's own life, seems . . . completely immaterial." As a justification he added: "Unless Homer was crazy, he could not possibly have believed his yarns of the Trojan War anymore than Klopstock the speeches of the angels," except, he insisted, that both have an "inner" truth (III:401).

The "inner truth" von Arnim constructs in **"Isabella"** blends history with legend, fact with fiction, and the old with the new in an attempt to draw attention to the issue of German national identity. He has no illusions about writing a serious history, at times urging the reader's acceptance of his version, at others warning against it. Upon the appearance of the tiny *Alraun,* the mandrake man given the imposing Roman name of Field-marshal Cornelius Nepos, the narrator interrupts to caution against connecting him with any historical person of that name (475). Yet at other times the same narrator strives to create at least an illusion of historical authenticity, as when, late in the novella, he claims Zacharias Taurinius as a source for his account of Isabella's death. Scholars have ascertained that, although in 1799 and 1800 Taurinius did publish a travelogue in two volumes titled *Beschreibung einiger See- und Landreisen nach Asien, Afrika und Amerika* (*Description of Several Ocean and Land Trips to Asia, Africa, and America*), Isabella's story has no place in it (Moering).

Most critics today, persuaded by Benedict Anderson's influential work, understand the concepts of nation and nationalism as "ideas," as imaginary constructs. As a spate of recent works attest, it was during the late eighteenth and early nineteenth centuries that the "idea" of nationhood took hold among German intellectuals.[14] In her comparison of five different forms of nationalism, Liah Greenfeld describes the German variant as an ethnic nationalism, a conception of belonging based on such factors as blood, common traditions, language, and religion rather than on a political constitution or other political forms of unification. Although she does not cite von Arnim, his **"Isabella of Egypt"** lends credence to her thesis. Von Arnim and those among his contemporaries who did provide her examples abhorred the long tradition of French cultural supremacy and were, especially after the Prussian defeat at Jena, increasingly driven to establish a German national identity in its stead. Lacking a political nation-state, however, they were forced to construct that identity according to ethnic rather than political criteria.[15] As the editors of *Nationalisms and Sexualities* conclude, "nationality is a relational term whose identity derives from its inherence in a system of differences . . . National identity is determined not on the basis of its own intrinsic properties but as a function of what it (presumably) is not" (5). In the Gypsies and their history, von Arnim found an element of alterity, that is, a mirror to help his German-speaking contemporaries define their own national characteristics and reflect on their dreams of a nation-state. In the "Ariel" frame to his 1809 novella collection *Der Wintergarten* (*The Winter Garden*), von Arnim's poet despairs: "We had hoped for a wonderful era for Germany . . . like a wonderful prismatic mirror she was to unite the whole world. But . . . the war came [and] shattered our mirror" (345). Von Arnim continued constructing mirrors, but instead of Germany as a grand mirror for the rest of the world, he found himself forced to create one for the Germans themselves.

\* \* \*

Since the late eighteenth century, cultures have never been described merely in terms of their variety, but within a hierarchy based on Western notions of developmental stages. They have been ranked according to their perceived ability to overcome a "natural" state and enter history as "developed" cultures. Gypsy culture has never been perceived as "developed" in the sense understood by Western critics. Especially since the Enlightenment, with its stress on values such as reason, progress, permanence, property, and the development of nations, Gypsies have come to be essentialized in the popular imagination as an ethnic group for whom these concerns matter little. They have come to be seen as a group out of time and out of history (Trumpener).[16] As such, they have been readily available to writers as an idealized or despised other, as a mirror through which writers can document their own opposition or allegiance to Western culture and its manifestations.[17] In either case, the writer has little interest in the Gypsies per se or in presenting anything resembling a balanced depiction of their actual existence or their very complex history.

As with the vast majority of other writers who have idealized Gypsies, what von Arnim idealizes in **"Isabella"** and elsewhere is a totalizing image he himself has created. In an essay published along with *Des Knaben Wunderhorn* (*The Boy's Magic Horn*) titled **"Von Volksliedern,"** he provides a prototypical example of what Edward Said has referred to as Orientalism, insisting, for example, on the Gypsies' child-like goodness, and claiming as well that although we unjustly persecute them, we owe the Gypsies "so many good and beneficial things. . . . Despite all their love, they find no home [*Heimat*] among us" (451-52). In other works of fiction, such as his novel *Die Kronenwächter,* he expresses a comparable understanding. Thus in "Isabella" the Gypsies are loyal to the wandering tribe; they are close to the organic processes of nature; their traditions are intact. Throughout, they are incorporated as a uniform representation of the more "natural," more mystical and spiritual aspects of human existence, the very aspects lacking in von Arnim's Karl V. Had Karl possessed them, the novel seems to infer, history might have been different. And were von Arnim's own compatriots possessed of these virtues, the inference continues, nationhood for Germans would be possible.

The categories von Arnim chooses for describing Gypsy existence are certainly not unfamiliar to feminist critics. They are by and large the same as those applied to women since the sex roles polarized toward the end of the eighteenth century: a spiritual, non-rational principle close to the processes of nature in contrast to the notions of progress, culture, and rationality typically associated with males. This role division also had implications for nationalist strivings. As the editors of *Nationalisms and Sexualities* phrased it in their introduction, crediting both George Mosse and Benedict Anderson, "nationalism favors a distinctly homosocial form of male bonding" (6). Nineteenth-century rhetoric generated a hierarchy that valued nations and the males who created them over females and "feminized" non-nations.

The rhetoric, however, also specified a role for women. A spiritual and maternal presence was also required as an accompaniment to the political male, if for no other reason than to secure a male-directed history (*Nationalisms,* 6). In von Arnim's case the evidence suggests that his glorification of women in **"Isabella"** was also an exuberant response to his 1811 marriage to Bettina Brentano. All three of the other works contained in the collection of 1812 in which **"Isabella"** appeared have female title characters.[18] The context is provided by the narrator's poem in the conclusion to **"Isabella"**:

Wo große Zeichen hin zur Zukunft deuten,
Da wollen wir nicht stets nach Männern schauen,
Es ändern sich auch einmal wohl die Zeiten:
Vielleicht beginnt nun bald die Zeit der Frauen!"

(557)[19]

Von Arnim's Isabella exhibits ideal love: she is "the only one in centuries" capable of a spiritual devotion devoid of the "lustfulness of her sex" (464). Even after her sexual encounter, actually seduction, of Karl V, she is touted as "deeply and profoundly innocent" (509). By the time of her death, she has been able to create something akin to an earthly paradise in Egypt, an accomplishment about which the narrator waxes particularly eloquent: through her efforts, there had emerged fertile gardens where happy children could play; there were now leaping fountains and brightly plumed birds where once crocodiles had basked in the sun and only the hissing of snakes had been heard (555).

This trope of the idealized, mediating female figured prominently in the works of other Romantic writers such as Novalis and Friedrich Schlegel, philosophers such as Franz von Baader, and artists such as Caspar David Friedrich, many of whom described their hopes and ideals in the language of androgynous perfection. Deploring their own one-sidedness, which they understood as a too strict adherence to the rational precepts of the Enlightenment, and premising their theories on the notion of rigidly polarized sexes, they posited in women all they deemed lacking in themselves. Thus glorified, women became the ideal partners through whom many early nineteenth-century artists and thinkers believed they could regain their own wholeness. Although their ideas were theoretically applicable to women's perfection as well, their works make clear that the wholeness they sought was for males alone; the female partners of their male protagonists often died or simply disappeared (see Friedrichsmeyer).

Isabella serves a similar utilitarian purpose for von Arnim. And just as von Arnim created her to reflect the spiritual love and the connection to the organic world missing in Karl's being, so did he attribute these same "female" qualities to the entire world of the Gypsies, who serve then as a mirror for a prospective German nation. But unlike many other writers, von Arnim does something else with his idealized mirror: he scratches and clouds it. In various ways he undercuts his idealization of the feminized and exotic Gypsies and their female redeemer, deliberately conditioning his reader to the impossibility of any lasting union between Karl and Isabella and attesting to the unbridgeable chasm separating Germans from Gypsies.

In addition to his narrator's partiality for Karl, von Arnim incorporates frequent, not so subtle reminders to his German-speaking audience of Isabella's and the Gypsies' fundamental otherness; frequently this is accomplished in terms of language, a key category in von Arnim's own understanding of what constitutes a *Volk*.[20] By the time Isabella forsakes Karl's bedroom, leaping out the window into the arms, literally, of her waiting people, they have sworn her their allegiance. Before repeating their song, however, the narrator interrupts the flow to delineate a linguistic boundary between the Gypsies and Isabella on the one hand and the Germans—author, narrator, and readers alike—on the other. For purposes of the story, he says, he will try to translate their "heartfelt greeting" (547). Her death scene, too, he feels moved to translate "into our German mother tongue" (555). Even in some of the most lyrical passages intoned to define Isabella's perfection, von Arnim inserts reminders of her difference, by linking her as she leaves Karl, for example, to *her* people, not to the Germans: "She belonged to the species of birds that, despite the tender care and loving attentions at the hands of kind people, cannot resist taking wing when it hears the call of its kin . . ." (548). We are assured that Isabella's "counterfeit marriage"—a misstep female literary characters have only in the late twentieth century been able to survive—did not disturb "the purity of *her* moral code" (548, my emphasis). In case we as readers have any lingering tendencies to look to Isabella as the nucleus of the story or as a model, the narrator intervenes quite directly to persuade us differently: the legends revolving around Isabella's life and death are acknowledged as "educational" (553), but, we are cautioned, "they do not belong in our European world" (553).

Von Arnim also provides his readers with the necessary insights to challenge Isabella's oft-proclaimed virtue. Thus, although Isabella is the titular and emotional center through much of the work, and although von Arnim is suggesting that at least some of the qualities associated with her Gypsy essence would have made Karl the kind of ruler who could have forged the all-important German nation, the reader is never allowed to settle into a fantasy of Isabella as the model for German womanhood. For that we have only to look to **Die Gräfin Dolores** (1810), where he preached his ideal of marital, monogamous, Christian love as a counter to Friedrich Schlegel's *Lucinde*. In addition to Isabella's distinctly unbourgeois sexual behavior, this supposed paragon is not adverse to the kind of material corruption von Arnim feared.[21] Although she lauds the poverty of her people (548), her whole purpose in creating Cornelius Nepos had been to get help in amassing the money necessary to attract Karl. Typically critics have blamed these and other blemishes on Braka, a judgment von Arnim encourages.[22] His narrator, for example, lingers on details as the old Gypsy woman instructs Isabella in the art of seduction. Similarly, it is Braka who convinces Isabella of the importance of money in attracting Karl and of her consequent need for the *Alraun* (463). But Isabella has other flaws too, and Braka cannot be implicated in all these thematic lines. She knowingly sacrifices her nearly human guard dog in the process of creating the *Alraun* (463-64), and later, when he is hungry, drowns a nursing kitten to make room for her tiny creation (472, 546). Thus, despite its idealization of Isabella, this novella should in no way be construed as intimating that von Arnim is dreaming of a woman to lead the German-speaking peoples to their destiny as a nation-state.

Nor, of course, are we to assume that the Gypsies are thoroughgoing models for Germanness. Although von Arnim idealizes the Gypsies, we know—as did readers of his day—that he is not recommending the Gypsy life style as a behavioral model for respectable Germanness. By presenting the Gypsies as so fairytale like, so much the outsiders, and so feminized, he infers the impossibility of anyone's taking them too seriously; by presenting them as exotic and childlike, he further removes them from the dimensions of history. Von Arnim, as his nonfictional writing makes clear, was a Prussian with a Protestant sense of morality,[23] dedicated to preserving the nonurban, noncapitalist, and male-oriented way of life he considered inherently German at a time when the upheavals following the French Revolution were threatening its demise. As such, his hopes fit the well-known pattern documented by Mosse, according to which nineteenth-century nationalism in Germany was very much in league with a desire for bourgeois morality and respectability. There was nothing nomadic, childlike, ahistorical, or even remotely sensual about the German nation for which von Arnim longed.

\* \* \*

Yet von Arnim succeeded in lulling successive generations of critics into an uncritical acceptance of his idealization of Isabella and the Gypsies. The trend was already there with Heine, who grounded his positive reception in part on his belief that "[t]his strange fairy-tale people, with their brown faces, friendly soothsayer eyes, and melancholy mysteriousness, comes to life. . . . Everything the excellent Arnim tells us about the gypsies is profoundly moving" (94-95). Even in 1992 Azade Seyhan wrote: "The exotic other, excluded and misunderstood, emerges as the representation of a higher truth" (129). Just as critics have generally accepted the exemplary nature of the Gypsies as von Arnim intended, so have they also taken von Arnim's word that Isabella is the pure and innocent redeemer. She is typically regarded as a utopian principle defined in opposition to Karl (Völker 118). Bernd Haustein's

description of her as the perfect synthesis of saint and human being (40), Werner Vordtriede's declaration that she is not involved in the "fall from grace caused by the worship of money" that he sees as the crux of the story (264), and Roland Hoermann's assessment of her as perhaps von Arnim's most attractive human figure, a *femme spirituelle* (65), are representative. Scholars have not protested the idealization, nor have they recognized that Isabella is declared "saintly" precisely because she can be instrumentalized by others. Braka, for example, uses her as a way of obtaining her own financial security, and Karl values her physical presence in part as a way to keep the *Alraun* in his services (542-43). Another good example of her malleability is provided by her dressing and cross-dressing. She is the compliant one, allegedly uninvolved in any long range plans; others dress her as part of their own power machinations. Early in the story, Braka instructs her in the art of feminine attire in order to attract Karl. Later Karl's aged and celibate tutor dresses her as a boy so she can be inconspicuously removed from the palace without damage to his own reputation (525). Later Karl dresses her again as a boy as part of his own joke on his tutor (536-38). Still later Karl has her dressed by one of the ladies of the court as befitting a princess, a move that ensures the court's accepting her as such.

If critics have been able to accept the allegedly purifying love of a gypsy seductress in the work of a Prussian moralist, they have done so, as did von Arnim, by measuring her and her people on a different scale. Now in one sense this is generous. By acknowledging that Gypsies live according to another code, von Arnim is indicating that he, like Herder, sees the relative merits of various ethnic groups, of their folk traditions, their language, their culture. But this is not the author's final assessment and neither should it be ours.

Ultimately, von Arnim's depiction of Isabella and the Gypsies is of a racial group so homogenous, so exotic, so radically other, and so "female" that its members cease to exist as human beings or subjects of their own history. At the same time, this treatment reflects an ethnic nationalism mired in illusions of exclusivity. This has been ignored by the critics, by Heine, who was usually looking for conservative credos and finding them in most works of German Romanticism, as well as by more contemporary critics presumably versed in the analytic strategies of feminist literary criticism or the ideologies of nationalism. There can be no question but that von Arnim's dream of nation, based here on distinct moral codes for distinct peoples, requires separate destinies for separate peoples. Consequently, the Gypsies and Isabella resemble a collective *deus ex machina*; having failed to perform their wonders, they can be dispatched on their way to Egypt—where they belong. Isabella's decision to return to Egypt is sanctimoniously described as an inevitability: "In Europe she was like a rare flower that opened only at night, because day was then dawning in her homeland" (548).

Fiction then has its benefits: the Gypsies willingly disappear as does Isabella, leaving Karl to ponder and rue his youthful indiscretions. The novella presumably left von Arnim's nineteenth-century German readers to mourn their lack of nation, to contemplate just what it was about Isabella and those Gypsies that won them their fictional homeland, and—perhaps—to make some adjustments in their own national character that could lead them in a similar direction. It leaves a late twentieth-century reader with a story, perhaps benign in itself, that, when viewed in its cultural and historical contexts, is one more disquieting document of the German dream of an ethnically pure nation-state forged by like-minded and like-blooded men, a homogenous homeland—and one certainly without Gypsies.

### Notes

1. For the scope of the discussion, see Haustein (v-xi); see also Hoffmann.

2. He advises his French audience to "[l]eave all these horrors of insanity, hallucination, and the spirit-world to us Germans," where they are at home. He has found at the French border, he reports, that "the sight of the tricolored flag frightens away ghosts of every sort" (98).

3. A reference with Roman numerals refers throughout this study to one of the 3 volumes of *Achim von Arnim und die ihm nahe standen.*

4. In 1960, Heinrich Henel commented that, had von Arnim been able to maintain the style and force of the first twenty pages, he would have written a masterpiece (91).

5. Parenthetical references to the novella are from the Migge edition. I have used the Pierce and Schneider translation where possible; other translations from the novella are my own.

6. Most critics cite Grellmann as von Arnim's main source for his eccentric "history" of the Gypsies (cf. Schürer; Neumann). In von Arnim's telling, the Jews have for centuries passed themselves off as Gypsies, resulting in great damage to the Gypsies' reputation (453-54). Few critics comment on the antisemitism of the novella.

7. Actually this prophecy is not fulfilled. It is Isabella who leads her people back.

8. Karl V (1500-58), well known from the equestrian portrait by Titian, was crowned Holy Roman Emperor in 1520 in Aachen. He was not successful in suppressing Protestantism, in part because he was continually drawn away from Germany by, among other pressures, the rivalry with France. He abdicated after the Religious Peace of Augsburg (1555), leaving the throne of Spain to Philipp II and the imperial crown to Ferdinand I, and withdrew to a monastery in Estremadura.

9. Riley's biography is the most recent.

10. They were so dedicated to promoting national unity that they refused, for example, to distinguish in *Des Knaben Wunderhorn* between songs from various geographic regions.

11. See Schürer and Haustein for a discussion of the novella in the context of the entire collection. The frame story establishes the connection to von Arnim's own day.

12. "*In your* minds the world of legend / Comes together as a complete whole, / My book on the contrary believes that many legends / Come back to life again in our times, / And many reveal themselves only in the future, / Now see if that can be the case for you."

13. See Kiermeier-Debre for a discussion of von Arnim's views on the limits of history vis-á-vis fiction; the study is based on the debate von Arnim and the Grimm brothers carried on in their letters after the publication of "Isabella."

14. In addition to Greenfeld, see, for example, Hobsbawm, Ignatieff, Brubaker, Connor.

15. On von Arnim's politics, see Knaack.

16. Acton, Hancock, Fraser, and Fonseca are perhaps the most important of recent writers to speak out against the prevailing representations and the homogenization such representations require. Although nomenclature remains problematic, Fonseca reports increasing acceptance of the term "Gypsy" by the people themselves (228) and uses it herself. I have chosen to use it because the other all-embracing term, "Roma," is confusing in a German context where it is used as the designation for a single Gypsy group.

17. Thomas Mann's caveat about the "gypsies in a green wagon" in "Tonio Kröger" is perhaps the best-known example of the former; Nicolaus Lenau's 1838 poem "Die Drei Zigeuner" illustrates the latter. Numerous other works are listed in Trumpener. See other examples in Djurić.

18. The others are: "Melück Maria Blainville, die Hausprophetin aus Arabien: Eine Anekdote," "Die

drei liebreichen Schwestern und der glückliche Färber: Ein Sittengemälde," and "Angelika, die Genueserin und Cosmus, der Seilspringer: Eine Novelle."

19. "Where great portents point to the future, / We do not want to focus constantly on men, / The times will probably be changing: / Perhaps the era of women will soon begin!"

20. He believed, for example, that the German language should be standardized and spread through Europe as the *lingua franca* that could unite popular culture with the arts and sciences. See discussion in Hoermann (20).

21. Haustein links these fears to von Arnim's anti-semitism (39-40).

22. Hoermann's comments are typical: when Karl strays into the neighborhood, "Braka quickly maneuvers the completely innocent Isabella into Charles's bedchamber" (92).

23. Von Arnim's Faust, for example, saves himself from the devil by printing the Bible and turning his back on fame (Streller).

## Bibliography

*Achim von Arnim und die ihm nahe standen.* Ed. Reinhold Stieg and Herman Grimm. 3 vols. Stuttgart: Cotta, 1894-1913.

Acton, Thomas. *Gypsy Politics and Social Change: The Development of Ethnic Ideology and Pressure Politics among British Gypsies from Victorian Reformism to Romany Nationalism.* London: Routledge, 1974.

Anderson, Benedict. *Imagined Communities: Reflections on the Origin and Spread of Nationalism.* London: Verso, 1983.

Arnim, Achim von. "Isabella of Egypt." *Fiction and Fantasy of German Romance. Selections from the German Romantic Authors, 1790-1830.* Ed. Frederick E. Pierce and Carl F. Schreiber. Trans. Carl F. Schreiber. NY: Oxford, 1927. 171-243.

———. "Isabella von Ägypten, Kaiser Karl des Fünften erste Jugendliebe." *Achim von Arnim: Sämtliche Romane und Erzählungen.* Ed. Walther Migge. Munich: Hanser, 1963. II:452-557.

———. "Der Wintergarten." *Achim von Arnim: Sämtliche Romane und Erzählungen.* Ed. Walther Migge. Munich: Hanser, 1963. II:123-435.

———. and Clemens Brentano. "Von Volksliedern." *Des Knaben Wunderhorn.* Berlin: Haude and Spener, 1928. I: 435-84.

Brubaker, Rogers. *Citizenship and Nationhood in France and Germany.* Cambridge: Harvard UP, 1992.

Connor, Walker. *Ethnonationalism: The Quest for Understanding.* Princeton: Princeton UP, 1994.

Djurić, Rajko. *Roma und Sinti im Spiegel der deutschen Literatur: Ein Essay.* Studien zur Tsiganologie und Folkloristik 13. Frankfurt a.M.: Lang, 1995.

Fonseca, Isabel. *Bury Me Standing: The Gypsies and Their Journey.* New York: Knopf, 1995.

Fraser, Angus. *The Gypsies.* 2nd ed. Oxford: Blackwell, 1995.

Friedrichsmeyer, Sara. *The Androgyne in Early German Romanticism: Friedrich Schlegel, Novalis, and the Metaphysics of Love.* Stanford German Studies 18. Bern: Lang, 1983.

Greenfeld, Liah. *Nationalism: Five Roads to Modernity.* Cambridge: Harvard UP, 1992.

Grellmann, H. M. G. *Dissertation on the Gipsies.* 2nd ed. [Trans. of *Historischer Versuch über die Zigeuner.* 1783.] London: Ballantine, 1807.

Hancock, Ian. *The Pariah Syndrome: An Account of Gypsy Slavery and Persecution.* Ann Arbor: Karoma, 1987.

Haustein, Bernd. *Romantischer Mythos und Romantikkritik in Prosadichtungen Achim von Arnims.* Göppinger Arbeiten zur Germanistik 104. Göppingen: Kümmerle, 1974.

Heine, Heinrich. "The Romantic School." *The Romantic School and other Essays.* Ed. Jost Hermand and Robert C. Holub. Trans. Helen Mustard. The German Library. Vol. 33. New York: Continuum, 1985. 1-127.

Henel, Heinrich. "Arnims 'Majoratsherren.'" *Weltbewohner und Weimaraner. Festschrift für Ernst Beutler.* Ed. B. Reifenberg and Emil Steiger. Zürich: Artemis, 1960. 73-104.

Herder, Johann Gottfried. *Reflections on the Philosophy of the History of Mankind.* Chicago: U of Chicago P, 1968.

Hobsbawm, E. J. *Nations and Nationalism Since 1780: Programme, Myth, Reality.* Cambridge: Cambridge UP, 1990.

Hoermann, Roland. *Achim von Arnim.* Twayne's World Authors Series. Ed. Ulrich Weisstein. Boston: Twayne, 1984.

Hoffmann, Volker. "Die Arnim-Forschung 1945-1972." *Deutsche Vierteljahrsschrift* 47 (Sonderheft 1973): 270-342.

Ignatieff, Michael. *Blood and Belonging: Journeys into the New Nationalism.* New York: Farrar, Straus and Giroux, 1994.

Kiermeier-Debre, Joseph. "'. . . was bloß erzählt und nicht geschehen . . .': Dichtung und Geschichte: Achim von Arnims Poetik im Einleitungstext zu seinem Roman *Die Kronenwächter.*" *Grenzgänge: Studien zu L. Achim von Arnim.* Ed. Michael Andermatt. Bonn: Bouvier, 1994. 117-46.

Knaack, Jürgen. *Achim von Arnim—Nicht nur Poet. Die politischen Anschauungen Arnims in ihrer Entwicklung.* Darmstadt: Thesen, 1976.

Lenz, Hans-Uffo. *Das Volkserlebnis bei Ludwig Achim von Arnim.* Germanische Studien 200. 1938. Nendeln: Kraus, 1967.

Moering, Renate. "Fremdsprachige Quellen zu Arnims Erzählungen." *Beiträge eines Wiepersdorfer Kolloquiums zu Achim und Bettina von Arnim.* Ed. Heinz Härtl and Hartwig Schultz. Berlin: de Gruyter, 1994. 103-16.

Mosse, George L. *Nationalism and Sexuality: Middle-Class Morality and Sexual Norms in Modern Europe.* Madison: U of Wisconsin P, 1985.

*Nationalisms and Sexualities.* Ed. Andrew Parker, et al. New York: Routledge, 1992.

Neumann, Peter Horst. "Legende, Sage und Geschichte in Achim von Arnims 'Isabella von Ägypten': Quellen und Deutung." *Jahrbuch der Deutschen Schillergesellschaft* 12 (1968): 296-314.

Riley, Helene M. Kastinger. *Achim von Arnim.* Reinbek bei Hamburg: Rowohlt, 1979.

Said, Edward. *Orientalism.* New York: Vintage Books, 1979.

Schürer, Ernst. "Quellen und Fluß der Geschichte: zur Interpretation von Achim von Arnims Isabella von Ägypten." *Lebendige Form: Interpretationen zur Deutschen Literatur. Festschrift für Heinrich Henel.* Ed. Jeffrey Sammons and Ernst Schürer. Munich: Fink, 1970. 189-210.

Seyhan, Azade. *Representation and Its Discontents.* Berkeley: U of California P, 1992.

Streller, Dorothea. "Achim von Arnim und 'Auch ein Faust.'" *Jahrbuch der Sammlung Kippenberg* 1 (1963): 150-62.

Trumpener, Katie. "The Time of the Gypsies: A 'People without History' in the Narratives of the West." *Critical Inquiry* 18.4 (summer 1992): 843-84.

Völker, Ludwig. "Naturpoesie, Phantasie und Phantastik: Über Achim von Arnims Erzählung *Isabella von Ägypten.*" *Romantik: Ein literaturwissenschaftliches Studienbuch.* Ed. Ernst Ribbat. Königstein/Ts: Athenäum, 1979. 114-37.

Vordtriede, Werner. "Achim von Arnim." *Deutsche Dichter der Romantik.* Ed. Benno von Wiese. Berlin: Schmidt, 1971. 253-79.

## Frederick Burwick and Roswitha Burwick (essay date 1998)

SOURCE: Burwick, Frederick and Roswitha Burwick. "*Hollin's Liebeleben*: Arnim's Transmutation of Science into Literature." In *The Third Culture: Literature and Science,* edited by Elinor S. Shaffer, pp. 103-52. Berlin: Walter de Gruyter, 1998.

[*In the following excerpt, Frederick and Roswitha Burwick discuss the parallels between science and literature as manifested in Arnim's* Hollins Liebeleben, *examining how Arnim's education in the sciences formed the basis of his literary works.*]

When he first turned to the task of writing a novel, Arnim was clearly determined to represent a broad range of thinking, feeling, and experiencing. For authenticity, he adapted from his own encounters and from the people and places he knew. Among the places in the novel are Halle und Göttingen,[1] where Arnim had studied from 1798 to 1801; Reichardt's estate at Giebichenstein, which he visited in 1799; the Harz Mountains through which he journeyed on foot in the spring of 1801, from the medieval town of Goslar, to the top of the Brocken, the Biehlshöhle, the valley of the Roßtrappe. The character of Poleni he based on his friend, Johann Friedrich Reichardt; the character of Rosalie is drawn from Reichardt's daughter Louise, with whom he shared an intimate friendship.[2] Poleni's daughter Bettine is recognizably Clemens Brentano's sister whom Arnim did not personally meet until the summer after the novel was completed, and whom he married nine years later, in 1811. The character of Roland reveals some of the traits of Brentano; Odoardo those of Friedrich Raumer. Arnim's love for Jeanette Dieterich—the wife of Heinrich Dieterich, in whose publishing house **Hollin** was printed—is reworked into Arnim's adaptation from **Werther.**[3] In his account of Hollin's suicide, Arnim has also interwoven recollections of Carl Franz von der Goltz, a school friend at the Joachimsthal Gymnasium whose suicide haunted Arnim throughout his life.[4] Stephan August Winkelmann, who oversaw the publication in Göttingen, wrote to Arnim that Jeanette Dieterich had requested that several sections of the book be omitted. She found certain episodes far too transparent to disguise the identity of the persons in-volved. On 26 Jan. 1802, Arnim responded to Winkel-mann's report of the deletions:

> Es ist keine Höflichkeit, wenn ich glaube, daß er eigentlich durch jede Weglassung die Du bestimmst gewinnen wirst, nur muß ich dir sagen, er ist mir durch manche seiner Fehler lieb und es würde mich kränken, wenn ich vieles darin vermisste, erlaube sie daher nicht weder die mit, noch weniger die gegen deinen Willen geschehen.[5]

When he later to wrote to Brentano (18 Nov. 1802), the book had already been published. Arnim candidly con-fessed the autobiographical echoes, and he lamented the sections that had been removed:

> Was mir an meinem Hollin gefiel, und ich könnte ihn zuweilen abgöttisch verehren, das ist nur für mich darin, es war eine Unvorsichtigkeit, ihn so drucken zu lassen. Der Stoff war gut, und ich habe damals gerade daraus weggelassen, was andre rühren könnte, 1. Mariens Tagebuch, 2. Die Voraus-Beurtheilungen des alten Schulrektors über Odoardo und Hollin, 3. Die Blätter aus dem Stammbuche eines alten Burschen, 4. Das Lied der drei rasenden Sänger—um all mein po-etisches Talent darauf zu verwenden, in eine erdichtete Geschichte allerlei wahre Scenen einzuflechten. An den Roman habe ich Talent verschwendet wie ein Weber, der künstlich ein changent Taft aus verschiedenem Auf-zuge und Einschlage gemacht, aber es so hinlegt, daß es nur von einer Seite, also nur in einer Farbe gesehen werden kann. Das ist mein Urteil über meinen Roman. [. . .] Für mich werde ich nie etwas Besseres schreiben, für *andre* nie etwas Schlechteres.[6]

Recent commentaries on **Hollin's Liebeleben,** notably those by Härtl und Lützeler,[7] have observed the com-plex structure and combination of literary genre. The novel consists of the following parts: 1. the foreword by the editor, Arnim, who is fulfilling a dying friend's last wish; 2. an address to the reader by Odoardo, Hol-lin's friend; 3. the correspondence between Odoardo and Hollin (11 letters), along with additional pages by Hollin, written as diary entries or unsent letters, and also interspersed by a letter from Hollin to Maria and another from Lenardo to Hollin; 4. an addendum, en-titled "Frank an den Herausgeber," to the collected cor-respondence between Hollin and Odoardo, which also contains passages interpolated verbatim from Schiller's *Maria Stuart*; 5. the biography of Saussure, entitled **"Erinnerung an Horace Benedikt von Saussure. Aus Odoardo's Papieren."** With the omission of the four additional parts, none of which were in the epistolary form, the work could readily be perceived as predomi-nantly an epistolary novel. Thus the work has been in-terpreted primarily in terms of the contrast between "Briefroman" und "Beilage," fiction and historical biog-raphy, ignoring the multiple generic form in the editor's

"Vorwort," Odoardo's "Anrede," and Frank's note to the editor. Such a reductive mode of reading would have been altogether impossible if the novel had re-tained the report from the school rector, the pages from an album, and the mad song of the three raving singers. The pages from Maria's diary (which, one suspects, were chief among the passages which Jeanette Dietrich found too revealing) were a significant loss to the novel, for they would have provided a counterbalance to the effusions in those pages from Hollin's desk that were also written as if they were entries from a diary or drafts of unsent letters.

Although it is not possible to reconstruct the omitted parts, it is clear that they added to the variety of prose "voices" that still remain in the published novel. The conventional form of the epistolary novel is disrupted, but not simply by the forewords and afterwords. Even in its formal "epistolary" section—the eleven letters—there is an obvious literary self-consciousness that moves beyond the monological constraints of the epis-tolary form into elaborations of setting and situation, dialogue and story-telling. Arnim's text is interwoven with personal autobiography, historical biography, abun-dant reference to and appropriation from other literary texts. These include not just the usual modicum of bib-lical and mythological allusions, but a programmatic aesthetic provided by the particular set of references to Tieck's *Magelone* and *Genoveva*, Rousseau's *Nouvelle Héloïse* and *Emile*, Goethe's *Werther, Faust. Ein Frag-ment*, and *Wilhelm Meister*, Haydn's *Schöpfung (Creation)*, Spinoza's *Ethics*, Schiller's *Maria Stuart*, Senebier's *Mémoire historique*.

It is necessary to take *cum grano salis* Arnim's remark that the "verdammte Werther" ("damned Werther") and his own "falsche Verehrung der Göthischen Formen" ("false reverence of Goethean forms") had seduced him into allowing the best passages to be cut from the novel to transform the narrative into the epistolary model. He resisted the editorial excisions at the publishing house, and it was important to him that his novel maintain its forthright "Tendenz."[8] To Goethe's *Werther*, as Lützeler rightly observes, Arnim was indebted for the particular form of the correspondence between Hollin and Odoardo as well as for the "Nachschrift an den Heraus-geber." Goethe, however, had but one fictive editor of Werther's letters; Arnim has three: Arnim himself serves as editor; Odoardo composes the address to the reader and the supplement on the Life of Saussure; Frank, whose relation to Hollin or Odoardo is not explained, writes the afterword to the editor. In Goethe's narrative the story progresses linearly through the epistolary monologues and the editor's stylistically homogeneous continuation; Arnim's narrative does not conform to the epistolary monologue, and within the correspondence are interspersed non-epistolary reports. Where Goethe's editor upheld the individual subjectivity of the protagonist, Arnim's several editors and many of his characters seem to move in and out of a pervasive and shared subjectivity, playing off one another as if they were facets of one diffuse consciousness. In *Werther,* the editor's brief foreword requests sympathy and understanding for the plight of the protagonist; the reader is asked not to withhold admiration and love for Werther's mind and character, nor tears for his sad fate. In very different terms, Arnim's editor wishes the reader every joy which "das Buch mit der Erinnerung an den Freund" may provide.[9] Odoardo's address to the reader, apparently written before his madness, introduces a sceptical antithesis to Hollin's "Liebeleben" when he asserts: "Unser Zeitalter ist gleich arm an Liebe wie in der Liebe."[10] Hollin's fate is traced through metaphors of nature, the recurring cycle of fruition and decay, temporal flux and change, recollections of youth and anticipations of death. Goethe presents a Werther who is so compulsively driven by his own feeling that he is incapable of coping with life; Arnim's Hollin is a character questing for knowledge and freedom, who is vanquished in his conflict between inner and outer forces.

Like Goethe's Lotte, Arnim's Maria is also a vaguely delineated female character, who lives only through the actions and reactions of the male characters. The scene in which Werther first beholds Lotte, as she slices bread for her younger brothers and sisters, has its parallel in the scene in which Hollin watches Maria as she serves tea in the forester's house:

> Ich muß mich empfindsam, sentimental schimpfen, aber nimm mich, wie ich bin. Sie entwickelte bei dieser einfachen Handlung des täglichen Lebens unzählbare reizende Bewegungen und Stellungen, die ich nie gesehen, nie geahndet hatte; die versorgenden, fragenden, die freundlichen Blicke alle dazu, ihr belebendes Gespräch während der geschäftigen Wendung des Körpers nach dem Kohlenbecken, der Aberglauben eine besondre Kunst dabei sich zuzuschreiben, um andern alle Bemühung verweisen zu können, es ist unwiderstehlich.[11]

Lotte must take on the responsibilities of mother for the orphaned children; in her bourgeois role she becomes for Werther an unattainable ideal. Arnim has created a very different character in Maria, who asserts her freedom even while conforming to the conventional expectations of her family. Maria, fully conscious of her femininity, attracts Hollin's love. Werther become enamoured of a Lotte whose feminine sexuality is innocently concealed in child's clothing. In a description of her that would apply as well to a child-woman in a painting by Jean-Baptiste Greuze, Goethe writes that she is a woman "von schöner Gestalt, mittlerer Größe,

die ein simples weißes Kleid, mit blaßroten Schleifen am Arm und Brust, anhatte" ("of a pretty figure, middle stature, who wore a simple white dress with pale red ribbons on the arm and bosom"). Maria, too, is described wearing a white dress as she steps forth into the sunrise on the Brocken. The "Brockenstrauß" which she carries in her hand is intended to reveal her harmony with nature and the specific place, the Brocken. Hollin observes her movements and gestures. She is aware of her body and her sexuality as well as of Hollin's desire. Werther's love for Lotte, in the first instance incestuous in its suggestion of her attraction as mother or sister, then (no longer as mere psychological nuance) adulterous as she becomes a married woman, is pathological precisely because it can never be fulfilled. Hollin's love, by contrast, is shown as the naturally developing response of a man to a woman. Both recognize the mutual attraction and eagerly desire its consummation, which, once Hollin has established a foundation for bourgeois propriety, can be legitimated in marriage. When Werther meets Lotte, he is the outsider who has entered into the bourgeois environment of her paternal home and later her husband's home. Hollin and Maria experience their emotional excitement in the midst of nature on their journey to the Brocken. It is in nature that their feelings are first aroused, and in nature that their love is consummated. In the scene in which he attempts to put her into a magnetic trance, the "passes" of his hands over her body arouses in them both a keen sexual awareness that is intensified by their response to the sublime apparitions of the Brocken and then culminates in their night of passion. The ecstasy of their physical union is transformed into a *unio mystica* in which nature opens wide "die Schranken des Lebens" and exalts their human love with the glory of divine love. It is a moment of absolute union in which all division, separation, and isolation are overcome.

The literary texts in Goethe's novel clearly document the aesthetic values of the period: Klopstock is honored for his "sensibility" ("Empfindsamkeit") in the relation of man to nature and in the celebration of love; an entire chapter is taken up with Werther reading to Lotte a passage from *Ossian* which celebrates nature in a lofty idealized manner. Although a great debate was raging over the authenticity of *Ossian,* which Macpherson claimed to have translated from ancient Celtic sources, Goethe's point was not to engage his characters in a literary discussion of its merits, but rather to have them respond emotionally to its language. Arnim, too, has interpolated literary texts into his novel, and once again it is evident that in **Hollin** he is striving against, rather than conforming to, the model of *Werther.* When Arnim introduces another literary text into his own, its presence is not to enhance aesthetic principles already endorsed and operative. The discussion reveals the ideas and ideals of the characters. Disagreement about literary merits is more important than enthusiastic approval, for the differences in aesthetic values derives precisely from a sense of otherness. The literary text is introduced as a foreign element to serve as a catalyst for action (Schiller's *Maria Stuart*; Goethe's *Faust. Ein Fragment*) or as a reagent to elicit contrary reactions (Rousseau's *Emile*; Tieck's *Die schöne Magelone*).

The first literary discussion occurs while Hollin sits at the bedside of Lenardo, whom he has wounded in a duel. The discussion of literature, Hollin acknowledges, brings the two into close friendship because it prompts them to recognize their similarities and differences. Not the study of handwriting nor the phrenological measuring of the skull, Hollin asserts, can reveal as much about our secret inner selves as do "die Bücher, die wir lieben." "Wir passen zu einander," Hollin declares, "wie Kern und Schale" ("We are suited to each other as seed and shell"). One of their university companions, known for his eccentric dress, sends them a copy of Rousseau's *La Nouvelle Heloise,* a book which Hollin found without "Spannung" and with "verschrobenen Ideen aller über Liebe und Ehe."[12] When he declares that it is a book in which one finds "mehr Worte als Gedanken," "more words than thoughts," Lenardo responds: "es hätte doch das allen dicken Büchern eigentümliche Interesse, was man selbst schlechten Gegenden abgewinnt, wenn man sich lang darin hat aufhalten müssen," "all thick books should have the inherent interest, that one acquires in bad neighborhoods where one has had to stay for a long time." What Hollin denounces as "verschrobene Ideen," "confused ideas," about love and marriage, Lenardo approves, saying that Julie, who marries de Wolmar instead of her lover Saint-Preux, was right in concluding, "daß die Ehe ohne Liebe sein müsse, weil sonst gegenseitiger Zwang in der Austeilung," "that marriage must be without love, otherwise [there would be] reciprocal force in the distribution,"[13] Hollin answers, "daß [. . .] ein Hingeben, ohne Liebe, wie Klare und Julie ihren Männern die meisten Ehen [schildern], die einzige, wahre unerlösliche Schändung sei, daß die ganze Verbildung und Unnatur unserer Zeit, ihre ganze geregelte Jämmerlichkeit dazu gehöre, mit dem Feuer der Haushaltung die Liebesfackel anzünden zu wollen."[14] In order to test the validity of his convictions, Lenardo tells Hollin, he will have to determine whether true love is possible. "And," as Rabelais said on such an occasion, "thereby hangs a tale."

In his reply to Hollin's letter, Odoardo continues the discussion of Rousseau. "Das Beispiel erzieht besser als die Vorschrift," "Example educates better than precept," a pedagogical exemplum appropriated from Rousseau's *Emile,* is undermined in Odoardo's corollary: "es hat doch keinen Wert und keine Dauer," "it has no worth and no duration." The "ewig geleitete und gefoppte Emil [. . .], zu dem selbst Sophie in der Liebe kein Zutrauen faßt," "Emil always led about and hoaxed [. . .], for whom even Sophie does not trust in love," is a fitting example of the instability of Rousseau's system.[15] "Die moralische Erziehung," Odoardo declares, "baut Kartenhäuser auf, die beim ersten Anstoße der Originalität zusammenstürzen."[16]

Literary texts, as it becomes clear in the discussion of Rousseau, are not simply read, they are experienced. They arouse an interaction of thought and feeling. Reading thick books, as Lenardo says, can be like spending a long time in a bad neighborhood—one acquires an interest in it. The influencing power which Arnim attributes to literature is replicated in the scene of mesmeric magnetism enacted on top of the Brocken. Although she denies that she has succumbed to a magnetic spell, Maria affirms the possibility of an aura of energy just beyond the threshold of normal sensory awareness:

> Wenn etwas daran wäre, meinte sie, so schiene es wohl darin zu liegen, daß unser Wesen nur in gewissem Sinne auf die Grenzen des Körpers eingeschränkt sei, daß es durch die ganze unendliche Kette seiner Bedingungen mit einem Körper verbunden in allen verteilt, besonders in der Luft, als der eigentlichen Werkstatt des Lebens, im schnellen Vorübergehen des befreundeten Lebens, das Verbinden des Getrennten, das Bild der Vereinigung alles Lebens erkennt.[17]

According to this doctrine of magnetic influence, the mind may be aroused to poetic inspiration and the sensual awareness heightened. As he passes his hands over Maria's body, Hollin, too, feels an erotic intensification: "das wundervolle Treiben des Bluts in der Nähe der Geliebten [. . .] wenn Du mit der ganzen Anspannung des geheimnisvollen Schwungs der magnetischen Bewegung über alle Schönheit zwischen Berührung und Nichtberührung mit dem Getast dahin schwebst." In the language of his electro-chemical experimentation, Arnim describes the effects as a galvanic attraction. For both Hollin and Maria it is a sensation, "die mit heiliger Wollust von außen nach innen und mit erneuerter Kraft von innen nach außen bis zu den stumpfesten Wurzelfasern alles Leben, Kindheit, Jugend, Alter, in den Genuß weniger Minuten zusammendrängt."[18]

The following morning, with the first rays of the rising sun, all nature is quickened with renewed life. Inspired by the "Himmelsröte," Maria begins to sing from Haydn's *Schöpfung* (*Creation*).[19] Her spontaneous celebration of divine creation is juxtaposed to Hollin's mythic vision of a primitive race of giants who piled the stones upon the mountain. Arnim also enhances the mythic moment with his reference to the singing stones of the Memnon colossi. The atmospheric phenomena of the so-called "Brocken Spectre," giant shadows cast by the sunrise against the bank of clouds to the west,[20] are described in greater detail in the version of the Hollin story which Arnim worked into ***Gräfin Dolores.***[21] Here Arnim virtually ignores the grand apparitions to describe, instead, how Maria und Hollin respond to the grandeur of the dawn.[22]

The group of students who had joined their company the previous evening, again gather for a literary discussion. Lopez, a theology student with poetic aspirations, reads a poem that he has just composed on the sunrise. The discussion of his poem quickly turns to a critique of contemporary literature. To the query whether he is familiar with Goethe's use of elegiac hexameters, the pretentious Lopez replies that he has long held Goethe in a degree of esteem, "ungeachtet seiner so zu sagen genialischen Fehler." He has even considered the possibility of producing a selection of Goethe's more successful pieces, omitting "die schlechten, wie den Faust und andre mehr, die gegen alle Regeln verstoßen."[23] By putting this criticism of *Faust. Ein Fragment* in the mouth of an arrogant amateur, Arnim avoids implicating himself directly in the negative appraisal of Goethe. But the criticism does not end with this explicit reference to the text; rather, Arnim goes on to adapt from Goethe's "Wald und Höhle" scene in a way that curiously anticipates Goethe's own elaboration of the *Fragment* in *Faust. Eine Tragödie,* first published in 1808. Sometime between 1797 and 1805 Goethe added the scene with the Walpurgis Night adventure on the Brocken.[24] Goethe's additions to *Faust* were unknown to Arnim when he wrote his novel in the Fall of 1801. Goethe, on the other hand, might well have read ***Hollin's Liebeleben.*** Arnim made Hollin's adventure on the Brocken a central moment in his plot, and it is in Hollin's account of the Walpurgis Night that Arnim reveals the delusions that take possession of his protagonist and ultimately bring about his self-destruction.

The opinions of the pompous would-be poet are to be understood as totally bereft of sensitivity and judgment. In addition to appraising Goethe as the bard of genial errors, Lopez goes on to rank Tieck among the worst poets of the age. Tieck's *Leben und Tod des heiligen Genoveva* (1800), like Goethe's *Faust. Ein Fragment* violates the rules of drama, and worse, by having a deer speak, supports pernicious superstition (41). Covertly in this discussion, a very different appraisal of Tieck's poetry is being shared: Hollin asks Maria in a whisper whether she has read Tieck's love story of *Die schöne Magelone* (1797). "Mit einem unbeschreiblich freudigen Blicke zog sie das Buch hervor. Zu meiner Erinnerung, sagte sie und steckte es mir heimlich zu."[25] In the very context of Lopez's repudiation of Tieck's poetry, Maria signals her love for Hollin by presenting him with her copy of Tieck's tale of two lovers steadfast in their love in spite of separation and hardship. Again, the discussion of literature becomes a motivating spring of action.

Hollin's love for Maria is to be tested by hardship largely of his own making, as confusion gives way to delusion and despairing jealousy. Maria, through no choice of her own, is set in a triad of Hollin's attraction to Hermine and Irene, whose echoing names link them together just as do the echoing names of Odoardo und Lenardo. The principle that Arnim has adapted from electro-physics ("Duplizität in Triplizität") is replicated in the constellation of characters: Hollin's longing for union with Maria ("Duplizität"), the tensions that arise when his love for Maria is confounded by the allure of Hermine and Irene ("Triplizität"), and his rivalry and friendship with Odoardo and Lenardo ("Triplizität"). Odoardo is earnest, rational, matter-of-fact, yet inclined to dwell on the past and subject to pessimism and melancholy; Lenardo, at the opposite pole, is spontaneous and readily caught up in the excitement of the moment. Hollin is a mid-point between these extremes: he is as emotional and impulsive as Lenardo; yet he can also be, as when he secures a position in order to become a proper suitor to Maria, as conscientious and rational as Odoardo. Essential to the fictional narrative, the triadic constellation Hollin/Odoardo/Lenardo is dissolved and realigned in terms of the biographical narrative in which Hollin's role is part of the triad which includes Hollin/Arnim/Saussure. In the character of Hollin, Arnim has represented his own restless ambition and his poetic talent; in Saussure, Arnim recognizes the model for practicality and dedication to science. Even in external appearance, Arnim is conscious of similarities, for Saussure and Hollin are described as handsome young men who quickly gain approval. They possess a quickness of mind that brings them success in their studies and promises professional success.

Similar cross-connections are also evident among the minor characters. Councillor Lenardo and his wife are representative of a narrowly conservative bourgeois society: for him nature and science are reduced to empirical observation and experiment, literature to practical education; for his wife there is no life or meaning beyond her domestic role. Countess Irene has a figure which reminds Hollin of Maria; her sensuality excites him physically, but without any deeper emotional bond. Hermine, as an actress, has none of the social advantages of the Countess; because she leads a life beyond the bourgeois norms, she represents for Hollin the freedom that the he must surrender in assuming his own position of bourgeois responsibility. Secondary characters, such as Baron Rüst, are made to contribute usefully to the narrative. The Baron's tale of the fate of the Swedish prisoner of state provides a narrative adjunct to the doubts disturbing Hollin whether love and fidelity can endure. The minor no less than the major characters are all caught up in the web of causality, all are involved in the circumstances that precipitate Hollin's suicide. Odoardo arouses Hollin's doubts in the constancy of love; it is Odoardo whom Hollin, in the turmoil of doubt, sees embracing Maria. Lenardo, in their early discussion of Rousseau, told Hollin how he once courted in disguise the woman who had pledged to him her "ewige Treue" and won from her the same oath for his second self. Misunderstandings multiply when Lenardo urges Hollin to appear in the play as an "Unknown" and forbids Maria to write letters to him. Hollin's flirtations with Irene and Hermine arouse Maria's doubts. A chain of unfortunate incidents, formed by the sequence of misunderstandings, ultimately binds Hollin to his tragic resolve.

As Arnim asserts in his scientific notes, the attraction between physical bodies has its parallel among human beings, who also seem to be governed by an "elective affinity" ("Wahlverwandtschaft"). It is a force, then, than can be expressed as love. In Hollin's words, "[. . .] verbrüdert uns nicht alle menschliche Gestalt, ist nicht die Liebe frei und ist es nicht die eigentlichste Sympathie, das innerste Band der Menschen, alles liebevoll zu umfassen und in sich aufzunehmen?"[26] Thus mere accidental conjunction can become the operative principle:

> Jedes Wesen hat seine sympathetische Richtung, eine freischwebende Erscheinung in der Außenwelt, sie ist der geheime Zug nach dem der glückliche Spieler die Karte aus dem Haufen zieht, die Täuschung die uns warnt nicht aus dem Bette zu fallen, die besonders das Kind, den Trunkenen, den Wahnsinnigen gegen Gefahren schützt, und die Liebe ist ihre eigentliche Erscheinung, von der wir nicht wissen von wannen sie kam.[27]

Hollin's very character is determined by this principle. His "Liebeleben" is not simply narrated, it is defined, interpreted, and explained through his interaction with the other characters. Just as Hollin is an incarnation of the sympathetic force of attraction, so Odoardo works as the contrary force of repulsion. Odoardo's very first words, in the address to the reader, are a denial of love's unifying attraction: "Unser Zeitalter ist gleich arm an Liebe wie in der Liebe." For Odoardo the cycle of nature is not an affirmation of eternal regeneration, but rather of inevitable mutability: the buds of spring will wither; the "helle blinkende Reif" will enfold the most beautiful blossoms in its embrace of death.[28] He beholds life as prolonged farewell, a melancholy remembrance

of loss. For him the phenomena of nature are beyond comprehension and remain the illusion of human fantasy; religion and poetry are the playthings of idle speculation.

> Die Philosophen kommen dazu und beweisen, daß alle Bewegung der Bewegung wegen sei, daß keine anfange, keine aufhöre; beweisen, daß insbesondre die Güte und also das Dasein Gottes aus der Schnelligkeit der Bewegung der Weltkugel folge, die keine Kegelkugel durch die stärkste Menschenhand erreichen könne.[29]

While Odoardo's gloomy scepticism stands in polar opposition to Lenardo's carefree attitude, it exercises a determinate pull upon Hollin's effort to affirm life and love and to pursue his future with optimism. The friendship between the physician Odoardo and the poet Hollin is defined by the tensions of attraction and repulsion:

> Doch vergesse ich sie nie, alle Eindrücke, die oft mit unerklärlicher Stärke mich ganz bestimmten, wie ich mich hingezogen fühlte zu Dir, bei Deinem ersten Anblicke, wie wohl mir ward mit Dir, wie ich allmählich aus Deinem frohen Mutwillen Mut zum Leben einsog; wie ich es mit Dir auszugleichen suchte, indem ich Ernst in Deine leichten Eingebungen des Augenblicks mischte.[30]

Together, Hollin and Odoardo could achieve a balance between their contrary natures; separated, each resorts to his natural tendency. Once he comes into contact with Lenardo, Hollin is pulled in the opposite direction. Hollin's compulsive drive for love, for freedom, defined by his own nature, has no inherent direction.

> Ringt nicht jedes Wesen nach seinem Gesetze, alles, vom Sonnenstäubchen an, nach Licht und Freiheit; [. . .] Und wir, frei aufgerichtet zur Mittagssonne, die einzig ausgezeichnet vor aller Kreatur, den Himmel vor uns und unter uns die träge Weltkugel schauen [. . .] unmöglich sollen wir den hohen, belebenden Trieb, die Fülle der schwellenden Kraft und Freude eindämmen [. . .].[31]

When he turns from the study of science to dedicate himself to philosophy and literature, he finds the determinate condition of life and science set in abeyance, and his own thought caught in the reversing polarity where playful jest becomes serious, and vice versa.

> Wissenschaft und wechselnd Leben buhlten um mich, da traten Philosophie und Poesie herbei, und Wissenschaft und Leben waren verschwunden, mit Blüten bekränzt war ernsthaft der Scherz und der Ernst Scherz geworden.[32]

His youthful political idealism goes awry when he joins a student fraternity and, misled by pseudo-patriotic maxims, finds himself engaged in a duel with Lenardo whom he has just met. Distraught after having almost killed Lenardo, Hollin's state of mind renders him incapable of expressing himself in terms of reason and natural law; he is compelled to adopt the language of poetic metaphor: "Auch Du ewige gütige Natur schreckst mich in deiner Trauer [. . .] Ich muß dem herrlichen Leben, der Freude des goldenen Lichts entsagen, ihm meine Augen schließen [. . .]."[33] Unable to determine his own direction, he followed his intellectual love of life into the study of natural science; led by a love of country he commits a senseless act in the name of patriotic zeal. Once he meets Maria, he experiences a more profound sense of love. United with her he is convinced that he can turn his intellectual abilities to proper use and, as husband and as citizen, fulfill both his personal and public aspirations.

With his farewell from N., however, he does not commence, as he hopes, the new life in which his dreams and ideals will be fulfilled.[34] He means to forge a career that will provide him the bourgeois status he needs to gain the approval of Maria's parents. In this very goal he experiences a paradoxical lack of purpose and suffers symptoms of isolation and estrangement. In vain he seeks to revive the sense of a union with nature which he felt upon Walpurgis Night;[35] nor can he in the embrace of Irene or Hermine conjure any semblance of his love for Maria. His poetic power, once animated by love, becomes pathologically perverted. He becomes victim of diseased fantasies, and his delusions begin to affect his response to those around him.

During the period in which his life was still motivated by love, he had a life most full of life ("das lebenvollste Leben"). Following their separation, life is reduced to deterministic action and reaction. Hollin loses his ability to control the antagonism of internal and external forces.[36] The knowledge that all nature obeys definite laws had once been, until his separation from Maria, a source of animating joy. Now he perceives only a cold determinism. The world becomes a stage upon which each individual can play only a given role, unable to alter the course of events. In an earlier letter, Hollin had cautioned Odoardo against the dark power of melancholy to compel one to suicide, if not to quaff the "huge beaker of poison" in a single draught, than more insidiously to swallow "the poison in a thousand little doses."

> Ich verdamme, ich verachte jene nicht, eben so wenig diese, es waltet ein mächtiges Schicksal über uns, in der Natur geht kein Leben unter, alles ersteht in erhöhter Organisation, aber keiner der noch Freundschaft, der Kraft zum Leben, Freude in der Natur fühlt, kann sich von allem gleichgültig trennen.[37]

According to Hollin's own definition, to commit suicide is to fall in battle against the forces of destiny. Over-

whelmed by his own exacerbated fantasies, he lost the ability to give his life the direction and purpose he desperately wanted. The memoire of Saussure, by contrast, recounts the course of one who recognized and overcame the antagonism and polar extremes, and who directed his own life with exemplary success. Hollin, too, had this potential, but he could not realize it.

Hollin pursues his "Liebeleben" through those stages in which his love for Maria is consummated and he experiences a mystical union with nature. Instead of developing from the natural sciences, to philosophy and poetry, and to a full comprehension of life, Hollin's intellectual and emotional growth are rent asunder. As soon as he has decided to dedicate himself to philosophy and poetry, science and rational objectivity are overthrown. Instead of complementing objectivity with subjectivity, he allows the inner realm of thought and feeling to dominate. No longer the object of scientific inquiry, nature is redefined as the arena in which the self participates in absolute freedom and may be absorbed into the all-pervading light and energy. With this realignment of self and nature comes a repudiation of the "träge Kleinmut des Bürgerlebens" which can only suffocate "allen kühnen, dehnenden, ausbreitenden Geist."[38]

His love for Maria aroused his poetic sensibilities. Her dawn song on the Brocken "erhob zuerst mein ganzes Innre in das heilige Reich der Töne; die wärmende Sonne weckte den ersten Ton in Memnons kalter Brust, in mir die leuchtende Liebe."[39] The image of the Memnon colossi, which Arnim repeats from his papers on the natural sciences, serves as symbol for the poetic power stimulated through its union with nature. But the image of the Memnon ruins suggests, as well, a sensitivity fragmented and imperilled. With Maria's love, Hollin acquires a poetic voice of enthusiasm and inspiration. Even in Hollin's rhapsodic effusions, however, Arnim undercuts the illusion of spontaneity by interweaving the apparently impromptu celebration with echoes from the "Wald und Höhle" scene of *Faust. Ein Fragment.* "Du, Geist der Erde, bist mir näher," "You, Spirit of the Earth, are nearer to me," Faust declares when he first conjures with the Sign of the Microcosm, "Schon fühl' ich meine Kräfte höher," "Already I feel my energies soar" ("Nacht," 107-108).[40] Later, he recalls this moment:

> Erhabener Geist, du gabst mir, gabst mir alles,
> Warum ich bath. Du hast mir nicht umsonst
> Dein Angesicht im Feuer zugewendet.
> Gabst mir die herrliche Natur zum Königreich,
> Kraft sie zu fühlen, zu genießen. [. . .]
>
> ("Wald und Höhle," 1890-94)[41]

Hollin, following his first night on the Brocken, expresses his love for Maria in an apostrophe to "erhabener Weltgeist": "was ich als Traum kaum konnte fassen, hast du in ihr, erhabener Weltgeist, mir geschaffen, mach das die Ahndung zur Gewißheit werde, und ich umfass' das Herrlichste der Erde."[42] "Sublime Spirit of the World" is not called upon in vain. Hollin's "Ahndung," (presentiment" becomes "Gewißheit," "certainty." Faust, in "Wald und Höhle," gives thanks to the "Erhabene Geist" for protection from the raging storm and for self-revelation:

> Und wenn der Sturm im Walde braus't und knarrt,
> Die Riesenfichte, stürzend, Nachbaräste
> Und Nachbarstämme, quetschend, nieder streift,
> Und ihrem Fall dumpf hohle der Hügel donnert;
> Dann führst du mich zur sichern Höhle, zeigst
> Mich dann mir selbst, und meiner eignen Brust
> Geheime tiefe Wunder öffnen sich
>
> (1901-07)[43]

Alone in the hut in the forest, Hollin gives expression to his passion for Maria with an intensity that echoes the tumultuous spirits of Walpurgis Night, an experience that also culminates in self-revelation:

> Stürmt Geister im pfeifenden Winde, hallt wilde Jäger im Walde, der Regen rauscht am Fenster hinab und stäubt durch die Spalten, es wankt mein Obdach und kracht, die Lichter flakern, doch liebevoll tragt ihr mein inneres Leben, die ewige Glut, die mich entzündet, dem Harrenden entgegen.[44]

Like Faust, Hollin too turns from external nature to "das innere Leben, die ewige Glut," "the inner life, the eternal passion." "Es facht in meiner Brust," Faust declares, "ein wildes Feuer" ("A wild fire is fanned within my breast").[45] In his transcendental apotheosis of the self, Hollin not only radiates outward as the light of love, he absorbs all that surrounds him into his own boundless identity: "Ich bin der ewge Quell, das ewge Öl der holden Flamme, in der ich nicht verbrenne, nicht vergehe, in deren Licht ich reingebrannt des Kampfes Wonne schmecke."[46] When Faust says that "ein wildes Feuer" burns within him, he does not succumb to the delusion of immanence. He distinguishes subjective from objective and knows what desires feed his internal flame: "So tauml' ich von Begierde zu Genuß, / Und im Genuß verschmacht' ich nach Begierde," "So I reel from lust to pleasure, / And in pleasure I languish for further lust," ll. 1923-24)." Hollin's ecstasy is not bound by flesh and physicality, it emanates with his own unrestrained subjectivity. His own consciousness replicates the organic vitality of external nature. He perceives the fecundity of nature as the impulse of his own love: "die süße Frucht ergetzt mich in den Blüten, in Früchten zeigt sich schon der Blüte ahndungsvolle Röte, es

strecken schon die neuen Knospen eröffnend ihren Götterkelch dem Licht entgegen, und tausendfach strebt alles Leben in ewger Kette wirkend fort."[47] Although his reference to life "in ewger Kette" echoes the language of electro-chemistry, Hollin endorses here the idea of the *catena aurea*. Empirical experience has been usurped by transcendental consciousness, a pervasive subjectivity that creates its own reality.

Once Hollin put aside the concerns of science, he allows only poetry and philosophy to direct his thoughts. Having rent asunder the intellectual disciplines, Hollin has limited the range of his own mind. He has estranged himself from the reality in which he nevertheless strives to establish himself in order to provide Maria a place as his bride. He loses his ability to distinguish subjective from objective. Entrapped by his own delusions, he can solve his problems only in that most solipsistic of all acts, suicide. The excerpts "Aus der Schreibtasche" reveal that Hollin, like the Sorcerer's Apprentice, has conjured a poetical-philosophical world far more powerful than he is capable of controlling. The light of love becomes burning fire that consumes him.

### Notes

1. In the retelling of the Hollin story in *Die Gräfin Dolores,* Arnim uses the abbreviations H. and G. instead of M. and N. (*Werke in sechs Bänden* vol. 1, p. 196); on 10 May 1798 he entered Halle as *studiosus iuris*; on 20 May 1800 he matriculated in Göttingen as a student of mathematics.

2. In her correspondence, Louise Reichardt expressed her deep feelings for Arnim, of which he was certainly aware; Renate Moering: "Arnims künstlerische Zusammenarbeit mit Johann Friedrich Reichardt und Louise Reichardt. Mit unbekannten Vertonungen und Briefen." Burwick/Fischer, eds.: *Neue Tendenzen der Arnimforschung,* pp. 209-17; pp. 253-69; see especially her letter of April 1811, written when Louise learned of Arnim's marriage to Bettina Brentano; on J. F. Reichardt and Giebichenstein, see p. 199.

3. Savigny und Winkelmann: *Der Briefwechsel (1800-1804) mit Dokumenten und Briefen aus dem Freundeskreis,* pp. 261, 264-265; Heinrich Dieterich comments laconically on his wife's interest in Arnim: "Sie fand, daß seine physischen und chemischen Studien einen zu unangenehmen Einfluß auf seine Atmosphäre hatten. Deshalb warf er alle bisherigen Beschäftigungen zur Seite, erneute seine Garderobe, versorgte sich mit wohlriechenden Essenzen und schrieb 'Holly's Liebeleben'." Raumer: *Lebenserinnerungen und Briefwechsel* vol. 1, p. 43.

4. In his letter to Bettina (27 Aug. 1806) Arnim wrote on the suicide of Günderode: "um einem drück-enden Lebensverhältnisse zu entgehen, das wohl so einem vereinsamten, gereizten Gemüthe im Augenblicke unendlich hoffnungslos scheinen mochte, das ist mehr Lebenskraft [. . .]." In the same letter he also mentioned Carl Franz von der Goltz, who studied with Arnim first at the Joachimsthal Gymnasium and subsequently in Halle: "Auch ich verlor einen Schulfreund und täglichen Bekannten auf gleiche Art vor sieben Jahren in Halle, [. . .] ich fühlte es, [. . .] daß der Zufall des Zusam-menlebens, nicht nothwendiges Vertrauen uns ver-bunden." Steig/Grimm: *Achim von Arnim und die ihm nahestanden* vol. 2, p. 41-2.

5. "I am not merely being polite when I believe that it [*Hollin*] will actually gain from every omission that you decide upon, but I must tell you, it is en-deared to me through many of its faults, and it would vex me, if I missed much of it; therefore do not let them happen, neither with nor, still less, against your approval" Savigny und Winkelmann: *Der Briefwechsel (1800-1804) mit Dokumenten und Briefen aus dem Freundeskreis,* pp. 264-65.

6. "What pleased me in my Hollin, and at times I could idolize him, is what I put into it only for myself; it was a lack of caution to allow it to be printed as it was. The subject was good, and I al-ready removed at the time what could touch oth-ers, 1. Maria's Diary, 2. The old School Rector's pre-judgment of Odoardo and Hollin, 3. the pages from the album of an old comrade, 4. The Song of the three raving singers—in order to turn all my poetic talent to interweaving a variety of true scenes in an fictional story. I squandered as much talent on the novel as a weaver, who artfully con-trives a *taffeta changeant* of various warp and weft, but then lays it out so that it can only be seen from one side, that is, in only one color. That is my judgment of my novel. [. . .] For myself I will never write anything better, for *others* never anything worse" (Steig/Grimm: *Achim von Arnim und die ihm nahestanden* vol. 1, p. 52).

7. Härtl: "Arnims kleiner Roman," p. 171; Lützeler, commentary to *Hollin's Liebeleben,* in Arnim: *Werke in sechs Bänden* vol. 1, pp. 709-16.

8. Steig/Grimm: *Achim von Arnim und die ihm nahe-standen* vol. 1, p. 24

9. Arnim: *Werke in sechs Bänden* vol. 1, p. 11.

10. Ibid., p. 12.

11. Ibid., p. 35: "I must accuse myself of sensibility and sentimentality, but take me as I am. At this simple task of daily life she displayed countless fascinating movements and poses which I had never seen or imagined; her caring, questioning, friendly looks, her animating talk while busily turning her body to the brazier, the superstition in attributing to herself a special art, in order to turn aside any assistance from the others; it is irresist-ible."

12. Ibid., p. 22.

13. Ibid., p. 23.

14. Ibid.: "that [. . .] a submission without love, as Clare and Julie [describe] most marriages to their husbands, is the sole, true irredeemable sacrilege; the proper response to that the entire malforma-tion and monstrosity of our time, its entire or-dained wretchedness, is to want to ignite with the match for the hearth the torch of love."

15. Ibid., p. 27.

16. Ibid.: "Moral education builds houses of cards which tumble down at the first touch of original-ity."

17. Ibid., pp. 37-38: "If there were something to it, she supposed, it would seem to be because our be-ing is limited only in a certain sense by the bound-aries of the body, that through the entire unending chain of its conditions it is connected with one body in all, especially in the air, as the actual workshop of life, in rapidly passing the life to which is allied, combining the divided, recognizes the image of the union of all life."

18. Arnim: *Werke in sechs Bänden* vol. 1, p. 37: "the wonderful surging of the blood near to your be-loved [. . .] when, with the entire harnessing of the secret verve of the magnetic pass, your hands hover between touching and not touching over all beauty," "which with holy lust from the outside inward and with renewed energy from the inside outward to the numbest roots of all life, child-hood, youth, age, compressed in the pleasure of a few minutes."

19. Haydn's *Die Schöpfung* was first performed at the Schwarzenberg Palace, Vienna, 29-30 April 1798; the English poem by Lidley was translated and adapted for the oratorio by Gottfried van Swieten.

20. M. Jordan's scientific account of the "Brocken Spectre" appeared in J. F. Gmelin's *Göttingen-sches Journal der Wissenschaften,* I, part iii (1798). The apparitions are most frequently seen at sunrise during April-May when the peak of the Brocken (1140 meters) is clear and shadows are

cast against the cloud bank gathered along the Abbenstein (769 meters) and Quitschenberg (882 meters).

21. Arnim: *Werke in sechs Bänden* vol. 1, p. 205.

22. *Hollin's Liebeleben,* ibid. vol. 1, p. 40.

23. Ibid., p. 41: "not counting his, so to speak, genial errors," "the bad pieces, such as Faust and many others, which trespass against all rules."

24. Goethe: *Werke (Hamburger Ausgabe)* vol. 3, p. 527; *Faust: Ein Fragment,* in *Sämtliche Werke: Gedenkausgabe der Werke, Briefe und Gespräche,* vol. 5, pp. 67-137. The only mention of Walpurgis in the 1790 version occurs at the close of the "Hexenküche," when Mephistopheles tells the witch, "Und kann ich dir was zu Gefallen thun, / So darfst du mir's auf Walpurgis sagen" (1052-1053). Goethe was apparently preparing to write the "Walpurgisnacht" episode in February, 1801, when he began borrowing books on witchcraft and magic from the Weimar Library; see: Keudell: *Goethe als Benutzer der Weimarer Bibliothek,* nos. 243-52; Goethe: *Goethe über seine Dichtungen* (ed. Gräf) vol. 2, 2, pp. 104-05.

25. Arnim: *Werke in sechs Bänden* vol. 1, p. 41: "With an indescribably happy look she drew forth the book. So that you will remember me, she said, and slipped it to me secretly."

26. Ibid., p. 16: "[. . .] doesn't the very human figure make us brothers, isn't love free and isn't it the most basic sympathy, the most inner bond of humanity, to embrace everything with love and make it one's own?"

27. Ibid., p. 43: "Every being has its sympathetic direction, a free-hovering apparition in the external world; it is the secret draw with which the lucky player picks the cards from the deck, the illusion that warns us not to fall out of bed, that protects especially the child, the drunk, the mad against danger, and its most essential manifestation is love, of which we never know whence it came."

28. Ibid., p. 12.

29. Ibid., p. 30: "The philosophers join in and prove that all motion is for the motion's sake, that none begins or ends; they prove that especially goodness and therefore the existence of God derives from the rapidity of the planet's motion, which no bowling ball from the strongest human hand could ever match."

30. Ibid., p. 14: "But I shall never forget them, all the impressions which often moved me with inexpli-

cable strength, how I felt myself attracted to you at first glance, how content I was being with you, how from your playful temperament I gradually derived courage for living; how I sought to reciprocate by mixing earnestness in your light inspirations of the moment."

31. Ibid., p. 15: "Doesn't every being, everything, from the smallest solar particle onward, according to its own law, struggle toward light and freedom; [. . .] And we, standing free in the midday sun, uniquely distinguished among all creatures, behold the heaven before us and beneath us the sluggish planet [. . .] it would be impossible for us to hold back the high, animating drive, the abundance of boundless energy and joy [. . .]."

32. Ibid.: "Science and mutable life vied around me, then came philosophy and poetry, and science and life were gone; crowned with blossoms, the jest became earnest and earnestness became a jest." Cf. Ricklefs: *Kunstthematik und Diskurskritik,* p. 18.

33. Arnim: *Werke in sechs Bänden* vol. 1, p. 19: "Even you, eternally blessed nature, terrify me in your mourning [. . .] I must renounce the magnificent life, and close my eyes to the joy of golden light [. . .]."

34. Ibid., p. 52.

35. Ibid., p. 53.

36. Ibid., p. 17.

37. Ibid., p. 31: "I do not damn, I do not despise one sort or the other. A mighty destiny rules over us; in nature no life perishes; everything arises in a higher organization; but no one, who still feels friendship, the energy to live, joy in nature, can depart from them all indifferently."

38. Ibid., p. 15.

39. Ibid., p. 60.

40. Goethe: *Sämtliche Werke: Gedenkausgabe der Werke, Briefe und Gespräche* vol. 5, *Faust. Ein Fragment* "Nacht," p. 72

41. Ibid., "Wald und Höhle," p. 130: "Sublime Spirit, you gave me, gave me all, / I asked for. It was not in vain / That you turned your face toward me in the flames. / You gave me glorious nature as my kingdom, / Strength to feel her and to enjoy her."

42. Arnim: *Werke in sechs Bänden* vol. 1, p. 39: "what I could scarcely comprehend as dream, you, sublime Spirit of the World, have created for me in her; grant me that my presentiment become a certainty, and I embrace what is most glorious on earth."

43. Goethe: *Sämtliche Werke: Gedenkausgabe der Werke, Briefe und Gespräche* vol. 5, pp. 130-31: "And when the storm roars in the woods and creaks, / The giant spruce, falling, strikes and smashes / Its neighbor's branches and its neighbor's trunk, / And with its fall the hill thunders a hollow thud; / Then you lead me to this secure cave, and show / Me to myself, and all the deep and secret wonders / Of my own breast are opened to me."

44. Arnim: *Werke in sechs Bänden* vol. 1, p. 48: "Spirits, storm in the whistling wind! You, Wild Hunter, echo in the woods! The rain splashes against the window and runs through the cracks, the roof over me shakes and creaks, the lamps flicker, yet lovingly you carry to me, waiting in anticipation, my inner life, the eternal passion which sets me aflame."

45. Goethe: *Sämtliche Werke: Gedenkausgabe der Werke, Briefe und Gespräche* vol. 5, p. 131.

46. Arnim: *Werke in sechs Bänden* vol. 1, p. 48: "I am the eternal source, the eternal oil of the lovely flame, in which I am not consumed and do not perish; in which light purified, I taste the joy of the struggle."

47. Ibid., p. 49: "the sweet fruit delights me in the blossom, in the fruit is already revealed a foreshadowing of the crimson blossom; the new buds when they open already stretch their holy chalice toward the light, and all life strives actively forth a thousandfold in the eternal chain."

## Bibliography

Arnim, Ludwig Achim von: *Hollin's Liebeleben: Ein Roman*. Neu hrsg. und mit einer Einleitung versehen von Jakob Minor. Tübingen: Mohr, 1883.

Arnim, Ludwig Achim von: *Werke in sechs Bänden*. Hrsg. von Roswitha Burwick, Jürgen Knaack, Paul Michael Lützeler, Renate Moering, Ulfert Ricklefs und Hermann F. Weiss. Vol. 1-6. Frankfurt a. M.: Deutsche Klassiker Verlag, 1989-1994 (Bibliothek deutscher Klassiker 39, 42, 55, 83, 72, 118).

Burwick, Roswitha, and Bernd Fischer, eds.: *Neue Tendenzen der Arnimforschung*. Bern, Frankfurt a. M., New York, Paris: Lang, 1990 (Germanic Studies in America. 60).

Goethe, Johann Wolfgang: *Goethe über seine Dichtungen*: Versuch einer Sammlung aller Äußerungen des Dichters über seine poetischen Werke. Hrsg. von Hans-Gerhard Gräf. Unveränd. Nachdruck der Ausgabe Frankfurt a. M. 1912-1914. Darmstadt: Wissenschaftliche Buchgesellschaft, 1968.

Goethe, Johann Wolfgang: *Sämtliche Werke: Briefe, Tagebücher und Gespräche*. Vierzig Bände, Hrsg. von Hendrik Birus u. a. I. Abteilung: Sämtliche Werke. Vol. 1-25. Frankfurt am Main: Deutscher Klassiker Verlag, 1985-1994 (Bibliothek deutscher Klassiker. 82).

Goethe, Johann Wolfgang von: *Sämtliche Werke: Gedenkausgabe der Werke, Briefe und Gespräche*. Bd. 1-24. Hrsg. von Ernst Beutlet. Zürich: Artemis, 1948-54.

Goethe, Johann Wolfgang von: *Werke*. Hamburger Ausgabe in 14 Bänden. Hrsg. von Erich Trunz. Vol. 1-14. Vol. 3: Dramatische Dichtungen 1. 10., überarb. Aufl. München: Beck, 1976.

Härtl, Heinz: "Ludwig Achim von Arnims kleiner Roman 'Hollins Liebeleben.' Zur Problematik seines poetischen Erstlings um 1800." *Wissenschaftliche Zeitschrift der Martin-Luther-Universität Halle-Wittenberg* 18:2 (1969):171-81.

Jordan, M: "Erscheinungen auf dem Brocken." *Cöttingensches Journal der Wissenschaften* (ed. J. F. Gmelin) 1:3 (1798).

Keudell, Elise von: *Goethe als Benutzer der Weimarer Bibliothek: Ein Verzeichnis der von ihm entliehenen Werke*. Hrsg. und mit einem Vorwort von Werner Deetjen. Weimar: Böhlau, 1931.

Raumer, Friedrich von: *Lebenserinnerungen und Briefwechsel*. Vol. 1-2. Leipzig: Brockhaus, 1861.

Ricklefs, Ulfert: *Kunstthematik und Diskurskritik: Das poetische Werk des jungen Arnim und die eschatalogische Wirklichkeit der "Kronenwächter."* Tübingen: Niemeyer, 1990.

Savigny, Friedrich Carl von, und Stephan August Winkelmann: *Der Briefwechsel (1800-1804) mit Dokumenten und Briefen aus dem Freundeskreis*. Hrsg. von Ingeborg Schnack. Marburg: Elwert, 1984.

Steig, Reinhold, and Herman Grimm, eds.: *Achim von Arnim und die ihm nahestanden*. Vol. 1-3. Stuttgart, Berlin: Cotta, 1894.

**Sheila Dickson (essay date summer 2000)**

SOURCE: Dickson, Sheila. "*An Apology for the Conduct of the Gordons*: *Dichtung* and *Wahrheit* in Achim von Arnim's *Mistris Lee*." *European Romantic Review* 11, no. 3 (summer 2000): 300-21.

*[In the following essay, Dickson examines the source behind Arnim's "Mistris Lee," which was based on an 1804 abduction case in England. In contrast to the*

*other stories in* Der Wintergarten, *which are inspired largely by German history and folk tales, "Mistris Lee" drew its material directly from contemporary events. Dickson reviews contemporary news accounts of the incident while analyzing the ways that Arnim adapted the material to suit his own work.*]

Achim von Arnim himself confirmed the factual source for his story **"Mistris Lee"** (published in 1809 as part of the collection **Der Wintergarten**) in a letter to Clemens Brentano as "durch einen Proceß veranlasst, den ich in England klagen hörte,"[1] and it has commonly been assumed that he was present at the trial of the Gordon brothers for the abduction of Mrs Lee which was held in Oxford in 1804. It is also known that he employed this source more than once: as an unfinished sketch in his notebook, with the title **"Der Zufall. Geschichte der Mrs Ligh,"** as part of an essay on English Law, and as the **"Novelle Mistris Lee."**[2] Arnim in his comments to Brentano identifies differences between the circumstances of the trial and his own story and highlights his difficulty in finding a believable way of getting the two main protagonists into bed together. Furthermore, the first version of the tale, in the sketch **"Der Zufall,"** displays important variations from the final, finished version in the **"Novelle,"** in which Lockhart forces his brother to carry out the abduction, the dream has a different content, and the innkeeper proves to be Mrs Lee's husband. These factors all seem to indicate that Arnim tried out different possibilities in his imagination, leaving the source behind him as no more than a starting point for fictional narrative, and for these reasons **"Mistris Lee"** has been treated as somewhat of an exception in **Der Wintergarten,** in which almost all the inset tales are re-workings of old sources.[3] In the light of these assumptions it is illuminating to look more closely than has been done previously at documents regarding the facts of the court case in England.

The trial of the brothers Loudoun and Lockhart Gordon at the Oxford Assizes in 1804 was reported on in detail by *The Morning Chronicle* and *The Sun* on Wednesday 7 March, by *The Times* on 7 and 8 March, and by *Bell's Weekly Messenger* and *The Weekly Dispatch* on Sunday 11 March. *The Times* provides us with the most information. On 7 March there are two full columns containing the Judge's address to the Grand Jury followed by reports on the examination of witnesses and the verdict. On 8 March three full columns provide "Further Particulars of the trial of the Gordons," a reflection of public interest in the case. This latter, more informative article contains references to facts which conform with details in Arnim's narrative, for example that Loudoun located Lee through information given by "Mr Blackett[4], a respectable apothecary," and quotations from the witnesses which appear in Arnim's story as dialogue, such as Lee's admission under cross-examination that

she commented as follows on Lockhart's failure to visit her: "I suppose that he has heard the report that I am a sceptic, and as he is a Clergyman, he don't like to come into my company; but you may assure him he need not be afraid, for if he comes I shall always avoid introducing the subject of religion" (compare Arnim 223[5]). Most interesting, perhaps, is the fact that Mrs Lee's dream, most easily identified as a Romantic motif and probably the most likely element to be accredited to Arnim's imagination, was actually documented as part of the court proceedings; *The Times* reports on 7 March the Learned Counsel's mention of "the accounts published in the newspapers [the gutter press: no such report exists in the broad-sheets], which he described as highly indecorous, and particularly mentioned a supposed interpretation of Mrs Lee's dream, for which, he said, there was not the least foundation." On leaving the courtroom it is reported that Lee was asked about her dream by a journalist or other onlooker and said that "the letter containing it was in the possession of Mr. Gordon, and he might produce it." On 8 March *The Times* repeats the Learned Counsel's warning to the Jury "against any impudent falsehoods or indecent statements which had been conveyed to the public through the medium of the newspapers. He mentioned this to fortify them against any prejudice they might have received from the erroneous accounts that came through the channel of the press, particularly Mrs Lee's dream, which had been grossly mis-stated."

The above serves to confirm Arnim's knowledge of the trial; which may be first-hand, and therefore his own information to Brentano, in other words the familiar view of the story's origins. However, the British Library holds two copies of a volume which was printed at least six times within the year 1804 and which represents a new and detailed source for Arnim's **Novelle.** The volume is entitled *An Apology for the Conduct of the Gordons containing the whole of their correspondence, conversation, &c. with Mrs Lee: to which is annexed, an accurate account of their examination at Bow Street, and their trial at Oxford,*[6] and the author is Loudoun Harcourt Gordon[7]. It contains exactly what the title proclaims. The Narrative of the apology or self-defence is prefixed by an Introduction, and followed by transcriptions of the "Examination before Mr Bond and Sir William Parsons, two of His Majesty's Justices of the Peace for the county of Middlesex," and of the trial at the Oxford Assizes. The credibility or otherwise of Loudoun's self-justification is unimportant here, but a comparison of this material with Arnim's **"Mistris Lee"** produces such overlapping of detail and of formulation that it must be taken as the major source from which Arnim drew, in many cases even translated,[8] and must revise our understanding of the status of the material in the text.

Arnim's narrator begins **"Mistris Lee"** with general remarks about the legal system in England. This material was also used in the sketch on English Law mentioned above and is based on Arnim's experiences in London. The narrator then gives his impression of his characters, impressions which could not be documented in the court case or in Loudoun's self-justification and which will form the basis for the particular interpretation given to the events that follow in Arnim's story (Arnim 219-20). The facts, however, of Lee's unhappy marriage are reported by Loudoun in his narrative (*Apology* 35), as are the circumstances surrounding Loudoun's return to London and his debts, which were, along with Lee's upbringing with the Gordons, her marriage, and her divorce settlement, common knowledge as a result of the trial. Loudoun begins his narrative with details of his first visit to Mrs Lee after his return from the West Indies, "about seven o'clock on the evening of Wednesday, the 14th of December, 1803" (*Apology* 35). Arnim is less exact with dates than Loudoun, but follows the sequence and time scale exactly. The former's description of this and of all subsequent meetings between the three characters is a translation of dialogue from Loudoun's *Apology* with the addition of a third-person narrator's interpretation of their thoughts and impressions.[9] This grants the reader insight into their perceptions and motivations in a far more subtle way than the comments of the first-person narrator of his own self-defence document Loudoun can afford: Loudoun mentions Lee's request at their first meeting to see Lockhart, her inquiries after his mother and sister, and her tears at the death of his sister Caroline (*Apology* 36). In the Introduction to his narrative he also mentions "the warm reception I received from Mrs Lee, [which] rekindled the latent flame" (*Apology* v), but interprets this, for his own reasons, as "my own inclination, united to the artful provocations made use of by Mrs Lee to affect her wishes, [which] soon deprived me of all power of resistance or reflection" (*Apology* v). Arnim's Loudon is captivated by her beauty, and at the beginning of his story Lee's character remains as enigmatic to the reader as it is to Loudon.[10]

Lee's interest in Lockhart is clearly documented by the author Loudoun, and when Loudoun visits for the third time alone he quotes her as saying that she believes his absence is due to his having heard that her "opinions are sceptical." Loudoun answered that his brother was very liberal and that he had "a larger acquaintance than he can possibly visit" (*Apology* 38). Lee mentioned her fear of being insulted at the theatre (*Apology* 39), and the conversation turned to the dream she had a few days before the appearance of the late meteor, "with which phenomenon Mrs Lee appeared to think her dream might have some connexion" (*Apology* 40). Loudoun asked for a copy of the dream, promising to show it to no-one other than his brother and Lee makes an

appointment for his next visit. Loudoun records his reaction that "it was not customary with me to be confined to any particular day to visit his friends, and that in the future I intended to call upon Mrs Lee occasionally" (*Apology* 40). In the parallel scene in Arnim's *Novelle,* the dialogue is almost an exact translation of the above, to which is added the narrator's information on Loudon's feeling that her behaviour and ideas are strange (Arnim 223), and his ironic comment on his character's ignorance as due to limited personal horizons resulting from reading sentimental novels and living as a soldier in the West Indies (Arnim 223).

The dream in its entirety is reproduced as follows in Loudoun's narrative

> At about three o'clock in the morning, as the Watchman afterwards informed me, and as I guessed, I thought I looked towards the South East and beheld the sun gloriously bright, rising amidst clouds tinted with gold. I never in my waking hours saw this phenomenon so beautiful. Gazing on it, I thought I exclaimed, "It is but three o'clock and quite dark in our hemisphere, yet the sun is rising! That is strange." As I was musing on this deviation from the usual course of nature, I directed my eyes towards the North East, and perceived the moon pale and rather clouded; but on each side were two luminaries like suns, which gradually enlightened her, till all the three bodies had the appearance of globes of fire. While I was observing them with peculiar delight, suddenly the most magnificent edifice that the human imagination can form, raised itself out of the three fiery orbs. Its columns were immense and roughly studded, in the way of fret work, with precious stones; the floor was glassy, but the roof and upper parts were so immensely high that I could not discern them; the architecture was complicated, and I had not time to analyze it; but never was my mind so strongly impressed with the ideas of beauty, grandeur and power. I was absorbed in deep meditation; when I opened my eyes and heard the Watchman call 'past three o'clock.' I had before mentioned the hour during my sleep, which is a very remarkable circumstance.

> (*Apology* 41-42)

In the Introduction to his narrative, Loudoun calls the dream "a parcel of nonsensical words, which will readily bear a most indecent interpretation" (*Apology* vi). He relates showing the dream to his brother, a clergyman, who "immediately told me it would bear a religious interpretation, and gave me the outline of that exposition which I afterwards transmitted to Mrs Lee and which is faithfully transcribed from the original manuscript, for the inspection of the public, in the following pages" (*Apology* vii). He claims that Lockhart's interpretation was the expression of a "sincere desire to point out to Mrs Lee . . . the weakness and wickedness of scepticism" (*Apology* viii). This version of events is obviously preferred by the Gordons, and is a possible scenario due to Lee's admitted scepticism, but Arnim had a different view of Lockhart, which can also be sustained with reference to the known facts of the trial. He has Loudon read the (same) dream to his brother (Arnim 223-24), whereupon Lockhart "machte eine zotenhafte Auslegung davon" (Arnim 224). This is a first indication of a crudeness of manner in this character, which will be developed in the course of the story.

The brothers' dream interpretation is also reproduced in full by Loudoun (*Apology* 42-45). Arnim leaves out some descriptive detail while remaining true to structure and content (compare Arnim 224-25):

December 27, 1803

DEAR MADAM.

Before I submit my thoughts to you upon the subject of the dream which you have done me the honour to communicate to me, allow me to assure you Madam, that it is not my intention to enter the lists as a champion for the truth of Christianity, which could gain nothing, and might be injured by my mistatement of those arguments, or misapplication of those evidences which certainly deserve our most serious consideration.

"The sun rising gloriously bright in the south East," exactly represents the first appearance of Jesus Christ in Judea. He is frequently stiled "the Sun of Righteousness," "the Light of the World," and "the True Light." "The clouds tinted with gold," pourtray the mental darkness and error, which at that time, with some few exceptions, degraded the whole human race. The "moon in the North East" exhibits the first promulgation of the Gospel; the North being the quarter of the globe always first named, may figuratively express the beginning of any thing; "the moon being pale and rather clouded" alludes to the temporary humiliation and sufferings of the Great Author of our religion. "The two luminaries, like suns on each side of her," are the Father and the Holy Ghost. "The gradual illumination of the Moon" shews the progress of the great work of the redemption of mankind in the person of Jesus Christ, after the completion of which, our Saviour ascended into heaven and became one of the "three globes of fire." "The globes of fire" most happily illustrate the only idea we can form of the Trinity; fire having been allowed to be in all ages the purest symbol of the deity. "The peculiar delight which you felt at observing" such glorious objects, is the natural effect upon the human mind, arising from the contemplation of the wonderful works of God. "The magnificent edifice which raised itself out of the three fiery orbs" is Christianity. "The immense columns" are the cardinal virtues; "their being roughly studded in the way of fret work" marks the difficulty of persevering in a virtuous course of life amidst the temptations and miseries of this world. "The precious stones" strikingly pourtray the innate beauty of virtue. "The glassy floor" beautifully symbolizes the tranquility and serenity of mind, which accompanies the true disciples of Christianity. "The roof and upper parts of the edifice being so immensely high that you were unable to discern them," shews us the weakness

and absurdity of our endeavouring to scan the ways of Providence, or to weigh the councils of omnipotence in the balance of poor human reason. No wonder Madam that "the architecture" of the great fabrick of revealed religion should have appeared "complicated" to you, and that "you should not have had time to analyze" those mysteries which "angels desire in vain to know," and which "the devils believe and tremble."

It is impossible to consider the doctrines of Christianity without being impressed as you were with the highest ideas, of which the human mind is susceptible of "the beauty, grandeur, and power" of the great author of our existence.

That frequent meditation upon this, of all other, most important subjects, may tranquilize your mind and make you as superior to the calamities which human mind is heir to, as your abilities are to the far greater part of mankind, is the sincere wish of, Dear Madam,

Your most faithful Servant,

L. H. Gordon.

P.S. Lockhart presents his respects to you Madam, and hopes that you will see him on Friday Morning next, when he proposes to do himself the honour of calling upon you.

I take the liberty of returning the paper which you did me the honour to entrust to my care.

In Loudoun's account of the visit on Friday 30 December Mrs Lee asked after Lockhart's mother. When Lockhart replied that she was well, we are told that Mrs Lee replied: "I am happy to hear it, for she is a most wonderful woman, but I think her principles are too rigid, do not you think so?" Lockhart replied, "I think it impossible that any principle can be too rigid with regard to virtue" (*Apology* 46). She reminded him that "he used to call her Dash, thunder at the door and say, 'Dash! I will come in.'" Lockhart replied that it had often given him pain at the recollection of how roughly he treated her, whereupon Lee said that she took it as mark of affection (*Apology* 46). After the visit, Loudoun reports his brother saying he "regretted having seen her, and was sorry for her unhappy situation, and that he would not on any account, now he had renewed the acquaintance, have Mrs Lee suppose that he treated her with neglect, and would leave his card at her house occasionally" (*Apology* 47). Arnim reproduces in translation these conversations, and his narrator adds his own interpretation of the characters: Loudon is unable to form a real impression of Lee or interpret her words and actions, on this occasion he notices that she seems more interested in his brother (Arnim 225). Of the latter we read the narrator's summary character reading: "Lockhart, wie alle rauhe Leute, wenn sie einmal erweicht [on being reminded of his boorish behaviour as a child], so bedauern sie es, nicht immer so gewesen zu sein" (Arnim 226).

The next document Loudoun transcribes is the letter he found on his return home after this visit (*Apology* 47-48). Arnim describes the same situation and reproduces the letter, again omitting some detail (compare Arnim 227):

> January 1, 1804
>
> Your interpretation to the dream is replete with ingenuity and good sense; the former abounds when you launch into the regions of fancy, the latter predominates when you confine yourself to probabilities. And here let me caution you against giving scope to "mimick fancy," which often whilst she flatters your vanity, and amuses your mind, is leading your senses astray.
>
> The epithet of "the Sun of Righteousness," though not new, is exceedingly beautiful, alluding no doubt to that person who certainly was a light to some of his followers, who for the most part were vicious and ignorant. Some of the early mystical writers have termed him "the Day spring." I am pleased with your remark upon "the immense columns." Your observation upon "the precious stones" is beautiful. The illustration of "the glassy floor" is very happy. I am fully convinced that virtue is congenial to the human mind; but in the present state of the world, the practice of it is attended with difficulty: I say in the present state of the world, for the serenity which accompanies virtue is so persecuted as almost to render it unattainable.
>
> Vain indeed! is our attempt to scan the ways of Providence; "the immense fabrick" has been adopted by its wise author for purposes only known to himself.
>
> The natural attraction which we feel towards those whom we have known in the days of childhood, induces me to express a wish to see you in the course of next week; with sincere good wishes, I subscribe myself,
>
> Yours truly,
>
> F. A. Lee.

The next visit is on Sunday 8 January. The date is given by Loudoun (*Apology* 52), Arnim's narrator interprets this gap, but is not certain of his character reading and therefore of the reason in this instance: "Er versäumte sie darauf ein paarmal, einmal wegen Beschäftigung, vielleicht auch aus Absicht, weil sie ihn einmal so kurz entlassen; sie schrieb ihm nochmals zu kommen und sie kamen acht Tage darauf zusammen" (Arnim 227). This visit was taken up with dream interpretation and Loudoun told Lee Alexander the Great's dream (Arnim 227). We read that Lee told Loudoun in the course of the conversation not to become enamoured of her but to suppose she was old and ugly, to which Loudoun replied that it was too late, that it was his "Most Unhappy day" when he heard of her marriage. Lee replied that she loved him, but that he could not live in the house with her as her husband resided within two streets of

her (*Apology* 52-53). Mrs Lee is quoted as saying, "So you really wish me to become your pretty little mistress?" to which Loudoun tells us he replied, "Human ties forbid you to be any thing else at present than the mistress of my soul" (*Apology* 54). Arnim's narrator reproduces the sequence and the details of the conversation, at the most dramatic point omitting the speech tags of narrative and presenting their direct speech in the form of dialogue in a play (Arnim 228): a shorthand device that clearly separates the source material from his own material at this juncture. The narrative perspective is widened in this scene and the narrator can give the reader insight into both characters' thoughts. We learn of Mrs Lee: "Es war der unschuldigste Augenblick ihres Lebens, es hatte sie alles überrascht, ohne sie zu erschrecken; der Zufall wollte es gut, aber der Mensch tut meist etwas zu viel" (Arnim 228-29), and of Loudon: "Er meinte, daß er etwas versäumt habe und lobte sich doch, daß er ihre Güte nicht mißbraucht" (Arnim 229).

That Loudoun/Loudon knocked at Lee's door around 11 o'clock the same day is reported by both Loudoun and Arnim's narrator, and that he was sent away by a manservant who said his mistress was in bed (*Apology* 55, Arnim 229). On his return the next day, Monday 9 January, the maidservant Davidson opened the door and put the following note in his hand (compare Arnim's translation 229):

> I can only attribute the rash action which you committed last night to intoxication; it is therefore impossible for me to see you until I receive an apology; indeed unless you intend to visit me as the friend of your infancy, perhaps it would be better, just at present, if you were to discontinue all personal intercourse.

Loudoun, on the evening of same day, gave the following letter to the manservant, who said Lee was very unwell (*Apology* 56).

> 9th January, 1804.
>
> DEAR MADAM,
>
> You do me justice by attributing the rash action which I unhappily committed last night to intoxication!!! to intoxication of my soul, Madam.—I dined at my brother's lodgings by myself, and drank no wine, as he was from home; but I had drank too freely in the morning of the most delicious potion which I shall ever taste, not to feel its effects, which will be fatal indeed, should they occasion your lasting displeasure.
>
> Forgive, Madam, the only action of my life which shall occasion your anger; do not drive me to despair; do but see me, and treat me like a dog as I deserve. I am,
>
> Dear Madam,
>
> Your most wretched servant,
>
> L. H. GORDON.

Arnim's gist translation cuts out some of Loudoun's verbiage, and his narrator comments that this was the last and worst of many letters he had written (compare Arnim 230).

The scene that follows is described in detail by Loudoun (*Apology* 57-62): After Lee read the letter, she requested Loudoun to come up. Loudoun knelt, took hold of her hand and looked earnestly into her face. Lee laughed "at so tragic-comic an attitude and said, 'Loudoun, it was not kind of you to call in the evening; why did you come so late?!'" Loudoun, "seeing her good humour and that the letter had been sufficient apology," kissed her hand and arose (*Apology* 57). The table divided them. Lee told Loudoun to move the chair. There followed salutations, embraces, and a plan of elopement over the course of three hours. Wales is mentioned, the question of an inn or a cottage, the question of taking servants, which Lee declined as "she can travel without and can procure Welch (sic) servants." Lee insisted that the elopement must take place without the knowledge of Davidson who is paid to spy upon her conduct. She claimed to have taken Davidson out of Mr Lee's family to show them that her conduct was such as not to fear the eye of scrutiny. She showed Loudoun the passage in her book stating: "It is my determination to pass the remainder of my life in the society of a male companion; and with him to follow the plan of a Sect in Germany, who lead a monastic life, with the exception of celibacy" (*Apology* 58-59).

Lee told Loudoun she had no money, as no dividends were due until February. Loudoun replied that he had funds and proposed to leave the next day, which prompted the reply from Lee: "You must have some presentiment of something evil about to befal me" (*Apology* 59). Loudoun denied this and explained that he was "convinced it was her wish and she had too much good sense not to lay aside dull forms and prudish ceremonies in the conclusion of an affair so intimately connected to their mutual happiness" (*Apology* 59). Lee asked for time to make arrangements and to consult a male friend. She then gave him her construction of her dream. The beginning must signify that "some immediate and material change is about to take place in my situation," which could allude to nothing less than her union with Loudoun (*Apology* 61). Loudoun writes that he has forgotten the remainder, but that it was favourable to their mutual wishes. He reports that Lee asked what his mother would think and repeatedly asked, "You really wish me to become your little mistress?" to which he replied, "The mistress of my soul, Mrs Lee" (*Apology* 61). The lovers exchanged handkerchiefs. Lee's was marked with "L.9" and Loudoun writes caustically in his *Apology* that this no doubt alluded to Lee's perfect love and submission: "Mrs Lee

has made some proficiency in the knowledge of the abstruse sciences" (*Apology* 62).

Arnim gives neither one the responsibility of thinking up the elopement plan, but accords Mrs Lee "was nie sein sollte, mehr Überlegung und Zuversicht dabei als er [i.e. Laudon]" (Arnim 230). He can tell us Lee's reason for showing Loudon her written intention to live according to the principles of a sect: "Sie wollte ihm damit beweisen, daß es überlegter Entschluß, kein Taumel" (Arnim 231). The narrator's response to the exchange of handkerchiefs is the ironic description of Loudon leaving Lee's house with "das mystische Halstuch vor seinem Munde, um die fremde Luft, die er einatmete, sich wert zu machen," followed by a generalised comment on the dangers of keeping secrets (Arnim 232).

During the following self-enforced absence of two days, and following a brief letter from Loudoun submitting to this test of his fortitude, Loudoun received the following letter from Lee (*Apology* 65-66):

> January 11 1804
>
> By my consenting to your proposal you will gain much and I shall lose the little which I still possess. Neither age nor situation can afford me the protection and support that will be necessary. Consult your heart, consult your reason. If pleasure were my object, neither my mind nor my body are at present in a state to make enjoyment pleasurable to me. You are well aware of the opinion the world will form of you and me. You say you are my friend: prove it by the sacrifice of a youthful passion. As a boy I thought you had a generous sentiment. Let me see that time has matured not destroyed it. You say that you will submit to my better judgement and discretion, I now exact from you the fulfilment of your promise. My determination is fixed, and those who will not second it are not my friends. Communicate this letter to your brother.

For Loudoun this letter was "merely intended to draw an answer from me and to implicate Lockhart in the elopement" (*Apology* xi). Arnim's narrator has now developed his, and so the reader's knowledge of the character Lee to the point where he can present this as "eine Antwort . . . , die wir uns sehr leicht erklären können" (Arnim 232). The explanation given is: "Sie war verheiratet, sehr unglücklich verheiratet gewesen und die Kraft der Unschuld schützte sie nicht mehr" (Arnim 232). Arnim's Mrs Lee is shown to be weak in character. She is weak enough to let her man of business dictate his translation of the above, to which he adds an opening sentence ("Sie haben an jenem Abend meine bedrängte Lage treu aufgefaßt") and changes another sentence slightly ("You are well aware of the opinion the world will form of you and me" becomes "wir beide müssen das Urteil der Welt höher achten" (Arnim 233).

On receipt of the letter, Arnim's Loudon misunderstands the meaning of the last words and there ensues a scene with no source in Loudoun's *Apology* between the two brothers in which ironically Loudon feels committed to go ahead as he believes she expects it, demonstrating his lack of perception and indecisiveness, and Lockhart is once again shown to be ill-mannered and foul-mouthed (Arnim 234).

As proof the elopement was planned on the Monday night (9 January), Loudoun quotes at this point in his narrative in a footnote a note from his brother accompanying a brace of pistols on Wednesday morning, 11 January (*Apology* 65):

> Let it be indelibly impressed on your mind, that the trifling present which accompanies this letter, was given you for the protection of your own honour, and the defence of an injured woman, who deserves your love, and commands your respect, by sacrificing every thing desirable in this world, for the sake of your society. Never argue, never dispute; avoid a first quarrel as you would a pestilence; sleep in different beds; never dress in the same room; observe the most scrupulous delicacy at all times and upon all occasions; enjoy, but do not abuse, the mystic rights of Venus.
>
> Believe that this advice is given you from an earnest wish for your future happiness, and is the result of much observation.

The letter is also presented as proof that it was not Lockhart's intention to participate in the elopement, "had not Mrs Lee by her artful letter of 11th and invitation of 12th induced him to do so" (*Apology* 65). Arnim integrates the note into a later scene after the elopement has taken place, in which he has Lockhart respond impatiently and rudely to Lee and Lee be hurt at his lack of interest in her opinion, and in her (it is at this point that she realises she loves him and not Loudon) (Arnim 240-41). In his translation of the letter he tones down "pestilence" to "Überdruß" and relates the point concerning delicacy to his own manner of self-expression ("sei auch im Sprechen zarter als ich" (Arnim 240-41).

The following letters are given to Lee in response to hers [*Apology* 67-68]).

MY DEAREST MADAM,

> If you assent to my proposition, I shall gain an inexhaustible source of felicity; you will lose the pity of the ignorant and the prejudiced. The protection that I have to offer you Madam, is the strength of body and mind, the courage and life of a man, not unused to danger. My age, Madam, has been matured by adversity, the only school of true philosophy; my situation, though it is not what I could wish, nor what my education and birth might have led me to expect, is rendered less irksome, by the possession and enjoyment of that inestimable treasure, *mens conscia recti,* which can neither be purchased nor stolen. I have consulted my heart, and would have plucked it out had it dared to think you less than the most perfect of human beings. I have consulted my reason in a low, but clear voice, it whispered praise. Pleasure, name it not my heart, for I have found no traces of you imprinted there. If the union of congenial souls can be rendered more complete by the union of their bodies, obey Madam the first mandate of God and of nature, or tremble at the thoughts of your disobedience. The world Madam is unworthy of you; the false opinion which it will probably form with regard to your conduct, will never be able to shake your constancy or fortitude. In obedience to your commands I have communicated your letter to my brother; he respects, he admires you, and he says that he will protect you at the hazard of his life and fortunes. I can feel, though I cannot express what I am to you, more than that I am,

My Dearest Madam,

Your sincere and affectionate,

L. H. Gordon.

MY DEAR MADAM,

> I consent with all my heart to every thought, word and expression contained in Loudoun's answer to your letter, which you did me the honour to desire him to communicate to me. If Loudoun deceives you Mrs Lee, I will certainly blow his brains out, and then we shall both be eternally damned as we shall most richly deserve. Strong feelings burst the fetters of ceremony, and express themselves in the untutored language of nature. Mrs Lee will find in Lockhart Gordon a friend who has a head to conceive, a heart to feel, and a hand to execute whatever may conduce to Mrs Lee's happiness.

I have the honour to be, &c.

L. Gordon.

In his translation, Arnim changes the first sentence of Loudoun's letter ("Mein Glück liegt in Deiner Bestimmung, das Vorurteil hast Du überwunden") and shortens his subsequent outpourings while remaining faithful to the tone of the letter (compare Arnim 234-35). He shortens the ceremonious address in Lockhart's first sentence ("Ich billige von ganzer Seele, was mein Bruder Ihnen sagt"), thus increasing the peremptory nature of his assurances (compare Arnim 235).

Lee's response to the letters in Loudoun's narrative was to tell Loudoun she had been dissuaded by her male friend to elope, but subsequently to convince him by her conversation that she was still willing (*Apology* 69). Arnim has Loudon's presence suppress the good advice (Arnim 235). Lee requested Loudoun to see her picture at Mr Cosway's the painter before he see her again (*Apology* 69); Arnim's Loudon "war wieder verwundert, daß sie noch für den Tag an so etwas dachte" (Arnim 235). Lee finally invited Lockhart and Loudoun to dinner on Sunday "to talk over the matter and settle it" (*Apology* 69-70).

Arnim invents a preamble to the next meeting: a conversation between the brothers which further illustrates and confirms their characters (Arnim 236). At dinner on Sunday 15 January in Loudoun's narrative, Lee asked Lockhart if he were surprised at the communication Loudoun had made to him. Lockhart's reply was that he was not surprised at anything so natural (*Apology* 71). Lee expressed the fear that "in a year Loudoun will run all over town after other women;" Lockhart answered: "Your beauty is sufficient security against that." He then commented that the best thing was to go out of town in a post chaise this evening, at which Lee laughed (*Apology* 91). Arnim's narrator adds the explanatory clause "sie hielt es für Scherz" (Arnim 236). A servant entering put an end to the conversation. Where Arnim has Mrs Lee exchange a "Freimaurergruß" with Lockhart (and, intriguingly, only then with Loudon) (Arnim 236), in Loudoun's *Apology* we read of a custom whereby two people drink to each other's health: "Mrs Lee hobbed a nob, as it is vulgarly called, with Lockhart, by placing the bottom of her glass on the top of Lockhart's, and vice versa; the same ceremony was repeated with Loudoun, and no doubt was symbolic of the union which it was then Mrs Lee's intention to complete that night" (*Apology* 71-72). The phrase is not explained in Loudoun's text and perhaps not translated for this reason, or perhaps Arnim has added the element of freemasonry from his own interest in the subject.

Loudoun's report of the elopement is as follows (*Apology* 72-75): at about 7 o'clock Lockhart said that the post chaise would be here presently. Lee asked, "What post chaise?" and Lockhart answered, "The one in which you and Loudoun are going to Wales." Lee laughed and asked Loudoun, "Is he in Earnest?" Loudoun said, "Yes, and I'm glad for we shall now be enabled to accomplish what we mutually wish, but want resolution to effect" (*Apology* 72). At this point Lockhart reminded Loudoun he had a present, a ring, and told Loudoun to put it on Lee's finger; Lee refused to accept it, and it remained upon the table. Lockhart assured Lee: "We are fully prepared, we have pistols for your protection" (*Apology* 73). Lee rose and felt Lockhart's pockets. Then she ran round the table to feel Loudoun's. Lockhart requested Lee to put her riding habit on, but she refused. Lockhart then told Loudoun to see if the post chaise was ready. Mrs Lee went upstairs and Lockhart told Loudoun not to leave her alone. She requested a manservant to send Loudoun to the drawing room. He found her kneeling on a chair with her face to the back of it. He saluted and embraced her

and said, "Come Mrs Lee, there is no time to be lost, pray put on your habit and take those things which you will more immediately require" (*Apology* 73-74). Mrs Lee's response, "I cannot go; I am not prepared," is interpreted as her displaying reluctance "which was to be expected of her when the eyes of the servants were upon her" (*Apology* 74). When Lockhart told her "The chaise is ready, come Mrs Lee, let us go," the maidservant Davidson is reported to have said, "My Mistress shall not go out of her house." However, writes Loudoun, Mrs Lee did go out, quietly (*Apology* 74). The female servants made a great outcry, and so Lockhart took a pistol out of his pocket to prevent noise. As Loudoun and Mrs Lee were walking to chaise, they met a man, "proved later to be Lord Stair's coachman," and Lee said: "Who are you, do you know me?" then asked Loudoun if he had locked the house (*Apology* 74-75). Lockhart's words on joining them: "Drive on or I'll shoot" is described by Loudoun as a phrase Lockhart as a sportsman "was apt to make use of" (*Apology* 75).

Arnim describes the same events, but the narrative perspective shifts again and the narrator now focuses on the thoughts and perception of Lee.[11] He thus shows Lee to be genuinely confused, a view that Loudoun wishes in his *Apology* to refute absolutely. Arnim expands on the scene upstairs with Lee on the chair and makes her try to pray (Arnim 237), where Loudoun's *Apology* and the reports of the trial make much of her lack of religious beliefs. The shift in narrative perspective mirrors a shift in narrative sympathy. The narrator shows compassion for Lee in her present position and criticises Loudon's lack of sensitivity in disturbing her in a moment of piety (Arnim 237).

In the post chaise Lee asked, "Do I not support my presence of mind wonderfully well?" and attempted to take the ring he had offered her off Loudoun's finger (*Apology* 75-76). He tried to put it on the fourth finger of her right hand, but she told him that was the wrong hand and said: "In compliance with the custom of the world I consent to wear this ring" (*Apology* 76). Lockhart expressed the hope that it fit and on Lee's affirmative commented that this was a good omen. Lee threw away her necklace, a charm against sensual pleasure, as she "no longer had any occasion for it." To her question "Do you think I'm right to fling it away?" Loudoun answered "Certainly" (*Apology* 77). When Lockhart said he should now return to London, Lee called this infamous and told him that "the world will never forgive you." Lockhart said he needed to be at a ball and Lee countered that he "will tell all the pretty misses I've eloped" (*Apology* 77). Lockhart insisted that it was in his own interest to be silent but there ensued a long argument, the culmination of which was that Lee made Lockhart promise to come to Wales and stay with them that night (*Apology* 78). Arnim's narrator presents this section too in shorthand form without narrative tag-clauses to increase the dramatic effect (Arnim 238-39). He comments, "Frauen in Not hören selten Gründe" and describes Lee as light-hearted and frightened in turn (Arnim 239). Arnim has Lockhart misinterpret Lee's need for comfort and security as crude sexual advances (Arnim 239). In this way he adds to our picture of all concerned in a way not possible or appropriate in his source work and in so doing creates a quite different constellation of characters.

In Tetsworth we are told that Lee ate a hearty supper and talked about "the Pyramids of Egypt, Grecian architecture and Hieroglyphicks" (*Apology* 80). For Loudoun this conversation is proof of her sanguine mood; Arnim uses it to illustrate the unease of all three protagonists (Arnim 239-40).[12] After Lee went to bed Loudoun sent a chambermaid to ask if she wanted anything and Lee is said to have replied, "Tell the gentleman to come to bed in ten minutes" (*Apology* 80-81). At this point Lockhart and Loudoun went to their room, Loudoun "was a long time fumbling about" and was told by Lockhart: "If you don't get out of the room I'll shoot you." He thereupon asked a chambermaid: "Did you ever see a fellow make such a piece of work about going to bed to his own wife?" (*Apology* 81). By this point Arnim's narrator is no longer interested in Loudon's character and so we do not learn much of his state of mind but are invited instead to appreciate and sympathise with the situation Lee finds herself in. The narrator describes the bedroom she is given (Arnim 239), and her shock at realizing she is to sleep alone (Arnim 240). This provides a motivation for her spending the night with Loudon that contradicts Loudoun's in his *Apology* and remains consistent with Arnim's characterisation of Mrs Lee.

At breakfast the next morning Loudoun describes how Lee continued to argue, claiming that Lockhart wished to go to London "to amuse pretty misses at her expense" (*Apology* 81). Lockhart assured her he was obliged to return to London to make interest for a family living. Lee complied but still, it is reported, believed he meant to expose her, and for that reason sent a note to Davidson: "No money, no cloaths, death or compliance" (*Apology* 82). Loudoun writes that Lee then told Mrs Edmonds, the innkeeper's wife, she had been forced from her house (*Apology* 82). When Mrs Edmonds supposed Mrs Lee would not go on, Lee replied, "Oh yes, I shall go on" and set out readily with Loudoun for Oxford (*Apology* 83). When the policeman Miller and the servant Davidson arrived with a warrant for Loudoun's arrest, Lee, in Loudoun's narrative, kissed Loudoun's hand saying, "He has done nothing" and called the arrest a "base and unwarrantable liberty"

(*Apology* 87). Miller is said to have told Mr Edmonds at Tetsworth that Mrs Lee loved Loudoun "like her own dear eyes" (*Apology* 91).

Arnim makes significant changes to this part of the story as his characters' motivations are quite different from those described by Loudoun. The narrator can now tell us everything, that is, account for Lee's puzzling behaviour here and throughout the story ("wir wollen das Rätsel lösen" [Arnim 241]). The "solution" is that Lee has realised that she actually loved Lockhart all along and does not want him to leave as she realises she will never see him again.[13] She has lost all interest in Loudon, indeed, he is offensive to her. She tells Mrs Edmonds she has been abducted because "sie konnte vor einer Frau sich nicht schuldig angeben" (Arnim 241). Arnim's conclusion is also fictional. He changes the court case, ironically always taken to be the source of his story, most radically and has the brothers condemned and sent to Botany Bay and Lee forced to return (pregnant) to her husband (Arnim 242-43). In fact, Mr Justice Lawrence ruled that no force had been used to bring Mrs Lee into the County of Oxford, and so the brothers were not guilty, although their "conduct had been disgraceful" (*The Times* 7 March).[14] Loudoun was detained for debt and therefore writes his *Apology* in prison (he dates it 7 April 1804 [*Apology* xxx]). Lee, as Arnim writes in his letter to Brentano, was almost attacked on leaving the courtroom. The newspapers were very exercised, not so much at her lack of morals in eloping, but at her lack of conventional religious belief. *The Weekly Dispatch* reported on Sunday 11 March:

> Mrs Lee's story affords a very delicate satire upon modern sceptics. This philosophical Lady, so much devoted to study and meditation, was much too wise, it seems, to believe in the Christian religion. Her enlightened mind and vigorous understanding rejected such doctrines as repugnant to her pure reason. Mark, however, the inconsistency of the female sage. She disbelieved Christianity, but she had a perfect faith that a bit of camphire attached to a steel necklace was an all-powerful charm to defend her virtue!—Truly has it been said, that infidels are the most credulous beings on earth, and believe any thing but the bible.

Loudoun presents himself in his *Apology* as a man in love, duped by "an artful and treacherous woman" (*Apology* ii); Arnim presents Loudon as unable to understand the woman he says he loves and indecisive, while being concerned to achieve his own desires. Loudoun defends his brother against the charge that his violent language was in fact threatening behaviour, as Lockhart was accused of this with reference to his command to the post-boy, "Drive on or I will shoot you" (the post-boy, according to Loudoun, gave evidence to the effect that he frequently addressed him in this way;

this is not reported in *The Times*) (*Apology* xx), and with reference to his compelling Loudoun to go to bed with Lee by telling him, "If you do not get out of this room I will shoot you," which Loudoun says was never spoken or taken seriously (*Apology* xxviii). (The prosecution claimed this as proof Loudoun did not love Lee as then he would not have hesitated [*Apology* 124]).[15] Arnim picks up these character traits of Lockhart and has no reason to excuse his behaviour. Arnim also invents an attempt by Lockhart to shoot Lee when they are discovered (Arnim 241-42)—a further illustration of his character's brutality and perhaps an allusion by Arnim to sexual tension between the two. He therefore presents Lockhart as an unpleasantly primitive, rude and self-centered individual, with a permanent curse on his lips.

A comparison of **"Mistris Lee"** with *An Apology for the Conduct of the Gordons* demonstrates that Arnim has based his characterisation of the Gordon brothers on reports of their "real" character in Loudoun's *Apology* (although in some cases they contradict Loudoun's own very subjective interpretation), in the newspapers, and perhaps also on his own impression of them in court. His narrator claims in his preamble that they are, in fact, easy to read: "Beide trugen ihren Charakter im Gesichte und in ihrer Haltung" (Arnim 220). Arnim's characterisation of Mrs Lee diverges most significantly from the source material available to him and as a result it is most complex and intriguing. The narrator indicates this with his remark, "ihren Charakter zu entwickeln mag die Geschichte dienen, sie werden bald finden, daß sie in die allgemeine Abteilung von gut und böse nicht passen will" (Arnim 220). Loudoun's presentation of Lee is of a clear-minded, selfish woman who was willing to elope with him and later lied to save her reputation. He vents his anger towards her by means of sarcastic comments and uncomplimentary descriptions, for example that during the elopement she "eat (sic) more every succeeding day than she had done the day before" (*Apology* xxv). The public seems to have agreed with this view, and condemned Lee's lack of religion while overlooking the actions of the clergyman Lockhart. In Arnim's **Novelle,** because of the way the narrative perspective changes in the course of the story, the narrator can give increasingly precise information on Lee's state of mind as the plot unfolds. For this reason we gain a picture of Arnim's Lee as confused, unhappy, and a victim of unpredictable moodswings. She lives off a literary diet of sentimental novels (as does Loudon), lets herself be pushed in different directions by stronger characters, and finally realises that she has eloped with the wrong man. This latter twist to the tale is prepared for by clues and hints in the narrative, some of which have been mentioned above,

and could be sustained in fact with reference to Loudoun's own documentation of her constant interest in Lockhart (for example he writes, "I submitted to the importunity with which Mrs Lee unceasingly endeavoured to persuade me to use my influence to induce Lockhart to visit her" (*Apology* v), and her ill-humour in Loudoun's account when he laughs at her appearance in the innkeeper's wife's dress (*Apology* xxvi).

Arnim indicates in his letter to Brentano that he has been most free in his interpretation of Lee: he calls her a "Hure", whom he tried to give an "unbestimmten, vollblütigen, halbkindischen Charackter" (*Freundschaftsbriefe* 2: 596), and in doing so juxtaposes contemporary public opinion of the person with his view of the fictional character he creates. However, the Mrs Lee who sat in the dock and claimed to have been "so much agitated as not to know what was going forward" and who "appeared to have frequently but a very vague recollection" when questioned about letters and visits from the Gordons, yet admits welcoming sensual pleasure in the chaise with her abductors (*The Times,* 8 March), and asked the brothers in the Hearing to "remember that it is not the first time that your lives have been in my power" (*Apology* 107), remains somewhat of an enigma. She simply disappeared from court, once the mob in front of the courtroom had been dispersed, and thereafter from historical view, into the realm of the creative imagination of a chance onlooker.

*Notes*

1. Letter of 19 Aug. 1809 (*Freundschaftsbriefe* 2: 595).

2. Commentary on "Mistris Lee" in Achim von Arnim, *Sämtliche Erzählungen 1802-1817,* 1061-62. Further references are made to this edition in the text of this article, prefixed by the author's name. The sketch *Der Zufall* is transcribed by Wingertszahn 82-83.

3. See, for example, the interpretations of Ziegler 169-186; Wingertszahn 75-84; Kastinger-Riley 76-86; and Staengle 85-87.

4. Arnim names "Herrn Blankett" (Arnim 221). This variance is perhaps due to a mistake by Arnim or to a misreading of Arnim's manuscript by the editor.

5. Arnim's text is easily accessible for purposes of comparison with the unknown source material, and for this reason, and for reasons of space, references to parallel passages in "Mistris Lee" are made without extensive quotation.

6. The British Library holds the second and the sixth editions, both published in 1804. References are

made to the second edition in the text of this article, prefixed by the shortened title *Apology.*

7. The form Loudoun rather than Loudon is not consistently employed, but is useful for the purposes of this article to avoid confusion between this individual and Arnim's character Loudon.

8. The accurateness of the translations may necessitate a reinterpretation of Arnim's knowledge of the English language during his stay in Britain. He claims in a letter to Brentano that he was unable to make himself understood during a boat-trip on the Thames (letter of 5 July 1803, Freundschaftsbriefe 1: 145), and this self-deprecating statement has been accepted by critics (see, for example, Moering 114).

9. The narrator is in fact a first-person narrator who re-tells "im Auszuge" (Arnim 219) a story told to him by another first-person narrator. However, within the inset tale, the narrative voice has the power to read thoughts and be present, invisibly, at private conversations, abilities we would expect a third-person narrator to possess. This exploitation of narrative levels calls all source material into question. On this point, see Dickson 158-165.

10. The narrator at this stage in the narrative views Lee through Loudon's perspective, for example: "ihm fiel nichts auf, als wie das kleine Mädchen so schön zugenommen und stark geworden" (Arnim 222); "aber sie war schön und immer schöner" (Arnim 223), and is not certain in his own interpretation of Lee. For example, "sich hingeben einer Liebe, hatte sie wohl in der Ehe verlernt," and "Mistris Lee schien auch an alle älteren Verhältnisse erinnert" (Arnim 222).

11. For example: "Die Verwirrung der armen Frau stieg aufs höchste; der ganze Entführungsgedanke war in ihr mehr ein bloßes Rettungsbild gewesen, sie hatte nie an die Gefahren der Ausführung gedacht" (Arnim 237).

12. There are also sexual undertones to this conversation and in the *Novelle* as a whole; see Wingertszahn 76-77.

13. This insight cannot so much explain her behaviour as highlight its oddness and inexplicablity, for example: "Sie wünschte sich beleidigt zu sein, um sich rächen zu können. Die Launen sind des Teufels Gewalt auf Erden" (Arnim 241). On this aspect of "Mistris Lee," see Dickson 85-86, 94. The fact that Lee has been in love with Lockhart while directing this love towards Loudon, who reminds her of him, is an example of misdirected perspective, discussed in the above study, 189-90.

14. Whether Lee had been forcibly removed from her home in London was outside the jurisdiction of the court, hence the concentration on her actions once in the chaise. The decisive evidence was, firstly, Lee admitting that she threw her "charm against pleasure" out of the chaise window and said, "The charm that has preserved my virtue hitherto is dissolved, now welcome pleasure" and, secondly, that she told the chambermaid in Tetsworth "to tell her husband that he might come to bed in ten minutes."

15. Loudoun also refers to a "report of [Lockhart] holding a pistol in one hand and a draft in the other to Mrs Lee for her signature" and explains that his brother was asking Lee to give him a note to her servants asking for clothes to be sent on (*Apology* 83).

Interestingly, in the initial Hearing of the case, Lee made the statement that she believed she was in danger from Lockhart and for that reason permitted Loudoun to come to bed with her (*Apology* 106).

*Works Cited*

*Achim von Arnim und Clemens Brentano. Freundschaftsbriefe.* Ed. Hartwig Schultz. 2 vols. Frankfurt/Main: Eichborn, 1998.

Arnim, Achim von. *Sämtliche Erzählungen* 1802-1817. Ed. Renate Moering. Frankfurt am Main: Deutscher Klassiker Verlag, 1990. Vol. 3 of *Achim von Arnim: Werke in sechs Bänden.* Ed. Roswitha Burwick, Jürgen Knaack, Paul Michael Lützeler, Renate Moering, Ulfert Ricklefs und Hermann F. Weiss. 6 vols. 1989-92.

Dickson, Sheila. *The Narrator, Narrative Perspective and Narrative Form in the Short Prose Works of the German Romantics.* Stuttgart: Hans-Dieter Heinz, 1994.

Loudoun, Harcourt Gordon. *An Apology for the Conduct of the Gordons containing the whole of their correspondence, conversation, &c. with Mrs Lee: to which is annexed, an accurate account of their examination at Bow Street, and their trial at Oxford.* 2nd ed. London, 1804.

Kastinger-Riley, Helene M. "Achim von Arnims Frauengestalten in *Mistris Lee, Die Frau von Saverne* und Die Verkleidungen des französischen Hofmeisters." *Neue Tendenzen der Arnimforschung.* Ed. Roswitha Burwick and Bernd Fischer. Bern: Peter Lang, 1990.

Moering, Renate. "Fremdsprachige Quellen zu Arnims Erzählungen." *Die Erfahrung anderer Länder.* Ed. Heinz Härtl and Hartwig Schultz. Berlin-New York: Walter de Gruyter, 1994.

Staengle, Peter. *Achim von Arnims Selbstbesinnung.* Frankfurt am Main: Peter Lang, 1988.

Wingertszahn, Christof. *Ambiguität und Ambivalenz im erzählerischen Werk Achim von Arnims.* St. Ingbert: W. J. Röhrig, 1990.

Ziegler, Vickie. "Arnims Amazonen." *Grenzgänge. Studien zu L. Achim von Arnim.* Ed. Michael Andermatt. Bonn: Bouvier, 1994.

**Sheila Dickson (essay date summer 2001)**

SOURCE: Dickson, Sheila. "The Body-Some Body-Any Body: Achim von Arnim and the Romantic Chameleon." *German Quarterly* 74, no. 3 (summer 2001): 296-307.

[*In the following essay, Dickson evaluates Arnim's place in the German Romantic movement of the early nineteenth century, examining the unique impact of his scientific background on the shaping of his literary sensibility.*]

The existence, composition and interaction of body and mind or soul were important notions in the Romantic era, and the artists and writers of the period had to come to terms with new philosophical and scientific debates surrounding them. Kleist's response to Kant's philosophy is one spectacular example, the automata and *doppelgänger* that populate E. T. A. Hoffmann's works provide further evidence, and Bonaventura's onion layers, peeling away to reveal an agonizing *Nichts,* is a nihilistic climax. The works of writer Achim von Arnim also present a reaction to the above which has, however, rarely been regarded as mainstream. This has been due primarily to a tenacious acceptance of the long-held view that Arnim's works lack the quality of, for example, those of Kleist or Hoffmann. A different, more defensible basis on which to differentiate Arnim from most other Romantic writers, however, is firstly the extent to which he was involved in scientific research and the seriousness with which he pursued these studies, contributing to learned journals alongside Schelling and Ritter and, like them, considered authoritative in the field, and secondly the fact that he did not lose this interest once he began to concentrate his energies on writing fiction. Recognition of the latter considerations in recent and ongoing research on Arnim offers scope for reinterpreting the former clichéd perception of Arnim as a second-rate Romantic by analyzing his creative writing as a response to contemporary scientific debate, in other words, by evaluating his works on his own terms. This paper aims to do this with specific reference to the presentation of body through the medium of the fictional characters in his short prose works.

A frequent criticism of Arnim's works has been that his characters are lifeless due to his (or his narrator's) Olympian detachment; it has been said that he treats his characters like a child his toys.[1] One of Arnim's first critics, Heinrich Heine, took this interpretation to an extreme in *Die Romantische Schule:* "Wenn [. . .] Arnim seine Toten beschwört, so ist es, als ob ein General Heerschau halte, und er sitzt so ruhig auf seinem hohen Geisterschimmel und läßt die entsetzlichen Scharen vor sich vorbeidefilieren."[2] It is easy to forge a link between these comparisons and a vision of Arnim the scientist, who watches from on high how his characters behave as if conducting a scientific experiment. The implication in each case being that Arnim's bodies have no soul (interpreted in this article as the spiritual part of a human being). Such statements are merely descriptive and not always perceptive. New scholarship on Arnim has greatly improved our awareness of the nature and quality of his work as a scientist and demonstrated its importance for his creative writing.[3] Roswitha Burwick argues in this context that Arnim's notions of nature, politics, history and human behavior are derived from his scientific studies.[4] In particular she argues that Arnim observed the empirical world and saw it and the bodies that populate it function according to physical and chemical forces and to actions and reactions that cannot always be perceived nor categorized and are unpredictable. Moreover, as matter is organic rather than static, nothing and no-body in the empirical world can ever remain the same over time, indeed, all matter changes every second. Klaus Stein identifies these principles as central to Romantic natural science: "Die Erklärbarkeit der qualitativen Verschiedenheit der Materie, des Werdens und Vergehens der Stoffe im chemischen Prozeß erwies sich als Crux der romantischen Naturphilosophie und -wissenschaft."[5] He quotes as follows from Schelling's *Ideen zu einer Philosophie der Natur als Einleitung in das Studium dieser Wissenschaft* (1797):

> Die Objekte selbst können wir nur als Produkte von *Kräften* betrachten, und damit verschwindet von selbst das Hirngespinst von *Dingen an sich,* die die Ursachen unserer Vorstellung seyn sollten [. . .]. Darum ist es *notwendig,* die Materie als ein Produkt von *Kräften* vorzustellen; denn *Kraft* allein ist das *Nichtsinnliche* an den Objekten, und nur was ihm selbst analog ist, kann der Geist *sich* gegenüberstellen.

> (Schelling's emphasis)[6]

While scientific experimentation within these parameters made Arnim aware of the complexity of all matter and proved to him that everything in the material world is a product of forces constantly in flux, acting and reacting to other forces, it also contributed specifically to his particular concept, both as scientist and artist, of human bodies. They are even more complex than organic or inorganic matter since they do not belong solely to this material world. They possess spirit, free will, imagination and unconscious desires, and as such they are subject to the widest imaginable range of both imminent and exterior forces and laws which can neither be understood nor explained by science. In the essay **"Dichtung und Geschichte"** Arnim asks: "Wäre dem Geist die Schule der Erde überflüssig, warum wäre er ihr verkörpert, wäre aber das Geistige je ganz irdisch geworden, wer könnte ohne Verzweiflung von der Erde scheiden?"[7] In other words, the human body as a material construct is only one side of an equation in which external forces interact with internal, and physical body with incorporeal soul.

Arnim gravitated away from science and the principles of scientific knowledge towards art in its widest sense because he came to believe that where the former was one-sided and could provide no or only limited certainty, the latter could, ideally, offer a synthesis of *Geist,* representing the spiritual, imaginative and artistic elements of human experience and cognition, and *Körper,* signifying the physical, historical and scientific. Art does not simply replace science in this process; rather, both elements must co-exist as Arnim's goal is for scientific observation of immediate, concrete, ever-changing reality to be complemented and completed by artistic vision of an ideal, eternal reality.[8] Arnim took this theme as the subject for his *Abiturrede* titled **"Das Wandern der Künste und Wissenschaften"** and held on completing his studies at the Joachimsthal *Gymnasium* in 1789. He returned to this model throughout his career, for example in **"Dichtung und Geschichte,"** the essay that introduces *Die Kronenwächter.* In a biography added as an appendage to *Hollin's Liebeleben,* Horace Benedict de Saussure is shown to unite the two in his life and work.[9]

Arnim's deliberations on the relationship of art to science must be placed within the general context of what Andrew Bowie has identified as the concern at the end of the eighteenth century for a new foundation for knowledge and the attempt in the face of the increasing importance of the sciences to integrate the scientific and the aesthetic. Bowie relates this concern to the realization, stemming from Kant's work, of the impossibility of separating imaginative and cognitive activity.[10] For Arnim, this—desirable—process of integration represented a perpetual challenge, as, having served his apprenticeship as scientist, he believed that only the spiritual can be wholly accessible. Also in **"Dichtung und Geschichte"** he writes: "Nur das Geistige können wir ganz verstehen und wo es sich verkörpert, da verdunkelt es sich auch" (*DKV* 2: 13).[11] For this reason the interrelation and interaction of *Geist* and *Körper* encapsulated in the body and soul of his characters is a crucial issue

in Arnim's works and its analysis can provide useful insight into his own particular program of Romantic aesthetics.

As a physical object of observation Arnim's bodies are indeed mysterious and elusive. For Arnim, as for other Romantic writers in the era immediately after Kant and Fichte, the role of the senses and the awareness of their limitations is a major matter of interest and great importance is accorded to what and how the characters see. Arnim the scientist also contributed to the debate on the eye and light.[12] In his works the characters constantly observe others in an attempt to understand them. Typical themes which underline this are the importance of appearance and beauty, the act of seeing, and spying.[13] In *Melück Maria Blainville* the gaze is used as a weapon that can physically wound the body (*DKV* 3: 760). The body assumes a complex function here: it gives the main information on characters to other characters and often also to the reader.[14] The observer has access only to the exterior yet must, or should, try to understand the person. The perception of behavior and behavior itself, however, prove very ambiguous. Characters change appearance, or seem to, as other characters watch.[15] As a result they cannot understand each other's actions (a central theme in *Melück Maria Blainville* and *Die Verkleidungen des französischen Hofmeisters*), and seemingly erratic behavior may even be condemned as madness (as is the case in *Der tolle Invalide* and *Frau von Saverne*). Characters consistently misinterpret the evidence of their senses even with respect to their own appearance.[16] Their wishes may override their senses at crucial moments, they may look at someone (usually an indifferent acquaintance) and think of someone else (usually the beloved), projecting their feelings for the latter onto the former.[17] On *Der Wintergarten* Arnim wrote to Clemens Brentano in 1809: "Es war mein Carneval mich in allerlei solche Historienmasken zu werfen, darum nannte ich sie meinen Wintergarten."[18] His characters perform this action in all stories and their disguised bodies distort our and other characters' perspectives, perhaps to extract information, hide, escape, or deceive.[19] This can degenerate to the level of the mask taking over one's character as is suggested at end of *Die Verkleidungen des französischen Hofmeisters*:

> Jetzt aber beruhigte sich meine Schwiegermutter mit dem Gedanken, der Mann sei gar nicht so ernster Entschlüsse wert gewesen, er sei nichts als ein Spaßmacher, ein Komödienspieler, eine Maske gewesen.
>
> Ich und meine Frau sind nicht dieser Meinung.
>
> (*DKV* 4: 373)

The human body is in fact many different bodies: the unity of person dissolves chameleon-like into a succession of individual moments of perception that are more confusing than coherent because, as matter, the body is subject to constant change and metamorphosis from within and outside itself. Arnim believed in this context in "die verschiedene Vorstellbarkeit des Verschiedenen."[20] A fragmented view of self and reality is a recurring idea in the Romantic period.[21] In recent criticism it has been compared with the twentieth-century poststructuralist notion of the incoherence of the subject. However, as we shall see, Arnim, like other Romantic writers, ultimately believed in and aspired to the harmony of one homogeneous, coherent reality as opposed to adopting a position of radical skepticism and perspectivism.[22]

Non-human bodies play an important part in some of Arnim's stories, particularly in *Isabella von Ägypten.* Significantly, there is not much difference between artificial and "real" characters: the Allraun and Golem fit into society quite easily (although the Allraun feels obliged to prove by petition that he is human).[23] In addition there are Arnim's dead bodies. Heine, quoted above, characterized all of his creations as dead bodies and in many cases the distinction between dead and living bodies is indeed unclear or non-existent. Statues come to life in *Der Wintergarten* and *Die Ehenschmiede* and statues are mistaken for people in *Raphael und seine Nachbarinnen.*[24] Society is criticized as rigid and boring through the motif of the living dead in *Fürst Ganzgott* (*DKV* 4: 67) and *Die Majorats-Herren* (*DKV* 4: 107, 110-11, 114). In *Isabella von Ägypten* the narrator makes the helpful suggestion that we should imagine that everyone around us is dead:

> [W]ie vergebens quält uns das Verhältnis zu manchem Menschen; könnten wir uns einbilden, er sei ein Toter, eine Erdscholle, eine Wurzel, [i.e. the Bärnhäuter, Golen and Allraun] unser Kummer und unser Zorn müßte verschwinden.

> (*DKV* 3: 691)

The Bärnhäuter in particular personifies the living dead, and he faces a dilemma over the two parts of his nature: "[Es] erhob sich zuweilen ein solcher Streit zwischen dem lebenden und verstorbenen Körper in ihm, daß es ihm über der ganzen Haut zuckte und juckte" (*DKV* 3: 672).[25] Such bodies are empty and so can be exchanged and manipulated to deliberately deceive the observer. They are a provocation to the characters and the reader as their existence questions human spirituality and humanity itself, but because they are a comparison not a norm, they confirm negatively the reality and desirability of another dimension to human existence by demonstrating that it is possible to survive without it.

The above examples are offered in evidence that the concept of the physical body is highly nebulous and incoherent in Arnim's work: it cannot, it seems, be fully understood if indeed it lives or has any substance or soul at all. It is a visible manifestation, physiologically accessible and available to scientific observation, if only indirectly and inadequately, yet at the same time it is, or should be, also a representation of self, of the union of the physical and the spiritual, and of the interaction of visible and invisible forces. Any knowledge of the body is thereby rendered questionable and, in the end, impossible. However, by foregrounding the physical body, Arnim is criticizing those who do not look beyond it but simply accept what they see without considering the unreliable nature of their information. Sensory deception in human experience is possible, perhaps even inevitable, because perception is fallible and because it is learned, which means that we often see what we expect to see. Nevertheless, certain characters' inability to recognize bodies with no inner core, or soul, is an indictment of the philistine who does not look beyond the outer shell. Karl, for instance, in *Isabella von Ägypten* condemns himself by mistaking Golem-Bella for the live Bella:

> Golem Bella antwortete auf das alles so natürlich, daß er keinen Argwohn schöpfte, sie selbst möchte diese Puppe sein: insbesondere da er die täuschende Kunst der Sinne für unfähig achtete, sein scharfes Auge zu täuschen.

> (*DKV* 3: 705)

The ironic repetition of "täuschen" speaks for itself. Arnim's reorientation away from science towards art was founded on a belief in the possibility of a different, more satisfactory and satisfying form of intelligence than this—a spiritual instead of scientific intelligence which the latter can make available through a particular kind of consciousness and which is described by the term "Ahndung":[26]

> [A]lle geistige Berührung ist nur Ahndung, wenn es sich darstellen sollte den Sinnen und das geschieht in der Kunst. Warum ist ein gutes Bildniß mehr als der Mensch selbst? Wie kann der Mensch darin eine ganze Welt zeigen? Weil inso fern ihm der ideelle Pol geöffnet der Mensch mehr umfaßt, als es um und in aller Welt sichtbar, er eröffnet allen Wesen diesen ideellen Pol.[27]

According to this theory it is possible for the artist, who does look beyond the empirical and tries to express what he sees for others, to overcome the fragmentation of the subject and to create in his work not just some body or any body but "the" body, whereby one particular body in the art form represents "eine ganze Welt," and all bodies exposed to the art form can participate in the privileged mode of insight of the "ideellen Pol," elsewhere called "ein Sehen höherer Art" (*DKV* 2:14) and "Urquell des höheren Lichtes" (*DKV* 3: 618).[28] This is because art, as opposed to science, permits a free play of imaginative associations generated by both external and internal stimuli such as historical, cultural and scientific experience, literature, myth and art, in conjunction with memory, intuition and creative fantasy. It creates links between the past and the present, between the other and the self in an attempt to portray artistically what we may, if we are responsive, sense intuitively, but which we cannot explain scientifically, with the aim of recreating a sense of wholeness and reestablishing contact with the original unity of the world: in effect, reuniting body and soul.[29]

Arnim is indebted in this goal to the idealism of the Classical Age, the optimism of the late Enlightenment, and the self-liberation and transcendence of Romanticism. In presenting the goal as a problem he is confronting the same fundamental existential and epistemological issues as his Romantic contemporaries. Arnim's personal aesthetic response, however, is unique and significant: he makes the fictional body, as the locus of a constant tension between the empirical and the spiritual, the fundamental principle and the subject matter of his art. The process of artistic creation is, accordingly, an important theme within the stories themselves. Just as the writer creates characters, the characters create characters too, using their imagination to give life to new, artificial and dead bodies.[30] The Jew who creates Golems claims that this is actually very easy:

> [D]er Mensch, der ein Ebenbild Gottes ist, kann etwas Ähnliches hervorbringen, wenn er nur die rechten Worte weiß, die Gott dabei gebraucht hat. Wenn es noch ein Paradies gäbe, so könnten wir so viel Menschen machen, als Erdklöße darin lägen.
>
> (*DKV* 3: 688)

In the same story the characters only have to mention the existence of the Bärnhäuter for his body to materialize (*DKV* 3: 656). In another related thematic strand some of Arnim's bodies themselves demonstrate the higher perception associated with the "ideellen Pol." For example, Melück has the power of prophecy, the Majoratsherr has "ein zweites Augenpaar" (*DKV* 4: 114), and the Allraun in *Isabella von Ägypten* has "[ein] ahndende[s] Augenpaar" (*DKV* 3: 647) as Isabella deliberately gives her creation the advantage of a second pair of eyes in the back of his head. For others, less fortunate, it is necessary to develop what Arnim once called the "Seelenorgan" to achieve this enhanced sensitivity (which in the case of the Allraun is degraded to cunning).[31] In *Die Majorats-Herren* he calls it simply imagination:

> [U]nd es erschien überall durch den Bau dieser Welt eine höhere, welche den Sinnen nur in der Phantasie erkenntlich wird: in der Phantasie, die zwischen den beiden Welten als Vermittlerin steht, und immer neu den *toten Stoff* der Umhüllung zu *lebendiger Gestaltung* vergeistigt, indem sie das Höhere verkörpert.
>
> (*DKV* 4: 142; my emphasis)

Through these themes of creation and higher perception, the works themselves describe the imaginative process of giving bodies life and soul that underpins artistic creativity: a self-reflection ("Poesie der Poesie") typical of Romanticism. Simultaneously, by a process of further self-reflection, Arnim challenges the reader as the body exposed to the motley collection of bodies that he creates in his works (so motley on occasion that the challenge must surely be deliberate) to use his imagination to initiate this process for himself, thus taking the work of art into the material world and vice-versa.[32] This is made clear in the definition of *Ahndung* already quoted:

> Warum ist ein gutes Bildniß mehr als der Mensch selbst? Wie kann der Mensch darin eine ganze Welt zeigen? Weil inso fern ihm der ideelle Pol geöffnet der Mensch mehr umfaßt, als es um und in aller Welt sichtbar, er eröffnet *allen Wesen* diesen ideellen Pol.[33]

If the reader succeeds in perceiving "the" body, he will participate in the insight of the "ideellen Pol"; if he fails or refuses, Arnim's bodies and Arnim's characters' bodies will remain artificial or dead for him. By making artistic creation and appreciation a central theme, Arnim is pursuing what he perceived to be the function and the justification of art: to educate the reader in particular and the people ("das Volk") in general, in this context to use their imagination. We can understand Arnim's editing of folk-tales in this same context. A work of art is for Arnim a monument to a cultural heritage and to the ideas of one or more individuals. It is a witness to an otherwise inaccessible past, but like a physical body, it is organic not static, and so it needs to be rewritten for the present time: the old must be renewed by the contemporary artist and the contemporary reader who should recognize elements with which they are familiar and project their own experience and feelings to create a new, ever-changing text.[34]

In these terms imagination is the most effective and productive organ of perception in the creation of the work of art, within the work of art, and in the response to the work of art. If artist (in this context the author), characters (who can also create as artists or authors), and readers do not restrict themselves to what they see and (think they) know, but give scope in addition to the creative fantasy of the mind, then they can unite the physical and spiritual worlds by means of the imaginative and artistic side of human experience and perception, represented by *Geist* in Arnim's work. The following quotations illustrate just how far this creative synthesis is removed from the principles of scientific observation:

> Die Lüge [ist] eine schöne Pflicht des Dichters.
>
> (*DKV* 2: 14)

> So täuschend und doch getäuscht und darum in der höchsten Wahrheit der Phantasie ist der Märchensinn der Kinder.
>
> (Steig 3: 224)

> Phantasie [ist] nur wahr, wenn sie täuschend sich selbst täuscht.
>
> (Steig 3: 242)

> Das Geistige wird Schein und Täuschung.
>
> (*DKV* 4: 289)

These statements demonstrate that in Arnim's aesthetic program the artist must achieve (self-)deception to create a true work of art and the reader must do the same to appreciate it. Deception, and the elusive nature of body, identified above, are therefore positive forces in art.[35] The fact that purely imaginative constructs such as Golems, Allrauns and the living dead in **Isabella von Ägypten** are treated as if they were part of the reality of the "real" characters may be an indictment of these characters, but it is a successful artist who persuades the reader to do likewise. This theme is clearly expressed through the character of the Majoratsherr, who sees things, including bodies, through imaginative self-deception as a creative process.[36] However, he is comically unable to deceive others.[37] The Majoratsherr claims, moreover, that he can differentiate clearly between what is perceived by the *Augen der Wirklichkeit* and the *zweites Augenpaar.* The reader is made to question this and can criticize the Majoratsherr as inept and inadequate, but in engaging with the text on these issues he is being invited, by implication, to address the question whether it is appropriate to construct such a clear distinction in art between reality and imagination. If the reader accepts an imaginative involvement in the work, he has already answered the question. For his part Arnim clearly believed and stoutly defended the (often grotesque) intermingling of reality, in the form of history—interpreted as the interaction of people in various kinds of social groupings and therefore representative of material reality—and fantasy in folk tales and in his own writing:[38]

> Nennen wir die heiligen Dichter auch Seher und ist das Dichten ein Sehen höherer Art zu nennen, so läßt sich die Geschichte mit der Kristallkugel im Auge zusammenstellen, die nicht selbst sieht, aber dem Auge notwendig ist, um die Lichtwirkung zu sammeln und zu vereinen.
>
> (*DKV* 2: 14)[39]

The decisive aesthetic criterion in Arnim's understanding of a work of art is the achievement of *getäuschte Täuschung* that removes the borders between imagination and reality. But, as the reactions to Arnim's works quoted at the beginning of this paper and the case of the Majoratsherr demonstrate, this is not always successful. So, if we now reconsider the possibility of integrating the two worlds represented by the terms *Geist* and *Körper* through this concept of art, we can reiterate that this was certainly Arnim's goal. More specifically his aim was always to enlighten and cultivate others, to influence their behavior through art. *Poesie* was to unite the people.[40] In practice, however, Arnim experienced repeatedly the lack of influence of art, and of his art, in the material, "real" world. In theory, every body created in a work of art must be some body, can be any body, but should achieve the privileged status of "the" body by portraying the "ideellen Pol" and giving others access to this through the imagination, but in practice Arnim was aware of the limitations of his own creations, and the limitations of his readers' understanding and appreciation of them. The negative assessment of Arnim's work was not a posthumous phenomenon. He was widely criticized even, if not especially, by his closest friends for being too subjective and self-indulgent. Brentano, for example, writes:

> Begreifst Du Deine Subjektivität? [. . .] Deine Verse sprechen sich nie aus, wer sollte sie nun aussprechen? Das ganze Leben um sie! Aber dazu müßten sie objektiver sein, sie sind aber keine unmittelbare Gedichte, sondern Du Dich unaussprechender bist ihr Mittel, und so muß man Dich kennen, um sie zu lieben.
>
> (Steig 1: 39)

Arnim can only defend himself (to the Grimms) thus:

> Darum ist auch die Dichterwelt in mir so und die historische außer mir mag auch wohl nach ihrer Art so seyn müssen, aber wie sie einander berühren und ob sie einander berühren, ist ebenso schwierig auszumitteln, wie der Zusammenhang zwischen Seele und Körper.[41]

This is a restatement of the principle taken as the starting point of our analysis: "Nur das Geistige können wir ganz verstehen und wo es sich verkörpert, da verdunkelt es sich auch." Imagination as an organ of perception can afford higher insight and a sense of regained wholeness and harmony of self and world, but this is wholly personal and cannot easily be subsumed into a general context within physical reality, particularly where the historical situation resists this.

Arnim's short prose works highlight the problematic nature of the process of artistic creation through additional layers of narrative self-reflection. This is the crux of this writer's individual response to the challenge of reuniting body and soul. Raphael in ***Raphael und seine Nachbarinnen*** creates the image of a woman from a male model. This is not misperception, but as art is almost totally imaginative: to a large extent it is a representation of "no body." For the great artist this subjectivity is a positive creative force and Raphael clearly can show through his work "eine ganze Welt" in which others can share: a perfect example of (self-)deception, but Arnim provides many examples of the results when a lesser mortal attempts the same. He thus creates a scale, and by implication places himself at some point on it. The created body can be no greater than its inspiration—"Der malende Affe" (alias Bäbe) copies Raphael's style but has none of his creativity or originality—his work is mostly poor imitation, where the worst aspects of the original become predominant: Golem-Bella is a copy of Bella, and of its Jewish creator, lacking any sparks of creative imagination:

> [E]ine zweite Bella stand vor beiden, die alles durch jenen Spiegel wußte, was Bella bis dahin erfahren, die aber nichts Eignes wollte, als was in des jüdischen Schöpfers Gedanken gelegen, nämlich Hochmut, Wollust und Geiz.
>
> (***DKV*** 3: 688-89)

The Allraun was created as a child and has only the worst attributes of any spoiled, selfish brat. Only Bella can love him because she created him ("es ist das Heiligste, diese Anhänglichkeit an alles, was wir schaffen" [***DKV*** 3: 644]).[42] The next stage of aesthetic self-reflection within the text is even more crass: the Allraun, himself a created body, creates a clay-Bella from the remains of the Golem, and is devoted to it, "denn was sie ist, das wurde sie durch ihn," but only he can love her or even recognize her as Bella: "Wer hätte aber in der langen Gurke, welche die Mitte des breiten Erdenkloßes bezeichnete, die feine zierlichgeschwungene Nase der schönen Bella erkannt" (***DKV*** 3: 729). We are presented here with the difference between true poetic imagination that continues and creates anew and mechanic skill (*Kunstfertigkeit*), creating for a purpose—usually deriving from self-interest—that can only reproduce copies of itself that are not merely limited, but also often dangerous and destructive (the Golem causes havoc at the court of Charles V in ***Isabella von Ägypten*** [***DKV*** 3: 737]).[43]

But Arnim does not merely accept criticism, he offers it too. This critical description of the Allraun's artistic creation is turned around into a jibe at the reader's inability to appreciate this highly personal art. Arnim defies anyone, any of the "kunstschwatzenden Menschen [. . .] mit ewig leerem Widerhall von griechischer Bildung [. . .] leeren Augen [. . .] leere[m] Herz" (in other words, dead bodies) to do better:

> Von euch ist aber nichts übergegangen zu den Göttern und von den Göttern nichts zu euch. Euch sind die kunstlebendigen Götterbilder Golems, und lösche ich euch die Worte aus, so sind sie euch in nichts zerfallen. Leugnet ihr das? Auf, so schafft etwas Eigenes, das ihr zu jenen stellen könt, ohne daß ihr selbst darüber lacht—aber eure Hände sind stets arm an Werken und euer Mund voll von Worten.
>
> (***DKV*** 3: 729)

Self-criticism is turned into self-defense. The statement from the same work, quoted above: "Wenn es noch ein Paradies gäbe, so könnten wir so viel Menschen machen, als Erdklöße darin lägen" continues "da wir aber ausgetrieben aus dem Paradiese, so werden unsre Menschen um so viel schlechter, als dieses Landes Leimen sich zum Leimen des Paradieses verhält!" (***DKV*** 3: 688). For Arnim this art is an expression of the human situation and a reflection of the cold, unimaginative materialism and utilitarianism of the early nineteenth century which restricted itself to the physical body and shut out the imagination, and which increasingly separated science and art into two mutually exclusive compartments, and through this imbalance and fragmentation denied the Romantic artist his goal of synthesis and harmony.[44] While Arnim believed in the "ideellen Pol," he also believed that art should not artificially create harmony, it should not be dishonest. He makes this premise clear in a letter to Wilhelm Grimm of 25 November 1812, in which he compares *Täuschung,* which, as indicated in quotations above, is the basis of all art that is "wahr" (true and real), with *Betrug,* which is deceitful: "Wenn ich nämlich von Täuschung als dem Anfang aller Dichtung rede, so ist es nicht jener Betrug, den Menschen etwas aufbürden zu wollen, was sie nicht gemeint, geglaubt haben—Täuschung ist Spiel, Betrug ist ernst" (Steig 3: 244). In the concluding discussion of ***Der Wintergarten*** he writes:

> Wie ist die Kunst zu schwach den Abgrund zu bedecken mit schönem Schein, doch diese Kunst ist schrecklich, die betrügt, die rechte Kunst ist wahr, sie heuchelt nie den Frieden, wo sie ihn doch nicht geben kann.
>
> (***DKV*** 3: 421)[45]

Arnim felt that in the present climate art could not, indeed, give more, which led to an increasingly resigned tone in his later work. For these reasons the tension between *Geist* and *Körper,* between artistic vision and empirical observation, remains unresolved in Arnim's writing. It underpins the problematic nature of his aesthetic program, and as I have tried to show, begs the question of the relationship between and identity of some body, any body, and the body in his work.

### Notes

1. Arnim treats his characters like puppets according to Ralph Tymms, *German Romantic Literature*

(London: Methuen, 1955) 285; he treats his work like his children in the judgment of Gerhard Rudolph, *Studien zur dichterischen Welt Achim von Arnims* (Berlin: de Gruyter, 1958) 54.

2. Manfred Windfuhr, ed., *Die Romantische Schule,* by Heinrich Heine (Hamburg: Hoffmann und Campe, 1979) 210, vol. 8/1 of *Historisch-kritische Gesamtausgabe der Werke.*

3. On the importance of science for Arnim's literary works, see Roswitha Burwick's monograph *Dichtung und Malerei bei Achim von Arnim* (Berlin: de Gruyter, 1989); her essays "Achim von Arnims Ästhetik. Die Wechselwirkung von Kunst und Wissenschaft, Poesie und Leben, Dichtung und Malerei," *Neue Tendenzen der Arnimforschung,* ed. Roswitha Burwick and Bernd Fischer (Berne: Peter Lang, 1990) 100 and "Physiology of Perception: Achim von Arnim's Practical and Historical Aesthetics," *The Romantic Imagination. Literature and Art in England and Germany,* ed. Frederick Burwick and Jürgen Klein (Amsterdam: Rodopi, 1996) 160; and the essay quoted in note 4. See also Frederick Burwick, "Elektrizität und Optik: Zu den Beziehungen zwischen wissenschaftlichen und literarischen Schriften Achim von Arnims," *Aurora* 44 (1986): 19-47.

4. Roswitha Burwick, "Achim von Arnim: Physiker und Poet," *Literaturwissenschaftliches Jahrbuch der Görres-Gesellschaft* ns 26 (1985): 125.

5. Klaus Stein, "'Die Natur, welche sich in Mischungen gefällt.' Philosophie der Chemie: Arnim, Schelling, Ritter," *"Fessellos durch die Systeme." Frühromantisches Naturdenken im Umfeld von Arnim, Ritter und Schelling,* ed. Walther Ch. Zimmerli, Klaus Stein and Michael Gerten (Stuttgart: frommann—holzboog, 1997) 144. See also Burwick, "Physiology of Perception" 161-62, who presents Arnim's argument that all substances are prone to constant flux, mutation and metamorphosis.

6. Stein 144. On this "Wechselwirkung aller Kräfte", see Burwick, "Arnims Ästhetik" 100.

7. Achim von Arnim, *Werke,* eds. Roswitha Burwick, Jürgen Knaack, Paul Michael Lützeler, Renate Moering, Ulfert Ricklefs and Hermann F. Weiss, 6 vols. (Frankfurt: Deutscher Klassiker Verlag, 1989-1994) 2: 13. Further references to this edition are made in the text with the abbreviation *DKV* followed by volume and page number.

8. Compare Burwick, "Arnims Ästhetik" 100: "Naturwissenschaft, noch als Empirismus verstanden und Wissenschaft, im allgemeinen als erlernbare handwerkliche und damit mechanische Fertigkeit aufgefaßt, erfahren erst durch das kreative Prinzip der Kunst Vollendung." See also Burwick, "Physiology of Perception" 157. Michael Gerten places similar emphasis on the fact that Arnim's goal was a unification not separation of all areas in human experience in "'Alles im Einzelnen ist gut, alles verbunden ist groß.' Ort und Methode der Naturforschung bei Achim von Arnim," Zimmerli, Stein and Gerten 96, 99.

9. This point is made by Burwick, *Dichtung und Malerei* 39-40. She analyzes this text in "'Sein Leben ist groß weil es ein Ganzes war.' Arnims Erstlingsroman *Hollin's Liebeleben* als 'Übergangsversuch' von der Wissenschaft zur Dichtung," Zimmerli, Stein and Gerten 49-89.

10. Andrew Bowie, *From Romanticism to Critical Theory. The philosophy of German literary theory* (London: Routledge, 1997) 61, 80, 58 respectively.

11. The use of the term "verstehen" could perhaps be compared with Wilhelm Dilthey's opposition of "verstehen" as the basis for the *Geisteswissenschaften,* and "erklären" as that of the natural sciences, see Bowie 146-48. Bowie also analyzes Schleiermacher's opposition of thinking and feeling, the latter being "immediate self-consciousness", the former reflected, and human thought being located between the two poles (Bowie 117-25).

12. Burwick, "Physiker und Poet" 135-45.

13. The heroines in *Gräfin Dolores,* "Mistris Lee," *Melück Maria Blainville* and the hero in *Owen Tudor* illustrate the importance of appearance and beauty; the act of seeing is emphasized particularly in *Gräfin Dolores* and *Melück Maria Blainville* and spying is a major theme in *Isabella von Ägypten, Die Majoratsherren,* and *Der tolle Invalide.*

14. For example the brothers in *Mistris Lee*: "Beide trugen ihren Charakter im Gesichte und in ihrer Haltung" (*DKV* 3: 220).

15. In *Die Ehenschmiede* Aura cannot remember people when they are not there (*DKV* 4: 898). It is also suggested she changes personality from day to day (*DKV* 4: 900).

16. In *Der Wintergarten* a statue comes to life (*DKV* 3: 78), in *Raphael und seine Nachbarinnen* Raphael mistakes a statue for Benedetta (*DKV* 4: 268), Frenel in *Melück Maria Blainville* mistakes a life-size doll for the *Graf* (*DKV* 3: 184). In *Die Ehenschmiede* a woman becomes a man, but was

in fact a man in the first place (*DKV* 4: 898-99). The Allraun in *Isabella von Ägypten* thinks he is handsome (*DKV* 3: 652), the Herzog in *Die Ehenschmiede* does not realize he is only half dressed until his wife shows him a mirror (*DKV* 4: 904).

17. This concept of misdirected looks is discussed in my dissertation; see Sheila Dickson, *The Narrator, Narrative Perspective and Narrative Form in the Short Prose Forms of the German Romantics* (Stuttgart: Heinz, 1994) 189-90.

18. Reinhold Steig and Herman Grimm, *Achim von Arnim und die ihm nahe standen,* 3 vols. (Stuttgart-Berlin: Cotta, 1894-1913) 1: 271. Further references to this text are given in the text with the abbreviation Steig followed by volume number and page number.

19. Dressing up is an important motif in *Die Verkleidungen des französischen Hofmeisters, Isabella von Ägypten,* and *Fürst Ganzgott und Sänger Halbgott.* In *Die Ehenschmiede* the characters also play roles from Shakespeare and quote Ovid to each other.

20. See Stein 154-55, 157, 178.

21. For a discussion of the fragmentation of self and world in Romantic narrative, see Dickson 30-42, 57-60.

22. For statements by Arnim indicating his belief in a single, meaningful reality, see Gerten 123-24, 158. On the problematic nature of equating Romantic and postmodernist concepts, see Ricarda Schmidt, "Narrative Strukturen romantischer Subjektivität in E. T. A. Hoffmanns *Die Elixiere des Teufels* und *Der Sandmann,*" *Germanisch-Romanische Monatsschrift* ns 49 (1999): 143-60.

23. The Allraun's petition is unsuccessful (*DKV* 3: 710). In the same work Cenrio puts a doll in Karl's bed to fool Adrian (*DKV* 3: 704). In *Die Ehenschmiede* Rennwagen constructs a "Sprachmaschine" that cannot be distinguished from himself (*DKV* 4: 900-01, 906-07).

24. See note 16 above.

25. A sensitive interpretation of this motif in *Isabella von Ägypten* is offered by Thomas P. Bonfiglio, "Electric Affinities: Arnim and Schelling's *Naturphilosophie,*" *Euphorion* 81 (1987): 217-39.

26. Burwick, "Physiker und Poet" 129, 150.

27. This unpublished manuscript is transcribed by Burwick, "Physiker und Poet" (149-50). She illustrates Arnim's theory by means of a diagram in *Dichtung und Malerei* (50-51). The use of *Geist* and *Seele* is quite different to that in this paper, however the dichotomy of physical and spiritual and the goal of uniting both is comparable.

28. Burwick quotes Arnim's comparison of existence in two, three and four dimensions (*Dichtung und Malerei* 50-54). The known, visible world is three-dimensional but certain people, in particular artists, and certain circumstances (such as dreams and the point of death), can have a fourth dimension. Arnim's concept of the "ideellen Pol" exists in these four dimensions, which he as artist can intuit ("ahnen") (Burwick, *Dichtung und Malerei* 51).

29. Compare note 11 on the difference between explanation and intuition. Gerten contrasts "abstraktwissenschaftliche[s] *Begreifen*" with "einer mehr intuitiven, ideellschöpferischen Sicht und künstlerischen *Darstellung* der Wirklichkeit" (Gerten 96; emphasis added by Gerten; see also 109-10). On art as recreating wholeness and re-establishing a link with a lost unity between man and nature, see Burwick, "Arnims Erstlingsroman" (62-63). She characterizes Arnim's writing (with specific reference to *Hollin's Liebeleben*) as "der Versuch [. . .], die wissenschaftlichen Probleme, die er als Naturforscher nur im Einzelnen zu lösen vermochte, als Dichter in ihrer Ganzheit aufzufassen und ästhetisch zu gestalten" Burwick, "Arnims Erstlingsroman" (56). Gerten quotes Arnim's unpublished essay "Verhältnis der chemischen Ausbildung zur poetischen" to illustrate this same point: "Daß der Chemiker die Natur anders ansieht als der Dichter im weitesten Sinne des Wortes bedarf keiner Erinnerung. Jenem erstirbt das Einzelne weil er es vom Ganzen getrennt und das Ganze weil er es vereinzelt hat, diesem lebt es stets in abwechselnder Gestalt" (Gerten 108-09).

30. Bonfiglio 225.

31. Burwick, "Physiker und Poet" 144-45.

32. Burwick describes this active reception in terms of a voltaic pile, where contact with the work of art produces a spark of inspiration ("Physiology of Perception" 167-68). On the interpretative demands placed on the reader in Romantic prose see Dickson 171-82.

33. See note 27. Emphasis added.

34. See Burwick, "Arnims Ästhetik" 107-08; Burwick, "Arnims Erstlingsroman" 65-66.

35. Compare the use of "täuschen" in the passage from *Isabella von Ägypten* quoted above (*DKV* 3: 705).

36. He sees "Plagegeister" instead of children (*DKV* 4: 115), "der Tod" followed by accusing spirits instead of the doctor (*DKV* 4: 116).

37. See his immediate reaction to his cousin's visions described in the previous note.

38. Burwick, "Physiker und Poet" 125.

39. Also: "es [hat] nie ein Gedicht gegeben, das historisch, und keins, das ohne Historie ist" (Steig 3: 204).

40. See, for example, Bernd Fischer, "Interpretation als Geschichtsschreibung: Zur poetischen Imagination Achim von Arnims," *Études Germaniques* (1988): 180, and Burwick, "Physiology of Perception" 166, who describes Arnim's ideal of the artist as aesthetic, ethical and moral educator, and of the non-artist as patron of art and culture. On Saussure see also Burwick, "Arnims Erstlingsroman" 51.

41. Transcribed in an unpublished dissertation by Dorothea Streller, "Arnim und das Drama," diss., U of Göttingen, 1972, 110.

42. See Bonfiglio 226.

43. Compare the text quoted by Gerten 109: in the comparison of art and chemistry in his essay "Verhältnis der chemischen Ausbildung zur poetischen," Arnim emphasizes that the former "hat keinen Zweck," and because of this it can create "ein Ganzes," "ein in sich vollständiges organisches System."

44. On the separation of science and art, compare the references in note 10, which refers to the situation at the turn of the century. Arnim lived and wrote during this seminal point of transition.

45. On Arnim's criticism of aesthetic dishonesty, see Fischer 183. On Arnim's belief that a work of art "involves the representation of the real as well as the ideal", see Burwick, "Physiology of Perception" 167.

## Fabian Lampart (essay date 2004)

SOURCE: Lampart, Fabian. "The Turn to History and the *Volk*: Brentano, Arnim, and The Grimm Brothers." In *The Literature of German Romanticism,* edited by Dennis F. Mahoney, pp. 171-89. Rochester, N.Y.: Camden House, 2004.

[*In the following essay, Lampart discusses the relationship between German Romanticism and folk literature. Lampart compares two crucial works in the tradition:* Des Knaben Wunderhorn, *a collection of German folk songs compiled by Arnim and Clemens Brentano, and the Grimm Brothers'* Kinder und Hausmärchen. *Taken together, these two works helped establish folklore as a vital element in German Romantic literature.*]

### FOLK SONGS AND FAIRY TALES: EXAMPLES OF FOLK LITERATURE

One salient feature of German Romanticism is the importance of "Volksdichtung" or "Volksliteratur" (folk literature). By this term the Romantics understood literature that has its origins in the collective memory of the people or even of one specific nation. "Volksliteratur" is part of a national or international cultural tradition, though it can be collected or even written down in a specific historical version by one single author.[1]

Johann Gottfried Herder (1744-1803) is a key figure in the process of propagating and diffusing the concept of *Volksliteratur* in Germany. In the 1760s, his function was restricted to a process of cultural transfer. Among German poets and intellectuals, Herder was the first to give an enthusiastic reception to James Macpherson's (1736-96) *Fragments of Ancient Poetry* (1760), which were said to have been created by the blind Gaelic bard Ossian. Later on, Herder was also the first to undertake an individual collection of folk songs in German. The *Volkslieder* (*Folk Songs,* 1778-79) are based on a multinational idea of folk literature. It is characteristic of his understanding of folk literature that Herder includes not only Nordic and Native American folk songs but also poems by Shakespeare and songs by Goethe. Some of the texts are written by contemporary authors, others are derived from the oral traditions of highly heterogeneous ethnic groups. Herder justifies such diversity by emphasizing their common origins in a living and vivid culture. In Herder's view, literature—folk poetry in particular—is created inside a collective tradition that is open to stimulation from different cultures.[2]

The Romantics based their ideas of *Volksliteratur* on Herder's concepts, but they modified it in two important ways. First, the term *Volk* no longer refers to an international collective as its foundation: folk poetry tends to be national and is limited to German traditions. Second, this collective foundation is no longer within reach but has become historicized: it belongs to a past age. Therefore, *Volksliteratur* is a part of history, and history has to be discovered by means of historical research. Accordingly, the Romantics began to collect the two folk genres, folk songs (*Volkslieder*) and fairy tales, with the aim of regaining and reconstructing lost national traditions.[3]

These ideas constitute the background for the origin of the two most famous and to this day immensely popular collections of Romantic *Volksdichtung*. Achim von

Arnim's (1781-1831) and Clemens Brentano's (1778-1842) *Des Knaben Wunderhorn: Alte deutsche Lieder (The Youth's Magic Horn: Old German Songs)* was published in three volumes between 1805 and 1808; Jacob Grimm (1785-1863) and his brother Wilhelm (1786-1859) published their collection of *Kinder und Hausmärchen (Children's and Household Tales)* in two volumes between 1812 and 1815.[4] Both books were neither the only nor the first collections. Arnim and Brentano as well as the Brothers Grimm began their work on the basis of prior collections, prior experiences, and thus prior ways of theorizing and systematizing the material. When Arnim and Brentano first made their still vague plans of a Romantic song book between 1801 and 1804, they faced the same problems Herder had encountered more than twenty years before their attempts, but at least Herder's (and others') solutions could serve them as a sort of compass.[5] Similarly, Jacob and Wilhelm Grimm were not the first to edit a collection of fairy tales. In the years before 1812, when the first volume of the *Kinder- und Hausmärchen* appeared, there had been several collections of fairy tales and legends. Not before the third edition in 1837 did their edition become the book it has remained ever since: the most famous collection of fairy tales in world literature.

With their two collections, Arnim, Brentano, and the Brothers Grimm shaped the image of Romantic *Volksliteratur.* The ideal of Romantic folk song in German literary or musical history is associated with the songs collected in *Des Knaben Wunderhorn,* while the term fairy tale all over the world is connected to the Brothers Grimm. Considering the prominent role played by the two collections in later definitions of *Volksliteratur,* it is even more remarkable that neither Arnim and Brentano nor Jacob and Wilhelm Grimm had a clearly defined concept of folk literature nor of how and where to discover and collect it. Thus, their books were works in progress in a practical and in a theoretical sense.

Arnim's and Brentano's first vague plan to collect folk songs dates back to the time of their voyage along the Rhine river valley in 1802, but not until 1805 did Brentano suggest to Arnim that they make a book of folk songs together. It was to replace and to succeed the older and, according to Arnim and Brentano, more commonplace collections—such as Herder's *Volkslieder* or the *Mildheimische Liederbuch (Mildheim Song Book,* 1799) by Rudolph Zacharias Becker—by means of the specific character of the songs. Soon Arnim and Brentano edited the first volume of their collection and found diligent collaborators in their research for folk songs all over Germany.[6] Two of the most zealous contributors were the Brothers Grimm. In October 1807, Arnim and Brentano were preparing the second volume of *Des Knaben Wunderhorn.* Brentano met Jacob and Wilhelm Grimm for the first time in Kassel and expressed his enthusiasm about their collections of folk poetry. As will be discussed later, the Brothers Grimm did not agree with Arnim's and Brentano's liberal view of what constituted *Volkslieder,* but collaborating in *Des Knaben Wunderhorn* was decisive for the development of their own interests in *Volksliteratur.* In 1807, the Brothers Grimm not only began to compile their own collection of folk songs, but also started to make excerpts from fairy tales and thus laid the foundations for the *Kinder-und Hausmärchen.*[7]

Contrary to Arnim and Brentano, the Brothers Grimm emphasized the authenticity and closeness of their collection to folk traditions. Whereas Arnim and Brentano revised and recomposed folk songs they found included in collections and books of the previous 300 years, the Brothers Grimm stuck to the importance of oral tradition. For Arnim and Brentano, it was natural to modify folk literature, but the Brothers Grimm criticized the procedure and claimed to keep strictly to the versions they collected from storytellers who had received the tales orally. The problems and implications of the debate centered upon the contradictory but at the same time correlative concepts of *Naturpoesie* and *Kunstpoesie* (natural and artistic poetry). Both terms are not merely aesthetic concepts. At the very least, they form essential ideas in the complex designs of the philosophy of history upon which Romantic thinking is based. *Naturpoesie* as well as *Kunstpoesie* represent different stages in the historical development of poetry with specific aesthetic and historical implications. Both of these collections are projected and realized in a period in which the concept of history as a complex context of political, philosophical, and cultural ideas—at least in intellectual discourse—turns out to be more and more problematic. The view of history as a process, as a growing consciousness of change, became a basic tendency of the age. The problem of history around 1800 will be treated in the ensuing section; the importance of *Kunstpoesie* and *Naturpoesie* in Romantic aesthetics and the philosophy of history will be discussed in the section dealing with *Volk* and *Poesie.* After the consideration of these premises, we can proceed with a general interpretation of *Des Knaben Wunderhorn* and the *Kinder- und Hausmärchen.*

### The Problem of History

Around 1800, the term *history* changed its meaning. Previously, history in intellectual discourse was an abstract concept, something far removed from concrete experience. Yet, at the beginning of the new century, it became more and more evident that there had been important transformations during the last decades all over

Europe. Differing from earlier revolutionary situations, these transformations were not limited just to abstract discussion, but were also closely connected with political and economic revolution. The new experience of history was a major turning point in European thinking. Reality itself, prior to this time a rather stable space of perceptions and experiences, became more and more insecure and unpredictable. These signs are indicative of an intellectual and cognitive crisis.[8]

As for Germany, the decisive event in this process of transformation can be reduced to one name: Napoleon. The German reaction to the French Revolution had been vivid and intense, particularly in the years between its outbreak in 1789 and the radical phase of the revolution in 1793-94, but it was to be Napoleon's role to spread the ideas of the Revolution all over Europe. Still more important than the revolutionary ideals of liberty, equality, and fraternity was the radical revolution of the political order in the countries of Western Europe. The Napoleonic Wars destroyed the system on which European politics had been based since the Thirty Years' War (1618-48). Territories like Italy or Germany, traditionally divided into a multitude of bigger and smaller states, were particularly affected by these changes. Centuries-old traditions and continuities were interrupted and brought to an end. It is symptomatic that Thomas Nipperdey opens his influential study of German history between 1800 and 1866 with the simple statement, "Am Anfang war Napoleon" (In the beginning, there was Napoleon).[9] Nipperdey thus underlines the absolutely fundamental role of Napoleon in the process of reshaping Germany between 1800 and 1815. But the revolutionary changes were not limited to politics and the economy; these were just one half of the phenomenon. The deep political changes and severe effects of the economic crisis had a direct impact on the everyday life of people, too. It was this experience of a profound crisis caused by the wars that finally rendered possible the feeling of history as a visible force even on the level of common life. Thus, history appeared as an irregular movement that was able to cancel all secure traditions and presumptions upon which life had been based in previous periods. History became a synonym for insecurity and contingency.

The new significance of history is symptomatic for the loss of metaphysical security that had already been described theoretically by thinkers of the Enlightenment period. The Neapolitan Giambattista Vico (1670-1744) in his *Scienza Nuova* (*New Science,* 1725-44) was one of the first philosophers to offer a definition of history that underlined its wholly secular character. According to Vico, there are different parts of creation. Whereas nature is made by God, civilization, politics, and culture are formed by human activity. Vico separates the secular world from Divine Creation, and, moreover, he entrusts the organization of this secular and historical world to human responsibility. The insecurity and contingency of history, according to Vico, is a problem to be resolved by mankind.[10]

Accordingly, the problem of how to cope with the new incalculability of the historical world also dominates philosophical thinking around 1800 in Germany. Johann Gottfried Herder made an important contribution to this discussion. In his *Ideen zur Philosophie der Geschichte der Menschheit* (*Ideas on the Philosophy of Human History,* 1784-91), he states a concept of history as progress toward the perfection of mankind. In Herder's view, history is a teleological process. It is directed toward human perfection, and its final scopes are ideals such as humanity, freedom, and universal happiness.[11] Immanuel Kant expressed similar ideas in his various essays on the philosophy of history.[12] Those concepts form important steps in resolving the problem of historical contingency and insecurity. By transforming history into a process that is clearly directed toward an ideal of humanity, it is possible to justify even contradictions and "dark ages" in the course of this development. In the end, humanity will reach providentially an ideal state of enlightened perfection. Providence in this post-Enlightenment view is no longer a religious category, but a wholly secular process; it is an historical law that leads mankind toward an age of perfect harmony.[13]

This utopian state of perfection is one of the basic concepts of historical thinking around 1800. If there is an end goal of history, then there is also a direct way to resolve the problems brought about by political, economic, or intellectual modernization. The question is how to find the right way to this ideal age. The answer is to look back to the ages before the present, ages in which man was not yet alienated from nature. Evidently, the philosophical theories of history develop in accordance with Jean Jacques Rousseau's (1712-78) thoughts about the evolution of man.[14] Starting from a state of natural harmony, with the development of notions of social propriety mankind enters an age of sociological and historical deformation. Furthermore, history as a modern state is characterized by the problematic contingency of human-made reality. But, contrary to Vico, Rousseau strongly emphasized the necessity to refer back to the ideal state of natural harmony prior to history in order to create the fundaments of a new utopian age.[15]

The result is a triadic scheme of history. In Romantic thought this triadic scheme became the basic mode of resolving and explaining the contradictions and problems of the discontinuous present. By looking back to the lost age of harmony, man could learn how to shape the future Golden Age. The triadic scheme is a recurrent structure in the different designs of philosophical descriptions of history from Herder and Kant through Schelling, Schiller, Hölderlin, and Novalis up to Hegel. There are vastly different ideological implications in these thinkers' conceptions of a secularized salvation history, but present in them all is the basic structure of an idealized prehistoric age, a present with clearly negative qualities, and an ideal future; there is always the final aim to discover paths to that ideal future by a roundabout route via the harmonious past.[16]

### THE RELATIONSHIP OF PEOPLE AND POESIE

The question of how to reconstruct the ideal and harmonious past is the focus of Romantic discussions on history. One of the most important answers is the concept of *Volk*. In one respect, the *Volk* (people or nation) is a reaction to the political ideas of the French Revolution. Romantic writers tried to answer the revolutionary ideas of a radical reorganization of society with alternative projects. In contrast to rapid political change, they emphasized the organic and natural evolution of social structures. The *Volk* was the focus of these conservative versions of a political and social revolution.

In accordance with Rousseau's and Herder's ideas, the *Volk* represents a collective individual. Comparable to a human being, it develops in several phases; it can and should be educated carefully in order to give shape to its specific abilities and to become, finally, a harmonious personality. Another analogy is more important: Romantic thinkers draw a comparison between the development of the individual *Volk* and the three ages of history. Therefore, childhood is more than the starting point of the collective social development that should be controlled and regulated carefully in order to prevent revolutionary convulsions. Both in the individual's life and in the evolution of the *Volk*, childhood is the anthropological state nearest to natural harmony, the first epoch in the triadic scheme. In childhood, man is not yet alienated from himself by education, and similarly, the childhood of a specific people or nation corresponds to a state not yet contaminated by civilization and historical development. Going back to the childhood of the *Volk*, man can rediscover some of the lost qualities of the ideal state before history.[17]

But how could it be possible to go back to an epoch removed from the present to such a degree that it lies literally beyond history? The Romantics give different answers, and in all of them *Poesie* plays a central part. In Romantic aesthetics, poesy is not merely poetry in the narrow sense of the word; rather, it represents a general force, a creative entity that synthesizes subjective and objective as well as individual and collective parts of reality. In the famous definition of Romantic poesy in *Athenaeum-Fragment no. 116,* Friedrich Schlegel's concept of "Universalpoesie" is characterized by a universal claim to unify the heterogeneous and contradictory aspects of reality (*KFSA* [*Kritische Friedrich-Schlegel-Ausgabe*] 2: 182-83). *Poesie* is an archetypal and anthropological force that can help to overcome the problematic fragmentation of the modern world.[18]

The central significance of *Poesie* is transformed in the different approaches of the Romantics. Whereas the Schlegel brothers, Schelling, and Novalis underline its general philosophic value as an absolute and unifying force, the second generation of Romantics tends to interpret the concept of *Poesie* in relation to history. For their part, Arnim and Brentano on the one hand, and the Brothers Grimm on the other, arrived at interpretations of poesy that differ in important respects. Consequently, one of the most important disputes of Romanticism arose from their rather opposite interpretations of *Poesie*.

In 1802, Arnim writes in a letter to Brentano the sentence which is to become the programmatic center of his poetic theory: "Alles geschieht in der Welt der Poesie wegen, die Geschichte ist der allgemeinste Ausdruck dafür" (Everything in the world happens due to poesy; history is the most common expression for that.).[19] The important point about the dichotomy concentrated in this program is the relation between poesy and history. Whereas poesy is a basic ontological force, history is a general term that refers to the temporality of human action. Everything that can be realized in a temporal reality is historical—forms of political and social organization as well as works of art. Thus, history is the most general visible expression of the creative force of poesy. Poesy is the moving element, and history is its manifestation in reality. Since the original forms of poesy are in the course of the centuries more and more covered by the sediments of history and thus, as it were, obscured, the Romantics seek ways to rediscover the invisible or almost lost poesy. Most evidently, it can be found in the living collective traditions of the people, as for example in legends or myths. Arnim and Brentano are convinced that the basic force of poesy can be found particularly well in the literature of the *Volk*, or as they define it, in the *Volkspoesie*.[20]

There is another aspect that needs to be considered. According to Arnim and Brentano, poetry (also in the narrower sense of the term) stands outside history and can realize itself in any historical epoch; thus, poetry is not restricted to prior ages and can be created as well in the present. Poetry recreated in the present is no longer a result of the collective and unconscious creativity of the people, but an individual creative act, yet it is still poetry. For Arnim and Brentano, there is no difference in the collectively created *Naturpoesie* and the individual creative act of *Kunstpoesie*. Both are just different ways of rediscovering the lost *Poesie*. Accordingly, in editing the folk songs of **Des Knaben Wunderhorn** it was not only natural but even necessary for Arnim and Brentano to revise and change profoundly the songs collected.[21] Therefore, Arnim's—and to a lesser extent, Brentano's—ideological and political attempt to discover a common ground for a future national identity in the legendary and mythical *Naturpoesie* cannot be a purely historical enterprise but has to be creative as well.[22] By changing, revising, and modifying ancient songs, legends, and myths—in short, by creating *Kunstpoesie*—it is no less possible to arrive at common national ground than through a strictly philological process as presumably practiced by the Grimm brothers.

Around 1806, the Brothers Grimm raised their protest. In several essays, they argued against Arnim and Brentano's liberal ideas about transforming older texts.[23] According to the Grimms, history and poetry have common origins in the collectivity of the nation, but these origins belong to a remote past. The exemplary form of *Volkspoesie* or *Naturpoesie* is a medieval epic such as the *Nibelungenlied*; like legends and myth it is created by the people. In the course of the centuries, historical thinking and poetry have been alienated from each other. Therefore, it is no longer possible to discover the foundations of a nation in collective creative acts. Individual creativity—*Kunstpoesie*—and collective poetry—*Volkspoesie*—at present are two highly different things. According to the Grimms, there is no way to create something like *Volkspoesie* individually under the conditions of modern life of around 1800. The only way to discover the original force of an intersubjectively created poetry is to go back to the origins and to collect carefully and correct philologically the remains of ancient *Volkspoesie*.

Under such conditions, it is obvious that the Grimm Brothers would oppose the "creative" editorial policies of Arnim and Brentano. In their view, there was no way to discover *Naturpoesie* if the original—and that meant orally transmitted—texts were manipulated. To the Grimms, Arnim and Brentano's revisions of the **Wunderhorn** songs were not acceptable. At least theoretically, *Volkspoesie* and *Kunstpoesie* were two different things for them, things that could by no means be united. To them, any arrangement of *Volkspoesie* was a destruction of its original qualities.[24] The surprising

practical consequences of these theoretical convictions will be discussed in the section about the *Kinder- und Hausmärchen*.

The idea of the *Volk* as a common ground for national identity in times of general historical crisis had a defensive character. The Romantics tried to develop literary concepts against what they regarded as politically wrong—the French occupation of Germany or at least of large parts thereof and the enactment of political reform in some German states, particularly in Prussia.[25] The Romantic ideal of reconstructing the foundations of a national identity in the collective memory of national literature had negative aspects, too. Even if the search for national traditions was no more than a starting point for the nationalism of the nineteenth and twentieth centuries, problematic aspects of Romantic ideas are already visible. Politically, the Romantics of Arnim and Brentano's generation tend to be rather conservative. Even if a close look at Arnim's political writings reveals rather refined concepts of reform politics attempting to integrate traditions, their basic tendency remains anti-revolutionary.[26] Another negative aspect of the return to the *Volk* is Romantic anti-Semitism.[27] In 1811, Arnim and Brentano were among the founders of the "Christlich-deutsche Tischgesellschaft" (Christian-German Dinner Society)—a gathering of aristocratic and bourgeois intellectuals in Berlin with the aim of cultivating patriotic thought. Among the members of the "Tischgesellschaft" were famous names of Prussian political and cultural life of the first decades of the nineteenth century.[28] Jews were not admitted, not even if they had converted to Christianity. This fact is all the more astonishing since the same members of the "Tischgesellschaft" were frequent visitors in the Berlin salon of the Jewish intellectual Rahel Levin (1771-1833). These contacts apparently couldn't prevent the members of the society from displaying their political and ideological convictions when they held their meetings. In March 1811, Brentano read to the society a satire[29] in which basic views of the Berlin Romantics—such as the superiority of Christianity, nationalistic feelings, and anti-Semitism—were united.[30] The reception was enthusiastic. Nationalist anti-Semitism at this early stage was not yet a violent political ideology, but the Romantics' connection between a presumed intellectual and artistic superiority and feelings of a conservative and elitist nationalism is problematic and sheds light on the explosive force inherent in a combination of aesthetics and politics.[31]

The dichotomy of *Volk* and *Poesie* is full of tensions. In a political context, the idea of a nation elevated by universal feelings of *Poesie* became one of the starting points for nationalist radicalism. In a literary perspective, the same idea is a basis for the poetic search or even philological research for collective national traditions. That brings us to the two most famous results of this creative research—*Des Knaben Wunderhorn* and *Die Kinder- und Hausmärchen.*

### ARNIM AND BRENTANO'S FOLK SONGS: TRADITION RECREATED

In 1805 Clemens Brentano suggested to Arnim that they edit a collection of Romantic folk songs together. Brentano wanted to edit a book that would replace former and, in his opinion, less satisfying collections of folk songs. In the letter to Arnim on 15 February 1805, he criticizes in particular the *Mildheimische Liederbuch* (1799), which in his view was superficial. In the same letter, Brentano defines the qualities he intends to realize in his and Arnim's song book: "[. . .] man könnte es abteilen in einen Band für Süddeutschland und einen für Norddeutschland, weil beide sich in ihren Gesängen notwendig trennen, es muß sehr zwischen den romantischen und alltäglichen [Gesängen] schweben, es muß geistliche, Handwerks-, Tagewerks-, Tageszeits-, Jahrzeits- und Scherzlieder ohne Zote enthalten, die Klage über das Mildheimische ist allgemein."[32] Brentano further provides philological and poetic guidelines for *Des Knaben Wunderhorn.* Nevertheless, his suggestions were to undergo significant transformations in the process of collating and editing the book.

This applies especially to his first point. Brentano held that the differences between song traditions in northern and southern Germany should remain visible in the division of the book into two separate volumes. Arnim was against this systematically justifiable division. He desired to emphasize the entire German tradition; for him, the collection was an element of cultural politics and should constitute an indirect contribution to national unification. In Arnim's view, the songs from all over Germany were a means to display common national traditions. The present state of political division and French occupation had to be overcome by referring back to a common national foundation that could be found in songs from all German regions. Thus, in the end, the collection replaced Herder's cosmopolitan approach to folk literature with a visibly national form.[33] Second, in his letter to Arnim, Brentano alludes to the general poetic character of the collection, saying that the book should hover between Romantic songs and songs treating everyday life and common experiences. With this expression, Brentano describes the singular poetic character of the *Wunderhorn* songs that often has been defined as their specific musicality. The program of a mixture between the Romantic and the commonplace may seem simple at first view, yet it leads to the key problem of the book. Arnim and Brentano intended to collate folk songs, but the question was how to edit them. They faced several problems. It was not so difficult to find songs and to discover older collections they could use; here they could base their proceedings on Herder's and on other predecessors' works. It was more problematic to find an agreement about the general aims of the collection. In an earlier project, Arnim and Brentano had interpreted the term *Volkslieder* as "songs for the people"—yet written by poets. Their idea was to produce *Kunstpoesie* in a folklore-like mode. When they began preparing the *Wunderhorn,* the former idea merged with the concept of collecting original folk songs. In 1805, they worked on at least three different levels. First, Arnim and Brentano began collecting songs from prior collections and older books. Second, they continued what they had already started during the voyage along the valley of the Rhine in 1802 and looked for original folk songs orally recorded among the people. With this field research at the basis of the *Volk,* they had helpers and contributors from all over Germany, among them the Brothers Grimm. Finally, Brentano and Arnim examined and revised the collected songs extensively and thus in many cases adjusted the material according to their specific idea of folk songs.[34]

Considering these different procedures it is possible to describe the particular character or "Volkston" of the *Wunderhorn* songs. On the one hand, Arnim and Brentano claimed that the oral origins of the songs were an important criterion for the collection. On the other, more than half of the songs are based on written sources. This contradiction between theory and practice is the point at which the aesthetics of *Des Knaben Wunderhorn* is concentrated. The dichotomy of orality and literality became for Arnim and Brentano the central poetic means in the process of adapting single songs to the whole collection. They created a sort of artistic orality. Since the publication of Heinz Rölleckes's critical edition of the *Wunderhorn,*[35] in which he provided the exact source of each song, it has been possible to examine precisely the editors' poetical treatment. The results are remarkable. Arnim's method of changing the original texts was quite different from Brentano's: whereas Brentano tried in many cases to stay as close as possible to the original texts, Arnim apparently was less careful and more individualistic in his approach. Songs that Brentano changed carefully and almost invisibly, Arnim edited by using less philologically exacting criteria—making songs more coherent, for example, and toning down colloquial and crude expressions. It is still remarkable that the book that, throughout the entire nineteenth century and perhaps to the present day, represents the quintessence of folk song is based upon the aesthetic reinvention of a tradition.

There is a third key question to which Brentano alludes in his letter: What kind of world is portrayed in the **Wunderhorn** songs? Like any work of art, **Des Knaben Wunderhorn** represents a single aesthetic reality. In the folk songs created by modern revisions, Arnim and Brentano give a fictional version of a factual world—a world that, according to the reality they found in the songs, should approximate the authentic past of the *Volk.* By listing the genres of the songs that should be integrated in the collection, Brentano also outlines structures of the **Wunderhorn** world. By defining the songs as "geistliche, Handwerks-, Tagewerks-, Tageszeits-, Jahrzeits- und Scherzlieder ohne Zote" (spirituals, songs of crafts and the day's work, the times of the day and year, and funny songs without obscenity; **KW** [**Des Knaben Wunderhorn**] 3: 563), he describes more than literary genres; he names the whole range of themes treated in **Des Knaben Wunderhorn.** The subjects of the songs refer to situations and emotions in the life of the *Volk.* On this basis, it is possible to attempt a general description of the collection.

The **Wunderhorn** songs treat archetypal structures of life in pre-modern society—that could be one approach of summing up the contents of the 723 *Volkslieder* of the collection. Gerhard Schulz names as recurrent motives birth, childhood, love, marriage, matrimony, and death, but there are also scenes from pre-industrial working life, historical ballads, and songs with a religious background about death and redemption. If there is something of a leitmotif behind the hundreds of songs of the **Wunderhorn,** it can be described, in the words of Schulz, as the cycle of being within a small family.[36] There is no logical structure in the succession of the songs, but behind the heterogeneity of the individual pieces, the reader can discover fragments of a universal narration in the lives of the people. By describing and varying the basic stages in the life of the small family, the collection comprises a mosaic image of the life of the *Volk.* This simple life of the people shows some qualities important to the Romantics, who lived in a time of insecurity and historical contingency, were in search of stable values, and preferred long-term gradual development to revolution. The life represented in **Des Knaben Wunderhorn** is regular and constant, and moves in the cyclical rhythms of nature.[37] This implies that there are still traces of a utopian and original life not yet contaminated by the degenerating impulses of political movements and modernization. There are several songs of the **Wunderhorn** that allude to the ideal of the *Volk* still far from the destructive influence of historical processes. Marriages or other celebrations are opportunities for discovering the original and natural humanity still vivid among the people. This can be seen in some songs that celebrate the biblical holiness of marriage, such as the first stanza of "Hochzeitmorgen" (Wedding-Day Morning):

Weil ich nun seh die goldnen Wangen
Der Himmelsmorgenröthe prangen,
So will auch ich dem Himmel zu,
Ich will der Leibsruh Abschied geben,
Und mich zu meinem Gott erheben,
Zu Gott, der meiner Seele Ruh.[38]

At the same time, the **Wunderhorn** by no means idealizes a past not yet destroyed by the problems of the modern present. The reality shown in the songs is imperfect and problematic, and the individuals do not live in a paradise. Yet, they try to resolve their problems and defend their way of life as free individuals comprising a part of a natural community. They face the problems of history, but at the same time they still have access to the utopian past.[39] This can be seen especially in the songs that deal with workers or craftsmen, that is, with the forms of work corresponding to the pre-industrial society that constitutes the socio-historical background of the songs. Miners, as in all Romantic poetry, play an important role. They are not yet alienated from the earth, but retain an intimate relation to stones and precious metals. Moreover, their profession is highly symbolic, representing one of the central motives of German Romanticism. Miners are nearer to center of the earth and thus to the essence of life.[40] In the song "Bergreihen," the miners are described as the men who have direct access to divine creation because, "Sie hauen das Silber aus der alten Wand, / Die Gott der Herr selbst gebauet hat, / Mit seiner selbst Gewalt" (They chip the silver from the old wall / That God himself hath made / With His own might; **KW,** 2: 409.). Other symbolically important professions are the millers and hunters; they represent the settled and the unsettled ways of life, respectively. Therefore, the songs reflect actual social problems. Whereas the miller signifies the life of the regular workingman, the hunter is associated with irresponsibility, lawlessness, and aristocratic privileges—and he is, last but not least, the seducer of girls. One concrete motif thus can allude to many different problems. **Des Knaben Wunderhorn** is not just a collection of different songs, but also a mirror of a past society in which the problems of the insecure reality around 1800 are reflected in the form of historical songs adjusted to contemporary experiences.

### THE GRIMMS' *FAIRY TALES*: ORAL NARRATION IN WRITTEN FORM

The Grimms' problems at the beginning of their work were similar to those faced by Arnim and Brentano while editing the **Wunderhorn** songs. But whereas Arnim and Brentano had emphasized the importance of their own creative part in the process of collating and editing folk songs from the very beginning, Jacob and Wilhelm Grimm considered themselves mainly collectors and philologists. Theoretically, they were strictly against Arnim and Brentano's technique of collecting and then remodeling the collected material.

Such a conviction was based upon their theoretical concepts, in which they strictly underline the difference between *Kunstpoesie* and *Volkspoesie*. The Brothers Grimm were serious in their aim to recover and reconstruct *Naturpoesie* in the collective memory of the people. For them, there was no creative way to get there; *Naturpoesie* could only be found by means of positivistic reconstruction. To the Grimms, that meant collecting and recording the fairy tales in exactly the same versions in which the people had told them.[41] The crucial point about the Grimms' theory about collecting fairy tales is how significantly it differs from the practice thereof. Their own description of their procedure and the way in which it actually evolved in their revisions of the earlier editions of the *Kinder- und Hausmärchen* constitute two contradictory aesthetic approaches.[42] The Grimms claimed to work strictly philologically, that is, without altering the original texts and recording the song with all its warts. Compared to Arnim and Brentano, they paid much more attention to the written records of literary texts. The activities of the Grimms were among the first important steps toward the development of a serious textual philology in German literary history. But in the particular case of the *Kinder- und Hausmärchen*, there were few written texts actually used as a basis. Therefore, the Grimms had to concentrate on oral tradition, on fairy tales told by people who—according to the idealized supposition— still lived and worked in the country, far from the modern life of the cities and thus nearer to the prior state of mythical harmony. Precision and accuracy of the sources were the main techniques employed in this task of collecting. That implied that the Grimms had to write down the fairy tales as they were told, changing as little as possible. Oral tradition was central in their concept. It was a measure of the archaic originality of the tales and thus a sign for their belonging to the *Volkspoesie*. According to Jacob and Wilhelm Grimm, Arnim and Brentano's editorial methodology was not only problematic but also fundamentally wrong. For them, the leading principle of any edition of folk poetry had to be fidelity to the oral traditions.[43]

Surprisingly, the claim for philological accuracy of oral sources in the Grimms' case is by no means less questionable than with Arnim and Brentano. Observing closely the different editions of the *Kinder- und Hausmärchen* that appear between 1819 and 1837, it becomes clear how important the literary arrangement of the single tales was even for Jacob and Wilhelm Grimm. Equally, examining the way the fairy tales actually were collected casts light on the alleged simplicity and originality of the first contributors from among the people.

First of all, the group of contributors did not consist of illiterate peasantry, country folk, or craftsmen, but for the most part of educated bourgeois ladies. Accordingly, the material of the fairy tales was by no means an immediate expression of the spirit of the *Volk* born from the depth of the past, but rather more a result of culti-

vated narration in society. The celebrated farmer's wife Dorothea Viehmann, mentioned in the preface of the second volume of the *Kinder- und Hausmärchen*, was in reality a tailor's wife and lived in Kassel. Furthermore, Dorothea Viehmann, as well as the Hassenpflug sisters who contributed to the Grimms' *Fairy Tales*, were of Huguenot origin and knew well the French fairy-tale tradition, particularly the *Fables* of Charles Perrault (1628-1703). Naturally, that does not mean that the fairy tales collected by Jacob and Wilhelm Grimm were derived from French fairy tales exclusively. Nevertheless, it shows that nearly all the contributors had a literary education and were quite capable of telling stories in a specific literary manner. In their first version, the tales collected in the *Kinder- und Hausmärchen* were less original expressions of a collective German *Volksgeist* than individual versions of tales belonging to the broader European fairy-tale tradition. (*KHM*, 3: 600-605)

In the second place, the fragile illusion of an oral tradition was modified again in the process of publishing the collection. In 1812 the first volume of the first edition of the *Kinder- und Hausmärchen* was published. This edition was still far from the version that currently offers the most extensive examples of classic fairy tales. In the course of the publication, Wilhelm, the younger of the two brothers, assumed full responsibility for the editing process. He is the one who brought about the stylistic changes that created the tone characteristic of fairy tales by today. Thus, he invented the classic introductory words, "Es war einmal . . ." (Once upon a time . . .), and similarly, he crafted the conclusion, since then classical: ". . . und sie lebten vergnügt bis an ihr Ende" (. . . and they lived happily ever after). The typical style of the fairy tales evolved between 1812 and 1837. Wilhelm Grimm produced metaphorical expressions that kept the balance between an assumed oral narration based on common speech and an archaic or epic tone. He thus created the characteristic narrative means for telling fairy tales. In the end, he had managed to connect the most contradictory elements in his narrative repertoire. Mythical origins and motifs of magical powers, atavistic and sometimes even cruel episodes were blended with folklore elements in a Romantic and Biedermeier atmosphere. Like Arnim and Brentano, Wilhelm Grimm tended at times to gloss over sexual allusions, but in other respects he rendered more visible the archaic elements. He managed to find stylistic and narrative approaches capable of creating entire texts out of different historical strata within fairy tales. The clearness and succinctness of his narrative style, the concentration on a single action, and his preference for extremes and contrasts were perhaps already traditional qualities of fairy tales. But it was the merit of the *Kinder- und Hausmärchen* to develop a style that was able to transport all these features successfully to a vast reading public.

The world represented in the *Kinder- und Hausmärchen* is the traditional world of the fairy tales.[44] They recount a conflict and its resolution. A problematic state at the beginning of the fairy tale is to be transformed into a harmonious or even utopian order at the end. Usually, that happens by means of a hero or heroine who has to accomplish a task. The hero moves through a reality in which natural laws are—or at least can be—suspended temporarily. Inside the world of the fairy tale, the miraculous and supernatural are normal and regular. Within that fictional frame, the hero can resolve his task. One decisive element of fairy-tale reality is the concise dualistic division between good and evil, beautiful and ugly, big and small, and aristocratic and common. Max Lüthi explains the importance of these fundamental structural dichotomies by pointing out the tendency of the fairy tale toward universality.[45] By displaying the most evident moral contrasts and values, the narrated world can claim to be a metaphorical equivalent to reality. The world of fairy tales—and that applies particularly to the *Kinder- und Hausmärchen*—may be limited to the sphere of the real and visible, but that limitation merely underlines the universal claim of the genre. In the narrative program of the fairy tale, a complicated, threatening, and dangerous reality becomes structured and rationalized through reduction to generic antagonisms. If reality is imperfect and fragile, then the fairy tale attempts to bring it to order, to make it conform to a utopian perspective. Therefore, it seems logical that the fairy tale's protagonists move in a straightforward, comprehensible world. In fairy-tale narration, experiences of the supernatural as well as existential problems are transformed into metaphorical figurations. In the fairy tale, dangerous changes—whether initially interior processes such as maturation or external changes like revolutions and historical progress—all are manageable.

How strongly the literary means of the *Kinder- und Hausmärchen* react to the discontinuous and problematic reality of the period around 1800 can be seen in the tale of "Dornröschen" ("Briar Rose," better known as "Sleeping Beauty"). It deals with the problem of time as a basic parameter of human life, as an anthropological condition that cannot be escaped. When the hundred-year sleep of Sleeping Beauty and the rest of the castle is ended, the characters proceed with a life that doesn't seem to have changed. In the tale, time as evolution, as a dangerous and progressive element of reality, is not accepted. When the population of the castle awakens, it achieves a state beyond the problems of history:

> Da gingen sie zusammen herab, und der König erwachte und die Königin und der ganze Hofstaat und sahen einander mit großen Augen an. Und die Pferde im Hof standen auf und rüttelten sich; die Jagdhunde sprangen und wedelten; die Tauben auf dem Dache zogen das Köpfchen unterm Flügel hervor, sahen umher und flogen ins Feld; die Fliegen an den Wänden krochen weiter; das Feuer in der Küche erhob sich, flackerte

und kochte das Essen; der Braten fing wieder an zu brutzeln; und der Koch gab dem Jungen eine Ohrfeige, daß er schrie; und die Magd rupfte das Huhn fertig. Und da wurde die Hochzeit des Königssohns mit dem Dornröschen in aller Pracht gefeiert, und sie lebten vergnügt bis an ihr Ende.[46]

In "Sleeping Beauty," the insecurity of human existence is suspended. The tale results in a tableau of timeless reality, and for a short, fictive moment, the problem of history is brought to a solution in the final utopian words (Schulz 2: 321).

The last example again renders evident what Jacob and especially Wilhelm achieved in their *Kinder- und Hausmärchen.* By means of the fiction of orality, they managed to create a coherent narrative mode in which fairy tales originating from different traditions could be told to a contemporary public. In re-narrating and re-modeling the ancient tales, the Brothers Grimm created a fictional reality that in itself reflected contemporary problems. Neither for Jacob and Wilhelm Grimm nor for Brentano and Arnim was the "turn to history and the *Volk*" an escape from their own contemporary problems. Nevertheless, it was a convincing literary reaction to their own modern experience of a fragile and shifting historical reality.

*Notes*

1. See "Volksdichtung," in Gero von Wilpert, *Sachwörterbuch der Literatur* (Stuttgart: Kröner, [8]2001), 886-7.

2. See Stefan Greif, "Märchen / Volksdichtung," in *Romantik-Handbuch,* edited by Helmut Schanze, (Stuttgart: Kröner, 1994), 257-67.

3. Detlef Kremer describes the aesthetic strategy to read German literature as "'altdeutschen' Traditionsraum" ("ancient-German" place of tradition), in Detlef Kremer, *Romantik* (Stuttgart: Metzler, 2001), 276-78.

4. Achim von Arnim, Clemens Brentano, *Des Knaben Wunderhorn: Alte Deutsche Lieder,* edited by Heinz Röllecke, 3 volumes (Stuttgart: Reclam, 1987), henceforth this work is cited as *KW*; Brüder Grimm, *Kinder- und Hausmärchen,* ed. by Heinz Röllecke (Stuttgart: Reclam., 1980), henceforth this work is cited as *KHM*.

5. See Gerhard Schulz, *Die deutsche Literatur* zwischen Französischer Revolution und *Restauration.* Vol 2: 1806-1830, (Munich: Beck, 1989), 696-708. (*Geschichte der deutschen Literatur,* ed. by Helmut de Boor and Richard Newald, vol. 7/2) Henceforth this work is cited as Schulz 2.

6. Heinz Röllecke, "Nachwort," in *KW,* 3: 557-81; here 564-65.

7. Röllecke, "Nachwort," in *KHM,* 3: 593-621; here 596-98.

8. See "Geschichte, Historie," in *Geschichtliche Grundbegriffe: Historisches Lexikon zur politisch-sozialen Sprache in Deutschland,* edited by Otto Brunner, Werner Conze, and Reinhart Koselleck, vol. 2 (Stuttgart: Klett-Cotta, 1975), 593-717, here 547-53; see also: Reinhart Koselleck, "Geschichte, Geschichten und formale Zeitstrukturen," in R. K., *Vergangene Zukunft: Zur Semantik geschichtlicher Zeiten* (Frankfurt: Suhrkamp, 1989 [¹1979]), 130-43.

9. Thomas Nipperdey, *Deutsche Geschichte 1800-1866: Bürgerwelt und starker Staat* (Munich: Beck, 1983), 11.

10. Giambattista Vico, *La scienza nuova* (Milan: Rizzoli, ⁴1993 [¹1977]), 231-32.

11. Johann Gottfried Herder, *Ideen zur Philosophie der Geschichte der Menschheit* (Stuttgart: Syndikat, 1985); J. G. Herder, *Auch eine Philosophie zur Geschichte der Bildung der Menschheit* (Stuttgart: Reclam, 1990).

12. Immanuel Kant, *Idee zu einer allgemeinen Geschichte in weltbürgerlicher Absicht,* in I. K., *Schriften zur Geschichtsphilosophie,* (Stuttgart: Reclam, 1992), 21-39.

13. "Die Geschichtsphilosophie [. . .] des späten 18. und des frühen 19. Jahrhunderts [. . .] hatte die Machbarkeit der Geschichte *nicht* vorausgesetzt. Sie suchte das die Aufklärer schockierende Phänomen zu verarbeiten, daß nun zwar die Menschen zunehmend besser die Natur beherrschen, daß sie immer mehr 'machen' können, daß sie mit all ihrem Können aber in einen sich beschleunigenden Prozeß hineingeraten sind, der sich jenseits ihrer Verfügung vollzieht" (The philosophy of history [. . .] of the late-eighteenth and early-nineteenth centuries [. . .] had not presupposed the makeability of history. It attempted to deal with the phenomenon that had so shocked Enlightenment thinkers: namely that people could now control nature increasingly better and "make" more and more, but that with all their abilities they had slipped into a self-accelerating process that was out of their control). Heinz Dieter Kittsteiner, *Listen der Vernunft: Motive geschichtsphilosophischen Denkens* (Frankfurt: Fischer, 1998), 8.

14. Jean-Jacques Rousseau, *Discours sur l'origine et les fondements de l'inégalité parmi les hommes* [1755]; *Du contrat social ou principes du droit politique* [1762], in J.-J. Rousseau, *Œuvres complètes, Du contrat social: Écrits politiques,* vol. 3, edited by Bernard Gagnebin, Marcel Raymond (Paris: Gallimard, 1964), 109-223; 347-470.

15. See Gerhard Schulz, *Die deutsche Literatur zwischen Französischer Revolution und Restauration.*

Vol 1: 1789-1806 (Munich: C. H. Beck, 1983), 181-89. (=*Geschichte der deutschen Literatur,* edited by Helmut de Boor and Richard Newald, vol. 7/1) Henceforth this work is cited as Schulz 1.

16. See Kremer, 74-78.

17. Gert Ueding, *Klassik und Romantik: Deutsche Literatur im Zeitalter der Französischen Revolution 1789-1815* (Munich & Vienna: Hanser, 1987), 117-20. (=*Hansers Sozialgeschichte der Deutschen Literatur,* edited by Rolf Grimminger, vol. 4)

18. Kremer, 90-92.

19. Achim von Arnim, Clemens Brentano, *Freundschaftsbriefe,* 2 volumes, edited by Hartwig Schultz (Frankfurt: Eichborn, 1998), 1: 21.

20. Achim von Arnim, "Von Volksliedern," in *KW,* 1: 379-414, here 403-4.

21. Paul Michael Lützeler, "Die Geburt der Kunstsage aus dem Geist der Mittelalter-Romantik: Zur Gattungsbestimmung von Achim von Arnims *Die Kronenwächter*" in *Aurora: Jahrbuch der Eichendorff-Gesellschaft* 46 (1986): 147-57, here 150-54.

22. Ueding, 758-59.

23. Jacob Grimm, *Gedanken, wie sich die Sagen zur Poesie und Geschichte verhalten* (1808), in J. G., *Kleinere Schriften,* vol. 1 (Berlin: Dümmler, 1879), 400-4. Jacob Grimm, *Von Übereinstimmung der alten Sagen* (1807); *Gedanken über Mythos, Epos und Geschichte* (1813), in J. G., *Kleinere Schriften IV, Recensionen und vermischte Aufsätze,* part 1 (Berlin: Dümmler, 1869), 9-12; 74-85. Wilhelm Grimm, *Über die Entstehung der altdeutschen Poesie und ihr Verhältnis zu der nordischen* (1808), in W. G., *Kleinere Schriften,* edited by Gustav Hinrichs (Berlin: Dümmler, 1881), 92-150.

24. Schulz 2: 263-68.

25. Ueding, 117-20; Kremer, 8-11.

26. See Jürgen Knaack, *Achim von Arnim—nicht nur Poet: Die politischen Anschauungen Arnims in ihrer Entwicklung* (Darmstadt: Thesen Verlag, 1976).

27. See Schulz 2: 146-56; Kremer, 14-15.

28. Also among the members of the "Tischgesellschaft" were Fichte, Savigny, Adam Müller, Kleist, Clausewitz, and the Brothers Grimm.

29. Clemens Brentano, *Der Philister vor, in und nach der Geschichte* (1811), in Clemens Brentano, *Werke,* vol. 2 (Darmstadt: Wissenschaftliche Buchgesellschaft, 1963), 959-1016.

30. See Schulz 2: 88-90; Kremer, 19.

31. See also Wolfgang Frühwald, "Antijudaismus in der Zeit der deutschen Romantik," in *Conditio Judaica: Judentum, Antisemitismus und deutschsprachige Literatur vom 18. Jahrhundert bis zum ersten Weltkrieg,* second part, edited by Hans Otto Horch and Horst Denkler (Tübingen: Niemeyer, 1989), 72-91.

32. "[. . .] one could divide it into one volume for southern Germany and one for northern Germany, for both are divided by their songs. It must certainly alternate between the Romantic and everyday [songs; F. L.]; it must contain spirituals, songs of crafts and the day's work, the times of the day and year, and funny songs without obscenity; complaint about the Mildheim Song Book is common." Quotation according to Heinz Röllecke, "Nachwort," in *KW,* 3: 557-81, here 563.

33. *KW,* 3: 565-67; Ueding, 756.

34. *KW,* 3: 567-71; Schulz 2: 699-700.

35. *Des Knaben Wunderhorn: Alte deutsche Lieder, gesammelt von L. A. v. Arnim und Clemens Brentano,* edited by Heinz Röllecke (Stuttgart: Kohlhammer, 1975). (=Clemens Brentano, *Sämtliche Werke und Briefe,* Historisch-Kritische Ausgabe, edited by Jürgen Behrens, Wolfgang Frühwald, and Detlev Lüders, volumes 6-9, 1-3.)

36. Schulz 2: 701.

37. Schulz 2: 704.

38. *KW,* 3: 209. "Because I now see the golden cheeks / Of heavenly dawn shine in splendor, / thus I too wish to rise heavenwards, / I want to take leave of bodily rest, / And lift myself to my God, / to God, who gives rest to my soul."

39. Schulz 2: 703.

40. See Theodore Ziolkowski, *German Romanticism and its Institutions* (Princeton: Princeton UP, 1990), 18-57.

41. Schulz 2: 266-67.

42. Schulz 2: 318-20.

43. For a general introduction see Heinz Röllecke, *Die Märchen der Brüder Grimm* (Munich: Artemis, 1985).

44. See "Märchen," in *Reallexikon der deutschen Literaturwissenschaft,* vol. 2, H-O, edited by Harald Fricke (Berlin & New York: de Gruyter: 2000), 513-17.

45. See Max Lüthi, *Das Märchen,* edited by Heinz Röllecke (Stuttgart: Metzler, $^9$1996), 29.

46. *KHM,* 1: 260. "Then they descended together, and the King awoke and so did the Queen and the entire kingdom, and all gazed at one another with great wonder. The horses in the stables stood up and shook themselves; the hunting dogs leapt and wagged their tails; the doves in the eaves lifted their gentle heads from under their wings, looked about and flew afield; and the flies on the walls crawled once more. The fire in the kitchen grew, flickered, and cooked the feast; the meat began to sizzle once again; and the cook boxed the boy's ears so that the boy shouted; and the maidservant plucked and prepared the chicken. And then the wedding of the King's son and Briar Rose was celebrated in utmost splendor, and they all lived happily ever after."

---

# FURTHER READING

## Criticism

Closs, August. *The Genius of the German Lyric: An Historic Survey of Its Formal and Metaphysical Values.* London: G. Allen & Unwin, 1938, 478 p.

Offers a brief assessment of Arnim's role in the Romantic movement, noting in particular his role in compiling the folk songs included in the *Wunderhorn.*

Dickson, Sheila. "Preconceived and Fixed Ideas: Self-Fulfilling Prophecies in *Der tolle Invalide auf dem Fort Ratonneau.*" *Neophilologus* 78, no. 1 (January 1994): 109-18.

Discusses the psychological aspects of Arnim's *Der tolle Invalide auf dem Fort Ratonneau,* evaluating the mental state of the protagonist within the framework of contemporary ideas concerning the human mind.

Duncan, Bruce. "Some Correspondences between Arnim's *Majoratsherren* and Fichte's Concept of the *Ich.*" *Monatshefte* 68, no. 1 (1976): 51-9.

Offers an analysis of Arnim's novella *Die Majoratsherren,* arguing that the tension between reality and fantasy embodied in the protagonist is rooted in Johann Fichte's notion of the *Ich.*

Feise, Ernst. "*Der Tolle Invalide* von Achim von Arnim." *Journal of English and German Philology* 53 (1954): 403-09.

Undertakes a close reading of Arnim's *Der Tolle Invalide.*

Gajek, Bernhard. "Achim von Arnim: Romantischer Poet und preußischer Patriot (1781-1831)." In *Sammeln und Sichten: Festschrift für Oscar Fambach zum 80,* edited by Joachim Krause, Norbert Oellers, and Karl Konrad Polheim, pp. 264-82. Bonn: Bouvier, 1982.

Discusses the link between Arnim's poetic language and his attitude toward German nationalism, paying particular attention to *Des Knaben Wunderhorn.*

Guignard, René. *Achim von Arnim, 1781-1831.* Paris: Société d'Édition "Les Belles Letters," 1936, 218 p.
　　Offers an evaluation of Arnim's life and work.

Hoermann, Roland. "The Romantic Golden Age in Arnim's Writings." *Monatshefte* 50 (January 1958): 21-9.
　　Evaluates the ways in which Arnim's work embodies some of the central themes of German Romanticism.

———. "Symbolism and Mediation in Arnim's View of Romantic Fantasy." *Monatshefte* 54 (May 1962): 201-15.
　　Examines the tension between rationality and idealism in Arnim's characters.

Holt, R. F. "Achim von Arnim and Sir Walter Scott." *German Life & Letters: A Quarterly Review* 26, no. 2 (January 1973): 142-60.
　　Debates Sir Walter Scott's influence on Arnim's historical novel *Die Kronenwächter.*

Howie, Margaret D. "Achim von Arnim and Scotland." *The Modern Language Review* 17 (1922): 157-64.
　　Discusses Achim von Arnim's brief journey to Scotland in 1803, evaluating its impact on such works as *Die Ehenschmiede, Owen Tudor,* and *Wintergarten,* among others.

Liedke, Herbert R. *Literary Criticism and Romantic Theory in the Work of Achim von Arnim.* New York: Columbia University Press, 1937, 187 p.
　　Provides a basic overview of Arnim's work within the context of German literary trends during the early nineteenth century.

Lokke, Kari E. "Achim von Arnim and the Romantic Grotesque." *Germanic Review* 58, no. 1 (winter 1983): 21-32.

Addresses prevailing critical assessments of Arnim's work, arguing that his anarchic narrative structures, extravagant conceits, and liberal mingling of history and fantasy are the very qualities that make his contribution to European Romantic literature so valuable.

Mornin, J. Edward. "National Subjects in the Works of Achim von Arnim." *German Life and Letters* 24 (1971): 316-27.
　　Examines the relationship between Arnim's political ideology and his writings, analyzing diverse patriotic themes and motifs that recur throughout Arnim's body of work.

Riley, Helen M. Kastinger. *Achim von Arnim in Selbstzeugnissen und Bilddokumenten.* Reinbek bei Hamburg: Rowohlt, 1979, 157 p.
　　Provides the first significant modern study of Arnim's life and work.

Stopp, Elisabeth. "Arnim's *Owen Tudor* and Its Background." *German Life and Letters* 29 (1975): 155-65.
　　Examines the various influences behind Arnim's *Owen Tudor,* including Arnim's travels in England and his extensive readings of medieval history.

Tymms, Ralph. *German Romantic Literature.* London: Methuen, 1955, 406 p.
　　Evaluates Arnim in relation to other German writers of his era, assessing Arnim's significance within the broader Romantic tradition.
　　Vordtriede, Werner. "Achim von Arnim." In *Deutsche Dichte der Romantik,* edited by Benno von Wiese, pp. 253-79. Berlin: Schmidt, 1971.

Offers a thorough and insightful survey of the author's major themes.

Weiss, Hermann F. "The Use of the Leitmotif in Achim von Arnim's Stories." *German Quarterly* 42 (1969): 343-51.

Examines Arnim's use of leitmotif as a means of providing structure to his fictional narratives.

---

**Additional coverage of Arnim's life and career is contained in the following sources published by Thomson Gale:** *Dictionary of Literary Biography,* **Vol. 90;** *Literature Resource Center;* *Nineteenth-Century Literature Criticism,* **Vol. 5; and** *Short Story Criticism,* **Vol. 9.**

# Augustus Baldwin Longstreet
## 1790-1870

American fiction writer, humorist, and essayist.

## INTRODUCTION

Augustus Baldwin Longstreet was one of the most important humorists to emerge out of the Southwestern frontier. He remains best known as the author of *Georgia Scenes* (1835), a collection of humorous sketches depicting the social customs and cultural mores of the American South in the early nineteenth century. Filled with regional idioms, detailed depictions of frontier life, and rowdy, masculine protagonists, the stories provide one of the earliest and most eloquent records of that period in Southern history. The work also helped shape the development of a distinctly American style of humor, one rooted in the folktales and oral storytelling traditions of the era. Among the authors influenced by Longstreet were Joseph Glover Baldwin, George Washington Harris, and Mark Twain. In addition to his accomplishments as writer of fiction, Longstreet also gained renown as a lawyer, politician and college president, and throughout his life he was a prominent figure in the South. An outspoken advocate of the Confederacy, Longstreet worked to defend the moral and cultural integrity of the region both before and during the Civil War.

## BIOGRAPHICAL INFORMATION

Longstreet was born on September 22, 1790, in Augusta, Georgia, the son of William Longstreet and Hannah Randolph, both of whom had originally come from New Jersey. He received his early education at home and then attended the academy of Moses Waddel in Willington, South Carolina, before transferring to Yale College. After graduating from Yale in 1813, he enrolled in nearby Reeve and Gould's Law School, earning his degree the following year. With a diverse, opinionated, and vocal student body from both Northern and Southern states, Reeve and Gould's exposed Longstreet to many of the cultural divisions that were beginning to emerge between the two regions, an experience that would help shape his mature political convictions. During these years Longstreet befriended John C. Calhoun, the noted lawyer and orator, with whom he shared a passionate devotion to Southern political principles.

After passing the Georgia bar in 1815, Longstreet entered into private practice. Two years later he married Frances Eliza Park, and he subsequently moved to Greensboro, where he earned election to the state legislature and later served as a superior court judge. In his travels throughout the state during this period, Longstreet began to collect the character observations and anecdotes that would later form the basis of *Georgia Scenes*. In 1827, he moved with his family to Augusta, where he once again started a private law practice while also becoming involved in the states' rights movement, contributing political articles to local newspapers. In 1834, Longstreet bought the Federalist *Augusta North American Gazette* and renamed it the *State Rights' Sentinel,* a newspaper devoted to the defense of Southern ideals against the growing influence of the federal government in local politics. During this period he also began writing short fiction for various periodicals, including his own. In 1835, Longstreet published a collection of these sketches under the title *Georgia Scenes.*

After the publication of *Georgia Scenes,* Longstreet produced little creative writing, devoting most of his subsequent career to political and social causes. His later writings, which largely consisted of letters and political tracts in defense of the Confederacy, included *A Voice from the South: Comprising Letters from Georgia to Massachusetts, and to the Southern States* (1847) and *Shall South Carolina Begin the War?* (1861). In 1839, Longstreet became president of Emory College, where he remained until 1848. He also served as president of the University of Mississippi (1849-56) and the University of South Carolina (1856-61). In 1864, Longstreet published his only novel, the semiautobiographical *Master William Mitten,* a work that failed to impress either readers or critics. During his remaining years Longstreet devoted his literary efforts to religious and political themes. He died in Oxford, Mississippi, on July 9, 1870.

## MAJOR WORKS

Longstreet's modern literary reputation is defined by a single work, the collection of sketches *Georgia Scenes.* The stories originally appeared in various Southern literary journals, beginning with the publication of "The Ball" in 1832. A number of other stories followed, most published under a pseudonym, among them "The Character of a Native Georgian" (1834) and "The Debating Society" (1835). In 1835, Longstreet collected nineteen sketches in a single volume, which he published under the title *Georgia Scenes, Characters, Incidents, &c. in the First Half Century of the Republic: By a Native Georgian.* In his preface to the work, Longstreet asserted that his purpose in writing *Georgia Scenes* was not to make a name for himself as an author—the fact that he published many of the pieces anonymously supports this claim—or even to entertain his readers. Rather, Longstreet aimed primarily to create a vital document of his life and times, one that would faithfully capture the spirit, attitudes, and day-to-day life of the Southwestern frontier. The stories are narrated by two distinctly Georgian characters: Lyman Hall, who recounts the twelve stories featuring male protagonists, and Abraham Baldwin, who relates the six stories concerning women. The remaining story, "The Militia Company Drill," was actually written by Oliver Hill Prince, a friend of Longstreet. The stories find unity in their simple, plainspoken diction, their colorful characters, and their morality. Such stories as "Georgia Theatrics" illustrate the tension between a coarse, often violent way of life and the austere demands of Christianity, a dichotomy in evidence throughout the Southwestern frontier during the period. Other sketches, notably "The Gander Pulling," contain oblique references to the ten-

sion building between Northern and Southern ways of life. In such tales as "The Horse Swap," Longstreet pits Southerner against Southerner, each exhibiting the qualities of guile, bombast, and pride with which the author usually characterized his peers. The sketches all share Longstreet's sardonic wit and keen ear for local idioms, and they unfold in a leisurely, relaxed manner reminiscent of the author's life and times.

## CRITICAL RECEPTION

Upon its original publication *Georgia Scenes* received high critical praise both in the North and in the South. Reviewing the work in the *Southern Literary Messenger,* Edgar Allan Poe lauded the work's humor as well as its realism, describing the collection as a vital contribution to the growing body of frontier literature. The first book-length study of Longstreet's career, Oscar P. Fitzgerald's *Judge Longstreet,* appeared in 1891. John Donald Wade's *Augustus Baldwin Longstreet: A Study of the Development of Culture in the South* (1924) remains a definitive twentieth-century critical biography. In the 1920s and 1930s critics such as Franklin J. Meine and Walter Blair began to regard *Georgia Scenes* as a landmark work in the canon of American humor writing, a point of departure for the later works of George Washington Harris and Mark Twain. Later in the twentieth century scholars began to pay closer attention to the literary merits of Longstreet's fictional style, citing his work as an early example of American literary realism. Recent critics have also drawn attention to the underlying political implications of the stories, regarding Longstreet's depictions of the South as part of a vigorous and creative defense of his native region against the encroachment of Union principles. Other interpretations have considered the subversive elements in *Georgia Scenes,* both in its use of irony and in its political undertones.

---

# PRINCIPAL WORKS

*State Rights' Sentinel* [editor and contributor] (journalism) 1834-36

*Georgia Scenes, Characters, Incidents, Etc. in the First Half Century of the Republic: By a Native Georgian* (short stories) 1835

*Letters on the Epistle of Paul to Philemon: Or, the Connection of Apostolical Christianity with Slavery* (prose) 1845

*A Voice from the South: Comprising Letters from Georgia to Massachusetts, and to the Southern States* (prose) 1847

---

# CRITICISM

## Edgar Allan Poe (review date March 1836)

SOURCE: Poe, Edgar Allan. Review of *Georgia Scenes.*
*Southern Literary Messenger* 2, no. 4 (March 1836):
287-92.

[*In the following review of Longstreet's* Georgia Scenes,
*Poe offers individual evaluations of each story, praising
the book's humor and wit, as well as its strikingly honest portrayal of Southern life.*]

This book has reached us anonymously—not to say
anomalously—yet it is most heartily welcome. The author, whoever he is, is a clever fellow, imbued with a
spirit of the truest humor, and endowed, moreover, with
an exquisitely discriminative and penetrating understanding of *character* in general, and of Southern character in particular. And we do not mean to speak of *human* character exclusively. To be sure, our Georgian is
*au fait* here too—he is learned in all things appertaining
to the biped without feathers. In regard, especially, to
that class of southwestern mammalia who come under
the generic appellation of "savagerous wild cats," he is
a very Theophrastus in duodecimo. But he is not the
less at home in other matters. Of geese and ganders he
is the La Bruyere, and of good-for-nothing horses the
Rochefoucault.

Seriously—if this book were printed in England it
would make the fortune of its author. We positively
mean what we say—and are quite sure of being sustained in our opinion by all proper judges who may be
so fortunate as to obtain a copy of the *Georgia Scenes,*
and who will be at the trouble of sifting their peculiar
merits from amid the *gaucheries* of a Southern publication. Seldom—perhaps never in our lives—have we
laughed as immoderately over any book as over the one
now before us. If these *scenes* have produced such effects upon *our* cachinnatory nerves—upon *us* who are
not "of the merry mood," and, moreover, have not been
unused to the perusal of somewhat similar things—we
are at no loss to imagine what a hubbub they would occasion in the uninitiated regions of Cockaigne. And
what would Christopher North say to them?—ah, what

would Christopher North say? that is the question. Certainly not a word. But we can fancy the pursing up of
his lips, and the long, loud, and jovial resonation of his
wicked, and uproarious ha! ha's!

From the Preface to the Sketches before us we learn
that although they are, generally, nothing more than
fanciful combinations of real incidents and characters,
still, in some instances, the narratives are literally true.
We are told also that the publication of these pieces was
commenced, rather more than a year ago, in one of the
Gazettes of the State, and that they were favorably received. "For the last six months," says the author, "I
have been importuned by persons from all quarters of
the State to give them to the public in the present form."
This speaks well for the Georgian taste. But that the
publication will *succeed,* in the bookselling sense of the
word, is problematical. Thanks to the long indulged literary supineness of the South, her presses are not as apt
in putting forth a *saleable* book as her sons are in con-
cocting a wise one.

From a desire of concealing the author's name, two different signatures, Baldwin and Hall, were used in the
original Sketches, and, to save trouble, are preserved in
the present volume. With the exception, however, of
one scene, "The Company Drill," all the book is the
production of the same pen. The first article in the list
is **"Georgia Theatrics."** Our friend *Hall,* in this piece,
represents himself as ascending, about eleven o'clock in
the forenoon of a June day, "a long and gentle slope in
what was called the Dark Corner of Lincoln County,
Georgia." Suddenly his ears are assailed by loud, profane, and boisterous voices, proceeding, apparently,
from a large company of ragamuffins, concealed in a
thick covert of undergrowth about a hundred yards from
the road.

> "You kin, kin you?
>
> "Yes I kin, and am able to do it! Boo-oo-oo-oo! Oh
> wake snakes and walk your chalks! Brimstone and fire!
> Dont hold me Nick Stova! The fight's made up, and
> lets go at it—my soul if I dont jump down his throat,
> and gallop every chitterling out of him before you can
> say 'quit!'
>
> "Now Nick, dont hold him! Jist let the wild cat come,
> and I'll tame him. Ned'll see me a fair fight—wont you
> Ned?
>
> "Oh yes; I'll see you a fair fight, my old shoes if I
> dont.
>
> "That's sufficient, as Tom Haynes said when he saw
> the Elephant. Now let him come!" &c. &c. &c.

And now the sounds assume all the discordant intonations inseparable from a Georgia "rough and tumble"
fight. Our traveller listens in dismay to the indications

of a quick, violent, and deadly struggle. With the intention of acting as pacificator, he dismounts in haste, and hurries to the scene of action. Presently, through a gap in the thicket, he obtains a glimpse of one, at least, of the combatants. This one appears to have his antagonist beneath him on the ground, and to be dealing on the prostrate wretch the most unmerciful blows. Having overcome about half the space which separated him from the combatants, our friend Hall is horror-stricken at seeing "the uppermost make a heavy plunge with both his thumbs, and hearing, at the same instant, a cry in the accent of keenest torture, 'Enough! My eye's out!'"

Rushing to the rescue of the mutilated wretch the traveller is surprised at finding that all the accomplices in the hellish deed have fled at his approach—at least so he supposes, for none of them are to be seen.

> "At this moment," says the narrator, "the victor saw me for the first time. He looked excessively embarrassed, and was moving off, when I called to him in a tone emboldened by the sacredness of my office, and the iniquity of his crime, 'come back, you brute! and assist me in relieving your fellow mortal, whom you have ruined forever!' My rudeness subdued his embarrassment in an instant; and with a taunting curl of the nose, he replied; you need'nt kick before you're spurred. There 'ant nobody there, nor ha'nt been nother. I was jist seein how I could 'a' *fout!* So saying, he bounded to his plow, which stood in the corner of the fence about fifty yards beyond the battle ground."

All that had been seen or heard was nothing more nor less than a Lincoln rehearsal; in which all the parts of all the characters, of a Georgian Court-House fight had been sustained by the youth of the plough *solus*. The whole anecdote is told with a raciness and vigor which would do honor to the pages of Blackwood.

The second Article is **"The Dance, a Personal Adventure of the Author"** in which the oddities of a backwood reel are depicted with inimitable force, fidelity and picturesque effect. **"The Horse-swap"** is a vivid narration of an encounter between the wits of two Georgian horse-jockies. This is most excellent in every respect—but especially so in its delineations of Southern bravado, and the keen sense of the ludicrous evinced in the portraiture of the steeds. We think the following free and easy sketch of a *hoss* superior, in joint humor and verisimilitude, to any thing of the kind we have ever seen.

> During this harangue, little Bullet looked as if he understood it all, believed it, and was ready at any moment to verify it. He was a horse of goodly countenance, rather expressive of vigilance than fire; though an unnatural appearance of fierceness was thrown into

it, by the loss of his ears, which had been cropped pretty close to his head. Nature had done but little for Bullet's head and neck, but he managed in a great measure to hide their defects by bowing perpetually. He had obviously suffered severely for corn; but if his ribs and hip bones had not disclosed the fact he never would have done it; for he was in all respects as cheerful and happy as if he commanded all the corn cribs and fodder stacks in Georgia. His height was about twelve hands; but as his shape partook somewhat of that of the giraffe his haunches stood much lower. They were short, straight, peaked, and concave. Bullet's tail, however, made amends for all his defects. All that the artist could do to beautify it had been done; and all that horse could do to compliment the artist, Bullet did. His tail was nicked in superior style, and exhibited the line of beauty in so many directions, that it could not fail to hit the most fastidious taste in some of them. From the root it dropped into a graceful festoon; then rose in a handsome curve; then resumed its first direction; and then mounted suddenly upwards like a cypress knee to a perpendicular of about two and a half inches. The whole had a careless and bewitching inclination to the right. Bullet obviously knew where his beauty lay, and took all occasions to display it to the best advantage. If a stick cracked, or if any one moved suddenly about him or coughed, or hawked, or spoke a little louder than common, up went Bullet's tail like lightning; and if the *going up* did not please, the *coming down* must of necessity, for it was as different from the other movement as was its direction. The first was a bold and rapid flight upwards usually to an angle of forty five degrees. In this position he kept his interesting appendage until he satisfied himself that nothing in particular was to be done; when he commenced dropping it by half inches, in second beats—then in triple time—then faster and shorter, and faster and shorter still, until it finally died away imperceptibly into its natural position. If I might compare sights to sounds, I should say its *settling* was more like the note of a locust than any thing else in nature.

**"The Character of a Native Georgian"** is amusing, but not so good as the scenes which precede and succeed it. Moreover the character described (a practical humorist) is neither very original, nor appertaining exclusively to Georgia.

**"The Fight"** although involving some horrible and disgusting details of southern barbarity is a sketch unsurpassed in dramatic vigor, and in the vivid truth to nature of one or two of the personages introduced. *Uncle Tommy Loggins,* in particular, an oracle in "rough and tumbles," and Ransy Sniffle, a misshapen urchin "who in his earlier days had fed copiously upon red clay and blackberries," and all the pleasures of whose life concentre in a love of fisticuffs—are both forcible, accurate and original generic delineations of real existences to be found sparsely in Georgia, Mississippi and Louisiana, and very plentifully in our more remote settlements and territories. This article would positively make the fortune of any British periodical.

**"The Song"** is a burlesque somewhat overdone, but upon the whole a good caricature of Italian bravura singing. The following account of Miss Aurelia Emma Theodosia Augusta Crump's execution on the piano is inimitable.

> Miss Crump was educated at Philadelphia; she had been taught to sing by Madam Piggisqueaki, who was a pupil of Ma'm'selle Crokifroggietta, who had sung with Madam Catalani; and she had taken lessons on the piano, from Signor Buzzifuzzi, who had played with Paganini.
>
> She seated herself at the piano, rocked to the right, then to the left,—leaned forward, then backward, and began. She placed her right hand about midway the keys, and her left about two octaves below it. She now put off the right in a brisk canter up the treble notes, and the left after it. The left then led the way back, and the right pursued it in like manner. The right turned, and repeated its first movement; but the left outrun it this time, hopt over it, and flung it entirely off the track. It came in again, however, behind the left on its return, and passed it in the same style. They now became highly incensed at each other, and met furiously on the middle ground. Here a most awful conflict ensued, for about the space of ten seconds, when the right whipped off, all of a sudden, as I thought, fairly vanquished. But I was in the error, against which Jack Randolph cautions us—'It had only fallen back to a stronger position.' It mounted upon two black keys, and commenced the note of a rattle-snake This had a wonderful effect upon the left, and placed the doctrine of snake charming beyond dispute. The left rushed furiously towards it repeatedly, but seemed invariably panic struck, when it came within six keys of it, and as invariably retired with a tremendous roaring down the bass keys. It continued its assaults, sometimes by the way of the naturals, sometimes by the way of the sharps, and sometimes by a zigzag, through both; but all its attempts to dislodge the right from its strong hold proving ineffectual, it came close up to its adversary and expired.

The **"Turn Out"** is excellent—a second edition of Miss Edgeworth's "Barring Out," and full of fine touches of the truest humor. The scene is laid in Georgia, and in the good old days of *fescues, abbiselfas,* and *anpersants*—terms in very common use, but whose derivation we have always been at a loss to understand. Our author thus learnedly explains the riddle.

> The *fescue* was a sharpened wire, or other instrument, used by the preceptor, to point out the letters to the children. *Abbiselfa* is a contraction of the words 'a, by itself, a.' It was usual, when either of the vowels constituted a syllable of a word, to pronounce it, and de-

note its independent character, by the words just mentioned, thus: 'a by itself *a,* c-o-r-n corn, *acorn*'—e by itself *e,* v-i-l vil, evil. The character which stands for the word '*and*' (&) was probably pronounced with the same accompaniment, but in terms borrowed from the Latin language, thus: '& *per se* (by itself) &.' 'Hence anpersant.'

This whole story forms an admirable picture of schoolboy democracy in the woods. The *master* refuses his pupils an Easter holiday; and upon repairing, at the usual hour of the fatal day, to his school house, "a log pen about twenty feet square," finds every avenue to his ingress fortified and barricadoed. He advances, and is assailed by a whole wilderness of sticks from the cracks. Growing desperate, he seizes a fence rail, and finally succeeds in effecting an entrance by demolishing the door. He is soundly flogged however for his pains, and the triumphant urchins suffer him to escape with his life, solely upon condition of their being allowed to do what they please as long as they shall think proper.

**"The Charming Creature as a Wife,"** is a very striking narrative of the evils attendant upon an ill-arranged marriage—but as it has nothing about it peculiarly Georgian, we pass it over without further comment.

**"The Gander Pulling"** is a gem worthy, in every respect, of the writer of **"The Fight,"** and **"The Horse Swap."** What a **"Gander Pulling"** is, however, may probably not be known by a great majority of our readers. We will therefore tell them. It is a piece of unprincipled barbarity not unfrequently practised in the South and West. A circular horse path is formed of about forty or fifty yards in diameter. Over this path, and between two posts about ten feet apart, is extended a rope which, swinging loosely, vibrates in an arc of five or six feet. From the middle of this rope, lying directly over the middle of the path, a gander, whose neck and head are well greased, is suspended by the feet. The distance of the fowl from the ground is generally about ten feet—and its neck is consequently just within reach of a man on horseback. Matters being thus arranged, and the mob of vagabonds assembled, who are desirous of entering the chivalrous lists of the **"Gander Pulling,"** a hat is handed round, into which a quarter or half dollar, as the case may be, is thrown by each competitor. The money thus collected is the prize of the victor in the game—and the game is thus conducted. The ragamuffins mounted on horseback, gallop round the circle in Indian file. At a word of command, given by the proprietor of the gander, the pulling, properly so called, commences. Each villain as he passes under the rope, makes a grab at the throat of the devoted bird—the end and object of the tourney being to pull off his head. This of course is an end not easily accomplished. The fowl is obstinately bent upon retaining his caput if possible—in which determination he finds a powerful adjunct in the grease. The rope, moreover, by the efforts of the human devils, is kept in a troublesome and tantalizing state of vibration, while two assistants of the proprietor, one at each pole, are provided with a tough cowhide, for the purpose of preventing any horse from making too long a sojourn beneath the gander. Many hours, therefore, not unfrequently elapse before the contest is decided.

"The Ball"—a Georgia ball—is done to the life. Some passages, in a certain species of sly humor, wherein intense observation of character is disguised by simplicity of relation, put us forcibly in mind of the Spectator. For example.

> "When De Bathle and I reached the ball room, a large number of gentlemen had already assembled. They all seemed cheerful and happy. Some walked in couples up and down the ball room, and talked with great volubility; but none of them understood a word that himself or his companion said.
>
> "Ah, sir, how do you know that?
>
> "Because the speakers showed plainly by their looks and actions, that their thoughts were running upon their own personal appearance, and upon the figure they would cut before the ladies, when they should arrive; and not upon the subject of the discourse. And furthermore, their conversation was like that of one talking in his sleep—without order, sense, or connexion. The hearer always made the speaker repeat in sentences and half sentences; often interrupting him with 'what?' before he had proceeded three words in a remark; and then laughed affectedly, as though he saw in the senseless unfinished sentence, a most excellent joke. Then would come his reply, which could not be forced into connexion with a word that he had heard; and in the course of which he was treated with precisely the civility which he had received. And yet they kept up the conversation with lively interest as long as I listened to them."

**"The Mother and her Child,"** we have seen before—but read it a second time with zest. It is a laughable burlesque of the baby 'gibberish' so frequently made use of by mothers in speaking to their children. This sketch evinces, like all the rest of the Georgia scenes—a fine dramatic talent.

**"The Debating Society"** is the best thing in the book—and indeed one among the best things of the kind we have ever read. It has all the force and freedom of some similar articles in the Diary of a Physician—without the evident straining for effect which so disfigures that otherwise admirable series. We will need no apology for copying **The Debating Society** entire.

> About three and twenty years ago, at the celebrated school in W———n, was formed a Debating Society, composed of young gentlemen between the ages of

seventeen and twenty-two. Of the number were two, who, rather from an uncommon volubility, than from any superior gifts or acquirements, which they possessed over their associates, were by common consent, placed at the head of the fraternity.—At least this was true of one of them: the other certainly had higher claims to his distinction. He was a man of the highest order of intellect, who, though he has since been known throughout the Union, as one of the ablest speakers in the country, seems to me to have added but little to his powers in debate, since he passed his twenty-second year. The name of the first, was Longworth; and Mc-Dermot was the name of the last. They were congenial spirits, warm friends, and classmates, at the time of which I am speaking.

It was a rule of the Society, that every member should speak upon the subjects chosen for discussion, or pay a fine; and as all the members valued the little stock of change, with which they were furnished, more than they did their reputation for oratory, not a fine had been imposed for a breach of this rule, from the organization of the society to this time.

The subjects for discussion were proposed by the members, and selected by the President, whose prerogative it was also to arrange the speakers on either side, at his pleasure; though in selecting the subjects, he was influenced not a little by the members who gave their opinions freely of those which were offered.

It was just as the time was approaching, when most of the members were to leave the society, some for college, and some for the busy scenes of life, that McDermot went to share his classmate's bed for a night. In the course of the evening's conversation, the society came upon the tapis. "Mac," said Longworth, "would'nt we have rare sport, if we could impose a subject upon the society, which has no sense in it, and hear the members speak upon it?"

"Zounds," said McDermot, "it would be the finest fun in the world. Let's try it at all events—we can lose nothing by the experiment."

A sheet of foolscap was immediately divided between them, and they industriously commenced the difficult task of framing sentences, which should possess the *form* of a debateable question, without a particle of the *substance*.—After an hour's toil, they at length exhibited the fruits of their labor, and after some reflection, and much laughing, they selected, from about thirty subjects proposed, the following, as most likely to be received by the society:

*"Whether at public elections, should the votes of faction predominate by internal suggestions or the bias of jurisprudence?"*

Longworth was to propose it to the society, and McDermot was to advocate its adoption.—As they had every reason to suppose, from the practice of the past, that they would be placed at the head of the list of disputants, and on opposite sides, it was agreed between them, in case the experiment should succeed, that they would write off, and interchange their speeches, in order that each might quote literally from the other, and thus *seem* at least, to understand each other.

The day at length came for the triumph or defeat of the project; and several accidental circumstances conspired to crown it with success. The society had entirely exhausted their subjects; the discussion of the day had been protracted to an unusual length, and the horns of the several boarding-houses began to sound, just as it ended. It was at this auspicious moment, that Longworth rose, and proposed his subject. It was caught at with rapture by McDermot, as being decidedly the best that had ever been submitted; and he wondered that none of the members had ever thought of it before.

It was no sooner proposed, than several members exclaimed, that they did not understand it; and demanded an explanation from the mover. Longworth replied, that there was no time then for explanations, but that either himself or Mr. McDermot would explain it, at any other time.

Upon the credit of the *maker* and *endorser,* the subject was accepted; and under pretence of economising time, (but really to avoid a repetition of the question,) Longworth kindly offered to record it, for the Secretary. This labor ended, he announced that he was prepared for the arrangement of the disputants.

"Put yourself," said the President, "on the affirmative, and Mr. McDermot on the negative."

"The subject," said Longworth "cannot well be resolved into an affirmative and negative. It consists more properly, of two conflicting affirmatives: I have therefore drawn out the heads, under which the speakers are to be arranged thus:

*Internal Suggestions. Bias of Jurisprudence.*

Then put yourself Internal Suggestions—Mr. McDermot the other side, Mr. Craig on your side—Mr. Pentigall the other side," and so on.

McDermot and Longworth now determined that they would not be seen by any other member of the society during the succeeding week, except at times when explanations could not be asked, or when they were too busy to give them. Consequently, the week passed away, without any explanations; and the members were summoned to dispose of the important subject, with no other lights upon it than those which they could collect from its terms. When they assembled, there was manifest alarm on the countenances of all but two of them.

The Society was opened in due form, and Mr. Longworth was called on to open the debate. He rose and proceeded as follows:

"*Mr. President*—The subject selected for this day's discussion, is one of vast importance, pervading the profound depths of psychology, and embracing within its comprehensive range, all that is interesting in morals, government, law and politics. But, sir, I shall not follow it through all its interesting and diversified ramifications; but endeavor to deduce from it those great and fundamental principles, which have direct bearing, upon the antagonist positions of the disputants; confining myself more immediately to its psychological influence when exerted, especially upon the *votes of faction*: for here is the point upon which the question mainly turns. In the next place, I shall consider the effects of those "suggestions" emphatically termed "*internal*" when applied to the same subject. And in the third place, I shall compare these effects, with "the bias of jurisprudence," considered as the only resort in times of popular excitement—for these are supposed to exist by the very terms of the question.

"The first head of this arrangement, and indeed the whole subject of dispute, has already been disposed of by this society. We have discussed the question, "are there any innate maxims? and with that subject and this, there is such an intimate affinity, that it is impossible to disunite them, without prostrating the vital energies of both, and introducing the wildest disorder and confusion, where, by the very nature of things, there exist the most harmonious coincidences, and the most happy and euphonic congenialities. Here then might I rest, Mr. President, upon the decision of this society, with perfect confidence. But, sir, I am not forced to rely upon the inseparable affinities of the two questions, for success in this dispute, obvious as they must be to every reflecting mind. All history, ancient and modern, furnish examples corroborative of the views which I have taken of this deeply interesting subject. By what means did the renowned poets, philosophers, orators and statesmen of antiquity, gain their immortality? Whence did Milton, Shakespeare, Newton, Locke, Watts, Paley, Burke, Chatham, Pitt, Fox, and a host of others whom I might name, pluck their never-fading laurels? I answer boldly, and without the fear of contradiction, that, though they all reached the temple of fame by different routes, they all passed through the broad vista of "*internal suggestions.*" The same may be said of Jefferson, Madison, and many other distinguished personages of our own country.

"I challenge the gentlemen on the other side to produce examples like these in support of their cause."

Mr. Longworth pressed these profound and logical views to a length to which our limits will not permit us to follow him, and which the reader's patience would hardly bear, if they would. Perhaps, however, he will bear with us, while we give the conclusion of Mr. Longworth's remarks: as it was here, that he put forth all his strength:

"*Mr. President,*—Let the bias of jurisprudence predominate, and how is it possible, (considering it merely as extending to those impulses which may with propriety be termed a *bias,*) how is it possible, for a government to exist, whose object is the public good? The marble hearted marauder might seize the throne of civil authority, and hurl into thraldom the votaries of rational liberty. Virtue, justice and all the nobler principles of human nature, would wither away under the pestilential breath of political faction, and an unnerved constitution be left to the sport of demagogue and parasite. Crash after crash would be heard in quick succession, as the strong pillars of the republic give way, and Despotism would shout in hellish triumph amidst the crumbling ruins—Anarchy would wave her bloody sceptre over the devoted land, and the blood-hounds of civil war, would lap the crimson gore of our most worthy citizens. The shrieks of women, and the screams of children, would be drowned amidst the clash of swords, and the cannon's peal: and Liberty, mantling her face from the horrid scene, would spread her golden-tinted pinions, and wing her flight to some far distant land, never again to re-visit our peaceful shores. In vain should we then sigh for the beatific reign of those "suggestions" which I am proud to acknowledge as peculiarly and exclusively 'internal.'"

Mr. McDermot rose promptly at the call of the President, and proceeded as follows:

"*Mr. President,*—If I listened unmoved to the very labored appeal to the passions, which has just been made, it was not because I am insensible to the powers of eloquence; but because I happen to be blessed with the small measure of sense, which is necessary to distinguish true eloquence from the wild ravings of an unbridled imagination. Grave and solemn appeals, when ill-timed and misplaced, are apt to excite ridicule; hence it was, that I detected myself more than once, in open laughter, during the most pathetic parts of Mr. Longworth's argument, if so it can be called.[1] In the midst of "crashing pillars," "crumbling ruins," "shouting despotism," "screaming women," and "flying Liberty," the question was perpetually recurring to me, "what has all this to do with the subject of dispute?" I will not follow the example of that gentleman—It shall be my endeavor to clear away the mist which he has thrown around the subject, and to place it before the society, in a clear, intelligible point of view: for I must say, that though his speech "*bears strong marks of the pen,*" (sarcastically,) it has but few marks of sober reflection. Some of it, I confess, is very intelligible and very plausible; but most of it, I boldly assert, no man living can comprehend. I mention this, for the edification of that gentleman, (who is usually clear and forcible,) to teach him, that he is most successful when he labors least.

"Mr. President: The gentleman, in opening the debate, stated that the question was one of vast importance; pervading the profound depths of *psychology,* and embracing, within its ample range, the whole circle of arts and sciences. And really, sir, he has verified his statement; for he has extended it over the whole moral and physical world. But, Mr. President, I take leave to differ from the gentleman, at the very threshhold of his remarks. The subject is one which is confined within very narrow limits. It extends no further than to the elective franchise, and is not even commensurate with this important privilege; for it stops short at the *vote of faction.* In this point of light, the subject comes within the grasp of the most common intellect; it is plain, simple, natural and intelligible. Thus viewing it, Mr. President, where does the gentleman find in it, or in all nature besides, the original of the dismal picture which he has presented to the society? It loses all its interest, and becomes supremely ridiculous. Having thus, Mr. President, divested the subject of all obscurity—having reduced it to those few elements, with which we are all familiar; I proceed to make a few deductions from the premises, which seem to me inevitable, and decisive of the question. I lay it down as a self-evident proposition, that faction in all its forms, is hideous; and I maintain, with equal confidence, that it never has been, nor ever will be, restrained by those suggestions, which the gentleman *"emphatically terms internal."* No, sir, nothing short of the bias, and the very strong bias too, of jurisprudence or the potent energies of the sword, can restrain it. But, sir, I shall here, perhaps, be asked, whether there is not a very wide difference between a turbulent, lawless faction, and the *vote* of faction? Most unquestionably there is; and to this distinction I shall presently advert and demonstrably prove that it is a distinction, which makes altogether in our favor."

Thus did Mr. McDermot continue to dissect and expose his adversary's argument, in the most clear, conclusive and masterly manner, at considerable length. But we cannot deal more favorably by him, than we have dealt by Mr. Longworth. We must, therefore, dismiss him, after we shall have given the reader his concluding remarks. They were as follows:

"Let us now suppose Mr. Longworth's principles brought to the test of experiment. Let us suppose his language addressed to all mankind—We close the temples of justice as useless; we burn our codes of laws as worthless; and we substitute in their places, the more valuable restraints of *internal suggestions.* Thieves, invade not your neighbor's property: if you do, you will be arraigned before the august tribunal of *conscience.* Robbers, stay your lawless hand; or you will be visited with the tremendous penalties of *psychology.* Murderers, spare the blood of your fellow creatures; you will be exposed to the excruciating tortures of *innate maxims—when it shall be discovered that there are any.* Mr. President, could there be a broader license to crime than this? Could a better plan be devised for dissolving the bands of civil society? It requires not the gift of prophecy, to foresee the consequences of these novel and monstrous principles. The strong would tyrannize over the weak; the poor would plunder the rich; the servant would rise above the master; the drones of society would fatten upon the hard earnings of the industrious. Indeed, sir, industry would soon desert the land; for it would have neither reward nor encouragement. Commerce would cease; the arts and sciences would languish; all the sacred relations would be dissolved, and scenes of havoc, dissolution and death ensue, such as never before visited the world, and such as never will visit it, until mankind learn to repose their destinies upon "those suggestions, *emphatically termed internal.*" From all these evils there is a secure retreat behind the brazen wall of the 'bias of jurisprudence.'"

The gentleman who was next called on to engage in the debate, was John Craig; a gentleman of good hard sense, but who was utterly incompetent to say a word upon a subject which he did not understand. He proceeded thus:

"*Mr. President,*—When this subject was proposed, I candidly confessed I did not understand it, and I was informed by Mr. Longworth and Mr. McDermot, that either of them would explain it, at any leisure moment. But, sir, they seem to have taken very good care, from that time to this, to have no leisure moment. I have inquired of both of them, repeatedly for an explanation; but they were always too busy to talk about it. Well, sir, as it was proposed by Mr. Longworth, I thought he would certainly explain it in his speech; but I understood no more of his speech than I did of the subject. Well, sir, I thought I should certainly learn something from Mr. McDermot; especially as he promised at the commencement of his speech to clear away the mist that Mr. Longworth had thrown about the subject, and to place it in a clear, intelligible point of light. But, sir, the only difference between his speech and Mr. Longworth's is, that it was not quite as flighty as Mr. Longworth's. I could n't understand head nor tail of it. At one time they seemed to argue the question, as if it were this: "Is it better to have law or no law?" At another, as though it was, "should factions be governed by law, or be left to their own consciences?" But most of the time they argued it, as if it were just what it seems to be—a sentence without sense or meaning. But, sir, I suppose its obscurity is owing to my dullness of apprehension, for they appeared to argue it with great earnestness and feeling, as if they understood it.

"I shall put my interpretation upon it, Mr. President, and argue it accordingly.

"'*Whether at public elections*'—that is, for members of Congress, members of the Legislature, &c. '*should the votes of faction*'—I don't know what '*faction*' has got to do with it; and therefore I shall throw it out. '*Should the votes predominate, by internal suggestions or the bias,*' I don't know what the *article* is put in here for. It seems to me, it ought to be, *be biased by* 'jurisprudence' or law. In short, Mr. President, I understand the question to be, should a man vote as he pleases, or should the law say how he should vote?"

Here Mr. Longworth rose and observed, that though Mr. Craig was on his side, he felt it due to their adversaries, to state, that this was not a true exposition of the subject. This exposition settled the question at once on his side; for nobody would, for a moment contend, that *the law* should declare how men should vote. Unless it be confined to the vote *of faction* and *the* bias of jurisprudence, it was no subject at all. To all this Mr. McDermot signified his unqualified approbation; and seemed pleased with the candor of his opponent.

"Well," said Mr. Craig, "I thought it was impossible that any one should propose such a question as that to the society; but will Mr. Longworth tell us, if it does not mean that, what does it mean? for I don't see what great change is made in it by his explanation."

Mr. Longworth replied, that if the remarks which he had just made, and his argument, had not fully explained the subject to Mr. Craig, he feared it would be out of his power to explain it.

"Then," said Mr. Craig, "I'll pay my fine, for I don't understand a word of it."

The next one summoned to the debate was Mr. Pentigall. Mr. Pentigall was one of those who would never acknowledge his ignorance of any thing, which any person else understood; and that Longworth and McDermot were both masters of the subject, was clear, both from their fluency and seriousness. He therefore determined to understand it, at all hazards. Consequently he rose at the President's command, with considerable self-confidence. I regret, however, that it is impossible to commit Mr. Pentigall's *manner* to paper, without which, his remarks lose nearly all their interest. He was a tall, handsome man; a little theatric in his manner, rapid in his delivery, and singular in his pronunciation. He gave to the *e* and *i,* of our language, the sound of *u*—at least his peculiar intonations of voice, seemed to give them that sound; and his rapidity of utterance seemed to change the termination, "*tion*" into "*ah.*" With all his peculiarities, however, he was a fine fellow. If he was ambitious, he was not invidious, and he possessed an amicable disposition. He proceeded as follows:

"*Mr. President,*—This internal suggestion which has been so eloquently discussed by Mr. Longworth, and the bias of jurisprudence which has been so ably advocated by Mr. McDermot—hem! Mr. President, in order to fix the line of demarkation between—ah—the internal suggestion and the bias of jurisprudence—Mr. President, I think, sir, that—ah—the subject must be confined to the *vote of faction,* and *the* bias of jurisprudence"———

Here Mr. Pentigall clapt his right hand to his forehead, as though he had that moment heard some overpowering news; and after maintaining this position for about the space of ten seconds, he slowly withdrew his hand, gave his head a slight inclination to the right, raised his eyes to the President as if just awakening from a trance, and with a voice of the most hopeless despair, concluded with "I don't understand the subject, Muster Prusidunt."

The rest of the members on both sides submitted to be fined rather than attempt the knotty subject; but by common consent, the penal rule was dispensed with. Nothing now remained to close the exercises, but the decision of the Chair.

The President, John Nuble, was a young man, not unlike Craig in his turn of mind; though he possessed an intellect a little more sprightly than Craig's. His decision was short.

"Gentlemen," said he, "I do not understand the subject. This," continued he, (pulling out his knife, and pointing to the silvered or *cross* side of it,) "is 'Internal Suggestions.' And this" (pointing to the other, or *pile* side,) "is 'Bias of Jurisprudence:'" so saying, he threw up his knife, and upon its fall, determined that 'Internal Suggestions' had got it; and ordered the decision to be registered accordingly.

It is worthy of note, that in their zeal to accomplish their purpose, Longworth and McDermot forgot to destroy the lists of subjects, from which they had selected the one so often mentioned; and one of these lists containing the subject discussed, with a number more like it, was picked up by Mr. Craig, who made a public exhibition of it, threatening to arraign the conspirators before the society, for a contempt. But, as the parting hour was at hand, he overlooked it with the rest of the brotherhood, and often laughed heartily at the trick.

"The Militia Company Drill," is not by the author of the other pieces but has a strong family resemblance, and is very well executed. Among the innumerable descriptions of Militia musters which are so rife in the land, we have met with nothing at all equal to this in the matter of broad farce.

**"The Turf"** is also capital, and bears with it a kind of dry and sarcastic morality which will recommend it to many readers.

**"An Interesting Interview"** is another specimen of exquisite dramatic talent. It consists of nothing more than a fac-simile of the speech, actions, and *thoughts* of two drunken old men—but its air of truth is perfectly inimitable.

**"The Fox-Hunt," "The Wax Works,"** and **"A Soge Conversation,"** are all good—but neither *as* good as many other articles in the book.

**"The Shooting Match,"** which concludes the volume, may rank with the best of the Tales which precede it. As a portraiture of the manners of our South-Western peasantry, in especial, it is perhaps better than any.

Altogether this very humorous, and very clever book forms an æra in our reading. It has reached us per mail, and without a cover. We will have it bound forthwith, and give it a niche in our library as a sure omen of better days for the literature of the South.

*Note*

1. This was extemporaneous, and well conceived; for Mr. McDermot had not played his part with becoming gravity.

## William Tappan Thompson (review date July 1840)

SOURCE: Thompson, William Tappan. Review of *Georgia Scenes. Southern Literary Messenger* 6, no. 7 (July 1840): 572-74.

[*In the following review of the second edition of* Georgia Scenes, *Thompson praises the satirical and subtle morality of the work while also admiring the unadorned directness and simplicity of Longstreet's prose.*]

We hail with pleasure the second edition of this justly popular book, though we were much disappointed at not finding in it the three numbers which appeared in this periodical after the first edition was printed. Two of them have been pronounced by good judges, fully equal, if not superior to any of the whole series, and the third (**"Little Ben"**) *when read by the author,* we have no hesitation in pronouncing the most laughter-provoking of all; but it loses almost all its interest on paper. *Apropos*: while speaking of "Little Ben" we may as well correct an error in regard to its origin. On our first perusal of the sketch, we were struck with the similarity between it and one of Mr. Matthews' popular Yankee-stories, which we had so often heard related on the stage by the *Zepheniah Tairall* of our playgoing days, Mr. Hill, in true Yankee style. On its publication, the "family resemblance" was pointed out to us by several of our readers, and though our knowledge of the author precluded the suspicion that he had put a plagiarism upon us, we were at a loss how to account for the "remarkable coincidence." We were however soon set aright on the subject, by one of the author's schoolfellows, who related to us the manner in which the author of the *Georgia Scenes* first came in possession of the story from the genuine original; how he afterwards went to Yale College, thence to the Law school at Litchfield, where the story, or rather his peculiar manner of telling it, became so popular, that Matthews, who shortly afterwards passed through the country, incorporated it with the budget of drolleries which he related to the public as "Yankee Stories," and thus gave it currency long before it appeared in print in its original form. This is the true history of **"Little Ben"**; but it is to be feared that no one will ever again enjoy the luxury of hearing it in its proper cadence, tone, emphasis and pronunciation, as the author since his entry upon the Ministry seems to have renounced all fellowship with this much admired offspring of his genius, and to have relinquished his professed design of carrying out his sketches of real life and character to all grades and conditions of society. We know not why, for there is nothing of an immoral tendency in the sketches, and (the opinion of the New Yorker to the contrary notwithstanding) we fearlessly assert that the "humor," instead of being "unrelieved by a single instance of beauty, sentiment or eloquence of style," is often relieved by all. As to the *style,* except when the author quotes the language of his characters, it is *throughout* remarkably pure, flowing and beautiful, and in some instances ascending high above its common level, and indeed above the common level of writers standing high in the literary world. We select a few passages from a vast number not behind them in any respect, in confirmation of our opinion. Take for instance the following description of a Southern winter's morning:

> I dressed myself, walked out, waked my servant and ordered my horse. Truly it was a lovely morning for the season of the year: December never ushered in one more lovely. Like a sheet of snow the frost overspread the earth!—Not a breath was stirring. The coming huntsman had sounded his horn upon a distant hill, and

its unrepeated notes had died away. A cloudless sky o'erspread the earth, as rich in beauty as ever won the gaze of mortal. Upon the western verge, in all his martial glory, stood Orion; his burnished epaulets and spangled sash with unusual brightness glowing. Capella glittered brighter still, and Castor, Procyon, and Arcturus rivalled her in lustre. But Sirius reigned the monarch of the starry host; and countless myriads of lesser lights glowed and sparkled, and twinkled o'er all the wide-spread canopy.

Or the following description of the chase, so easy and natural, and yet so full of animation:

> How, or why, I am unable to tell, but truth constrains me to say, that for some moments I was enraptured with the sport. The fox obliqued towards us, and entered a field of which our position commanded a full view. He must have left his covert with reluctance, for he was not more than a hundred paces ahead of the hounds when he entered the field. First of the pack, and side by side, the heroes of the clamorous band rose the fence. Then followed, in thick array, the whole troop; and close on their rear, Crocket burst through the copsewood and charged the fence without a pause. Around me, in every direction, I could see the huntsmen sweeping to the choir; and as, emerging from the forest or gaining the heights around, they caught the first glimpse of the gallant pack, they raised a shout which none but the overcharged heart can give, and none but the lifeless heart receive unmoved.

As a specimen of the author's descriptive style, we will take the following description of a woodland scene. Is not the change portrayed quite visible?

> The classic hut occupied a lovely spot, overshadowed by majestic hickorys, towering poplars, and strong-armed oaks. The little plain on which it stood was terminated, at the distance of about fifty paces from its door, by the brow of a hill, which descended rather abruptly to a noble spring, that gushed joyously forth from among the roots of a stately beech at its foot. The stream from this fountain scarcely burst into view before it hid itself beneath the dark shade of a field of cane, which overspread the dale through which it flowed, and marked its windings, until it turned from the sight among vine-covered hills, at a distance far beyond that to which the eye could have traced it without the help of its evergreen belt. A remark of the captain's as we viewed the lovely country around us, will give the reader my apology for the minuteness of the foregoing description.

* * *

> Forty-two years afterwards, I visited the spot on which he stood when he made the remark. The sun poured his whole strength upon the bald hill which once supported the sequestered school-house, many a deep-washed gully met at a sickly bog where gushed the limpid fountain; a dying willow rose from the soil which nourished the venerable beech; flocks wandered among the dwarf pines, and cropped a scanty meal from the vale where the rich cane bowed and rustled to every breeze, and all around was barren, dreary and cheerless.

Our space will not permit us to extend our extracts, and we must be content with one more, a compliment to the character of our countrywomen, than whom none better merit such an encomium.

> Their life is a life of good offices. At home they are patterns of industry, care, economy and hospitality; abroad they are ministers of comfort, peace, and consolation. Where affliction is, there are they to mitigate its pains. Nor night, nor day, nor summer's heat, nor winter's cold, nor angry elements, can deter them from scenes of suffering and distress. They are the first at the fevered couch, and the last to leave it. They hold the first and last cup to the parched lip. They bind the aching head, close the dying eye, and linger in the death-stricken habitation, to pour the last drop of consolation into the afflicted bosoms of the bereaved. I cannot, therefore, ridicule them myself, nor bear to hear them ridiculed in my presence.

If there be any thing defective in this style, if it be not really beautiful, we confess that we are much wanting in taste. True, it is destitute of the false gloss and affected sentimentalism so lavishly employed by a certain school of modern writers, whose chief claim to distinction, consists in the facility with which they crowd their sentences with redundant superlatives and words of original coinage. We confess that we have not yet arrived at that perfection of refinement, which relishes such strained and artificial style in preference to the pure, flowing mother English of our author.

The *moral* of the pieces when not professedly drawn by the author, as is frequently the case, is to be found in the delicate satire which runs through the whole descriptions and delineations.

It may be proper to remark that the author, A. B. Longstreet, Esq., formerly of this place, now President of Emory College, was not a clergyman when the pieces were written. Though earnestly and repeatedly pressed by men of the soundest morals, to continue the sketches, he could not be prevailed upon to favor the public with a single number after he entered the desk. We have understood, however, that before he engaged in his new avocation, he had promised the Harpers to correct the work for their press. If so, we have no doubt but that he will do it. Indeed we are informed that he has said since the appearance of the second edition, that as there is no stopping the work, he will immediately set about correcting and improving it, so that if it goes to another edition, it may at least be free from many errors that are in this edition. We understand the author has by him several numbers finished or unfinished, which have never been published. We earnestly entreat him to favor the public with these in the third edition. Having long known him, having labored in his office for several years, and been intimate with him for many since, we know from his character that there is nothing in the unpublished numbers which can savor of immorality; and we hope he will give them to the public. We learn that he says they are too light and trifling for his present station and calling; and this would silence us, if they were mere *fancy sketches,* as some of the northern critics seem to think. But they are not—they are faithful delineations of real scenes and characters; which as we have heard the author say more than once, when we have conversed with him on the subject, he meant to carry through all grades of society, (beginning with those which were fast changing and fading away, and ending with those which are alike in all ages and countries,) so that if his book survived, we might be seen and heard by our posterity two hundred years hence just as we are—to leave a record in which we might be seen in all the relations and walks of life. "We have," said he, "histories of Greece and Rome, but they never descend into private life. They tell you of the public games, &c., but they do not let you hear, in their own vernacular, the wits and wags who assembled there. They tell you how a distinguished character was brought up, but they do not introduce you into his mother's nursery, or tell you any thing of parental government generally, &c. &c. Now I propose to exhibit Georgia just as it is; not only as to population and character, but as to terrestrial scenery, so that those who come after us may know not only the changes which have taken place in the character and dialect of the people, but in the face of the country."

Now if in carrying out this design it becomes necessary for the author to describe the ludicrous, or even the profane, can any person be so fastidious as to censure him, or transfer to *him* the levity which appears in *his characters*? And is this laudable design to be abandoned by perhaps the only man living who can faithfully execute it, and doubtless by the only one who ever will attempt it, (for few would be willing to follow him in the same path,) because his sketches must at times be humorous? We hope not; and we hope that some of his pious friends will join us in endeavoring to prevail upon the author to go on with his work to its completion.

Of the illustrations which accompany the present edition, we have a word to say. It is to be regretted that the artist has so widely mistaken his subject. He seems to have confounded our true piney-woods Georgian with the Orange street loafer of New York, whose universal characteristics are a grotesque physiognomy and dilapidated apparel. This is a great mistake, and inasmuch as it tends to destroy the true intention and design of the sketches, should have been studiously avoided. Such sprouts as Ransy Sniffle, Bill Stallions, Bob Durham, Blossom, or the hero of the Lincoln Rehearsal, would be sought for in vain among the vagabond assemblage which daily pay their court at the New York Police Of-

fice, from whence it would seem the artist has drawn his inspiration. We are the more surprised at the broad miss of the artist when we consider the graphic descriptions of the text. Not a character or scene but there stands forth in bold, original, truthful delineation, and in the hands of a Cruikshank, or our own American Johnson, would have shown forth the very embodiment of the author's conception. The "Lincoln Rehearsal," to our notion, is the best picture of the bunch—the only defect in which is, that the hero of that desperate encounter is not represented in the full indulgence of his propensity for gouging out the "owl-eyes" of his passive antagonist. "Blossom and His Horse Bullet," which comes next in order, is a decided failure. Blossom, who professed to be "perhaps a *leetle,* jist a *leetle* of the best man at a horse-swap that ever stole *cracklins* out of his mammy's fat gourd," is represented as a sort of ragged rowdy, mounted on a nag resembling any thing else but the sprightly, ambling *Bullet,* whose tail, instead of flaring up like a sky-rocket, as represented in the picture, "was," says the author, "nicked in superior style, and exhibited the line of beauty in so many directions, that it could not fail to hit the most fastidious taste in some of them. From the root it dropped into a graceful festoon; then rose in a handsome curve; then resumed its first direction; and then mounted suddenly upward like a cypress knee to a perpendicular of about two and a half inches. The whole had a careless and bewitching inclination to the right." "Ned Brace at Church" would do, had note books been in fashion in those days. Ned, whom it will be recollected, "had not the gift of singing," is truly represented as joining in the psalm "with one of the loudest, hoarsest, and most discordant voices that ever annoyed a solemn assembly." *Ransy Sniffle,* as represented by the artist, is, barring the head, no more the little clay-eating, ague-faced Ransy Sniffle, described by the author, than any one else. "Michael St. John the Schoolmaster effecting an entrance by storm," will do—so will the illustration to **"The Charming Creature as a Wife."** "The Militia Drill," is a good picture of a militia parade the world over, though the uniform of the officer is not exactly adapted to the age. The same may be said of "Hurrying to the Races." Hardy, Slow, and Tobias Swift, in the **"Interesting Interview,"** are quite passable. **"The Fox Hunt"** is by no means in accordance with the description. **"The Wax Works"** is better, and conveys some idea of the scene presented at the breaking up of the show.

On the whole, we hope to see the third edition accompanied with better and more illustrations, as there are some subjects which are not illustrated in the present volume. We doubt not that the rapid sale of the book will encourage the Harpers to issue another edition speedily, when we hope to see **"Darby Anvil," "The Family Picture,"** and **"Little Ben"** added to the collection, should they not be able to prevail upon the author to furnish them with more of his inimitable sketches, which we understand he has in his possession.

## Carl J. Weber (essay date spring 1936)

SOURCE: Weber, Carl J. "A Connecticut Yankee in King Alfred's Country." *Colophon* 1, no. 4 (spring 1936): 525-35.

[*In the following essay, Weber discusses the controversy surrounding the 1880 publication of Thomas Hardy's novel* The Trumpet-Major, *one chapter of which bears striking similarities to "The Militia Company Drill" (initially attributed to Longstreet but later shown to be the work of Oliver Hillhouse Prince). Weber argues that the publicity surrounding this incident did much to revive public interest in Longstreet's work.*]

On November 4th, 1905, *The New York Times* published (in its Saturday Supplement) a question addressed to it by a correspondent who wished to know whether the works of A. B. Longstreet were still in print. To this inquiry the editor replied: "We find no record in Allibone or elsewhere of this author." Since then thirty years have slipped by with little reason to recall the name of Longstreet. Yet since he was the author of a once-famous American book, we may use the recent centenary of its first appearance as an opportunity for trying to clear up a literary mystery that has remained unsolved for over half a century.

Augustus B. Longstreet was the author of *Georgia Scenes,* which first saw the light slightly over one hundred years ago in Augusta, Georgia. It was printed at the office of the *States Rights Sentinel,* a newspaper edited at that time by Longstreet. The book was "entered in the Clerk's Office for the District of Georgia, in conformity to the act of Congress to secure copy rights, etc.," late in 1835, probably in December. The exact date cannot be given. A recent check of the copyright records of the Federal District Courts of Georgia, now held in the office of the Register of Copyrights in the Library of Congress, reveals that there are no records for the years prior to 1845, nor has the Register of Copyrights been able to ascertain where such records may now be located.

Although Longstreet's name did not appear in the volume, he was locally known as the author; and the success of that first edition of 1835 was so great that Longstreet found himself carried far along the road to fame. When he became a Methodist minister in 1838 and declined to have anything more to do with his book and

its accounts of prize-fights, horse-races, and other such snares of the devil, Harpers hired an artist (E. H. Hyde) and proceeded to issue a second and illustrated edition of *Georgia Scenes* in New York in 1840. Between that date and the end of the century eleven other editions were offered to a moderately eager public. Edgar Allan Poe gave his judgment of the book in March, 1836:

> If this book were printed in England, it would make the fortune of its author. We positively mean what we say,—and are quite sure of being sustained in our opinion by all proper judges who may be so fortunate as to obtain a copy of the *Georgia Scenes.*

Longstreet died in 1870. Before he had been dead a year, another author issued *his* first book—like Longstreet's, anonymously—an English author who was destined to bring the American book back into public attention again. In 1871 Thomas Hardy published his first novel, and it was Hardy who, curiously enough, gave Longstreet a temporary reprieve from oblivion and called forth three more editions of *Georgia Scenes.* The reason may be briefly explained.

In 1880 Hardy's *The Trumpet-Major* appeared and was shortly read by, among others, Charles P. Jacobs of Indianapolis, Indiana. Mr. Jacobs' own words tell the rest of the story:

> In the twenty-third chapter of *The Trumpet-Major,* Mr. Hardy sets out to describe a drill of the rustic militia in England. . . . The commanding officer, who has put his men through the evolutions and dismissed them, calls them again into ranks, and gives them a second lesson.—As I read this, I remembered that I had in my library an old book entitled *Georgia Scenes,* which contained, among other things, a humorous sketch of a drill of the rural militia. . . . From this sketch I make a few extracts for the purpose of comparison with the quotation from *The Trumpet-Major:*

> Hardy

> "Men, I dismissed ye too soon—parade, parade again, I say," he cried. "My watch is fast, I find. There's another twenty minutes afore the worship of God commences. Now all of you that ha'n't got fawlocks, fall in at the lower end. Eyes right and dress!"

> As every man was anxious to see how the rest stood, those at the end of the line pressed forward for that purpose, till the line assumed the form of a horseshoe.

> "Look at ye now! Why, you are all a crooking in. Dress, dress!"

> They dressed forthwith; but impelled by the same motive they soon resumed their former figure, and so they were despairingly permitted to remain.

> "Now, I hope you'll have a little patience," said the sergeant, as he stood in the centre of the arc, "and pay particular attention to the word of command, just ex-

actly as I give it out to ye; and if I should go wrong, I shall be much obliged to any gentleman who'll put me right again, for I have only been in the army three weeks myself, and we are all liable to mistakes."

"So we be, so we be," said the line heartily.

"'Tention, the whole, then. Poise fawlocks! Very well done!"

"Please, what must we do that haven't got no fire-locks?" said the lower end of the line in a helpless voice.

"Now, was ever such a question! Why, you must do nothing at all, but think *how* you'd poise 'em *if* you had 'em. You middle men, that are armed with hurdle-sticks and cabbage-stalks just to make believe, must of course use 'em as if they were the real thing. Now then, cock fawlocks! Present! Fire! (Not shoot in earnest, you know; only make pretence to.) Very good—very good indeed; except that some of you were a *little* too soon, and the rest a *little* too late" . . .

"I must dismiss ye," said the sergeant . . . "'Tention! To the right—left wheel, I mean—no, no—right wheel. Mar—r—r—rch!'"

Some wheeled to the right and some to the left, and some obliging men, including Cripplestraw, tried to wheel both ways.

"Stop, stop; try again. Gentlemen, unfortunately when I'm in a hurry I can never remember my right hand from my left, and never could as a boy. You must excuse me, please. Practice makes perfect, as the saying is; and, much as I've learnt since I 'listed, we always find something new. Now then, right wheel! march! halt! Stand at ease! dismiss! I think that's the order o't, but I'll look in the Gover'ment book afore Tuesday."

### Longstreet

'Look to the right and dress!' They were soon, by the help of the noncommissioned officers, placed in a straight line, but as every man was anxious to see how the rest stood, those on the wings pressed forward for that purpose till the whole line assumed nearly the form of a crescent.

'Why look at 'em,' says the captain; 'why, gentlemen, you are all a crooking in at both *eends,* so that you will get out to me by and by! Come, gentlemen, *dress! dress!*'

This was accordingly done; but impelled by the same motives as before, they soon resumed their former figure, and so they were permitted to remain.

'Now, gentlemen,' says the captain, 'I am going to carry you through the *revolutions* of the manual exercise; and I want you, gentlemen, if you please, to pay particular attention to the word of command, just exactly as I give it out to you. I hope you will have a little patience, gentlemen, if you please; and if I should be a going wrong, I will be much obliged to any of you, gentlemen, to put me right again, for I mean all for the best, and I hope you will excuse me if you

please. Come, boys, come to a shoulder . . . *Poise foolks!* [A note appended here says: 'A contraction and corruption of "firelock." Thus, "firelock," "f'lock," "foolk".'] *Cook foolk!* Very handsomely done . . . *Tention the whole!* Please observe, gentlemen, that at the word fire, you must fire; that is, if any of your guns are loaded, you must not shoot in yearnest, but only make pretence, like, and you, gentlemen fellow-soldiers, who's armed with nothing but sticks, riding-switches, and corn-stalks, needn't go through the firings, but stand as you are, and keep yourselves to yourselves. *Half cock foolk!* Very well done . . . Draw rammer! Those who have no rammers to their guns need not draw, but only make the motion; it will do just as well, and saves a great deal of time . . . *Order foolk!* Handsomely done, gentlemen! Very handsomely done! And all together, too, except that one half of you were a *leetle* too soon, and the other half a *leetle* too late . . . *Tention the whole! To the left—left, no—right, that is, the left—I mean the right—left wheel, march!'*

In this he was strictly obeyed; some wheeling to the right, some to the left, and some to the right-left, or both ways.

'Stop! Halt! Let us try it again! I could not just then tell my right hand from my left! You must excuse me, if you please. Experience makes perfect, as the saying is. Long as I have served, I find something new to learn every day: but all's one for that. Now, gentlemen, do that motion once more.'

It will need no acuteness of vision to see that there is something more than an accidental similarity between the description given by Mr. Hardy . . . and the American sketch. . . . It will, I think, bother the novelist's friends to prove prior invention for him.

Mr. Jacobs sent his charge of plagiarism to *The Critic,* and this New York magazine printed it on January 28th, 1882. The deadly parallels were reprinted in *The Academy* in London on February 18th, but Hardy ignored the charge both at home and abroad. Critics could only make their own guesses. Professor W. P. Trent, for example, wrote (in *Southern Writers,* 1905, p. 122):

> One of the most humorous papers in **Georgia Scenes** . . . is "The Militia Drill," much read abroad, which the distinguished English novelist, Mr. Thomas Hardy, has either directly imitated or else strikingly paralleled in an unconscious fashion in his charming novel *The Trumpet-Major.*

In the opinion of another American, Lyndon Orr, there is no such thing as unconscious assimilation by one author of the work or thought of another. Orr wrote to *The Bookman* (New York, February, 1906):

> That Augustus Baldwin Longstreet is so entirely forgotten . . . may account for the fact that no one . . . has noticed the inspiration drawn from him by a famous English novelist. Let us compare a passage from

. . . Hardy's *The Trumpet-Major* . . . with a passage from Longstreet's **Georgia Scenes.** . . . The comparison is interesting, but it needs no comment.

The editor of *The Bookman,* after publishing Mr. Orr's "disclosure," remarked (April, 1906):

> It is inconceivable that a writer so distinguished as Hardy should have consciously plagiarized anybody's book. . . . A learned friend of ours suggests that the passage may have been included in some English school reader, and that Hardy may have had to con it over many times when a boy, so that it became fixed in his mind, even to the phraseology. Then, thirty years or more afterwards . . . the Georgia novelist's sentences may have welled up into his mind by a process of unconscious memory. . . . We give this explanation for what it is worth; and as a matter of fact, we have no other.

Four years later Professor John Erskine guardedly remarked (in *Leading American Novelists,* 1910, p. 326):

> About 1840 appeared Augustus Baldwin Longstreet's **Georgia Scenes,** which seems to have had the good fortune of influencing a scene in Mr. Thomas Hardy's *The Trumpet-Major.*

Hooper Alexander, of Atlanta, Georgia, saw no need, after Hardy's death, for the caution of the professors. Writing in the *New Republic* (February 29, 1928), he declared:

> The sketch was beyond question an adaptation, indeed it might be said to be an almost literal lifting, of a passage in the **Georgia Scenes.**

Now the curious fact is that Hardy never saw Longstreet's **Georgia Scenes.** He said as much, and the truth of his statement can be proved. In spite of all that has been said about Longstreet, Hardy was in no way indebted to the American author. The most that can be claimed is that his book must be given credit for the detection of plagiarism on Hardy's part. For plagiarism there was, even though it was not from **Georgia Scenes.**

When *The Critic* first published the charge against Hardy in 1882, it did so under the heading, "Will Mr. Hardy Explain?" When *The Bookman* repeated the charge in 1906, it concluded: "We rather wish that Mr. Hardy would condescend to put in a reply."

As a matter of fact Hardy had by that time replied. But he had done it so guardedly that few persons recognized it as a reply, and perhaps no one among those few fully understood it. When Hardy's successful career as a novelist led his London publishers to issue a new uniform edition of his works, he provided a preface for the new printing of *The Trumpet-Major.* This preface still appears in the modern reprints of the novel, so that all may now read:

> "The drilling scene of the local militia received some additions from an account given in so grave a work as Gifford's 'History of the Wars of the French Revolution' (London, 1817). But on reference to the History I find I was mistaken in supposing the account to be advanced as authentic, or to refer to rural England."

Nothing here, you see, about Longstreet or **Georgia Scenes.** Not a word to attract the attention of any English reader as yet unfamiliar with the charge printed in America. No wonder the editor of *The Critic* was not satisfied. On May 9, 1896, he remarked editorially:

> The new edition of *The Trumpet-Major* contains a preface by the author, dated October, 1895, which contains, however, neither explanation of nor reference to the charge of plagiarism made by *The Critic* on 28 January 1882. . . . Thus the matter stands. Mr. Hardy has ignored the charge.

A month later Hardy broke silence, and on July 4th, 1896, his reply to the renewed attack appeared. He wrote:

> To the Editor of *The Critic*:—
>
> Sir:—My publishers have just sent me a cutting from *The Critic* of May 9, which contains a paragraph on a resemblance between the drilling scene in *The Trumpet-Major* and a scene in an American book published in 1840. I know nothing of the latter work. . . . Some of the details of this particular militia drill . . . were suggested by a similar description in Gifford's *History of the War with Napoleon,* published in London in 1817—a description which I understood to refer to the English peasantry. This book and the Army Regulations . . . were the only printed matter I used. . . .
>
> Yours faithfully,
>
> Thomas Hardy
>
> London, June 9, 1896.

The editor of *The Critic* commented:

> It would seem to be neither impossible nor improbable that Judge Longstreet . . . was indebted to the same original—a most natural method of accounting for the remarkable similarity between the two descriptions. . . . It would be interesting to compare these parallels with the corresponding passage in Gifford's *History of the War with Napoleon.* Unfortunately the book is not to be found at either the Astor or the Lenox Library.

And there *The Critic* dropped the matter, though American literary historians went right on, as we have seen, accusing Hardy of stealing from **Georgia Scenes,** in spite of his specific declaration, "I know nothing of the latter work." Had it, however, been possible for the editor of *The Critic* to obtain a copy of Gifford's book, a careful examination would have shown him that the sketch in the *History of the Wars Occasioned by the French Revolution* (the correct title), in two volumes, London, 1817, was *not* the original. *The Critic*'s surmise that Longstreet and Hardy had both used Gifford as a common source is easily discredited. In presenting a description of the "United States of America, Character of the Americans," etc., C. H. Gifford includes (in Volume II, Book XI, Chapter 9, p. 967) a "Satire upon American Discipline." This he quoted from an unnamed source, carefully putting it all within quotation marks, and declaring that this account of how one Captain Clodpole drilled his men would "give some idea of American tactics." How Thomas Hardy could read this and "understand it to refer to the English peasantry" is hard to fathom. The sketch is indexed on page 1729 of Gifford under "American discipline" and under no other heading.

It is at once obvious that Gifford could not have quoted in London in 1817 a sketch by Longstreet not printed until 1835 in America. Nor was Longstreet copying from Gifford. Neither was quoting the other, but *both were using an anonymous American pamphlet of 1815.* Longstreet, like Gifford, had frankly indicated his borrowing. A footnote to "The Militia Company Drill" stated: "This is from the pen of a friend . . . and published about twenty years ago."

This footnote is now over one hundred years old, but it has been so generally ignored that Longstreet's name has constantly figured in the story of Hardy's plagiarism. Judge Richard H. Clark made the first attempt to give the true author due credit. In *Memoirs* (1898) he declared:

> The discussion of the plagiarism has produced a curiosity to pursue **Georgia Scenes,** and in some of the bookstores it can be found alongside of *The Trumpet-Major.* . . . But Longstreet did not write "The Militia Company Drill." . . . Every old Georgian knows as well who the author was, as if it had been expressly stated. . . . The author was and is known to be Oliver H. Prince.

Professor Trent recorded the same ascription:

> One of the most humorous papers in **Georgia Scenes** is said to have been written by . . . Oliver Hillhouse Prince (1787-1837).
>
> (*Southern Writers,* 1905, p. 122.)

Oliver Prince was a native of Connecticut. Early in life he left his Yankee birthplace and went to Georgia. There he became a lawyer and in the course of time became known as the author of two digests of the laws of Georgia. The second appeared in 1837 and was the only digest of the laws in use in Georgia up to 1851. It is this digest alone which today keeps the name of Oliver Hillhouse Prince in the catalogues of American libraries, but in his own day he was known as the author of a number of anonymous writings. He became quite celebrated for his wit and humor, of which "The Militia Company Drill" gives some illustration. His fate was a sad one. In 1837 he went to New York to superintend the publication of the second edition of his digest, and while returning to his home in Macon he was lost at sea in the wreck off the coast of North Carolina of the new steamship *Home.*

Early evidence of the wide-spread fame of Prince's military sketch is available. According to S. F. Miller (*Bench and Bar of Georgia,* 1858, I, 341), Governor George R. Gilmer wrote, under date of September 4, 1851: "Mr. Prince . . . wrote 'Captain Clodpole . . .' which was republished throughout the United States and in some parts of Europe." *Appleton's Cyclopaedia of American Biography* (1888) recorded: "Oliver Hillhouse Prince . . . was the author of many humorous sketches, one of which, giving an account of a Georgia militia muster, was translated into several languages." This statement was repeated in the *National Cyclopaedia of American Biography* in 1901, and again in *Lamb's Biographical Dictionary of the United States* in 1907. Prince's authorship was also known to the editor of *The Bookman,* who wrote (April, 1906): "In the literary forum, the case is really not Longstreet vs. Hardy, but rather Prince vs. Hardy."

If a copy of Prince's pamphlet were still extant, this half-century-old case might now be regarded as definitely closed. In his biography of Longstreet (1924), John D. Wade reported (p. 179) having seen a copy fifteen years ago, but all recent attempts to locate it have been unavailing. Even so, a recent examination of Gifford and Longstreet side by side in the Harvard Library makes it possible to state with sufficient certainty what happened. The Connecticut Yankee Prince published his "Captain Clodpole" anonymously in 1815. A copy (or a reprint) of it came into the hands of C. H. Gifford in London, and he carefully copied it into his *History* in 1817. Then in 1835, in Georgia, Longstreet also copied it into the pages of the book whose centenary occurred late in 1935. Longstreet's transcription was a careless one; there are seventy-nine verbal departures, some of them sense-destroying, from the text as recorded by Gifford. In 1840 and frequently thereafter Harper & Brothers reprinted **Georgia Scenes** and thus made "The Militia Company Drill" widely enough known, so that

Hardy's unacknowledged adaptation could be easily recognized when it appeared in the pages of *The Trumpet-Major* in 1880.

Hardy professed to regard it all as very insignificant, and wrote *The Critic* "apologizing for occupying your space with such a trivial matter as a few sentences in a novel written twenty years ago." But his "few sentences"—actually about two hundred and sixty words, together with the general purport of three full pages— are today the chief reason for being interested in the recent centennial of a once-famous American book with its chapter by a Connecticut Yankee.

### James B. Meriwether (essay date fall 1982)

SOURCE: Meriwether, James B. "Augustus Baldwin Longstreet: Realist and Artist." *Mississippi Quarterly: The Journal of Southern Culture* 35, no. 4 (fall 1982): 351-64.

[*In the following essay, Meriwether contends that literary scholarship has unjustly categorized Longstreet as a regional writer while ignoring his more significant contributions to the development of American literary realism.*]

Augustus Baldwin Longstreet, author of the 1835 collection of stories *Georgia Scenes,* seems to me to be both misunderstood and underrated today. The two points are connected: if he is generally underrated as a literary artist, as I think he is, it is at least in part because literary critics and literary historians have long tended, and today tend increasingly, to cast him in an inappropriate role. In brief, I want to argue first, that it does Longstreet a major disservice to consider him a "Southwestern humorist," the category in which he is almost universally placed at present; and second, that by relegating him to this category, and then considering only those stories which confirm that categorization, we can very quickly lose sight of the literary artistry which he displays at his best.

Let me begin by very briefly summarizing his career.[1] He was born in Augusta, Georgia, in 1790. Both his parents came from New Jersey. Following in the footsteps of John C. Calhoun, with whom his family was acquainted, young Longstreet attended for four years (1808-1811) the distinguished school at Willington, in upcountry South Carolina, of which Moses Waddel, later President of the University of Georgia, was head; he was admitted to the junior class at Yale College and graduated with the class of 1813; subsequently he studied law with Judge Tapping Reeve in Litchfield, Con-

necticut, and returning to Georgia, passed his bar examination in 1815. He was elected to the General Assembly of Georgia in 1821, was elected Judge of the Superior Court in 1822, and in 1824 ran for Congress.

Grief at the death of his first-born son caused him to withdraw from the congressional race, and not long afterward he joined the Methodist church. In 1829 he was licensed to preach. In 1833 he sought, unsuccessfully, appointment to a professorship at the University of Georgia. In 1833-34 he published in the Milledgeville, Georgia, *Southern Recorder* eight of the sketches and stories which were to go into *Georgia Scenes,* using the two pseudonyms "Hall" and "Baldwin." Later in 1834 he republished these sketches in the Augusta *State Rights' Sentinel,* which he had bought and was now editing. Later in 1834 and in 1835 he continued the series with original contributions to the *Sentinel,* and late in 1835 he brought it out in book form, printed and published at the press of his own newspaper. The book preserved the two pseudonyms of the newspaper sketches, and further concealed Longstreet's connection with the work by identifying the author on the title-page only as "a native Georgian." During this same period, 1834-1836, he used another pseudonym, "Bob Short," for a series of brief political satires in the columns of the *Sentinel.*

Though he sold his newspaper in 1836, for several years after the original publication of *Georgia Scenes* Longstreet continued to bring out more stories, most of them identified as belonging to the same series and intended for a revised and expanded edition. Some of them appeared in *The Augusta Mirror* and in *The Southern Miscellany,* both edited by his friend and former associate at the *Sentinel,* William Tappan Thompson; others appeared, later, in *The Magnolia,* when it was under the editorship of William Gilmore Simms. However, in 1839 he had become junior pastor in a Methodist church in Augusta, and later that year he became president of Emory College in Oxford, Georgia—the first of four college presidencies he was to hold in his career, including the University of Mississippi and South Carolina College. A second edition of *Georgia Scenes* appeared in 1840 in New York; in a prefatory note the publishers, Harper and Brothers, stated that they had "been unable to prevail upon the author to revise the work." Though by this time Longstreet was widely known to be the author, the pseudonym of "a native Georgian" was preserved on the title-page of this second edition.

Longstreet's abundant literary energies were largely devoted to educational, religious, and political writings for the remainder of his career, but he did publish in

1864 a novel, **Master William Mitten,** greatly inferior to *Georgia Scenes* as fiction, save for the interest supplied by several chapters concerning the school at Willington.

Though there is much to be learned about Longstreet (and his times) from his later writings, nothing that he wrote after **"The Shooting-Match,"** the last sketch of the 1835 *Georgia Scenes,* can be said to enhance his literary reputation or increase our respect for his abilities as an artist.

Let me deal now with the problem of defining Longstreet's work—or his best work. If he is mis-defined and mis-categorized and mis-pigeonholed by being called a Southwestern humorist, wherein does the error lie? First, we might ask, what is Southwest about Georgia? An Atlantic seaboard state, one of the original thirteen colonies, is it to be usefully classified as Southwestern? Perhaps the western portion of the state, in its early days, had enough in common with old Southwestern states like Alabama, Mississippi, and Louisiana to make this classification attractive—but Longstreet belongs to Augusta, on the Savannah River, the easternmost portion of the state; and further, his orientation was even more eastward: towards South Carolina and Connecticut. I grant that there *is* a perspective from which all Georgia—and the non-seaboard areas of South and North Carolina and Virginia too—can be considered Southwestern. New York City might afford such a perspective—or Richmond, where Edgar Allan Poe, reviewing *Georgia Scenes* for the *Southern Literary Messenger,* praised Longstreet's depiction of Southwestern characters and characteristics.[2] But we should not confine ourselves, today, to the geographical (or chronological) perspective of the young editor of the *Southern Literary Messenger*—and we might recall, too, that if Poe referred to some aspects of *Georgia Scenes* as Southwestern, he also was careful to apply the adjectives "Southern" and "Georgian" to it, and to emphasize the ways in which the book deals with the universal rather than with the local or regional.

There is an unfortunate tendency to think of Southwestern humor as a literary category so firmly centered in the old Southwest that it is therefore proper to include in it a variety of figures who are only marginally Southwestern, if at all, geographically speaking. The truth is that the origins of this humor, like the language of the plain people in which it is grounded, is to be found in the Southeast, from Virginia to South Carolina.[3] If eventually it flourished most notably in the more western of the Southern states, there were still a number of Southeasterners, including William Gilmore Simms, who played an important part in it. Even George Washington

Harris, we might recall, was from *eastern* Tennessee. I do not propose that we establish a separate category of Southeastern humor, to go with Southwestern; but it seems to me more appropriate to refer to simply as Southern humor, the humor written by Longstreet and Simms, Harris, and all their like. At any rate, I see no benefit to be derived from calling *Georgia Scenes* an example of Southwestern humor; if one needs to subdivide the American humor, or Southern humor, of that period, the proper category to put it in would be backwoods or upcountry humor. (I shall make only one brief comment here about the even worse misrepresentation of Longstreet that is achieved by calling him a "frontier" humorist; the region of Augusta, Georgia, in the period from 1790 to 1835 had its problems, but it wasn't anywhere close to the frontier.)

But though the category Southern humor is broader than Southwestern humor, it is still too narrow for Longstreet, as Longstreet himself, and his contemporaries and reviewers and early readers, were all certainly aware. Poe did praise the book's humor, of course,—but his remarks are generally quoted out of context—out of the context of the entire review, that is, which repeatedly praises *Georgia Scenes* for its faithfulness in delineating the customs and language and characters of the plain people of Georgia. Mingled with his comments on the humor are such phrases as "dramatic vigor" and "raciness and vigor" (the narration); "inimitable force, fidelity and picturesque effect" (the descriptions); and "forcible, accurate and original generic delineations of real existences. . . ." Poe saw immediately that the humor was inseparable from the more serious intent of the work, referring to its "joint humor and verisimilitude," and to its "sly humor, wherein intense observation of character is disguised by simplicity of relation," which reminded Poe of *The Spectator.*

Longstreet himself might well have thought that he had made his intentions perfectly clear in the preface to his book, where he makes no mention of humor at all, and stresses his purpose as being that of a social historian, recording the fast-changing manners and ways of the people of his time and place.[4]

He made his purpose even plainer, though, in a letter he wrote to T. W. White, owner and publisher of the *Southern Literary Messenger,* in response to Poe's review (which Longstreet clearly thought had been written by White himself).[5]

> I am continuing the Scenes, as I can snatch time from my pressing avocations; and hope to have another volumn, of larger size, completed by the close of the year. The leading object of the **Georgia Scenes,** is to enable those who came after us, to see us *precisely as we are.*

If my life be spared; they will [be] carried through all ranks of society. I have often desired to see the Greeks and Romans, as they saw each other—To be present at their amusements—hear their wits and wags—enter their dwellings—see their tables—witness their paternal and maternal government—hear their children—look into their schools and &c. &c. The time will come perhaps, when the same desire will be felt to know all about us; and to gratify that desire, I am now writing.

Now let me quote from an important review of the second edition of *Georgia Scenes,* one which is much less well known than Poe's, unfortunately. This was by Longstreet's associate William Tappan Thompson. It appeared in the *Augusta Mirror,* which he was then editing, in 1840.[6]

Thompson expressed regret that the second edition had not been revised and expanded, as it had been the author's original intention to do. Since Longstreet had entered the ministry, said Thompson, he

seems to have renounced all fellowship with this much admired offspring of his genius, and to have relinquished his professed design of carrying out his sketches of real life and character to all grades and conditions of society. . . .

He went on to say that

We understand the author has by him several numbers finished or unfinished, which have never been published. We earnestly entreat him to favor the public with these in the third edition. Having long known him, having labored in his office for several years, and been intimate with him for many since, we know from his character that there is nothing in the unpublished numbers which can savor of immorality; and we hope he will give them to the public. We learn that he says they are too light and trifling for his present station and calling; and this would silence us, if they were mere *fancy sketches,* as some of the northern critics seem to think. But they are not—they are faithful delineations of real scenes and characters. . . .

Thompson quoted Longstreet as having said that he intended, in a revised *Georgia Scenes,* to describe the character of the countryside itself:

Now I propose to exhibit Georgia just as it is; not only as to population and character, but as to terrestrial scenery, so that those who come after us may know not only the changes which have taken place in the character and dialect of the people, but in the face of the country.

Not a word here, you note, about humor: instead, Longstreet, from the first edition to the plans for a third, in his preface to the book and as quoted by his close friend and professional associate, emphasizes that his purpose is to be a realist—or a realistic social historian.

Let me now comment briefly upon the literary technique of *Georgia Scenes,* in justification of my statement that Longstreet's artistry has not yet received its due.[7] Certain features of his skill as a writer were recognized from the beginning, of course, with Poe's review leading the way in showing appreciation of his skill in dialogue and of the realism and humor with which he rendered the characters of his plain people. But Longstreet deserves praise, even higher praise, for two further strengths as a writer, two elements in his artistry, which have been generally ignored or not commented upon by even his warmest admirers, from Poe and Thompson to the present. These two strengths of *Georgia Scenes* are first, the handling of point of view; and second, structure—that is, the structure of *Georgia Scenes* as a book, as at least a relatively unified whole. These two elements in Longstreet's artistry are closely connected; in fact, they function together as almost a single device for giving cumulative point, progression, and finally, a considerable degree of unity, to this book of fiction. But let me begin by discussing the narrative point of view by itself.

Or rather, his narrative points of view by themselves. In his preface, Longstreet calls attention to an element in his work which is of great importance, if we are to understand what he was doing—though its significance for the book as a whole appears to have been generally overlooked. Longstreet tells us that when he first wrote and published the sketches which went into the volume, he was "extremely desirous" of concealing his authorship; and that in order to accomplish his purpose, he had used two pseudonyms. For sketches in which men are the principal actors, he says, he uses the name Hall; for those in which women are the most prominent, he writes under the name Baldwin. A third pseudonym occurs in the book: Timothy Crabshaw, which is signed to the sketch "The Militia Company Drill." This is not by Longstreet, he explains in his preface, but by a friend; it was included in order to fill out the portrait of middle Georgia Longstreet was attempting to provide in the book as a whole—and we can assume that he found it sufficiently consonant with the rest of the book, in style, in point of view, and in subject matter, to add it confidently to his own work.[8] Granted Longstreet's historical purpose in writing the book, we can appreciate his intention in so including this piece by his fellow lawyer Oliver Hillhouse Prince. But at the same time we might regret that its inclusion may serve as an excuse to undervalue the unity of *Georgia Scenes* and to distract the reader from seeing how carefully Longstreet was working, in the book as a whole, to give it coherence through the narratives—and characterizations—of Hall and Baldwin.

Omitting "The Militia Company Drill," we have eighteen sketches or stories in the volume: twelve by Hall, six by Baldwin. Longstreet's prefatory comment about the division of the sketches between the two narrators is a little misleading; for not only is Hall given twice as many of the sketches as is Baldwin; Hall begins the volume with **"Georgia Theatrics"** and ends it with **"The Shooting-Match,"** besides having a majority of the best of the sketches, including the most elaborate and thematically most complex of them. The six "Baldwin" sketches, by their subject matter and by the persona of their narrator, serve as occasional interludes, used for change of pace and variety of subject matter. The dominant figure of the book is Hall; his friend Baldwin—for the two are acquainted, and appear together in several of the sketches—Hall's friend Baldwin simply serves as a foil to the ultimately much more masculine and successful Lyman Hall.

In one of the Baldwin sketches, **"The Song,"** Baldwin refers to Hall as his room-mate (p. 72), though apparently this arrangement didn't last very long, for there is no reference to it elsewhere. Hall is apparently a lawyer; Baldwin emphatically is not (p. 84). The friends are linked by their common interest in human character and social history but are dissimilar in some important ways. Hall is more than a little prudish, compared to Baldwin; in **"The Song"** Baldwin notes his friend's disapproval of Miss Crump's decolleté and his subsequent mutterings about the need for more "republican simplicity" (p. 68). Both like music; but Baldwin describes himself as "extravagantly fond" of it (p. 65), and Miss Crump's pianistic and vocal villainies drive him out of the house, while Hall is still able to endure them. Hall is less sensitive, more stable emotionally than Baldwin; yet in the earlier chapters he is shown to be somewhat squeamish, as his reaction to the violence and cruelty of **"The Horse Swap"** and **"The Fight"** makes clear. Baldwin is the more moody and emotional; at one point Hall asks a singer for a "lively air" to cheer up his friend, who had been strongly affected by a pathetic song. Early in the book Baldwin reveals a better sense of humor than does Hall; but his sensitivity leads him toward misanthropy, and frequently he is too easily discouraged and cast down, as he is in **"The Dance,"** for example. When his old sweetheart doesn't recognize him, in fact doesn't even recall his name, his pleasure in the innocent, rustic simplicity of the occasion is quite spoiled. In his last sketch of the volume, **"A Sage Conversation,"** Baldwin is reduced to being a passive observer and hearer of the conversation among three "aged matrons"—a conversation elicited by his friend Ned Brace's mention of "marriage" between two men. Homosexuality, transvestitism, seduction and betrayal are the dark underlying themes of this sketch,

skillfully and delicately handled (of necessity) by Longstreet, and Baldwin makes his exit from the book on a note of futility and passivity.

As soon as we perceive Hall to be the major character of the book as well as its chief narrator, we can understand the principal device used to give unity to the volume. For Hall changes and grows during the work. In **"Georgia Theatrics"** he begins as a greenhorn as well as a spectator of events. Professor Leo Lemay has made a recent comment on this which I take pleasure in quoting. He refers to **"Georgia Theatrics"** as a parable, and a masterpiece, and says that its

> real meaning lies in Longstreet's satire of the horrified persona [that is, Hall] who expects to see an example of the violent, eye-gouging fights that exist in his imagination and who discovers that the fighting sounds emanate from a lone adolescent boy acting out how he could have fought. Longstreet's underlying target is human nature: the reader tends to identify with the persona and thus to reveal his own yearning for violence. Longstreet (correctly, I believe) thought such an appetite was to be found in all readers, although his more obvious targets were those people who, like the persona, believed in the especial violence of the Old South.[9]

Hall, in this first sketch, is making his way on horseback along a country road when he hears the sounds of the imitation battle that so misleads him. In the last sketch, **"The Shooting-Match"**—for me, with **"The Turn Out,"** one of the two best pieces of the book—in **"The Shooting-Match,"** Hall is also making his way on horseback along a country road. But this is a different part of Georgia; and almost a quarter of a century has elapsed. Hall is now a mature man, who reveals his total understanding of the ways of the country people, especially those folkways that govern the reaction of a rural community to a stranger. He proves himself to be very much a man of the people by the way he handles himself in an encounter with Billy Curlew, a back-countryman who is on his way to a shooting match and who, when convinced that Hall won't disgrace his host, invites him to attend and participate. At the match Hall, though out of practice, shoots well enough to win second place among a group of skilled marksmen. He modestly pleads good luck; and perhaps luck was involved, too: but Hall knows shooting as well as he does shooters, and since on two previous occasions he had shown his skill in "lucky" shots, we may fairly conclude that Hall is a born shooter, a natural good shot. The story and the book end on a happy note: Billy Curlew and his friends tell Hall that they'll vote for him if he "offers" for anything. They have sized him up, correctly, as a man of means and education who has not lost the common touch. Longstreet makes it clear that the judgment of these people is to be respected and if Hall will accept such responsibilities he will be an able and successful public official.

In addition to the unity provided by the principal narrator and his related function as a character who moves from the role of passive and naive observer to active participant in the life of his people, Longstreet develops several related themes which bind together many of the separately plotted sketches. Among these I have time to mention only what seem to me the two most important—though they are so closely related that they might be better considered two aspects of a single strand of thematic material, which Longstreet weaves throughout all the sketches, from first to last. These two themes (or two aspects of one theme) are Longstreet's view of human nature; and his belief in progress. *Georgia Scenes* provides abundant evidence that Longstreet thought that impulses towards savagery and violence were to be found not far from the surface in many men, perhaps most of them; and that it is the function of human laws and institutions to restrain, discipline, and civilize these impulses and to make good citizens out of barbarians. His chief method of showing the possibility of progress is to trace, as he does throughout the book, the way in which man's natural violence and aggressiveness can be properly brought under control. Thus the unrestrained pride and competitiveness, barbarity and cruelty of man to man in **"The Fight,"** early in the volume, give way to the organized sport of **"The Gander Pulling,"** still cruel to the animal world but surely an improvement over human eye-gouging and nose-biting; and after the mockery of militarism in "The Militia Company Drill" we end with the elaborate sport, governed by strict rules (including several varieties of verbal gamesmanship) that provides the substance of **"The Shooting-Match."**

Longstreet, however, is always too much the realist to sentimentalize his people, whether individuals or sexes or communities or a whole society. **"The Turn Out,"** for example, celebrates the role of personal example and formal education in the making of future citizens; but this story of sturdy republican ideals in the year 1790 is set in a later narrative context which enables Hall to give a grim description of the wasteland which eroded soil and poor stewardship of land have made of the once fruitful fields around the old schoolhouse. The admirable Captain Griffen had predicted in 1790 "These Lands . . . will never wear out. Where they lie level, they will be as good fifty years hence as they are now." Returning to the scene forty-two years later, Hall finds "many a deep-washed gully . . . and all around was barren, dreary, and cheerless" (p. 76). The contrast is more than a commentary upon mutability and the uncertainty of progress; revealing Captain Griffen as a

very poor prophet, Hall also reveals himself as a man who can accept such changes without the bitterness and despair to which his friend Baldwin yields.

This is the darker side of the picture, or the warning that Longstreet offers, occasionally didactically but usually indirectly, to those men and women who are unrealistic or irresponsible, whether as private citizens or public officials.

*Georgia Scenes* is primarily a work of fictional realism, secondarily one of humor—though it might be more accurate to call it a work of realism which often employs the various means of humor toward the ends of realism. It is an ambitious and an accomplished book, the artistry of which is easy to overlook—especially if one is familiar only with excerpts. Taken as a whole the work shows particular skill in its handling of narration and narrative distance, with the double focus of the Hall/ Baldwin narrators and their growth or change used to mirror and to judge the progress of this particular part of the republic, in its first half-century. Point of view is treated with great complexity and sophistication—some of which may be less than deliberate and conscious on the part of the author. The gradual evolution of the volume must inevitably have produced a certain amount of complexity, in the contrasting characterizations of the two narrators and their relationship with each other, not part of the original scheme. But even if this complexity is a by-product of the carrying-out of the plan of the volume, it cannot be overlooked as a significant feature of the finished work. The author had the fortune to be working in a literary tradition of great richness and resource: an oral tradition of tale-telling which made available to him a great many devices of narration that were firmly rooted in the English vernacular long before tales were told in middle Georgia. And Longstreet, we remember, had the reputation all his life of being an exceptionally good *raconteur.*

In a general essay on American humor, a few years ago, James M. Cox called *Georgia Scenes* "as 'good' a book as Hawthorne's *Twice-Told Tales,* published two years later. It has as much art, imagination, perception, and insight as Hawthorne's early work possesses."[10] I agree, of course; and I will go further and say that it is not only as good a work of fiction as Hawthorne's first collection; as a whole, it is at least as good a book of fiction as had yet been written in America—that is, by the year 1835.

Later on, not much later on, to be sure, there would be works of fiction by Hawthorne, Poe, and Melville that would be artistically superior to Longstreet's book; and the sum total of the fictional accomplishment of a Cooper or a Simms would of course be very much greater. But in 1835 Longstreet was a rather lonely pioneer of literary realism, one whose accomplishment was not easy to measure, then—or, apparently, since; certainly his artistic superiority to most of his immediate predecessors and contemporaries has not been more readily apparent to later generations. He lies buried in St. Peter's Cemetery, in Oxford, Mississippi, not far from the grave of William Faulkner, another Southern writer who made notable artistic and technical contributions to our literature by his handling of point of view, and by the making of a unified work of fiction from a collection of seemingly independent stories. I am not being facetious when I suggest that we may learn something from thinking of Longstreet and Faulkner together—or that the accidental juxtaposition of their graves may remind us of a literary relationship that is not in the least accidental. For Faulkner learned a great deal from Longstreet and the other antebellum Southern writers who, after *Georgia Scenes,* worked with the rich Southern materials of the small farm and the small town, the yeoman farmer and his urban opposite number. And in turn perhaps we can learn something from the author of *As I Lay Dying* and *The Hamlet* about how to read Longstreet—read him, as so many generations of critics have not, with a deep appreciation of his best qualities, qualities which for so long were out of critical fashion, but which we have no excuse to overlook now. Perhaps then we can hope for sustained critical examinations of Longstreet on the high level of those incidental comments by Leo Lemay and James Cox; and our literary histories and textbooks will come closer to doing justice to the deceptively simple-seeming accomplishment of *Georgia Scenes,* with its dark but undespairing view of human nature, its vigorous and tough-minded realism, its sophistication in handling narrative point of view and thematic unity in an episodic book of fiction, and finally, its celebration of the Southern plain people and their folkways and their humor and above all their language, as being appropriate for a work of high literary ambition.

### Notes

1. There is no adequate biography of Longstreet. John Donald Wade's pioneering *Augustus Baldwin Longstreet: A Study of the Development of Culture in the South,* New York, 1924 (a Columbia University doctoral dissertation directed by W. P. Trent), is highly inaccurate and badly outdated. J. R. Scafidel's "The Letters of Augustus Baldwin Longstreet" (diss. University of South Carolina 1977), provides essential biographical and bibliographical data in its notes; see also the "Chronology," pp. xx-xxiii. Dr. Scafidel contributed the biographical sketch of Longstreet to *Lives of Mis-*

*sissippi Authors, 1817-1967,* ed. James B. Lloyd, University Press of Mississippi, 1981. See also his "Augustus Baldwin Longstreet: Native Augustan," in *Richmond County History,* 2 (summer 1979), 19-29; and "A Georgian in Connecticut: A. B. Longstreet's Legal Education," in *Georgia Historical Quarterly,* 61 (fall 1977), 222-231. See also the biographical sketch by Kimball King in *Dictionary of Literary Biography,* III, "Antebellum Writers in New York and the South," ed. Joel Myerson, Detroit, 1979, pp. 204-210.

2. Review of *Georgia Scenes* in the *Southern Literary Messenger,* 2 (March 1836), 287-292. Scafidel, pp. 98-101, includes an important letter from Longstreet to T. W. White, the publisher of the *Messenger,* whom Longstreet obviously takes to be the author of this anonymous review. Disagreeing with Longstreet, I follow several generations of Poe scholars in attributing the review to Poe.

3. Not only can all the elements now generally accepted as defining "Southwestern humor" be found in the old Southeast; most of them can be traced further to the old Northeast, to New England and eastern Canada, and thence across the Atlantic to Great Britain.

4. Longstreet's brief preface is an important critical document in its own right, even apart from its significance for *Georgia Scenes.* He defends the realism of the work, including occasional coarseness of language, on the grounds that he is writing, as a historian, for posterity, rather than for his contemporaries. And he occasionally has his narrators, in the sketches themselves, make the same points he did in the preface. Baldwin, speaking of his intentions in telling "A Sage Conversation," says "Certainly the amusement of the readers of my own times is not the leading object of it, or of any of the "Georgia Scenes;" forlorn as may be the hope that their main object will ever be answered" (p. 187).

5. See fn. 2. In the letter Longstreet also calls attention to a serious printer's error in the preface; where he had intended to say that his "art," in the sketches, "consists of nothing more than fancifully combining real incidents & characters," the printer has him declaring that the sketches themselves consist of nothing more than such "fanciful combinations" (Scafidel, pp. 99-100).

6. No copy of this issue of the *Augusta Mirror* has been located; the passages from the review quoted here are taken from the *Southern Literary Messenger,* 4 (July 1840), 572-574, which reprinted it.

7. Virtually nothing has been written about Longstreet's specific literary skills and achievement in *Georgia Scenes,* though he has not lacked for general praise. I am indebted to seminar discussions with a number of my graduate students at the University of South Carolina, over the years, and particularly to Mr. George Ellison and Dr. J. R. Scafidel, which have helped to shape my ideas about Longstreet.

8. Longstreet, *Georgia Scenes,* New York, 1840, p. iv. I have used this edition (hereafter cited in the text) for convenience, since the original 1835 edition, though textually superior, is very rare. A new edition, based on a careful study of the *State Rights' Sentinel* newspaper texts and the original 1835 book version, is badly needed. See J. R. Scafidel's review of the 1975 Beehive Press edition, *Mississippi Quarterly,* 29 (winter 1975-76), 136-142.

9. Lemay, review of *Violence and Culture in the Antebellum South,* by Dickson D. Bruce, Jr., in *Early American Literature,* 15 (1980), 199.

10. James M. Cox, "Humor and America: The Southwestern Bear Hunt, Mrs. Stowe, and Mark Twain," *Sewanee Review,* 83 (October-December 1975), 588.

## Wilson Snipes (essay date winter 1985-86)

SOURCE: Snipes, Wilson. "The Humor of Longstreet's Persona: Abram Baldwin in *Georgia Scenes.*" *Studies in American Humor* 4, no. 4 (winter 1985-86): 277-89.

[*In the following essay, Snipes examines how Longstreet employs the character of Abram Baldwin as a means of transforming tragic elements of human life into satire.*]

In *Georgia Scenes* Augustus Baldwin Longstreet, frequently identified as the father of Southwest humor, created the personae Abram Baldwin and Lyman Hall, the first a tragic figure and primarily a social satirist, the second a realist, romantic, and humorist. Longstreet used the Baldwin persona for six of the sketches, mostly devoted to the social life of the times with one, **"A Sage Conversation,"** in part devoted to a practical joke played by the character Ned Brace. In twelve of the sketches Longstreet used Hall as a persona, sketches in the main devoted to the habits and customs of the rural and frontier people of Georgia. Exceptions include **"The Character of a Native Georgian"** which portrays a series of practical jokes played in Savannah by Ned Brace,

**"The Turf"** in which Hall is accompanied by Baldwin to a horse race and observes the behavior of ladies and gentlemen as well as others of the society, **"The Fox Hunt"** in which Hall uses himself as the butt of humor when he discovers that his romanticized anticipations of the pleasures of a fox hunt are contrary to the realities, and **"The Debating Society"** which he acknowledges is not strictly a Georgia scene but is introduced since the "chief actors" in it are Georgians.[1] Longstreet's reputation as a Southwest humorist rests primarily on the rural and frontier sketches signed by Hall, since those by Baldwin are usually dismissed as little more than Addisonian imitations.[2]

In the "Preface" to the 1835 edition of **Georgia Scenes,** Longstreet is explicit about the distinction between the two narrators:

> From private considerations, I was extremely desirous of concealing the author, and the more effectually to do so, I wrote under two signatures. *Hall* is the writer of those sketches in which *men* appear as the principal actors and *Baldwin* of those in which *women* are the predominant figures.[3]

To identify Hall with those sketches devoted to men and Baldwin with those devoted to women does little toward characterizing and defining the personae, but it establishes the author's commitment to two distinct characters, personalities, and perspectives of "the peculiarities of the age" (pp. 116, 147).[4] Unfortunately this distinction has been neglected or minimized generally in Longstreet criticism.[5] The following remarks will be devoted to a brief examination of the humorous nature of the persona Abram Baldwin.

Baldwin describes himself as a person with "a native propensity to extract amusement from all that passes under [his] observation," but he is more definite when he states that the amusement of the readers of his own day "is not the leading object" "of any of the **Georgia Scenes**; [sic] forlorn as may be the hope that their main object will ever be answered" (pp. 172-3). Perhaps the main object of Baldwin's purpose is better expressed through a dialogue between Baldwin and Hall in **"The Turf,"** a dialogue written by Hall. In this sketch Baldwin invites Hall to accompany him to the local horse races, an event of no interest to either. Baldwin explains to Hall that their joint observations will provide "many instructing, interesting, or amusing incidents" which neither alone might perceive. But his strongest argument is intellectual and didactic: "I visit it to acquire a knowledge of the human character, as it exhibits itself in the various scenes of life, and with the hope of turning the knowledge thus acquired to some good account" (p. 138). Despite Baldwin's disavowal of amusement as his primary purpose in writing scenes, readers have obviously found their greatest enjoyment in the humor, the "native propensity" of the narrator, not in the moral aims which may be Baldwin's "forlorn" main object.

The subjects and situations Baldwin treats are much more limited than those considered by Hall.[6] In fact, in three of the six sketches, **"The Dance," "The Song,"** and **"The Ball,"** Baldwin makes himself and his reactions the focus and subject of the humor. In **"The 'Charming Creature' as a Wife"** he focuses on the life and fatal marriage of his nephew George Baldwin, but his presence as narrator is pronounced throughout the sketch not only in his way of telling the story but through his comments and judgments. So too in **"A Sage Conversation"** he establishes his voice and attitudes as the standard against which the contrasting conversations of the aged, rural matrons will be considered. Only in **"The Mother and Her Child"** does he allow the sketch to proceed primarily by its own weight, but even here he establishes an overview, that the mother's way of talking to the child is an example of "gibberish," an illustration and exhibition of "one of the peculiarities of the age." Baldwin's character and personality essentially dominate his sketches. Beneath this humorous domination may lie pathos and tragedy, perhaps Baldwin's main object, perceptions of the superficiality of human nature and the human condition; but on the more obvious level the sketches are amusing, funny, ridiculous, satirical, ironic, for we rarely lose sight of Baldwin, as essayist and narrator selecting details, making judgments, describing his own thoughts and feelings, and directing responses.

As narrators, both Baldwin and Hall use themselves as objects of humor, both relate a Ned Brace story, both relate observed experiences, both find amusement in dialect stories, both satirize the manners and habits of the ladies and gentlemen of their own society, and both are self-revelatory in their ways of telling stories. But of the two, Baldwin is the more personal, more autobiographical, more emotional; he is more a disconsolate observer and participant than a member of society. A social critic, some of his sketches have a bite absent from those of Hall, his sense of humor mitigated in part by his self-perception that his life has been a failure, "little more than an unbroken scene of disaster, disappointment, vexation and toil" (p. 9). Baldwin is explicit in **"The Dance"** in developing this pessimistic view of his own life: "And now, when I was too old to enjoy the pleasures which I had discarded, I found that my aim [for Fame] was absolutely hopeless; and that my pursuits had only unfit me for the humbler walks of life, and to exclude me from the higher" (pp. 9-10). A sense of tragedy underlies his humorous exterior. He perceives himself as one who is outside society, a con-

dition brought on by his own failings, a person not comfortable with himself nor with the life of those around him. From this perspective his sense of humor should be considered.

He is a highly opinionated narrator, expressing strong views on the kind of music he enjoys, the character of women who are "charming creatures," the kinds of dancing appropriate for society, the proper decorum people should observe in polite and courteous relationships, the horrors of drinking. He even disdains Hall's "rude" comment on the extent to which a woman should or should not "expose an unmantled bosom" (p. 57). For example, he dislikes French music, detests Italian music, and finds German music "scarcely sufferable," but he enjoys the music of Scotland and Ireland, that of Burns, Ramsay, and Tannahill (pp. 55-6). He regrets that people forego their own judgments of what music is excellent while deferring to German, French, and Italian performers, *the most expert,* as if they "must be the best judges of music, and must make the best selections. . . ." He ironically finds this "fashionable music of the day" "tolerable; just as has [the society found] the use of tobacco or ardent spirits." Baldwin knows his own mind.

He is also a reflective man, ruminating over his past life and failures, recalling with affection and respect the dead Negro fiddler, Billy Porter, comparing the dancers of a frontier county with those of his own generation, expressing regret that Tannahill's publishers had neglected the composer's genius. In **"The 'Charming Creature' as a Wife,"** to illustrate, he recalls the life of his nephew from youth to death and draws a moral from this life, that no man should marry a self-centered woman. Throughout the sketches he introduces details and events from his earlier life to enhance his perceptions of the present.

But Baldwin portrays himself primarily as a sensitive social critic and satirist, as a man who finds in the day-to-day actions, incidents, and situations of life a failure to recognize and express meaningful and significant human and humane values. He is a kindly and perceptive man—witness his serious praise of Miss Mary Williams' voice in **"The Song"** and his idealized portrait of his brother's wife in **"A 'Charming Creature' as a Wife"**—but far more frequently his observations and comments carry the bite of satire and criticism.

The two characters he develops most fully in his sketches are Miss Aurelia Emma Theodosia Augusta Crump in **"The Song"** and Miss Evelina Caroline Smith in **"The 'Charming Creature' as a Wife,"** the latter portrait drawn as a combination of moral condemnation, satire, and bitterness. His judgment of Miss Smith, who ruined his nephew's life, is that she was, even before her marriage, "an accomplished hypocrite, with all her other foibles" (p. 74). At the conclusion of this sketch, he states his moral thesis: ". . . let the fate of my poor nephew [who "died the drunkard's death"] be a warning to mothers against bringing up their daughters to be 'CHARMING CREATURES'"(p. 96). In **"The Dance"** he identifies a charming creature as a girl from the city who is "weakly, sickly, delicate, useless, affected" as well as "charming" (p. 5).

Baldwin's most devastating satire of such "creatures" is reserved for Miss Crump. In his satire Baldwin comments on everything about her from her Philadelphia musical education to her barnyard performance at an evening's "entertainment." She is socially pretentious, a reluctant performer at the piano until her mother intervenes, a young woman who affects a preference for reading Dante and Racine over practicing at the piano, a person of no musical or vocal talent, ultimately making her a perfect creature for Baldwin's satire, a person with no self-recognition of her limitations and inabilities.[7]

Baldwin expresses his contempt for her musical education in the Theophrastian names he invents for her teachers in Philadelphia: "Madam Piggisqueaki, who was a pupil of Ma'm'selle Crokifroggietta, who had sung with Madam Catalani; and she had taken lessons on the piano from Seignor Buzzifussi, who had played with Paganini" (p. 58). With the exception of the composer and violinist Paganini (1782-1840) Baldwin's prejudices against Miss Crump's musical training under Italian, French, and Spanish teachers offer a satirical heritage: pigs squeak, frogs croak, insects buzz.

Miss Crump lives up to her background and conceit. Her singing is "compounded of a dry cough, a grunt, a hiccough, and a whisper" (p. 59). Baldwin represents her initial playing as a horse-race and battle between her right and left hands, each attempting to overcome the other. Later in her performance she "charged the piano": "She boxed it, she clawed it, she raked it, she scraped it" (p. 60). To this she added her "unearthly howls": "she screamed, she howled, she yelled, cackled. . . ." Mr. Jenkins from Philadelphia and Nick Truck from Lincoln County, who had once been to Bordeaux, found Miss Crump's performance transforming, but Baldwin "in convulsions" ran home from the scene, "took sixty drops of laudanum [enough opium to knock him out for a considerable length of time] and fell asleep" (p. 60).

Later Baldwin dreams that Miss Crump as Hecate pursues him and commands beasts and birds to tear him to pieces, but his friend Hall awakens him from this dream,

and he learns that Miss Crump is still playing after midnight, with Jenkins and Truck still transported. Baldwin completes the sketch, upon learning that she was playing yet another Italian piece, and with a swoon "heard no more," his satire complete.

As a satirist Baldwin allows his imagination to work with realities, offering images that must be seen through his eyes and mind as he extrapolates and transforms each scene. He does not provide a "realistic" description or image, but a transformed one, a mixture of the fanciful and the imaginary with the real, as Longstreet described the overall method in the "Preface."[8] At every turn Baldwin's character and personality, as the teller of the tale, offers an implied or unstated norm to which the fanciful, imaginary, and real are held in varying relationships, thereby offering a dual or multiple viewpoint for purposes of contrast, incongruity, exaggeration, satire, and irony.

The distinction between Baldwin as humorist and Baldwin as satirist may be illustrated by two lengthy but necessary descriptions he offers of the boys and girls dancing in one of the frontier counties, from **"The Dance,"** and the ladies and gentlemen attending a ball "in the city of _____," from **"The Ball"**—the former dancing a "good old republican reel," the latter a "cotillon," the reel of Scottish, the cotillon of French ancestry. In describing the dancing of the rural boys and girls Baldwin draws humorous parallels between the dancers of his youth and those he observed at the Jackson dance:

> Jim Johnson kept up the double shuffle from the beginning to the end of the reel: and here was Jim over again in Sammy Tant. Bill Martin always set to his partner with the same step; and a very curious step it was. He brought his right foot close behind his left, and with it performed precisely the motion of the thumb in cracking that insect which Burns has immortalized; then moved his right back, threw his weight upon it, brought his left behind it, and *cracked* with that as before; and so on alternately. Just so did Bill Kemp, to a nail. Bob Simons danced for all the world like a "Suple Jack" (or, as we commonly call it, a *Suple* Sawney"), when the string is pulled with varied force, at intervals of seconds: and so did *Jake* Slack. Davy Moore went like a suit of clothes upon a clothing line on a windy day: and here was his antitype in Ned Clark. Rhoda Noble swam through the reel like a cork on wavy waters; always giving two or three pretty little perchbite *diddles* as she rose from a coupee: Nancy Ware was her very self. Becky Lewis made a business of dancing; she disposed of her part as quick as possible, stopped dead short as soon as she got through, and looked as sober as a judge all the time; even so did Chloe Dawson. I used to tell Polly Jackson that Becky's countenance, when she closed a dance, always seemed to say, "Now, if you want any more dancing, you may do it yourself."

(p. 8)

In this description Baldwin is nostalgic and sentimental, while humorously but kindly observing the dancers before him: for example, Davy Moore's movements are like those of "a suit of clothes upon a clothing line on a windy day," those of Rhoda Noble like those of "a cork on wavy water, and Becky Lewis through her movements" making "a business of dancing" while appearing "sober as a judge." The humorous image on the whole is a kindly one of these rural young people being themselves and enjoying the dance.

However, when Baldwin in **"The Ball"** portrays the dancing of the ladies and gentlemen of his own social circle, he is not so kindly but holds them up to ridicule. In part in this sketch their "general depression of spirits" had been brought on by the conflict between the late arrivals, Misses Gilt and Rino, and the manager of the dance, Mr. Crouch.

> The dancing of the ladies was, with few exceptions, much after the same fashion. I found not the least difficulty in resolving it into the three motions of a turkey-cock strutting, a sparrow-hawk lighting, and a duck walking. Let the reader suppose a lady beginning a strut at her own place, and ending it (precisely as does the turkey-cock) three feet nearer the gentleman opposite her; then giving three sparrow-hawk bobs, and then waddling back to her place like a duck; and he will have a pretty correct idea of their dancing. Not that the three movements were blended at every turn of the dance, but that one or more of the three answered to every turn. The strut prevailed most in balancing; the bobs, when balanced to; and the waddle, when going around. To all this Mrs. Mushy was an exception. When she danced, every particle of her danced, in spite of herself.
>
> There was as little variety in the gentlemen's dancing as there was in the ladies'. Any one who has seen a gentleman clean mud off his shoes on a door mat, has seen nearly all of it; the principal difference being, that some scraped with a pull of the foot, some with a push, and some with both.
>
> "I suppose," said I to a gentleman, "they take no steps because the music will not admit of them?"
>
> "Oh no," said he; "it's quite ungenteel to take steps." I thought of the wag's remarks about Miss Crump's music. "If this be their dancing," thought I, "what must their *mourning* be!"
>
> (pp. 114-15)

The "lady" dancers remind Baldwin of the barnyard and the antics of the fowl with Mrs. Mushy so fat that her body goes in every direction during the dance. The "gentlemen" danced as if they were cleaning mud off their shoes on a door mat, scraping by pushing or pulling or both. The explanation for their dancing is that it is "quite ungenteel to take steps." The image Baldwin creates through his description is one of strutting, lighting, waddling, and scraping, a satirical picture of people conducting themselves as if they were turkeys, chickens, sparrow hawks, and ducks in a barnyard, not ladies and gentlemen at a dance.

Throughout the sketches Baldwin uses familiar literary techniques to heighten the nature of his humor and satire. He will exaggerate the size of Jim Johnson's foot after Jack Slack has stumbled over it during a dance: he had, "in truth, a prodigious foot" (p. 9). He will slip into the text in passing a humorous incongruity: Mrs. Gibson "possessed a lovely disposition, which marriage could not spoil" (p. 13). Or he will contrast country girls greeting one another with handshakes with an exaggerated religious allusion on the more fashionable custom of greeting one another with a kiss: "The custom of kissing, as practised in these days by the *amiables,* is borrowed from the French, and by them from Judas" (p. 6). He will represent himself as absurdly trying to repeat "the double crosshop" he danced in his youth followed by the realistic humor of his second thoughts: "the first experiment convinced me of three things at once: 1st. That I could not have used the step in this way in my best days; 2nd. That my strength would not more than support it in its proper place for the remainder of the reel; and 3rd. If I tried it again in this way, I should knock my brains out against the puncheons . . ." (p. 12).

He will use the familiar idiom to describe an activity, such as Billy Porter the Negro fiddler having been drinking before playing, "taking a turn with the brethren (the Bar)" (p. 5). He will offer a contrast between the fashions of the country girls and those of the city ladies while disavowing any satirical purpose:

> They [the country girls] carried no more cloth upon their arms or straw upon their head than was necessary to cover them. They used no artificial means of spreading their frock tails to an interesting extent from their ankles. They had no boards laced to their breasts, nor any corsets laced to their sides; consequently, they looked for all the world, like human beings, and could be distinctly recognized as such at the distance of two hundred paces . . .
>
> (p. 6)

He continues with a Ciceronian disavowal, "Let me not be understood as interposing the least objection to any lady in this land of liberty dressing as she pleases," and thereby heightens the satire:

> If she choose to lay her neck and shoulders bare, what right have I to look at them? much less to find fault with them. If she choose to put three yards of muslin in a frock sleeve, what right have I to ask why a little

strip of it was not put in the body? If she like the pattern of a hoisted umbrella for a frock, and the shape of a cheese-cask for her body, what is all that to me?

(p. 6)

The exaggerated disavowal is just the point: ladies' fashions in dress are incomprehensible to Baldwin's more pragmatic, male mind.

One of the strategies Baldwin adapts to his humorous and satirical purpose is that of re-creating varieties of speech or styles as indicative of various social positions and human interrelationships, usually represented in contrast to the primary speech and style of the normative spokesman, Baldwin himself. These varieties include at least six distinct types: Baldwin's own speech, the affected speech of the socially pretentious ladies and gentlemen, the exaggerated speech of the recently educated, the "gibberish" of a mother to her infant, the Negro speech of the domestics, and the rural or frontier speech of the Georgia natives.[9] Baldwin himself, in a parenthetical remark, distinguishes between his own acquired or educated and his native speech: "to speak in my native dialect, I was 'mortal tired'" (p. 13). Perhaps the most efficient way to suggest the humor among these varieties of speech may be realized through brief, representative selections of each.

In **"The Ball,"** a satire on the conduct of the local fashionable ladies and gentlemen, one of the guests responds to the suggestion that he is not fond of dancing:

> "You quite misapprehend me, sir," returned Mr. Noozle. "Mine was not a declaration touching in the remotest degree my personal predilections or antipathies, but a simple interrogatory to Miss Feedle. No, sir; though I cannot lay claim to the proficiency of Noverre in the *saltant* art, I am, nevertheless, extravagantly fond of dancing; too much so, I fear, for one who has but just commenced the *veginti lucubrationes annorum,* as that inimitable and fascinating expositor of the elements of British jurisprudence, Sir William Blackstone, observes. To reach these high attainments in forensic—"

(p. 110)

Mr. Noozle's pomposity, Latinized diction, circumlocutions, self-perceptions, classical quotation, and social insensitivity all identify him as an object of satire; he is an affected idiot without knowing it.

The exaggerated speech of the Princeton-educated George Baldwin to the Philadelphia-educated Miss Evelina Caroline Smith, the rich young woman George Baldwin chooses to court, illustrates the social artificiality of the man, a fact he himself quickly acknowledges:

> "Believe me, Miss Smith," said he, as if he were opening a murder case, "believe me, there are fascinations about this hospitable dome, in the delicate touches of

the pencil which adorn it, and in the soft breathings of the piano, awaked by the hand which I have just relinquished, which will not permit me to delay, as heretofore, those visits which professional duty requires me to make to your kind parent (your father) a single moment beyond the time that his claims to my respects become absolute. Good evening, Miss Smith."

> "Did ever mortal of common sense talk and act so much like an arrant fool as I have this evening!" said George, as the veil of night fell upon the visions which had danced before his eyes for the four preceding hours.

(p. 78)

The "fascinations" this smitten lover has discovered in Miss Smith lead to his hyperbolic and euphemistic remarks about her home as a "hospitable dome," her paintings and playing as "delicate touches" and "soft breathing," and his intention of pursuing the courtship. He is an "arrant fool" and knows it. Baldwin intensifies the satire through his comments that George spoke to the lady "as if he were opening a murder case," an extremely serious formality, and through his cliche-ridden "veil of night" falling followed by "visions" dancing in the smitten lover's head. The narrator repeatedly satirizes not only the artificialities of the "sociables" and "amiables" of society, their dress, manners, affectations, and expressions, but the pomposities of the recently educated.

The ridiculous "gibberish" of a mother, Mrs. Slang, to her eight-month old infant offers a sharp contrast to the self-conscious, pretentious, affected, and exaggerated speech of the socially ambitious and the educated:

> "Muddy's baby was hongry. Dat was what ails muddy's darling, thweety ones. Was cho hungry, an' nobody would givy litty darling any sings 't all for eaty?" (*loosing her frock bosom.*) "No, nobody would gim thweety ones any sings fo' eat 't all." (*Offers the breast to the child, who rejects it, rolls over, kicks, and screams worse than ever.*)

> "Hush! you little brat! I believe it's nothing in the world but crossness. Hush!" (*shaking it*), "hush, I tell you." (*Child cries to the NE PLUS ULTRA.*)

(p. 117)

Through the contrasts between Mrs. Slang's gibberish to the child, and her normal though exasperated voice, "Hush! you little brat!" Baldwin portrays the inanity of adult behavior in dealing with a wailing child.

Although Baldwin offers no extended speeches or conversations by Negroes, the following remarks by the maid Rose from **"The Mother and Her Child"** is representative of Baldwin's re-creation of Negro speech. Rose is both pitiful because she is defenseless and comical, in a sense, in view of the situation.

140

"Why, what upon earth ails the child? Rose, you've hurt this child somehow or other!"

"No, ma'am, 'cla' I didn't; I was just sitt'n down dar in the rock'n-chair all 'long side o' Miss Nancy's bureau, an' wa'n't doin' noth'n' 't all to him, jis playin' wid him, and he jis begin to cry heself, when nobody wa'n't doin' nothin' 't all to him, and nobody wa'n't in dar nuther sept jis me and him, and I was—"

(p. 117)

The speech includes pronunciations, such as "dar" for there, "jis" for just, "wid" for with, "nuther" for neither, "wa'n't" for wasn't; it also includes the dropping of syllables such as "cla" for declare, "sept" for except, "'long" for along; the "ing" form is abbreviated in such words as "sitt'n," "rock'n," "noth'n'," "playin'," "doin',"; "at" is rendered as "'t"; subject-verb disagreement is represented by "he jis begin"; the neologism "heself" is introduced, probably for emphasis; except for the opening denial the speech is an extended run-on sentence. The narrator represents Rose as an amusing figure, repetitiously denying her responsibility for the infant's discomfort.

Of course Longstreet is particularly recognized as a Southwest humorist for his reproduction of rural and frontier speech, but such speech appears in only two of Baldwin's stories, **"The 'Charming Creature' as a Wife"** and **"A Sage Conversation,"** the latter involving a Ned Brace practical joke. The following excerpt of Mrs. Barney's observations on a neighbor's sickness and death is representative:

M<small>RS.</small> R.

What ailment did Lucy die of, Mis' Barney?

M<small>RS.</small> B.

Why, first she took the *ager* and fever, and took a *'bundance* o' doctor's means for that. And then she got a *powerful* bad cough, and it kept *gittin'* worse and worse, till at last it turned into a consumption, and she jist *nat'ly wasted away,* till she was *nothing but skin and bone,* and she died; but, poor *creater,* she died mighty happy; and I think, in my heart, she made the prettiest corpse, *considerin',* of anybody I most ever seed.

(p. 177)

Her pronunciations include "ager" for ague, "jist" for just, "creater" for creature, and "seed" for saw; she drops syllables from "'bundance," for abundance, "o'" for of, and "nat'ly" for naturally; she drops the "g" from her pronunciations of "gettin'"and "considerin'"; she uses the euphemism "wasted away" and the cliche "nothing but skin and bone"; her diction includes the adjectival use of "'bundance" to modify "o' doctor's

means" and "powerful" to modify "bad cough."[10] Her speech includes both simple and compound sentences as well as an extended run-on sentence. Despite Baldwin's Ciceronian disavowal of intending any ridicule of the rural matrons in the sketch, the above illustration holds Mrs. Barney up to ridicule, not because of her sentiments but because of her native way of expressing them.

In each instance of varieties of speech, the character and personality of the speaker is seen from and through the perspective of the standard represented by the Baldwin persona. His attitudes, values, behaviors, and perspectives dominate each sketch and contain a stated or implied judgment of the characters and situation represented. From Baldwin's point of view Mr. Noozle is a pompous idiot; George Baldwin, a fool to be taken in by "a charming creature"; Mrs. Slang, ridiculous in the speech she uses with her child; the Negro Rose, amusing in her protestations of having caused the baby's discomfort; the rural matrons, both funny and absurd in being taken in by Ned Brace's practical joke about two men getting married and in their characteristic dialect.

Baldwin's humor and satire are based on subjects and situations easily adapted to purposes of amusement, characters who lend themselves to ridicule and exaggeration, individuals and communities who offer contrasts between social backgrounds and manners, techniques that heighten the distinctions between and among individuals and society, and varieties of speech prevalent among the people of the time. But the primary basis for the humor and satire rests on the character and personality of the narrator, Abram Baldwin, his personal way of perceiving himself and the life around him, and his ways of describing his dominant point of view. Baldwin is a moral and didactic man, a highly opinionated and reflective person, a narrator who has the capacity to see himself with a degree of objectivity, but he is primarily a tragic figure who employs the modes of the humorist and satirist, extracting and transforming his own life and that around him into the amusing, funny, ridiculous, and absurd.

He anticipated with hope that posterity would see beyond his surface humor and satire into the deeper, more moral and meaningful nature of the human predicament, as he himself does in part through reflections on his own life. Poe understood this when he complimented the author of the ***Scenes*** as "a clever fellow, imbued with a spirit of the truest humor, and endowed, moreover, with an exquisitely discriminative and penetrating understanding of *character* in general, and of Southern character in particular."[11] Baldwin's "truest humor" and "understanding of character" emerge from his own self-perceptions initially, from his acknowledgment of his own failure in life, from a self-perceived tragic view that embraces and encompasses a humorous view. That he saw the warp and woof of the *Scenes* as much more than amusing and mere entertaining sketches written for a popular audience of the day perhaps best explains his pessimistic hope that his "forlorn" purpose might perhaps someday be realized.

*Notes*

1. A nineteenth sketch entitled "The Militia Company Drill" was written by Oliver Prince and signed by the persona Timothy Crabshaw.

2. See Walter Blair, *Native American Humor* (1800-1900) (1937; rpt. San Francisco: Chandler Publishers, 1960), p. 76, where he identifies all of the sketches written by Baldwin as "Americanized *Spectator* papers."

3. Augustus B. Longstreet, *Georgia Scenes [,] Character, Incidents &c. in the first half of the Republic* with an introduction by Richard Harwell (1835; rpt. Savannah: The Beehive Press, 1975), p. 2.

4. Both Baldwin and Hall use this phrase. All parenthetical textual notes refer to the McElderry edition of *Georgia Scenes*. A. B. Longstreet, *Georgia Scenes*, with an Introduction by B. R. McElderry, Jr. (1835; rpt. New York: Sagamore Press Inc., 1957).

5. For a recent instance see James B. Meriwether, "Augustus Baldwin Longstreet: Realist and Artist," *Mississippi Quarterly*, 35 (fall 1982), 359: "The six 'Baldwin' sketches, by their subject matter and by the persona of their narrator, serve as occasional interludes, used for change of pace and variety of subject matter. The dominant figure of the book is Hall; his friend Baldwin—for the two are acquainted, and appear together in several of the sketches—. . . simply serves as a foil to the ultimately much more masculine and successful Lyman Hall."

6. For brief listings of the subjects treated by Southwest humorists see Franklin J. Meine, "Tall Tales of the Southwest," reprinted in *The Frontier Humorists*, edited by M. Thomas Inge (Hamden, Connecticut: Archon Books, 1975), pp. 24-5, and Henning Cohen and William B. Dillingham, "Introduction," *Humor of the Old Southwest* (Boston: Houghton Mifflin Company, 1964), pp. xii-xiii. That the character of the persona is not included among the lists is surprising.

7. It is worth noting that Baldwin's literary references are not as extensive as those in Hall's sketches.

8. Longstreet, Harwell, p. 1.

9. Hall far more than Baldwin recreates the rural and frontier speech of the age.

10. Adiel Sherwood lists four pages of objectionable Georgia "Provincialisms," including "ager" and "seed," in *A Gazetteer of the State of Georgia*, third edition (Washington City: Force, 1837), pp. 69-72. His purpose in offering the list, he states, is that "seeing them printed, we shall forbear to drag them into service." Longstreet, of course, justifies the usages in terms of verisimilitude.

11. Edgar Allan Poe, "*Georgia Scenes*," [*The Frontier Humorists: Critical Views*, 1975] Inge[, Thomas, ed.], p. 85.

## Keith Newlin (essay date winter 1987-88)

SOURCE: Newlin, Keith. "*Georgia Scenes*: The Satiric Artistry of Augustus Baldwin Longstreet." *Mississippi Quarterly: The Journal of Southern Culture* 41, no. 1 (winter 1987-88): 21-37.

[*In the following essay, Newlin argues that Longstreet's* Georgia Scenes, *long regarded by scholars as little more than frontier humor, actually played a key role in the emergence of American satire.*]

In the preface to *Georgia Scenes*, Augustus Baldwin Longstreet notes that he has "used some little art in order to recommend [*Georgia Scenes*] to the readers of my own times."[1] Yet this collection of sketches has had to wait until the 1980s to receive any real appreciation of its artistry. In the past, most scholars have emphasized Longstreet's contribution to the development of Southwestern humor by discussing only those sketches in *Georgia Scenes* that are similar to subsequent frontier sketches—principally **"Georgia Theatrics," "The Fight," "The Gander Pulling," "The Horse Swap"** and **"The Character of a Native Georgian"**—ignoring or at best only briefly acknowledging the existence of the other fourteen scenes, which are more Addisonian than "Southwest humorist."

Kenneth Lynn, for example, in *Mark Twain and Southwestern Humor*, traces the development of the "frame" structure in **"Georgia Theatrics," "The Fight,"** and **"The Horse Swap"**; Franklin J. Meine, in *Tall Tales of the Southwest*, emphasizes the "realism" of *Georgia Scenes*: the sketches "showed red-necked Georgia crackers in eye-gouging, nose-biting fights, in coarse horse trade wrangles, and in capers which even invaded funeral processions."[2] And Walter Blair, whose discussion in *Native American Humor* ranges beyond Longstreet's frontier sketches, still is more impressed by Longstreet's depiction of the rougher rural life than the Addisonian essays which make up half the book. These sketches, he explains, "are the least admirable in the book; and one regrets their frequency—not because they are bad but because Longstreet's predecessors did such things better."[3] Moreover, this emphasis on Longstreet's frontier sketches extends to the various anthologies of Southwestern humor. Such collections as Henning Cohen and William B. Dillingham's *Humor of the Old Southwest,* V. L. O. Chittick's *Ring-Tailed Roarers,* and Blair's *Native American Humor* reprint only the "frontier" scenes and none of the Addisonian satires.

This critical tunnel vision badly skews the way *Georgia Scenes* is read, for the book is not primarily a work in the Southern humorist tradition, although it helped form that tradition. As James B. Meriwether has recently pointed out, Longstreet in his preface and his letters emphasizes his role as "a social historian, recording the fast-changing manners and ways of the people of his time and place."[4] While Meriwether argues at length the impropriety of classifying Longstreet as a "Southwestern" or "frontier" writer, or even as a "humorist," his argument does not sufficiently account for Longstreet's purpose in *Georgia Scenes.* In his materials and literary methods, Longstreet is primarily a mannerist in the fashion of Addison and Irving, who happens to sketch "frontier" incidents in only one half of *Georgia Scenes*; the other half has more in common with the *Spectator* and Irving's *Sketch Book* than with subsequent books such as Johnson Jones Hooper's *Some Adventures of Captain Simon Suggs* (1845), Thomas Bangs Thorpe's *Mysteries of the Backwoods* (1846), or George Washington Harris's *Sut Lovingood's Yarns* (1867).

In a passage quoted by Oscar Fitzgerald, Longstreet's first biographer, Longstreet seems to anticipate the trend in Southwestern humor scholarship and tries to correct potential misunderstanding. He writes,

> The design of the *Georgia Scenes* has been wholly misapprehended by the public. It has been invariably received as a mere collection of fancy sketches, with no higher object than the entertainment of the reader, whereas the aim of the author was to supply a chasm in history which has always been overlooked—the manners, customs, amusements, wit, dialect, as they appear in all grades of society to an ear and eye witness of them.[5]

Much of the scholarship has overlooked Longstreet's satires of the upper class and the role these sketches play in the composition of *Georgia Scenes.* Like Addison, Longstreet ridicules pretentious courtship rituals, foppish behavior that passes for "elegant" society—

indeed, the range of decorous behavior. And like much of the Augustan literature which provided his model, Longstreet's satiric purpose is to instruct by illustrating the foibles in "all grades of society," and to correct through ridicule the cruelty that lies behind much social interaction. Yet this critical neglect of Longstreet's satires on manners is understandable, for his sketches of rural life are what influenced subsequent writers. But focusing only on the folk humor elements in selected sketches misses a good deal of what Longstreet intended and misses completely the artistry of *Georgia Scenes.*

For Longstreet clearly intended *Georgia Scenes* to be read as a unified work, despite his somewhat misleading explanations in the preface. The scenes had previously appeared in the Milledgeville *Southern Recorder* and his own *State Rights Sentinel,* published under two pseudonyms, "Hall" and "Baldwin." These dual pseudonyms, Longstreet writes, "have now become too closely interwoven with the sketches to be separated from them, without an expense of time and trouble which I am unwilling to incur. *Hall* is the writer of those sketches in which *men* appear as the principal actors, and *Baldwin* of those in which *women* are the prominent figures" (p. iv). But the preface also tells us that "For the last six months I have been importuned by persons from all quarters of the State to give them to the public in the present form" (p. iii). The significance of this explanation to the composition of *Georgia Scenes* has been overlooked. Although it is not clear when Longstreet first collected his sketches into the arrangement that was to become *Georgia Scenes,* three of his sketches—**"The Debating Society," "A Sage Conversation,"** and **"The Shooting Match"**—contain internal references to *Georgia Scenes* as a collection, typically a doubt about the suitability of a scene for inclusion (pp. 133, 187, 200). And since these three scenes were first published in February and March 1835, it is likely that Longstreet wrote them with the entreaties of his friends in mind, for **"A Sage Conversation"** and **"The Shooting Match"** are also the last two scenes Longstreet wrote and appear last in *Georgia Scenes.* As we shall see, in these two sketches Longstreet brings to a close the principal themes in the book.

Longstreet achieves some unity in *Georgia Scenes* through the sequence of the sketches, although the arrangement may not have been intentional. While Kimball King argues that *Georgia Scenes* follows a "pattern of rural-urban contrasts,"[6] there are too many anomalies in this sequence to sustain such a pattern, for most of the sketches are set in towns of some sort, and it is not clear which town is "urban" and which "rural." Longstreet's division of scenes along sex lines is only moderately helpful for understanding the sequence of sketches, for men are the principal actors in **"The Dance"** and **"The Song"** (Baldwin himself), and in **"The 'Charming Creature' as a Wife," "The Ball,"** and **"The Sage Conversation,"** men figure as prominently as do the women. What Longstreet probably meant is that the Baldwin sketches are comedies of manners, satirizing male-female relations, whereas the Hall sketches are predominantly moral fables, emphasizing the cruelty inherent in competition. The purpose of both types, in good Addisonian fashion, is to instruct while amusing, for the pretense and frivolity of the upper classes that Baldwin typically describes are just as destructive to the social order as the barbarities and competition that Hall depicts.

Yet this division of topics is not entirely sustained in *Georgia Scenes,* for a sketch assigned to Hall occasionally satirizes manners (**"The Character of a Native Georgian," "The Debating Society," "The Turf," "The Fox-Hunt"**), and a sketch assigned to Baldwin will moralize about competition and cruelty (**"The Mother and her Child"**). The scenes are thus sequenced neither by a contrast between rural or urban setting, nor by a strict division by gender. A more consistent unifying principle is the oscillation of satirical targets: between moralizing about some form of competition, cruelty, or deception and ridiculing some form of foppery, pretension, or hypocrisy. In short, *Georgia Scenes* alternates between portraying the cruelty inherent in encounters between common people and satirizing the no less cruel behavior of the supposed social elite. And this oscillating pattern becomes more persuasive as a unifying device when one notes that the sketches are placed in *Georgia Scenes* without regard to the original publication date; early scenes appear late; late scenes appear early. A brief table charting the pattern of contrasts might be useful:

*Scene (First Published)*[7]: *Satirical Target*

**"Georgia Theatrics"** (1833): competition between youth and imaginary opponent.

**"The Dance"** (10/29/33): FOLLY OF PRIDE.

**"The Horse Swap"** (11/13/33): competition over ability to sustain deception.

**"The Character of a Native Georgian"** (1/8/34): FOLLY OF UNRESTRAINED PASSION.

**"The Fight"** (11/27/33): competition to determine best man.

**"The Song"** (11/8/33): COMPLACENCY WITH EUROPEAN VALUES.

**"The Turn Out"** (12/11/33): competition between pupils and teacher—a rite of passage.

**"The 'Charming Creature' as a Wife"** (4/14/34): FOLLY OF BASING MARRIAGE ON SURFACE APPEARANCE.

**"The Gander Pulling"** (1/15/34): cruelty within a peculiar competitive contest.

**"The Ball"** (3/6/34): FOPPERY OF "MODERN" DANCE.

**"The Mother and her Child"** (6/2/34): cruelty lurking behind competition between mother and nanny.

**"The Debating Society"** (3/5/35): FRIVOLITY OF COLLEGE DEBATES.

**"The Militia Drill"** (5/15/34): struggle to impose order on chaos.

**"The Turf"** (11/20/33): RACING AS UNGENTLEMANLY.

**"An Interesting Interview"** (1834): drunkenness as self-destructive.

**"The Fox Hunt"** (2/12/35): PRETENTIOUSNESS OF THE HUNT.

**"The Wax Works"** (2/19/35): the con game.

**"A Sage Conversation"** (3/17/35): GOSSIP/GULLIBILITY.

**"The Shooting Match"** (Feb. 1835): competition for "best shot."

The satirical target in such scenes as **"The Horse Swap," "The Fight," "The Gander Pulling,"** and **"The Shooting Match"** is readily apparent even in a cursory reading, for these tales focus on the competitive contest itself: the best horse-trader, the best fighter, the best goose-neck wringer, and the best shot. Similarly, the more Addisonian scenes emphasize the effects of pretense or foppery on others: in **"Native Georgian,"** Ned Brace's pretended barbaric table manners stem from his own "ungovernable proclivity" and horrify all around him; **"The Ball"** illustrates the pretentiousness of "modern" dance; and **"A Sage Conversation"** details the triviality inherent in gossip. Of course, for some of the scenes the contrasting pattern is more obvious than for others, but such scenes as **"The Mother and her Child,"** "The Militia Drill," and **"An Interesting Interview"** have more in common with what I've categorized as "competitive scenes" than with those that stress manners, for each focuses on a form of one-upmanship. Moreover, scenes like **"The Turf"** and **"The Fox-Hunt"** share an emphasis on decorous behavior with such similar manners scenes as **"The Ball"** and **"The 'Charming Creature' as a Wife."**

But more than the sequence of scenes, Longstreet relies on the portrayal of the narrators to unify *Georgia Scenes.* For the majority of the scenes, the narrator is not always what Kenneth Lynn terms "the Self-controlled Gentleman," "Outside and above the comic action . . . morally irreproachable" due to the distancing device of the frame.[8] Indeed, Hall and Baldwin frequently become the center of our interest by taking part in the scenes and thereby revealing their own weaknesses. In short, both Hall and Baldwin become characters as well as narrators.

The first two sketches are important for their depiction of the characters (as opposed to narrators) Hall and Baldwin. In both **"Georgia Theatrics"** and **"The Dance,"** each narrator is portrayed as gullible and proud, and each becomes embarrassed by his naiveté. **"Georgia Theatrics"** opens with Hall "Rapt with the enchantment" of the natural purity surrounding the town of Lincoln. Amid his contemplations he hears what appears to be an eye-gouging fight. Filled with righteous indignation at both what he hears and the desecration of his meditations, he calls out to the "ruffian" in "a tone imboldened by the sacredness of my office and the iniquity of his crime, 'Come back, you brute! and assist me in relieving your fellow-mortal, whom you have ruined for ever!'" (p. 11). When Hall discovers that the eye-gouging is only a mock fight, he is chagrined and turns to examine the ground, where he notes two thumb prints "about the distance of a man's eyes apart." Aside from the humor in this bit of rustic duplicity, the scene is important for what it reveals about Hall as a character: he is morally righteous, easily duped, and prone to act on insufficient information; in short, Hall is himself a rube in the backwoods, a stranger to what he observes.

Like **"Georgia Theatrics,"** **"The Dance"** introduces Baldwin as a naive narrator. While the first sketch satirizes Hall's pride in his moral superiority, **"The Dance"** mocks Baldwin's sense of self-importance. More than in the first sketch, the narrator's perceptions dominate; Baldwin's tone throughout is nostalgic and melancholy, regretful of years misspent in the city away from the wholesomeness of the country. Baldwin reflects, "But I was foolishly told that my talents were of too high an order to be employed in the drudgeries of a farm, and I more foolishly believed it. I forsook the pleasures which I had tried and proved, and went in pursuit of those imaginary joys which seemed to encircle the seat of Fame" (p. 18). With the knowledge of his wasted life before him, Baldwin recognizes a former "sweetheart," Polly Gibson, his memories surface, and he tries to recapture his lost youth. Longstreet sets up Baldwin for disappointment by satirizing his prideful assumption that he is as unforgettable to Polly as she is to him. Receiving permission from Gibson to dance with Polly, Baldwin proclaims, "'But don't get jealous, squire, if she seems a little too glad to see me'" (p. 16). Baldwin asks Polly to dance "in a voice audible to most of the assembly" (p. 19), yet finds that Polly does not remember him. Thus publicly embarrassed by her faulty

memory, he decides that she'll recognize him "as soon as she sees the *double crosshop*" (p. 20), a maneuver he used to dance with her, but he misses his chance when Polly is distracted by a thieving dog. The joke, of course, is that Polly—who has not left the country and therefore has no reason to relish past memories—has forgotten him. The sketch concludes with Baldwin unrecognized and "petulant," like Hall a bit wiser amid his chagrin.

With these two sketches Longstreet has inaugurated a pattern that informs all of *Georgia Scenes.* As a character, Hall gradually becomes less naive, less overtly moralistic, and matures from a self-righteous observer to an accepted part of the events he witnesses and takes part in. Baldwin, however, due to the nature of the sketches he appears in, never really changes: he remains an outsider, ridiculing pretension and frivolity. Because Baldwin has left the country and received a city education, he applies city standards to what he observes—thus his emphasis on manners.

Perhaps the most significant characteristic of the Hall sketches is that Hall is a stranger who intrudes into the society he describes. And as Kenneth Lynn has observed, Hall as narrator is the chief device by which Longstreet can distance himself from what he portrays in his role as social historian. Yet for all this supposed distance, Hall emerges, not as a "Gentleman [who] was as completely in control of the situation he described as he was of himself,"[9] but as a fictional character who, at times, becomes overwhelmed by the events he observes and comes to participate in. Indeed, by the close of *Georgia Scenes,* Hall becomes fully assimilated into society, his capacity for moral evaluation diminished by his acquiescence.

In the early scenes, however, Hall is successful in maintaining his distance; aware that he is an intruder into a society with which he is unfamiliar, he refrains from taking part in the events he witnesses. Instead, Longstreet emphasizes Hall's "observations," and he is particularly careful to underscore the accuracy of those observations. In the opening paragraph of **"The Horse Swap,"** for instance, Hall notes that "I like to see all that is passing" and he approaches a quickly forming crowd to examine the scene "with the strictest scrutiny" (p. 23). Because he is a stranger, Hall is not able to appreciate the one-upsmanship of the horse trade, and when Peter Ketch reveals a large sore previously hidden under a blanket, Hall moralizes: "My heart sickened at the sight; and I felt that the brute who had been riding him in that situation deserved the halter." Yet since he is an accurate observer, Hall next notes: "The prevailing feeling, however, was that of mirth" (p. 30).

As an outsider, Hall is unable to appreciate this mirth, and his moral condemnation serves both to express Longstreet's central theme of the cruelty inherent in all such popular amusements and to illustrate Hall's own naïveté, for although he examines the scene with the "strictest scrutiny," he misses crucial details. Longstreet thus at once depicts Hall as a self-conscious observer alert to minutia and underscores his gullibility, for Hall, like the crowd, gets sucked in by the deception.

In **"The Gander Pulling,"** a sketch describing the apparently common sport of pulling off the greased heads of geese, Hall becomes more intimately involved in the events he describes. Longstreet relies on the weight of accumulated detail, as well as Hall's reactions, to condemn this activity. After arriving at the scene of the contest, Hall observes that while people from all social strata are present, "few females were there, however; and those few were from the lowest walks of life" (p. 113). Hall thus sets the scene by underscoring the disreputable quality of the sport. Hall is so amazed at what unfolds that he dwells upon the irony of the mechanics of greasing, for a "gourd of *goose*-grease" supplies the lubricant, and at this sight, Hall notes, "my thoughts took a melancholy turn. They dwelt in sadness upon the many conjugal felicities which had probably been shared between *greasess* and *greassee*" (pp. 113-114). In an extended analogy, Hall personifies the plight of the gander, horrified at the irony of the scene:

> And now, alas! an extract from the smoking sacrifice of his bosom friend was desecrated to the unholy purpose of making his neck "a fit object" for Cruelty to reach "her quick, unerring fingers at." Ye friends of the sacred tie! judge what were my feelings when, in the midst of these reflections, the voice of James Prator thundered on mine ear, "Darn his old dodging soul; brother Ned! grease his neck till a fly can't light on it!"
>
> (p. 114)

Despite the sport's inherent cruelty, Longstreet is able to wrench comedy from it through the juxtaposition of James Prator's crude speeech with Hall's more genteel reflections. Yet amusing though the characters' subsequent actions may be, Longstreet emphasizes through Hall's descriptions that the common people lack a suitable moral standard for which to strive. The disparity between their references to each other as "gentlemen" and their behavior and dialect points to the dominant theme underlying Hall's sketches: the common people act as they do not so much because they are cruel but because they lack moral guidance.

This theme is developed further in **"The Turf,"** in which Hall accompanies Baldwin to the races. Longstreet frames the sketch through Baldwin, who here acts as Longstreet's spokesman. They are going, Baldwin pompously tells Hall, only to "'acquire a knowledge of the human character, as it exhibits itself in the various scenes of life, and with the hope of turning the knowledge thus acquired to some good account'" (p. 152). With Longstreet's didactic purpose stated, the narrators occupy themselves with "making observations," and the objects of their observations provide examples of the lesson Longstreet wishes to teach. In addition to a Major Close, who gambles away the money he needs to pay his bills, Hall observes assorted drunks, cruel treatment of horses, even crueler threats to jockeys, and so forth. As in **"The Gander Pulling,"** Longstreet emphasizes through ironic contrast that such sport exists because the people who participate in it—here, "persons, of all ages, sexes, conditions, and complexions" (p. 152)—need moral arbiters to set standards of behavior. Two interludes at the end of the scene illustrate Longstreet's theme. In the first, two small boys fight while grown-ups cheer them on, only to fight among themselves later; in the second, a horse falls and kills his rider. A Mrs. Blue remarks that "'had it not been for that little accident, the sport would have been delightful,'" and a General Grubbs adds, "'What a pity it is . . . that this amusement is not more encouraged!'" (p. 160). Longstreet thus suggests that even the supposedly well-bred—women and military officers—are hypocrites and lack the moral judgment to guide their own behavior, let alone that of others.

As James Meriwether accurately observes, Longstreet's theme is "that impulses towards savagery and violence were to be found not far from the surface in many men, perhaps most of them; and that it is the function of human laws and institutions to restrain, discipline, and civilize these impulses." Yet the scenes themselves do not provide much evidence of any successful restraint offered by human law, for the cruelties Hall notes occur within a framework of rules. Meriwether sees organized sport as Longstreet's solution to check man's proclivity toward barbarism, even suggesting that the sport in **"The Gander Pulling"** is "surely an improvement over human eye-gouging and nose-biting."[10] Longstreet's emphasis in these scenes, however, is not one of approbation but of disapproval, and this condemnation serves to underscore the need for better moral education of the citizenry since the laws are not curtailing the incidence of cruelties.

In these sketches Hall has served primarily as Longstreet's didactic spokesman, and the emphasis on Hall's voyeurism extends through most of his scenes. Yet in two sketches—**"The Fox-Hunt"** and **"The Shooting Match"**—Hall escapes from his role as moral commentator to become a full-fledged character, the center of the reader's interest. And it is in these two sketches that

Hall matures from an aloof moral judge to an accepted part of the society he has previously condemned.

**"The Fox-Hunt"** is a well-crafted, pivotal scene in Hall's journey toward assimilation. It is also a parody of fox-hunting rituals and indicts through its parody the cruelty inherent in a sport in which gentlemen romanticize killing. The sketch begins with a lengthy quotation from William Somerville's "The Chase," whose poetry, Hall tells us, "sanctifies the sport" and is "calculated to inspire" (pp. 166, 167). The selection describes the fox as a "felon vile," who steals "the poor defenceless lamb," and is consequently pursued by the hunter on his "clean, generous steed." The diction is elevated, the sentiment heroic, the sport glorified. Kimball King believes Longstreet's inclusion of the quotation to be an instance of "some rather obvious padding" and "a good example of indiscriminant use of literary allusion."[11] However, Longstreet includes the selection because the structure of the scene depends upon it. As Hall begins the fox hunt, his head filled with visions inspired by "The Chase," he learns from practical experience how pretentious and hypocritical the sport is, and his education is accomplished through an inversion of the conventions expressed in "The Chase."

Whereas the speaker of the poem awakens at dawn, full of vigor, and arrives on time with a reliable horse, Hall awakens in the dark, mistakenly blows his hunting horn in the house, causing his sensible landlady to remark, "'I can't see what any man of common sense wants to be gitting up this time of night for, in such cold weather, just to hear dogs run a fox.'" Hall thinks to himself, "It struck me there was a good deal of sound philosophy in the good lady's remarks; but she was a *woman,* and she had never read Somerville" (p. 168). The balance of the sketch is designed to show the wisdom of the landlady's observation and the folly of fox hunting.

The "generous steed" of "The Chase" becomes in Smoothtooth an old, broken-down, temperamental slowpoke, given to sudden stops and starts, completely unsuitable for the hunt. The true-nosed hounds become a mangy mob, given to false starts and wrong scents. The "dangerous course," filled with obstructions that the hunters easily surmount, becomes in Hall's experience a quagmire of noose-like vines, obstructing logs, and impenetrable trees. In the midst of the hunt, Hall comes to his senses. Inspired this time by the December cold (which doesn't exist in Somerville's romantic poem), Hall wonders "'Why seek amusement in the tortures of a poor unoffending animal! In this country, at least, I never heard of a single loss from a farmyard which could be fairly traced to the fox; not even of a goose, much less of a lamb. . . . Folly! madness in the

extreme!'" (p. 173). Despite his condemnation of the sport, Hall discovers that "for some moments I was enraptured with the sport" (p. 176). His distance as a moral critic decreasing, Hall finds himself becoming one of the boys, so intoxicating is the excitement of the chase. The sketch ends with Hall "perfectly satisfied with fox-hunting," now a confirmed participant in what he had hitherto only observed.

**"The Shooting Match"** concludes Hall's appearance in *Georgia Scenes,* and in this sketch Hall becomes fully assimilated into the society he has been observing and commenting on from a distance. Hall proves himself to the simple folk by getting the upper hand in introductory joking with Billy Curlew, by engaging in tall talk, and by winning second place in the contest, despite his doubts. His repartee with his fellow shooters reveals his new-found ease with their society, so much so that Billy invites him home to share supper and others offer to vote for him should he ever run for office. Hall has thus matured from the moralizing intruder of **"Georgia Theatrics"** to the harshly condemnatory judge of **"The Gander Pulling"** to a full-fledged member of the society he had formerly criticized.

Longstreet extends his condemnation of cruelty and its potential to destroy social order to Baldwin's scenes, where Baldwin's satiric commentary illustrates that even the supposedly well-bred cannot provide the moral guidance the common people need. Although disparaged for their emulation of British models by critics such as Walter Blair, the Baldwin scenes display considerable artistry in their composition, with delightful characterization, more than a little wit, and a command of imagery that suggests Longstreet's familiarity with Augustan satire. And as in the satires of Pope and Swift, Longstreet's purpose is to instruct through ridicule, showing that the pretense and frivolity of the well-bred invalidate their supposed social superiority.

**"The Song"** is one of the more carefully structured scenes of this group and is representative of all the Baldwin sketches in method and theme. Its purpose is to satirize Georgian society's preference for Continental singing and its reliance upon Europe for standards of taste. Since **"The Dance"** has portrayed Baldwin as a disaffected city dweller who prefers the simpler values of the country, it is no surprise that he regards the "French and Italian style of singing and playing" as "European abominations" (p. 66).

As he does in most of the Baldwin sketches, Longstreet first frames **"The Song"** by describing a general deficiency in manners and then following with an extended example illustrating how the social barbarism affects his more cultivated taste. He begins by comparing French and Italian music to that of Scotland, which "has escaped the corruptions which have crept into the empire of music, and, consequently, her music recommends itself, with irresistible charms, to every ear which is not vitiated by the senseless rattle of the Continent." "Ireland," he notes, "is a little more contaminated," but it retains enough "primitive simplicity and sweetness to entitle [its compositions] to the patronage of all who would cultivate a correct taste" (p. 65). Baldwin then describes the "tortures" he suffers when he must listen to unpractised amateurs further mangling what to his ears already is "manslaughter."

With this general deficiency in taste defined, Baldwin next presents two contrasting examples: the first illustrates "correct taste" in music—Miss Mary Williams' recital of Burns and Tannahill; the second Miss Aurelia Emma Theodosia Augusta Crump's attempts at the Italian style. Here as in other sketches the length and artificiality of Miss Crump's name is an emblem of her pretentiousness, and Baldwin consistently refers to her as "Miss" throughout to underscore the satire (Miss Williams, in contrast, is always simply "Mary").

Baldwin's brief description of Mary's recital provides a paradigm of which the lengthy description of Miss Crump's playing is a satirical inversion. Baldwin begins by inviting Mary to play.

> She rose promptly at my request, without any affected airs, and with no other apology than that "she felt some diffidence at playing in the presence of *Miss Crump*." . . . Mary seated herself at [the piano], and, after a short but beautiful prelude, she commenced one of Burns's plaintive songs. . . . The composer and the poet were both honoured by the performer. Mary's voice was inimitably fine. Her enunciation was clear and distinct, with just emphasis enough to give the verse its appropriate expression, without interrupting the melody of the music; and her modulations were perfect.
>
> (p. 67)

In contrast to Mary's immediate, unaffected response to Baldwin's request, Miss Crump disdains to play, declaring that "she was entirely out of practice," that "she scarcely ever touched the piano," and so forth. Baldwin's presentation of Miss Crump's eventual acquiescence reveals both the insincerity of Miss Crump and Longstreet's wit:

> "Augusta, my dear [interposes Mrs. Crump], go and play a tune or two: the company will excuse your hoarseness."
>
> Miss Crump rose immediately at her mother's bidding, and moved to the piano, accompanied by a large group of smiling faces.

"Poor child," said Mrs. Crump . . . she is frightened to death. I wish Augusta could overcome her diffidence."

(p. 69)

Miss Crump's performance is also in pointed contrast to Mary's. Longstreet's selection of exaggerated images to portray the assault on Baldwin's sensibilities is reminiscent of Pope. Miss Crump's playing is first compared to a race: her right hand moves "in a brisk canter up the treble notes, and the left after it. The left hand then led the way back, and the right pursued it in like manner. The right turned, and repeated its first movement; but the left outran it this time, hopped over it, and flung it entirely off the track" (p. 69). The competition between hands develops into a battle; the hands "became highly incensed at each other, and met furiously on the middle ground . . . a most awful conflict ensued . . . the right whipped off all of a sudden . . . fairly vanquished." The left hand, however, "continued its assaults, sometimes by the way of the naturals, and sometimes by the way of the sharps, and sometimes by a zigzag through both" until finally "it came close up to its adversary and expired" (pp. 69-70).

But poor Baldwin's agony is not over, for Miss Crump begins to sing: "my ear caught, indistinctly, some very curious sounds, which appeared to proceed from the lips of Miss Augusta: they seemed to be compounded of a dry cough, a grunt, a hiccough, and a whisper" (p. 70). At the climax of the song, in marked contrast to Mary's singing "with just emphasis enough," Miss Crump accompanies her playing with "a squall of a pinched cat . . . she screamed, she howled, she yelled, cackled, and was in the act of dwelling upon the note of a screech-owl" when Baldwin can stand no more and quits the performance (p. 71). So affected is he that despite "sixty drops of laudanum" he sees Miss Crump in his dreams "flying through the air towards the city" to "the cry of 'Hecate is coming!'" (p. 72).

**"The Song"** thus illustrates that the Miss Crumps of the world do not hold the solution to the problem of moral guidance. Through the device of contrast, Longstreet also shows that European standards are not suitable for regulating behavior, for the very artificiality of the "French and Italian style" has little relevance for Georgian society. Baldwin's preference for the simpler Scottish and Irish music indicates that the moral arbiters the people need require a blend of education and common sense, achieved not through isolation (reflected in the nationalism of French or Italian music), but through compromise. As in the Hall scenes, the thematic purpose of **"The Song"** is to offer an argument for assimilation, a cultural compromise.

While Longstreet consistently portrays Baldwin as an aloof critic of upper-crust Georgian society, his portrayal of Hall is problematic. On the one hand, Hall functions as a moral critic, showing through his reactions the sort of moral guidance society needs. On the other hand, Hall eventually becomes assimilated into that society, and he thus loses his critical distance. Longstreet also loses his critic, for without the requisite *"cordon sanitaire,"* in Kenneth Lynn's phrase, Hall's impressions become suspect (and, indeed, Hall has suspended his criticism in **"The Shooting Match"**). The problem, then, is that Longstreet has unintentionally compromised his moral arbiter by having him engage with and eventually become accepted into the very society he wishes to satirize. Of course, Longstreet may have intended his readers to recognize Hall's slip and laugh at his inadvertent hypocrisy, but it is also likely that Longstreet simply lost sight of Hall's role as moral commentator in his development of Hall's character. Despite this flaw—if it is a flaw—*Georgia Scenes* remains an engaging satire of an evolving frontier.

## Notes

1. Augustus Baldwin Longstreet, *Georgia Scenes,* facsimile rpt. of 2nd ed. (Upper Saddle River, N.J.: Gregg Press, 1969), p. iii. Subsequent references are cited in text.

2. Franklin J. Meine, *Tall Tales of the Southwest* (New York: Knopf, 1930), p. xvii.

3. Walter Blair, *Native American Humor* (New York: American Book Co., 1937), p. 77.

4. James B. Meriwether, "Augustus Baldwin Longstreet: Realist and Artist," *Mississippi Quarterly,* 35 (1982), 355.

5. Oscar Penn Fitzgerald, *Judge Longstreet: A Life Sketch* (Nashville: Methodist Episcopal Church, South, 1891), p. 164.

6. Kimball King, *Augustus Baldwin Longstreet* (Boston: Twayne, 1984), p. 83.

7. All dates are from King, pp. 56-89, 146-147.

8. Kenneth Lynn, *Mark Twain and Southwestern Humor* (Boston: Little, Brown, 1959), p. 64.

9. Lynn, p. 64.

10. Meriwether, p. 361.

11. King, p. 86.

## Carolyn S. Brown (essay date 1987)

SOURCE: Brown, Carolyn S. "Flush Times: Varieties of Written Tales." In *The Tall Tale in American Folklore and Literature,* pp. 39-73. Knoxville: University of Tennessee Press, 1987.

[*In the following excerpt, Brown examines how Longstreet's sketches, with their innovative narrative style and distinctive sense of humor, exerted an impact on the later emergence of the American "tall tale."*]

> A new vein of literature, as original as it is inexhaustible in its source, has been opened in this country within a very few years, with the most marked success.
>
> —William T. Porter, 1843

Whether in a barroom or at a boys' summer camp, the yarnspinner who knows how to tell a good lie creates not just a tale, not just a comic exaggeration, but also a character, be he wit, hero, fool or rogue; and he also creates a distinct, peculiar relationship with his auditors, be they strangers, acquaintances, enemies, or lifelong friends. So too, the writer who would successfully adapt the tall tale to print must make his tale-teller not just a type or a dialect-speaking voice, but a realizable character. And he must evoke (perhaps create, since he is a writer and not a folk narrator) an implicit set of values and a common experience which can be stretched and exaggerated, creating that tall world which exists at the border between the credible and the incredible, pushing sometimes slightly and sometimes very far beyond that implied normal experience. In the best tall tale literature, the author does even more: he or she creates this tall tale atmosphere and establishes the tall tale relationship not simply among the characters but between the author and the readers. In the nineteenth century, particularly during the flush times of 1831 to 1860, a long and numerous procession of writers flooded America's periodicals, almanacs, and books with written tall tales which created compelling tall narrators and established this tall tale relationship in varying, complex, comic ways.

Certainly there were signs and beginnings and even full-fledged tall tales in print before 1831. Americans were telling tall tales all along in their homes, taverns, stages, and camps, and the tallness occasionally slipped into print. In 1728 William Byrd's *History of the Dividing Line betwixt Virginia and North Carolina* described and exaggerated what the Virginia gentleman saw as the extraordinary indolence of the North Carolinians.[1] Benjamin Franklin, whose humor concentrated on homely aphorisms, crackerbarrel philosophy, and sophisticated imitations of the *Spectator,* nonetheless understood and occasionally captured in print his countrymen's delight in tall humor. In one newspaper spoof he claimed that the American sheep's "very tails are so laden with Wool, that each has a Car or Waggon on four little Wheels to support and keep it from trailing on the Ground." He then described the preparations for a cod and whale fishery in the Great Lakes, and claimed that "the grand leap of the Whale . . . up the Fall of Niagara is esteemed by all who have seen it, as one of the finest Spectacles in Nature."[2] Though this kind of humor appears infrequently in Franklin's writing, such well-turned tales must have been created by a man practiced in the art of oral yarnspinning.

By the early nineteenth century, the tall talk of real-life southwesterners began to be recorded in popular literature. In a travel book published in 1810, Christian Schultz reported an exchange of boasts between two riverboatmen;[3] in 1821 Alphonso Wetmore depicted the tall-talking boatman Mike Fink in *The Peddlar*; and in 1822 the song "the Hunters of Kentucky" caught the national imagination as an expression of exuberant patriotism. Clearly business was picking up.

By 1830 the idea of distinct, stereotypical regional characters was firmly established, available to be thrown in the face of European cultural snobbery, as in Paulding's *The Lion of the West* (1831); contrasted with other regional characters, as in many of the *Spirit of the Times* sketches; or set against a genteel norm, as in Longstreet's sketches of Georgia scenes (originally published 1827-35). During the next several decades, newspapers like the *New Orleans Picayune,* the *St. Louis Reveille,* and the (New York) *Spirit of the Times,* along with almanacs and popular anthologies, overflowed with tall literature from every section of the country. Most of the writers were professional men—lawyers, soldiers, editors—intent on recording the language, habits, and humor of peculiar local types and characters. Their most difficult task was to create, from the regional stereotypes, individual, compelling characters and to capture in print the maneuvering, manipulating, challenging, and entertaining relationship between tale-teller and audience. Some of them stuck very close to actual tales heard, reporting rather than inventing. Others created characters, tales, and tale-telling situations from a combination of memories and personal fancy. Among them, they developed a corpus of forms and techniques for creating the literary tall tale.

## The Sketch

Protesting that he presented nothing more than "fanciful *combinations* of *real* incidents and characters," Augustus Baldwin Longstreet—lawyer, judge, newspaper editor, and later college president—in 1835 published a collection of sketches and essays that inaugurated the flush times of the American literary tall tale. Originally published separately in Georgia newspapers, the collected *Georgia Scenes* were immediately popular in both the South and the North; Longstreet came to be classified among the distinguished southern writers; and later sketch writers excused their backwoods subject matter by citing the example of "the great Longstreet."[4] These fanciful combinations of real incidents are not exclusively tall tales. The book's sections are too dis-

parate, and it owes too much to literary tradition, especially to the Addisonian essay, for any such simple classification. But in the combination of Baldwin and Hall, in the contrast of city and backwoods, in the conjoining of elevated prose and rustic dialect, Longstreet creates a Georgia out of which tallness can, and occasionally does, grow.

Longstreet establishes the potential for a tall tale relationship first by indicating the credentials of the author and his two narrators. The title page ascribes the book simply to "A Native Georgian." Among Georgians, this sobriquet establishes the author as an insider, free to criticize, joke, and yarn about his native region. To outsiders, the "native Georgian" is one who ought to know (and claims, in the Preface, to tell) the truth about a state which, to the antebellum North, seemed mysterious and uncivilized. The individual sketches are signed, as they were in the original newspaper publication, with either of two pseudonyms: Baldwin or Hall. Lyman Hall and Abraham Baldwin take their names from two early Georgia patriots[5] and thus possess the right to describe, explain, criticize, and exaggerate. Their snatches of autobiography reveal that both grew up with the maturing civilization on the frontier and abandoned the rural life in search of education, culture, and fame. Both thus exercise a dual vision: an acquired taste for civilization, enlivened by a sentimental attachment to and a real appreciation of rustic simplicity and vigor. Baldwin and Hall between them create a world of values upon which the tall tale can operate.

Baldwin is conservative, commonsensical, Addisonian.[6] His gently moralistic essays probe the foibles of polite society by sketching type characters: a mother silly with her child but rude to her servant, a young lady who is a "Charming Creature" but a miserably incompetent wife, travelers who become enamoured of cacophonous French and Italian music, young fops who duel over an imagined insult to a vain young lady. Though his tone is not strident, he pokes and prods thoughtless social conventions, imitativeness, and self-centered posing:

> Here the seconds separated, and soon after the principals met; and Crouch shot Noozle, in due form and according to the latest fashion, through the knees. I went to see him after he had received his wound; and, poor fellow, he suffered dreadful tortures. So much, said I, for a young lady's lingering from a ball an hour too long, in order to make herself conspicuous.
>
> ("The Ball")[7]

Baldwin's disapproval of modern music, dancing, fashions, and manners is offset by his admiration for amiable and competent housewives; plainspoken, hardworking farmers; and modest but forthright country girls. Observing the preparations for a country dance, he poses the rhetorical question, "Which is entitled to the most credit; the young lady who rises with the dawn, and puts herself and whole house in order for a ball four hours before it begins, or the one who requires a fortnight to get herself dressed for it?" (13). As the dance guests arrive, Baldwin demonstrates a clear distaste for "the refinements of the present day in female dress": the country girls "carried no more cloth upon their arms or straw upon their heads than was necessary to cover them. They used no artificial means of spreading their frock tails to an interesting extent from their ankles. They had no boards laced to their breasts, nor any corsets laced to their sides; consequently, they looked, for all the world, like human beings, and could be distinctly recognised as such at the distance of two hundred paces" (14). In Baldwin's view, modern civilization, as represented by Europe, the northern cities, and their southern imitators, does not necessarily confer superiority of morality or sense. Longstreet, we must remember, originally published many of these sketches in his paper, the *State Rights Sentinel,* and was a fervent advocate first of nullification and later of secession. His Baldwin sketches call for a culture based not on imitation of the North but on an indigenous southern dignity and simplicity. His contrast of excessive cultivation and rustic simplicity provides a two-layered vision of reality and normalcy against which Longstreet's tall tale Georgia can press.

Lyman Hall's vision is more complex, for he speaks in several voices. In **"A Native Georgian," "The Wax Works,"** and **"The Debating Society,"** he gaily describes the masculine recreations (mostly practical jokes) of his own class. His appreciation of **"The Horse Swap"** as a recreation for the rural lower class is similarly undiluted; but in other portrayals of backwoods pastimes—**"Georgia Theatrics," "The Fight,"** and **"The Gander Pulling"**—he alternates vivid description with overly sentimental, moralistic reactions. This last is Longstreet's tall tale voice.

Longstreet's contrast between imported civilization and the more indigenous rustic society is based on the cliché, widely believed among his northern contemporaries, that the South was culturally backward and morally depraved. Letters and diaries of antebellum northerners explicitly reveal their preconceptions, their fear of southern violence and their belief in southern impetuosity. Upon arriving in New Orleans in 1841, for example, a young New Englander confided to his diary that, for the purpose of "money getting," he was "going regardless of consequences, into an unhealthy climate amongst lawless and vicious men."[8] Fifty years after Longstreet, a more famous southerner living in the North recalled the brutality of the stereotypical backwoods poor white of that period. He spoke through the voice of Huck Finn:

> There couldn't anything wake them up all over, and make them happy all over, like a dog-fight—unless it might be putting turpentine on a stray dog and setting fire to him, or tying a tin pan to his tail and see him run himself to death.[9]

Longstreet, who studied at Yale and amused his friends there with anecdotes about Georgia, was well aware of his region's reputation.[10] His gander-pulling, eye-gouging, nose-biting Georgians elaborate the stereotype, filling it out with realistic detail. Having already baited the reader with claims of historical accuracy, the author then lulls him with a cultural cliché, and thus sets him up for a sell.

**"Georgia Theatrics,"** which was written toward the middle of the series but placed first in the book, is something of a microcosm of Hall's work as a whole. It begins with the kind of precise detail more typical of the tall tale than the humorous essay, followed immediately by a statement of the narrator's moral preconceptions:

> If my memory fail me not, the 10th of June, 1809 found me, at about 11 o'clock in the forenoon, ascending a long and gentle slope in what was called "The Dark Corner" of Lincoln. I believe it took its name from the moral darkness which reigned over that portion of the country at the time of which I am speaking. If in this point of view it was but a shade darker than the rest of the country, it was inconceivably dark.
>
> (p. 9)

The narrator's graceful prose aligns him with a world of order, optimism, and conventional feelings:

> . . . its natural condition was anything but dark. It smiled in all the charms of spring; and spring borrowed a new charm from its undulating grounds, its luxuriant woodlands, its sportive streams, its vocal birds, and its blushing flowers.
>
> (p. 9)

Borrowing his imagery and diction from eighteenth-century poetry, the narrator characterizes himself as a man who sees the world through literary conventions that are soon to prove inadequate. The voices emerging from a nearby grove, in contrast, speak with the poetry of folk speech—sharp rhythmic bursts, alliteration, curses, and startling imagery:

> Oh, wake snakes, and walk your chalks! Brimstone and—fire! Don't hold me, Nick Stoval! The fight's made up, and let's go at it.—my soul if I don't jump down his throat, and gallop every chitterling out of him before you can say 'quit!'
>
> (p. 9)

Hurrying toward the fight, our gentleman apparently arrives too late to prevent the victor from gouging out his opponent's eye. As he approaches, the "accomplices in the hellish deed" seem all to have fled. He sees only the victor retreating from the spot. Even in his horror and anger, his speech is conventional and stilted: "Come back, you brute! and assist me in relieving your fellow mortal, whom you have ruined for ever!" (p. 11). This fight, however, turns out to have been only a game, a play with all the parts acted by a youth of eighteen, who was "just seein' how I could'a' *fout*." Though the youth's moral vision undoubtedly is dark, the narrator has been taken in, deceived by his own preconceptions about the southern backwoods way of life. Although some eye gouging probably did occur in the Georgia of 1809,[11] Longstreet's purpose is not to document it or to say how common he believed it to be. Instead, he warns us against passing judgments based on ignorance and narrow preconceptions. And he has introduced us into a world at the limits of our knowledge, where fact and fantasy are difficult to distinguish, and where ordinary reactions and judgments may be inapplicable.

The gander pulling was a nineteenth-century pastime well documented by contemporary writers, and Longstreet's sketch on the subject casts no doubt upon its nature or the fact of its existence. He does, however, contrast this rowdy and to many sensibilities brutal recreation with an overly sentimental regard for the sport's innocent victim:

> The devoted gander was now produced; and Mr. Prator, having first tied his feet together with a strong cord, proceeded to the *neck-greasing*. Abhorrent as it may be to all who respect the tenderer relations of life, Mrs. Prator had actually prepared a gourd of *goose* grease for this very purpose. For myself, when I saw Ned dip his hands into the grease, and commence stroking down the feathers from breast to head, my thoughts took a melancholy turn. They dwelt in sadness upon the many conjugal felicities which had probably been shared between the *greasess* and the *greasee*. I could see him as he stood by her side, through many a chilly day and cheerless night. . . . Ye friends of the sacred tie! judge what were my feelings when, in the midst of these reflections, the voice of James Prator thundered on mine ear, "Darn his old dodging soul; brother Ned! grease his neck till a fly can't light on it!"
>
> (pp. 113-14)

The abrupt switch to coarse dialogue brings the reader back to the idea of sport, with a jolt and perhaps a laugh. The narrator's true jocularity has already leaked out in his reference to "the greasess and the greasee" and it is now fully developed in his comic characterization of the competitors' horses.

> Gridiron was a grave horse; but a suspicious eye which he cast to the right and left, wherever he moved, showed that "he was wide awake," and that "nobody

better not go fooling with him" as his owner sometimes used to say. . . . Off they went, Miss Sally delighted; for she now thought the whole parade would end in nothing more nor less than her favourite amusement, a race. But Gridiron's visage pronounced this the most nonsensical business that ever a horse of sense was engaged in since the world began. . . . Gridiron, who had witnessed Miss Sally's treatment with astonishment and indignation, resolved not to pass between the posts until the whole matter should be explained to his satisfaction. He therefore stopped short, and, by very intelligible looks, demanded of the whippers whether, if he passed between them, he was to be treated as Miss Spitfire had been? . . . In the midst of the conference, Gridiron's eye lit upon the oscillating gander. . . . After a short examination, he heaved a sigh, and looked behind him to see if the way was clear. It was plain that his mind was now made up; but, to satisfy the world that he would do nothing rashly, he took another view, and then wheeled and went for Harrisburg as if he had set in for a year's running. Nobody whooped at Gridiron, for all saw that his running was purely the result of philosophic deduction.

(pp. 115-17)

When the gander's head has come off and the prize has been awarded, the winner and losers are reconciled by joking, drinking, and fighting, "after which all parted good friends." If the sketch has a moral, it is not that gander pulling is barbaric, for by the end the agony of the gander is long forgotten. If it has a meaning within the structure of the book, it is that an outsider's ordinary tastes and sentiments may not be competent to judge the frontier life, and that the rewards of contact with the frontier come not from piously condemning but from accepting and appreciating the frontier and frontier tales on their own terms.

A sketch narrator who expresses and even seems to believe in conflicting values does not necessarily write tall tales, of course. In his discussion of Washington Irving's Geoffrey Crayon sketches, William Hedges explains that in most American sketches (as in much of American literature) the narrator's response to people and places is of greater interest than the people and places are in themselves. Ultimately, the sketch reveals as much about the narrator as about his subject. In the case of Geoffrey Crayon, it reveals "a personality which does not fully comprehend itself" and its own conflicts, a personality caught between the two extremes of European cultivation, dignity, and respectability and, on the other hand, American individualism, freedom, even irresponsibility.[12] The narrator of **"The Gander Pulling"** likewise feels the tug of conflicting value systems but has loaded his language in favor of the rough and ready frontier. He deliberately establishes the conflict in order to tease the reader, to make the reader himself feel that conflict, and to encourage him to choose, for the moment of the tale at least, tall humor over civilized notions of social responsibility.

One of Longstreet's most popular pieces, **"The Fight,"** increases the frontier violence and so increases the potential for conflict between the narrator's stated values and his enjoyment of rough tales. **"The Fight"** depicts in great detail the kind of courthouse battle that was only imagined in **"Georgia Theatrics."** Having read the earlier sketch, do we now rush in, morally indignant like the narrator of **"Georgia Theatrics,"** and condemn the characters? Do we treat this as documentary evidence that such fights commonly occurred with the full approval of families, friends, and peace officers? Do we swallow whole the narrator's claims of indignation? More likely we approach the sketch with skepticism and a sense of humor.

To establish his law-and-order pose, and perhaps to mollify any somber Georgians who might otherwise take offense, Longstreet opens and closes with assurances that his sketch is set "in the younger days of the Republic" and that "such scenes of barbarism and cruelty . . . are now of rare occurrence." This temporal and moral distancing superficially free him of responsibility for an incident he delights in describing.

The narrator, Hall, clearly admires Billy Stallings and Bob Durham as physical specimens:

> Billy ruled the upper battalion, and Bob the lower. The former measured six feet and an inch in his stockings, and, without a single pound of cumbrous flesh about him, weighed a hundred and eighty. The latter was an inch shorter than his rival, and ten pounds lighter; but he was much the most active of the two. In running and jumping he had but few equals in the county; and in wrestling, not one. In other respects they were nearly equal. Both were admirable specimens of human nature in its finest form.
>
> (p. 53)

Despite their positions as leaders of rival "battalions," Billy and Bob "were always very friendly; indeed, at their first interview, they seemed to conceive a wonderful attachment to each other." Hall deliberately demonstrates their lack of moral viciousness by contrasting them with Ransy Sniffle, a comic figure, degenerate both physically and morally:

> Now there happened to reside in the county just alluded to a little fellow by the name of Ransy Sniffle; a sprout of Richmond, who, in his earlier days, had fed copiously upon red clay and blackberries. This diet had given to Ransy a complexion that a corpse would have disdained to own, and an abdominal rotundity that was quite unprepossessing. Long spells of the fever and ague, too, in Ransy's youth, had conspired with clay

and blackberries to throw him quite out of the order of nature. His shoulders were fleshless and elevated; his head large and flat; his neck slim and translucent; and his arms, hands, fingers, and feet were lengthened out of all proportion to the rest of his frame. . . . His height was just five feet nothing; and his average weight in blackberry season, ninety-five. I have been thus particular in describing him, for the purpose of showing what a great matter a little fire sometimes kindleth. There was nothing on the earth which delighted Ransy so much as a fight. He never seemed fairly alive except when he was witnessing, fomenting, or talking about a fight. . . . Ransy had been kept for more than a year in the most torturing suspense as to the comparative manhood of Billy Stallings and Bob Durham. He had resorted to all his usual expedients to bring them in collision, and had entirely failed.

> (pp. 54-55)

When a fight between Bob and Billy finally occurs, inspired by a quarrel between their wives and enflamed by Ransy Sniffle, they are surrounded by a cheering, tall-talking crowd. "Hurra, my little hornet!" they cry. "Oh, my little flying wild-cat, hold him if you can! and, when you get him fast, hold lightning next." As Bill and Bob tear at one another, biting off ears, flesh, and fingers, the crowd responds with joy and more tall talk:

> "Look yonder!" cried the west; "didn't I tell you so! He hit the ground so hard it jarred his nose off. Now ain't he a pretty man as he stands? He shall have my sister Sal just for his pretty looks. I want to get in the breed of them sort o' men, to drive ugly out of my kinfolks."
>
> (p. 62)

Finally, with Bob atop him grinding dirt into his eyes, Bill cries "ENOUGH!" Meeting again two months after the fight, Bob and Billy shake hands and declare the dispute settled fairly:

> "Bobby, you've *licked* me in a fair fight; but you wouldn't have done it if I hadn't been in the wrong. I oughn't to have treated your wife as I did; and I felt so through the whole fight; and it sort 'o cowed me."
>
> "Well, Billy," said Bob, "let's be friends. Once in the fight, when you had my finger in your mouth, and was pealing me in the face and breast, I was going to halloo; but I thought of Betsy, and knew the house would be too hot for me if I got whipped when fighting for her after always whipping when I fought for myself."
>
> (p. 64)

Though the fight between Bob and Billy is neither more nor less rational, the violence neither more nor less defensible, than the pistol duel in **"The Ball,"** Longstreet shows that here, at least, a primitive kind of justice has been done.

The extraordinary strength and agility of the heroes, the tall talk, and the savoring of his region's supposed flaws, all indicate the inspiration of the oral tall tale—the triumph, indeed of tall tale over historical sketch. The closing sanctimonious judgment is by this point in *Georgia Scenes* formulaic:

> Thanks to the Christian religion, to schools, colleges, and benevolent associations, such scenes of barbarism and cruelty as that which I have been just describing are now of rare occurrence, though they may still be occasionally met with in some of the new counties. Wherever they prevail, they are a disgrace to that community. The peace-officers who countenance them deserve a place in the Penitentiary.
>
> (p. 64)

Though it partly reveals a genuine conflict in the mind of the sketch writer, this facade of moral outrage corresponds to the oral narrator's poker face: it is a disguise which, when penetrated by the clever, the open-minded, or the initiated, reveals humor. The notion that the dull, the narrow-minded, and the naïve might mistake these sketches for undiluted history and humorless moralizing adds another layer of humor—at least for Longstreet's Georgians, the real insiders to this joke. **"The Fight"** is, of course, a fiction, and in it Longstreet has created a self-consistent fictional world in which Billy and Bob are not villains or bullies but heroes whose strength, dignity, and good nature justify their violence, and a world in which Ransy Sniffle and the hypocritical Squire Loggins, safely fictional, can be safely laughed at.

Hall's clearest revelation of himself as a yarnspinner occurs at the very end of the last sketch in the book, **"The Shooting Match."** Traveling on horseback through a rural county, Hall falls in with a young man named Billy Curlew. Eyeing Hall's good horse and fine clothes, Billy attempts a traditional country man's ploy to assert his superiority over snoopy, upperclass strangers. We know it today primarily as the "Arkansas Traveler." Hall, a former country man himself, turns the game back on Billy.

> "Good morning, sir!" said I, reining up my horse as I came up beside him.
>
> "How goes it stranger?" said he, with a tone of independence and self-confidence that awakened my curiousity to know a little of his character.
>
> "Going driving?" inquired I.
>
> "Not exactly," replied, he, surveying my horse with a quizzical smile; "I haven't been a driving *by myself* for a year or two; and my nose has got so bad lately, I can't carry a cold trail *without hounds to help me.*"
>
> Alone, and without hounds as he was, the question was rather a silly one; but it answered the purpose for which it was put, which was only to draw him into conversation, and I proceeded to make as decent a retreat as I could.

> "I didn't know," said I, "but that you were going to meet the huntsmen, or going to your stand."
>
> "Ah, sure enough," rejoined he, "that *mout* be a bee, as the old woman said when she killed a wasp. It seems to me I ought to know you."
>
> "Well, if you *ought,* why don't you?"
>
> "What *mout* your name be?"
>
> "It might be anything," said I, with borrowed wit, for I knew my man, and knew what kind of conversation would please him most.
>
> "Well, what *is* it, then?"
>
> "It *is* Hall," said I; "but you know it might as well have been anything else."
>
> "Pretty, digging!" said he. "I find you're not the fool I took you to be; so here's to a better acquaintance with you."
>
> (pp. 197-98)

Billy is in fact on his way to a shooting match. And Hall, it turns out, is the very man Billy's "daddy used to tell [him] about," who as a boy won prizes in shooting matches against grown men. According to Billy, Hall "was born a shooting, and killed squirrels before he was weaned." Hall protests that his entire reputation was based upon two chance shots, one of which won a handkerchief for Billy's mother. He agrees, nonetheless, to accompany Billy to the match, only to find that Billy insists he take a shot. Though at first "thunder-struck" by the idea of shooting in the match, Hall finally resolves "to throw [him]self upon a third chance shot," insisting always to the reader upon his inability and embarrassment. After all the other shots have been made, Lyman Hall takes his turn:

> Policy dictated that I should fire with a falling rifle, and I adopted this mode; determining to fire as soon as the sights came on a line with the diamond, *bead* or no *bead.* Accordingly, I commenced lowering old Soap-stick; but in spite of all my muscular powers, she uniformly accelerated velocity. Before I could arrest her downward flight, she had not only passed the target, but was making rapid encroachments on my own toes. . . . I now, of course, determined to reverse the mode of firing, and put forth all my physical energies to raise Soap-stick to the mark. The effort silenced Billy, and gave tongue to all his companions. I had just strength enough to master Soap-stick's obstinate proclivity, and consequently, my nerves began to exhibit palpable signs of distress with her first imperceptible movement upward. A trembling commenced in my arms; increased, and extended rapidly to my body and lower extremities; so that, by the time that I had brought Soap-stick up to the mark, I was shaking form head to foot, exactly like a man under the continued action of a strong galvanic battery. . . . As soon as I found that Soap-stick was high enough (for I made no farther use of the sights than to ascertain this fact), I pulled trigger, and off she went.

After this display of weakness and ineptitude, the other men (and probably the reader) are astonished to discover that Hall's shot is second best—he has driven the cross at the center of the bull's eye. Hall jokes about the technique of shooting "with the double wabble," and expresses disappointment that his shot was only second best, but finally claims again that the shot was nothing more than good luck.

At this point, many readers may still be inclined to believe in their seemingly reliable narrator, especially since he makes himself out to be so humble and good-natured. We are amused, even, at Billy's simple-minded insistence on Hall's skill. But the closing paragraphs undercut our confidence, and suggest a new understanding of the story by revealing a new meaning in the narrator's name. The name Lyman Hall is taken from an early Georgian who signed the Declaration of Independence, and Georgia readers would initially have accepted the historical allusion and sought no further meaning. We find at the end, however, that this Ly-man may be a man who lies.

> "Tell your mother," said I, "that I send her a quarter of beef, which I won, as I did the handkerchief, by nothing in the world but mere good luck."
>
> "Hold your jaw, Lyman!" said Billy; "I an't a gwine to tell the old woman any such lies; for she's a *rael* reg'lar built Meth'dist."

The sketch then ends with an apparently unrelated remark. As Hall turns to leave, one of the men asks what office he is campaigning for. Though Hall assures him that he is not candidate, the man insists that all the "boys" will support him.

> "Yes," said Billy, "dang old Roper if we don't go our death for you, no matter who offers. If ever you come out for anything, Lyman, jist let the boys of Upper Hogthief know it, and they'll go for you to the hilt, against creation, tit or no tit, that's the *tatur.*"
>
> I thanked them kindly, but repeated my assurance. The reader will not suppose that the district took its name from the character of the inhabitants. In almost every county in the state there is some spot or district which bears a contemptuous appellation, usually derived from local rivalships, or from a single accidental circumstance.

Upper Hogthief may have earned its name or reputation through a single accidental circumstance. But is Hall named Lyman by accident, and did he earn his reputation as a marksman with three chance shots? This final emphasis on lies, names, reputations, and accidents casts doubt back upon the entire sketch, emphasizing the question of the narrator's reliability without ever settling it. The oral tall tale seldom settles such matters, either: the listener must not expect to know at exactly what point and in what manner literal fact has given way to fiction.

Hall is, in the end, a yarnspinner who elaborates for the sake of a good story, who insists upon historical fidelity and then chooses a tall subject, who flaunts his region's flaws and treats them as strengths, who toys with the distinctions between cultural stereotypes and individual reality, and who genially challenges outsiders to distinguish among all of these.

Joining the tall tale and the Addisonian essay into one book, Longstreet depicted a Georgia of contrasts—a growing, changing state not to be easily classified or simplistically understood. He shows a region in flux, flowing and maturing from wildness to civilization, where there are still wild stretches awash with reckless fun and violence as well as overly "civilized" inlets encrusted with pretensions and imported corruptions. Between them he implies, and partly depicts, a moderate course, an American (though perhaps only Southern) golden mean of homespun virtues, healthy recreations, and practical jokes that stop short of violence. But he makes clear that his ideal of ethical and aesthetic moderation embraces the humor of straight-faced comic exaggeration, for he is a yarnspinner himself whose fictions pose as facts to catch the unwary and delight the knowing.

*Notes*

1. *William Byrd's Histories of the Dividing Line Betwixt Virginia and North Carolina,* ed. William K. Boyd (New York: Dover, 1967). See, for example, p. 54 and pp. 90-92.

2. Letter in the *Public Advertiser,* May 22, 1765, rpt. in *Benjamin Franklin's Letters to the Press, 1758-1775,* ed. Verner W. Crane (Chapel Hill: Univ. of North Carolina Press, 1950), 33-34.

3. Christian Schultz, Jr., *Travels on a Inland Voyage through the Territories of Indiana, Louisiana, Mississippi and New Orleans, Performed in the Years 1807 and 1808* (1810; facsimile rpt. University Microfilms, 1979), II, 145.

4. John Donald Wade, *Augustus Baldwin Longstreet: A Study of the Development of Culture in the South* (New York: Macmillan, 1924), 149-56.

5. Ibid., 150.

6. Edgar Allan Poe was probably the first critic to point out Longstreet's debt to the *Spectator,* in his highly complimentary review of *Georgia Scenes* in the *Southern Literary Messenger,* 2 (1836), 287-92.

7. Augustus Baldwin Longstreet, *Georgia Scenes: Characters, Incidents, &c., in the First Half Century of the Republic by a Native Georgian,* 2nd ed. (New York: Harper, 1840), 129. Parenthetical references will be to this edition.

8. Quoted by Lewis O. Saum in *The Popular Mood of Pre-Civil War America,* Contributions in American Studies, 46 (Westport, Conn.: Greenwood Press, 1980), 171.

9. Mark Twain, *The Adventures of Huckleberry Finn,* ed. Scully Bradley et al. (New York: Norton, 1961), 113.

10. Wade, 148.

11. For a discussion of actual "rough and tumble" fighting in the Old Southwest see Elliot Gorn, "'Gouge and Bite, Pull Hair and Scratch': The Social Significance of Fighting in the Southern Backcountry," *American Historical Review,* 90 (1985), 18-43. According to Gorn, "Foreign travelers might exaggerate and backwoods storytellers embellish, but the most neglected fact about eye-gouging matches is their actuality" (33).

12. William L. Hedges, *Washington Irving: An American Study, 1802*-1832 (Baltimore: Johns Hopkins Press, 1965), 98, 105, 146, 157-58.

## Scott Romine (essay date spring 1996)

SOURCE: Romine, Scott. "Negotiating Community in Augustus Baldwin Longstreet's *Georgia Scenes.*" *Style* 30, no. 1 (spring 1996): 1-27.

[*In the following essay, Romine investigates the various tensions that exist between different social classes in Longstreet's* Georgia Scenes. *Analyzing the sketches from socioeconomic, cultural, and moral perspectives, Romine argues that Longstreet's fiction in fact represents a complex integration of various groups into a single cohesive community, even while Longstreet tacitly acknowledges and accepts the dominant social hierarchy of the antebellum South.*]

Commonly considered to be the first work of Southwestern humor, Augustus Baldwin Longstreet's *Georgia Scenes* (1835) has long been exiled to the margins of antebellum Southern literature, which, in turn, occupies a marginal position of its own. In his 1993 *Yeoman versus Cavalier,* Richie Devon Watson banishes Southwestern humor to a subliterary "generic cordon sanitaire" isolated from the more central plantation tradition (57-58). Besides being misleading on its own terms,

Watson's assertion that in their own time "southwest humorists were simply not considered legitimate writers" (57) has tended, as a general critical view, to legitimate the dismissal of Longstreet and his fellow Southwestern humorists as literary dabblers whose ideological work is crudely simplistic and easily apprehended.[1] Much of this neglect can be traced to the highly reductive critical lens through which *Georgia Scenes* (and, indeed, Southwestern humor as a genre) has been viewed: Kenneth Lynn's theory of the *cordon sanitaire,* a paradigm that pits gentleman narrators against bumbling and sometimes sinister yokels in a relentlessly repetitive and monological justification of class privilege. But a reconsideration of Longstreet's symbolic organization of collective experience, paying particular attention to a network of tropes—of economy, nature, representation, and language games—implicates Longstreet in a complex negotiation of class roles. Exploring the response of Longstreet's primary narrator, Lyman Hall, to the dialogic imperative of the lower class and tracing the development of what I will call his socionarrative style (by which I mean a social style reflected in narrative stylistics), I shall demonstrate how Longstreet legitimates the social relationships presumed to exist in the ideal (and even utopian) Georgia community.

Since his stated explanation of his narrative project focused exclusively on issues of preservation and realism, Longstreet himself would probably have been skeptical of such a project. He wrote of *Georgia Scenes* that "the aim of the author was to supply a chasm in history which has always been overlooked—the manners, customs, amusements, wit, dialect, as they appear in all grades of society to an ear and eye witness of them" (qtd. in Fitzgerald 164). In his preface to *Georgia Scenes,* he claimed to have used "some little art" only to "recommend [the sketches] to the readers of my own times" in the hope that their initial popularity would increase "the chance of their surviving the author" until a day "when time would give them an interest" (1).[2] Critics such as Kimball King have justly praised Longstreet for his work as a social historian (137-40), and James E. Kibler has argued for *Georgia Scenes* as a seminal work in the development of American realism (viii-xiii). Nevertheless, few critics have questioned the general position argued by Robert L. Phillips, Jr., who claims that Longstreet's "realism" is at least complicated by the narrative values implicit, and sometimes quite explicit, in the tales themselves (28-53, 137-50). The concept of a realistic narrative—in the sense of narrative being somehow objective or value-neutral—has, of course, been discredited at least since Wayne Booth's *Rhetoric of Fiction,* and even had it not, such a concept has little relevance for *Georgia Scenes,* a work in which social valuation is perhaps *the* fundamental textual activity. On a formal level, however, *Georgia Scenes* fulfills Roman Jakobson's criterion that metonymy provide the symbolic substructure of realist narrative. Longstreet's description of his sketches as "fanciful *combinations* of *real* incidents and characters" points to a deep structure in which contiguity is privileged over similarity as the dominant organizing principle of his narrative, which, following Jakobson's formulation. "metonymically digresses from the plot to the atmosphere and from the characters to the setting in space and time" (255). More significantly, this formal metonymic structure is replicated on the level of social interaction. As Jakobson reminds us, a "competition" between metaphor and metonymy "is manifest in any symbolic process, be it intrapersonal or social" (258). In *Georgia Scenes,* this "competition" manifests itself in the kind of knowledge Hall has of the lower-class white; as the narrative progresses. Hall's analogical equation of poor white and animal is replaced by a metonymic knowledge through which a mutually recognized relationship between the classes is finally established. It is in this context of symbolic competition that the archival nature of *Georgia Scenes*—its status as a repository of a historically located discursive paradigm—can be most fully appreciated.

In his 1959 *Mark Twain and Southwestern Humor,* Kenneth Lynn provides an alternative, but fundamentally flawed, paradigm.[3] Lynn's contribution was his historicization of a framed narrative said to represent the reaction of the Whig gentleman to the uncouth backwoodsman associated with Jacksonian democracy. According to Lynn, "Longstreet and his successors found that the frame was a convenient way of keeping their first person narrators outside and above the comic action, thereby drawing a *cordon sanitaire,* so to speak, between the morally irreproachable Gentleman and the tainted life he describes" (64). This *cordon sanitaire,* according to Lynn, exists on both a moral and a linguistic plane: the vernacular formally announces the moral inferiority of the "tainted" poor white "Clown" Conversely, the "Self-Controlled Gentleman" employs a literate style that provides a normative ground from which didactic evaluation and ultimately control of the lower class is made possible (64-65, 68-69). Thus, the narrator's language and the lower-class vernacular are rigidly separated, and never the twain shall meet—that is, until Mark Twain. Although Lynn is clearly correct in recognizing a class distinction, his scheme represents a radical reduction of the complexities inherent in the encounter between gentleman narrators and lower-class whites. The *cordon sanitaire* relies on a social model in which class relationships are unequivocally antagonistic; the cultural work performed by Southwestern humor, according to Lynn, is little more than a Whiggish

attempt to quash the political claims of the Jacksonian democrat symbolically represented by the uncouth backwoodsman.[4] Yet as we begin to examine Longstreet's corpus, we find that, far from asserting his moral superiority to these "tainted" characters, Longstreet's narrator is more likely to elide the social distance between himself and his subject in an effort to negotiate consensual participation in a common social field.

**"Georgia Theatrics,"** which Lynn takes as an epitome of the *cordon sanitaire,* will serve as a useful point of entry into our examination of Longstreet's narrative dynamics. In this short sketch, which opens *Georgia Scenes,* Lyman Hall (whom Lynn inexplicably calls a minister) recounts an 1809 visit he made to Lincoln County, Georgia. Walking in the countryside "[r]apt with the enchantment of the season" (4), Hall overhears what is apparently a vicious fight between two ruffians. Horrorstruck upon hearing that one of the combatants has lost an eye, he runs to the spot, where he encounters the "victor":

> He looked excessively embarrassed, and was moving off, when I called to him, in a tone emboldened by the sacredness of my office, and the iniquity of his crime, "Come back, you brute! and assist me in relieving your fellow mortal, whom you have ruined for ever!"
>
> My rudeness subdued his embarrassment in an instant; and with a taunting curl of the nose, he replied, "You needn't kick before you're spurr'd. There a'nt nobody there, nor ha'nt been nother. I was jist seein' how I could 'a' *fout.*
>
> (6)

Indeed, as Hall informs his "gentle reader," "his report was true," and the young farmer returns to his plow having performed "nothing more nor less than a Lincoln rehearsal" (6). Lynn presents the sketch as a quintessential example of the "Self-Controlled Gentleman" confronting the "youthful Clown" from the moral distance provided by the *cordon sanitaire* of the frame. Thus, Lynn locates the narrative discourse at a strictly normative level, a level from which the boy's use of the vernacular and his "iniquitous crime"—read here as psychological neurosis—mark him as wholly deviant (66-69). Lynn's rigid hierarchy hardly holds up under scrutiny, however, as several critics have noted: Newlin, for one, writes that Hall shows himself to be "morally righteous, easily duped, and prone to act on insufficient information; in short, Hall is himself a rube in the backwoods, a stranger to what he observes" (27).

Having kicked, as the boy memorably puts it, before he is spurred, Hall asserts his moral authority in an "emboldened" tone that embodies his tendency to assign morality strictly according to class. This tendency is evident from the opening lines of the sketch, in which he gives the locale as "The Dark Corner" of the frontier county of Lincoln, explaining, "I believe it took its name from the moral darkness, which reigned over that portion of the county, at the time of which I am speaking. If in this point of view, it was but a shade darker than the rest of the county, it was inconceivably dark" (3). Claiming that in the meantime (the sketch is ostensibly written in the early 1830s) the area had "become a living proof 'that light shineth in darkness'" (3), Hall becomes absorbed in his pastoral reveries until startled by the "loud, profane, and boisterous voices": "In Mercy's name! thought I, what band of ruffians has selected this holy season, and this heavenly retreat, for such Pandæmonian riots!" (4-5). As he approaches, he notes that the "accomplices in this hellish deed" had fled (11). Hall's diction ("[m]oral darkness," "profane" voices, "Pandæmonian riots," "hellish deed") suggests a rigid moral binarism that legitimates his act of social authority; as righteous stroller in his "heavenly retreat," he appropriates the moral right to intervene in the fracas. Because his narrative style projects moral values onto his narrative landscape, it *predicts* his social style, which likewise "finds" moral values (or their conspicuous absence) in the situation he encounters. When he does intervene, he invokes his hierarchical privilege by calling the boy a "brute" who (illogically) is "morally" bound to return and aid his "fellow-mortal." Thus, in relation to Hall, the boy is characterized as "bestial"—an identification reinforced when Hall says that the ground looked "as if two Stags had been engaged upon it" (6)—while in relation to his imaginary antagonist, he becomes "human," and thus subject to Hall's moral code.

Hall's unresolved contradiction is contingent upon two unmediated versions of the "natural." A term with important implications throughout *Georgia Scenes,* the "natural" invokes (1) the nature of pastoral reverie (equated with heaven and the gentleman) and (2) the proto-Darwinian nature of survival of the fittest (equated with hell and the poor white). While the former nature is regulated by implicit moral rules ("natural law"), the latter is marked, from Hall's perspective, by a sinister inversion of normative morality. Thus, the boy's bestiality represents an inversion of the natural scene of "sportive streams," "vocal birds," and "blushing flowers" Hall observes during his heavenly retreat. (Not coincidentally, Hall begins his description of the countryside with the claim that "[w]hatever may be said of the *moral* condition of the Dark Corner, at the time just mentioned, its *natural* condition was any thing but dark" [4].) Moreover, the boy's metaphoric status as "animal" symbolically *contaminates* the contexts in which he appears: as a metonymic stand-in for place (the "Dark Corner") and a synedochic representative of class (poor whites), the boy. Hall implies, cannot be expected to act morally, despite being "obligated" to do so. One might say that from Hall's perspective, the boy is acting according to *his* nature instead of Hall's. In symbolically organizing the situation, Hall simultaneously creates and legitimates his social authority. Yet this authority fails in two respects. First, Hall's "opponent" is revealed to be exclusively the result of symbolic actions occurring at the level of his subjective consciousness. What purports to be "found" is shown to be "constructed," and in this sense, his opponent is quite as imaginary as the boy's. Second, the boy utterly refuses to recognize, and thereby subverts, whatever social authority Hall represents, a subversion that notably involves another animal metaphor (a spurred horse).

The failure of Hall's socionarrative style in **"Georgia Theatrics"** results from the absence of dialogic class negotiation; both Hall and the farmboy fail to recognize their common involvement in the same social field or community. To put the matter this way, however, raises two potentially questionable issues. First, one could argue that the narrative itself does not recognize this common involvement, that the gentleman narrator wants nothing to do with the poor white trash other than to poke fun at him for the reader's amusement or as a justification of the cultural status quo (this, as we have seen, is Lynn's argument). Secondly, one could argue that such common involvement is merely an illusion engendered by a narrative designed to serve the interests of an upper class. Such an argument rests on the premise that community is an epiphenomenon of class structure that functions to conceal "real" social contradictions. The first criticism is much easier to answer than the second since all that must be shown is a style that dialogically takes into account the voice of the Clown rather than monologically consigning that voice to communal exile. The second is much harder to answer; in some respects, it cannot be answered. Longstreet's negotiation of community is demonstrably dialogic in nature; to use Bakhtin's language, Longstreet's "world is full of other people's words [which the artist must] introduce . . . into the plane of his own discourse, but in such a way that this plane is not destroyed" (*Problems* 201). Yet at the same time, there is no way absolutely to counter the objections of Lennard J. Davis, who claims that, while actual conversation is dialogic in Bahktin's sense of the word, "dialogue in novels lacks this crucial and democratic strand—everything that comes from the author is autocratically determined" (177-78). In many instances, Longstreet's dialogism is autocratic in precisely the way Davis uses the term; the issue then becomes whether Longstreet's integration of the Clown's voice into the plane of his own discourse can be considered *legitimate.*

Because I essentially want to bracket Longstreet's rhetoric rather than restore its material context. I will concentrate on his narrative legitimation rather than its legitimacy *per se*. In going about this, I would like first to consider the negotiation-based model of social relations proposed by Theodore B. Leinwand, who conceives of social power as a continual discourse of "[c]ompromise, negotiation, exchange, [and] give and take" (479). Leinwand deemphasizes conflict as an inherent "operator" in the field of "sociopolitical and cultural practices," arguing instead that the win-lose/subversion-containment terminology of Foucauldian discourse fails to account for the complexity of social relations as they actually exist and are modified over time (478).[5] Leinwand's model is especially relevant to *Georgia Scenes,* a work in which exchange constitutes an important trope. Throughout the work we find horses, money, promises, oaths, curses, blows, insults, and so on being exchanged, often after a period of literal negotiation. In examining individual sketches. I want to argue generally that such exchanges provide the opportunity for the negotiation of communal norms, and further, that the final horizon of this negotiation is the relationship between the gentleman narrator and the lower-class whites he encounters. Briefly, I will define negotiation as legitimate when it performatively establishes consensus regarding social organization. This definition, of course, relies on consensus as it is represented by the gentleman narrator and thus can be called into question as an ideologically motivated resolution in the same sense that community can be considered epiphenomenal. But before discussing how Longstreet naturalizes his narrative negotiation, let me briefly note that his rhetoric of realism can be construed as an attempt to answer such objections, as can his attempt, which I discuss later in this essay, to legitimate his authority to "represent" the lower-class whites in both the political and narrative senses of the word.

Longstreet's narrative negotiation is in some ways "built upon" a rhetoric of nature, a trope which finds exaggerated form in both its pastoral and bestial incarnations. As in **"Georgia Theatrics,"** Hall's effete, highly stylized characterization of nature constitutes one pole of this trope; the other consists of the rather Hobbesian "nature" of the Georgia poor white. As the narrative progresses, Hall increasingly comes to find a style of narration that will negotiate these two poles and appear normal (natural) in contrast to their excesses, which find verbal form in the raw vernacular of the backwoodsman and the effete moral rhetoric of the dandy. The effect of this juxtaposition is the unnatural, a category that defines the "natures" of both the poor white and the dandy. Contapunctal to the opposition between natural and unnatural is a second opposition between

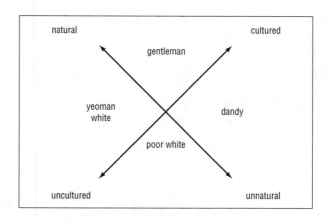

cultured and uncultured, categories oriented along class lines. Schematized in a Greimas rectangle, the structuring oppositions of *Georgia Scenes* look like this: [see above figure]

The organizing structure of *Georgia Scenes* thus produces four types of characters: the yeoman white, the poor white, the gentleman, and the dandy. To briefly schematize the two axes, we might note that the natural-unnatural axis orients itself according to issues of norms and normalcy, of morality, and of behavior; this axis is primarily egalitarian, applying equally to all member of the community, defining what are "right" and "wrong" actions. Conversely, the cultured-uncultured axis orients itself according to issues of propriety, status, and manners; this axis is primarily hierarchical, defining what are "proper" and "improper" actions. As the narrative negotiation of *Georgia Scenes* unfolds, we find the initially dominant term (cultured) apparently being superseded by the term that allows wider communal participation (natural), it having more to do with social behavior than birthright. At the same time, Longstreet's attempt to preserve and legitimate the concept of "natural" hierarchy through the mechanism of representation is far from disinterested, and the utopian vision of community portrayed in **"The Shooting Match,"** the final episode of the book, should be interpreted as an ideologically motivated resolution to pressing (and perhaps intractable) social tensions.[6]

### LYMAN HALL AND THE DIALOGIC IMPERATIVE

As the narrative progresses, Hall becomes more deeply integrated within his community, his narrative style finally coming to represent a sort of communal voice, a perspective from which class tensions are resolved even if such a resolution is far from the natural process implied in his narrative closure. Indeed, much of the rhetorical energy of Hall's narrative is devoted to effacing the very idea of class, of which he rarely demonstrates a conceptual awareness. This apparent ignorance of class relationships, however, must be heavily qualified since Hall finally displays an ignorance of the content of class rather than the social forms associated with it; to use Michael Polanyi's terminology, class remains an integral component of his "tacit knowledge" even though it rarely serves as a focal point. This distinction, in turn, is a lesson he learns in due course; his mistake in **"Georgia Theatrics"** is precisely a matter of form (here taken as a position within a social hierarchy) and content (the characteristics associated with that position): in short, Hall mistakenly assumes that the poor white living in the "Dark Corner" of Lincoln will act out his depraved moral nature. Yet if Hall stumbles in **"Georgia Theatrics,"** he nevertheless avoids the kind of withdrawal that defines the socionarrative style of his fellow narrator, Baldwin; in Hall's defense, moreover, it might be said that at least he publicly vocalizes his assumptions about social relationships and thereby allows the possibility of correction and modification.

Consciousness that he too provides a figure to be interpreted by others becomes for Hall an important point of departure in his evolution toward a more egalitarian socionarrative style. Hall's second sketch, **"The Horse Swap,"** begins with Hall noticing a man "cavorting" on horseback in front of an impassive crowd. As Hall approaches, he relates that the man "eyed me closely" before "he fetched a whoop, and swore that 'he could outswap any live man, woman or child, that ever walked these hills, or that ever straddled horse flesh since the days of old daddy Adam.' 'Stranger,' said he to me, 'did you ever see the *Yellow* Blossom from Jasper?'" (20-21). After being assured by the man that he is, in fact, the celebrated personage in question, Hall relates, "I began to feel my situation a little awkward" until an older gentleman named Peter Ketch "relieves" him by drawing the attention of the Yellow Blossom and engaging him in a horse swap. After an almost ritualistic series of offers, counteroffers, rhetorical feints, and insults, Ketch and the Blossom finally agree to swap horses. When Bullet, the horse Ketch has obtained, is discovered to have a huge sore on his back, it appears that Ketch has been fooled—that is, until his young son reveals that Blossom's new beast, Kit, is both blind and deaf.

In an important essay on the role of games in Southwest humor, Michael Oriard notes that what Ketch actually gains in the exchange is "stature in the eyes of the townspeople" (14). "An audience," Oriard says, "whether simply readers like ourselves or bystanders at the scene, is essential to such contests . . . because it provides the context in which the stake of the game is meaningful" (14). Ketch's rhetorical strategy makes particularly shrewd use of the crowd, relying as it does on the audience's ability to unpack his layered and sometimes subtle ironies. Unlike Blossom, whose hyperbolic self-proclamations are designed to create a dis-

tance between himself and those around him, Ketch has a rhetorical style that implicates and involves his audience. When, for example, Blossom comments on the "curious look" in Kit's eyes, Ketch responds, "Oh yes, sir, . . . just as blind as a bat. Blind horses always have clear eyes. Make a motion at his eyes, if you please, sir." When Kit jerks back, Ketch continues, "Stone blind, you see, gentlemen . . . but he's just as good to travel of a dark night as if he had eyes" (26). Finally, when Blossom grumbles, "Blame my buttons . . . if I like them eyes," Ketch responds gracefully, "No . . . nor I neither. I'd rather have 'em made of diamonds; but they'll do, if they don't show as much white as Bullet's." In each instance, Ketch employs what Wayne Booth calls stable irony—that is, irony that relies on shared assumptions and contexts to communicate its message. When Ketch refers to Bullet's eyes or when he ironically (but truthfully) announces that Kit is "stone blind," he is not merely bargaining with Blossom; rather, he is bargaining with the assembled audience, winning it to his side through a shrewd series of rhetorical moves. Thus, when Blossom threatens to end the bargaining, Ketch refers to the figure he attempts to project to the townsfolk: "I didn't care about trading; but you cut such high shines, that I thought I'd like to back you out; and I've done it. Gentlemen, you see I've brought him to a hack" (27). And later, when negotiations stall for a second time, Hall reports that "it was pretty unanimously decided that the old man had backed Blossom out" (28) until the young trader backs down and agrees to Ketch's terms. In both instances, Ketch's strategy pays concrete dividends; because he is able to create consensus by manipulating audience reactions, he can bring communal sentiment to bear upon Blossom, whose image as "a leetle of the best man, at a horse swap, that ever trod shoe leather" (21) requires that the community recognize his prowess with each trade.

In the end, however, the joke is on Blossom, for he has utterly failed to read the situation correctly. This episode mirrors countless incidents in Southwestern humor; indeed, the very nature of the horse swap and its equivalents (gambling episodes, confidence games, swindles) throughout the genre revolves around each participant's ability both to interpret competently and to externalize himself so as to deny this ability to others. While in many cases this process works to undermine communal stability—one thinks of Johnson Jones Hooper's Simon Suggs, for instance—Longstreet tends, in *Georgia Scenes* at least, to posit some congruity between communal health and the kind of uncertainty created when a character like Ketch misrepresents himself and his immediate situation. If in Longstreet's ideal community each man should be easily apprehended and roles mutually accepted, a corollary truth is that a measure of uncertainty and instability—in short, a measure of play—is no less necessary for the maintenance of communal norms and values. Indeed, when we note the numerous cases of false impersonation or misrepresentation in the pages of *Georgia Scenes*—a list that would include, besides Peter Ketch, the character of Ned Brace in both **"The Character of a Native Georgian"** and **"A Sage Conversation,"** the young gentlemen of **"The Wax Works,"** the debaters in **"The Debating Society,"** and Hall himself in **"The Shooting Match"**—we come to realize that the trope is an important one in Longstreet's (and particularly Hall's) narrative world. A composite picture of Longstreet's quasi-trickster figure would reveal a gentleman who has mastered the language games of his native community to such an extent that he can foresee the social implications of his verbal self-projection. Peter Ketch, for example, is marked by his dialect as being of a higher social class than Blossom; although clearly not an aristocrat, his speech and general manner have enough polish to establish him firmly as a middle-class yeoman. As we have seen, his rhetorical appeal to the community places him in an advantageous position vis-à-vis the exchange he negotiates, an exchange which furthermore is more social than economic since his increased stature works to reaffirm preexisting communal hierarchies.[7] The wild backwoods youth, Hall lets us realize, returns to the countryside having received something of an education from the older town-dweller.[8]

The ability to gauge one's audience and rhetorically mislead it works performatively to establish the preexisting social hierarchy; indeed, one might say that a facility to mislead is equivalent to the (natural) ability to lead. From the narrative perspective, such verbal facility represents a special kind of social power and as such must be used responsibly. As Jürgen Habermas remarks.

> Thanks to the creativity of natural language the native speaker gains a unique power over the practical consciousness of the members of a community. The career of sophistry reminds us that it can be used for mindfogging agitation as well as for enlightening people.
>
> There is, however, another side to this power: the specific lack of power of the speaking subject vis-à-vis habitualized language-games: they cannot be modified unless one participates in them. This in turn can be successful only to the extent that the rules which determine a language-game have been internalized To enter into a linguistic tradition necessitates, at least latently, the efforts of a process of socialization: the "grammar" of language-games has to become part of the personality structure.
>
> (184)

Habermas's equation of language games and socialization processes provides a useful way of approaching Hall's sketches since his dialogic encounters during the course of the book necessitate an internalization of language-game "grammar" before he can actively perform and negotiate his social authority, a position from which, in turn, social consensus can be established and mutually affirmed. In such early sketches as **"The Horse Swap."** Hall plays a more or less passive role, allowing someone like Ketch, who functions almost as a surrogate, to enter into the language game with all the cultural implications that attend it. As his monological narrative perspective begins to admit the language of the lower class. Hall demonstrates a willingness to perceive, narrate, and finally engage in the verbal exchanges and language games that define and maintain social order.

As he engages the social economy of his community through its language games. Hall retains as a rhetorical subtext the trope of nature we have already noted. Most of Hall's sketches, including **"The Horse Swap," "The Fight," "The Turn-Out," "The Gander Pulling," "The Turf," "The Fox Hunt,"** and **"The Shooting Match,"** focus upon gatherings in which characters establish social status through a game or contest of some sort. As they are represented diachronically, these contests mediate the nature-culture opposition that permeates *Georgia Scenes* and, in doing so, work to naturalize the cultural positions they produce. In **"The Fight,"** we find hierarchy established through physical combat; although the two combatants, Bob Durham and Billy Stallions, are described as "admirable specimens of human nature in its finest form" (56), Hall is quick to denounce the fight as a "scen[e] of barbarism and cruelty . . . now of rare occurrence" (70). Social hierarchy performatively established through physical combat thereby partakes of the rhetoric of bestial nature we noted in **"Georgia Theatrics,"** a "nature" furthermore constructed as an anachronism, it having been suppressed by cultural institutions, including "the Christian religion," "schools, colleges, and benevolent associations" (35). Hall makes a similar temporal contrast in **"Georgia Theatrics,"** for between the erstwhile "moral darkness" of Lincoln and its present respectability, he claims, "I could adduce from this county instances of the most numerous and wonderful transitions, from vice and folly, to virtue and holiness, which have ever perhaps been witnessed since the days of the apostolic ministry" (3).

Nevertheless, this preference for the present over the past is offset by several passages in which Hall makes the opposite comparison. In **"The Turn Out,"** for example, Hall interrupts the tale to describe the lush countryside he and Captain Griffin see as they walk to the schoolhouse. Apologizing to his reader for the "minuteness of the foregoing description," Hall justifies himself by passing along the Captain's remark that the surrounding lands "will never wear out" (83). Hall then relates that forty-two years later he visited the same site, which by that point had become "barren, dreary and cheerless" (84). This passage subtly emphasizes the loss of the "natural" that Hall laments on several occasions: he begins the tale, for example, by describing the "Georgia Welcome of 1790" that he fears "Georgia will know . . . no more"—a clear comparison between present decadence and sophistication and the natural hospitality of what he unself-consciously calls the "good old days" (80). A similar passage occurs later in the tale, when "the *ruffle-shirted* little darlings of the present day" compare unfavorably with the "hardy sons of the forest" he encounters as he visits Captain Griffin (90). Thus, unlike his fellow narrator Baldwin, for whom the present is always a sorry substitute for the irredeemable past. Hall demonstrates a divided temporal preference: on the one hand, he characterizes the past as simple and natural and the present as precious and decadent; on the other, he characterizes the past as bestial and uncouth and the present as civilized.

While this construction may appear to be simply inconsistent, I would contend that, instead, it helps delineate the abstract categories necessitating narrative resolution. Referring back to the categories discussed earlier, we find that within the opposing pairs of terms, cultured-uncultured and natural-unnatural, the historical progression unfolding within Hall's narrative is positive in the former case and negative in the latter. In other words, as the community of *Georgia Scenes* matures, it simultaneously becomes less "bestial" and less "pastoral," these terms implying qualities obverse to those in "nature." A closer examination of these passages, moreover, reveals a class context at work; when Hall prefers the present, he is generally speaking about the lower class, while his preference for the past usually indicates that the upper class is the topic of discussion. Thus, as the community of *Georgia Scenes* develops over time, the frontier excesses of the poor white tend to disappear as part of the same cultural shift that produces a more decadent and sophisticated upper class. This construction provides a key to Longstreet's negotiation of social relationships: the ostensible collapse of the social distance between the "natural" versions of the gentleman and the lower-class white necessitates a renegotiation of their mutual roles, a negotiation that, to reiterate, occurs largely within the context of communal contests.

Among the most complex of Hall's later tales dealing with ritualistic gatherings that reinforce shared communal experience, **"The Gander Pulling"** shows Hall's narrative style becoming less rigid in how it evaluates the lower class. In this ritual, a heavily greased gander is hung upside-down from a loose rope under which competitors pass mounted on horseback. The horseman who pulls the greased fowl's head from his body is declared the winner. As he describes the greasing of the gander, Hall shifts from an objective point of view to a morally interested one:

> Abhorrent as it may be, to all who respect the tenderer relations of life, *Mrs.* Prator had actually prepared a gourd of *goose*-grease for this very purpose. For myself, when I saw Ned dip his hands into the grease, and commence stroking down the feathers, from breast to head, my thoughts took a melancholy turn—They dwelt in sadness upon the many conjugal felicities which had probably been shared between the *greasess* and the *greasee*. . . . And now alas! an extract from the smoking sacrifice of his bosom friend, was desecrated to the unholy purpose of making his neck "a fit object" for Cruelty to reach "her quick, unerring fingers at." Ye friends of the sacred tie! judge what were my feelings, when in the midst of these reflections, the voice of James Prator thundered on mine ear, "Durn his old dodging soul; brother Ned! grease his neck till a fly can't light on it!"

(128-29)

In this passage, the dialogic juxtaposition of styles—as well as of perception—works to bridge the social boundary separating Hall from the yeoman white within a context that occurs in several of Hall's sketches: the context of cruelty to animals. In **"The Horse-Swap,"** cruelty to animals allows Hall to assert the moral distance between himself and the lower classes; after the sore on Bullet's back is exposed, Hall "felt that the brute who had been riding him in that situation, deserved the halter" (28). In the passage above, however, Hall presents the same conflation of human and animal attributes ironically; we have little difficulty in perceiving that Hall's overblown rhetoric of moral concern is just as exaggerated as Prator's blunt outburst. The ironic opacity of Hall's rhetoric indicates a language that is no longer a transparent vehicle of absolute social authority. Likewise, his exaggerated sentimentality serves to subvert his metaphoric characterization of both the birds and their tormenters, the latter of whom, unlike Blossom and the farmboy of **"Georgia Theatrics,"** escape being consigned to the category of brute beast. Less concerned with judging the behavior of the lower class, Hall becomes more engaged in the ritualistic negotiation of social relationships.

Yet while Hall is not as eager to condemn the morals of the lower class, he is equally unwilling to dispense entirely with class distinctions. Early in the sketch, he notes that the "few females" in attendance "were from the lowest walks of life" (128), and later, as the gander pulling commences with the cry "Now blaze away!," he parenthetically glosses the command as the one used "for an onset of every kind, with people of this order" (131). Moreover, the issue of class seems to qualify Hall's attitude toward the fighting and drinking that follow the gander pulling, neither of which elicits, as we might expect, his moral condemnation. Instead, we find Hall sympathetically portraying the man who brings about these potential transgressions, one Fat John Fulger, the winner of the gander pulling who is colorfully described by one spectator as "that *gourd* o' hog's *lard*" (133). Though not among the more skilled contestants, Fulger caps his victory with a speech Hall initially characterizes as being "little calculated to reconcile [the losers and those who had staked bets on them] to their disappointment" (133). "*Boys,*" Fulger begins, "don't pull with *men* any more. I've *just* got my hand in; I wish I had a pond full o' ganders here now, jist to show how I could make their heads fly—Bet all I've won, you may hang three upon that rope, and I'll set Slouch at full speed, and take off the heads of all three, with the first grab; two with my hands, and one with my teeth" (134). This mock self-aggrandizement, Hall explains, "was all fun, for John knew, and all were convinced that he knew, that his success, was entirely the result of accident. John was really a 'good natured fellow,' and his *cavorting* had an effect directly opposite to that which the reader would suppose it had—it reconciled all to their disappointment, save one" (134).⁹ What Fulger accomplishes through his ironic self-portrayal is a rhetorical resolution to the real tensions accompanying his victory; in a sense, his skill at language games makes up for his ineptitude at gander pulling. In employing stable irony, as Hall is careful to explain to his reader, Fulger reestablishes harmony in an audience seething with potential violence, the result of accident marring a social ritual in which consensus—here concerning the probable winners, Odum and Bostwick—had already been achieved. From Hall's point of view, Fulger's ability to reestablish the consensus he had disrupted qualifies the morally dubious actions that follow when he spends his winnings treating the company to drinks, "and thereby produced four Georgia rotations [fights]; after which all parted good friends" (134).

Notably absent is any narrative moralizing, especially since Hall condemns both fighting and drinking on other occasions. Indeed, a later sketch entitled **"An Interesting Interview"** is devoted entirely to protraying the ill effects of "the all-destroying vice" of drunkenness. At the beginning of this tale, which relates a drunken conversation of two "industrious, honest, sensible farmers, when sober" (185), Hall looks forward to the day ten years hence when he hopes to "see [drunkenness] driven

entirely, from the higher walks of life at least, *if not from all grades of society*" (184; my emphasis). This divided sense of class expectation similarly informs the ending of **"The Gander Pulling,"** where instead of judging them for their drunken, brawling ways. Hall instead presents the lower-class folk sympathetically. Moreover, Hall presents drinking and fighting not as threats to normative communal relationships, but rather as means of establishing legitimate relationships—among people of a certain sort. If, as one of his drunkards claims, "circumstances alter cases" (186), Hall's narrative perspective proves flexible enough to recognize and even sanction the positive consequences of drinking and fighting within the community-building context of the gander pulling. If the participants in the gander pulling do not quite live up to Hall's gentlemanly ideals, they nevertheless engage in a way of negotiating social relationships that Hall is reluctant to condemn outright. At the same time, Hall's situational ethics with respect to drinking and fighting legitimate the social hierarchy evident within his narrative community. In not holding the yeoman white to a strict or absolute morality, Hall engages in a strategy of containment that leaves unspoken its conceptual articulation. Thus, while Hall includes the yeoman whites of **"The Gander Pulling"** in the collective experience of Georgia culture, they enter the community positionally—that is, as members who are neither required nor expected to participate fully within the value system at work at the ultimate level of communal morality, a value system that in turn legitimates class distinctions between gentleman and yeoman white. This sense of inclusion, then, while broadening the parameters of communal participation, nevertheless fails to eliminate class distinctions.

### The Political Closure of "The Shooting Match"

The maintenance of community requires a socionarrative style flexible enough to sustain engagement with the lower class while simultaneously perpetuating the social gradations that inform *Georgia Scenes* from the beginning. This tension between "common ground" and class distinction constitutes the dominant problem to be resolved through Hall's narrative negotiation. Given Longstreet's lifelong devotion to the ideals of Jeffersonian democracy, class distinction proves particularly troubling since what must finally be justified is how, in a society in which all men are created equal, some are more equal than others. In a 17 April 1834 editorial in the *State Rights' Sentinel,* the Augusta newspaper he owned and edited, Longstreet confronted the issue of class in the context of American violence. Longstreet wondered how Americans could be as violent as Europeans, or perhaps even more so, given that the former had no extremes of grandeur or poverty, of aristocracy and peasantry—no feudal barbarian distinctions of vassal, as in Europe; and that the great mass and bulk of the population are, it may be said, of the middling class, and placed upon an equality of condition—certainly as respects their political rights, and in the aggregate they are so also in respect to their morals, their education, and their rank in society.

("Causes" 1)

Although Longstreet's language subtly subverts his homage to a (nearly) classless society—equality of "rank in society" in the aggregate" is an utterly meaningless entity—it is interesting to note how, following Longstreet's logic, social hierarchy might (as in Europe) "legitimately" fuel violence. Longstreet resolves this issue by privileging political equality, the mechanism through which *all* Americans are "placed upon an equality of condition." Since political equality, by which Longstreet means suffrage, does not, however, preclude a hierarchical organization of those representing and those being represented, in a post-*Georgia Scenes* sketch entitled **"Darby, The Politician,"** Longstreet describes the social chaos resulting from an unfit yeoman white's being elected to office.[10] The trope of representation permeates *Georgia Scenes* as well. In **"The Fight,"** for example, we find surprisingly little narrative scorn directed at the combatants themselves; instead, the conniving Ransy Sniffle and the combatants' wives (who initiate the fight with their own quarrel) receive the most outspoken narrative censure, and in his moralistic coda to the tale, Hall explicitly condemns the peace officers who "countenance" such "disgrace[s] to the community," asserting that they "deserve a place in the Penitentiary" (70). Thus, Hall reserves his harshest comments for what we might call inverted representatives (the morally inferior wives and Ransy Sniffle "standing in" for the parties concerned) and delinquent representatives (the peace officers who fail to represent community interests).[11] Perhaps more than any other sketch, **"The Fight"** demonstrates the need for the legitimate representation we find in **"The Shooting Match,"** where Hall's moral fitness to represent the yeoman whites resolves class tension by producing consensual, tacit agreement about class roles.

While such a resolution will necessarily be ideologically interested, it is nonetheless achieved through negotiation—the dialogic give-and-take that legitimates social relationships—rather than unilateral imposition. The integrated morality at work in **"The Gander Pulling"** suggests the ability of Hall's later narrative style to effect this negotiation; as the narrative progresses, we infer a tacit belief system that tends to naturalize both the interaction between Hall as narrator and his narrative object and the negotiated exchange taking place

within the narrative field. The culmination of this pattern comes in **"The Shooting Match,"** the concluding sketch of *Georgia Scenes,* where we find Hall's narrative negotiation actively engaging issues of class.[12] Traveling in a frontier county, Hall comes upon a "swarthy, bright-eyed smerky little fellow," whom he asks if he is "going driving" (229).

"Not exactly," replied he, surveying my horse with a quizzical smile, "I have n't been driving *by myself* for a year or two, and my nose has got so bad lately I can't carry a cold trail *without hounds to help me.*"

Alone, and without hounds, as he was, the question was rather a silly one; but it answered the purpose for which it was put, which was only to draw him into conversation, and I proceeded to make as decent a retreat as I could.

"I did n't know," said I, "but that you were going to meet the huntsmen, or going to your stand."

"Ah, sure enough," rejoined he, "that *mout* be a bee, as the old woman said when she killed a wasp. It seems to me I ought to know you."

"Well, if you *ought,* why *don't* you?"

"What *mout* you name be?"

"It *might* be any thing," said I, with borrowed wit; for I knew my man, and knew what kind of conversation would please him most.

"Well, what *is* it then?"

"It *is,* Hall," said I; "but you know it might as well have been any thing else."

"Pretty digging!" said he. "I find you're not the fool I took you to be; so here's to a better acquaintance with you."

(229-30)

Although the language game between Hall and Billy Curlew ends in mutual respect, its unstated rules suggest an initial unwillingness to engage the other as a social equal; for Billy, this unwillingness is clearly represented as class resentment. According to the unstated rules of the game, hierarchy is established by attributing literal significance to a word or phrase where none is intended; by thus improperly attributing literality to the other's language, Billy and Hall are able in turn to make the other look the fool. The antagonistic dialogism suggested by the mutual reluctance to "share a language"—that is, to interpret intentional rather than literal meaning—is resolved when the two characters implicitly agree to play the game as a game; thus, after Hall has demonstrated that he is no fool, Billy is able to renew the banter as a means of affirming mutual respect. When Hall asks Billy to "give me your name," the latter replies, "To be sure I will, my old coon—take it—take it, and welcome. Any thing else about me you'd like to have?" (230). In the end, the dialogic instability of language works not to create difference, but to define mutual participation within a community.

Hall's willingness thus to engage a member of the lower class signals an important shift in *Georgia Scenes,* for while his initial tendency to moralize from on high has been heavily modified since **"Georgia Theatrics,"** he nevertheless fails to establish consensus with the lower classes until **"The Shooting-Match."** While Hall's narrative perspective increasingly shows that he recognizes the social value of the lower class's "uncouth" ways, he does not enter into a dialogic relationship as a *member* of the community until this concluding sketch. At various points in **"The Shooting Match,"** Hall's comments to the reader systematically indicate that he is highly conscious of the way he establishes discursive relationships with members of the lower class: he relates that his initial "silly" question "answered the purpose for which it was put, which was only to draw him into conversation"; he comments that "I knew my man, and knew what kind of conversation would please him most"; and shortly thereafter, upon meeting Squire Sims, he explains, "I am always free and easy with those who are so with me, and in this course I rarely fail to please" (233). Having thus internalized the rules of the language games governing communal interaction, Hall orients his language toward his audience so as to make negotiated exchange possible, a circumstance that in turn is predicated on his acknowledging that he is likewise available to the evaluation of members of the lower class. As Bakhtin explains, the speaker's

> orientation toward the listener is an orientation toward a specific conceptual horizon, toward the specific world of the listener; it introduces totally new elements into his discourse; it is in this way, after all, that various different points of view, conceptual horizons, systems for providing expressive accents, various social "languages" come to interact with one another. . . . The speaker breaks through the alien conceptual horizon of the listener, constructs his own utterance on alien territory, against his, the listener's, apperceptive background.
>
> (*Dialogic* 282)

That Billy represents an alien conceptual horizon is made clear at several points in the tale; even after he and Hall establish mutual respect, Billy guesses that "you hardly ever was at a shooting match, stranger, from the cut of your coat" (230). Thus marked as an alien, Hall is nevertheless able to engage Billy's "apperceptive background"—that is, the tacit assumptions that permit him to judge Hall on the basis of a coat that acts here as a metonymic indicator of class. (Billy's prejudice is that Hall—and by extension, all men of his social standing—is, so to speak, an empty coat.) When

Hall relates that he has not only been to shooting matches, but "won beef" at one as a child, Billy is incredulous until he realizes that Hall is the very man of whom his father, who had won a bet on Hall's shooting, has spoken "many a time" (231-32). Knowing that he can count on the other fellows to make, as he has done, a metonymic association between clothing and character, Billy hopes to "tear the lint off the boys" by betting on Hall at the shooting match. As he tells Hall. "They'll never 'spect such a looking man as you are of knowing any thing about a rifle" (232), a class prejudice he reaffirms shortly thereafter when he introduces Hall to Squire Sims, telling him, "for all you see him in the fine clothes, he's a *swinge*-cat—a darned sight cleverer fellow than he looks to be" (233).

The narrative emphasis on reciprocal valuation indicates how substantially the framing dynamics have become elaborated within the intratextual sphere of action, where interpretation is no longer available solely to the gentleman narrator. We have seen in **"Georgia Theatrics"** how Hall's initial moralizing socionarrative style, when enforced as a "Sacred Office," leads to a subversion of social authority. Conversely, **"The Shooting Match"** shows an ahenated and alienating style giving way to active externalization on Hall's part; no longer a mere moralizing spectator, he actively participates in communal ritual, gladly accompanying Billy to the shooting match when invited to do so. This physical act is significant, for here we see a negotiated settlement of potentially divisive class boundaries being effected—literally and figuratively—on common ground. If Hall's subjective style had previously been, as in **"Georgia Theatrics"** and **"The Fight,"** alien to the lower-class whites he encountered, **"The Shooting Match"** shows an integration of Hall's subjectivity and his external negotiation of social order.

Not that any such order is apparent upon Hall's arrival at the shooting match; indeed, the very opposite is true, as Hall finds himself, after Billy enters him in the competition and brags of his shooting prowess, the object of intense and generally skeptical scrutiny. As Hall relates, "Every inch of me was examined with the nicest scrutiny; and some plainly expressed by their looks, that they never would have taken me for such a bite" (235). Unwilling to wound Billy's feelings by either shooting by proxy (Hall explains that "by all rules of breeding I was bound to shoot in person") or refusing to shoot at all, Hall reluctantly enters the contest, holding out for the last shot. During the intervening rounds of shooters, Hall describes in minute detail the rules of the shooting match, its history in the state of Georgia, the types of weapons used, and especially the verbal gamesmanship of the various participants. As in several earlier sketches, insults and word play replace the actual contest as the primary site of competition: Mealy Whitecotton's frail physique, Zeb Dagget's weak boasts, and Simon Stow's ineffectual deliberateness all receive sarcastic commentary from the crowd. When Hall's turn comes, he too becomes the butt of his fellow shooters' comments, for in spite of Billy's assurances that he is a shooter of great renown. Hall finds that he can hardly raise the yeoman's heavy rifle. Haplessly attempting to raise the piece amid the men's clever sarcasm (one man explains that Hall "used to shoot well . . . but can't now nor never could," while another warns those standing near the target, "for I'll be dod durned if Broadcloth don't give some of you the dry gripes if you stand too close thare" [244-45]). Hall fires blindly and immediately begins saving face through self-deprecation. Having learned a lesson from Fat John Fulger of **"The Gander Pulling,"** Hall explains that "I have always found that the most credible way of relieving myself of derision, was to heighten it myself as much as possible. It is a good plan in all circles, but by far the best which can be adopted among the plain rough farmers of the country" (245). Fully conscious of his audience's language games and the potential resentment they harbor, Hall facetiously swears never to shoot for beef again if the cross is not knocked out, then provides a ludicrous explanation of the single and double wabble—shooting techniques, he explains, well known to all the best marksmen. As the men tending the target approach, the irony of Hall's discourse has become apparent to his fellow shooters, who are no longer interested in the accuracy of his shot, since Hall's "airs and harangue" have "put the thought to flight" (246). Astonishingly, however, the men tending the target arrive with the news that Hall's shot is, as one puts it, "only second best after all the fuss" (246), to which Hall exclaims "with uncontrollable transports," "Second best!" From their distant perspective, Hall relates, the combination of Billy's boasting, the courtesy extended to him, and his struggles with the rifle ("taken as the flourishes of an expert who wished to 'astonish the natives'") have conspired to create in them the expectation of a skilled shot. Although these men are disappointed with Hall's marksmanship, those who have witnessed firsthand his shooting and his facetious rhetoric are incredulous, and their astonishment, Hall explains, "blinded [them] to the real feelings with which the exclamation ["Second best!"] was uttered, and allowed me sufficient time to prepare myself for making the best use of what I had said before, with a very different object" (247).

Because its illocutionary meaning is open to dual interpretations, Hall's exclamation allows him the opportunity to lament "with an air of despondency" that he is "getting too old and dim sighted to shoot a rifle" (247). Although he later asserts that, in fact, the shot had been

the result of pure luck, Hall demonstrates his facility at communal language games; marked as different by his clothing and fancy speech, Hall adapts his speech so as to show that he is "one of them." James Kibler thus acts as Longstreet's ideal reader in claiming that, despite "superficial" differences, Hall and the shooters "find common ground." Kibler continues, "[t]here is absolutely no class 'struggle' or resentment because these 'simple' men have the dignity of possessing values in common with the 'high and mighty of land,'—the same values that matter more than the trappings of wealth, power, and fame. It is thus finally these shared values that bond them and bind the community into an organic whole. From this common ground, the one 'class' can regard the other with genuine respect across their superficial 'barriers'" (xviii). In asserting that class "barriers" are superficial while community is organic, Kibler affirms the utopian resolution provided through Hall's narrative negotiation, as does Billy Curlew, who invites Hall home to "swap lies," an offer, he asserts, that "won't cost [Hall] a cent" (248). Yet however utopian, the ending of the sketch demonstrates that this resolution nevertheless restricts the yeoman farmer to a positional entrance into the community. As he is preparing to leave, Hall is stopped by a member of the crowd and asked what he is "offering for." When Hall assures him that he is not a candidate for office, the man replies, "Oh . . . if you're up for any thing you need'nt be mealy-mouthed about it, 'fore us boys; for we'll all go in for you here up to the handle," a sentiment endorsed by Billy, who affirms that if Hall ever should, the "boys of Upper Hogthief" will "go for you, to the hilt, against creation, tit or no tit, that's the *tatur*" (249).

This reference to political patronage coupled with a severe juxtaposition of high and low dialects suggests the integral role political representation plays in bridging tacit social boundaries and thereby legitimating the organic community. Simply put, Hall is able to achieve a social style capable of creating consensus, a style that encompasses the yeoman farmers of Upper Hogthief as citizens—that is, as functioning members of a political culture—rather than frontier curiosities but recently evolved from the half-horse, half-alligator. **"The Shooting Match"** performs the essential cultural work of reclaiming the poor white of the Dark Corner as the yeoman white of Upper Hogthief, yet it does so with the tacit understanding that the political role of the latter is defined in relation to that of the gentleman.[13] This unspoken agreement is a key example of what Jameson calls the *ideologeme,* that rhetorical construct "susceptible to both a conceptual description and a narrative manifestation all at once" (87). Displayed here in its narrative manifestation, which Jameson describes as "a kind of ultimate class fantasy about the 'collective characters' which are the classes in opposition" (87), the ideologeme of political representation tacitly delimits cultural roles; there is no question of either Hall's fitness to represent or the yeoman's lack thereof. Nor is this resolution presented conceptually, since we have no rationalization for why this fitness should be the case. In this respect, we must view Hall's narrative resolution as more a matter of form than of content since interclass relationships are established and mutually affirmed without, and almost at the expense of, an explanation regarding (to use Hayden White's phrase) the content of the form.

The tacit resolution provided by **"The Shooting Match"** simultaneously legitimates Hall's ability to represent, both politically and narratively, the yeomen of Upper Hogthief. In other words, his subjective knowledge of them "as they are" validates, as they recognize, his ability to represent them in a political context. As Kenneth Burke reminded us many years ago, it is "no mere accident of language that we use the same word for sensory, artistic, and political representation" (26) since each realm constitutes a mode of symbolic action. Yet, as in most Jeffersonian rhetoric, the representative relationship here is not strictly synecdochic in the sense that the "whole" Hall represents is monolithic, although the yeomen's perception that Hall is "one of them" tends to elide class distinctions, as does Hall's narrative style itself. Nevertheless, the relative disappearance of Hall as a moralistic narrator—which Newlin, approaching the text via Lynn's paradigm, has characterized as an outright flaw—and the consequent emphasis on Hall as character does not bring about a total collapse of the narrative frame.[14] Instead, since the narrative dynamics of **"The Shooting Match"** represent the elaboration of the moral values associated with Hall's narrative style within the social field of his narrative, we may say that his narrative style, having been dialogically modified over the course of the book, has become a social style and thus can be put into play as speech that has social value as a unit of exchange. That exchange—the verbal give-and-take between Hall and his fellow shooters— nevertheless takes place within a narrative medium in which Hall on several occasions assumes the role of commentator—that is, metonymically digressing to provide information or interpretation not explicitly germane to the action being described. In many instances, such digressions show Hall, in his role as a social historian, providing historical contexts unavailable to the narratee or presumably to the folk of Upper Hogthief. With respect to the latter, Hall occasionally invokes his wider field of perception, as when, on three occasions, he introduces a particular character and then describes the class or type the man represents. He introduces Squire Sims, for example, as having been "a Justice of the Peace in his day; (and where is the man of his age in Georgia who has not?)" (232), a formulation that quickly fixes the Squire in the reader's mind as a minor official and a good fellow. He describes Moses Firmby, one of the better shooters, as "a tall, slim man of rather sallow complexion; and it is a singular fact, that . . . the mountaineers have not generally robust frames or fine complexions: they are, however, almost inexhaustible by toil" (240). Thus Hall effortlessly shifts from describing an individual to what many will recognize as a specific Southern type, as he does with Mealy Whitecotton, who is introduced as "another Ransy Sniffle" (233). In the sphere of what we might call social synecdoche, Hall moves with confidence; there is no question, as in **"Georgia Theatrics,"** of his categorical expectations—his social taxonomy—being subverted. Indeed, the reader is not surprised to learn that Mealy Whitecotton is numbered among those few who remain contemptuous of Hall to the end.

Hall's ability thus to quickly and efficiently categorize these minor characters represents a kind of social authority resulting from the fact that they are, in a deep sense, *familiar* to him. As he attains a style through which the previously alien and threatening members of the community have been domesticated, Hall tacitly legitimates his authority to organize his culture symbolically. The authority to interpret embedded in these ostensibly offhand comments represents a kind of social power. For example, Hall's categorization of Mealy Whitecotton—notice that it is done with just three words—is also a way of controlling him; unlike our previous Ransy Sniffle, whose ability to fuel violence *via* the mechanism of inverted representation constitutes a real threat to community stability, Mealy is easily dealt with. On a more complex level, Hall's social authority is elaborated in his relationship with Billy Curlew, who fully represents Jameson's collective character. Hall's narrative relationship with Billy is, on two occasions, literally that of an interpreter—one who decodes the dialect message of the yeoman white. In the first instance, Hall glosses Billy's invitation to the shooting match, a "short sentence . . . replete with information for me," thereby demonstrating his intimate knowledge of the social context in which the offer had been extended. In the second, which occurs just after the shooting match, Hall relates how Billy "begged me to go home with him for the night, or as he expressed it, 'to go home with him and swap lies that night, and it should'nt cost me a cent,' the true reading of which, is, that if I would go home with him, and give him the pleasure of an evening's chat about old times, his house should be as free to me as my own" (248). This dialogic encounter demonstrates how completely Hall's gentlemanly style has absorbed the yeoman's raw vernacular. In socializing Billy's coarse economic metaphors, Hall "restores" the social meaning implicit in the proffered exchange.

Although somewhat redundant, because this translation of economic terminology into the language of community epitomizes the narrative work of *Georgia Scenes,* it represents the final, utopian horizon on which the exchanges between Hall and the yeoman white are simultaneously socialized and naturalized. In conclusion, let me suggest that one of the most important elements of Longstreet's narrative negotiation is its distinctively Southern resolution of contradictions inherent in Republican ideology. With one foot in the era of Jefferson and the other in the antebellum era, *Georgia Scenes* retains a commitment to class hierarchy even as it defines a collective experience. The tenuous nature of this resolution can perhaps best be gauged by its eventual demise in the postbellum era, when political pressures produced a more rigid—and in many respects more hostile—demarcation between the upper and lower class, the latter of which, with the rise of populists and their demagogic descendants, was less likely to submit to aristocratic political leadership. Yet there is another sense in which the community produced by *Georgia Scenes* survives well into the twentieth century and which indeed may be intrinsic to the experience of community in general. In conceptually repressing how he legitimates the social organization of his community, Hall engenders a consensus that rests largely on tacit and unspoken agreement, suggesting perhaps that, in the final analysis, we cannot know the symbolic procedures through which we resolve social contradiction and experience community.

## Notes

1. For a discussion that shows how highly Longstreet was regarded by both critics and the reading public, see John Donald Wade, 151-60. Of particular interest among the responses to Longstreet's work is a laudatory review in the *Southern Literary Messenger* in which Edgar Allan Poe praises the work as "a sure omen of better days of the literature of the South" (104). Nevertheless, Watson is certainly correct in differentiating Southwestern humor from more polite literature in terms of the cultural role each played. Much work remains to be done on the relationship between Southwestern humor and print culture.

2. I have used the Beehive Press edition of *Georgia Scenes* because it is the only modern edition based on the original 1835 edition. The 1840 Harper's edition, used as the copy text for all other modern editions, employed the Harper's house style, which eliminated much of Longstreet's idiosyncratic grammar, spelling, and punctuation.

3. With Longstreet in particular, Lynn's thesis is often treated as a given. William B. Lenz, for example, offers a typical assessment:

> The frame technique establishes a comic, aesthetic distance between the author's narrative personae, "Hall" and "Baldwin," and his dialect-speaking characters; the reader joins the cultured narrator in laughing at the rude talk and crude manners of the country folk he describes. The structure also insists on an even greater moral distance, one not always apparent in oral tales, that suggests the moral alignment of author, audience, and narrator in contrast with the comically antisocial prancing, snorting, and swearing vernacular characters.

(315)

Keith Newlin modifies Lynn's thesis only to argue that when the gentlemen violate the *cordon sanitaire,* they reveal "their own weaknesses" (27). Newlin comes perilously close to a critical anachronism: that Longstreet's violation of Lynn's paradigm constitutes a flaw on the author's part. C. Hugh Holman writes that Longstreet's "detached view . . . established a vantage point which gave aesthetic distance to his portraits of the cruel, unlearned, but shrewd denizens of the piedmont, weighing these people against the implicit concept of the ordered seaboard society which [he] revered. As a result the figures in *Georgia Scenes* are comic grotesques" (71-72). Although he seconds the presence of Holman's "aesthetic distance," King is more sensitive to the nuances of Hall's perspective (see especially 58-59). See Kibler and James B. Meriwether for implicit critiques of Lynn's paradigm. Although in this essay I confine my revision of Lynn to the context of *Georgia Scenes,* see my essay-review of Hennig Cohen and William B. Dillingham's *Humor of the Old Southwest* for a more general critique. In their seminal essay on Southwestern humor, Cohen and Dillingham recognize exceptions to the *cordon sanitaire* elsewhere in the genre—as have other critics (notably Walter Blair in his 1943 discussion of "The Big Bear of Arkansas")—yet they too cite Longstreet as an author who places himself "above and apart" from "the lowly characters of *Georgia Scenes*" (xxx).

4. Lynn modifies his argument somewhat in later claiming that "[i]n his best work, however, Longstreet buries his meanings deep within the concrete action of the comedy. His finest stories are parables, not tracts" (66). Although Lynn's distinction between mimesis and diagesis in Long-

street's fiction is useful, the concrete action to which Lynn refers merely replicates the antagonistic relationship between the Clown and Self-Controlled Gentleman, the latter of whom simply perceives the Clown's innate depravity rather than having to comment upon it. In short, Lynn argues that whether primarily mimetic or diagetic in orientation, the narrative frame provides an absolute perspective from which the Clown is measured, evaluated, and found wanting.

5. In terms of our immediate topic, let me briefly note that conflict (rather than negotiation) is the explicit "operator" in Lynn's discursive model. Although applied in the context of Renaissance drama, Leinwand's model may actually have more relevance for American literature in general and *Georgia Scenes* in particular, given that both rely on a republican context in which political power is literally determined by negotiation and consensus-building.

6. See Kibler and Meriwether for persuasive discussions of how Baldwin serves as foil for Hall. Even in praising the virtues of the yeoman white in sketches such as "The Dance" and "A Sage Conversation," Baldwin manifests an alienated and alienating narrative perspective. Unwilling to externalize himself, he pontificates on the virtues of simplicity through the mediated language of literary pastoralism (significantly, his favorite poet is Robert Burns).

7. Perhaps we can more clearly recognize the latent social significance of what we might call Ketch's boundary defense by contrasting Blossom with a character who would appear in print over a century later—Faulkner's Flem Snopes, another horse-trading swindler whose facility at manipulating social convention confounds whatever feeble attempts the town can muster to keep him within the relatively safe confines of Frenchman's Bend.

8. A similar instance of misrepresentation occurs in "The Character of a Native Georgian." Hall describes the story's protagonist Ned Brace as a man who "seemed to live only to amuse himself with his fellow beings": "The beau in the presence of his mistress, the fop, the pedant, the purse-proud, the over-fastidious and sensitive, were Ned's favorite game. These never passed him uninjured; and against such, he directed his severest shafts. . . . He was admirably fitted to his vocation. He could assume any character which his humor required him to personate, and he could sustain it to perfection" (31). Although Hall asserts

this social value, the sketch itself consists of sometimes mean-spirited practical jokes at the expense of the gullible. Indeed, in his final prank, Brace constitutes a social threat as he interrupts a line of water buckets being carried to fire so that he can get a drink (54-55). See Wade 171-72 for a persuasive explanation of the schizophrenic nature of the sketch.

9. The one exception is a poor white named Billy Mixen, who, like Ransy Sniffle, the instigator in "The Fight," is described as a "huckleberry eater." Longstreet refers to this character type again in "The Shooting Match"; see the discussion of Mealy Whitecotton below.

10. The title character is designated in the first sentence of the tale as "the first man who, without any qualifications for the place, was elected to the Legislature of Georgia" (50). Although Darby is well-suited to his role as small merchant, his entry into politics is presented in sinister terms, especially since Longstreet repeatedly refers to his "shrewdness," "low cunning," and his knowledge of "the prejudices and weaknesses of the common people of the country, [of which he] had no little tact in turning . . . to his own advantage" (53). After shrewdly arranging for his friends to urge him to enter the race, Darby eventually debates his gentleman rivals, Smith and Jones. Playing the role of the populist demagogue to the hilt, Darby leads his rivals into a rhetorical trap by forcing them first to agree that the poor are just as free as the rich and then to defend freehold suffrage, which dictated that only landowners could vote. Although Smith and Jones eloquently (though feebly) attempt to argue their way out, Darby has effectively—in the minds of the gathered farmers, at least—appropriated for his own sinister ends the idea that all men are created equal. Republican ideology, then, serves as a kind of master code through which social discourse must be channeled, and the rhetorical effort expended by Darby and his rivals serves chiefly to gain primary access to it. Unlike those of "The Shooting Match," the contradictions of republican ideology in this sketch are resolved, according to Fredric Jameson's formulation, "only through intervention of praxis" (here, Darby's sordid political career) because Darby's rhetoric forces them into the form of "logical scandal or double bind." See Jameson 82-83.

11. In "The Turn Out," Hall's next sketch, we find a healthier form of transgression sanctioned by a higher level of communal authority. The context of the tale is a schoolboy revolt sanctioned by

Captain Griffin, who contains what potential violence might erupt. Urging the "young Washingtons" in their battle against the schoolmaster, Griffin uses the carnivalesque inversion of authority as an opportunity to instill republican virtues in the young combatants.

12. That this dialogic imperative affects the mode of narration is a point made explicitly by Longstreet in his preface to the book. Addressing those who "have taken exceptions to the coarse, inelegant, and sometimes ungrammatical language, which *the writer* represents *himself* as occasionally using [my emphasis]," Longstreet asserts unequivocally that "*it is language accommodated to the capacity of the person to whom he represents himself as speaking* [Longstreet's emphasis]" (2). Although critics have almost universally interpreted this statement as a justification, on realistic grounds, for the coarse dialect found throughout the book, Longstreet clearly feels compelled to explain only the coarseness of "the writer's" language *as speech*—that is, the language of either Baldwin or Hall. The opening pages of "The Shooting Match" provide the most concrete evidence for Hall's acceptance of the dialogic imperative, for there we find his speech tangibly modified to suit his audience.

13. Hall concludes "The Shooting Match" with a digression that signals a marked shift in how he has come to interpret morality and place metonymically. Unlike the Dark Corner of "Georgia Theatrics," a name, he had assumed, that accurately depicted the morality of its inhabitants, "Upper Hogthief" receives the following authorial commentary: "The reader will not suppose that the district took its name from the character of its inhabitants. In almost every county in the State, there is some spot, or district, which bears a contemptuous appellation, usually derived from local rivalships, or from a single accidental circumstance" (249). So ends *Georgia Scenes* on a note of class reconciliation.

14. Newlin writes of "The Fox Hunt" and "The Shooting Match" that "Longstreet has unintentionally compromised his moral arbiter [Hall] by having him engage with and eventually become accepted into the very society he wishes to satirize" (36). In accounting for this "flaw," Newlin suggests that Longstreet either "intended his readers to recognize Hall's slip and laugh at his inadvertent hypocrisy" or "simply lost sight of Hall's role as moral commentator in his development of Hall's character" (36-37).

*Works Cited*

Bakhtin, Mikhail. *Problems of Dostoevsky's Poetics.* Ed. and trans. Caryl Emerson. Minneapolis: U of Minnesota P, 1984.

———. *The Dialogic Imagination.* Ed. and trans. Michael Holquist and Caryl Emerson. Austin: U of Texas P, 1981.

Blair, Walter. "The Technique of 'The Big Bear of Arkansas.'" *Southwest Review* 28 (1943): 426-35.

Booth, Wayne C. *The Rhetoric of Fiction.* Chicago: U of Chicago P, 1961.

———. *A Rhetoric of Irony* Chicago: U of Chicago P, 1974.

Burke, Kenneth. *The Philosophy of Literary Form.* Berkeley: U of California P, 1973.

Cohen, Hennig, and William B. Dillingham, eds. *Humor of the Old Southwest.* 3rd ed. Athens: U of Georgia P, 1994.

Davis, Lennard J. *Resisting Novels: Ideology and Fiction.* New York: Methuen, 1987.

Fitzgerald, O. P. *Judge Longstreet: A Life Sketch.* Nashville: Publishing House of the Methodist Episcopal Church, 1891.

Habermas, Jürgen. *Communication and the Evolution of Society.* Trans. Thomas McCarthy. Boston: Beacon, 1979.

Holman, C. Hugh. *The Roots of Southern Writing.* Athens: U of Georgia P, 1972.

Jakobson, Roman. "Two Aspects of Language and Two Types of Aphasic Disturbances." *Selected Writings.* Vol. 2. The Hague: Mouton, 1971. 239-59. 7 vols. 1962-85.

Jameson, Fredric. *The Political Unconscious: Narrative as a Socially Symbolic Act.* Ithaca: Cornell UP, 1981.

Kibler, James E., Jr. Introduction. *Georgia Scenes.* Nashville: J. S. Sanders, 1992. vii-xxii.

King, Kimball. *Augustus Baldwin Longstreet.* Boston: Twayne, 1984.

Leinwand, Theodore B. "Negotiation and the New Historicism." *PMLA* 105 (May 1990): 477-89.

Lenz, William B. "Augustus Baldwin Longstreet." *Fifty Southern Writers before 1900.* Ed. Robert Bain and Joseph M. Flora. Westport: Greenwood, 1987. 312-22.

Longstreet, Augustus B. "The causes of the frequency of Murders, Suicides, and Insanity in the United States." *State Rights' Sentinel* 17 April 1834: 1.

———. "Darby, The Politician." *Stories with a Moral.* Ed. Fitz R. Longstreet. Philadelphia: John C. Winston, 1912. 50-87.

———. *Georgia Scenes: Characters, Incidents, &c. in the First Half Century of the Republic.* 1835. Savannah: Beehive, 1975.

Lynn, Kenneth. *Mark Twain and Southwestern Humor.* 1959. Westport: Greenwood, 1972.

Meriwether, James B. "Augustus Baldwin Longstreet: Realist and Artist." *Mississippi Quarterly* 35 (1982): 351-64.

Newlin, Keith. "Georgia Scenes: The Satiric Artistry of Augustus Baldwin Longstreet." *Mississippi Quarterly* 41 (1987-88): 21-37.

Oriard, Michael. "Shifty in a New Country: Games in Southwestern Humor." *Southern Literary Journal* 12 (1980): 3-28.

Phillips, Robert L., Jr. *The Novel and the Romance in Middle Georgia Humor and Local Color.* Diss, U of North Carolina at Chapel Hill, 1971.

Poe, Edgar Allan. "Georgia Scenes." *The Frontier Humorists: Critical Views.* Ed. M. Thomas Inge. Hamden: Archon, 1975. 85-104.

Polanyi, Michael. *The Tacit Dimension.* Garden City: Doubleday, 1966.

Romine, Scott. "Texts, Types, and Southwest Humor." *Mississippi Quarterly* 49 (1995-96): 99-108.

Wade, John Donald. *Augustus Baldwin Longstreet: A Study in the Development of Culture in the South.* New York: Macmillan, 1924.

Watson, Richie Devon. *Yeoman versus Cavalier: The Old Southwest's Fictional Road to Rebellion.* Baton Rouge: Louisiana State UP, 1993.

## David Rachels (essay date fall 1998)

SOURCE: Rachels, David. "Oliver Hillhouse Prince, Augustus Baldwin Longstreet, and the Birth of American Literary Realism." *Mississippi Quarterly: The Journal of Southern Culture* 51, no. 4 (fall 1998): 603-19.

[*In the following essay, Rachels briefly discusses the controversy surrounding the publication of Thomas Hardy's 1880 novel* The Trumpet-Major *and its alleged plagiarism of a sketch from* Georgia Scenes. *Rachels points out that Longstreet himself "borrowed" the sketch from Oliver Hillhouse Prince, who published "The Militia Company Drill" in 1807 under the name Timothy Crabshaw. Rachels examines the place of Prince's story within the larger body of moral satire published during the era and the influence it exerted on the young Longstreet.*]

In 1882, a sharp-eyed reader noticed a disturbing similarity between some pages in Thomas Hardy's most recent novel, *The Trumpet-Major* (1880), and a selection called "The Militia Company Drill" in an older book, **Georgia Scenes,** which had been copyrighted in 1840.[1] Charles P. Jacobs was certain that Hardy had plagiarized, and he promptly said so in a letter to *The Critic,* a New York literary magazine. But Jacobs was not sure from whom Hardy had stolen. Who had written "The Militia Company Drill"? Jacobs wrote, "[A] note appended to it says: 'This is from the pen of a friend. . . . It was published about twenty years ago.' The article is signed 'Timothy Crabshaw,' though the book, I have been informed, was written by Judge Longstreet, who died many years ago." Jacobs had been informed correctly. Although Augustus Baldwin Longstreet's name did not appear in **Georgia Scenes, Characters, Incidents, &c. in the First Half Century of the Republic**— the book was credited to "A Native Georgian"—it was known to be his work. Today, of course, Longstreet's volume is recognized as the first major work of American literary realism.[2] But to Jacobs, it had no such significance.

Displaying the texts side-by-side, Jacobs showed what Hardy had done. He wrote, "It will need no acuteness of vision to see that there is something more than an accidental similarity between the description given by Mr. Hardy (in the left-hand column) and by 'Timothy Crabshaw' (in the right)."[3] This is part of Jacobs's exhibit:

### Mr. Hardy

'*Look to the right, and dress!* They were soon, by the help of the noncommissioned officers, placed in a straight line; but as every man was anxious to see how the rest stood, those on the wings pressed forward for that purpose till the whole line assumed nearly the form of a crescent.

'Why look at 'em,' says the captain: 'why, gentlemen, you are all a crooking in at both *eends,* so that you will get on to me by and by! Come, gentlemen, *dress! dress!*

### 'Timothy Crabshaw'

'Men, I dismissed ye too soon; parade, parade again I say,' he cried. 'My watch is fast, I find.' There is another twenty minutes afore the worship of God commences. Now, all of you that han't fawlocks, fall in at the lower end. Eyes right, and dress!'

As every man was anxious to see how the rest stood, those at the end of the line pressed forward for that purpose, till the line assumed the form of a horse-shoe.

'Look at ye now! Why you are all a crooking in, Dress! dress!'

In the ensuing controversy, many readers came to Hardy's defense; they could not believe that such a famous writer had done anything wrong. One defended Hardy by pointing out how much the British author had improved the American original. Unfortunately, the printer had accidentally reversed Jacobs's columns (I have duplicated the mistake above), and Hardy's defender had unwittingly argued that Hardy had ruined the American original.[4] Another came to Hardy's defense, ironically, by denigrating the plagiarized passage in his book: "[T]he passage in *The Trumpet Major,* which bears so striking a resemblance to the one in *Georgia Scenes* is, after all, not sufficiently remarkable to tempt another novelist to convey it bodily."[5] Hardy himself denied any knowledge of *Georgia Scenes.* He did, however, admit that he was indebted to a more obscure work, C. H. Gifford's *History of the Wars Occasioned by the French Revolution,* which had been published in 1817. Learning this, the editor of *The Critic* returned to *Georgia Scenes,* where Longstreet had noted that "The Militia Company Drill" had first been published "about twenty years ago." Was Gifford's book this publication? Was he the author of "The Militia Company Drill":

In fact, "The Militia Company Drill" was written by Oliver Hillhouse Prince ("Timothy Crabshaw" was Prince's pseudonym), and in the following years a number of writers pointed this out.[6] The relationship between Prince, Longstreet, and *Georgia Scenes* is in one respect simple: of the nineteen items in *Georgia Scenes,* Prince wrote one, and Longstreet wrote the rest. But this is a curious and confusing fact. *Georgia Scenes* is a collection of Longstreet's writing, originally published by Longstreet himself. Why did Longstreet include Prince's sketch? Imagine how strange it would seem today if John Updike, in his new collection of short stories, included a story by Joyce Carol Oates that he thought particularly fine. This strangeness may partly explain the sloppy scholarship that has grown up around Prince and Longstreet. For example, one encyclopedia of literary biography identifies Longstreet as a "humorist, jurist, and educator, who sometimes wrote over the signature 'Timothy Crabshaw.'"[7] Another reference work (1974) takes this mistake to an embarrassing extreme, asserting that all of Longstreet's original *Georgia Scenes* were published under Prince's pseudonym.[8] On the whole, Longstreet's use of "The Militia Company Drill" has generated little recognition for Prince while causing a great deal of confusion. This is a pity. Through his influence on Longstreet, Prince played a vital part in the founding of American literary realism.

## PRINCE'S NARRATIVE

On June 6, 1807, in the small town of Washington, Georgia, Sarah Hillhouse, the state's first woman newspaper editor, published the 329th issue of her family's weekly, the *Monitor.* On this day, the first two of the *Monitor*'s four pages were given over almost entirely to an item written by Sarah's nephew, twenty-four-year-old Oliver Hillhouse Prince.[9] This piece consisted of two letters, one framing the other. The framework was addressed to "the body aggregate" and was signed "Fugitas." The letter within this letter, which purported to describe the recent muster of a Georgia militia company, was addressed to Fugitas ("Dear Fugey") and was signed "Timothy Crabshaw." Removed from its frame, this narrative was an immediate success, as reprintings spread throughout the United States and then across the Atlantic.

In thinking about the place of Prince's militia narrative in American literary history, we may usefully begin by considering a better-known work that was published in the same year, William Irving, James Kirke Paulding, and Washington Irving's *Salmagundi; or The Whimwhams and Opinions of Launcelot Langstaff, Esq. & Others.* The *Salmagundi* papers, which were issued in New York on an irregular basis from January 24, 1807, to January 25, 1808, appeared in the wake of similar works in American periodicals such as Joseph Dennie's *Port Folio* (1801-1807), John Howard Payne's *Thespian Mirror* (1805-1806), and Charles Brockden Brown's *Literary Magazine and American Register* (1803-1807). In addition, the first issue of *Salmagundi* was partially a response to *The Town,* a New York magazine that published its only five issues in the first two weeks of 1807.[10] The most prominent British influences on *Salmagundi* were Joseph Addison and Richard Steele, whose *Spectator* papers were reissued in a bestselling, eight-volume edition in Philadelphia in 1803.[11] In the first number of the *Spectator,* which was originally published in London in 1711, Addison declared the periodical to have a high moral purpose: "I have often been told by my Friends, that it is Pity so many useful Discoveries which I have made, should be in the Possession of a Silent Man. For this Reason therefore, I shall publish a Sheet-full of Thoughts every Morning, for the Benefit of my Contemporaries; and if I can any way contribute to the Diversion or Improvement of [Great Britain], I shall leave it, when I am summoned out of it, with the secret Satisfaction of thinking that I have not Lived in vain."[12] Similarly, the authors of *Salmagundi* set out "to instruct the young, reform the old, correct [New York] and castigate the age. . . ."[13]

Of course, readers purchased *Salmagundi* not for castigation but for entertainment, leading Irving, Paulding, and Irving to worry that "many people read our numbers, merely for their amusement, without paying any attention to the serious truths conveyed in every page." The *Salmagundi* authors risked only amusing their readers because they chose to convey their "truths" with humor: "It is one of our indisputable facts," they wrote, "that it is easier to laugh ten follies out of countenance than to coax, reason, or flog a man out of one" (p. 227). This principle was employed as well by Prince in his militia narrative. In the frame to that narrative, we see Prince attempting to coax, reason, and frog Georgians into recognizing a serious problem: he argues that if the rag-tag Georgia militia should ever face a well-trained army, the Georgians would either flee or be slaughtered; Georgia, therefore, had better fix this problem or else be left to rely upon "an extraordinary providence," the "justice of nations," or "the mercy of a conqueror."[14] In the militia narrative itself, however, we see Prince attempting to laugh readers out of this folly, much as Irving, Paulding, and Irving had advised. In a noteworthy coincidence—if it be a coincidence at all—in the *Salmagundi* of March 7, 1807, William Irving had satirized a local militia drill:

> The commanding officer ordered his men to wheel and take [the pump] in flank—the army accordingly wheeled, and came full butt against it in rear exactly as they were before:—"wheel to the left," cried the officer: they did so, and again, as before, the inveterate pump intercepted their progress. "Right about, face!" cried the officer; the men obeyed, but bungled—they *faced back to back.*
>
> (p. 118)

Prince's satire, which was published three months later, is similar:

> 'Tention the whole! *To the right! wheel!*
>
> Each man faced to the right about.
>
> Why gentlem[e]n! I did'nt mean for every man to stand still and turn *nay*turally right round; but when I told you to wheel to the right, I intended for you to wheel round to the right as it were. Please to try that again gentlemen; every right-hand man must stand fast, and only the others turn round.
>
> In a previous part of the exercise, it had, for the purpose of sizing them, been necessary to denominate every second person a 'right-hand-man.' A very natural consequence was, that on the present occasion, those right-hand-men maintained their position and all the intermediate ones faced about as before.

Each narrative has fun with the futile efforts of an incompetent commander drilling an incompetent militia. A major difference, however, is the voice that Prince's narrator allows his subjects. Both Prince's narrator, Crabshaw, and Irving's narrator, Mustapha, consider themselves superior to the characters they describe, but

Crabshaw's words serve primarily to frame the words of the militia captain, whose hopeless orders drive the narrative. Mustapha, on the other hand, does not report the words of his subjects. Beyond "wheel to the left" and "right about, face," readers hear almost no voice other than Mustapha's, as he, like the other *Salmagundi* narrators, would rather summarize than let another character speak. As a result, Irving's work seems more an essay or sketch in the mode of Addison and Steele, while Prince's work, filled with the speech of a common Georgian, seems more a realistic short story.

We must remember, of course, that Prince's militia narrative was not originally a discrete story but was embedded in a long-winded, two-part editorial. The story became popular because editors reprinted it without its ponderous frame and without the passages of explicit editorializing that appeared in the story itself.[15] This pruning left a work that one critic has identified as the first example of Old Southwest Humor. This distinction alone should earn Prince a footnote in every history of American literature.[16] Prince deserves more than a footnote, however, for the effect that his narrative had on one reader.

### PRINCE AND LONGSTREET

The early lives of Prince (1782-1837) and Longstreet (1790-1870) were much the same. In 1784, Longstreet's parents migrated to Georgia from New Jersey; in 1796, Prince's family migrated to Georgia from Connecticut. Both men were followers of Georgia governor George M. Troup's political party, and both had daughters named Virginia and Frances. Each man was, in the same order, a lawyer, a politician, and a newspaper editor. Of the careers they shared, Prince and Longstreet found their greatest successes as lawyers. Prince was so highly esteemed that the state legislature selected him to author the first digest of Georgia state law. Longstreet published *Review of the Decision of the Supreme Court of the United States in the Case of McCulloch vs. the State of Maryland* (1819; now lost), and took at least one case to the Supreme Court himself.

Among their contemporaries, however, the reputations of Prince and Longstreet rested largely upon their wit.[17] Stories of Longstreet's humor have been preserved primarily by John Donald Wade in his *Augustus Baldwin Longstreet: A Study of the Development of Culture in the South* (1924). Fewer stories of the lesser-known Prince survive. One is retold by Virginia King Nirenstein in her chronicle of the Princes, *With Kindly Voices: A Nineteenth-Century Georgia Family*:

> One day in Mrs. [Nicholas] Johnson's parlor a spirited discussion broke out concerning Sir Walter Scott's poetry. Prince and his friend Judge Augustin Clayton, an-

other of the circuit's notable wits, maintained that the revered Sir Walter's poetry was doggerel which could have been written by anyone. To prove this point Prince rapidly reeled off a string of sentences, to which Judge Clayton added a postscript in the style of Scott.

> The subject of the simulated poetry was Brownlee [*sic*], the cow Colonel Johnson kept in the front yard where a green lawn naturally resulted.

(p. 5)[18]

It is interesting to note Prince's apparent disdain for Scott, a figure later held in contempt by another Southern American realist, Mark Twain.[19]

For the lawyers of Prince and Longstreet's era, wit was important as much outside as inside the courtroom. Wisecracks, jokes, anecdotes, and stories were primary sources of entertainment as the legal brethren rode their circuit and spent their nights together in taverns, inns, and makeshift hotels. Prince was admitted to the bar in 1806, one year before the publication of his militia narrative. Over the course of this year, he perhaps had opportunities to refine his storytelling skills with his fellow lawyers. Longstreet at this time was nothing but a sixteen-year-old schoolboy. There is, however, some reason to believe that he was among the first readers of Prince's narrative.

Early in life, Longstreet had not read much, but when he was fifteen, his mother had taken in a young boarder named George McDuffie, a future United States congressman, United States senator, and South Carolina governor. Under McDuffie's influence, Longstreet's reading habits turned for the better, McDuffie was a voracious reader whose habit of reading aloud at first irritated Longstreet. But as Longstreet gradually learned to enjoy McDuffie's performances, he learned to enjoy reading as well, and a sort of competition developed: "I observed that when we read the same books and papers," Longstreet recalled, "he always knew twice as much of their contents as I did. I determined to match him if possible, and I commenced reading with care, and in a measure studying what I read." Given that McDuffie "devoured every . . . newspaper with greediness that he could lay his hands on," it seems certain that he and Longstreet read the *Monitor,* as they lived in Augusta while the Prince family paper was published in nearby Washington. The *Monitor* would have especially interested the politically minded young men because on January 4, 1805, it had won the contract to publish the proceedings of the Georgia state legislature.[20] To any alert reader, Prince's militia narrative, written in common language about common Georgians, would have seemed different from the things that ordinarily appeared in the newspapers. Years later, when he was explaining the intent of his own literary work, Longstreet wrote that

the aim of the author was to supply a chasm in history which has always been overlooked—the manners, customs, amusements, wit, dialect, as they appear in all grades of society to an ear and eye witness of them. But who ever tells us of the comments of the wits and the ways of the common walks of life, in their own dialect . . . ?[21]

One answer would have been Oliver Hillhouse Prince.

In 1821, six years after his own admission to the bar, Longstreet was elected to the state legislature in Milledgeville. During Longstreet's term, Prince visited Milledgeville to see to the publication of the first edition of his *Digest of the Laws of the State of Georgia* (1822). The two men may have first met at this time (Nirenstein, pp. 14-15, 66). If, in fact, Longstreet had missed seeing Prince's militia narrative when it debuted in 1807, it is difficult to imagine that he had also missed the many reprintings of the subsequent fifteen years. A last chance to read the work before Prince's Milledgeville visit came on January 7, 1822, when the narrative appeared under Prince's name as "Militia Muster" in the *Augusta Chronicle & Georgia Gazette.* In any case, whenever Prince and Longstreet did first meet, we may fairly assume that Longstreet knew of Prince not only as a fellow lawyer but also as a wit and an author.[22] Thus, when Longstreet began writing his **Georgia Scenes** around 1830 (p. 145), he had two sources from which to take his cues: the oral literature of the circuit riders and the written example of Prince.

On January 5, 1832, Prince became co-editor of the Milledgeville *Georgia Journal.* By this time, the literary seed he had planted twenty-five years earlier was showing growth in a variety of humorous, realistic narratives. One popular example of this new realism, Ham Jones's "Cousin Sally Dilliard," had appeared in *Atkinson's Saturday Evening Post* on August 6, 1831.[23] On February 23, 1832, the *Georgia Journal* reprinted Jones's sketch on its front page with this note: "The following exquisite morceau has already appeared in a neighboring paper; but we readily adopt the suggestion of a friend to treat our patrons with a republication of it. The fidelity of the copy will recommend it to many a reader, who has probably seen many originals, that might have sat for the portrait." In other words, the strength of "Cousin Sally Dilliard" was its realism. As co-editor of the *Georgia Journal,* Prince could have defined his place in this burgeoning literary revolution, but he appears to have devoted his energies to the paper's central concern: politics. In fact, politics was the central concern of all Georgia newspapers in 1832. The state's first literary journal—William Tappan Thompson and James McCafferty's *Augusta Mirror*—would not appear until 1838, the year after Prince's death.[24] For the *Georgia Journal* (and other Georgia newspapers of the time), fiction served as filler. Sometimes, as in the case of "Cousin Sally Dilliard," this filler could be "exquisite," but it was filler all the same.

Tradition has it that Prince wrote more fiction than just his militia story. For example, *Appleton's Cyclopædia of American Biography* (1888) recorded that "Oliver Hillhouse Prince was the author of many humorous sketches. . . ." But in the extant files of the *Monitor,* there are no other humorous sketches that can be traced to Prince. In fact, nowhere in the surviving issues of the paper is there any other item that might fairly be described as a "humorous sketch." The nearest to that description are short jokes and anecdotes that serve as filler.[25] Similarly, if Prince wrote any fiction for the *Georgia Journal,* it was short and unsigned. One obvious candidate for his authorship is "A Militia Training," a narrative written entirely in dialogue, which appeared on November 12, 1832. But why would Prince have bothered to write a sketch that so plainly rehashed his best-known work? More likely, he re-printed "A Militia Training" for readers-in-the-know to see a clear example of his continuing influence.[26] Of the other unsigned items in the *Georgia Journal,* "Free Inquiry" is among the most substantial. This is the work in its entirety:

> In times of religious excitement, evening meetings are not unfrequently held, called meetings of "free inquiry." Where one of these excitements prevailed, lived Jock Pettibone and Nat Pease; they were ungodly fellows, and more apt to be excited by rum than by religion—one evening Jock being about three sheets in the wind was looking about for his usual companion to help him keep up the *Spree* as he called it, he strolled about, but Nat was no where to be found—at length seeing a crowd of people collected and not exactly aware of the nature of the meeting, he entered and took a seat among the rest in hopes to spy out his friend in the midst of [the] multitude. Soon Mr. Higginson the minister arose and observed—"This is a meeting where every person is free to speak; if any of you have any thing on your minds, or any inquiries to make, there is perfect liberty.["] Upon this, Jock got up and steadying himself as well as he could by the bench, began "Mr.—Higgin—son,—I—should—like—to—make—one—inquiry,—if—it—be—in—order."
>
> "Certainly, Mr. Pettibone, this is a meeting of "free inquiry," ask any question you think proper—I am very glad to perceive that you manifest an inquiring spirit."
>
> "Well—then,—since—you—are—so—good—as—to—allow—me—to—speak—freely—I—would—just ask—you—whether—[you've] seen any thing of NAT PEASE?"[27]

"Free Inquiry" appeared on January 29, 1834. Less than two months later, in his own newspaper, Longstreet published **An Interesting Interview,** a Georgia Scene that, like "Free Inquiry," relied on drunken speech for its humor. Here is an excerpt:

> Why, Nancy! what, in, the worl' has got into you! Is you drunk too? Well, 'pon, my word, and honor, I, b'lieve, every body, in this town, is, got drunk to-day. Why, Nancy! I never, did, see, you, in, that fix, before, in, all, my, live, long, born, days.[28]

While no one remembers "Free Inquiry" today, **"An Interesting Interview"** is lauded for its realism in dealing with alcohol and drunken speech. The praise began with Poe: "'*An Interesting Interview*' is [a] specimen of exquisite dramatic talent. It consists of nothing more than a fac-simile of the speech, actions, and *thoughts* of two drunken old men—but its air of truth is perfectly inimitable."[29] By his own account, Longstreet had aimed at such a facsimile. He wanted to preserve the lives of ordinary people for posterity:

> I have often desired to see the Greeks and Romans, as they saw each other—To be present at their amusements—hear their wits and wags—enter their dwellings—see their tables—witness their paternal & maternal government—hear their children—look into their schools &c. The time will come, perhaps, when the same desire will be felt to know all about us: and to gratify that desire. I am now writing.
>
> ("Letters," p. 100)

To fulfill this purpose. Longstreet realized that he ought to take his Georgia Scenes from their newspaper columns and collect them into a book, and it was, of course. *Georgia Scenes* that kept **"An Interesting Interview"** from the anonymous fate of "Free Inquiry."

On October 30, 1833, while Prince was co-editing the *Georgia Journal.* Longstreet published his first Georgia Scene in a different Milledgeville newspaper, the *Southern Recorder.* We do not know whether Longstreet first offered his sketches to Prince. If he did, it is difficult to imagine that Prince would have refused them, as he often scrambled to fill his columns with fiction of various sorts. It may be that the editors of the *Southern Recorder* got wind of Longstreet's work, and the **Georgia Scenes** were solicited rather than offered. In any event, there does not appear to have been a rift between Longstreet and Prince: in January 1834, when the first issue of Longstreet's paper, the Augusta *State Rights' Sentinel,* appeared, the editors of the *Georgia Journal* welcomed the efforts of their "old friend Judge Longstreet; a gentleman whose talents and attainments need no testimony from us. We greet him as an acquisition to the corps Editorial; and we do this with the more pleasure from thinking (if the vanity and egotism may be pardoned,) that there is some similarity in our tastes and temper, and habits, as well as politics."[30]

As an editor, Longstreet, like Prince, scrambled to fill columns with type. On one occasion, he filled space by giving Prince's militia narrative yet another reprinting—a fact that establishes beyond any doubt Longstreet's knowledge of Prince's sketch. What is positively startling, however, is Longstreet's decision to publish Prince's work *as a* Georgia Scene once he had Prince's permission to do so.[31] Why did Longstreet publish another man's work almost as if it were his own? The answer, in part, is that "The Militia Company Drill" (as Longstreet gave the title) fit the purpose of his literary endeavor, which was to depict ordinary life as it really was. Prince's account of a militia muster had, according to Longstreet, "[saved him] the trouble and mortification of describing the same thing in a worse style." Indeed, Longstreet found Prince's work to be even more realistic than much of his own. In his preface to *Georgia Scenes,* Longstreet explained that since pure realism can be "dull and insipid," he had "used some little art in order to recommend [his sketches] to the readers of [his] own times." Later, in defending the realism of these sketches, Longstreet explained that "The Militia Company Drill" was real life unembellished: "**'The Wax Works'** & **'Fox Hunt'** [two other *Georgia Scenes*] are nearly literally true. 'The Company Drill,' is even without coloring."[32]

In fact, "The Militia Company Drill" could easily pass as a work written by Longstreet. The story is narrated by a passive outsider. Timothy Crabshaw is a traveler who bemusedly describes the chaos of a Georgia militia drill. The narrators of Longstreet's stories find themselves in similar situations. In **"The Fight,"** Lyman Hall watches with fascination and horror as two toughs have it out. He stands as a genteel outsider, a role that he also plays in such stories as **"The Horse Swap,"** **"The Turf,"** and **"The Gander Pulling."** Longstreet's other narrator, Abraham Baldwin, plays a similar role in such stories as **"The Dance"** and **"The Song."** The three narrators—Crabshaw, Hall, and Baldwin—are united by their purpose of realistic reportage.

This goes some distance toward explaining Longstreet's publication of another man's work in *Georgia Scenes.* Since Prince's literary aesthetic of 1807 had become Longstreet's own, perhaps Longstreet saw nothing strange about borrowing his friend's work. Yet modern critics have increasingly seen *Georgia Scenes* not as a haphazard collection of sketches but as a unified work, and this unity is provided in large part by the development of Longstreet's two narrators. Baldwin and Hall. Would Longstreet not have recognized that the inclusion of a third narrator would compromise the integrity of his book? Perhaps, but this would have been a secondary concern. Longstreet's primary concern would have been preserving the slice of Georgia history pre-

sented in "The Militia Company Drill." Furthermore, by including "The Militia Company Drill" in *Georgia Scenes,* Longstreet may have been acknowledging his debt to Prince, and he may also have been smoothing ruffled feathers. Perhaps Prince resented Longstreet's success in Prince's area of literary innovation. Could there have been a rift after all? Looking back in 1896, another Georgian, Joel Chandler Harris, wrote that

> A great deal of the humor that originated in Georgia has been printed in books. We find it in Judge Longstreet's *Georgia Scenes,* in [William Tappan Thompson's] Major Jones's "Travels," in Colonel Richard Malcolm Johnston's "Stories of Georgia Life," and in other volumes that have attracted public attention. But the best of it has been lost. It originated when the lawyers were riding about on horseback or in buggies from court to court, and tradition has only preserved a small part of it.[33]

Longstreet ranks ahead of Thompson and Johnston, also purveyors of humorous realism, in part because he published first. It was Longstreet who first thought that the tales of the lawyers might be worth preserving. (As Arthur Palmer Hudson put it, Longstreet "had the wit to realize that something old in talking might look new in writing."[34]) But as we have seen. Prince beat Longstreet into print by a considerable margin. Might Prince have resented that Longstreet's achievement was eclipsing his own?

There is circumstantial evidence for this. The *Georgia Journal,* while it reprinted a wide variety of fiction, both American and European, never reprinted a Georgia Scene. This is extraordinary for a paper whose editors found "Cousin Sally Dilliard" to be "exquisite" and claimed to share Longstreet's "tastes and temper." Indeed, the *Georgia Journal* and *State Rights' Sentinel* often reprinted the same brief filler items. For example, the same anecdote of a young boy visiting the post office appeared in Prince's paper on August 27, 1834, and in Longstreet's paper on the following October 9. Why did this shared editorial taste not extend to the *Georgia Scenes*? We know that the editors of the *Georgia Journal* received Longstreet's paper on a regular basis, as they reprinted, among other things, no fewer than seven of the political satires that Longstreet wrote under the pseudonyms of "e. Prater" and "Bob Short." Yet the *Georgia Scenes* appear not even to have been mentioned in the pages of the *Georgia Journal.* If Prince was in fact jealous or resentful of the *Georgia Scenes,* this might explain how the earliest of them ended up in the Milledgeville *Southern Recorder* rather than the Milledgeville *Georgia Journal.*

If Longstreet's inclusion of "The Militia Company Drill" in *Georgia Scenes* was meant to give Prince his due, then the gesture, as we have seen, has been both a success and a failure. Longstreet has succeeded in bringing Prince's sketch to thousands of new readers, but Prince himself has generally failed to receive credit. Most readers have taken "The Militia Company Drill" as just another Georgia Scene, paying little attention to Longstreet's statement, which appears twice in the book, that "The Militia Company Drill" is the work of a different author. It is easy to imagine careless readers forgetting the disclaimer in the book's preface or passing over the footnote attached to Prince's sketch. It is also easy to imagine readers not taking these disclaimers seriously. Longstreet identified Prince in neither his newspaper nor his book. The differences between the headnote that preceded Prince's narrative in the *Augusta Chronicle & Georgia Advertiser* and the headnote that preceded it in Longstreet's own paper are instructive:

*Augusta Chronicle & Georgia Advertiser* January 7, 1822.

The following exquisite piece of humor, was written by OLIVER H. PRINCE, Esq. of Washington, Wilkes County, in this State. It was first published in the Monitor, about 10 or 15 years ago, has since been re-printed in many of the periodical works in this Country and in England; and has even, we understand, been translated into French—And yet, the Author has been in a great measure unknown: for it goes very hard with people living beyond the Savannah River, to believe that any thing like Mind can exist in Georgia.

(p. 2)

*Augusta State Rights' Sentinel* May 15, 1834

For the following amusing, graphic, yet faithful description of a COMPANY DRILL in this State, I am indebted to a gentleman who has long been known as the author of it. It was taken from the life, about twenty years ago, and made its first appearance in the Washington Monitor, from which it was copied into almost every gazette in the United States. Hence it passed over to Europe, where it appeared in every language spoken on the Continent. The author has granted me permission to place it among the *Georgia Scenes*—a permission of which I gladly avail myself, because it saves me the trouble and mortification of describing the same thing in a worse style. HALL.

(p. 3)

For Longstreet's purposes, it was important to describe Prince's sketch not merely as a "piece of humor" but as an "amusing, graphic, yet faithful description." In keeping with Longstreet's view that his *Georgia Scenes* were primarily history, his headnote aligns Prince's intent with his own. But why is Prince's name missing from Longstreet's headnote? When Longstreet requested permission to borrow the sketch. Prince may have asked his friend not to call him by name. It seems just as likely, however, that Longstreet simply followed the practice he had already established for his own name.

In the *Georgia Scenes.* "Abraham Baldwin" and "Lyman Hall" were fronting for Longstreet: so, when "The Militia Company Drill" became a Georgia Scene, "Timothy Crabshaw" fronted for Prince. (Longstreet's own charade even included exchanging letters with "Baldwin" and "Hall" in the pages of his newspaper.) Thus, by signing his headnote "Hall," Longstreet doubly obscured Prince's identity. Longstreet did not deny writing the sketch; Hall did. It would be natural, then, for Longstreet's readers to assume that "Hall" was introducing yet another pseudonym for the single author of the *Georgia Scenes.*

When Longstreet included "The Militia Company Drill" in his book, he again disclaimed Prince's sketch, but again his disclaimer was pseudonymous: Longstreet published *Georgia Scenes* as "A Native Georgian," and the book's preface was signed "The Author." With so many pseudonyms about, and no real names, the book's readers may have assumed—and some may continue to assume—that Crabshaw, Hall, Baldwin, A Native Georgian, and The Author are all the same man.

In the spring of 1837, two years after the first edition of *Georgia Scenes* had been published. Oliver Hillhouse Prince and his wife, Mary Norman Prince, traveled north to New York and Boston, where Prince delivered to a printer the manuscript of his revised and enlarged law digest. The second edition of *A Digest of the Laws of the State of Georgia* appeared later that year, but Prince never saw it. On October 9, as the Princes made their way home, their steamship, the *Home,* was caught in a storm off the North Carolina coast. Mary was washed overboard. Oliver, who had taken command of efforts to pump out the leaking vessel, went down with the ship. He could little have imagined the enduring importance of his modest contribution to American letters.

*Notes*

1. This is the date of the second edition of *Georgia Scenes,* which was published by Harper & Brothers of New York.

2. Longstreet has been named as a founder (if not *the* founder) of American literary realism by critics such as John Donald Wade ("First American Realist," *Atlanta Journal Magazine,* June 30, 1935, pp. 64) and James B. Meriwether ("Augustus Baldwin Longstreet: Realist and Artist," *Mississippi Quarterly,* 35 [fall 1982], 351-364).

3. Charles P. Jacobs, "Will Mr. Hardy Explain?" *The Critic,* January 28, 1882, pp. 25-26.

4. See "A Card from Mr. Hardy," *The Critic,* July 4, 1896, p. 8.

5. "Longstreet vs. Hardy," *The Bookman: A Magazine of Literature and Life,* April 1906, p. 121.

6. See, for example, *Memoirs of Judge Richard H. Clark,* ed. Lollie Belle Wylie (Atlanta: Franklin Printing and Publishing Company, 1898), p. 237; W. P. Trent, *Southern Writers: Selections in Prose and Verse* (New York: Macmillan, 1905), p. 122; "Longstreet vs. Hardy," *The Bookman,* April, 1906, pp. 121-122; John Donald Wade, *Augustus Baldwin Longstreet: A Study of the Development of Culture in the South* (New York: Macmillan, 1924), p. 178; and Carl J. Weber, "A Connecticut Yankee in King Alfred's Country," *Colophon,* n.s. 1 (1936), 525-535.

7. Stanley J. Kunitz and Howard Haycraft, eds., *American Authors 1600-1900: A Biographical Dictionary of American Literature* (New York: The H. N. Wilson Company, 1938), p. 479.

8. Frank N. Magill, ed., *Cyclopedia of World Authors* (revised edition, Englewood Cliffs, New Jersey: Salem Press, Incorporated, 1974), II, 1095.

9. See Virginia King Nirenstein, *With Kindly Voices: A Nineteenth-Century Georgia Family* (Macon: Tullous Books, 1984), pp. 4-5.

10. Bruce I. Granger, introduction to *Letters of Jonathan Oldstyle, Gent.* and *Salmagundi; or the Whim-whams and Opinions of Launcelot Langstaff, Esq. & Others* by Washington Irving (Boston: Twayne Publishers, 1977), pp. xx-xxi.

11. Frank Luther Mott, *Golden Multitudes: The Story of Best Sellers in the United States* (New York: Macmillan, 1947), p. 305.

12. *The Spectator,* ed. Donald F. Bond (Oxford: Oxford University Press, 1965), I, 5.

13. Washington Irving, [William Irving, and James Kirke Paulding], *Salmagundi; or The Whim-whams and Opinions of Launcelot Langstaff, Esq. & Others,* ed. Bruce I. Granger and Martha Hartzog. *The Complete Works of Washington Irving,* ed. Richard Dilworth Rust (Boston: Twayne Publishers, 1977), VI, 67.

14. The entire article appeared in two parts: [Oliver Hillhouse Prince], "For the Monitor," Washington (Georgia) *Monitor,* June 6, 1807, pp. 1-2, and [Prince], "For the Monitor (Concluded from Our Last)," *Monitor,* June 13, 1807, pp. 1-2.

15. This editorializing is summarized in *Augustus Baldwin Longstreet's Georgia Scenes Completed: A Scholarly Text,* ed. David Rachels (Athens: University of Georgia Press, 1998), pp. 311-312.

16. Prince has received passing notice in out-of-the-way places. Howard S. Mott writes that Prince's militia narrative "may be the first American short story classic" (*Collecting Southern Amateur Fiction of the Nineteenth Century: An Address before the Bibliographical Society of the University of Virginia, November 7, 1951* [Charlottesville: Bibliographical Society of the University of Virginia, 1952], p. 3), and H. Prentice Miller, who discovered the original publication of Prince's story in a file of the *Monitor* at the University of North Carolina, names Prince's work as "[t]he earliest important example of Southern humor" ("Ante-Bellum Georgia Humor and Humorists," *Emory University Quarterly,* 5 [June 1949], 86).

17. In *Reminiscences of an Old Georgia Lawyer* (1870; reprint, Atlanta: Cherokee Publishing Company, 1984), Garnett Andrews remarked that "the popular taste appreciates wit more than any other talent; comedy above tragedy, and laughter above thought." Prince, Andrews recalled, was "a man of infinite jest"; Longstreet, he said, was "kind-hearted and sunny" (pp. 41, 42, 68). In Stephen F. Miller's *The Bench and Bar of Georgia: Memoirs and Sketches,* (Philadelphia: Lippincott, 1858), Philip Clayton placed Prince and Longstreet together in "a galaxy of wit that has never had its equal in any generation of lawyers that have graced the Georgia bar" (I, 173), and in *The Memories of Fifty Years* (Philadelphia: Claxton, Remsen & Haffelfinger, 1870), W. H. Sparks remembered Prince and Longstreet as "chosen spirits of fun" (p. 482).

18. This anecdote earlier appeared in George R. Gilmer's *Sketches of Some of the First Settlers of Upper Georgia, of the Cherokees, and the Author* (New York: D. Appleton and Company, 1855). Gilmer's gloss on Brownee is rather different: "[Col. Johnson] used to shirtee his fields along the public road with cow-pens, so as to make the corn which was seen in passing by exhibit a very luxuriant appearance, and so create the opinion in the lookers-on that his land was very productive. His orders to the cowboys were, that the cattle must never leave the pen in the morning until they had added to its fertility. A neighbor passing by found a boy running a cow, and crying as if his heart would break. Being a very kind man, he stopped to inquire what was the matter, and received for answer that Brownee would not do what master ordered" (p. 118). According to Gilmer, Prince and Clayton's parody of Scott involved Brownee and this "little negro cowboy." Gilmer also notes that the parody was later published in a paper ed-

ited by David Hillhouse in Columbia, South Carolina (p. 122).

19. Years later, while Prince was co-editor of the *Georgia Journal,* that newspaper reprinted an item that lamented the end of Scott's Waverly series. It is impossible to know whether Prince approved of this bit of filler. See "Waverly Series Ended," Milledgeville *Georgia Journal,* March 8, 1832, p. 2.

20. A. B. Longstreet. "Old Things Become New." *The XIX Century,* April 1870, p. 840; Nirenstein, p. 5.

21. Quoted in O. P. Fitzgerald, *Judge Longstreet: A Life Sketch* (Nashville: Publishing House of the Methodist Episcopal Church, South, 1891), p. 164.

22. Much of the evidence connecting Prince and Longsteet is only circumstantial because few of their papers survive. As an old man during the Civil War, Longstreet watched Union soldiers burn his house with his papers as their kindling. A fair number of his letters survive, scattered in various libraries across the country. None, however, dates before 1829, probably seven years after he first met Prince. The only extant Longstreet letter that mentions Prince does so only in passing. See *The Letters of Augustus Baldwin Longstreet,* ed. James R. Scafidel (Diss., University of South Carolina, 1977), p. 115. A small number of Prince's papers are preserved at the University of Georgia. Unfortunately, none sheds light on his literary career or on his friendship with Longstreet. There are as well a few Prince papers among those of his son, who also was named Oliver Hillhouse Prince. These are held in the Jackson and Prince Family Papers at the University of North Carolina at Chapel Hill. Of related interest are the Alexander and Hillhouse Family Papers, which also are held at Chapel Hill.

23. Hamilton C. Jones, *Ham Jones, Ante-Bellum Southern Humorist: An Anthology,* ed. Willene Hendrick and George Hendrick (Hamden, Connecticut: Archon, 1990), p. 33.

24. Bertram Holland Flanders. *Early Georgia Magazines: Literary Feriodicals to 1865* (Athens: University of Georgia Press, 1944), p. 30.

25. See, for example. "The Sick Wife Cured in Revenge." Washington (Georgia) *Monitor.* August 2, 1806, p. 3, and "Military Anecdote." Washington (Georgia) *Monitor,* November 21, 1807, p. 3. Both of these items are unattributed. "Fugitas" published a number of additional editorials in the *Monitor,* including one other that framed a letter from "Tim Crabshaw" ("Electioneering," Wash-

ington [Georgia] *Monitor.* September 19, 1807, p. 2). On another occasion, there appeared a letter addressed to "Fugitas" and signed "Timothy" ("For the Monitor," Washington [Georgia] *Monitor,* April 1, 1809, p. 2).

26. "A Militia Training." *Georgia Journal.* November 12, 1832, p. 3. In addition, the *Georgia Journal* reprinted an item from the *Nashville Banner* that recalls Prince's original militia editorial in the *Monitor.* "The Military System" remarks that the "farces, called '*musters*' . . . have long been complained of as useless and ridiculous. . . ." These meetings are occasions of "vice, riot, and disorder" ("The Military System." *Georgia Journal.* December 2, 1834, p. 3).

27. "Free Inquiry," *Georgia Journal,* January 29, 1834, p. 2.

28. [A. B. Longstreet], "An Interesting Interview," Augusta *State Rights' Sentinel,* March 17, 1834, p. 3.

29. [Edgar Allan Poe], review of *Georgia Scenes* [by A. B. Longstreet], *The Southern Literary Messenger,* March 1836, p. 292.

30. "Editorial Changes," *Georgia Journal,* January 15, 1834, p. 2.

31. See Longstreet's prefatory note to "The Militia Company Drill" in the Augusta *State Rights' Sentinel,* May 15, 1834, p. 3. which is reprinted later in this essay.

32. [A. B. Longstreet]. *Georgia Scenes, Characters, Incidents, &c. in the First Half Century of the Republic* (Augusta: Printed at the S. R. Sentinel Office, 1835), p. [iii]; "Letters," p. 99.

33. Joel Chandler Harris, *Stories of Georgia* (New York: American Book Company, 1896), p. 250.

34. Arthur Palmer Hudson, *Humor of the Old Deep South* (New York: Macmillan, 1936), pp. 16-17.

## Ahmed Nimeiri (essay date spring 2001)

SOURCE: Nimeiri, Ahmed. "Play in Augustus Baldwin Longstreet's *Georgia Scenes.*" *Southern Literary Journal* 33, no. 2 (spring 2001): 44-61.

[*In the following essay, Nimeiri examines the various aspects of "play" present in Longstreet's* Georgia Scenes. *Nimeiri regards Longstreet's sense of play as an essential civilizing device in the Southern frontier, asserting that the humor of the sketches in fact con-*

*ceals a darker, more savage reality that lies just below the surface. According to Nimeiri, Longstreet viewed games, sports, and role playing as means of transcending the social schisms inherent in antebellum society, thus enabling a metaphoric transformation of that society in the process.*]

The distinguishing feature of Augustus Baldwin Longstreet's *Georgia Scenes* is its depiction of play—in its two senses of contesting and role playing—as the hallmark of antebellum southern life. The titles of the sketches indicate that they are predominantly concerned with games, sports and artistic performances, and in every sketch there is some form of play, from the obvious forms of sport and role playing to, in a few sketches, the more complicated social games and rituals. In most cases Longstreet presents characters as behaving in life as if they were performing on a stage. These characters range from the young man in **"Georgia Theatrics,"** who rehearses a courthouse fight, to Ned Brace who assumes different characters in pursuit of humor, to Miss Crump and her affectations, to a group of young men pretending to be wax figures, to the narrators, Hall and Baldwin, taking part in activities that are essentially role playing. Characters that act directly and immediately without a sense of a deliberate performance are scarce.

Few critics have noted the importance of play in *Georgia Scenes*. The pioneering effort in this respect is that of Michael Oriard in his essay on games in southwestern humor. Oriard observes that "in Southwestern humor the center appears to be play and games" (4). The games collectively reveal "the fact that game-playing was virtually a mode of existence for many of the frontier denizens described in hundreds of humorous tales, a mode that captured the imaginations of the writers that recorded them" (5). More recently, Scott Romine commented on Longstreet's tendency to connect communal harmony with play. He states, "If in Longstreet's ideal community each man should be easily apprehended and roles mutually accepted, a corollary truth is that a measure of uncertainty and instability—in short, a measure of play—is no less necessary for the maintenance of communal norms and values" (9).

Apt and revealing though these commentaries on play may be, they broach the subject rather broadly and generally. A detailed discussion of play in *Georgia Scenes* is needed if Longstreet's achievement in this book is to be properly assessed. The first thing to note is that Longstreet does not present play simply as a significant activity in the southern society of the early nineteenth century, but depicts it as the essence of the life of that society. He focuses on it to such a degree that it becomes identical with life or a substitute for it. The sketches contain examples of play that comprehend the significant aspects of the antebellum southern society, such as trade, education, politics, and interpersonal relationships in general. In these examples, typical activities are presented without the seriousness and logic that normally define them. They are divested of moral and rational elements in order to become flexible enough to exist in contexts from which they are normally excluded.

*Georgia Scenes* shows clearly that forms of play are useful in transforming or, at least, channeling violence, cruelty and similar negative impulses into harmless (if not, altogether, meaningful and creative) action. In these forms of play, there are two possible effects. The obvious and the predominant one is the catharsis that a player experiences as a result of directing his negative and antisocial impulses to the object of play and using them up in a contest instead of directing them at other people. The cathartic effect, as we shall see, is possible even in fights between men in which violence is displayed, because violence, in this case, occurs in a context that ultimately transforms it into play. The other effect, which is less frequent and sometimes overlaps with the first one, may be described as the affirmative effect. This is produced by the kind of play which is designed to affirm the values of society and educate its members into the significance of these values.

James B. Meriwether states that "*Georgia Scenes* provides abundant evidence that Longstreet thought impulses towards savagery and violence were to be found not far from the surface in many men, perhaps most of them; and it is the function of human laws and institutions to restrain, discipline and civilize these impulses and to make good citizens out of barbarians" (361). The statement would be true if "play" were substituted for "human laws and institutions." The function of play in *Georgia Scenes* is, in effect, similar to that of laws and institutions. Play, however, is the stage of civilization that precedes any formalized rules or laws. It provides a more natural, if less effective, restraint than they do because it caters for the emotions and the imagination while they express the mind and apply its rules to experience. *Georgia Scenes* is, obviously, more about play than it is about "the restraints of human laws and institutions." The first sketch, **"Georgia Theatrics,"** brings together a lawyer and a player when Hall, on his way to court, observes a rehearsal of a courthouse fight. In the last sketch, **"The Shooting Match,"** the lawyer becomes a player who performs admirably in verbal games and a shooting match. The metamorphosis of the lawyer into a player is what *Georgia Scenes* is essentially about and, in an important sense, it expresses Longstreet's own metamorphosis, after the failure of his quest for a political career, from an espouser of states' rights and nullification into an artist who seeks meaning and comfort in literature.[1] The metamorphosis may seem to be a brief and not spectacular one, but undoubtedly it constitutes a significant improvement on Longstreet's biography. Although he did not develop his literary career after *Georgia Scenes,* he secured with this one book a place in the American literary canon. Humor and realism have been generally regarded as constituting the book's claim to a major literary status, but it is really Longstreet's vision of the antebellum South and of human life in general that makes his book continue to be a significant text. By placing play at the heart of human life, Longstreet distinguishes himself from the Transcendentalists, the Romantics, and the heirs of Puritanism. He makes clear in this book that he does not view man as naturally good or innately depraved but regards the man who plays as capable of changing inner evils into overt good or, at least, harmless behavior. Nevertheless, he is aware of the negative sense of play, which he perceives in actions without sense or purpose such as affectations, pretenses and the social and psychological games that turn any situation and, life itself, into an empty affair.

Play, ultimately, serves as an effective metaphor that enables Longstreet to transcend the limitations of a narrow conservative vision of the antebellum South developed in response to his time and place, to a liberating sense of man and human experience. Jessica Wegmann has shown that racism and sexism are glaringly present in the stories of *Georgia Scenes.* Yet the stories are redeemed not just by wit and humor but also, more importantly, by what they reveal of the creative potential in the individual and the possibility of a human community. It is not true, as Wegmann contends, that Longstreet "constructed the narratives to argue his position on race and gender" (25). It would be more just to say that his sexism and racism constitute an aspect of his vision of the South—an aspect that should not be ignored but, at the same time, should not be exaggerated.

The idea of play is present in all the nineteen sketches of *Georgia Scenes,* and it gives the book a thematic unity. Generally speaking, the positive aspect of play is expressed in the sketches narrated by Hall while the negative sense is explored in Baldwin's sketches. The narrators reflect the degree of their involvement in their milieu by the part they take in its play. Hall becomes aware of and, afterwards, involved with the rural community first by observing some of its roughest play and tolerating it, then by gradually appreciating country sports and amusements, and finally by participating in the games and social rituals of rustic people. Baldwin,

on the other hand, expresses his rejection of the society of the city, which forces him to shrink into himself, in distaste for its songs, balls, and social games.

Taken together, the sketches depict the agrarian southern society of the early nineteenth century as gradually becoming urban. Longstreet does not simply satirize town life in the few Baldwin sketches, but he projects urbanization throughout the book as an inevitable and sinister reality encroaching on the South and divesting the life of the individual and society of meaning and cohesiveness.[2] He expresses his sense of the new reality in stark and uncompromising terms in **"The 'Charming Creature' as Wife"** when he describes the society of the city as one of a rising middle class that impoverishes the South economically and morally, represented here by Mr. Smith, the illiterate merchant who has made his fortune "rather by good luck than good management" (84). The moral deterioration and death of George Baldwin, the narrator's nephew, are inevitable consequences of succumbing to the influence of the urban milieu while the bankruptcy of Mr. Smith, which is also inevitable, expresses the moral bankruptcy of the emerging southern urban middle class and its mismanagement of the economic life of the South.

In such a context, play reveals the effort of the southern gentleman to make sense of and to come to terms with his society at that point in the history of South. It is significant that Longstreet should employ two narrators, instead of one, to dramatize that effort. In the preface to the first edition of *Georgia Scenes,* he explains this bifurcation:

> From private considerations, I was extremely desirous of concealing the author, and, the more effectually to do so, I wrote under two signatures. These have now become too closely interwoven with the sketches to be separated from them, without expense of time and trouble which I am unwilling to incur. *Hall* is the writer of those sketches in which *men* appear to be the principal actors, and *Baldwin* of those in which *women* are the prominent figures.

> (xxiv)

But it is difficult, after reading *Georgia Scenes,* to accept any part of this reasoning. If the choice of the names was not deliberate it must have been, at least, intuitive, because the two names have unmistakable thematic implications. In one sense, they have made the narrators representative characters exhibiting the broad qualities of their prototypes and expressing the two facets of the southern elite: the potential for action that leads to a positive engagement with others and the tendency to fall back on sensibility and retreat into the self.[3] The sketches bring out clearly the success of the effort of the man of action to ingratiate himself with the rural community and the failure of the man of sensibility to end his estrangement in the emerging urban South. Hall moves largely in a setting of rural and backwoods characters. He begins in **"Georgia Theatrics," "The Horse Swap,"** and **"The Fight"** by misunderstanding and disapproving—although he is obviously fascinated by—rural life but gradually he comes to terms with it and is accepted in it in **"The Shooting Match."** Baldwin, who has estranged himself from his rural origins, tries to extricate himself from urban sophistication and return to the country in **"The Dance,"** but he fails to get recognition there and is, therefore, forced back to the city where he is condemned to live as a peevish outsider. While Hall observes and comments on action—the prime aspect of the experience of the country—and through understanding of and finally engagement in action (although in almost all cases it is play) is able to come to terms with the rural society, Baldwin is repeatedly discomfited by the superficial culture and sophistication that rule city life. In a sense, the fact that Hall has twelve sketches while Baldwin has half that number attests to the breadth of Hall's sphere of action and the success of his effort to interact meaningfully with the community he is involved with, and indicates the narrowness of Baldwin's life and his failure to develop and achieve significance in his society.

Longstreet suggests in this book that play is the effective way to end the southern gentleman's alienation and bring him close to the positive aspects of southern life located in what remained of the rural society of the Old South. Hall and Baldwin are conditioned by their education and training, which are based on reason and morality, as well as their upbringing, which inculcates moral and rational precepts, and it is this conditioning that accounts for their detachment and their inability to respond adequately to the life around them. In order, therefore, to come closer to that life, they must be free of the influences of that conditioning. But since it is inconceivable to live overtly and frankly without the moral and the rational restrictions that make social intercourse possible and the individual's life meaningful, even if regimented, the gentleman can only resort to play to achieve any degree of freedom from the imposed limitations of his life. This is what Baldwin tries but fails to do when he dances in the country and what Hall succeeds in accomplishing at the end of his endeavor when he plays the games of the backwoodsman. *Georgia Scenes* makes clear that the liberating kind of play is available in the countryside and backwoods, not in towns, and that this kind of play may shake and even disrupt the gentleman's character, but ultimately it broadens the scope of his experience.

Eight of Hall's sketches deal directly or indirectly with the countryside or the backwoods, either by depicting typical rural characters and activities or by expressing themes peculiar to rural areas. The other four sketches—**"The Character of a Native Georgian," "The Debating Society," "The Turf,"** and **"The Wax-Works"**— have their setting in the town but they have an obvious thematic connection with the first group of sketches. Hall's sketches treat play mainly as role-playing and, to a minor degree, as organized sport, and they stress the idea that play is the essence of the experience of the rural community so much that most of them read like burlesques where there is only a travesty of action. In the first four sketches, for example, the courthouse fight is not a real fight, the horse swap is a hoax, Ned Brace's character is made up of antics and pranks, the fight between Billy Stallings and Bob Durham has a theatrical quality about it, and the turn-out of the teacher by the pupils is a ritualistic game. Action, in these sketches, like the sentence that Longworth and McDermot frame in **"The Debating Society,"** "possesses the form . . . without a particle of the substance" (134).

The first five of Hall's sketches bring out the main sense of play as it is expressed in role-playing. In the deceptively simple first sketch, **"Georgia Theatrics,"** Longstreet recounts the gentleman's discovery of play in the agrarian society and hints at a change of heart as a result of this discovery. The contrast that develops, in Hall's mind, between the moral and the natural conditions of Lincoln Corner and his characterization of the imaginary fighters and their activity as a "band of ruffians" and "Pandemonium riots" that disturb and disfigure nature, described as "holy" and "heavenly," indicate the kind of notions the southern gentleman has about the agrarian society and that have set him apart from that society. Hall's discovery that what he has assumed to be a real fight is only a rehearsal of a courthouse fight is the turning point in his experience and it leads to a significant change in his perspective on the South. The truth that is driven home to Hall, at the end of the sketch, is that violence in the agrarian society of the South is, generally, not real but it is play and make-believe. The discovery of the rehearsal effectively redefines for Hall the agrarian society as a society that has succeeded in transforming the harsh realities of its life into meaningful and constructive experiences. It is this discovery that vindicates the claim that the agrarian South has undergone a momentous change from barbarism to civilization, with which *Georgia Scenes* opens and which dominates the book:

> Could I venture to mingle the solemn with the ludicrous, even for the purposes of honourable contrast, I could adduce from this county instances of the most numerous and wonderful transitions, from vice and folly to virtue and holiness, which have ever, perhaps, been witnessed since the days of the apostolic ministry.
>
> (9)

The incident of the imaginary fight and Hall's response to it express from the outset the vision that Longstreet coins to make his endorsement of the Old South tenable. That "the most numerous and wonderful transitions" are not necessarily always brought about by heroic feats or great spiritual experiences, but also, and in an important sense, as Hall insinuates, by the more accessible human effort to integrate play into everyday life, is what makes it possible, ultimately, to perceive country folks' play as constituting a civilized endeavor.

Role-playing makes up the essence of the major activities in folk life in Hall's next four sketches and, in a curious way, it produces social harmony and a sense of well being. In **"The Horse-Swap,"** play-acting is established as a necessary adjunct to individual and social experience because it produces the humor that tones down the harsh commercialism of the urban society and the puritan social ethics that justify it. The curious transaction that involves the swapping of a defective horse for a more defective one is a parody of trade and the transactional activity that are distorted into commercialism. The whole incident gives an emphatic sense of a theatrical act. All those present, including the horses, play-act in an obvious sense—Bullet's tail movement is evidence. It becomes clear, in the end, that the transaction is a game in which each participant displays his skill and acumen and where material gain and loss are not of primary significance. Such a transaction, however, is possible only in the context of the rustic society where economics is subordinated to spirit and where morality is occasionally replaced by humor in order to do justice to the complexity of life. The rustics understand and accept that the disfigurement of nature and dispossession of people in commercial transactions are daily occurrences that may be necessary for survival. But in order to make these realities palatable they place them within a context of play and humor.

Longstreet insists that agrarian play and humor are not superfluous or absurd. Their value and their positive effect on a community would be appreciated if one looked at the city where their absence only accentuates the emptiness and oppressiveness of its life and drives a "native," like Ned Brace in **"The Character of a Native Georgian,"** to pursue them in curious and desperate ways in order to maintain the authenticity and vitality of his character. Ned's pranks, played in an obvious and crude manner, indicate that his quest goes beyond humor to making a travesty of his acquired social character and ridiculing acceptable social behavior. The fact that his role-playing is often gratuitous and is continued in spite of its sinister implications indicates a persistent effort to break away from social intercourse and interpersonal relationships and to negate the possibility of a fixed identity. That is, Ned strives to subvert the newly acquired urban character in order to revive and maintain "the character of a native Georgian." His actions are targeted against things not native—hotels, table manners, foreigners, the blurring of racial and social differences—implying perhaps the narrowest sense of the southern identity. To stress this sense of a separate identity, Longstreet implies in the uncritical manner in which he presents Ned's excesses and absurdities that his infantilism, racism, and xenophobia are appropriate reactions to a way of life that is neither authentic nor original. Ned, in fact, expresses better than any other character in *Georgia Scenes* Longstreet's conservatism, and Ned's oddities and absurdities give the sense of being stretched to mask his closeness to his creator.[4] But, in an important sense his pranks and jokes also are carried to an offensive extreme to smooth the way for an acceptance of rough country play in the next sketch. Longstreet stresses, in this sketch, that play in the city is a disturbing activity that nullifies social values. This is the opposite of the situation in the country where play is an integral part of life and where the country community constantly provides games, contests and rituals that help free the individual of negative impulses and integrate him into rural society.

Communal play is the subject of the rest of Hall's sketches. In **"The Fight"** this kind of play is introduced, in an intensely dramatic form, as a means of liberating the rural character of impulses that threaten the very basis of social life. The fight between Billy Stallings and Bob Durham, in which eyes are gouged, ears are torn, fingers are bitten off, and ribs are broken, can hardly be called play. Yet, the fight has about it the sense of play—both as a game and a theatrical performance—that the careful reader cannot miss. It is a thing that the people have wanted to happen in order to determine who is the better man. Ransy Sniffle exhibits this curiosity and need for a spectacle in an extreme form and his behavior emphasizes the idea that, for the community, the fight is a performance like that in a ring. He has longed for the fight to take place and has made effort to make it happen and he finally succeeds in bringing it about by telling Bob Durham of Billy Stalling's insult to his wife. The quality of stage performance is brought out when Squire Loggins, an authority on such fights whose predictions always come true, uses characteristic terms that apply to the action of a play to describe the imminent fight: "Sammy, watch Robert Durham close at the beginning of the fight; take care of William Stallions in the middle of it; and see who has the wind at the end" (58). The fight has clearly the two effects of play. The cathartic effect is exhibited by Ransy Sniffle who has been restless and agitated and who is at peace only after the fight has taken place. Ransy represents the dark aspects of the communal psyche and its negative impulses. His physical emaciation and his uncanny aspect suggest a level of the psyche untouched by civilization and morality. Alive only in the middle of feuds and strife and playing the role of the devil in his effort to bring about the fight, Ransy also represents the demonic in the rural character. That the fight gives Ransy and the community complete satisfaction is sufficient indication that the wild, hostile and aggressive impulses that disturb social intercourse have been acted out and are now under control. The affirmative aspect of play is expressed in the result of the fight which stresses that superiority is essentially moral superiority as Billy Stalling's final didactic comment indicates: "Bobby you licked me a fair fight; but you wouldn't have done if I hadn't been in the wrong. I oughtn't to have treated your wife as I did; and I felt so through the whole fight; and it sort o' cowed me" (64). Longstreet, obviously, tries to appease and reassure readers of his own background and class, who may not accept the idea of the psychically cathartic role of rough country play, by the inconsistently didactic conclusion of the sketch. But, in a more important sense, the didacticism that controls and closes the sketch functions as an index of Hall's development and shows his struggle to maintain his gentlemanly identity in the face of the disruptive realities of country life. The gentlemanly reservations expressed in **"The Fight"** become minimal in **"The Turn Out"** where Hall is an approving observer of another form of country play in which a significant group of the country community is involved. The pupils' barring of their schoolmaster from the schoolhouse is play—a deliberate performance and a game—that has become an approved communal ritual with an obvious educative purpose. The fact that the game takes place inside the schoolhouse indicates that it is an educational activity complementary to, but certainly more effective than, the formal instruction offered in that schoolhouse. By playing this game with their teacher, the boys acquire a sense of the necessity and limit of authority and rebellion and learn the need and value of compromise as a practical measure in coming to terms with experience. This kind of play is appreciated by the gentleman not only because he can perceive its moral purpose but also because of his sense that its ritualistic aspect gives it a dignity that approaches that of serious art, as the references to Pope, Swift and other poets at the end of the sketch suggest.

The other Hall sketches that deal with role-playing— **"The Debating Society," "An Interesting Interview,"** and **"The Wax-Works"**—as well as "The Militia Company Drill," the sketch narrated by Timothy Crawshaw and written by Longstreet's friend Oliver Hillhouse Prince, consist of little more than pointless arguments, antics, absurd behavior, and sheer awkward movement, things which readers of the time seem to appreciate, as Poe's comments on the **"Debating Society"** and "The Militia Company Drill" indicate (Inge 92). The sense of travesty and burlesque is emphatic in these sketches and, placed at the end of the book, they have the effect of intensifying the sense of the apocryphal superseding the actual in Hall's sketches and thus mellowing it or altogether doing away with its severity.

The four sketches whose subject is organized sport enhance the significance of play—both as role-playing and organized sport—and emphasize its pivotal position in the Old South. Although the four sketches describe sports characteristic of the time, they focus on instances in the games and contests that bring out not the typical character of the community and the individual but their aberrations, limitations, and failures. When Baldwin asks Hall to go with him to the turf in the sketch which bears that name, Hall tells him that he has "no interest in its amusements." Baldwin then answers, "Nor do I . . . but I visit it to acquire knowledge of the human character" (152). The "human character" that is revealed in these sketches is a character that has become liberated from social restraints by its presence in a context of play. Both players and spectators engage and indulge in forms of play that may not be tolerated outside the particular context of sports, such as jokes, antics, mimicry, and buffoonery. The humor that their actions produce approaches, sometimes, the raw humor of Simon Suggs and Sut Lovingood, although it is often checked by authorial interference or the general moral tone that pervades these sketches. But notwithstanding the humor, the four sketches treat some of the harsh realities of southern life, such as violence, cruelty (especially to animals), and moral callousness. As in the first five Hall sketches, but less successfully, Longstreet places these realities within a context of play to suggest that that is the effective way of dealing with them. Violence and cruelty are prominent features of "gander pulling" in the sketch that describes that sport. Hall is at first disturbed and disgusted by the mistreatment of the animal but he is gradually reconciled to the sport when he perceives its effect on the spectators. People "of different ages, sexes, sizes and complexions" (113) develop a spirit of fellowship and become animated as they watch the sport and cheer the participants, and the gander pulling with all its roughness has the obvious cathartic effect of working out antisocial impulses in both participants and spectators. That effect, however, as Longstreet shows in **"The Turf,"** may be found in a minimal degree and an almost unrecognizable form in city sports. The turf breaks down the barriers between the self-encapsulated and morally indifferent people of the city and makes them, at least during the time they are watching that sport, accessible to each other, but it also brings out the social and moral evils of the city. Longstreet makes clear, by the critical and satirical tone that Hall maintains throughout the sketch, that whatever positive effect that or any sport may have is determinedly dispelled by the general discord in the urban scene.

The other two sketches about organized sports, **"The Fox-Hunt"** and **"The Shooting Match,"** express the possibility of the gentleman participating in folk life and thus bring to a completion Hall's development. In both sketches Hall changes his position from that of an observer of play to a player who takes part in games and plays roles. It is a sign of his changed position that he himself generates the humor that attend country play and it is effectively this humor that brings him close to country folk. In **"The Fox-Hunt,"** Hall, a gentleman who gets his sense of life from books, comes in touch with physical and sensuous experience when he hunts in an inept and comic way on a lazy horse. But it is in **"The Shooting Match,"** in which Hall uses play and humor successfully to end his detachment from the agrarian community, that Longstreet asserts clearly the feasibility of gentlemanly involvement in the agrarian South. The sketch mainly recounts Hall's effort to replace his gentlemanly image with an image the country community may relate to more comfortably. His effort to come close to country people amounts to almost a change of identity as he strives to subvert the forbidding image of himself that sets him apart from that community. Hall adopts the backwoodsman's idiom and manners to break down the barriers between himself and Billy Curlew, created by Hall's position and dress. But no sooner does Billy concede that Hall is not the "fool [he] took [him] to be" (198) and gives him his hand in acknowledgement than he recognizes Hall as the shot who, as a boy, performed legendary feats, thus creating another forbidding image that might isolate him from the participants in the shooting match. Hall, however, tries to make himself accessible to the rustics by performing in the peculiar manner he does, and in this he succeeds. His awkwardness and weakness are aspects of a persona he puts on to negate the image of excellence Billy Curlew draws of him and tries to impress on the consciousness of the country community. Significantly, Hall wins second place in the shooting match, a position not too high or too low to set him apart from the country folk. But Hall does not become, as Newlin states, "assimilated into that society" (360), since it is only through play that he can interact with it. Longstreet, obviously, checks the implications of his romantic vision when he stresses that the gentleman's involvement in folk life does not constitute a forfeiture of his gentlemanly identity. Thus the rustics' reading of Hall's play-acting as a political act is plausible since the practical involvement of the gentleman in their life is often political and at the end Hall comes out as the gentleman he has always been.

In Baldwin's sketches artistic performances take the place of country and backwoods games, contests, and pranks. These sketches form a necessary complement to Hall's sketches. First, they stress the reality of the urban society and demonstrate that it is not possible to achieve a complete view of the South without taking into account that society. Second, they justify and make viable the romantic vision expressed in Hall's sketches. Hall's progress, in the agrarian society, would be too romantic without Baldwin's frustration and failure in the city. Interspersed among Hall's sketches, Baldwin's sketches have the effect of staying the reader from developing a final view of the world presented by Hall. They usually follow after the harsh aspects of the agrarian society are accented in Hall's sketches, ostensibly placed in this manner to dispel the effect of that harshness by depicting the mellow refinement of the city. But, in fact, they present an image of an empty life that makes the country seem, even when violence and cruelty are prominent in it, more appropriate for human beings. Hence **"The Song"** comes after **"The Fight,"** and **"The Ball"** follows **"The Gander Pulling,"** but instead of indicating alternatives of humanizing sophistication that free the mind of the possibilities of violence and cruelty suggested in Hall's sketches, these Baldwin sketches depict a life that, in its deadening effect, makes rural roughness almost desirable.

Baldwin's sketches show clearly the effect of the emerging urban society on the southern gentleman's retreat into isolation and cynicism. They depict activities which, in normal circumstances, bring the individual into harmony with himself and his world—such as the ball, the song, and the conversation—as having become, in the city, play in the most negative sense. What becomes painfully clear in these pretenses at sophistication are the rarefaction and devitalization of the urban character and the inadequacy of the urban response to experience. Each Baldwin sketch focuses on an activity which is essentially play and which, directly or indirectly, exposes the dehumanizing elements of the urban southern society. The pivotal point in the first sketch he narrates is the dance, which becomes, effectively, an act that defines both the individual and the community and tests their claims to genuineness and integrity. That the country dance takes place in the morning, a time urbanites regard as unsuited for dancing, indicates that the country people have made it an integral part of their life and given it a place equal to that of work and worship. Baldwin obviously oversimplifies the urban-rural opposition, and in his discourse, which at this point consists of familiar thought and rhetoric, the rural community emerges as totally right and wholesome. Nevertheless, he expresses strongly his sense of having lost his true identity through prolonged contact with the society of the city. The more important point of the sketch, however, is Baldwin's failure to win his youthful sweetheart's recognition and redeem himself after his distinguished performance in the dance, an experience which foreshadows and parallels Hall's successful performance and the consequent recognition he wins in **"The Shooting Match."** Thus Baldwin provides the justification and rationale for Hall's involvement in the rural community and makes Hall's success in that community a desirable goal for the southern gentleman.

The manner in which Baldwin narrates his sketches, his caustic satire, and his increasing detachment from the experiences he recounts reflects his extreme isolation in the city. The sketches have often an abstract quality of parable that makes them look contrived and only distantly and tenuously related to the actual. The quality is clear even in **"The 'Charming Creature' as Wife,"** a sketch which purports to be a true account of the tragic marriage of Baldwin's nephew. However true the story Baldwin tells, it is more significant as an illustration of his idea of the "charming creature" than an account of the tragedy of his nephew. Baldwin, that is, turns the story of his nephew into an apocryphal experience in order to rationalize his rejection of the city. But the idealization of Baldwin's nephew's mother and setting her and her farmer's values as the norm against which the character and conduct of her son's wife are assessed, in order to bring out the failures of the wife and dismiss her liberal values, succeed only in baring the complacent narrowness of Longstreet's sense of the southern character.

The sense of parable is evident in **"The Mother and her Child"** and **"A Sage Conversation,"** two minor efforts that seem abstract and unrelated to the other Georgia scenes, but placed in the context of Baldwin's sketches they will be seen to comment on the emptiness and absurdity of the urban social discourse. Baldwin describes gibberish as "one of the peculiarities of the age" (130) and conveys, through the parable-like story of the mother and her child, his sense of the isolation of people in that society and the inefficacy of the discourse they develop in ending that isolation. Equally, the wisdom that that society can boast of, represented comically by the aged matrons in **"A Sage Conversation,"** is facetiously inadequate in the face of the dark realities that beset social intercourse. Baldwin's and Ned Brace's stopping at the aged matrons' house is a comic visit to a comic oracle, with the aged matrons as priestesses that the two men consult about the mysteries of urban life. Ned Brace's story of two men marrying each other and raising children produces, among the matrons, an interminable conversation that touches on such taboo subjects as homosexuality and transvestitism without ever hinting at their significance or implications.

The parables in Baldwin's sketches crystallize Longstreet's characteristic effort, in *Georgia Scenes,* to use art to keep his perceptions of the reality of his society from overwhelming his consciousness. His highly didactic art derives from the sense that play, in his society, has become so rigidly formalized into spiritless ritual that, instead of dispelling or, at least, minimizing the horrors at the heart of southern social life, it intensifies its nightmarish quality. Baldwin is more traumatized by the artistic performances he attends than he is by the reality around him. In his satires of such performances, in **"The Song"** and **"The Ball,"** he exposes the perversion of art in the urban South. The singing of Miss Aurelia Emma Theodosia Augusta Crump is dissonance and pretentious affectation while the ball is a chaotic farce where conflicts and feuds flourish. People seem to dehumanize themselves and trivialize and vulgarize social intercourse when they take part in these amusements. The cynicism and the unmistakable sense of the absurdity of both reality and art that close Baldwin's part of the book result essentially from his failure to use art effectively to come to terms with his society—precisely the fate Longstreet tries to avoid by writing *Georgia Scenes.*

Significantly, *Georgia Scenes* concludes not with Baldwin's cynicism but with Hall's affirmation of the value of the experience of the agrarian society of the South. The romantic vision that this conclusion confirms is manifestly complex. Longstreet does not simply reject the city in favor of the country but bases his endorsement and celebration of the agrarian South on a view of the relationship of reality and art and the implications of that view on the situation of the southern gentleman at the beginning of the nineteenth century. By suggesting that play constitutes the significant aspect of rustic life and by insinuating, at the same time, that reality can be properly apprehended and lived when it is turned into art, Longstreet is able to present the agrarian society as a civilized haven in which involvement is possible and rewarding for the gentleman. But he makes it clear that this involvement can only be achieved through art. *Georgia Scenes* is an expression of such gentlemanly involvement. It is a southern gentleman's effort to come to terms with the rugged reality of the South "in the first half century of the Republic,"[5] which his upbringing and education would have led him to dismiss and insulate himself against but which he came to think of as the source of meaning and vitality lacking in contemporary urban life.

*Georgia Scenes* reflects clearly its author's progressive appreciation of unpolished folks and his decreasing interest in gentility and sophistication. The superior vantage point and aesthetic distance observed in the sketches and stories of the other southern humorists is not found in the same manner in *Georgia Scenes.* Hall and Baldwin are not content with the role of observer. Occasionally, they are central characters in the sketches they narrate, and often they try to influence the action they describe or record its effect on them or, at least, maintain a moral tone that indicates an active presence.

It is because Longstreet is generally lumped with the "southwestern humorists" that the distinctive aspects of his work—the postulation of play as the hallmark of the antebellum South and his affirmation of gentlemanly involvement in country life—are missed. But Longstreet is significantly different from those humorists in the way he perceives reality and in the manner he delineates it. The humorists may distance themselves from the crude life they depict, by assuming a detached or neutral stance or by using a highly stylized language, but what they present always purports to be real life, not the imitation or travesty that the depiction of play, in *Georgia Scenes,* suggests. Their characters do not act in the deliberate and theatrical manner of Longstreet's characters, but, in spite of their comic behavior, they respond spontaneously to the situations in which they are involved. The antebellum humorists are, in fact, realists who depict, neutrally and objectively, a neglected or excluded aspect of the experience of the antebellum South. They and their narrators are minimally present in their own narratives and rarely interfere to influence the action or furnish a perspective for viewing or judging it. Longstreet, on the other hand, uses literature to express a personal vision of the South. This purpose could not have been served by realism.[6] In *Georgia Scenes,* he obviously finds it difficult to affirm and celebrate, in a realistic fashion, a way of life that could not be historically justified. Therefore, he identifies the agrarian South almost exclusively with play, its most palatable aspect, to make possible the expression of his vision.

### Notes

1. Longstreet, a great nullification enthusiast, started to publish the sketches that he later collected in *Georgia Scenes* in the *Southern Recorder* in 1833 when the nullification controversy was heading to an end and when hopes for nullification grew weak. Between 1833 and 1834, he published twelve sketches in the *Southern Recorder.* In January 1834, he owned, published, and edited the *States Rights' Sentinel.* The six remaining sketches were published in the *Sentinel* between 1834-1836 (King 56-90). The sketches were written at a time when Longstreet was disappointed with and withdrawing from politics. He ran three times for office: twice he withdrew and once he was defeated. Although he published the *Sentinel* to champion states' rights, his waning interest in politics was becoming evident as time went on. Wade remarks, "Editorially, Longstreet wrote about politics at first with almost exclusive attention, but as the active hope for nullification subsided he became less interested in politics and more interested in life in general" (136).

2. Kimball King is the only critic to use the word "urban" in relation to *Georgia Scenes* when he speaks of a "pattern of urban-rural contrasts" in the book (83). The idea of an urban South, in the nineteenth century, has always been denied, especially in the South. Lawrence H. Larsen remarks that "the view remained widely accepted that the region had little in the way of urban foundations and that the existing cities bore only a slight relationship or relevance to the nascent agrarian civilization that would serve as the foundation of the Confederate States of America" (2-3). But Larsen states that "certainly, the South, both antebellum and postbellum, was predominantly rural. Nevertheless, from the earliest days of settlement, Southern development bore an urban physiognomy" (3).

3. The biographical sketches of Lyman Hall and Abraham Baldwin, in the *Dictionary of American Biography,* depict Hall as a man who had an active life, both in the North and the South, and who was noted for his initiative and independent mind (1:531-532), while Baldwin is described as having had a relatively quieter life, devoting it mostly to educational projects (4:139-140).

4. When *Georgia Scenes* was first published in 1835 the author was identified, in the title page, as "a Native Georgian." It would not have been possible, then, not to think of a connection between the author and Ned Brace.

5. The full title of the 1835 edition of the book is *Georgia Scenes: Characters, Incidents &c. in the First Half Century of the Republic. By a Native Georgian.*

6. The tendency to elevate *Georgia Scenes* on the basis of realism has been part of the assessment of Longstreet's literary career and the discussion of the book since its publication in 1835. Longstreet was the first to stress that realism was the hallmark of his book. In his preface to the first edition of the book, he remarks that the sketches "consist of little more than fanciful combinations of real incidents" (xxiii), and he states, in a letter to T. W. White, the publisher of *The Southern Literary Messenger,* that his purpose in writing *Georgia Scenes* "is to enable those who come after us, to see us *precisely as we are*" (Scafidel 100). Criticism of the book has been essentially a repetition or paraphrasing of this idea, combining or replacing it, occasionally, with an emphasis on humor. Few critics expressed doubts about or objected to the view that realism was the main aspect of the book. Robert L. Philips, for example, states, "Although Longstreet has been recognized as an im-

portant early realist in American fiction, there is a strong element of romance in his writing, which grows out of his narrators' seeming unwillingness to present humanity objectively and let the reader draw his own conclusions" (148). Recently, Jessica Wegmann contended that "the critical treatment of [the stories] as pure descriptive realism unaccompanied by discussion of the construction of their didacticism" was the cause of the modern reader's discomfort with them and the decline in their popularity (14).

## Works Cited

Inge, M. Thomas, ed. *The Southern Humorists: Critical Views.* Hamden: Archon Books, 1975.

Johnson, Allen, ed. *Dictionary of American Biography.* Vol. 1. New York: Charles Scribner's Sons, 1964.

———, and Dumas Malone, eds. *Dictionary of American Biography.* Vol. 4. New York: Charles Scribner's Sons, 1960.

King, Kimball. *Augustus Baldwin Longstreet.* Boston: Twayne Publishers, 1984.

Larsen, Lawrence H. *The Urban South.* Lexington: UP of Kentucky, 1990.

Longstreet, Augustus Baldwin. *Georgia Scenes.* Nashville: J. S. Sanders, 1992.

Meriwether, James B. "Augustus Baldwin Longstreet: Realist and Artist." *Mississippi Quarterly* 35 (1982): 351-364.

Newlin, Keith S. "The Satiric Art of Augustus Baldwin Longstreet." *Mississippi Quarterly* 41 (1987): 21-37.

Oriard, Michael. "Shifty in a New Country: Games in Southwestern Humor." *Southern Literary Journal* 12 (1980): 3-28.

Phillips, Robert L. "The Novel and the Romance in Middle Georgia Humor and Local Color." Diss. U of North Carolina at Chapel Hill, 1971.

Romine, Scott. "Negotiating Community in Augustus Baldwin Longstreet's *Georgia Scenes.*" *Style* 30 (1996): 1-27.

Scafidel, J. R. "The Letters of Augustus Baldwin Longstreet." Diss. U of South Carolina, 1976.

Wade, John Donald. *Augustus Baldwin Longstreet: A Study of the Development of Culture in the South.* Athens: U of Georgia P, 1959.

Wegmann, Jessica. "'Playing in the Dark' with Augustus Baldwin Longstreet's *Georgia Scenes*: Critical Reception and Reader Response to the Treatment of Race and Gender." *Southern Literary Journal* 30 (1997): 13-26.

## Kurt Albert Mayer (essay date 2001)

SOURCE: Mayer, Kurt Albert. "Augustan Nostalgia and Patrician Disdain in A. B. Longstreet's *Georgia Scenes.*" In *The Humor of the Old South,* edited by M. Thomas Inge and Edward J. Piacentino, pp. 101-12. Lexington: University Press of Kentucky, 2001.

[*In the following essay, Mayer examines* Georgia Scenes *in relation to Longstreet's career as an author, lawyer, and politician, as well as within the framework of the larger body of Southern literary humor.*]

Although they are usually allotted no more than a brief mention in most surveys of American literature, Augustus Baldwin Longstreet and his *Georgia Scenes* are regularly credited as having initiated Southwestern humor on which Twain and Faulkner were to feed copiously. Detailed examinations of Longstreet's only notable literary achievement are comparably scarce; moreover, they seem to be preoccupied with determining whether in fact the sketches may be regarded as social history—whether, in literary terms, the book is protorealist. Easy launches for arguments along those lines were provided by the inflated subtitle of the volume, *Characters, Incidents, &c. in the First Half Century of the Republic,* by a Native Georgian; and by the preface appended to the first edition, which appeared anonymously in 1835. As the secret of authorship was soon out, the assertions contained in the opening paragraph of the preface were duly rehearsed—that "some little art" was used in crafting the sketches, which were "nothing more than fanciful *combinations* of *real* incidents and characters," though "some of the scenes are as literally true as the frailties of memories would allow them to be" (*Georgia Scenes Completed* 3).[1]

Highlighting set phrases of authorial prefatory tiptoeing, the debate has gone wrong, misled by statements Longstreet made in later years. An 1836 letter, for instance, claimed: "The design of the *Georgia Scenes* has been wholly misapprehended by the public. It has been invariably received as a mere collection of fancy sketches, with no higher object than the entertainment of the reader, whereas the aim of the author was to supply a chasm in history which has always been overlooked—the manners, customs, amusements, wit, dialect, as they appear in all grades of society to an ear and eye witness of them" (qtd. in Rachels, xlviii).

The question is not whether *Georgia Scenes* is social history, but how it is to be read as social history. Longstreet attempted a partial answer in the last paragraph of the preface: "I cannot conclude these introductory remarks without reminding those who have taken exception to the coarse, inelegant, and sometimes ungrammatical language which the writer represents himself as occasionally using, *that it is language accommodated to the capacity of the person to whom he represents himself as speaking*" (**GSC** [*Georgia Scenes Completed*] 3-4, emphasis in the original).

The ambiguities culminating in the italicized passage are a final twirl of authorial prefatory tiptoeing. Repetition of the word "represent" invokes the political dimension of the sketches, and the pun on "to whom" makes clear that the pieces were meant as direct addresses to readers rather than as social history—that is, disinterested texts, accounts once removed. James M. Cox has noted that Longstreet's "weakness came from leaning too much toward refinement, politeness, and culture" (110). In other words, the clumsiness compounded in the final sentence of the preface results less from "ignorance of the implications of using frontier materials and oral narrative techniques" (Lenz 316) or an inadequately realized "aesthetic distance" (Holman 7) bu, more fundamentally, from an uncertainty with respect to notions of social difference.[2]

This essay argues that when writing *Georgia Scenes,* Longstreet was a frustrated politician turned temporary artist by accident, rather than exemplifying "the drift from art to politics" Richard M. Weaver regards as characteristic of most antebellum Southern humorists (80; cf. Lynn, *Twain* 116). Social difference is a major determinant of Longstreet's *Georgia Scenes,* which originated as occasional items in the local press, while their author, a jack-of-all-trades but not really a writer, was hotly engaged in day-by-day politics. The sketches are held together mainly by their common setting; as Franklin J. Meine (xvi), Walter Blair (65), and Van Wyck Brooks (240) have remarked, they are provincial, wholly and intensely local. They are also intensely political, drawing on the context of the debates coming to the hilt in the 1830s. The region depicted, Middle Georgia, was a middle ground, contested economically, socially, culturally, and politically. There, the ways of the tidewater aristocracy crossed those of the yeomanry peopling the red hills of the upcountry. The area had experienced spectacular economic growth as the center of the cotton belt during the 1820s; but by the 1830s the boom was over, having moved west. As signs of stagnation were noticeable, the antagonism crested in controversies over the tariff, nullification and states' rights, the institution of slavery, and the urge for democratic reform of local and state governments.

**"Georgia Theatrics,"** the sketch opening Longstreet's collection, stages that antagonism as an incongruous confrontation, a clash of cultures cast in part as a class conflict. A gentleman by the name of Hall remembers a foray into Lincoln County, thirty miles northwest of Augusta. Conscious of his social and moral superiority, he expends a good deal of rhetoric on creating the narrative distance he deems appropriate: "If my memory fail me not, the 10th of June, 1809, found me, at about 11 o'clock in the forenoon, . . . in what was called 'The Dark Corner' of Lincoln. I believe it took its name from the moral darkness which reigned over that portion of the county at the time of which I am speaking" (*GSC* 4).

The incident about to be related is tucked away safely in the past and in a far corner of the locale, not yet penetrated by the light of culture. Hall is hardly within, and much less of, the world he presents. His bland imitation of Augustan essayists contributes to opening a gap Longstreet himself identified unwittingly as "a chasm in history" and Kenneth S. Lynn termed a *"cordon sanitaire"* (*Twain* 64), set up against a tale of a brief encounter that happened long ago. Riding in that Dark Corner, Hall suddenly heard strange noises from a thicket, voices that seemed to emanate from a "band of ruffians" engaged in "Pandæmonian riots." Finally, a single youth emerges, embarrassed by the inadvertent witness. The young man is immediately classed by the vernacular put in his mouth, even if he seemingly has the punch line of the sketch. "'You needn't kick before you're spurr'd. There a'nt nobody there, nor ha'nt been nother. I was jist seein' how I could 'a' *fout*.'" The words take on portent in terms of class when the narrator realizes that the "Lincoln rehearsal" was staged in preparation for a fight in front of the courthouse, the sociopolitical center of the county. Even if it was just a rehearsal, the historionics were all the more intimidating because of the social difference Hall established so deftly. "I went to the ground from which he had risen, and there were the prints of his two thumbs, plunged up to the balls in the mellow earth, about the distance of a man's eyes apart" (*GSC* 5-6).

The social polarization and the latent violence contained in the narrative invoke notions of class struggle—or at least the fear of it. Lynn cites **"Georgia Theatrics"** as evidence in support of his thesis that the antebellum humorists were mostly Whigs who wrote with a strongly aristocratic bias. In particular, he points to "the conservative political allegory inherent in the sketch," for the narrator "embodies a conservative political ideal," and "the violent boy represents what to the Whig mind was the central quality of Jacksonianism" (*Twain* 67-68). But the opposition of gentleman versus yokel, Georgia style, is too clear-cut. Longstreet cannot be tucked away as a Whig aristocrat. His political views, Lynn concedes, were "Whig *manqué*" (*Twain* 57); beyond those, Longstreet was a planter patrician only by marriage. Legend has it that upon his wedding he did not have money enough to buy proper clothes or pay the fee to the officiating minister. His parents had come from New Jersey a few years before their fourth son Gus was born in Augusta in 1790. They were yeoman farmers who struggled at times to make ends meet but managed to provide Gus with the best education that could be had. At age eighteen, he was sent to Moses Waddel's academy in Willington, South Carolina, then one of few schools of note in the whole South.

More profitable than the learning Longstreet acquired were the social connections gained. Waddel's institution was attended by many a future congressman, senator, and governor of Georgia and South Carolina. Boarding with a brother of John Calhoun, Gus shared a room with George McDuffie, who had already been a boarder of the Longstreets and who would become governor and U.S. senator of South Carolina, "perhaps the boldest of the loquacious tribe of Fire Eaters" (Parrington 2:62). Thus, it was early on when Gus Longstreet befriended the two men who were to be the leading figures in his political life. Recalling them four years after the end of the Civil War, he termed Calhoun "matchless" and regarded McDuffie as "hardly inferior to him in anything" (qtd. in Wade, 123).[3]

Gus followed the educational path of John Calhoun to Yale and on to Tapping Reeve's law school in Litchfield. In the fall of 1814, Gus returned to his home state, took the bar examination, and commenced riding the circuit as a lawyer on the western tier. The area was settled only recently; social stratification had not yet had time to consolidate. The introduction of cotton as the cash crop supplanting tobacco promised easy fortunes but entailed social upheaval, for the economic urge towards bigger farms demanded more and more slaves while driving out many dispossessed whites.

Longstreet was "a young man . . . looking to popular confidence as his sole means of advancement," writes John D. Wade, his biographer (51). And everybody, it seems, liked him. He soon married—"up." Eliza Parke's dowry amounted to a handsome fortune—two thousand dollars in cash and thirty slaves, whose renting out netted their owner another fifteen hundred dollars annually. Gus did well with his wife's money, as he bought six hundred acres of land near his in-laws at the prospering county seat of Greensboro. Greene County soon elected him captain of the militia, a hub of the social and intellectual life of the community. In 1821, he was chosen as a representative to the state assembly and elected Judge of the Superior Court in the following year. He had risen to chairman of the Judiciary Committee of the Georgia assembly when in 1824 he ran for Congress,

but dropped out of the race after his first-born son and his mother-in-law died within two days of each other. When the states' righters suffered defeat in the 1825 state assembly elections, Longstreet fell victim to the spoils system; turned out of office, the judge was left with no more than the title he proudly retained until his death. The personal losses incurred a religious conversion—characteristically an undogmatic one—to Methodism. Conceivably, the ousting from politics nourished his radicalism as well as his increasing vindictiveness.

In 1827 the Longstreets moved to Augusta. He "commenced planting and lawing," as an autobiographical sketch for the Yale alumni paper has it (qtd. in Wade, 117). The residence purchased was ostentatious, located on a large tract of land not far from the city named Westover and built by one of the Byrds of Virginia. The oligarchic airs Longstreet affected scarcely concealed inherent contradictions; the pose resembled the pretensions of many a self-made planter aristocrat of Middle Georgia. Well-educated by the standards of his time, he was "not in any sense a cultured man," according to the estimate of a well-meaning acquaintance (qtd. in Hubbell, 667).[4] The judge, losing money on the plantation, soon sold all his slaves; more successful in auctioning off his land as real estate, he remained a fervent propagandist of slavery. In the 1840s he would advance the foundation of a separate Southern Methodist church and publish *Letters on the Epistle of Paul to Philemon or The Connection of Apostolical Christianity with Slavery,* a pamphlet calling upon the Bible to defend "the peculiar institution." On other grounds, Longstreet became active in the temperance movement even though he always liked his glass of wine with dinner.

Augusta was more inviting than the upcountry and its federalist yeomanry, for an advocate of states' rights could expect support from beyond the Savannah River, where the prophets of the creed had their home base. Longstreet leaned strongly towards the extreme tenets pronounced by McDuffie and eventually by Calhoun—he indeed preceded both of his idols in advancing those tenets—but the stance was precarious, for nullifiers found little backing outside South Carolina (cf. Cooper and Terrill 165). In summer 1832, as the dispute over nullification neared frenzy, Longstreet announced his bid for a seat in the state assembly but withdrew when he realized that the sentiment in Georgia was overwhelmingly pro-union and he had no chance of winning.

Dreams of office thwarted, he turned to the press. The move was propitious as the cultural climate of the South was ripe with a sudden flourish of periodical publications. The first eight of the sketches came out originally in the *Milledgeville Southern Recorder,* a paper historians consult chiefly as a lode of radical states' rights journalism. Drafts of scenes may have begun as early as 1830 but were only printed late in 1833, a few weeks before Longstreet acquired his own outlet for his writings. The takeover of a languishing federalist weekly was surely meant as a political gesture. The *Augusta North American Gazette,* promptly renamed *State Rights Sentinel,* became the mouthpiece of his opinions in editorials that, for Kenneth Lynn, "screamed political and moral outrage" ("Longstreet" 57). Wade, too, emphasizes the "extreme political view-point of the paper," which regularly and prominently featured "announcements about runaway slaves" (133, 135).

Since the collected *Georgia Scenes* are attributed to "A Native Georgian," the title of the opening sketch, **"Georgia Theatrics,"** adverts to authorial theatrics as well. Elaborate guises accompanied the piecemeal publication of what in less than two years' time would surprisingly amount to a book. The sketches in the *Southern Recorder* were ascribed to two different authors whose pen names, Hall and Baldwin, recalled two early Georgia patriots. Lyman Hall signed the Declaration of Independence and served as governor in 1783-1784; Abra(ha)m Baldwin signed the Constitution and was the first Georgian to win recognition as a congressman. Once the scenes appeared in the *State Rights Sentinel,* the author's masks were upheld, though they were no longer urgent. The differentiation between Baldwin and Hall was subjected to the overall bent of the paper, which was voiced by a third pseudonymous spokesman—Bob Short, a diehard nullifier expounding his convictions in numerous squibs. "My friend Jack wishes to know at what age he should marry. Answer.—If he be a States' Rights man he should marry at twenty-five; but if he be a D.U. [Democratic Union] Republican he should not marry before he attain[s] the age of eighty-five" (qtd. in Rachels, xxiv).

The preface of the book concedes that the distinction between Hall and Baldwin is a leftover undermining the unity of the volume: "I was extremely desirous of concealing the author, and, the more effectually to do so, I wrote under two signatures. These have now become too closely interwoven with the sketches to be separated from them, without an expense of time and trouble which I am unwilling to incur. *Hall* is the writer of those sketches in which men appear as the principal actors, and *Baldwin* of those in which women are the prominent figures" (*GSC* 3).

A reminder that *Georgia Scenes* are gendered in awkward ways, the assertion makes too much of keeping the two narrators apart. Their notions of social differ-

ence, for one, diverge on irrelevant matters at best.[5] Baldwin, a respectable, stiff and prudish urbanite of indefinite interests, is always out on some unspecified business. Hall is a judge riding the circuit, conscious of the gravity of his office and forever embarrassed by crudities. The two men meet on occasion and seem closer to each other than to anyone else in the book.

Two narrators allow for a certain latitude of presentation and variety of scenery, yet the perspective never varies. Looking down on practically all others, Longstreet's observers of "the 'civilizing' process" (Kibler xvi) perceive mainly differences between their caste and those below, while conflating the disparities among those dismissed as inferior. **"The Fight"** offers a case in point. Hall virtually disappears from the set he laid out so carefully. Ransy Sniffle, the epitome of the dirt eater, is all over the place to get the fight started yet does not associate with the narrator observing the scene from increasing distance. Early on, though, Sniffle is close enough for a detailed portrait that becomes a vicious caricature of a déclassé. Bill and Bob may be "the very *best men* in the county . . . , in the Georgia vocabulary" (*GSC* 33); the mutilations they inflict upon each other make them appear more grossly distorted than Sniffle. The graphic quality of the descriptions and the inherent verbal violence betray that, for all his efforts at dissociating himself from the scene, Hall is a voyeur, whose pangs of conscience are woven into the moralizing closure of the frame, an insufferable affirmation of low-to-middle-brow culture.

**"The Gander Pulling,"** the last sketch to appear in the *Milledgeville Southern Recorder* and among the first to be printed in the *State Rights Sentinel,* combines Hall's social and political views most explicitly. Removed to a distant past, "the year 1798" (*GSC* 73), it opens with a lengthy digression on the prehistory of Augusta, declaring that then four villages competed for primacy in the region. Making his case "from conjecture" (*GSC* 74), the erstwhile resident of the city presents the rivalry as an extended analogy of national affairs in the early 1830s.[6] The account teems with catch-phrases of political doctrine of the day—*"single body," "public welfare," "Social Compact," "separate bodies," "private welfare"*—all italicized so as to make sure that the reader will not miss the point, and capped with the assertion that in due course one of the towns "was literally *nullified.*" Advocating a confederacy, not a union, Hall bespeaks his commitment to states' rights, supposing that his audience share that position. As he introduces the central episode of the story proper, the gander-pulling contest, by quoting an "'*advurtyzement*' . . . to All woo mout wish to purtak tharof" (*GSC* 74), he does not even pretend to imitate speech but exaggerates the distance between himself and the objects of narration.

When describing his arrival on the scene where the atrocious spectacle is to take place, he quickly sets himself apart from those who have gathered: "a considerable number of persons, of different ages, sexes, sizes, and complexions, . . . from the rival towns, and the country around. But few females were there however, and those few, were from the lowest walks of life." After some remarks on the gander—once "moving with patriarchal dignity," it was now reduced to "a fit object for 'cruelty'" (*GSC* 76)—the emphasis on social difference is maintained in the rendition of the participants, for they are reduced to mere names, owners of horses which in turn are depicted in mocking detail. In the end, the winner by luck turns out to be Fat John Fulger, whose "own voice condemns him as a hopeless vulgarian" (Silverman 549); and Hall's concluding remarks bristle with unmitigated condescension for all involved. If, as Kenneth Silverman contends, **"The Gander Pulling"** posits "the crackers" as the "real enemies" of Longstreet's South (549), then *Georgia Scenes* must be seen as reflecting not so much "an interest in the common man," as Gretlund suggests (127), but a patrician disdain of poor-white ambitions.

Frankly self-congratulatory about his mission as a vanguard of civilization, Hall is less certain if the culture he imported has been beneficial in all respects. Rather than facing the present, he relishes nostalgic glimpses of the days when the frontier was still a presence on the western tier of Middle Georgia and the unpleasant realities of the contemporary world had not yet mushroomed. **"The Turn-Out"** reminisces about "the good old days," when a visit Hall paid to "my friend Captain Griffin . . . and his good lady" was met "with a *Georgia welcome* of 1790" (*GSC* 47). This dating of what is chronologically the first sketch marks the year of Governor Hall's death and Longstreet's birth as a seamless transition. The nostalgia blurs social differences as it limns an idealized harmony in Edenic surroundings. Yet, Griffin's idyll vanished with the illusion that the lands were inexhaustible. The Captain had boasted that "they will be as good fifty years hence as they are now." Hall records a return to the spot, "forty two years afterward," finding the place "barren, dreary and cheerless" (*GSC* 49-50). The reader is left to infer that soil erosion resulting from abuse of the land, the wastefulness of the plantation system, had a share in the destruction of the pastoral.[7]

Yearning for the good, simple country life is Hall's province, though Baldwin resorts to it as well. In **"The Dance, A Personal Adventure of the Author,"** a nostalgic lens glorifies a county magistrate's family of five, who live content and happy in a one-room log cabin. They comport themselves with natural dignity and ease, unhampered by social etiquette. Even Billy Porter, the

African American scratching the fiddle at the frolic, is awarded an approving nod, for he knows his assigned place and assumes it willingly. Baldwin's nod comes easily as it is granted to one who at the time of narration is already dead. The treatment of Porter and the marginalization of African Americans—who made up about one-third of the population in Middle Georgia but are hardly mentioned in the *Georgia Scenes*—suggest that in his thinking of race Longstreet upheld the dogma of the benevolent subservience of slave to master. He was about to make the turn from negro bondage as a necessary evil to slavery as a positive good.[8]

Baldwin is given only six pieces to Hall's twelve, but his sketches balance the distribution of rural and urban Georgia scenes. Nearly half of the sketches contained in the book have an urban setting, focusing largely on the upper segment of society. Baldwin is as prone to moralizing as Hall, while his insights in the dwellings of well-to-do burghers are more easily given to satire. Foppishness is targeted in **"The Ball,"** where Misses Feedle, Deedle, Gilt, and Rhino congregate with gentlemen like Crouch, Flirt, Boozle, and Noozle. They pretend not "to ape the indecencies of Europe's slaves" and abstain from "mathematical cotillons . . . immodest waltzes . . . detestable, disgusting gallopades" (*GSC* 80); instead, Baldwin has them perform indigenous movements, "the three motions of a turkey-cock strutting, a sparrow-hawk lighting, and a duck walking" (*GSC* 86).

Baldwin's notions of social rank receive fullest treatment in **"The 'Charming Creature,' as a Wife."** The longest piece of the collection displays, according to Jessica Wegmann, "Longstreet's careful construction of what he considers correct social hierarchy" (19). Preachy and remonstrative, the sketch ends by recapitulating its moral, "a warning to mothers, against bringing up their daughters to be 'Charming Creatures'" (*GSC* 73). The note of caution is accentuated by personal connection. George Baldwin, the central character, is identified as the narrator's nephew. His parents are all modesty and moderation: the mother, "the repository of all feminine virtue"; the father, "a plain, practical, sensible farmer," bettered by no one of "those who move in his sphere of life" (*GSC* 53-54). George, an aspiring lawyer, deviates from the model path laid out by his elders when he falls for the "charming Evelina" (*GSC* 63). Her beauty blinds him to social difference—which the narrator expounds in a lengthy portrait of Evelina's father, a wealthy, unlettered cotton merchant. She is spoiled since she never received a proper domestic education; "pride and vanity became at an early age the leading traits of the child's character." She matures to "an accomplished hypocrite, with all her other foibles" (*GSC* 56). George insists on marrying her and finds an early grave.

The moral is unrelenting: Do not stray from your social roots. Beware of deception by superficial glamor. Virtue elevates, not wealth. Baldwin advocates benevolent paternalistic control and would have the proper position of women defined entirely by their subservience to fathers and husbands. Wegmann concludes, "when either wife or slave attempts to subvert the hierarchy of white male superiority, all lose and become miserable" (23). The observation is valid for issues of social difference as well.[9]

Toward the latter part of his career as an editor, political opponents accused Longstreet of having lost his old democratic faith (cf. Wade 137). His hardening conservatism, discernible in the progression of *Georgia Scenes,* resulted from the realization that nullification was a lost cause and further effort vain. Disenchanted with the course of affairs, his interest in journalism faded; in the summer 1836, he sold the paper that, as Longstreet would claim in his autobiographical sketch, had caused "much loss of time, and some loss of money" (qtd. in Wade, 138). The flow of scenes petered out once the book collection was printed in September 1835; only a few more sketches were published in the following years, not collected until 1998. Ascribed mostly to Baldwin, they were hastily written, sententious tracts rather than composed scenes, their flimsy story lines mere pretexts for sermonizing.

**"Darby Anvil"** is exemplary. In Wade's opinion, it "proclaims Longstreet's complete abandonment of any but the most conservative democracy" (205). Written late in 1838, when Longstreet decided to take up the ministry, it poses as an autobiographical obituary of Baldwin's life in politics—which, the sketch insinuates, was ended by the likes of Darby Anvil. Those populists appealing to the class from which they emerged were invited to usurp power when in 1835 Georgia opened floodgates by formally abandoning freehold suffrage.

"I well remember," Baldwin begins, "the first man who, without any qualifications for the place, was elected to the legislature of Georgia. He was a blacksmith by trade, and Darby Anvil was his name" (*GSC* 162). The title character turns into a negative image lacking in all that is deemed necessary and expedient for the tasks coming with public office. Social difference is a major distinctive category, defined by cultural prerogative rather than by ownership of property. Anvil's deficit is that he is unlettered, "ignorant in the extreme," the

want squared by "some shrewdness, and much low cunning" (*GSC* 163). When he announces his candidacy, he cannot even comprehend the basics of states' rightism. "'I know I'm nothin' but a poor ign'ant blacksmith that dont know nothin' no how'" (*GSC* 167). The thick accent classes, and is classed; it is "to demonstrate," Kenneth S. Lynn has noted, "the social and political incapacities of the barbarous Democracy" (*Twain* 68-69). So as to make sure that the reader will not miss the point, Baldwin inserts a lengthy portrait of Darby Anvil as a Ransy Sniffle done over before he exposes the unabashed populism and "electioneering harangues" (*GSC* 165) that secure Darby's election.

Anvil's sudden political rise is propelled by overreaching ambition, the cause of his subsequent fall. He ends ignominiously, an alcoholic. The narrator, a captive of the worldview of his author, cannot muster any sympathy but castigates Darby for having set a detrimental precedent. The final paragraph of the sketch swells to a farewell address not easily surpassed in pathos. "The penalties of these acts are now upon our heads; and upon our children's children will they descend with unmitigated vigor. I forbear to follow the consequences farther—in charity to my native land I forbear" (*GSC* 178).

Baldwin's announcement that he will quit politics follows a pattern of vindictive withdrawals characteristic of Augustus Longstreet, in whose disposition there was an anticipation of the morbid sensitivity and touchy pride ascribed to southern politicians in the late antebellum.[10] Longstreet was moved by temper, not by intellect. The *Georgia Scenes* betray that shifty base in oscillations from queasiness to ebullience in diction. If the structural unity of the book is haphazard, a clear pattern can be made out with respect to social difference. The background of Longstreet's thought was vaguely, if fiercely, Jeffersonian agrarian; rural life was theoretically the best and most normal (cf. Parrington 2:170). In keeping with that particularly southern brand of conservatism that meandered from John Randolph to John Calhoun, his ideal society is patriarchal, biblical, as John D. Wade has noted (60). It subscribes fully to Calhoun's notions of a "white democracy," including all its contradictions.[11] Calhoun maintained he "had always been . . . a staunch supporter of the interests of his state, his class, and his region" (Niven 2). Intensely concerned with the South's social order, he was a Republican hostile to the democratic principle of numerical majority.

Eugene D. Genovese contends that "[e]ducated Southerners, as self-proclaimed heirs to medieval chivalry, understood true nobility to rest on virtue" (49). Politics becomes a question of morals, and on that, Longstreet was unrelenting, even if at times he propounded a rather hollow moralism. Devoted to Calhoun, he was not a vigorous intellectual or a profound thinker like the Carolinian. "His mind was of a literal cast" (Wade 93). A countryman at heart, he had a strong desire for social order. His *Georgia Scenes* attempted to fix that social order in writing. The result was a dirge for a world gone under, a prelapsarian pastoral, with planter society and slavery written out of the sketches. Longstreet is a realist only in that for him it is important that his writing establishes relations to an empirical reality. His negotiations of that reality more often than not give in to the prescriptive ordering of Augustan ideals.

Judge Longstreet comes remarkably close to James Henry Hammond, Calhoun's firebrand votary in the House of Representatives. An upwardly mobile lawyer, erstwhile schoolmaster and newspaper editor, Hammond became a plantation owner in 1831, when he married the heiress of Silver Bluff, an estate of over ten thousand acres located about a dozen miles southeast of Augusta. The diary he kept meticulously documented his learning of the ways of a planter politician; the book complements *Georgia Scenes* while sharing most premises. Hammond, an editor of the diary concludes, "seems to have succumbed to the myth of the Old South even before the South was old and before there was a myth" (Bleser 304).

### Notes

1. When Sydnor (312ff.) and Hubbell (666ff.) elevated Longstreet to an early prototype of the local color writer, this was ostensibly to balance the portrait presented by Longstreet's first biographer, Bishop Oscar Penn Fitzgerald of the Methodist Episcopal Church, South, whose *Judge Longstreet, A Life Sketch* emphasized the career in education and the church while it barely mentioned political ambitions. The tag of "proto-local-colorist" became a catch phrase used by almost everyone writing on Longstreet; it indeed grew to the central argument of fairly recent works by Meriwether, Newlin, and Kibler, where a political dimension is explicitly denied. Only in the last few years have essays come out, notably the ones by Smith and Wegmann, that challenge those traditionalist views of Longstreet and *Georgia Scenes*.

2. I use the term "social difference" rather than "class" because of ideological implications. While I follow Althusser and Jameson in their belief that the perception of reality is always already an interpretive act that is prefigured by a collective discourse that is produced by the combination of material and social conditions, my disuse of the term "class" is to signal that I share the doubts Derrida phrased in *Specters of Marx*. There, Derrida claims he is "suspicious of the simple opposition of *dominant* and *dominated,* or even of the final determination of the forces in conflict" (55). Society is not necessarily defined by head-on antagonisms of rival groups; rather, oppositions are manifold, mostly gradual, and only rarely polar. And, to avoid an overload of ideological import, I have settled on the term "social difference," which has the advantage of denoting neither a binary opposition nor a hierarchic structure but a bundle of differences, albeit fundamental ones.

3. Longstreet's late assertion of his deliberately staking out his future course by following Calhoun and McDuffie exemplifies Derrida's tenet that social difference, as part of one's inheritance, is not received but assumed. "Inheritance is never *a given,* it is always a task. . . . *To be* . . . means . . . to inherit[;] . . . the *being* of what we are *is* first of all inheritance, whether we like it or know it or not. . . . An inheritance is always the reaffirmation of a debt, but a critical, selective, and filtering reaffirmation" (54, 91-92).

4. Parrington's appellation of "so vigorous a plebeian" (2:167) diminishes Longstreet's patrician prepossessions. More to the point is Carr's summary: "enamored by wealth and power, [Longstreet] very early adopted, and throughout his life maintained, the conservative philosophy of those politicians with whom he was in constant association" (25).

5. Hamlin Hill regards Hall and Baldwin bluntly as "two sanctimonious halves of a single personality" (qtd. in Lilly, 278).

6. Silverman (548) offers a persuasive reading of the elaborate analogy.

7. Since "The Gander Pulling" alludes to the days of "Tobacco, then the staple of Georgia" (*GSC* 75), as an historical "other," "The Turn-Out" may well be read as an implicit criticism of the heedless expansion of the plantation system after cotton replaced tobacco as the leading cash crop.

8. For a detailed evaluation of Longstreet's condescending depiction of African Americans, see Wegmann (14-18), who picks up a remark made by Rachels: "readers will notice that the word 'slave' appears only once in the book [and 'slaves' once as well], and it does not refer to African-American slavery. Despite the obvious importance of slavery to Georgia social life, Longstreet discusses it nowhere in *Georgia Scenes*" (xcviii; the parenthetical addition is Wegmann's [14]).

9. The very title and didacticism of "The 'Charming Creature,' as a Wife" have the sketch appear as if it were a chapter of a gentleman's conduct book. That this may indeed have been part of Longstreet's intention—that the *Georgia Scenes* were to set examples by which young southern gentlemen in search of cultivation could orient themselves—can also be inferred from "The Character of a Native Georgian." That sketch portrays the central figure, Ned Brace, in less than commendable terms. He is anything but a gentleman, but rather a trickster "marked by a desire to put self above society regardless of the social costs of doing so" (Bruce 229).

10. Longstreet seems like a prototype of the southerner described by Tocqueville, who noted a "deep-seated uneasiness and ill agitation which are observable in the South," a region that, "peopled with ardent and irascible men, is becoming more and more irritated and alarmed" (1:418).

11. See Gray (34-45) for an evaluation of Calhoun's ability to talk in two ways at once.

### Works Cited

Blair, Walter. *Native American Humor, 1800-1900.* New York: American Book Co., 1937.

Bleser, Carol, ed. *Secret and Sacred: The Diaries of James Henry Hammond, a Southern Slaveholder.* New York: Oxford Univ. Press, 1988.

Brooks, Van Wyck. *The World of Washington Irving.* New York: Dutton, 1944.

Bruce, Dickson D., Jr. *Violence and Culture in the Antebellum South.* Austin: Univ. of Texas Press, 1979.

Carr, Duane. *A Question of Class: The Redneck Stereotype in Southern Fiction.* Bowling Green, Ohio: Bowling Green State Univ. Popular Press, 1996.

Cooper, William J., Jr., and Thomas E. Terrill. *The American South. A History.* New York: McGraw-Hill, 1991.

Cox, James M. "Humor of the Old Southwest." *The Comic Imagination in American Literature.* Louis D. Rubin, ed. Voice of America Forum Series. Washington: USIA, 1974. 105-16.

Derrida, Jacques. *Specters of Marx. The State of the Debt, the Work of Mourning, and the New International.* Peggy Kamuf, tr. New York: Routledge, 1994.

Fitzgerald, Oscar Penn. *Judge Longstreet. A Life Sketch.* Nashville, Tenn.: Publishing House of the Methodist Church, South, 1891.

Genovese, Eugene D. *The Southern Tradition. The Achievement and Limitations of an American Conservatism.* Cambridge, Mass.: Harvard Univ. Press, 1994.

Gray, Richard. *Writing the South. Ideas of an American Region.* Cambridge, UK: Cambridge Univ. Press, 1986.

Gretlund, Jan Nordby. "1835: The First Annus Mirabilis of Southern Fiction." *Rewriting the South: History and Fiction.* Lothar Hönnighausen and Valeria Gennaro Lerda, eds. Tübingen, Germany: Francke, 1993. 121-30.

Holman, C. Hugh. *The Roots of Southern Writing.* Athens: Univ. of Georgia Press, 1972.

Hubbell, Jay B. *The South in American Literature, 1607-1900.* Durham, N.C.: Duke Univ. Press, 1954.

Kibler, James E., Jr. Introduction. Augustus Baldwin Longstreet. *Georgia Scenes.* Nashville, Tenn: J. S. Sanders, 1992. vii-xxii.

Lenz, William E. "Augustus Baldwin Longstreet (1790-1870)." *Fifty Southern Writers Before 1900. A Bio-Bibliographical Sourcebook.* Westport, Conn: Greenwood, 1987. 312-22.

Lilly, Paul R., Jr. "Augustus Baldwin Longstreet." *American Humorists, 1800-1950.* Part I: A-L. DLB 11. Stanley Trachtenberg, ed. Detroit, Mich.: Gale Research, 1982. 276-83.

Longstreet, Augustus Baldwin. *Georgia Scenes Completed.* David Rachels, ed. Athens: Univ. of Georgia Press, 1998. [GSC]

Lynn, Kenneth S. *Mark Twain and Southwestern Humor.* Westport, Conn.: Greenwood Press, 1976. (Boston: Little, Brown, 1960.)

———. "A. B. Longstreet." *The Comic Tradition in America.* New York: Norton, 1958. 55-58.

Meine, Franklin J., ed. *Tall Tales of the Southwest.* New York: Knopf, 1930.

Meriwether, James B. "Augustus Baldwin Longstreet: Realist and Artist." *Mississippi Quarterly* 35 (1982): 351-64.

Newlin, Keith. "Georgia Scenes: The Satiric Artistry of Augustus Baldwin Longstreet." *Mississippi Quarterly* 41 (1987-1988): 21-34.

Niven, John. *John C. Calhoun and the Price of Union.* Baton Rouge: Louisiana State Univ. Press, 1988.

Parrington, Vernon Louis. *Main Currents in American Thought.* 2 vols. New York: Harcourt, Brace, and Co., 1927.

Rachels, David. "Introduction." Augustus Baldwin Longstreet. *Georgia Scenes Completed.* David Rachels, ed. Athens: Univ. of Georgia Press, 1998. xi-lxvii.

Silverman, Kenneth. "Longstreet's 'The Gander Pulling.'" *American Quarterly* 18 (1966): 548-49.

Smith, Stephen A. "The Rhetoric of Southern Humor." *The Future of Southern Letters.* Jeffrey Humphreys and John Lowe, eds. New York: Oxford Univ. Press, 1996. 170-85.

Sydnor, Charles S. *The Development of Southern Sectionalism.* Baton Rouge: Louisiana State Univ. Press, 1949.

Tocqueville, Alexis de. *Democracy in America.* Henry Reeve and Francis Bowen, trans. Phillips Bradley, ed. 2 vols. New York: Knopf, 1945.

Wade, John Donald. *Augustus Baldwin Longstreet: A Study in the Development of Culture in the South.* M. Thomas Inge, ed. Athens: Univ. of Georgia Press, 1969. (New York: Macmillan, 1924.)

Weaver, Richard M. *The Southern Tradition at Bay: A History of Post-Bellum Thought.* George Core and M. E. Bradford, eds. New Rochelle, N.Y.: Arlington House, 1968.

Wegmann, Jessica. "'Playing in the Dark' with Longstreet's *Georgia Scenes*: Critical Reception and Reader Response to Treatments of Race and Gender." *Southern Literary Journal* 30 (1997): 13-26.

## David Rachels (essay date 2001)

SOURCE: Rachels, David. "A Biographical Reading of A. B. Longstreet's *Georgia Scenes.*" In *The Humor of the Old South,* edited by M. Thomas Inge and Edward J. Piacentino, pp. 113-29. Lexington: University Press of Kentucky, 2001.

[*In the following essay, Rachels analyzes* Georgia Scenes *as a work of social history while examining the numerous autobiographical aspects of the work.*]

> Judge Longstreet was born on Monday, the 22d of September, 1790. Where he was born is not so easy to say. Duyckink, in his *Cyclopædia of American Literature,* says he was born in Richmond County, near Augusta, Georgia. Appleton's *New American Cyclopædia* says he was born in Augusta, Georgia. Judge Longstreet himself says he was born in Edgefield District, South Carolina.
>
> James Wood Davidson, *The Living Writers of the South* (1869)[1]

Whenever Augustus Baldwin Longstreet discussed the impetus behind *Georgia Scenes, Characters, Incidents, &c. in the First Half Century of the Republic* (1835), he insisted the work was more than "a mere collection of fancy sketches." His motivation, he claimed, was a "higher object than the entertainment of the reader." This object "was to supply a chasm in history which has always been overlooked—the manners, customs, amusements, wit, dialect, as they appear in all grades of society to an ear and eye witness of them."[2] Thus, Longstreet thought of *Georgia Scenes* not as humor but as social history.

One puzzling fact is that Longstreet found so much of this social history an embarrassment. *Georgia Scenes* is cluttered with his apologies for and condemnations of the very behaviors that he felt compelled to record for posterity. The first sketch in the book, **"Georgia Theatrics,"** is set in Lincoln, Georgia, in 1809. At this time, Lincoln was a town of "[inconceivable] moral darkness," but Longstreet's narrator, Lyman Hall, assures his readers that Lincoln has since become "a living proof 'that light shineth in darkness.'"[3] The only "darkness" in "Georgia Theatrics" is a one-man fight in which an eighteen-year-old practices eye gouging by jamming his thumbs into the earth. Elsewhere, however, Hall describes and condemns an actual rough-and-tumble fight. In addition, he depicts lower-class Georgians swearing, gambling, and drinking to excess. Longstreet's other narrator, Abraham Baldwin, criticizes upper-class Georgians for impractical dress, bad marriages, poor taste in music, miseducation of their children, and a variety of pretentious behaviors. Why would Longstreet, a proud Georgian, have wanted to preserve these myriad faults for the ages?

The answer may be that the subject of *Georgia Scenes* is not only "characters, incidents, &c. in the first half century of the republic" but, more specifically, Longstreet himself. Like the young man in **"Georgia Theatrics,"** Longstreet grew up in a lower-class world where social status was earned with one's fists. By virtue of his education at Willington Academy, Yale College, and Litchfield Law School, however, he was able to establish himself among the upper classes. *Georgia Scenes,* then, is Longstreet's attempt to negotiate a social position in keeping with his ambitions while not forgetting his origins.

The autobiographical elements of *Georgia Scenes* have been overlooked by critics who have accepted orthodox views of antebellum southern humorists. In his genre-defining anthology, *Tall Tales of the Southwest* (1930), Franklin J. Meine painted this group of writers in broad strokes: "They were not professional humorists, but debonair settlers engaged in various tasks: lawyers, newspaper editors, country gentlemen of family and fortune, doctors, army officers, travellers, actors—who wrote for amusement rather than for gain." Meine singles out Longstreet as "a prominent young lawyer and newspaper editor." In another important early anthology, *Native American Humor* (1937), Walter Blair expands Longstreet's résumé to "lawyer, legislator, judge, and editor."[4] These biographies are accurate as far as they go, but readers cannot appreciate Longstreet's work if they imagine that his birth was coincident with his bar exam.[5]

Meine and Blair gave currency to the belief that antebellum southern humorists, if not always "debonair," were professional men who described from a safe distance the strange behavior of the "crackers" around them. In his influential analysis of antebellum southern humor, Kenneth S. Lynn described this distance as a *"cordon sanitaire"* (quarantine line) provided by framed narratives:

> That the frame device eventually became the structural trademark of Southwestern humor is because it suited so very well the myth-making purposes of the humorists. For Longstreet and his successors found that the frame was a convenient way of keeping their first-person narrators outside and above the comic action, thereby drawing a *cordon sanitaire,* so to speak, between the morally irreproachable Gentleman and the tainted life he described. . . . However hot-tempered the author might be in private life, the literary mask of the Southwestern humorists was that of a cool and collected personality whose own emotions were thoroughly in hand.

Lynn singles out Hall of **"Georgia Theatrics"** as a "Self-controlled Gentleman" narrator. Then, in a summary of the story remarkable for its misleading omissions, Lynn obscures the fact that Hall becomes the butt of the story's joke precisely because he *lacks* self-control.[6] Rushing to the scene of the supposed fight, Hall commands the fleeing youth: "'Come back, you brute! and assist me in relieving your fellow mortal, whom you have ruined forever!'" The young man replies with a taunt that "'you need n't kick before you're spur'd. There an't nobody there, nor ha'nt been nother. I was jist seein' how I could 'a' *fout*'" (5). Lynn's "Self-controlled Gentlemen" now seems an impulsive fool.

As *Georgia Scenes* progresses, the dominant narrative and thematic threads are provided by the book's narrators, Hall and Baldwin, and the ways in which they react to and interact with the people around them. Though many critics of *Georgia Scenes* have taken Lynn's *cordon sanitaire* as a given, only oversimplification or misrepresentation can sustain the notion throughout a full reading of the book.[7] Unfortunately, widespread acceptance of Lynn's analysis has further obscured the connection between Longstreet's life and work. In a striking example, Henning Cohen and William B.

Dillingham, in their discussion of the frameworks employed by antebellum southern humorists, conclude that "[i]t is as hard to identify Longstreet with the lowly characters of *Georgia Scenes* as it is to link [Frank] Norris with his brute dentist [McTeague]."[8]

My argument is that it is not difficult to identify Longstreet with his "lowly characters" and that the reasons for doing so predate his legal career. Portrayals of Longstreet as a "gentleman" imply that he was born into his social position. This was not the case. Longstreet was born in Augusta, Georgia, in 1790 to William Longstreet and Hannah Randolph Longstreet who, circa 1784, had moved to Georgia from New Jersey in search of a better life. There is evidence that William Longstreet was a well-regarded member of his community: in 1794, he served as a justice of the peace; in 1794-1795, he served as a representative in the state legislature; and, when Augusta was incorporated in 1798, he was elected one of six city commissioners.[9]

It is not clear, however, how the elder Longstreet supported his family. In a brief biography that Augustus wrote of William, he identifies his father as "an American inventor."[10] Unfortunately, all of the inventions that Augustus describes were financial failures. His father devised a method of propelling a boat by steam, but Robert Fulton undercut him. He invented a new roller for ginning cotton, which "promised him a fortune," but his two steam-powered mills burned within a week. He later erected a new set of steam mills, but the British burned them during the War of 1812. Augustus concludes that "[t]hese disasters exhausted his resources and discouraged his enterprise, though he was confident that steam would soon supersede all other motive powers."[11]

William Longstreet's failed inventions, particularly his steamboat, made him something of a laughingstock. According to tradition, he was so obsessed with his boat that he "was ridiculed by his neighbors and friends." A letter that he wrote in 1790 to Edward Telfair, the governor of Georgia, hints that tradition may be near the truth. Hoping to win the governor's patronage, Longstreet first attempts to forestall the reaction to which he seems accustomed: "Sir:—I make no doubt but that you have often heard of my steamboat, and as often heard it laughed at." This was written four days after Augustus was born. Thus, given that William worked at his steamboat well into the next century, Augustus grew up with a father who was, paradoxically, a well-respected joke.[12]

William Longstreet's reputation could not have been helped by his support of the Yazoo Act, which one historian has called "the greatest fraud that Georgia was ever to know." This act, passed by the Georgia assembly in 1794, provided for the sale of at least 35 million acres of land to four companies for only $500,000. In return for their votes, legislators were to receive generous grants of land. Longstreet himself offered a bribe of 100 thousand acres to a fellow legislator. The act became law in 1795, and a political firestorm soon followed. Many legislators were voted out of office; at least one angry community forced its representative to leave the state. This may explain the brevity of William Longstreet's political career. The act was repealed in 1796; every mention of it was deleted from state records; and all paperwork associated with it was burned. Thus, William Longstreet failed in another attempt to support his family.[13]

Fortunately, Hannah Longstreet had the greater influence on the life of young Augustus. Longstreet's mother wrote to a relative that she was determined "to give [her children] a good education as it [was] all [they] could] do for them." Longstreet's first school was Augusta's Richmond Academy, which had opened in 1785. At the end of 1798, however, decaying buildings and a lack of money forced the school to close.[14] Longstreet was eight years old and had no school. This may have been the family's motivation for moving a short distance away. About 1800, they crossed the Savannah River into Edgefield District, South Carolina.

According to Edgefield historian John A. Chapman, this was a period of "great demoralization" in the district. Chapman writes, "The great besetting sin was the too free use of whiskey or rum; and to this may be added their usual accompaniments, card-playing, profanity and the disregard of the Sabbath. Many persons now living [in 1897] can remember when there was a grog-shop at every cross road, and sometimes between, when the cross roads were too far apart." Chapman records that it was not until 1809—well after the Longstreets had returned to Georgia—that a religious revival swept through Edgefield and morals began to improve.[15]

With or without religion, murder was so common in the district that it earned the reputation of "Bloody Edgefield." One historian describes the "Edgefield tradition" as "[standing] for the syndrome of violence and extremism that until recent times was thought to epitomize the South Carolina spirit."[16] While Edgefield had less crime than average for South Carolina, it had nearly double the number of homicides. So violent was the district that Thomas Jefferson Mackey, a judge whose circuit included Edgefield, joked, "I am going to hold court in Edgefield, and I expect a somewhat exciting term, as the fall shooting is about to commence."[17]

But not all Edgefield deaths were shootings. Some doubtless came as a result of the backcountry's tradition of rough-and-tumble fighting. Fighting was such a problem in South Carolina that in 1786, following the lead of North Carolina and Virginia, the state made "premediated mayhem" punishable by death. This law prohibited gouging out eyes and biting off fingers, but not the severing of ears and noses. Ears and noses remained fair game because their loss did not prevent hearing and smelling. A pair of eye gouges, on the other hand, would blind an opponent, and thus—legal codes notwithstanding—it became, according to Elliott J. Gorn, "the sine qua non of rough-and-tumble fighting, much like the knockout punch in modern boxing." The prevalence of eye gouging in South Carolina led an amazed judge to declare, "Before God, gentlemen of the jury, I never saw such a thing before in the world. There is a plaintiff with an eye out! A juror with an eye out! And two witnesses with an eye out!"[18]

In this environment Longstreet spent, in his words, "two or three happy years." So happy were these years that later in life he would sometimes claim to have been born in Edgefield. But his birth there was only spiritual. His departure from Augusta and school was "a joyous release." Longstreet records that in Edgefield his "highest ambition was to out-run, out-jump, out-shoot, throw down and whip, any man in the district."[19] This was no small ambition given that in 1790 Edgefield counted 2,333 free white male citizens aged sixteen and up.[20] Longstreet claims that when "the heart-sinking order" came that he must return to school in Augusta, "[he] was giving fair promise of attaining [his] ends."[21] Of course, "attaining his end" of whipping any man in Edgefield would have required proficiency in eye gouging, the very skill that the eighteen-year-old young man practices in **"Georgia Theatrics."** It is interesting to note that **"Georgia Theatrics"** is set in the spring of 1809—when Longstreet himself would have been eighteen.

But the ambitions of Longstreet's youth were squelched by his mother—it was she, Longstreet remembered, who "kept him resolutely to his tasks"—and he did not end up an eighteen-year-old rough-and-tumble fighter.[22] Longstreet returned to Richmond Academy sometime after it reopened on November 1, 1802, and the age of eighteen found him enrolled in Moses Waddel's academy in Willington, South Carolina. From there he attended Yale College and then Litchfield Law School. When he passed his bar exam in 1815, he became the gentleman familiar to students of southern literature. As a circuit-riding lawyer encountering citizens of all classes, Longstreet would have had opportunities to gather material for *Georgia Scenes*. Critics have also stressed the importance of the legal profession's tradition of oral storytelling, which provided method and material to Longstreet and other lawyer-humorists.[23]

In Longstreet's case, however, the telling of his stories predates law school. Longstreet recalled that he "projected [the Georgia Scenes] in Judge [Jonathan] Ingersoll's parlor in New Haven" while a student at Yale. Obviously, the sources for these stories must predate 1813, when Longstreet left New Haven. Given the intensity of life in Edgefield in combination with the joy that he experienced there, Longstreet would naturally have drawn on his years in the district when he regaled his Yankee friends with tales of the southern backcountry. As well, Longstreet would have had difficulty escaping the influence of Edgefield even when the ostensible subject of his storytelling was Georgia. Looking back on his life, Longstreet observed that "South Carolina and Georgia have been twin nurses of me and twin sisters in my affections."[24]

It has been easy to for critics to assume a cause-and-effect relationship between Longstreet's legal career and his fiction writing, as the first Georgia Scene was published in 1833, more than eighteen years after his bar exam. Longstreet had made a good marriage in 1817, and now, with careers in law and politics, he was solidly established in the upper class. To a casual observer, he would indeed have seemed a man apart from many of the lower-class characters about whom he wrote. Furthermore, another important change had taken place in his life: in 1827 he had joined the Methodist Church, and in 1829 he had become licensed to preach (though he would not become a full-time minister until 1838, more than three years after the publication of *Georgia Scenes*). Thus, while Longstreet might fondly remember sowing the wild oats of his youth, and while he might enjoy observing life in the Georgia backcountry, he now felt that he could describe these scenes only with disclaimers attached. He might relish the details of a rough-and-tumble fight, but those "peace officers who countenance them, deserve a place in the Penitentiary" (41). He might be amused by the inane banter of two drunken men, but he "hope[s] the day is not far distant, when drunkenness will be unknown in our highly favored country" (109).

Longstreet's uneasy relationship with his material led him to publish the Georgia Scenes anonymously. When he gathered them for a book, he offered this explanation: "From private considerations, I was extremely desirous of concealing the author, and the more effectually to do so, I wrote under two signatures. . . . *Hall* is the writer of those sketches in which *men* appear as the principal actors, and *Baldwin* of those in which *women* are the prominent figures" (3). Having adopted a pair of personae, Longstreet was able to play out contrasting scenarios as Hall and Baldwin negotiate their class relationships. Like Longstreet, Hall and Baldwin are upper-class men of lower-class origin. Hall, whose narratives explore mostly the masculine world of the frontier, manages to reestablish a relationship of mutual respect with the lower classes, while Baldwin, whose narratives explore mostly the feminized world of the upper classes, becomes a social outcast. In the end, Longstreet finds less to admire in his present station in life than in his humble origins.

When Longstreet published the first Georgia Scenes in the *Milledgeville Southern Recorder,* he began by running through the possibilities afforded by his narrators: Baldwin narrates **"The Dance"**; Baldwin narrates **"The Song,"** with Hall appearing in the sketch; Hall narrates **"The Horse Swap"**; and Hall narrates **"The Turf,"** with Baldwin appearing in the sketch.[25] But as sketches continued to appear, Hall became the dominant voice of the series. Thus, when Longstreet rearranged the sketches for *Georgia Scenes,* he used a sketch narrated by Hall—**"Georgia Theatrics"**—to open the book.

In **"The Dance,"** we learn that Baldwin, like Longstreet, was a man of humble origin who aspired to a higher station. As a young man he quit farm life, and he appears to have become a professional, though the nature of his profession is never made clear. At the start of **"The Dance,"** he has been "called by business to one of the frontier counties," where he must "enlist the services of . . . one of the magistrates of the county" (6). Lest readers should think Baldwin is a lawyer, in a later sketch he makes clear that he is not (55). Beyond this, information about his "business" is scarce. In any case, his aspirations, whatever they were, have turned out to be misguided. At a country dance, he encounters an old flame:

> I thought of the sad history of many of her companions and mine, who used to carry light hearts through the merry dance. I compared my after life with the cloudless days of my attachment to Polly. Then I was light hearted, gay, contented and happy; I aspired to nothing but a good name, a good wife, and an easy competency. The first and last were mine already, and Polly had given me too many little tokens of her favor, to leave a doubt now, that the second was at my command. But I was foolishly told that my talents were of too high an order to be employed in the drudgeries of a farm, and I more foolishly believed it. I forsook the pleasures which I had tried and proved, and went in pursuit of those imaginary joys which seemed to encircle the seat of Fame. From that moment to the present, my life had been little else than one unbroken scene of disaster, disappointment, vexation and toil— and now when I was too old to enjoy the pleasures which I had discarded, I found that my aim was absolutely hopeless, and that my pursuits had only served to unfit me for the humbler walks of life, and to exclude me from the higher.
>
> (10)

Baldwin suffers because he feels no sense of belonging to any class, high or low. Ostensibly, he may now belong to the upper class, but as we will see in his later sketches, his encounters with the upper class revolt him. In **"The Dance,"** he tries to recapture, however briefly, "the pleasures which [he has] discarded." His attempt hinges upon a theatrical revelation of his identity to his old flame Polly. When Polly does not recognize his name, he joins the dance and attempts to perform "the double cross hop," a difficult dance step, which, in Baldwin's youth, "was almost exclusively [his] own" (11). Unfortunately for Baldwin, Polly leaves just before he dances. After she returns, he shares with her his memories of the friends of their youth. Polly remembers them all—but she does not remember Baldwin. Like Hall at the end of **"Georgia Theatrics,"** Baldwin seems a fool.

Having failed to recapture his past, Baldwin spends most of the rest of *Georgia Scenes* languishing in the miserable present and satirizing the pretensions of the upper classes. While **"The Dance"** was set "[s]ome years ago" (6), his next sketch, **"The Song,"** is set only "a few evenings ago" (43). **"The Song"** bears our Baldwin's claim that his "pursuits" have in some sense "exclude[d]" him from the higher classes. On the surface of things, this would not seem to be the case: he finds himself not at a country "frolick" but at a sophisticated party given by Mrs. B—. After tea and conversation, the entertainment is music, and two Georgia belles play the piano and sing. Mary Williams performs so beautifully that Baldwin cries. He cannot, however, abide the performance of the pretentious Aurelia Emma Theodosia Augusta Crump. Her performance drives Baldwin from the party "in convulsions" (46).

Also at the party is Hall. Ironically, Longstreet's narrator of the masculine frontier is better suited for the evening's entertainment. When he sees Baldwin crying, he comes to his aid by requesting that Miss Mary play "some lively air" (43), and he has no difficulty enduring the onslaught of Miss Crump. Though he wishes not to leave while Miss Crump is playing, he finally departs near midnight. Fittingly, Baldwin turns out to be his roommate, and Hall's arrival wakes him from a nightmare starring Miss Crump. When Baldwin learns that Miss Crump is still performing, he does something even more stereotypically feminine than cry—he swoons. It seems that Baldwin is too feminine even for the feminine world that he inhabits.

In **"The Dance,"** Baldwin appears as a participant—albeit in some sense a failed participant—in the action of the story. In **"The Song,"** Baldwin withdraws his participation from an already passive activity. In the remaining four sketches that he narrates, Baldwin participates even less. He plays no part at all in **"The 'Charming Creature,' as a Wife"** but to tell the cautionary tale of his nephew, George Baldwin.

The trajectory of George Baldwin's life resembles that of his uncle: the son of a successful though uneducated farmer, George shows great promise as a lawyer until his life is derailed by the "charming creature" whom he chooses for a wife. Miss Evelina Caroline Smith possesses a good mind and, what is infinitely more important to her nouveau riche parents, good looks. Such superficial priorities have led the Smiths to ruin their daughter. Between the ages of six and fourteen, Evelina received no education beyond praise for her beauty and instruction in exhibiting herself to best advantage. Then, when Evelina was fourteen, her parents—purely in an effort to keep up with the Joneses—sent her north for an education. When a solid education was grafted onto Evelina's superficial personality, the result was an upper-class nightmare: Longstreet describes her as proud, vain, and hypocritical (56).

By parroting the "modest, sensible" views that she has learned by rote, Evelina snares George without even trying (57). Beyond her beauty, however, she is nothing that she appears to be. Though formally educated, Evelina uses her knowledge only to manipulate others, and after she has married George, she proves wholly incapable of managing a household. George's mother, by contrast,

> was pious, but not austere; cheerful, but not light; generous, but not prodigal; economical, but not close; hospitable, but not extravagant. In native powers of mind, she was every way my brother's equal—in acquirements she was decidedly his superior.—To this I have his testimony, as well as my own; but it was impossible to discover in her conduct, any thing going to shew that she coincided with us in opinion. To have heard her converse, you would have supposed she did nothing but read—to have looked through the departments of her household, you would have supposed she never read. Every thing which lay within her little province, bore the impress of her own hand, or acknowledged her supervision. Order, neatness, and cleanliness prevailed every where.
>
> (54)

She seems to be Longstreet's ideal woman, a perfect balance of upper-class education and lower-class practicality.

While Longstreet's portrayal of Evelina is unsympathetic, even hostile, he sees George as the unfortunate victim of one bad decision. However, when Mr. Dawson, a dear old friend of the Baldwins, insults Evelina, readers may feel their sympathies begin to shift. When Evelina tries to defend herself, her father-in-law does not take up her case. Rather, he explains to Mr. Dawson, "'She is unused to our country manners, and therefore does not understand them'" (66). To Evelina, he tries to explain that Dawson's acerbic insults were actually jokes. George, for his part, does not utter a syllable in defense of his wife. Later, during their first evening in their new home together, when George tells Evelina that he wants her to become just like his mother, readers may feel their sympathies shift even more still. For the modern reader, the balance may finally tip in Evelina's favor when she defends her treatment of their slaves: "Well, really, I can't see any great harm in treating aged people with respect, even if their skins are black." George, unfortunately, may speak for Longstreet: "I wish you had thought of that when you were talking to old Mr. Dawson. I should think he was entitled to as much respect as an infernal black wench!" (69)

George eventually succumbs to alcoholism and dies, and the sketch concludes with his uncle's injunction to mothers "against bringing up their daughters to be 'Charming Creatures'" (73). Just as Abraham Baldwin is undone by "pursuit of those imaginary joys which seemed to encircle the seat of Fame," George Baldwin is undone by pursuit of those imaginary joys which seemed to encircle Evelina. As for Evelina's fate, Longstreet's sympathies rest with her husband—he does not bother to tell what becomes of her.

How, then, is a man to avoid marrying an Evelina? In 1817, Longstreet too had been a promising young barrister in search of a helpmate. What led him to propose to his wife, Frances Eliza Parke? In an 1842 letter, Longstreet, perhaps speaking from experience, advised the son of his wife's stepfather to "marry some handsome, intelligent, industrious girl; and if she should withal happen to be rich, why dont refuse her on that account." This could well describe Longstreet's wife, an attractive woman who had inherited a substantial dowry from a grandfather, her father, and a brother. Longstreet biographer James R. Scafidel cynically wonders, "Who could resist her (and her wealth)?" Evelina, like Longstreet's wife, was a beautiful, wealthy woman. Longstreet could easily have made the same mistake as George Baldwin, but he did not. He and Eliza were married, by Longstreet's own count, for "fifty years, seven months, and ten days."[26] Perhaps, then, **"The 'Charming Creature,' as a Wife"** is the literary equivalent of an extended sigh of relief.

In Baldwin's next sketch, **"The Ball,"** our narrator again crosses paths with someone from his humble past. He is invited to the ball by Jack DeBathle, of whom he writes, "Jack had been the companion of my childhood, my boyhood, and my early manhood, and through many a merry dance had we hopt, and laughed and tumbled down together, in the morning of life" (80). His memories of Jack recall his embarrassing reunion with Polly Gibson in **"The Dance."** Though the two men are reunited for a different sort of dance, Baldwin's meeting with an old friend might afford him a chance to renew his interest in the business of living. Instead, Baldwin passively observes and reports what he sees: a superficial world in which the women are vain and the men are effete. It is the antithesis of **"The Dance"** and the world that he has lost.

Baldwin's penultimate sketch, **"The Mother and Her Child,"** is his slightest. Again he passively reports what he sees. Here he is critical of baby talk, "the gibberish which is almost invariably used by mothers and nurses to infants" (87). The narrative—focusing as it does on a mother, her baby, *and* the baby's nurse—implies that this offensive "gibberish" is the domain of the upper classes. However, this is a difficult distinction to make, for we have seen that in *Georgia Scenes* upper class tends to go hand in hand with feminine.

**"A Sage Conversation"** is Baldwin's final and most interesting narrative. He begins the sketch as something of a participant. He is traveling with his friend Ned Brace—whose character Longstreet based in part on Edmund Bacon, a lawyer from Edgefield—when the men stop for the night at a house where three elderly women are keeping company. An inveterate joker, Brace decides to have some fun with the women; just before he and Baldwin retire for the evening, he tells of two men he knew "who became so much attached to each other that they actually got married" (129). Even more remarkably, he reveals that the two men raised children together. When Brace asks his friend if he knew these men and their children, Baldwin plays along with the joke. With the old women amazed and confused, Brace and Baldwin retreat to bed.

Now Baldwin resumes his role of passively observing and reporting, but his method of observation takes a new form. In four of his five previous sketches—**"The Dance," "The Song," "The Ball,"** and **"The Mother and Her Child"**—Baldwin openly observed the activity about him. In **"A Sage Conversation,"** by contrast, he is reduced to "casting an eye through the cracks of [a] partition." Baldwin explains, "I could not resist the temptation. . . . From my bed it required but a slight change of position to see any one of the group at pleasure" (130). Thus, Baldwin spends the majority of his last sketch as an emasculated Peeping Tom. He entered *Georgia Scenes* dancing with "fine bouncing, ruddy cheeked girls" in the morning (7). He exits peeping at three old women and eavesdropping on their conversation at night.

The women are unable to solve the riddle of the men who married and raised children together. Their best guess is that one of the men was a woman in disguise. In the morning they press Ned Brace for an explanation. He responds that the men were widowers who had children from their earlier marriages (presumably, to women). Thus, they were able to raise children together. But the original oddity remains unexplained: Did two men really want to marry one another—and was this actually allowed?

James B. Meriwether first noted that the themes of **"A Sage Conversation"** include homosexuality and transvestitism.[27] The juxtaposition of these themes with Baldwin the latter-day Peeping Tom is suggestive. Baldwin is a bachelor with no visible prospects, and as *Georgia Scenes* progresses, his chances of a relationship with a woman seem increasingly remote. With **"The Dance,"** he begins the book with the hope of rekindling, in some small way, his relationship with the elder Polly Gibson. Though he fails, he does keep company with fine young women. He dances with the daughters of his contemporaries in **"The Dance,"** and then he is deeply moved by the singing of Miss Mary Williams in **"The Song."** After the performance of Miss Aurelia Emma Theodosia Augusta Crump, however, Baldwin turns misogynistic. He shows nothing but contempt for the "charming creature" who ruined the life of his nephew George Baldwin and for the "charming creatures" who populate **"The Ball."** Mrs. Slang of **"The Mother and Her Child"** appears only in her role as the mother of another man's son, and in **"A Sage Conversation"** Baldwin is reduced to peeping at the oldest women in the book. Perhaps, then, Ned Brace's story of the married men is a dig at Baldwin. At this stage in his life, Baldwin's only meaningful relationships are with other men—Jack DeBathle in **"The Ball,"** Mr. Slang in **"The Mother and Her Child,"** and his roommate Hall in **"The Turf"** (narrated by Hall). In his final sketch, it is Ned Brace—a man—with whom he retires for bed. Thus, Baldwin stands as Longstreet's worst-case scenario for upward mobility. Indeed, we might consider him a worst-case scenario for what could have become of Longstreet himself.

Baldwin, however, is not the dominant voice of the book. Longstreet reserves that role for Lyman Hall, who narrates twelve sketches to Baldwin's six.[28] Hall has no relationships with women worth mentioning, nor does he seem to need any. His domain is the masculine world of the backcountry. In his last sketch in *Georgia*

*Scenes,* he succeeds in doing what Baldwin failed to do in his first sketch: he recaptures his place among the common people of Georgia.

Like Baldwin, Hall appears to be a professional. Lynn, in his reading of **"Georgia Theatrics,"** takes Hall to be a minister. But the evidence for this, which Lynn does not discuss, is only circumstantial. In the opening paragraph of the story, Hall refers to Judas and the apostolic ministry, and he quotes John 1:5 (4). In addition, he uses such phrases as "In Mercy's name" and "hellish deed," and he describes the setting as a "heavenly retreat, for such Pandæmonian riots" (5).[29] The most compelling evidence may be Hall's explanation that when he confronted the young fighter he felt "emboldened by the sacredness of [his] office" (5), but this passage is open to at least a pair of interpretations. Hall is traveling on horseback, and "the sacredness of [his] office" may confirm that he is, indeed, a circuit-riding minister. It seems equally plausible, however, that "the sacredness of [his] office" refers merely to the moral urgency of having encountered a "hellish deed." Meriwether takes Hall for a lawyer, though, like Lynn, he does not explain his deduction.[30] Either profession, minister or lawyer, would of course link Hall to his creator.

We have already seen that in **"Georgia Theatrics"** Hall begins *Georgia Scenes* on a shaky note. Like Baldwin, his initial brush with the lower classes leaves him looking foolish. Also like Baldwin, his reaction is to become more passive in his next sketches. It seems natural to trace the evolution of Hall just as we have done with Baldwin, beginning with his first sketch and concluding with his last. But this strategy for interpreting *Georgia Scenes* has one serious problem. As Longstreet prepared to publish his sketches as a book, he arranged them for artistic effect. This arrangement, however, is not chronological. For example, **"Georgia Theatrics,"** set in 1809, is not the earliest sketch that Hall narrates. Nor is his final sketch, **"The Shooting Match,"** which is set "about a year ago," his most recent (136).[31]

Critics can defend the practice of giving interpretive precedence to the arrangement of Longstreet's sketches if they are willing to consider the circumstances under which he published *Georgia Scenes.*[32] The project of writing the sketches evolved haphazardly, and the collected and rearranged sketches were published in haste. Longstreet took the time to do some revision, though not as much as he would have preferred.[33] Indeed, it is surprising that Longstreet revised as much as he did, given, as he states in the book's preface, that he could not afford the time to read proof. If Longstreet had actually produced the revised edition of *Georgia Scenes* that he planned, he may well have harmonized the dating of the sketches with their arrangement.[34]

Appropriately, the earliest dateable sketch is set in 1790, the year of Longstreet's birth. Hall narrates **"The Turn-Out,"** which is set at a country school. Scafidel suspects a link between this school and Willington Academy; he notes the similarities between the setting for **"The Turn-Out"** and Longstreet's later description of Willington in his 1841 eulogy for Moses Waddel.[35] In **"The Turn-Out,"** the school is set near "the brow of a hill which descended rather abruptly to a noble spring, that gushed joyously forth." In Longstreet's eulogy for Waddel, he sets Willington Academy near "the brow of [a] gentle eminence . . . [that] descends, to a bold gushing fountain at its foot." Both idyllic descriptions give way to more somber thoughts. In **"The Turn-Out,"** Captain Griffin opines, "These lands will never wear out. Where they lie level they will be as good fifty years hence as they are now." But Hall reports that when he returned to the site of the school in 1832, he found "many a deep washed gully met at a sickly bog, where gushed the limpid fountain" (49-50). Similarly, Longstreet describes that in Willington "the beautiful rivulet that laved [the students'] feet, now darkly flows through an artificial channel, bordered on either side with a treacherous morass."[36] Such similarities suggest that **"The Turn-Out"** may be a paean to the joy of Longstreet's youth. In **"The Turn-Out,"** this joy takes a mischievous form: the schoolboys barricade themselves inside the schoolhouse before the schoolmaster arrives in hopes of winning a holiday. Neither Hall nor Captain Griffin condemns this troublemaking. Griffin, in fact, encourages it.

Longstreet's other tale of schoolboys is also narrated by Hall. **"The Debating Society"** is set in about 1812, and it is the most explicitly autobiographical *Georgia Scene,* as Longstreet explained in an 1836 letter: "'**The Debating Society**' is as literally true, as the frailty of memory would allow it to be. McDermot, is His Excellency George McDuffie, present Governor of South Carolina: and Longworth, is your humble servant. The scene of the debate, was Willington Academy, Abbeville District, So. Carolina; then under the superintendence of the Rev. Dr. Moses Waddel."[37] In this sketch, the young Longstreet and his accomplice McDuffie trick their debating society into arguing a nonsensical question. The sketch ends with the other boys "[laughing] heartily at the trick" (98). Thus, in both **"The Debating Society"** and **"The Turn-Out,"** schoolboys thwart the upper-class business of education, and neither sketch condemns this behavior. These are the only sketches in *Georgia Scenes* that portray upper-class activity in a wholly positive light, and in both cases the activity in question succumbs to anarchy.

Here Longstreet remembers his education with fondness. He was being initiated into the upper classes, but the wildness of Edgefield had not yet been subdued. Longstreet's schoolboy sketches support Scott Romine's observation that "when Hall prefers the present, he is generally speaking about the lower class, while his preference for the past usually indicates that the upper class is the topic of discussion."[38] We can reduce this to a cliché: the grass is always greener on the other side. Longstreet's fondness for the upper class was strongest when he was young and still working to earn his place in the world, and his fondness for the lower class intensified when he was no longer one of them.

As strong as his feelings for the present-day lower class may have been, when Longstreet looked back in time— that is, when he looked back at his own history—his feelings were often ambivalent. **"The Fight,"** for example, is set in "the younger days of the Republic" (33) and thus may predate **"The Turn-Out."** Its plot centers on Billy Stallings and Bob Durham and their long-anticipated battle to determine the "best man" in the county. Stallings and Durham represent the very type of man whom Longstreet idolized as a boy. Longstreet's ambition to "throw down and whip, any man in the district" meant that he wanted to be the victor in his own version of the Stallings-Durham fight: Longstreet wanted to be the "best man" in Edgefield. Many years removed from Edgefield, Longstreet still finds the spectacle of rough-and-tumble fighting fascinating—as much he may now claim to disapprove of "such scenes of barbarism and cruelty," he cannot look away. And when Longstreet offers his disclaimer at the end of the sketch, he refuses to single out his heroes, Stallings and Durham, for censure. Instead, he scapegoats the "peace officers" who look the other way (41).

Over the course of *Georgia Scenes,* Hall becomes more at home among the lower classes, and Meriwether traces a corresponding change in the violence he encounters: the savagery of man against man in **"The Fight"** gives way to the cruelty of man against animal in **"The Gander Pulling,"** which in turn gives way to the bloodless sport of **"The Shooting Match."**[39] Remarkably, these sketches appear to fall in chronological order: **"The Fight"** occurs in the "younger days of the Republic"; **"The Gander Pulling"** takes place in 1798; and **"The Shooting Match"** concludes *Georgia Scenes* "about a year ago." Therefore, it seems that if Hall is to regain his place among the humbler classes, then they must meet his half way. Only when the revolting spectacle of a rough-and-tumble fight is a thing of the past—fascinating though the spectacle may be—can he recapture his place in that past.

**"The Shooting Match"** is Hall's triumph and Longstreet's best-case scenario for upward mobility. Hall holds his own in a friendly verbal sparring match with a "swarthy, bright-eyed, smerky little fellow" named Billy Curlew (136), and then he holds his own with a rifle as well. Hall's final sketch is an inversion of Baldwin's first. In **"The Dance,"** Baldwin revealed his humble origins and then failed to recapture them. Hall, on the other hand, does not reveal his own humble origins until his final sketch, when he is able to recover the very skill that made him renowned as a boy:

> [Curlew:] "I reckon you hardly ever was at a shooting match, stranger, from the cut of your coat?"
>
> [Hall:] "Oh yes," returned I, "many a time. I won beef at one, when I was hardly old enough to hold a shotgun off-hand."
>
> "*Children* don't go to shooting matches about here," said he, with a smile of incredulity. "I never heard of but one that did, and he was a little *swinge*-cat.—He was born a shooting, and killed squirrels before he was weaned."
>
> "Nor did *I* ever hear of but one," replied I, "and that one was myself."
>
> (137)

Further conversation confirms that Hall is indeed the prodigy whom Curlew has heard about.

**"The Shooting Match"** is the only sketch in *Georgia Scenes* that Longstreet did not first publish in his newspaper. He appears to have written it specifically to conclude his book. Hall ends *Georgia Scenes* with the moral victory of a second-place finish in the shooting match, a victory that Longstreet may well have imagined for himself. Hall's youthful talent was among Longstreet's youthful talents: Longstreet wrote that in his youth he was "expert as a cotton picker, a wrestler, and a marksman."[40] Neither Longstreet nor Hall could have held his own picking cotton or wrestling with Billy Stallings or Billy Curlew. Marksmanship, by comparison, offers an easy bridge to the past. Hall needs only one lucky shot, and his opponents recognize him as one of their own—yet they cannot overlook that he is a man above them. Should he ever run for office, they all swear to vote for him.

As Lyman Hall returns to his roots in **"The Shooting Match,"** so did A. B. Longstreet return to his roots in *Georgia Scenes.* He never forgot how he loved the freedom of Edgefield. When he was forced to return to Richmond Academy, it became, in his words, his "hated penitentiary," where he was "considered by [his] preceptors a dunce . . . and treated accordingly." Longstreet's behavior on the dunce stool, as recorded by George W. Williams, may serve as a metaphor for his literary career:

> The teacher thought he would break the spirit of the fun-loving and mischief-making young man. . . . It was like the boy who attempted to punish the rabbit by turning it loose in a brier patch. . . .

> The six foot gawky boy enacted a monkey show that made the school boys wild. There the "dunce" sat with the side of his face exposed to the master's view, as quiet, placid and respectful as if he had been in a church.
>
> By some legerdemain he distorted the other side of his face. The school was thrown into uncontrollable confusion, so ridiculous was his appearance while grinning, winking and blinking at the boys; in spite of the anger and hickory switch of the master, they laughed, whooped, breaking up in a general stampede. There sat young Longstreet on the dunce box, quiet and calm, with only the school master for an audience.[41]

Just as there were two Longstreets as a youth—the serious façade offered his teacher and the devil-may-care cut-up revealed only to his classmates—there were two Longstreets as an adult. On the one hand, there was Longstreet of Yale, who argued a case before the Supreme Court and who published the *Augusta State Rights' Sentinel.* On the other, there was Longstreet of Edgefield, who recalled and rekindled the spirit of his wild youth in *Georgia Scenes.* And, just as Longstreet the youth hid half his face from his teacher, so did Longstreet the adult think it wise to hide half his face from the public. Thus, he published *Georgia Scenes* anonymously.

*Notes*

1. James Wood Davidson, *The Living Writers of the South* (New York: Carleton, 1869), 340.

2. Longstreet quoted in O. P. Fitzgerald, *Judge Longstreet: A Life Sketch* (Nashville: Publishing House of the Methodist Episcopal Church, South, 1891), 164.

3. A. B. Longstreet, *Augustus Baldwin Longstreet's Georgia Scenes Completed: A Scholarly Text,* ed. David Rachels (Athens: Univ. of Georgia Press, 1998), 4. Hereafter cited parenthetically in the text.

4. Franklin J. Meine, *Tall Tales of the Southwest: An Anthology of Southern and Southwestern Humor 1830-1860* (New York: Alfred A. Knopf, 1930), xvi, xvii; Walter Blair, *Native American Humor (1800-1900)* (New York: American Book Company, 1937), 63.

5. The standard anthology of recent decades, Henning Cohen and William B. Dillingham's *Humor of the Old Southwest* (1964, 1975, 1994), continues in the same vein, asserting that the "typical Old Southwestern humorist . . . was a man of education and breeding." As for Longstreet himself, Cohen and Dillingham leapfrog from his birth in Augusta, Georgia, to his education at Willington Academy in South Carolina (*Humor of the Old Southwest,* 3rd ed. [Athens: Univ. of Georgia Press, 1994], xx, 29).

6. Kenneth S. Lynn, *Mark Twain and Southwestern Humor* (Boston: Little, Brown, 1959), 64, 66-67.

7. Lynn's reading of *Georgia Scenes* has been attacked most extensively (and successfully) by Scott Romine in "Negotiating Community in Augustus Baldwin Longstreet's *Georgia Scenes*," *Style* 30.1 (1996): 1-27.

8. Cohen and Dillingham, *Humor of the Old Southwest,* xxx.

9. James R. Scafidel, unfinished Longstreet biography, James R. Scafidel Papers, South Carolina Historical Society, 3. Hereafter cited as Scafidel. Scafidel's manuscript, which carries Longstreet to 1835, is the best source available for information about Longstreet's early life. The only complete biographies of Longstreet are inadequate: O. P. Fitzgerald's *Judge Longstreet: A Life Sketch* (1891) and John Donald Wade's *Augustus Baldwin Longstreet: A Study of the Development of Culture in the South* (1924).

10. For the origins of this biographical sketch, see Fitzgerald, 199, and "The Letters of Augustus Baldwin Longstreet," ed. James R. Scafidel (Ph.D. diss., University of South Carolina, 1977), 581. The latter is hereafter cited as "Letters."

11. [A. B. Longstreet], "William Longstreet," in *The New American Cyclopædia: A Popular Dictionary of General Knowledge,* ed. George Ripley and Charles A. Dana (New York: D. Appleton, 1867), 646.

12. Joel Chandler Harris, *Stories of Georgia* (New York: American Book Company, 1896), 165; William Longstreet to Edward Telfair, September 26, 1790, quoted in Edward Mayes, *Genealogy of the Family of Longstreet* ([Jackson, MS?]: [Hederman Brothers?], [1893?]), 23.

13. Kenneth Coleman, *Georgia History in Outline* (Athens: Univ. of Georgia Press, 1978), 31; Scafidel, 7.

14. Hannah Longstreet to Rebekah Hendrickson, May 12, 1807, Augustus Baldwin Longstreet Papers, Manuscript Division, South Caroliniana Library, Univ. of South Carolina; Charles G. Cordle, "The Academy of Richmond County," *Richmond County History* 1.1 (1969): 26-27. Cordle's essay first appeared in the February 1939 issue of the *Southern Association Quarterly.*

15. John A. Chapman, *History of Edgefield County from the Earliest Settlements to 1897* (Newberry, S.C.: Elbert H. Aull, 1897), 73.

16. Fox Butterworth, *All God's Children: The Bosket Family and the American Tradition of Violence* (New York: Alfred A. Knopf, 1995), 7; Richard Maxwell Brown, *Strain of Violence: Historical Studies of American Violence and Vigilantism* (New York: Oxford Univ. Press, 1975), 83.

17. Jack Kenny Williams, *Vogues in Villainy: Crime and Retribution in Ante-Bellum South Carolina* (Columbia: Univ. of South Carolina Press, 1959), 3-4; Thomas Jefferson Mackey quoted in U. R. Books, *South Carolina Bench and Bar,* vol. 1 (Columbia, S.C.: The State Company, 1908), 199.

18. Williams, *Vogues in Villainy,* 33; Elliot J. Gorn, "'Gouge and Bite, Pull Hair and Scratch': The Social Significance of Fighting in the Southern Backcountry," *American Historical Review* 90 (Feb. 1985), 20; Judge Aedamus Burke, quoted in Gorn, 33.

19. A. B. Longstreet, "Old Things Become New," *The XIX Century,* April 1870, 839.

20. Bureau of the Census, *Heads of Families at the First Census of the United States Taken in the Year 1790: South Carolina* (Washington, D.C.: Government Printing Office, 1908), 9.

21. Longstreet, "Old Things Become New," 839.

22. [A. B. Longstreet], "Augustus Baldwin Longstreet," in *The New American Cyclopædia: A Popular Dictionary of General Knowledge,* ed. George Ripley and Charles A. Dana (New York: D. Appleton, 1867), 646. For the origins of this autobiographical sketch, see Fitzgerald, 199, and "Letters," 581.

23. See, for example, Blair, *Native American Humor,* 70ff.

24. "Letters," 145, 662.

25. These sketches appeared over four weeks in 1833: "The Dance" appeared on October 30; "The Song," on November 6; "The Horse Swap," on November 13; and "The Turf," on November 20.

26. "Letters," 135, 656; Scafidel IV-3.

27. James B. Meriwether, "Augustus Baldwin Longstreet: Realist and Artist," *Mississippi Quarterly* 35 (1982): 359-60.

28. The nineteenth sketch in *Georgia Scenes,* "The Militia Company Drill," was written by Longstreet's friend Oliver Hillhouse Prince. For a discussion of Longstreet's motivations for including this sketch in his book, see David Rachels, "Oliver Hillhouse Prince, Augustus Baldwin Longstreet, and the Birth of American Literary Realism," *Mississippi Quarterly* 51 (1998): 603-19.

29. Though it is probably a coincidence, it is interesting to note that in 1816, eighteen years before Longstreet first published "Georgia Theatrics," an-

other minister, Mason Locke Weems, compared Longstreet's old home Edgefield to Pandemonium: "Oh mercy! . . . Old Edgefield again! Another murder in Edgefield! . . . For sure it must be Pandemonium itself, a very District of Devils" (Mason Locke Weems, *The Devil in Petticoats or God's Revenge against Husband Killing* (1816; rep., Edgefield: Bacon and Adams, 1878), 3.

30. Lynn, *Mark Twain and Southwest Humor,* 66; Meriwether, "Augustus Baldwin Longstreet: Realist and Artist," 359.

31. The business of tracing Baldwin's evolution is also complicated by the fact that his sketches are not arranged chronologically. "The Dance," which is set "[s]ome years ago," is followed by "The Song," which is set only "a few evenings ago" (6, 43). Next, "The 'Charming Creature,' as a Wife," though given no specific date, is the earliest of Baldwin's sketches, as it traces the life of Baldwin's nephew, who is ten years younger than his middle-aged uncle and who died as a young man. Baldwin's fourth sketch, "The Ball," is set "about ten years ago," and his fifth, "The Mother and Her Child," only "[a] few days ago" (80, 88). Finally, his last sketch, "A Sage Conversation" is not his most recent, as it is set "many years since" (128).

32. Recent critics have focused mostly on the arrangement of the sketches while generally ignoring their chronological order. See, for example, Meriwether, "Augustus Baldwin Longstreet: Realist and Artist," 360-61; Patricia Beam, "The Theme and Structure of *Georgia Scenes*," *Journal of English* 15 (1987): 68-79; and Keith Newlin, "*Georgia Scenes*: The Satiric Artistry of Augustus Baldwin Longstreet," *Mississippi Quarterly* 41 (1987-1988): 24ff.

33. For a catalog of Longstreet's revisions, see *Georgia Scenes Completed* (279-331). Longstreet particularly regretted that he did not have a chance to thoroughly revise "The Character of a Native Georgian" ([William W. Mann], "Who Is 'Ned Brace?'" *Southern Field and Fireside,* October 8, 1859, 156).

34. Longstreet mentions his plans for a revised *Georgia Scenes* in an 1842 letter to James Barton Longacre ("Letters" 140). Years later, he may have been planning to revise and enlarge the book ([Mann], "Who Is 'Ned Brace?'" 156).

35. Scafidel, II-12.

36. A. B. Longstreet, *Eulogy on the Life and Public Services of the Late Rev. Moses Waddel* (Augusta, Ga.: Published at the Chronicle and Sentinel Office, 1841), 7-8.

37. "Letters," 98-99.

38. Romine, "Negotiating Community in Augustus Baldwin Longstreet's *Georgia Scenes,*" 12.

39. Meriwether, "Augustus Baldwin Longstreet: Realist and Artist," 361. In his analysis, Meriwether includes "The Militia Company Drill," which I have omitted because it was not written by Longstreet and does not concern Hall.

40. [Longstreet], "Augustus Baldwin Longstreet," 646.

41. Longstreet, "Old Things Become New," 839; George W. Williams, *Advice to Young Men, and Nacoochee and Its Surroundings* (Charleston, S.C.: Walker, Evans & Cogswell Co., 1899), 108. Williams places the dunce-stool story *before* the Longstreets moved to Edgefield, but his chronology and dating of events is confused. See Scafidel, 9-13.

---

## FURTHER READING

### Bibliography

Griffith, Nancy Snell. *Humor of the Old Southwest: An Annotated Bibliography of Primary and Secondary Sources.* New York: Greenwood, 1989, 220 p.

    Includes an overview of source materials relating to Longstreet and his work.

### Biographies

Johnson, John W., and F. A. P. Barnard. "Biographical Sketches of Judge A. B. Longstreet." *Mississippi Historical Society Publications* 12 (1912): 122-47.

    Details the major events in the life of Augustus Longstreet, from his early school days to his career as an author, educator, and judge.

Lenz, William E.. "Augustus Baldwin Longstreet (1790-1870)." In *Fifty Southern Writers before 1900: A Bio-Bibliographical Sourcebook,* edited by Robert Bain and Joseph M. Flora, pp. 312-22. Westport, Conn.: Greenwood, 1983.

    Includes an entry on Longstreet's life and work.

### Criticism

Beam, Patricia. "The Theme and Structure of *Georgia Scenes.*" *Journal of English* 15 (1987): 68-79.

    Offers an analysis of the characters in *Georgia Scenes* while examining the ways that Longstreet incorporates them into the narrative structure of the work.

Downs, Robert B. "Yarns of Frontier Life." In *Books That Changed the South,* pp. 74-81. Chapel Hill: University of North Carolina Press, 1977.

> Evaluates the broader significance of Longstreet's stories, both as historical chronicles of the Southeast frontier and as early examples of a distinctly American style of humor.

Ford, Thomas W. "Ned Brace of *Georgia Scenes.*" *Southern Folklore Quarterly* 29 (1965): 220-27.

> Discusses the influence of early American folklore, notably the oral storytelling tradition of the Southeast frontier, on the distinctive humor and style that characterize Longstreet's work.

Gribben, Alan. "Mark Twain Reads Longstreet's *Georgia Scenes.*" In *Gyascutus: Studies in Antebellum Southern Humorous and Sports Writing,* pp. 103-11. Atlantic Highlands, N.J.: Humanities, 1978.

> Examines the influence of Longstreet's sketches on Mark Twain through an analysis of Twain's notebooks from the 1880s.

Hamilton, Kristie. "Toward a Cultural theory of the Antebellum Literary Sketch." *Genre* 23 (1990): 297-323.

> Analyzes Longstreet's writings within the context of American society following the War of 1812, comparing Longstreet's efforts to chronicle these changing times with the writings of Washington Irving, Nathaniel Hawthorne, and others.

Lenz, William E. "Longstreet's *Georgia Scenes*: Developing American Characters and Narrative Techniques." *Markham Review* 11 (1981): 5-10.

> Analyzes the unique combination of literary convention and frontier vernacular that characterize Longstreet's writings.

Link, Samuel Albert. *Pioneers of Southern Literature, Volume 2.* Nashville, Tenn.: M. E. Church, 1899, 599 p.

> Devotes a chapter to Longstreet's life and literary career, comparing his writings with the works of other Southern humorists such as Baldwin, Hooper, W. T. Thompson, and Davy Crockett.

Mayfield, John. "The Theatre of Public Esteem: Ethics and Values in Longstreet's *Georgia Scenes.*" *Georgia Historical Quarterly* 75 (1991): 566-86.

> Explores the many ways in which Longstreet's humor both celebrates and satirizes the cultural and social values of the Old South.

Scafidel, James R. "A. B. Longstreet and Secession: His Contributions to Columbia and Charleston Newspapers, 1860-1861." In *South Carolina Journals and Journalists,* edited by James B. Meriwether, pp. 77-87. Columbia, S.C.: Southern Studies Program, 1975.

> Provides a survey of Longstreet's journalistic writings from the Civil War era, chronicling his complex opinions concerning secession and war.

———. "A Georgian in Connecticut: A. B. Longstreet's Legal Education." *Georgia Historical Quarterly* 61 (1977): 222-37.

> Examines how Longstreet's years at Tapping Reeve's Law School in Connecticut, where ideological differences between Northern and Southern students contributed to a tense social atmosphere, played a significant role in shaping Longstreet's mature intellectual and political beliefs.

Silverman, Kenneth. "Longstreet's 'The Gander Pulling.'" *American Quarterly* 18 (1966): 548-49.

> Examines the political overtones of Longstreet's "The Gander Pulling," asserting that the story reflects many of the tensions that existed between the North and South in the years leading up to the Civil War.

Smith, Gerald J. "Augustus Baldwin Longstreet and John Wade's 'Cousin Lucius.'" *Georgia Historical Quarterly* 61 (1972): 276-81.

> Argues that John Wade's title character in the short story "The Life and Death of Cousin Lucius" is based largely on Longstreet.

Wade, John Donald. *Augustus Baldwin Longstreet: A Study of the Development of Culture in the South.* 1924. Reprint, edited by M. Thomas Inge. Athens: University of Georgia Press, 1969, 392 p.

> Chronicles the author's long career against the backdrop of antebellum society and culture.

Wegmann, Jessica. "'Playing in the Dark' with Longstreet's *Georgia Scenes*: Critical Reception and Reader Response to Treatments of Race and Gender." *Southern Literary Journal* 30, no. 1 (fall 1997): 13-26.

> Evaluates *Georgia Scenes* within the context of social attitudes in the antebellum South, focusing in particular on Longstreet's treatment of slavery and sexism.

---

**Additional coverage of Longstreet's life and career is contained in the following sources published by Thomson Gale:** *Dictionary of Literary Biography,* **Vols. 3, 11, 74, 248;** *Literature Resource Center;* **and** *Reference Guide to American Literature,* **Ed. 4.**

# Studies in the History of the Renaissance

## Walter Pater

A groundbreaking, unconventional, and controversial critical exploration of some of the most influential personalities and works of art from the Renaissance era.

The following entry presents criticism of Pater's collection of essays *Studies in the History of the Renaissance* (1873). For information on Pater's complete career, see *NCLC,* Volumes 7 and 90.

## INTRODUCTION

Walter Pater first published his *Studies in the History of the Renaissance* in 1873. The original edition of the book included eight essays, five of them published previously, as well as the "Preface" and the "Conclusion." As a work of history, the study proved unconventional in many respects, particularly because of its impressionistic prose style as well as for the highly subjective nature of its scholarship. Perhaps the most radical characteristic of the book was its conception of the Renaissance itself, which Pater interpreted not as a historical period but as a vital spirit, one that had originated in the Middle Ages and extended through the European Enlightenment, with traces reaching even into the modern era. For these reasons the book divided critics upon its original publication. Older, more established scholars censured the unorthodoxy of Pater's approach, while younger intellectuals, notably Oscar Wilde and William Butler Yeats, hailed the work as a radical declaration of a modern aesthetic theory. Of all the essays in the book, the "Conclusion" attracted the most attention, primarily for its seeming espousal of hedonism as well as for its anti-Christian stance. Ostensibly wishing to avoid further controversy, Pater suppressed the "Conclusion" from the next edition of the work, which appeared in 1877 under the revised title *The Renaissance: Studies in Art and Poetry.* Some critics have suggested that the change in title was prompted by Mrs. Mark Pattison's review of the first edition, in which she complained about the lack of conventional historical considerations in the work. A third edition, which included a new essay entitled "The School of Giorgioni" as well as a restored, slightly modified version of the "Conclusion," was published in 1888. A

fourth printing, the last to appear in Pater's lifetime, followed in 1893. Through all of these printings the author made constant revisions to the essays, so that no two editions of the work are the same. The poetic, enigmatic nature of Pater's literary style, as well as his iconoclastic approach to art history, helped define the debate over modern art that arose in the decades after his death, and *The Renaissance* had a powerful impact on such modernist pioneers as Wallace Stevens, James Joyce, Virginia Woolf, Ezra Pound, and T. S. Eliot, among others.

## CONTENT AND STRUCTURE

In the "Preface" to *Studies in the History of the Renaissance,* Walter Pater defines the critic not as a chronicler of historical or artistic fact but rather as a unique interpreter of beauty. Indeed, the book arose out of Pater's interest in questions of aesthetics, in particular as these are related to the notion of the individual creative genius. For Pater the importance of the Renaissance for late Victorian England lay not in its historical epoch or even in the works of art themselves. Rather, in his study Pater attempts to identify the underlying spirit of the Renaissance as it is embodied in its most accomplished artists and thinkers. Although Pater clearly regards the Renaissance as a triumphant era in the history of Western culture, a period in which the Hellenic ideal of beauty attained its most powerful and far-reaching expression, he also views it as a conceptual framework for discussions of art and culture in the modern age. As such, Pater's study is concerned not so much with the history of the Renaissance than with his own notion of a "Renaissance spirit," and his ruminations on the nature of art and life say as much about his own times as they do about the Renaissance era. This radical new approach to the subject of Renaissance art, heightened by Pater's highly subjective, emotion-driven prose style, is what makes the work so difficult to classify.

The scope of Pater's book extends beyond traditional notions of the Renaissance period, both chronologically and geographically. Though the majority of the essays concern Italian artists, the book includes an examination of medieval French literature as well as a lengthy analysis of the life of the German archaeologist and historian Johann Joachim Winckelmann, whose groundbreaking investigations of Greek art and culture in the eighteenth century helped create the modern study of antiquity. Indeed, *Studies in the History of the Renaissance* is particularly noteworthy for articulating the notion that the Renaissance effectively resuscitated the concept of Hellenic beauty, in the process forming a bridge between the classical world and the modern age.

The individual essays in the book contain a variety of critical approaches and demonstrate the diverse nature of Pater's own aesthetic passions. In his essay on Michelangelo, for example, Pater pays little attention to the artist's paintings and sculptures, for which he remains most famous. Instead, Pater focuses on Michelangelo's sonnets, which he regards as critical to understanding the essence of the artist. Pater's essay on Botticelli is considered a seminal work on the painter, and it helped usher in a revival of interest in the artist's work. In the essay "Two Early French Stories," Pater identifies aspects of medieval French art and literature that prefigure the humanistic spirit of the Renaissance, concluding that the Middle Ages embodied a significant aesthetic awakening in its own right. In "Leonardo da Vinci" Pater discusses the painting *La Gioconda* (*Mona Lisa*) in idolatrous terms, describing the woman in the picture as a timeless, almost otherworldly being, at once a Greek goddess, a saint, and a "vampire" who embodies all of the diverse, conflicting passions of human existence. The description stands as one of Pater's best known and provocative pieces of writing, and it represents a radical break from traditional pictorial analysis. The book's "Conclusion," originally published as part of the 1868 essay "Poems by William Morris," represents Pater's most radical statement of his aesthetic philosophy, as it enjoins the reader to devote his or her life, without compromise, to the pleasure of art. The essay, and *The Renaissance,* concludes with the line "For art comes to you proposing frankly to give nothing but the highest quality to your moments as they pass, and simply for those moments' sake."

## MAJOR THEMES

At the core of Pater's study of the Renaissance lies the maxim *l'art pour l'art,* or "art for art's sake." Originally championed by nineteenth-century French aesthetes, this notion of art as an end in itself helped shape Pater's conception of a life dedicated to aesthetic appreciation. In Pater's view the importance of the Renaissance, as of all culture, lies in its power to stimulate the human spirit, to inspire the individual to make the most of his or her life. By establishing a critical relationship with the Renaissance that is in many ways deeply personal, Pater in essence makes it his own and reshapes it according to his own unique interpretations. At the same time, throughout the work Pater suggests that any philosophical, ethical, or social system that requires the individual to sacrifice his or her subjective appreciation of the world is false and not worth inhabiting. *The Renaissance,* then, is primarily a statement of Pater's unique passion for art.

Pater's aesthetic philosophy finds its most eloquent articulation in the book's "Conclusion." Here Pater sets forth his personal interpretation of the meaning and purpose of art. In this brief essay he wistfully describes modern life as transitory and indefinite, a realm in which Christian notions of redemption and moral value have become increasingly out of place. In such an uncertain spiritual existence, according to Pater's view, qualities of excitement, stimulation, and pleasure become paramount. For Pater these sensations find their truest realization in the appreciation of art. In this way his book not only creates a framework for further study of Renaissance art but also serves as a profound statement on the nature of human existence, and the book serves both as a work of art history and of philosophy. Pater's *The Renaissance* stands on the threshold between Romanticism and modernism, embodying the deeply personal considerations of the former while presaging much of the experimentation and ambiguity of the latter.

## CRITICAL RECEPTION

*The Renaissance* sparked considerable critical debate upon its original publication. The book's "Conclusion" in particular aroused controversy for its apparent repudiation of Christian notions of life and death, and many critics and scholars attacked what they perceived to be the work's distinct pagan elements. Even those contemporary critics who seemed willing to forgive Pater his apparent heterodoxy still took him to task for the style of the work. One contemporary critic, Mrs. Mark Pattison, observed that Pater's book had little to do with history in the traditional sense of the word. Margaret Oliphant went even further with her criticism, declaring the work "pretentious" and without real substance. Still, Pater had his champions, and many reviewers in both England and the United States had high praise for the elegance of his prose, for the perspicuity of his critical insights, and above all for his passion. In the twentieth century scholars have examined various parallels between *The Renaissance* and modern art and literature, noting that the ambiguity of Pater's style and approach embodies many of the central ideas of high modernism. Critics like Denis Donohue have argued that Pater's prose style exerted a powerful impact on the development of twentieth-century literature, an influence that is still evident today. A number of scholars, notably Paul Barolsky, have examined the notion of subjectivity in *The Renaissance,* asserting that the personal nature of Pater's approach represents a conjoining of subject and style that was radical for its time. Other theoretical approaches to the work have explored such topics as the relationship between biography and art, the conflict between subjectivity and objectivity inherent in the creation of critical texts, and the role of politics and morality in aesthetic concerns.

## PRINCIPAL WORKS

*Studies in the History of the Renaissance* (essays) 1873; republished as *The Renaissance: Studies in Art and Poetry,* 1877

*Marius the Epicurean: His Sensations and Ideas* (novel) 1885

*Imaginary Portraits* (prose) 1887

*Appreciations: With an Essay on Style* (essays) 1889

*Plato and Platonism: A Series of Lectures* (essays) 1893

*An Imaginary Portrait* (prose) 1894; republished as *The Child in the House,* 1895

*Greek Studies: A Series of Essays* (essays) 1895

*Miscellaneous Studies: A Series of Essays* (essays) 1895

*Essays from the "Guardian"* (essays) 1896

*Gaston de Latour: An Unfinished Romance* (unfinished novel) 1896

*Uncollected Essays* (essays) 1903

*New Library Edition of the Works of Walter Pater.* 10 vols. (essays, novel, unfinished novel, and prose) 1910

*Walter Pater: Selected Works* (essays, novel, and prose) 1948

*Letters of Walter Pater* (letters) 1970

## CRITICISM

***The Atlantic Monthly* (review date October 1873)**

SOURCE: Review of *The Renaissance. The Atlantic Monthly* 32, no. 192 (October 1873): 496-98.

[*In the following review, the author has high praise for Pater's literary style, extolling its elegance, subtlety, and passion. The review, however, questions whether Pater's high level of subjectivity is suitable for a work of criticism, remarking that the book's lack of intellectual rigor ultimately diminishes the persuasiveness of Pater's arguments.*]

Considered as an application of the old saying that it takes nine tailors to make a man, the most noteworthy product of the Centenary celebration of Alexander Von Humboldt's birth is the piece of literary patchwork edited by Karl Bruhns, and styled "a life" of the great traveller, in which four German professors have united to sketch his career, and eight more to catalogue and criticise his works,—a combination curious even in these days of literary partnership, and typical of the character of the subject. The German book was printed in three volumes last year, and the merely biographical part of it has been promptly made available to English and American readers, through a translation in two volumes by the sisters Lassell, which deserves credit for not repeating the idioms of the German language.

The first volume, compiled wholly by Julius Löwenberg, describes Humboldt's youth and early manhood, his family, education, official service in the bureau of mines, connection with the society of Jena and Weimar, projects of travel, and presentation at the court of Aranjuez in 1799; and then sketches in two monographs his journeys in America (1799-1804), and preparations (1804-1808) for publishing their results, and his travels in Asia in 1829. The second volume opens with a monograph, by Robert Avé-Lallemant, of Humboldt's sojourn in Paris from 1808 to 1827, comprising brief accounts of his scientific companions at the French capital, and references to his diplomatic services during that period; and ends with a critical narration, by Alfred Dove, of the decline of Humboldt's life at Berlin, from 1827 to 1859, including details of his association with the Prussian kings, and the conception, preparation, and publication of the Kosmos. An extraordinary list of Humboldt's writings, with which the second volume of the German book concludes, has been omitted by the translators; and they have not attempted to add or even epitomize the scientific essays of the eight professors, which form the third volume.

None of the natural defects of such a work have been remedied by the supervision of Professor Bruhns. Each compiler measures Humboldt with a different gauge, and describes him by a different method. Herr Löwenberg is more enthusiastic than critical; Dr. Avé-Lallemant is uncritically statistical; and Dr. Dove is more critical than enthusiastic. This shifting of standard and style is as vexatious to the reader as sudden changes of conveyance to a tourist. Löwenberg, for instance, says that, "highly gifted as Humboldt was with mental power, he was not less endowed with moral excellence"; while Dove denies to him "any perceptible development of moral culture." Nevertheless, the book is deeply interesting, and a valuable contribution to literature, for it contains much new information, and shows (especially on the part of Dr. Dove) much nice discernment. During the half century since Humboldt became a household name in the United States, the American conception of him has been derived from the effusions of popular scientists, and the fugitive correspondence of the press, and has always been remarkably vague and blindly enthusiastic. The present work, without detracting from the full measure of his glory, will do something to inform the English-reading public of the contradictions of his character, and to clarify, even if it lessens, their admiration of his virtues and achievements. And this is the more important, since he must ever be a unique and romantic figure in the history of physical science; for the almost completed exploration of the surface of the planet, and the growing tendency of the age to specialties, will render the reproduction of such a man impossible. The fact marks an epoch in the world's progress, that no future traveller can ever reveal so much of the new and strange, nor any future intellect grasp so nearly the whole knowledge of its era. Dr. Dove says truly that, "the honors profusely showered upon the author of Kosmos may, after all, be regarded merely as the homage offered by the men of the nineteenth century, proud of the grand achievements of modern science, to their own comprehensive genius, impersonated, in a manner not granted to every age, in a living representative gifted with a mind alike distinguished for power of arrangement and universality of comprehension."

One omission in Dr. Dove's summary of Humboldt's character is remarkable. He refuses to attempt a definition of Humboldt's religious faith, "leaving it," he says, "to the hyenas of orthodoxy to drag from the grave of the dead that which he, to some extent, kept concealed from himself,"—an unfortunate expression, unjust alike to the memory of the dead and to the natural and reasonable desire of mankind to be instructed by the opinions of a great intellect, which was devoted, throughout a life of extraordinary length, to studying the manifestations of an Intelligence in Nature. All the world knows that the abstinence of the evangelical clergy (with a single exception) from any share in the ceremonies of Humboldt's funeral was, perhaps, its most remarkable feature; and this fact is duly chronicled by Dr. Dove, who elsewhere alludes to the assertion by "an authority otherwise trustworthy," that Alexander von Humboldt confessed to a "heresy," similar to his brother William's, in that, besides two things that passed his comprehension, namely, romantic love and music (which last Alexander was accustomed to style the *calamité sociale*), there was a third, namely, orthodox piety. Granting that the opinions of historical personages on all matters of belief are not rightful property of the public, yet a book is defective which undertakes to tell the whole story of a life, and expressly leaves its religious faith to doubtful inference. It is no definition to describe it generally as a "System of Pantheism or Naturalism," nor any excuse that the subject of the biography "held himself aloof from any attempt to reduce it to formulæ." When so much is hinted, it is better to ascertain and tell the whole. If the religious opinions of Humboldt were nowhere positively asserted by himself, they are nevertheless discoverable by any willing biographer from his criticisms of the beliefs of others. It is pitiful to see a writer who does not scruple to unveil a hundred petty instances of the sarcasm and vanity of his hero, nor even to recount all the sorry correspondence with Uhland about the Order of Merit, pretend that delicacy forbids a disclosure of his honest theory of the sustaining principle of the Universe.

—As Mr. Pater several times explains, both in the preface and the body of his work, his ***Studies in the History of the Renaissance*** do not relate merely to that period when Gothic art in Italy yielded to the reviving taste for the classic forms. The Renaissance he thinks a process so gradual, and of such vague limits, that it may be traced far back into the dark ages, when the sense of beauty first began to stir after the fall of Greek art and letters. In this he seems right enough; but it is only giving a more general meaning to a word which was specifically used before. Nothing new is established; and we doubt if the cultivated reader of Mr. Pater's agreeable essays will learn from them to see the Renaissance in a light different from that in which it had already appeared to him; while we think he will feel that Mr. Pater has strained some points in making Du Bellay and kindred French poets active elements of the Renaissance, though it undoubtedly found its literary consummation in Winckelmann and Goethe. We do not undervalue the particular services that Mr. Pater renders the student of the Renaissance; there is hardly a page which does not suggest or present some acceptable view of some phase of the subject. Perhaps this is all that he hoped to accomplish; at any rate it is a very great deal; and his essays are written with so much toleration and decency that he might seem to be treating of anything but matters of art, which inflame controversy as nothing else but matters of religion can. Imagine a manner as unlike Ruskin's as possible, and you have Mr. Pater's manner. His essays are on the old French poem, Aucassin and Nicollette, in the gay sensuousness of which he fancies the beginning of a return to the Greek spirit; on Pico della Mirandula, the first of the Italian Platonists, who dreamed of identifying the truth and beauty of paganism with those of Christianity; on Sandro Botticelli, in whose paintings the love of unreligious beauty is manifest; on Luca della Robbia, whose place in art is midway between the system of the Greeks and that of Michael Angelo, who partakes of the universalizing tendency of the former and the individualizing tendency of the latter; on Michael Angelo, on Lionardo da Vinci, and on Winckelmann, whose relation to the Renaissance is evident, and on Joachim du Bellay, who is not so evidently related to it, though he may be claimed for it, if one likes.

One of the best of these essays is that on Da Vinci. It is constant enough to all the known facts of Lionardo's career, and where those are wanting it supplies them by reasonable conjecture, or, rather, question. Yet much is to be forgiven to all writers on art, who oblige themselves to see more in the great *chefs d'œuvre* than the honest old masters ever put there; and Mr. Pater requires clemency in this way with the rest. Here, for example, is what he writes of one of the most famous of Da Vinci's pictures.

"'La Gioconda' is in the truest sense Lionardo's masterpiece, the revealing instance of his mode of thought and work. In suggestiveness, only the Melancholia of Dürer is comparable to it; and no crude symbolism disturbs the effect of its subdued and graceful mystery. We all know the face and hands of the figure, set in its marble chair, in that cirque of fantastic rocks, as in some faint light under the sea. . . . The presence that thus so strangely rose beside the waters is expressive of what in the ways of a thousand years men had come to desire. Hers is the head upon which all "the ends of the world are come"; and the eyelids are a little weary. It is a beauty wrought out from within the flesh, the deposit, cell by cell, of strange thoughts and fantastic reveries and exquisite passions. Set it for a moment beside one of those white Greek goddesses or beautiful women of antiquity, and how they would be troubled by this beauty, into which the soul with all its maladies has passed! All the thoughts and experiences of the world have etched and moulded therein that which they have of power to refine and make expressive the outward form, the animalism of Greece, the lust of Rome, the reverie of the middle ages with its spiritual ambition and imaginative loves, the return of the Pagan world, the sins of the Borgias. She is older than the rocks amidst which she sits; like the vampire, she has been dead many times, and learned the secrets of the grave; and has been a diver in deep seas, and keeps their fallen days about her; and trafficked for strange webs with Eastern merchants; and, as Leda, was the mother of Helen of Troy, and, as Saint Anne, the mother of Mary; and all this has been to her but as the sound of lyres and flutes, and lives only in the delicacy with which it has moulded the changing lineaments and tinged the eyelids and hands. The fancy of a perpetual life, sweeping together ten thousand experiences, is an old one; and modern thought has conceived the idea of humanity as wrought upon by, and summing up in itself, all modes of thought and life. Certainly, Lady Lisa might stand as the embodiment of the old fancy, the symbol of the modern idea."

She might, but does she? There is really nothing to prove that Lionardo, who lived before the modern thought, had the old fancy in his mind. In fact, there is nothing to show that he had any purpose, save to make the most beautiful picture he could of a strangely beautiful woman. But modern art-criticism is attributive when it supposes itself interpretative. The sight of an old painting inspires the critic with certain emotions, and these he straightway seizes upon as the motives of the painter. It *may* happen that both are identical; or it may happen that the effect produced was never in the painter's mind at all. Very likely it was not; but this vice, which Mr. Ruskin invented, goes on perpetuating itself; and Mr. Pater, who is as far from thinking with Mr. Ruskin as from writing like him, falls a helpless prey to it. Yet, as Mr. Pater deals more with the general character of the painter than with his intentions in particular works, his offence is far less than that of his original in this respect, and he does really give us an almost satisfactory impression of a genius as grand as it was fine, as profound as it was various, in his study of Lionardo.

His theory of Michael Angelo, as the last rather than the first of his kind, has also much to support it; and the idea that he is to be understood through those sculptors who went before him, and some modern authors and artists, and not through his immediate successors or his school, is quite acceptable. His "professed disciples are in love with his strength only, and seem not to feel his grave and temperate sweetness. Theatricality is their chief characteristic; and that is a quality as little attributable to Michael Angelo as to Minor or Luca Signorelli. With him as with them, all is passionate, serious, impulsive. . . . That strange interfusion of sweetness and strength is not to be found in those who claimed to be his followers, but it is found in many of those who worked before him, and in many others down to our own time,—in William Blake, for instance, and in Victor Hugo, who, though not of his school, and unaware, are his true sons, and help us to understand him, as he in turn interprets and justifies them. Perhaps this is the chief use in studying old masters."

It is Mr. Pater's delicate suggestiveness in this place and in other places that makes him useful in the study of a subject which, if you do not limit it by the exactest statement, has no limits. His Renaissance is a larger affair than the Renaissance of most writers and thinkers, but it is also vastly vaguer, and his thoughts about it partake in general of this vagueness. One follows him well pleased with his style, and grateful for his clear perception of particular aspects and characteristics; yet doubtful after all whether much that he calls Renaissance was not merely ripe and perfect Gothic in literature and art. That it is at least as much the one as the other may be safely maintained. In fact, until we come to Winckelmann, we are not certain that it is the Renaissance which we have had to do with. But Winckelmann became so truly Hellenic that there can be no question but we lay fast hold upon the Renaissance in him. Coming long after the mystical middle ages, he is no more of them than if he had gone before them with the other Greeks; and as Mr. Pater says in one of the finest passages of his book, "with the sensuous element in Greek art he deals in the pagan manner; and what is implied in that? It has sometimes been said that art is a means of escape from the tyranny of the senses. It may be so for the spectator; he may find that the spectacle of supreme works of art takes from the life of the senses something of its turbid fever. But this is possible for the spectator only because the artist in producing these works has gradually sunk his intellectual and spiritual ideas in sensuous form. He may live, as Keats lived, a pure life; but his soul, like that of Plato's false astronomer, becomes more and more immersed in sense until nothing else has any interest for him. How could such a one ever again endure the grayness of the ideal or spiritual world?. . . . To the Greek the immersion in the sensuous was indifferent. Greek sensuousness, therefore, does not fever the blood; it is shameless and childlike. But Christianity, with its uncompromising idealism, discrediting the slightest touch of sense, has lighted up for the artistic life, with its inevitable sensuousness, a background of flame. 'I did but taste a little honey with the end of the rod that was in mine hand, and lo, I must die!' It is hard to pursue that life without something of conscious disavowal of a spiritual world; and this imparts to genuine artistic interests a kind of intoxication. From this intoxication Winckelmann is free; he fingers those pagan marbles with unsinged hands, with no sense of shame or loss. That is to deal with the sensuous side of art in the pagan manner."

And this was the true, the perfect Renaissance. But it came in a critic, it seems, and not in an artist.

### The Nation: A Weekly Journal Devoted to Politics, Literature, Science & Art (review date 9 October 1873)

SOURCE: Review of *The Renaissance. The Nation: A Weekly Journal Devoted to Politics, Literature, Science & Art* 17, no. 432 (9 October 1873): 243-44.

[*In the following review, the author, though highly praising Pater's prose, questions most of his assertions about Renaissance history and art, concluding that the book fails to express anything particularly original about the subject.*]

Mr. Pater, in a book which on the whole deserves the epithet fascinating, shows a power of expression and a subtlety of analysis which at first reading disposed us to admit him to a place among the best critics; but when we return to study out the meaning unfolded and measure our acquisitions, we find we must change the word. Much is enfolded and much is told that is admirable in telling, but not so much of the theme as of Mr. Pater himself; of him we obtain a very distinct and pleasing notion in general, but of his nominal subject we hardly know more than before we read his *Studies.* The author is too much of an artist to be a good critic, and hardly attempts to disguise the fact that he is more interested in the perfection of his own style than in the mysteries of the art on which his studies are based. In fact, he sets out with a fallacy which shows clearly enough that "diletto" rather than "cognosco" is the root of his thinking. "Such discussions [on beauty in the abstract, etc.] help us very little to enjoy what has been well done in art or poetry, to discriminate between what is more and what is less excellent in them, or to use words like beauty, excellence, art, or poetry with more meaning than they would otherwise have. Beauty, like all other qualities presented to human experience, is relative, and the definition of it becomes unmeaning and useless in proportion to its abstractness. To define beauty, not in the most abstract, but in the most concrete terms possible, not to find a universal formula for it, but the formula which expresses most adequately this or that special manifestation of it, is the aim of the true student of æsthetics." And having thus broadly stated his creed, which is that of most dilettanti, viz., that there is no standard, that there are no fundamental principles in art, but simply recognitions of personal sympathies and expressions of personal delights, he goes on to define with a logic not so successful as his rhetoric what the æsthetic critic has to do with.

The simple fact is that for want of definitions, formulas, abstract terms, and all those precise and "metaphysical" distinctions which our author holds in defiance, if not in abhorrence, the criticism of art is all afloat—is in effect nothing but the unreasoning and generally unreasonable expression of individual preferences or tastes, which may to-day be adopted as the standard from the personal prestige of the holder and to-morrow be rejected because another has supplanted him; and in this field he is king who has most power of persuasion, not he who has most reason. The habitual critic is simply a dilettante with more or less experience of art, with a set of rules which are pure assumption, and which contribute in no degree to establish taste on a sounder basis. What is wanted to render criticism a science and make even dilettantism certain and progressive, is a thorough nomenclature of art and definition of all its qualities in the abstract; and a declaration that any such attainments are either hopeless or useless, or in any degree inapplicable, is a confession of individual incapacity to attain to or make use of them.

To assert that art and beauty have not laws capable of rigid definition, and as rigid application to all cases which can ever come under them, is equivalent to asserting that there is no such thing as beauty, and that art is whatever any one chooses to call it. Art, speaking in the distinctive sense of that term in which it is used when considered in reference to the expression of an ideal, is purely and only the metrical, rhythmical, harmonic (what the Greeks termed musical, pertaining to any of the Muses), or concordant expression of emotion, whether it be in poetry, painting, music, dancing, or any other conceivable way of opening the soul to influences above and beyond it; and to say that any of the arts thereby evolved is incapable of as absolute analysis and as abstract definition as music or color, is to confess a voluntary and factitious limit to the powers of the human intellect. The arts are but different forms of the

same thing, and the analogies are so absolute and coherent that to have analyzed one is to have shown the way to analyze the whole.

It is true that in the moment of the enjoyment of any art-expression the analysis is, if not impossible, at least destructive of the completeness of the enjoyment, except to highly trained and peculiarly fitted minds; and the recognition of this half-truth is what Mr. Pater, like almost all dilettante critics, means by his statement. The absolute definition and embodiment in laws (not rules) of the principles which lie at the root of art is not only possible, but as indispensable to its complete and final development as the laws which govern the heavenly bodies are to the calculation of eclipses. It does not follow that art can be evoked by knowledge or application of rules, but that it cannot be fully understood and most effectively cultivated without that knowledge and application.

Mr. Pater takes with the word *renaissance* a liberty which, though very common, is historically and logically inadmissible. The word does not mean a revival, but a new birth, and was applied to a phase of art which its votaries believed to be the re-creation of Greek art. Its proper and technical meaning is in the resumption of classical *forms* of art-expression, as seen in Raphael's later work, Michael Angelo, and the indefinite horde who followed, amongst whom we notice most commonly Poussin, etc., etc.—an art which, far from being a new birth or even a revival, was, in its substitution of the borrowed and imitated themes which it effected, in reality the decay of art—that inevitable decay which accompanies the substitution of a reflected and imitative enthusiasm for genuine emotions which compel their own rhythmical expression and develop their own forms. If the term "renaissance" is in any way applicable to Italian art, it belongs to Giotto, who first went frankly to the original springs of art, the pure beauty of nature; but it is very doubtful if there was ever any suspense or renaissance in art, since when it subsided in one form it broke out in another, and the spirit was always the same, and immortal. A peculiar national temperament develops one form; change the nature of its emotions and the form of the art changes; but so long as there is genuine and lofty emotion, there will be art, be there schools or no schools. Nature is herself the great mistress—not, as the German critics have it, external and material nature, but the universal human-divine nature, in which are born and nourished every aspiration and emotion the embodiment of which becomes art.

The ***Studies*** have the coherence which might be expected from separate essays on kindred topics, but written without any central thought; they are full of thought and suggestion, and abound in evidence of culture and accomplishment, but they must be taken not as a book, but each on its distinct merits. The last on Winckelmann is perhaps one of the completest expressions of the dilettante view of that celebrated art-writer which we can expect to have. It takes Winckelmann's side of Winckelmann, who was an art-critic in the sense that German painters are idealists when they *try* to be ideal, who confounded artifice with art, the form of things with their substance, and, like all worshippers of the renaissance, died in the worship of form and accident, not of substance and law. He was a narrow-minded man, whose nature was only open to reflected (and hence artificial) emotions, and the rigid forms of Greek art appealed to his narrow side—the nature which was the source of Greek art he had no eye for. He sought for the secret of the perfection of that art in a hypothetical and visionary physical perfection amongst the Greeks instead of where it really was, in the serene and exalted character of the Greek intellect, healthy and happy, full of sublime passions, with a remarkable freedom from sensuality, with a tranquil faith, and lives singularly free from what we may call worldly ambitions. If the whole known *répertoire* of Greek sculpture were alive and walking amongst us to-day, we should no more develop great sculptors than we do, because the temper in which that was conceived and born does not exist in modern times. This Winckelmann and his followers do not comprehend; they do not see that all the copying and imitation of antique statues which doomsday will permit will no more make an artist than the study of Greek hexameters will make another Homer. Art that looks back ceases to be art, and becomes artifice; a renaissance that is the renewal of dead forms is not a new birth, it is a galvanic resuscitation; and the modern sympathy (like Winckelmann's) with the Renaissance so-called, is but a morbid abhorrence of life and health, and fondness for death and artifice.

But we must not leave Mr. Pater with our differences alone adjusted. Differ in opinion with him we must, and continually, yet with profound respect for his opinion. The essay on **"Pico Della Mirandola"** is so full of genuine appreciation, so complete, so comprehensive, that, without having previous knowledge of Mirandola, one feels that, if living, he would say that Mr. Pater has told him better than he could have told himself. And generally the essays on literary themes are better than those on artistic (using the word in its narrow, common sense), for the simple reason that without being to a certain extent an artist it is absolutely impossible to be a comprehensive critic of art. In poetry, Mr. Pater is one of the cognoscenti; in painting, as we have said, only a dilettante. His conception of literary qualities seems clear and definite, but that of pictorial character evasive

and indefinite, like a picture drawn by an untrained talent, with a vague, unincisive touch. But in whichever theme, his power, individuality, and charm of style are such as to make his book one of the best acquisitions which art-literature has made of late.

### Arthur Symons (essay date 1932)

SOURCE: Symons, Arthur. "Chapter Two." In *A Study of Walter Pater,* pp. 20-32. London: Charles J. Sawyer, 1932.

[*In the following excerpt, Symons evaluates Pater's responses to some of the great Renaissance paintings. Symons asserts that Pater's passion for the work he is describing, along with the eloquence of his prose, expresses a profound truth about the nature of art itself, even when his declarations are factually incorrect.*]

II

Turning from the criticisms of literature to the studies in painting, we see precisely the same qualities, but not, I think, precisely the same results. In a sentence of the essay on **"The School of Giorgione,"** which is perhaps the most nicely balanced of all his essays on painting, Walter Pater defines, with great precision:

> In its primary aspect, a great picture has no more definite message for us than an accidental play of sunlight and shadow for a few moments on the wall or floor: is itself, in truth, a space of such fallen light, caught as the colours are caught in an Eastern carpet, but refined upon, and dealt with more subtly and exquisitely than by nature itself.

But for the most part it was not in this spirit that he wrote of pictures. His criticism of pictures is indeed creative, in a fuller sense than his criticism of books; and, in the necessity of things, dealing with an art which, as he admitted, has, in its primary aspect, no more definite message for us than the sunlight on the floor, he not merely divined, but also added, out of the most sympathetic knowledge, certainty. It is one thing to interpret the meaning of a book; quite another to interpret the meaning of a picture. Take, for instance, the essay on Botticelli. That was the first sympathetic study which had appeared in English of a painter at that time but little known; and it contains some of Pater's most exquisite writing. All that he writes, of those angels 'who, in the revolt of Lucifer, were neither for Jehovah nor for His enemies,' of that sense in the painter of 'the wistfulness of exiles,' represents, certainly, the impression made upon his own mind by these pictures, and, as such, has an interpretative value, apart from its beauty as a piece of writing. But it is, after all, a speculation before a canvas, a literary fantasy; a possible interpretation, if you will, of one mood in the painter, a single side of his intention; it is not a criticism, inevitable as that criticism of Wordsworth's art, of the art of Botticelli. Botticelli has the secret of the Greek rhythm and nothing in his feeling comes to disturb that rhythm. Whether he paints the Birth of Venus or of Christ, he has the same pure curiosity and indifference: each to him is a picture and nothing more than a picture. The pensive unconcern in the Virgin's face is an expression chosen for its melancholy grace and wistful charm. And this picture is created by one who gave his genius equally, it might be, to Venus rising naked out of the waves, and to the Virgin enthroned and indifferent among indifferent angels. Judith, leaving the tent of Holofernes whom she has slain, is seen going home in the midst of her enemies with the olive-branch and the sword held in her hand. All his figures are hypnotised by that magic of his which is perverse and subtle: and all these, enduring the pressure of an immense weariness, have in their eyes the look of those who do or who endure great things in a dream.

Had Walter Pater devoted himself exclusively to art criticism, there is no doubt that, in a sense, he would have been a great art critic. There are essays—such as his unsurpassable **"Leonardo da Vinci,"** his lovely and all but final interpretation of Botticelli, and his **"School of Giorgione"**—in which the essential principles of the art of painting are divined and interpreted with extraordinary subtlety. I remember hearing him say that, as he grew older, books interested him less and less, pictures delighted him more and more. Yet, even in that admirable essay on Giorgione, he left out all mention of *The Geometricians* in the Vienna Gallery. So, writing subtly on Coleridge, he left out *Kubla Khan*. As it was, he corrected many of the hasty and generous errors of Ruskin and helped to bring criticism to a wiser and more tolerant attitude towards the Arts.

In his essay on Giorgione, in which he came perhaps nearer to a complete and final disentangling of the meaning and functions of the Arts than any writer on æsthetics has yet done, we are told: 'All art constantly aspires towards the condition of music'; and again—

> It is the art of music which most completely realises this artistic ideal, this perfect identification of matter and form. In its consummate moments, the end is not distinct from the means, the form from the matter, the subject from the expression; they inhere in and completely saturate each other; and to it, therefore, . . . all the arts may be supposed constantly to tend and aspire. In music, then, rather than in poetry, is to be found the true type or measure of perfected art.

This is the beginning of Pater's essay:

It is the mistake of much popular criticism to regard poetry, music, and painting—all the various products of art—as but translations into different languages of one and the same fixed quantity of imaginative thought, supplemented by certain technical qualities of colour, in painting; of sound, in music; of rhythmical words, in poetry. In this way, the sensuous element in art, and with it almost everything in art that is essentially artistic, is made a matter of indifference; and a clear apprehension of the opposite principle—that the sensuous material of each art brings with it a special phase or quality of beauty, untranslatable into the forms of any other, an order of impressions distinct in kind—is the beginning of all true æsthetic criticism.

In writing of the school of Giorgione, Pater, unfortunately, relied upon criticism of so devastating a nature as to have reduced the painter's surviving work almost to a solitary picture—'like Sordello's one fragment of lovely verse.' Of the 'six or eight famous pictures at Dresden, Florence, and the Louvre' that had been attributed to him he says, 'It is now known that only one is certainly from Giorgione's hand,' and, 'What remains of the most vivid and stimulating of the Venetian masters, a live flame, as it seemed, in those old shadowy times, has been reduced almost to a name by his most recent critics.'

Opinions will always differ as to the pictures that can, with certainty, be assigned to Giorgione; but my own list, drawn up after having visited all the Galleries of Europe, including the Hermitage and the Prado, amounts to eleven in all, and they are—the *Trial of Moses, Judgment of Solomon,* and *Knight of Malta,* in the Uffizzi; the *Portrait of a Lady* in the Borghese Gallery; the *Sleeping Venus* at Dresden; the *Geometricians* (also known as *The Three Philosophers*) at Vienna; the picture from the Palazzo Giovanelli at Venice exhibited at Burlington House in 1930 as *The Tempest,* but which I prefer to call *The Gipsy Madonna*; the *Madonna with St Roch and St Francis* in the Prado, Madrid; a *Portrait of a Man*—perhaps Antonio Brocardo—at Budapest; the Castelfranco altar-piece, *The Virgin and Child with St Francis and St Liberale*; and *Le Fête Champêtre* in the Louvre.

Pater's false guides led him to believe that the wonderful *Concert* in the Pitti Palace, certainly painted by Titian when under the influence of Giorgione, was 'undoubtedly Giorgione's,' and to acclaim it as 'the standard of Giorgione's genuine work,' a claim that cannot now be supported; but it seems to me inconceivable that Pater should have been so misled as to accept the attribution of one of the artist's most wonderful pictures, the *Fête Champêtre,* to 'an imitator of Sebastiano del Piombo.' And yet, relying on his instinct, he wrote beautifully about it, referring to a 'favourite picture in the Louvre, the subject of a delightful sonnet by a poet whose own painted work often comes to mind as one ponders over these precious things,' Rossetti. And of it he writes: 'the presence of water—the well or marble-rimmed pool, the drawing or pouring of water, as the woman pours it from a pitcher with her jewelled hand in the *Fête Champêtre,* listening, perhaps, to the cool sound as it falls, blent with the music of the pipes—is as characteristic, and almost as suggestive, as that of music itself.'

A beautiful passage which Pater left out when he reprinted his essay on Giorgione is worth while giving here:

> Who, in some such perfect moment, when the harmony of things inward and outward beat itself out so truly and with a sense of receptivity, with entire inaction on our part, some messenger from the real soul of things must be on his way to one, has not felt the desire to perpetuate all that, just so, to suspend it in every particular circumstance, with the portrait of just that one spray of leaves lifted just so high against the sky, above the well, for ever? A desire how bewildering with the question whether there be indeed any place wherein these desirable moments take permanent refuge. Well! in the school of Giorgione you drink water, perfume, music, lie in receptive humour thus for ever, and the satisfying moment is assured.

How often have I not fallen into that mood of pure idleness and pure receptivity when in Venice under the intense heat I used to lie back in a gondola, feeling myself at every instant in harmony with its rhythm as it glided along the lagoons and then shot suddenly round corner after corner, from a narrow canal to a narrower one, without as much as grazing the prow of the gondola which meets you. So I felt in 1894, when I had the luck of seeing the great *serenata* when the late King of Italy and the present ex-Kaiser of Germany played that little Masque of Kings. The *galleggiata* with its five thousand lights, a great floating dome of crystals, started from the Rialto; the luminous house of sound floated slowly, almost imperceptibly, down the Grand Canal, a black cluster of gondolas before it and behind it. And as we floated imperceptibly down it seemed as if the palaces on each side of us were afloat too, drifting past us, to the sound of music, through a night brilliant with strange fires. And that, certainly, might well be called a night of receptivity.

### III

I have always thought that Pater's Conclusion to his book on the Renaissance is one of the most imaginative and perfect and intensely personal confessions that he ever wrote. I have never forgotten such sentences as these:

Not the fruit of experience, but experience itself, is the end. A counted number of pulses only is given to us of a variegated, dramatic life. . . . How shall we pass most swiftly from point to point, and be present always at the focus where the greatest number of vital forces unite in their purest energy? To burn always with this hard, gem-like flame, to maintain this ecstasy, is success in life.

Pater refers here to the awakening of the literary sense in Rousseau, and how

> an undefinable taint of death had always clung about him. . . . He asked himself how he might make as much as possible of the interval that remained; and he was not biased by anything in his previous life when he decided that it must be by intellectual excitement, which he found just then in the clear, fresh writings of Voltaire.

To Pater it was, in fact, 'in the terrible tragedy of Rousseau that French romanticism, with much else, begins: reading his *Confessions* we seem actually to assist at the birth of this new, strong spirit on the French mind.' And in this sordid and eloquent figure he saw his strangeness, his distortion; the *cor laceratum.* And this is he who begins his *Confessions* with the proclamation of his ego: that he desires to show to his equals a man in all the truth of nature: '*et cet homme, ce sera moi. Moi seul.*' He says also, 'I am not made like anyone else I have ever seen; yet, if I am not better, at least I am different.'

## Graham Hough (essay date 1949)

SOURCE: Hough, Graham. "Pater." In *The Last Romantics,* pp. 134-74. London: Gerald Duckworth & Co. Ltd., 1949.

[*In the following excerpt, Hough examines the controversy surrounding Pater's original conclusion to* The Renaissance. *Pondering the oblique, somewhat tentative quality of Pater's prose, Hough asserts that the indirect nature of Pater's argument actually reinforces the essay's central themes—that reality is essentially unknowable and that human existence is marked primarily by conditions of inconstancy and impermanence.*]

That Pater himself feared that his ethic might be a subversive one is evident from the fate of the conclusion to **The Renaissance.** This, which is probably the frankest and certainly the extremest version of his creed, was suppressed in the second edition, as it "might possibly mislead some of those young men into whose hands it might fall". This nervousness about presenting the findings of his own heart and his own conscience is characteristic of Pater; and it is probably responsible for the extremely compressed and elliptical form in which this short conclusion is presented. Whether Pater always realises how much he is saying is doubtful, but he is actually saying a great deal, and the wistful sigh of his sentences is apt to make us feel that they are more tenuous, more empty of content than they really are. When he worked and reworked these carefully moulded phrases, he was not concerned only with the minutiae of style, but with a prolonged and genuine development of feeling. In the case of this appendix to *The Renaissance,* we have to expand almost every paragraph by reference to pages in other essays and other books if we are to see what its real implications are; and Pater was perhaps not unwilling that his whole thought should only become apparent in this indirect and allusive way. Positivist assurance about the nature of things was deeply distasteful to him, almost as distasteful as controversy; he would rather suppress a passage than have to argue about it or defend it, and if there was one attitude he would have abhorred it was that of the overt revolutionary. He is therefore frequently guilty of that tiresome kind of reticence that consists in not following out the implications of what he says; or that even more tiresome kind that consists in giving reasons for what he says other than the fundamental ones. If therefore we want to find exactly how far he might have misled the young men, or in what direction, we must do a certain amount of piecing together of passages from different portions of his work.

When he prefaces the conclusion with a quotation from the *Cratylus,* λεγει που 'Ηράκλειτος ὅτι πάντα χωρεῖ καὶ οὐδ᾽ἐν μενει, and proceeds to discuss, in a brief couple of pages, the doctrine of the perpetual flux, we have to turn for further elucidation to the other place where he uses the same quotation, to the chapter in *Plato and Platonism* on the Doctrine of Motion. The Heraclitean πάντα ῥεῖ is fundamental to Pater's creed, and we find it appearing in one form or another throughout his writings. He does not, however, produce it as a piece of ancient wisdom; he regards the doctrine of Heraclitus as an early intuitive guess at a truth which modern philosophy and science have confirmed. He begins the conclusion to *The Renaissance* by saying "to regard all things and principles of things as inconstant modes or fashions has more and more become the tendency of modern thought". He means in the first place, it appears, scientific thought. The physical realities which we regard as actual are only the momentary combinations of forces that are perpetually at work and perpetually in motion in all nature and in all life. "That clear, perpetual outline of face and limb is but an image of ours, . . . a design in a web, the actual threads of which pass out beyond it." Pater seems quite happy

about this. He shows no nostalgia for a more stable world-picture; and he is equally content to accept the complete continuity of man with nature. There is none of the Tennysonian discomfort about the scientific view of man's place in the natural world.

He then proceeds to reduce, in the manner of the eighteenth-century empiricists, material objects to sense-impressions; then to point out that the impressions are confined within "the narrow chamber of the individual mind"; and then to destroy the substantiality of the individual mind by suggesting that it reduces itself to the contents of consciousness, that these are only momentary impressions, the only continuity being given by "a relic, more or less fleeting, of such moments gone by". There is, of course, nothing particularly "modern" about this; we appear to have reached a radical scepticism like that of Hume, and as usual in such a situation, we begin to wonder where we go from here. But Pater does not really mean it. It is difficult to see where this atomised and solipsist epistemology is leading in the realm of conduct; probably nowhere. If the self is reduced in this way to a series of momentary impressions, each containing only a fleeting relic of such moments gone by, the elementary conditions for a philosophy of value disappear. And this is not what Pater intends at all. Like other sceptics before him, Pater is forced to rebuild with different materials the edifice he has just destroyed: like Hume he is destroying our supposed intellectual certainties in order to replace them by the authority of feeling.

In fact these introductory paragraphs of the conclusion to *The Renaissance* are little more than a pseudo-philosophical preamble; by painting a picture of dissolution and fluidity they set the emotional tone for what is to follow, but intellectually their connection with it is very slight. In the first chapter of *Plato and Platonism* Pater develops the idea of the Heraclitean flux in quite a different direction, and one which corresponds much more closely with his real intentions:

> πάντα χωρεῖ, πάντα ῥεῖ—it is the burden of Hegel on the one hand, to whom nature and art and polity, aye and religion too, each in its long historic series are but so many conscious movements in the secular process of the eternal mind; and on the other hand of Darwin and Darwinism, for which "type" itself properly is not, but is only always becoming. The bold paradox of Heraclitus is, in effect, repeated on all sides, as the vital persuasion just now of a cautiously reasoned experience, and in illustration of the very law of change which it asserts, may itself presently be superseded as a commonplace.
>
> Nay, the idea of development (that, too, a thing of growth, developed in the process of reflexion) is at last invading one by one, as the secret of their explanation,

all the products of mind, the very mind itself, the abstract reason; our certainty, for instance, that two and two make four.[1]

What Pater wants to attack is not the existence of material objects apart from their being perceived, or causality, or the substantial existence of the self; or if he does want to attack these things, it is only as a mildly antidogmatic flourish. What he really wants to attack is the notion of an absolute and unchanging truth; and for this he wants to substitute a theory of development or emergence. He has in mind, vaguely enough, no doubt, some kind of evolutionism in ideas, an essentially historical way of thought which teaches "that nothing man has projected from himself is really intelligible except at its own date, and from its proper point of view in the 'secular process', the solidarity of the intellectual life with common or general history."[2] It is no use the young scholar asking himself whether Plato's opinions are or are not true in any absolute or final sense, he can only try to understand them in the setting of their own age; and as for the business of judging them, it is simply a matter of deciding what they mean to oneself in the setting of one's own age. The question of absolute truth is as irrelevant in philosophy as it is in literary criticism, where metaphysical questions are "as unprofitable as metaphysical questions elsewhere".

Braced by our bath in the eternal flux and lightened of the burden of metaphysics, we can now proceed to the next paragraph of the conclusion to *The Renaissance.* "The service of philosophy, of speculative culture, towards the human spirit, is to rouse, to startle it to a life of constant and eager observation." Philosophy cannot lead us to absolute truth, since there is no absolute truth; its pretensions in this respect are no more than moderately respectable delusions; but what it can do is to make us more aware of our immediate experience. It is not clear how philosophy does this; in the Winckelmann essay we are told that it is "by suggesting questions which help one to detect the passion, the strangeness and the dramatic contrasts of life". Pater does not elaborate the point; and in other places he frequently suggests that philosophy tends to lead us away from actual experience into a world of boojums, which are not real experience at all.

> Of course we are not naturally formed to love, or be interested in, or attracted towards, the abstract as such; to notions, we might think, carefully deprived of all the incident, the colour and variety, which fits things—this or that—to the constitution and natural habit of our minds, fits them for attachment to what we really are.[3]

### Notes

1. [*Plato and Platonism* (Library Edition, 1910)] pp. 19 and 20.

2. ibid., p. 10.

3. ibid., p. 155.

## Geoffrey Tillotson (essay date 1951)

SOURCE: Tillotson, Geoffrey. "Arnold and Pater: Critics Historical, Aesthetic, and Unlabelled." In *Criticism and the Nineteenth Century,* pp. 96-123. London: The Athlone Press, 1951.

[*In the following excerpt, Tillotson examines the numerous contradictions in Pater's* The Renaissance. *Although Tillotson concludes that the book fails as art criticism, he is impressed by Pater's insistence on interpreting a painting through a careful study of its concrete elements rather than attempting to decipher it in terms of theoretical abstractions. To Tillotson this attitude reflects a deliberate effort to transform the role of the critic from a passive stance to an active one by stressing the inherent strength and power of emotional responses to works of art.*]

### II

Walter Pater followed Arnold in honouring 'the object as in itself it really is'.

He quoted the phrase in the preface to the book we have come to call *The Renaissance,* his first book, and that which had more effect on his contemporaries than any later book of his:

> 'To see the object as in itself it really is', has been justly said to be the aim of all true criticism whatever. . . .[1]

And the sentence proceeds to include in the category of 'all true criticism whatever'—is it a wide or a narrow category?—that sort of criticism of which Pater himself, to take him at his word, was a practitioner: the category of 'aesthetic' criticism.

We might well have expected from Peter a preference for the object as it *was.* Since 1877 when his book attained its second edition, it has borne the title *The Renaissance: Studies in Art and Literature,* but when first published in 1873 its title promised more of the historical: *Studies in the History of the Renaissance.* Pater, then, began by offering himself as an historian, and several passages in the works repeat the offer. Moreover, in the course of the first essay in his book, **'Aucassin and Nicolette'**[2] he produced the following:

> To say of an ancient literary composition that it has an antiquarian interest, often means that it has not distinct æsthetic interest for the reader of to-day. Antiquarian-

ism, by a purely historical effort, by putting its object in perspective and setting the reader in a certain point of view from which what gave pleasure to the past is pleasurable for him also, may often add greatly to the charm we receive from ancient literature. But the first condition of such aid must be a real, direct, æsthetic charm in the thing itself; unless it has that charm, unless some purely artistic quality went to its original making, no merely antiquarian effort can ever give it an æsthetic value or make it a proper object of æsthetic criticism. These qualities, when they exist, it is always pleasant to define, and discriminate from the sort of borrowed interest which an old play, or an old story, may very likely acquire through a true antiquarianism.[3]

Here Pater offered a certain encouragement to the historian. Provided the historian chose his object well, he could 'add greatly to the charm we receive from ancient literature.' He could not create 'charm' where none of that 'one thing needful' seemed to exist already, but where it did, he could add more. There is no reason to quarrel with this. Pater was speaking as Arnold was to,[4] of the critic, not of the historian, and no critic, however well versed in history, is going to work on an object that looks unpromising when there exist so many that, before he begins, look 'charming' and that promise to prove so more and more as he comes to see them as belonging more intimately to their time. Here there was encouragement to the historian. And elsewhere. For instance,

> every intellectual product must be judged from the point of view of the age and the people in which it was produced.[5]

Or this smile at the 'scholars of the fifteenth century':

> They lacked the very rudiments of the historic sense, which by an imaginative act throws itself back into a world unlike one's own, and judges each intellectual product in connection with the age which produced it.[6]

All such remarks were encouraging to the scholar-critic. But, alas, they lacked the support of Pater's practice. In the paragraph immediately following the last quotation Pater twice used the word 'strange' and twice the word 'quaint', words, that is, which no one uses who has made an effort to throw himself back into a former age. One recalls the opening of Kittredge's book on Chaucer with its good-humoured pillorying of 'quaint' and other terms of patronage and antipathy.[7] In practice, more often than not, the past is served up by Pater as if it were the present. Far from going back to the Renaissance through the crooked corridors of time, he preferred to see it as it had wound its way through them into his beloved present.

### III

Take his remarks on pictures. Pater liked pictures not as they were left by the artist, but as they had survived.

He liked them, that is, 'embrowned'. His taste, therefore, defeated what we can go so far as to call his adequate knowledge of the facts.

The only source of the embrownment of Renaissance pictures is varnish and the changes worked on it by time. To begin with, no doubt, varnish was applied as we apply it to modern pictures, as a preservative that is seen as both necessary and defiling. But at some time we conveniently think of as the eighteenth century, it was applied for its own sake, as an enrichment, and applied generously as basting to a duck. In other words, it was applied by some painters to their new pictures, and by dealers and by owners to old pictures. By the eighteenth century, varnish had become a prime pigment. And the poets promoted it to a grade still higher. They saw the autumnal effect it had on paintings as an effect unconnected with chemicals and the hand of man, as an effect that time had produced unaided on the picture as the painter left it. This is what Dryden told Kneller to expect from a beneficent future:

> More cannot be by Mortal Art exprest;
> But venerable Age shall add the rest.
> For Time shall with his ready Pencil stand;
> Retouch your Figures with his ripening Hand,
> Mellow your Colours, and imbrown the Teint,
> Add every Grace, which Time alone can grant;
> To future Ages shall your Fame convey;
> And give more Beauties, than he takes away.[8]

As well as from the varnish pot, embrownment came to be asked of the palette. Even so late as the close of the eighteenth century, Sir George Beaumont was busy advising Constable to give his landscapes the glow of 'an old Cremona fiddle'.[9] In 1873, Pater was still admiring the fictions of varnish. It does not seem to have crossed his mind that his love for the 'minor tones'[10] of Renaissance pictures was a love for the tricks of dealers who were administering to a particular taste active well after the close of the period the 'history' of which he was making his 'study'. If it had, he might have been more eager to seek the object of the historian, the object as it *was* at first. If not, he could only have stuck to his love for the minor tones of Renaissance pictures as a man sticks to a woman who has deceived him, that is cynically and with what strong-minded pleasures come from the complexities of lost innocence. Certainly, Pater loved complexities. Even though he did not know about varnish, he contrived as much complexity as he could for the aesthetic benefit of his Renaissance pictures. For though ignorant of the last and sobering deception, he knew that time had worked changes. And he made the most of them—when he cared to, and for his particular purposes. He saw to it that he had enough knowledge to flirt with.

The embrownment of Time and his 'pencil'—Dryden's words are wise to both sources of change—was hugged by Dryden as a warmth. Pater, in one sentence and part of a footnote, felt it as a chill. Or so he said. At the beginning of his meditation on the Mona Lisa he remarked that

> Perhaps of all ancient pictures time has chilled it least.[11]

Apart from 'perhaps' (which is no great fault, if we consider the difficulty of certitude in the matter) that sentence is worthy of the historian Pater had given himself out to be. 'Ancient' and 'time' show him taking the first step necessary for the historian, the step backwards; while 'chilled' shows him going still further and acknowledging time's changes; and further still, and acknowledging that the changes time works on a material object are changes to be deplored—acknowledging it apparently as a move towards remedying the damage by an exercise of the historical imagination. And there is another touch of the historical imagination in the footnote to this same sentence. Pater added the footnote at some point during the preparation of his manuscript—it is there in the article as first published, in the *Fortnightly Review*:[12]

> Yet for Vasari there was some further magic of crimson in the lips and cheeks, lost for us.[13]

I find this note disingenuous. Pater speaks as if he would like to have seen what Vasari saw. But if that crimson had survived till his day, what would have become of the minor tones of his description? Would the Mona Lisa have kept as much fallen day about her, would the eyelids have had the same weariness, if the cheeks had retained the merriness of those of Hogarth's Shrimp Girl? 'Perhaps of all ancient pictures time has chilled it least.' But time had chilled it enough, fortunately for Pater, to allow him to write a poem on *la femme fatale,* as it also had chilled the roses of Botticelli's Birth of Venus to the exquisite point at which Pater could describe them as 'embrowned a little, as Botticelli's flowers always are'.[14] He banished from the body of his paragraph the crimson he knew of as the original, the Renaissance, colour. It was not, however, banished from his book. It was made to peep up into the minor tones which, if Pater had been an historian, it would have been made to banish as the usurpers they were. Pater knew history, that is, for his own ambiguous ends.

Pater quoted Vasari and made some use of him. Vasari's account of the picture takes us as near as we can get to knowing how Leonardo's picture was first received. Vasari considered it a most remarkable instance of a painter's fidelity to the appearance of a certain beautiful woman, whom he himself knew, or whom he knew by repute, and as a picture affording an intellectual satisfaction—the satisfaction of confirming the Aristotelian account of art as *mimesis*. And when Vasari did use his imagination, it was merely to imagine that the painting was real flesh with the pulse of blood in it:

> This head is an extraordinary example of how art can imitate Nature, because here we have all the details painted with great subtlety. The eyes possess that moist lustre which is constantly seen in life, and about them are those livid reds and hair which cannot be rendered without the utmost delicacy. The lids could not be more natural, for the way in which the hairs issue from the skin, here thick and there scanty, and following the pores of the skin. The nose possesses the fine delicate reddish apertures seen in life. The opening of the mouth, with its red ends, and the scarlet cheeks seem not colour but living flesh. To look closely at her throat you might imagine that the pulse was beating.[15]

No doubt this account, even at the time, was an inadequate one. Even from the start any observer must have been taken by the picture as a record of character and personality. But here was a contemporary criticism, and one would have expected a *soi-disant* historian to have schooled himself to approach his picture in accordance with its principles: Browning, one recalls, knew better: for the nonce he made himself a Vasari:

> That's my last Duchess painted on the wall,
> Looking as if she were alive. I call
> That piece a wonder, now. . . .

Vasari's criticism of the Mona Lisa amounted to the means of unvarnishing it. Pater saw that this was so, but through eyes deliberately kept half shut. In his own account all things needful for a right historical judgment existed: he knew that the Mona Lisa was old and that it had changed. All things needful existed, but to be perverted. Pater confused them all together in the interests of an ambiguous material lying halfway between history and the last exciting moment of the present. Speaking of his morality, Henry James was to say that he hunted with the hounds and ran with the hare.[16] The same was true of his historical criticism.

Pater, then, was not much more of an historian than Arnold was. We read him as we read Arnold, for his own sake rather than for the sake of understanding his object. Take away the object and there remain all the splendours of Pater. He is, for instance, a writer making constant use of similes. The major term to which they are tied may have been wrongly conceived, but the life in the minor term is unforgettable:

> The white light on [the face of the Botticelli's Madonnas] is cast up hard and cheerless from below, as when snow lies upon the ground, and the children look up with surprise at the strange whiteness of the ceiling.[17]

The same life is in his metaphors. His imagery usually leaves art for external nature. In that field time has had nothing to say—or rather, nothing to say to poets. And so nothing to say to Pater. Men, and what they have made, confuse him, but his eye for what comes issued from the hand of nature, as it is nature external to man, is a clear one. He is, therefore, more a painter-like poet than a critic. His claim to be an historian is mainly that time has thrust history upon him, as on any writer. His account of the Mona Lisa witnesses not so much to Leonardo as to the nineteenth-century idea of the fatal woman, and to the thorough poeticising of works of art which Gautier seems to have been the first to practise, and, falling between him and Pater, Swinburne.[18]

IV

Pater quoted Arnold's phrase, but he did not apply it to aesthetic criticism without stating it with a difference:

> in æsthetic criticism the first step towards seeing one's object as it really is, is to know one's own impression as it really is, to discriminate it, to realise it distinctly.

The difference lay in that epistemological term 'impression'. It had not occurred to Arnold to use the term. As a critic, if not always as a poet, Arnold's business was with the world of every-day. And so with the common reader. 'The great art of criticism', he said on one occasion, 'is to get oneself out of the way and to let humanity decide'.[19] The words came oddly from one who was always fighting his fellows, but not oddly in that to fight them was to honour them as worth fighting. In a later essay, that excellent piece introducing his edition of six of *The Lives of the Poets,* Arnold paid delighted homage to Johnson, to whose criticism he found himself coming back repeatedly as to a *point de repère.* There is nothing surprising in this homage. Johnson was a critic who could say 'I rejoice to concur with the common reader.'[20] If on occasions he could not get himself out of the way and let humanity decide, the occasions, important as some of them were, were exceptions. Usually Johnson stood with the common reader, whom he defined as using 'common sense' (i.e., drawing on the sense he shared with his fellows), as being 'uncorrupted with literary prejudices' and as holding opinions which remained firm 'after all the refinements of subtlety and the dogmatism of learning.'[21] This was a good description of Johnson himself. And a fair one of Arnold. When Arnold spoke of the object as in itself it really is he meant the object as it is seen by the common reader, who by definition has no more party and sectarian prejudice than he has refinements and dogmatism. In the eighteenth century, the number of such readers was as high as it ever was, and in the nineteenth century—such were the intellectual, political, religious divisions of the time—as low. Nevertheless, the count of common readers was only low comparatively. In standing among them, Arnold had a cheering sense of numbers. Like Johnson, he expressed his own distrust of the 'personal' estimate. I have quoted his dismissal of the 'historic estimate', and on the heels of that follows his dismissal of the 'personal':

> a poet or a poem may count to us on grounds personal to ourselves. Our personal affinities, likings, and circumstances, have great power to sway our estimate of this or that poet's work, and to make us attach more importance to it as poetry than in itself it really possesses, because to us it is, or has been, of high importance. Here also we over-rate the object of our interest, and apply to it a language of praise which is quite exaggerated.[22]

In preferring what he called the 'real estimate', he was preferring the estimate of the common reader who, again by definition, knows nothing of the associations which, falling to a single reader, fall to one who is uncommon. Arnold's dismissal of the personal estimate was his dismissal—perhaps a conscious one—of the theories of Pater.

Pater's use of the word 'impression' indicated that, for his part, he was moving away from Arnold and the common reader. That, at bottom, is why he invoked epistemology. By profession he was a purveyor of philosophy: his book on Plato was a printed version of lectures given at Oxford. And he was interested in philosophy more generally than a profession always guarantees: witness the use made of it in *Marius* and in his essay on Coleridge. Not that he needed these credentials—those epistemological matters were by that time common knowledge. In choosing to speak of impression along with object he was appealing to Locke and the rest. And as Locke did he thought of impression and object as both being real. For Locke the object existed to be known, and so on several occasions for Pater. It was in this domain of external fact that Pater saw the scientist as employed—the artist and writer of literature being employed in another domain, their 'sense of fact'.[23] For Pater this domain of fact had even a vigorous life of its own: even colour—that favourite quality of things for Pater—has such a life:

> the more you come to understand what imaginative colouring really is, that all colour is no mere delightful quality of natural things, but a spirit upon them by which they become expressive to the spirit, the better you will like this peculiar quality of colour [in Botticelli's 'Venus rising from the sea'].[24]

The external world, then, had its own existence, and for their knowledge of that existence men were indebted in the first place to their senses. Pater remembered the 'impression' that Locke and other psychologists had spoken of, and added it to the 'object' spoken of by Arnold. He would have forgotten epistemology as completely as Arnold had done unless it had suited his purpose to remember it. He sought the impression because, if one chose to insist, no one could deny that it existed in a private sanctum. When Locke spoke of impressions he was not concerned with the privacy of one man's as against another's. He was, like any philosopher, generalising; he was trying to show how all human beings enter into their knowledge. Pater, on the other hand, was insisting on the uniqueness of the impressions to every individual man. He spoke not of impressions but of 'one's own impressions'. And in the same paragraph of the Preface to **The Renaissance** from which I have been quoting, he even allowed himself one of his rare italics in asking

> What is this song or picture, this engaging personality presented in life or in a book, to *me*? What effect does it really produce on me? Does it give me pleasure? and if so, what sort or degree of pleasure?[25]

And further, he went on to invoke a concept invoked only by those who see mankind as divided up, the concept of 'temperament': he concluded his brief argument with

> What is important, then, is . . . that the critic should possess . . . a certain kind of temperament.

Pater could rest content now that impression and temperament were enthroned.

The word 'temperament' indicated how far and how quickly Pater had left Arnold behind. Arnold's phrase 'the object as in itself it really is' was for rescuing the object from the clutches of the individual. Pater was for clutching it closer. Arnold had sought to disencumber the object of any 'individual fancy', but here was Pater exalting temperament, the very hive of such fancies; we cannot see him trying to get himself out of the way and let humanity decide. For Arnold the object lay in the external world sharply clear for anybody who had not blinded himself with some insular or provincial zeal or other. For Pater the object as it really is lay in the privacy of the individual impression of it. Obviously, the way to see an object more for what it is in itself is not to centre attention in the impression it makes so much as to go on collecting impressions of it till they cease to show enough new differences to make further collection worth while. Then you may feel satisfied that you are being fair to the object, as fair as in you lies. But it seems that Pater had little interest in this sort of fairness. We can see him as one who got an impression quickly enough to get it more as he wanted it, to get it while it was still fluid enough to be workable and trans-

formable. He wished it to be Paterine as much as possible, more Paterine than objective. We are left wondering why he quoted Arnold's phrase at all. And the explanation may well be more to his credit as a man than as a critic—he liked Arnold's criticism and liked it too indiscriminately, and liked also to show his liking.

We can see how disproportionate was the contribution that Pater's encouraged temperament made to his criticism if we contrast Ruskin's way of describing a picture with Pater's. Here is Ruskin's description of Botticelli's 'Crowning of the Madonna':

> [The Madonna] is surrounded by a choir of twelve angels, not dancing, nor flying, but carried literally in a whorl, or vortex, whirlwind of the breath of heaven; their wings lie level, interwoven among the clouds, pale sky of intense light, yet darker than the white clouds they pass through, their arms stretched to each other, their hands clasped—it is as if the morning sky had all been changed into marble, and they into living creatures; they are led in their swift wheel by Gabriel, who is opposite to you, between the Christ and the Madonna; a close rain of golden rays falls from the hand of Christ, He placing the crown on the Virgin's head; and Gabriel is seen through it as a white bird through rain, looking up, seeing the fulfilment of his message.[26]

As well as to indicate his own evaluation of the object, Ruskin intended his description to serve as a second-best for those who lacked opportunity to see the object itself: and his editors in 1906 noted how much more satisfactory is his description even than the excellent photographic reproduction which by that date they had by them. Ruskin's description is humbly tendering us the means of seeing an object as in itself it really is. Ruskin suppressed his own rich originality—his originality, that is, at the degree at which the originality of anybody becomes noticeable—in the interests of our seeing the picture for what it really is.

There was still another limitation recommended by Pater. Not a limitation, however, taking him further into himself, but one operating on the object. The impression fondled by the temperament was to be an impression of an object that was beautiful. The 'certain kind of temperament' recommended for the critic was 'the power of being deeply moved by the presence of beautiful objects', and it took some authority from 'the words of a recent critic of Sainte-Beuve'[27]:

> De se borner à connaître de près les belles choses, et à s'en nourrir en exquis amateurs, en humanistes accomplis.[28]

Pater's sanctum might be a private one but it was not without its window. And of necessity. Only through an inlet would the objects get at Pater to produce their impressions on him. Pater had perforce to be accessible. But if so, only to beautiful things.

The thing was as important to Pater as its beautifulness. He could not breathe among abstractions. For all his interest in philosophy he distrusted everything except the concrete. So to some extent did Arnold who, on one occasion, even went so far as to recommend that poetry should be tested touchstone-wise by means of supreme single lines. As the opening paragraph of his Preface to **The Renaissance,** Pater placed this persuasive argument against abstraction:

> Many attempts have been made by writers on art and poetry to define beauty in the abstract, to express it in the most general terms, to find a universal formula for it. The value of such attempts has most often been in the suggestive and penetrating things said by the way. Such discussions help us very little to enjoy what has been well done in art or poetry, to discriminate between what is more and what is less excellent in them, or to use words like beauty, excellence, art, poetry, with more meaning than they would otherwise have. Beauty, like all other qualities presented to human experience, is relative; and the definition of it becomes unmeaning and useless in proportion to its abstractness. To define beauty not in the most abstract, but in the most concrete terms possible, not to find a universal formula for it, but the formula which expresses most adequately this or that special manifestation of it, is the aim of the true student of æsthetics.[29]

Many years later he was to ask:

> Who would change the colour or curve of a rose-leaf for that οὐσία ἀχρώματος, ἀσχημάτιστος, ἀναφής— that colourless, formless, intangible, being—Plato put so high?[30]

And though 'beauty' remained one of Pater's favourite words, it was often given some sort of a footing in the concrete when he provided it with 'this or that special manifestation' in his favourite adjectives: *blithe, delicate, strange, comely, fresh, sweet, quaint, grave,* and so on.

## VI

When once Pater had withdrawn into the private sanctum of the impression and the temperament, a sanctum giving on to beautiful objects, he was no less busy than Arnold. He differed, therefore, from the 'aesthete' as he, or it, is conceived by the popular imagination. This, a century earlier, had been Burke's account of how men are affected in body and mind when beholding a thing sufficiently beautiful:

> When we have before us such objects as excite love [i.e., 'love in the mind'] and complacency; the body is affected, so far as I could observe, much in the following manner: the head reclines something on one side; the eye-lids are more closed than usual, and the eyes roll gently with an inclination to the object; the mouth is a little opened, and the breath drawn slowly, with now and then a low sigh; the whole body is composed, and the hands fall idly to the sides. All this is accompanied with an inward sense of melting and languor. These appearances are always proportioned to the degree of beauty in the object, and of sensibility in the observer. And this gradation from the highest pitch of beauty and sensibility even to the lowest of mediocrity and indifference, and their correspondent effects, ought to be kept in view, else this description will seem exaggerated, which it certainly is not . . . a relaxation somewhat below the natural tone seems to me to be the cause of all positive pleasure.[31]

And, in mockery of Pater's 'Conclusion', there soon came Mr. Rose in Mallock's *New Republic*:

> '. . . the aim of culture . . . is indeed to make the soul a musical instrument, which may yield music either to itself or to others, at any appulse from without; and the more elaborate a man's culture is, the richer and more composite can this music be. The minds of some men are like a simple pastoral reed. Only single [*sic*] melodies, and these unaccompanied, can be played upon them—glad or sad; whilst the minds of others, who look at things from countless points of view, and realise, as Shakespeare did, their composite nature—their minds become, as Shakespeare's was, like a great orchestra. Or sometimes', said Mr. Rose dreamily, as if his talk was lapsing into a soliloquy, 'when he is a mere passive observer of things, letting impressions from without move him as they will, I would compare a man of culture to an Æolian harp, which the winds at will play through . . . wandering in like a breath of air amongst the chords of his soul, touching note [*sic*] after note into soft music, and at last gently dying away into silence'

—a reverie which is broken into, 'in a very matter-of-fact tone,' by one of the company who

> saw that Mr. Rose's dreamy manner always tended to confuse Lady Ambrose.[32]

But though Pater's aesthetic critic might look supremely and even morbidly idle, incapacitated, decadent, Pater saw him as intensely occupied. The imagery in which Pater described him is kinetic.

An interest in power was strong during the nineteenth century, and in claiming power for his temperament Pater stood among the many disciples of Wordsworth.[33] In the 'Essay, Supplementary to the Preface [of 1815]', Wordsworth thundered against those who gave the word 'taste' (when used in the sense of a refined liking for the arts) a denotation that was passive:

> It is a metaphor, taken from a *passive* sense of the human body, and transferred to things which are in their essence *not* passive,—to intellectual *acts* and *operations.*

And he concluded:

> without the exertion of a co-operating *power* in the mind of the Reader, there can be no adequate sympathy with [great poetry].[34]

In his turn, therefore, Pater came to unite passive and active in that remarkable phrase, the 'power of being deeply moved'. He also described the aesthetic critic as one

> who experiences these impressions *strongly,* and *drives directly at* the discrimination of them.[35]

This is the sort of masculine temperament that overtook the tender impression. And when for one moment Pater represented the mind as harbouring an impression passively, the impression being the active force—'How is my nature modified by its presence, and under its influence?'—on that occasion, instead of thinking of Mr. Rose, we retort with 'Yes, but how is its nature modified by yours?' For Pater's power of modifying impressions was a power like that of lust.

## VII

It was perhaps because there was all this power available that the critic who proclaimed his limitation to the impression of objects that are beautiful made so many predatory raids on objects whose prime quality is not aesthetic. If Pater did not insist that 'beauty is truth', he was inclined to insist that truth—or goodness or wisdom or thinking—is beauty. In his Preface he listed the following as objects giving pleasure to the aesthetic critic:

> the picture, the landscape, the engaging personality in life or in a book, La Gioconda, the hills of Carrara, Pico of Mirandula, are valuable for their virtues,[36] as we say in speaking of a herb, a wine, a gem; for the property each has of affecting one with a special, unique impression of pleasure.[37]

The predatory instincts of the aesthetic critic were to be made clearer still in a hoveringly daring sentence given to Mr. Rose:

> To the eye of true taste, an Aquinas in his cell before a crucifix, or a Narcissus gazing at himself in a still fountain, are—in their own ways, you know—equally beautiful.[38]

On several other occasions Mallock quietly copied Pater's way of listing incompatibles as if they were all on the same footing. One such list I reserved on transcribing the dreamy disquisition of Mr. Rose:

> a beautiful face, a rainbow, a ruined temple, a death-bed, or a line of poetry.

As satiric method it is consummate. By doing nothing more than make a list such as Pater himself might have made Mallock makes Pater's lists look silly: the only difference is that Mallock's list is compiled with the tongue in the cheek.

The attempt to absorb other categories into the aesthetic was one that Pater vividly encouraged rather than originated. In the nineteenth century attempts were often made to absorb the beautiful into whatever category was preferred. What remained constant throughout the rearrangements was the beautiful, whether absorbed or absorbing. Wordsworth had made it the victim of an absorption effected by a sort of pagan religiosity: as a human being he had been prompted to thoughts too deep for tears by a flower, by 'the meanest flower that blows'. On the other hand Keats pulled the beautiful near to man—to man who had no religion except a love of beauty—as if it were a fur coat. He showed no decided sense of the difference between a warmth supplied him by a flower (not the meanest) and that supplied him by a human being:

> . . . when the melancholy fit shall fall . . .
> Then glut thy sorrow on a morning rose,
>   Or on the rainbow of the salt sand-wave,
>   Or on the wealth of globed peonies;
> Or if thy mistress some rich anger shows,
>   Emprison her soft hand, and let her rave,
>   And feed deep, deep upon her peerless eyes.[39]

I used the word 'man' in my description of Keats. But the term was too generous: the figures of the last three lines are dolls: 'Among the objects', commented Bridges, 'on which a sensitive mind is recommended to indulge its melancholy fit, the anger of his mistress is enumerated with roses, peonies, and rainbows, as a beautiful phenomenon plainly without respect to its cause, meaning or effect.'[40] Keats's list of incompatibles was seized on and made into a formula. Then there was the famous list drawn up by one of Browning's bishops, a list which scarcely had an ecclesiastical authority:

> how can we guard our unbelief,
> Make it bear fruit to us?—the problem here.
> Just when we are safest, there's a sunset-touch,
> A fancy from a flower-bell, some one's death,
> A chorus-ending from Euripides—
> And that's enough for fifty hopes and fears. . . .[41]

Here the objects of painter, poet, ordinary man, scholar are all merged as equally prompting religious enquiry. And it was from this list that Mallock took his most shockingly incongruous item. Repeated criticism of these pleasant confusions came from Newman. He pilloried a string of them in the Appendix to his *Discourses on the Scope and Nature of University Education*—the work which we now read as it ended its textual history in *The Idea of a University*.[42] In that Appendix Newman illustrated various points in his lectures by widely ranging quotations. Among them is one from a translated volume of Tieck which shows the hero beside himself with erotic ecstasy while participating in the devotions of his mistress:

> It seemed to him as if, from the wounds of longing, his existence was bleeding away in ardent prayers. Every word of the priest thrilled through him; every tone of the music gushed devotion into his bosom; his lips quivered, as the fair one pressed the Crucifix of her rosary to her rosy mouth.

And so on. Newman turns from his transcript with the comment:

> Which is the object of worship here—the true Incarnate Lord, or the dust and ashes?[43]

Pater's confusions were subtler and more fastidious than this German carnival, but confusion no less. Under the thickest bank of garden flowers Mallock's arm was long enough to find the serpent. Nor was Henry James more merciful. Mallock had substituted a clear moral line for a blur, but had left undisturbed the high level on the social and intellectual scale: his story takes place among notables in an English country house; he made the confusion look comic but kept it fashionable and English. Henry James, ignoring the moral ambiguity, enlarged the discredit by exhibiting an early convert, one of 'the children of this world'[44], in the person of his Mrs. Church. This American lady, travelling Europe, had found in the 'Conclusion' of *The Renaissance* (and in Arnold's boosting of 'the best') a gospel delightfully easy to follow:

> . . . Mrs. Church was as gracious as I could have desired; she put her marker into her book, and folded her plump little hands on the cover . . . she embarked . . . upon those general considerations in which her refined intellect was so much at home.

> 'Always at your studies, Mrs. Church', I ventured to observe.

> 'Que voulez-vous? . . . Do you know my secret?' she asked, with an air of brightening confidence. And she paused a moment before she imparted her secret—'To care only for the *best*! To do the best, to know the best—to have, to desire, to recognise, only the best. That's what I have always done, in my quiet little way. I have gone through Europe on my devoted little errand, seeking, seeing, heeding, only the best. . . . That's the real secret—to get something everywhere. . . . Sometimes it has been a little music, sometimes a little deeper insight into the history of art; every little counts you know. Sometimes it has been just

a glimpse, a view, a lovely landscape, an impression. We have always been on the look-out. Sometimes it has been a valued friendship, a delightful social tie.[45]

### VIII

An 'Appreciation' by Pater was sometimes another name for an attempt to claim territory for the aesthetic critic which belongs rightfully, or belongs in the first place, to literary criticism in general. On this head Pater's worst offence, so far as English literature goes, was the Appreciation entitled **'Wordsworth.'** That Appreciation begins by announcing a concern with 'the true aesthetic value' of Wordsworth's poetry. Any one, however, who brings such a concern to Wordsworth's poetry is doomed to an early disappointment or to an early conversion; if he continues in his reading it will be to discover other things. Wordsworth was not Keats. His sense of beauty was merely a minor function, cowed by his sense of the sublime. His poetry concerned things which, even if they are beautiful, are valued first of all because they interest, interpret, console or ennoble mankind; or if not always mankind, Wordsworth. The Wordsworth that Pater built up is not the Wordsworth as (in his life and works) he really was in his own time, was in Pater's, or is in ours. He is made out as too exquisite, too tremulously sensitive, too freely passionate. Pater spoke of his 'life of much quiet delicacy', and described his imagery also as 'delicate'. Then the fellowship Wordsworth discovered between man and such a thing as a lichened stone is called 'weird', many of his effects called 'strange', and the 'mysticism' of 'Daffodils' and 'Two April Mornings' 'half playful'. These qualities of delicacy, weirdness, strangeness, are not cardinal qualities of Wordsworth's poetry, even if they exist there at all. And Pater found them because he was looking for beauty. It may be noted that the Wordsworth presented here and there in the Appreciation of Coleridge is much truer both as to life and as to poems: e.g., Pater forgot himself enough to perceive Wordsworth's 'fine mountain atmosphere of mind'.[46] Truer also is the Wordsworth occupying a page of the Preface to *The Renaissance.* The Wordsworth of the Appreciation bearing his name is a scented Wordsworth. In making him an aesthete, Pater was as far astray as when he compared 'Resolution and Independence' with 'The Eve of St. Agnes' in respect of 'fullness of imagery'.[47] And he was far astray because he was near home: he applied to Wordsworth the epithets denoting the qualities that delighted himself, and that delighted himself in things that were beautiful. His Wordsworth was too much like Pater. He strikes one as a mixture of Gissing's Henry Ryecroft and Mr. Walter de la Mare. Here the temperament got the better of the object. After perverting it into the beautiful, it annexed it.

## IX

Pater, then, extended the bounds of the aesthetic critic illegitimately. But to transgress a bad law is to obey a better one. And the beneficent result of the transgression was that in practice Pater's limitation of his object was not so drastic as he had advertised. And sometimes there was a cleaner emancipation. Sometimes Pater took over objects not mainly, or in the first place, beautiful, and did not degrade them by ignoring all but their beauty. On these occasions he went out into the object, shedding his aesthetics as he went. When he forgot that the aesthetic bounds existed, his criticism was not aesthetic criticism at all, except as any and every sort of criticism is so. Pater rightly saw that beauty was a constant in literature—classical literature exhibiting beauty with order, and romantic literature beauty with strangeness.[48] But this beauty, as Pater also saw, was not invariably fierce and claimant. It was often merely beautiful to the pitch of providing the pleasure that readers had always asked of literature—a pleasure that is usually a mild one. Every critic is aware of the need for literature to provide this degree of beauty, however vague his awareness of it, and whatever other qualities he attends to mainly or in the first place. Pater, therefore, is sometimes no more an aesthetic critic than other critics are.

To some extent, Pater's confusions may have been due to the uncertain meaning of the very term he paraded on his banner. The term 'aesthetic' has been a hard one to pin down to one meaning—witness its history as given in the *Oxford English Dictionary*. Not concerned with its use by the epistemologists, Pater considered it as pertaining to 'taste'. Even so he did not limit its application to the beautiful objects on which 'taste' is properly exercised—that is, to aspects of external nature and to the 'fine' arts. He allowed it to stray into literature. And to leave plains and mountains, pictures and music, for literature is to leave objects in which beauty may be allowed on occasions and for most men to be supreme for objects in which beauty is almost always submerged or outfaced by admixture with the human, and so with the moral, social, political and what not. Literature deals with man, and though it is beautiful, beauty is seldom its prime characteristic.

Pater had the good sense to see this, if not always squarely. From the start his objects included man. When he represented the aesthetic critic as asking 'Does [this object] give me pleasure?' he included among the possible givers of that pleasure objects other than objects of 'taste'. 'The objects with which aesthetic criticism deals' were made to include from the start, 'artistic and accomplished forms of human life', and 'engaging personalit[ies] presented in life or in a book'—those as well as 'music', 'poetry', 'song' and 'picture'. Of course he claimed all these things and persons as aesthetic. But his interest did not stop at the aesthetic when as always his human objects had other claims on him. When he spoke of men 'artistic', 'accomplished' and 'engaging', he was not so much limiting the interest these objects provided *qua* men, as ruling out certain sorts of men altogether—we cannot see him writing on the Borgias, Machiavelli or Henry VIII. When he put certain Renaissance figures in 'the *House Beautiful*', they included 'saints' as well as the painters of certain beautiful pictures. In the second edition of **The Renaissance,** among other passages, this was added:

> For in the *House Beautiful* the saints too have their place; and the student of the Renaissance has this advantage over the student of the emancipation of the human mind in the Reformation, or the French Revolution, that, in tracing the footsteps of humanity to higher levels, he is not beset at every turn by the inflexibilities and antagonisms of some well-recognised controversy, with rigidly defined opposites, exhausting the intelligence and limiting one's sympathies. That opposition of the professional defenders of a mere system to the more sincere and generous play of the forces of human mind and character, which I noted as the secret of Abelard's struggle, is indeed always powerful. But the incompatibility of souls really 'fair' is not essential; and within the enchanted region of the Renaissance, one needs not be for ever on one's guard; here there are no fixed parties, no exclusions; all breathes of that unity of culture in which whatsoever things are comely are reconciled, for the elevation and adornment of our spirits. And just in proportion as those who took part in the Renaissance become centrally representative of it, just so much the more is this condition realised in them. The wicked popes, and the loveless tyrants, who from time to time become its patrons, or mere speculators in its fortunes, lend themselves easily to disputations, and, from this side or that, the spirit of controversy lays just hands on them. But the painter of the *Last Supper,* with his kindred, live in a land where controversy has no breathing-place, and refuse to be classified.[49]

Though Pater excluded from consideration certain sorts of men, he did not exclude men. And though he might often speak of such human matters as 'self-restraint', 'austerity', and 'human feeling'[50] as if they were flowers, he did not always do so. His total response was other than the aesthetic, and being other was deeper—deeper, that is, as depth is measured by mankind as a whole. Some of the works he singled out for aesthetic criticism were works that had little to offer such criticism. In so far as English literature went, they included Shakespeare's histories (which though they have no wicked popes, have loveless tyrants in plenty and in addition have Falstaff, Doll Tearsheet and Pistol) and *Measure for Measure* (a play which is squarely based on the matter and morals of sexual relationships); and he wrote on Sir Thomas Browne who wrote on vulgar errors. As Pater well knew, a critic cannot live by cake alone. And the non-aesthetic exists so plentifully in Pater's objects that we should be ready to overlook his self-elected title, and read his writings as unlabelled criticism, taking whatever they give. It was seldom that he allowed his title to restrict him. In his essay on Botticelli, he threw it over and spoke of himself as providing 'general criticism', and what was more, general criticism on 'a secondary painter'. And towards the end of his essay on Winckelmann, there was an unaesthetic blast that might have come straight from Arnold:

> The aim of a right criticism is to place Winckelmann in an intellectual perspective, of which Goethe is the foreground. For, after all, he is infinitely less than Goethe; it is chiefly because at certain points he comes in contact with Goethe that criticism entertains consideration of him.[51]

Here aesthetic criticism was conveniently forgotten in a larger if less manageable interest. In that late essay on style he was to write that

> the chief stimulus of good style is to possess a full, rich, complex matter to grapple with.[52]

Here was the kinetic imagery which Pater first enlisted for the aesthetic critic, but serving now other ends. Even from the start, however, Pater had had the good sense not to deny himself his share of interest in those ends. And to call those ends aesthetic would be to slight them.

## Notes

1. *Studies in the History of the Renaissance,* 1873, p. viii. All further quotations from this book are taken from this edition and, unless otherwise stated, from this page.

2. In the second edition, 1877, this essay was expanded into 'Two Early French Stories'.

3. *The Renaissance,* pp. 9 f.

4. Arnold's dismissal of the 'historic estimate' came eight years later.

5. *The Renaissance,* p. 22.

6. Ibid.

7. 'There is no great harm in the air of patronage with which our times, in their self-satisfied enlightenment, address the great who were of old; but we do use droll adjectives! If these great ancients show the simplicity of perfect art, we call them *naïf,* particularly when their irony eludes us; if they tickle our fancy, they are *quaint*; if we find them altogether satisfactory, both in form and sub-

stance, we adorn them with the epithet *modern,* which we somehow think is a superlative of eminence. . . .' (*Chaucer and his Poetry,* Cambridge, Mass., 1933 edition, p. 3).

8. 'To Sir Godfrey Kneller, Principal Painter to His Majesty', ll. 174 ff.

9. 'Sir George thought Constable too daring in the modes he adopted to obtain the [quality of freshness]; while Constable saw that Sir George often allowed himself to be deceived by the effects of time, of accident, and by the tricks that are, far oftener than is generally supposed, played by dealers, to give mellowness to pictures. . . . Sir George had placed a small landscape by Gaspar Poussin on his easel close to a picture he was painting, and said, "Now, if I can match these tints I am sure to be right." "But suppose, Sir George," replied Constable, "Gaspar could rise from his grave, do you think he would know his own picture in its present state? Or if he did, should we not find it difficult to persuade him that somebody had not smeared tar or cart-grease over its surface, and then wiped it imperfectly off?" At another time, Sir George recommended the colour of an old Cremona fiddle for the prevailing tone of everything, and this Constable answered by laying an old fiddle on the green lawn before the house. Again, Sir George, who seemed to consider the autumnal tints necessary, at least to some part of a landscape, said, "Do you not find it very difficult to determine where to place your brown tree?" And the reply was, "Not in the least, for I never put such a thing into a picture".' (C. R. Leslie, *Life and Letters of John Constable,* 1896 edition, pp. 140 f.)

I am indebted for the reference to this passage to E. W. Manwaring's *Italian Landscape in Eighteenth Century England,* 1925, p. 16. Though Constable was rebelling against this age-old provision of brown colours, he retained a certain love for at least brownishness.

Ruskin in his brilliant discussion of the use of the word 'brown' by poets and the use of the colour by 'Sir George Beaumont and his colleagues' notes the remark of 'one of our best living modern colourists' that 'there is no brown in Nature[.] What we call brown is always a variety either of orange or purple' (*Modern Painters,* IV. v. §10).

10. *The Renaissance,* p. 49. Pater's love of minor tones, while not exclusive, was stronger than A. C. Benson could understand: 'He was fond . . . of insisting upon some altogether unimportant detail . . . he used to pretend that he shut his eyes in crossing Switzerland, on his journeys to and

from Italy, so as not to see the "horrid pots of blue paint", as he called the Swiss lakes.' (*Walter Pater,* 1906, p. 191.) In approving shades of blue, Pater went as far as he could when he furnished his rooms with blue and white china.

11. *The Renaissance,* p. 116. 'Chill' in this sense Pater seems to have borrowed from Ruskin's *Modern Painters* (*Works,* iii. 249 n.).

12. 1869, p. 506.

13. Pater does not say 'some crimson' but 'some further magic of crimson'. Mr. Empson has noted the Elizabethan fondness for such a construction:

> What means [the warning of] this trumpet's sound?

(*Seven Types of Ambiguity,* 1930, p. 112.) Pater's uses of it would call for subtle analysis.

14. *The Renaissance,* p. 49.

15. *Leonardo da Vinci,* Phaidon Press, 1943, p. 11.

16. I cannot recall the source of this quotation.

17. *The Renaissance,* p. 46.

18. See George Boas, 'The Mona Lisa in the History of Taste', *Journal of the History of Ideas,* New York, i (1940), 207 ff.

19. *Essays in Criticism,* p. 208.

20. *The Lives of the Poets,* iii. 441.

21. ibid.

22. *Essays in Criticisin: Second Series,* p. 7.

23. *Appreciations,* pp. 3 f.

24. *The Renaissance,* p. 48.

25. We can see this as in part a protest against the communal emotions aimed at by the Utilitarians: as F. H. Bradley was soon to say:

> 'The end for modern Utilitarianism is not the pleasure of one, but the pleasure of all, the maximum of pleasurable, and minimum of painful, feeling in all sentient organisms, and not in my sentient organism. . . .' (*Ethical Studies,* 1876, p. 80.)

26. *Works,* xxiii. 273 f.

27. I have made no attempt to discover his identity.

28. *The Renaissance,* p. ix.

29. *The Renaissance,* p. vii. The wording was slightly revised in 1877 and again in 1888.

30. *Appreciations,* p. 67.

31. *A Philosophical Inquiry into the Origin of our Ideas of the Sublime and the Beautiful* (*Works,* 1845, i. 182 f).

32. *The New Republic,* ii. 23 f. I have marked the mistaken references to music. If they are intended as mistakes they sharpen the mockery of Pater, whose own references to music trespass beyond his knowledge. See p. 139 below, n. 2.

33. 'Power' and 'might', and words formed from them, are among those most characteristic of Wordsworth. Keats learned Wordsworth's usage. On occasions the debt is a subtle one: Keats' 'taste the sadness of her might' ('Ode on Melancholy', l. 29) is derived from such expressions as 'the might of joy' ('Resolution and Independence', ll. 22 f.).

34. *Poetical Works,* ed. cit., ii. 427.

35. My italics.

36. That is, their 'powers and forces'.

37. p. ix.

38. *The New Republic,* ii. 129.

39. 'Ode on Melancholy', ll. 11 ff.

40. *Collected Essays, Papers &c.,* iv (1929), p. 163.

41. 'Bishop Blougram's Apology'.

42. The best brief account of the text of Newman's writings is that indispensable essay, 'On Reading Newman' which Fr. Tristram contributed to *Newman Centenary Essays,* 1945, pp. 223 ff.

43. Op. cit., 1852, p. 438.

44. See p. 133 below.

45. *Washington Square: The Pension Beaurepas . . .* 1881, ii. 173 f.

46. *Appreciations,* p. 87.

47. Op. cit., p. 43. Pater calls Keats's poem by the title of one of Tennyson's, 'Saint Agnes' Eve'.

48. *Appreciations,* p. 248.

49. 1877 edition, pp. 28 f.

50. *Appreciations,* pp. 14, 32, 103.

51. *The Renaissance,* p. 200.

52. *Appreciations,* p. 12.

## Iain Fletcher (essay date 1959)

SOURCE: Fletcher, Iain. "Walter Pater." In *Walter Pater,* pp. 14-22. London: Longmans, Green & Co., 1959.

[*In the following excerpt, Fletcher analyzes Pater's unique interpretation of the Renaissance, suggesting that Pater's focus on the Renaissance artist, rather than merely the work of art itself, reflects his belief that the personal judgments of the critic play a vital role in the appreciation of art.*]

## IV

**The Renaissance** was intended as a prolegomenon to a new age: an age whose choicer spirits might achieve oneness with themselves through aesthetic contemplation. The topics dealt with range from the thirteenth to the eighteenth centuries. For Pater, the Renaissance was not a phenomenon confined narrowly to one place or period, but a widespread, discontinuous and prolonged movement of the European spirit. Its essence was the vivid and disruptive impact of the values of Greek life, thought and art on the jaded or one-sided local traditions of European culture. Pater thought of these jaded and one-sided traditions as mainly those of the Christian Middle Ages, but not wholly so; for he saw Winckelmann, the eighteenth-century German Hellenist, who is the subject of one of his best essays, as reacting not against Christianity, but against the decadence of early Humanism itself, against a sterile neo-Classical eighteenth-century orthodoxy, and as seeking out the reality, rather than the conventional picture, of ancient Greece. Yet Winckelmann is a little set apart from Pater's other Renaissance types. They all, painters and poets, had the sense of discovering in the classical world something *new,* and the possibility of renewed creation. Winckelmann, their belated descendant, had the sense, rather, of recovering something *lost.* The Hellenistic past, for Winckelmann, becomes the starting point of a mode of contemplation, rather than of creation. He anticipates the critical attitude which, for Pater, was the attitude of the nineteenth-century mind at its best.

To the historians of the eighteenth century, the Renaissance suggested mainly the re-acquisition of classical learning, the new taste for Roman (rather than Greek) antiquities that marks the fifteenth and sixteenth centuries, first in Italy, and then through the other civilized parts of Europe. It meant the rise of the Humanists and the fall of the Schoolmen. But Pater's own century had acquired a more subtle, vivid and objectively defined historical sense. The Renaissance was now seen as the re-birth of Man, a re-birth of individuality, the beginning, in fact, of the Modern World. In Pater's own age, this wistfulness about a past, now for the first time so sharply conceived by historians that it could be explored, in imagination, as the present can be conceived, combined with a typical Victorian unease. This led many to project an 'ideal moment' into the past. But the views of writers who romantically idealized selected portions of the past were often quite unrelated to historical actualities; Pater wrote as a scholar.

Pater's method, in **The Renaissance,** of exploring not so much a period as a movement of history through selected individuals, places him in line with Michelet, with the German romantic historians, and in a sense even with Carlyle. History for him has both a dramatic interest and a practical bearing. In Burckhardt's famous *Civilization of the Renaissance* (1860) Pater discovered a method of concentrating on sudden luminous moments of a period, of a movement, rather than attempting to draw a flat systematic map of it. This approach had an obvious attraction for a writer who believed passionately both in the fruitfulness of the tentative approach, and in the isolation of all individuals within the 'flux'. There is, however, one important difference between Burckhardt and Pater. Burckhardt tended to insist over-sharply on distinctions between 'historical periods', periods which, we are more and more realizing, are less realities than conveniences of the historian. Pater emphasized the essential continuity of the Renaissance with the Middle Ages on the one hand, and with modern times on the other, and in this he is in line with present historical research. Pater also differed from the leading historians of his time in the special nature of his interest in the individual. For him, as for Sainte Beuve, it is rather the man behind a work of art or literature (rather than, for instance, the 'style of an age') that gives a work unity. Art, for him, existed for personality's sake; and he saw the shaping of personality, through the creation and appreciation of art, as, in a sense, the highest kind of art. It is here that he is fundamentally a moralist, not a mere (or pure) critic of literature or art.

The "Preface" summarizes Pater's critical method. Pater begins with Arnold's definition of the critic's first duty as being 'to see the object as in itself it really is', but significantly adds 'in aesthetic criticism the first step towards seeing one's object as it really is, is to know one's own impression as it really is'. For Pater, the impression is our sole contact with anything external to ourselves. Pater parts company from Arnold in stressing Hellenism exclusively, and not even paying lip-service to Hebraism. Whereas both Pater and Arnold use literature as the basis for a theory of life, Pater follows much more consistently the corollary of culture as an inward process. Arnold is too glib when he relates the instinct for the good life to literature as represented by the submission to 'the best that has been thought and said' and to the problem of the good life in relation to others. For Pater this is not possible: believing as he does that man is fundamentally isolated, and that the senses are all that men have in common. Culture at this stage appears only as a harmony of sensations in the individual life, and for this reason he extends (Arnold was indifferent to the other arts) Arnold's concern with literature to painting and sculpture.

Pater's method of greater receptivity and intensification of personality through contemplation of the work of art is an ideal for the few, not the many, in his own age, and in its insistence on the appreciative approach offers a consumer's rather than a producer's view of art. Here is a typical passage:

> The aesthetic critic, then, regards all the objects with which he has to do, all works of art, and the fairer forms of nature and human life, as powers or forces producing pleasurable sensations, each of a more or less peculiar . . . kind. This influence he feels, and wishes to explain, analysing and reducing it to its elements. To him, the picture, the landscape, the engaging personality in life or in a book, *La Gioconda,* the hills of Carrara, Pico of Mirandola, are valuable for their virtues, as we say, in speaking of a herb, a wine, a gem; for the property each has of affecting one with a special, a unique impression of pleasure. Our education becomes complete in proportion as our susceptibility to these impressions increases in depth and variety.

A certain looseness in the texture of his argument is typical of Pater. He tends to use abstract concepts decoratively; to isolate ideas rather than to relate them, and when he ascribes so much to the 'fineness of truth' of the single word, he often treats it, or other fragments or details of larger wholes (a piece of decorative or symbolic detail in a painting, say) as if it were an aesthetic sufficiency. Yet the apparent want of discrimination between the different levels of pleasure there gives a misleading impression of Pater's total attitude. The mention of *persons* as well as *things* must involve the moral dimension, since the aesthetic critic is contemplating what is *responsive*. The impressions, also, received from even the simplest objects of contemplation which Pater lists here—a herb, a wine, a gem—are, in fact, complex. The 'unique' impression is the uniqueness of a complex whole; whose elements, or some of them, may be broadly or closely similar to elements of other complex wholes. By not adverting to this point, Pater seems to leave out from the critic's function the task of comparison, and grading, of broadly or partly similar wholes, and the notion of a hierarchy of different kinds of wholes.

The chief qualifications of the aesthetic critic are, for Pater, alertness, openness, a clear notion of what he is trying to isolate. But Pater was not primarily concerned with pure aesthetic theory, he is a practical critic: he feels that the man who 'experiences impressions strongly, and drives directly at the analysis and discrimination of them, has no need to trouble himself with the abstract question of what beauty is in itself or what is its exact relation to truth or experience'. Yet, though he appears to isolate Beauty in an uncompromising Art for Art's sake fashion, Pater had to admit that the perfection of oneself in relation to beautiful objects must at least indirectly involve the moral perfection of oneself in relation to others, for among 'the objects with which criticism deals' are 'artistic and accomplished forms of human life'.

The single essay in *The Renaissance* which deals most directly with 'artistic and accomplished forms of human life' is that on Winckelmann, with whom Pater felt a profound personal sympathy. Winckelmann grew up in eighteenth-century Germany without any advantages, was largely self-taught, and dedicated himself passionately to the study of Greek antiquity. His example was the foundation of Goethe's struggle to acquire a classical balance between breadth of culture and intensity of feeling: 'One *learns* nothing from him, but one *becomes* something.' And in this sense Winckelmann is the supreme example of the transmission of culture through temperament. Pater saw in Wincklemann's story the example of a life full of 'distinguishing intensity', a life of rich being, not of mere doing. As an art critic, also, Pater admired Winckelmann for his feeling for the concrete, his lack of shame in handling the sensuous side of Greek art. For the spectator, Pater noted approvingly, the intellectual and the spiritual are properly merged in the sensuous. Yet from the example of Winckelmann, Pater realized the sacrifice involved in the aesthetic life.

From this stringent ideal of the cultivated man as receptive spectator rather than violent originator, Pater arrives at the theory of the conduct of life he inculcates in the "Conclusion" to *The Renaissance.* This is a highly compressed, evocative document. Pater gives, first, his own version of Hume's and Mill's phenomenalism. The sole unit of experience is 'the impression'. All that is actual is a single sharp moment, gone before it can be said to be. Yet there lingers inexplicably within that moment the relic, more or less fugitive, of other such moments gone by. These moments are in perpetual flight, but their onset can be 'multiplied', and their impact made more vivid by 'the high passions'. As the moment is isolated by analysis from its context, so the observer is abstracted from his social frame: he is cut off alike from the solidity of the world and from social solidarity:

> Experience, already reduced to a swarm of impressions, is ringed round for each one of us by that thick wall of personality through which no real voice has ever pierced on its way to us, or from us to that which we can only conjecture to be without. Every one of those impressions is the impression of the individual in his isolation, each mind keeping as a solitary prisoner its own dream of a world.

The price to be paid for the freedom of the human sensibility to seek first and foremost the heightening of its sensations is a high one. The solid world, the social world, even the vague assurance of something beyond the veil, all go. The purpose of such language with its melancholy emphasis on dissolution and isolation is to set the stage for the real message of the "Conclusion." This is that we should multiply and intensify our sensations at all cost: that not the wisdom of experience, but the excitement of experiencing, is the one thing necessary:

> Not to discriminate every moment some passionate attitude in those about us, and in the very brilliancy of their gifts some tragic dividing of forces on their ways, is, on this short day of frost and sun, to sleep before evening. . . . We have an interval . . . and then our place knows us no more. . . . Our one chance lies in expanding that interval, in getting as many pulsations as possible into the given time. High passions may give us this quickened sense of life, ecstasy and sorrow of love, the various forms of enthusiastic activity. . . . Of this wisdom, the poetic passion, the desire of beauty, the love of art for its own sake has most. For art comes to you, proposing frankly to give nothing but the highest quality to your moments as they pass, and simply for those moments' sake.

This is not, however, the mere creed of Art for Art's sake: it is Art for the sake of a specially conceived morality. For Pater, as Professor Kermode has pointed out, 'art is what is significant in life, and so sensibility or insight, corruptible as it is, is the organ of moral knowledge, and art, for all its refusal to worship the idola of vulgar morality, is the only true morality; indeed it is nothing less than life itself'. Intensities, for Pater, were not all in one narrowly monotonous key, the key, for instance, of sublimated or tantalized sexuality: making love was an intense experience, so was a mystic's vision, so were the overtones of 'a chorus-ending in Euripides'. (For all his talk about intensifying and multiplying sensations, he does not quite cultivate them for their own sake: he seeks through them rather the unification of personality.) Yet, after Pater wrote, it was impossible for critics and artists to continue in the naïvely moralistic view of art that had marked even a great critic like Ruskin or a painter of genuine integrity like Holman Hunt.

### V

In *The Renaissance* Pater had been trying to fix the secret individual experiences of a few personalities who in his scheme of values mattered supremely, by attempting to define in them some central quality, some fixed point in the flux. That fixed point was best illustrated in Michelangelo by the Biblical phrase 'Out of the strong came forth sweetness'. In Leonardo, the fixed point was the conflict between the scientist's curiosity and the artist's love of beauty; and so on. But there was one great objection to making ideal types out of actual historical personages. Anybody who has actually existed remains, even after his death, subject to the flux. New scholarly discoveries have altered. For instance, since Pater's time, our view of Giorgione, of whom Pater accepted only two pictures as provenly authentic; and even where there has not been this type of development, we cannot help seeing Pater's Leonardo or his Botticelli as doubly distant in time from us; as presented to us through the subtly distorting medium of Pater's own late nineteenth-century sensibility (and our view of that sensibility is itself a subtly distorted mid-twentieth-century view). It was Pater's awareness of this fundamental flaw in the notion of making art out of history that turned him from writing about historical figures, idealized into types, and towards writing, as in *Imaginary Portraits* and *Marius the Epicurean,* about imaginary figures who could be, without possibility of reduction, ideal types. He decided to create characters who had no historical existence, who could still, like the characters in *The Renaissance,* be incarnations of the unending development of culture, but who could be fixed, like works of art. There are likely to be no such shifts in our evaluations of Pater's purely imaginary characters. What they have in common is that they are all gifted or dedicated natures, born out of due time. Duke Karl is the herald of a serene neo-classicism in a Germany desolated by religious wars; Sebastian van Storck is torn between the life of feeling and the passion for metaphysics, and chilled by the abstractions of Spinozan philosophy. In other such stories (some of them were published posthumously) we find buried Hellenism irrupting into the Gothic twilight. Brother Apollyon is really Apollo in exile, while Denys of Auxerre re-enacts the ritual death of Dionysus as Lord of Misrule, so playing out Pater's notion that ritual remains, while beliefs falter. All the subjects of Pater's *Imaginary Portraits* are destroyed by the age in which they live, but remain unchanged at the centre; portents of change, they are themselves unchanging; all of them die unreasonably and almost casually, drastically, yet in a way that seems irrelevant to their life-patterns. The effect of these 'imaginary portraits' is curiously cold, though impressive. We do not feel our way into these stories; rather we reflect on them from a distance. Perhaps we are supposed to have heard them before (as in the case of Dionysus and Apollo, with their harsh cycles, we certainly are) but told in another tone of voice. They reflect Pater's own predicament; images of himself projected into history, full of the sense of exile, never communicating.

### Solomon Fishman (essay date 1963)

SOURCE: Fishman, Solomon. "Walter Pater." In *The Interpretation of Art: Essays on the Art Criticism of John Ruskin, Walter Pater, Clive Bell, Roger Fry, and*

Herbert Read, pp. 43-72. Berkeley: University of California Press, 1963.

[*In the following essay, Fishman examines the moral and philosophical implications of Pater's theory of aesthetics. The critic asserts that Pater's criticism is defined primarily by the subjective quality of its prose rather than its insight into art history. Fishman finds that Pater's essays on the Renaissance are valuable not as works of art criticism in the traditional sense but as unique personal reflections on the power of art to transform people's lives. In this light the principal function of Pater's criticism is to inspire a similar capacity for appreciation in the reader.*]

Walter Pater is not usually bracketed with the art critics. We think of him primarily as a man of letters—the master of an exquisite, though excessively labored style—who incidentally possessed a taste for the visual arts. Even as a literary man, he casts a vague image, his criticism verging on poetic creation, his fiction tending toward the reflective, philosophical essay. The image is persistent, however, and has survived nearly a half-century of neglect. It is best defined in Iain Fletcher's brief but excellent monograph:

> He remains the classic example of a type of temperament in whom we can recognize certain subdued and almost inexpressible moments of the self, its moments of wistfulness and hesitation and its partial triumphs of perception; and more than Marius, or any of those shadowy half-created characters in the *Imaginary Portraits,* he has created himself for us in his *oeuvre* as a permanently significant symbolical figure: the most complete example, the least trivial, of the aesthetic man.[1]

Pater's essays on Renaissance art and Greek sculpture are no longer seriously regarded as a reliable source either of historical information or aesthetic enlightenment, and yet there were innumerable young men in the last century and the early part of this whose interest in the visual arts was first aroused by reading them. For Oscar Wilde, *The Renaissance* was "my golden book," and Arthur Symons, William Sharp, Lionel Johnson, and William Butler Yeats regarded him as master. Bernard Berenson acknowledged his debt to Pater as his first mentor on early Florentine and Venetian art, but long after he had outstripped Pater in knowledge of painting he continued to accept *Marius* as a guide to the art of life—"the art, namely, of so reliving the ideal or poetic traits, the elements of distinction in our everyday life . . . that the unadorned remainder of it, the mere drift and debris of our days, comes to be as though it were not."[2]

Although Pater's writings on art do not rank with Ruskin's work as a major contribution to aesthetics or art criticism, they served to crystallize and make explicit an outlook only latent in Ruskin—the conviction that art represents the highest value in existence—which, once its full implications became clear, was repugnant to Ruskin. Having awakened his audience to the full imaginative and emotional potential of the visual arts, Ruskin was the involuntary progenitor of the aestheticism with which the name of Pater is associated. The phrase "art for art's sake" is highly ambiguous; in the context of literary criticism it has acquired an almost totally pejorative connotation. Applied to Pater, it has a double sense. If it refers to aestheticism as a theory of the conduct of life, a mode of achieving perfection of the self by means of a balance of culture and feeling, it should be interpreted as meaning art for the sake of a highly specialized morality. In the narrower context of aesthetics, insofar as it specifies the ontology of art, art for art's sake has a certain validity on purely empirical grounds, since the central fact concerning modern art is the assumption, whether overt or concealed, that the work of art requires no justification other than its own existence. As a critical doctrine, art for art's sake implies that the work of art be apprehended and judged on its own terms rather than by extrinsic standards.

It is unfair to saddle Pater with responsibility for the excesses of art for art's sake, specifically with the advocacy of a complete divorce of art and life. In the essay on **"Style"** (1888), he himself reverted to the traditional view that the judgment of the literary work must ultimately be a moral judgment transcending aesthetic criteria. Actually the "Preface" and "Conclusion" to *The Renaissance* (1873), upon which Pater's fame as an aesthete was based, do not stipulate the autonomy of the work of art. The "Preface," an exposition of critical method, deliberately renounces concern with fundamental aesthetic questions, with the nature and function of art:

> In aesthetic criticism the first step towards seeing one's object as it really is, is to know one's own impression as it really is, to discriminate it, to realize it distinctly . . . he who experiences these impressions strongly . . . has no need to trouble himself with the abstract question what beauty is in itself, or what its exact relation to truth or experiences—metaphysical questions, as unprofitable as metaphysical questions elsewhere.[3]

The "Conclusion" has even less to say concerning aesthetics; in it Pater placed aesthetics within the sphere of ethics, exhorting the reader to pursue a way of life in which aesthetic experience has the highest value, but making no specifications concerning the nature of that experience.

Although the "Preface" and "Conclusion" do not formally commit Pater to art for art's sake, he cannot be exonerated from a charge of aestheticism. There is little doubt that he was predisposed to it by temperament and background. One cannot help feeling, furthermore, that the tone of the essays which constitute the body of *The Renaissance* was to some extent determined by Ruskin's presence at Oxford as Slade Professor. Whatever subtlety Ruskin's views on the relation of art to morality may have once possessed, it was no longer in evidence in his Oxford lectures; Ruskin's heavy-handed moralizing may well have provoked an extreme reaction in Pater. Quite apart from the explicit repudiation of moral judgment, there is another circumstance which tended to confirm the aestheticism of *The Renaissance.* The original title, *Studies in the History of the Renaissance,* led a contemporary reviewer, Mrs. Mark Pattison, to complain that the work failed to point out the vital relationships between Renaissance art and the main movements—social, political, and intellectual—of the period. Although it was not Pater's intention to write either a history of the Renaissance or a history of Renaissance art, the critique does point to a serious shortcoming in his critical procedure. Just as his critical theory dispenses with philosophical knowledge, his art criticism makes little use of his extensive historical culture. He disavows interest in "periods, types, schools of taste," preferring to locate the specific virtue of the work of art in its direct commerce with the sensibility of the spectator. He makes a broad generalization to the effect that fifteenth-century Italian art owes its specific quality to an "intimate alliance with mind, participation in the best thoughts which the age produced," but in the essays devoted to the Renaissance painters, he links the specific aesthetic virtue to the personality of the artist rather than to the age in which he lived.

Although Pater manifested little or no interest in social and political questions, historical or contemporary, it would be unfair to tax him with an indifference to ideas, but it must be admitted that for him even ideas possess a quasi-aesthetic quality. He is inclined to savor the temper of a philosopher or the intellectual tone of a religious system as he would a work of art. Pater's reserve and decorum strike us as being infinitely more civilized than Ruskin's inspired though manic preaching, his relativism and skepticism more congenial to our age than Ruskin's dogmatism. But even if aesthetic experience is the highest form of experience for Pater, he fails to give a sense of the importance of art which Ruskin conveys. The reason for this lies, I think, in the fact that Pater is too much concerned with the spectator's role in the aesthetic transaction, the heightened intensity of the viewer's experience, rather than with the life and intensity inherent in the work itself.

To some extent this deficiency resulted from Pater's lack of technical knowledge, which deprived him of the means for designating the specifically formal elements which are the proper subject of aesthetic criticism. Pater eventually recognized the need for a technical, formalist approach, but in the "Preface" to *The Renaissance* "aesthetic criticism" signifies impressionistic criticism. The role of the amateur, more evident in his writings on art than in his literary criticism, precluded his sharing, even imaginatively, in the creative act. The word "passion," which occurs frequently in Pater's account of aesthetic experience, refers to the spectator's response to the work rather than to the artist's attitude. Pater's real gift is for the discernment of the delicate nuance rather than of power; he is more successful in dealing with Luca della Robbia than with Michelangelo. By taste and temperament he was inclined toward refinement rather than robustness, toward the contemplative rather than the dramatic. Unfortunately, Pater's personal predilections were confused with his aesthetic theories; the penchant for decadence, more discernible in *The Renaissance* than in his later work, was readily assimilable with the atmosphere of the Aesthetic Movement of the eighties and nineties. Pater, more than most literary figures, has suffered from the excesses of his followers. The irony lies in the fact that the aura of abandon should have lent itself to one whose personal life was so circumspect, so retiring.

The cloistered quality of Pater's existence is, unfortunately, communicated to his writings on art, and vitiates his work to some extent. Both art and literature were sometimes regarded by him as mere appurtenances of culture:

> Different classes of persons at different times, make, of course, very various demands upon literature. Still, scholars, I suppose, and not only scholars, but all disinterested lovers of books, will always look to it, as to all other fine art, for a refuge, a sort of cloistral refuge, from a certain vulgarity in the actual world. A perfect poem like *Lycidas,* a perfect fiction like *Esmond,* the perfect handling of a theory like Newman's *Idea of a University,* has for them something of the use of a religious "retreat."[4]

This attitude has been used against Pater as a warrant of his incompetence, his refusal to deal with literature as an embodiment of reality. Perhaps this attitude is not so offensive with respect to the visual arts, where realism, though it has its adherents, is no longer the leading cry.

The effect of Pater's dilettantism might have been mitigated had he chosen to deal with contemporary art as well as with the art of antiquity and the Renaissance. Pater makes glancing references to contemporary artists, to Ingres and Legros among others, which indicate a receptivity to the art of his time. His review of George Moore's *Modern Painting* reveals an open mind toward the French Impressionists, if not an actual knowledge of their work. But in the main his all-absorbing interest was in art remote from his own time, and hence from the "actual world." Purged of its associations with decadence and escapism, Pater's point of view emphasizes the significant contemplative element in aesthetic experience, which had been clearly recognized in the eighteenth century but tended to be slighted in the more pragmatic atmosphere of his time, as it is in ours. At any rate, Pater did not share the current view that the hedonistic aspects of aesthetic experience somehow detract from the dignity and significance of art.

I have noted as one of Ruskin's critical shortcomings his tendency to concern himself with matters that are involved in the genesis of the work but not actually visible or demonstrable in the work. If, according to an influential segment of current critical doctrine, aesthetic criticism is "intrinsic," that is, addresses itself to the concrete phenomena embodied in the work itself, Ruskin is guilty of the "genetic fallacy," as are all critics who devote themselves to the psychology of the artist or to his social milieu. Inasmuch as Pater's studies are an inquiry into the personalities of the Renaissance painters, he is also culpable. His essay on Leonardo da Vinci centers on the "mystery in his work, and something enigmatical beyond the usual measure of great men." Pater's procedure seems very odd in an age familiar with a psychological approach to art: "A lover of strange souls may still analyse for himself the impression made on him by those works, and try to reach through it a definition of the chief elements of Leonardo's genius."[5] Pater proposes an analysis, not of the works, but of his subjective impressions of them. In terms of the intrinsic approach, this constitutes the affective fallacy in criticism.

The most flagrant example of the affective fallacy in Pater is his description of "La Gioconda," the climax of his essay on Leonardo and probably the most famous piece of art criticism in English, though it is an early work (1869) and not truly representative of Pater's critical abilities. After the statement concerning the "unfathomable smile, always with a touch of something sinister in it" the palpable work is abandoned for a purely lyric flight, a prose poem bearing only a most tenuous relationship to its subject:

> The presence, that thus rose as strangely beside the waters, is expressive of what in the ways of a thousand years men had come to desire . . . She is older than the rocks among which she sits; like a vampire, she has been dead many times, and learned the secrets of the grave . . . and all this has been to her but as the sound of lyres and flutes . . . The fancy of a perpetual life, sweeping together ten thousand experiences is an old one; and modern thought has conceived the idea of hu-

manity as wrought upon by and summing up in itself all modes of thought and life. Certainly Lady Lisa might stand as the embodiment of the old fancy, the symbol of the modern idea.[6]

The extraordinary success of the passage suggests that it manages, perhaps by means of prose cadence and imagery, to express more than a subjective impression, that is, to capture some quality inherent in the picture. One cavils only at its inclusion within the category of criticism, even of impressionist criticism.

The critical program announced in the Preface to *The Renaissance,* though frankly and necessarily subjective, does not give license for wayward flights of fancy. "To know one's own impression as it really is, to discriminate it, to realise it distinctly" would appear to be indispensable conditions of a valid criticism of the visual arts, inasmuch as the object must be apprehended by means of sense impressions. To know one's own impression is equivalent to the act of seeing. From the point of view of the twentieth-century formalists, the further requirements, those of discriminating and realizing the visual impression, would nearly exhaust the critic's functions. The formalist critic does not rely on pure sensibility, of course, but on a sensibility operating through some visual system or scheme by means of which he can describe, analyze, and interpret sense impressions. Pater, as I have already noted, did not possess the technical knowledge necessary for the formulation of such a system. His art criticism is therefore limited by his equipment for verbalizing the product of a refined and acute visual sensibility—that of a literary man. Inasmuch as it was a translation of pictorial elements in literary terms, Pater's critical practice, with a few exceptions to be noted, violated the formalists' prohibition of "literary" interpretation. Yet the theory, particularly the theory of pictorial form he outlined in **"The School of Giorgione,"** is an important document in formalist criticism. Ruskin possessed the technical information and the capacity for describing art in visual terms which are required in formalist criticism, but the formalists denied the relevance of the ethical and social content of his criticism to aesthetics.

Without speculating on the autonomous character of aesthetic experience, Pater attempted to view the work of art as it really is, disencumbered of extrinsic considerations:

> The aesthetic critic, then, regards all the objects with which he has to do, all works of art, and the fairer forms of nature and human life, as powers or forces producing pleasurable sensations, each of a more or less peculiar and unique kind . . . And the function of the aesthetic critic is to distinguish, analyze, and separate from its adjuncts, the virtue by which a picture, a

landscape, a fair personality in life or in a book, produces this special impression of beauty or pleasure, to indicate what the source of that impression is, and under what conditions it is experienced. His end is reached when he has disengaged that virtue and noted it, as a chemist notes some natural element, for himself and others. . . . What is important, then, is not that the critic should possess a correct abstract definition of beauty for the intellect, but a certain kind of temperament, the power of being deeply moved by the presence of beautiful objects.[7]

Although it obviates such distractions to aesthetic criticism as social and ethical matters and even aesthetic preconceptions, the critical procedure outlined here surrenders too readily the possibility of objectivity, "to see the object as it really is." Later formalist critical theory concedes the inevitability of personal predilection in aesthetic emotion, but holds out the promise of formal analysis which minimizes subjective preferences. The essays on Leonardo, Botticelli, and Michelangelo are primarily studies of personality as reflected in works of art. It is not Pater's inclination to locate the source of the specific aesthetic "virtue" of an artist's work in his personality, nor the fact that he is drawn toward certain artists by temperamental affinity, that is at fault, but his tendency to identify himself with his subjects, to view them as exensions of his own personality. Pater did eventually hit upon a literary form, the imaginary portrait, which suited his gifts more perfectly than the critical essay.

Although Pater's reputation is that of an aesthete—one whose sensibilities are highly developed and who devotes his life to their cultivation—his ultimate concern was ethical, growing out of his personal predicament with respect to the religious crisis of his age. Ruskin's most vigorous writing on art coincided with the period of his most ardent religious faith. And although that faith was subject to several transformations during his lifetime, his constant practice was to subsume his aesthetics under a theistic outlook. For Pater the subordination of aesthetic emotion to religious feeling was no longer possible. As T. S. Eliot observed in his essay on Pater, the effect of his writings was to extend to the field of art Matthew Arnold's concept of culture as a substitute for religion. Whether or not Eliot's contention ignores the authenticity of religious feeling in *Marius the Epicurean,* it is borne out by the "Conclusion" to *The Renaissance.* The argument of the "Conclusion" issues from a virtually total religious skepticism. Human knowledge is reduced to the operations of the universe of matter. From an atomistic hypothesis of flux, change, and impermanence is deduced the inexorable isolation of the individual consciousness—the thick wall of personality. It should be noted that Pater's sense of isolation was deeply rooted in his tempera-

ment, and that the philosophical hypothesis, though sincere, is probably the rationalization of a serious emotional lack on Pater's part, revealed by his incapacity after childhood to experience an intimate relationship.

The exhortation to burn with a "hard gem-like flame" follows from the philosophical premise. From the phenomenalism of modern science, which reduces experience to a series of discrete sensations, Pater argues that true economy in the ethical sense calls for the greatest possible cultivation of sensuous awareness. The emphasis is on quantity as well as on quality of aesthetic experience, on its intensity and variety:

Only be sure it is passion—that it does yield you this fruit of a quickened, multiplied consciousness. Of this wisdom, the poetic passion, the desire of beauty, the love of art for art's sake, has most; for art comes to you professing frankly to give nothing but the highest quality to your moments as they pass, and simply for these moments' sake.[8]

In this context, "art for art's sake" has little or no critical relevance. It refers neither to the internal constitution of the work of art, nor to its production. Applied to the practitioner, the "religion of art"—the justification of the superiority of art to all other experience and hence of a life devoted exclusively to art—has a certain ethical validity. It was the creed, moreover, which was adopted almost wholesale by the most genuinely creative visual artists of the past century. But the doctrine of art for art's sake adumbrated in the Conclusion is mainly concerned with the appreciation of art. The great deficiency of Pater's writing on art, so evident in contrast with Ruskin, is its emphasis on receptivity, on the passive response of art. This aspect of Pater's art criticism is intensified by his almost exclusive concern with the firmly established art of the past. In theory at least, Pater's attitude encouraged receptivity to the new and experimental, as the following indicates:

For us the Renaissance is the name of a many-sided but yet united movement, in which the love of the things of the intellect and the imagination for their own sake, the desire for a more liberal and comely way of concerning life, make themselves felt, urging those who experience this desire to search out first one and then another means of intellectual and imaginative enjoyment, and directing them not merely to the discovery of old and forgotten sources of this enjoyment, but to divine new sources of it, new experiences, new subjects of poetry, new forms of art.[9]

Pater's relativism and his strictures against the formation of habit should have reinforced this attitude. Herbert Read, for one, believes that Pater would have welcomed the radical art of the twentieth century—Proust and Kafka, Bartok and Stravinsky, Picasso and Henry

Moore. Yet while there is no definite evidence to disprove Read's contention, one nevertheless senses in Pater a nostalgia for the past more pervasive than a sympathy for contemporary work.

Whereas Ruskin was drawn to early Renaissance and Gothic art, Pater's tastes are more conventional. He is attracted mainly to classical art, to Greek sculpture, and to the classical element in Renaissance art. He manages to work into his Renaissance studies an essay on Winckelmann, the great eighteenth-century German art historian, a figure with whom Pater cannot help identifying himself. What appeals to Pater in both the personality and work of Winckelmann is the frank affirmation of the pagan outlook, the affirmation of the sensuous element in the life of the imagination:

> Winckelmann here reproduces for us the earlier sentiment of the Renaissance. On a sudden the imagination feels itself free. How facile and direct, it seems to say, is this life of the senses and the understanding, when once we have apprehended it! Here, surely, is the more liberal life we have been seeking so long . . . How mistaken and roundabout have been our effort to reach it by mystic passion and monastic reverie; how they have deflowered the flesh; how little they have emancipated us.[10]

The classical tradition in the visual arts represented for Pater as it did for Winckelmann the norm by which all subsequent art is to be measured and according to which nearly all other art is in a sense and a degree decadent: "The longer we contemplate that Hellenic ideal, in which man is at unity with himself, with his physical nature, with the outward world, the more we may be inclined to regret that he should ever have passed beyond it, to contend for a perfection that makes the blood turbid, and frets the flesh, and discredits the actual world about us. . . ."[11] Although Pater shares Winckelmann's nostalgia for a "golden age" of art, represented by what both of them conceived to be the greatest period of Greek sculpture—that of the fifth century—he adopts a more "advanced" point of view in deprecating Winckelmann's inability to appreciate nonclassical art—"the subtle and penetrative, but somewhat grotesque art of the modern world." In spite of his admiration for the pagan ideal, frankly sensual and unclouded by doubt, conflict, and melancholy, Pater's real affinity was precisely for that aspect of Renaissance art in which the Hellenistic element is in conflict with the Christian. The charm of Leonardo, Michelangelo, and Botticelli for him lies in a certain mysterious, ambiguous, and, we might say, "decadent" quality. Here, perhaps, Pater is too prone to romanticize the Renaissance, to read into it the dichotomies of his own state of mind. He discerns the specific aesthetic quality or "virtue" of Leonardo's art to be its modernity, the intrusion of spirit into the classic world of sense:

> Sometimes this curiosity came into conflict with the desire of beauty; it tended to make him go too far below that outside of things in which art begins and ends. The struggle between the reason and its ideas, and the senses, the desire of beauty is the key to Leonardo's life at Milan . . . Now he was to entertain in this narrow medium those divinations of a humanity too wide for it, that larger vision of the opening world, which is not only too much for the great irregular art of Shakespeare.[12]

Botticelli also, in Pater's angle of vision, is an artist torn between two world-views, between the simplicities of religion and naturalism and a "modern" introspection and subtlety. From this conflict arises "the peculiar sentiment with which he infuses his profane and sacred persons, comely, and in a certain sense like angels, but with a sense of displacement or loss about them—the wistfulness of exiles, conscious of a passion and energy greater than any known issue of them explains, which runs through all his varied work with a sentiment of ineffable melancholy."[13]

It is evident from these passages, as it is from all the central essays on the visual arts including **"The School of Giorgione,"** which postulates a conception of pictorial form as independent of subject matter, that Pater is concerned primarily with representational elements. In this respect, there is no radical difference between the aesthetic outlook of Ruskin and Pater. Nor is there a great divergence in matters of taste. Although Pater exhibits a predilection for the morbid and decadent, his preferences, so far as period is concerned, are more conventional than Ruskin's. The contrast in their personalities could hardly be greater, and yet it is fairly clear that Pater's visual response to painting was determined by Ruskin. One concludes that, despite a fundamental disagreement concerning the ethical import of art, Pater's art criticism is a direct continuation of Ruskin's. Yet Pater maintains a curious silence about Ruskin's influence—indeed, about Ruskin's existence. The only recorded reference betrays a sharp note of rivalry, even of hostility; "A friend remembers that he [Pater] was once talking of the artistic perceptions of Ruskin, and said suddenly with a show of impatience, 'I cannot believe that Ruskin saw more in the church of St. Mark than I do.'"[14] Pater's biographer reveals what one had already suspected, that the only definite artistic influence was that of Ruskin, whom Pater had read at the age of nineteen.

It would be absurd to imply that before Ruskin, cultured Englishmen had been completely insensitive to the visual arts. What Ruskin perceived and what Pater learned from him was that the real significance of the visual arts derived neither from technical skill in representation nor from the grandeur of the subject matter but from the capacity to convey emotion by means of an imaginative transformation of the data of visual appearances. Pater's hedonism, it is hardly necessary to explain, does not counsel submission to undefined sensuous experience, but to the life of the senses transformed into art by what Pater called "imaginative reason." Despite his revolt against a puritanical culture, which took the form of nostalgia for an uninhibited paganism, he valued a work of art primarily as an expression of the human spirit, embracing emotion, intellect, and imagination.

The precursor of both Ruskin's and Pater's aesthetic views was the romantic doctrine of imagination. The romantic strain in Ruskin's art theory was strongly conditioned, as I have already observed, by a religious dogma which imposed certain limits on the scope of the visual arts, principally the requirement of naturalism, the definition of which varied considerably in his work, but otherwise remained constant. It should also be remembered that Ruskin's social theories were motivated by religious conviction and that his social interests tended to modify his theory of art. Pater, on the other hand, represents a secular version of the romantic theory of art; he is much closer than Ruskin to Baudelaire and the Symbolists on the question of naturalism. Pater is relatively cautious concerning the prerogative of the artist to transform natural facts in the interests of imaginative vision. He does not actually go as far as Whistler in this respect. It is his attitude toward the relationship of art and nature which constitutes his divergence from Ruskin. For Ruskin art is subordinate to nature and is to be judged by its conformity to what he conceived of as natural laws. Pater, on the other hand, was inclined to view nature through the medium of art. The role of nature in art does not figure in his aesthetic doctrine; his attitude can be deduced from his aesthetic interests:

> . . . nature is to him always a setting, a background, subordinated to the human interest . . . The home, the house, the room, the furniture and decoration, the garden . . . , all these were nearer to his heart than nature in her wilder and sterner aspects, because the thought and hand of humanity had passed over them, writing its care and its dreams legibly on cornice and lintel, on panel and beam, on chest and press, on alley and bower, on border and fountain.[15]

Although Pater's interest in the art of the human figure was far greater than in landscape, here also he was not at all concerned with the problem of representational accuracy. The idealized human figure of classical sculpture constituted for him the norm of beauty as it had done for eighteenth-century art criticism. He is not, therefore, committed to a canon of realism and recognizes deviations from it as an expressive device. The discussion of Renaissance sculpture in **"Luca della Robbia"** points, in a most tentative manner, toward the notion of abstract art. Pater is speaking of the special limitation of sculpture which results from the material conditions of the medium, tending toward a hard realism verging on caricature: "Against this tendency to the hard presentment of mere form trying vainly to compete with the reality of nature itself, all noble sculpture constantly struggles; each great system of sculpture resisting it in its own way, etherealizing, spiritualizing, relieving its hardness, its heaviness, and death."[16] The terminology is highly reminiscent of Ruskin, and indeed there is no basic discrepancy between Ruskin's and Pater's attitude toward realism insofar as they both subscribe to the central tenet of romantic expressionist theory—that the main business of art is not the imitation of objective reality but the projection of an inner vision or emotion.

Ruskin, of course, did not completely resolve the tension between expressionism and the mimetic doctrine imposed by his theology. The role of nature is less ambiguous in Ruskin's aesthetics than in his art criticism. According to *Modern Painters,* volume II, beauty is an objective phenomenon independent of the beholder, existing in the forms of nature, which can be arranged in a hierarchy headed by organic forms. The beauty of a work of art is therefore derivative, depending on a correspondence with natural forms. While Ruskin fully recognizes the function of the imagination in art, he attributes to it an intuitive grasp of natural forms. Now Pater is noncommittal in the realm of aesthetics:

> Beauty, like all other qualities presented to human experience, is relative; and the definition of it becomes unmeaning and useless in proportion to its abstractness. To define beauty, not in the most abstract, but in the most concrete terms possible, to find not a universal formula for it, but the formula which expresses most adequately this or that special manifestation of it, is the aim of the true student of aesthetics.[17]

Pater's relativism is not so thorough-going in practice as in theory; he consistently associates artistic excellence with "strangeness." This might be ascribed simply to a preference for the exotic—a variant of the romantic love of the remote and the irregular, except that Pater converts it into an aesthetic principle:

> A certain strangeness, something of the blossoming of the aloe, is indeed an element in all true works of art; that they shall excite and surprise us is indispensable. But that they shall give pleasure and exert a charm over us is indispensable too; and this strangeness must be sweet also—a lovely strangeness. . . .[18]

The strangeness so highly valued by Pater is closely related to the expressive element, that inward vision or emotion which is objectified in the work of art. Pater undoubtedly owes this aspect of his critical theory to the romantic movement in literature of which he is an heir. His distinction lies in his peculiar susceptibility to expressive elements in the visual arts. The passage on strangeness, which occurs in the essay on Michelangelo, may be elucidated and amplified by another reference to the same artist:

> When Michelangelo came, with a genius spiritualized by the reverie of the middle age, penetrated by its spirit of inwardness and introspection, living not a mere outward life like the Greek, but a life full of inward experiences, sorrows, consolations, a system which sacrificed so much of what was inward and unseen could not satisfy him. To him, lover and student of Greek sculpture as he was, work which did not bring what was inward to the surface, which was not concerned with individual expression, with individual character and feeling, the special history of the special soul was not worth doing at all . . . he secured for his work individuality and intensity of expression, while he avoided a too hard realism, that tendency to harden into caricature which the representation of feeling must always have.[19]

The reference to caricature shows Pater's tendency to associate expressiveness in the visual arts with facial expression. While his reaction to the enigmatic smile of "Mona Lisa" or the peevish-looking Madonnas of Botticelli are memorable, his concept of expressiveness is not confined to the literary, anecdotal, or psychological content of painting. Michelangelo's expressiveness is explained in formal terms. The rough texture of his sculpture which is actually perfect finish, the apparent incompleteness of nearly all of it, has an effect comparable to that of time and accident on certain classical works, and is actually a technical equivalent of color, a means of imparting vitality to the hardness of the medium. Thus by a deliberate formal device the artist achieves what Pater calls spirituality.

Even in his early essays on art Pater was not given to assigning the significance of a work to its literary or anecdotal subject matter—the paramount offense in art criticism according to the current view, upon which formalism has left its mark even when it is no longer regarded as an adequate basis for a total account of art. In distinguishing between Botticelli's treatment of religious subjects and the simple naturalism of his predecessors, he notes that the real matter of Botticelli is not the iconographic content, which is merely the ostensible subject, but the undercurrent of feeling portrayed. Although his observations on Renaissance sculpture appear to prefigure a formal approach which was more clearly defined in his later work, he is still primarily concerned with those elements of expression which could be apprehended in psychological rather than formal terms. The significant duality at this point was feeling vs. subject matter rather than form vs. content.

The transition to a full-fledged formalism can be discerned in the essay on **"Style."** It is significant that here Pater is dealing with literary style, a topic on which he possessed the kind of expert knowledge which he lacked in the field of visual art. In designating style as an aesthetic differentia, perhaps the most essential, since of all aesthetic elements it is most intimately connected with personality, Pater invokes the term "truth," which is omnipresent in Ruskin but which Pater had hitherto scrupulously avoided. Pater is discussing the difference between communicative and imaginative discourse. He concedes to the former a modest aesthetic function, and along with it a limited merit to the truth to fact which occupies so prominent a place in Ruskin's art theory:

> For just in proportion as the writer's aim, consciously or unconsciously, comes to be the transcribing, not of the world, not of mere fact, but of his sense of it, he becomes an artist, his work *fine* art; and good art (as I hope ultimately to show) in proportion to the truth of his presentment of that sense; as in those humbler or plainer functions of literature also, truth—truth to bare fact, there—is the essence of such artistic quality as they may have. Truth! there can be no merit, no craft at all without that. And further, all beauty is in the long run only fineness of truth, or what we call expression, the finer accommodation of speech to that vision within . . . Literary art, that is, like all art which is in any way imitative or reproductive of fact—form, or colour, or incident—is the representation of such fact as connected with soul, of a specific personality, in its preference, its volition and power. Such is the matter of imaginative or artistic literature.[20]

Without actually renouncing the mimetic or representational function of art, Pater unequivocally subordinates it to expression, regarded as the specifically aesthetic attribute; furthermore, by identifying expression with style, the emphasis is placed on the formal element, or perhaps more accurately, on the indissoluble bond between form and subject matter. Pater guards against the assumption that style is a superficial or adventitious quality of the work of art. For, if it is the product of subjective emotion or vision, it is not dependent on the caprice of the individual artist and therefore to be regarded as mere mannerism; the stipulation of truth guarantees its authenticity. Pater's proposition concerning the inner necessity, the inevitability, of style is demonstrated by an examination of Flaubert's idea of *le mot juste,* one of the salient examples of the aesthetic approach to literary art. Pater's version of expressionism, based on an absolute correspondence between the aesthetic element and the vision within, bears a certain resemblance to Benedotto Croce's identification of expression and intuition. Yet Pater, for all his fascination with the manifestations of personality in the work of the Renaissance painters, is too deeply committed to the classical tradition which stresses structure and volition—"which foresees the end in the beginning and never loses sight of it"—to subscribe fully either to an intuitive or a transcendental theory of art. He rejects Coleridge's idea of the imagination, which for modern critics is the central statement of romantic aesthetics:

> What makes his view a one-sided one is, that in it the artist has become almost a mechanical agent; instead of the most luminous and self-possessed phase of consciousness, the associative act in art or poetry is made to look like some blindly organic process of assimilation. The work of art is likened to a living organism. That expresses truly the sense of a self-delighting, independent life which the finished work of art gives us; it hardly figures the process by which such a work was produced . . . The philosophic critic, at least, will value, even in works of imagination, seemingly the most intuitive, the power of understanding in them, their logical processes of construction, the spectacle of supreme intellectual dexterity which they afford.[21]

The traditionalism of the essay on **"Style"** is most pronounced in its final paragraphs, in which Pater makes amends for the aestheticism which had outraged many of his contemporaries. Here he limits the capacities of aesthetic criticism to a primary stage in the whole critical process, which is completed by an ethical judgment. This act of recantation is not necessarily to be viewed as concession to his detractors nor as a renunciation of his former views, since it largely exempts the nonliterary arts:

> The distinction between great art and good art depending immediately, as regards literature at all events, not on its form, but on the matter . . . It is on the quality of the matter it informs or controls, its compass, its variety, its allegiance to great ends, or the depth of the note of revolt, or the largeness of hope in it, that the greatness of literary art depends.[22]

The essay on **"Style"** represents a significant alteration in Pater's critical theory from the overstated impressionism of the Preface—a prime example of the "affective fallacy"—toward the "intrinsic" approach, which in our own time places high value on stylistic analysis. Had Pater been able to apply the insights of this essay to the visual arts, his stature as an art critic would have been immeasurably increased. Ideally, Pater should have developed the principal idea of **"The School of Giorgione"** concerning the importance of medium in determining the formal constitution of the work of art into a conception of pictorial style, in which the formal elements are seen as the embodiment of the painter's inner vision. But to perceive Giorgione's achievement in terms of style would have required the kind of connoisseurship and technical and historical knowledge that Pater simply did not possess. He would have had to place Giorgione's individual style in relation to the Ve-

netian school in particular, to Italian Renaissance painting in general, and ultimately to the whole history of art conceived of in terms of the evaluation and transmission of styles.

Nevertheless **"The School of Giorgione,"** as far as it goes, is a notable document in art criticism, providing the rationale, if not the means, for the formal analysis of style. It is a carefully reasoned work, the major part of which is devoted to relatively abstract critical theory, and not at all characteristic of the impressionist approach announced in the Preface. Pater begins in the vein of Lessing's *Laocöon* by enforcing the distinction between the visual arts and literature and by protesting the traditional kind of literary treatment of painting. Unlike Lessing, who makes the mimetic capability the distinguishing factor, Pater concentrates on the sensuous appeal of the medium, on aesthetic surface:

> For, as art addresses not pure sense, still less the pure intellect, but the "imaginative reason" through the senses, there are differences of kind in aesthetic beauty, corresponding to differences in kind of the gifts of sense themselves. Each art, therefore, having its own special mode of reaching the imagination, its own special responsibilities to its material. One of the functions of aesthetic criticism is to define these limitations; to estimate the degree in which a given work of art fulfills its responsibilities to its special material; to note in a picture that true pictorial charm, which is neither a mere poetical thought or sentiment, on the one hand, nor a mere result of communicable skill in colour or design, on the other.[23]

This may appear to be rudimentary to us, but we must recall that in Pater's earlier writing on art and most of Ruskin's, pictures were interpreted in terms of their illustrative values. Ruskin was not entirely consistent on this point, but he often assumed the substance of painting and poetry to be identical, and the difference in medium a minor difference in "language." Pater is now very explicit in ruling out a literary approach:

> It is in the criticism of painting that this truth most needs enforcing for it is in popular judgments of pictures that false generalization of all art into forms of poetry is most prevalent. To suppose that all is mere technical acquirement in delineation or touch, working through and addressing itself to the intelligence, on the one side, or a merely poetical, or what may be called literary interest, addressed also to the pure intelligence, on the other;—this is the way of most spectators, and of many critics, who have never caught sight, all the time, of that true pictorial quality which lies between (unique pledge of the possession of the gift) the inventive or creative handling of pure line and colour, which, as almost always in Dutch painting, as often also in the works of Titian and Veronese, is quite independent of anything definitely poetical in the subject it accompanies. It is the *drawing*—the design projected from that

peculiar pictorial temperament or constitution, in which while it may possibly be ignorant of true anatomical proportions, all things whatever, all poetry, every idea however abstract or obscure, floats up as a visible scene or image; it is the colouring—that weaving of just perceptible gold threads of light through the dress, the flesh, the atmosphere in Titian's *Lace-girl*—the staining of the whole fabric of the thing with a new delightful physical quality. This drawing, then—the arabesque traced in the air by Tintoret's flying figures, by Titian's forest branches; this colouring—the magic conditions of light and hue in the atmosphere of Titian's *Lace-girl* or Rubens' *Descent from the Cross*:—these essential pictorial qualities must first of all delight the sense, delight it as directly and sincerely as a fragment of Venetian glass; and through this delight only like the medium of whatever poetry or science may be beyond them, in the intention of the composer. In its primary aspect, a great picture has no more definite message for us than an accidental play of sunlight and shadow for a moment, on the wall or floor.[24]

In designating the essential pictorial quality to lie midway between technique of execution and literary interest, Pater has defined the area which was to absorb the attention of the formalist critics of the present century—the area of "significant form," perhaps the most problematic question in modern art criticism. Pater specifies both the creative and the essential aspects of pictorial form, but he does not actually succeed in linking form and expression. A lacuna exists between the formalist approach implicit in the Giorgione essay and the idea of style he formulated later in connection with literary art.

It will be noted that Pater makes a reservation concerning formalism, that it constitutes a primary, in the sense of preliminary, stage of criticism, that from this primary and essential "condition" we may proceed to the literary or scientific interest of the picture. This caution is due to a certain conservatism on Pater's part which can be explained by the nature of the art with which he is dealing—representational art containing a relatively high degree of naturalism. It is all the more remarkable, then, that he proceeds to what is actually propaganda for an art of pure form, in which the pictorial qualities are primary in the sense of principal. Pater's rationale is based on the analogy of music, an idea which was widespread in nineteenth-century Symbolist aesthetics, and recurs in certain twentieth-century theories of nonfigurative art. Pater's remains the classic statement of the case:

> All art constantly aspires towards the condition of music. For while in all other works of art it is possible to distinguish the matter from the form, and the understanding can always make this distinction, yet it is the constant effort of art to obliterate it. That the mere matter of a poem, for instance—its subject, its given inci-

dents or situations; that the mere matter of a picture—the actual circumstances of an event, the actual topography of a landscape—should be nothing without the form, the spirit, of the handling, that this form, this mode of handling should become an end in itself, should penetrate every part of the matter:—this is what all art constantly strives after, and achieves in different degrees.[25]

The idea of "form as an end in itself" is much more important both historically and critically than that of art for art's sake, with which Pater is usually associated. For though one may regard the doctrine of pure poetry as a minor or negligible literary phenomenon, one cannot take a comparable attitude toward the parallel movement in the visual arts. It is possible to take issue with the statement that all art constantly aspires toward the condition of music. For stylistic reasons, perhaps, Pater employs the declarative rather than the optative form, thereby making it more absolute than he intended. He is voicing an hypothesis which, though not eccentric, does not adequately account for the historical development of the visual arts. Furthermore, analogy with music is ambiguous, in that the status of musical form and content remains a baffling problem in aesthetics. If one regards music as an art of pure form devoid of content, Pater's statement looks forward to the nonobjective art of our time. But it is more likely, in the light of the application of his theory to the school of Giorgione, that Pater thinks of music as embodying fusion of form and content so complete that neither can be extricated from the other. While the notion of an organic fusion of form and content is one of the most fruitful discoveries of modern critical theory and one that is almost universally accepted, it is a difficult hypothesis to demonstrate. An obvious example is the interaction of meter and meaning in a poem. We may be intuitively convinced of a unified effect, but, as I. A. Richards has observed, the metrical and the semantic analysis must proceed on planes which never actually converge. The interaction of matter and form in representational art may be more intimate than in poetry, but it still presents great difficulties for critical analysis. One rather dramatic solution of the problem is to declare the irrelevance of subject matter. In practice, the nonformal elements keep intruding themselves, as Roger Fry discovered. At any rate a purely formalistic approach would appear to operate best on purely formal art.

Pater's version of formalism is handled with considerable discretion and tact. Far from arguing the irrelevance of subject matter, he demonstrated that in the case of Giorgione, the formal aim, which is the principal or even exclusive aim, is achieved by the control of subject matter. Giorgione's distinction is his discovery of *genre,* a special kind of subject matter wholly amenable to the formal ends of the artist, since it makes no historical, theological, literary, or naturalistic claims on his fantasy. It is significant, in the light of twentieth-century aesthetics, that Pater traces the formalist motive of Giorgione to its origin in Byzantine art:

> The beginnings of Venetian painting link themselves to the last, stiff , half-barbaric splendors of Byzantine decoration, and are but the introduction into the crust of marble and gold on the walls of *Duomo* of Murano, or of Saint Marks, of a little more human expression. And throughout the course of its later development, always subordinate to architectural effect, the work of the Venetian school never escaped from the influence of its beginnings. Unassisted, and therefore unperplexed, by naturalism, religious mysticism, philosophical theories, it had no Giotto, no Angelico, no Botticelli. Exempt from the stress of thought and sentiment, which taxes so severely the resources of the generations of Florentine artists, those earlier Venetian painters down to Carpaccio and Bellini, seem never for a moment to have been tempted even to lose sight of their art in its strictness, or to forget that painting must be before all things decorative, a thing for the eye, a space of colour on the wall, only more dexterously blunt than the markings of its precious stone or the chance interchange of sun and shade upon it—this to begin and end with—whatever higher matter of thought, or poetry, or religious reverie, might play its part therein, between.[26]

Pater's criticism of the visual arts encompasses both of the dominant aesthetic approaches of our own time—the expressionist and the formalist—but does not really succeed in achieving a synthesis. His idea of expressiveness is primarily the product of his literary experience, his idea of form that of his visual sensibility. He does not find Giorgione's work to be less expressive than that of the Florentines: the difference lies in the degree to which formal and expressive elements are fused. For him, Giorgione's pictures constitute "painted poems," in which the literary element is so refined, so idealized (so remote from actuality) that it is no longer felt to be an intrusion upon the purely visual, or "decorative," element. Pater appears to be on the verge of "significant form," but it is doubtful that without the example of Post-Impressionist art he could have arrived at the absolute formalism of Clive Bell and Roger Fry, or without a knowledge of nonobjective art at the synthesis or formalism and expressionism which is the singular achievement of Sir Herbert Read.

### Notes

1. Iain Fletcher, *Walter Pater,* Writers and Their Work series, no. 114 (London: Longmans, Green, 1959), p. 36.

2. Quoted in Sylvia Sprigge, *Berenson: A Biography* (Boston: Houghton Mifflin, 1960), p. 48.

3. Walter Pater, *The Renaissance* (London: Macmillan, 1888), p. x.

4. Walter Pater, "Style," *Appreciations* (London: Macmillan, 1897), p. 14.

5. Pater, *The Renaissance,* p. 103.

6. *Ibid.,* p. 129.

7. *Ibid.,* pp. xi-xii.

8. *Ibid.,* p. 252.

9. *Ibid.,* p. 2.

10. *Ibid.,* p. 193.

11. *Ibid.,* p. 234.

12. *Ibid.,* p. 116.

13. *Ibid.,* p. 57.

14. A. C. Benson, *Walter Pater* (New York: Macmillan, 1906), p. 185.

15. *Ibid.,* p. 206.

16. Pater, *The Renaissance,* p. 67.

17. *Ibid.,* p. ix.

18. *Ibid.,* p. 75.

19. *Ibid.,* p. 69.

20. Pater, *Appreciations,* p. 6.

21. *Ibid.,* pp. 80-81.

22. *Ibid.,* p. 35.

23. Pater, *The Renaissance,* p. 135.

24. *Ibid.,* pp. 136-137.

25. *Ibid.,* p. 140.

26. *Ibid.,* p. 145.

### Richard S. Lyons (essay date autumn 1972)

SOURCE: Lyons, Richard S. "The 'Complex, Many-Sided' Unity of *The Renaissance.*" *Studies in English Literature: 1500-1900* 12, no. 4 (autumn 1972): 765-81.

[*In the following essay, Lyons examines Pater's* The Renaissance *within the context of the nineteenth-century aesthetic movement. The author analyzes the various moral concerns that form the foundation of Pater's theory of art.*]

The identification of Walter Pater with a few notorious phrases from the Conclusion to *The Renaissance* seems to have ended. Recent studies of Pater have been mainly concerned with the *Imaginary Portraits* and *Marius the Epicurean.* The relative position of *The Renais-*

*sance* in Pater's writings has changed; the emphasis is now on its introduction of themes later treated in the fiction or its exaggeration of attitudes qualified or abandoned in *Marius* and the late essays.[1] This concern for Pater's fictional world and the more precise discrimination of his development are unquestionably valuable and yet it would be unfortunate if *The Renaissance* were really neglected, for it remains central for Pater and one of the important English books of its time. It presents a complex of attitudes—aesthetic, cultural, moral—that has relevance beyond the enthusiasms of the *fin de siècle*. This relevance is being widely recognized and is linked to the redefinition of the range of views loosely labelled "aesthetic."[2] The present essay is a contribution to that collective effort; it proposes to elucidate the aesthetic, cultural and moral attitudes of *The Renaissance* and to show their interconnections as well as some of the contradictions and ambiguities latent within them. The relationships are easily stated in general terms: *The Renaissance* is a work of aesthetics based upon a concept of culture and animated by a moral ideal. The immediate concern of the book is with art; but this concern serves as the basis for culture, and this "aesthetic" culture is defended by a moral vision. The aesthetic ideas are best approached through Pater's notion of *expression*; the idea of culture gets its most important treatment in the essay on Winckelmann, and the moral ideal is presented most explicitly in the Conclusion. These are the focal points of the discussion, but the emphasis throughout will be on their interdependence.[3]

Pater's famous statement that "in aesthetic criticism the first step towards seeing one's object as it really is, is to know one's own impression as it really is, to discriminate it, to realize it distinctly" is clearly a "first step," and the critic's goal, as the phrase from Arnold indicates, is to return to the work of art itself with a more precise understanding.[4] For Pater, the question, "What is this song or picture, this engaging personality presented in life or in a book, *to me?*" (viii), has as its ultimate aim a more subtle awareness of the distinguishing qualities of that to which one is responding. In fact, Pater is less likely to move from the work to the beholder than from the work to its creator, using the life of the artist to approach the work from the other side. Here too, however, the return is always to the object itself. Even when our main interest is the artist, it is the work of art which unites the beholder with the creator and it does so precisely by those virtues or qualities the critic must discriminate. To understand properly this relationship we must consider Pater's idea of *expression,* the central aesthetic formulation of *The Renaissance.*

Pater defines *expression* in the essay on Della Robbia as "some subtler sense of originality—the seal on a man's work of what is most inward and peculiar in his moods, and manner of apprehension" (71). What Pater means by "subtler" is indicated when he compares *expression* to "the passing of a smile over the face of a child, the ripple of the air on a still day over the curtain of a window ajar" (65). As the Preface instructs us, it is to such apprehensions that the aesthetic critic must be attuned, and the quality of Pater's prose is perfectly suited to rendering them. The very fineness of the discriminations may be misleading, however, suggesting that *expression* is a matter of a special finish or a superadded grace. For Pater, *expression* is not some further refinement of art; it is its quintessence. Rare as it may be, Pater claims that "essentially, perhaps, it is the quality which alone makes works in the imaginative and moral order really worth having at all" (72). Despite the "perhaps," we must recognize the magnitude of the claim. To grant the statement its full seriousness, however, it is necessary to understand the relation of the idea of *expression* to Pater's whole enterprise in *The Renaissance.*

Both the choice and treatment of his subject show Pater's aesthetic principles at work. Pater sees in the period of the Renaissance and the particular artists he discusses a peculiar fitness for his concerns. As he explains, the artists of the fifteenth century gave their work expression in an "unmistakable way" (72). Since Pater's search is not for those qualities which an artist shares with others of his time, but for his unique contribution, it is significant that he is not led to bizarre or eccentric artists. He chooses artists firmly within the central tradition. Given his critical aims, this choice helps explain why Pater's treatment seems at times thin, even attenuated. It is not merely, as Pater explains in the Preface, that few artists leave "only what the heat of their imagination has wholly fused" (x). To the historically aware, much of any art lies in its traditions, and what is original may be seen only in some subtle modification of what the artist has received. In such circumstances, the distinguishing features must necessarily be slight, only noticeable to the attentive eye, like that tremor of the curtain on a still day.

It is extremely important that the distinguishing qualities of the artists Pater discusses are not glaring, that they hint and suggest, always with something of the mysterious, the finally unresolvable, about their proffered insights. The edge of discrimination is only sharpened by some strain of attention or discipline of perception, that "nicety" of which Pater speaks in the Preface. Perhaps more importantly, the focus must always be on the object itself and the precise value of its revelations comes from the fact that they are unavailable by any other means. Therefore, however, they can never be corroborated, never validated and finally known. It is significant that, despite the biographical form of the essays, works of art are rarely explained or interpreted by biographical detail. Rather the biography is given as a shadowy background into which the works cast some fitful light. Pater often prefers legend to fact, as in the case of Leonardo; here the legend itself becomes a kind of work of art, evidence of a "comely life" which has its privileged revelations to offer, its own *expression* we may seize upon. For the historical movement of the Renaissance as well, Pater is at pains to reduce the singularity of the movement, to stress its lines of continuity with the Middle Ages and the Enlightenment. Still, these artists taken together have their *expression*; on them is impressed "what is most inward in [the] moods, and manner of apprehension" of the age. Moreover, it is implied that the insight they offer, however much it may be reinforced by other studies, remains unique, their special and irreplaceable contribution.

This fact reconciles what might be an apparent conflict between aesthetic and historical response in Pater. In one sense, Pater's criticism is resolutely historical: it is one of the central tenets of the book that every artist is a reflection of the currents of thought and feeling of his age. The questions in the Preface: "In whom did the stir, the genius, the sentiment of the period, find itself? where was the receptacle of its refinement, its elevation, its taste?" (x) reflect Pater's true bias. Yet Pater is in many respects unhistorical; in fact, the real effort of the historical critic, to put his "object in perspective, and [set] the reader in a certain point of view, from which what gave pleasure to the past is pleasurable for him" (19), serves Pater as a definition of antiquarianism, which has interest only if a real, direct aesthetic charm exists in the work itself. That an object has only antiquarian interest for Pater really means that it has no *expression*, that it can be invested with interest by applying to it our knowledge of a past age but that it does not in itself have any special revelation, any "virtue" for which it may be prized. The historical and aesthetic responses in Pater cannot really be distinguished because the historical awareness comes only aesthetically; the aesthetic quality in a work or a life becomes the capacity to evoke our sense of some special quality of the artist or the age of which it is a product. By the same token, the historical context in Pater is always dim, impressionistic, because our subtle response to the work of art or the shape of a life is our only means of really knowing the secret it holds of the past.

Pater's aesthetic principles are revealed through his choice of subject in yet another way. One of the requisites for *expression* is a sense of unity, and Pater finds in the "many-sided" movement of the Renaissance a

unity which, if nowhere stated, is everywhere implied. Similarly, with each artist Pater discusses, he finds a leading motive, an inspiriting principle, what Pater was elsewhere to call his *vraie vérité*, as the key to his life and works. The unity that Pater seeks in the age or in individual artists regularly derives from a resolution or reconciliation of opposing forces or tendencies. Pater speaks, for example, of that unity of culture in which "'whatsoever things are comely' are reconciled" (27), and the same association of unity and reconciliation recurs in the opening pages of the essay on Pico della Mirandola. Pater finds this unity most often in moments of transition. Much of the book is taken up with the early Renaissance and its sources in the Middle Ages and a long section is devoted to the afterglow in the life of Winckelmann. The central chapters on Michelangelo and Leonardo deal with the artists' beginnings and endings and with those features in their work which set them apart or link them to traditions not usually associated with them; Michelangelo becomes the forerunner of Blake and Victor Hugo, and Leonardo is seen in his late medieval origins and as a fascinating precursor of modern, romantic ideas. One of the chief effects of this emphasis on beginnings and endings is a curious foreshortening so that even the amazingly long and crowded artistic lives of Michelangelo and Leonardo are made to appear momentary and curiously insubstantial. Witness the strange description of the massive and passionate Michelangelo in the incredible artistic vigor of his late years as a *revenant,* "a ghost out of another age, in a world too coarse to touch his faint sensibilities very closely" (90). Leonardo's life is so shrouded in mystery by Pater that it figures as a kind of dream, tantalizing but timeless. The other artists are frankly treated as representing a moment of transition, capturing in a somewhat tentative way a new mode of feeling or expression. We may take Pater's remark on Botticelli as representative: "He has the freshness, the uncertain and diffident promise, which belong to the earlier Renaissance itself, and make it perhaps the most interesting period in the history of the mind" (61-62).

That the unity which is the requisite for the supreme aesthetic quality of *expression* should be most perfectly apprehended at moments of transition suggests that this unity is evanescent, the result of a precarious balance that may soon shift and fall. One effect of such an emphasis might be to give a sense of change, of a continuing evolutionary or dialectical process. Occasionally, Pater's statements about organic development and evolutionary growth seem to imply such a view, but the primary effect in **The Renaissance** is the opposite: whether in dealing with individual artists or with the historical movement as a whole, our sense of time is reduced to a moment, so that a work of art, a life, a whole sweep of history may be apprehended by a single perception. We return to the shifting of the curtain or the passing smile on the child's face.

There is a connection between Pater's interest in "our moments of play, [when] we are surprised at the unexpected blessedness of what may seem our least important part of time" (151) and his concern for moments of transition, particularly the "freshness, the uncertain and diffident promise" of early manhood he notes in Botticelli and the Renaissance itself. In both instances, the relief from intensely felt stresses and conflicts, whether of life or history, comes not so much by the active struggle of dialectic as by a relaxation of striving, allowing those unexpected moments of *bien-être* for which Pater claims it was Leonardo's peculiar genius to learn to wait. So, for example, Marius achieves his most perfect vision in a privileged hour of unexpected delay and at precisely that point when he is moving from the authority of Marcus Aurelius to that of Cornelius and Cecilia.[5] The connection of these moments with times of transition makes them at once more precious and more precarious, capturing that ambivalence in the emphasis on the moment that Barbara Charlesworth has pointed out.[6] The finest example of this special sense of equilibrium is the passage in **"The School of Giorgione"** linking Giorgione's painting with dramatic poetry. Though long, it is worth quoting in its entirety:

> Now it is part of the ideality of the highest sort of dramatic poetry, that it presents us with a kind of profoundly significant and animated instants, a mere gesture, a look, a smile, perhaps,—some brief and wholly concrete moment—into which, however, all the motives, all the interests and effects of a long history have condensed themselves, and which seem to absorb past and future in an intense consciousness of the present. Such ideal instants the school of Giorgione selects, with its admirable tact, from that feverish, tumultuously coloured world of the old citizens of Venice— exquisite pauses in time, in which, arrested thus, we seem to be spectators of all the fulness of existence, and which are like some consummate extract or quintessence of life.
>
> (150).

All that has been noted about *expression*—its capacity for unique revelation, its momentary quality, its harmonizing of several impulses—is implicit in the passage although the term is never used.

Pater's idea of *expression* grants to aesthetic contemplation a privileged role in human experience. How important a role is suggested by the phrases "the fulness of life" and "quintessence of life." Pater means more than the imitation in a work of art of life that is full and passionate; the fulness of life resides in the art itself. For Pater works of art at their perfect moments become the only avenues to an awareness of the most essential qualities of life. No higher claim could be made for art. Yet there is a crucial problem in this position; the viewers are, after all, only spectators, and the life of which the work presents the quintessence is not itself either art or the apprehension of it (although when Pater speaks of Giorgione's pictures as portraying life itself as a kind of listening, we come close to this view). The problem is central to the whole concept of aesthetic culture on which **The Renaissance** is based, since the claim Pater makes for the book as a whole in its relation to the "complex, many-sided movement" of the Renaissance is analogous to that made for works of art in relation to the "fulness of life." Pater faces the problem in the essay on Winckelmann; there he defines the concept of culture on which the book is based and explores indirectly the contradictions inherent in it.

Pater begins the essay on Winckelmann by alluding to Goethe's description "of the teacher who had made his career possible" as "an abstract type of culture" (177). The purpose of the essay becomes defining the culture which Winckelmann represents and placing it in relation both to the supreme figure of Goethe himself and to the "modern world." Winckelmann is the type of an aesthetic culture in two senses. First, the field of his knowledge is severely restricted to art, more especially to the art of Greece. Pater calls this limitation "a step forward in culture" because it meant that Winckelmann "multiplied his intellectual force by detaching from it all flaccid interests" (181). Part of the aim of the essay is to show with what success this total absorption in a limited range of the arts was able to sustain and nourish a life otherwise doomed to be constricted and ineffectual. But Winckelmann's culture was aesthetic in a more profound sense. His response to the pagan world was essentially the kind of response that Pater offers as proper to works of art: he reacted with extraordinary intensity to the *expression* in Greek art and so was able to divine (Pater speaks of his "divinatory power") the Greek spirit in the full and untranslatable way that is available only through art. The keynote of Pater's treatment of Winckelmann is his insistence on the special character of Winckelmann's response to the ancient world; he responded not only with his intelligence but with his passion and temperament. His massive erudition is subordinated to his intuitive response. The central unifying feature of Winckelmann's life becomes the consistency of his aesthetic response. What makes Winckelmann's achievement the more remarkable is that he had available so little of the central Greek tradition. Perhaps one should say that this fact validates the aesthetic quality of his understanding—we recall the fine discrimination needed to single out the virtue of the work from its dross, or the acute awareness needed to catch the passing smile or the tremor of the curtain. The central pages of the essay, in which Pater tries to define the Hellenic spirit, seem intrusive, despite the brilliance of some of their formulations, precisely because they are an attempt to translate the aesthetic response into scholarly terms.

The definition of Hellenism has another ostensible purpose: to explain Winckelmann's importance for Goethe by revealing that the Hellenic element in Goethe's culture was made accessible to him by Winckelmann. In fact, Winckelmann's importance has already been established in the essay by rendering his life in terms appropriate to a work of art. Out of the singleness of Winckelmann's culture, and as by a happy blending of its subject and form, come the qualities of "balance, unity with oneself, consummate Greek modelling" (228). Elsewhere Pater speaks of Winckelmann's single-mindedness as casting off interests "which in most men are the waste part of nature" (185), and we recall the language Pater uses in the Preface to describe artists casting off all debris in their works. Winckelmann's aesthetic culture becomes, therefore, not only a model, the type of culture on which *The Renaissance* is based, but itself an object of contemplation, having its own form and *expression*.

Yet Pater's explicit claim is that "the aim of a right criticism is to place Winckelmann in an intellectual perspective, of which Goethe is the foreground. For, after all, he is infinitely less than Goethe; it is chiefly because at certain points he comes in contact with Goethe, that criticism entertains consideration of him" (226). I think this statement of Pater's is best understood as a recognition of a fundamental contradiction in the concept of culture which Winckelmann represents. The contradiction is clearer if we consider Arnold's two-sided definition of culture in *Culture and Anarchy*. Arnold establishes the grounds for culture in his elevated sense of the word "curiosity" and chooses for its motto Montesquieu's words, "to render an intelligent being yet more intelligent." Yet there is a second motive for culture which Arnold offers: the study of perfection. For this motive Arnold chooses as a motto, "To make reason and the will of God prevail."[7]

This second motive for culture differs from the first in two respects: the study of perfection involves more of our nature than the scientific passion and, preeminently, it aims to issue in action. It is almost the whole of Arnold's rhetorical purpose in *Culture and Anarchy* to argue that because culture studies *perfection* it must not rush too hastily into doing; it must learn to *know* reason and the will of God before trying to make them prevail, but there is no question that the ultimate claim on action, as well as the involvement of the full range of human concerns, is what gives to culture, in Arnold's view, its final dignity and seriousness. The culture that Winckelmann represents has two distinguishing features: its unity and balance are achieved at the cost of severely limiting the range of its interests, and it issues not in action but in a passionate contemplation. Pater describes Winckelmann's temperament as a "moral sexlessness, a kind of ineffectual wholeness of nature, yet with a true beauty and significance of its own" (221).[8] Yet the culture proposed by *The Renaissance* is justified by Pater as putting us in touch with life, even the fulness of life, in a unique and irreplaceable way. That is why the emphasis in the discussion of Winckelmann falls on his passion, his temperament, the dynamics of a life which viewed from another standpoint seems to static and removed.

Goethe offers Pater an apparent reconciliation of this contradiction for his culture fits the Arnoldian idea perfectly, having both breadth of interest and a call to action: "Goethe's culture . . . ever emerged in the practical functions of art, in actual production" (230). The trouble is that Goethe is *not* in the foreground of the essay on Winckelmann; what he represents cannot be assimilated to the idea of culture that lies behind not only that essay but the book as a whole. It is significant that the description of culture which is represented to be a description of Goethe's higher life, is precisely an intensified and extended version of the kind of culture Winckelmann represents and, indeed, might serve as the definition of the aim towards which the entire development of *The Renaissance* is directed. The essence of this culture is its spectatorial role, active only in the fact that it requires a constant discrimination and selection. Confronted by partial cultures, "arising out of the intense, laborious, one-sided development of some special talent," it rigorously avoids commitment to any of them. What it searches for is the satisfaction of its self-awareness. "But the pure instinct of self-culture cares not so much to reap all that these forms of culture can give, as to find in them its own strength." The ultimate goal is a vision of life: "It [the intellect] struggles with those forms till its secret is won from each, and then lets each fall back into its place, in the supreme artistic view of life" (229).

Goethe reconciles the "supreme, artistic view of life" with action of a special kind: creating works of art. These works of art have a particular role to play in "the service of culture," that is, the kind of culture that Winckelmann and *The Renaissance* exemplify. In explaining this role, Pater makes one of his crucial formulations and gives a significant insight into the reason for contradictions in his idea of culture and for the moral ambiguities that are related to them. "What modern art has to do in the service of culture is so to rearrange the details of modern life, so to reflect it, that it may satisfy the spirit. And what does the spirit need in the face of modern life? The sense of freedom" (230-231). The *sense* of freedom because freedom itself does not exist; necessity controls all our actions; law, the "army of unalterable law" rules everywhere. The sense of freedom resolves itself into an attitude: "there is still something in the nobler or less noble attitude with which we watch their fatal combinations" (231). It is against this vision of the nature of modern life, or rather of modern awareness, that we must set the idea of culture offered in the essay on Winckelmann. Put this way, however, the issue becomes a moral one, at least in the Arnoldian sense that the question "how to live" is a moral question. The notorious Conclusion to **The Renaissance** is Pater's attempt to face directly the moral issues involved.[9]

The opening pages of the Conclusion are Pater's attempt to show what "the tendency of modern thought" does to our sense of life. The historical relativism that informs the attitude of the aesthetic critic as outlined in the Preface is here allied with the spirit of scientific analysis to serve as a solvent of any sense of continuity or stability in experience. Pater moves from "inconstant modes or fashions" to the ceaseless "combination of natural elements" with no effort of transition. Pater is simply evoking in this opening paragraph the general complex of positivistic attitudes so widely pervasive in late-nineteenth-century writers.[10] The difference lies in the use to which these attitudes are put. Other writers, George Eliot for example, used the connection between natural law and historical change to suggest a principle of stability and order in human experience. Pater, typically, derives the reverse effect. As tradition loses its permanence, so objects lose their solidity. All nature, man included, becomes only the "concurrence, renewed from moment to moment, of forces parting sooner or later on their ways" (239). A third tendency of modern thought, that of introspective reflection, is evoked to complete the destructive analysis. Man's inner life loses its continuity; not only are we cut off from others but from ourselves. All that is real in our life is finally reduced to barely apprehensible moments, "to a single sharp impression."[11]

We have seen this same attitude all through **The Renaissance**; what marks off the Conclusion is the new intensity of language. Having reduced all experience to a succession of moments, Pater tries to expand these moments to their fullest and in the process a new sense of urgency comes into the prose. In fact, however, the approach to experience at large is exactly analogous to the aesthetic attitudes embodied in Pater's idea of *expression*. The same reduction to the moment, to the unique and untranslatable (unanalyzable) revelation that constitutes the essential reality of art for Pater, is here applied to all experience. The difference in tone derives partly from the fact that the emphasis in the rest of **The Renaissance** falls on the rarity, and thereby the preciousness of *expression* in art, whereas in the Conclusion the awareness of *expression* would be constant. What Pater offers in these closing pages is a vision of life as *continuous* aesthetic experience. When we consider what Pater has said about the difficulty of pure aesthetic achievement for the artist, and about the fine pitch of discrimination needed to apprehend *expression,* we can acknowledge that the extremity of language is at least partly justified by the exalted vision proposed. Yet we must remember what Pater evidently feared the "young men" would not notice, that this language of passion and intensity is applied to an attitude fundamentally contemplative, not active. When Pater says that "not the fruit of experience, but experience itself is the end" he is speaking of experience as "sharp and eager observation," the ability to "discriminate every moment." When he speaks of touching as well as seeing and of "great passions" and "the various forms of enthusiastic activity," it *is* the "fruit" we seek: a "quickened, multiplied consciousness." It is supremely true of works of art that the experience of them is an end in itself; indeed, as we have seen, the experience of art defines the kind of experience Pater is advocating.

Impassioned contemplation is called the ideal of culture in Pater's essay on Wordsworth, and Wordsworth's moral value is seen as deriving from his ability to evoke and sustain such an ideal; that great and serious essay has a sureness of tone that the slightly feverish Conclusion lacks, but the positions are essentially the same.[12] There are, however, latent contradictions in the Conclusion that need examination. The first and most obvious has already been discussed in relation to both aesthetics and culture: the ideal Pater calls for depends upon its not being generally accepted. "Those about us" must furnish the spectacle we are to watch with that impassioned contemplation Pater advocates, and they can only offer us the chance to exercise our discrimination by themselves participating in life, even as creators of those works of art that afford us our supreme experiences. Even those philosophical theories which we must be testing and casting aside derive ultimately from a conviction to which the aesthetic attitude is foreign. It is unfair to be superior to Pater on this point. His sense of the corrosive effect of historical relativism and scientific analysis seems truer than even the guarded meliorism of George Eliot. Moreover, both the ambiguity of Pater's position and some of the extravagance of his rhetoric, so easy a mark for mockery, derive from his refusal to surrender entirely the sense of reality in both actions and objects. Though his analysis of the tendency of modern thought leads him to an ideal of contemplation, he believes in the reality of what is contemplated and, indeed, tries to invoke the "splendour of our experience" even as he explains it away.

There is a second moral ambiguity in the Conclusion, however, and one that is related to its subversive tendencies even more profoundly than its misleading language of passion. Pater's analysis of experience denies the possibility of any real knowledge of others like ourselves. Each person is isolated, "each mind keeping as a solitary prisoner its own dream of a world" (235). The moral isolation such a view implies, the perfect egocentricity it accepts, is nowhere in the Conclusion contradicted or qualified. Yet elsewhere in *The Renaissance* Pater tries to mitigate this egoism and, in fact, claims the moral ideal of sympathy as the inspiriting force in the humanism he writes about and endorses.

This ideal of sympathy is most fully stated at the close of the essay on Pico della Mirandola: "For the essence of humanism is that belief of which he seems never to have doubted, that nothing which has ever interested living men and women can wholly lose its vitality—no language they have spoken, nor oracle beside which they have hushed their voices, no dream which has once been entertained by actual human minds, nothing about which they have ever been passionate, or expended time and zeal" (49). The passage serves as a kind of credo for *The Renaissance* in its entirety. The note struck in the passage is a call to our feelings, hence the words "vitality," "passionate," "zeal." The way out of our isolation is in a sympathetic vibration to the emotion of others; if we cannot *know* a world outside ourselves, at least we can imagine what it feels like. So stated, Pater's humanism seems not so far from George Eliot's ideal of sympathy, yet the very catholicity of interest in Pater betrays a fundamental difference between the two writers. For George Eliot our sympathy should be strongest for those closest to us because it can shape our actions towards them. The sympathy of Pater, on the other hand, can be all inclusive because it is, ironically, allied with self-preoccupation and detachment; whatever moral implications it has derive not from the way it can direct our actions but from the way it deepens our feelings. Thus the moral vision of the book is perfectly consistent with the aesthetic and cultural attitudes; indeed, the passage on Pico is also a definition of the ideal of culture expressed in the essay on Winckelmann. Moreover, there is a connection between the way the critic's concentration upon his own impression becomes the way to understanding the reality of the work of art and the way the self-culture of a Winckelmann

puts him in contact with the reality of the classical world and, indeed, allows him to open for others "a new organ of feeling." The aesthetic, cultural, and moral ideals of *The Renaissance* are finally one vision—a vision that with its ambiguities and contradictions has considerable coherence and depth.

Both the consistency and the contradictions in *The Renaissance* are important. There has been in the study of Pater a great deal of emphasis on the peculiarities of his temperament, and Pater's own statements, particularly in *Marius the Epicurean,* about the importance of temperament in shaping each person's vision of the world have given sanction to this approach. Certainly much of the tone of Pater's writings derives from the odd combination of passion and reserve in the fastidious and inward don. Yet the complex of attitudes represented in *The Renaissance* transcends mere temperament; it had sufficient coherence and depth to remain important for English literature for forty and more years; it is relevant to the work of the finest writers of the end of the nineteenth and the beginning of the twentieth centuries— Yeats, James, Conrad, Forster. Pater's emphasis upon "being" rather than "doing," his attempt to find in art a "new organ of feeling," his refinement (or attenuation) of the mid-century ideal of sympathy from its practical moral bias to its emotional value—all have significance far beyond the usual line of Wilde, Symonds, and the minor decadents. Above all, the attempt in *The Renaissance* to establish an ideal of culture based upon the enrichment of personal sensibility that would give at least a "sense of freedom" in the midst of an intellectual atmosphere increasingly bleak and a society increasingly hostile and destructive to the spirit is reflected in work after work of the decades that followed. As Graham Hough has argued, these attitudes have their roots in the work of the first Romantics; but in Pater, and in *The Renaissance* in particular, they stand divorced from appeals to metaphysical, theological and even moral traditions that are drawn upon by earlier writers. It is the degree to which Pater accepts the conclusions of modern thought even as he attempts to counteract its effects that accounts for much of the integrity and, also, the narrowness of his vision. If, as David De-Laura has claimed, Pater's "House Beautiful" is the "unique product of a passing stage of culture," the stage did not pass quickly, and if it "lies in ruins" it took a great storm to accomplish its destruction.[13]

If the consistency of Pater's vision accounts in part for its extended relevance, the contradictions latent within it account in part for its continuing interest. Pater's failures as a writer may come less from inconsistencies in his vision than from his inability to dramatize effectively or embody in symbol and image the conflicts inherent in it. Where Pater succeeds, the contradictions themselves become the subject of his art. For example, the essential contradiction involved in Pater's attempt to invest the detached and contemplative mode with the sense of "the fulness of life" as well as the ambiguities latent in the emphasis on the moment as the focus of all experience are related to the persistent concern of Pater with childhood—as play and as promise—and with death, especially with death as a return. In one sense, both the innocence of childhood and the fulfillment of death seem to solve the problem of action and to offer supreme moments when experience really is *being* rather than *doing* and the "sense of freedom" either as promise or release is most fully felt. The joining of the two moments, however, makes clear the ambiguities of feeling attached to them, and this joining is beautifully accomplished in the persistent figure of exile in Pater's work in which the exile is ended only with the return in death to childhood.[14] Pater's most perfect artistic accomplishment, the story **"The Child in the House,"** depends upon these contradictions and ambiguities and gathers them up in the images and pattern of the story.

Pater is a minor writer and the aesthetic movement in the narrow sense in which it is usually considered is a minor literary episode. Yet Pater, for all his lines of connection with earlier writers, may usefully be placed near the beginning of a "movement" aesthetic in the broadest and yet perhaps most pertinent sense. The story of the movement's development and collapse has yet to be told, though the growing interest in the era from 1870 to 1914 is preparing the way. It is in this larger movement that Pater's writings will find their true place and ***The Renaissance*** its lasting importance.

## Notes

1. See for clear examples: U. C. Knoepflmacher, *Religious Humanism and the Victorian Novel* (Princeton, 1965), and Gerald C. Monsman, *Pater's Portraits: Mythic Pattern in the Fiction of Walter Pater* (Baltimore, 1967).

2. See *Edwardians and Late Victorians: English Institute Essays 1959* (New York, 1960), particularly Ruth Z. Temple, "The Ivory Tower as Lighthouse," and Richard Ellmann, "The Two Faces of Edward," and, for an extension of the term back into earlier writers, William A. Madden, *Matthew Arnold: A Study of the Aesthetic Temperament in Victorian England* (Bloomington, 1967).

3. *The Renaissance* is, of course, a collection of articles written over a number of years. The unity of the book derives then, not from a single plan of composition but from the consistency of Pater's viewpoint during the years from the middle 1860's to 1873. Pater rearranged the articles out of the order of their composition, transposed pages from other articles (the Conclusion was largely taken from a review of William Morris's poetry; pages of "Winckelmann" derive from the early essay "Diaphaneite") and, in the third edition (1888), added "The School of Giorgione" (1878). The present essay will treat the work as a whole in its final form as the finest crystallization of the attitudes it represents. Clearly, a genetic approach would better reveal the convergence of Pater's views in the early years, and a restriction to the first edition would be more accurate in gauging the book's immediate influence. As a work representative of the aesthetic attitude, however, the final edition is the most authoritative and complete.

4. *The Renaissance: Studies in Art and Poetry* (London, 1910), p. viii. Hereafter page references to this edition will be given in parentheses after the quotations.

5. *Marius the Epicurean: His Sensations and Ideas* (London, 1910), II, 62 ff.

6. *Dark Passages: The Decadent Consciousness in Victorian Literature* (Madison, 1965), pp. 41-44 *et passim*.

7. *Culture and Anarchy,* ed. J. Dover Wilson (Cambridge, 1950), pp. 44, 45.

8. The phrases are from an early essay, "Diaphaneite," *Miscellaneous Studies* (London, 1910), p. 253. The character Pater describes in the essay is offered as an example of "the mental attitude, the intellectual manner of perfect culture" (p. 250).

9. The contradiction between the necessity for detachment and the rhetoric of the "fulness of life" is very well explored by David J. DeLaura in "The 'Wordsworth' of Pater and Arnold: 'The Supreme Artistic View of Life,'" *Studies in English Literature,* VI (1966), 651-667. Mr. DeLaura fails to take sufficiently into account, I believe, the degree to which this contradiction turns on Pater's acute awareness of the implications of the "positivistic" viewpoint of science. Hence, he attaches more weight to Pater's lack of concern for society than to his philosophical dilemma.

10. The best summary of these attitudes is found in Bernard J. Paris, *Experiments in Life: George Eliot's Quest for Values* (Detroit, 1965), chs. i-v.

11. Cf. Charlesworth, *Dark Passages,* pp. 41-42.

12. *Appreciations* (London, 1910), p. 62. See DeLaura, "The 'Wordsworth' of Pater and Arnold," 660, for the connections between *The Renaissance* and the essay on Wordsworth.

13. "Pater and Newman: The Road to the Nineties," *Victorian Studies,* X (1966-67), 67.

14. The image of exile and return is discussed from a different point of view in Monsman, *Pater's Portraits,* pp. 211-213.

## Lawrence F. Schuetz (essay date 1974)

SOURCE: Schuetz, Lawrence F. "The Suppressed 'Conclusion' to *The Renaissance* and Pater's Modern Image." *English Literature in Transition* 17, no. 4 (1974): 251-58.

[*In the following essay, Schuetz analyzes the various factors behind Pater's decision to remove his infamous "Conclusion" from the 1877 edition of* The Renaissance, *among them Pater's sensitivity to the potential impact of critical censure on his reputation. Schuetz also examines the controversy surrounding the original publication of the essay, as well as subsequent negative reactions to Pater's decision to suppress it.*]

Pater's suppression of the "Conclusion" in the second edition of *The Renaissance* (1877) has long elicited critical speculation about his motives and his character in general. Pater's enigmatic and uneventful life, further obscured by generally unsatisfactory biographies, inevitably invites such speculation. With relatively few verifiable facts available, established opinion has focused on his sensitivity to adverse criticism, particularly W. H. Mallock's caricature of Mr. Rose in *The New Republic,* or on Pater's concern for reputation and his position in Oxford as leading motives for the suppression. Neither view affords a very favorable image of Pater, and neither accords proper significance to his stated motive for withdrawing the piece. In a note to the restored "Conclusion" (third edition, 1888), Pater expresses his ethical concern that its philosophy had been misinterpreted: "This brief 'Conclusion' was omitted in the second edition of this book, as I conceived it might possibly mislead some of those young men into whose hands it might fall. On the whole, I have thought it best to reprint it here, with some slight changes which bring it closer to my original meaning. I have dealt more fully in *Marius the Epicurean* with the thoughts suggested by it."[1] The wording of the note clearly reflects that of a letter to Pater from John Wordsworth, in which Wordsworth criticized the philosophy of the "Conclusion" on the basis of a misinterpretation of its principles. This letter and the position it represented were probably the central consideration in Pater's decision to withdraw the "Conclusion" and certainly influenced his overall revaluation of its thought. Pater's decision was determined by the high seriousness with which he approached the substance of his work and the form in which it was expressed, not by the weakness of character implied by the widely accepted views of his motivation. The implications of this apparently minor point, moreover, extend beyond simple speculation over problematical motives, for much of the critical discussion of the "Conclusion's" suppression both reflects and fosters the predominantly negative modern image of Pater.

The influence of Mallock's *New Republic* has been suggested most authoritatively by Geoffrey Tillotson in "Pater, Mr. Rose, and the 'Conclusion' of the *Renaissance,*"[2] This scrupulously fair article examines Mallock's methods of parodying Pater and offers a balanced analysis of the "Conclusion" itself. Tillotson concludes that although "Mallock said that his portrait of Pater, like that of each of his speakers, was a portrait both individual and typical, . . . Pater had to bear the full brunt of both the individual and the typical."[3] The article suggests that Mallock's misinterpretation of the "Conclusion," rather than the satire per se, may have influenced Pater's decision: "Pater must have numbered Mallock among these misled; for Mr. Rose is a sensualist, at least in mind. Pater dropped his 'Conclusion,' the main source and excuse for Mr. Rose, and by the time it reappeared it had been revised."[4] Tillotson does justice to both Mallock and Pater in indicating that *The New Republic* may have been a contributing—though hardly sufficient—cause for the suppression of the "Conclusion."

The difficulty arises from the extension of such implications to an interpretation of Pater's character in general. Jerome Buckley, for example, asserts that "Pater may have feared his detractors not less than he was shortly to resent his admirers, and that the 'misled' young men may have been those already contemning his manner and attitudes."[5] Buckley finds in Mallock's Mr. Rose the "immediate and specific cause" of the "Conclusion"'s suppression and concludes that "Pater may, therefore, very well have decided after due deliberation that an expurgated edition of *The Renaissance* might prove the most effective answer to his 'misled' assailant and forestall future attack of a similar kind." This implies that Pater was willing to modify his principles in response to Mallock's criticism. But Buckley further impugns Pater's integrity by stating: "How characteristically 'unWildean' was the willingness to withdraw what constituted in essence a declaration of art's amoral self-sufficiency . . . he was, I believe, definitely deferring in a quite 'unaesthetic' way to a rather conservative criticism."[6] Thus we see Pater finally as a hypersensitive ego unable to withstand the mockery of a Mallock and totally lacking the courage of his convictions.

Yet Thomas Wright long ago discounted any such influence by Mallock on Pater, his thought or his career. But Wright, characteristically, exaggerates: "We are able to declare positively," Wright states, "that, instead of suffering distress, he took [*The New Republic*] as a compliment, thoroughly enjoyed it and laughed heartily at the passages that went nearest the truth. Pater was troubled, indeed, not because people might recognise the portrait, but because he feared they might not recognise it. . . . We would also point out that he was a man who did not care one straw what anybody said of him—being in this respect not in the least sensitive."[7] This is patently an overstatement, based simply on Pater's alleged remark that he was "pleased to be called Mr. Rose—the rose being the queen of flowers."[8] Even if Wright's quotation is accurate, his conclusion is hardly justified by such a casual remark. Pater was in fact sensitive to criticism. He changed the title of the second edition of *The Renaissance,* for example, because critics such as Mrs. Pattison had objected to the misleading use of "History" in the original title, ***Studies in the History of the Renaissance.***[9] Similarly, like many contemporary writers, Pater "leaked" an advance copy of ***Marius*** to William Sharp to assure a favorable review.[10]

This is not, however, the virtually neurotic sensitivity of a D. G. Rossetti, nor does it substantiate the influence of Mallock. Pater's correspondence with his publisher, Macmillan, suggests that he decided sometime prior to 15 November 1876 to withdraw the "Conclusion." In a note to Pater two days prior to that date, Macmillan proposed a new edition of *The Renaissance,* and Evans notes that "Pater had apparently spoken to him previously of making some alterations, the most important of which was to be the dropping of the 'Conclusion.'"[11] In his reply to Macmillan on the fifteenth, Pater writes: "I shall be very glad to have a new and revised edition of my essays, adding a small quantity of new matter, and making a good many alterations, so that the new book would be of the size of the present."[12] Since there is no specific reference to the "Conclusion" in any of the correspondence concerning the second edition of *The Renaissance,* the precise chronology of Pater's decision to drop the piece cannot be established definitely. However, Pater's revisions do not appreciably shorten the text of *The Renaissance,* and his concern for maintaining the "size" of the book can only mean that he had made the decision by this time. Moreover, he seems already to have well in mind, if not actually completed, the expansion of **"Aucassin and Nicolette"** to fill the "Conclusion's" place.

The chronology of Pater's decision to withdraw the "Conclusion," then, further calls into question the extent of Mallock's influence. While *The New Republic* had, of course, appeared serially in *Belgravia* from June to December of 1876, it is hardly realistic to rate the impact of the initial installments, either on public opinion or on Pater, as strong enough to force withdrawal of so important a statement as the "Conclusion." Furthermore, Mallock's primary target in the novel is Jowett (Dr. Jankinson), and Mr. Rose is a relatively minor figure who appears but seldom in the opening episodes. The satire on Rose, hardly scathing, consists mainly of mocking the "dreamy" nature of his aestheticism and rather accurately parodying Pater's style. Mallock's most significant misinterpretation of *The Renaissance* is reflected in Rose's exaggeration of Pater's views on religion, but Rose himself points out that his audience "slightly misrepresents" his views.[13] Thus, if Mallock did indeed influence Pater's decision, it was probably because Pater simply considered him another of those "misled young men."

Wright, however, is responsible for a yet more deleterious view of Pater's motives. Having dismissed Mallock's influence out of hand, he strongly implies that "Jowett's Salutary Whip" was responsible for Pater's overall revision of *The Renaissance.* In February of 1874, shortly after the initial publication of *The Renaissance,* Pater was to have had the Junior Proctorship of Oxford. But Jowett, "distinctly displeased" by the book and Pater's ideas in general, opposed him, and Pater lost the post. "Henceforth," Wright maintains, "he kept a very wayward tongue under stricter control; and one may allocate to this period the beginning of a nobler Pater."[14] In spite of Wright's confident assertions, however, the details of the Proctorship incident have not been established. Jowett's mistrust of aestheticism in any form, and Pater's in particular, is well known, but the exact nature and extent of his influence on the election remain obscure.[15] More important, Wright stresses that Pater was moved to revise his views by the loss of the post's three hundred pound stipend, upon which he had "already calculated." This explanation hardly jibes with Pater's rather spartan lifestyle, his fondness for continental travel notwithstanding. In none of his correspondence with Macmillan does Pater ever quibble over money or press for larger editions to promote his reputation; in fact, he took upon himself a loss of thirty-five pounds for cancelling a proposed edition of his essays which he found "inadequate."[16] The loss of the Proctorship surely must have been a bitter blow to Pater, but Wright's view probably overemphasizes the role of Jowett and certainly distorts Pater's motives. Although the importance of Jowett's opposition should not be overlooked, the election probably had its greatest impact on Pater because it constituted a stinging rebuff by his peers, the very group he sought to influence with *The Renaissance.*

All of these factors—Mallock's Mr. Rose, Pater's general sensitivity to criticism, and especially the Proctorship incident—may have indeed contributed to the suppression of the "Conclusion." But Pater's primary concern from the very beginning was that his principles had been misinterpreted, as indeed they had. The *Blackwood's* review, for example, charged that *The Renaissance* was a "pretentious volume" which purveyed "delicate atheisms" and an "elegant materialism," and it finally dismissed the "Conclusion" as simply "in bad taste" in a critical work.[17] Pater expressed his genuine ethical concern over such misinterpretations in a letter of 1 April 1873 to John Morley, in which he thanks Morley for a sympathetic review of *The Renaissance,* and specifically for his "explanation of my ethical point of view, to which I fancy some readers have given a prominence I did not intend."[18]

Amidst the more general criticism, Pater was probably most deeply affected by the letter of 17 March 1873 from John Wordsworth, his friend, former pupil, and fellow tutor.[19] More important than their personal relationship, Wordsworth had been elected to the Proctorship for which Pater had been rejected, and the position stated in his letter undoubtedly represented to Pater the views of many of his colleagues.[20] Wordsworth praises *The Renaissance*'s "beauty of style and the felicity of thought" but takes issue with the "Conclusion": "I cannot disguise from myself that the concluding pages adequately sum up the philosophy of the whole; and that that philosophy is an assertion, that no fixed principles either of religion or morality can be regarded as certain, that the only thing worth living for is momentary enjoyment and that probably or certainly the soul dissolves at death into elements which are destined never to reunite." He goes on to suggest to Pater, "Could you indeed have known the dangers into which you were likely to lead minds weaker than your own, you would, I believe, have paused. Could you have known the grief your words would be to many of your Oxford contemporaries, you might even have found no ignoble pleasure in refraining from uttering them."[21] The similarity between the wording of Wordsworth's letter and that of Pater's 1888 note, together with the clear anticipation of Pater's action, seems more than coincidental.

The relationship between the letter and the note suggests that Wordsworth's dangerously "misleading" misinterpretation of the "Conclusion" may have been the determining factor in Pater's decision to withdraw the piece. Reinforcing the general criticism and the result of the Proctorship election, Wordsworth's letter brought home immediately to Pater that his ethical principles had indeed been widely misinterpreted, particularly among the very audience to which he had specifically addressed *The Renaissance,* his "Oxford contemporaries" and the rising young leaders of "culture." It is these "young men" that Pater may have had in mind in the note to the restored "Conclusion." The critical commonplace that the note refers specifically to Oscar Wilde and his "school" could hardly apply to the decision to withdraw the "Conclusion," for Pater evidently did not know Wilde even by reputation until several months after the second edition of *The Renaissance* had been published. In a letter of 14 July 1877 to Wilde, Pater wrote: "Your excellent article on the Grosvenor Gallery . . . makes me much wish to make your acquaintance."[22] The wording of the letter indicates that Pater knew of Wilde at this time only because of the article. Pater may have numbered Wilde among those "misled" by 1888, when the "Conclusion" was restored, but this is highly unlikely since their relationship remained cordial until at least 1890, when Wilde published *The Picture of Dorian Gray*. In perhaps his most sharply critical review, Pater condemned the book's rather questionable morality and dissociated himself from Wilde's views.[23] Thus, although the individual impact of these various factors, culminating in the Wordsworth letter, cannot be gauged precisely, together they underscore the fact that Pater's decision to withdraw the "Conclusion" was based primarily on the highest ethical motives.

The withdrawal of the "Conclusion," moreover, was but the first step in Pater's continuing effort to clarify his position. As Germaine d'Hangest has pointed out, the entire period from 1874 to 1885 was, for complex reasons, one of revaluation, a *"retour sur soi,"* for Pater.[24] During this time, he published only fifteen scattered articles, and he resigned his tutorship in 1880 in order to devote more time to carefully preparing *Marius,* his fullest clarification of the principles set forth in the "Conclusion." Wordsworth's misinterpretation of the "Conclusion," particularly the assertions of hedonism and the dissolution of the soul, was certainly an important factor in Pater's revaluation of his thought. Wordsworth reminded him that *The Renaissance* was taken "as the mature result of your studies in an important period of history,"[25] and Pater could hardly have failed to realize the shortcomings of the "Conclusion" which allowed such misinterpretation. Thus, he took great pains in *Marius* to refute the charges of hedonism, materialism and amorality, which had been brought by other critics as well, and to clarify his own ethical principles in Marius' rigorous intellectual and aesthetic *"ascesis."*[26]

Amidst the complexities of subsidiary factors, Pater's genuine ethical concerns in withdrawing the "Conclusion" are frequently overlooked. As a result, the adverse speculation over his motives has reinforced our negative image of Pater. We see him at best as a delicate sensibility willing to sway with the wind of popular opinion, a fine stylist with little to say; at worst as a neurotic dilettante anxious to preserve ego and position at the cost of repudiating his principles. When it has not produced outright neglect of Pater, this image has too often influenced critical analysis of his work. Edmund Chandler, for example, candidly admits his "antipathy" toward Pater and adopts an attitude similar to Buckley's in analyzing revisions of **Marius.** He discovers an attempt to camouflage an "innate element of sadism in Pater's own personality" in the excision of a passage on the burning of a cat by Commodus.[27] Chandler fails to consider, however, that the passage may have been designed to "distance" the reader from the sumptuous scene of Commodus' banquet in honor of Apuleius, and that upon reconsideration Pater may simply have found the passage *de trop.* This can hardly be considered "evidence of emotional abnormality."[28] Chandler finally concludes that "every instance" of revision affecting thought in **Marius** "was probably demanded by considerations external to the work,"[29] considerations such as whether a passage "gave offense to his contemporaries, or whether Pater later thought that it was in a way blasphemous."[30]

Even among avowed partisans of Pater, the image has its effects. Richmond Crinkley sees **Marius** simply as an attempt to present the "Conclusion's" philosophy "in a mode more acceptable to his contemporaries. Reputation was important to the reticent don."[31] Similarly, Gerald Monsman, an astute Paterian, speculates: "Hardly two weeks after he had been elected a fellow of Brasenose College, Pater read an essay on Fichte's Ideal Student to the Old Mortality. One wonders if Pater would have been so candid as to read a controversial paper of this kind before his election."[32] The impression thus created distorts the value of Pater's thought and hardly encourages in the student, the general reader, and particularly the non-specialist a serious and objective reading of Pater's works.

Certainly Pater has his faults: the early works are marred by occasional rash assertions and inconsistencies, the later by overly cautious qualifications which sometimes obscure the meaning. His personality may indeed have had its eccentricities. Nevertheless, in view of his significant contributions to literature, criticism, the history of ideas and "culture" in its highest sense, Pater's image needs and deserves remodelling. In spite of a recent renewal of critical interest in him, our perspective of Pater seems inevitably to be colored by the yellow filter of Wilde and the excesses of the Nineties when he ought to be seen in the clear light of objective critical judgment.

*Notes*

1. *The Renaissance* (Lond: Macmillan, 1900), p. 233.

2. In *Essays and Studies by Members of the English Association,* XXXII (1946), 44-60.

3. Ibid, pp. 48-49. Tillotson previously (p. 44) quotes Mallock, *Memoirs of Life and Literature* (NY: Harper, 1920), pp. 87-88, on his intentions in *The New Republic.*

4. Ibid, p. 50.

5. "Pater and the Suppressed 'Conclusion,'" *Modern Language Notes,* LXV (1950), 250.

6. Ibid, p. 251.

7. *The Life of Walter Pater* (Lond: Everett, 1907), II, 17-18. In contrast, A. C. Benson (*Walter Pater* [Lond: Macmillan, 1906], p. 54) had earlier maintained that "the satire caused Pater considerable distress" but made no connection with the suppression of the "Conclusion."

8. Ibid, II, 18.

9. See *Letters of Walter Pater,* ed by Lawrence Evans (Oxford: Clarendon P, 1970), p. 18, n. 2.

10. Ibid, "Introduction," p. xxii. Evans examines Pater's general "defensiveness" in pp. xii-xiv.

11. Ibid, p. 18, n. 1.

12. Ibid, Letter to Alexander Macmillan, pp. 17-18, n. 26.

13. *Belgravia,* XXX (Sept 1876), 343-51. The passage appears virtually unchanged as Bk. IV, Ch. I in the novel's final form.

14. *Life of Pater,* I, 259.

15. Again contradicting Wright, Benson (pp. 54-55) condemned Jowett's action but gave no further specific details and made no mention of the "Conclusion." Even the latest biography of Jowett, Geoffrey Faber's *Jowett: A Portrait with Background* (Cambridge, Mass: Harvard UP, 1957), pp. 376-84, adds little to clarify the matter.

16. See the letters to Macmillan, *Letters,* p. 34, n. 55, and pp. 35-36, n. 57: for a list of the proposed contents, see p. 32, n. 52. Pater was probably dissatisfied because the essays' subjects, ranging from Demeter to Shakespeare and Lamb, lacked any central focus.

17. *Blackwood's Magazine,* CXIV (Nov 1873), 604-9. Even the generally favorable reviews showed a lack of understanding. E.g., *Athenaeum,* no. 2383

(28 June 1873), 829, oddly, praised *The Renaissance* but pointed out that "the true Renaissance aimed at something else than enjoying itself in this life . . . but [Pater] does not seem, to us, sufficiently affected by its nobler qualities."

18. *Letters,* p. 14, n. 21. Morley's review, "Mr. Pater's Essays," appeared in *Fortnightly Review,* XIX (April 1873), 469-77.

19. The actual personal relationship between Wordsworth and Pater is difficult to establish. The notoriously unreliable Wright states that they became "fast friends" when Wordsworth was Pater's private pupil (I, 239-40). But E. W. Watson maintains that Wordsworth showed little interest in Pater's tuition, and Watson says nothing of any further personal relationship. The two men do seem to have respected each other, however, for Wordsworth opens his letter by acknowledging that "I owe so much to you in time past, and have so much to thank you for as a colleague more recently, that I am very much pained in making this avowal" (*Letters,* p. 13, n. 20).

20. Wordsworth, son of the influential Bishop of Lincoln, was considered a leader of the more conservative faction among the younger Oxford men and was active in religious controversies beginning in 1869. He rose rapidly to be made Bishop of Salisbury in 1885 (see Watson, pp. 66-76). There is no evidence of any collusion or even a particularly cordial relationship between Wordsworth and Jewett in the Proctorship matter. Watson maintains, in fact, that a series of Wordsworth's 1870 lectures "contradicted Jewett's theory of education" (pp. 50-52).

21. *Letters,* pp. 13-14, n. 20.

22. Ibid, pp. 24-25, n. 37. Wilde had sent the article, which appeared in *Dublin University Magazine,* XC (July 1877), 118-26, to Pater.

23. See Evans, "Introduction," pp. xli-xlii. Pater's review, "A Novel by Mr. Oscar Wilde," appeared in *Bookman* (Lond), I (Nov 1891), 59-60.

24. *Walter Pater: L'homme et l'oeuvre* (Paris: Didier, 1961), I, 220-40. The quotation is the title of Ch. 2, Pt. III.

25. Letters, p. 13, n. 20.

26. See especially Ch. XVI ("Second Thoughts").

27. "Pater on Style," *Anglistica,* XI (Copenhagen: Rosenkilde & Bagger, 1958), p. 78. The "cat" passage occurs in the first ed of *Marius* (Lond: Macmillan, 1885), II, 99. It is important to note that

Apuleius had earlier been Marius' literary ideal, and that the entire banquet scene shows that Marius has passed beyond this stage.

28. Ibid. Chandler cites as further "evidence" the passage describing the Roman Games (Ch. XIV), which serves a similar function in distancing the reader from Aurelius' philosophy.

29. Ibid, p. 86.

30. Ibid, p. 72.

31. *Walter Pater: Humanist* (Lexington: University of Kentucky P, 1970), p. 138.

32. "Pater, Hopkins, and Fichte's Ideal Student," *South Atlantic Quarterly,* LXX (Summer 1971), 366. The paper referred to is evidently an early version of "Diaphaneite," hardly one of Pater's more shocking essays.

### Billie Andrew Inman (essay date spring 1975)

SOURCE: Inman, Billie Andrew. "Pater's Conception of the Renaissance: From Sources to Personal Ideal." *The Victorian Newsletter,* no. 47 (spring 1975): 19-24.

[*In the following essay, Inman discusses Pater's contention that the essence of the Renaissance lay in its liberal and creative use of diverse aspects of history, philosophy, and culture, a form of borrowing that helped lend Renaissance art its richness and complexity. Inman argues that this eclectic character of the Renaissance finds a distinct parallel in the form and style of Pater's study, which itself draws from a wealth of cultural influences.*]

If Pater can be considered a writer of genius, he was at the time he published ***Studies in the History of the Renaissance,*** the type of genius-as-critic that Arnold had described in "The Function of Criticism at the Present Time"—one who drew upon a fresh intellectual current for ideas and transformed these ideas into works of art. The shaping fire was another idea, stated explicitly sixteen years later in "Postscript": ". . . in literature as in other matters it is well to unite as many diverse elements as may be."[1] Whether this idea too was borrowed is open to question. Borrowed or not, it became Pater's leading apprehension. It was not, however, the open-ended idea that it is usually assumed to be. Pater's conception of the function of art, which he imposed upon his own work, set a limitation to the types of diverse elements that may be combined. It is my purpose to show that the borrowed ideas, developed in the light of the leading apprehension as limited by the conception of the function of art, constitute the basic lines of Pater's vision of the Renaissance, a personal ideal by which he thought art of the nineteenth century could be judged.

According to Arnold, "for the creation of a masterwork of literature two powers must concur, the power of the man and the power of the moment."[2] For Pater the moment was indeed crucial. If he had been old enough in the 1840s to write a book about the period immediately following the Middle Ages, he would have inherited, as Ruskin did, a conception of the post-medieval period created by German philosophers and critics in the early nineteenth century and transmitted by Alexis François Rio—a period of decline, in which pure Christian faith and native, national art were corrupted by alien pagan elements. That he could have accommodated himself to such a conception is doubtful; certainly, he could not have produced the book that he published in 1873. By an accident of chronology, Pater formed his idea of the Renaissance in the 1860s, when Michelet's and Burckhardt's descriptions of the period were available. Though Michelet and Burckhardt differed much in their thinking, neither regarded the medieval period as the golden age, as the German critics had done in the Romantic period. Both saw the Renaissance as a step forward that broke the tyranny of a repressive medieval culture: Michelet, a step toward greater geographical and scientific knowledge, greater human freedom, and universal sympathy; Burckhardt, toward greater political freedom, the discovery of natural beauty and the discovery of man, and the realization of the many-sided individual.

Michelet, the first historian to define and describe the Renaissance as a period in history as distinct from merely a rebirth of classical knowledge and art,[3] published his *XVI^e Siècle: La Renaissance,* in 1855, the seventh volume in his *Histoire de France.* Pater was reading Michelet in 1870 and again in 1872.[4] Three of Pater's basic ideas in **The Renaissance** describing the Renaissance as a period in history had been set forth by Michelet: (1) that the Renaissance began in France in the twelfth century (p. 1); (2) that the most definitive characteristics of Renaissance expression were "liberty of the heart" and "liberty of the intellect" (pp. 3-4); and (3) that the Middle Ages and the Renaissance overlapped (pp. 2-3). With regard to the last, Pater expresses approval of the "theory of a Renaissance within the middle age" that heals "that rupture between the middle age and the Renaissance which has so often been exaggerated" (p. 3). Michelet had summarized his discussion of the overlapping of the two periods by saying that it took the Renaissance three hundred years to be born because it took the oppressive Middle Ages three hundred years to die.[5] To both Pater and Michelet, Abelard was one of the first heroes of the Renaissance

within the Middle Ages (pp. 3-4), and in his discussion of Abelard Pater suggests his source by referring to a passage in Michelet's history (p. 5).[6]

To Burckhardt's *Die Kultur der Renaissance in Italien* (1860), a landmark in *Kulturgeschichte,* Pater was indebted for three ideas developed in **The Renaissance,** the first two stated in the Preface and the third in **"Two Early French Stories"**: (1) that "the fifteenth century in Italy . . . is an age productive in personalities, many-sided, centralised, complete" (p. xiv); (2) that artists, scholars, and men of the world were able to "breathe a common air, and catch light and heat from each other's thoughts" (p. xiv); and (3) that the Renaissance was an age of synthesis (pp. 1-2). Burckhardt's description of the reconciliation in the fifteenth century between pagan and Christian rituals and ideas is similar to that which Pater developed at length in **The Renaissance** and other works. Burckhardt states that in a number of the most widespread Catholic rites there are "remnants of pagan ceremonies," but that in Italy in the fifteenth century "we find instances in which the affiliation of the new faith with the old seems consciously recognized."[7] Pico della Mirandola, Pater's chief reconciler of pagan and Christian motifs, was one of Burckhardt's heroes, too. Burckhardt praises him for being "the only man who loudly and vigorously defended the truth and science of all ages against the one-sided worship of classical antiquity."[8] Burckhardt's synthesis was much broader, however, than the reconciliation of pagan and Christian rituals and ideas. In his Introduction to Part III: **"The Revival of Antiquity,"** he states: "We must insist upon it, as one of the chief propositions of this book, that it was not the revival of antiquity alone, but its union with the genius of the Italian people, which achieved the conquest of the Western world."[9] The following statement from Pater's **"Two Early French Stories"** is an indirect acknowledgment of Burckhardt's influence: "The word *Renaissance* . . . is now generally used to denote not merely the revival of classical antiquity which took place in the fifteenth century, and to which the word was first applied, but a whole complex movement, of which that revival of classical antiquity was but one element or symptom" (pp. 1-2). Burckhardt believed that the unifying spirit of this complex culture was the spirit of individualism, which made its representative persons "in religion, as in other matters, altogether subjective."[10]

Pater was concerned not with distinctions between Michelet's overlapping of ages and Burckhardt's synthesis, but with the similarity: the idea that the Renaissance was an eclectic period combining medieval (largely Christian) and classical elements. This idea jibed with that part of Hegel's conception of history that Pater could accept, the idea that in the process of history the present holds within itself elements of the past.[11] It could be related by analogy to Darwin's idea that "nature makes no sudden starts."[12] So many lines of thought converging at one point constitute for a skeptical mind like Pater's a high degree of probability that the idea is true. His summary definition of the Renaissance in **"The Early French Stories"** is a combination of and interpretation of Burckhardt's "subjectivism" and Michelet's "liberty": "For us the Renaissance is the name of a many-sided but yet united movement, in which the love of the things of the intellect and the imagination for their own sake, the desire for a more liberal and comely way of conceiving life, make themselves felt, urging those who experience this desire to search out first one and then another means of intellectual or imaginative enjoyment" (p. 2).

A different type of person might have looked upon the blending of cultural strains in life and art as anathema. Ruskin, for example, felt that any artist who could mingle ideas and sentiments from Christianity and paganism in his philosophy or religion did not believe in either and that for this reason neither could provide real inspiration for his work. With vital belief gone, Ruskin thought, the artist becomes altogether absorbed in technique and the result is the decline of art. To him, therefore, the Renaissance was a "foul torrent," its religion hollow and its art corrupt.[13] But the idea of the composite culture was very appealing to Pater. He assumed that the blending of seemingly disparate cultural elements meant enrichment—in the culture of an age or of an individual. The kind of freedom implied in the choice of diverse elements, which to Ruskin meant loss of faith in everything, seemed to Pater the freedom to appreciate individual things—ideas, experiences, works of art—for their own sake, that is, for the pleasure or significance they hold for the individual, without reference to a larger context or a creed.

Pater probably did not independently reach the conclusion that a composite culture is desirable. This conclusion, too, was in the fresh intellectual current. It had been well expressed by Mme de Staël in *On Germany*: "Undoubtedly, as I have constantly reiterated in the course of this work, it is desirable that modern literature be based upon our history and our creed. But the point is not that we should be forcing art backward in time but that we should combine, as much as possible, the various fine qualities displayed by the human mind in all eras."[14] However Pater acquired this judgment, it became integral to *The Renaissance* and to all of his subsequent works.

Though Pater assumed when writing *The Renaissance*, as thereafter, that eclectic culture or eclectic art can be consciously formed through selection of diverse ele-

ments, he is never as direct as de Staël in suggesting a qualitative selectivity. His reference in "Postscript" to "as many diverse elements as may be" is vague. In his definition in **"Pico della Mirandola"** of a term that seems synonymous with eclectic culture, *humanism,* he suggests no qualitative selection: "For the essence of humanism is that belief of which he [Pico] seems never to have doubted, that nothing which has ever interested living men and women can wholly lose its vitality—no language they have spoken, nor oracle beside which they have hushed their voices, no dream which has once been entertained by actual human minds, nothing about which they have ever been passionate, or expended time and zeal" (*Renaissance,* p. 49). But, ironically, de Staël's recommendation that "fine qualities" be selected represents Pater's practice better than his own statements.[15] His own principles of selectivity in *The Renaissance* can be seen behind his 1875 criticism of Symonds' *Renaissance in Italy: The Age of the Despots*:

> The spirit of the Renaissance proper, of the Renaissance as a humanistic movement, on which it may be said this volume does not profess to touch, is as unlike the spirit of Alexander VI. as it is unlike that of Savonarola. Alexander VI. has more in common with Ezzelino da Romano, that fanatical hater of human life in the middle age, than with Tasso or Lionardo [sic]. The Renaissance is an assertion of liberty indeed, but of liberty to see and feel those things the seeing and feeling of which generate not the "barbarous ferocity of temper, the savage and coarse tastes" of the Renaissance Popes, but a sympathy with life everywhere, even in its weakest and most frail manifestations. Sympathy, appreciation, a sense of latent claims in things which even ordinary good men pass rudely by—these on the whole are the characteristic traits of its artists, though it may be still true that "aesthetic propriety, rather than strict conceptions of duty, ruled the conduct even of the best. . . ."[16]

Burckhardt had described the tempestuous, sometimes violent, energy, the brutality, the egotism, the materialism, the gross immorality that existed in the Renaissance along with intellectual and aesthetic brilliance and humane sensitivities. Pater, however, excluded the gross and violent aspects of the age in his selection of diverse elements. In stating his purpose in writing *The Renaissance,* he testifies to selectivity, but, again, does not make his principle of selection clear: "The subjects of the following studies are taken from the history of the *Renaissance,* and touch what I think the chief points in that complex, many-sided movement" (p. xi). In what sense are the "points" that are treated "chief"? They are not chief if the book is to be judged as history or even if it is to be judged as art history. What Pater called points are really qualities of mind and art, and they were selected because they constitute an ideal eclectic culture that Pater wanted to recommend to his readers—to recommend without seeming didactic.

Pater's purpose is elucidated by his own conception of the function of art, for he certainly considered himself an artist. To Pater art was a refuge from the world, or, better, a transcendence of the world, with its materialistic vulgarity, its depressing sense of determinism, its violence, ugliness, and grossness. He believed that the best art creates an ideal that is elevating and refreshing to the human spirit.[17] In **"Dante Gabriel Rossetti,"** he states that "poetry, at all times, exercises two distinct functions: it may reveal, it may unveil to every eye, the ideal aspects of common things . . . or it may actually add to the number of motives poetic and uncommon in themselves, by the imaginative creation of things that are ideal from their very birth" (*Appreciations,* p. 218). Pater illustrates in **"Demeter and Persephone"** the difference between the less desirable aspects of reality and an artistic ideal:

> . . . the myth of Demeter, like the Greek religion in general, had its unlovelier side, grotesque, unhellenic, unglorified by art, illustrated well enough by the description Pausanias gives us of his visit to the cave of the Black Demeter at Phigalia . . . he tells us enough about it to enable us to realise its general characteristics, monstrous as the special legend with which it was connected, the black draperies, the horse's head united to the woman's body, with the curved reptiles creeping about it. If, with the thought of this gloomy image of our mother the earth, in our minds, we take up one of those coins which bear the image of Kore or Demeter, we shall better understand what the function of sculpture really was, in elevating and refining the religious conceptions of the Greeks.

> (*Greek Studies,* pp. 137-38)

The "quickened, multiplied consciousness" of the Conclusion to *The Renaissance* is not an immersion in life but a type of transcendence through the selection of the most exquisite sensations from life: "While all melts under our feet, we may well grasp at any exquisite passion, or any contribution to knowledge that seems by a lifted horizon to set the spirit free for a moment . . ." (p. 237).

Each of the Renaissance essays presents a quality or a blend of qualities that Pater thought necessary to an ideal, eclectic age and to an eclectic art. (He never sharply distinguished between life and art.) One of these qualities directly reflects the master idea of the book, that the Renaissance combines medieval and classical elements. This quality is a blend of strength, which Pater thought medieval, and sweetness, which he thought classical. In **"Two Early French Stories,"** he generalizes upon this blend: ". . . the Renaissance has not only the sweetness which it derives from the classical world, but also that curious strength of which there are great resources in the true middle age [the pre-Gothic dark ages]" (p. 15). *Strength,* as Pater defines it in **"The Poetry of Michelangelo,"** is fanciful energy, wild imagination that produces that which is "singular or strange" (*Renaissance,* p. 73). It has the power to surprise and excite. Pater thought that if unenlightened, medieval strength could be dark, monstrous, and forbidding. He was to typify it in **"Vézelay"** (1894) in his description of the Romanesque Cluniac monastery: "In its mortified light the very soul of monasticism, Roman and half-military, as the completest outcome of a religion of threats, seems to descend upon one" (*Misc. Studies,* p. 133). Vézelay seems to Pater an "iron place" (p. 133); its decoration has about it a frightful savagery: "Of sculptured capitals . . . there are nearly a hundred, unwearied in variety, unique in the energy of their conception, full of wild promise in their coarse execution, cruel, you might say, in the realisation of human form and features" (p. 134). The main theme of this decoration, Pater states, is punishment of wicked persons for their sins, and it is often satiric, even "merry" in its brutality: "how adroitly the executioner planted knee on the culprit's bosom, as he lay on the ground, and out came the sinful tongue, to meet the iron pincers" (p. 135).

Pater felt that what *strength* needed to keep it from running to extremes was *sweetness.* As used in *The Renaissance, sweetness* is approximately synonymous with *tender emotion that springs from sympathy with humanity in its most fundamental experiences.* In **"The Poetry of Michelangelo"** Pater gives his fullest definition of it. It means, first, the gentle wonder that people naturally feel when contemplating the creation of new life. Pater says that Michelangelo's favorite pagan story was the myth of Leda, in which "the delight of the world" breaks from a bird's egg, and that the theme of *The Last Judgment* is not really judgment, but resurrection (p. 76). He implies that the *Creation of Man* in the Sistine Ceiling has a strong *natural* appeal, stating that Adam is "rude and satyrlike" as he awaits the quickening touch (p. 75). Michelangelo captures this tender emotion, also, by leaving many of his statues incomplete, the figures just emerging into life from the rough stone (p. 76). In the second sense, *sweetness* means the profound and wholly human pity that a skeptical person feels in contemplating sorrow occasioned by death. To Pater there is no morbidity or grotesqueness in Michelangelo's treatment of death, nothing to suggest the *Danse Macabre* (p. 93). Michelangelo depicts the dead in their dignity, but the viewer is inspired to pity because he knows that the dignity of the dead body is brief and because to him there is no assurance of a future life. In Michelangelo's representations of the *Pietà,* Pater sees not a special and divine sorrow, but "the pity of all mothers over all dead sons"—"a hopeless, rayless, almost heathen sorrow" (p. 94). Again, in the sacristy of San Lorenzo, according to Pater, "mere human nature" stirs pity (p. 94). He contrasts Dante's childlike belief in a "precise and firm" immortality with Michelangelo's skeptical speculation about the dead, represented by the restless, indeterminate figures in San Lorenzo. ". . . in Michelangelo you have maturity . . . dealing cautiously and dispassionately with serious things; and what hope he has is based on the consciousness of ignorance—ignorance of man, ignorance of the nature of the mind, its origin and capacities" (p. 95). In short, in Pater's interpretation, Michelangelo humanizes the traditional medieval themes of Creation and Entombment and thereby achieves *sweetness.*

Pater added a discussion of *Li Amitiez de Ami et Amile* to the second edition of *The Renaissance* to illustrate medieval strength in a pure form, or as he terms it, "the early strength of the Renaissance" (p. 15).[18] In the second and subsequent editions, he introduces *Aucassin et Nicolette* as a story that illustrates the "early sweetness, a languid excess of sweetness even" (p. 15).[19] To illustrate the combination of strength and sweetness in the early Renaissance, he refers to the poetry of Provence and to Gothic architecture—a blend of Romanesque strength and classical sweetness, not, to him, the pure medieval form that Ruskin and other devotees of the Gothic thought (*Renaissance,* p. 2). In the High Renaissance, it was Michelangelo, according to Pater, who combined medieval strength and classical sweetness to perfection. In **"Pico della Mirandola,"** Pater describes approvingly the "picturesque union of contrasts" in the *Holy Family* (*tondo Doni*), in which "Michelangelo actually brings the pagan religion, and with it the unveiled human form, the sleepy-looking fauns of a Dionysiac revel, into the presence of the Madonna, as simpler painters had introduced there other products of earth, birds or flowers, while he has given to that Madonna herself much of the uncouth energy of the older and more primitive 'Mighty Mother'" (*Renaissance,* p. 48). The theme of **"The Poetry of Michelangelo"** is that Michelangelo became a great artist and, at long last, an admirable man by sweetening his great strength. As far as thematic significance is concerned, **"The Poetry of Michelangelo"** is the central essay in the book, because it describes the basic blend of classical and medieval qualities.

Other characteristic qualities of the Renaissance besides the blend of strength and sweetness are (1) a combined "liberty of the heart" and "liberty of the intellect," like Abelard's; (2) a sympathy that of itself is morality, like Botticelli's; (3) a conciliatory spirit like Pico della Mirandola's that will not let any system of thought deprive one of a beautiful idea belonging to another system of thought; (4) a blend of simplicity and expressiveness, like Luca della Robbia's[20]; (5) a blend of curiosity and the love of beauty, like Leonardo's; (6) a perfect blend of matter and form, like Giorgione's; (7) the only purely aesthetic quality, a perfect manner in art, like Joachim du Bellay's, that delights the receiver in and of itself when the matter may be only the inconsequential moods of the artist; and (8) a temperamental affinity with a past mode, like Winckelmann's with Hellenism, so strong that it rediscovers the life in that mode and transmits it to the present.

In the concluding paragraph of **"The Poetry of Michelangelo,"** Pater reveals his purpose in serving as an aesthetic critic for readers of the Renaissance essays, presumably artists, lovers of art, and choice spirits who wish to live life as an art. By discussing "old masters" and defining "those characteristics, and the law of their combination" by which the old masters achieved their effects—in short, their *formulas,* he was setting standards by which to interpret, judge, and, by implication, refine modern art (*Renaissance,* p. 96). One might say that he was elucidating, not specific passages from great authors to be used as touchstones, as Arnold was to do, but the characterizing elements in the works of great artists, to be so used. To illustrate the recurrence of a Renaissance formula in the nineteenth century, he notes that the "strange interfusion of sweetness and strength" exemplified in the High Renaissance by Michelangelo can be found in the works of William Blake and Victor Hugo. To Pater, the nineteenth century, which had no dominant creed, was, like the Renaissance, an eclectic age—intellectually curious, broadly sympathetic, and responsive to the art of all ages.[21] Its artists, with not only modern reality but also the whole heritage of Western civilization to draw upon, could extract and combine splendid, often diverse, qualities in the creation of an artistic ideal of culture that would refresh the human spirit. Under the gentle guidance of the aesthetic critic, appreciators of art could refine their senses so that in their assessment of modern art they would know where "the stir, the genius, the sentiment of the period" reside, or "where the greatest number of vital forces unite in their purest energy" (*Renaissance,* pp. x, 236).

### Notes

1. *Appreciations, with an Essay on Style,* in *The Works of Walter Pater,* Library Ed., 10 vols. (London, 1910), p. 261. The Library Edition is used exclusively in this paper for works included in the edition with the title of each work referred to and the page number given in the text. Works not included in the Library Edition are acknowledged by notes.

2. "The Function of Criticism at the Present Time," in *Matthew Arnold: Lectures and Essays in Criticism*, ed. R. H. Super (Ann Arbor, 1960), p. 261.

3. Wallace K. Ferguson, *The Renaissance in Historical Thought: Five Centuries of Interpretation* (Boston, 1948), p. 173.

4. No full account exists of Pater's reading during these or other years, but Bruce E. Vardon lists in his dissertation, "Variant Readings in Walter Pater's *Studies in the History of the Renaissance*" (University of Chicago, 1950), books borrowed by Pater from the Taylor Institution at Oxford between 1865 and 1873. Pater borrowed Volume 10 of Michelet's *Histoire de France* in November 1870, and Volumes 11 and 12 in April 1872 (Vardon, p. 366). It seems that he had read the preceding volumes earlier and was finishing the work in these years.

5. *XVI^e Siècle: La Renaissance,* in *Histoire de France*, VII (Paris: Librairie Internationale, 1876), pp. 105-7.

6. Michelet discusses Abelard in *La Renaissance,* pp. 29-30.

7. *The Civilization of the Renaissance in Italy,* trans. S. G. C. Middlemore (London, 1929), p. 464.

8. *Ibid.,* p. 210.

9. *Ibid.,* p. 175.

10. *Ibid.,* p. 473.

11. In "History as Palingenesis in Pater and Hegel," *PMLA,* 86 (May 1971), William Shuter ably discusses the influence of this idea of Hegel's upon Pater, but he does not make clear the differences between Pater's conception of history and Hegel's, which are as important to an understanding of Pater as the similarities.

12. In *Plato and Platonism,* Pater relates the idea of historical continuity to evolution: "With the world of intellectual production, as with that of organic generation, nature makes no sudden starts. *Natura nihil facit per saltum*; and in the history of philosophy there are no absolute beginnings" (p. 5). Darwin had used a very similar Latin statement— *Natura non facit saltum*—in his discussion of natural selection (*The Origin of Species* [Chicago: Encyclopaedia Britannica, Inc., 1952], p. 235).

13. Ruskin refers to "the foul torrent of the Renaissance" in *The Seven Lamps of Architecture,* in *Complete Works of John Ruskin,* ed. E. T. Cook and Alexander Wedderburn, Library ed. (London, 1903-1912), VIII, 98.

14. *Madame de Staël on Politics, Literature, and National Character,* trans. and ed. Morroe Berger (Garden City, 1964), p. 318. Pater seems to have been well acquainted with Mme de Staël's works. In his first two published essays he refers to statements of hers ("Coleridge's Writings," *Westminster Review,* 85 [January 1866], 113; "Winckelmann," *Westminster Review,* 87 [January 1867], 87). And he checked out the first volume of her *Oeuvres Complètes* in the winter of 1869 from the Taylor Institution (Vardon, p. 366).

15. In *Walter Pater: Humanist,* Richard Crinkley sees cultural synthesis as the main theme of *The Renaissance*; however, he takes the definition of *humanism* at face value as the principle behind the synthesis, without considering the discrepancy between the definition and Pater's actual syntheses in *The Renaissance, Marius,* and *Gaston de Latour,* which are selective ([Lexington, 1970], pp. 3-4, 61).

16. Pater's review appeared in the *Academy,* 7 (July 31, 1875); rpt. *Uncollected Essays by Walter Pater* (Portland, Maine, 1903), pp. 6-7.

17. To some critics who have observed his tendency to idealize, Pater is simply an escapist. Ruth C. Child states in *The Aesthetic of Walter Pater*: "[even] Pater's mature philosophy of life . . . is, in large part, an escape philosophy. The artist is to create an ideal world which shall afford a refuge from the world as it is" ([New York, 1940], p. 142). To Charles du Bos, Pater's tendency to escape was based on fear—"expressed in the refusal to accept in his work and its artistic form, life in its raw state." (Quoted from du Bos's *Journal 1926-27,* p. 45, by Angelo P. Bertocci, in "French Criticism and the Pater Problem," *Boston University Studies in English,* 1 [autumn 1955], 184.) To Gerald C. Monsman, however, Pater's selectivity is not escapism but a kind of transcendence that breaks the time barrier ("Pater's Aesthetic Hero," *University of Toronto Quarterly,* 40 [winter 1971], 145-46).

18. *The Renaissance: Studies in Art and Poetry,* 2nd ed. (London, 1877), p. 16.

19. *Ibid.*

20. To Richard S. Lyons, in "The 'Complex, Many-Sided' Unity of *The Renaissance*," *SEL,* 12 (autumn 1972), the idea of expressiveness, as developed in "Luca della Robbia," is "the central aesthetic formulation of *The Renaissance*" (p. 767). It is *expressiveness,* "that intimate impress of an indwelling soul" (*Renaissance,* p. 63), that

makes a work of art valuable and gives it the power to survive in even a hostile culture. Though we approach the book differently, Lyons also concludes that Pater was trying "to establish an ideal of culture" (p. 779).

21. Pater discusses the nineteenth century in "Prosper Mérimée," *Misc. Studies,* p. 11; "Postscript," *Appreciations,* pp. 260-61; *Plato and Platonism,* pp. 20-21; and the Introduction to *Purgatory of Dante Alighieri,* trans. Charles L. Shadwell (London, 1892), p. xv; rpt. in *Uncollected Essays,* p. 147.

## Lawrence F. Schuetz and Ian Small (essay date 1976)

SOURCE: Schuetz, Lawrence F. and Ian Small. "Pater and the Suppressed 'Conclusion' to *The Renaissance*: Comment and Reply." *English Literature in Transition* 19, no. 4 (1976): 313-21.

[*In the following essay, Small reacts to a 1974 essay by Lawrence F. Schuetz ("The Suppressed 'Conclusion' to* The Renaissance *and Pater's Modern Image"), and Schuetz replies. Small contends that Schuetz ignores several key factors behind Pater's decision to suppress the conclusion, notably the numerous accusations of moral indecency and "effeminacy" that were leveled at him and his aesthetic theories throughout the 1870s. In his response Schuetz counters that Small's argument is based on a number of fallacious assumptions, in particular the notion that Pater was consistently and universally persecuted during this period.*]

### 1. IAN SMALL COMMENTS

In a recent article ("The Suppressed 'Conclusion' to *The Renaissance* and Pater's Modern Image," *ELT* [*English Literature in Transition*], XVII: 4 [1974], 251-58), Lawrence Schuetz discussed the circumstances of Pater's decision to omit the "Conclusion" in the second edition of *The Renaissance* in 1877. He concluded that "established criticism" has attributed the decision to Pater's "sensitivity to adverse criticism" (in particular to W. H. Mallock's *The New Republic*) and to Pater's concern for his reputation at Oxford. He argued that "neither view afforded a very favorable image of Pater, and neither accords proper significance to his stated motive for withdrawing the piece." Schuetz discounted the effect of Mallock's work on Pater, arguing that the work was published too late in 1876 to affect Pater's decision; he went on to assert that Pater's decision, influenced by the unfavourable reaction of John Wordsworth to parts of the first edition of *The Renaissance,* and Pater's failure to obtain the Junior Proctorship at Oxford

in 1874, was one motivated above all by "genuine ethical concerns." However, when Pater's action is seen in the light of other contemporary evidence—principally when considered against his reputation among undergraduates at Oxford—it appears much less laudable, but perhaps more understandable; and Schuetz's interpretation of that action much less plausible.

We have good evidence that Pater planned to meet Edmund Gosse in the early months of 1877[1]—the time of the serialisation of *The New Republic*; and we know that Gosse in *Critical Kit Kats* (1896) remembered that Pater had been "ruffled" by the publication of *The New Republic,* but also by certain "newspaper articles." It is those newspaper articles that finally provide the key to the real reasons for Pater's omission of the "Conclusion" to *The Renaissance,* but Gosse's collocation is revealing. Mallock started work on *The New Republic* while he was at Oxford and, he claimed, rewrote the work up to seven times:[2] one can perhaps, then, safely conclude that there were early manuscript drafts of the work available in Oxford in 1875, the year of the Oscar Browning scandal (Pater had known Browning since 1868 and was associated with him by, among others, Mark Pattison).[3] The date is significant, because the charge that Mallock made publicly in *The New Republic* was that Mr. Rose's (i.e. Pater's) aestheticism was connected with, or another aspect of, unnatural sexual proclivities and an interest in the erotic generally. These, obviously, weren't light charges, and some reviewers accused Mallock of publishing a portrait of Pater that was malevolent.[4] But really all Mallock had done was to familiarise a wide public with charges that were then being made at Oxford, charges that, indeed, had been made for some time.

Now the reputation of Pater at Oxford between the years 1873 and 1877 was closely involved with that of John Addington Symonds. Their work was reviewed together and they were represented (unfairly and inaccurately, as it turned out) as upholding and propounding the same aesthetic principles; that aesthetic creed, it was asserted, involved "effeminacy" and (though, of course, matters were never described so bluntly) homosexuality. For example, *The Quarterly Review* in 1876 made the crude accusation that Pater was the "most thoroughly representative" contemporary proponent of an "emasculated" Romantic tradition.[5] The frequent allegation of "effeminacy" gives a context to otherwise cryptic accounts of the reception of *The Renaissance* in Oxford in 1873. Mrs. Humphry Ward claimed somewhat mysteriously in 1918 there had been "various attempts at persecution."[6] Ingram Bywater, one of Pater's closest friends at Oxford, was to write to a Dr. H. Diels in Berlin claiming that in Pater's work there was "a certain sympathy with a certain aspect of Greek life [which] was not confined to him." Little wonder that W. W. Jackson, Bywater's biographer, was to assert that there was "a storm of criticism at Oxford":

Dr. Mackarness, then Bishop of Oxford, in his "Charge to the Clergy of the Diocese" shortly afterwards delivered in Cathedral of Christ Church, not unnaturally fastened on the most pronounced passages of the Studies, and dwelt upon what he considered to be an imminent danger, viz., that . . . Oxford tutors . . . would instil the principles of the book into the minds of their young men.[7]

*The Examiner* of March 1873, too, bore testimony to the kind of impression that Pater's thought made in Oxford in the early 'seventies.

Now the history of the accusations of moral irresolution gives meaning to Pater's actions in late 1876 and early 1877. In November 1876 Pater accepted the offer made by Macmillan of a new edition of *The Renaissance.* By late January 1877 the book was in print; by the end of February or the beginning of March, Pater had corrected proofs, and by 26 April 1877 the book was binding.[8] What Mr. Schuetz neglects to note is that these dates coincide exactly with the climax of renewed controversy at Oxford in which Pater was again deeply concerned and which made very explicit what had been darkly hinted at in the years since the publication of the first edition of *The Renaissance*: the assertion that certain aesthetic beliefs implied effeminacy and homosexuality. The event that occasioned the allegations was the election of the Professor of Poetry at Oxford.[9] In January 1877 Henry Sidgwick urged John Addington Symonds to allow himself to be nominated. On 8 February 1877 *The Oxford and Cambridge Undergraduates' Journal* announced the candidacy of both Symonds and Pater—but in the same number it advocated the literary merits of a lesser man, the Reverend A. J. D. D'Orsey. Towards the end of April the journal carried an article which accused Pater of being a subversive force and which noted in passing the paganism (another euphemistic reference to homosexuality) in some English public schools. In April 1877, Pater withdrew from the election; but, as a parting shot, in May *The Oxford and Cambridge Undergraduates' Journal* published "Muscular Christianity," a fierce diatribe by Edward Cracroft Lefroy, which attacked the intellectual claims of Pater and Symonds, and much more viciously, questioned their moral probity. Lefroy accused them of atheism and effeminacy and "the worst passions and the most carnal implications of humanity."[10] That month Symonds also withdrew from the election.

*The Oxford and Cambridge Undergraduates' Journal* reflected, of course, undergraduate gossip; that is, it made public what would have been known already to a few—and that few, in Oxford in the early 'seventies, obviously included the young Mallock. It is evidence of the sort of contempt in which Pater was held in some circles. That the publication of Mallock's work coincides with the outbursts in the *Journal* is significant; but the coincidence of Pater's revisions with the climax of virulent national and local personal attacks hardly needs labouring. Perhaps the main point, then, that one should make about the revisions of *The Renaissance,* is simply that Pater showed prudence. Indeed, his decision had been timely, for in March 1877 the criticisms were taken up by a more authoritative figure than either Mallock or the editor of *The Oxford and Cambridge Undergraduates' Journal.* The Reverend Richard St. John Tyrwhitt, who had stood for the Slade professorship in 1869, hinted in *The Contemporary Review* at a connection between Aestheticism and homosexuality, accusing the proponents of Aestheticism of advocating the "total denial of any moral restraint."[11] In the light of this sort of evidence, it seems to be unnecessary to try and find other motives for Pater's decision to appear less controversial. Surely men less sensitive to criticism than Pater would have done the same, especially since most of the hostility implied accusations of sexual perversion?

### 2. Lawrence F. Schuetz Replies

In an article in the present issue of this journal, Ian Small has questioned the interpretation of Pater's motives for withdrawing the "Conclusion" to *The Renaissance* which I set forth in an earlier article ("The Suppressed 'Conclusion' to *The Renaissance* and Pater's Modern Image," *ELT,* XVII: 4 [1974], 251-58). Small seeks to show that "contemporary evidence" indicates that Pater withdrew the piece not because of any ethical concern that it had been misinterpreted but because of his concern for his reputation, particularly in the face of what Small contends were persistent allegations of homosexuality. This argument, however, appears to rest upon several questionable interpretations and assumptions.

The initial appearance of *The Renaissance* did, of course, spark controversy in Oxford. But several contemporaries, including Benson and Mrs. Humphrey Ward, have pointed out that "the younger generation was thrilled with a sense of high artistic possibilities" by the book.[12] Thus, even among undergraduates, the initial response was not as completely negative as Small implies. Moreover, Pater's reaction to the early criticism is particularly important. Small cites Mrs. Ward's "mysterious" allusion to "various attempts at persecution" but fails to note that in the very next sentence she states: "The author of the book [Pater] was quite unmoved."[13] Similarly, Small cites Edmund Gosse as stating that Pater was "ruffled" by Mallock's *New Republic.* The full context is as follows:

It has been represented that he suffered violent distress from this parody of his style and manner, that it caused him to retire from society and to abandon the prosecution of literature. Nothing in the world could be further from the truth. He thought the portrait a little unscrupulous, and he was discomposed by the freedom of some of its details. But he admired the promise and cleverness of the book, and it did not cause him to alter his mode of life or thought in the smallest degree. He was even flattered, for he was an author much younger and more obscure than most of those who were satirised, and he was sensible that to be thus distinguished was a compliment. What he liked less, what really did ruffle him, was the persistence with which the newspapers at this time began to attribute to him all sorts of "aesthetic" follies and extravagances. He said to me, in 1876: "I wish they wouldn't call me a 'hedonist'; it produces such a bad effect on the minds of people who don't know Greek." And the direct result of all these journalistic mosquito-bites was the suppression of the famous "Conclusion" in the second (1877) edition of his *Renaissance.*[14]

As my earlier article sought to point out, Gosse's conclusion is probably erroneous. Nevertheless, Pater's genuine ethical concern over misinterpretations of the "Conclusion" is again reflected in the above statement.

Most of the reviews of *The Renaissance* were, in fact, rather bland and somewhat mystified, and their criticisms of the "Conclusion" were comparatively mild. The *Quarterly Review* article cited by Small is highly eccentric in its virulence and expresses an unusually Philistine attitude. In essence, the article propagates a moral aesthetic and deplores the "analytical spirit" of modern poetry, attacking Pater as its "mouthpiece." The reviewer's position is sufficiently indicated by his assertion that "the true spirit of poetry" is expressed in "the poetry of instinct, patriotism, and religion." He goes so far as to condemn Browning's poetry as "prose in convulsions."[15] Such vehemence is hardly typical of the reviews of Pater's work.

The question of Mallock's "charges" against Pater in *The New Republic* is also significant. Mallock's main attacks are directed at Pater's "morbid" interest in the relationship of beauty and death (Bk. IV, Ch. II); Pater's affected mannerisms and disdain for anything new (Bk. IV, Ch. I): and, most seriously, Pater's relativism in religion and fondness for aesthetically appealing rituals rather than their religious content (Bk. IV, Ch. II). The only passage that in any way implies "Unnatural sexual proclivities" is the episode in which Mr. Rose offers 30f for a copy of "Cultes Secrets des Dames Romaines" (Bk. IV, Ch. II). The episode is treated in a humorous fashion and is, indeed, precisely the sort of off-color joke at which the typical undergraduate might snigger. It hardly constitutes a serious "charge" of moral turpitude. The fact that reviewers of Mallock's work recognized that the portrait of Mr. Rose was "an injustice" and "undeserved" hardly supports Small's contention that *The New Republic* had "widespread" influence on public opinion.[16]

Manuscripts of *The New Republic* were undoubtedly circulated among undergraduates before it was published, but Wright, Benson and Gosse all point out that Pater was disinterested in college business and virtually oblivious to students except in terms of their immediate work under his tutelage.[17] Is it not more probable, then, that Pater's decision to drop the "Conclusion" was influenced to a far greater extent by the serious misinterpretations of his thought by his peers, as expressed in the Wordsworth letter?[18] Moreover, it should be noted that the publications which Small cites as reflections of undergraduate opinion, as well as the election for Professor of Poetry which "occasioned the allegations," all came about well after Pater had made his decision and the second edition was already in the process of being printed.[19]

Small's most serious allegation, that these 1877 publications in fact accused Pater of homosexuality, is questionable. Lefroy's charge that the aestheticism of Symonds and Pater implied "a total denial of any moral restraint" refers specifically to his view that they advocated "a philosophy which bade each man follow freely the bent of his own unchastened disposition, or encouraged the cultivation of merely sensual faculties, without an equal training of man's diviner instincts."[20] Lefroy—like Mallock and, indeed, John Wordsworth—was extremely conservative in his religious views, and his attack illustrates the same misinterpretation of Pater's philosophy as that set forth in Wordsworth's letter. Small's interpretation of Tyrwhitt's "The Greek Spirit in Modern Literature" as accusing Pater of homosexuality raises a more difficult issue. Tyrwhitt does indeed, in the most circumspect and polite manner, point out the homosexual implications of Symonds' position. However, these charges are directed specifically at the concluding chapter of Symonds' *Studies of the Greek Poets*: the article does not once mention Pater's name, nor does it allude in even the most veiled fashion to any of Pater's works. While the philosophies of Symonds and Pater were to some extent identified, these specific charges against Symonds can no more be applied to Pater than to Matthew Arnold, to whom Tyrwhitt devotes two-thirds of his article.[21]

Finally, Small's interpretation of the terms "effeminate" and "paganism" as euphemisms for homosexuality is also open to question. While "effeminate" may have had connotations of sexual perversion, it appears to have referred in the publications of the time primarily to a "feminine" weakness of moral will, a lack of strong moral standards, a dilettantish preciosity of sensibility, and an affectation of superficial mannerisms (cf. the affected posturings attributed to Mr. Rose by Mallock). Similarly, "paganism" generally referred to a lack of moral standards and Christian restraint in conjunction with a *carpe diem* philosophy. For example, in an 1895 review of Symonds' and Pater's works, entitled "Latter-day Pagans," W. F. Barry defined "paganism" as "moral relaxation, effeminacy, sickly self-consciousness, morbid tastes, *tedium vitae*; the hope of annihilation which had rather die than live; complete dissolution of soul; 'moments' only, not even the 'states' which materialism would grant—how much less energy, or sovereign self-direction according to the moral law, or life everlasting."[22] Reflecting his general attitude, Barry equates "paganism" with "humanism." It should further be noted that he condemns Symonds but frequently praises Pater by comparison, especially for the moral position set forth in *Marius*. Moreover, even Gosse applies these terms to Pater in a completely innocent context. Noting Pater's distaste for controversy, he points out that "in the old days, Pater, startled by strangers, was apt to seem affected: he retreated as into a fortress, and enclosed himself in a sort of solemn effeminacy. . . . It was put on entirely for the benefit of strangers, and to his inner circle of friends it seemed like a joke."[23] Gosse further notes that "when I had first known him he was a pagan, without any guide but that of the personal conscience; years brought gradually with them a greater and greater longing for the supporting solace of a creed."[24] The veracity of any allegations of homosexuality against Pater hardly require comment.

Small's attitude toward Pater reflects precisely the type of negative image that my earlier article sought to counter. Far from seeking "other" or "less controversial" motives, that article sought simply to focus attention on perhaps the most valid of sources, Pater's own statements. Because we know so little of him as a private man, the question of Pater's motivation in withdrawing the "Conclusion" will quite probably never be resolved satisfactorily. However, Small's "contemporary evidence" reflects perhaps more validly the broad conflicts of the times, the conflicting forces which Arnold categorized as Hebraism and Hellenism, and which Pater himself sought to reconcile in his later work. *Marius the Epicurean,* the work Pater wrote specifically to clarify the "Conclusion," deals with the problems of discovering stable moral standards in a relativistic world, and with the role of aesthetic sensibility in developing these standards amidst the increasingly rapid flux of human experience. There is absolutely no indication in the handling of the novel that Pater was concerned in the least with allegations of homosexuality or effeminacy; indeed, he makes the central representative of Christianity not the "muscular" Cornelius but the compassionate and sensitive Cecilia. The conclusion of the novel is a direct response to Wordsworth's charge that Pater believed in "the dissolution of the soul at death." The depth and seriousness of the novel's material, together with its pains-taking care in construction and style, is a far cry from the sniggering of the undergraduate—or the self-righteous extremism of the Philistine.

## Notes

1. See L. Evans (ed), *Letters of Walter Pater* (Oxford: Oxford UP, 1970), p. 28, henceforth referred to as *Letters.*

2. W. H. Mallock, *Memoirs of Life and Literature* (Lond: Chapman & Hall, 1920), p. 66. On the preceding page Mallock claimed that as early as his "second year of residence" he was "constantly engaged in tentative sketches of a book in which I hoped some day to give a comprehensive account of the moral and intellectual condition to which my Oxford experiences had by that time reduced or raised me."

3. See Oscar Browning, *Memoirs of Sixty Years at Eton, Cambridge and Elsewhere* (Lond: John Lane, 1910), p. 182; and *Letters,* pp. 16-17. Browning's biographer, H. E. Wortham, claimed that soon after his dismissal from Eton, Browning stayed with Pater in Oxford. See H. E. Wortham, *Victorian Eton and Cambridge* (Lond: Arthur Baker, 1927), p. 150.

4. See the unsigned review of the third edition of *The New Republic* in *Contemporary Review,* XXX (1877), 1099. The reviewer obviously knew some of the subjects of Mallock's book. Thus: "It is impossible to help being tickled with the imitation (which, by the way, contains too much actual extract) of "Critical Essays on the Renaissance" in Mr. Rose's reflections on the ideal of modern Love. But this identifies the author of those essays, in a manner quite undeserved and uncalled for, with the character of Mr. Rose; which is made the only dark one in the book, by certain traits and speeches. It may be right enough to have an exponent of certain tendencies of modern aestheticism, and some sayings and doings of that school may be none the worse for a little castigation . . . [but the] author of the Essays . . . is not to be held to say, or to think, that it [art] is atheistic or immoral."

See also the unsigned review of *The New Republic* in *Athenaeum,* no. 2578 (24 March 1877), 378, which, at one point, obviously alludes to the unfair attacks on Pater: "There are some touches in one character which cannot but be regarded as the gravest possible offences against good taste, good manners and fair play." The reviewer was probably Theodore Watts-Dunton, hence the criticism of Mallock.

5. See an unsigned review of Alexander Grosart's *The Prose Works of William Wordsworth,* in *Quarterly Review,* CXLI (1876), 132. It is interesting that the reviewer saw fit to move from a discussion of classicism and romanticism in verse to a thorough denunciation of the works of Symonds and Pater.

6. Mrs. Humphry Ward, *A Writer's Recollections* (Lond: W. Collins Sons, 1918), p. 120.

7. See W. W. Jackson, *Ingram Bywater: The Memoirs of An Oxford Scholar,* (Oxford: Clarendon P, 1917), pp. 10, 77-9. Jackson claimed that Pater was defended publicly by Dr. Ince, the subrector of Exeter, in an address to the Church Congress.

8. See *Letters,* pp. 18-24.

9. Some of the details are related in Phyllis Grosskurth, *John Addington Symonds* (Lond: Longmans, 1964), pp. 168-172.

10. See *The Oxford and Cambridge Undergraduates' Journal,* 19 April 1877, p. 291; and especially Edward Cracroft Lefroy's essay "Muscular Christianity," *The Oxford and Cambridge Undergraduates' Journal,* 31 May 1877, p. 450. See also John Addington Symonds' recollection of the affair in *In the Key of Blue* (Lond: Mathews & Lane, 1893), p. 90.

11. See Richard St. John Tyrwhitt, "The Greek Spirit In Modern Literature," *Contemporary Review,* XXIX (1876-77), 558. Tyrwhitt's polemic was directed against Symonds' *Studies of the Greek Poets.* He discussed and rejected Symonds' celebration of Greek homosexual love. Ironically (for some of his readers, at least) Tyrwhitt recommended Jowett's work as offering the proper account of Greek homosexuality.

12. A. C. Benson, *Walter Pater* (Lond: Macmillan, 1906), p. 52.

13. *A Writer's Recollections* (Lond: Collins, 1918), p. 120.

14. *Critical Kit-Kats* (Lond: Heinemann, 1896), pp. 257-58.

15. "Wordsworth and Gray," *Quarterly Review,* CXLI (Jan 1976), 55-71.

16. "Essays and Notices," *Contemporary Review,* XXX (Nov 1877), 1098-99.

17. Thomas Wright, *The Life of Walter Pater* (Lond: Everett, 1907), II, 118; Benson, *Walter Pater,* p. 20; Gosse, *Critical Kit-Kats,* p. 260.

18. See *Letters of Walter Pater,* ed by Lawrence Evans (Oxford: Clarendon P, 1970), p. 13, n. 20.

19. *The Academy*'s notice of the Professor of Poetry election (XI [Feb 24, 1877], 160) favored the Bishop of Derry, "a poet, and, what is perhaps as important, an ecclesiastic," thus revealing its moral bias. Nevertheless, the article comments: "Mr. Pater we hope to see some day in one of the Slade chairs of Fine Art," a just estimation of where Pater's talents lay and hardly the completely negative attitude Small leads us to assume.

20. Quoted in J. A. Symonds, *In the Key of Blue* (NY: Macmillan, 1918), pp. 92-93. Regrettably, I have been unable to obtain the complete text of Lefroy's article.

21. *Contemporary Review,* XXIX (March 1877), 552-66. Tyrwhitt extensively analyzes Arnold's concepts of Hebraism and Hellenism, attempting to show that they are not in conflict but are essentially identical, and sees Symonds' position as a perversion of Arnold's Hellenism.

22. *Quarterly Review,* CLXXXII (July 1895), 31-58.

23. *Critical Kit-Kats,* pp. 266-67.

24. Ibid, p. 260.

## Robert Peters (essay date November 1981)

SOURCE: Peters, Robert. "The Cult of the Returned Apollo: Walter Pater's *Renaissance* and *Imaginary Portraits.*" *Journal of Pre-Raphaelite Studies* 2, no. 1 (November 1981): 53-69.

[*In the following essay, Peters discusses aspects of sexuality in* The Renaissance *and* Imaginary Portraits. *Peters traces the root of Pater's notion of sexuality to classical Greek civilization, in particular the Apollonian ideal of beauty. For Peters the essence of Pater's sexuality was androgyny, a paradigm that admits all forms of aesthetic and physical sensuality.*]

Walter Pater's peculiar fusion of art, sensuousness, and Greek idealism provided an esthetic-philosophical framework for younger men seeking alternatives to a suffocating Victorian England. When Pater's **Studies in the History of the Renaissance** were published in 1874, his most flamboyant follower, Oscar Wilde, declared that with the book's appearance the world should have ended: Wilde would then have an eternity for savoring the marvellous "golden book." The **Renaissance** inspired generations of late Victorian youths, and led them to an art of nerves, a special attenuation of sense and esthetic feeling new in English literature. Central was the image of the androgynous male—Apollo returned to life to inspirit an insipid bourgeois age.

Early in his famous "Preface" to the **Renaissance,** Pater explained that one of the functions of "the aesthetic critic" is to regard all objects, including both works of art and "the fairer forms of nature and human life," as producible of "pleasurable sensations, each of a more or less peculiar or unique kind." Once one is struck by the *temperament* of beautiful personalities or beautiful objects, one defines his pleasure by analyzing the influence conveyed by these phenomena. Each "fair personality," each picture, each landscape, has its *virtue,* wrote Pater—or that power generating "special impressions" on the sensitive critic/viewer/perceiver. Pater's critic is utterly catholic; all periods and schools of taste are equal. "Genius," Pater concluded, "is always above its age."

## I

For Pater the Italian Renaissance was particularly momentous. For the first time in Europe, after the ancient Greeks, cults of the personality flowered—"the care for physical beauty" and "the worship of the body" broke down limits imposed by the rigorous Christianity of the Middle Ages. Pater saw parallels between fifteenth and sixteenth century Italy and the age of Periclean Athens; both were periods "productive in personalities, many-sided, centralised, complete." The blonde youths of the Renaissance, stunning in bodily beauty, agility, and their power to inspirit less-beautiful mortals around them, were kin to the youths of Athens—rendered, of course, in what remains to us of Greek sculpture (and in Roman copies), and in the descriptions by Plato and the Greek poets.

In **"Two Early French Stories,"** an early chapter of **Renaissance,** Pater's Aucassin, a "slim, tall, debonair *dansellon*" with curly yellow locks and "eyes of *vair,*" leads his people, inspiring them by his "sweet grave figure" in its "dainty, tight-laced armor." Aucassin was, said Pater, "the very image of the Provençal love-god," a version of the ancient Eros-Apollo.

In another essay, **"Pico della Mirandola,"** Apollo relives his ancient life as keeper of Admetus' cows by returning to Lower Austria to live as a shepherd. Tending his flocks, he sings so sweetly that a suspicious monk

recognizes him as the pagan god and, much fearing and distressed, delivers the youth to a spiritual tribunal. On the torture rack, the youth confesses that he is indeed Apollo. His only wish before his execution is that he be allowed once more to play his lyre. The wish is granted. He plays so magically that all the women present weep, many of them falling ill because his music is to be silenced. The youth is executed and buried. When the citizens wish to assure his never returning again to earth (they are plagued by his beauty and his musicianship), they open his grave intending to drive a stake through his heart. They find an empty grave. The god, maintaining his ancient pattern, has disappeared. Eventually, again like Apollo, he will return in some new guise, in some unexpected place, to work his charm.

Pater knew that an ordinary human sensibility was incapable of assimilating the generative force of such Apollonian beauty, and would in fact seek to destroy it, dismembering Apollo and scattering his parts, hoping they would never recombine to plague the world again. Repeatedly in Pater's stories and essays mobs slaughter androgynous youths; to love Apollo means that you accept (and love) your own mixed sexuality, a fact Pater seemed to sense, anticipating twentieth-century psychology.

Obviously, works of art and artists themselves risk destruction at the hands of the masses. The homosexual mode in life and art symbolizes for Pater an expanding consciousness, one moving towards idealized, rare feelings, towards what Pater called *Allgemeinheit.* By providing this conceptual framework for Uranian feelings, Pater helped his followers accept their troubling sexuality. When one is struck by physical beauty in another person he can interpret his pleasure as evidence of his ability to respond to an androgynous ideal.

This "hermaphroditism" Pater detected in various of Leonardo da Vinci's works. Pater alludes to Leonardo's rendering of a "curious beauty" emanating from persons of doubtful gender. Leonardo plunged into human personality, said Pater, and modelled faces more revealingly than any other painter had done, juxtaposing a fascination with death with a thirst for an ambivalent sexual beauty. Leonardo's perpetual retouchings, "his odd experiments with colour," Pater felt, evidenced his exacting struggle after such beauty. Around his sitters "powers" work in the common air unfelt by others. Leonardo's figures are the receptacles of these powers, which they transmit "in a chain of secret influences." Here, indeed is that Gospel of Intensity so much a feature of the decadent and esthetic modes of the eighteen-nineties—simply with a gaze you plumb the recesses of another person's soul.

One of Leonardo's drawings in particular intrigued Pater: the head of a young man. Pater speculated that this was a portrait of Andrea Solaino, Leonardo's favorite pupil and servant, loved "for his curled and waving hair." Leonardo, it seems, usually chose his pupils for "some natural charm of person or intercourse." His favored youths had "just enough genius to be capable of initiation into Leonardo's secret, his homosexuality. The ambience is clearest, Pater felt, in *St. John the Baptist,* at the Louvre. Of this rendering, one of the few totally naked figures Leonardo ever painted, Pater observed that one would never enter a wilderness, hoping to find such "delicate brown flesh and woman's hair." John, "whose treacherous smile would have us understand something far beyond the outward gesture or circumstance," is really a decayed god; his strangeness reflects the *Bacchus* hanging nearby. We are carried, as we are with so many of Leonardo's works, past the range of "conventional associations."

Pater here suggests that Leonardo was in fact painting his own sexuality, reflecting subtle, transcendental notions of truth and beauty. Throughout Pater's essays there is a sanctioning of elitist values: "a chain of secret influences" binds men together, forging a strength against a Philistine culture. Certainly, sensitive young Victorian males reading Pater's essays could now more readily accept and live out their own "secrets," with Pater's blessing—and with Leonardo's.

## II

To enrich his concept of transformed sexual passion, Pater found allusions to music helpful. The enlightened Paterian soul, quivering in response to Beauty, yearns after "the condition of music." Art, Pater explained in one of his most influential dictums, strives always to free itself from "the mere intelligence, to become a matter of pure perception." The gross materials of art, its "constituent elements" of subject matter and material, are utterly refined. The intellect—the force that translated material and subject into *form*—now blends with *form* into a single effect, termed by Pater "the imaginative reason."

Of all the arts, music most perfectly realizes this "identification," or blending of matter and form. Here, in consummation, abstract but at the same time elevating, matter and form "inhere in and completely saturate each other." To this condition, Pater speculated, all the arts constantly "tend and aspire." Obviously, to sense physical beauty in a youth is to locate one's self already on the ladder of "imaginative reason." By immersing one's sensate mind totally in earthly beauty, one begins to transmute that mind into a more abstract and purer feeling. To be alert is to be *intense*. To be intense is evidence that you are one of a blessed aristocracy of esthetes: you are among the purest of all lovers of art and life.

As one might expect, in his theorizing Pater continuously drew parallels with ancient Greece. In his second essay, on the great early eighteenth-century art historian and archeologist Johann Joachim Winckelmann (1717-1768) whose *Geschichte der Kunst des Alterthums* (1764) transformed European thinking about Greek art, Pater explored connections between *intensity* and Periclean Athens. Pater's treatment of Winckelmann's sexuality is veiled rather than straightforward. Yet it is there, including allusions to the archeologist's murder under suspicious circumstances, in 1768, in Trieste. Winckelmann had stopped on his way home from Vienna where he had been honored by Queen Maria Theresa with medals. He made the mistake of showing them to a fellow-traveller, one Archangeli, who apparently out of greed garroted Winckelmann.

At the outset of his lengthy essay, Pater described Winckelmann's interpretations of Plato: earlier commentators (among them Christian Wolff) had regarded Plato as "no longer pagan" but "spiritual," and, hence, broadly Christian. Winckelmann insisted on Plato's wholly Greek nature, denying any easy Christian parallels. This "Greek quality," Winckelmann felt, derived from Plato's love for youths. As he often did, Pater sent up smoke, to dissuade us from lingering over Winckelmann's animal delight in these youngsters: they were idealized innocents, "still uninfected by any spiritual sickness, finding the end of all endeavour in the aspects of the human form, the continual stir and motion of a comely human life." "Stir and motion" suggest the cult of the idealized athlete—that magnetic, vibrant, male form of Greek sculpture. To find "the end of all endeavour," as Pater implied that Winckelmann had, in the turn of a golden thigh, the slabs of a superbly plated chest with nipples erect, or the muscular structure of a powerful neck, is to see the sexual as indeed a primary element of art and beauty. If we are to find emancipation through Art, Pater insisted, we must resurrect Winckelmann's belief in the primacy of immediate "sight and touch" over "abstract theory."

When Winckelmann abandoned "the crabbed Protestantism" of his youth, became a Roman Catholic convert, and entered Rome—with Voltaire's works under his arm—his absorption of ancient Greek art and mores waxed more single-minded than ever. His homosexuality flourished: he formed numerous liaisons with young men, finding many of them, Pater observed, "more beautiful than Guido's archangel." These relationships, wrote Pater, brought the archeologist "into contact with the pride of human form, and staining the thoughts with its bloom, perfected his reconciliation to the spirit of Greek sculpture." Pater quotes from a letter Winckelmann wrote to a young nobleman, Friedrich von Berg: "The first time I saw you, the affinity of our spirits was revealed to me: your culture proved that my hope was not groundless; and I found in a beautiful body a soul created for nobleness, gifted with the sense of beauty." Parting from von Berg was intensely painful. Later friendships with men merely recalled that pain, the worst of Winckelmann's life.

Like Pater, Winckelmann translated his homosexual feelings into theories about art and life. Writing again to von Berg, Winckelmann was surprisingly straightforward: "As it is confessedly the beauty of man which is to be conceived under one general idea, so I have noticed that those who are observant of beauty only in women, and are moved little or not at all by the beauty of men, seldom have an impartial, vital, inborn instinct for beauty in art. To such persons the beauty of Greek art will ever seem wanting, because its supreme beauty is rather male than female." He pursued two provocative speculations: first, if one is to find art in these exquisite male forms, "a higher sensibility" is required than sensual attraction." Beauty, Winckelmann continued, "like tears shed at a play, gives no pain, is without life, and must be awakened and repaired by culture." The great cultural awakener is to worship athletes. Why? Obviously, says Winckelmann, "the spirit of culture is much more ardent in youth than in manhood." Our instinct for beauty "must be exercised and directed to what is beautiful, before that age is reached at which one would be afraid to confess that one had no taste for it."

An interesting syllogism is implicit here, one that undoubtedly appealed to Pater and other sensitive Victorians, both Uranian and non-Uranian, who sought in art a spiritual antithesis to the smug materialistic society around them. The syllogism runs something like this: the pursuit of Art is the highest of all human ventures. Men who observe beauty equally in males and females are more innately suited to experience art than men who limit their responses to female beauty. Thus, to experience Art cultivates a sensitivity for male beauty.

It is possible, of course, that when Pater wrote **The Renaissance** he was winsomely naive about the real implications of much of his theorizing; perhaps that is why he later modified the work, deleting the famous "Conclusion" from the second edition. When he restored it in subsequent editions, he still omitted the few passages he felt were potentially damaging to the morals of young, impressionable readers. Somewhat primly

STUDIES

*IN THE HISTORY OF THE*

RENAISSANCE

BY

WALTER H. PATER

FELLOW OF BRASENOSE COLLEGE, OXFORD

London

MACMILLAN AND CO.

1873

[*All rights reserved*]

*Title page for the 1873 first edition of* Studies in the History of the Renaissance.

he defended his suppressions: the passages, he said, might possibly mislead some of those young men "into whose hands **The Renaissance** might fall." Pater's hermit-like life at Oxford, where he was a classics scholar, is well-known. He seems to have enjoyed few liaisons with either males or females. But, to return to the question of Pater's naivete: I think he saw the sexual implications of his writings. His messages, though muffled in a gossamer style, were consciously sent. Even his original speculations about the continuing influence of Classical art had its overtly homosexual frame. He wrote of "the Hellenic element" always present in European cultures. "Hellenism," he wrote, "is not merely an absorbed element in our intellectual life; it is a conscious tradition in it." And while the art of any age is colored by the *individual* geniuses of that age, there remains always "an element of permanence, a standard of taste, which genius confesses." So it is with Hellenic art—its influence continues through extant sculptures, mosaics, and literary works. These "supreme artistic products" are "a series of elevated points" forming a standard of taste as meaningful to the present as it was to the past. Greek art is sensuous; Christian art is mystical, forever struggling "to express thoughts beyond itself." On the other hand, Greek sculpture symbolizes nothing "beyond its own victorious fairness." The spiritual element in Greek sculpture is so refined and blent with the sensuous that the Greek mind begins and completes itself with a finite image, an athletic human body, and, as such, reflects the "perfect animal nature of the Greeks." Here thought balances and never outstrips or lies beyond "the proper range of its sensible embodiment." Greek sculpture is an exercise in *tact,* of forms in motion, with energies reserved and seldom committed to any definite action; the "moulding of the bodily organs is still as if suspended between growth and completion, indicated but not emphasized; where the transition from curve to curve is so delicate and elusive, that Winckelmann compares it to a quiet sea, which, although we understand it to be in motion, we nevertheless regard as an image of repose."

The youths on horseback, of the Panathenaic frieze, provided Pater with a superb example of Greek idealism mirrored in sculpture. In fact, Pater said, if one work and only one should have survived from Hellenic art this should have been the one: ". . . that line of youths on horseback, with their level glances, their proud, patient lips, their chastened reins, their whole bodies in exquisite service. This colourless, unclassified purity of life, with its blending and interpenetration of intellectual, spiritual, and physical elements, still folded together, pregnant with the possibilities of a whole world closed within it, is the highest expression of the indifference which lies beyond all that is relative or partial."

Pater capped his enthusiasm for the Hellenic in his famous "Conclusion." The modern Hellenist, he explained, should see his life in a series of moments, some relaxed, some intense; his primary knowing will happen according to the number of sense impressions he is able to transmute. Furthermore, in a single lifetime, the Hellenist can expect only "a counted number of pulses" as his own. The problem is to experience, via the senses, what is beautiful and hence eternal in these impressions. If we are to realize pleasure from these sensations, we must "burn always," Pater declared, with a "hard gemlike flame." The world of such sensations is a perpetually shifting place; it slips from beneath us at the very moment we feel most secure on it. Understandably, the *fixed* in our experience contains those impressions we are able to capture and hold, however fleetingly: "We may well grasp at any exquisite passion, or any contribution to knowledge that seems

by a lifted horizon to set the spirit free for a moment, or any stirring of the senses, strange dyes, strange colours, and curious odours, or work of the artist's hands, or the face of one's friend." Nuances abound. They will elude us unless we generate "great passions," nonconventional passions, to receive and nourish these fleeting moments. No culture, Pater felt, better illuminated this truth than that of Periclean Athens. And no figure in that culture better synthesized that truth than the Apollonian youth, the athlete burgeoning into manhood, hyacinthine-curled, bronzed, red-lipped, muscular, delicate. Given these primary themes from *The Renaissance,* we can easily understand Pater's fascination with the motif of the returned Apollo, a motif weaving throughout one of his rather neglected yet most important works—his series of *Imaginary Portraits* (1877). Since these tales are out of print and difficult of access, I shall paraphrase them.

### III

Duke Carl of Rosenmold, in Pater's portrait of the same name, is a composite of Johann Winckelmann and the homosexual Bavarian king, Ludwig II, who ruled Bavaria from 1864, at age 17, to 1886, when he drowned under still-mysterious circumstances. Ludwig saw himself as a synthesizer of the arts, a genius, if you will, who kept aloof from the rest of humanity, finding his equal in Richard Wagner and a series of male lovers, some titled, some not. Ludwig supported Wagner lavishly on Bavarian public money for several years. Without Ludwig's support there would have been no *Ring* cycle. In 1878, after the cooling of his obsessive friendship with Wagner, Ludwig began to build his famous castles: Linderhof, Neuschwanstein, and Herrenchiemsee. The costs of the castles resulted in such vigorous complaints from the ministers of state that Ludwig was eventually deposed as insane.

In Pater's story, the young Duke Carl awakens to Greek culture by reading a Sapphic ode in *Ars Versificandi: the Art of Versification,* by Conrad Celtes, possibly printed by Dürer in 1486. This ode was for Carl "the pearl, the golden nugget" of the entire volume. In the poem, Celtes prayed, urging Apollo to visit Germany, bringing his lyre with him: "The god of light coming to Germany from some more favoured world beyond it, over leagues of rainy hill and mountain, making soft day there: that had ever been the dream of the ghost-ridden yet deep-feeling and certainly meek German soul; of the great Dürer. . . . And it was precisely the aspiration of Carl himself."

Like the real-life King Ludwig II, whose absolute hero and model was Louis XIV, the French Sun-King, Duke Carl imagined his Apollo appearing in Germany dressed like Louis XIV, whose court was the ultimate in refinement and aesthetic embellishments. Soon Duke Carl's acquaintances began to call him "the northern Apollo." He was greatly flattered, and roamed his dukedom, inviting all people he met, somewhat unrealistically perhaps, to share the honey of art with him. He knew music, drama, sculpture, and painting. He played the violin. He loved florid styles, and much preferred French literature to German, finding the latter hopelessly dull. Like Ludwig II extolling Wagner's music, Duke Carl believed that the Germany of the new spirit would build itself to the sound of music, a kind of Wagnerian *Gesamtkunstwerk.*

Duke Carl's obsessions chilled him; he could gladden others and irradiate them with his inner light, but he himself was increasingly chilled. He craved to visit Greece. In preparation he fantasized that his ancestors actually were southern. How else, he wondered, could he explain his "strange restlessness, like the imperfect reminiscence of something that had passed in earlier life." This German Apollo never visited Greece though; rather, he travelled compulsively throughout the German landscape—as Ludwig II had done. Strenuous exercise alone alleviated his melancholy. Only his organist Max, and Fritz the treble-singer, along with himself, of course, were worthy of a new age. His people were hopelessly prosaic, their lives despicable.

Carl grew obsessed with death and decay. As a bizarre test of his power, he commanded that his people bury him, with much pomp and circumstance, so that he could then witness his "resurrection." He composed his own dirge: the true artist to the very end. While his "death" and "burial" had absurdist overtones, they were symbols for the Duke, now considered quite Mad. The ceremony allowed him to feel more than ever estranged from his people: the empty coffin "served as a kind of symbolic coronation incident," marking off his almost total withdrawal from public life. His days were spent in wild pursuits (one assumes they were sexual) with his youthful favorites. His obsession with Apollo persisted.

At Strasbourg, Carl "became fairly captive" to the Middle Ages. An illumination occurred. He was visited by the veritable Apollo, god of light. He no longer felt bewildered by the whence and the how of the coming national *Eclaircissement,* the *Aufklärung.* When this great event occurred, "the spirits of distant Hellas would reawake in the men and women of little German towns. Distant times, the most alien thoughts, would come near together, as elements in a great historic symphony." Carl felt a new and ardent patriotism. He fell in love with the Alps, symbols of his new Germany. He re-

turned home filled with fervor, and in the midst of enjoying his own elaborate marriage ceremonies, was slaughtered by the officers of a victorious army moving across Germany. The German Apollo was dead, his mission unfulfilled.

**"Sebastian van Storck,"** the next tale from *Imaginary Portraits,* is a complex psychological (and speculative) study of an Apollonian Dutch youth whose beauty becomes a curse; his psyche contained a *mysterious* element. Winter was his season. He loved cold and ice, empty landscapes adjoining wintry seas. His sport was ice-skating. His genealogy was a blend of two disparate, contrasting European cultures—an intriguing problem for Pater, fascinated as he was (as was Ruskin) by contrasts between southern and northern European temperaments. Sebastian's mother was Spanish and Catholic. His father was Dutch and Protestant.

Sebastian was a dreamer and meditator. Intellectually he was so brilliant his tutor sent him home, afraid to teach him, refusing to "disturb too early" the boy's fine intelligence. Sebastian seemed a prototype of the impressionable young men Pater feared were following his own philosophy of the "hard gemlike flame." Sebastian's tutor regretted that his charge was too impressed by "the doctrines of a surprising new philosophy." Later, we discover that Sebastian had indeed entertained a view of life as a series of fleeting impressions, a Paterian-like flux. Sebastian, though, behaved in quite un-Paterian fashion by rejecting all of the arts, declaring them painful and useless since they merely added "to the monotonous tide of competing, fleeting existence." He also rejected women, schooling, and finally his own beauty.

When Thomas de Keyser, the painter, desired to paint Sebastian, Sebastian declined, later shredding the only portrait of him ever made. He sensed de Keyser's sexual attraction, was dismayed at a party to find the painter by stealth drawing him, and refused again ever to allow de Keyser near him. When his mother, arguing filial duty, asked him to sit for a family portrait, he refused. "There are duties towards the intellect," he said, "which woman can but rarely understand." The only woman he noticed, Mlle. van Westerheene, sought to excite him, failed, and in good nineteenth-century fashion crept off and died.

Sebastian's philosophy was rigorously logical. A saying of Spinoza had turned his head: "Whoso loveth God truly must not expect to be loved by Him in return." The antidote, Sebastian felt, was to cultivate "an intellectual disinterestedness," to achieve an entirely unimpassioned mind, and to suppress one's subjective side entirely. The world, he concluded, "is but a thought, or a series of thoughts." One should, therefore, cultivate no feelings but submit to one's intellect, "whithersoever it might lead." It led Sebastian to "zero."

Winter, for Sebastian symbolized that zero. The "pallid Arctic sun, disclosing itself over the dead level of a glacial, a barren and absolutely lonely sea," was an image for a life with all purpose frozen out of it. In that still, drowsy, spellbound world of perpetual ice he found a necessary charm.

Like all returned Apollos, Sebastian too must die young, and tragically. Ironically, this strange denier, or *no-sayer*, drowns during a flood trying to save a child. He was on one of his philosophical retreats to a desolate coastal landscape, in pursuit of *nothing*. When he saved the child, whom he swaddled in his furs and placed in the upper room of a tower, he himself died of exposure. The child lived. His parents, believing him bent on suicide, were glad to find his death the result of a humanitarian act. A physician comforted his mother by saying that her son would have died soon anyway, perhaps painfully, of a disease newly imported to Europe, a disease "begotten by the fogs of that country . . . on people grown somewhat over-delicate in their nature by the effects of modern luxury."

Obviously, Pater sermonizes here: read "London fogs" for Dutch fogs. Read "hyper-contemporary civilization" for "modern luxury." A curious twist? We should not overlook the austerity behind Pater's thought. His Hedonism was, in substance, a fairly Spartan reflection of the ancient philosophers he loved. If life is a matter of selecting the best among a plethora of sense experiences, we must choose only those capable of enhancing our spiritual fiber. Hedonism, as Pater amply demonstrated in his novel **Marius the Epicurean,** is a rigorous and demanding philosophy.

At the same time, Pater's Sebastian is the extreme of the Wildean personality patterning itself after Pater's theories in **The Renaissance.** By reducing the hedonist philosophy of the senses to absolutes, you do face *zero.* And, since you are capable of determining which sense impressions to experience, you may easily suspect all impressions, and reject all. But the true Wildean seeks to experience *all,* and his pursuit of as many sensations as possible is also a kind of mortal *No;* for he eschews choice, fuzzing and distorting his senses so that he becomes the victim rather than the orchestrator of experience. Thus, the cult of the exquisite youth, as it derived from ancient Greek art, reappears in late Victorian England in two possible guises: an Apollo so balanced and so self-controlled that he dismisses feeling for an inte-

rior "well-reasoned nihilism"; or an Apollo orchestrating his senses and enlivening his soul with glorious earthly music. Pater's Apollos are seldom able to accept and assimilate their beauty. His Apollos must die young, their unearthly beauty an obsession and a curse, a warning to insufficiently cautious hedonists.

Pater's most thoroughgoing treatment of the Apollo-returned motif appears in **"Denys l'Auxerrois."** Denys is Apollo the archetypal artist; like other Apollos his exceptional beauty and haunting inner drives lead to tragedy. The story is very consciously wrought. Pater uses a picture, a device later popularized by Oscar Wilde in *The Portrait of Dorian Gray,* to launch the tale.

Among the riches and treasures of Auxerre Cathedral, an edifice containing a variety of Gothic styles from the Pointed to the latest Flamboyant, is a splendor of late-Gothic stained glass. One of the windows has lines of pearly white running "hither and thither, with a delightful distant effect, upon ruby and dark blue." This is a "Travellers' window." The strange lines of white are the long walking-staves of Abraham, Raphael, the Magi, and other saintly patrons of journeys.

Once, visiting this medieval cathedral and city, Pater's narrator enters the priest's house, a small Gothic building near the village church. Here he finds a gathering of exceptional tapestries, celebrating a theme he had observed in a fragment of stained glass, possibly coming from the cathedral itself, earlier in an old bric-a-brac shop. In both glass and tapestry, the growth of music was the theme: pipes, cymbals, and long reed-like trumpets—and the building of a great organ, oddly resembling the ancient instrument present in the old priest's library.

Listeners, embroidered in the tapestry, seemed to hear the silent rapturous organ music. A "sort of mad vehemence" prevailed: "delicate bewilderments . . . giddy dances, wild animals leaping, above all perpetual wreathings of the vine, connecting, like some mazy arabesque, the various presentations of the one oft-repeated figure, translated here out of the clear-coloured glass into the sadder, somewhat opaque and earthen hues of the silken threads." That "oft-repeated" figure was the organ-builder, a flaxen-haired youth "sometimes well-nigh naked among the vine-leaves, sometimes muffled in skins against the cold, sometimes in the dress of a monk, but always with a strong impress of real character and incident from the veritable streets of Auxerre."

The narrator is struck by what appeared to be "a suffering, tortured figure," with the beauty of "a pagan god." Intrigued by the contrasts implicit in this creature, so seemingly tragic yet surrounded by incredible accessories—clothing, flowers, jewels—the narrator spins out his tale of Apollo returned to mid-thirteenth century France.

During the building of the great Cathedral at Auxerre, in the Champagne country near Troyes, workmen unearthed an ancient, finely-sculptured Greek stone coffin. Inside was a flask of green glass, resembling a great emerald. It had once held Roman wine. Some sediment remained, and was enjoyed at a supper celebrating the conclusion of the masons' labors. The drinkers were stirred to feel that "a sort of golden age" was about to occur—a blessed time of beauty and renewed paganism. There ensued a series of remarkable wine seasons. Even poor men enjoyed the surplus. Arts and crafts flourished as they never had within memory.

One Easter, the canons of the Cathedral observed an old ritual of playing ball inside the Cathedral. Choir boys flung the ball along the vaulted roof of the central aisle until it reached the canons waiting near the altar. Among this gathering, Denys appeared, leaping in, dominating the game and stimulating the participants: "The boys played like boys, the men almost like madmen, and all with a delightful glee which became contagious, first in the clerical body, and then among the spectators. The aged Dean of the Chapter . . . held up his purple skirt a little higher, and stepping from the ranks with an amazing levity, as if suddenly relieved of his burden of eighty years, tossed the ball with his foot to the venerable capitular Homilist, equal to the occasion. And then, unable to stand inactive any longer, the laity carried on the game among themselves, with shouts of not too boisterous amusement; the sport continuing till the flight of the ball could no longer be traced along the dusky aisles."

The mysterious youth was of suspect parentage. None seemed to know why or from whence Denys had appeared. Gossip said that his father was the powerful Count of Auxerre who had impregnated a country girl. She, terrified by a storm, about to have her child, sought refuge with the Count, reached his door, was struck by lightning, and delivered her child as she died. Denys grew to become an incredible gardener—Apollo among the flowers; and he supported himself by selling his produce in the local market, exotic produce quite suitable for a gardener-god: pomegranates, melons, flower seeds, and honey.

Again, like Sebastian van Storck and the young Duke Carl of Rosenmold, Denys' androgynous beauty impressed both sexes. Whenever they saw him, women basked in his beauty. Men were ensnared by a strange power "hidden under the white veil of that youthful form." Seeing him rejuvenated old people. "This was a period," Pater gravely reports, "of young men and men's influence." Denys loosed "a new spirit": "The hot nights were noisy with swarming troops of dishevelled women and youths with red-stained limbs and faces, carrying their lighted torches over the vine-clad hills, or rushing down the streets, to the horror of timid watchers, towards the cool spaces by the river. A shrill music, a laughter at all things, was everywhere. And the new spirit repaired even to church to take part in the novel offices of the Feast of Fools. Heads flung back in ecstasy—the morning sleep among the vines, when the fatigue of the night was over—dew-drenched garments—the serf lying at his ease at last: the artists, then so numerous at the place, caught what they could, something, at least, of the richness, the flexibility of the visible aspects of life, from all this."

Denys even influenced nature: "It seemed there would be winter no more." He was inordinately fond of grotesque children and strange animals. He healed crippled children. A tamed wolf kept him company. Of all creatures he abhorred the owl. He dominated a yearly ritual procession, a morality play depicting the God of wine riding in triumph from the east. As the wine god, Denys wore soft silk and rode on a painted chariot. For a headdress he wore an elephant scalp with gilded tusks—paganism rampant.

Throughout all such festivities and, indeed, in daily life, Denys remained entirely aloof from other men. He slept with no one, he was intimate with no one. His transforming powers seemed to emanate from his presence alone. Enamored with him, people turned their erotic frenzies on one another, as a kind of sublimation of the terrible energies Denys' beauty provoked.

As the years passed, Denys maintained his youth. The citizens surmised that his simple rustic life kept him young. Like a seasonal creature (following the pattern of the original Apollo), he began to disappear as winter approached, visiting regions to the south. At Marseilles, he reportedly "trafficked with sailors." In the spring he returned to Auxerre, displaying a plethora of exotic goods never before seen in the town—"seeds of marvellous new flowers, creatures wild and tame, new pottery painted in raw gaudy tints, the skins of animals, meats fried with unheard of condiments." Local artists were particularly impressed. The local grape-vine dresser stopped dressing vines and founded an art school. Inspired by Denys's exoticism, the director and his artisans formed an aristocracy, a veritable *gens fleur-de-lisés,* as they worked together to decorate the great church "and a hundred other places beside."

Paradoxically, as the region waxed in its zest and color, Denys was increasingly plagued. Like the ancient wine god who had his dark, antipathetic side, Denys had his. He abandoned his strict vegetarianism and began to devour flesh, with "an almost savage delight." Rumor said that he had axed someone to death in a vineyard, for the sheer pleasure of killing. (The old Apollo had not hesitated to flay Marsyas alive for beating him in a musical competition). Women reportedly spawned his illegitimate children, again, according to rumor, drowning them in lakes or hanging them in dark cellars. Gradually, fearing and despising his sorcery, the citizens forced him into hiding.

Though concealed in a monastery, Denys's influence for destruction continued. The times grew foul, crops failed, vineyards were diseased, misery was rampant. To stem these evils, the Bishop visited Auxerre and decided to exhume the corpse of an ancient saint buried beneath the Cathedral. Relics of the corpse might reverse Auxerre's bad luck. After much random excavating, bones were retrieved, as Denys unobserved stood by. As the Bishop drew the skeleton forth, every feature of the corpse's face was, to Denys, "traceable in a sudden oblique ray of ghastly dawn." Denys was transformed; he seemed no longer mad and had become "a subdued, silent, melancholy creature." He unobtrusively took one of the saint's bones to wear about his neck, left Auxerre, and was received secretly by an order of artisan monks nearby. Here he became famous. In cowl and with tonsured head, he "leaned over the painter, and led his work, by a kind of visible sympathy, often unspoken, rather than by any formal comment."

The monks wished to develop musical instruments "of a freer and more various sacred music than had been in use hitherto—a music that might express the whole compass of their souls. Denys made the consummation possible, imagining a combination of all musical instruments then in use in the structuring of a single organ. "Like the wine god of old," he had always loved the pipe, in all its forms, from the simple and pastoral— "like the piping of the wind itself from off the distant fields"—to pipes producing a "wild, savage din" capable of driving excitable people mad. This first organ was to be an exact reflection of Denys's own spiritual and earthly history, with all its sorrows and delights. Further, by completing the organ, Denys and his workmen would symbolically unify all the arts, and, hence, the entire range of human emotions: "It was the triumph of all the various modes of the power of the pipe, tamed, ruled, united. Only, on the painted shutters of the organ-case Apollo with his lyre in his hand, as lord of the strings, seemed to look askance on the music of the reed, in all the jealousy with which he put Marsyas to death so cruelly."

The people of Auxerre seemed to have completely forgotten Denys, sequestered as he was—until the day the Bishop blessed the foundation for a new bridge. At the core of the central pile, the skeleton of a child placed there in Roman days was exhumed. Denys, watching, was suddenly spied by various citizens who shouted and rushed at him. He flung himself into a river and disappeared: another of Apollo's mysterious withdrawals from the visible world.

Denys, in fact, survived his plunge and returned to the anonymity of the cloister, where he worked further on the organ. He seemed now increasingly obsessed with death.

Finally the great organ was completed, and the public heard it for the first time at a religious festival celebrating the demise of winter. During a secular pageant, Winter was to be hunted blindfolded through the streets. Hoping to restore some of his former influence over the town, Denys secretly assumed the central role. As he lowered Winter's ashen mantle over his body, a point of haircloth scratched his lip, drawing blood. The blood enraged the spectators, who sensed that this was the despised and feared Denys. They seized him and tore him into pieces. The men "stuck little shreds of his flesh, or, failing that, of his torn raiment, into their caps; the women lending their long hair-pins for the purpose." Next day, the monk Hermes sought in vain for his friend's remains. He failed. At midnight, however, a stranger brought him Denys's heart, which the monk buried under a stone marked with a cross in a dark corner of the cathedral.

IV

As in most mythic survival tales, the heart, or some other relevant limb or organ, remains to allow the reemergence of the myth figure at some future time, in some later culture. A recombination of body parts, a renewal of flesh and bone, produces a spring season, and a vibrant return of the god to earth. So far so good. There are other intriguing ramifications illuminating Pater's own homosexuality and, more generally, the problem of nineteenth-century homosexual artists. Social repressions have traditionally led these men to conceal their real predilections behind such devices as switched genders (John Addington Symonds, for example wrote numerous love sonnets to men, and by using the female pronoun pretended they were for women) and a suggestive, classically-rendered hermaphroditism (Simeon Solomon's designs and Oscar Wilde's representations of young androgynous males are notable). At the risk of psychologizing, one can, I think, read the violence in Pater's tales as a reflection of Pater's own guilt feelings, subconscious perhaps, about being homosexual.

The rending of Apollo is a symbolic act of self-laceration blent with a paradoxical defiance against a persecuting society: the Apollo does return, and, by extension, the homosexual may eventually have his day. Further, the translation of these feelings into classical terms was a sanitizing of them through art: purged of all kinkiness, stale odors, sweat, and blemishes, loving occurs between Greek statues come to life, idealized to the highest realms of art and beauty. Obviously, such sanitizing enabled these men, if they so chose, to accept their homosexuality without suffering the full measure of guilt induced by public disapprobation. At the same time, such concealments had a propagandistic side: first, these works contained sensitive messages to suffering readers wrestling with their homosexuality; and, second, the straight world enticed by the beauty of these poems, stories, and pictures might be more tolerant once they realized that homosexual love engendered this beauty.

The Apollo theme is, then, central to Pater's thought. The motif informs his novel *Marius the Epicurean,* which I have not discussed here. Marius is a youth of surpassing physical beauty who wanders in a world of beautiful males, pursuing religious values and love. Certainly the impact of *The Renaissance* on younger Victorian writers and artists was magnetic and has been well-documented. Any history of late Victorian art aspiring to completeness must account for its influence. In his fascination with portraits of the returned Apollo as a driven, tragic figure, Pater did understand, and underlined, the risks of allowing one's aberrational passions to unbridle and enervate one's choice-making faculties. One must fear being destroyed by some winsome youth, idolized as a prototypical Apollo. For one, Oscar Wilde failed to read Pater's warning sufficiently, preferring to accept only part of Pater's dicta, that the pursuit of art via the passions meant taking destructive risks. There is, finally, an ambivalence in Pater's writings, as there most probably was in his private life. His comprehension of the difficult problem of the outcast homosexual (and artist) was pioneering; and, despite the persecutions persisting into our own day, reading these essays and tales can still inspire males seeking to deal creatively with their Apollonian selves.

## Paul Barolsky (essay date fall 1982)

SOURCE: Barolsky, Paul. "Walter Pater and the Poetry of Nothingness." *Antioch Review* 40, no. 4 (fall 1982): 469-78.

[*In the following essay, Barolsky discusses the relationship between Pater's writings and the emergence of modernism. At the heart of Pater's modernity, Barolsky claims, is his keen grasp of the abstract elements in a work of art, an idea that found its most eloquent expression in* The Renaissance. *Describing the book as a "prose poem," Barolsky argues that Pater's literary style, more than the work's content, foreshadows many of the fundamental principles of modern art.*]

Walter Pater was once regarded primarily as the very type of Victorian culture, his accomplishment seen as the epitome of the nineteenth-century aspiration to commemorate the great art and literature of the past. This view still obtains, but our literary perspective has changed; and as his writings have receded into the past they have also come to be regarded increasingly as a primary source of modernist literature. Such books as *The Renaissance, Imaginary Portraits,* and *Plato and Platonism,* all published during the last three decades of the century, are now closely studied for their influences on Yeats, Pound, and Eliot, on Joyce, Woolf, and Stevens. Yet Pater's writings are not characterized, it is said, by the formal innovations that mark the works of those modernists who came under his spell.

Granted that this is so, the modernity of his book *The Renaissance* is nonetheless far greater than is now generally supposed. Perhaps Pater's ostensible concern with a historical topic has deflected attention from the implicit theme of his book, which is abstraction, and from his own abstract means of rendering this void. Kenneth Clark has justly suggested that Pater's appreciation of the abstract qualities of painting was to influence the modern criticism of art, especially the writings of Roger Fry. What has escaped attention, however, is the fact that, from his verbal palette, Pater created his own abstract art. *The Renaissance* not only stresses the fundamental tendency of the arts toward abstraction, as is well known, but expresses or embodies this very tendency—if in an oblique manner. The full extent of the book's abstractness becomes evident to us only upon careful examination of its form and imagery.

It is strange that the form of *The Renaissance* has never been considered in any detail, since Pater himself was preoccupied with the forms of literature and of the arts in general. In recent essays, I have suggested that like modernity and consciousness, which are major themes of Pater's writing, the form of his book is perpetually changing, "re-forming itself." If his book is ostensibly a series of biographies of central types of the Renaissance—Pico, Botticelli, Della Robbia, Michelangelo, Giorgione, Leonardo, Du Bellay—it is more than this, becoming a meditation on universal history from antiquity to the present. Strictly speaking, however, it is not considered a history. Strongly colored by Pater's own sentiments, his "lives" are autobiographical, but they do not become autobiography per se. Informed by a unifying consciousness, the characters are protean manifestations of a single fictional protagonist, not unlike Marius in Pater's subsequent novel. But *The Renaissance* is scarcely fiction as we understand this term. Pater's book is also poetical, and sometimes either individual passages or even chapters have been called poetry, though the book in its entirety is not generally regarded as a poem.

Yet I think we can consider *The Renaissance* most effectively as poetry, or rather, as a prose poem. Before writing it, Pater had written poetry of no distinction, most of which he burned, but following the example of Baudelaire, he developed as an essayist into a superb prose poet. In the "Preface" to *The Renaissance,* Pater speaks of art "casting off all debris, and leaving us only what the heat of the imagination has wholly fused and transformed." Pater's own exquisitely wrought prose poetry is such a creation or transformation, intricate, but spare and refined. It stands apart in this respect from the more exuberant and profuse poetical prose of Ruskin or Carlyle, and his essays are united to each other through the nuances of poetical imagery into a network of subtle interrelations that we do not find in the collected essays of Hazlitt, Lamb, Swinburne, and Arnold. All of these writers influenced Pater's prose, but in contrast to them, Pater weaves his essays on the Renaissance together into a unified, extended poem. Not the poetry of nature as in Wordsworth, nor the poetry of myth à la Keats, Pater's prose poetry is neither Browning's poetry of situations, nor Rossetti's and Morris's "aesthetic poetry." Neither is it quite the sensuous abstraction of Swinburne, nor the eclecticism of Matthew Arnold—though it is indebted to all of these poets. The subject of Pater's prose poem, instead, is the history or motions of a disembodied spirit—"the Platonic dream of the passage of the soul through one form of life after another."

If we associate *The Renaissance* with Yeats's comparable *A Vision,* written under Pater's spell, we find that the poetical accomplishment of Pater's prose is far richer than that in Yeats's influential book. As an essayist, T. S. Eliot also never rivaled the lyrical finesse of Pater's prose, and although Virginia Woolf could, she did not gather her essays into the same kind of unity that Pater aspired to in the "poem" called "The Renaissance." One might say that whereas Swinburne, Arnold, Eliot, and Woolf, among artists who were major critics, realized their artistic powers most fully in their own poetry or fiction, Pater treated the essay, far more than these literary artists, as art. Even more than Hazlitt, Lamb, Ruskin, and Carlyle, all writing prose inspired by romantic poetry, Pater sought to transform the essay into poetry, extending the sequence of essays into a sustained poetical narrative.

Pater's poetry is of an abstract type. All of the principal characters in his book fuse into a single being living through all of time. Impersonally and transparently rendered, this consciousness is, of course, Pater's idealized self. We gain insight into both the unity and abstraction of Pater's prose poem if we follow this abstracted, ideal being, ever re-forming itself, from the very beginnings of the book through its conclusion. Doing so, we come to see the ways in which Pater's writing relates to the modernism of nineteenth-century art and literature, prefiguring the aesthetics of our own century as well. We should remain attentive, throughout, to Pater's own language—not only in order to savor its precious rhythmical cadences and poetical effects, but to see how both his diction and elliptical manner of expression contribute to the carefully controlled, over-all effect of abstract art, a poetry of nothingness.

At the outset of this journey of the mind, consciousness first manifests itself as Abelard. He lives in "dreamy tranquillity" in "a world something like shadows"—an "uncertain twilight." And he knows "so well how to assign its exact value to every abstract thought." Speaking of his subsequent writings, Pater once remarked: "Child in the House: voilà, the germinating, original source, specimen, of all my *imaginative* work." Yet already in the essay on medieval French literature and in the other essays of *The Renaissance,* first written in the 1860s, Pater had produced the seed of his imaginative writing. Abelard and the subsequent Renaissance manifestations of dreamy idealism are prototypes of the Paterian child in the house, of Marius the Epicurean, of Sebastian Storck, and other imaginary types.

Like Abelard, who journeyed to Rome, the Neoplatonic Pico is a "knight-errant of philosophy." His life, similar to that of all of Pater's selves, is perceived as many wanderings, "wanderings of the intellect as well as physical journeys." There is "something not wholly earthly" about this "mystic," "as if the chilling touch of the abstract and disembodied beauty" of the Platonists had passed over him. Indoctrinated with Pythagoras in "mysteries," Pico is a "master of silence," and for him and his Neoplatonic fellows, the word *mystic* means *"shutting the eyes,* that one may see the more inwardly." Although Pater praises the humanist culture of Pico and his contemporaries, his panegyric is euphuistically presented in the language of negatives: "For the essence of humanism is that belief of which he seems *never* to have doubted, that *nothing* which has ever interested living men and women can wholly *lose* its vitality—*no* language they have spoken, *nor* oracle beside which they have *hushed* their voices, *no dream* which has once been entertained by actual human minds, *nothing* about which they have ever been passionate or *expended* time and zeal [italics added]."

A "visionary" counterpart to the Neoplatonists, Botticelli creates an art of "wan," "cold," and "cadaverous" colors, circumscribed by "abstract lines." His abstraction is not only formal but psychological. His characters are infused with "the wistfulness of exiles," with "a sense of displacement or loss." Botticelli's own life is "colourless," like the lives and works of the Tuscan sculptors, in which "all tumult of sound and colour has passed away." Like Abelard, these sculptors exist in shadow, and "one asks in vain for more than a shadowy outline of their actual days." Their art suggests "the wasting and etherealization of death." This quality is symbolized even later in Michelangelo's snow man made for Piero de' Medici—an art of "incompleteness, which suggests rather than realizes actual form." The sculpture of the Tuscans is rooted in Greek sculpture, which is Platonically "like some subtle extract or essence, or almost like pure thoughts or ideas." It still has in it the "pure form" and "abstraction" of Greek art from which "mere accidents of particular time and place" are purged away. Working in this "abstract art of sculpture," Luca della Robbia and the other sculptors of his school bring a profound expressiveness to their art, like "the passing of a smile over the face of a child, the ripple of the air on a still day over the curtain of a window ajar."

The art of Della Robbia is "midway" between the "pure" sculpture of the Greeks and the even more abstract work of Michelangelo. In its very strangeness Michelangelo's art has "something of the blossoming of the aloe" about it. The creation of life "is in various ways the motive of all Michelangelo's art," and we feel in it "that power which we associate with all the warmth and fullness of the world." But discovering this emergent force in "the cold and lifeless stone," Michelangelo expresses the creativity of nature, without rendering its elements, all of which "disappear"—"woods, clouds, seas, and mountains." He "has traced no flowers" in this primordial world, filled but with "blank ranges of rocks, and dim vegetable forms as blank." "Incompleteness" is central to Michelangelo's art, and one "trusts to the spectator to complete the half-emergent form." Michelangelo's is a world of "dreams and omens"; his "capacity for profound dreaming" is embodied in the *Bacchus.* Like Pico, he is a Platonic wanderer, and his madrigals express the sentiments of such a "wanderer returning home." As in Della Robbia's sculpture, his drawings capture fleeting moments; his "unfinished sketches" arrest "some salient feeling or

unpremeditated idea" as it passes. He is drawn to the "shadowy" figure, Vittoria Colonna, meeting with her in an "empty church" in Rome, tasting there "the sunless pleasures of weary people." Ever seeking the pure, abstract, divine ideal, he remains homeless, like "a traveller might be resting for one evening in a strange city." A "ghost," a "*revenant,*" as the French say, he is always "dreaming" in a "worn out society . . . on the morning of the world's history, on the primitive form of man." No less does Michelangelo dwell on death and its effect: "the lines become more simple and dignified; only the abstract lines remain in great indifference." Death, in its abstract purity, is the theme of Michelangelo's "hopeless, rayless" *Pietàs.* It is the subject of the sacristy in San Lorenzo, filled with "vague fancies," which are "defined and fade again" when one tries to "fix" on the "surroundings of the disembodied spirit." Pondering death, Michelangelo returns to a "previous state of existence," penetrating the very "formlessness" that preceded life, "far off, thin and vague."

As if upon Paterian "wings of the dove," we next approach Leonardo. In his youth, Leonardo trained with Verrocchio, whose studio was filled with "things for sacred or household use . . . with the reflexion of some far-off brightness." Seeking to fathom the powers of nature through art and science, "he seemed to those about him as one listening to a voice silent for other men." Yet the "mystery" of Leonardo's "over-clouded" life never quite lifts, and "we but dimly see his purpose." His character is marked by "restlessness," his art by "retouchings," his life by "years of wandering," from Florence to "fugitive, changeful, and dreamlike" Milan and back, on to Rome and then France, where he enters the "vague land" of death. The leitmotif of Leonardo's life is motion; "all the solemn effects of moving water" are the source of continual fascination to him. It flows endlessly through his paintings, "springing from its distant source among the rocks on the heath of the *Madonna of the Balances,* passing, as a little fall, into the treacherous calm of the *Madonna of the Lake,* as a goodly river next, below the cliffs of the *Madonna of the Rocks,* washing the white walls of its distant villages, stealing out in a network of divided streams in *La Gioconda* to the seashore of *Sainte Anne*—that delicate place, where wind passes like the hand of some fine etcher over the surface, and the untorn shells are lying thick upon the sand, and the tops of the rocks, to which the waves never rise, are green in the grass, grown fine as hair." The "perpetual motion" that we experience in Leonardo's art is the very passage of time—a "stream" of "impressions" or the "stream of consciousness," as William James was to call it, in Pater's wake.

Leonardo's landscapes are "places far withdrawn," for it is through the "strange veil of sight" that things appear to him: "in no ordinary night or day, but as in faint light of eclipse, or in some brief interval of falling rain at daybreak or through deep water." Like Michelangelo, Leonardo attends the very "refinement of the dead," rendering its "abstract grace" in his art. He draws the head of a child whose skull within is "as thin and fine as some sea shell worn by the wind." He renders "the Daughters of Herodias, with their fantastic head-dresses knotted and folded so strangely to leave the dainty oval of the face disengaged." His figures of "some inexplicable faintness . . . feel powers at work in the common air unfelt by others," passing "them on to us in a chain of secret influences." Under his spell, Leonardo's protégés are "ready to efface their individuality," and in Leonardo's own "fugitive" manuscripts and sketches—these "stray jottings"—we discern his own "self-forgetfulness," combined with the "solitary" culture of beauty. Like the exiled gods of antiquity, living still in disguise during the Christian epoch, Leonardo is an alien in his own age, and his "strange" *St. John* appears as if an exiled Bacchus. Such symbolic transformations are "the starting point of a train of sentiment, subtle and vague as in a piece of music." This imagery always "carries one altogether beyond the range of its conventional associations."

Leonardo's life is defined by negation—"this perpetual delay" gives him an "air of weariness and *ennui*." We find him "refusing" to work upon the *Last Supper* "except at the moment of invention." His technique is so "refined" that within fifty years the fresco had fallen into "decay." His Eucharistic image has the "unreality" of the school of Perugino. "Finished or unfinished"—and we remain in doubt as to whether the central head of Christ was ever finished—the "whole company" of Apostles are "ghosts . . . faint as the shadows of the leaves upon the wall on autumn afternoons." The figure of Christ is "the faintest, the most spectral of them all." Leonardo's art of "faint light" and "fantastic rocks" is a sort of "after-dreaming": from childhood we find the image of the "unfathomable smile" "defining itself on the fabric of his dreams," present "incorporeally" in Leonardo's brain, absorbed finally into the *Mona Lisa.* "By what strange affinities had the dream and the person grown up thus apart, and yet so closely together," we might ask. The very strangeness of Leonardo is epitomized in the *Medusa,* then thought to be a painting by Leonardo; it is "like a great calm stone against which the wave of the serpents break." The head that transforms the beholder into stone is itself transformed here into stone. Like the waving of hair that Leonardo so loved, the serpents become, finally, the waves of the unfathomable sea—the vast waters that are the very type of Leonardo's endless curiosity and consciousness.

Dependent on "colouring," the "weaving of light as of just perceptible gold threads," the painting of Giorgione and his school is no less abstract than Leonardo's. Above all "a thing for the eye," any great picture is indeed abstract, "has no more definite message for us than an accidental play of sunlight and shadow for a few moments on the wall or floor." It is like "a space of such fallen light caught as the colours are in an Eastern carpet" or a Japanese fan painting, dependent on "abstract-colour." This "abstract language" is most complete in music where the distinction between form and matter is obliterated. In the musical painting of the Venetians, "mere light and shade," backgrounds retain "certain abstracted elements only of cool colour and tranquillizing line." Informed by "passing light," this "music" occurs when a "momentary tint of stormy light" invests "a homely or too familiar scene with a character which might well have been drawn from the deep places of the imagination." In poetry this pure music is expressed by a "certain suppression or vagueness of subject," and in the painted poetry of Giorgione, which serves "neither for uses of devotion nor of allegorical or historical teachings," the subjects are refined "till they seem like glimpses of life from afar." As in his art, the "true outlines" of Giorgione's own life and person are "obscured"; he is thus like Abelard, Pico, Botticelli, and Leonardo, all living lives either colorless or in shadow. His musical art is about music itself, and with an "unearthly glow" he captures the "waves of wandering sound." This vague effect is that of "a momentary touch of an instrument in the twilight, as one passes through some unfamiliar room in a chance company," and one seems to hear the silence of "time as it flies."

Similar to the music of Giorgione, the poetry of the French poet Du Bellay is one in which "the matter is almost nothing, and the form almost everything." His poetical work, like the art of sixteenth-century France in general, exhibits a "fleeting splendour," an "aerial touch." He writes in "transparent" prose expressive of a "weird foreign grace," and the poetry of his times is of "an exquisite faintness"—"fantastic, faded rococo." His life is made up of "slow journeys," his poetry of regrets, longings that certain moments or accidents "may happen again." His creations are touched by a "sense of loss" and "homesickness," further tinged "by the sentiment of the grandeur of nothingness—*la grandeur du rien.*"

If Abelard's life and writings prefigure the Renaissance, Winckelmann's career still commemorates the classical tradition. Like Du Bellay and Michelangelo, ghosts and exiles, Winckelmann has about him "a wistful sense of something lost to be regained." He considers himself a "stranger," who has "come into the world and into Italy too late." The "corpse-like" ideal of the Middle Ages and the "vagueness" of Oriental art both stand apart from the "abstract world" of Hellenic art to which Winckelmann aspires. But this "pure form" and "colourless abstraction" of the "sexless" Greek gods already has "a touch of the corpse in it," prefiguring the art of the Middle Ages. Like Helen of Troy, these "abstracted gods," "wander as the specters of the Middle Ages" and they become the symbol of the modern "exile"—of Winckelmann and of Pater himself, lost in the "perpetual flight of modernity."

Pater's idealism, his tendency toward abstraction, was nurtured by literature. Above all, the idealism of Plato and Platonism, from Plotinus to Pico, Ficino, and finally Winckelmann, informs Pater's own creation of "pure form." But this vision is also enriched by numerous modern writings. Kant's philosophy of "pure reason," Schiller's recognition that fine art annihilates "the material by means of the form" are part of Pater's perception. His tendency toward dream or reverie was encouraged by Romantic literature in general—for example, Keats, DeQuincy, and Ruskin—but especially by Baudelaire. And the abstracting sensuousness of Pater's own style, its tendency toward the poetry of nothingness, owes much to Gautier, Rossetti, and especially Swinburne. Pater's literary vision is itself closely related to the art of his age. His perpetual picturing of changing sensations and impressions in an impalpable world of dissolving form and flux is strikingly akin to the Impressionism practiced by French painters at the very time he was writing *The Renaissance.* In fact, for all the differences of temperament between, say, Monet and Pater, it can be argued that Pater's is one of the first, most coherent literary formulations of Impressionism—not just as a critical position but as a continuous analysis of consciousness in a world of continual change. This Impressionism is not merely expressed in the infamous conclusion of his book but, as we have observed, is sustained throughout, each chapter flowing into the next. The suggestiveness of Pater's tone also intersects with Symbolist art. His ethereal beings, pale or nearly colorless, isolated and in silence or inward vision, are remarkably close literary analogues to the disappearing faces rendered in faint, refined pastels by Redon—symbolic of silence and of a vision beyond sight. And although the refinement and exquisite intricacy of Pater's writing stand apart from the bold energy of Rodin's art, Pater's emphasis on the aesthetics of the "half-emergent form," of "incompleteness," prefigures the related concern in the works of the great French sculptor, in which form seems to come into being before our own eyes. Pater's writings also anticipate the stress on "pure form" in the criticism of modern art. His influence is echoed and re-echoed in writings on abstract art from Roger Fry to Clement Greenberg and his followers, all of whom, like Pater, justly emphasize the "solution of purely artistic problems."

It has recently been said that although "nothingness" or the "void"—the nonentity "nil"—was a dominant theme of French and American literature in the nineteenth century, it was not a topic of importance in English writing of the period. Yet we come to see that nothingness is central to the creation of *The Renaissance.* Pater's abstract art is a perpetual taking away, purging, and refining. The world he envisions inwardly is pure, empty, abstract, blank, shut, and silent. Etherealized and siderealized, it is inhabited by an alien—a stranger and pilgrim—who wanders continuously in dream, in the vague twilight of passing instants, fleeting, momentary, and wandering impressions and stray sensations. He experiences isolation, the continuous effect of accident or change, and the sense of loss that is ever defined in negative terms of renunciation, retreat, disembodiment, displacement, and disappearance. Houseless and restless, this exile moves through an environment that is noiseless, rayless, and colorless. As if itself effaced, this consciousness becomes faceless, helpless, even sexless. Confronting formlessness, it is unfixed in unreality; homeless, its journey is always unfinished. Incompleteness is the essence, incorporeally and inexpressibly experienced in invisibility.

Before Pater, Flaubert had aspired "to write a book about nothing . . . a book which would have almost no subject matter or at least whose subject would be invisible if that is possible." Following his great French master, Pater himself achieved such a *grandeur du rien,* as he calls it in Du Bellay's apposite phrase. Concerned with countless themes, Pater's book, at bottom, has "no subject matter" precisely because its ever-changing form and imagery dissolve the thematic matter into a vast void. What Pater says, discussing Michelangelo, is true of himself and indissolubly of his book, like "a dream that lingers a moment, retreating in the dawn, incomplete, aimless, helpless: a thing with faint hearing, faint memory, faint power of touch; a breath, a flame in the doorway, a feather in the wind." In the root sense, poetry is making, and in the poetry of Walter Pater, we discover the endless fabrication of "airy nothingness." Woven within a web of wonder, it is neither fiction, nor exactly nonfiction. For all its similitude to the literature that influenced it and to writings afterward, *The Renaissance* stands alone as one of the eeriest lyrics in all of modern literature—the pathetic vision of nature, man, and history "vanishing away" in a white light, distant and pale.

## Paul Barolsky (essay date 1984)

SOURCE: Barolsky, Paul. "From Mannerism to Modernism: The Playful Artifice of Walter Pater." *University of Hartford Studies in Literature* 16, nos. 2-3 (1984): 47-57.

*[In the following essay, Barolsky discusses Pater's attitude toward Mannerism while asserting that Pater's writing contains many distinct Mannerist qualities. Barolsky goes on to assert that Pater's analysis of Mannerist art played a pivotal role in sparking renewed interest in the period among artists and critics in the early twentieth century.]*

### I

Mannerism, the elegant style of sixteenth-century art and literature, is especially notable for its playful artifice and is thus especially appealing to the highly self-conscious modern temper. After centuries of neglect or ridicule, it was rediscovered or appreciated anew by art historians writing at the beginning of this century. Like Metaphysical poetry, closely related to it and also rescued from oblivion and ridicule in the same period, Mannerism is a style of exquisite wit through which words and images alike are elegantly wrought into texts and objects of precious complexity. If Mannerism was eventually given historical definition by scholars of our century, the foundations for the revival of interest in it were laid in the nineteenth century by aesthetic critics who appreciated, in Gautier's words, *"l'art pour l'art"*—"art for art's sake."

Gautier himself admired the refined art of the sixteenth century, and in his neglected guide book to the Louvre, he marks the qualities of the Mannerists, particularly of Parmigianino: "The elegant slenderness, the coquettish poses, the somewhat affected, inclined heads, the turn of the hands, the slender fingers, the delicate oval faces, the lips with their sinuous smiles, the eyes with their lustrous glances, have a charm of their own, especially when it is Mazzola's [Il Parmigianino's] brush that has prepared the feast." Gautier's taste for Mannerism was shared by his protégés the Goncourts, who described the Harlequin by their beloved Watteau "posed as if by a pen-stroke of Parmigianino," and by such critics as Geffroy and Plon, who wrote admiringly of the elegant works of Palissy and Cellini.

The appetite for such preciosity also informs the writings of Gautier's principal English follower, Swinburne. In his notes on the drawings in the Uffizi, the poet describes a mannered study of Cleopatra, then thought to be by Michelangelo, in an appropriately artificial and admiring prose: "Here also the electric hair, which looks as though it would hiss and glitter, if once touched, is wound up to a tuft with serpentine plaits and involutions." In a similar way, Henry James was captivated by the refinements of Bronzino's *maniera,* the elegant ideals of which are reflected in his fiction, for example, in the Bronzinesque literary portraiture of the *Portrait of a Lady.* But perhaps of all observations on Mannerism by

nineteenth-century writers, the most generalized and, at the same time, most pointed are those made by Walter Pater in the essay on Joachim Du Bellay, in his classic book of 1873, *The Renaissance.* Like Swinburne, Pater admired Gautier, and along with both of these poets, he was drawn to the *recherché* sixteenth century art of extreme artificiality. Pater does not speak of "Mannerism" as such; however, he clearly defines its characteristics, and, even though his observations have escaped the attention of virtually all students of Mannerist art and literature, his sense of this style still obtains in the formidable scholarship of S. J. Freedberg and John Shearman.

Like many art-historians after him, Pater recognizes that the French art and literature of the sixteenth century has its origins in the "French daintiness" of the Middle Ages and that this refinement is blended with an imported "Italian *finesse.*" Already in the first essay of his book, **"Two Early French Stories,"** to which the chapter on Du Bellay is a pendant, Pater had stressed the "continuity" between the Middle Ages and the Renaissance (and that phase of the period we now call Mannerist), remarking upon the "connection" between "the sculpture of Chartres, the windows of Le Mans, and the work of the later Renaissance, the work of Jean Cousin and German Pilon" (*Renaissance* 2). As if reacting to Jacob Burckhardt's *Civilization of the Renaissance in Italy,* a work which rather sharply defines the Renaissance as a break with the Middle Ages, Pater suggests that this purported rupture "has so often been exaggerated," and in doing so he introduces the theme embellished by Johan Huizinga in *The Waning of The Middle Ages.* Pater observes: "What is called the Renaissance in France is thus not so much the introduction of a wholly new taste ready-made from Italy, but rather the finest and subtlest phase of the middle ages itself, its fleeting splendour and temperate Saint Martin's summer" (*Renaissance* 123-24). This is precisely the historical notion of continuity that Huizinga appropriated from Pater, though the great Dutch scholar focused instead on the court of Burgundy in the fifteenth century as the site of this medieval sunset.

Pater stresses the continuity between the Middle Ages and the sixteenth century—what he calls the "comely decadence" or later Renaissance, what we call the period of Mannerism—by observing the "daintiness of hand" in the intermediary art and literature of the fifteenth century: the poetry of Villon and the *Hours of Anne of Brittany.* This aerial delicacy and elegance, *une netteté remarquable d'exécution,* as he calls it, presages the art of the sixteenth century, the "nicety" of Clouet's polished work, of Ronsard's and Du Bellay's refined poetry. Eventually the Italian taste begins to permeate the arts of France, the "attenuated grace of Italian ornament" veiling the Gothic in the chateaux of Chenonceáux, Blois, Chambord." The "correlative" to this Italianate architecture in painting is the work of *"Maître Roux* [Rosso Fiorentino] and the masters of the school of Fontainbleau" who bring a certain "Italian voluptuousness" to their exquisite work. As the "seriousness" of the French aesthetic recedes, "only the elegance, the aerial touch, the perfect manner remains" (**Renaissance** 123-125).

Unequivocally celebrating the aesthetics of Mannerism, Pater asserts that "this elegance, this manner, this daintiness of execution are consummate, and have an unmistakable aesthetic value." He elaborates on this proposition when he speaks of the poetry of Ronsard and of the *Pléiade,* observing further that the interest of Mannerist literature depends on the fact "that it was once poetry *à la mode,* that it is part of the manner of a time—a time which made much of manner, and carried it to a high degree of perfection." This poetry, he adds, "is one of the decorations of an age which threw a large part of its energy into the work of decoration" (**Renaissance** 131-132). The poetry of Ronsard is a poetry "not for the people, but for a confined circle, for courtiers, great lords and erudite persons, who desire to be humoured, to gratify a certain refined voluptuousness they have in them." Like the poetry of the Middle Ages, Ronsard's work is "to be entertained not for its matter only, but chiefly for its manner; it is *cortois,* it tells us, *et bien assis*" (**Renaissance** 14). Not marked by vigor or originality, it is nevertheless "full of the grace which comes of long study and reiterated refinements, and many steps repeated and many angles worn down, with an exquisite faintness, *une fadeur éxquise,* a certain tenuity and caducity, as for those who can bear nothing vehement or strong; for princes weary of love, like Francis the First, or of pleasure, like Henry the Third, or of action, like Henry the Fourth." It is as if Pater were describing Mannerist portraits of "grace and finish, perfect in minute detail," depicting courtiers and rulers "a little jaded," who "have a constant desire for a subdued and delicate excitement, to warm their creeping fancy a little"—the highly refined portraits by Parmigianino, Bronzino, and Salviati, the exquisite effigies of Clouet, Moro, and Hilliard (**Renaissance** 135).

Stressing the grace, elegance, decoration, delicacy, finesse, and studied artifice of this "manner," Pater is using the very language Vasari employed in the sixteenth century, in his *Lives* of the artists, to describe the "*grazia,*" "*finezza,*" and "*delicatezza*" of the "*maniera.*" And what is "nicety" of execution in Pater's term, or "*netteté,*" is "*nettezza*" or "*pulitezza*" in Vasari's vocabulary, this "daintiness of hand" or "aerial touch" being what Vasari calls a certain "*piumosità*" or featheriness of the artist's stroke.

If Pater is the first modern critic of Mannerism on the one hand, he is, on the other, a latter-day Mannerist, still writing self-consciously in the tradition of those Mannerists whom he admired. To use his own characterization of Plato, with whom he feels kinship, Pater is "artist and critic at once." In his *Confessions* Rousseau spoke of how he learned to read books by becoming their very authors, and in a similar way, Pater becomes the writers he reads by writing as they do. He interprets them not by detailed analysis but by writing in their manner—by parodying them, in the Renaissance sense of the word, which intends emulation rather than mockery. It has been observed that the "Euphuism" of John Lily is a characteristic manifestation of Mannerism in Elizabethan literature, and we find that Pater extols this style in the chapter "Euphuism" of **Marius the Epicurean,** writing himself euphuistically. Here Pater discusses the history of Euphuism from Roman Euphuism to the "Euphuism of the Elizabethan age, and of the modern French romanticists," foreshadowing E. R. Curtius's discussion in *European Literature and the Latin Middle Ages* of Mannerism as a recurrent tendency of literature. It is with such manner that Pater describes Flavian's literary ideals:

> It is certainly the most typical expression of a mood, still incident to the young poet, as a thing peculiar to his youth, when he feels the sentimental current setting forcibly along his veins, and so much as a matter of purely physical excitement, that he can hardly distinguish it from the animation of external nature, the upswelling of the seed in the earth, and of the sap through the trees. Flavian, to whom, again, as to his later euphuistic kinsmen [and Pater, as we have observed, is among them], old mythology seemed as full of untried, unexpressed motives and interest as human life itself, had long been occupied with a kind of mystic hymn to the vernal principle of life in things; a composition shaping itself, little by little, out of a thousand dim perceptions, into singularly definite form (definite and firm as fine-art in metal, thought Marius) for which, as I said, he had caught his "refrain," from the lips of the young men, singing because they could not help it; in the streets of Pisa.

(**Marius** 76-77)

Pater exhibits skill as a Mannerist writer throughout his entire *oeuvre,* sometimes commenting on the very themes of Mannerism. It is widely recognized that Mannerist artists and writers alike developed the "grotesque" to a fine art, and Pater re-creates their grotesques in words: "Just so the grotesque details of the charnel-house nest themselves, together with birds and flowers and the fancies of the pagan mythology, in the traceries of the architecture of the time, which wantons in its graceful arabesques with the images of old age and death" (**Renaissance** 135). Pater also creates his own Mannerist conceits or *concetti,* as in this architectural fantasy: "and [one] often finds a true poetry, as in those strangely twisted staircases of the *châteaux* of the country of the Loire, as if it were intended that among their odd turnings the actors in a theatrical mode of life might pass each other unseen" (*Renaissance* 105). The artists of the cinquecento aspired to the *figura serpentinata*, and Pater finds such twisting forms in the spiral staircases of the period, recreating them in his own serpentine "literary architecture."

The subtle wit of Pater's staircase, which exists somewhere between actual architecture and Pater's fancy, is typical of his irony, for we are made to envision ghostly beings, unbeknownst to each other, spiraling upward and downward. Pater's playful invention is in sympathy with the very playfulness of Mannerist art, based on delightful surprises and soaring to strange effects and subtle irony. Such playfulness is found, for example, in Giulio Romano's bizarre treatment of architecture and grotesque frescoes in the Palazzo del Te, built for the court of Mantua. Strangely enough, although Pater's contemporaries sometimes commented on his sense of humor, and although *The Renaissance* is permeated by the appreciation of play, wit, and humor, the playful aspect of his own art is everywhere ignored, rendered all but invisible, perhaps, by the studied gravity and the fastidious morbidity that rises in his prose between his readers and their recognition of its buried life of play.

## II

Pater's own sense of humor is continuously stirred by other artists and writers. He is thus charmed by the "child-like humor in the quaint figure of Mary" painted by Titian in the *Presentation of the Virgin* (*Renaissance* 104). He delights in the "burlesque element" of Provencal poetry in which "one hears the faint, far-off laughter still." **"Aucassin and Nicolette"** is "tinged with humour," and morsels of it pass "into burlesque" (*Renaissance* 14). Sometimes Pater's sense of playfulness is roused by images devoid of humor but which seem child-like and thus charming in their naiveté. The medieval fresco in the Camposanto of Pisa depicting the "system of the world, held, as a great target or shield in the hands of the creature Logos" is a "childish dream" and seems to Pater "like a painted toy" (*Renaissance* 32). Ancient mythology, although a subject both weighty and serene for the Italian poets, is also a "toy" in the hands of the French, and in their poetry, it is filled with "play" (*Renaissance* 134). Also a sort of sculptural toy is the snowman made for Piero de' Medici by Michelangelo, presumably "a work extracted from him half in derision" (*Renaissance* 53).

For Pater, Leonardo typifies the very spirit of play—the very play of the mind. He shares with Leonardo "the love of beautiful toys," those charming *objets* which come from his studio. Whereas "it is not in play that Leonardo painted that other *Medusa*" (the painting in the Uffizi no longer considered to be by Leonardo), the earlier picture of the same subject was, by contrast, the epitome of play. This picture, now lost but described by Vasari, was prepared as a "surprise" for Leonardo's father. Upon seeing it he "pretended astonishment," or so Pater claims (or pretends). Thus in the play of Pater's imagination, Leonardo's father joined in his son's little illusionistic game. Speaking of Leonardo as a musician, Pater observes that he was a "player on the harp," amusing himself with the double sense of the word, for Leonardo both played the instrument and played with its very form, creating "a strange harp of silver of his own construction, shaped in some curious likeness to a horse's skull." The play of Leonardo's mind is intertwined with his "love of the impossible—the perforation of mountains, changing the course of rivers, raising great buildings such as the church of *San Giovanni*, in the air." Leonardo's sense of humor (or actually Pater's) is of the subtlest kind—expressed in Pater's appreciation of the "half-humorous pathos of the diminutive, rounded shoulders of the child" in Leonardo's paintings. Even in the very last years of his life Leonardo surrounded himself with humorous devices or inventions, especially "strange toys that seemed alive of wax and quicksilver": for example, the grotesque beast invented by Leonardo in the Vatican, one of the artist's "*pazzie*," as Vasari called them (*Renaissance* 77-101).

Perhaps of all Pater's allusions to play none is more fundamental to his own art than his pastoral prose poem in celebration of Giorgionesque idylls:

> In these then, the favorite incidents of Giorgione's school, music or the musical intervals in our existence, life itself is conceived as a sort of listening—listening to music, to the reading of Bandello's novels, to the sound of water, to time as it flies. Often such moments are really our moments of play, and we are surprised at the unexpected blessedness of what may seem our least important part of time; not merely because play is in many instances that to which people really apply their own best powers, but also because, at such times, the stress of our servile, everyday attentiveness being relaxed, the happier powers in things without are permitted free passage, and have their way with us. And so, from music, the school of Giorgione passes often to the play which is like music; to those masques in which men avowedly do but play at real life, like children "dressing-up," disguised in the strange old Italian dresses, parti-coloured, or fantastic with embroidery and furs, of which the master was so curious a designer, and which, above all the spotless white linen at wrist and throat, he painted so dexterously.

> (*Renaissance* 119-120)

Pater's specific comparison of Giorgionesque actors to children at play is still Wordsworthian, but even more specifically his association of their performances to "masques" can be likened to Rossetti's shrewdly apposite description in his sonnet on Botticelli's *Primavera,* of the painting as a "masque." In the play of art, "the stress of our servile, everyday attentiveness" is relaxed, for as Pater asserts elsewhere, art is "an equivalent for the sense of freedom." His view of the pageantry of Renaissance art is not unlike that of Burckhardt, and may even depend on the Swiss scholar's emphasis on it. However, his own focus on play as an expression of freedom pre-figured and probably influenced Johan Huizinga, who wrote on the "play-forms in art" in *Homo Ludens: A Study of the Play-Element in Culture.* Asserting, as if in the manner of Pater, that "the first main characteristic of play" is "that it is free," Huizinga is somewhat less skeptical than Pater, who insists not that play is freedom but, more exquisitely, that it is an equivalent for the "sense" of such freedom.

It is a commonplace in the writings on Pater that he becomes all of his subjects—that Pico, Della Robbia, Botticelli, Leonardo, Michelangelo, Giorgione, Du Bellay, and Winckelmann are Pater's own personae. Just as the actors of Giorgionesque pictures play the role of courtier, shepherd, and nymph, Pater becomes, for example, Giorgione, wearing the mask of the painter. Disguised as Giorgione, he writes a lyrical or Giorgionesque appreciation or re-creation of Giorgione's idylls. Like Michelangelo, whom Pater calls a *revenant* in the manner of the French, Pater is a ghost who passes through all of history, assuming the identities of each of its prominent cultural heroes from Plato to Goethe and Hugo.

This play of identity is linked to Pater's play with the very forms of his book, for just as Pater becomes all of his subjects, he adapts all of their forms, both literary and visual. I have previously suggested that Pater's book is essay, philosophy, biography, autobiography, history, art criticism, literary criticism, and poetry; that, metaphorically, Pater regards his prose, if one can even call it that, as a form of architecture, sculpture, painting, and music. By playing with the forms of his literary art, Pater treats it as if it were a sort of artistic "toy." Leonardo, as Pater asserts, perpetually transformed nature in his drawings, and Pater, in analogous fashion, is constantly transforming art. For example, the essay on the school of Giorgione can be read as a philosophical treatise on the forms of art and their limits, schematically as a biography of Giorgione, and, to the extent that Pater identifies himself with the painter's ideals, as an autobiographical reflection—a hint at Pater's own life of the mind. Contributing to our understanding of Renaissance culture, by commenting on the courtly social ethos of Giorgionesque art, this essay is also history. Illuminating the creator's role as pastoral

painter and celebrating the very pleasures of Giorgione's idylls, their tranquillity and harmony of vision, it is also both art history and criticism. When he celebrates the color and deft touch of the Venetians, Pater becomes, himself, a painter in words, and achieves the very "*colour*" of Giorgione, in words woven of golden threads. Like Giorgione he transforms art into music, reverberating in the very sonorities of his own prose which emulates the sound of pipes. The forms and imagery of the essay on Giorgione are related to those in the rest of the book in the very proportioned and ordered manner of what Pater calls "literary architecture," and finally, Giorgione is "moulded," as are all of Pater's subjects, into aggrandized imaginary statuary, placed in niches of his literary Walhalla.

As we read ***The Renaissance,*** we join in Pater's play, reading it now as one genre, now as another, or yet, simultaneously as combinations of such genres. One of the special delights of Pater's book is that it can be read and reread in so many different ways as its various structures sharpen, dissolve, and reform. We can read it as a verbal equivalent of the visual arts or as literature. The literary forms a divided into sub-genres such as the pastoral. In every chapter Pater describes flowers, gardens, vast panoramas, or "morsels" of landscape—for example, Botticelli's "hillsides with pools of water" or the *Fête Champêtre,* "a landscape full of clearness, of the effects of water"—and we thus come to perceive his work as, itself, a sustained pastoral. To the extent that ***The Renaissance*** is an idealized "community" or "intellectual commonwealth," purged of controversy or discord, it is, like the world of Castiglione's *Il Cortegiano,* a species of utopia—the dream of the Renaissance as a Golden Age.

Pater's pastoral and utopian vision is tinged, however, by the "tragic" consciousness of death, the awareness that this perfection cannot endure. "*Et ego in Arcadia fui,*" as Pater says, in the last chapter on Winckelmann (***Renaissance*** 141). Death, too, comes to Arcady, and as Pater's book unfolds, it becomes yet another genre of literature, an *ars moriendi*—a preparation for death. The very title of ***The Renaissance*** alludes to this theme of mortality, and Pater considers the lives of others as a "meditation on death." Preparing himself for his own end, Pater ponders death in every chapter, from the deaths of Amis and Amile, "united," to the murder of Winckelmann, meditating on the iconography of death in the texts, tombs, and effigies of Dante, Boccaccio, Botticelli, Rossellino, Savonarola, Dürer, and Michelangelo: "*Outre-tombe! Outre-tombe!*—is the burden of their thoughts" (***Renaissance*** 72-73). For Leonardo, as for Pater in anticipation, death is the "last curiosity," and almost as in a Northern print, the figure of Death looms behind all of Pater's historical selves. At the very last, when his consciousness of its imminence is intensified, he exclaims, "Well! we are all *condamnés,* as Victor Hugo says: 'we are all under sentence of death but with a sort of indefinite reprieve'" (***Renaissance*** 190).

No wonder we fail to see the play of Pater, for it is completely intertwined with and nearly disguised by his morbid sense of fatality. Whereas Renaissance art and literature is typified by a serious play, the *serio ludere* of Erasmus, Michelangelo, Rabelais, and Montaigne, Pater's play might more appropriately be called a type of *ludere sollemnis.* In the kaleidoscope of his literary art, all of the pieces of colored glass are tinted in subtle gradations of black. We recall that as a child Pater "played at being a priest, using sermons and costumed processions."

The basic game that Pater plays in ***The Renaissance*** and in all of his writings is that of finding the "mid-point" between opposites. This is the procedure or "method," as Pater tells us in ***Plato and Platonism,*** of Plato, who invented the dialogue as the very means of articulating this dialectic. ***The Renaissance*** is a diaphanous "dialogue of the mind with itself," and just as Plato reconciled the "Absolute Being" of Parmenides and the "flux" of Heraclitus, Pater re-creates this unity in his own work. He simultaneously establishes the unity of all beings in an all-embracing historical structure, while reflecting on the dissolution of this totality, on the isolation of the individual. In ***Plato and Platonism,*** Pater speaks of Plato's love of paradox, of his irony, commenting implicitly on his own play between opposites, for he both builds up a whole in ***The Renaissance*** and shows how it vanishes in a "whirlpool." Type and antitype, classical and romantic, freedom and necessity; the finite and the infinite, the abstract and the concrete, passion and moderation; unity and discord, curiosity and ennui, birth and death; home and exile, youth and age, permanence and change; attraction and repulsion, soul and body, perfection and imperfection— these are but a few of the seemingly infinite but finite dualities or oppositions that Pater unifies in his dialogue with himself, creating a larger unity or "identity" from their totality which nonetheless approaches "nothingness" in its very schematism. Pater ironically grasps "*la grandeur du rien*" paradoxically contained within "*le grand tout,*" and this identity or unity of antitheses is the correlative to his playful fusion of all genres of art, the identity of all of its forms. Pater's "Mona Lisa" is the very icon of his paradoxical method, for she is "all modes of thought and life," becoming abstract, as "all this" has been but music to her. She is the symbol of Pater's double-self, her smile being the symbol of his

ironic vision, and perhaps, too, we can see this smile as an expression of the bemused pleasure Pater takes in the play of his own mind or consciousness.

### III

Although ***The Renaissance*** is dialogue, *ars moriendi,* pastoral, and utopia, it is no less a disguised novel. Pater becomes all of his subjects, and, as they live through history, their lives become the stages in the life of his transparent protagonist. He is the exiled pagan gods alive in the Middle Ages, then a series of Renaissance artists, and writers, before becoming Winckelmann, Goethe, and Hugo in the modern world. The evolution of this single being is the development of Pater's own consciousness. If for Pico, or the Paterian protagonist at an earlier stage of development, "the world is a limited place," for Pascal, or the Paterian hero at a more sophisticated stage of consciousness, the universe is infinite. The incipiently novelistic structure of ***The Renaissance*** is one which Pater would elaborate in ***Marius the Epicurean*** and in ***Gaston De Latour,*** novels in which the hero lives through important transitional moments in history. But since these works are more limited in their chronological scope, they are less fantastic than ***The Renaissance.***

It has been observed that Pater's fiction was a source of inspiration to Virginia Woolf when she composed her novel *Orlando,* the lyrical story or fantasy of a character who lives through history from the Renaissance to the twentieth century, changing sex from male to female during this journey. Even more than Pater's novels or his ***Imaginary Portraits,*** however, ***The Renaissance*** provides the over-all structure for *Orlando,* for whereas the characters in Pater's fictions belong to a particular period, the protagonist of ***The Renaissance,*** like Orlando, lives through history. Just as Orlando is an Elizabethan courtier, poet, ambassador, wife, and contemporary woman, living through the Elizabethan period, the Restoration, the Enlightenment, and the Romantic age, Pater's character, as we have already observed, lives through history, changing identities as time passes. It has been remarked that Pater's Mona Lisa, a symbol of multiple selves who lives through all ages, is, so to speak, the Ur-Orlando. When we see that in his fiction, Pater became the Mona Lisa, thus undergoing a change of sex, the transformation, in reverse, of Orlando seems almost to be a spoof of Pater. Woolf's fictional sex-change appears to be a playful travesty (in the root sense of the word, from *travestir*) of Pater's "dressing-up," disguised in the "strange old Italian dresses" of the Mona Lisa. In a sense Woolf is the first critic of Pater's disguised fiction, recognizing the way this fiction is woven into the seamless fabric of his book.

Orlando is conspicuously Paterian in various respects. If Pater rather somberly and meticulously ponders the problem of multiple selves, Woolf does so with comic abandon, observing "these selves of which we are built up, one on top of another as plates are piled on a waiter's hand." Just as Pater's painters and poets are seers or visionaries, Orlando is endowed with (what Pater himself would have called) "the capacity of the eye"—for, as Woolf says, "sights exalted him." The Paterian protagonist is an alien or stranger, an exotic set apart, and, likewise, as Woolf delights in telling us with exaggerated emphasis, Orlando loves "to feel himself for ever and for ever and for ever alone." Toward the end of Woolf's novel, as the flux of history and consciousness accelerates in a markedly Paterian way, "all is movement and confusion" to Orlando. In the very caricatural pace of her motor trip through London, Orlando seems to swirl in the Paterian whirlpool of impressions. As time passes faster and faster, her clock ticks "louder and louder," and as the flux of time and consciousness reaches a pitch, she is filled with mock "desperation," lest she "fall into the raging torrent beneath." Her mind has become "a fluid," like the incessant "flood" or "stream" of Pater's impressions. Against this "continual vanishing away" the Paterian self seeks "profoundly significant moments," "exquisite pauses in time." To counteract this flux, Pater's personae aspire to the "ecstasy" or "exquisite passion" of art. And this is what Orlando achieves at the end, in an epiphany of epiphanies (far greater than anything in Wordsworth, Pater, Joyce, or even Proust): the pulsating moment of vision of a toy boat on the Serpentine. "Ecstasy," Orlando cries, "ecstasy: 'A toy boat, a toy boat, a toy boat,' she repeated." Here, then, in a consummate mock-pastoral of pastorals, is the *reductio ad absurdum* of Pater's vision of the work of art as "toy." For the metaphor of the toy has been made literal, and how perfect is this mockery, since the boat floats above water—symbol for Pater of the time and consciousness momentarily arrested in this farcical rapture!

Making parody of these themes of flux, consciousness, and self, Woolf illuminates the multiple selves in Pater's work. Although Pater's writing is grave, Woolf nevertheless recognizes the very playfulness beneath the somber surface of Pater's work—the way in which, dressed up and disguised, Pater playfully assumes his various identities. The theme of "identity" is central to modernist literature, and just over a decade after the publication of *Orlando,* Vladimir Nabokov played with it far more self-consciously in his first novel written in English, *The Real Life of Sebastian Knight*—the novel in which the narrator V. attempts to correct the misleading biography by the critic Mr. Goodman of V.'s half-brother, the novelist Sebastian Knight. As if by coinci-

dence—and how Nabokov loved coincidence!—Sebastian had planned to write a fictional biography with photographs illustrating the subject at different phases of his life: the very format of Woolf's recent book. Indeed V., Sebastian, and Goodman's Sebastian, all intertwined, are in a sense all Nabokov's selves in just the same way that the various Orlandos are Woolf or, for that matter, Pater's quasi-historical, quasi-fictional subjects are his own identities. V. concludes: "I am Sebastian, or Sebastian is I, or perhaps we are both someone whom neither of us knows." They are like those *Doppelgänger* who, each unconscious of the other, pass on the spiral staircase of Pater's consciousness.

The highly contrived literary games that Nobokov plays are grounded in the playfulness of modern aestheticism. Teasing with ambiguities of self and reality, exquisitely playing with language, Nabokov belongs to what we might speak of as a modern current of Mannerism. It once seemed that the advent of Expressionism accounted primarily for the rediscovery of sixteenth-century Mannerism, but it should by now appear that the sheer artifice and self-reflecting ludic character of nineteenth- and twentieth-century literature collectively contributed to the reevaluation of the earlier style. Seen in the broad context of modernist art and literature—not merely in the narrow context of the historiography of art—Pater's appreciation of form, artifice, and manner, of Mannerism, seems scarcely anomalous. Just as the impersonal sitters of Bronzino's portraits and Parmigianino, in his much admired *Self-Portrait in a Convex Mirror,* are, ironically, both present and concealed beneath their mask-like faces, Pater is disguised in his literary portraits, for ever so artfully he plays the roles of the various subjects in his "gallery" of Renaissance heroes. Virginia Woolf's parody of Pater's mannered self-consciousness and manipulation of multiple identities or selves irresistibly draws our attention to the spirit continuously at play in Pater's refined and mannered prose—a spirit in quest of those fragile moments of "unexpected blessedness" that Nabokov called "aesthetic bliss."

## Bibliography

Burckhardt, Jacob. *The Civilization of the Renaissance in Italy,* trans. S. G. C. Middlemore. London: Phaidon, 1960.

Curtius, E. R. *European Literature and the Latin Middle Ages,* trans. Willard R. Trask. New York: Pantheon, 1953.

Freedberg, S. J. *Painting in Italy: 1500-1600.* Harmondsworth: Penguin, 1971.

Gautier, Théophile. *The Complete Works,* trans. F. C. De Sumichrast, Vol. 5. New York: Bigelow, Smith, and Company, 1910.

Huizinga, Johan. *Homo-Ludens: A Study of the Play-Element in Culture.* Boston: Beacon, 1950.

Huizinga, Johan. *The Waning of the Middle Ages.* Garden City: Doubleday, 1954.

Nabokov, Vladimir. *The Real Life of Sebastian Knight.* Norwalk: New Directions, 1941.

Pater, Walter. *The Renaissance: Studies in Art and Poetry,* ed. Donald L. Hill. Berkeley: Univ. of California, 1980.

Pater, Walter. *Marius the Epicurean.* London: Macmillan, 1893.

Shearman, John. *Mannerism.* Harmondsworth: Penguin, 1971.

Swinburne, Algernon Charles. *Essays and Studies.* London: Chatto and Windus, 1876.

Woolf, Virginia. *Orlando: A Biography.* New York: Harcourt, Brace, 1956.

## Ross Borden (essay date fall 1985)

SOURCE: Borden, Ross. "Pater's Temporizing: The 'Conclusion' to *The Renaissance*." *The Victorian Newsletter,* no. 68 (fall 1985): 29-31.

[*In the following essay, Borden compares the original version of Pater's famous "Conclusion," first published in the 1868 essay "Poems of William Morris," with the later, revised version, which appeared in the 1888 edition of* The Renaissance. *Through a close reading of both texts, Borden argues that the revision represents Pater's bolder, more assertive vision of life and art.*]

In *The Westminster Review* of October 1868 appeared a review without a signature, entitled **"Poems by William Morris."** If it was the author who decided the title, he may have intended a challenge to the ignorant and a promise to the informed: his own style of poetry would not remain anonymous. We shall find that masks of a near transparency are characteristic of Pater, early and late. In 1873 the concluding pages of the unsigned review appeared again, somewhat altered, this time as the "Conclusion" to Walter Pater's **Studies in the History of the Renaissance.** The book was adored by the young, but attacked by the old guard at Oxford, above all for its aesthetic climax. Pater suffered a time of perplexity, which he converted, as usual, into a form of ingenuity. He omitted the troublesome "Conclusion" from the second edition, in 1877. He also changed the title to **The Renaissance: Studies in Art and Poetry.** Since our subject is the historical imagination, we may note that Pa-

ter seems to have abandoned History in favor of Art and Poetry. The new title may indicate a surrender to caution, consistent with suppressing the "Conclusion," which had historicized everything, the world without and the world within. But it is possible to read the new title in a different light, as compensating for the suppression and, indeed, vindicating the "Conclusion." For Pater allows the book to announce itself as history, as an event with the ghostliest effects. The title now has the very outline of the "Conclusion": a moment of history, perfected in art. The contour of a phrase gives a cold sort of comfort, which Pater knew best of all how to cherish. Students who missed the grand statement could find it, now glorified, circulating through Oxford. This episode prepares the way for the next and nearly the last: his restoring the "Conclusion" in the 1888 edition. Most of the changes make a show of moderation, and they seem to have fooled no one, though some critics take pleasure from his apparent cowardice. The large fact, however, is that Pater did reprint the "Conclusion." As in the altered title, we may detect in this version signs of a secret triumph.

To order the evidence, it may serve to try the perspectives of a hostile reader, then a sympathetic reader, and last a reader thankful not to be cheated of a legitimate terror, but amazed by the resources of anarchy in Pater's art. Now in our hostile mood, we delight to find Pater recanting. The best evidence is his new tenderness toward religion. In 1868 he wrote:

> The service of philosophy, and of religion and culture as well, to the human spirit, is to startle it into a sharp and eager observation.

This is to place religion on a level with culture, to subordinate both to philosophy, and to enlist all three in the service of the human spirit as it seeks experience in the sensuous world. In 1888 Pater writes:

> The service of philosophy, of speculative culture, towards the human spirit is to rouse, to startle it into sharp and eager observation.

This leaves religion out of reach and unbruised. Here the human spirit is roused before it is startled: given a soft warning, alerted to the surprise. The object is no longer "*a* sharp and eager observation," a momentary impression. It has become a life of constant observation, an ideal of conduct binding each moment to the next. Earlier, the service of philosophy was "*to* the human spirit." Once he settled on "to rouse, to startle it," Pater thought to avoid an unwanted echo by writing "towards the human spirit." The new preposition sounds mistaken, under an alien constraint. It betrays the tendency of Pater's revisions to lift the spirit above the present moment. A soul roused to vigilance appears safe enough.

There are three other modifications of this sort, at the level of whole sentences. Our unfriendly critic may content himself with one more, to establish that the first is not an exception.[1] In 1868 Pater wrote:

> Well, we are all *condamnes,* as Victor Hugo somewhere says: we have an interval, and then we cease to be.

The "somewhere" suggests more than casual scholarship. Not Pater but Victor Hugo has lost his place, undergone dissolution. The flippant turn of phrase indicates a grave prospect. Pater dwells on this view in 1888, but he deletes the adverb as if it were misleading:

> Well! we are all *condamnes,* as Victor Hugo says: we are all under sentence of death but with a sort of indefinite reprieve—*les hommes sont tous condamnes a mort avec des sursis indefinis*: we have an interval, and then our place knows us no more.

Pater weakens the sentence by trying to buttress it with solemn repetitions. He extends the quotation in French and throws the burden of his meaning across the Channel. In a favorite touch he adds an exclamation point to show that he himself is taken aback. The sentence is badly altered by the end: "and then we cease to be" is translated into biblical language, "and then our place knows us no more." Everyone here, artistic or not, is assured of surviving elsewhere.

To continue with censure, we may glance at the difference a single word can make. Pater urged us in 1868 to discard any "morality . . . not identified with ourselves." He changes the word in 1888:

> The theory or idea or system which requires of us the sacrifice of any part of this experience, in consideration of some interest into which we cannot enter, or some abstract *theory* we have not identified with ourselves, or what is only conventional, has no real claim upon us. [my italics]

Morality escapes criticism now. But the repetition of "theory" short-circuits the sentence, with the result that its finer discriminat ions, of theory or idea or system, of "some interest . . . or what is only conventional," look elaborately haywire.

Finally, at the heart of his sensibility, Pater recommended in 1868 "any stirring of the senses, strange dyes, strange flowers and curious odours." The plurals, yielding to one another, make a single rapture. In 1888 Pater replaces "flowers" with "colours"; and he adds a comma after it, so that "strange colours" is now a discrete image. The revision helps to interpret "strange dyes," which must represent a texture. Liquid or woven, it is an appeal to touch as "strange colours" is an appeal to sight. "Strange dyes, strange colours, and curious odours" falls into a pattern of touch, sight, and smell. But in the earlier version "strange flowers" crosses these boundaries to assimilate the senses in a central, unstable moment. After this "strange colours" seems only to repeat "strange dyes" in a duller phase. The additional comma taps on the flaw and shivers the ecstasy.

A sympathetic reader admits the new moderation, but interprets it differently—in the light of Pater's story, his footnote to the revised "Conclusion." The second edition of the **Renaissance,** though it lacked a rallying chapter, did not still the commotion at Oxford. Pater declined to be the rage. In 1881 he resigned his position as tutor, to spend the next three years clarifying his position as critic. This image of himself he called **Marius the Epicurean: His Sensations and Ideas,** published in 1885. It was intended to show that passionate observation, Pater's program in the **Renaissance,** is consistent with social values, even with some forms of Christianity.[2] Once he had corrected the hedonistic tendencies of his argument, he could reprint the "Conclusion." He had only to make "slight changes":

> This brief "Conclusion" was omitted in the second edition of this book, as I conceived it might possibly mislead some of those young men into whose hands it might fall. On the whole, I have thought it best to reprint it here, with some slight changes which bring it closer to my original meaning. I have dealt more fully in **Marius the Epicurean** with the thoughts suggested by it.

A reader may accept this view from the highest authority. It would appear that the modifications demonstrate Pater's sense of responsibility.

I should like to press the point harder than friendly critics have done as a way of transforming it into our last, appalled perspective. Edmund Chandler has observed of **Marius,** revised like the **Renaissance** in its third edition (1892): "By the time of the later edition Pater was more firmly confident and emphatic in his own aesthetic attitude, though more discreet in his recommendation of it to others" (74). We can hear the note of confidence in the new "Conclusion." Pater begins by accepting responsibility, which has the desired effect: it allows him to sound responsible. Yet he accepts responsibility for nothing other than his "original meaning"—the review of 1868—and for "those young men" who have it by heart.

To a wary reader the changes of 1873 and 1888 together show a weird assurance. Pater has added a great deal of punctuation, which is read as emphasis rather than hesitation. For instance, all but one of the following commas are missing from the review:

Not to discriminate every moment some passionate attitude in those about us, and in the brilliancy of their gifts some tragic dividing of forces on their ways, is, on this short day of frost and sun, to sleep before evening.

A critic intent on Pater's self-betrayal would argue that these changes, and others like them, soften the effect of time passing, which Pater rendered acutely in the first version. Yet the discrimination of moments, the brief arrest of time, is just the measure of success for Pater, his avowed ideal of art.

The "Conclusion" of 1888 begins to appear less concessive, more assertive than before. A large difference is the deletion of a paragraph from the 1868 text:

Such thoughts seem desolate at first; at times all the bitterness of life seems concentrated in them. They bring the image of one washed out beyond the bar in a sea at ebb, losing even his personality, as the elements of which he is composed pass into new combinations. Struggling, as he must, to save himself, it is himself that he loses at every moment.

This is a vision of warning, fashioned from a vision of Pater himself. He had cancelled the passage in 1873, probably with the idea of disowning so desolate a prophecy. In 1888 the idea seems still more confident: rather than caution his reader, he offers a new self-image.

Has Pater revised the text according to his "original meaning" or according to the "thoughts suggested by it?" He directs some readers to the 1868 review and others to **Marius the Epicurean.** The footnote to the "Conclusion" is the most significant change, the highest note of triumph and literally the lowest, in its radical division of self the most startling. In each of the previous essays Pater disguised himself as the artist he was praising. As essay followed essay, the identification and the praise became fainter. In the body of the "Conclusion" there is no self-portrait of this kind. Once the drowning swimmer is gone, there is only the mask of style. But in the footnote Pater appears in his own right, as the leader of a new generation. It is typical of him that he arrives by indirection, claiming that he cannot possibly mislead. To appreciate the bitterness of this self-projection, the motive for it and the license it gave Pater to continue writing, it is important to recall that in 1885, when the two volumes of **Marius** were complete, Ruskin resigned as Slade Professor of Fine Art, Pater proposed himself and Oxford chose a safer man.

We discover allusions to the event in sentences that we have considered empty of self. In fact, they declare a personal resistance. For example,

Well! we are all *condamnes,* as Victor Hugo says: we are all under sentence of death but with a sort of indefinite reprieve—*les hommes sont tous condamnes a mort avec des sursis indefinis*: we have an interval, and then our place knows us no more.

The exclamation marks the point of identification. The persistent translation invites us to read deeper. The repetitions do not void the meaning: they signal a hidden, worried significance. With a fellowship at Brasenose, without a chair at the University, Pater feels "under sentence of death but with a sort of indefinite reprieve." The sentence revolves around a lack of definition, a center of indifference not Pater's. The "but," unmatched in the French, expresses the irony of his situation at Oxford, which would not know him.[3]

To recover himself, Pater begins a different school: "of this wisdom . . . the love of art for art's sake." Here is his largest self-assertion:

for art comes to you *professing* frankly to give nothing but the highest quality to your moments as they pass, and simply for those moments' sake. [my italics]

As ever, the "you" designates an "I" in front. The class of young men is at the end of a term, about to enroll in another. The text of 1893, the last to be supervised by Pater, shows the context to be altered yet again. He comes to write "proposing frankly," as if after all he had lost his hope of a profession and an academy. Even this change has a double aspect, however. By granting so much to time, Pater is forever conjuring the possibility of a second Renaissance. With all the ceremony of a marriage vow, he proposes so odd an affair.

By comparing two sentences within the 1873 text, we may harmonize our discrepant conclusions. In the first chapter Pater defines the Renaissance:

For us the Renaissance is the name of a many-sided but yet united movement, in which the love of the things of the intellect and the imagination for their own sake, the desire for a more liberal and comely way of conceiving life, make themselves felt. . . .

This may be compared with the last sentence of the **Renaissance**:

Of this wisdom, the poetic passion, the desire of beauty, the love of art for art's sake, has most; for art comes to you professing frankly to give nothing but the highest quality to your moments as they pass, and simply for those moments' sake.

The second statement is different from the first, as one would expect of Pater, so sensitive to changes from moment to moment that every sentence has the look of a separate undertaking, doomed as soon as it reaches completion. More striking perhaps than the differences is the high level of similarity between the two statements, occurring at opposite ends of a book that propounds incessant change. But the swift unweaving of every moment requires Pater to weave it once more, to re-form it as best he can, "with a sense in it, a relic more or less fleeting, of such moments gone by." The power of time to undo everything forces Pater to do everything again, only with a harder polish, the high finish of a desperate art. And the similarity between one sentence and another throws their differences into relief, making the slightest shade of qualification look brilliant. By the time we reach the "Conclusion," "the things of the intellect and the imagination" have lost whatever solidity had been given them by Pater's language, to be apprehended now as the quality of a moment, no more than the epiphany of art. We have learned to recognize the play of sameness and difference everywhere in language, to identify it with the production of all significance. It seems to have attracted Pater with unusual force, nearly to having riveted him as a stylist, perhaps because he was so conventional, desiring to be the same as other men with intense diffidence, and yet so singular, even to the point of cultivating his strangeness. Self-divided, he exploited a principle of language to rare effect, through the attenuation of monotony happening again and again upon the finest discriminations. He temporized for a double reason: to suit the time and to gain time for himself.

### Notes

1. In addition to those cited:

   a) 1868: "Some spend this interval in listlessness, some in high passions, the wisest in art and song."

   1888: "Some spend this interval in listlessness, some in high passions, the wisest, at least among 'the children of this world,' in art and song."

   The allusion is to Luke 16:8, and the application is difficult: "And the Lord commended the unjust steward, because he had done wisely: for the children of this world are in their generation wiser than the children of light."

   b) 1868: "High passions give one this quickened sense of life, ecstasy and sorrow of love, political or religious enthusiasm, or the 'enthusiasm of humanity.'"

   1888: "Great passions may give us this quickened sense of life, ecstasy and sorrow of love, the various forms of enthusiastic activity, disinterested or otherwise, which come naturally to many of us."

2. An echo of my reading which I have been unable to locate, probably in Stein.

3. Pater first expanded the quotation in 1873:

   "Well, we are all *condamnes,* as Victor Hugo says: *les hommes sont tous condamnes a mort avec des sursis indefinis*: we have an interval, and then our place knows us no more."

   Here the context is different: Pater was in line to receive a position as University proctor, which he would fail to win the following year, probably on account of the "Conclusion." His expectations make the passage less fretful and the allusion less pointed than it would become in 1888. Indefiniteness in Pater is sometimes soothing, sometimes threatening.

### Works Cited

Chandler, Edmund. *Pater on Style*. Copenhagen: Rosenkilde and Bagger, 1958.

[Pater, Walter H.] "Poems by William Morris." *The Westminster Review* 34 n.s. (1868): 300-312.

Pater, Walter, H. *The Renaissance: Studies in Art and Poetry*. London: and New York: Macmillan, 1888.

———. *The Renaissance: Studies in Art and Poetry*. London and New York: Macmillan, 1893.

———. *Studies in the History of the Renaissance*. London: Macmillan, 1873.

Stein, Richard. *The Ritual of Interpretation*. Cambridge, Harvard UP, 1975.

## Wendell V. Harris (essay date winter 1988)

SOURCE: Harris, Wendell V. "Ruskin and Pater—Hebrew and Hellene—Explore the Renaissance." *Clio: A Journal of Literature, History, and the Philosophy of History* 17, no. 2 (winter 1988): 173-85.

[*In the following essay, Harris examines Pater's and Ruskin's opposing views on art and morality.*]

If there is such a thing as the spirit of an age, it can only be the incredibly complex sum of innumerable vectors of cultural force. Retrospective *zeitgeists* are reconstructions of an earlier spirit known through fragmentary evidences seen through the assumptions of later milieus—and achieved by individual minds pursuing their own purposes. Mine is a reconstruction of two minds' nineteenth-century reconstructions of evidences of the dominant tendencies of incalculable numbers of minds over several centuries and across a diversity of European cultures. I take my framework from Matthew Arnold, or from my view of the significance of certain of his insights.

By the time Victoria came to the throne, the enormous intellectual excitement of the Renaissance had been damped by the religious and political struggles of the seventeenth century, tamed by the eighteenth and diluted by the nature worship and sentiment of the Romantic movement. When later in the century the word "renaissance" was finally being assimilated into English, the period to which it referred was a foreign domain, its various regions—philosophical, religious, aesthetic, political—to be explored, or ignored, according to one's preoccupations.

Not everyone who might be expected to be was actually much interested in the endeavor. Arnold congratulated the Renaissance on its discovery of the thought and poetry of classical antiquity but preferred to give his attention to the original rather than the revival. Carlyle, always more interested in assessing the heroic man and dramatic event than in characterizing whole ages, took his heroes indifferently from the middle ages, Renaissance, and more recent times. After all, though Carlyle was fascinated by history, that is, by "the Letter of Instructions, which the old generations write and posthumously transmit to the new," that Letter "comes to us in the saddest state; falsified, blotted out, torn, lost and but a shred of it in existence . . ."[1] It was therefore better not to extrapolate too far from the individual man or event.

No longer an active force, the Renaissance was eminently available to Victorians as a symbol to be shaped to one's purposes. The two best-known Victorian uses are Ruskin's *Stones of Venice* and Pater's **The Renaissance.** The opposition between Ruskin and Pater is patent—as Pater presumably intended that it should be. As everyone knows, Ruskin's variously phrased denunciations of the Renaissance centuries are well summed up in the seven words from the first volume of *The Stones of Venice*: "The Renaissance frosts came, and all perished" (9:278).[2] Pater simply swept that Ruskinian judgment aside: "For us the Renaissance is the name of a many-sided but yet united movement, in which the love of the things of the intellect and the imagination for their own sake, the desire for a more liberal and comely way of conceiving life, make themselves felt . . ." (2).[3] Graham Hough pointed out long ago that Pater simply reversed the relation between morality and aesthetic taste so influentially proclaimed by Ruskin, and Richard Ellmann comments that Pater's **Renaissance** is *The Stones of Venice* inverted. "Pater is all blend where Ruskin is all severance." Michael Levey writes that where Ruskin had "laid out a strict, ethical garden of art with defined flowerbeds and a large amount of forbidden, poisonous fruit," Pater "turned it into a jungle rich and rank, where anyone was free to wander as he liked."[4]

We can well imagine how the two men might have expressed their judgments on each other and, indeed, on themselves:

Ruskin on Pater:

> Here we see luxury of ornament, the more pernicious as it gilds the ashes of unbelief. There is no love of God's creation here, only distorted reflections given specious interest by hectic, unnatural tints.

Ruskin on Ruskin:

> All honor to the man who praises that which is praiseworthy and withholds it from that which elevates the works of man above those of his God. What though such a champion weary of chronicling the infidelity and baseness of spirit of the Renaissance, and lose himself in the difficulties of achieving a right understanding of the grotesque; he has followed his task where it has led him, not, like the haughty sixteenth-century architect, sacrificed the soul of his work to symmetry.

Pater on Ruskin:

> In all the eloquent pages this driven spirit gave the world, strength puts sweetness to flight, and urgency overcomes contemplation. Strange by-roads offer unexpected but unassimilable splendors distracting the eager mind from the exalted purpose and rigorous pilgrimage on which it set out.

Pater on Pater:

> The strange beauty in these portraits arises from the blending of curious colors folded within an evanescent form whose very instability gives a subtle charm which is just the reflex of their own so fleeting passage.

As these mock quotations are contrived to suggest, the difference lies not in the qualities Ruskin and Pater found in the Renaissance; if we abstract their descriptions of what was characteristic of the Renaissance from the normative frameworks in which they appear, their Renaissances are quite similar. To adapt Arnoldian terminology to our own purposes, the object as it is in itself is not what their disagreements—nor the world's disagreements generally—are about. It is when Pater translates the question of "the object as in itself it really is" into "what is this song or picture . . . to *me*?" (viii) that he moves toward the ground on which most conflict lies. "What does this mean to me?" very quickly signifies "what use can my mind make of this?"

Pater and Ruskin equally recognized the classical influences, the surging individualism, the explicit pursuit of pleasure, the rise of science, the growth of a class of men of refined, if selfish and worldly, aesthetic sensibilities. One finds them in general agreement about the intellectual temper of the centuries in question, just as one finds agreement about a number of general principles. Pater's well-known preoccupation with the evanescent moment, "the sudden act, the rapid transition of thought, the passing expression" (150) was preceded by Ruskin's own interest in the fugacious: "But what we want art to do for us is to stay what is fleeting. . . . The dimly seen, momentary glance, the flitting shadow of faint emotion, the imperfect lines of fading thought . . ." (11:62). Though both were apparently fascinated by metaphysics, both in their own ways warned against its claims. "Nay, I believe that metaphysicians and philosophers are, on the whole, the greatest troubles the world has got to deal with," pronounces Ruskin (5:334). "But a taste for metaphysics may be one of those things which we must renounce, if we mean to mould our lives to artistic perfection" suggests Pater (229-30). Both placed execution below conception, though Ruskin tended to call the latter "soul" while Pater called it "spirit." There was no disagreement about the appeal of Renaissance art to the learned and refined—though where Ruskin deplored the haughtiness of Renaissance architecture that appealed only to the few (10:243-44), Pater constantly addressed himself to the refined intelligence. Of course they disagreed about the value of Grecian models; Ruskin lamented that "the classical enthusiasm had destroyed the best types of architectural form" (11:16) while Pater proclaimed, "The standard of taste . . . was fixed in Greece, at a definite historical period" (199). But the right evaluation of the art of Greece and Rome was secondary to their larger purposes.

Ruskin and Pater, then, saw very much the same Renaissance while using it wholly differently. Their responses represent the most obvious alternative uses to which the Renaissance could be put. The nineteenth century's awakened sense that its own culture descended directly from the Renaissance seemed to many to disqualify that age as a model for the revitalization or reform of society, but if radical cultural changes were necessary, it could well represent that which was to be repudiated. The historical ideal, if it had ever in fact existed, must lie in those centuries between imperial Rome and the enthusiastic rediscovery of the Greek and Roman cultures. When Ruskin became one of those for whom the middle ages embodied a desirable "dream of order," his genius, energy, and opportunity to devote himself to observation and thought produced the fullest development of the Gothic alternative.

On the other hand, the Renaissance could also be seen as a treasure-trove of fascinating personalities, splendid works of art, and intriguing philosophical speculations. As such it offered God's plenty to one like Browning who sought pleasure in meditating on the special qualities ("virtues") of individual personalities, moments, and events rather than edifying homilies. We may chucklingly pass beyond Wilde's comment that "Meredith is a prose Browning, and so was Browning" to recognize that Pater has a literal claim to be "Browning in prose."[5] Like Browning, Pater set himself to give new interest to the past by emphasizing the complex strangeness of particular aspects and individual personalities.

Ruskin's and Pater's alternative views reflect unusually pure forms of the opposed intellectual tendencies Matthew Arnold called "Hebraism" and "Hellenism." To write as did Arnold of these two forces as "rivals dividing the empire of the world between them" has an old-fashioned ring, but we can rechristen them "terministic screens" if we like Kenneth Burke's terminology, or "internalized perspectives" if we prefer the vocabulary of the sociology of knowledge.[6] One knows that Arnold would not have been pleased to call Pater a Hellene; Pater was too much the apostle of sweetness and too little concerned with championing the light of reason or bringing it to bear on contemporary sociopolitical problems. Arnold would probably have equally questioned how the Ruskin who helped engender the aesthetic movement and enlisted the sympathies of Oscar Wilde could be regarded as the epitome of the Hebraic. But though Arnold gave the terms currency, the two great bents of mind he so designates need not be bound by Arnold's own applications; while remembering what Arnold meant by them, we can employ them for our own purposes. The organizing notions of the Hebraic and the Hellenic will help us see the extent to which the rival evaluations of the Renaissance gave it different symbolic roles. At the same time, the roles assigned these contrasting symbols clarify the operation of the Hellenic and Hebraic casts of mind.

Ruskin may have been the most thorough-going Hebraist to think deeply about aesthetic theory. Though his views of the relation between art, religion, and society are notoriously subject to modification and redaction from book to book, an overarching continuity results from a powerful Hebraism that not only gives primacy to moral judgments but holds that all judgments are ultimately moral. Looking back over the five volumes of *Modern Painters* published between 1843 and 1860, Ruskin wrote in the Preface to the fifth volume that the book was a declaration of "the perfectness and eternal beauty of the work of God; and tests all work of man by concurrence with, or subjection to that" (7:9). The difficulty is that though his standard remained the same, his tests varied, as did, therefore, his resulting assessments. While the first volume of *Modern Painters* is content to evaluate landscape painting on the basis of its truth to the natural world—a reasonable ground on which to pursue his original intention of defending the painting of Turner—the second begins to exalt the religious art of Fra Angelico, Giotto, and Ghirlandajo. The first reference to Ruskin's preferences for Gothic (especially Venetian Gothic) does not appear until near the end of Volume 2 (4:305). Before he had written the third volume of *Modern Painters* his interest in architecture produced *The Seven Lamps of Architecture,* which exhibits the elements of Ruskin's central judgment of the Renaissance in suspension just before they come together. Thus we find the shift of interest from painting (where his admiration for Tintoretto, Titian and Veronese made it impossible for him to be consistent in denouncing Renaissance art) to architecture (in which field his overriding admiration for Gothic led to no such conflict), an increasing conviction that architecture reflected the moral and religious health of a culture, and the beginning of a concern for the conditions under which the individual workman labors.[7] These coalesce, of course, in *The Stones of Venice* under the pressure of the Hebraic need to define all things in moral terms. There the characteristic aspects of the Renaissance become moral transgressions that can be assigned to the cardinal sin of pride. It is not until the subsequently published Volume 3 of *Modern Painters* that the terms "Renaissance" and "medieval" enter, and only there will Ruskin declare "there is *no* entirely sincere or great art in the seventeenth century" (5:400).

The same driving force that made it necessary for Ruskin to reorient his scale of values with his discovery of early Christian painting between 1843 and 1846 lies behind the transformation of a preference for Gothic architecture into a prolonged denunciation of the whole fabric of Renaissance life and thought. It equally lies behind the great reversal of 1858 when he was able fully to accommodate his admiration for artists like Titian and Tintoretto within his ethical worldview by recognizing "things done delightfully and rightly are always done by the help and in the Spirit of God" (35:496) and the final adjustment in 1874 when he was able to place Giotto high once again by distinguishing technical knowledge from spiritual vision. Ruskin's movement from a strict protestantism to rejection of specifically theological dogma in favor of a kind of religion of humanity, thence to a possible flirtation with Roman Catholicism, and finally to a comfortable, vaguely Christian theism never touched the Hebraic core of his thought—through it all he never doubted that all judgments, all discriminations, reflected ultimate moral differences.

Ever serving a Hebraism that seeks to weigh all things in the same balance, Ruskin could never rest in a mere historical analysis or aesthetic judgment. The absolute dichotomy between virtue and evil demands cognate dichotomies: all man's works are pious or impious, noble or base; they are acts of worship or acts that scorn God. Accurate delineation of the gulf between demanded criteria and categorization: not only do we have seven lamps of architecture but six elements of Gothic architecture and three kinds of ornament, etc. This, even though Ruskin is scornful of the prevalence of rules and systems in the Renaissance. As he writes in the third volume of *The Stones of Venice*: "wheresoever we find the system and formality of rules much dwelt upon, and spoken of as anything else than a help for children, there we may be sure that noble art is not even understood, far less reached" (11:118). Where distinctions become complicated and difficult to discern, Ruskin labors all the harder—as in the tortuous explanation of the nature of the grotesque that occupies an entire chapter of the third volume of *Stones of Venice.* Moreover, if there are to be absolute judgments, there must be a common quality in all great art. Though always on his guard against reductionism, Ruskin must posit something as this necessary property; he chooses the presentation of noble truths and the arousal of noble emotions representing "unchanging love of all things God has created to be beautiful, and pronounced to be good" (5:43).

Where a single principle is made the source or ground of all lesser criteria of judgment, it is easy for that principle to be used to rationalize judgments actually made on quite other grounds. Thus Ruskin's overarching evaluative question—"does this (whatever it may be) glorify God?"—notoriously serves to justify judgments made on the basis of personal preference. If an artist gives a painting a high degree of finish, one may condemn him for pride, for attempting a perfection beyond what is appropriate to human effort. Alternatively, one may praise him for developing his God-given powers to the full. The proper deduction of subordinate principles from an ultimate one is a tricky business: does one best praise God's creation by eschewing such subjects as dirty beggar boys,[8] or might it be that to paint them well is to see creation whole? Ruskin's Hebraism never wavers in its conception of the highest principle, but one often is dubious of its application.

In sum, it is impossible to know how much of Ruskin's admiration for the middle ages resulted from that revival of interest in Gothic already in progress thanks to Pugin, Scott, and romanticism generally, how much from quite personal aesthetics responses, and how much from the order in which he came to know particular works of art and architecture. (He, more than George Moore even, "conducted his education in public" as his knowledge of art expanded beyond Turner and the collections of the National Gallery and Dulwich Gallery.) The resulting collocation of aesthetic response and ethical principle is in a way quite arbitrary: a Hebraist equally as uncompromising as Ruskin could have argued that the Renaissance was more moral than the middle ages, that it saw God's world more directly, rejoiced in that world more fully, recognized the individuality of each human being He put on earth more clearly. But Ruskin's vision, however exaggerated and wrongheaded portions of it might be, consistently made the Renaissance a vast symbol of impious pride.

Where Ruskin's invariant Hebraism analyzes in order to judge, Pater's relativistic Hellenism analyzes in order to experience a thing as fully as possible. In the Winckelmann essay, Pater seems to echo Arnold in making Hellenism "the principle pre-eminently of intellectual light" (190), but within that essay, partly concealed by the indirection and reservation of Paterian prose, lies a three-fold meaning of the light metaphor which subverts the Arnoldian scheme. The "sharp edge" of Hellenic light that cuts through melancholy, mysticism, and gloom (204) is Greek thought; the simple perfection of a sun-lit statue "taking no colour from any one-sided experience" (219) is the ideal of Greek art. We cannot return to the first nor rest content with the second. But, thirdly, the Hellenic light also represents the never-satisfied, never-resting enthusiasm which "struggles" with each form of culture, each manifestation of genius "till its secret is won" (229). In this third sense it is an attitude toward experience that may be obtained always and anywhere. One's eager immersion seeks not to discover general laws or their consequences, but rather to engage in what Charles Sanders Peirce called "abduction," the reasoning from effect to cause, where "cause" is not conceived as a general law but as a unique convergence of causes (or, in Paterian terms, "forces"). An illuminating parallel can be found, rather surprisingly, in the kind of mind Conan Doyle gives Sherlock Holmes. Thomas Sebeok has cleverly portrayed Holmes as the master, not of deduction, but of Peircean "abduction."[9] Holmes seeks every bit of evidence about a crime (in the same way the connoisseur or critic seeks to be attentive to every detail in a work of art) and then seeks to reconstruct the particular set of circumstances that could have produced the totality of that evidence. Where Ruskin's thrust is always toward presumably universal principles implied by a single sovereign principle, Pater's is toward the discovery of a unique constellation of causes. Or, as Pater explains in two well-known sentences:

> The aesthetic critic, then, regards all the objects with which he has to do, all works of art, and the fairer forms of nature and human life, as powers or forces producing pleasurable sensations, each of a more or less peculiar or unique kind. This influence he feels, and wishes to explain, by analyzing and reducing it to its elements.
>
> (ix)

That discovery of the constituents of the particular "virtue" of the work, we come to recognize the more we read Pater, is the goal itself. Like Sherlock Holmes, the Paterian reader finds exhilaration in the challenge, the process of careful exploration of the evidence (the work itself) and the opportunity to employ the full powers of intelligence and (here perhaps art has the advantage over crime) esthetic sensibility. When Arnold wrote, "The uppermost idea with Hellenism is to see things as they really are,"[10] he further assumed the Socratic belief that one who truly knows the right will do it. But knowing things as they in themselves are does not necessarily lead to knowing what it is right that one should do. Let us then provisionally distinguish between three activities, the first two of which Arnold conflates: knowing the thing as it is, making a normative judgment about it, and saluting the causes, the forces upon whose momentary conjunction depends the uniqueness of the thing contemplated. The last is Paterian.

Pater, like Ruskin, is comfortable distilling sweeping characterizations of the Greek, medieval, Renaissance, and modern mind and art from individual instances. Ruskin can read the transition from true to false workmanship in the capitals of the Ducal Palace (9:54-55 and 11:9-11); Pater reads the qualities of Hellenic art out of the Panathenaic frieze or the Berlin "*adorante*" (218). But the same instance may speak very differently to each of them. Both cite the pair of Raphael's frescoes in the Vatican. "On one wall of that chamber he placed a picture of the World or Kingdom of *Theology*, presided over by *Christ*. And on the side wall of that same chamber he placed the World or Kingdom of *Poetry*, presided over by *Apollo*," wrote Ruskin. "And from that spot, and from that hour, the intellect and the art of Italy date their degradation" (12:148). To Pater, however, these frescoes demonstrate the fruitful coexistence of two traditions (197-98). And where Ruskin strides from the exemplary instance toward statements of principles *beyond* any age, seeking always universality, Pater drives toward as full an evocation of the artist as possible. That is why the essays of the *Renaissance* are essentially portraits. Uniqueness, the peculiar virtue of the individual work, becomes of interest rather than the ways in which it is typical of its age. What is for Ruskin one great text for a massively extended sermon on the wages of sin becomes for Pater a gallery of variegated moments. That perhaps is why, for all his care in choosing the most accurate and evocative word in describing particular moments, Pater's choice of characterizing adjectives for the historical periods under discussion—"strong" for the middle ages, "sweet" for the Renaissance—are so oddly imprecise (2). While he enthusiastically pursues the special qualities of individual works or artists, those of a historical age are too complex for any but very general description.

Moreover, in the very process of playing about an idea or work of art, Pater's Hellenism tends to break down rigidities of definition as in his softening of the distinction between prose and poetry and classicism and romanticism.[11] Even the opposition between the Renaissance and the middle ages, he finds, is artificial. Accepting the term "Renaissance," he nevertheless is interested in erasing boundaries and tracing continuities. Too often, writes Pater,

> the Renaissance is represented as a fashion which set in at a definite period. That is the superficial view: the deeper view is that which preserves the identity of European culture. The two are really continuous: and there is a sense in which it may be said that the Renaissance was an uninterrupted effort of the middle age, that it was ever taking place.

(225-26)

Regarded as "ever taking place," the Renaissance is transmuted from a historical period to the symbol of an attitude toward experience. That is why a portion of Pater's 1868 review of William Morris could serve as the Conclusion to his treatment of it. The attitude it symbolizes seeks widely for its sources of pleasure, inspiration, and wisdom, denies any single set of norms, and regards the flow of time and change as both inevitable and fascinating. Both Ruskin and Pater saw history as made up of successive series of cultivation, culmination, and collapse. For Ruskin this is a sombre truth; for Pater it is the greatest source of history's savor. Pater simply takes it as a law that *ennui* "ever attaches itself to realisation" (222). Greek thought and art must grow troubled, give way to the medieval, which will be metamorphosed in the Renaissance, and transmogrified first by romanticism and then by modern relativism. The human mind—both intellect and sensitivity—becomes ever richer *not* because it advances toward an external set of truths but simply because it incorporates all that went before.[12] Beliefs therefore cannot stand in static opposition but are continually modifying one another.[13] Throughout Pater's work, Hough notes, "We find the same tendency to hail the deliquescence of all rigid forms of belief" (138). Pater's solvent was his sense of the enriching complications of historical change. Pater writes that all moments of transition are of particular interest: "Theories which bring into connexion with each other modes of thought and feeling, periods of taste, forms of art and poetry, which the narrowness of men's minds constantly tends to oppose to each other, have a great stimulus for the intellect" (3). But as the Conclusion to the *Renaissance* proclaims, all moments are actually transitional.

The works and artists that make up the Renaissance represent less a historical period than the ever-present possibility of a personal renaissance, that is, of revitalization. Pater substitutes a dream of vitality for the "dream of order." On the other hand, Ruskin seems to accept the label "Renaissance" without probing its appropriateness—for him the return to the art of antiquity included in the concept of a rebirth was mingled with an already advancing corruption of spirit that rendered the pagan influence virulent. For Pater the sense of a "return" was subordinated to a strong sense of revitalization. What Pater celebrates in the *Renaissance* are instances of that assertion of individuality that Burckhardt had already made the essence of the Renaissance spirit. Pater believes that assertion possible not only to the artist but to those who devote themselves to the appreciation of the unique moment conserved in a work of art. Winckelmann found Greek sculpture personally revitalizing; Pater demonstrates that such rejuvenation may be found through study of the Renaissance; Pater's reader may find it in Greek sculpture, or the Renaissance, or in many another place, including the prose of Pater. The subtitle of the essay on Winckelmann, "Et Ego in Arcadia Fui," has broad application: Arcadia awaits all those who seek it in art.

Which leads us to a final set of oppositions arising out of apparently similar goals. Both Ruskin and Pater taught the full development of the individual as the path to the fullest happiness. But if, while cultural epochs come and go, it is possible in every age for the individual to achieve a quickened sense of life and find delight in self-culture, the improvement of the age is an illusory, or at best partial, goal. The purer the Hebraism, the more it must seek to lead (or force) society toward a vision of a complete life in which humanity achieves as much righteousness as possible. The purer the Hellenism, the less concern with the improvement of society, the more with perfection of the individual.

Pater's ideal appeals to us because it is both broad and flexible: after all, the Hellene can savor Ruskin as well as Pater, but the Hebrew (not only a Ruskin but a Carlyle, or Newman, or Eliot) must set his face almost wholly against Pater's Hellenism. But in the sure revolutions of the world the time may well come when the majority of readers will again insist on resting in Hebraic certainty. While Pater's Hellenism permits an unflurried acceptance of the widest variety of aesthetic and intellectual pleasures, the principle also makes an imperious demand: as soon as the "virtue" of a work or a conception of life is plumbed, it must be abandoned. If history is necessarily a series of revitalizations, the fullest form of human life is equally a set of renewals. A higher, fuller, whole life "means the life of one for whom, over and over again, what was once precious has become indifferent" (228). Pater has translated the historical Renaissance into a symbol of an intellectual curiosity that can never rest content in *any* Renaissance, personal or historical.

Pater's symbolism is no less arbitrary than Ruskin's. The Renaissance seems to us the great example of rebirth, of revitalization. But if Hellenism of the Paterian kind celebrates subtle analysis and the cultivation of pleasure through richly conjectural meditation, an argument can equally be made for taking the "monkish" middle ages as its symbol. Indeed, once one turns one's mind that way, one can better imagine Pater leading a life of asceticism, ritual, and curious study in the cloister than Ruskin. And would not Ruskin actually have been happier in the Renaissance than in the medieval period? One can readily imagine him eagerly trying to master the manifold new intellectual currents—even if only to assess their moral value—but he would have withered behind monastery walls.

Which of these estimates of the Renaissance do we accept today? Though Hebraism and Hellenism divide the world between them, most minds are compounded of both and give total allegiance to neither. If we look with distaste at that graceless pile, the Escorial, we will think, Ruskin-like, that those who commanded it and those who designed it were proud and ostentatious even in building for religious uses, and believe that its workmen could have taken no pleasure in their task. If, on the other hand, we turn from a gallery of medieval paintings to even minor Renaissance works with a feeling that we are moving among fresher, richer currents— and most of us today do—we will agree with Pater about the value of those artists who "have a distinct quality of pleasure which we cannot get elsewhere" and very possibly that the early Renaissance is "perhaps the most interesting period in the history of the mind."[14]

For the greater part of the late-twentieth-century men and women who are interested in such matters at all, these two Victorian Renaissances have mingled comfortably enough. Pater's *Renaissance* was published when he was 34, the age at which Ruskin had published the third volume of *The Stones of Venice.* Neither book can be argued to represent its author's final view of the relation between art, life, and morality, but each book represents a symbolic framework essential both to Victorian thought and to the twentieth century's hardly self-consistent view of the Renaissance.

Given the present literary-philosophic climate, we may well ask if what I have called the relativity of Ruskin's and Pater's judgments about and use of the Renaissance are not further evidence of the indeterminacy of all language. What could it have meant to talk about "the Renaissance" in, say, 1888 (the year in which the third version of *The Renaissance* and the final volumes of *Praeterita* were appearing), if that word was being used so differently? What indeed can the word mean today if most of us use it at times in a Ruskinian, at times in a Paterian sense? The answer is, first, that Ruskin and Pater would pretty much have agreed that they were talking about the same phenomena. And as for the differences in their evaluative judgments, that we are quite able to distinguish them evidences their determinacy. We define and judge all concepts according to our purposes; we understand others' purposes through our ability to recognize the differences between their definitions and between their judgments. A concept like "the Renaissance" is revitalized each time a speaker or writer conveys his or her unique use of it. In that sense, Pater had the best of it: revitalizations, renaissances, of a concept like "the Renaissance" are ever occurring.

*Notes*

1. Thomas Carlyle, "On History Again," *Complete Works,* Sterling Edition, 20 vols. (Boston: Estes and Lauriat, 1885), 15:74, 75.

2. All parenthetical Ruskin references are to *The Works of John Ruskin,* eds. E. T. Cook and A. D. O. Wedderburn, 39 vols. (London: George Allen, 1902-1912). The volumes of the *Works* cited are:

   Vols. 3-7: Vols. 1-15 *Modern Painters* (1843-60)

   Vol. 8: *The Seven Lamps of Architecture* (1849)

   Vols. 9-10: Vols. 1-3 *The Stones of Venice* (1851-53)

   Vol. 12: *Lectures on Architecture and Painting* (1854)

   Vol. 35: *Praeterita* (1885-89)

3. Parenthetical references to Walter Pater's *The Renaissance: Studies in Art and Poetry* (1873; London: Macmillan, 1910).

4. Graham Hough, *The Last Romantics* (London: Duckworth, 1947), 18; Richard Ellmann, *Golden Codgers* (London: Oxford, 1973), 51; Michael Levey, *The Case of Walter Pater* (London: Thames and Hudson, 1978), 23.

5. Oscar Wilde, *Complete Works* (London: Collins, 1948), 1013.

6. Kenneth Burke, *Language as Symbolic Action* (Berkeley: U of California P, 1966), 44-57. Peter L. Berger and Thomas Luckman, *The Social Construction of Reality: A Treatise in the Sociology of*

*Knowledge* (Garden City: Doubleday Anchor, 1967), 129-33.

7. For the last point see *The Seven Lamps of Architecture* (8:263-265).

8. Ruskin can write: "But look at these two ragged and vicious vagrants that Murillo has gathered out of the street. You smile at first, because they are eating so naturally and their roguery is so complete. But is there anything else than roguery there, or was it well for the painter to give his time to the painting of those repulsive and wicked children?" (10:228) Pater uses Murillo's beggar boys as a standard of "life-like charm" with which to compare the vividness of certain scenes in Plato's dialogues in *Plato and Platonism* (1893; London: Macmillan, 1910), 128.

9. Thomas Sebeok, "'You Know My Method': A Juxtaposition of Charles S. Peirce and Sherlock Holmes" in *The Play of Musement* (Bloomington: Indiana UP, 1981), 17-52.

10. Matthew Arnold, *Culture and Anarchy*, ed. R. H. Super (Ann Arbor: U of Michigan P, 1965), 165.

11. There is a curious symmetry to *Appreciations*: the opening of the first essay, "Style," asserts the value of recognizing the difference between poetry and prose and then erodes it; the "Postscript" performs the same maneuver with "classical" and "romantic."

12. This sense of change as a process in which new qualities are gained at the expense of the loss of others while the cumulative total of possible aesthetic experiences increases runs through *Greek Studies* (1895) as well as the Winckelmann essay dating from 1867. It was of course a commonplace of the time, to be found in Arnold, Carlyle, and Newman as well. For a succinct statement we may turn to J. A. Symonds, the third of the influential nineteenth-century English writers on the Renaissance. "Has any solid gain of man been lost in the stream of time to us-ward? We doubt that. Has anything final and conclusive been arrived at? We doubt that also. The river broadens as it bears us on": *The Renaissance in Italy,* 7 vols. (London: Smith, Elder, 1875-86), 7:436-37.

13. Pater was in fact trying to do for philosophical thought generally what Thomas Kuhn did for the philosophy of science in *The Structure of Scientific Revolutions* (Chicago: U of Chicago P, 1962). Cf. *Plato and Platonism*, 36-37.

14. Perhaps it is only a reflection of the taste of our time, but, like Ruskin, most of us find it easier to elevate Gothic architecture above that of the Renaissance than to prefer medieval to Renaissance painting.

## Lesley Higgins (essay date fall 1989)

SOURCE: Higgins, Lesley. "Concluding or Occluding Gestures: How Appropriate Is Pater's 'Conclusion' to *The Renaissance*?" *Dalhousie Review* 69, no. 3 (fall 1989): 349-56.

[*In the following essay, Higgins examines Pater's* The Renaissance *as both a work of art criticism and a philosophical meditation. Higgins focuses on the book's famous "Conclusion," asserting that its placement seems at odds with the rest of the book, both stylistically and on the level of content. A closer reading, however, reveals that this contrast provides a glimpse into Pater's true ambition: to integrate aspects of Hellenism, the Renaissance, and the modern age into a comprehensive statement about the nature of art and human existence.*]

With an appropriateness that I hope will become manifest in the course of my argument, this discussion of Walter Pater's seminal study ***The Renaissance***[1] is a self-constituted *doppelgänger*: it is "twin-born," to borrow Pater's term (***Renaissance*** 109), in order to highlight the competing preoccupations—aesthetic criticism and the criticism of life—which inform the text as a whole. This is not to suggest, however, that ***The Renaissance*** is hopelessly self-divided. The student of Pater must, out of necessity, become a student of Heraclitus—and the pre-Socratic sage teaches that only from the conflict of elements can true harmony arise. ***The Renaissance,*** I will argue, achieves such a "picturesque union of contrasts" (37), but the nature and degree of union cannot be ascertained until the contrasts are understood.

The "Conclusion" figures prominently in such a project because it seems, at first glance, to derail Pater's carefully-crafted ***Studies in the History of the Renaissance***—to pursue new, tangential avenues of thought and expression rather than summarize the essays which precede it. With its gem-like flames, moments of vision, and appeals for ecstasy, the "Conclusion" is a brilliant bravura performance, a frank and engaging response to the "forces" of modern life as Pater knew them. At face value, however, the personal philosophy of flux and response articulated in the "Conclusion" tells us a great deal about Walter Pater the man and his sense of the *zeitgeist*, but little about his knowledge of Renaissance culture. It seems to occlude, to obstruct, our appreciation of the earlier essays; the discrimination and clarity of **"Leonardo"** and **"The School of Giorgione"** give way to a darkling scepticism and hedonism of experience "for its own sake" (190).

Take away the "Conclusion," one could argue, and what remains is a highly selective, thoughtfully idiosyncratic aesthetic study, one in which each chapter may be read as an episode in Pater's dramatic and self-dramatizing quest for meaning through art. Each artist or connoisseur presented—della Robbia, da Vinci, or Winckelmann—reenacts this aesthetic adventure. "Take away" the final pages of **The Renaissance** was precisely the hue and cry of many of its first readers—remove them, destroy them, keep them away especially from impressionable young people. An Oxford bishop, John Fielding Mackarness, denounced the pages publicly[2], as did the *London Quarterly Review*[3]; George Eliot's declaration that they, along with the whole book, were "poisonous" was typical of numerous private responses (Haight V:455). (These vehemently negative views recall the initial reactions of Christian ascetics when the "relics" of classical art resurfaced in the Middle Ages: it was, to quote the **"Winckelmann"** essay, "as if an ancient plague-pit had been opened" [180].)

When revising his **Studies in the History of the Renaissance** in late 1876 and early 1877, to prepare a second edition, Pater bowed to the pressures of censure (and the threats of Benjamin Jowett) and removed the "Conclusion." His official "reasons" for doing so are noted in the third and fourth editions: "This brief 'Conclusion,'" he explains, "was omitted in the second edition of this book, as I conceived it might possibly mislead some of those young men into whose hands it might fall" (186n).

Did this most careful and fastidious of writers then write a new conclusion for his book? He did not. This may have been, in part, a political gesture: he had allowed himself to be partially silenced, but would draw attention to the censorship by leaving the work conclusionless. Nevertheless, the second edition, as it stands, seems to substantiate the claim that Pater's **The Renaissance: Studies in Art and Poetry** (its new and abiding name) is perfectly coherent and unified without the "Conclusion." It is still a tribute to "the susceptible and diligent eye" of artist and critic alike; it remains an accomplished aesthetic study which performs the double-natured theory of perception articulated in its "Preface" (what is the object "as in itself it really is," what is this object "to *me*?"). After all, the "Preface" claims that the "true student of aesthetics" will "define beauty, not in the most abstract but in the most concrete terms possible" (xix). Yet the "Conclusion" delineates, in highly abstract terms, what "the spirit need[s] in the face of

modern life" (184); the "desire of beauty" is only mentioned in the penultimate sentence as one example of the "great passions" that will bring "the highest quality to your moments as they pass" (190).

Should this, then, be our final position on the "Conclusion," words to the effect that, captivating and rebellious as it is, this late-Victorian *cri de coeur* wrenches the reader from the glories of the Renaissance to the problems of modernity; it obscures the carefully-nuanced considerations of specific artists and individual works by invoking both the disturbing truths of contemporary science (Spencer, Darwin, Tyndall) and the distressing conjectures of post-Renaissance philosophy (Hume, Kant, Hegel, Fichte).[4] Such a view, I would suggest, implies that **The Renaissance** is a single-minded, single-purposed text, one which surveys the past solely for the pleasures of its artifacts. Pater's project, however, is much grander and multifaceted. Overtly, he challenges then-contemporary notions of historiography, the need to fix dates and delineate historical "periods," by dissolving periodization: he identifies instead a Renaissance *impulse* which can be traced as far back as twelfth-century France (**"Two Early French Stories"**) and as far forward as late eighteenth-century Germany (**"Winckelmann"**). Covertly, he reinvents the framework within which we are to experience and evaluate all of Western culture. His explicit topic is The Renaissance, but his implicit subject is the rebirth, the revival of Hellenism—the history of its "strange, perpetual weaving and unweaving" throughout the fabric of Western civilization.

He *is* writing a history, but history as enactment, not "mere antiquarianism." The spectre of "antiquarianism" is invoked throughout **The Renaissance** (14-15, 78, 101, 143) to describe a sterile, specialized, non-participatory process of cataloguing the past, organizing its dates, anecdotes, and artifacts. A "busy" antiquarian produces records and Gradgrind-like "facts"; a true historian "vitalizes his subject" and brings it within the realm of the reader's experience (Pater, **"William Morris"** 146). The latter phrase appears, not in **The Renaissance,** but in Pater's October 1868 review of **"Poems by William Morris."** What Pater especially lauds in Morris is his resourcefulness in revivifying both the Middle Ages and the "antique" classical world. In this way, the nineteenth-century "aesthetic" artist becomes a renascence man: one "who, while he handles an ancient subject, never becomes an antiquarian, but vitalizes his subject by keeping it always close to himself" (Pater, **"William Morris"** 146). He is, in fact, a "Hellenist of the middle age" (146).

**"Poems by William Morris"** is not only an early workshop-essay in which Pater ponders aesthetic theory and articulates his methodology, it is the originative moment of *The Renaissance: Studies in Art and Poetry.* The "Conclusion" to *The Renaissance* is actually a revised version of the final seven paragraphs of **"Poems by William Morris."** From the outset, then, Pater was shaping his essays, his studies, in terms of history as the manifestation of a shared—that is, Hellenistic—sensibility, an "outbreak of the human spirit" (Pater, *Renaissance* xxii) possible at any propitious time, in any receptive culture.

Systems and dogmas were anathema to Pater; a systematized, rigidly proscribed view of history he particularly decried. **"Two Early French Stories,"** the first essay in *The Renaissance,* sounds the alarm concerning the "ignorant worship of system for its own sake" (6); the "Conclusion" echoes and amplifies the warning:

> The theory or idea or system which requires of us the sacrifice of any part of . . . experience, in consideration of some interest into which we cannot enter, or some abstract theory we have not identified with ourselves, or of what is only conventional, has no real claim upon us.

(189)

However, if the Hellenistic-Renaissance "spirit" cannot be reduced to abstract theorems, how are we to judge a true "outbreak" from a false? In the "Preface" Pater introduces his notion of an active, affective principle which resides within the object, "the virtue by which," he insists, "a picture, a landscape, a fair personality in life or in a book, produces this special impression of beauty or pleasure" (xx-xxi). The responsive critic, he believes, internalizes the "primary data" of impressions and sensations, and exposes them to the subjective influences of his or her cognitive processes. This conflation of memory, reason, imagination, emotion, "discrimination and analysis" (xx) then results in a new level of aesthetic "consciousness." Subsequent to this "interfusion" of a work's virtue and the individual's perceptive faculties, the critic reconstitutes the experience verbally and thereby renders it accessible to a sensitive reader. From this deduction, Pater generalizes further: not only does each object have such a virtue, each cultural experience embodies an "essential truth, the *vrai verité*" (122). Therefore, at strategic points throughout *The Renaissance,* Pater pauses to identify the virtues of Hellenism as they are revived throughout Europe.

Each such revival, one could say, constitutes a privileged cultural moment, a moment when, through *ascesis* (refinement) and *aesthesis* (sensory perception), the "hard gem-like flame" of Hellenism is rekindled. Pater's essays celebrate these temporally-flexible, always exhilarating "moments" of "intense consciousness,"

"exquisite pauses in time, in which, arrested thus, we seem to be spectators of all the fullness of existence, and which are like some consummate extract or quintessence of life" (118). The "Conclusion" then reiterates, with hectic and hypnotic urgency, the need to cherish and cultivate such moments, to grasp "at any exquisite passion, or any contribution to knowledge that seems by a lifted horizon to set the spirit free" and achieve, however fleetingly, a "quickened sense of life" (189-190).

Pater's vision of Hellenism reborn is expressed in two ways in *The Renaissance*: mythically, through a subtext which synthesizes Heraclitus and Coleridge; and metaphorically, through a painting of Botticelli. Mythically, this unified and unifying cultural experience is figured as an "under-current," an inspirational stream which has as its source the sacred "waters of Castalia" on Mt. Parnassus (157). This "river [which makes] glad" (157) any receptive city or citizen is, however, essentially Heraclitean: in the words of the "Conclusion," it displays not "the movements of the shore-side, where the water flows down indeed, though in apparent rest—but the race of the mid-stream, a drift of momentary acts of sight and passion and thought" (187). Reassuringly, though, this Hellenistic stream also has a Coleridgian aspect, as we might expect from a man whose first publication, in January 1866, was a review of **"Coleridge's Writings."** Like "Alph, the sacred river" of Xanadu, the stream of universal Hellenism sometimes flows through "caverns measureless to man," only to resurface, unexpectedly, in local fountains throughout Europe. Each new spring refreshes and "quickens" the lives of those who drink from it. What the "Conclusion" promises, despite its "whirlpool" of scientific and philosophical near-chaos, is that this "interfusion" of universal virtues and local sympathies can occur in the "modern" world—the world of late nineteenth-century England.

Pater's visual and verbal "correlative" for this promise of rebirth and renewal is Botticelli's painting, "The Birth of Venus." (The layering and conflation of time in this splendid passage is particularly revealing.)

> [One finds the] most complete expression [of Botticelli's artistry, Pater writes, in the] Venus rising from the sea, in which the grotesque emblems of the middle age, and a landscape full of peculiar feeling, and even its strange draperies, powdered all over in the Gothic manner with a quaint conceit of daisies, frame a figure that reminds you of the faultless nude studies of Ingres. At first, perhaps, you are attracted only by a quaintness of design, which seems to recall all at once whatever you have read of Florence in the fifteenth century; afterwards you may think that this quaintness must be incongruous with the subject, and that the colour is ca-

daverous or at least cold. And yet, the more you come to understand what imaginative colouring really is, that all colour is no mere delightful quality of natural things, but a spirit upon them by which they become expressive to the spirit, the better you will like this peculiar quality of colour; and you will find that quaint design of Botticelli's a more direct inlet into the Greek temper than the works of the Greeks themselves even of the finest period. Of the Greeks as they really were, of their difference from ourselves, of the aspects of their outward life, we know far more than Botticelli, or his most learned contemporaries; but for us long familiarity has taken off the edge of the lesson, and we are hardly conscious of what we owe to the Hellenic spirit. But in pictures like this of Botticelli's you have a record of the first impression made by it on minds turned back towards it, in almost painful aspiration, from a world in which it had been ignored so long; and in the passion, the energy, the industry of realisation, with which Botticelli carries out his intention, is the exact measure of the legitimate influence over the human mind of the imaginative system of which this is perhaps the central subject.

(*Renaissance* 45-46)

Impression, passion, energy, an "almost painful aspiration"—the words enter the mind quietly at first, but accrue force and meaning with each new essay, gathering strength from such congruent terms as consciousness, fusion, flux, and the moment. The crescendo of signification is heard in the "Conclusion," when Pater dislodges the reader from the comfortable position of armchair aestheticism. (It is very easy to think of *The Renaissance* as a Palace of Art, and each essay as a separate collection of artifacts within that palace or gallery.) Pater disrupts any complacency, any dispassionate non-involvement with his words, by stripping away the illustrations and confronting us instead with the spartan, chastening text: "we are all *condamnés*," the "Conclusion" reminds us, "we are all under sentence of death but with a sort of indefinite reprieve" (189). Aesthetic criticism has resurfaced as the criticism of life; we are once again conscious of what we owe to the Hellenic spirit. The "Conclusion" is not a mirror-image of the preceding essays, but their *doppelgänger*; an "inward similitude" (7) ensures that "every thought and feeling" of the "Conclusion" is "twin-born with its sensible analogue or symbol" in the essays proper (109).

As a manual for aesthetic criticism, the success of *The Renaissance: Studies in Art and Poetry* depends on the reader's willingness to respond to Pater's impressions and observations. As a manual for living in the "modern" world, the success of *The Renaissance* depends on the reader's willingness to respond to and then act upon Pater's vision of Hellenic regeneration. His strategy of bringing together the abstract entreaties of the late 1860s with the concrete fruits of those speculations—essays

written from 1867 to 1877—underlines, I would suggest, both the continuity and the boldness of Pater's vision. The decision to grant his entreaties the last word in *The Renaissance* signals the urgency of his mission. Nonetheless, the act of entitling the final paragraphs "Conclusion" reveals the perverseness of Pater's penetrating wit. The text as a whole invites the reader—compels the reader—to acknowledge that Hellenism lives. It was not some episode in the pageant of human history that has long since concluded. On the contrary it is, Pater insists, an abiding virtue of the human spirit, "the greatest number of vital forces unite[d] in their purest energy" (*Renaissance* 188).

Pater was a great reader of Francis Bacon—and Bacon, he knew, spoke of "conclusions" in terms of inclusiveness, and new experiments. Many of those who would praise, in isolation, the rhetoric and substance of the "Conclusion" find its position, if not its presence, in *The Renaissance* illogical. But Pater, the product of Oxford's rigorous, if old-fashioned, classical training, was schooled in logic. He knew that a conclusion, in the latter sense, was the last of three propositions forming a syllogism. *The Renaissance: Studies in Art and Poetry* is a historical syllogism. The first proposition is Hellenism; the second, the Renaissance. The third and most comprehensive proposition, the concluding gesture which springs from its antecedents, is "modern life."

*Notes*

1. Although the "standard" edition for all Pater texts is the 1910 Macmillan Library series, most commentators agree that the best extant version of *The Renaissance* is to be found in Donald Hill's presentation of the 1893 (that is, the fourth) edition. My argument, therefore, takes as its copy-text the fourth edition of *The Renaissance,* the last version which Pater saw through the press. The evolution of *The Renaissance* is pertinent to my argument. When *Studies in the History of the Renaissance* was published in 1873, it contained: "Preface," "Aucassin and Nicolette," "Pico della Mirandola," "Sandro Botticelli," "Luca della Robbia," "The Poetry of Michelangelo," "Leonardo da Vinci," "Joachim Du Bellay," "Winckelmann," and the "Conclusion." The second edition of 1877 was renamed *The Renaissance: Studies in Art and Poetry,* a title which Pater then retained. The second edition did not include the "Conclusion"; "Aucassin and Nicolette" had been substantially revised, and renamed "Two Early French Stories." The "Conclusion" was restored in the third edition of 1888, and "The School of Giorgione" was added. The fourth edition of 1893 consisted of: "Preface," "Two Early French Stories," "Pico della

Mirandola," "Sandro Botticelli," "Luca della Rob-
bia," "The Poetry of Michelangelo," "Leonardo da
Vinci," "The School of Giorgione," "Joachim Du
Bellay," "Winckelmann," and the "Conclusion."
The essays should also be considered in their or-
der of composition and/or original publication:
"Winckelmann" (October 1867), "Conclusion"
(originally, the concluding paragraphs of "Poems
by William Morris," October 1868); "Leonardo da
Vinci" (November 1869); "Sandro Botticelli"
(August 1870); "Pico della Mirandola" (October
1871); "The Poetry of Michelangelo" (November
1871); "Luca della Robbia," 1872; "Aucassin and
Nicolette," 1872; "Joachim Du Bellay," 1872;
"Preface," 1873; "The School of Giorgione"
(October 1877).

2. Mrs. Humphry Ward recalls "very clearly the effect of [*The Renaissance*] . . . of its entire aloofness also from the Christian tradition of Oxford,
its glorification of the higher and intenser forms
of aesthetic pleasure, of 'passion' in the intellectual sense—as against the Christian doctrine of
self-denial and renunciation. It was a doctrine that
both stirred and scandalized Oxford. The bishop
of the diocese thought it worth while to protest.
There was a cry of Neo-paganism, and various attempts at persecution." (Ward I:161).

3. For a complete survey of the initial reviews, consult Seiler, 47-112.

4. For a survey of the reading which Pater synthesizes in his "Conclusion," see Inman.

### Works Cited

Coleridge, Samuel Taylor. "Kubla Khan." *Selected Poetry and Prose.* Ed. Elisabeth Schneider. 2nd ed. New
York: Holt, Rinehart and Winston, 1971. 120-22.

Haight, Gordon S., ed. *The George Eliot Letters.* 7 vols.
New Haven: Yale UP, 1954-56.

Inman, Billie Andrew. "The Intellectual Context of
Walter Pater's 'Conclusion.'" *Journal of Prose Studies*
4.1 (1981); rpt. in Bloom, Harold, ed. *Walter Pater.*
Modern Critical Views. New York: Chelsea House,
1985. 131-50.

Pater, Walter. "Poems by William Morris." *Westminster
Review* XC (1868): 144-49.

———. *The Renaissance: Studies in Art and Poetry.*
Ed. Donald L. Hill. Berkeley: U of California P, 1980.

Seiler, R. M., ed. *Walter Pater: The Critical Heritage.*
London: Routledge & Kegan Paul, 1980.

Ward, Mrs. Humphry. *A Writer's Recollections.* 2 vols.
New York: Harper and Brothers, 1918.

**Jeffrey Wallen (essay date winter 1999)**

SOURCE: Wallen, Jeffrey. "Alive in the Grave: Walter
Pater's Renaissance." *ELH* 66, no. 4 (winter 1999):
1033-51.

[*In the following essay, Wallen analyzes the evolution of
Pater's critical thinking during his composition of* The
Renaissance, *contrasting his subjective approach to art
criticism with the absolutist models of John Ruskin and
Matthew Arnold. Wallen argues that Pater's work is
less a study of the Renaissance than a treatise on a
radical new aesthetic theory.*]

> The historical training of our critics prevents their hav-
> ing an influence in the true sense—an influence on life
> and action.
>
> —Friedrich Nietzsche, *On the Uses and
> Disadvantages of History for Life*

In 1873, when Walter Pater's first book was published,
it bore the title **Studies in the History of the Renaissance.** When the second edition was published four
years later, the title was changed to **The Renaissance:
Studies in Art and Poetry.**[1] It is not surprising that the
word "History" drops out, since there is so little conventional history in this book. One of the book's earliest reviewers, a friend of Pater's, Mrs. Pattison (Emilia
Frances Strong), remarked:

> The title is misleading. The historical element is pre-
> cisely that which is most wanting, and its absence
> makes the weak place of the whole book . . . the work
> is in no wise a contribution to the history of the Re-
> naissance. For instead of approaching the subject,
> whether Art or Literature, by the true scientific method,
> through the life of the time of which it was an out-
> come, Mr. Pater prefers in each instance to detach it
> wholly from its surroundings, to suspend it isolated be-
> fore him, as if it were a kind of air-plant independent
> of ordinary sources of nourishment. The consequence
> is that he loses a great deal of the meaning of the very
> objects which he regards most intently. This is espe-
> cially noticeable when he passes from the examination
> of fragments to deal with the period as a whole. . . .
> Mr. Pater writes of the Renaissance as if it were a kind
> of sentimental revolution having no relation to the con-
> ditions of the actual world.[2]

I have quoted this passage at length in order to raise the
question of what we learn about the history of the Renaissance—or about history or the Renaissance—from
Pater's book. Why has Pater chosen to write about Renaissance artists? Do his critical views really have much
to do with the Renaissance at all? Most discussions of
Pater's work attend to its aesthetic rather than its historical implications, and one might well read this book
as a manifesto of aesthetic criticism. Moreover, Pater

published his first essay in 1866, on Coleridge, and his next two essays, published in yearly intervals, were on Winckelmann (which he used as the last chapter of *The Renaissance*) and on the poems of William Morris (the last half of that essay was employed almost without change as the "Conclusion" to *The Renaissance*). Only in 1869, after laying down the gauntlet for a new mode of criticism in these essays, which, in contrast to his later ones, were published anonymously, did he begin to publish the essays on Leonardo, Botticelli, Pico della Mirandola, and Michelangelo that form the kernel of *The Renaissance*.[3]

In order to answer these questions, I want to start by laying out Pater's critical preoccupations and aims, to see how they influence and connect with his interpretation of the Renaissance. One approach would be to contrast Pater's views on art and his use of the Renaissance with that of Matthew Arnold, and especially with that of John Ruskin, the two major critics of the era. In the first sentence of the "Preface" to *The Renaissance* Pater rejects Ruskin's attempts to "define beauty in the abstract, to express it in the most general terms, to find some universal formula for it," and a few sentences later he ironically quotes Arnold's dictum "to see the object as in itself it really is" in order to disparage it with his own twist: "in aesthetic criticism the first step towards seeing one's object as it really is, is to know one's own impression as it really is, to discriminate it, to realise it distinctly."[4] Against these concerns with properly defining and knowing the artwork, Pater shifts his attention to the impressions and pleasures of the critic. Yet rather than using as a point of departure what Pater is *not* doing—not adhering to conventional Victorian notions of history, not engaging in the moral and cultural criticism of Arnold and Ruskin—I want instead to begin at least with an attempt to follow Pater: to "distinguish" the particular virtues of his criticism and to explore his choice of the Renaissance as the period for studying works of art that affect "one with a special, a unique impression of pleasure" (*R* [*The Renaissance*], xx).

In the "Preface" to *The Renaissance,* Pater sets out his idea of aesthetic criticism. He writes that the "objects with which aesthetic criticism deals—music, poetry, artistic and accomplished forms of human life—are indeed receptacles of so many powers or forces" (*R* [*The Renaissance*], xix). I want to highlight this inclusion of "forms of human life" in a list of types of art, since we will see repeatedly a troubling of the distinctions between work and life, object and subject, artist and critic. Pater next says that we should ask of such an object, "How is my nature modified by its presence, and under its influence?" (*R,* xx). The power or force of the artwork then is primarily an ability to "influence." The

aesthetic objects with which Pater concerns himself have not only *had* the capacity to influence later artists, or to affect the broader culture of their time—this would be a more conventional and limited notion of influence—they still have the power to modify the present and to shape our nature. Their "influence" is what still lives on, and they are to be judged according to how they *impress* (in all the senses of this word) the critic.

Pater turns to the Renaissance because the artworks and the artists of the period still have the power to influence (in other words, they are not merely of "antiquarian" interest, of interest only to those who specialize in classifying old objects), and also because he conceives the Renaissance itself as characterized by processes of influence: what Pater studies are instances of undergoing and transmitting influence.[5] Pater asserts that the "Venus" of Botticelli provides "a more direct inlet into the Greek temper than the works of the Greeks themselves," and that "the passion, the energy, the industry of realisation, with which Botticelli carries out his intention, is the exact measure of the legitimate influence over the human mind of the imaginative system of which this is perhaps the central subject" (*R,* 46). Botticelli's passion, energy, and industry are his response to, and a return of, "the Hellenic spirit." The influence of the Greeks is of course a standard topos of the Renaissance, but Pater is less interested in "the Greeks as they really were, of their difference from ourselves, of the aspects of their outward life"—of all that comprises a knowledge of the Greeks—than in the fresh contact with, and the re-experiencing of, what was essential to their "temper." For this purpose, Botticelli offers "a more direct inlet . . . than the works of the Greeks themselves even of the finest period." Pater's Renaissance is a series of inlets.

Giorgione, in contrast, provides a first glimpse into the "essence of what is pictorial in a picture," and is described as the "initiator" of an art striving "towards the perfect identification of matter and form" (*R,* 111). Rather than helping us to become "conscious of what we owe to the Hellenic spirit" (*R,* 46), Giorgione exemplifies a new consciousness about art. Pater writes:

> For the aesthetic philosopher, therefore, over and above the real Giorgione and his authentic extant works, there remains the *Giorgionesque* also—an influence, a spirit, a type in art, active in men so different as those to whom many of his supposed works are really assignable. . . . Giorgione thus becomes a sort of impersonation of Venice itself, its projected reflex or ideal, all that was so intense or desirable in it crystallising about the memory of this wonderful young man.
>
> (*R,* 116-17)[6]

Giorgione provides not simply a new way of painting, or even a new way of seeing, but rather a crystallization and personification of the spirit of the time. Pater resorts to tropes of embodiment to characterize and convey that which Giorgione *transmits* to others. Giorgione, as a "crystal man," enables us to see "a spirit, a type in art," and it is this which lives on, even now when most of his paintings have been attributed to others.[7]

Pater's aesthetic project and his conception of the Renaissance are congruent; each are a probing, an undergoing, and an embodying of influence. The Winckelmann essay, "not incongruous with the studies which precede it" (*R*, xxiv), according to Pater, is therefore crucial, as it offers the opportunity for unifying these dual views of the Renaissance as process and product, as subject and object, as the creation and the reception of art. Winckelmann, a re-discoverer and theorist of Greek art, "reproduces for us the earlier sentiment of the Renaissance" (*R*, 146)—the sentiment of being deeply moved by contact with "the buried fire of ancient art" (*R*, 146)—as he too experiences "a new channel of communion" (*R*, 146) with a prior way of life.

Yet for all the mentions of "influence" throughout *The Renaissance*—and there are dozens—there is little discussion of where these influences ought to lead. We do not get a reworking of Schiller for example (a new conception of *The Aesthetic Education of Man*), nor a depiction of the trajectory that these influences might have on the course of a life.[8] Pater omitted the "Conclusion" from the second edition of *The Renaissance* as he "conceived that it might possibly mislead some of those young men into whose hands it might fall" (*R*, 186). There is a lot to say about this phrase, but I will only add here that Pater, in response to his critics, may fear misleading young men, but he has no plans or directions for leading them.[9] In the "Preface," Pater moves into a vocabulary of education—which we might expect, since education is typically viewed as directing the modification and maturation of our "nature"—but he offers an unusual version: "Our education becomes complete in proportion as our susceptibility to these impressions [impressions of pleasure] increases in depth and variety" (*R*, xx). This is Pater's odd response to notions of *Bildung,* the German idea of formation, cultivation, "the ennoblement of character," education.[10] Education is defined here as the development of susceptibility to impressions, and in art he seeks "impressions of pleasure" rather than "the best that is known and thought in the world," as Matthew Arnold would have it.[11] It is precisely this relation to art—undergoing an influence, susceptibility to impression—that Max Nordau will stigmatize twenty years later as the key traits of "degeneration."[12]

Since what is at issue for Pater is not a consideration of the proper directions that influence ought to take (he does not look to the Renaissance for models to emulate, or for a book of virtues in William Bennett's sense), we need to look at the modes by which influence takes effect, rather than at the ends that are to be achieved. We need to explore the forces that are at work here, rather than question their teleology. Throughout the book, Pater is fascinated by moments of contact and transmission, by possibilities of combination and reconciliation, and especially, by instances of re-vitalization. These moments let us enter into the experiences of others (by breaking the rigid frames of our contemporary world), or they let us bring together that which has been separated by our reified categories of understanding (the body and the intellect, the pagan and the Christian, the strange and the sweet), or they let us explore the borders between the living and the dead, the animated body and the corpse.

I want to suggest that these modes of influence, these powers that can "deeply move" us, are also the primary tropes *of* the Renaissance for Pater. That is, the instances of contact, re-configuration, and transmission which Pater explores in his essays are the defining features of the Renaissance, as well as the means by which these "works of art, and . . . fairer forms of human life" can still modify us, still put us "under [their] influence." Yet I also want to suggest that any congruence between Pater's aesthetic criticism and his understanding of the Renaissance complicates any easy characterization of such notions as connection, unification, and revitalization. In particular, I will therefore examine those instances where the dualities that are unified or reconciled by a vision of the "Renaissance" come into crisis, and where these figures of contact and influence become unstable. For it is these instances which will force us to rethink Pater's Renaissance.

I will first lay out some basic responses to the question of what the powers and "influences" of the Renaissance are for Pater. In the odd opening chapter of the book, **"Two Early French Stories,"** which situates us in France rather than Italy, and in the thirteenth century rather than the fifteenth, Pater retells the fictional stories of Aucassin and Nicolette and of Amis and Amile, as well as the historical story of Abelard and Heloise, and he puts forward several preliminary definitions and basic conceptions about the Renaissance. Pater speaks of "the desire for a more liberal and comely way of conceiving life" (*R*, 1), and this liberality ("assertion of the liberty of the heart" [*R*, 18]) takes the form of connecting things that heretofore have been separated: bringing "into connexion with each other modes of thought and feeling, periods of taste, forms of art and poetry, which the narrowness of men's minds constantly tends to oppose to each other" (*R*, 2). Both the rigidity of abstract systems and the stratification of history into discrete periods are to be overcome by a more antinomian spirit that can encompass the full range of human experience. Pater also states that Abelard:

> prefigures the character of the Renaissance, that movement in which, in various ways, the human mind wins for itself a new kingdom of feeling and sensation and thought, not opposed to but only *beyond* and independent of the spiritual system then actually realised.
>
> (*R*, 5, my emphasis)

The Renaissance is conceived as the possibility of cultural unification and reconciliation, and as a movement beyond the usual constraints and limits. A new vitality is achieved by forging new connections, which unify or go beyond the opposing currents that have narrowed men's minds. Pater writes that "In their search after the pleasures of the senses and the imagination, in their care for beauty, in their worship of the body, people were impelled beyond the bounds of the Christian ideal" (*R*, 18-19), and he offers a fanciful portrait of "the enchanted region of the Renaissance . . . Here are no fixed parties, no exclusions: all breathes of that unity of culture in which 'whatsoever things are comely' are reconciled, for the elevation and adorning of our spirits" (*R*, 20-21). Even the two impulses of "elevation" and "adornment," often at odds with each other in Romantic poetry, are here reconciled. It is such synthetic and typical depictions, with only the occasional odd Paterian twist of conjoining "liberty" and "comely," that lead Bill Readings to claim that "the Renaissance . . . actually took place in the nineteenth century as the nostalgia of Burckhardt, Pater, and Michelet for an originary moment of cultural reunification."[13]

Readings's argument is a powerful one, and he describes nostalgia as seeking "to redeem epistemological uncertainty by recourse to the plenitude of aesthetic sensation."[14] One can find passages throughout Pater's writing to support this claim, and the "Conclusion" to ***The Renaissance*** offers the key example: "analysis leaves off" with "that continual vanishing away, that strange, perpetual, weaving and unweaving of ourselves," and gives way to the insight that "To burn always with this hard, gem-like flame, to maintain this ecstacy, is success in life" (*R*, 188-89). Readings also argues that the history of the university in the nineteenth century "is that of modernity's encounter with culture, where culture is positioned as the mediating resynthesis of knowledges, returning us to the primordial unity and immediacy of a lost origin."[15] In what ways then does the "Renaissance" function for Pater as an originary moment of cultural unification, and as a means for conceiving culture as that which will provide a synthesis of all that has been disassociated and fragmented? And how are we to read all the figures of connection, transmission, vitality, and living on? Are we to read them as signs of nostalgia and as efforts "to redeem epistemological uncertainty by recourse to the plenitude of aesthetic sensation"?

This is certainly one story that could be told, but I want to complicate it with other versions as well. The stories that Pater tells in this opening chapter, the historical tale of Abelard and Heloise, and the fictional ones of Aucassin and Nicolette, and of Amis and Amile, are about unification, perhaps, but the characters are united only in death. Rather than images of plenitude and primordial unity, we get images of separation, cutting, violence, dismemberment, and blood: Amile is re-united with Amis when he beheads his own children and bathes Amis in their blood, and again in death, when his body and coffin are miraculously transported next to that of Amis. The harmony is finally that of two corpses. The most striking moment in Pater's retelling of *Aucassin et Nicolette* is when Aucassin "rides all day through the forest in search of Nicolette, while the thorns tear his flesh, so that one might have traced him by the blood upon the grass," and he "weeps at even-tide because he has not found her" (*R*, 18). The coupling of Abelard and Heloise is less fortunate, and Pater writes that the "opposition into which Abelard is thrown . . . breaks his soul to pieces" (*R*, 6)—to say nothing of his body, castrated by Heloise's relatives. He communicates with Heloise only through letters; they are re-united and re-entombed in 1817, as part of an effort to make the new, out-of-the-way, Père Lachaise cemetery a fashionable place to be buried. Throughout the book we will see instances of Pater's fascination with blood and corpses, and these elements disturb any vision of "that unity of culture in which 'whatsoever things are comely' are reconciled."

I will not take the space to provide a fuller interpretation of Pater's re-telling of these stories; I only want to suggest that there are several currents at work here, and that in reading Pater we need to do more than just look at his definitions of the Renaissance.[16] In other words, when Pater characterizes the Renaissance as bringing "into connexion with each other modes of thought and feeling, periods of taste, forms of art and poetry, which the narrowness of men's minds constantly tend to oppose to each other," we should not interpret these connections simply as processes of unification, of harmony and reconciliation, or even as transporting us beyond fixed oppositions. We are presented with discomforting juxtapositions and violations of boundaries, and what lingers on in these essays are troubled and troubling images (most famously, "The presence that rose thus so strangely beside the waters, is expressive of what in the ways of a thousand years men had come to desire" [*R*, 98]; thus begins Pater's evocation of the Mona Lisa), rather than ones portraying a "unity of culture." Both Pater's view of the Renaissance and his conception of the aesthetic are at stake here: the aesthetic object is often characterized as achieving a form of union—between the particular and the universal, the sensual and the noumenal, the transitory and the permanent, appearance and essence—and we shall see how Pater invokes and also disturbs these conceptions of an aesthetic ideal.

Pater's book hardly has the shape of a conventional narrative, and as I mentioned, several of these essays were first published in journalistic form, and not in the order that they appear when published together. Yet I want to proceed a little longer in following the progression of these essays step by step, and to elaborate further Pater's notions of connection and reconciliation in the Renaissance by looking at the next essay, on **"Pico della Mirandola,"** for there is a definite trajectory to this book.[17] Pater begins the essay on Pico with the statement: "No account of the Renaissance can be complete without some notice of the attempt made by certain Italian scholars of the fifteenth century to reconcile Christianity with the religion of ancient Greece" (**R**, 23). Pater presents a nuanced reading of this attempt, and he differentiates modern scholarly methods with their "historic sense" that emphasizes successive stages of development and "estimates every intellectual creation in its connexion with the age from which it proceeded" (**R**, 26), from the Renaissance forms of interpretations in which the religions of the world were seen "as subsisting side by side," (**R**, 26) and in which interpreters were "thus thrown back upon the quicksand of allegorical interpretation" (**R**, 26).

The project of reconciling, or at least bringing into connection, Christianity and ancient Greece informs much work in the latter half of the nineteenth century (Matthew Arnold's *Culture and Anarchy* is a prime example), but Pater disparages the "possible reconciliation[s]" that Pico arrives at, and he is uninterested in anything that Pico actually has to say about Christianity or ancient Greece.[18] Pater writes: "And yet to read a page of one of Pico's forgotten books is like a glance into one of those ancient sepulchres, upon which the wanderer in classical lands has sometimes stumbled, with the old disused ornaments and furniture of a world wholly unlike ours still fresh in them" (**R**, 31-32). It is hard to distinguish, in this description of the experience of reading Pico's books, between what is sepulchral and what is "fresh"; yet what engages Pater is not the scholarly product, whether sepulchral book or fresh ornament, but the effect "of the attempt made . . . to reconcile Christianity with the religions of ancient Greece" on Pico himself: "This picturesque union of contrasts, belonging properly to the art of the close of the fifteenth century, pervades, in Pico della Mirandola, an

actual person, and that is why the figure of Pico is so attractive" (**R**, 37). Pater repeats this displacement from "work" to "life" several times in the essay: "it is because this life is so perfect a parallel to the attempt made in his writings to reconcile Christianity with the ideas of paganism, that Pico, in spite of the scholastic character of those writings, is really interesting" (**R**, 34). Although Pater actually tells us little of Pico's life, the move from the artifacts that have survived to "the figure of Pico"—the imaginative reconstruction of "an actual [living] person" and of a beautiful appearance (of "a young man fresh from a journey, 'of feature and shape seemly and beauteous'"; [**R**, 28])—is Pater's attempt to make vital again "the spirit of order and beauty in knowledge" (**R**, 38) that has modified Pico's nature, and that in turn may affect our own. Pater states that Pico's "story is a sort of analogue or visible equivalent to the expression of this purpose [the 'reconciliation of the gods of Greece with the Christian religion'] in his writings" (**R**, 27), and Pater's literary portrait, his attempt to render palpable again this "visible equivalent," also aims at re-enacting "the essence of humanism," the belief "that nothing which has ever interested living men and women can wholly lose its vitality" (**R**, 38).

In each of his essays Pater presents a literary portrait of an individual, and it is only through some evocation of the life of the artist that Pater explores the "powers or forces" of the aesthetic object. As Denis Donoghue puts it, speaking for Pater:

> A work of art is an object added to the world, but not merely that; it is the outward sign of a type of life that may be new, an original self-creation. Leonardo, Botticelli, Michelangelo, and Giorgione are names of new types of life. Many forces went into their making, but finally each created himself through these semblances.[19]

In antithesis to Ruskin, for whom an organic community is the true source of great art, it is "strange souls," or "a type of life that may be new," which interest Pater. Yet there is something uncanny about the life of Pico as Pater invokes it: the work is not an "outward mode" that can always be seen "in strict connexion with the spiritual condition which determined it," as Pater writes of Charles Lamb, but an "ancient sepulchre."[20] Pater concludes:

> while his actual work has passed away, yet his own qualities are still active, and himself remains, as one alive in the grave, *caesiis et vigilibus oculis* [his eyes grey, and quick of look], as his biographer describes him, and with that sanguine, clear skin, *decenti rubore interspersa* [intermingled with comely reds], as with the light of morning upon it.
>
> (**R**, 38)

The portrait of Pico, then, is finally of "one alive in the grave"—the life that remains, the vitality of human interests and passions that is "the essence of humanism" and central to the Renaissance, is here framed by the grave (which is figured by "his actual work" that "has passed away," rather than by the death of his body—he is entombed by his own writings!). We might interpret this passage as suggesting that amidst the "death" of Pico's works (their failure to provide a satisfactory solution to the tension between pagan and Christian), there is still available for us the vitality that produced them, the animating spirit that seeks to reconcile the major currents of the time. Yet the vitality of whatever "qualities are still active" from the Renaissance is tinged by decay, and inextricably linked to its own passing: the place of life, where Pico "himself remains," is the home of death. For Pater the *frisson* of pleasure, from Pico, and as we will see more widely, from the Renaissance, comes from "finding the ideal of that youth still red with life in the grave" (*R,* 167), as he writes of Winckelmann. Here, the signs of life are only "that sanguine, clear skin," "intermingled with comely reds"—Pico as he first appeared to Marsilio Ficino, but now haunted by the knowledge that this comely appearance persists only in the words of others.

The reception of the Renaissance for Pater—the effects that it produces, the pleasures that it gives—is always haunted by the knowledge of another time. Pico is for us "alive in the grave," which suggests a disparity between an existential and a temporal mode—he has lived on past his own period. A common figure for this state is of course the vampire, and in the most famous passage of *The Renaissance,* Pater explicitly compares Mona Lisa to a vampire: "She is older than the rocks among which she sits; like the vampire, she has been dead many times, and learned the secrets of the grave" (*R,* 99).[21] It is not only the passage of time since the Renaissance that creates a vampiric existence for what survives from this period: this dual temporality is a key trait of everything that Pater finds there. Near the beginning of the essay on Pico Pater quotes a long passage from Heinrich Heine's "The Gods in Exile," one of his favorite texts, in which the Greek gods are forced to assume disguises and take on odd jobs in order to survive the "triumph of Christianity."[22] They are now "unfortunate emigrants," and Apollo, suspect "on account of his beautiful singing," (*R,* 24) is believed to be a vampire, and the last words Pater quotes are "But they found the grave empty" (*R,* 25) (the villagers had gone to drive a stake through the body of the entombed Apollo, recently executed for being a pagan god). The Renaissance, for Pater, may consist of a rediscovery, even a bringing back to life, of a Greek spirit—"the care for physical beauty, the worship of the body" (*R,* xxii)—but life is now also an experience of exile and estrangement, which no return voyage of Odysseus can

ever overcome. We will need to rethink such ideas as "the worship of the body" under an awareness of exile and displacement; for Pater, it leads to a fascination with sculpted figures, purged of "the commonness of the world" (*R,* 172), and with corpses, drained of "turbid" blood.

In contrast to the two models of historical thinking that Pater has outlined, of viewing the varied beliefs and outlooks of different times "as successive stages in a regular development," or as "subsisting side by side, and substantially in agreement with each other," his essays offer a different experience of history, in which the present is haunted by the past, and by the passing of time and the passage from life to death. The figures that structure these essays—the vampire, the god in exile, the revenant ("a ghost out of another age" [*R,* 71]), the clairvoyant, the specter—all radically confuse the boundaries between historical eras, and between what is living and what has passed on. Pater writes that "we can hardly imagine how deeply the human mind was moved, when, at the Renaissance, in the midst of a frozen world, the buried fire of ancient art rose up from under the soil" (*R,* 146), but the "fire of ancient art" has a different vitality in the modern era, even as it thaws "a frozen world." The song of Apollo may be heard again, but he is now a disguised God, hunted and persecuted for his singing, and no matter what our degree of sympathy, we can only hear this song as displaced from the vital ground of its own soil, and as living beyond the time it recalls.

Michelangelo is described in surprisingly similar terms. Although Pater begins with the standard depiction of "convulsive energy" (*R,* 57), this energy, even when brought to the "creation of life," expresses "mere expectancy and reception," not "a self-contained, independent life," as do the Elgin marbles: "With him the beginning of life has all the characteristics of resurrection; it is like the recovery of suspended health or animation" (*R,* 59).[23] Pater thus speaks of "the impression in him of something flitting and unfixed, of the houseless and complaining spirit, almost clairvoyant through the frail and yielding flesh" (*R,* 69). Neither the era nor the physical body are adequate containers for this "spirit," and Pater states that Michelangelo "lingers on; a *revenant,*" "beyond his time in a world not his own" (*R,* 71). Both the artist and the artwork only problematically embody "a spirit of the age." And as we have seen, whatever vitality remains of Pico's experiences comes to us already framed by its failures, by the passing into desuetude of whatever incarnations its "spirit of order and beauty in knowledge" had achieved.

Pater turns to the life of the artist in each essay in order to provide a subjective medium with which to explore all the thoughts, passions, and tensions of which the work is only "an outward sign," a "semblance" (as Donoghue states, ventriloquizing Pater), and with which to impart to us the powers of influence that it still retains for the receptive critic. Yet for Pater what is influential is precisely what is vampiric: not simply the pleasure, or even the forces, of another era, but these forces as having survived their own displacement, passing, and disembodiment. Any simple harmony of work and life, of "l'homme et l'oeuvre" in Sainte-Beuve's terms, is always already disrupted.

Sainte-Beuve, the dominant mid-nineteenth-century French critic, seeks to explain the work by first understanding the man, and to do this he gathers information about the descent and the family of the writer, about his earliest society and friends, and about the reactions and opinions of all who knew him. He asserts: "Examined in this fashion, restored to its historic frame of time and place, attended by all the circumstances surrounding its birth, each literary work reveals its full meaning, both historical and literary."[24] The man and the work together come out of a specific "milieu," an "historic frame of time and place," and it is this common grounding in a discrete, unified moment that allows the work to be understood as a transparent incarnation of the life. But for Pater, the "milieu" is itself a sedimentation of many times, and the attempt to apply "the true scientific method" as described by Mrs. Pattison, of approaching art and literature "through the life of the time of which it was an outcome," goes awry, since the "life of the time" in the modern era is, for Pater, precisely a life *not* of the time: analysis yields only "a continual vanishing away" (*R*, 188), or "a chain of secret influences" (*R*, 91).

When Pater analyzes Leonardo's portraits, he tells us nothing of the "milieu" or "the life of the time," and insists that these portraits of women "are not of the Christian family, or of Raphael's" (*R*, 91). He describes them instead as "Daughters of Herodias" (the daughter of Herodias of course is Salome, who asks for the beheading of John the Baptist), and as "clairvoyants"[25]:

> They are the clairvoyants, through whom, as through delicate instruments, one becomes aware of the subtler forces of nature, and the modes of their action, all that is magnetic in it, all those finer conditions wherein material things rise to that subtlety of operation which constitutes them spiritual, where only the finer nerve and the keener touch can follow. It is as if in certain significant examples we actually saw those forces at their work on human flesh. Nervous, electric, faint always with some inexplicable faintness, these people seem to be subject to exceptional conditions, to feel powers at work in the common air unfelt by others, to become, as it were, the receptacle of them, and pass them on to us in a chain of secret influences.
>
> (*R*, 91)

This passage echoes and radically reconceptualizes Plato's notion of art in the *Ion*, as a "divine power that moves [us], as a 'Magnetic' stone moves iron rings."[26] In contrast to Plato, there is no origin, no Muse that inspires and possesses the poet, and no endpoint to this chain of iron rings, no final destination in either the spectator or the enthusiast. Rather than a series of individual portraits, or a series of visions of what these clairvoyants have seen, Pater describes the magnetic power of art itself, "all those finer conditions wherein material things rise to that subtlety of operation which constitutes them spiritual." This "magnetic power" provides an undercurrent, an exception to the tides of history and to the dominant families, whether of religion or art. For Pater, Leonardo's portraits are not delimited by the material image or the temporal moment; they do not contain an individual life, and do not follow the "ideal art" of the Greeks, "in which the thought does not outstrip or lie beyond the proper range of its sensible embodiment" (*R*, 165). We see instead "those forces at their work on human flesh." This discomforting, decomposing, disfiguring image re-defines the portrait as both the receptacle, and the vehicle for the passing on, of "powers at work in the common air unfelt by others."

There are many other passages in *The Renaissance* where Pater's insights about art and about the "powers or forces" that live on from this historical period go against Mrs. Pattison's understanding of "the historical element." Pater's essays suggest that following such a "scientific method" would only be to misinterpret the art and literature of the Renaissance, drawing on too simple a notion of "the life of the time" to guide our understanding. Pater's work also points to the difficulty of viewing the Renaissance as "an originary moment of cultural reunification," to use Bill Readings's terms, since the vision of the Renaissance that these essays present is always also vampiric, displaced, and haunted by exile and death. The Renaissance has strong powers of "influence," but that which remains vital, that which is re-born and lives on, is "still active . . . as one alive in the grave." Pater writes: "It has been said that all the great Florentines were pre-occupied with death. *Outre-tombe! Outre-tombe!* is the burden of their thoughts, from Dante to Savonarola" (*R*, 72-73). He asserts that they "must often have leaned over the lifeless body, when all was at length quiet and smoothed out" (*R*, 74), and he writes that "the entombment," for Michelangelo, "is the subject of predilection": "but always as a hopeless, rayless, almost heathen sorrow—no divine sorrow, but mere pity and awe at the stiff limbs and colourless lips" (*R*, 74). Yet how are we to understand Pater's own "predilection," and his own fascination with the Renaissance? I do not want to conclude with the idea that Pater is really so morbid, and that "outre-tombe! outre-tombe!" (this sounds like Chateaubriand) is really the sole burden of his thoughts. Throughout these essays there is an uneasy intertwining of vitality and death, incarnation and disembodiment, heat and cold, pleasure and pain, passion and its sublimation. In the closing essay on Winckelmann, Pater attempts to stabilize these tensions by splitting them into almost separable images of early and modern, pagan life and the German scholar, Greek sculpture and the belated critic.

Pater describes Winckelmann's discovery of Greek sculpture as the pivotal moment in his life:

> And now a new channel of communion with the Greek life was opened for him. Hitherto he had handled the words only of Greek poetry, stirred indeed and roused by them, yet divining beyond the words some unexpressed pulsation of sensuous life. Suddenly he is in contact with that life, still fervent in the relics of plastic art. Filled as our culture is with the classical spirit, we can hardly imagine how deeply the human mind was moved, when, at the Renaissance, in the midst of a frozen world, the buried fire of ancient art rose up from under the soil. Winckelmann here reproduces for us the earlier sentiment of the Renaissance. On a sudden the imagination feels itself free. How facile and direct, it seems to say, is this life of the senses and the understanding, when once we have apprehended it! Here, surely, is that more liberal mode of life we have been seeking so long, so near to us all the while.

> (*R,* 146)

Is what attracts Pater here the "fire," the "pulsation of sensuous life," and a new "life of the senses and the understanding," all represented by the Greeks? Or is he more compelled by the contrast between fire and ice, by the spectacle of "buried fire" rising up from under the soil, and by the contact with relics, with the physical remains of an earlier life? Is Pater hoping to open up a "new channel of communion of Greek life," or does he instead take pleasure in juxtaposition, in an abrupt contact with "the first naïve, unperplexed recognition of man by himself" (*R,* 170), and in the modern world, "with its conflicting claims, its entangled interests, distracted by so many sorrows, with many preoccupations" (*R,* 182)?

I think both the Hellenic and the decadent impulses are everywhere at work in this essay, and it is their interconnection that makes Pater's discussion of sculpture here so intriguing. Pater almost entirely ignores sculpture in *The Renaissance,* discussing the bas-reliefs of Luca della Robbia, and only the poetry of Michelangelo. Greek sculpture offers Pater the opportunity to gaze on the living body, but turned to stone; life and death are united in art. Moreover, sculpture allows Pater

to contemplate the naked male physique, yet without fear of response, and without the uncanniness of gazing at corpses.[27] In this most homoerotic of his essays, Pater describes Greek sculptures as they have come down to us, stripped of color: "That white light, purged from the angry, bloodlike stains of action and passion, reveals, not what is accidental in man, but the tranquil godship in him, as opposed to the restless accidents of life" (*R,* 170). Pater states that Winckelmann's "romantic, fervent friendships with young men," "bringing him into contact with the pride of human form, and staining the thoughts with its bloom, perfected his reconciliation to the spirit of Greek sculpture" (*R,* 152). It is reconciliation which Pater seeks in turn. Greek sculpture purges away the "bloodlike stains," and, according to Pater, frees Winckelmann from "intoxication": "he fingers those pagan marbles with unsinged hands, with no sense of shame or loss. That is to deal with the sensuous side of art in the pagan manner" (*R,* 177). The language here is unconvincing; Pater is neither free from intoxication nor shame; and perhaps this is all the heat that Pater's fingers can bear. The essay on Winckelmann, rather than resolving the tensions that haunt and invigorate Pater's Renaissance, only "reproduces for us the . . . sentiment" of the modern critic.

For Pater, conflict is the condition of modernity, yet he does not seek to evade "so bewildering an experience, the problem of unity with ourselves," through his evocation of Winckelmann. He writes:

> the problem of unity with ourselves, in blitheness and repose, is far harder than it was for the Greek within the simple terms of antique life. Yet, not less than ever, the intellect demands completeness, centrality. It is this which Winckelmann imprints on the imagination of Goethe, at the beginning of life, in its original and simplest form, as in a fragment of Greek art itself, stranded on that littered, indeterminate shore of Germany in the eighteenth century.

> (*R,* 182)

Winckelmann serves as the forerunner for Goethe; imprinting both his reception of earlier powers and forces and his own fragmentation on some later mind. This, too, is finally the influence that Pater seeks to have for some "young men into whose hands [his book] might fall."

*Notes*

1. Throughout this essay, I will be referring to Pater's book simply as *The Renaissance.*

2. Emilia Pattison, "unsigned review in the *Westminster Review,*" in *Walter Pater: The Critical Heritage,* ed. R. M. Seiler (London: Routledge & Kegan Paul, 1980), 71-72.

3. Laurel Brake, in her *Walter Pater* (Plymouth: Northcote House Publishing, 1994), offers further details on Pater's early publishing history:

> Pater's earliest published work appeared in one of the older quarterlies, the Westminster Review, which persisted with anonymity, even in 1866 when anonymity was on the decline in magazine journalism. Between 1866 and 1868 Pater's "Coleridge's Writings," "Winckelmann," and "Poems by William Morris" were all included in its pages as unsigned reviews, for quarterlies normally consisted of essays framed as "reviews" which were linked to the book trade and current publication lists. When in 1869 Pater transferred his work to a new monthly periodical, the Fortnightly Review, he was able to abandon anonymity and reviewing at once, for one of the platforms of the new Fortnightly in 1865 had been the policy of signature. Moreover, although it called itself a review, like the new market of the monthlies it had dispensed with reviews and published free-standing articles.
>
> (16)

4. Walter Pater, *The Renaissance: Studies in Art and Poetry* (1893), ed. Donald L. Hill (Berkeley: Univ. of California Press, 1980), xix. Hereafter cited parenthetically in the text and abbreviated *R*. Donald Hill's scholarly edition, which contains excellent textual and explanatory notes, is based on the 1893 text (the fourth edition), and is the last which Pater revised himself. Hill remarks in his explanatory notes to the opening lines of *The Renaissance*:

> Pater's readers would recall that one of these writers was John Ruskin, who had made elaborate efforts to define beauty in abstract terms, notably in the earlier volumes of *Modern Painters* (1843-60). But this reference would include also the more systematic treatises on aesthetics produced chiefly by German philosophers since the mid-eighteenth century.
>
> (*R*, 294)

Pater's privileging of the Renaissance can also be seen as a rejoinder to Ruskin's enthusiasm for the Gothic, such as in his *The Stones of Venice*.

Arnold's definition of the "critical effort" first appears in "On Translating Homer" (1862), and is taken up again at the beginning of "The Function of Criticism at the Present Time" (1864). Pater's re-phrasing of and response to Arnold has received a great deal of commentary. Denis Donoghue offers one of the best glosses of how these few words reveal the stakes and differences between Arnold and Pater in his *Walter Pater: Lover of Strange Souls* (New York: Knopf, 1995), 123-25. Harold Bloom, in his introduction to his edition of Pater's writings, notes that Oscar Wilde, "attempting to complete his master [Pater], charmingly amended" the phrase to "the primary aim of the critic is to see the object as in itself it really is not" ("Introduction," *Selected Writings of Walter Pater* [New York: Columbia Univ. Press, 1974], viii).

5. Pater often uses the term "antiquarian" disparagingly. In the first essay of *The Renaissance,* "Two Early French Stories," he writes: "Antiquarianism, by a purely historical effort, by putting its object in perspective, and setting the reader in a certain point of view, from which what gave pleasure to the past is pleasurable for him also, may often add greatly to the charm we receive from ancient literature. But the first condition of such aid must be a real, direct, aesthetic charm in the thing itself" (*R,* 14-15). Nietzsche, in *On the Uses and Disadvantages of History for Life* (1874), provides an interesting critique of the "antiquarian" approach to history.

6. The essay "The School of Giorgione" first appeared in the *Fortnightly Review* in 1877, and was included in the third edition of *The Renaissance* in 1888.

7. Pater expounds his notion of the "crystal man" in his early essay "Diaphaneitè," unpublished in his lifetime.

8. Schiller, in contrast to Pater, places aesthetic experience in the service of education, and finally in the service of the State.

9. I have discussed some of Pater's fears of misleading young men, and his explorations, especially in *Marius the Epicurean,* of the future consequences of influences and of the "susceptibility to influence," in my unpublished essay, "Walter Pater's Conversations with the *Fin de siècle.*"

10. In his excellent discussion of *Bildung* in *The University in Ruins,* Bill Readings glosses it as "the ennoblement of character" (*The University in Ruins* [Cambridge: Harvard Univ. Press, 1996], 65).

11. In "The Function of Criticism at the Present Time" Arnold writes: "But criticism, real criticism, is essentially the exercise of this very quality [curiosity]. It obeys an instinct prompting it to try to

know the best that is known and thought in the world, irrespectively of practice, politics, and everything of the kind; and to value knowledge and thought as they approach this best, without the intrusion of any other considerations whatever," Matthew Arnold, *Essays in Criticism,* First Series, ed. Sister Thomas Marion Hoctor (Chicago: Univ. of Chicago Press, 1964), 17. He develops this idea much further in *Culture and Anarchy.*

12. Pater's ideas about the influence of aesthetic impressions are certainly very different from Nordau's, yet they share a common vocabulary, and they also have some similar concerns about the possible effects of these influences. See Nordau's *Degeneration,* intro. George L. Mosee (Lincoln: Univ. of Nebraska Press, 1993).

13. Readings, 169.

14. Readings, 171.

15. Readings, 169.

16. Re-telling stories as a means of exploring their influence and power is one of Pater's favorite modes of narration. It is central to Pater's critical writing, and even more important for the imaginative writing of *Marius the Epicurean* and the "Imaginary Portraits."

17. Within Pater's book, there is a progression from earliness to decadence, from simplicity to complexity, and a probing of loss and belatedness that not only parallels the trajectory of the Renaissance, but that also takes up and develops in greater complexity the critical problems raised in the earlier chapters. It would be possible, and worthwhile, to read *The Renaissance* as an allegory of the development of the aesthetic critic.

18. Pater states that Pico della Mirandola is "an early instance of those who, after following the vain hope of an impossible reconciliation from system to system, have at last fallen back unsatisfied on the simplicities of their childhood's belief" (*R,* 30). Pater also writes that "he wins one on, in spite of one's self, to turn again to the pages of his forgotten books, although we know already that the actual solution proposed in them will satisfy us as little as perhaps it satisfied him" (*R,* 37).

19. Donoghue, 310.

20. Walter Pater, "Charles Lamb" (1878), in *Walter Pater: Three Major Texts (The Renaissance, Appreciations, and Imaginary Portraits),* ed. William E. Buckler (New York: New York Univ. Press, 1986), 463. I discuss further Pater's essay on Lamb, and his practice of literary portraiture, in "Between Text and Image: The Literary Portrait," *a/b: Auto/Biography Studies* 10 (1995): 50-65.

21. A comparison with the writings of Edgar Allan Poe, Bram Stoker, or others in the nineteenth century who blur the line between the living and the dead would not be out of place.

22. There is no evidence of a sense of humor in Pater, which makes his great appreciation for Heine, or at least of this text, all the more striking. In his notes to *The Renaissance* Donald Hill remarks that in the midst of his lengthy quotation, "Pater omits one of Heine's sarcasms: 'als der wahre Herr der Welt sein Kreuzbanner auf die Himmelsburg pflanzte . . .' [when the true lord of the world planted his crusading banner on the castle of heaven]." Hill continues: "Heine's fantasy of the gods in exile took a strong hold on Pater's imagination. He refers to it again and again in later works and carries out aspects of the notion in two stories, 'Denys l'Auxerrois' (1886) and 'Apollo in Picardy' (1893)" (*R,* 322).

23. Pater's ideas are close to Baudelaire's descriptions in "Le Peintre de la Vie Moderne": "Supposez un artiste qui serait toujours, spirituellement, à l'état du convalescent, et vous aurez la clef du caractère de M. G." [Now imagine an artist perpetually in the spiritual condition of the convalescent, and you will have the key to the character of M. G.] (*Curiosités esthétiques, L'Art romantique, et autres Oeuvres critiques,* ed. Henri Lemaitre [Paris: Garnier Frères, 1962], 461). Pater often borrows from Baudelaire without attribution, and passages and ideas from this essay show up elsewhere in his writings.

24. Charles-Augustin Sainte-Beuve, *Literary Criticism of Sainte-Beuve,* ed. and trans. Emerson R. Marks (Lincoln: Univ. of Nebraska Press, 1971), 7.

25. The figure of Salome is extremely popular in the nineteenth century, and appears prominently in the work of Heinrich Heine, Gustave Flaubert, Gustave Moreau, Joris-Karl Huysmans, Stéphane Mallarmé, and Pater's student, Oscar Wilde. Herodias and Salome have sometimes been fused together, such as in Mallarmé's "Hérodiade."

In other passages in *The Renaissance,* it is the artist, Michelangelo or Leonardo, who is described as the clairvoyant, rather than the subject of the portrait. The notion of the clairvoyant troubles any simple conception of agency, in which it would be easy to determine who it is that is seeing clearly. Here are some other references to the clairvoyant. In "The Poetry of Michelangelo," Pater writes: "And this gives the impression in him of something flitting and unfixed, of the houseless and complaining spirit, almost clairvoyant through the frail and yielding flesh" (*R,* 69). While earlier in the "Leonardo" essay, he says: "The science of that age was all divination, clairvoyance, unsubjected to our exact modern formulas, seeking in an instant of vision to concentrate a thousand experiences" (*R,* 83). Finally, in the "Leonardo" essay, Pater notes: "To him philosophy was to be something giving strange swiftness and double sight, divining the sources of springs beneath the earth or of expression beneath the human countenance, clairvoyant of occult gifts in common or uncommon things, in the reed at the brookside, or the star which draws near to us but once in a century" (*R,* 84). Pater's mode of seeing aspires to that of the clairvoyant, "wherein material things rise to that subtlety of operation which constitutes them spiritual."

26. Plato, *Two Comic Dialogues: Ion and Hippias Major,* trans. Paul Woodruff (Indianapolis: Hackett Publishing Company, 1983), 25.

27. In later writings, Pater often mentions gazing at corpses. In "The Child in the House," (in *Walter Pater: Three Major Texts*) his somewhat autobiographical, first "imaginary portrait" he writes: "For with this desire of physical beauty mingled itself early the fear of death—the fear of death intensified by the desire of beauty. Hitherto he had never gazed upon dead faces, as sometimes, afterwards, at the *Morgue* in Paris, or in that fair cemetery at Munich, where all the dead must go and lie in state before burial, behind glass windows, among the flowers and incense and holy candles—the aged clergy with their sacred ornaments, the young men in their dancing-shoes and spotless white linen—after which visits, those waxen, restless faces would always live with him for many days, making the broadest sunshine sickly" (233).

## J. B. Bullen (essay date 1999)

SOURCE: Bullen, J. B. "Pater, Mill, Mansel and the Context of the Conclusion to *The Renaissance.*" *Nineteenth-Century Contexts* 21, no. 1 (1999): 1-15.

[*In the following essay, Bullen evaluates the relationship between Pater's "Conclusion" and the prevailing intellectual climate of his age. Bullen argues that Pater's conception of subjective human experience, and of the prerogative of human beings to pursue a life of pure aesthetic pleasure, represents a radical, and in many respects incendiary, departure from the dominant spiritual and moral tenets of his day.*]

The "Conclusion" to Pater's *Renaissance*—rightly described by Linda Dowling as "that most disturbing and invigorating passage of all his prose"[1]—has attracted, Donald Hill tells us, "more attention than any of Pater's other writings over the past hundred years."[2] That "attention" has taken many forms, ranging from George Eliot's famous denunciation of its "false principles of criticism and false conceptions of life"[3] to Billie Inman's detailed analysis of the "intellectual context" which determined Pater's reading in the 1860s.[4]

In the early years, criticism of Pater focused on what appeared to be his doctrines of selfishness and self-cultivation. In the 1870s, the Oxford pulpits rang to sermons preached against his "poor philosophy of life which would concentrate all efforts upon self"[5] and his "lack of self restraint and self sacrifice,"[6] while in the press Margaret Oliphant and others inveighed against his "grand pursuit of self culture."[7] Modern critics have concentrated on the Conclusion as one of the founding texts of aestheticism, and writers from Geoffrey Tillotson to Germain d'Hangest have stressed its "essential and decisive role" in the Aesthetic Movement.[8] More recently, Carolyn Williams remarked that it is his most "controversial piece" and the one which "inaugurated the career of public notoriety which he both invited and evaded,"[9] and when Billie Inman prised open the text to discover reminiscences, echoes and reminders of Goethe, Renan, Fichte, Hume, Spencer, Tyndall, Hegel, Aristippus, Plato, Morris, and Baudelaire lurking "beneath the surface"[10] of the Conclusion, one might have thought that the last word had been said about the nature of that notoriety. Yet even now something might be added to explain why Pater seemed such a provocative writer in the 1870s.

It has been the fate of the Conclusion to be treated in isolation from its context. It was first published anonymously in 1868 as the last quarter of what was ostensibly a review of William Morris's poetry and was then printed as the last section of the set of essays on Renaissance subjects. Early critics, scandalised by its profligate hedonism, were blinded to its philosophical force, and later critics, amazed by its originality, saw in it the beginnings of a whole wave of aesthetic writing. Neither group, however, reflected much upon the significance of what Pater has to say about Morris, nor what the poetry of Morris has in common with Pater's notion of the Renaissance. Furthermore, Billie Inman, for all her remarkable industry, in focusing on local effects and influences, has missed the most immediate and significant philosophical source for Pater's ideas. Carolyn Williams in her minute deconstruction of the Conclusion rightly notices that the second paragraph "falls squarely in the philosophical tradition of Johnson kicking a rock to prove Berkeley wrong."[11] But in common with other scholars, she has overlooked Pater's contribution to a now forgotten, but much more recent and extremely contentious, debate which was disturbing not only the quiet world of Oxford academic life, but whose clamour reached even as far as Russia.

The questions which Pater addresses in the Conclusion are: what does philosophy and science tell us of the nature of sentient experience, and how does art, the most graphic record of sentient experience, enable us to reflect more clearly upon it? In both the Morris review and *The Renaissance* Pater proceeds from his analysis of works of art and literature to the philosophical implications of that analysis, and in both pieces he makes a transition from art to what he calls "the sad-coloured world of abstract philosophy."[12] But when Pater asks his readers to "see what modern philosophy" has to say about the nature of consciousness he is entering territory which was certainly familiar to many of those readers and which had been already been explored, as Peter Dale points out, by a number of the leading intellectuals of the period.[13]

The issue as to whether consciousness is a purely material phenomenon, or whether our understanding of the external world is merely an illusion of consciousness goes back to Plato's cave and beyond, but it was reanimated in the mid-nineteenth century by two key texts—J. H. Mansel's Bampton Lectures of 1858, entitled *The Limits of Religious Thought,* and John Stuart Mill's *An Examination of Sir William Hamilton's Philosophy* published in 1865.

Mansel, the Waynflete Professor of Moral and Metaphysical Philosophy at Oxford was a neo-Kantian and follower of Sir William Hamilton, whose life-long effort was to reconcile the ideas of moral philosophy with those of revealed religion. Much of the substance both of his Bampton Lectures and of his book, *Metaphysics* (significantly subtitled *The Philosophy of Consciousness, Phenomenal and Real*) of 1860, was devoted to the question: "Does there exist in the human mind any direct faculty of religious knowledge, by which . . . we are enabled to decide what is the true nature of God and the manner in which He must manifest Himself to the world?"[14] Like Hamilton before him, Mansel concluded that the human mind was able to accommodate only what Kant called phenomena, and that noumena were finally inaccessible to it. It was in this latter realm, the realm of the ideal, the infinite or what Hamilton

called the "Unconditioned" that God resided. "This doctrine" said Mansel, "brings Ontology into contact with Theology; and it is only in relation to theology that ontology acquires a practical importance."[15] The seriousness of deciding upon the exact limits of our sensory perception was given added *gravitas* because, he claimed, "it is possible . . . to make the relation between the human mind and its objects the type and image of that between the universe and its first principle."[16] Summing up his own position within philosophical theology from St Augustine onwards Mansel said: "We believe that God in His own nature is absolute and unconditioned; but we can only positively conceive Him by means of relations and conditions suggested by created things." Like Hamilton before him he concluded that "the Unconditioned is incognisable and inconceivable" by the rational human mind and was comprehended only through revelation, faith, and intuition.[17]

Mansel's conclusions were seized upon with delight by his opponents amongst sceptics and free-thinkers. "Never was an amiable and intelligent divine," wrote the philosopher W. H. Smith, "betrayed by his own ingenuity, and the energy of argument, into an error more patent or more to be regreted."[18] Herbert Spencer's *First Principles* (1862) paid ironic tribute to Hamilton and Mansel in underlining the fact that the absolute is inconceivable to the intellect; the same ideas lent retrospective support to work of the psychologist Alexander Bain, whose *The Senses and the Intellect* of 1855 had already promulgated an exclusively material basis for human experience, but above all, it led John Stuart Mill to mount a combined attack on both Hamilton and Mansel from a materialist and empiricist view in his notoriously icono-clastic *Examination of Sir William Hamilton's Philosophy.*

Where Hamilton and Mansel stressed the absolute and the Unconditioned, Mill stressed the empirical and the relative. The words with which Pater opened his Conclusion: "To regard all things and principles of things as inconstant modes or fashions has more and more become the tendency of modern thought"[19] is certainly a reference to what Mill called the doctrine of "The Relativity of Human Knowledge." Pater had already engaged with this issue in his essay on Coleridge where, in his first published words, he pointed out that "modern thought is distinguished from ancient by its cultivation of the 'relative' spirit in place of the 'absolute.'" "To the modern spirit," he added, "nothing is, or can be rightly known, except relatively and under conditions."[20] For Mill, the Relativity of Human Knowledge meant that "an object is to us nothing else than that which affects our senses in a certain manner . . . that even an imaginary object is but a conception . . . so that our knowledge of objects, and even our fancies about objects, consist of nothing but the sensations which they excite, or which we imagine them exciting, in ourselves."[21]

What had happened in the 1850s and 1860s was that scientific investigation had reanimated the debate about the limits of sensory experience in such a way that the findings of what was early psychology opened up discussions of a moral and metaphysical nature. As Pater himself put it in **"Coleridge's Writings"**: "The moral world is ever in contact with the physical; [and] the relative spirit has invaded moral philosophy from the ground of the inductive sciences."[22] In this way Pater wrote as one in a long line of thinkers, all of them concerned with the world, as he put it, "not of objects" but of "impressions, unstable, flickering, [and] inconsistent."[23]

Thus in their different ways, Herbert Spencer and Alexander Bain, the historian George Grote, the alienist, Henry Maudsley, the philosophers Mark Pattison, James McCosh, and William Henry Smith together with many others in the 1860s were concerned with the problem about the way in which the evidence of our senses bore upon our belief in God and the moral consequences of the belief. It was Mill's work, however, which served to polarise attitudes. Having established to his own satisfaction "the entire inaccessibility to our faculties of any other knowledge of Things than that of the impressions which they produced in our mental consciousness,"[24] Mill went on to ask "Have we, or have we not, an immediate intuition of God [?]" "The name of God is veiled," he went on, "under two extremely abstract phrases, "The Infinite" and "The Absolute," perhaps from a reverential feeling: such, at least, is the reason given by Sir William Hamilton's disciple, Mr. Mansel, for preferring the more vague expression."[25]

The controversy that surrounded the "two philosophies" as David Masson called them at the time,[26] were as much political as they were intellectual or theological, with conservative Churchmen taking the high ground of metaphysics and intuitionism alongside Mansel, and the sceptics and radicals siding with Mill. Pater's friend Mark Pattison, the rector of Lincoln College, was a free-thinker and bitter enemy of Mansel, and in an article published in *The Reader* of 1865, he was one of the first to welcome the demise of what he described as moribund theologism. On his side, Mansel was supported by James McCosh in his book *In Defence of Fundamental Truth* of 1866, in which McCosh attacked Mill for what he called his "Humeanism and Comtism"—a snide reference to his atheism and dubious French politics. Mansel himself came back at Mill in a long and important article entitled *The Philosophy of the Conditioned* also published in 1866.

In *The Philosophy of the Conditioned* Mansel set out two of the current positions on the nature of consciousness with which he was in conflict—what he called "Materialism" and "Idealism." "Mr Mill," he said, "is one of the most distinguished representatives of that school of Materialism which Sir W. Hamilton denounced as virtual Atheism,"[27] and Mansel's explanation of the two positions closely resembles Pater's succinct account of the two views of the mind/body relations in the Conclusion. Mansel writes; "Either the *ego* may be represented as a mode of the *non-ego*, or the *non-ego* of the *ego* . . . In other words: it may be maintained, *first*, that matter is the only real existence; mind and all the phenomena of consciousness being really the result solely of material laws; the brain, for example, secreting thought as the liver secretes bile; and the distinct personal existence of which I am apparently conscious being only the result of some such secretion."[28] Which Pater renders in the form of the question: "What is the whole physical life . . . but a combination of natural elements to which science gives their names? . . . Our physical life is a perpetual motion of them . . . processes which science reduces to simpler and more elementary forces."[29] Mansell then describes what he calls "Idealism" where the "mind is the only real existence; the intercourse which we apparently have with a material world being really the result solely of the laws of our mental constitution,"[30] which becomes in Pater "the inward world of thought and feeling . . . the race of the midstream, a drift of momentary acts of sight and passion and thought." "At first sight," Pater continues, "experience seems to bury us under a flood of external objects, pressing upon us with a sharp, and importunate reality,"[31] a form of scepticism which, said Mansel, "makes man the slave and not the master of nature; passively carried along in the current of successive phenomena; unable, by any act of free will, to arrest a single wave in its course . . ."[32]

This debate was no local skirmish, and by the time that *The Renaissance* was published in 1873 the controversy about the limits of consciousness had spread throughout Europe and beyond. Indeed such common currency had it become that Tolstoy mentions it in *Anna Karenina* which appeared in 1875. Sergey Ivanovitch, Levin's brother, responding to the remarks of a well-known Professor of philosophy who had come from Harkov expressly to clear up a difference that had arisen between them says:

> "I cannot admit . . . that my whole eonception of the external world has been derived from perceptions."

> "Yes," replies the Professor, "but they—Wurt, and Knaust, and Pripasov—would answer that your consciousness of existence is derived from the conjunctions of all your sensations, that that consciousness of

existence is the result of your sensations. Wurt, indeed, says plainly that assuming there are no sensations, it follows that there is no idea of existence."[33]

Like most of his contemporaries, Levin, who has been listening to this exchange is most concerned about its metaphysical implications. He "noticed that they connected these scientific questions with those spiritual problems, that at times they almost touched on the latter."[34]

Back in England the disagreement between Mansel's party and Mill's party also focused most intensely on what Levin called "spiritual problems." The issue of how we understand the world was rather an academic one; the problem of how we have knowledge of God was much more immediate. So from Moscow to Oxford the question remained, how, by means of the limited nature of sensory experience do we comprehend the numinous, and how through those same senses, we are able to understand the purposes of the Almighty? At this point the vexed issue of morality entered in. W. H. Smith summarised the problem thus: "Mr Mansel has unhappily said the moral attributes of God do, or may, differ from those of man, not in *degree* only but in *kind,* leaving the human reason (in the face of any assertion made of God) without any guidance whatever. Into this unhappiness the metaphysics of the Oxford preacher has beguiled him. . . . If goodness in God is not what we call goodness, we are left without any power of estimating and *feeling* the moral attributes of God—without any power of framing for ourselves, or understanding when revealed, a conception worthy of our worship."[35] Mill pounced upon Mansel's idea that since God is unknowable, there is no necessary conjunction between Divine and human morality. "If in ascribing goodness to God I do not mean what I mean by goodness," he asked, "what do I mean by calling it goodness? and what reason have I for venerating it?" "Whatever power such a being may have over me," he went on, "there is one thing which he shall not do: he shall not compel me to worship him. I will call no being good, who is not what I mean when I apply that epithet to my fellow creatures; and if such a being can sentence me to hell for not so calling him, to hell I will go."[36]

Intelligent readers of the 1860s sensitised to attacks on religious orthodoxy by writers as diverse as Lyell, Darwin, and Jowett, would have detected in Mill's attack on Hamilton another blow—this time from the ground of philosophy. But Mill's attack was two-fold. He pointed up not only the contradictions into which contemporary theology had fallen about man's access to any understanding of God, but he also questioned the validity of a moral code which was derived from such

religious beliefs. Pater's audience, too, would have recognised where he stood in this debate. Believing that metaphysical questions were, as he put it, "unprofitable"[37] the whole issue of the existence of God is conspicuously absent from his argument—an absence easily overlooked by the modern reader who might well fail to read Pater's accounts of Materialism and Idealism in terms of its theological context. But Pater both ironises and aestheticises the impact of science on "modern philosophy." In contrast to the carefully structured logical prose of Mill or Mansel, Pater's language is terse, dense, and image laden. His rendition of the "outer world" and the "inner world" as perceived through the eyes of modern philosophy is not a summary or a precis; it is, instead, an impression rather than an argument (as Hardy once wrote); it is a moving metaphorical, lyrical and aesthetic evocation of a problem which half-accepts the premises, while distancing the conclusions. "With this sense of the splendour of our experience," he wrote, "and of its awful brevity, gathering all we are into one desperate effort to see and touch, we shall hardly have time to make theories about the things we see and touch" and rounding on his philosophical and theological contemporaries, claims that "the theory of idea or system which required of us the sacrifice of any part of this experience . . . has no real claim upon us."[38] But Pater moves in a direction neither touched upon, nor contemplated either by Mansell or Mill and in doing so intensifies his heresy. For Pater, it is not God and his nature that is the highest object which our senses can contemplate, for God is absent from his discussion. His place is taken by aesthetic experience and by art. Indeed, it is not our knowledge or ignorance of the numinous, so critical to Mill and Mansel, that preoccupies Pater, it is art, and it is not God which gives meaning and definition to our conscious life, it is, instead, the "quickened, multiplied consciousness," as he puts it, achieved through the contemplation of works of art.

The offence given by Pater's **Renaissance** as Mrs Humphrey Ward accurately pointed out was "its entire aloofness from the Christian tradition of Oxford [and] its glorification of the higher and intenser forms of aesthetic pleasure."[39] Pater's originality was to argue his case, not like Mill and Mansel in abstract or logical terms, but in a form of language which enacted its own conclusions—a species of "aesthetic poetry"—and to deflect the tendency of that argument away from the "unprofitable" area of metaphysics and towards that most powerful, immediate repository of human sentient experience—art.

One of those much involved with the Mill/Mansel controversy was the famous proto-psychiatrist Henry Maudsley, and in a chapter entitled "On the Method and Study of the Mind" in his book *The Physiology and Pathology of the Mind* (1867) Maudsley suggests that the examples of history might be of importance in constructing what he calls "a positive mental science." He says that, "freed from the many disturbing conditions which interfere so much with his observation of the individual, the philosopher may perhaps in history discover the laws of human progress in their generality and simplicity."[40] Though Maudsley had neither the knowledge nor the skill to do this, Pater had, and in his essay on Morris he integrates art and history by contrasting the two modes of Morris's "aesthetic poetry" in the context of a historical framework in order to furnish a wider theory of the development of consciousness. As Carolyn Williams so luminously puts it: "In Pater, the 'aesthetic' is generated as a distinctly historical phenomenon."[41]

On the one hand there is the mode which Morris adopts in *The Defence of Guenevere* and which Pater links to the poetry of medieval France; on the other hand there is the mode which he adopts in *The Life and Death of Jason* and *The Earthly Paradise* which Pater likens to the fifteenth-century rediscovery of the classical past. Pater's approach to Morris's poetry is less literary than phenomenological. He interprets Morris's style as two independent mental states, each of which he expresses as a relationship between the mind and the economy and the erotics of the sentient body.[42]

Morris's title poem, *The Defence of Guenevere*, he writes, is "a thing tormented and awry with passion, like the body of Guenevere defending herself from the charge of adultery."[43] This he likens to the erotic religion of the middle ages, with its "hundred sensuous images" and its "choice" between "Christ and a rival lover." But Morris's poetry, like Provençal verse, expresses a kind of mental erotic "idolatory" into which "earthly love enters" but as a guilty extramarital perverse passion full of "chastisement" and "reconciliation."[44] The feeling of "wild, convulsed sensuousness" in medieval poetry is replicated, Pater claims, in the earlier work of Morris, whose poems he categorises in terms of a delirious mind infected with bodily states of disease and disorder. The colouring of "King Arthur's Tomb," he writes, is "feverish" and "delirious" suggestive of a "poison in one's blood," and the "sickening of life and all things." "Galahad" acts as a "strong narcotic," and in the "Blue Closet," "delirium reaches its height." Like the poetry of the middle ages, says Pater, the poems that comprise *The Defence of Guenevere* are "wild," "convulsed" and sensuous; they are characterised by "reverie, illusion, delirium," and they represent, he says, "a beautiful disease or disorder of the senses."[45]

In contrast *The Life and Death of Jason* resembles, for Pater, the healthy waking after a night of fever: a return to the life of the body and mental recruitment after diseased sleep. It is a shift from the complex and convoluted to the simple—the "simple elementary passions, anger, desire, regret, pity and fear" and what corresponds to them in the sensuous world, "bare, abstract fire, water, air, tears, sleep, silence."[46] The change of style, he says, resembles a reaction from dreamlight to daylight—a species of enlightenment; it is the "surprise" of "people first waking from the golden age, at fire, snow, wine, the touch of water as one swims, the salt taste of the sea."[47] The erotic is located now, not in the world of guilt, sin, and shame but in the open acceptance of bodily desire. "Desire," he says, "here is towards the body of nature for its own sake, not because a soul is divined through it.

As Pater describes it Morris's style has undergone a transformation similar to that experienced by the artists and writers of the early Renaissance. The "reaction from dreamlight to daylight" is important, Pater claims, "not merely for the sake of the individual poet . . . but chiefly because it explains through him a transition which, under many forms, is one law of the life of the human spirit, and of which what we call the Renaissance is only a supreme instance."[48]

For Pater the Renaissance is not a period, it is a state of consciousness and its principal record is to be found in works of art. In this sense he has historicised and aestheticised a debate about the status of consciousness which had been going on at least since Mansel's Bampton Lectures of 1858. He has also eroticised and embodied it. In the debate between Mansel and Mill, consciousness was experienced exclusively as a series of mental acts, and in their discussions the body functions as a lay figure, a mere adjunct, a conduit of sensation between phenomena and mind; for Pater consciousness is a transaction between mind and body, and is as much corporeal as it is mental. Pater expanded upon this in the first essay of **The Renaissance** when, in a passage of remarkable explicitness, he identified his own agenda with that of the antinomianism of the early Renaissance poets, and their "spirit of rebellion and revolt against the moral and religious ideas of the time." "In their search after the pleasures of the senses and the imagination," he wrote, "in their care for beauty, in *their worship of the body,* people were impelled beyond the bounds of the Christian ideal; and their love became sometimes a strange idolatry, a strange rival religion."[49]

As Carolyn Williams puts it, "Pater has characterized "modern thought" and the "medieval mind" as suffering from the same problem and needing the same "sense of escape" that aesthetic poetry provides," and she adds that there exists a "homology between the dialectic of self-consciousness and [Pater's] strategies for representing history."[50] In the metonymic relationship between Morris's poetry and the development of consciousness Pater outlines a programme for himself and his contemporaries faced with the dilemma posed by the current tendencies of science and metaphysics.

In Pater's review of Morris we can see very clearly the germs of *Studies in the History of the Renaissance,* and we can see, too, the explosive nature of its subsequent development. First he suppressed the highly charged material on Morris, and published it many years later in the first edition of *Appreciations* in 1889. But even then it was too hot to handle and he removed it from subsequent editions. But the sentiments remained, masked as "history" and distributed through a series of Renaissance studies which, involving strange unorthodox loves, beautiful men and boys, emerging fully developed in the Greek passion of Winckelmann. But "Greekness" as Linda Dowling has shown, took many forms in the late nineteenth century from Mill's to Arnold's and Jowett's to Symonds'. The most threatening was, of course, the homo-erotic version, and when reviewers such as the anonymous "Z" in *The Examiner* linked Pater's Conclusion with Aristippus's Cyrenianism we are approaching the point of enthroning "delirious debauchery in the seat of virtue."[51]

The true nature of Pater's offence in the eyes of his early readers is now a little clearer. In drawing directly on "what modern philosophy, when it is sincere, really does say about human life" Pater is closer to Mill and the freethinkers than to his colleagues the Oxford theologians. But the philosophical evidence is frighteningly solipsistic reducing life to a neo-medieval "disease or disorder of the senses." So to the young men whom he projects as his audience Pater offers, instead, the Renaissance model, with its love of art, its "great passions," its "ecstasy and sorrow of love," its Greekness and its "worship of the body." In this way, Mill and his controversy with Hamilton and Mansel offered Pater a point of departure. Since God was "unknowable," and orthodox morality based upon shaky foundations, our pulsations were all that remained to us. In this way Pater was able to theorise and justify first his reading of Morris's poetry and then the findings of his Renaissance essays in terms which prioratised the life of the body expressed in art. Art, for Pater, was erotic in a way in which it was erotic for Rossetti, Swinburne, or Simeon Solomon, so when contemporary theologians described Pater's "attempt to destroy the moral and religious basis of character"[52] perhaps they were being less hysterical than we, at this distance, might think.

### Notes

1. Dowling, Linda, *Hellenism and Homosexuality in Victorian Oxford* (Ithaca, 1993), p. 98.

2. Pater, Walter, *The Renaissance: Studies in Art and Poetry,* Ed. Donald L. Hill (Berkeley, 1980), p. 450. Henceforth cited as *The Renaissance.*

3. *The George Eliot Letters,* Ed. Gordon S. Haight (New Haven and London, 1955), 5, 455.

4. Inman, Billie Andrew, "The Intellectual Context of Pater's 'Conclusion,'" in P. Dodd (Ed.), *Walter Pater: An Imaginative Sense of Fact* (London, 1981), pp. 12-30.

5. W. W. Capes, *Oxford Undergraduates' Journal* (November, 1873), pp. 98-99.

6. Mackernass, John Fielder, Bishop of Oxford, *A Charge Delivered to the Clergy of Oxford . . . in the Cathedral Church of Christchurch, April 20, 1875* (Oxford, 1875), p. 15.

7. Margaret Oliphant, "Pater's History of the Renaissance," *Blackwoods Magazine,* 114 (1873), 605.

8. Geoffrey Tillotson, "Pater, Mr. Rose and the 'Conclusion' of *The Renaissance,*" *Essays and Studies by Members of the English Association, 1946,* 32 (Oxford, 1947), 44-60 and Germain, d'Hangest, 'La Place de Walter Pater dans le Movement Esthétique', *Etudes Anglaises,* 27 (1947), 160.

9. Carolyn Williams, *Transfigured World: Walter Pater's Aesthetic Historicism* (Ithica, 1989), p. 11.

10. Inman (1981), p. 28.

11. Williams (1989), p. 21. She mentions, in passing, (p. 51n) Mill's *An Examination of Sir William Hamilton's Philosophy* but does not discuss its wider impact on Pater's Conclusion.

12. Walter Pater, "Poems by William Morris," *Westminster Review,* NS 34 (1868), 309. Henceforth cited as "William Morris."

13. Peter Allan Dale, *The Victorian Critic and the Idea of History: Carlyle, Arnold, Pater* (Cambridge Mass, 1977), pp. 174-76. Dale in pointing out that the doctrine of the relativity of human knowledge was one of the cornerstones of empiricism, is one of the few critics to recognise the importance of Mill's work for Pater.

14. H. L. Mansel, *The Limits of Religious Thought: The Bampton Lectures* (1858; 4th edn., 1859), p. xliii.

15. H. L. Mansel, "The Philosophy of the Conditioned: Sir William Hamilton and John Stuart Mill—Part 1," *Contemporary Review,* 1 (1866), 192.

16. Ibid., p. 33.

17. Ibid., p. 33.

18. W. H. Smith, "J. S. Mill on our Belief in the External World," *Blackwoods Magazine*, 99 (1866), 24.

19. "William Morris," pp. 309-10.

20. Pater, "Coleridge's Writings," *Westminster Review*, NS 29 (1866), 107.

21. John Stuart Mill, *An Examination of Sir William Hamilton's Philosophy*, ed. J. M. Robson, in *The Collected Works of John Stuart Mill* (Toronto, 1979), ix, 6. Henceforth cited as *An Examination*.

22. "Coleridge's Writings," p. 107.

23. "William Morris," p. 310.

24. *An Examination*, p. 10.

25. Ibid., p. 34.

26. David Masson in *Recent British Philosophy* (1865).

27. H. L. Mansel, "The Philosophy of the Conditioned," p. 47.

28. Ibid., p. 33.

29. "William Morris," p. 310.

30. "The Philosophy of the Conditioned," p. 33.

31. "William Morris," p. 310.

32. "The Philosophy of the Conditioned," p. 48.

33. Leo Tolstoy, *Anna Karenina* trans. Constance Garnett (New York, 1950), Chap. 7, p. 31.

34. *Anna Karenina*, pp. 30-1.

35. Smith, "J. S. Mill," p. 24.

36. *An Examination*, p. 102 and p. 103.

37. *The Renaissance*, p. xx.

38. "William Morris," p. 312.

39. Mrs. Humphry Ward, *A Writer's Recollections* (London, 1918), 1, 161.

40. Henry Maudsley, *The Physiology and Pathology of the Mind* (1867), p. 28.

41. Williams (1989), p. 59.

42. Pater's unusual treatment of these poems is pointed up by comparison with Swinburne's exclusively linguistic and technical treatment of the same works in the previous year. Swinburne is interested in what he calls "the descriptive and decorative beauties" of the verse; it is essentially literary criticism, the poet reading the work of another poet. See: Swinburne, "Morris's 'Life and Death of Jason,'" *Fortnightly Review*, 8 (1867), 19-28.

43. "William Morris," p. 301.

44. Ibid., pp. 301-2.

45. Ibid., p. 302.

46. Ibid., p. 305.

47. Ibid., p. 306.

48. Ibid., p. 305.

49. *The Renaissance*, pp. 18-19. My emphasis.

50. Williams (1989), p. 66 and p. 68.

51. Z, "Modern Cyrenaicism," *Examiner*, 12 April, 1873. Reprinted in *Walter Pater: The Critical Heritage*, Ed. Robert M. Seiler (1980), p. 75.

52. William W. Jackson, *Ingram Bywater: The Memoir of an Oxford Scholar, 1840-1914* (London, 1917), p. 77.

## David Carrier (essay date spring 2001)

SOURCE: Carrier, David. "Walter Pater's 'Winkelmann.'" *The Journal of Aesthetic Education* 35, no. 1 (spring 2001): 99-109.

[*In the following essay, Carrier offers a close reading of Pater's essay on the German art historian Johann Joachim Winckelmann. Carrier draws numerous parallels between Pater and the philosopher Alexander Nehamas, notably the notion that philosophical beliefs are inextricably linked to an author's literary style and that this unity is what provides the most compelling portrayal of a subject.*]

"We're condemned to be interpreters."

Alexander Nehamas[1]

In his recent book, *The Art of Living: Socratic Reflections from Plato to Foucault*, Alexander Nehamas presents an original provocative argument. He contrasts two conceptions of philosophy—philosophy as a theoretical discipline concerned to offer arguments; and the interest of Socrates, Montaigne, and also (so he argues) Nietzsche and Foucault in the art of living. "The philosophers of the art of living . . . consider the self to be not a given but a constructed unity. . . . When the work is finished . . . the elements that constitute the individual produced are all part of an orderly, organized whole" (*AL*, 4).[2] Building on his *Nietzsche: Life as Lit-*

*erature,* Nehamas claims that constructing a self is both "a literary and philosophical accomplishment" (*AL,* 2-3). It is a philosophical accomplishment because it requires holding views about philosophical issues. And it is a literary accomplishment "because the connection between those philosophical views is not only a matter of systematic logical interrelations but also, more centrally, a matter of style" (*AL,* 3).

I want to test Nehamas's claims by applying them to a writer he does not discuss in *The Art of Living.* Walter Pater's **"Winckelmann,"** the last essay in his ***The Renaissance,*** sets the life of Johann Joachim Winckelmann in an account of the rebirth of antiquity in France and Italy.[3] Pater develops views about philosophical issues using a literary structure I will reconstruct. As there is currently great interest in Pater's work, Nehamas's argument offers an original way of understanding that writer's arguments.

What separates Nehamas from his colleagues who treat philosophy as a theoretical discipline is concern for the literary dimensions of expression of philosophical ideas. Do philosophers make claims that can be paraphrased? If so, then literary style in philosophy is merely an embellishment. Alternatively, does the way in which a writer's claims are presented unavoidably influence our evaluation of that argument? How we answer these questions tells what importance we give to style. Pater's view is that philosophical and literary concerns are inextricably bound together. Like Nehamas, he is a philosopher interested in the art of living.

Here I do a close reading of part of **"Winckelmann."** My analysis is best read alongside Pater's text. Much can be learned in this way.

Does Winckelmann, a historian of classical antiquity, belong in ***The Renaissance***? "It was a blunder on the part of Walter Pater to include a chapter on Winckelmann in his work on the Renaissance. Winckelmann's study of Greek art was not at all like that of Renaissance scholars."[4] True enough—but Pater argues that although Winckelmann was an eighteenth-century art historian, "by his Hellenism, his life-long struggle to attain to the Greek spirit, he is in sympathy with the humanists of the previous century" (***TR*** [***The Renaissance***], xxv). Pater uses his sources—Renaissance painting and poetry, English and German aesthetic theory and creative writing, and Winckelmann's writings—in highly complex ways.[5] Working without footnotes, he borrows from, sometimes misquotes, and usually transforms earlier accounts. Concerned here only with the implications of Pater's argument, I say little about how he handles the writings of Goethe and Hegel; nor do I discuss the adequacy of his account of Greek sculpture.[6] Read in relation to *The Art of Living,* Pater's essay poses deep, as yet unresolved questions about the nature of aesthetic experience. His analysis, purporting to deal with historical issues, speaks to our concerns.

An apt epigraph concisely characterizes the text it introduces—telling us what attitude to take toward its argument. It is natural to imagine the epigraph of **"Winckelmann,"** *Et ego in Arcadia fui,* spoken by the man the essay is about (*TR,* 141; printed in italics directly under the title). After a difficult youth in Germany, Winckelmann managed to live in his ideal world, Italy, immersed in his favored activity, the study of antique art. He thus might have said, "I too have been in Arcadia." Pater imitates Goethe, whose epigraph for *Italian Journey,* "*et in Arcadia ego,*" certainly describes the poet's life in Italy.[7] It is natural that Pater borrows from Goethe in this way, for Goethe's relation to Winckelmann is one central concern of **"Winckelmann."** Unlike Winckelmann and Goethe, Pater does not claim to have been in Arcadia. Pater thus follows Goethe's text as—so **"Winckelmann"** claims—Goethe in his writing follows Winckelmann; but Goethe is speaking about his own life while Pater is only describing Winckelmann's. The self-effacing Pater brings together who cultural heroes, Winckelmann and Goethe, leaving himself out of the story. Who can imagine Pater asserting, "I too was in Arcadia?" Pater visited Italy, but for him the ideal world remained in the past. In the modern world, he could find no such place.

In commentary on Erwin Panofsky's famous account of Nicolas Poussin's painting, *The Arcadian Shepherds,* the phrase *et in Arcadia ego* has been much discussed.[8] Panofsky noted that the Latin can be translated, "death is even in Arcadia." Inscribed on the tomb in Poussin's painting, these words may either be read as spoken by a dead man who once lived in Arcadia or as asserting death is even in that ideal world. Winckelmann both lived in an ideal world and found that there is death even in Arcadia. **"Wickelmann"** supports that reading of the phrase. Winckelmann's entire aesthetic was permeated by awareness of death.

*Ut in Arcadia ego,* Panofsky argues, can refer either to a Utopia distant in space or to an ideal place distant in time. This is why the divisions in **"Winckelmann"** are both geographic and temporal—there are two ways to locate the ideal place and, by contrast, identify the site of banal everyday life. Winckelmann, born in the North, was at home only in the South; like Goethe, another Northerner, he found himself only in Italy. This South/North opposition appears also a contrast between hot bright ancient Greece and the cold modern North—

whether that modern site be Italy, where the rebirth of antiquity took place, or Germany. "At the Renaissance, in the midst of a frozen world, the buried fire of ancient art rose up from under the earth" (*TR*, 146).

Winckelmann did not return home—he was murdered in Trieste, an Italian city between the North and the South. Goethe came back from his Italian journey. Winckelmann the art lover could only live in the past; Goethe learned to reconcile admiration for the classical world with living and working in the present. Pater's geographic division thus stands also for the temporal contrast between classical antiquity and the modern world. Winckelmann, backward looking in his aesthetic, could be happy only in Italy; Goethe brought home to Germany knowledge of how to live and work productively in the modern world.

The first part of **"Winckelmann"** describes Winckelmann, who failed to understand the modern world. The second part discusses Goethe, who learned to make art adequate to our post-antique culture. Past and present; South and North: these two oppositions appear within an essay with two parts. **"Winckelmann"** recounts the art historian's life and surveys Hegel's aesthetic, which was influenced by Winckelmann's writing. The essay originally was published as a review of two books whose titles were listed at the beginning, a life of Winckelmann and a translation of Wickelmann's *The History of Ancient Art among the Greeks,* but that does not explain why it has these two parts, or how they are related. Pater does not summarize these books he supposedly is reviewing. When the essay was reprinted in **The Renaissance** the names of the books were removed.

This transition in **"Winckelmann"** is signaled by a detail occurring at the start of the second part. Pater describes two famous Raphaels in the Vatican, *Disputa* and *Parnassus.* One shows Christian history, the other Greek mythology, "Dante alone appearing in both" (*TR,* 157).[9] As Pater explains just before this transition, Winckelmann stood to Goethe as did Virgil to Dante—a man associated with pagan antiquity (Winckelmann, Virgil) guided a poet of the modern Christian era (Goethe, Dante). That Goethe appears in both parts of **"Winckelmann,"** as Dante is represented in both frescoes, exemplifies the central theme of Pater's book. The Renaissance both breaks with and builds upon antiquity. **The Renaissance** is about transitions—its argument that the Renaissance is a transition both preserving and transcending antiquity is presented in the form of its literary structure.

**"Winckelmann"** begins and ends with a discussion of Winckelmann's effect on Goethe. The poet, we are told at the beginning, compared Winckelmann to inexhaust-

ibly suggestive artworks. Goethe's own modernist art, we learn at the end, surpasses the Greek ideal of Winckelmann's theorizing. Initially Winckelmann is described as a great writer who, after difficult struggles, succeeds in getting to Rome. But after discussion of Hegel's aesthetic theory, which goes beyond Winckelmann's, a different view emerges. Wickelmann, a historian, was not actively engaged with the present. Hegel was, and so his theory of art's history is infinitely more suggestive. In Hegel's aesthetics, Winckelmann's history is but one stage in the dialectic. Winckelmann failed to understand even the whole of the Greek achievement, the way in which "the supreme and colorless abstraction of those divine forms . . . is also a premonition of the fleshless, consumptive refinements of the pale, medieval artists" (*TR,* 179). He thus is ultimately "chiefly" interesting because "at certain points he comes in contact with Goethe" (*TR,* 181).

We expect a modernist artist to express himself in his art, projecting outward in what he makes his inward feelings: "Just as the artist is made up of a physiognomic exterior and an inner psychological space, the painting consists of a material surface and an interior which opens illusionistically behind that surface."[10] Because the artist has an inner life which is expressible outwardly, we can ask if his art corresponds truthfully to his inner feelings. The possibility of skepticism—the question, is this act of expression truthful?—arises in modern Romantic art because there is something concealed from public view. "In antique art . . . as Pater described it in his essay on Winckelmann, there is no inner self-awareness to fuse with an outer world."[11] There is an analogy between this inner and outer distinction and the interpretation of ironical words. Irony, Nehamas argues, "involves saying something other than, and not just contrary to, what one means" (*AL,* 56). Because there is a speaker's intention, his audience may give some other sense to his words.

In the chapter on Socrates in his **Plato and Platonism,** Pater discusses irony:

> The irony, the humor, for which he (Socrates) was famous—the unfailing humor which some have found in his very last words—were not merely spontaneous personal traits, or tricks of manner; but an essential part of the dialectical apparatus as affording a means of escape from responsibility, convenient for one who has scruples about the fitness of his own thoughts for the reception of another, doubts as to the power of words to convey thoughts, such as he thinks cannot after all be properly conveyed to another, but only awakened, or brought to birth in him, out of himself—who can tell with what distortions in that secret place?[12]

He cannot tell whether the thoughts he inspires are identical with his own. Socrates would like to avoid claiming responsibility for his words—as, famously, Pater worried about taking responsibility for the conclusion to *The Renaissance,* which was read to challenge Christian morality in the name of aesthetic values.

As art writer, Winckelmann turns away from the present to look back to antiquity. But in his life he is a modernist—"the last fruit of the Renaissance" (*TR,* xxv). His creative work is less expressive than his life. That Winckelmann, who lived in Rome, in his writing showed so little understanding of the Christian art of that city is disappointing. Too narrowly focused on the distant past he, unlike Pater, was unable to recognize that antiquity prepared for the Renaissance. Winckelmann did not produce a theory of modernism. That task was left, Pater says, to Goethe, Victor Hugo and some other (unnamed) writers. Certainly Baudelaire—one of Pater's essential sources—is among those successful modernists. "Quel est celui de nous qui n'a pas . . . rêve le miracle d'une prose poétique, musicale sans rythme et sans rime, assez souple et assez heurtée pour s'adapter aux mouvements lyriques de l'lâme" [which of us has never imagined . . . the miracle of a poetic prose, musical though rhythmless and rhymeless, flexible enough to identify with the lyrical impulses of the soul].[13] Pater also is a modernist. Supple as Baudelaire's prose poems, **"Winckelmann"** is flexible enough to identify the lyrical impulses of Winckelmann's soul—as Winckelmann's own prose was not.

Winckelmann was "like a relic of classical antiquity laid open to accident to our alien, modern atmosphere" (*TR,* 175). Goethe agrees: "eine solche antike Natur war, insofern man es nur von einem unserer Zeitgenoses behaupten kann, in Winckelmann wieder erschienen" [the reincarnation of ancient man, insofar as that may be said of anyone in our time].[14] They describe the man Winckelmann as if he were one of the antique sculptures he loved, artifacts buried until the Renaissance. The gay Winckelmann understood the Greeks because of "his own nature" (*TR,* 175). But he was not merely a passive re-creator of the era he loved. "Penetrating into the antique world by his passion," involved in "a constant handling of the antique" (*TR,* 176, 145). Winckelmann had an affinity with the era he loved which was "not merely intellectual, that . . . is proved by his romantic, fervent friendships with young men" (*TR,* 152).

Goethe and Winckelmann never met. Because it appears at the start of the essay so inevitable that these kindred souls will become friends, the disjointed transition in **"Wickelmann"** expresses the real character of their relationship, as is it identified by the end of Pater's narrative. While Goethe awaited Wincklemann's return to Germany from Rome, the historian was mur-

dered. A great potential relationship thus never was realized—but this is not entirely regrettable. Winckelmann's image survives in Goethe's creative writing. Since Goethe's themes transcend those of Greek art, meeting would have led to misunderstandings. Perhaps their relationship would have been like the stormy friendships recorded in Winckelmann's letters, which Pater notes, are unlike the accounts of the calm Greeks in *History of Art.* Winckelmann's death was tragic, but insofar as it helped make him into a modernist work of art, that should not be regretted. "Who, if he saw through all, would fret against the chain of circumstance which endows one at the end with those great experiences?" (*TR,* 185). The form of Winckelmann's tragic life gives readers of **"Winckelmann"** pleasure. Untimely death may be the price of life in Arcadia. For an aesthete art gives "nothing but the highest quality to your moments as they pass, and simply for those moments' sake" (*TR,* 190). Pater treats Winckelmann's murder as giving form to this narrative of the historian's relationship with Goethe. The aesthete's living for the here-and-now can appear cruel.

Pater implies that Winckelmann's life is a critique of his writings. There was more to him than appears in the aesthetic theory presented in his books. The ancients, connoisseurs of surfaces, lacked an inner self-awareness: "The mind begins and ends with the finite image . . . it has not yet become too inward; the mind has not yet learned to boast of its independence of the flesh" (*TR,* 164). Discovery of inwardness is an achievement of Christian culture in which artworks are "overcharged symbols, a means of hinting at an idea which art cannot fitly or completely express" (*TR,* 164). The lack of correspondence between Winckelmann's classical writings and his Romantic life anticipates the art and life of Pater's wayward follower Oscar Wilde. Wickelmann, too, put his genius into his life, and only his talent into his works. "Not of the modern world . . . although so much of his outer life is characteristic of it" (*TR,* 181), unable to bring his inner life, his experience of classical art, into correspondence with his outer everyday modern life, Winckelmann fails to achieve that unity of great artworks which express outwardly their creator's culture. *Mona Lisa,* for example, according to Pater, expresses Leonardo da Vinci's life and the history of painting. Winckelmann's *History of Art,* by contrast, does not represent its author's modernist personality.

*The Renaissance* displays the continuities of European culture, the ways in which treating pagan and Christian art in opposition is a "superficial view" (*TR,* 180). For Pater, Winckelmann was a limited historian because in his writings Greek and modern art are opposed. The very style of his prose shows his limitations as a commentator on modern art. "Occupied ever with himself

. . . he was ever jealously refining his meaning into a form, express, clear, objective" (**TR,** 176). He was qualified to write about classical art because it was like Winckelmann himself. But as Baudelaire noted, a modernist must go outside of himself. The disjointed narrative of **"Winckelmann"** gives a better picture of Wickelmann than does Winckelmann's own prose. When Pater speaks of "a moral sexlessness, a kind of ineffectual wholeness of nature," it is unclear whether he describes Winckelmann or Winckelmann's account of Greek art (**TR,** 176). Ultimately that distinction is not important—Winckelmann is like the Greek art he describes.

Nehamas asserts that "the features that characterize oneself and one's life are similar to the features of literary works. The virtues of life are comparable to the virtues of good writing—style, connectedness, grace elegance—and also, we must not forget, sometimes getting it right."[15] Winckelmann possessed style, grace, and elegance—but in one way connectedness and "getting it right" were not his virtues. His inner life and its outer expression in his writing were not connected; he failed "to get" the art of his own day. His life becomes a work of art only when described by Goethe and Pater, who recognize (as Winckelmann did not) that today the world of Hellenism has become distant.

For Goethe, Winckelmann was like "a fragment of Greek art itself, stranded . . . [in] Germany in the eighteenth century" (**TR,** 182). Goethe's own Hellenism involved "wholeness, good, beauty" (**TR,** 182). The question he poses, "can the blitheness and universality of the antique ideals be communicated to artistic productions, which shall contain the fullness of the experience of the modern world?" (**TR,** 184) is akin to Nehamas's question—is it possible today to practice the Socratic art of living? Pater asks, if "breadth, centrality, with blitheness and repose, are the marks of Hellenic culture," then "is such culture a lost art?" (**TR,** 181). In the modern world, Pater says, "the problem of unity with ourselves . . . is far harder than it was for the Greek within the simple terms of antique life" (**TR,** 182). And yet we too, like the ancients, demand completeness and centrality. Goethe learned the art of living from Winckelmann. As Pater quotes him to say, "'One learns nothing from (Winckelmann) . . . but one becomes something" (**TR,** 147).

Present day commentators, justly sensitive to the importance of Pater's homosexuality, say less about his attachment to Christianity. They tend to emphasize Pater's identification with Winckelmann; I rather would note the ways in which Pater emphasized the distance between himself and his subject. "Christian asceticism

. . . has from time to time provoked into strong emphasis the contrast or antagonism to itself, or the artistic life, with its inevitable sensuousness" (**TR,** 177). Awareness of what Pater calls "the modern world" (**TR,** 184), the ways in which Christianity transformed the pagan sensibility, is not Winckelmann's concern. For Pater, this is a real limitation of Winckelmann. Winckelmann's "serenity . . . is the absence of any sense of want, or corruption, or shame" (**TR,** 176), qualities central to **The Renaissance.** Pater shares more with Goethe—they both are Romantics who, admiring Wickelmann, grasp his limitations.

Scholars who today discuss Panofsky and Ernst Gombrich may indicate in passing how personal experiences influenced these men. But we do not expect that the lives of these historians be works of art. Study of art does not turn a person into an artwork. Pater is concerned not only with Winckelmann's writings, but also with treating his life as a work of art. Often we are interested in how Pater anticipates the concerns of present day art history. Judged by our standards, his writings may seem unsatisfactory:

> Walter Pater is ultimately disappointing as a critic of the arts. His output was limited, his characterization of individual works of art is tentative, and for someone so concerned with the personality in art he was mysteriously casual about attribution.[16]

His proto-psychoanalytic account of Leonardo da Vinci is sketchy; his beautiful essay on Giorgione's style merely suggestive; his remarks on Winckelmann's theories only schematic. But if we evaluate Pater by his own standards, the standards defined by his writing, then this judgment will seem mistaken. Here again, Nehamas's distinction between two conceptions of philosophy is extremely helpful. Just as treating the philosophers of the art of living as concerned only with contributing to a theoretical discipline is to distort and diminish their real accomplishment, so to think of Pater as merely anticipating modern art history writing is to adopt a very misleading perspective on his goals and his achievement.

Like the sculptures of Luca della Robbia and Michelangelo, the paintings of Leonardo and the school of Giorgione and the French literature discussed in **The Renaissance,** Winckelmann's life is a work of art. On one reading, that is an uncontroversial way to describe **"Winckelmann."** Pater is a biographer. Some biographies display literary distinction. To thus associate his life of Winckelmann with these sculptures, paintings, and poems is only to say that Pater describes all of these entities in his literary style. But that reading trivializes my claims. Describing something in stylish prose does not transform it into a work of art; only the description, and not what it describes, is an artwork. The more interesting but problematic claim is that Winckelmann's life itself is a work of art. Lives, as much as sculptures, paintings, and poems, can be artworks. That life itself, apart from how it is described by a skilled biographer, achieves style, connectedness, and grace—Winckelmann's life exemplifies elegance and getting it right.

What today maybe makes the idea of the art of living seem archaic is the sense that the aesthete belongs to a now vanished culture—and that the aesthete was a morally irresponsible privileged person. These two ideals are connected—for the aesthete cannot be too much concerned with working. This model for the aesthete is described by Meyer Schapiro:

> Bernard Berenson, inspired by Walter Pater's books, wished to make of his life a work of art. He had two ideals: to live aesthetically, at the height of sensibility to art and nature; and to lead an aristocratic existence as the master of a big house, holding court for the elegant, the worldly, the famous, and the gifted.[17]

However we judge Berenson's particular interpretation of Pater's book, there is more to Pater's (and Nehamas's) vision of life as a work of art than this. Pater certainly does not think that only aristocrats can live aesthetically. Most of his literary characters do not hold court. Nehamas is concerned with "the individualist strain of the tradition of philosophy as the art of living" (*AL,* 169), but for him, as for Pater, an aesthete need not necessarily be economically privileged.

Identifying the traditional close tie between the cultivation of aesthetic sensitivity and aristocratic existence thus does not to show the narrowness of the aesthete's ways of life. Rather, the intrinsic value of an aesthete's life can be used to make a political point. Just as in today's museums art originally produced mostly for elites is accessible to the public, so in a just society it might be possible for anyone to become an aesthete. Because traditional societies allow only a privileged few to practice the art of living, those societies are unjust. An adequate theory of justice must defend the right to aesthetic experience. When Nehamas questions any "strong distinction between the private project of making something out of ourselves and the public goal of changing the lives of others," he hints at how such an argument might be developed.[18]

Today Pater's concern with the art of living makes **"Winckelmann"** seem exotic—as exotic as *The Art of Living.* "If I do have a public message," Nehamas says, "it is that aesthetic facts—beauty, style, and elegance,

grace, and connectedness—are crucial to life."[19] When denuded of its historical associations, this art of living may be highly relevant to the present. One way to see the potential force of Nehamas's political claim is to note how many 1960s artists thought (in ways very different from Berenson!) about making their lives into art. In conceptual art of that era, attention was drawn to the aesthetic qualities of the most banal everyday actions. For example, in a performance Scott Burton faced

> the audience, stage center, wearing a shirt and pair of pants the same color, color A. He removes the shirt, revealing under it an identical shirt of color B. He removes the pants, revealing under the an identical pair of color B. He removes the shirt, revealing an identical shirt of color A. He removes the shirt, revealing an identical shirt of color B. He removes the pants, revealing an identical pair of color B.[20]

Burton's way of turning life into art, differs as much from Berenson's as does Marcel Proust's prose from Samuel Beckett's. Just as there are diverse styles of good writing—and thus many ways of achieving style, connectedness, grace, elegance, and getting it right—so there are many ways of turning one's life into art. The variety of possible ways of pursuing the art of living corresponds to range of literary styles in which the unity of the self can be described.

The belief that aesthetes are morally irresponsible is heavily influenced by the popular images of Pater such as are provided by Berenson's life—and also by a common reading of the "Conclusion" of *The Renaissance.* "Every moment some form grows perfect . . . for that moment only. Not the fruit of experience, but experience itself, is the end" (*TR,* 188). I have elsewhere shown that this popular view is deeply misleading. Pater is essentially a moralist, and as such

> finds danger in narrow preoccupation with the aesthetic. Pater . . . sees the transcendent as imminent in everyday life; he found religion "a transcendent version representation . . . of human life and its familiar or exceptional incidents . . . a mirror, towards which men might . . . see themselves as angels, with the daily meat and drink, even, become a kind of sacred transaction"

> (*Marius the Epicurean*)[21]

*The Renaissance* describes the transition from pagan antiquity to the modern Romantic world; taking as given that transition, *Marius the Epicurean* adopts a modern perspective on antiquity to identify the positive contribution made by Christian morality, and to criticize Pater's own society.

A development of those claims would provide a highly suggestive perspective on Nehamas's argument. And it would show why the argument **"Winckelmann"** is of more than merely academic interest. But that is the task for another occasion.

This essay is for Alexander Nehamas.[22]

*Notes*

1. See my "Talking with Alexander Nehamas," *Bomb* 65, no. 41 (fall 1998).

2. Alexander Nehamas, *The Art of Living: Socratic Reflections from Plato to Foucault* (Berkeley: University of California Press, 1998). This book will be cited as *AL* in the text for all subsequent references. A related perspective on these claims is provided by Arthur C. Danto, "In Their Own Voice: Philosophical Writing and Actual Experience," reprinted in his *The Body/Body Problem: Selected Essays* (Berkeley: University of California Press, 1999), chap. 12.

3. I use the annotated edition by Donald L. Hill, *The Renaissance* (Berkeley: University of California Press, 1980). This book will be cited as *TR* in the text for all subsequent references.

4. R. G. Collingwood, *The Idea of History,* ed. Jan van der Dussen (Oxford: Oxford University Press, 1993), 88, n. 1.

5. Alex Potts, *Flesh and the Ideal: Winckelmann and the Origins of Art History* (New Haven: Yale University Press, 1994), 238-25; Denis Donoghue, *Walter Pater: Lover of Strange Souls* (New York: Alfred A Knopf, 1995), chap. 14; Wolfgang Leppmann, *Winckelmann* (London: Victor Gallancs, 1970). I discuss "Winckelmann" in my *Principles of Art History Writing* (University Park: Pennsylvania State University Press, 1991), chap. 6. The Pater scholar who has most influenced me is Paul Barolsky.

6. Pater's account of Greek art is found in the unfinished sequence of essays published in his *Greek Studies: A Series of Essays* (London: Macmillan, 1901).

7. Johann Wolfgang von Goethe, *Italian Journey. 1786-1788,* trans. W. H. Auden and Elizabeth Mayer (New York: Schocken, 1968), 1.

8. See my *Poussin's Paintings: A Study in Art-Historical Methodology* (University Park: Pennsylvania State University Press, 1993), 29-35.

9. "Raphael's painting of the *Flaying of Marsyas* is placed in the corner between the *Parnassus* and the *Disputa* . . . flanked on either side by the figure of Dante. . . . In the entire cycle . . . Dante is the only author represented twice: and since his two portraits appear at the corner in which Theology and Poetry are joined, it is only consistent that the picture in that corner is an example of Poetic Theology"; Edgar Wind, *Pagan Mysteries in the Renaissance,* rev. ed. (New York: W. W. Norton, 1968).

10. Rosalind E. Krauss, *Passages in Modern Sculpture* (New York: Viking, 1977), 256.

11. Gerald Monsman, *Walter Pater's Art of Autobiography* (New Haven: Yale University Press, 1980), 46.

12. Walter Pater, *Plato and Platonism: A Series of Lectures* (London: Macmillan, 1901), 88.

13. Baudelaire, *The Poems in Prose,* trans. Francis Scarfe (London: Anvil Press, 1980), 24-25.

14. *Goethes Werks* (Hamburg: Christian Wegner, 1967), vols. 12, 99; Johann Wolfgang von Goethe, *Essays on Art and Literature,* ed. John Gearey, trans. Ellen von Nardroff and Ernest H. von Nardroff (New York: Suhrkamp, 1986), 101.

15. "Talking with Alexander Nehamas," 41.

16. Richard Wollheim, "Walter Pater: From Philosophy to Art," *Comparative Criticism,* ed. E. S. Shaffer (Cambridge: Cambridge University Press, 1995), 37.

17. Meyer Schapiro, "Mr. Berenson's Values," *Encounter* 16 (1961). See also Franklin E. Court, "The Matter of Pater's 'Influence' on Bernard Berenson: Setting the Record Straight," *English Literature in Transition* 26, 1 (1983): 16-22.

18. Alexander Nehamas, "Nietzsche, Modernity, Aestheticism," *The Cambridge Companion to Nietzsche,* ed. Bernd Magnus and Kathleen M. Higgins (Cambridge: Cambridge University Press, 1996), 237.

19. "Talking with Alexander Nehamas," 41.

20. Lucy R. Lippard, *Six Years: The Dematerialization of the Art Object from 1966 to 1972* (1973; reprint Berkeley: University of California Press 1997), 96.

21. "Baudelaire and the Origins of Formalist Art Criticism," *Comparative Criticism. An Annual Journal,* ed. E. S. Shaffer, 17 (Cambridge: Cambridge University Press, 1995): 118. See also the title essay of my *The Aesthete in the City: The Philosophy and Practice of American Abstract Painting in the 1980s* (University Park: Pennsylvania State University Press, 1994); and my *England and its Aes-*

*thetes: Biography and Taste* (Amsterdam: Gordon and Breach, 1997).

22. I thank Paul Barolsky, Bill Berkson and Alexander Nehamas for comments on earlier drafts.

## Damon Franke (essay date spring 2004)

SOURCE: Franke, Damon. "The 'Curious' Pagan Spirit of Pater's *The Renaissance*." *Nineteenth-Century Prose* 31, no. 1 (spring 2004): 170-90.

[*In the following essay, Franke argues that Pater's* The Renaissance *aims primarily to exhort readers to cultivate a more open, "inclusive" conception of art and culture. According to Franke, Pater admired Renaissance artists because of their mastery of a range of expressive forms and particularly for their ability to unite pagan and Christian ideas of art and life. In Franke's view this reconciliation of paganism and Christianity reflects Pater's broader ambition to integrate Renaissance ideals with principles of modern aestheticism.*]

Of the many famous dicta born with Pater's "Conclusion" to *The Renaissance,* perhaps the most subversive of his mandates for aesthetic criticism overtly calls for a consistent questioning of authority: "What we have to do is to be for ever curiously testing new opinions and courting new impressions, never acquiescing in a facile orthodoxy, of Comte, or of Hegel, or of our own" (189).[1] Pater's plea yokes together two terms to privilege the paganism that he finds subtly apparent in Christian iconography. To be "curious" in the face of "orthodoxy" is both what Pater values in his chosen Renaissance artists and what he strove for in his own life. Indeed, Pater's projection of autobiographical concerns onto his subjects (as William Sharp first pointed out) emphasizes his desire for harmony between an artist's life and work. In his treatment of Pico della Mirandola, Leonardo da Vinci and Johann Winckelmann, Pater admires most in them the principle that the artist's work relates to his life, and asserts that the form of his artwork should also convey the array of sentiments associated with its historical and philosophical content. For Pater, this principle of *Andersstreben,* first posited by Baudelaire, explains both how the particular historical quality of the Renaissance, a pagan sensibility, appears in art and how correspondent aesthetic qualities become sublimated in the person. In his discussion of Giorgione, Pater explains his usage of *Andersstreben* in describing the relation between painting and music: "each art may be observed to pass into the condition of some other art, by what German critics term an *Anders-streben*—a partial alienation from its own limitations, through which the

arts are able, not indeed to supply the place of each other, but reciprocally to lend each other new forces" (105).[2] Pater's argument throughout *The Renaissance* implies that a similar productive dynamic undergirds the historical relation between Christianity and paganism, and his defense of "curiosity" and a "pagan spirit" distinguish the work as a cohesive, unified treatise delineating in component parts the historical, aesthetic, and political relations between paganism and Christianity.

As a correlative of *Andersstreben,* the prominent metaphor and preeminent form of art in *The Renaissance* is music, an artform in which it is impossible "to distinguish matter from the form."[3] Pater declares, therefore: "*All art aspires towards the condition of music*" (106). Analogously for the religious concerns of *The Renaissance,* Pater tries to bring to the foreground the pagan "matter" repressed historically in the "forms" of Christian symbols and tradition. Pater finds that the unique dialogue between paganism and Christianity in Renaissance art is its masterstroke, in that they too "lend each other new forces." Curiosity is the driving force behind this genius. While criticism has generally seen *The Renaissance* as a disjointed collection of essays, the reciprocal function of curiosity and a pagan sensibility constitutes a dominant, consistent argument throughout Pater's work. In the third (1888) and fourth (1893) editions, Pater's inclusion of **"The School of Giorgione"** and the discussion of Amis and Amile within **"Two Early French Stories,"** and the restoration of the "Conclusion" cultivate the coherence of a curious, pagan spirit. As part of this thesis, Pater argues that a curious, pagan spirit achieves a "serenity" and potentially harmonizes form and content through a desire for beauty and a search for historical and aesthetic continuities between paganism and Christianity.

The emphatic rhetoric of the first sentence of the essay on Pico della Mirandola equally applies to a predominant theme subtending Pater's work: "No account of the Renaissance can be complete without some notice of the attempt made by certain Italian scholars of the fifteenth century to reconcile Christianity with the religion of ancient Greece" (23). Pater suggests that any historical harmonization of Western religions must reconcile Christianity with paganism, even at the expense of orthodoxy.[4] As a result, Pater's "Conclusion" elicited a stern rebuke from the Bishop of Oxford, and "scandalous" and "notorious" came to be mentioned in the same breath as the "Conclusion." Pater's paganism informs both the contemporaneous debates between established religion, comparative anthropology, and evolutionary thought, and T. S. Eliot's later attempt to debunk Pater's view of form and content. In defending the Christian tradition as the "true" content of art, T. S.

Eliot continued the charges against Pater who "knew almost nothing" about "the essence of the Christian faith" and only offers a "degradation of philosophy and religion" ("Arnold and Pater" 388-91). In fact, Pater champions "curiosity" as the relentless, unsettling characteristic of artists who challenge the thoughtless acceptance of "tradition." Pater suggests that the unmitigated love of beauty accompanying any "proper" aesthetics far outweighs the threat to orthodoxy concomitant with the resurfacing of potentially oppositional internal elements. A curious look at Pater's **"Poems by William Morris,"** an October 1868 review of Morris' *The Earthly Paradise,* helps to clarify the fact that the orthodoxy "of our own" that Pater is questioning is indeed Christianity.[5]

In its previously published form, the "Conclusion" occupied a similar structural position in the unsigned Morris review. Of interest, then, are the tone and subject matter that led Pater initially to such controversial remarks that promote "the love of art for its own sake" and declaim the "conventional" as having "no real claim upon us" (189-90). What follows is the paragraph in the review that immediately precedes the seven paragraphs that later comprise the "Conclusion":

> One characteristic of the pagan spirit these new poems have which is on their surface—the continual suggestion, pensive or passionate, of the shortness of life; this is contrasted with the bloom of the world and gives new seduction to it; the sense of death and the desire of beauty; the desire of beauty quickened by the sense of death. "*Arriéré*" you say, "here in a tangible form we have the defect of all poetry like this." The modern world is in possession of truths; what but a passing smile can it have for a kind of poetry which, assuming artistic beauty of form to be an end in itself, passes by those truths and the living interests which are connected with them, to spend a thousand cares in telling once more these pagan fables as if it had to but choose between a more and a less beautiful shadow? It is a strange transition from the earthly paradise to the sad-coloured world of abstract philosophy. But let us accept the challenge; let us see what modern philosophy, when it is sincere, really does say about human life and the truth we can attain in it, and the relation of this to the desire of beauty.
>
>                                                                     (89)

Denis Donoghue believes that when Pater transposed the review into the "Conclusion," "he excised the passage about the pagan spirit, presumably because it was too closely attached to his broodings on Morris's poems" (53). Donoghue could not be more wrong here. The "pagan spirit" also best describes Pater's heretical stance that subtends *The Renaissance.* At once, the "shortness of life" and "sense of death" emphasized in the passage elucidates the inspired *carpe diem* motif of the "Conclusion" and suggests that a "pagan spirit" can

provide insight into the relation between beauty and truth. One senses that Pater is not satisfied with the Keatsian proposition of the Grecian Urn: "Beauty is truth, truth beauty, that is all / Ye know on earth, and all ye need to know." For Pater's curiosity is especially aroused by those artists who do "spend a thousand cares in telling . . . pagan fables." Here Pater hints at a nuanced reasoning behind his recurrent use of the word "curiosity." Etymologically, "curiosity" derives from the Latin *curiosus,* "full of cares" or "careful." Moreover, among the many theories of development blossoming in the 1860s, the discipline of etymology (<Gr. *etumos,* "truth, what is") began to promote an intersection of history and language as the "study of truth." One of Pater's colleagues at Oxford, Max Müller, reinserted the importance of etymology in philological studies and put forth "the notion that the meaning of a word was equivalent to its whole etymological history." Incidentally, Müller also equated "the spirit of religion with its history" (Burrow 200). In its multitiered linguistic history, the word "curiosity" plays several roles in *The Renaissance,* often denoting alternately "inquisitiveness" or "an interesting object," but never excluding any of its associated meanings.

By the time Pater wrote the bulk of the essays that comprise *The Renaissance,* Matthew Arnold's *Culture and Anarchy* (1869) had exerted considerable influence in critical studies of culture. The first words of the famous first chapter on "Sweetness and Light" claim that the "disparagers of culture make its motive curiosity" (204). Arnold believes that this has happened because, in English usage, the word "curiosity" solely conveys pejorative connotations. However, as he had noted in "The Function of Criticism at the Present Time" (1865), other languages use the term "to mean, as a high and fine quality of man's nature, just the disinterested love of a free play of the mind on all subjects." In this positive sense, curiosity is the controlling motive of cultural criticism (141). By combining this view of culture with the belief that societies try to improve culture and perform "the will of God," Arnold believes that "culture" then is "*a study of perfection*" ("Sweetness" 205). Though Pater would refrain from thinking of "the will of God," this form of the word "curiosity" similarly continues, for Pater, to carry all of its varied historical significances. Thinking of the "truth" linguistically buried in "etymology" sheds light on the passage from the Morris review: "The modern world is in possession of truths; what but a passing smile can it have for a kind of poetry which, assuming artistic beauty of form to be an end in itself, passes by those truths and the living interests which are connected with them" (89). Again Pater evokes the idea that language carries history residually and keeps the past alive. In miniature, hearing all the voices of a word exemplifies his humanist belief that "nothing which has ever interested living men and women can wholly lose its vitality," including any "language they have spoken" (38). Pater uses "curiosity" as a keyword to reveal and underscore a similar historical development from paganism to Christianity. More importantly, Pater struggles to show the need for the recognition and persistence of the pagan spirit.

In "Dallying nicely with words," John Hollander argues that, in a cross-section of writers from Shakespeare to Hopkins, "words are often like some agents in a larger fiction, not so much an epic or drama, but more a complex romance, of language" (123). In this light, Pater's use of the word "curiosity" becomes an example of what Hollander calls "an allegorising of the etymological process" (130). Hollander suggests that literature, in a "recognisably Miltonic kind of move," can play "on English word and Latin etymon" and become a "valorisation of the relation between past and present usage" (130). Uncovering the etymological layers of the word "curious" would take us from "an object arousing interest" to "a desire to know or learn" to a process "full of cares" or of "healing."[6] When Petronius alludes to Horace's *curiosa felicitas,* he is referring to this linguistic dimension of "curiosity" by implying an "elaborate and painstaking care in composition" (Arrowsmith 185). The last sense, "healing," shows the word's cognate relationship with "cure." (On another level, the connotations of "curiosity" associated with "pornography" or "strangeness" speak to the homoerotics Pater often cultivates vis-à-vis his subjects, especially Leonardo.)[7] By extension, the thought processes involved in such a search for roots and "truth" represent to Pater a convalescence that at least tries to harmonize Christian icons with analogous pagan symbols. Implicit in this approach is a sentiment that finds a malaise or loss of integration in the present. Hoping to revive the healing serenity of "*Heiterkeit,* that pagan blitheness" (180), Pater promotes, throughout *The Renaissance,* a willful and independent inquisitiveness as a means to restore this "cheerful" contentment in humanity.

In his repetitive, incantatory use of the word "curiosity," Pater draws attention to the word itself as an object of interest and as an illustration of how dormant and archaic meanings of any word or practice can be recovered. The word informs *The Renaissance* from the "curious strength" and "curious interest" of **"Two Early French Stories"** (7-11) to the "curiosity, the initiatory idea," of **"Pico della Mirandola"** (25) to the call in the Conclusion "to be for ever curiously testing new opinions" (189). However, clearly the most playful repetition of the word occurs in **"Leonardo da Vinci."** Pater describes the genius of Leonardo as "composed, in almost equal parts, of curiosity and the desire of

beauty, to take things as they came" (86). Pater then unfolds the dynamic between these traits by repeating the terms with slight variation for the rest of the essay. Once, the terms fuse into "curious beauty" (90), and, in the following sentence, Pater nearly begs the question in explicating the synthesis of the terms: "Curiosity and the desire of beauty—these are the two elementary forces in Leonardo's genius; curiosity often in conflict with the desire of beauty, but generating, in union with it, a type of subtle and curious grace" (86). Here we have the three central meanings of "curiosity" playing off each other, and, in the process, creating a dialectical system. Pater suggests that the general desire to know engages a particular object, arouses interest, and consequently generates a "curious grace" or healing power. If there were any doubt as to the importance of curiosity to Pater, the conclusion of the Leonardo essay, the purple patch for curiosity, speculates how Leonardo dies looking "forward now into the vague land, and experienced the last curiosity" (101).

Reading the layered meanings of curiosity in *The Renaissance* becomes a key that demonstrates the parallel endeavor of the work to use a historical process to reconcile the Christian present with its pagan past. To be constantly curious presents a direct threat to authority; curiosity not only challenges authority, but the progressive, continuative nature of inquisitive searching precludes the establishment of any fixed forms or orthodox doctrine. As Richard Dellamora argues, for Pater, a "curious" "cultivation of self implies religious unbelief" ("Modernism" 137). From the "Preface" to the "Conclusion," Pater emphasizes the durative process of searching far above the need for any final answers. One of the few qualities that Pater does want to achieve—the healing serenity of *Heiterkeit*—would not curtail curiosity in its attainment. Conversely, a serenity would be incorporated into curiosity and replace the angst-ridden concern for origins burgeoning in Pater's time.

While the role of "curiosity" plays a subtle role in linking the essays in *The Renaissance,* the prevalence of pagan issues more overtly harmonizes the collection. The echo of pagan practices and images in the essays builds on the call to reconcile past and present and gradually culminates in the challenge to Christian orthodoxy in the "Conclusion." Pater particularly takes interest in the appropriation of pagan gods and symbols by Christianity. In the two chapters highly concerned with cultivating a methodology for linking past and present, content and form, Pater stresses Pico's listing of correspondences between the Greek and Christian religions and Giorgione's "'imaginative reason,' that complex faculty for which every thought and feeling is twin-born with its sensible analogue or symbol" (109). In the *Doni* Madonna, for another example, "Michelangelo actually brings the pagan religion . . . into the presence of the Madonna" and gives her "much of the uncouth energy of the older and more primitive 'Mighty Mother'" (37). And, in Leonardo's *La Gioconda,* Pater sees in Mona Lisa all "the thoughts and experience of the world" including "the return of the Pagan world" (98). In these works and in the "strange likeness" between Leonardo's paintings of Saint John and Bacchus, Pater invokes "Heine's notion of decayed gods, who, to maintain themselves, after the fall of paganism, took employment in the new religion" (93).[8] Pater, as a Platonist, is drawn to those art forms that slightly reveal this transmogrification by foregrounding a residue of an earlier connotation of the subject. Furthermore, the idea of former pagan gods lying fallow in Christianity leads Pater to make the bold claim in **"Winckelmann"** that "the broad foundation . . . of all religions as they exist for the greatest number, is a universal pagan sentiment, a paganism which existed before the Greek religion, and has lingered far onward into the Christian world, ineradicable" (160).

Consequently, criticism that speaks of paganism in *The Renaissance* generally focuses on **"Winckelmann."** Paul Jordan-Smith calls the essay Pater's "remarkable confession of faith," which "would bring back the spirit of paganism with its earthliness, its naturalness, and unite it to the gentleness and sympathy of Christian thought" (242). In his exhaustive study of the persistence of ancient Greek influence in Victorian Britain, Frank Turner interprets Pater's discernment of a "universal pagan sentiment" to indicate "humankind's acute awareness of its vulnerability in the natural world"; consequently, through "the myths, human beings sought to make themselves less estranged from nature and by religious ritual to exercise some vague control over it" (98). Moreover, Turner finds that Pater values the ability of paganism to adapt and foster "an ideal art that was appropriate to the finitude of the human situation" (99). Turner, Donoghue, Michael Levey, and David De-Laura, who emphasizes the paganism of Hellenism, most extensively discuss the pagan elements in Pater's writings. **"Winckelmann"** and, appropriately, his novel *Marius the Epicurean* (1885) receive most of the attention. Richard Dellamora, though, in discussing the Leonardo essay specifically, contrasts John Ruskin's love of medieval Christian art with Pater's work, which "prefers 'pagan' to 'Christian' art precisely because it is 'pagan.'" Dellamora also argues that Pater's method "discloses processes basing and shaping Leonardo's art which afford guidance to contemporary artists in creating new forms." Consequently, he believes that "Pater's work does not merely mark the advent of modernism; it is itself modernist" ("Modernism" 136).

Early on in the Preface, Pater argues that the actual value of trying to develop a universal formula for art arises concomitantly "in the suggestive and penetrating things said by the way" (xix). By valorizing the very process of aesthetic criticism, Pater seeks no other goal than the constancy of reinvestigation and the questioning of accepted norms. In his egalitarian and unrigid approach, Pater underscores the naive attempts of Pico della Mirandola (1463-1494) to come to terms with historical process. Though Pater believes that Pico exemplifies the idea that "the Renaissance of the fifteenth century was, in many things, great rather by what it designed or aspired to do, than by what it actually achieved," Pater claims that it "remained for a later age to conceive the true method of effecting a scientific reconciliation of Christian sentiment with the imagery, the legends, the theories about the world, of pagan poetry and philosophy." During the Renaissance, Pater finds that the "only possible reconciliation was an imaginative one" (36), but suggests the modern possibility of synthesizing science and religion through a "proper" Hegelian historical sense. A proper historical summary or philosophy of the world also synthesizes "all modes of thought and life" (99). With an application of the "true" historical sense, built on the idea of process, Pater feels that he can fulfill this task.

In a striking passage from the first essay in *The Renaissance,* **"Two Early French Stories,"** Pater sets forth the internal dynamics of his hermeneutics for thinking about the period. For any interpretation of the amalgam of Christian and pagan sentiments seen in Renaissance art, Pater suggests that the three methodological desiderata are an affinity for the sensuous, a willingness to be unorthodox, and an application of the historical sense.[9] In this light, **"The Early French Stories"** serves as an overture for the central themes of *The Renaissance.* By establishing a "continuity" between twelfth century France and fifteenth century Italy, Pater believes his approach will effect a "*healing* [of] that rupture between the middle age and the Renaissance which has so often been exaggerated" (2, italics added). Here, in the opening pages of the book, Pater foreshadows his use of the word "curiosity" and responds to Ruskin's recent praise of a sparse, sublime Gothic art antithetical to the decadent effusions of the Renaissance.

The Oxford Movement had also revived medievalism at Pater's institution, so his valorization of the successive period in history and its particular paganism confronted both established religion and aesthetics. However, in adopting a view of history as a constantly unfolding process, Pater clearly identifies with the developmental theories prevalent in his time. By supporting a methodology that casts suspicion on the immutability of the word of God, *The Renaissance* executes a critique of the idea of any *lex eterna*. In the following passage from **"Two Early French Stories,"** Pater supports the particular challenge to the law of the church by lauding the heresy of antinomianism:

> One of the strongest characteristics of that outbreak of the reason and the imagination, of that assertion of the liberty of the heart, in the middle age, which I have termed a medieval Renaissance, was its antinomianism, its spirit of rebellion and revolt against the moral and religious ideas of the time. In their *search* after the pleasures of the senses and the imagination, in their *care* for beauty, in their worship of the body, people were impelled beyond the bounds of the Christian ideal; and their love became sometimes a strange idolatry, a strange rival religion. It was the return of that ancient Venus, not dead, but only hidden for a time in the caves of the Venusberg, of those old pagan gods still going to and fro on the earth, under all sorts of disguises.

(18-19, italics added)

As this passage reveals, Pater's preoccupations in *The Renaissance* are foreshadowed again by **"Poems by William Morris."** In addition to stressing the terminology, "a medieval Renaissance," he champions once more a "spirit of rebellion" in confronting the hegemonic religion of the time. Curiosity, though unsaid directly in the passage, remains the central subversive element. In the "search" that has a "care for beauty" (two senses of "curiosity") "people were impelled beyond the bounds of the Christian ideal." The opposition of Christianity and curiosity clearly echoes the call in the "Conclusion" to be "curiously testing" "orthodoxy." The French stories become an example for Pater of how to revive dormant pagan gods. While a desire to see historical elements in present appearances will discover the gods in their "disguises," Pater underscores the primary need for a vigorous antinomian ethics. Antinomians preach a doctrine that frees Christians, saved by grace, from the observance of moral law. Etymologically, they are "against" the "law." Finding antinomianism "crucial" to the Paterian aesthetic, Donoghue claims that "Pater had an interest in finding, below the surface of an apparently unified society, intimations of visionary dissent" (134). Though, as Donoghue argues, Pater had no illusions about a pagan revolution, he wanted to serve "a quiet rebuke to the certitude with which modern orthodoxy acts in the world" (136).

Prior to the call to "burn" with a "hard, gem-like flame," Pater's "Conclusion" highlights "the tendency of modern thought" to regard both the physical world and the human psyche as fundamentally mutable and fleeting. In each case, the "Conclusion" responds to the germination in the 1850s and '60s of Higher Criticism and evolutionary thought, the seeds for what became the "modernist" crisis in the Catholic Church. Inspired by the lessons of Darwin's *Origin of Species* (1859) and *The Descent of Man* (1871), various scholars began applying notions of process and development to language, historical texts, and even, in bold moves, the Old Testament and the Gospels. Pater similarly opposes the static tenets needed by orthodoxy with the contemporary view of "physical life" as "a perpetual motion" of "elements, phosphorus and lime and delicate fibres," which "are present not in the human body alone" (186). The interconnectedness of the material world humbles humanity, and viewing human beings as part of an evolving, internecine web of nature focuses attention on "this" world. In terms of the psyche, Pater notes that "the inward world of thought" illustrates that the "whirlpool is still more rapid." The experience of "this" world becomes a linguistic and impressionistic function that isolates the individual and leads to Pater's *carpe diem* conclusion to observe as many of these "unstable, flickering, inconsistent" impressions as possible (187). Pater's definition of "success in life" directly opposes orthodox views of morality and destiny that require "the sacrifice of any part of this experience." For the Oxford don, asceticism and living with a goal of achieving heaven "have no real claim upon us" (189). While the implications of this perspective led to Pater's apotheosis during the "art for art's sake" movement of the decadent decade, the influences informing his school of thought should not be separated from those that elicited the "modernist" crisis.

While the "modernist" threat to orthodoxy did not weigh as heavily on Protestantism (having already left the Catholic Church), all Christian sects still were brought into the imbroglio perpetuated by a skeptical interpretation of the Bible. For instance, the Bishop of Oxford, John Fielder Mackarness, followed the strategic response of Catholicism by defaming Pater as an internal dissenter whose philosophies should be quelled. On April 25, 1875, the Bishop spoke on the religious skepticism being promoted at Oxford: "To speak the simple truth, a considerable number of Graduates who hold office in the University, or Fellowships in the Colleges, have ceased to be Christians in anything but name;—in some cases, even the name is repudiated, when arguments based upon its retention are pressed" (qtd. in Seiler 95). Though he did not cite Pater by name, the Bishop quoted three passages from the "Conclusion" to *The Renaissance* as examples of the emphasis that skeptics place on the ephemerality of life and the consequent need for reaping a manifold set of experiences.[10] Additionally, the Bishop critiqued the rise of a scientific historical method: "The historical facts of Christianity fare no better than its precepts: deference to scientific criticism (whatever that may mean), forbids them to be taken for true" (qtd. in Seiler 95). As a result of this form of education, the Bishop believed that wayward youths would develop a "selfishness of character" and lose "all motive for serious action" (qtd. in Seiler 96). In contrast, for Pater, Pico della Mirandola presents a serious attempt to synthesize all forms of thought out of a magnanimous, humanist gesture.

In the essay on Pico, Pater uses his compelling but failed attempt to reconcile paganism and Christianity as an illustration of the need for a proper historical criticism. Still, Pico's endeavor to list 900 theses arguing that all Western philosophy and religions share the same underlying truths led Pater to consider the Renaissance humanist scholar his spiritual precursor, who also personified "curiosity" and believed "that nothing which has ever interested living men and women can wholly lose its vitality" (38). He had a "desire . . . to hear all voices" (27). Above all, Pater finds Pico to be an attractive figure because he is a "picturesque union of contrasts" himself, and a person who "wins one on, in spite of one's self, to turn again to the pages of his forgotten books" (37). A figure like Pico who was so desirous of all forms of knowledge inspires others to be so curious. Indeed, Pater certainly thinks of himself as continuing the approach of Pico, who was "one of the last who seriously and sincerely entertained the claim on men's faith of the pagan religions" (33). In 1486, Pico planned on debating his 900 interdisciplinary theses at a conference to which he invited scholars from across Europe; however, Pope Innocent VIII declared thirteen of his theological theses to be heretical. When Pico avoided being burned at the stake by withdrawing the plans for his conference and acquiescing to work in a Dominican order, his life, according to Pater and his view of *Andersstreben,* became "so perfect a parallel to the attempt made in his writings to reconcile Christianity with the ideas of paganism" (34). Still holding a "tenderness" for his earlier life, Pico wrote *Heptaplus, or Discourse on the Seven Days of Creation* (1490), a series of sonnets which strives to harmonize the works of Plato and Moses through an "unbroken system of correspondences" and, of particular interest to Pater, a rigorous and inspired analysis of the "double meanings of words" (34-35).

Despite admiring Pico's intentions, Pater hints that a "modern scholar" occupied by a similar problem would not treat religious traditions as hermetically sealed texts and divorce them from their cultural contexts. By placing the varied contexts at hand in light of the "gradual education of the human mind," Pater declares that the "basis of the reconciliation of the religions of the world would thus be the inexhaustible activity and creativeness of the human mind itself, in which all religions alike have their root, and in which all alike are reconciled" (26). However, the historical sense required for this type of methodology would not develop until at least Hegel. During the Renaissance, Pater finds that scholars, despite exemplifying "a curiosity of the human mind" to compare religions, had to rely on the "quicksand of allegorical interpretation" (25-27). Lacking historical tools and stuck within a geocentric view of the universe, fifteenth-century scholars tried to reconcile religions, "not as successive stages in a regular development of the religious sense, but as subsisting side by side." As a result of such a spatial methodology, the interpretations tended to "misrepresent" the material because, set "side by side, the mere surfaces could never unite in any harmony of design" (26). Thus Pater pokes at Pico's overly-nuanced attempt to force a harmonization where none exists. Nevertheless, he feels that the results of such an endeavor, successful or not, are chiefly important for the loss of the "religious significance" and the rise of treating "the subject" as "purely artistic or poetical." Foreshadowing his call in the "Conclusion" for the love of art for its own sake, Pater claims that "the natural charm of pagan story" caused Renaissance artists, unlike their scholarly counterparts, to value the beauty of the Greek gods solely out of aesthetic appreciation (23). In contrast to the wrongheaded attempts of scholars of the period to collocate the pagan and Christian as distinct complements, the art of the Renaissance cultivates a "practical truce and reconciliation of the gods of Greece with the Christian religion" (27). Here Pater foregrounds the capacity of the Renaissance artists to capture what their contemporary scholars could not—the method by which the past subtly persists in the present.

Owing much unacknowledged debt to Pater, T. S. Eliot refines the idea of a living past in his landmark essay "Tradition and the Individual Talent" (1919) with the famous line that "the historical sense invokes a perception, not only of the pastness of the past, but of its presence" (4).[11] In his perspective on the Victorians, Eliot stridently heeds his own advice that a poet should distance himself "from his predecessors, especially his immediate predecessors" ("Tradition" 4). In his 1930 essay on Arnold and Pater, Eliot attacks them for replacing "Religion" with "Culture" and, in Pater's case, for emphasizing a subjective impression-ism in aesthetic interpretation. Eliot opposes their mutual "curiosity" that might uncover historical material unflattering or antithetical to Christianity. Eliot then quickly devolves into a personal attack on Pater's mental faculties and ultimately tries to decanonize him. Since Pater was "incapable of sustained reasoning," Eliot believes that his work will not influence "a single first-rate mind of a later generation" ("Arnold and Pater" 390-92). The attempt to disempower Pater's influence by and large succeeded, for as Nathan Scott points out, Eliot's *ad hominem* attack on Pater's aestheticization of religion, though "utter nonsense," "proved over the span of a generation to be something like a benchmark for contemporary criticism" of Pater because of the "immense prestige he [Eliot] commanded" (64). In lambasting Pater's portrayal of Marius' casual conversion to Christianity, Eliot clearly has in mind his own recent conversion when claiming that Pater has no "realization of the chasm to be leapt between the meditations of Aurelius and the Gospels" ("Arnold and Pater" 392). On 29 June 1927, Eliot was baptized into the Church of England, and his writings from then on overtly promote Christianity.[12] Yet Eliot steadfastly maintains his critical position on the dynamic between the past and present—content and form. Consequently, and this can be seen in "Arnold and Pater," Eliot endeavors to promulgate Christianity as *the* Western tradition.

The very distinctions made in the process of defining "tradition" mark the difference between Pater and Eliot. In each of their forms of rhetoric, the diverging pasts that they privilege illustrate the recurrently contested realm of canon-formation. For Eliot, the new work of art must "conform" to the "existing monuments" that "form an ideal order among themselves" ("Tradition" 5). While he states that the individual artist must make the canon alter "ever so slightly," a collapse of the pagan/Christian dyad would not entail, especially for the post-1927 Eliot, "conformity between the old and new" ("Tradition" 5). In contrast to Eliot's privileging of a self-consciously Christian presence, Pater, as we have seen, stresses the pagan sentiment, which is "a part of the eternal basis of all religions, modified indeed by changes of time and place, but indestructible, because its root is so deep in the earth of man's nature" (160). In a wonderfully evocative description, DeLaura proclaims that Pater's writings strive to move beyond the "inevitably inhibiting Victorian timidity and fear of paganism" in order "to provide a new spiritual basis for modern life which incorporates nothing less than a 'comprehensive' view of the totality of man's past" (*Hebrew* 181). Indeed, Eliot responds so vehemently to Pater because he needs to counter a previous aesthetic critic who pre-empted his ideas of form and content, but with an oppositional viewpoint on what composed the tradition. In Pater's vision, the canon needs to be expanded in a more inclusive gesture.

The gesture would heal what Pater sees as the rupture between the medieval period and the Renaissance and concomitantly reveal the shared origins of paganism and Christianity. In his discussion of **"Winckelmann,"** which propels his thesis beyond the Renaissance, Pater points at the fluid inclusivity of history: "Pagan and Christian art are sometimes harshly opposed, and the Renaissance is represented as a fashion which set in at a definite period. That is the superficial view: the deeper view is that which preserves the identity of European culture. The two are really continuous; and there is a sense in which it may be said that the Renaissance was an uninterrupted effort of the middle age." Still, Pater finds that the temperament of the modern age would benefit from the example of Winckelmann and his "*Heiterkeit,* that pagan blitheness" (180) that reflects "a kind of ineffectual wholeness of nature, yet with a beauty and significance of its own" (176). In the rhapsodic denouement of **"Winckelmann,"** Pater calls for an attempt to re-achieve the Hellenic healing ideals of serenity, balance, and unity. As opposed to the art of Christian asceticism, treating "art in the pagan manner" is to handle the subject "with no sense of shame or loss" (177). In kindling sensuousness, this serenity creates the paradox of being a "negative quality" in its "absence of any sense of want, or corruption or shame" (176). With the revival of pagan subjects in art, the Renaissance world, according to Pater, awoke "with eyes refreshed, to those ancient, ideal forms" (181). At last, the curiosity for this task would be satisfied. A return of the pagan allows for a persistence of Christian forms while recalling the pagan past buried below much of Christian doctrine and tradition. A pagan renaissance delivers a blow to the canonized relations of form and content instantiated by Eliot. Conformity need not be a mandate for art, for content can be changed. The historically-documented appropriation of pagan rituals testifies to that.

*Notes*

1. Quotations are drawn from the fourth edition of *The Renaissance* (1893), the last, revised edition published in Pater's lifetime.

2. Here, Pater without acknowledgement quotes from Baudelaire's essay "L'Oeuvre et la vie d'Eugène Delacroix" (1863).

3. According to Pater, in music, the note simultaneously denotes both form and content, and they cannot be detached from one another. A song (a ballad), then, compounds the levels of relations between form and content by yoking together music, which has its own internal relations, and words, which can vary verse by verse. With each verse, the song must reconfigure itself to make the repetitive rhythm cohere with the new sequence of words.

4. Paterian criticism is acutely aware of his attacks on Christianity, as Denis Donoghue reminds us that Gerard Manley Hopkins noted in his journal of "Pater talking two hours against Xianity" (33). Levey also finds that Pater's approach to religious

orthodoxy was one to "pepper ironically the target of Christianity—and religious systems of all kinds—with the intention of provoking thought" (82). At a fundamental level, Pater suggests the process of rumination will ultimately undermine dogmatic Christianity.

5. Moreover, Pater shows an affinity with Morris in wanting to take heart in the sufferings of others and work against the progression of linear history.

6. The first definition in the *OED* of "curious" used as a subjective quality of persons is: "Bestowing care or pains." Demonstrating the relation of "curious" to "cure," John Ayto states that the "Latin adjective curiosus originally meant 'careful,' a sense preserved through Old French *curios* into English *curious* but defunct since the 18th century. The secondary sense 'inquisitive' developed in Latin, but it was not until the word reached Old French that the meaning 'interesting' emerged" (150).

7. For a rich discussion of homoeroticism in Pater's writings, see Richard Dellamora's *Masculine Desire*. Dellamora pursues the idea that Pater reads Leonardo's *Head of the Medusa* "as a sign of male-male desire in which self-awareness takes the form of a rhetorical wish to be woman" (130).

8. In "Pico della Mirandola," Pater quotes a lengthy passage from Heine's *Gods in Exile* (1853-54) to put forth the idea that, after the triumph of Christianity, pagan gods "had then to take flight ignominiously, and hide themselves among us here on earth, under all sorts of disguises" (24). For Pater, the role of the art critic is to decipher these disguises.

9. Donoghue also adds that Pater uses a reference to Joachim of Flora following the passage I have quoted as a further aesthetic endeavor to see "modernity" as "the supersession of religion by art" (137).

10. Wolfgang Iser stresses that the "skepticism of Pater's first essay [on Coleridge] remained fundamental to all his writings" (17). Moreover, Iser finds that Pater's type of skepticism bears relation on the role of "curiosity" discussed here, for Iser describes it as "skepticism in the old classical sense of 'spying out, investigating, searching examining'" (16).

11. In his essay on the subtextual Paterian echoes in Eliot's criticism, David DeLaura finds that, in "Sandro Botticelli," Pater "had given several hints which suggest a source for the criterion of the 'objective correlative'" ("Pater and Eliot" 428).

12. For further information on Eliot's conversion experience and its effects on his writings, see Lyndall Gordon, *Eliot's New Life* (New York: Farrar, Straus & Giroux, 1988).

## Works Cited

Arnold, Matthew. "The Function of Criticism at the Present Time." 1865. *Matthew Arnold: Selected Prose.* Ed. P. J. Keating. New York and London: Penguin, 1987. 130-57.

———. "Sweetness and Light." 1869. *Matthew Arnold: Selected Prose.* Ed. P. J. Keating. New York and London: Penguin, 1987. 204-27.

Arrowsmith, William. "Notes to *The Satyricon.*" Petronius. *The Satyricon.* Tr. William Arrowsmith. New York: Meridian, 1987. 166-92.

Ayto, John. *Dictionary of Word Origins.* New York: Little, Brown and Company, 1990.

Burrow, J. W. "The Uses of Philology in Victorian England." *Ideas and Institutions of Victorian Britain.* Ed. Robert Robson. New York: Barnes and Noble, 1967: 180-204.

DeLaura, David J. *Hebrew and Hellene in Victorian England.* U of Texas P, 1969.

———. "Pater and Eliot: The Origin of the 'Objective Correlative.'" *Modern Language Quarterly* 26.3 (September 1965): 426-31.

Dellamora, Richard. *Masculine Desire: The Sexual Politics of Victorian Aestheticism.* U of North Carolina P, 1990.

———. "Pater's Modernism: The Leonardo Essay." *University of Toronto Quarterly* 47.2 (winter 1977/78): 135-50.

Donoghue, Denis. *Walter Pater: Lover of Strange Souls.* New York: Alfred A. Knopf, 1995.

Eliot, T. S. "Arnold and Pater." *Selected Essays of T. S. Eliot.* 1932. New York: Harcourt, 1964. 382-93.

———. "Tradition and the Individual Talent." *Selected Essays of T. S. Eliot.* 1932. New York: Harcourt, 1964. 3-11.

Hollander, John. "Dallying nicely with words." *The Linguistics of Writing: Arguments between Literature and Language.* Ed. Nigel Fabb *et al.* New York: Methuen, 1987. 123-34.

Iser, Wolfgang. *Walter Pater: The Aesthetic Moment.* Cambridge UP, 1987.

Jordan-Smith, Paul. *On Strange Altars.* New York: Albert & Charles Boni, 1924.

Levey, Michael. *The Case of Walter Pater.* London: Thames and Hudson, 1978.

Pater, Walter. "Poems by William Morris." *William Morris: The Critical Heritage.* Ed. Peter Faulkner. London: Routledge & Kegan Paul, 1973. 79-92.

———. *The Renaissance: Studies in Art and Poetry,* 4th Edition. 1893. Ed. Donald L. Hill. U of California P, 1980.

Scott, Jr., Nathan A. *The Poetics of Belief.* U of North Carolina P, 1985.

Seiler, R. M. *Walter Pater: The Critical Heritage.* London: Routledge & Kegan Paul, 1980.

Turner, Frank M. *The Greek Heritage in Victorian Britain.* Yale UP, 1981.

---

# FURTHER READING

## Criticism

Barolsky, Paul. *Walter Pater's Renaissance.* University Park: Pennsylvania State University Press, 1987, 214 p.

Discusses the intimate relationship between Walter Pater's lyrical prose style and his subjective approach to art criticism, examining how this relationship lies at the core of *The Renaissance.*

Bellringer, Alan W. "The 'Conclusion' to *The Renaissance*: Pater's Original Meaning." *Prose Studies 1800-1900* 1, no. 1 (1977): 45-55.

Compares Pater's first version of the "Conclusion" with his subsequent revisions of the essay, arguing that the original text represents the author's clearest, most emphatic statement of his aesthetic principles.

Bockley, Jerome Hamilton. "Pater and the Suppressed 'Conclusion.'" *Modern Language Notes* 65, no. 4 (April 1950): 249-51.

Examines some possible motives behind Pater's decision to leave his "Conclusion" out of the second edition of *The Renaissance.*

Buckler, William E. "The Renaissance." In *Walter Pater: The Critic as Artist of Ideas,* pp. 72-81. New York: New York University Press, 1987.

Discusses Pater's essay on Michelangelo.

Child, Ruth C. *The Aesthetic of Walter Pater.* New York: The Macmillan Company, 1940, 157 p.

Outlines the evolution of Pater's critical approach over the course of his career, from his early essays on the Renaissance through his later fictional works.

Crawford, Robert. "Pater's *Renaissance,* Andrew Lang, and Anthropological Romanticism." *ELH* 53, no. 4 (winter 1986): 849-79.

Discusses Pater's friendship with the anthropologist Andrew Lang, as well as the impact of recent advances in the field of anthropology on the development of Pater's modernist literary and intellectual sensibility.

Daruwala, Maneck Homi. "'The Discerning Flame': Of Pater and *The Renaissance.*" *VIJ: Victorians Institute Journal* 16 (1988): 85-127.

Analyzes Pater's preoccupation with the role of the artist's personality in the creation of art, evaluating the influence of this concept on later writers such as Oscar Wilde and William Butler Yeats.

Dellamora, Richard. "Pater's Modernism: The Leonardo Essay." *University of Toronto Quarterly* 47, no. 2 (winter 1977-78): 135-50.

Examines how Pater's analysis of Leonardo da Vinci, with its emphasis on the artist's individuality and unique creative genius, demonstrated a distinctly modern critical approach and marked a radical departure from existing scholarship on Renaissance art.

Donoghue, Denis. *Walter Pater: Lover of Strange Souls.* New York: Alfred A. Knopf, 1995, 364 p.

Argues for Pater's indispensable role in the development of modernism, notably through his espousal of radically subjective forms of expression and thought.

Inman, Billie Andrew. "The Intellectual Context of Walter Pater's 'Conclusion.'" *Journal of Prose Studies* 4, no. 1 (May 1981): 12-30.

Examines the various literary and philosophical influences behind the "Conclusion" by conducting a thorough evaluation of the books Pater was reading at the time of its composition.

Malley, Shawn. "Walter Pater's Heroic Nostos: The Underworld Journey in *The Renaissance.*" *Nineteenth-Century Prose* 21, no. 1 (spring 1994): 1-16.

Evaluates Pater's unique concept of artistic inspiration and provides an in-depth analysis of Pater's attitudes toward the Renaissance and Hellenism.

Nash, Jerry C. "'The Poet of One Poem': Du Bellay, Walter Pater, and Modern Aesthetic Criticism." *Oeuvres and Critiques* 20, no. 1 (1995): 113-19.

Examines Pater's appraisal of French author Joachim du Bellay within the context of Renaissance developments in sixteenth-century France.

Oliphant, Margaret. "Pater's *History of the Renaissance*." *Blackwood's Edinburgh Magazine* 114, no. 697 (November 1873): 604-09.

Describes Pater's study as "pretentious," asserting that the work's ornate style serves only to mask its lack of substance.

Østermark-Johansen, Lene. "Serpentine Rivers and Serpentine Thought: Flux and Movement in Walter Pater's Leonardo Essay." *Victorian Literature and Culture* 30, no. 2 (2002): 455-82.

Analyzes the relationship between Pater's prose and his subject in his essay on Leonardo da Vinci, while also examining Pater's attitude toward Leonardo's theories concerning human physiology, motion, and water.

Sullivan, William H. "Four Early Studies from Pater's *The Renaissance*: The Aesthetics for a Humanist Myth." *The Victorian Newsletter,* no. 40 (fall 1971): 1-7.

Asserts that Pater's principal goal in *The Renaissance* is to set forth a "humanist myth" for art.

Symonds, J. A. Review of *The Renaissance. Academy* 4 (March 15, 1873): 103-05.

Offers an insightful and candid critique of Pater's landmark work.

Teukolsky, Rachel. "The Politics of Formalist Art Criticism: Pater's 'School of Giorgioni.'" In *Walter Pater: Transparencies of Desire,* edited by Laurel Brake, Lesley Higgins, and Carolyn Williams, pp. 151-69. Greensboro, N.C.: ELT Press, 2002.

Discusses the political ramifications of Pater's formalist approach to art criticism, examining how Pater's aesthetic theories corroborated and also rebelled against dominant aspects of Victorian culture.

Tucker, Paul. "'Reanimate Greek': Pater and Ruskin on Botticelli." In *Walter Pater: Transparencies of Desire,* edited by Laurel Brake, Lesley Higgins, and Carolyn Williams, pp. 119-132. Greensboro, N.C.: ELT Press, 2002.

Compares Pater's and Ruskin's views on the painter, while also examining Botticelli's role in the development of Renaissance art.

---

**Additional coverage of Pater's life and career is contained in the following sources published by Thomson Gale:** *British Writers,* **Vol. 5;** *Concise Dictionary of British Literary Biography,* **1832-1890;** *Dictionary of Literary Biography,* **Vols. 57, 156;** *Literature Resource Center*; *Nineteenth-Century Literature Criticism,* **Vols. 7, 90;** *Reference Guide to English Literature,* **Ed. 2; and** *Twayne's English Authors.*

# How to Use This Index

## The main references

Calvino, Italo
1923-1985 ....... CLC **5, 8, 11, 22, 33, 39,
73; SSC 3, 48**

**list all author entries in the following Gale Literary Criticism series:**

*AAL* = *Asian American Literature*
*BG* = *The Beat Generation: A Gale Critical Companion*
*BLC* = *Black Literature Criticism*
*BLCS* = *Black Literature Criticism Supplement*
*CLC* = *Contemporary Literary Criticism*
*CLR* = *Children's Literature Review*
*CMLC* = *Classical and Medieval Literature Criticism*
*DC* = *Drama Criticism*
*HLC* = *Hispanic Literature Criticism*
*HLCS* = *Hispanic Literature Criticism Supplement*
*HR* = *Harlem Renaissance: A Gale Critical Companion*
*LC* = *Literature Criticism from 1400 to 1800*
*NCLC* = *Nineteenth-Century Literature Criticism*
*NNAL* = *Native North American Literature*
*PC* = *Poetry Criticism*
*SSC* = *Short Story Criticism*
*TCLC* = *Twentieth-Century Literary Criticism*
*WLC* = *World Literature Criticism, 1500 to the Present*
*WLCS* = *World Literature Criticism Supplement*

## The cross-references

See also CA 85-88, 116; CANR 23, 61;
DAM NOV; DLB 196; EW 13; MTCW 1, 2;
RGSF 2; RGWL 2; SFW 4; SSFS 12

**list all author entries in the following Gale biographical and literary sources:**

*AAYA* = *Authors & Artists for Young Adults*
*AFAW* = *African American Writers*
*AFW* = *African Writers*
*AITN* = *Authors in the News*
*AMW* = *American Writers*
*AMWR* = *American Writers Retrospective Supplement*
*AMWS* = *American Writers Supplement*
*ANW* = *American Nature Writers*
*AW* = *Ancient Writers*
*BEST* = *Bestsellers*
*BPFB* = *Beacham's Encyclopedia of Popular Fiction: Biography and Resources*
*BRW* = *British Writers*
*BRWS* = *British Writers Supplement*
*BW* = *Black Writers*
*BYA* = *Beacham's Guide to Literature for Young Adults*
*CA* = *Contemporary Authors*
*CAAS* = *Contemporary Authors Autobiography Series*
*CABS* = *Contemporary Authors Bibliographical Series*
*CAD* = *Contemporary American Dramatists*
*CANR* = *Contemporary Authors New Revision Series*
*CAP* = *Contemporary Authors Permanent Series*
*CBD* = *Contemporary British Dramatists*
*CCA* = *Contemporary Canadian Authors*
*CD* = *Contemporary Dramatists*
*CDALB* = *Concise Dictionary of American Literary Biography*
*CDALBS* = *Concise Dictionary of American Literary Biography Supplement*
*CDBLB* = *Concise Dictionary of British Literary Biography*

**CMW** = *St. James Guide to Crime & Mystery Writers*
**CN** = *Contemporary Novelists*
**CP** = *Contemporary Poets*
**CPW** = *Contemporary Popular Writers*
**CSW** = *Contemporary Southern Writers*
**CWD** = *Contemporary Women Dramatists*
**CWP** = *Contemporary Women Poets*
**CWRI** = *St. James Guide to Children's Writers*
**CWW** = *Contemporary World Writers*
**DA** = *DISCovering Authors*
**DA3** = *DISCovering Authors 3.0*
**DAB** = *DISCovering Authors: British Edition*
**DAC** = *DISCovering Authors: Canadian Edition*
**DAM** = *DISCovering Authors: Modules*
   **DRAM:** *Dramatists Module;* **MST:** *Most-studied Authors Module;*
   **MULT:** *Multicultural Authors Module;* **NOV:** *Novelists Module;*
   **POET:** *Poets Module;* **POP:** *Popular Fiction and Genre Authors Module*
**DFS** = *Drama for Students*
**DLB** = *Dictionary of Literary Biography*
**DLBD** = *Dictionary of Literary Biography Documentary Series*
**DLBY** = *Dictionary of Literary Biography Yearbook*
**DNFS** = *Literature of Developing Nations for Students*
**EFS** = *Epics for Students*
**EXPN** = *Exploring Novels*
**EXPP** = *Exploring Poetry*
**EXPS** = *Exploring Short Stories*
**EW** = *European Writers*
**FANT** = *St. James Guide to Fantasy Writers*
**FW** = *Feminist Writers*
**GFL** = *Guide to French Literature,* Beginnings to 1789, 1798 to the Present
**GLL** = *Gay and Lesbian Literature*
**HGG** = *St. James Guide to Horror, Ghost & Gothic Writers*
**HW** = *Hispanic Writers*
**IDFW** = *International Dictionary of Films and Filmmakers: Writers and Production Artists*
**IDTP** = *International Dictionary of Theatre: Playwrights*
**LAIT** = *Literature and Its Times*
**LAW** = *Latin American Writers*
**JRDA** = *Junior DISCovering Authors*
**MAICYA** = *Major Authors and Illustrators for Children and Young Adults*
**MAICYAS** = *Major Authors and Illustrators for Children and Young Adults Supplement*
**MAWW** = *Modern American Women Writers*
**MJW** = *Modern Japanese Writers*
**MTCW** = *Major 20th-Century Writers*
**NCFS** = *Nonfiction Classics for Students*
**NFS** = *Novels for Students*
**PAB** = *Poets: American and British*
**PFS** = *Poetry for Students*
**RGAL** = *Reference Guide to American Literature*
**RGEL** = *Reference Guide to English Literature*
**RGSF** = *Reference Guide to Short Fiction*
**RGWL** = *Reference Guide to World Literature*
**RHW** = *Twentieth-Century Romance and Historical Writers*
**SAAS** = *Something about the Author Autobiography Series*
**SATA** = *Something about the Author*
**SFW** = *St. James Guide to Science Fiction Writers*
**SSFS** = *Short Stories for Students*
**TCWW** = *Twentieth-Century Western Writers*
**WLIT** = *World Literature and Its Times*
**WP** = *World Poets*
**YABC** = *Yesterday's Authors of Books for Children*
**YAW** = *St. James Guide to Young Adult Writers*

# Literary Criticism Series
# Cumulative Author Index

**20/1631**
See Upward, Allen

**A/C Cross**
See Lawrence, T(homas) E(dward)

**Abasiyanik, Sait Faik** 1906-1954
See Sait Faik
See also CA 123

**Abbey, Edward** 1927-1989 ........ **CLC 36, 59; TCLC 160**
See also AMWS 13; ANW; CA 45-48; 128; CANR 2, 41, 131; DA3; DLB 256, 275; LATS 1:2; MTCW 2; TCWW 2

**Abbott, Edwin A.** 1838-1926 ........ **TCLC 139**
See also DLB 178

**Abbott, Lee K(ittredge)** 1947- .......... **CLC 48**
See also CA 124; CANR 51, 101; DLB 130

**Abe, Kobo** 1924-1993 ...... **CLC 8, 22, 53, 81; SSC 61; TCLC 131**
See also CA 65-68; 140; CANR 24, 60; DAM NOV; DFS 14; DLB 182; EWL 3; MJW; MTCW 1, 2; RGWL 3; SFW 4

**Abe Kobo**
See Abe, Kobo

**Abelard, Peter** c. 1079-c. 1142 ..... **CMLC 11, 77**
See also DLB 115, 208

**Abell, Kjeld** 1901-1961 ...................... **CLC 15**
See also CA 191; 111; DLB 214; EWL 3

**Abercrombie, Lascelles**
1881-1938 .............................. **TCLC 141**
See also CA 112; DLB 19; RGEL 2

**Abish, Walter** 1931- ........... **CLC 22; SSC 44**
See also CA 101; CANR 37, 114; CN 7; DLB 130, 227

**Abrahams, Peter (Henry)** 1919- ......... **CLC 4**
See also AFW; BW 1; CA 57-60; CANR 26, 125; CDWLB 3; CN 7; DLB 117, 225; EWL 3; MTCW 1, 2; RGEL 2; WLIT 2

**Abrams, M(eyer) H(oward)** 1912- ... **CLC 24**
See also CA 57-60; CANR 13, 33; DLB 67

**Abse, Dannie** 1923- .......... **CLC 7, 29; PC 41**
See also CA 53-56; CAAS 1; CANR 4, 46, 74, 124; CBD; CP 7; DAB; DAM POET; DLB 27, 245; MTCW 1

**Abutsu** 1222(?)-1283 ...................... **CMLC 46**
See also Abutsu-ni

**Abutsu-ni**
See Abutsu
See also DLB 203

**Achebe, (Albert) Chinua(lumogu)**
1930- ..... **BLC 1; CLC 1, 3, 5, 7, 11, 26, 51, 75, 127, 152; WLC**
See also AAYA 15; AFW; BPFB 1; BRWC 2; BW 2, 3; CA 1-4R; CANR 6, 26, 47, 124; CDWLB 3; CLR 20; CN 7; CP 7; CWRI 5; DA; DA3; DAB; DAC; DAM MST, MULT, NOV; DLB 117; DNFS 1; EWL 3; EXPN; EXPS; LAIT 2; LATS

1:2; MAICYA 1, 2; MTCW 1, 2; NFS 2; RGEL 2; RGSF 2; SATA 38, 40; SATA-Brief 38; SSFS 3, 13; TWA; WLIT 2; WWE 1

**Acker, Kathy** 1948-1997 ........... **CLC 45, 111**
See also AMWS 12; CA 117; 122; 162; CANR 55; CN 7

**Ackroyd, Peter** 1949- ......... **CLC 34, 52, 140**
See also BRWS 6; CA 123; 127; CANR 51, 74, 99, 132; CN 7; DLB 155, 231; HGG; INT CA-127; MTCW 1; RHW; SATA 153; SUFW 2

**Acorn, Milton** 1923-1986 .................. **CLC 15**
See also CA 103; CCA 1; DAC; DLB 53; INT CA-103

**Adamov, Arthur** 1908-1970 ......... **CLC 4, 25**
See also CA 17-18; 25-28R; CAP 2; DAM DRAM; EWL 3; GFL 1789 to the Present; MTCW 1; RGWL 2, 3

**Adams, Alice (Boyd)** 1926-1999 .. **CLC 6, 13, 46; SSC 24**
See also CA 81-84; 179; CANR 26, 53, 75, 88; CN 7; CSW; DLB 234; DLBY 1986; INT CANR-26; MTCW 1, 2; SSFS 14

**Adams, Andy** 1859-1935 ................. **TCLC 56**
See also TCWW 2; YABC 1

**Adams, (Henry) Brooks**
1848-1927 ................................. **TCLC 80**
See also CA 123; 193; DLB 47

**Adams, Douglas (Noel)** 1952-2001 .. **CLC 27, 60**
See also AAYA 4, 33; BEST 89:3; BYA 14; CA 106; 197; CANR 34, 64, 124; CPW; DA3; DAM POP; DLB 261; DLBY 1983; JRDA; MTCW 1; NFS 7; SATA 116; SATA-Obit 128; SFW 4

**Adams, Francis** 1862-1893 ............. **NCLC 33**

**Adams, Henry (Brooks)**
1838-1918 .......................... **TCLC 4, 52**
See also AMW; CA 104; 133; CANR 77; DA; DAB; DAC; DAM MST; DLB 12, 47, 189, 284; EWL 3; MTCW 1; NCFS 1; RGAL 4; TUS

**Adams, John** 1735-1826 ............... **NCLC 106**
See also DLB 31, 183

**Adams, Richard (George)** 1920- ... **CLC 4, 5, 18**
See also AAYA 16; AITN 1, 2; BPFB 1; BYA 5; CA 49-52; CANR 3, 35, 128; CLR 20; CN 7; DAM NOV; DLB 261; FANT; JRDA; LAIT 5; MAICYA 1, 2; MTCW 1, 2; NFS 11; SATA 7, 69; YAW

**Adamson, Joy(-Friederike Victoria)**
1910-1980 ................................. **CLC 17**
See also CA 69-72; 93-96; CANR 22; MTCW 1; SATA 11; SATA-Obit 22

**Adcock, Fleur** 1934- ........................... **CLC 41**
See also CA 25-28R, 182; CAAE 182; CAAS 23; CANR 11, 34, 69, 101; CP 7; CWP; DLB 40; FW; WWE 1

**Addams, Charles (Samuel)**
1912-1988 .................................. **CLC 30**
See also CA 61-64; 126; CANR 12, 79

**Addams, (Laura) Jane** 1860-1935 . **TCLC 76**
See also AMWS 1; CA 194; DLB 303; FW

**Addison, Joseph** 1672-1719 .................. **LC 18**
See also BRW 3; CDBLB 1660-1789; DLB 101; RGEL 2; WLIT 3

**Adler, Alfred (F.)** 1870-1937 ........... **TCLC 61**
See also CA 119; 159

**Adler, C(arole) S(chwerdtfeger)**
1932- ....................................... **CLC 35**
See also AAYA 4, 41; CA 89-92; CANR 19, 40, 101; CLR 78; JRDA; MAICYA 1, 2; SAAS 15; SATA 26, 63, 102, 126; YAW

**Adler, Renata** 1938- ...................... **CLC 8, 31**
See also CA 49-52; CANR 95; CN 7; MTCW 1

**Adorno, Theodor W(iesengrund)**
1903-1969 .............................. **TCLC 111**
See also CA 89-92; 25-28R; CANR 89; DLB 242; EWL 3

**Ady, Endre** 1877-1919 .................... **TCLC 11**
See also CA 107; CDWLB 4; DLB 215; EW 9; EWL 3

**A.E.** ............................................... **TCLC 3, 10**
See Russell, George William
See also DLB 19

**Aelfric** c. 955-c. 1010 .................... **CMLC 46**
See also DLB 146

**Aeschines** c. 390B.C.-c. 320B.C. ... **CMLC 47**
See also DLB 176

**Aeschylus** 525(?)B.C.-456(?)B.C. .. **CMLC 11, 51; DC 8; WLCS**
See also AW 1; CDWLB 1; DA; DAB; DAC; DAM DRAM, MST; DFS 5, 10; DLB 176; LMFS 1; RGWL 2, 3; TWA

**Aesop** 620(?)B.C.-560(?)B.C. ......... **CMLC 24**
See also CLR 14; MAICYA 1, 2; SATA 64

**Affable Hawk**
See MacCarthy, Sir (Charles Otto) Desmond

**Africa, Ben**
See Bosman, Herman Charles

**Afton, Effie**
See Harper, Frances Ellen Watkins

**Agapida, Fray Antonio**
See Irving, Washington

**Agee, James (Rufus)** 1909-1955 ...... **TCLC 1, 19**
See also AAYA 44; AITN 1; AMW; CA 108; 148; CANR 131; CDALB 1941-1968; DAM NOV; DLB 2, 26, 152; DLBY 1989; EWL 3; LAIT 3; LATS 1:2; MTCW 1; RGAL 4; TUS

**Aghill, Gordon**
See Silverberg, Robert

**al-Hariri, al-Qasim ibn 'Ali Abu Muhammad al-Basri**
1054-1122 .......................... **CMLC 63**
See also RGWL 3

**Ali, Ahmed** 1908-1998 ...................... **CLC 69**
See also CA 25-28R; CANR 15, 34; EWL 3

**Ali, Tariq** 1943- ............................... **CLC 173**
See also CA 25-28R; CANR 10, 99

**Alighieri, Dante**
See Dante

**Allan, John B.**
See Westlake, Donald E(dwin)

**Allan, Sidney**
See Hartmann, Sadakichi

**Allan, Sydney**
See Hartmann, Sadakichi

**Allard, Janet** ..................................... **CLC 59**

**Allen, Edward** 1948- .......................... **CLC 59**

**Allen, Fred** 1894-1956 ...................... **TCLC 87**

**Allen, Paula Gunn** 1939- ......... **CLC 84, 202; NNAL**
See also AMWS 4; CA 112; 143; CANR 63, 130; CWP; DA3; DAM MULT; DLB 175; FW; MTCW 1; RGAL 4

**Allen, Roland**
See Ayckbourn, Alan

**Allen, Sarah A.**
See Hopkins, Pauline Elizabeth

**Allen, Sidney H.**
See Hartmann, Sadakichi

**Allen, Woody** 1935- ............. **CLC 16, 52, 195**
See also AAYA 10, 51; CA 33-36R; CANR 27, 38, 63, 128; DAM POP; DLB 44; MTCW 1

**Allende, Isabel** 1942- ... **CLC 39, 57, 97, 170; HLC 1; SSC 65; WLCS**
See also AAYA 18; CA 125; 130; CANR 51, 74, 129; CDWLB 3; CLR 99; CWW 2; DA3; DAM MULT, NOV; DLB 145; DNFS 1; EWL 3; FW; HW 1, 2; INT CA-130; LAIT 5; LAWS 1; LMFS 2; MTCW 1, 2; NCFS 1; NFS 6, 18; RGSF 2; RGWL 3; SSFS 11, 16; WLIT 1

**Alleyn, Ellen**
See Rossetti, Christina (Georgina)

**Alleyne, Carla D.** ............................. **CLC 65**

**Allingham, Margery (Louise)**
1904-1966 ...................................... **CLC 19**
See also CA 5-8R; 25-28R; CANR 4, 58; CMW 4; DLB 77; MSW; MTCW 1, 2

**Allingham, William** 1824-1889 ...... **NCLC 25**
See also DLB 35; RGEL 2

**Allison, Dorothy E.** 1949- ......... **CLC 78, 153**
See also AAYA 53; CA 140; CANR 66, 107; CSW; DA3; FW; MTCW 1; NFS 11; RGAL 4

**Alloula, Malek** ................................. **CLC 65**

**Allston, Washington** 1779-1843 ....... **NCLC 2**
See also DLB 1, 235

**Almedingen, E. M.** ........................... **CLC 12**
See Almedingen, Martha Edith von
See also SATA 3

**Almedingen, Martha Edith von** 1898-1971
See Almedingen, E. M.
See also CA 1-4R; CANR 1

**Almodovar, Pedro** 1949(?)- ........... **CLC 114; HLCS 1**
See also CA 133; CANR 72; HW 2

**Almqvist, Carl Jonas Love**
1793-1866 ................................... **NCLC 42**

**al-Mutanabbi, Ahmad ibn al-Husayn Abu al-Tayyib al-Jufi al-Kindi**
915-965 ...................................... **CMLC 66**
See also RGWL 3

**Alonso, Damaso** 1898-1990 .............. **CLC 14**
See also CA 110; 131; 130; CANR 72; DLB 108; EWL 3; HW 1, 2

**Alov**
See Gogol, Nikolai (Vasilyevich)

**al'Sadaawi, Nawal**
See El Saadawi, Nawal
See also FW

**Al Siddik**
See Rolfe, Frederick (William Serafino Austin Lewis Mary)
See also GLL 1; RGEL 2

**Alta** 1942- ............................................. **CLC 19**
See also CA 57-60

**Alter, Robert B(ernard)** 1935- .......... **CLC 34**
See also CA 49-52; CANR 1, 47, 100

**Alther, Lisa** 1944- ........................... **CLC 7, 41**
See also BPFB 1; CA 65-68; CAAS 30; CANR 12, 30, 51; CN 7; CSW; GLL 2; MTCW 1

**Althusser, L.**
See Althusser, Louis

**Althusser, Louis** 1918-1990 ............. **CLC 106**
See also CA 131; 132; CANR 102; DLB 242

**Altman, Robert** 1925- ................. **CLC 16, 116**
See also CA 73-76; CANR 43

**Alurista** ............................................. **HLCS 1**
See Urista (Heredia), Alberto (Baltazar)
See also DLB 82; LLW 1

**Alvarez, A(lfred)** 1929- ................. **CLC 5, 13**
See also CA 1-4R; CANR 3, 33, 63, 101, 134; CN 7; CP 7; DLB 14, 40

**Alvarez, Alejandro Rodriguez** 1903-1965
See Casona, Alejandro
See also CA 131; 93-96; HW 1

**Alvarez, Julia** 1950- .......... **CLC 93; HLCS 1**
See also AAYA 25; AMWS 7; CA 147; CANR 69, 101, 133; DA3; DLB 282; LATS 1:2; LLW 1; MTCW 1; NFS 5, 9; SATA 129; WLIT 1

**Alvaro, Corrado** 1896-1956 ............ **TCLC 60**
See also CA 163; DLB 264; EWL 3

**Amado, Jorge** 1912-2001 ... **CLC 13, 40, 106; HLC 1**
See also CA 77-80; 201; CANR 35, 74; CWW 2; DAM MULT, NOV; DLB 113, 307; EWL 3; HW 2; LAW; LAWS 1; MTCW 1, 2; RGWL 2, 3; TWA; WLIT 1

**Ambler, Eric** 1909-1998 .............. **CLC 4, 6, 9**
See also BRWS 4; CA 9-12R; 171; CANR 7, 38, 74; CMW 4; CN 7; DLB 77; MSW; MTCW 1, 2; TEA

**Ambrose, Stephen E(dward)**
1936-2002 .................................. **CLC 145**
See also AAYA 44; CA 1-4R; 209; CANR 3, 43, 57, 83, 105; NCFS 2; SATA 40, 138

**Amichai, Yehuda** 1924-2000 .. **CLC 9, 22, 57, 116; PC 38**
See also CA 85-88; 189; CANR 46, 60, 99, 132; CWW 2; EWL 3; MTCW 1

**Amichai, Yehudah**
See Amichai, Yehuda

**Amiel, Henri Frederic** 1821-1881 .... **NCLC 4**
See also DLB 217

**Amis, Kingsley (William)**
1922-1995 ...... **CLC 1, 2, 3, 5, 8, 13, 40, 44, 129**
See also AITN 2; BPFB 1; BRWS 2; CA 9-12R; 150; CANR 8, 28, 54; CDBLB 1945-1960; CN 7; CP 7; DA; DA3; DAB; DAC; DAM MST, NOV; DLB 15, 27, 100, 139; DLBY 1996; EWL 3; HGG; INT CANR-8; MTCW 1, 2; RGEL 2; RGSF 2; SFW 4

**Amis, Martin (Louis)** 1949- .... **CLC 4, 9, 38, 62, 101**
See also BEST 90:3; BRWS 4; CA 65-68; CANR 8, 27, 54, 73, 95, 132; CN 7; DA3; DLB 14, 194; EWL 3; INT CANR-27; MTCW 1

**Ammianus Marcellinus** c. 330-c.
395 .......................................... **CMLC 60**
See also AW 2; DLB 211

**Ammons, A(rchie) R(andolph)**
1926-2001 ...... **CLC 2, 3, 5, 8, 9, 25, 57, 108; PC 16**
See also AITN 1; AMWS 7; CA 9-12R; 193; CANR 6, 36, 51, 73, 107; CP 7; CSW; DAM POET; DLB 5, 165; EWL 3; MTCW 1, 2; PFS 19; RGAL 4

**Amo, Tauraatua i**
See Adams, Henry (Brooks)

**Amory, Thomas** 1691(?)-1788 .............. **LC 48**
See also DLB 39

**Anand, Mulk Raj** 1905-2004 ...... **CLC 23, 93**
See also CA 65-68; CANR 32, 64; CN 7; DAM NOV; EWL 3; MTCW 1, 2; RGSF 2

**Anatol**
See Schnitzler, Arthur

**Anaximander** c. 611B.C.-c.
546B.C. ...................................... **CMLC 22**

**Anaya, Rudolfo A(lfonso)** 1937- ...... **CLC 23, 148; HLC 1**
See also AAYA 20; BYA 13; CA 45-48; CAAS 4; CANR 1, 32, 51, 124; CN 7; DAM MULT, NOV; DLB 82, 206, 278; HW 1; LAIT 4; LLW 1; MTCW 1, 2; NFS 12; RGAL 4; RGSF 2; WLIT 1

**Andersen, Hans Christian**
1805-1875 ....... **NCLC 7, 79; SSC 6, 56; WLC**
See also AAYA 57; CLR 6; DA; DA3; DAB; DAC; DAM MST, POP; EW 6; MAICYA 1, 2; RGSF 2; RGWL 2, 3; SATA 100; TWA; WCH; YABC 1

**Anderson, C. Farley**
See Mencken, H(enry) L(ouis); Nathan, George Jean

**Anderson, Jessica (Margaret) Queale**
1916- ....................................... **CLC 37**
See also CA 9-12R; CANR 4, 62; CN 7

**Anderson, Jon (Victor)** 1940- ............. **CLC 9**
See also CA 25-28R; CANR 20; DAM POET

**Anderson, Lindsay (Gordon)**
1923-1994 .................................. **CLC 20**
See also CA 125; 128; 146; CANR 77

**Anderson, Maxwell** 1888-1959 ........ **TCLC 2, 144**
See also CA 105; 152; DAM DRAM; DFS 16, 20; DLB 7, 228; MTCW 2; RGAL 4

**Anderson, Poul (William)**
1926-2001 .................................. **CLC 15**
See also AAYA 5, 34; BPFB 1; BYA 6, 8, 9; CA 1-4R; 181; 199; CAAE 181; CAAS 2; CANR 2, 15, 34, 64, 110; CLR 58; DLB 8; FANT; INT CANR-15; MTCW 1, 2; SATA 90; SATA-Brief 39; SATA-Essay 106; SCFW 2; SFW 4; SUFW 1, 2

**Anderson, Robert (Woodruff)**
1917- ....................................... **CLC 23**
See also AITN 1; CA 21-24R; CANR 32; DAM DRAM; DLB 7; LAIT 5

**Anderson, Roberta Joan**
See Mitchell, Joni

**Anderson, Sherwood** 1876-1941 .. **SSC 1, 46; TCLC 1, 10, 24, 123; WLC**
See also AAYA 30; AMW; AMWC 2; BPFB 1; CA 104; 121; CANR 61; CDALB 1917-1929; DA; DA3; DAB; DAC; DAM MST, NOV; DLB 4, 9, 86; DLBD 1; EWL 3; EXPS; GLL 2; MTCW 1, 2; NFS 4; RGAL 4; RGSF 2; SSFS 4, 10, 11; TUS

**Andier, Pierre**
See Desnos, Robert

**Andouard**
See Giraudoux, Jean(-Hippolyte)

Austin, Mary (Hunter) 1868-1934 . **TCLC 25**
See Stairs, Gordon
See also ANW; CA 109; 178; DLB 9, 78,
206, 221, 275; FW; TCWW 2

Averroes 1126-1198 .......................... **CMLC 7**
See also DLB 115

Avicenna 980-1037 .......................... **CMLC 16**
See also DLB 115

Avison, Margaret (Kirkland) 1918- .. **CLC 2,
4, 97**
See also CA 17-20R; CANR 134; CP 7;
DAC; DAM POET; DLB 53; MTCW 1

Axton, David
See Koontz, Dean R(ay)

Ayckbourn, Alan 1939- ...... **CLC 5, 8, 18, 33,
74; DC 13**
See also BRWS 5; CA 21-24R; CANR 31,
59, 118; CBD; CD 5; DAB; DAM DRAM;
DFS 7; DLB 13, 245; EWL 3; MTCW 1,
2

Aydy, Catherine
See Tennant, Emma (Christina)

Ayme, Marcel (Andre) 1902-1967 ... **CLC 11;
SSC 41**
See also CA 89-92; CANR 67; CLR 25;
DLB 72; EW 12; EWL 3; GFL 1789 to
the Present; RGSF 2; RGWL 2, 3; SATA
91

Ayrton, Michael 1921-1975 ................. **CLC 7**
See also CA 5-8R; 61-64; CANR 9, 21

Aytmatov, Chingiz
See Aitmatov, Chingiz (Torekulovich)
See also EWL 3

Azorin ................................................ **CLC 11**
See Martinez Ruiz, Jose
See also EW 9; EWL 3

Azuela, Mariano 1873-1952 .. **HLC 1; TCLC
3, 145**
See also CA 104; 131; CANR 81; DAM
MULT; EWL 3; HW 1, 2; LAW; MTCW
1, 2

Ba, Mariama 1929-1981 ...................... **BLCS**
See also AFW; BW 2; CA 141; CANR 87;
DNFS 2; WLIT 2

Baastad, Babbis Friis
See Friis-Baastad, Babbis Ellinor

Bab
See Gilbert, W(illiam) S(chwenck)

Babbis, Eleanor
See Friis-Baastad, Babbis Ellinor

Babel, Isaac
See Babel, Isaak (Emmanuilovich)
See also EW 11; SSFS 10

Babel, Isaak (Emmanuilovich)
1894-1941(?) .. **SSC 16, 78; TCLC 2, 13**
See Babel, Isaac
See also CA 104; 155; CANR 113; DLB
272; EWL 3; MTCW 1; RGSF 2; RGWL
2, 3; TWA

Babits, Mihaly 1883-1941 ............... **TCLC 14**
See also CA 114; CDWLB 4; DLB 215;
EWL 3

Babur 1483-1530 ................................. **LC 18**

Babylas 1898-1962
See Ghelderode, Michel de

Baca, Jimmy Santiago 1952- . **HLC 1; PC 41**
See also CA 131; CANR 81, 90; CP 7;
DAM MULT; DLB 122; HW 1, 2; LLW 1

Baca, Jose Santiago
See Baca, Jimmy Santiago

Bacchelli, Riccardo 1891-1985 ......... **CLC 19**
See also CA 29-32R; 117; DLB 264; EWL
3

Bach, Richard (David) 1936- ............ **CLC 14**
See also AITN 1; BEST 89:2; BPFB 1; BYA
5; CA 9-12R; CANR 18, 93; CPW; DAM
NOV, POP; FANT; MTCW 1; SATA 13

Bache, Benjamin Franklin
1769-1798 ..................................... **LC 74**
See also DLB 43

Bachelard, Gaston 1884-1962 ...... **TCLC 128**
See also CA 97-100; 89-92; DLB 296; GFL
1789 to the Present

Bachman, Richard
See King, Stephen (Edwin)

Bachmann, Ingeborg 1926-1973 ....... **CLC 69**
See also CA 93-96; 45-48; CANR 69; DLB
85; EWL 3; RGWL 2, 3

Bacon, Francis 1561-1626 .............. **LC 18, 32**
See also BRW 1; CDBLB Before 1660;
DLB 151, 236, 252; RGEL 2; TEA

Bacon, Roger 1214(?)-1294 ........... **CMLC 14**
See also DLB 115

Bacovia, George 1881-1957 ........... **TCLC 24**
See Vasiliu, Gheorghe
See also CDWLB 4; DLB 220; EWL 3

Badanes, Jerome 1937-1995 .............. **CLC 59**

Bagehot, Walter 1826-1877 ........... **NCLC 10**
See also DLB 55

Bagnold, Enid 1889-1981 .................. **CLC 25**
See also BYA 2; CA 5-8R; 103; CANR 5,
40; CBD; CWD; CWRI 5; DAM DRAM;
DLB 13, 160, 191, 245; FW; MAICYA 1,
2; RGEL 2; SATA 1, 25

Bagritsky, Eduard ......................... **TCLC 60**
See Dzyubin, Eduard Georgievich

Bagrjana, Elisaveta
See Belcheva, Elisaveta Lyubomirova

Bagryana, Elisaveta ......................... **CLC 10**
See Belcheva, Elisaveta Lyubomirova
See also CA 178; CDWLB 4; DLB 147;
EWL 3

Bailey, Paul 1937- ............................ **CLC 45**
See also CA 21-24R; CANR 16, 62, 124;
CN 7; DLB 14, 271; GLL 2

Baillie, Joanna 1762-1851 ...... **NCLC 71, 151**
See also DLB 93; RGEL 2

Bainbridge, Beryl (Margaret) 1934- . **CLC 4,
5, 8, 10, 14, 18, 22, 62, 130**
See also BRWS 6; CA 21-24R; CANR 24,
55, 75, 88, 128; CN 7; DAM NOV; DLB
14, 231; EWL 3; MTCW 1, 2

Baker, Carlos (Heard)
1909-1987 ............................... **TCLC 119**
See also CA 5-8R; 122; CANR 3, 63; DLB
103

Baker, Elliott 1922- ............................ **CLC 8**
See also CA 45-48; CANR 2, 63; CN 7

Baker, Jean H. ........................... **TCLC 3, 10**
See Russell, George William

Baker, Nicholson 1957- ............. **CLC 61, 165**
See also AMWS 13; CA 135; CANR 63,
120; CN 7; CPW; DA3; DAM POP; DLB
227

Baker, Ray Stannard 1870-1946 .... **TCLC 47**
See also CA 118

Baker, Russell (Wayne) 1925- ........... **CLC 31**
See also BEST 89:4; CA 57-60; CANR 11,
41, 59; MTCW 1, 2

Bakhtin, M.
See Bakhtin, Mikhail Mikhailovich

Bakhtin, M. M.
See Bakhtin, Mikhail Mikhailovich

Bakhtin, Mikhail
See Bakhtin, Mikhail Mikhailovich

Bakhtin, Mikhail Mikhailovich
1895-1975 ............... **CLC 83; TCLC 160**
See also CA 128; 113; DLB 242; EWL 3

Bakshi, Ralph 1938(?)- ...................... **CLC 26**
See also CA 112; 138; IDFW 3

Bakunin, Mikhail (Alexandrovich)
1814-1876 ......................... **NCLC 25, 58**
See also DLB 277

Baldwin, James (Arthur) 1924-1987 . **BLC 1;
CLC 1, 2, 3, 4, 5, 8, 13, 15, 17, 42, 50,
67, 90, 127; DC 1; SSC 10, 33; WLC**
See also AAYA 4, 34; AFAW 1, 2; AMWR
2; AMWS 1; BPFB 1; BW 1; CA 1-4R;
124; CABS 1; CAD; CANR 3, 24;
CDALB 1941-1968; CPW; DA; DA3;
DAB; DAC; DAM MST, MULT, NOV,
POP; DFS 11, 15; DLB 2, 7, 33, 249, 278;
DLBY 1987; EWL 3; EXPS; LAIT 5;
MTCW 1, 2; NCFS 4; NFS 4; RGAL 4;
RGSF 2; SATA 9; SATA-Obit 54; SSFS
2, 18; TUS

Baldwin, William c. 1515-c. 1563 ...... **LC 113**
See also DLB 132

Bale, John 1495-1563 .......................... **LC 62**
See also DLB 132; RGEL 2; TEA

Ball, Hugo 1886-1927 .................... **TCLC 104**

Ballard, J(ames) G(raham) 1930- . **CLC 3, 6,
14, 36, 137; SSC 1, 53**
See also AAYA 3, 52; BRWS 5; CA 5-8R;
CANR 15, 39, 65, 107, 133; CN 7; DA3;
DAM NOV, POP; DLB 14, 207, 261;
EWL 3; HGG; MTCW 1, 2; NFS 8;
RGEL 2; RGSF 2; SATA 93; SFW 4

Balmont, Konstantin (Dmitriyevich)
1867-1943 ............................... **TCLC 11**
See also CA 109; 155; DLB 295; EWL 3

Baltausis, Vincas 1847-1910
See Mikszath, Kalman

Balzac, Honore de 1799-1850 ... **NCLC 5, 35,
53, 153; SSC 5, 59; WLC**
See also DA; DA3; DAB; DAC; DAM
MST, NOV; DLB 119; EW 5; GFL 1789
to the Present; LMFS 1; RGSF 2; RGWL
2, 3; SSFS 10; SUFW; TWA

Bambara, Toni Cade 1939-1995 ........ **BLC 1;
CLC 19, 88; SSC 35; TCLC 116;
WLCS**
See also AAYA 5, 49; AFAW 2; AMWS 11;
BW 2, 3; BYA 12, 14; CA 29-32R; 150;
CANR 24, 49, 81; CDALBS; DA; DA3;
DAC; DAM MST, MULT; DLB 38, 218;
EXPS; MTCW 1, 2; RGAL 4; RGSF 2;
SATA 112; SSFS 4, 7, 12

Bamdad, A.
See Shamlu, Ahmad

Bamdad, Alef
See Shamlu, Ahmad

Banat, D. R.
See Bradbury, Ray (Douglas)

Bancroft, Laura
See Baum, L(yman) Frank

Banim, John 1798-1842 .................. **NCLC 13**
See also DLB 116, 158, 159; RGEL 2

Banim, Michael 1796-1874 ............. **NCLC 13**
See also DLB 158, 159

Banjo, The
See Paterson, A(ndrew) B(arton)

Banks, Iain
See Banks, Iain M(enzies)

Banks, Iain M(enzies) 1954- ............. **CLC 34**
See also CA 123; 128; CANR 61, 106; DLB
194, 261; EWL 3; HGG; INT CA-128;
SFW 4

Banks, Lynne Reid ........................... **CLC 23**
See Reid Banks, Lynne
See also AAYA 6; BYA 7; CLR 86

Banks, Russell (Earl) 1940- ....... **CLC 37, 72,
187; SSC 42**
See also AAYA 45; AMWS 5; CA 65-68;
CAAS 15; CANR 19, 52, 73, 118; CN 7;
DLB 130, 278; EWL 3; NFS 13

Banville, John 1945- ................... **CLC 46, 118**
See also CA 117; 128; CANR 104; CN 7;
DLB 14, 271; INT CA-128

Banville, Theodore (Faullain) de
1832-1891 ................................... **NCLC 9**
See also DLB 217; GFL 1789 to the Present

**Baraka, Amiri** 1934- .... **BLC 1; CLC 1, 2, 3, 5, 10, 14, 33, 115; DC 6; PC 4; WLCS**
See Jones, LeRoi
See also AFAW 1, 2; AMWS 2; BW 2, 3; CA 21-24R; CABS 3; CAD; CANR 27, 38, 61, 133; CD 5; CDALB 1941-1968; CP 7; CPW; DA; DA3; DAC; DAM MST, MULT, POET, POP; DFS 3, 11, 16; DLB 5, 7, 16, 38; DLBD 8; EWL 3; MTCW 1, 2; PFS 9; RGAL 4; TUS; WP

**Baratynsky, Evgenii Abramovich** 1800-1844 .................... **NCLC 103**
See also DLB 205

**Barbauld, Anna Laetitia** 1743-1825 ................................. **NCLC 50**
See also DLB 107, 109, 142, 158; RGEL 2

**Barbellion, W. N. P.** .......................... **TCLC 24**
See Cummings, Bruce F(rederick)

**Barber, Benjamin R.** 1939- ............. **CLC 141**
See also CA 29-32R; CANR 12, 32, 64, 119

**Barbera, Jack (Vincent)** 1945- ......... **CLC 44**
See also CA 110; CANR 45

**Barbey d'Aurevilly, Jules-Amedee** 1808-1889 .................... **NCLC 1; SSC 17**
See also DLB 119; GFL 1789 to the Present

**Barbour, John** c. 1316-1395 .......... **CMLC 33**
See also DLB 146

**Barbusse, Henri** 1873-1935 ............. **TCLC 5**
See also CA 105; 154; DLB 65; EWL 3; RGWL 2, 3

**Barclay, Alexander** c. 1475-1552 ....... **LC 109**
See also DLB 132

**Barclay, Bill**
See Moorcock, Michael (John)

**Barclay, William Ewert**
See Moorcock, Michael (John)

**Barea, Arturo** 1897-1957 ................ **TCLC 14**
See also CA 111; 201

**Barfoot, Joan** 1946- ............................ **CLC 18**
See also CA 105

**Barham, Richard Harris** 1788-1845 ................................. **NCLC 77**
See also DLB 159

**Baring, Maurice** 1874-1945 ............. **TCLC 8**
See also CA 105; 168; DLB 34; HGG

**Baring-Gould, Sabine** 1834-1924 ...... **TCLC 88**
See also DLB 156, 190

**Barker, Clive** 1952- .... **CLC 52, 205; SSC 53**
See also AAYA 10, 54; BEST 90:3; BPFB 1; CA 121; 129; CANR 71, 111, 133; CPW; DA3; DAM POP; DLB 261; HGG; INT CA-129; MTCW 1, 2; SUFW 2

**Barker, George Granville** 1913-1991 ................................ **CLC 8, 48**
See also CA 9-12R; 135; CANR 7, 38; DAM POET; DLB 20; EWL 3; MTCW 1

**Barker, Harley Granville**
See Granville-Barker, Harley
See also DLB 10

**Barker, Howard** 1946- ...................... **CLC 37**
See also CA 102; CBD; CD 5; DLB 13, 233

**Barker, Jane** 1652-1732 ................. **LC 42, 82**
See also DLB 39, 131

**Barker, Pat(ricia)** 1943- ...... **CLC 32, 94, 146**
See also BRWS 4; CA 117; 122; CANR 50, 101; CN 7; DLB 271; INT CA-122

**Barlach, Ernst (Heinrich)** 1870-1938 ................................. **TCLC 84**
See also CA 178; DLB 56, 118; EWL 3

**Barlow, Joel** 1754-1812 .................... **NCLC 23**
See also AMWS 2; DLB 37; RGAL 4

**Barnard, Mary (Ethel)** 1909- ........... **CLC 48**
See also CA 21-22; CAP 2

**Barnes, Djuna** 1892-1982 .... **CLC 3, 4, 8, 11, 29, 127; SSC 3**
See Steptoe, Lydia
See also AMWS 3; CA 9-12R; 107; CAD; CANR 16, 55; CWD; DLB 4, 9, 45; EWL 3; GLL 1; MTCW 1, 2; RGAL 4; TUS

**Barnes, Jim** 1933- ............................... **NNAL**
See also CA 108; 175; CAAE 175; CAAS 28; DLB 175

**Barnes, Julian (Patrick)** 1946- . **CLC 42, 141**
See also BRWS 4; CA 102; CANR 19, 54, 115; CN 7; DAB; DLB 194; DLBY 1993; EWL 3; MTCW 1

**Barnes, Peter** 1931-2004 ............... **CLC 5, 56**
See also CA 65-68; CAAS 12; CANR 33, 34, 64, 113; CBD; CD 5; DFS 6; DLB 13, 233; MTCW 1

**Barnes, William** 1801-1886 ............ **NCLC 75**
See also DLB 32

**Baroja (y Nessi), Pio** 1872-1956 ........ **HLC 1; TCLC 8**
See also CA 104; EW 9

**Baron, David**
See Pinter, Harold

**Baron Corvo**
See Rolfe, Frederick (William Serafino Austin Lewis Mary)

**Barondess, Sue K(aufman)** 1926-1977 .................................... **CLC 8**
See Kaufman, Sue
See also CA 1-4R; 69-72; CANR 1

**Baron de Teive**
See Pessoa, Fernando (Antonio Nogueira)

**Baroness Von S.**
See Zangwill, Israel

**Barres, (Auguste-)Maurice** 1862-1923 .............................. **TCLC 47**
See also CA 164; DLB 123; GFL 1789 to the Present

**Barreto, Afonso Henrique de Lima**
See Lima Barreto, Afonso Henrique de

**Barrett, Andrea** 1954- ..................... **CLC 150**
See also CA 156; CANR 92

**Barrett, Michele** ............................. **CLC 65**

**Barrett, (Roger) Syd** 1946- .............. **CLC 35**

**Barrett, William (Christopher)** 1913-1992 .................................... **CLC 27**
See also CA 13-16R; 139; CANR 11, 67; INT CANR-11

**Barrett Browning, Elizabeth** 1806-1861 ... **NCLC 1, 16, 61, 66; PC 6, 62; WLC**
See also BRW 4; CDBLB 1832-1890; DA; DA3; DAB; DAC; DAM MST, POET; DLB 32, 199; EXPP; PAB; PFS 2, 16; TEA; WLIT 4; WP

**Barrie, J(ames) M(atthew)** 1860-1937 ......................... **TCLC 2, 164**
See also BRWS 3; BYA 4, 5; CA 104; 136; CANR 77; CDBLB 1890-1914; CLR 16; CWRI 5; DA3; DAB; DAM DRAM; DFS 7; DLB 10, 141, 156; EWL 3; FANT; MAICYA 1, 2; MTCW 1; SATA 100; SUFW; WCH; WLIT 4; YABC 1

**Barrington, Michael**
See Moorcock, Michael (John)

**Barrol, Grady**
See Bograd, Larry

**Barry, Mike**
See Malzberg, Barry N(athaniel)

**Barry, Philip** 1896-1949 .................. **TCLC 11**
See also CA 109; 199; DFS 9; DLB 7, 228; RGAL 4

**Bart, Andre Schwarz**
See Schwarz-Bart, Andre

**Barth, John (Simmons)** 1930- ... **CLC 1, 2, 3, 5, 7, 9, 10, 14, 27, 51, 89; SSC 10**
See also AITN 1, 2; AMW; BPFB 1; CA 1-4R; CABS 1; CANR 5, 23, 49, 64, 113; CN 7; DAM NOV; DLB 2, 227; EWL 3; FANT; MTCW 1; RGAL 4; RGSF 2; RHW; SSFS 6; TUS

**Barthelme, Donald** 1931-1989 ... **CLC 1, 2, 3, 5, 6, 8, 13, 23, 46, 59, 115; SSC 2, 55**
See also AMWS 4; BPFB 1; CA 21-24R; 129; CANR 20, 58; DA3; DAM NOV; DLB 2, 234; DLBY 1980, 1989; EWL 3; FANT; LMFS 2; MTCW 1, 2; RGAL 4; RGSF 2; SATA 7; SATA-Obit 62; SSFS 17

**Barthelme, Frederick** 1943- ...... **CLC 36, 117**
See also AMWS 11; CA 114; 122; CANR 77; CN 7; CSW; DLB 244; DLBY 1985; EWL 3; INT CA-122

**Barthes, Roland (Gerard)** 1915-1980 ........ **CLC 24, 83; TCLC 135**
See also CA 130; 97-100; CANR 66; DLB 296; EW 13; EWL 3; GFL 1789 to the Present; MTCW 1, 2; TWA

**Bartram, William** 1739-1823 ....... **NCLC 145**
See also ANW; DLB 37

**Barzun, Jacques (Martin)** 1907- ..... **CLC 51, 145**
See also CA 61-64; CANR 22, 95

**Bashevis, Isaac**
See Singer, Isaac Bashevis

**Bashkirtseff, Marie** 1859-1884 ....... **NCLC 27**

**Basho, Matsuo**
See Matsuo Basho
See also PFS 18; RGWL 2, 3; WP

**Basil of Caesaria** c. 330-379 .......... **CMLC 35**

**Basket, Raney**
See Edgerton, Clyde (Carlyle)

**Bass, Kingsley B., Jr.**
See Bullins, Ed

**Bass, Rick** 1958- ......... **CLC 79, 143; SSC 60**
See also ANW; CA 126; CANR 53, 93; CSW; DLB 212, 275

**Bassani, Giorgio** 1916-2000 ................. **CLC 9**
See also CA 65-68; 190; CANR 33; CWW 2; DLB 128, 177, 299; EWL 3; MTCW 1; RGWL 2, 3

**Bastian, Ann** ..................................... **CLC 70**

**Bastos, Augusto (Antonio) Roa**
See Roa Bastos, Augusto (Antonio)

**Bataille, Georges** 1897-1962 ............ **CLC 29; TCLC 155**
See also CA 101; 89-92; EWL 3

**Bates, H(erbert) E(rnest)** 1905-1974 ...................... **CLC 46; SSC 10**
See also CA 93-96; 45-48; CANR 34; DA3; DAB; DAM POP; DLB 162, 191; EWL 3; EXPS; MTCW 1, 2; RGSF 2; SSFS 7

**Bauchart**
See Camus, Albert

**Baudelaire, Charles** 1821-1867 . **NCLC 6, 29, 55, 155; PC 1; SSC 18; WLC**
See also DA; DA3; DAB; DAC; DAM MST, POET; DLB 217; EW 7; GFL 1789 to the Present; LMFS 2; PFS 21; RGWL 2, 3; TWA

**Baudouin, Marcel**
See Peguy, Charles (Pierre)

**Baudouin, Pierre**
See Peguy, Charles (Pierre)

**Baudrillard, Jean** 1929- ..................... **CLC 60**
See also DLB 296

**Baum, L(yman) Frank** 1856-1919 .. **TCLC 7, 132**
See also AAYA 46; BYA 16; CA 108; 133; CLR 15; CWRI 5; DLB 22; FANT; JRDA; MAICYA 1, 2; MTCW 1, 2; NFS 13; RGAL 4; SATA 18, 100; WCH

**Bertrand, Louis oAloysiusc**
See Bertrand, Aloysius
See also DLB 217
**Bertran de Born** c. 1140-1215 ........ **CMLC 5**
**Besant, Annie (Wood)** 1847-1933 ..... **TCLC 9**
See also CA 105; 185
**Bessie, Alvah** 1904-1985 .................... **CLC 23**
See also CA 5-8R; 116; CANR 2, 80; DLB 26
**Bestuzhev, Aleksandr Aleksandrovich**
1797-1837 ................................ **NCLC 131**
See also DLB 198
**Bethlen, T. D.**
See Silverberg, Robert
**Beti, Mongo** ......................... **BLC 1; CLC 27**
See Biyidi, Alexandre
See also AFW; CANR 79; DAM MULT; EWL 3; WLIT 2
**Betjeman, John** 1906-1984 ...... **CLC 2, 6, 10, 34, 43**
See also BRW 7; CA 9-12R; 112; CANR 33, 56; CDBLB 1945-1960; DA3; DAB; DAM MST, POET; DLB 20; DLBY 1984; EWL 3; MTCW 1, 2
**Bettelheim, Bruno** 1903-1990 .......... **CLC 79; TCLC 143**
See also CA 81-84; 131; CANR 23, 61; DA3; MTCW 1, 2
**Betti, Ugo** 1892-1953 ........................ **TCLC 5**
See also CA 104; 155; EWL 3; RGWL 2, 3
**Betts, Doris (Waugh)** 1932- ..... **CLC 3, 6, 28; SSC 45**
See also CA 13-16R; CANR 9, 66, 77; CN 7; CSW; DLB 218; DLBY 1982; INT CANR-9; RGAL 4
**Bevan, Alistair**
See Roberts, Keith (John Kingston)
**Bey, Pilaff**
See Douglas, (George) Norman
**Bialik, Chaim Nachman**
1873-1934 ................................ **TCLC 25**
See also CA 170; EWL 3
**Bickerstaff, Isaac**
See Swift, Jonathan
**Bidart, Frank** 1939- .......................... **CLC 33**
See also CA 140; CANR 106; CP 7
**Bienek, Horst** 1930- ...................... **CLC 7, 11**
See also CA 73-76; DLB 75
**Bierce, Ambrose (Gwinett)**
1842-1914(?) ..... **SSC 9, 72; TCLC 1, 7, 44; WLC**
See also AAYA 55; AMW; BYA 11; CA 104; 139; CANR 78; CDALB 1865-1917; DA; DA3; DAC; DAM MST; DLB 11, 12, 23, 71, 74, 186; EWL 3; EXPS; HGG; LAIT 2; RGAL 4; RGSF 2; SSFS 9; SUFW 1
**Biggers, Earl Derr** 1884-1933 ........ **TCLC 65**
See also CA 108; 153; DLB 306
**Billiken, Bud**
See Motley, Willard (Francis)
**Billings, Josh**
See Shaw, Henry Wheeler
**Billington, (Lady) Rachel (Mary)**
1942- ........................................ **CLC 43**
See also AITN 2; CA 33-36R; CANR 44; CN 7
**Binchy, Maeve** 1940- ...................... **CLC 153**
See also BEST 90:1; BPFB 1; CA 127; 134; CANR 50, 96, 134; CN 7; CPW; DA3; DAM POP; INT CA-134; MTCW 1; RHW
**Binyon, T(imothy) J(ohn)** 1936- ....... **CLC 34**
See also CA 111; CANR 28
**Bion** 335B.C.-245B.C. .................... **CMLC 39**

**Bioy Casares, Adolfo** 1914-1999 ... **CLC 4, 8, 13, 88; HLC 1; SSC 17**
See Casares, Adolfo Bioy; Miranda, Javier; Sacastru, Martin
See also CA 29-32R; 177; CANR 19, 43, 66; CWW 2; DAM MULT; DLB 113; EWL 3; HW 1, 2; LAW; MTCW 1, 2
**Birch, Allison** .................................... **CLC 65**
**Bird, Cordwainer**
See Ellison, Harlan (Jay)
**Bird, Robert Montgomery**
1806-1854 ................................... **NCLC 1**
See also DLB 202; RGAL 4
**Birkerts, Sven** 1951- ........................ **CLC 116**
See also CA 128; 133, 176; CAAE 176; CAAS 29; INT CA-133
**Birney, (Alfred) Earle** 1904-1995 .. **CLC 1, 4, 6, 11; PC 52**
See also CA 1-4R; CANR 5, 20; CP 7; DAC; DAM MST, POET; DLB 88; MTCW 1; PFS 8; RGEL 2
**Biruni, al** 973-1048(?) .................... **CMLC 28**
**Bishop, Elizabeth** 1911-1979 ..... **CLC 1, 4, 9, 13, 15, 32; PC 3, 34; TCLC 121**
See also AMWR 2; AMWS 1; CA 5-8R; 89-92; CABS 2; CANR 26, 61, 108; CDALB 1968-1988; DA; DA3; DAC; DAM MST, POET; DLB 5, 169; EWL 3; GLL 2; MAWW; MTCW 1, 2; PAB; PFS 6, 12; RGAL 4; SATA-Obit 24; TUS; WP
**Bishop, John** 1935- .......................... **CLC 10**
See also CA 105
**Bishop, John Peale** 1892-1944 ..... **TCLC 103**
See also CA 107; 155; DLB 4, 9, 45; RGAL 4
**Bissett, Bill** 1939- .................. **CLC 18; PC 14**
See also CA 69-72; CAAS 19; CANR 15; CCA 1; CP 7; DLB 53; MTCW 1
**Bissoondath, Neil (Devindra)**
1955- ...................................... **CLC 120**
See also CA 136; CANR 123; CN 7; DAC
**Bitov, Andrei (Georgievich)** 1937- ... **CLC 57**
See also CA 142; DLB 302
**Biyidi, Alexandre** 1932-
See Beti, Mongo
See also BW 1, 3; CA 114; 124; CANR 81; DA3; MTCW 1, 2
**Bjarme, Brynjolf**
See Ibsen, Henrik (Johan)
**Bjoernson, Bjoernstjerne (Martinius)**
1832-1910 ............................ **TCLC 7, 37**
See also CA 104
**Black, Robert**
See Holdstock, Robert P.
**Blackburn, Paul** 1926-1971 .......... **CLC 9, 43**
See also BG 2; CA 81-84; 33-36R; CANR 34; DLB 16; DLBY 1981
**Black Elk** 1863-1950 ......... **NNAL; TCLC 33**
See also CA 144; DAM MULT; MTCW 1; WP
**Black Hawk** 1767-1838 ...................... **NNAL**
**Black Hobart**
See Sanders, (James) Ed(ward)
**Blacklin, Malcolm**
See Chambers, Aidan
**Blackmore, R(ichard) D(oddridge)**
1825-1900 ................................ **TCLC 27**
See also CA 120; DLB 18; RGEL 2
**Blackmur, R(ichard) P(almer)**
1904-1965 ................................ **CLC 2, 24**
See also AMWS 2; CA 11-12; 25-28R; CANR 71; CAP 1; DLB 63; EWL 3
**Black Tarantula**
See Acker, Kathy
**Blackwood, Algernon (Henry)**
1869-1951 ................................... **TCLC 5**
See also CA 105; 150; DLB 153, 156, 178; HGG; SUFW 1

**Blackwood, Caroline** 1931-1996 .... **CLC 6, 9, 100**
See also BRWS 9; CA 85-88; 151; CANR 32, 61, 65; CN 7; DLB 14, 207; HGG; MTCW 1
**Blade, Alexander**
See Hamilton, Edmond; Silverberg, Robert
**Blaga, Lucian** 1895-1961 .................. **CLC 75**
See also CA 157; DLB 220; EWL 3
**Blair, Eric (Arthur)** 1903-1950 .... **TCLC 123**
See Orwell, George
See also CA 104; 132; DA; DA3; DAB; DAC; DAM MST, NOV; MTCW 1, 2; SATA 29
**Blair, Hugh** 1718-1800 .................... **NCLC 75**
**Blais, Marie-Claire** 1939- .... **CLC 2, 4, 6, 13, 22**
See also CA 21-24R; CAAS 4; CANR 38, 75, 93; CWW 2; DAC; DAM MST; DLB 53; EWL 3; FW; MTCW 1, 2; TWA
**Blaise, Clark** 1940- .......................... **CLC 29**
See also AITN 2; CA 53-56; CAAS 3; CANR 5, 66, 106; CN 7; DLB 53; RGSF 2
**Blake, Fairley**
See De Voto, Bernard (Augustine)
**Blake, Nicholas**
See Day Lewis, C(ecil)
See also DLB 77; MSW
**Blake, Sterling**
See Benford, Gregory (Albert)
**Blake, William** 1757-1827 . **NCLC 13, 37, 57, 127; PC 12, 63; WLC**
See also AAYA 47; BRW 3; BRWR 1; CD-BLB 1789-1832; CLR 52; DA; DA3; DAB; DAC; DAM MST, POET; DLB 93, 163; EXPP; LATS 1:1; LMFS 1; MAI-CYA 1, 2; PAB; PFS 2, 12; SATA 30; TEA; WCH; WLIT 3; WP
**Blanchot, Maurice** 1907-2003 ......... **CLC 135**
See also CA 117; 144; 213; DLB 72, 296; EWL 3
**Blasco Ibanez, Vicente** 1867-1928 . **TCLC 12**
See also BPFB 1; CA 110; 131; CANR 81; DA3; DAM NOV; EW 8; EWL 3; HW 1, 2; MTCW 1
**Blatty, William Peter** 1928- ................ **CLC 2**
See also CA 5-8R; CANR 9, 124; DAM POP; HGG
**Bleeck, Oliver**
See Thomas, Ross (Elmore)
**Blessing, Lee** 1949- .......................... **CLC 54**
See also CAD; CD 5
**Blight, Rose**
See Greer, Germaine
**Blish, James (Benjamin)** 1921-1975 . **CLC 14**
See also BPFB 1; CA 1-4R; 57-60; CANR 3; DLB 8; MTCW 1; SATA 66; SCFW 2; SFW 4
**Bliss, Frederick**
See Card, Orson Scott
**Bliss, Reginald**
See Wells, H(erbert) G(eorge)
**Blixen, Karen (Christentze Dinesen)**
1885-1962
See Dinesen, Isak
See also CA 25-28; CANR 22, 50; CAP 2; DA3; DLB 214; LMFS 1; MTCW 1, 2; SATA 44; SSFS 20
**Bloch, Robert (Albert)** 1917-1994 .... **CLC 33**
See also AAYA 29; CA 5-8R; 179; 146; CAAE 179; CAAS 20; CANR 5, 78; DA3; DLB 44; HGG; INT CANR-5; MTCW 1; SATA 12; SATA-Obit 82; SFW 4; SUFW 1, 2
**Blok, Alexander (Alexandrovich)**
1880-1921 ...................... **PC 21; TCLC 5**
See also CA 104; 183; DLB 295; EW 9; EWL 3; LMFS 2; RGWL 2, 3

**Blom, Jan**
See Breytenbach, Breyten
**Bloom, Harold** 1930- ............... **CLC 24, 103**
See also CA 13-16R; CANR 39, 75, 92, 133; DLB 67; EWL 3; MTCW 1; RGAL 4
**Bloomfield, Aurelius**
See Bourne, Randolph S(illiman)
**Bloomfield, Robert** 1766-1823 ..... **NCLC 145**
See also DLB 93
**Blount, Roy (Alton), Jr.** 1941- ......... **CLC 38**
See also CA 53-56; CANR 10, 28, 61, 125; CSW; INT CANR-28; MTCW 1, 2
**Blowsnake, Sam** 1875-(?) .................... **NNAL**
**Bloy, Leon** 1846-1917 ..................... **TCLC 22**
See also CA 121; 183; DLB 123; GFL 1789 to the Present
**Blue Cloud, Peter (Aroniawenrate)**
1933- ............................................. **NNAL**
See also CA 117; CANR 40; DAM MULT
**Bluggage, Oranthy**
See Alcott, Louisa May
**Blume, Judy (Sussman)** 1938- .... **CLC 12, 30**
See also AAYA 3, 26; BYA 1, 8, 12; CA 29-32R; CANR 13, 37, 66, 124; CLR 2, 15, 69; CPW; DA3; DAM NOV, POP; DLB 52; JRDA; MAICYA 1, 2; MAICYAS 1; MTCW 1, 2; SATA 2, 31, 79, 142; WYA; YAW
**Blunden, Edmund (Charles)**
1896-1974 ....................... **CLC 2, 56; PC 66**
See also BRW 6; CA 17-18; 45-48; CANR 54; CAP 2; DLB 20, 100, 155; MTCW 1; PAB
**Bly, Robert (Elwood)** 1926- ....... **CLC 1, 2, 5, 10, 15, 38, 128; PC 39**
See also AMWS 4; CA 5-8R; CANR 41, 73, 125; CP 7; DA3; DAM POET; DLB 5; EWL 3; MTCW 1, 2; PFS 6, 17; RGAL 4
**Boas, Franz** 1858-1942 .................... **TCLC 56**
See also CA 115; 181
**Bobette**
See Simenon, Georges (Jacques Christian)
**Boccaccio, Giovanni** 1313-1375 ... **CMLC 13, 57; SSC 10**
See also EW 2; RGSF 2; RGWL 2, 3; TWA
**Bochco, Steven** 1943- .......................... **CLC 35**
See also AAYA 11; CA 124; 138
**Bode, Sigmund**
See O'Doherty, Brian
**Bodel, Jean** 1167(?)-1210 ............... **CMLC 28**
**Bodenheim, Maxwell** 1892-1954 .... **TCLC 44**
See also CA 110; 187; DLB 9, 45; RGAL 4
**Bodenheimer, Maxwell**
See Bodenheim, Maxwell
**Bodker, Cecil** 1927-
See Bodker, Cecil
**Bodker, Cecil** 1927- ........................... **CLC 21**
See also CA 73-76; CANR 13, 44, 111; CLR 23; MAICYA 1, 2; SATA 14, 133
**Boell, Heinrich (Theodor)**
1917-1985 ..... **CLC 2, 3, 6, 9, 11, 15, 27, 32, 72; SSC 23; WLC**
See Boll, Heinrich
See also CA 21-24R; 116; CANR 24; DA; DA3; DAB; DAC; DAM MST, NOV; DLB 69; DLBY 1985; MTCW 1, 2; SSFS 20; TWA
**Boerne, Alfred**
See Doeblin, Alfred
**Boethius** c. 480-c. 524 .................... **CMLC 15**
See also DLB 115; RGWL 2, 3
**Boff, Leonardo (Genezio Darci)**
1938- ............................... **CLC 70; HLC 1**
See also CA 150; DAM MULT; HW 2

**Bogan, Louise** 1897-1970 ....... **CLC 4, 39, 46, 93; PC 12**
See also AMWS 3; CA 73-76; 25-28R; CANR 33, 82; DAM POET; DLB 45, 169; EWL 3; MAWW; MTCW 1, 2; PFS 21; RGAL 4
**Bogarde, Dirk**
See Van Den Bogarde, Derek Jules Gaspard Ulric Niven
See also DLB 14
**Bogosian, Eric** 1953- .................. **CLC 45, 141**
See also CA 138; CAD; CANR 102; CD 5
**Bograd, Larry** 1953- .......................... **CLC 35**
See also CA 93-96; CANR 57; SAAS 21; SATA 33, 89; WYA
**Boiardo, Matteo Maria** 1441-1494 ........ **LC 6**
**Boileau-Despreaux, Nicolas** 1636-1711 . **LC 3**
See also DLB 268; EW 3; GFL Beginnings to 1789; RGWL 2, 3
**Boissard, Maurice**
See Leautaud, Paul
**Bojer, Johan** 1872-1959 .................. **TCLC 64**
See also CA 189; EWL 3
**Bok, Edward W(illiam)**
1863-1930 ............................... **TCLC 101**
See also CA 217; DLB 91; DLBD 16
**Boker, George Henry** 1823-1890 . **NCLC 125**
See also RGAL 4
**Boland, Eavan (Aisling)** 1944- .. **CLC 40, 67, 113; PC 58**
See also BRWS 5; CA 143, 207; CAAE 207; CANR 61; CP 7; CWP; DAM POET; DLB 40; FW; MTCW 2; PFS 12
**Boll, Heinrich**
See Boell, Heinrich (Theodor)
See also BPFB 1; CDWLB 2; EW 13; EWL 3; RGSF 2; RGWL 2, 3
**Bolt, Lee**
See Faust, Frederick (Schiller)
**Bolt, Robert (Oxton)** 1924-1995 ....... **CLC 14**
See also CA 17-20R; 147; CANR 35, 67; CBD; DAM DRAM; DFS 2; DLB 13, 233; EWL 3; LAIT 1; MTCW 1
**Bombal, Maria Luisa** 1910-1980 .... **HLCS 1; SSC 37**
See also CA 127; CANR 72; EWL 3; HW 1; LAW; RGSF 2
**Bombet, Louis-Alexandre-Cesar**
See Stendhal
**Bomkauf**
See Kaufman, Bob (Garnell)
**Bonaventura** .................................... **NCLC 35**
See also DLB 90
**Bond, Edward** 1934- .......... **CLC 4, 6, 13, 23**
See also AAYA 50; BRWS 1; CA 25-28R; CANR 38, 67, 106; CBD; CD 5; DAM DRAM; DFS 3, 8; DLB 13; EWL 3; MTCW 1
**Bonham, Frank** 1914-1989 ................ **CLC 12**
See also AAYA 1; BYA 1, 3; CA 9-12R; CANR 4, 36; JRDA; MAICYA 1, 2; SAAS 3; SATA 1, 49; SATA-Obit 62; TCWW 2; YAW
**Bonnefoy, Yves** 1923- . **CLC 9, 15, 58; PC 58**
See also CA 85-88; CANR 33, 75, 97; CWW 2; DAM MST, POET; DLB 258; EWL 3; GFL 1789 to the Present; MTCW 1, 2
**Bonner, Marita** .................................... **HR 2**
See Occomy, Marita (Odette) Bonner
**Bonnin, Gertrude** 1876-1938 ............. **NNAL**
See Zitkala-Sa
See also CA 150; DAM MULT
**Bontemps, Arna(ud Wendell)**
1902-1973 ..... **BLC 1; CLC 1, 18; HR 2**
See also BW 1; CA 1-4R; 41-44R; CANR 4, 35; CLR 6; CWRI 5; DA3; DAM MULT, NOV, POET; DLB 48, 51; JRDA; MAICYA 1, 2; MTCW 1, 2; SATA 2, 44; SATA-Obit 24; WCH; WP

**Boot, William**
See Stoppard, Tom
**Booth, Martin** 1944-2004 .................. **CLC 13**
See also CA 93-96; 188; 223; CAAE 188; CAAS 2; CANR 92
**Booth, Philip** 1925- .......................... **CLC 23**
See also CA 5-8R; CANR 5, 88; CP 7; DLBY 1982
**Booth, Wayne C(layson)** 1921- ......... **CLC 24**
See also CA 1-4R; CAAS 5; CANR 3, 43, 117; DLB 67
**Borchert, Wolfgang** 1921-1947 ........ **TCLC 5**
See also CA 104; 188; DLB 69, 124; EWL 3
**Borel, Petrus** 1809-1859 ................. **NCLC 41**
See also DLB 119; GFL 1789 to the Present
**Borges, Jorge Luis** 1899-1986 ... **CLC 1, 2, 3, 4, 6, 8, 9, 10, 13, 19, 44, 48, 83; HLC 1; PC 22, 32; SSC 4, 41; TCLC 109; WLC**
See also AAYA 26; BPFB 1; CA 21-24R; CANR 19, 33, 75, 105, 133; CDWLB 3; DA; DA3; DAB; DAC; DAM MST, MULT; DLB 113, 283; DLBY 1986; DNFS 1, 2; EWL 3; HW 1, 2; LAW; LMFS 2; MSW; MTCW 1, 2; RGSF 2; RGWL 2, 3; SFW 4; SSFS 17; TWA; WLIT 1
**Borowski, Tadeusz** 1922-1951 ........... **SSC 48; TCLC 9**
See also CA 106; 154; CDWLB 4; DLB 215; EWL 3; RGSF 2; RGWL 3; SSFS 13
**Borrow, George (Henry)**
1803-1881 ............................... **NCLC 9**
See also DLB 21, 55, 166
**Bosch (Gavino), Juan** 1909-2001 ..... **HLCS 1**
See also CA 151; 204; DAM MST, MULT; DLB 145; HW 1, 2
**Bosman, Herman Charles**
1905-1951 ............................... **TCLC 49**
See Malan, Herman
See also CA 160; DLB 225; RGSF 2
**Bosschere, Jean de** 1878(?)-1953 ... **TCLC 19**
See also CA 115; 186
**Boswell, James** 1740-1795 ... **LC 4, 50; WLC**
See also BRW 3; CDBLB 1660-1789; DA; DAB; DAC; DAM MST; DLB 104, 142; TEA; WLIT 3
**Bottomley, Gordon** 1874-1948 ..... **TCLC 107**
See also CA 120; 192; DLB 10
**Bottoms, David** 1949- ....................... **CLC 53**
See also CA 105; CANR 22; CSW; DLB 120; DLBY 1983
**Boucicault, Dion** 1820-1890 ........ **NCLC 41**
**Boucolon, Maryse**
See Conde, Maryse
**Bourdieu, Pierre** 1930-2002 ............ **CLC 198**
See also CA 130; 204
**Bourget, Paul (Charles Joseph)**
1852-1935 ............................... **TCLC 12**
See also CA 107; 196; DLB 123; GFL 1789 to the Present
**Bourjaily, Vance (Nye)** 1922- ........ **CLC 8, 62**
See also CA 1-4R; CAAS 1; CANR 2, 72; CN 7; DLB 2, 143
**Bourne, Randolph S(illiman)**
1886-1918 ............................... **TCLC 16**
See also AMW; CA 117; 155; DLB 63
**Bova, Ben(jamin William)** 1932- ...... **CLC 45**
See also AAYA 16; CA 5-8R; CAAS 18; CANR 11, 56, 94, 111; CLR 3, 96; DLBY 1981; INT CANR-11; MAICYA 1, 2; MTCW 1; SATA 6, 68, 133; SFW 4
**Bowen, Elizabeth (Dorothea Cole)**
1899-1973 . **CLC 1, 3, 6, 11, 15, 22, 118; SSC 3, 28, 66; TCLC 148**
See also BRWS 2; CA 17-18; 41-44R; CANR 35, 105; CAP 2; CDBLB 1945-

**Breton, Andre** 1896-1966 .. **CLC 2, 9, 15, 54; PC 15**
See also CA 19-20; 25-28R; CANR 40, 60; CAP 2; DLB 65, 258; EW 11; EWL 3; GFL 1789 to the Present; LMFS 2; MTCW 1, 2; RGWL 2, 3; TWA; WP

**Breytenbach, Breyten** 1939(?)- .. **CLC 23, 37, 126**
See also CA 113; 129; CANR 61, 122; CWW 2; DAM POET; DLB 225; EWL 3

**Bridgers, Sue Ellen** 1942- .................. **CLC 26**
See also AAYA 8, 49; BYA 7, 8; CA 65-68; CANR 11, 36; CLR 18; DLB 52; JRDA; MAICYA 1, 2; SAAS 1; SATA 22, 90; SATA-Essay 109; WYA; YAW

**Bridges, Robert (Seymour)**
1844-1930 ..................... **PC 28; TCLC 1**
See also BRW 6; CA 104; 152; CDBLB 1890-1914; DAM POET; DLB 19, 98

**Bridie, James** ................................. **TCLC 3**
See Mavor, Osborne Henry
See also DLB 10; EWL 3

**Brin, David** 1950- ............................... **CLC 34**
See also AAYA 21; CA 102; CANR 24, 70, 125, 127; INT CANR-24; SATA 65; SCFW 2; SFW 4

**Brink, Andre (Philippus)** 1935- . **CLC 18, 36, 106**
See also AFW; BRWS 6; CA 104; CANR 39, 62, 109, 133; CN 7; DLB 225; EWL 3; INT CA-103; LATS 1:2; MTCW 1, 2; WLIT 2

**Brinsmead, H. F(ay)**
See Brinsmead, H(esba) F(ay)

**Brinsmead, H. F.**
See Brinsmead, H(esba) F(ay)

**Brinsmead, H(esba) F(ay)** 1922- ...... **CLC 21**
See also CA 21-24R; CANR 10; CLR 47; CWRI 5; MAICYA 1, 2; SAAS 5; SATA 18, 78

**Brittain, Vera (Mary)** 1893(?)-1970 . **CLC 23**
See also BRWS 10; CA 13-16; 25-28R; CANR 58; CAP 1; DLB 191; FW; MTCW 1, 2

**Broch, Hermann** 1886-1951 ........... **TCLC 20**
See also CA 117; 211; CDWLB 2; DLB 85, 124; EW 10; EWL 3; RGWL 2, 3

**Brock, Rose**
See Hansen, Joseph
See also GLL 1

**Brod, Max** 1884-1968 ..................... **TCLC 115**
See also CA 5-8R; 25-28R; CANR 7; DLB 81; EWL 3

**Brodkey, Harold (Roy)** 1930-1996 .. **CLC 56; TCLC 123**
See also CA 111; 151; CANR 71; CN 7; DLB 130

**Brodsky, Iosif Alexandrovich** 1940-1996
See Brodsky, Joseph
See also AITN 1; CA 41-44R; 151; CANR 37, 106; DA3; DAM POET; MTCW 1, 2; RGWL 2, 3

**Brodsky, Joseph** . **CLC 4, 6, 13, 36, 100; PC 9**
See Brodsky, Iosif Alexandrovich
See also AMWS 8; CWW 2; DLB 285; EWL 3; MTCW 1

**Brodsky, Michael (Mark)** 1948- ....... **CLC 19**
See also CA 102; CANR 18, 41, 58; DLB 244

**Brodzki, Bella** ed. ............................ **CLC 65**

**Brome, Richard** 1590(?)-1652 .............. **LC 61**
See also BRWS 10; DLB 58

**Bromell, Henry** 1947- ......................... **CLC 5**
See also CA 53-56; CANR 9, 115, 116

**Bromfield, Louis (Brucker)**
1896-1956 ................................. **TCLC 11**
See also CA 107; 155; DLB 4, 9, 86; RGAL 4; RHW

**Broner, E(sther) M(asserman)**
1930- ...................................... **CLC 19**
See also CA 17-20R; CANR 8, 25, 72; CN 7; DLB 28

**Bronk, William (M.)** 1918-1999 ........ **CLC 10**
See also CA 89-92; 177; CANR 23; CP 7; DLB 165

**Bronstein, Lev Davidovich**
See Trotsky, Leon

**Bronte, Anne** 1820-1849 ..... **NCLC 4, 71, 102**
See also BRW 5; BRWR 1; DA3; DLB 21, 199; TEA

**Bronte, (Patrick) Branwell**
1817-1848 ................................. **NCLC 109**

**Bronte, Charlotte** 1816-1855 ...... **NCLC 3, 8, 33, 58, 105, 155; WLC**
See also AAYA 17; BRW 5; BRWC 2; BRWR 1; BYA 2; CDBLB 1832-1890; DA; DA3; DAB; DAC; DAM MST, NOV; DLB 21, 159, 199; EXPN; LAIT 2; NFS 4; TEA; WLIT 4

**Bronte, Emily (Jane)** 1818-1848 ... **NCLC 16, 35; PC 8; WLC**
See also AAYA 17; BPFB 1; BRW 5; BRWC 1; BRWR 1; BYA 3; CDBLB 1832-1890; DA; DA3; DAB; DAC; DAM MST, NOV, POET; DLB 21, 32, 199; EXPN; LAIT 1; TEA; WLIT 3

**Brontes**
See Bronte, Anne; Bronte, Charlotte; Bronte, Emily (Jane)

**Brooke, Frances** 1724-1789 ............. **LC 6, 48**
See also DLB 39, 99

**Brooke, Henry** 1703(?)-1783 ................. **LC 1**
See also DLB 39

**Brooke, Rupert (Chawner)**
1887-1915 ..... **PC 24; TCLC 2, 7; WLC**
See also BRWS 3; CA 104; 132; CANR 61; CDBLB 1914-1945; DA; DAB; DAC; DAM MST, POET; DLB 19, 216; EXPP; GLL 2; MTCW 1, 2; PFS 7; TEA

**Brooke-Haven, P.**
See Wodehouse, P(elham) G(renville)

**Brooke-Rose, Christine** 1926(?)- ..... **CLC 40, 184**
See also BRWS 4; CA 13-16R; CANR 58, 118; CN 7; DLB 14, 231; EWL 3; SFW 4

**Brookner, Anita** 1928- .. **CLC 32, 34, 51, 136**
See also BRWS 4; CA 114; 120; CANR 37, 56, 87, 130; CN 7; CPW; DA3; DAB; DAM POP; DLB 194; DLBY 1987; EWL 3; MTCW 1, 2; TEA

**Brooks, Cleanth** 1906-1994 . **CLC 24, 86, 110**
See also AMWS 14; CA 17-20R; 145; CANR 33, 35; CSW; DLB 63; DLBY 1994; EWL 3; INT CANR-35; MTCW 1, 2

**Brooks, George**
See Baum, L(yman) Frank

**Brooks, Gwendolyn (Elizabeth)**
1917-2000 ... **BLC 1; CLC 1, 2, 4, 5, 15, 49, 125; PC 7; WLC**
See also AAYA 20; AFAW 1, 2; AITN 1; AMWS 3; BW 2, 3; CA 1-4R; 190; CANR 1, 27, 52, 75, 132; CDALB 1941-1968; CLR 27; CP 7; CWP; DA; DA3; DAC; DAM MST, MULT, POET; DLB 5, 76, 165; EWL 3; EXPP; MAWW; MTCW 1, 2; PFS 1, 2, 4, 6; RGAL 4; SATA 6; SATA-Obit 123; TUS; WP

**Brooks, Mel** .................................. **CLC 12**
See Kaminsky, Melvin
See also AAYA 13, 48; DLB 26

**Brooks, Peter (Preston)** 1938- ........... **CLC 34**
See also CA 45-48; CANR 1, 107

**Brooks, Van Wyck** 1886-1963 ........... **CLC 29**
See also AMW; CA 1-4R; CANR 6; DLB 45, 63, 103; TUS

**Brophy, Brigid (Antonia)**
1929-1995 .............. **CLC 6, 11, 29, 105**
See also CA 5-8R; 149; CAAS 4; CANR 25, 53; CBD; CN 7; CWD; DA3; DLB 14, 271; EWL 3; MTCW 1, 2

**Brosman, Catharine Savage** 1934- ..... **CLC 9**
See also CA 61-64; CANR 21, 46

**Brossard, Nicole** 1943- ............ **CLC 115, 169**
See also CA 122; CAAS 16; CCA 1; CWP; CWW 2; DLB 53; EWL 3; FW; GLL 2; RGWL 3

**Brother Antoninus**
See Everson, William (Oliver)

**The Brothers Quay**
See Quay, Stephen; Quay, Timothy

**Broughton, T(homas) Alan** 1936- ..... **CLC 19**
See also CA 45-48; CANR 2, 23, 48, 111

**Broumas, Olga** 1949- ...................... **CLC 10, 73**
See also CA 85-88; CANR 20, 69, 110; CP 7; CWP; GLL 2

**Broun, Heywood** 1888-1939 ......... **TCLC 104**
See also DLB 29, 171

**Brown, Alan** 1950- ............................ **CLC 99**
See also CA 156

**Brown, Charles Brockden**
1771-1810 ............... **NCLC 22, 74, 122**
See also AMWS 1; CDALB 1640-1865; DLB 37, 59, 73; FW; HGG; LMFS 1; RGAL 4; TUS

**Brown, Christy** 1932-1981 ................ **CLC 63**
See also BYA 13; CA 105; 104; CANR 72; DLB 14

**Brown, Claude** 1937-2002 ... **BLC 1; CLC 30**
See also AAYA 7; BW 1, 3; CA 73-76; 205; CANR 81; DAM MULT

**Brown, Dan** ........................................ **CLC 209**
See also AAYA 55; CA 217; MTFW

**Brown, Dee (Alexander)**
1908-2002 ............................ **CLC 18, 47**
See also AAYA 30; CA 13-16R; 212; CAAS 6; CANR 11, 45, 60; CPW; CSW; DA3; DAM POP; DLBY 1980; LAIT 2; MTCW 1, 2; NCFS 5; SATA 5, 110; SATA-Obit 141; TCWW 2

**Brown, George**
See Wertmueller, Lina

**Brown, George Douglas**
1869-1902 ................................. **TCLC 28**
See Douglas, George
See also CA 162

**Brown, George Mackay** 1921-1996 ... **CLC 5, 48, 100**
See also BRWS 6; CA 21-24R; 151; CAAS 6; CANR 12, 37, 67; CN 7; CP 7; DLB 14, 27, 139, 271; MTCW 1; RGSF 2; SATA 35

**Brown, (William) Larry** 1951-2004 . **CLC 73**
See also CA 130; 134; CANR 117; CSW; DLB 234; INT CA-134

**Brown, Moses**
See Barrett, William (Christopher)

**Brown, Rita Mae** 1944- ........ **CLC 18, 43, 79**
See also BPFB 1; CA 45-48; CANR 2, 11, 35, 62, 95; CN 7; CPW; CSW; DA3; DAM NOV, POP; FW; INT CANR-11; MTCW 1, 2; NFS 9; RGAL 4; TUS

**Brown, Roderick (Langmere) Haig-**
See Haig-Brown, Roderick (Langmere)

**Brown, Rosellen** 1939- .............. **CLC 32, 170**
See also CA 77-80; CAAS 10; CANR 14, 44, 98; CN 7

**Brown, Sterling Allen** 1901-1989 ...... **BLC 1; CLC 1, 23, 59; HR 2; PC 55**
See also AFAW 1, 2; BW 1, 3; CA 85-88; 127; CANR 26; DA3; DAM MULT, POET; DLB 48, 51, 63; MTCW 1, 2; RGAL 4; WP

**Brown, Will**
See Ainsworth, William Harrison

**Burroughs, William S(eward)**
1914-1997 .. **CLC 1, 2, 5, 15, 22, 42, 75, 109; TCLC 121; WLC**
See Lee, William; Lee, Willy
See also AAYA 60; AITN 2; AMWS 3; BG 2; BPFB 1; CA 9-12R; 160; CANR 20, 52, 104; CN 7; CPW; DA; DA3; DAB; DAC; DAM MST, NOV, POP; DLB 2, 8, 16, 152, 237; DLBY 1981, 1997; EWL 3; HGG; LMFS 2; MTCW 1, 2; RGAL 4; SFW 4

**Burton, Sir Richard F(rancis)**
1821-1890 .................................. **NCLC 42**
See also DLB 55, 166, 184

**Burton, Robert** 1577-1640 ................... **LC 74**
See also DLB 151; RGEL 2

**Buruma, Ian** 1951- .......................... **CLC 163**
See also CA 128; CANR 65

**Busch, Frederick** 1941- ... **CLC 7, 10, 18, 47, 166**
See also CA 33-36R; CAAS 1; CANR 45, 73, 92; CN 7; DLB 6, 218

**Bush, Barney (Furman)** 1946- .......... **NNAL**
See also CA 145

**Bush, Ronald** 1946- ........................... **CLC 34**
See also CA 136

**Bustos, F(rancisco)**
See Borges, Jorge Luis

**Bustos Domecq, H(onorio)**
See Bioy Casares, Adolfo; Borges, Jorge Luis

**Butler, Octavia E(stelle)** 1947- .. **BLCS; CLC 38, 121**
See also AAYA 18, 48; AFAW 2; AMWS 13; BPFB 1; BW 2, 3; CA 73-76; CANR 12, 24, 38, 73; CLR 65; CPW; DA3; DAM MULT, POP; DLB 33; LATS 1:2; MTCW 1, 2; NFS 8; SATA 84; SCFW 2; SFW 4; SSFS 6; YAW

**Butler, Robert Olen, (Jr.)** 1945- ...... **CLC 81, 162**
See also AMWS 12; BPFB 1; CA 112; CANR 66; CSW; DAM POP; DLB 173; INT CA-112; MTCW 1; SSFS 11

**Butler, Samuel** 1612-1680 ............. **LC 16, 43**
See also DLB 101, 126; RGEL 2

**Butler, Samuel** 1835-1902 ......... **TCLC 1, 33; WLC**
See also BRWS 2; CA 143; CDBLB 1890-1914; DA; DA3; DAB; DAC; DAM MST, NOV; DLB 18, 57, 174; RGEL 2; SFW 4; TEA

**Butler, Walter C.**
See Faust, Frederick (Schiller)

**Butor, Michel (Marie Francois)**
1926- ............... **CLC 1, 3, 8, 11, 15, 161**
See also CA 9-12R; CANR 33, 66; CWW 2; DLB 83; EW 13; EWL 3; GFL 1789 to the Present; MTCW 1, 2

**Butts, Mary** 1890(?)-1937 .............. **TCLC 77**
See also CA 148; DLB 240

**Buxton, Ralph**
See Silverstein, Alvin; Silverstein, Virginia B(arbara Opshelor)

**Buzo, Alex**
See Buzo, Alexander (John)
See also DLB 289

**Buzo, Alexander (John)** 1944- .......... **CLC 61**
See also CA 97-100; CANR 17, 39, 69; CD 5

**Buzzati, Dino** 1906-1972 .................... **CLC 36**
See also CA 160; 33-36R; DLB 177; RGWL 2, 3; SFW 4

**Byars, Betsy (Cromer)** 1928- ........... **CLC 35**
See also AAYA 19; BYA 3; CA 33-36R, 183; CAAE 183; CANR 18, 36, 57, 102; CLR 1, 16, 72; DLB 52; INT CANR-18; JRDA; MAICYA 1, 2; MAICYAS 1; MTCW 1; SAAS 1; SATA 4, 46, 80; SATA-Essay 108; WYA; YAW

**Byatt, A(ntonia) S(usan Drabble)**
1936- .............................. **CLC 19, 65, 136**
See also BPFB 1; BRWC 2; BRWS 4; CA 13-16R; CANR 13, 33, 50, 75, 96, 133; DA3; DAM NOV, POP; DLB 14, 194; EWL 3; MTCW 1, 2; RGSF 2; RHW; TEA

**Byrd, Willam II** 1674-1744 ................. **LC 112**
See also DLB 24, 140; RGAL 4

**Byrne, David** 1952- ........................... **CLC 26**
See also CA 127

**Byrne, John Keyes** 1926-
See Leonard, Hugh
See also CA 102; CANR 78; INT CA-102

**Byron, George Gordon (Noel)**
1788-1824 ..... **DC 24; NCLC 2, 12, 109, 149; PC 16; WLC**
See also BRW 4; BRWC 2; CDBLB 1789-1832; DA; DA3; DAB; DAC; DAM MST, POET; DLB 96, 110; EXPP; LMFS 1; PAB; PFS 1, 14; RGEL 2; TEA; WLIT 3; WP

**Byron, Robert** 1905-1941 ............... **TCLC 67**
See also CA 160; DLB 195

**C. 3. 3.**
See Wilde, Oscar (Fingal O'Flahertie Wills)

**Caballero, Fernan** 1796-1877 ......... **NCLC 10**

**Cabell, Branch**
See Cabell, James Branch

**Cabell, James Branch** 1879-1958 .... **TCLC 6**
See also CA 105; 152; DLB 9, 78; FANT; MTCW 1; RGAL 4; SUFW 1

**Cabeza de Vaca, Alvar Nunez**
1490-1557(?) .................................. **LC 61**

**Cable, George Washington**
1844-1925 ..................... **SSC 4; TCLC 4**
See also CA 104; 155; DLB 12, 74; DLBD 13; RGAL 4; TUS

**Cabral de Melo Neto, Joao**
1920-1999 ................................ **CLC 76**
See Melo Neto, Joao Cabral de
See also CA 151; DAM MULT; DLB 307; LAW; LAWS 1

**Cabrera Infante, G(uillermo)** 1929- . **CLC 5, 25, 45, 120; HLC 1; SSC 39**
See also CA 85-88; CANR 29, 65, 110; CD-WLB 3; CWW 2; DA3; DAM MULT; DLB 113; EWL 3; HW 1, 2; LAW; LAWS 1; MTCW 1, 2; RGSF 2; WLIT 1

**Cade, Toni**
See Bambara, Toni Cade

**Cadmus and Harmonia**
See Buchan, John

**Caedmon** fl. 658-680 ........................ **CMLC 7**
See also DLB 146

**Caeiro, Alberto**
See Pessoa, Fernando (Antonio Nogueira)

**Caesar, Julius** ................................ **CMLC 47**
See Julius Caesar
See also AW 1; RGWL 2, 3

**Cage, John (Milton, Jr.)**
1912-1992 ..................... **CLC 41; PC 58**
See also CA 13-16R; 169; CANR 9, 78; DLB 193; INT CANR-9

**Cahan, Abraham** 1860-1951 .......... **TCLC 71**
See also CA 108; 154; DLB 9, 25, 28; RGAL 4

**Cain, G.**
See Cabrera Infante, G(uillermo)

**Cain, Guillermo**
See Cabrera Infante, G(uillermo)

**Cain, James M(allahan)** 1892-1977 .. **CLC 3, 11, 28**
See also AITN 1; BPFB 1; CA 17-20R; 73-76; CANR 8, 34, 61; CMW 4; DLB 226; EWL 3; MSW; MTCW 1; RGAL 4

**Caine, Hall** 1853-1931 .................... **TCLC 97**
See also RHW

**Caine, Mark**
See Raphael, Frederic (Michael)

**Calasso, Roberto** 1941- ................... **CLC 81**
See also CA 143; CANR 89

**Calderon de la Barca, Pedro**
1600-1681 .......... **DC 3; HLCS 1; LC 23**
See also EW 2; RGWL 2, 3; TWA

**Caldwell, Erskine (Preston)**
1903-1987 .... **CLC 1, 8, 14, 50, 60; SSC 19; TCLC 117**
See also AITN 1; AMW; BPFB 1; CA 1-4R; 121; CAAS 1; CANR 2, 33; DA3; DAM NOV; DLB 9, 86; EWL 3; MTCW 1, 2; RGAL 4; RGSF 2; TUS

**Caldwell, (Janet Miriam) Taylor (Holland)**
1900-1985 ........................ **CLC 2, 28, 39**
See also BPFB 1; CA 5-8R; 116; CANR 5; DA3; DAM NOV, POP; DLBD 17; RHW

**Calhoun, John Caldwell**
1782-1850 ................................ **NCLC 15**
See also DLB 3, 248

**Calisher, Hortense** 1911- ..... **CLC 2, 4, 8, 38, 134; SSC 15**
See also CA 1-4R; CANR 1, 22, 117; CN 7; DA3; DAM NOV; DLB 2, 218; INT CANR-22; MTCW 1, 2; RGAL 4; RGSF 2

**Callaghan, Morley Edward**
1903-1990 ..... **CLC 3, 14, 41, 65; TCLC 145**
See also CA 9-12R; 132; CANR 33, 73; DAC; DAM MST; DLB 68; EWL 3; MTCW 1, 2; RGEL 2; RGSF 2; SSFS 19

**Callimachus** c. 305B.C.-c.
240B.C. .................................... **CMLC 18**
See also AW 1; DLB 176; RGWL 2, 3

**Calvin, Jean**
See Calvin, John
See also GFL Beginnings to 1789

**Calvin, John** 1509-1564 ...................... **LC 37**
See Calvin, Jean

**Calvino, Italo** 1923-1985 .... **CLC 5, 8, 11, 22, 33, 39, 73; SSC 3, 48**
See also AAYA 58; CA 85-88; 116; CANR 23, 61, 132; DAM NOV; DLB 196; EW 13; EWL 3; MTCW 1, 2; RGSF 2; RGWL 2, 3; SFW 4; SSFS 12

**Camara Laye**
See Laye, Camara
See also EWL 3

**Camden, William** 1551-1623 ............... **LC 77**
See also DLB 172

**Cameron, Carey** 1952- ...................... **CLC 59**
See also CA 135

**Cameron, Peter** 1959- ...................... **CLC 44**
See also AMWS 12; CA 125; CANR 50, 117; DLB 234; GLL 2

**Camoens, Luis Vaz de** 1524(?)-1580
See Camoes, Luis de
See also EW 2

**Camoes, Luis de** 1524(?)-1580 . **HLCS 1; LC 62; PC 31**
See Camoens, Luis Vaz de
See also DLB 287; RGWL 2, 3

**Campana, Dino** 1885-1932 ............. **TCLC 20**
See also CA 117; DLB 114; EWL 3

**Campanella, Tommaso** 1568-1639 ....... **LC 32**
See also RGWL 2, 3

**Campbell, John W(ood, Jr.)**
1910-1971 .................................... **CLC 32**
See also CA 21-22; 29-32R; CANR 34; CAP 2; DLB 8; MTCW 1; SCFW; SFW 4

**Campbell, Joseph** 1904-1987 ........... **CLC 69; TCLC 140**
See also AAYA 3; BEST 89:2; CA 1-4R; 124; CANR 3, 28, 61, 107; DA3; MTCW 1, 2

**Campbell, Maria** 1940- ....... **CLC 85; NNAL**
See also CA 102; CANR 54; CCA 1; DAC

Campbell, (John) Ramsey 1946- ..... CLC 42;
  SSC 19
    See also AAYA 51; CA 57-60, 228; CAAE
    228; CANR 7, 102; DLB 261; HGG; INT
    CANR-7; SUFW 1, 2
Campbell, (Ignatius) Roy (Dunnachie)
  1901-1957 .................................. TCLC 5
    See also AFW; CA 104; 155; DLB 20, 225;
    EWL 3; MTCW 2; RGEL 2
Campbell, Thomas 1777-1844 ....... NCLC 19
    See also DLB 93, 144; RGEL 2
Campbell, Wilfred ........................... TCLC 9
    See Campbell, William
Campbell, William 1858(?)-1918
    See Campbell, Wilfred
    See also CA 106; DLB 92
Campion, Jane 1954- ....................... CLC 95
    See also AAYA 33; CA 138; CANR 87
Campion, Thomas 1567-1620 ............. LC 78
    See also CDBLB Before 1660; DAM POET;
    DLB 58, 172; RGEL 2
Camus, Albert 1913-1960 ...... CLC 1, 2, 4, 9,
    11, 14, 32, 63, 69, 124; DC 2; SSC 9,
    76; WLC
    See also AAYA 36; AFW; BPFB 1; CA 89-
    92; CANR 131; DA; DA3; DAB; DAC;
    DAM DRAM, MST, NOV; DLB 72; EW
    13; EWL 3; EXPN; EXPS; GFL 1789 to
    the Present; LATS 1:2; LMFS 2; MTCW
    1, 2; NFS 6, 16; RGSF 2; RGWL 2, 3;
    SSFS 4; TWA
Canby, Vincent 1924-2000 ................ CLC 13
    See also CA 81-84; 191
Cancale
    See Desnos, Robert
Canetti, Elias 1905-1994 .. CLC 3, 14, 25, 75,
    86; TCLC 157
    See also CA 21-24R; 146; CANR 23, 61,
    79; CDWLB 2; CWW 2; DA3; DLB 85,
    124; EW 12; EWL 3; MTCW 1, 2; RGWL
    2, 3; TWA
Canfield, Dorothea F.
    See Fisher, Dorothy (Frances) Canfield
Canfield, Dorothea Frances
    See Fisher, Dorothy (Frances) Canfield
Canfield, Dorothy
    See Fisher, Dorothy (Frances) Canfield
Canin, Ethan 1960- ............. CLC 55; SSC 70
    See also CA 131; 135
Cankar, Ivan 1876-1918 ................ TCLC 105
    See also CDWLB 4; DLB 147; EWL 3
Cannon, Curt
    See Hunter, Evan
Cao, Lan 1961- ............................... CLC 109
    See also CA 165
Cape, Judith
    See Page, P(atricia) K(athleen)
    See also CCA 1
Capek, Karel 1890-1938 ........ DC 1; SSC 36;
    TCLC 6, 37; WLC
    See also CA 104; 140; CDWLB 4; DA;
    DA3; DAB; DAC; DAM DRAM, MST,
    NOV; DFS 7, 11; DLB 215; EW 10; EWL
    3; MTCW 1; RGSF 2; RGWL 2, 3; SCFW
    2; SFW 4
Capote, Truman 1924-1984 . CLC 1, 3, 8, 13,
    19, 34, 38, 58; SSC 2, 47; TCLC 164;
    WLC
    See also AMWS 3; BPFB 1; CA 5-8R; 113;
    CANR 18, 62; CDALB 1941-1968; CPW;
    DA; DA3; DAB; DAC; DAM MST, NOV,
    POP; DLB 2, 185, 227; DLBY 1980,
    1984; EWL 3; EXPS; GLL 1; LAIT 3;
    MTCW 1, 2; NCFS 2; RGAL 4; RGSF 2;
    SATA 91; SSFS 2; TUS
Capra, Frank 1897-1991 ................... CLC 16
    See also AAYA 52; CA 61-64; 135

Caputo, Philip 1941- ....................... CLC 32
    See also AAYA 60; CA 73-76; CANR 40,
    135; YAW
Caragiale, Ion Luca 1852-1912 ...... TCLC 76
    See also CA 157
Card, Orson Scott 1951- ....... CLC 44, 47, 50
    See also AAYA 11, 42; BPFB 1; BYA 5, 8;
    CA 102; CANR 27, 47, 73, 102, 106, 133;
    CPW; DA3; DAM POP; FANT; INT
    CANR-27; MTCW 1, 2; NFS 5; SATA
    83, 127; SCFW 2; SFW 4; SUFW 2; YAW
Cardenal, Ernesto 1925- .......... CLC 31, 161;
    HLC 1; PC 22
    See also CA 49-52; CANR 2, 32, 66; CWW
    2; DAM MULT, POET; DLB 290; EWL
    3; HW 1, 2; LAWS 1; MTCW 1, 2;
    RGWL 2, 3
Cardinal, Marie 1929-2001 ............. CLC 189
    See also CA 177; CWW 2; DLB 83; FW
Cardozo, Benjamin N(athan)
    1870-1938 ................................. TCLC 65
    See also CA 117; 164
Carducci, Giosue (Alessandro Giuseppe)
    1835-1907 ................... PC 46; TCLC 32
    See also CA 163; EW 7; RGWL 2, 3
Carew, Thomas 1595(?)-1640 . LC 13; PC 29
    See also BRW 2; DLB 126; PAB; RGEL 2
Carey, Ernestine Gilbreth 1908- ...... CLC 17
    See also CA 5-8R; CANR 71; SATA 2
Carey, Peter 1943- ......... CLC 40, 55, 96, 183
    See also CA 123; 127; CANR 53, 76, 117;
    CN 7; DLB 289; EWL 3; INT CA-127;
    MTCW 1, 2; RGSF 2; SATA 94
Carleton, William 1794-1869 ........... NCLC 3
    See also DLB 159; RGEL 2; RGSF 2
Carlisle, Henry (Coffin) 1926- .......... CLC 33
    See also CA 13-16R; CANR 15, 85
Carlsen, Chris
    See Holdstock, Robert P.
Carlson, Ron(ald F.) 1947- ............... CLC 54
    See also CA 105, 189; CAAE 189; CANR
    27; DLB 244
Carlyle, Thomas 1795-1881 ..... NCLC 22, 70
    See also BRW 4; CDBLB 1789-1832; DA;
    DAB; DAC; DAM MST; DLB 55, 144,
    254; RGEL 2; TEA
Carman, (William) Bliss 1861-1929 ... PC 34;
    TCLC 7
    See also CA 104; 152; DAC; DLB 92;
    RGEL 2
Carnegie, Dale 1888-1955 ............... TCLC 53
    See also CA 218
Carossa, Hans 1878-1956 ............... TCLC 48
    See also CA 170; DLB 66; EWL 3
Carpenter, Don(ald Richard)
    1931-1995 ................................... CLC 41
    See also CA 45-48; 149; CANR 1, 71
Carpenter, Edward 1844-1929 ....... TCLC 88
    See also CA 163; GLL 1
Carpenter, John (Howard) 1948- ... CLC 161
    See also AAYA 2; CA 134; SATA 58
Carpenter, Johnny
    See Carpenter, John (Howard)
Carpentier (y Valmont), Alejo
    1904-1980 . CLC 8, 11, 38, 110; HLC 1;
    SSC 35
    See also CA 65-68; 97-100; CANR 11, 70;
    CDWLB 3; DAM MULT; DLB 113; EWL
    3; HW 1, 2; LAW; LMFS 2; RGSF 2;
    RGWL 2, 3; WLIT 1
Carr, Caleb 1955- ............................. CLC 86
    See also CA 147; CANR 73, 134; DA3
Carr, Emily 1871-1945 .................... TCLC 32
    See also CA 159; DLB 68; FW; GLL 2
Carr, John Dickson 1906-1977 .......... CLC 3
    See Fairbairn, Roger
    See also CA 49-52; 69-72; CANR 3, 33,
    60; CMW 4; DLB 306; MSW; MTCW 1,
    2

Carr, Philippa
    See Hibbert, Eleanor Alice Burford
Carr, Virginia Spencer 1929- ........... CLC 34
    See also CA 61-64; DLB 111
Carrere, Emmanuel 1957- ............... CLC 89
    See also CA 200
Carrier, Roch 1937- ..................... CLC 13, 78
    See also CA 130; CANR 61; CCA 1; DAC;
    DAM MST; DLB 53; SATA 105
Carroll, James Dennis
    See Carroll, Jim
Carroll, James P. 1943(?)- ............... CLC 38
    See also CA 81-84; CANR 73; MTCW 1
Carroll, Jim 1951- ..................... CLC 35, 143
    See also AAYA 17; CA 45-48; CANR 42,
    115; NCFS 5
Carroll, Lewis ..... NCLC 2, 53, 139; PC 18;
    WLC
    See Dodgson, Charles L(utwidge)
    See also AAYA 39; BRW 5; BYA 5, 13; CD-
    BLB 1832-1890; CLR 2, 18; DLB 18,
    163, 178; DLBY 1998; EXPN; EXPP;
    FANT; JRDA; LAIT 1; NFS 7; PFS 11;
    RGEL 2; SUFW 1; TEA; WCH
Carroll, Paul Vincent 1900-1968 ...... CLC 10
    See also CA 9-12R; 25-28R; DLB 10; EWL
    3; RGEL 2
Carruth, Hayden 1921- ..... CLC 4, 7, 10, 18,
    84; PC 10
    See also CA 9-12R; CANR 4, 38, 59, 110;
    CP 7; DLB 5, 165; INT CANR-4; MTCW
    1, 2; SATA 47
Carson, Anne 1950- ........... CLC 185; PC 64
    See also AMWS 12; CA 203; DLB 193;
    PFS 18
Carson, Ciaran 1948- ..................... CLC 201
    See also CA 153; CA-Brief 112; CANR
    113; CP 7
Carson, Rachel
    See Carson, Rachel Louise
    See also AAYA 49; DLB 275
Carson, Rachel Louise 1907-1964 .... CLC 71
    See Carson, Rachel
    See also AMWS 9; ANW; CA 77-80; CANR
    35; DA3; DAM POP; FW; LAIT 4;
    MTCW 1, 2; NCFS 1; SATA 23
Carter, Angela (Olive) 1940-1992 ...... CLC 5,
    41, 76; SSC 13, 85; TCLC 139
    See also BRWS 3; CA 53-56; 136; CANR
    12, 36, 61, 106; DA3; DLB 14, 207, 261;
    EXPS; FANT; FW; MTCW 1, 2; RGSF 2;
    SATA 66; SATA-Obit 70; SFW 4; SSFS
    4, 12; SUFW 2; WLIT 4
Carter, Nick
    See Smith, Martin Cruz
Carver, Raymond 1938-1988 ..... CLC 22, 36,
    53, 55, 126; PC 54; SSC 8, 51
    See also AAYA 44; AMWS 3; BPFB 1; CA
    33-36R; 126; CANR 17, 34, 61, 103;
    CPW; DA3; DAM NOV; DLB 130;
    DLBY 1984, 1988; EWL 3; MTCW 1, 2;
    PFS 17; RGAL 4; RGSF 2; SSFS 3, 6,
    12, 13; TCWW 2; TUS
Cary, Elizabeth, Lady Falkland
    1585-1639 ................................... LC 30
Cary, (Arthur) Joyce (Lunel)
    1888-1957 ........................... TCLC 1, 29
    See also BRW 7; CA 104; 164; CDBLB
    1914-1945; DLB 15, 100; EWL 3; MTCW
    2; RGEL 2; TEA
Casal, Julian del 1863-1893 ......... NCLC 131
    See also DLB 283; LAW
Casanova de Seingalt, Giovanni Jacopo
    1725-1798 ................................. LC 13
Casares, Adolfo Bioy
    See Bioy Casares, Adolfo
    See also RGSF 2

**Casas, Bartolome de las** 1474-1566
See Las Casas, Bartolome de
See also WLIT 1

**Casely-Hayford, J(oseph) E(phraim)**
1866-1903 .................. **BLC 1; TCLC 24**
See also BW 2; CA 123; 152; DAM MULT

**Casey, John (Dudley)** 1939- ............. **CLC 59**
See also BEST 90:2; CA 69-72; CANR 23, 100

**Casey, Michael** 1947- ........................ **CLC 2**
See also CA 65-68; CANR 109; DLB 5

**Casey, Patrick**
See Thurman, Wallace (Henry)

**Casey, Warren (Peter)** 1935-1988 .... **CLC 12**
See also CA 101; 127; INT CA-101

**Casona, Alejandro** .......................... **CLC 49**
See Alvarez, Alejandro Rodriguez
See also EWL 3

**Cassavetes, John** 1929-1989 ............. **CLC 20**
See also CA 85-88; 127; CANR 82

**Cassian, Nina** 1924- ............................ **PC 17**
See also CWP; CWW 2

**Cassill, R(onald) V(erlin)**
1919-2002 ........................ **CLC 4, 23**
See also CA 9-12R; 208; CAAS 1; CANR 7, 45; CN 7; DLB 6, 218; DLBY 2002

**Cassiodorus, Flavius Magnus** c. 490(?)-c. 583(?) ........................... **CMLC 43**

**Cassirer, Ernst** 1874-1945 ............... **TCLC 61**
See also CA 157

**Cassity, (Allen) Turner** 1929- ....... **CLC 6, 42**
See also CA 17-20R; 223; CAAE 223; CAAS 8; CANR 11; CSW; DLB 105

**Castaneda, Carlos (Cesar Aranha)**
1931(?)-1998 ...................... **CLC 12, 119**
See also CA 25-28R; CANR 32, 66, 105; DNFS 1; HW 1; MTCW 1

**Castedo, Elena** 1937- .......................... **CLC 65**
See also CA 132

**Castedo-Ellerman, Elena**
See Castedo, Elena

**Castellanos, Rosario** 1925-1974 ....... **CLC 66; HLC 1; SSC 39, 68**
See also CA 131; 53-56; CANR 58; CDWLB 3; DAM MULT; DLB 113, 290; EWL 3; FW; HW 1; LAW; MTCW 1; RGSF 2, 3

**Castelvetro, Lodovico** 1505-1571 ........ **LC 12**

**Castiglione, Baldassare** 1478-1529 ...... **LC 12**
See Castiglione, Baldesar
See also LMFS 1; RGWL 2, 3

**Castiglione, Baldesar**
See Castiglione, Baldassare
See also EW 2

**Castillo, Ana (Hernandez Del)**
1953- ...................................... **CLC 151**
See also AAYA 42; CA 131; CANR 51, 86, 128; CWP; DLB 122, 227; DNFS 2; FW; HW 1; LLW 1; PFS 21

**Castle, Robert**
See Hamilton, Edmond

**Castro (Ruz), Fidel** 1926(?)- ............... **HLC 1**
See also CA 110; 129; CANR 81; DAM MULT; HW 2

**Castro, Guillen de** 1569-1631 ............. **LC 19**

**Castro, Rosalia de** 1837-1885 ... **NCLC 3, 78; PC 41**
See also DAM MULT

**Cather, Willa (Sibert)** 1873-1947 . **SSC 2, 50; TCLC 1, 11, 31, 99, 132, 152; WLC**
See also AAYA 24; AMW; AMWC 1; AMWR 1; BPFB 1; CA 104; 128; CDALB 1865-1917; CLR 98; DA; DA3; DAB; DAC; DAM MST, NOV; DLB 9, 54, 78, 256; DLBD 1; EWL 3; EXPN; EXPS; LAIT 3; LATS 1:1; MAWW; MTCW 1, 2; NFS 2, 19; RGAL 4; RGSF 2; RHW; SATA 30; SSFS 2, 7, 16; TCWW 2; TUS

**Catherine II**
See Catherine the Great
See also DLB 150

**Catherine the Great** 1729-1796 .......... **LC 69**
See Catherine II

**Cato, Marcus Porcius**
234B.C.-149B.C. ..................... **CMLC 21**
See Cato the Elder

**Cato, Marcus Porcius, the Elder**
See Cato, Marcus Porcius

**Cato the Elder**
See Cato, Marcus Porcius
See also DLB 211

**Catton, (Charles) Bruce** 1899-1978 . **CLC 35**
See also AITN 1; CA 5-8R; 81-84; CANR 7, 74; DLB 17; SATA 2; SATA-Obit 24

**Catullus** c. 84B.C.-54B.C. .............. **CMLC 18**
See also AW 2; CDWLB 1; DLB 211; RGWL 2, 3

**Cauldwell, Frank**
See King, Francis (Henry)

**Caunitz, William J.** 1933-1996 ......... **CLC 34**
See also BEST 89:3; CA 125; 130; 152; CANR 73; INT CA-130

**Causley, Charles (Stanley)**
1917-2003 ................................ **CLC 7**
See also CA 9-12R; 223; CANR 5, 35, 94; CLR 30; CWRI 5; DLB 27; MTCW 1; SATA 3, 66; SATA-Obit 149

**Caute, (John) David** 1936- ................ **CLC 29**
See also CA 1-4R; CAAS 4; CANR 1, 33, 64, 120; CBD; CD 5; CN 7; DAM NOV; DLB 14, 231

**Cavafy, C(onstantine) P(eter)** ........... **PC 36; TCLC 2, 7**
See Kavafis, Konstantinos Petrou
See also CA 148; DA3; DAM POET; EW 8; EWL 3; MTCW 1; PFS 19; RGWL 2, 3; WP

**Cavalcanti, Guido** c. 1250-c. 1300 ........................... **CMLC 54**
See also RGWL 2, 3

**Cavallo, Evelyn**
See Spark, Muriel (Sarah)

**Cavanna, Betty** ........................... **CLC 12**
See Harrison, Elizabeth (Allen) Cavanna
See also JRDA; MAICYA 1; SAAS 4; SATA 1, 30

**Cavendish, Margaret Lucas**
1623-1673 .............................. **LC 30**
See also DLB 131, 252, 281; RGEL 2

**Caxton, William** 1421(?)-1491(?) ......... **LC 17**
See also DLB 170

**Cayer, D. M.**
See Duffy, Maureen

**Cayrol, Jean** 1911- ............................ **CLC 11**
See also CA 89-92; DLB 83; EWL 3

**Cela (y Trulock), Camilo Jose**
See Cela, Camilo Jose
See also CWW 2

**Cela, Camilo Jose** 1916-2002 ....... **CLC 4, 13, 59, 122; HLC 1; SSC 71**
See Cela (y Trulock), Camilo Jose
See also BEST 90:2; CA 21-24R; 206; CAAS 10; CANR 21, 32, 76; DAM MULT; DLBY 1989; EW 13; EWL 3; HW 1; MTCW 1, 2; RGSF 2; RGWL 2, 3

**Celan, Paul** ........ **CLC 10, 19, 53, 82; PC 10**
See Antschel, Paul
See also CDWLB 2; DLB 69; EWL 3; RGWL 2, 3

**Celine, Louis-Ferdinand** .. **CLC 1, 3, 4, 7, 9, 15, 47, 124**
See Destouches, Louis-Ferdinand
See also DLB 72; EW 11; EWL 3; GFL 1789 to the Present; RGWL 2, 3

**Cellini, Benvenuto** 1500-1571 ................ **LC 7**

**Cendrars, Blaise** ........................ **CLC 18, 106**
See Sauser-Hall, Frederic
See also DLB 258; EWL 3; GFL 1789 to the Present; RGWL 2, 3; WP

**Centlivre, Susanna** 1669(?)-1723 ....... **DC 25; LC 65**
See also DLB 84; RGEL 2

**Cernuda (y Bidon), Luis**
1902-1963 ..................... **CLC 54; PC 62**
See also CA 131; 89-92; DAM POET; DLB 134; EWL 3; GLL 1; HW 1; RGWL 2, 3

**Cervantes, Lorna Dee** 1954- ..... **HLCS 1; PC 35**
See also CA 131; CANR 80; CWP; DLB 82; EXPP; HW 1; LLW 1

**Cervantes (Saavedra), Miguel de**
1547-1616 .... **HLCS; LC 6, 23, 93; SSC 12; WLC**
See also AAYA 56; BYA 1, 14; DA; DAB; DAC; DAM MST, NOV; EW 2; LAIT 1; LATS 1:1; LMFS 1; NFS 8; RGSF 2; RGWL 2, 3; TWA

**Cesaire, Aime (Fernand)** 1913- ......... **BLC 1; CLC 19, 32, 112; DC 22; PC 25**
See also BW 2, 3; CA 65-68; CANR 24, 43, 81; CWW 2; DA3; DAM MULT, POET; EWL 3; GFL 1789 to the Present; MTCW 1, 2; WP

**Chabon, Michael** 1963- ... **CLC 55, 149; SSC 59**
See also AAYA 45; AMWS 11; CA 139; CANR 57, 96, 127; DLB 278; SATA 145

**Chabrol, Claude** 1930- ..................... **CLC 16**
See also CA 110

**Chairil Anwar**
See Anwar, Chairil
See also EWL 3

**Challans, Mary** 1905-1983
See Renault, Mary
See also CA 81-84; 111; CANR 74; DA3; MTCW 2; SATA 23; SATA-Obit 36; TEA

**Challis, George**
See Faust, Frederick (Schiller)
See also TCWW 2

**Chambers, Aidan** 1934- ..................... **CLC 35**
See also AAYA 27; CA 25-28R; CANR 12, 31, 58, 116; JRDA; MAICYA 1, 2; SAAS 12; SATA 1, 69, 108; WYA; YAW

**Chambers, James** 1948-
See Cliff, Jimmy
See also CA 124

**Chambers, Jessie**
See Lawrence, D(avid) H(erbert Richards)
See also GLL 1

**Chambers, Robert W(illiam)**
1865-1933 ......................... **TCLC 41**
See also CA 165; DLB 202; HGG; SATA 107; SUFW 1

**Chambers, (David) Whittaker**
1901-1961 ............................ **TCLC 129**
See also CA 89-92; DLB 303

**Chamisso, Adelbert von**
1781-1838 ............................. **NCLC 82**
See also DLB 90; RGWL 2, 3; SUFW 1

**Chance, James T.**
See Carpenter, John (Howard)

**Chance, John T.**
See Carpenter, John (Howard)

**Chandler, Raymond (Thornton)**
1888-1959 ............... **SSC 23; TCLC 1, 7**
See also AAYA 25; AMWC 2; AMWS 4; BPFB 1; CA 104; 129; CANR 60, 107; CDALB 1929-1941; CMW 4; DA3; DLB 226, 253; DLBD 6; EWL 3; MSW; MTCW 1, 2; NFS 17; RGAL 4; TUS

**Chang, Diana** 1934- ............................ **AAL**
See also CA 228; CWP; EXPP

Chang, Eileen 1921-1995 ......... **AAL; SSC 28**
See Chang Ai-Ling; Zhang Ailing
See also CA 166
Chang, Jung 1952- ............................ **CLC 71**
See also CA 142
Chang Ai-Ling
See Chang, Eileen
See also EWL 3
Channing, William Ellery
1780-1842 ................................. **NCLC 17**
See also DLB 1, 59, 235; RGAL 4
Chao, Patricia 1955- ....................... **CLC 119**
See also CA 163
Chaplin, Charles Spencer
1889-1977 ................................. **CLC 16**
See Chaplin, Charlie
See also CA 81-84; 73-76
Chaplin, Charlie
See Chaplin, Charles Spencer
See also DLB 44
Chapman, George 1559(?)-1634 . **DC 19; LC 22, 116**
See also BRW 1; DAM DRAM; DLB 62, 121; LMFS 1; RGEL 2
Chapman, Graham 1941-1989 ......... **CLC 21**
See Monty Python
See also CA 116; 129; CANR 35, 95
Chapman, John Jay 1862-1933 ....... **TCLC 7**
See also AMWS 14; CA 104; 191
Chapman, Lee
See Bradley, Marion Zimmer
See also GLL 1
Chapman, Walker
See Silverberg, Robert
Chappell, Fred (Davis) 1936- .... **CLC 40, 78, 162**
See also CA 5-8R, 198; CAAE 198; CAAS 4; CANR 8, 33, 67, 110; CN 7; CP 7; CSW; DLB 6, 105; HGG
Char, Rene(-Emile) 1907-1988 .... **CLC 9, 11, 14, 55; PC 56**
See also CA 13-16R; 124; CANR 32; DAM POET; DLB 258; EWL 3; GFL 1789 to the Present; MTCW 1, 2; RGWL 2, 3
Charby, Jay
See Ellison, Harlan (Jay)
Chardin, Pierre Teilhard de
See Teilhard de Chardin, (Marie Joseph) Pierre
Chariton fl. 1st cent. (?)- ............... **CMLC 49**
Charlemagne 742-814 .................... **CMLC 37**
Charles I 1600-1649 ............................ **LC 13**
Charriere, Isabelle de 1740-1805 .. **NCLC 66**
Chartier, Alain c. 1392-1430 ............... **LC 94**
See also DLB 208
Chartier, Emile-Auguste
See Alain
Charyn, Jerome 1937- .............. **CLC 5, 8, 18**
See also CA 5-8R; CAAS 1; CANR 7, 61, 101; CMW 4; CN 7; DLBY 1983; MTCW 1
Chase, Adam
See Marlowe, Stephen
Chase, Mary (Coyle) 1907-1981 ........... **DC 1**
See also CA 77-80; 105; CAD; CWD; DFS 11; DLB 228; SATA 17; SATA-Obit 29
Chase, Mary Ellen 1887-1973 .......... **CLC 2; TCLC 124**
See also CA 13-16; 41-44R; CAP 1; SATA 10
Chase, Nicholas
See Hyde, Anthony
See also CCA 1
Chateaubriand, Francois Rene de
1768-1848 ......................... **NCLC 3, 134**
See also DLB 119; EW 5; GFL 1789 to the Present; RGWL 2, 3; TWA

Chatterje, Sarat Chandra 1876-1936(?)
See Chatterji, Saratchandra
See also CA 109
Chatterji, Bankim Chandra
1838-1894 ................................. **NCLC 19**
Chatterji, Saratchandra ............... **TCLC 13**
See Chatterje, Sarat Chandra
See also CA 186; EWL 3
Chatterton, Thomas 1752-1770 ....... **LC 3, 54**
See also DAM POET; DLB 109; RGEL 2
Chatwin, (Charles) Bruce
1940-1989 ...................... **CLC 28, 57, 59**
See also AAYA 4; BEST 90:1; BRWS 4; CA 85-88; 127; CPW; DAM POP; DLB 194, 204; EWL 3
Chaucer, Daniel
See Ford, Ford Madox
See also RHW
Chaucer, Geoffrey 1340(?)-1400 .. **LC 17, 56; PC 19, 58; WLCS**
See also BRW 1; BRWC 1; BRWR 2; CD-BLB Before 1660; DA; DA3; DAB; DAC; DAM MST, POET; DLB 146; LAIT 1; PAB; PFS 14; RGEL 2; TEA; WLIT 3; WP
Chavez, Denise (Elia) 1948- ................ **HLC 1**
See also CA 131; CANR 56, 81; DAM MULT; DLB 122; FW; HW 1, 2; LLW 1; MTCW 2
Chaviaras, Strates 1935-
See Haviaras, Stratis
See also CA 105
Chayefsky, Paddy ............................ **CLC 23**
See Chayefsky, Sidney
See also CAD; DLB 7, 44; DLBY 1981; RGAL 4
Chayefsky, Sidney 1923-1981
See Chayefsky, Paddy
See also CA 9-12R; 104; CANR 18; DAM DRAM
Chedid, Andree 1920- ...................... **CLC 47**
See also CA 145; CANR 95; EWL 3
Cheever, John 1912-1982 ..... **CLC 3, 7, 8, 11, 15, 25, 64; SSC 1, 38, 57; WLC**
See also AMWS 1; BPFB 1; CA 5-8R; 106; CABS 1; CANR 5, 27, 76; CDALB 1941-1968; CPW; DA; DA3; DAB; DAC; DAM MST, NOV, POP; DLB 2, 102, 227; DLBY 1980, 1982; EWL 3; EXPS; INT CANR-5; MTCW 1, 2; RGAL 4; RGSF 2; SSFS 2, 14; TUS
Cheever, Susan 1943- .................. **CLC 18, 48**
See also CA 103; CANR 27, 51, 92; DLBY 1982; INT CANR-27
Chekhonte, Antosha
See Chekhov, Anton (Pavlovich)
Chekhov, Anton (Pavlovich)
1860-1904 ....... **DC 9; SSC 2, 28, 41, 51, 85; TCLC 3, 10, 31, 55, 96, 163; WLC**
See also BYA 14; CA 104; 124; DA; DA3; DAB; DAC; DAM DRAM, MST; DFS 1, 5, 10, 12; DLB 277; EW 7; EWL 3; EXPS; LAIT 3; LATS 1:1; RGSF 2; RGWL 2, 3; SATA 90; SSFS 5, 13, 14; TWA
Cheney, Lynne V. 1941- ...................... **CLC 70**
See also CA 89-92; CANR 58, 117; SATA 152
Chernyshevsky, Nikolai Gavrilovich
See Chernyshevsky, Nikolay Gavrilovich
See also DLB 238
Chernyshevsky, Nikolay Gavrilovich
1828-1889 ................................... **NCLC 1**
See Chernyshevsky, Nikolai Gavrilovich
Cherry, Carolyn Janice 1942-
See Cherryh, C. J.
See also CA 65-68; CANR 10

Cherryh, C. J. ................................ **CLC 35**
See Cherry, Carolyn Janice
See also AAYA 24; BPFB 1; DLBY 1980; FANT; SATA 93; SCFW 2; SFW 4; YAW
Chesnutt, Charles W(addell)
1858-1932 .... **BLC 1; SSC 7, 54; TCLC 5, 39**
See also AFAW 1, 2; AMWS 14; BW 1, 3; CA 106; 125; CANR 76; DAM MULT; DLB 12, 50, 78; EWL 3; MTCW 1, 2; RGAL 4; RGSF 2; SSFS 11
Chester, Alfred 1929(?)-1971 ........... **CLC 49**
See also CA 196; 33-36R; DLB 130
Chesterton, G(ilbert) K(eith)
1874-1936 . **PC 28; SSC 1, 46; TCLC 1, 6, 64**
See also AAYA 57; BRW 6; CA 104; 132; CANR 73, 131; CDBLB 1914-1945; CMW 4; DAM NOV, POET; DLB 10, 19, 34, 70, 98, 149, 178; EWL 3; FANT; MSW; MTCW 1, 2; RGEL 2; RGSF 2; SATA 27; SUFW 1
Chettle, Henry c. 1564-c. 1606 .......... **LC 112**
See also DLB 136; RGEL 2
Chiang, Pin-chin 1904-1986
See Ding Ling
See also CA 118
Chief Joseph 1840-1904 ...................... **NNAL**
See also CA 152; DA3; DAM MULT
Chief Seattle 1786(?)-1866 .................. **NNAL**
See also DA3; DAM MULT
Ch'ien, Chung-shu 1910-1998 .......... **CLC 22**
See Qian Zhongshu
See also CA 130; CANR 73; MTCW 1, 2
Chikamatsu Monzaemon 1653-1724 ... **LC 66**
See also RGWL 2, 3
Child, L. Maria
See Child, Lydia Maria
Child, Lydia Maria 1802-1880 .. **NCLC 6, 73**
See also DLB 1, 74, 243; RGAL 4; SATA 67
Child, Mrs.
See Child, Lydia Maria
Child, Philip 1898-1978 ............... **CLC 19, 68**
See also CA 13-14; CAP 1; DLB 68; RHW; SATA 47
Childers, (Robert) Erskine
1870-1922 ................................. **TCLC 65**
See also CA 113; 153; DLB 70
Childress, Alice 1920-1994 . **BLC 1; CLC 12, 15, 86, 96; DC 4; TCLC 116**
See also AAYA 8; BW 2, 3; BYA 2; CA 45-48; 146; CAD; CANR 3, 27, 50, 74; CLR 14; CWD; DA3; DAM DRAM, MULT, NOV; DFS 2, 8, 14; DLB 7, 38, 249; JRDA; LAIT 5; MAICYA 1, 2; MAIC-YAS 1; MTCW 1, 2; RGAL 4; SATA 7, 48, 81; TUS; WYA; YAW
Chin, Frank (Chew, Jr.) 1940- ...... **CLC 135; DC 7**
See also CA 33-36R; CANR 71; CD 5; DAM MULT; DLB 206; LAIT 5; RGAL 4
Chin, Marilyn (Mei Ling) 1955- ......... **PC 40**
See also CA 129; CANR 70, 113; CWP
Chislett, (Margaret) Anne 1943- ...... **CLC 34**
See also CA 151
Chitty, Thomas Willes 1926- ............. **CLC 11**
See Hinde, Thomas
See also CA 5-8R; CN 7
Chivers, Thomas Holley
1809-1858 ................................. **NCLC 49**
See also DLB 3, 248; RGAL 4
Choi, Susan 1969- ......................... **CLC 119**
See also CA 223
Chomette, Rene Lucien 1898-1981
See Clair, Rene
See also CA 103

**Conrad, Robert Arnold**
See Hart, Moss
**Conroy, (Donald) Pat(rick)** 1945- ... **CLC 30, 74**
See also AAYA 8, 52; AITN 1; BPFB 1; CA 85-88; CANR 24, 53, 129; CPW; CSW; DA3; DAM NOV, POP; DLB 6; LAIT 5; MTCW 1, 2
**Constant (de Rebecque), (Henri) Benjamin** 1767-1830 .................................. **NCLC 6**
See also DLB 119; EW 4; GFL 1789 to the Present
**Conway, Jill K(er)** 1934- ................. **CLC 152**
See also CA 130; CANR 94
**Conybeare, Charles Augustus**
See Eliot, T(homas) S(tearns)
**Cook, Michael** 1933-1994 .................. **CLC 58**
See also CA 93-96; CANR 68; DLB 53
**Cook, Robin** 1940- .............................. **CLC 14**
See also AAYA 32; BEST 90:2; BPFB 1; CA 108; 111; CANR 41, 90, 109; CPW; DA3; DAM POP; HGG; INT CA-111
**Cook, Roy**
See Silverberg, Robert
**Cooke, Elizabeth** 1948- .................... **CLC 55**
See also CA 129
**Cooke, John Esten** 1830-1886 .......... **NCLC 5**
See also DLB 3, 248; RGAL 4
**Cooke, John Estes**
See Baum, L(yman) Frank
**Cooke, M. E.**
See Creasey, John
**Cooke, Margaret**
See Creasey, John
**Cooke, Rose Terry** 1827-1892 ...... **NCLC 110**
See also DLB 12, 74
**Cook-Lynn, Elizabeth** 1930- ............ **CLC 93; NNAL**
See also CA 133; DAM MULT; DLB 175
**Cooney, Ray** ........................................ **CLC 62**
See also CBD
**Cooper, Anthony Ashley** 1671-1713 .. **LC 107**
See also DLB 101
**Cooper, Dennis** 1953- ....................... **CLC 203**
See also CA 133; CANR 72, 86; GLL 1; St. James Guide to Horror, Ghost, and Gothic Writers.
**Cooper, Douglas** 1960- ...................... **CLC 86**
**Cooper, Henry St. John**
See Creasey, John
**Cooper, J(oan) California** (?)- .......... **CLC 56**
See also AAYA 12; BW 1; CA 125; CANR 55; DAM MULT; DLB 212
**Cooper, James Fenimore** 1789-1851 ...................... **NCLC 1, 27, 54**
See also AAYA 22; AMW; BPFB 1; CDALB 1640-1865; DA3; DLB 3, 183, 250, 254; LAIT 1; NFS 9; RGAL 4; SATA 19; TUS; WCH
**Cooper, Susan Fenimore** 1813-1894 .................................. **NCLC 129**
See also ANW; DLB 239, 254
**Coover, Robert (Lowell)** 1932- ...... **CLC 3, 7, 15, 32, 46, 87, 161; SSC 15**
See also AMWS 5; BPFB 1; CA 45-48; CANR 3, 37, 58, 115; CN 7; DAM NOV; DLB 2, 227; DLBY 1981; EWL 3; MTCW 1, 2; RGAL 4; RGSF 2
**Copeland, Stewart (Armstrong)** 1952- .................................................. **CLC 26**
**Copernicus, Nicolaus** 1473-1543 ....... **LC 45**
**Coppard, A(lfred) E(dgar)** 1878-1957 ................... **SSC 21; TCLC 5**
See also BRWS 8; CA 114; 167; DLB 162; EWL 3; HGG; RGEL 2; RGSF 2; SUFW 1; YABC 1
**Coppee, Francois** 1842-1908 .......... **TCLC 25**
See also CA 170; DLB 217

**Coppola, Francis Ford** 1939- ... **CLC 16, 126**
See also AAYA 39; CA 77-80; CANR 40, 78; DLB 44
**Copway, George** 1818-1869 ............... **NNAL**
See also DAM MULT; DLB 175, 183
**Corbiere, Tristan** 1845-1875 .......... **NCLC 43**
See also DLB 217; GFL 1789 to the Present
**Corcoran, Barbara (Asenath)** 1911- ........................................... **CLC 17**
See also AAYA 14; CA 21-24R, 191; CAAE 191; CAAS 2; CANR 11, 28, 48; CLR 50; DLB 52; JRDA; MAICYA 2; MAICYAS 1; RHW; SAAS 20; SATA 3, 77; SATA-Essay 125
**Cordelier, Maurice**
See Giraudoux, Jean(-Hippolyte)
**Corelli, Marie** ............................... **TCLC 51**
See Mackay, Mary
See also DLB 34, 156; RGEL 2; SUFW 1
**Corinna** c. 225B.C.-c. 305B.C. ...... **CMLC 72**
**Corman, Cid** ..................................... **CLC 9**
See Corman, Sidney
See also CAAS 2; DLB 5, 193
**Corman, Sidney** 1924-2004
See Corman, Cid
See also CA 85-88; 225; CANR 44; CP 7; DAM POET
**Cormier, Robert (Edmund)** 1925-2000 ......................... **CLC 12, 30**
See also AAYA 3, 19; BYA 1, 2, 6, 8, 9; CA 1-4R; CANR 5, 23, 76, 93; CDALB 1968-1988; CLR 12, 55; DA; DAB; DAC; DAM MST, NOV; DLB 52; EXPN; INT CANR-23; JRDA; LAIT 5; MAICYA 1, 2; MTCW 1, 2; NFS 2, 18; SATA 10, 45, 83; SATA-Obit 122; WYA; YAW
**Corn, Alfred (DeWitt III)** 1943- ....... **CLC 33**
See also CA 179; CAAE 179; CAAS 25; CANR 44; CP 7; CSW; DLB 120, 282; DLBY 1980
**Corneille, Pierre** 1606-1684 ... **DC 21; LC 28**
See also DAB; DAM MST; DLB 268; EW 3; GFL Beginnings to 1789; RGWL 2, 3; TWA
**Cornwell, David (John Moore)** 1931- .......................................... **CLC 9, 15**
See le Carre, John
See also CA 5-8R; CANR 13, 33, 59, 107, 132; DA3; DAM POP; MTCW 1, 2
**Cornwell, Patricia (Daniels)** 1956- . **CLC 155**
See also AAYA 16, 56; BPFB 1; CA 134; CANR 53, 131; CMW 4; CPW; CSW; DAM POP; DLB 306; MSW; MTCW 1
**Corso, (Nunzio) Gregory** 1930-2001 . **CLC 1, 11; PC 33**
See also AMWS 12; BG 2; CA 5-8R; 193; CANR 41, 76, 132; CP 7; DA3; DLB 5, 16, 237; LMFS 2; MTCW 1, 2; WP
**Cortazar, Julio** 1914-1984 ... **CLC 2, 3, 5, 10, 13, 15, 33, 34, 92; HLC 1; SSC 7, 76**
See also BPFB 1; CA 21-24R; CANR 12, 32, 81; CDWLB 3; DA3; DAM MULT, NOV; DLB 113; EWL 3; EXPS; HW 1, 2; LAW; MTCW 1, 2; RGSF 2; RGWL 2, 3; SSFS 3, 20; TWA; WLIT 1
**Cortes, Hernan** 1485-1547 ................... **LC 31**
**Corvinus, Jakob**
See Raabe, Wilhelm (Karl)
**Corwin, Cecil**
See Kornbluth, C(yril) M.
**Cosic, Dobrica** 1921- ........................ **CLC 14**
See also CA 122; 138; CDWLB 4; CWW 2; DLB 181; EWL 3
**Costain, Thomas B(ertram)** 1885-1965 .................................. **CLC 30**
See also BYA 3; CA 5-8R; 25-28R; DLB 9; RHW
**Costantini, Humberto** 1924(?)-1987 . **CLC 49**
See also CA 131; 122; EWL 3; HW 1

**Costello, Elvis** 1954- .......................... **CLC 21**
See also CA 204
**Costenoble, Philostene**
See Ghelderode, Michel de
**Cotes, Cecil V.**
See Duncan, Sara Jeannette
**Cotter, Joseph Seamon Sr.** 1861-1949 .................... **BLC 1; TCLC 28**
See also BW 1; CA 124; DAM MULT; DLB 50
**Couch, Arthur Thomas Quiller**
See Quiller-Couch, Sir Arthur (Thomas)
**Coulton, James**
See Hansen, Joseph
**Couperus, Louis (Marie Anne)** 1863-1923 ................................ **TCLC 15**
See also CA 115; EWL 3; RGWL 2, 3
**Coupland, Douglas** 1961- ........... **CLC 85, 133**
See also AAYA 34; CA 142; CANR 57, 90, 130; CCA 1; CPW; DAC; DAM POP
**Court, Wesli**
See Turco, Lewis (Putnam)
**Courtenay, Bryce** 1933- ..................... **CLC 59**
See also CA 138; CPW
**Courtney, Robert**
See Ellison, Harlan (Jay)
**Cousteau, Jacques-Yves** 1910-1997 .. **CLC 30**
See also CA 65-68; 159; CANR 15, 67; MTCW 1; SATA 38, 98
**Coventry, Francis** 1725-1754 ............... **LC 46**
**Coverdale, Miles** c. 1487-1569 ............ **LC 77**
See also DLB 167
**Cowan, Peter (Walkinshaw)** 1914-2002 ...................................... **SSC 28**
See also CA 21-24R; CANR 9, 25, 50, 83; CN 7; DLB 260; RGSF 2
**Coward, Noel (Peirce)** 1899-1973 . **CLC 1, 9, 29, 51**
See also AITN 1; BRWS 2; CA 17-18; 41-44R; CANR 35, 132; CAP 2; CDBLB 1914-1945; DA3; DAM DRAM; DFS 3, 6; DLB 10, 245; EWL 3; IDFW 3, 4; MTCW 1, 2; RGEL 2; TEA
**Cowley, Abraham** 1618-1667 .............. **LC 43**
See also BRW 2; DLB 131, 151; PAB; RGEL 2
**Cowley, Malcolm** 1898-1989 ............. **CLC 39**
See also AMWS 2; CA 5-8R; 128; CANR 3, 55; DLB 4, 48; DLBY 1981, 1989; EWL 3; MTCW 1, 2
**Cowper, William** 1731-1800 ..... **NCLC 8, 94; PC 40**
See also BRW 3; DA3; DAM POET; DLB 104, 109; RGEL 2
**Cox, William Trevor** 1928-
See Trevor, William
See also CA 9-12R; CANR 4, 37, 55, 76, 102; DAM NOV; INT CANR-37; MTCW 1, 2; TEA
**Coyne, P. J.**
See Masters, Hilary
**Cozzens, James Gould** 1903-1978 . **CLC 1, 4, 11, 92**
See also AMW; BPFB 1; CA 9-12R; 81-84; CANR 19; CDALB 1941-1968; DLB 9, 294; DLBD 2; DLBY 1984, 1997; EWL 3; MTCW 1, 2; RGAL 4
**Crabbe, George** 1754-1832 .... **NCLC 26, 121**
See also BRW 3; DLB 93; RGEL 2
**Crace, Jim** 1946- ............. **CLC 157; SSC 61**
See also CA 128; 135; CANR 55, 70, 123; CN 7; DLB 231; INT CA-135
**Craddock, Charles Egbert**
See Murfree, Mary Noailles
**Craig, A. A.**
See Anderson, Poul (William)
**Craik, Mrs.**
See Craik, Dinah Maria (Mulock)
See also RGEL 2

**Curtis, Price**
See Ellison, Harlan (Jay)
**Cusanus, Nicolaus** 1401-1464 ............. **LC 80**
See Nicholas of Cusa
**Cutrate, Joe**
See Spiegelman, Art
**Cynewulf** c. 770- ........................... **CMLC 23**
See also DLB 146; RGEL 2
**Cyrano de Bergerac, Savinien de**
1619-1655 ............................... **LC 65**
See also DLB 268; GFL Beginnings to
1789; RGWL 2, 3
**Cyril of Alexandria** c. 375-c. 430 . **CMLC 59**
**Czaczkes, Shmuel Yosef Halevi**
See Agnon, S(hmuel) Y(osef Halevi)
**Dabrowska, Maria (Szumska)**
1889-1965 ................................. **CLC 15**
See also CA 106; CDWLB 4; DLB 215;
EWL 3
**Dabydeen, David** 1955- ..................... **CLC 34**
See also BW 1; CA 125; CANR 56, 92; CN
7; CP 7
**Dacey, Philip** 1939- ......................... **CLC 51**
See also CA 37-40R; CAAS 17; CANR 14,
32, 64; CP 7; DLB 105
**Dacre, Charlotte** c. 1772-1825? ... **NCLC 151**
**Dafydd ap Gwilym** c. 1320-c. 1380 ..... **PC 56**
**Dagerman, Stig (Halvard)**
1923-1954 ............................... **TCLC 17**
See also CA 117; 155; DLB 259; EWL 3
**D'Aguiar, Fred** 1960- ....................... **CLC 145**
See also CA 148; CANR 83, 101; CP 7;
DLB 157; EWL 3
**Dahl, Roald** 1916-1990 ....... **CLC 1, 6, 18, 79**
See also AAYA 15; BPFB 1; BRWS 4; BYA
5; CA 1-4R; 133; CANR 6, 32, 37, 62;
CLR 1, 7, 41; CPW; DA3; DAB; DAC;
DAM MST, NOV, POP; DLB 139, 255;
HGG; JRDA; MAICYA 1, 2; MTCW 1,
2; RGSF 2; SATA 1, 26, 73; SATA-Obit
65; SSFS 4; TEA; YAW
**Dahlberg, Edward** 1900-1977 .. **CLC 1, 7, 14**
See also CA 9-12R; 69-72; CANR 31, 62;
DLB 48; MTCW 1; RGAL 4
**Daitch, Susan** 1954- ......................... **CLC 103**
See also CA 161
**Dale, Colin** ................................... **TCLC 18**
See Lawrence, T(homas) E(dward)
**Dale, George E.**
See Asimov, Isaac
**Dalton, Roque** 1935-1975(?) ..... **HLCS 1; PC 36**
See also CA 176; DLB 283; HW 2
**Daly, Elizabeth** 1878-1967 ................. **CLC 52**
See also CA 23-24; 25-28R; CANR 60;
CAP 2; CMW 4
**Daly, Mary** 1928- ........................... **CLC 173**
See also CA 25-28R; CANR 30, 62; FW;
GLL 1; MTCW 1
**Daly, Maureen** 1921- ....................... **CLC 17**
See also AAYA 5, 58; BYA 6; CANR 37,
83, 108; CLR 96; JRDA; MAICYA 1, 2;
SAAS 1; SATA 2, 129; WYA; YAW
**Damas, Leon-Gontran** 1912-1978 .... **CLC 84**
See also BW 1; CA 125; 73-76; EWL 3
**Dana, Richard Henry Sr.**
1787-1879 ............................... **NCLC 53**
**Daniel, Samuel** 1562(?)-1619 ............... **LC 24**
See also DLB 62; RGEL 2
**Daniels, Brett**
See Adler, Renata
**Dannay, Frederic** 1905-1982 ............. **CLC 11**
See Queen, Ellery
See also CA 1-4R; 107; CANR 1, 39; CMW
4; DAM POP; DLB 137; MTCW 1
**D'Annunzio, Gabriele** 1863-1938 ... **TCLC 6, 40**
See also CA 104; 155; EW 8; EWL 3;
RGWL 2, 3; TWA

**Danois, N. le**
See Gourmont, Remy(-Marie-Charles) de
**Dante** 1265-1321 .... **CMLC 3, 18, 39, 70; PC 21; WLCS**
See also DA; DA3; DAB; DAC; DAM
MST, POET; EFS 1; EW 1; LAIT 1;
RGWL 2, 3; TWA; WP
**d'Antibes, Germain**
See Simenon, Georges (Jacques Christian)
**Danticat, Edwidge** 1969- ........... **CLC 94, 139**
See also AAYA 29; CA 152, 192; CAAE
192; CANR 73, 129; DNFS 1; EXPS;
LATS 1:2; MTCW 1; SSFS 1; YAW
**Danvers, Dennis** 1947- ..................... **CLC 70**
**Danziger, Paula** 1944-2004 ................. **CLC 21**
See also AAYA 4, 36; BYA 6, 7, 14; CA
112; 115; 229; CANR 37, 132; CLR 20;
JRDA; MAICYA 1, 2; SATA 36, 63, 102,
149; SATA-Brief 30; WYA; YAW
**Da Ponte, Lorenzo** 1749-1838 ........ **NCLC 50**
**Dario, Ruben** 1867-1916 ....... **HLC 1; PC 15; TCLC 4**
See also CA 131; CANR 81; DAM MULT;
DLB 290; EWL 3; HW 1, 2; LAW;
MTCW 1, 2; RGWL 2, 3
**Darley, George** 1795-1846 ............... **NCLC 2**
See also DLB 96; RGEL 2
**Darrow, Clarence (Seward)**
1857-1938 ............................... **TCLC 81**
See also CA 164; DLB 303
**Darwin, Charles** 1809-1882 ........... **NCLC 57**
See also BRWS 7; DLB 57, 166; LATS 1:1;
RGEL 2; TEA; WLIT 4
**Darwin, Erasmus** 1731-1802 ......... **NCLC 106**
See also DLB 93; RGEL 2
**Daryush, Elizabeth** 1887-1977 ...... **CLC 6, 19**
See also CA 49-52; CANR 3, 81; DLB 20
**Das, Kamala** 1934- ............. **CLC 191; PC 43**
See also CA 101; CANR 27, 59; CP 7;
CWP; FW
**Dasgupta, Surendranath**
1887-1952 ............................... **TCLC 81**
See also CA 157
**Dashwood, Edmee Elizabeth Monica de la
Pasture** 1890-1943
See Delafield, E. M.
See also CA 119; 154
**da Silva, Antonio Jose**
1705-1739 ............................... **NCLC 114**
**Daudet, (Louis Marie) Alphonse**
1840-1897 ............................... **NCLC 1**
See also DLB 123; GFL 1789 to the Present;
RGSF 2
**d'Aulnoy, Marie-Catherine** c.
1650-1705 ............................... **LC 100**
**Daumal, Rene** 1908-1944 ................. **TCLC 14**
See also CA 114; EWL 3
**Davenant, William** 1606-1668 ............. **LC 13**
See also DLB 58, 126; RGEL 2
**Davenport, Guy (Mattison, Jr.)**
1927-2005 ......... **CLC 6, 14, 38; SSC 16**
See also CA 33-36R; CANR 23, 73; CN 7;
CSW; DLB 130
**David, Robert**
See Nezval, Vitezslav
**Davidson, Avram (James)** 1923-1993
See Queen, Ellery
See also CA 101; 171; CANR 26; DLB 8;
FANT; SFW 4; SUFW 1, 2
**Davidson, Donald (Grady)**
1893-1968 ......................... **CLC 2, 13, 19**
See also CA 5-8R; 25-28R; CANR 4, 84;
DLB 45
**Davidson, Hugh**
See Hamilton, Edmond
**Davidson, John** 1857-1909 ............. **TCLC 24**
See also CA 118; 217; DLB 19; RGEL 2

**Davidson, Sara** 1943- ......................... **CLC 9**
See also CA 81-84; CANR 44, 68; DLB
185
**Davie, Donald (Alfred)** 1922-1995 .... **CLC 5, 8, 10, 31; PC 29**
See also BRWS 6; CA 1-4R; 149; CAAS 3;
CANR 1, 44; CP 7; DLB 27; MTCW 1;
RGEL 2
**Davie, Elspeth** 1919-1995 ................... **SSC 52**
See also CA 120; 126; 150; DLB 139
**Davies, Ray(mond Douglas)** 1944- ... **CLC 21**
See also CA 116; 146; CANR 92
**Davies, Rhys** 1901-1978 ................. **CLC 23**
See also CA 9-12R; 81-84; CANR 4; DLB
139, 191
**Davies, (William) Robertson**
1913-1995 ....... **CLC 2, 7, 13, 25, 42, 75, 91; WLC**
See Marchbanks, Samuel
See also BEST 89:2; BPFB 1; CA 33-36R;
150; CANR 17, 42, 103; CN 7; CPW;
DA; DA3; DAB; DAC; DAM MST, NOV,
POP; DLB 68; EWL 3; HGG; INT CANR-
17; MTCW 1, 2; RGEL 2; TWA
**Davies, Sir John** 1569-1626 ................. **LC 85**
See also DLB 172
**Davies, Walter C.**
See Kornbluth, C(yril) M.
**Davies, William Henry** 1871-1940 ... **TCLC 5**
See also CA 104; 179; DLB 19, 174; EWL
3; RGEL 2
**Da Vinci, Leonardo** 1452-1519 ..... **LC 12, 57, 60**
See also AAYA 40
**Davis, Angela (Yvonne)** 1944- .......... **CLC 77**
See also BW 2, 3; CA 57-60; CANR 10,
81; CSW; DA3; DAM MULT; FW
**Davis, B. Lynch**
See Bioy Casares, Adolfo; Borges, Jorge
Luis
**Davis, Frank Marshall** 1905-1987 ...... **BLC 1**
See also BW 2, 3; CA 125; 123; CANR 42,
80; DAM MULT; DLB 51
**Davis, Gordon**
See Hunt, E(verette) Howard, (Jr.)
**Davis, H(arold) L(enoir)** 1896-1960 . **CLC 49**
See also ANW; CA 178; 89-92; DLB 9,
206; SATA 114
**Davis, Natalie Z(emon)** 1928- ......... **CLC 204**
See also CA 53-56; CANR 58, 100
**Davis, Rebecca (Blaine) Harding**
1831-1910 .................. **SSC 38; TCLC 6**
See also CA 104; 179; DLB 74, 239; FW;
NFS 14; RGAL 4; TUS
**Davis, Richard Harding**
1864-1916 ............................... **TCLC 24**
See also CA 114; 179; DLB 12, 23, 78, 79,
189; DLBD 13; RGAL 4
**Davison, Frank Dalby** 1893-1970 ..... **CLC 15**
See also CA 217; 116; DLB 260
**Davison, Lawrence H.**
See Lawrence, D(avid) H(erbert Richards)
**Davison, Peter (Hubert)** 1928- ......... **CLC 28**
See also CA 9-12R; CAAS 4; CANR 3, 43,
84; CP 7; DLB 5
**Davys, Mary** 1674-1732 .................. **LC 1, 46**
See also DLB 39
**Dawson, (Guy) Fielding (Lewis)**
1930-2002 ............................... **CLC 6**
See also CA 85-88; 202; CANR 108; DLB
130; DLBY 2002
**Dawson, Peter**
See Faust, Frederick (Schiller)
See also TCWW 2, 2
**Day, Clarence (Shepard, Jr.)**
1874-1935 ............................... **TCLC 25**
See also CA 108; 199; DLB 11
**Day, John** 1574(?)-1640(?) ................... **LC 70**
See also DLB 62, 170; RGEL 2

**Denmark, Harrison**
See Zelazny, Roger (Joseph)
**Dennis, John** 1658-1734 ........................ **LC 11**
See also DLB 101; RGEL 2
**Dennis, Nigel (Forbes)** 1912-1989 ...... **CLC 8**
See also CA 25-28R; 129; DLB 13, 15, 233;
EWL 3; MTCW 1
**Dent, Lester** 1904-1959 .................. **TCLC 72**
See also CA 112; 161; CMW 4; DLB 306;
SFW 4
**De Palma, Brian (Russell)** 1940- ...... **CLC 20**
See also CA 109
**De Quincey, Thomas** 1785-1859 ..... **NCLC 4,
87**
See also BRW 4; CDBLB 1789-1832; DLB
110, 144; RGEL 2
**Deren, Eleanora** 1908(?)-1961
See Deren, Maya
See also CA 192; 111
**Deren, Maya** ............................. **CLC 16, 102**
See Deren, Eleanora
**Derleth, August (William)**
1909-1971 .................................. **CLC 31**
See also BPFB 1; BYA 9, 10; CA 1-4R; 29-
32R; CANR 4; CMW 4; DLB 9; DLBD
17; HGG; SATA 5; SUFW 1
**Der Nister** 1884-1950 ...................... **TCLC 56**
See Nister, Der
**Der Stricker** c. 1190-c. 1250 ......... **CMLC 75**
**de Routisie, Albert**
See Aragon, Louis
**Derrida, Jacques** 1930-2004 ....... **CLC 24, 87**
See also CA 124; 127; CANR 76, 98, 133;
DLB 242; EWL 3; LMFS 2; MTCW 1;
TWA
**Derry Down Derry**
See Lear, Edward
**Dersonnes, Jacques**
See Simenon, Georges (Jacques Christian)
**Desai, Anita** 1937- ......... **CLC 19, 37, 97, 175**
See also BRWS 5; CA 81-84; CANR 33,
53, 95, 133; CN 7; CWRI 5; DA3; DAB;
DAM NOV; DLB 271; DNFS 2; EWL 3;
FW; MTCW 1, 2; SATA 63, 126
**Desai, Kiran** 1971- ........................... **CLC 119**
See also BYA 16; CA 171; CANR 127
**de Saint-Luc, Jean**
See Glassco, John
**de Saint Roman, Arnaud**
See Aragon, Louis
**Desbordes-Valmore, Marceline**
1786-1859 ................................. **NCLC 97**
See also DLB 217
**Descartes, Rene** 1596-1650 ........... **LC 20, 35**
See also DLB 268; EW 3; GFL Beginnings
to 1789
**Deschamps, Eustache** 1340(?)-1404 .. **LC 103**
See also DLB 208
**De Sica, Vittorio** 1901(?)-1974 ......... **CLC 20**
See also CA 117
**Desnos, Robert** 1900-1945 ............. **TCLC 22**
See also CA 121; 151; CANR 107; DLB
258; EWL 3; LMFS 2
**Des Roches, Catherine** 1542-1587 ..... **LC 117**
**Destouches, Louis-Ferdinand**
1894-1961 ............................... **CLC 9, 15**
See Celine, Louis-Ferdinand
See also CA 85-88; CANR 28; MTCW 1
**de Tolignac, Gaston**
See Griffith, D(avid Lewelyn) W(ark)
**Deutsch, Babette** 1895-1982 ............. **CLC 18**
See also BYA 3; CA 1-4R; 108; CANR 4;
79; DLB 45; SATA 1; SATA-Obit 33
**Devenant, William** 1606-1649 ............. **LC 13**
**Devkota, Laxmiprasad** 1909-1959 . **TCLC 23**
See also CA 123

**De Voto, Bernard (Augustine)**
1897-1955 ................................. **TCLC 29**
See also CA 113; 160; DLB 9, 256
**De Vries, Peter** 1910-1993 ..... **CLC 1, 2, 3, 7,
10, 28, 46**
See also CA 17-20R; 142; CANR 41; DAM
NOV; DLB 6; DLBY 1982; MTCW 1, 2
**Dewey, John** 1859-1952 .................. **TCLC 95**
See also CA 114; 170; DLB 246, 270;
RGAL 4
**Dexter, John**
See Bradley, Marion Zimmer
See also GLL 1
**Dexter, Martin**
See Faust, Frederick (Schiller)
See also TCWW 2
**Dexter, Pete** 1943- ......................... **CLC 34, 55**
See also BEST 89:2; CA 127; 131; CANR
129; CPW; DAM POP; INT CA-131;
MTCW 1
**Diamano, Silmang**
See Senghor, Leopold Sedar
**Diamond, Neil** 1941- ........................... **CLC 30**
See also CA 108
**Diaz del Castillo, Bernal**
1496-1584 ..................... **HLCS 1; LC 31**
See also LAW
**di Bassetto, Corno**
See Shaw, George Bernard
**Dick, Philip K(indred)** 1928-1982 ... **CLC 10,
30, 72; SSC 57**
See also AAYA 24; BPFB 1; BYA 11; CA
49-52; 106; CANR 2, 16, 132; CPW;
DA3; DAM NOV, POP; DLB 8; MTCW
1, 2; NFS 5; SCFW 1, 2; SFW 4
**Dickens, Charles (John Huffam)**
1812-1870 .... **NCLC 3, 8, 18, 26, 37, 50,
86, 105, 113; SSC 17, 49; WLC**
See also AAYA 23; BRW 5; BRWC 1, 2;
BYA 1, 2, 3, 13, 14; CDBLB 1832-1890;
CLR 95; CMW 4; DA; DA3; DAB; DAC;
DAM MST, NOV; DLB 21, 55, 70, 159,
166; EXPN; HGG; JRDA; LAIT 1, 2;
LATS 1:1; LMFS 1; MAICYA 1, 2; NFS
4, 5, 10, 14, 20; RGEL 2; RGSF 2; SATA
15; SUFW 1; TEA; WCH; WLIT 4; WYA
**Dickey, James (Lafayette)**
1923-1997 .... **CLC 1, 2, 4, 7, 10, 15, 47,
109; PC 40; TCLC 151**
See also AAYA 50; AITN 1, 2; AMWS 4;
BPFB 1; CA 9-12R; 156; CABS 2; CANR
10, 48, 61, 105; CDALB 1968-1988; CP
7; CPW; CSW; DA3; DAM NOV, POET,
POP; DLB 5, 193; DLBD 7; DLBY 1982,
1993, 1996, 1997, 1998; EWL 3; INT
CANR-10; MTCW 1, 2; NFS 9; PFS 6,
11; RGAL 4; TUS
**Dickey, William** 1928-1994 ........... **CLC 3, 28**
See also CA 9-12R; 145; CANR 24, 79;
DLB 5
**Dickinson, Charles** 1951- ................. **CLC 49**
See also CA 128
**Dickinson, Emily (Elizabeth)**
1830-1886 ... **NCLC 21, 77; PC 1; WLC**
See also AAYA 22; AMW; AMWR 1;
CDALB 1865-1917; DA; DA3; DAB;
DAC; DAM MST, POET; DLB 1, 243;
EXPP; MAWW; PAB; PFS 1, 2, 3, 4, 5,
6, 8, 10, 11, 13, 16; RGAL 4; SATA 29;
TUS; WP; WYA
**Dickinson, Mrs. Herbert Ward**
See Phelps, Elizabeth Stuart
**Dickinson, Peter (Malcolm de Brissac)**
1927- ..................................... **CLC 12, 35**
See also AAYA 9, 49; BYA 5; CA 41-44R;
CANR 31, 58, 88, 134; CLR 29; CMW 4;
DLB 87, 161, 276; JRDA; MAICYA 1, 2;
SATA 5, 62, 95, 150; SFW 4; WYA; YAW
**Dickson, Carr**
See Carr, John Dickson

**Dickson, Carter**
See Carr, John Dickson
**Diderot, Denis** 1713-1784 .................... **LC 26**
See also EW 4; GFL Beginnings to 1789;
LMFS 1; RGWL 2, 3
**Didion, Joan** 1934- . **CLC 1, 3, 8, 14, 32, 129**
See also AITN 1; AMWS 4; CA 5-8R;
CANR 14, 52, 76, 125; CDALB 1968-
1988; CN 7; DA3; DAM NOV; DLB 2,
173, 185; DLBY 1981, 1986; EWL 3;
MAWW; MTCW 1, 2; NFS 3; RGAL 4;
TCWW 2; TUS
**di Donato, Pietro** 1911-1992 ......... **TCLC 159**
See also CA 101; 136; DLB 9
**Dietrich, Robert**
See Hunt, E(verette) Howard, (Jr.)
**Difusa, Pati**
See Almodovar, Pedro
**Dillard, Annie** 1945- .............. **CLC 9, 60, 115**
See also AAYA 6, 43; AMWS 6; ANW; CA
49-52; CANR 3, 43, 62, 90, 125; DA3;
DAM NOV; DLB 275, 278; DLBY 1980;
LAIT 4, 5; MTCW 1, 2; NCFS 1; RGAL
4; SATA 10, 140; TUS
**Dillard, R(ichard) H(enry) W(ilde)**
1937- ....................................... **CLC 5**
See also CA 21-24R; CAAS 7; CANR 10;
CP 7; CSW; DLB 5, 244
**Dillon, Eilis** 1920-1994 ..................... **CLC 17**
See also CA 9-12R; 182; 147; CAAE 182;
CAAS 3; CANR 4, 38, 78; CLR 26; MAI-
CYA 1, 2; MAICYAS 1; SATA 2, 74;
SATA-Essay 105; SATA-Obit 83; YAW
**Dimont, Penelope**
See Mortimer, Penelope (Ruth)
**Dinesen, Isak** ..... **CLC 10, 29, 95; SSC 7, 75**
See Blixen, Karen (Christentze Dinesen)
See also EW 10; EWL 3; EXPS; FW; HGG;
LAIT 3; MTCW 1; NCFS 2; NFS 9;
RGSF 2; RGWL 2, 3; SSFS 3, 6, 13;
WLIT 2
**Ding Ling** .......................................... **CLC 68**
See Chiang, Pin-chin
See also RGWL 3
**Diphusa, Patty**
See Almodovar, Pedro
**Disch, Thomas M(ichael)** 1940- ... **CLC 7, 36**
See Disch, Tom
See also AAYA 17; BPFB 1; CA 21-24R;
CAAS 4; CANR 17, 36, 54, 89; CLR 18;
CP 7; DA3; DLB 8; HGG; MAICYA 1, 2;
MTCW 1, 2; SAAS 15; SATA 92; SCFW;
SFW 4; SUFW 2
**Disch, Tom**
See Disch, Thomas M(ichael)
See also DLB 282
**d'Isly, Georges**
See Simenon, Georges (Jacques Christian)
**Disraeli, Benjamin** 1804-1881 ... **NCLC 2, 39,
79**
See also BRW 4; DLB 21, 55; RGEL 2
**Ditcum, Steve**
See Crumb, R(obert)
**Dixon, Paige**
See Corcoran, Barbara (Asenath)
**Dixon, Stephen** 1936- ......... **CLC 52; SSC 16**
See also AMWS 12; CA 89-92; CANR 17,
40, 54, 91; CN 7; DLB 130
**Dixon, Thomas** 1864-1946 ............. **TCLC 163**
See also RHW
**Djebar, Assia** 1936- ......................... **CLC 182**
See also CA 188; EWL 3; RGWL 3; WLIT
2
**Doak, Annie**
See Dillard, Annie
**Dobell, Sydney Thompson**
1824-1874 ............................... **NCLC 43**
See also DLB 32; RGEL 2

**Dr. A**
See Asimov, Isaac; Silverstein, Alvin; Silverstein, Virginia B(arbara Opshelor)

**Drabble, Margaret** 1939- ...... **CLC 2, 3, 5, 8, 10, 22, 53, 129**
See also BRWS 4; CA 13-16R; CANR 18, 35, 63, 112, 131; CDBLB 1960 to Present; CN 7; CPW; DA3; DAB; DAC; DAM MST, NOV, POP; DLB 14, 155, 231; EWL 3; FW; MTCW 1, 2; RGEL 2; SATA 48; TEA

**Drakulic, Slavenka** 1949- ................ **CLC 173**
See also CA 144; CANR 92

**Drakulic-Ilic, Slavenka**
See Drakulic, Slavenka

**Drapier, M. B.**
See Swift, Jonathan

**Drayham, James**
See Mencken, H(enry) L(ouis)

**Drayton, Michael** 1563-1631 .................. **LC 8**
See also DAM POET; DLB 121; RGEL 2

**Dreadstone, Carl**
See Campbell, (John) Ramsey

**Dreiser, Theodore (Herman Albert)** 1871-1945 .... **SSC 30; TCLC 10, 18, 35, 83; WLC**
See also AMW; AMWC 2; AMWR 2; BYA 15, 16; CA 106; 132; CDALB 1865-1917; DA; DA3; DAC; DAM MST, NOV; DLB 9, 12, 102, 137; DLBD 1; EWL 3; LAIT 2; LMFS 2; MTCW 1, 2; NFS 8, 17; RGAL 4; TUS

**Drexler, Rosalyn** 1926- ................... **CLC 2, 6**
See also CA 81-84; CAD; CANR 68, 124; CD 5; CWD

**Dreyer, Carl Theodor** 1889-1968 ...... **CLC 16**
See also CA 116

**Drieu la Rochelle, Pierre(-Eugene)** 1893-1945 ................................. **TCLC 21**
See also CA 117; DLB 72; EWL 3; GFL 1789 to the Present

**Drinkwater, John** 1882-1937 .......... **TCLC 57**
See also CA 109; 149; DLB 10, 19, 149; RGEL 2

**Drop Shot**
See Cable, George Washington

**Droste-Hulshoff, Annette Freiin von** 1797-1848 .......................... **NCLC 3, 133**
See also CDWLB 2; DLB 133; RGSF 2; RGWL 2, 3

**Drummond, Walter**
See Silverberg, Robert

**Drummond, William Henry** 1854-1907 ................................... **TCLC 25**
See also CA 160; DLB 92

**Drummond de Andrade, Carlos** 1902-1987 .............. **CLC 18; TCLC 139**
See Andrade, Carlos Drummond de
See also CA 132; 123; DLB 307; LAW

**Drummond of Hawthornden, William** 1585-1649 ...................................... **LC 83**
See also DLB 121, 213; RGEL 2

**Drury, Allen (Stuart)** 1918-1998 ....... **CLC 37**
See also CA 57-60; 170; CANR 18, 52; CN 7; INT CANR-18

**Druse, Eleanor**
See King, Stephen (Edwin)

**Dryden, John** 1631-1700 ..... **DC 3; LC 3, 21, 115; PC 25; WLC**
See also BRW 2; CDBLB 1660-1789; DA; DAB; DAC; DAM DRAM, MST, POET; DLB 80, 101, 131; EXPP; IDTP; LMFS 1; RGEL 2; TEA; WLIT 3

**du Bellay, Joachim** 1524-1560 ............. **LC 92**
See also GFL Beginnings to 1789; RGWL 2, 3

**Duberman, Martin (Bauml)** 1930- ..... **CLC 8**
See also CA 1-4R; CAD; CANR 2, 63; CD 5

**Dubie, Norman (Evans)** 1945- .......... **CLC 36**
See also CA 69-72; CANR 12, 115; CP 7; DLB 120; PFS 12

**Du Bois, W(illiam) E(dward) B(urghardt)** 1868-1963 ..... **BLC 1; CLC 1, 2, 13, 64, 96; HR 2; WLC**
See also AAYA 40; AFAW 1, 2; AMWC 1; AMWS 2; BW 1, 3; CA 85-88; CANR 34, 82, 132; CDALB 1865-1917; DA; DA3; DAC; DAM MST, MULT, NOV; DLB 47, 50, 91, 246, 284; EWL 3; EXPP; LAIT 2; LMFS 2; MTCW 1, 2; NCFS 1; PFS 13; RGAL 4; SATA 42

**Dubus, Andre** 1936-1999 ..... **CLC 13, 36, 97; SSC 15**
See also AMWS 7; CA 21-24R; 177; CANR 17; CN 7; CSW; DLB 130; INT CANR-17; RGAL 4; SSFS 10

**Duca Minimo**
See D'Annunzio, Gabriele

**Ducharme, Rejean** 1941- ................... **CLC 74**
See also CA 165; DLB 60

**du Chatelet, Emilie** 1706-1749 ............ **LC 96**

**Duchen, Claire** ................................... **CLC 65**

**Duclos, Charles Pinot-** 1704-1772 ......... **LC 1**
See also GFL Beginnings to 1789

**Dudek, Louis** 1918-2001 ............. **CLC 11, 19**
See also CA 45-48; 215; CAAS 14; CANR 1; CP 7; DLB 88

**Duerrenmatt, Friedrich** 1921-1990 ... **CLC 1, 4, 8, 11, 15, 43, 102**
See Durrenmatt, Friedrich
See also CA 17-20R; CANR 33; CMW 4; DAM DRAM; DLB 69, 124; MTCW 1, 2

**Duffy, Bruce** 1953(?)- ......................... **CLC 50**
See also CA 172

**Duffy, Maureen** 1933- ......................... **CLC 37**
See also CA 25-28R; CANR 33, 68; CBD; CN 7; CP 7; CWD; CWP; DFS 15; DLB 14; FW; MTCW 1

**Du Fu**
See Tu Fu
See also RGWL 2, 3

**Dugan, Alan** 1923-2003 ................... **CLC 2, 6**
See also CA 81-84; 220; CANR 119; CP 7; DLB 5; PFS 10

**du Gard, Roger Martin**
See Martin du Gard, Roger

**Duhamel, Georges** 1884-1966 ............. **CLC 8**
See also CA 81-84; 25-28R; CANR 35; DLB 65; EWL 3; GFL 1789 to the Present; MTCW 1

**Dujardin, Edouard (Emile Louis)** 1861-1949 ................................. **TCLC 13**
See also CA 109; DLB 123

**Duke, Raoul**
See Thompson, Hunter S(tockton)

**Dulles, John Foster** 1888-1959 ....... **TCLC 72**
See also CA 115; 149

**Dumas, Alexandre (pere)** 1802-1870 .............. **NCLC 11, 71; WLC**
See also AAYA 22; BYA 3; DA; DA3; DAB; DAC; DAM MST, NOV; DLB 119, 192; EW 6; GFL 1789 to the Present; LAIT 1, 2; NFS 14, 19; RGWL 2, 3; SATA 18; TWA; WCH

**Dumas, Alexandre (fils)** 1824-1895 ...... **DC 1; NCLC 9**
See also DLB 192; GFL 1789 to the Present; RGWL 2, 3

**Dumas, Claudine**
See Malzberg, Barry N(athaniel)

**Dumas, Henry L.** 1934-1968 ......... **CLC 6, 62**
See also BW 1; CA 85-88; DLB 41; RGAL 4

**du Maurier, Daphne** 1907-1989 .. **CLC 6, 11, 59; SSC 18**
See also AAYA 37; BPFB 1; BRWS 3; CA 5-8R; 128; CANR 6, 55; CMW 4; CPW; DA3; DAB; DAC; DAM MST, POP; DLB 191; HGG; LAIT 3; MSW; MTCW 1, 2; NFS 12; RGEL 2; RGSF 2; RHW; SATA 27; SATA-Obit 60; SSFS 14, 16; TEA

**Du Maurier, George** 1834-1896 ..... **NCLC 86**
See also DLB 153, 178; RGEL 2

**Dunbar, Paul Laurence** 1872-1906 ... **BLC 1; PC 5; SSC 8; TCLC 2, 12; WLC**
See also AFAW 1, 2; AMWS 2; BW 1, 3; CA 104; 124; CANR 79; CDALB 1865-1917; DA; DA3; DAC; DAM MST, MULT, POET; DLB 50, 54, 78; EXPP; RGAL 4; SATA 34

**Dunbar, William** 1460(?)-1520(?) ........ **LC 20**
See also BRWS 8; DLB 132, 146; RGEL 2

**Dunbar-Nelson, Alice** ........................... **HR 2**
See Nelson, Alice Ruth Moore Dunbar

**Duncan, Dora Angela**
See Duncan, Isadora

**Duncan, Isadora** 1877(?)-1927 ....... **TCLC 68**
See also CA 118; 149

**Duncan, Lois** 1934- ........................... **CLC 26**
See also AAYA 4, 34; BYA 6, 8; CA 1-4R; CANR 2, 23, 36, 111; CLR 29; JRDA; MAICYA 1, 2; MAICYAS 1; SAAS 2; SATA 1, 36, 75, 133, 141; SATA-Essay 141; WYA; YAW

**Duncan, Robert (Edward)** 1919-1988 .... **CLC 1, 2, 4, 7, 15, 41, 55; PC 2**
See also BG 2; CA 9-12R; 124; CANR 28, 62; DAM POET; DLB 5, 16, 193; EWL 3; MTCW 1, 2; PFS 13; RGAL 4; WP

**Duncan, Sara Jeannette** 1861-1922 ................................. **TCLC 60**
See also CA 157; DLB 92

**Dunlap, William** 1766-1839 ............. **NCLC 2**
See also DLB 30, 37, 59; RGAL 4

**Dunn, Douglas (Eaglesham)** 1942- .... **CLC 6, 40**
See also BRWS 10; CA 45-48; CANR 2, 33, 126; CP 7; DLB 40; MTCW 1

**Dunn, Katherine (Karen)** 1945- ....... **CLC 71**
See also CA 33-36R; CANR 72; HGG; MTCW 1

**Dunn, Stephen (Elliott)** 1939- .. **CLC 36, 206**
See also AMWS 11; CA 33-36R; CANR 12, 48, 53, 105; CP 7; DLB 105; PFS 21

**Dunne, Finley Peter** 1867-1936 ...... **TCLC 28**
See also CA 108; 178; DLB 11, 23; RGAL 4

**Dunne, John Gregory** 1932-2003 ..... **CLC 28**
See also CA 25-28R; 222; CANR 14, 50; CN 7; DLBY 1980

**Dunsany, Lord** ........................... **TCLC 2, 59**
See Dunsany, Edward John Moreton Drax Plunkett
See also DLB 77, 153, 156, 255; FANT; IDTP; RGEL 2; SFW 4; SUFW 1

**Dunsany, Edward John Moreton Drax Plunkett** 1878-1957
See Dunsany, Lord
See also CA 104; 148; DLB 10; MTCW 1

**Duns Scotus, John** 1266(?)-1308 ... **CMLC 59**
See also DLB 115

**du Perry, Jean**
See Simenon, Georges (Jacques Christian)

**Durang, Christopher (Ferdinand)** 1949- ..................................... **CLC 27, 38**
See also CA 105; CAD; CANR 50, 76, 130; CD 5; MTCW 1

**Duras, Claire de** 1777-1828 ......... **NCLC 154**

**Ekwensi, Cyprian (Odiatu Duaka)**
1921- ............................... **BLC 1; CLC 4**
See also AFW; BW 2, 3; CA 29-32R;
CANR 18, 42, 74, 125; CDWLB 3; CN
7; CWRI 5; DAM MULT; DLB 117; EWL
3; MTCW 1, 2; RGEL 2; SATA 66; WLIT
2

**Elaine** .......................................... **TCLC 18**
See Leverson, Ada Esther

**El Crummo**
See Crumb, R(obert)

**Elder, Lonne III** 1931-1996 ..... **BLC 1; DC 8**
See also BW 1, 3; CA 81-84; 152; CAD;
CANR 25; DAM MULT; DLB 7, 38, 44

**Eleanor of Aquitaine** 1122-1204 ... **CMLC 39**

**Elia**
See Lamb, Charles

**Eliade, Mircea** 1907-1986 ................. **CLC 19**
See also CA 65-68; 119; CANR 30, 62; CD-
WLB 4; DLB 220; EWL 3; MTCW 1;
RGWL 3; SFW 4

**Eliot, A. D.**
See Jewett, (Theodora) Sarah Orne

**Eliot, Alice**
See Jewett, (Theodora) Sarah Orne

**Eliot, Dan**
See Silverberg, Robert

**Eliot, George** 1819-1880 ...... **NCLC 4, 13, 23,
41, 49, 89, 118; PC 20; SSC 72; WLC**
See Evans, Mary Ann
See also BRW 5; BRWC 1, 2; BRWR 2;
CDBLB 1832-1890; CN 7; CPW; DA;
DA3; DAB; DAC; DAM MST, NOV;
DLB 21, 35, 55; LATS 1:1; NFS 17;
RGEL 2; RGSF 2; SSFS 8; TEA;
WLIT 3

**Eliot, John** 1604-1690 ............................. **LC 5**
See also DLB 24

**Eliot, T(homas) S(tearns)**
1888-1965 ...... **CLC 1, 2, 3, 6, 9, 10, 13,
15, 24, 34, 41, 55, 57, 113; PC 5, 31;
WLC**
See also AAYA 28; AMW; AMWC 1;
AMWR 1; BRW 7; BRWR 2; CA 5-8R;
25-28R; CANR 41; CDALB 1929-1941;
DA; DA3; DAB; DAC; DAM DRAM,
MST, POET; DFS 4, 13; DLB 7, 10, 45,
63, 245; DLBY 1988; EWL 3; EXPP;
LAIT 3; LATS 1:1; LMFS 2; MTCW 1,
2; NCFS 5; PAB; PFS 1, 7, 20; RGAL 4;
RGEL 2; TUS; WLIT 4; WP

**Elizabeth** 1866-1941 ......................... **TCLC 41**

**Elkin, Stanley L(awrence)**
1930-1995 .. **CLC 4, 6, 9, 14, 27, 51, 91;
SSC 12**
See also AMWS 6; BPFB 1; CA 9-12R;
148; CANR 8, 46; CN 7; CPW; DAM
NOV, POP; DLB 2, 28, 218, 278; DLBY
1980; EWL 3; INT CANR-8; MTCW 1,
2; RGAL 4

**Elledge, Scott** .................................... **CLC 34**

**Elliott, Don**
See Silverberg, Robert

**Elliott, George P(aul)** 1918-1980 ....... **CLC 2**
See also CA 1-4R; 97-100; CANR 2; DLB
244

**Elliott, Janice** 1931-1995 ................... **CLC 47**
See also CA 13-16R; CANR 8, 29, 84; CN
7; DLB 14; SATA 119

**Elliott, Sumner Locke** 1917-1991 ..... **CLC 38**
See also CA 5-8R; 134; CANR 2, 21; DLB
289

**Elliott, William**
See Bradbury, Ray (Douglas)

**Ellis, A. E.** ........................................... **CLC 7**

**Ellis, Alice Thomas** ......................... **CLC 40**
See Haycraft, Anna (Margaret)
See also DLB 194; MTCW 1

**Ellis, Bret Easton** 1964- ...... **CLC 39, 71, 117**
See also AAYA 2, 43; CA 118; 123; CANR
51, 74, 126; CN 7; CPW; DA3; DAM
POP; DLB 292; HGG; INT CA-123;
MTCW 1; NFS 11

**Ellis, (Henry) Havelock**
1859-1939 ................................. **TCLC 14**
See also CA 109; 169; DLB 190

**Ellis, Landon**
See Ellison, Harlan (Jay)

**Ellis, Trey** 1962- ................................. **CLC 55**
See also CA 146; CANR 92

**Ellison, Harlan (Jay)** 1934- ... **CLC 1, 13, 42,
139; SSC 14**
See also AAYA 29; BPFB 1; BYA 14; CA
5-8R; CANR 5, 46, 115; CPW; DAM
POP; DLB 8; HGG; INT CANR-5;
MTCW 1, 2; SCFW 2; SFW 4; SSFS 13,
14, 15; SUFW 1, 2

**Ellison, Ralph (Waldo)** 1914-1994 .... **BLC 1;
CLC 1, 3, 11, 54, 86, 114; SSC 26, 79;
WLC**
See also AAYA 19; AFAW 1, 2; AMWC 2;
AMWR 2; AMWS 2; BPFB 1; BW 1, 3;
BYA 2; CA 9-12R; 145; CANR 24, 53;
CDALB 1941-1968; CSW; DA; DA3;
DAB; DAC; DAM MST, MULT, NOV;
DLB 2, 76, 227; DLBY 1994; EWL 3;
EXPN; EXPS; LAIT 4; MTCW 1, 2;
NCFS 3; NFS 2; RGAL 4; RGSF 2; SSFS
1, 11; YAW

**Ellmann, Lucy (Elizabeth)** 1956- ..... **CLC 61**
See also CA 128

**Ellmann, Richard (David)**
1918-1987 ................................. **CLC 50**
See also BEST 89:2; CA 1-4R; 122; CANR
2, 28, 61; DLB 103; DLBY 1987; MTCW
1, 2

**Elman, Richard (Martin)**
1934-1997 ................................. **CLC 19**
See also CA 17-20R; 163; CAAS 3; CANR
47

**Elron**
See Hubbard, L(afayette) Ron(ald)

**El Saadawi, Nawal** 1931- ................. **CLC 196**
See al'Sadaawi, Nawal; Sa'adawi, al-
Nawal; Saadawi, Nawal El; Sa'dawi,
Nawal al-
See also CA 118; CAAS 11; CANR 44, 92

**Eluard, Paul** ................. **PC 38; TCLC 7, 41**
See Grindel, Eugene
See also EWL 3; GFL 1789 to the Present;
RGWL 2, 3

**Elyot, Thomas** 1490(?)-1546 ................. **LC 11**
See also DLB 136; RGEL 2

**Elytis, Odysseus** 1911-1996 ........ **CLC 15, 49,
100; PC 21**
See Alepoudelis, Odysseus
See also CA 102; 151; CANR 94; CWW 2;
DAM POET; EW 13; EWL 3; MTCW 1,
2; RGWL 2, 3

**Emecheta, (Florence Onye) Buchi**
1944- ............... **BLC 2; CLC 14, 48, 128**
See also AFW; BW 2, 3; CA 81-84; CANR
27, 81, 126; CDWLB 3; CN 7; CWRI 5;
DA3; DAM MULT; DLB 117; EWL 3;
FW; MTCW 1, 2; NFS 12, 14; SATA 66;
WLIT 2

**Emerson, Mary Moody**
1774-1863 ................................. **NCLC 66**

**Emerson, Ralph Waldo** 1803-1882 . **NCLC 1,
38, 98; PC 18; WLC**
See also AAYA 60; AMW; ANW; CDALB
1640-1865; DA; DA3; DAB; DAC; DAM
MST, POET; DLB 1, 59, 73, 183, 223,
270; EXPP; LAIT 2; LMFS 1; NCFS 3;
PFS 4, 17; RGAL 4; TUS; WP

**Eminescu, Mihail** 1850-1889 .. **NCLC 33, 131**

**Empedocles** 5th cent. B.C.- ........... **CMLC 50**
See also DLB 176

**Empson, William** 1906-1984 ... **CLC 3, 8, 19,
33, 34**
See also BRWS 2; CA 17-20R; 112; CANR
31, 61; DLB 20; EWL 3; MTCW 1, 2;
RGEL 2

**Enchi, Fumiko (Ueda)** 1905-1986 ..... **CLC 31**
See Enchi Fumiko
See also CA 129; 121; FW; MJW

**Enchi Fumiko**
See Enchi, Fumiko (Ueda)
See also DLB 182; EWL 3

**Ende, Michael (Andreas Helmuth)**
1929-1995 ................................. **CLC 31**
See also BYA 5; CA 118; 124; 149; CANR
36, 110; CLR 14; DLB 75; MAICYA 1,
2; MAICYAS 1; SATA 61, 130; SATA-
Brief 42; SATA-Obit 86

**Endo, Shusaku** 1923-1996 ..... **CLC 7, 14, 19,
54, 99; SSC 48; TCLC 152**
See Endo Shusaku
See also CA 29-32R; 153; CANR 21, 54,
131; DA3; DAM NOV; MTCW 1, 2;
RGSF 2; RGWL 2, 3

**Endo Shusaku**
See Endo, Shusaku
See also CWW 2; DLB 182; EWL 3

**Engel, Marian** 1933-1985 .... **CLC 36; TCLC
137**
See also CA 25-28R; CANR 12; DLB 53;
FW; INT CANR-12

**Engelhardt, Frederick**
See Hubbard, L(afayette) Ron(ald)

**Engels, Friedrich** 1820-1895 .. **NCLC 85, 114**
See also DLB 129; LATS 1:1

**Enright, D(ennis) J(oseph)**
1920-2002 .......................... **CLC 4, 8, 31**
See also CA 1-4R; 211; CANR 1, 42, 83;
CP 7; DLB 27; EWL 3; SATA 25; SATA-
Obit 140

**Enzensberger, Hans Magnus**
1929- ............................... **CLC 43; PC 28**
See also CA 116; 119; CANR 103; CWW
2; EWL 3

**Ephron, Nora** 1941- ..................... **CLC 17, 31**
See also AAYA 35; AITN 2; CA 65-68;
CANR 12, 39, 83

**Epicurus** 341B.C.-270B.C. ............. **CMLC 21**
See also DLB 176

**Epsilon**
See Betjeman, John

**Epstein, Daniel Mark** 1948- ............... **CLC 7**
See also CA 49-52; CANR 2, 53, 90

**Epstein, Jacob** 1956- .......................... **CLC 19**
See also CA 114

**Epstein, Jean** 1897-1953 ................. **TCLC 92**

**Epstein, Joseph** 1937- ............... **CLC 39, 204**
See also AMWS 14; CA 112; 119; CANR
50, 65, 117

**Epstein, Leslie** 1938- ......................... **CLC 27**
See also AMWS 12; CA 73-76, 215; CAAE
215; CAAS 12; CANR 23, 69; DLB 299

**Equiano, Olaudah** 1745(?)-1797 . **BLC 2; LC
16**
See also AFAW 1, 2; CDWLB 3; DAM
MULT; DLB 37, 50; WLIT 2

**Erasmus, Desiderius** 1469(?)-1536 ..... **LC 16,
93**
See also DLB 136; EW 2; LMFS 1; RGWL
2, 3; TWA

**Erdman, Paul E(mil)** 1932- .............. **CLC 25**
See also AITN 1; CA 61-64; CANR 13, 43,
84

**Erdrich, Louise** 1954- ........ **CLC 39, 54, 120,
176; NNAL; PC 52**
See also AAYA 10, 47; AMWS 4; BEST
89:1; BPFB 1; CA 114; CANR 41, 62,
118; CDALBS; CN 7; CP 7; CPW; CWP;
DA3; DAM MULT, NOV, POP; DLB 152,

102; DLBD 2; DLBY 1986, 1997; EWL
3; EXPN; EXPS; LAIT 2; LATS 1:1;
LMFS 2; MTCW 1, 2; NFS 4, 8, 13;
RGAL 4; RGSF 2; SSFS 2, 5, 6, 12; TUS

**Fauset, Jessie Redmon**
1882(?)-1961 .. **BLC 2; CLC 19, 54; HR
2**
See also AFAW 2; BW 1; CA 109; CANR
83; DAM MULT; DLB 51; FW; LMFS 2;
MAWW

**Faust, Frederick (Schiller)**
1892-1944(?) ............................. **TCLC 49**
See Austin, Frank; Brand, Max; Challis,
George; Dawson, Peter; Dexter, Martin;
Evans, Evan; Frederick, John; Frost, Fred-
erick; Manning, David; Silver, Nicholas
See also CA 108; 152; DAM POP; DLB
256; TUS

**Faust, Irvin** 1924- ................................. **CLC 8**
See also CA 33-36R; CANR 28, 67; CN 7;
DLB 2, 28, 218, 278; DLBY 1980

**Faustino, Domingo** 1811-1888 ...... **NCLC 123**

**Fawkes, Guy**
See Benchley, Robert (Charles)

**Fearing, Kenneth (Flexner)**
1902-1961 ................................. **CLC 51**
See also CA 93-96; CANR 59; CMW 4;
DLB 9; RGAL 4

**Fecamps, Elise**
See Creasey, John

**Federman, Raymond** 1928- .......... **CLC 6, 47**
See also CA 17-20R, 208; CAAE 208;
CAAS 8; CANR 10, 43, 83, 108; CN 7;
DLBY 1980

**Federspiel, J(uerg) F.** 1931- .............. **CLC 42**
See also CA 146

**Feiffer, Jules (Ralph)** 1929- ...... **CLC 2, 8, 64**
See also AAYA 3; CA 17-20R; CAD; CANR
30, 59, 129; CD 5; DAM DRAM; DLB 7,
44; INT CANR-30; MTCW 1; SATA 8,
61, 111

**Feige, Hermann Albert Otto Maximilian**
See Traven, B.

**Feinberg, David B.** 1956-1994 .......... **CLC 59**
See also CA 135; 147

**Feinstein, Elaine** 1930- ...................... **CLC 36**
See also CA 69-72; CAAS 1; CANR 31,
68, 121; CN 7; CP 7; CWP; DLB 14, 40;
MTCW 1

**Feke, Gilbert David** .......................... **CLC 65**

**Feldman, Irving (Mordecai)** 1928- ..... **CLC 7**
See also CA 1-4R; CANR 1; CP 7; DLB
169

**Felix-Tchicaya, Gerald**
See Tchicaya, Gerald Felix

**Fellini, Federico** 1920-1993 ......... **CLC 16, 85**
See also CA 65-68; 143; CANR 33

**Felltham, Owen** 1602(?)-1668 .............. **LC 92**
See also DLB 126, 151

**Felsen, Henry Gregor** 1916-1995 ..... **CLC 17**
See also CA 1-4R; 180; CANR 1; SAAS 2;
SATA 1

**Felski, Rita** ...................................... **CLC 65**

**Fenno, Jack**
See Calisher, Hortense

**Fenollosa, Ernest (Francisco)**
1853-1908 ................................. **TCLC 91**

**Fenton, James Martin** 1949- .... **CLC 32, 209**
See also CA 102; CANR 108; CP 7; DLB
40; PFS 11

**Ferber, Edna** 1887-1968 .............. **CLC 18, 93**
See also AITN 1; CA 5-8R; 25-28R; CANR
68, 105; DLB 9, 28, 86, 266; MTCW 1,
2; RGAL 4; RHW; SATA 7; TCWW 2

**Ferdowsi, Abu'l Qasem** 940-1020 . **CMLC 43**
See also RGWL 2, 3

**Ferguson, Helen**
See Kavan, Anna

**Ferguson, Niall** 1964- ...................... **CLC 134**
See also CA 190

**Ferguson, Samuel** 1810-1886 ......... **NCLC 33**
See also DLB 32; RGEL 2

**Fergusson, Robert** 1750-1774 .............. **LC 29**
See also DLB 109; RGEL 2

**Ferling, Lawrence**
See Ferlinghetti, Lawrence (Monsanto)

**Ferlinghetti, Lawrence (Monsanto)**
1919(?)- ..... **CLC 2, 6, 10, 27, 111; PC 1**
See also CA 5-8R; CANR 3, 41, 73, 125;
CDALB 1941-1968; CP 7; DA3; DAM
POET; DLB 5, 16; MTCW 1, 2; RGAL 4;
WP

**Fern, Fanny**
See Parton, Sara Payson Willis

**Fernandez, Vicente Garcia Huidobro**
See Huidobro Fernandez, Vicente Garcia

**Fernandez-Armesto, Felipe** ............. **CLC 70**

**Fernandez de Lizardi, Jose Joaquin**
See Lizardi, Jose Joaquin Fernandez de

**Ferre, Rosario** 1938- ...... **CLC 139; HLCS 1;
SSC 36**
See also CA 131; CANR 55, 81, 134; CWW
2; DLB 145; EWL 3; HW 1, 2; LAWS 1;
MTCW 1; WLIT 1

**Ferrer, Gabriel (Francisco Victor) Miro**
See Miro (Ferrer), Gabriel (Francisco
Victor)

**Ferrier, Susan (Edmonstone)**
1782-1854 ................................. **NCLC 8**
See also DLB 116; RGEL 2

**Ferrigno, Robert** 1948(?)- ................. **CLC 65**
See also CA 140; CANR 125

**Ferron, Jacques** 1921-1985 ............... **CLC 94**
See also CA 117; 129; CCA 1; DAC; DLB
60; EWL 3

**Feuchtwanger, Lion** 1884-1958 ........ **TCLC 3**
See also CA 104; 187; DLB 66; EWL 3

**Feuerbach, Ludwig** 1804-1872 ..... **NCLC 139**
See also DLB 133

**Feuillet, Octave** 1821-1890 ............ **NCLC 45**
See also DLB 192

**Feydeau, Georges (Leon Jules Marie)**
1862-1921 ................................. **TCLC 22**
See also CA 113; 152; CANR 84; DAM
DRAM; DLB 192; EWL 3; GFL 1789 to
the Present; RGWL 2, 3

**Fichte, Johann Gottlieb**
1762-1814 ................................. **NCLC 62**
See also DLB 90

**Ficino, Marsilio** 1433-1499 ................. **LC 12**
See also LMFS 1

**Fiedeler, Hans**
See Doeblin, Alfred

**Fiedler, Leslie A(aron)** 1917-2003 ..... **CLC 4,
13, 24**
See also AMWS 13; CA 9-12R; 212; CANR
7, 63; CN 7; DLB 28, 67; EWL 3; MTCW
1, 2; RGAL 4; TUS

**Field, Andrew** 1938- ......................... **CLC 44**
See also CA 97-100; CANR 25

**Field, Eugene** 1850-1895 ................... **NCLC 3**
See also DLB 23, 42, 140; DLBD 13; MAI-
CYA 1, 2; RGAL 4; SATA 16

**Field, Gans T.**
See Wellman, Manly Wade

**Field, Michael** 1915-1971 ................ **TCLC 43**
See also CA 29-32R

**Field, Peter**
See Hobson, Laura Z(ametkin)
See also TCWW 2

**Fielding, Helen** 1958- ...................... **CLC 146**
See also CA 172; CANR 127; DLB 231

**Fielding, Henry** 1707-1754 ....... **LC 1, 46, 85;
WLC**
See also BRW 3; BRWR 1; CDBLB 1660-
1789; DA; DA3; DAB; DAC; DAM
DRAM, MST, NOV; DLB 39, 84, 101;
NFS 18; RGEL 2; TEA; WLIT 3

**Fielding, Sarah** 1710-1768 ............. **LC 1, 44**
See also DLB 39; RGEL 2; TEA

**Fields, W. C.** 1880-1946 ................. **TCLC 80**
See also DLB 44

**Fierstein, Harvey (Forbes)** 1954- ..... **CLC 33**
See also CA 123; 129; CAD; CD 5; CPW;
DA3; DAM DRAM, POP; DFS 6; DLB
266; GLL

**Figes, Eva** 1932- .............................. **CLC 31**
See also CA 53-56; CANR 4, 44, 83; CN 7;
DLB 14, 271; FW

**Filippo, Eduardo de**
See de Filippo, Eduardo

**Finch, Anne** 1661-1720 ............. **LC 3; PC 21**
See also BRWS 9; DLB 95

**Finch, Robert (Duer Claydon)**
1900-1995 ................................. **CLC 18**
See also CA 57-60; CANR 9, 24, 49; CP 7;
DLB 88

**Findley, Timothy (Irving Frederick)**
1930-2002 ........................... **CLC 27, 102**
See also CA 25-28R; 206; CANR 12, 42,
69, 109; CCA 1; CN 7; DAC; DAM MST;
DLB 53; FANT; RHW

**Fink, William**
See Mencken, H(enry) L(ouis)

**Firbank, Louis** 1942-
See Reed, Lou
See also CA 117

**Firbank, (Arthur Annesley) Ronald**
1886-1926 ................................. **TCLC 1**
See also BRWS 2; CA 104; 177; DLB 36;
EWL 3; RGEL 2

**Fish, Stanley**
See Fish, Stanley Eugene

**Fish, Stanley E.**
See Fish, Stanley Eugene

**Fish, Stanley Eugene** 1938- ............. **CLC 142**
See also CA 112; 132; CANR 90; DLB 67

**Fisher, Dorothy (Frances) Canfield**
1879-1958 ................................. **TCLC 87**
See also CA 114; 136; CANR 80; CLR 71,;
CWRI 5; DLB 9, 102, 284; MAICYA 1,
2; YABC 1

**Fisher, M(ary) F(rances) K(ennedy)**
1908-1992 ........................... **CLC 76, 87**
See also CA 77-80; 138; CANR 44; MTCW
1

**Fisher, Roy** 1930- .............................. **CLC 25**
See also CA 81-84; CAAS 10; CANR 16;
CP 7; DLB 40

**Fisher, Rudolph** 1897-1934 .... **BLC 2; HR 2;
SSC 25; TCLC 11**
See also BW 1, 3; CA 107; 124; CANR 80;
DAM MULT; DLB 51, 102

**Fisher, Vardis (Alvero)** 1895-1968 .... **CLC 7;
TCLC 140**
See also CA 5-8R; 25-28R; CANR 68; DLB
9, 206; RGAL 4; TCWW 2

**Fiske, Tarleton**
See Bloch, Robert (Albert)

**Fitch, Clarke**
See Sinclair, Upton (Beall)

**Fitch, John IV**
See Cormier, Robert (Edmund)

**Fitzgerald, Captain Hugh**
See Baum, L(yman) Frank

**FitzGerald, Edward** 1809-1883 ...... **NCLC 9,
153**
See also BRW 4; DLB 32; RGEL 2

**Fox, William Price (Jr.)** 1926- .......... **CLC 22**
See also CA 17-20R; CAAS 19; CANR 11;
CSW; DLB 2; DLBY 1981

**Foxe, John** 1517(?)-1587 ........................ **LC 14**
See also DLB 132

**Frame, Janet** .. **CLC 2, 3, 6, 22, 66, 96; SSC 29**
See Clutha, Janet Paterson Frame
See also CN 7; CWP; EWL 3; RGEL 2;
RGSF 2; TWA

**France, Anatole** ............................ **TCLC 9**
See Thibault, Jacques Anatole Francois
See also DLB 123; EWL 3; GFL 1789 to
the Present; MTCW 1; RGWL 2, 3;
SUFW 1

**Francis, Claude** ................................ **CLC 50**
See also CA 192

**Francis, Richard Stanley** 1920- ... **CLC 2, 22, 42, 102**
See also AAYA 5, 21; BEST 89:3; BPFB 1;
CA 5-8R; CANR 9, 42, 68, 100; CDBLB
1960 to Present; CMW 4; CN 7; DA3;
DAM POP; DLB 87; INT CANR-9;
MSW; MTCW 1, 2

**Francis, Robert (Churchill)**
1901-1987 ...................... **CLC 15; PC 34**
See also AMWS 9; CA 1-4R; 123; CANR
1; EXPP; PFS 12

**Francis, Lord Jeffrey**
See Jeffrey, Francis
See also DLB 107

**Frank, Anne(lies Marie)**
1929-1945 ...................... **TCLC 17; WLC**
See also AAYA 12; BYA 1; CA 113; 133;
CANR 68; CLR 101; DA; DA3; DAB;
DAC; DAM MST; LAIT 4; MAICYA 2;
MAICYAS 1; MTCW 1, 2; NCFS 2;
SATA 87; SATA-Brief 42; WYA; YAW

**Frank, Bruno** 1887-1945 ................. **TCLC 81**
See also CA 189; DLB 118; EWL 3

**Frank, Elizabeth** 1945- ..................... **CLC 39**
See also CA 121; 126; CANR 78; INT CA-126

**Frankl, Viktor E(mil)** 1905-1997 ...... **CLC 93**
See also CA 65-68; 161

**Franklin, Benjamin**
See Hasek, Jaroslav (Matej Frantisek)

**Franklin, Benjamin** 1706-1790 .......... **LC 25; WLCS**
See also AMW; CDALB 1640-1865; DA;
DA3; DAB; DAC; DAM MST; DLB 24,
43, 73, 183; LAIT 1; RGAL 4; TUS

**Franklin, (Stella Maria Sarah) Miles**
**(Lampe)** 1879-1954 ................... **TCLC 7**
See also CA 104; 164; DLB 230; FW;
MTCW 2; RGEL 2; TWA

**Franzen, Jonathan** 1959- ................. **CLC 202**
See also CA 129; CANR 105

**Fraser, Antonia (Pakenham)** 1932- . **CLC 32, 107**
See also AAYA 57; CA 85-88; CANR 44,
65, 119; CMW; DLB 276; MTCW 1, 2;
SATA-Brief 32

**Fraser, George MacDonald** 1925- ...... **CLC 7**
See also AAYA 48; CA 45-48; 180; CAAE
180; CANR 2, 48, 74; MTCW 1; RHW

**Fraser, Sylvia** 1935- ........................... **CLC 64**
See also CA 45-48; CANR 1, 16, 60; CCA 1

**Frayn, Michael** 1933- . **CLC 3, 7, 31, 47, 176**
See also BRWC 2; BRWS 7; CA 5-8R;
CANR 30, 69, 114, 133; CBD; CD 5; CN
7; DAM DRAM, NOV; DLB 13, 14, 194,
245; FANT; MTCW 1, 2; SFW 4

**Fraze, Candida (Merrill)** 1945- ........ **CLC 50**
See also CA 126

**Frazer, Andrew**
See Marlowe, Stephen

**Frazer, J(ames) G(eorge)**
1854-1941 ................................. **TCLC 32**
See also BRWS 3; CA 118; NCFS 5

**Frazer, Robert Caine**
See Creasey, John

**Frazer, Sir James George**
See Frazer, J(ames) G(eorge)

**Frazier, Charles** 1950- ..................... **CLC 109**
See also AAYA 34; CA 161; CANR 126;
CSW; DLB 292

**Frazier, Ian** 1951- ............................. **CLC 46**
See also CA 130; CANR 54, 93

**Frederic, Harold** 1856-1898 .......... **NCLC 10**
See also AMW; DLB 12, 23; DLBD 13;
RGAL 4

**Frederick, John**
See Faust, Frederick (Schiller)
See also TCWW 2

**Frederick the Great** 1712-1786 .......... **LC 14**

**Fredro, Aleksander** 1793-1876 ......... **NCLC 8**

**Freeling, Nicolas** 1927-2003 .............. **CLC 38**
See also CA 49-52; 218; CAAS 12; CANR
1, 17, 50, 84; CMW 4; CN 7; DLB 87

**Freeman, Douglas Southall**
1886-1953 ................................. **TCLC 11**
See also CA 109; 195; DLB 17; DLBD 17

**Freeman, Judith** 1946- ..................... **CLC 55**
See also CA 148; CANR 120; DLB 256

**Freeman, Mary E(leanor) Wilkins**
1852-1930 ............. **SSC 1, 47; TCLC 9**
See also CA 106; 177; DLB 12, 78, 221;
EXPS; FW; HGG; MAWW; RGAL 4;
RGSF 2; SSFS 4, 8; SUFW 1; TUS

**Freeman, R(ichard) Austin**
1862-1943 ................................. **TCLC 21**
See also CA 113; CANR 84; CMW 4; DLB
70

**French, Albert** 1943- ......................... **CLC 86**
See also BW 3; CA 167

**French, Antonia**
See Kureishi, Hanif

**French, Marilyn** 1929- .. **CLC 10, 18, 60, 177**
See also BPFB 1; CA 69-72; CANR 3, 31,
134; CN 7; CPW; DAM DRAM, NOV,
POP; FW; INT CANR-31; MTCW 1, 2

**French, Paul**
See Asimov, Isaac

**Freneau, Philip Morin** 1752-1832 .. **NCLC 1, 111**
See also AMWS 2; DLB 37, 43; RGAL 4

**Freud, Sigmund** 1856-1939 ............ **TCLC 52**
See also CA 115; 133; CANR 69; DLB 296;
EW 8; EWL 3; LATS 1:1; MTCW 1, 2;
NCFS 3; TWA

**Freytag, Gustav** 1816-1895 .......... **NCLC 109**
See also DLB 129

**Friedan, Betty (Naomi)** 1921- ........... **CLC 74**
See also CA 65-68; CANR 18, 45, 74; DLB
246; FW; MTCW 1, 2; NCFS 5

**Friedlander, Saul** 1932- ..................... **CLC 90**
See also CA 117; 130; CANR 72

**Friedman, B(ernard) H(arper)**
1926- ............................................ **CLC 7**
See also CA 1-4R; CANR 3, 48

**Friedman, Bruce Jay** 1930- ...... **CLC 3, 5, 56**
See also CA 9-12R; CAD; CANR 25, 52,
101; CD 5; CN 7; DLB 2, 28, 244; INT
CANR-25; SSFS 18

**Friel, Brian** 1929- .... **CLC 5, 42, 59, 115; DC 8; SSC 76**
See also BRWS 5; CA 21-24R; CANR 33,
69, 131; CBD; CD 5; DFS 11; DLB 13;
EWL 3; MTCW 1; RGEL 2; TEA

**Friis-Baastad, Babbis Ellinor**
1921-1970 ................................. **CLC 12**
See also CA 17-20R; 134; SATA 7

**Frisch, Max (Rudolf)** 1911-1991 ... **CLC 3, 9, 14, 18, 32, 44; TCLC 121**
See also CA 85-88; 134; CANR 32, 74; CD-
WLB 2; DAM DRAM, NOV; DLB 69,
124; EW 13; EWL 3; MTCW 1, 2; RGWL
2, 3

**Fromentin, Eugene (Samuel Auguste)**
1820-1876 ....................... **NCLC 10, 125**
See also DLB 123; GFL 1789 to the Present

**Frost, Frederick**
See Faust, Frederick (Schiller)
See also TCWW 2

**Frost, Robert (Lee)** 1874-1963 .. **CLC 1, 3, 4, 9, 10, 13, 15, 26, 34, 44; PC 1, 39; WLC**
See also AAYA 21; AMW; AMWR 1; CA
89-92; CANR 33; CDALB 1917-1929;
CLR 67; DA; DA3; DAB; DAC; DAM
MST, POET; DLB 54, 284; DLBD 7;
EWL 3; EXPP; MTCW 1, 2; PAB; PFS 1,
2, 3, 4, 5, 6, 7, 10, 13; RGAL 4; SATA
14; TUS; WP; WYA

**Froude, James Anthony**
1818-1894 ................................. **NCLC 43**
See also DLB 18, 57, 144

**Froy, Herald**
See Waterhouse, Keith (Spencer)

**Fry, Christopher** 1907- ........... **CLC 2, 10, 14**
See also BRWS 3; CA 17-20R; CAAS 23;
CANR 9, 30, 74, 132; CBD; CD 5; CP 7;
DAM DRAM; DLB 13; EWL 3; MTCW
1, 2; RGEL 2; SATA 66; TEA

**Frye, (Herman) Northrop**
1912-1991 ........ **CLC 24, 70; TCLC 165**
See also CA 5-8R; 133; CANR 8, 37; DLB
67, 68, 246; EWL 3; MTCW 1, 2; RGAL
4; TWA

**Fuchs, Daniel** 1909-1993 .............. **CLC 8, 22**
See also CA 81-84; 142; CAAS 5; CANR
40; DLB 9, 26, 28; DLBY 1993

**Fuchs, Daniel** 1934- ......................... **CLC 34**
See also CA 37-40R; CANR 14, 48

**Fuentes, Carlos** 1928- .. **CLC 3, 8, 10, 13, 22, 41, 60, 113; HLC 1; SSC 24; WLC**
See also AAYA 4, 45; AITN 2; BPFB 1;
CA 69-72; CANR 10, 32, 68, 104; CD-
WLB 3; CWW 2; DA; DA3; DAB; DAC;
DAM MST, MULT, NOV; DLB 113;
DNFS 2; EWL 3; HW 1, 2; LAIT 3; LATS
1:2; LAW; LAWS 1; LMFS 2; MTCW 1,
2; NFS 8; RGSF 2; RGWL 2, 3; TWA;
WLIT 1

**Fuentes, Gregorio Lopez y**
See Lopez y Fuentes, Gregorio

**Fuertes, Gloria** 1918-1998 ................... **PC 27**
See also CA 178; 180; DLB 108; HW 2;
SATA 115

**Fugard, (Harold) Athol** 1932- . **CLC 5, 9, 14, 25, 40, 80, 211; DC 3**
See also AAYA 17; AFW; CA 85-88; CANR
32, 54, 118; CD 5; DAM DRAM; DFS 3,
6, 10; DLB 225; DNFS 1, 2; EWL 3;
LATS 1; MTCW 1; RGEL 2; WLIT 2

**Fugard, Sheila** 1932- ......................... **CLC 48**
See also CA 125

**Fukuyama, Francis** 1952- .............. **CLC 131**
See also CA 140; CANR 72, 125

**Fuller, Charles (H.), (Jr.)** 1939- ......... **BLC 2; CLC 25; DC 1**
See also BW 2; CA 108; 112; CAD; CANR
87; CD 5; DAM DRAM, MULT; DFS 8;
DLB 38, 266; EWL 3; INT CA-112;
MTCW 1

**Fuller, Henry Blake** 1857-1929 .... **TCLC 103**
See also CA 108; 177; DLB 12; RGAL 4

**Fuller, John (Leopold)** 1937- ........... **CLC 62**
See also CA 21-24R; CANR 9, 44; CP 7;
DLB 40

**Garrigue, Jean** 1914-1972 ............... **CLC 2, 8**
See also CA 5-8R; 37-40R; CANR 20

**Garrison, Frederick**
See Sinclair, Upton (Beall)

**Garrison, William Lloyd**
1805-1879 .............................. **NCLC 149**
See also CDALB 1640-1865; DLB 1, 43, 235

**Garro, Elena** 1920(?)-1998 .. **HLCS 1; TCLC 153**
See also CA 131; 169; CWW 2; DLB 145; EWL 3; HW 1; LAWS 1; WLIT 1

**Garth, Will**
See Hamilton, Edmond; Kuttner, Henry

**Garvey, Marcus (Moziah, Jr.)**
1887-1940 ....... **BLC 2; HR 2; TCLC 41**
See also BW 1; CA 120; 124; CANR 79; DAM MULT

**Gary, Romain** ................................. **CLC 25**
See Kacew, Romain
See also DLB 83, 299

**Gascar, Pierre** ............................. **CLC 11**
See Fournier, Pierre
See also EWL 3

**Gascoigne, George** 1539-1577 ............ **LC 108**
See also DLB 136; RGEL 2

**Gascoyne, David (Emery)**
1916-2001 ................................. **CLC 45**
See also CA 65-68; 200; CANR 10, 28, 54; CP 7; DLB 20; MTCW 1; RGEL 2

**Gaskell, Elizabeth Cleghorn**
1810-1865 .... **NCLC 5, 70, 97, 137; SSC 25**
See also BRW 5; CDBLB 1832-1890; DAB; DAM MST; DLB 21, 144, 159; RGEL 2; RGSF 2; TEA

**Gass, William H(oward)** 1924- . **CLC 1, 2, 8, 11, 15, 39, 132; SSC 12**
See also AMWS 6; CA 17-20R; CANR 30, 71, 100; CN 7; DLB 2, 227; EWL 3; MTCW 1, 2; RGAL 4

**Gassendi, Pierre** 1592-1655 ................. **LC 54**
See also GFL Beginnings to 1789

**Gasset, Jose Ortega y**
See Ortega y Gasset, Jose

**Gates, Henry Louis, Jr.** 1950- ... **BLCS; CLC 65**
See also BW 2, 3; CA 109; CANR 25, 53, 75, 125; CSW; DA3; DAM MULT; DLB 67; EWL 3; MTCW 1; RGAL 4

**Gautier, Theophile** 1811-1872 .. **NCLC 1, 59; PC 18; SSC 20**
See also DAM POET; DLB 119; EW 6; GFL 1789 to the Present; RGWL 2, 3; SUFW; TWA

**Gawsworth, John**
See Bates, H(erbert) E(rnest)

**Gay, John** 1685-1732 ........................... **LC 49**
See also BRW 3; DAM DRAM; DLB 84, 95; RGEL 2; WLIT 3

**Gay, Oliver**
See Gogarty, Oliver St. John

**Gay, Peter (Jack)** 1923- ................... **CLC 158**
See also CA 13-16R; CANR 18, 41, 77; INT CANR-18

**Gaye, Marvin (Pentz, Jr.)**
1939-1984 ................................. **CLC 26**
See also CA 195; 112

**Gebler, Carlo (Ernest)** 1954- ......... **CLC 39**
See also CA 119; 133; CANR 96; DLB 271

**Gee, Maggie (Mary)** 1948- ................ **CLC 57**
See also CA 130; CANR 125; CN 7; DLB 207

**Gee, Maurice (Gough)** 1931- ............ **CLC 29**
See also AAYA 42; CA 97-100; CANR 67, 123; CLR 56; CN 7; CWRI 5; EWL 3; MAICYA 2; RGSF 2; SATA 46, 101

**Geiogamah, Hanay** 1945- ................... **NNAL**
See also CA 153; DAM MULT; DLB 175

**Gelbart, Larry (Simon)** 1928- .... **CLC 21, 61**
See Gelbart, Larry
See also CA 73-76; CANR 45, 94

**Gelbart, Larry** 1928-
See Gelbart, Larry (Simon)
See also CAD; CD 5

**Gelber, Jack** 1932-2003 ...... **CLC 1, 6, 14, 79**
See also CA 1-4R; 216; CAD; CANR 2; DLB 7, 228

**Gellhorn, Martha (Ellis)**
1908-1998 ............................. **CLC 14, 60**
See also CA 77-80; 164; CANR 44; CN 7; DLBY 1982, 1998

**Genet, Jean** 1910-1986 . **DC 25; CLC 1, 2, 5, 10, 14, 44, 46; TCLC 128**
See also CA 13-16R; CANR 18; DA3; DAM DRAM; DFS 10; DLB 72; DLBY 1986; EW 13; EWL 3; GFL 1789 to the Present; GLL 1; LMFS 2; MTCW 1, 2; RGWL 2, 3; TWA

**Gent, Peter** 1942- ............................. **CLC 29**
See also AITN 1; CA 89-92; DLBY 1982

**Gentile, Giovanni** 1875-1944 ......... **TCLC 96**
See also CA 119

**Gentlewoman in New England, A**
See Bradstreet, Anne

**Gentlewoman in Those Parts, A**
See Bradstreet, Anne

**Geoffrey of Monmouth** c.
1100-1155 .............................. **CMLC 44**
See also DLB 146; TEA

**George, Jean**
See George, Jean Craighead

**George, Jean Craighead** 1919- ......... **CLC 35**
See also AAYA 8; BYA 2, 4; CA 5-8R; CANR 25; CLR 1; 80; DLB 52; JRDA; MAICYA 1, 2; SATA 2, 68, 124; WYA; YAW

**George, Stefan (Anton)** 1868-1933 . **TCLC 2, 14**
See also CA 104; 193; EW 8; EWL 3

**Georges, Georges Martin**
See Simenon, Georges (Jacques Christian)

**Gerald of Wales** c. 1146-c. 1223 ... **CMLC 60**

**Gerhardi, William Alexander**
See Gerhardie, William Alexander

**Gerhardie, William Alexander**
1895-1977 ................................... **CLC 5**
See also CA 25-28R; 73-76; CANR 18; DLB 36; RGEL 2

**Gerson, Jean** 1363-1429 ...................... **LC 77**
See also DLB 208

**Gersonides** 1288-1344 .................... **CMLC 49**
See also DLB 115

**Gerstler, Amy** 1956- ......................... **CLC 70**
See also CA 146; CANR 99

**Gertler, T.** ...................................... **CLC 34**
See also CA 116; 121

**Gertsen, Aleksandr Ivanovich**
See Herzen, Aleksandr Ivanovich

**Ghalib** ...................................... **NCLC 39, 78**
See Ghalib, Asadullah Khan

**Ghalib, Asadullah Khan** 1797-1869
See Ghalib
See also DAM POET; RGWL 2, 3

**Ghelderode, Michel de** 1898-1962 ..... **CLC 6, 11; DC 15**
See also CA 85-88; CANR 40, 77; DAM DRAM; EW 11; EWL 3; TWA

**Ghiselin, Brewster** 1903-2001 .......... **CLC 23**
See also CA 13-16R; CAAS 10; CANR 13; CP 7

**Ghose, Aurabinda** 1872-1950 ......... **TCLC 63**
See Ghose, Aurobindo
See also CA 163

**Ghose, Aurobindo**
See Ghose, Aurabinda
See also EWL 3

**Ghose, Zulfikar** 1935- ................. **CLC 42, 200**
See also CA 65-68; CANR 67; CN 7; CP 7; EWL 3

**Ghosh, Amitav** 1956- ................. **CLC 44, 153**
See also CA 147; CANR 80; CN 7; WWE 1

**Giacosa, Giuseppe** 1847-1906 .......... **TCLC 7**
See also CA 104

**Gibb, Lee**
See Waterhouse, Keith (Spencer)

**Gibbon, Edward** 1737-1794 ................ **LC 97**
See also BRW 3; DLB 104; RGEL 2

**Gibbon, Lewis Grassic** .................... **TCLC 4**
See Mitchell, James Leslie
See also RGEL 2

**Gibbons, Kaye** 1960- ........... **CLC 50, 88, 145**
See also AAYA 34; AMWS 10; CA 151; CANR 75, 127; CSW; DA3; DAM POP; DLB 292; MTCW 1; NFS 3; RGAL 4; SATA 117

**Gibran, Kahlil** 1883-1931 . **PC 9; TCLC 1, 9**
See also CA 104; 150; DA3; DAM POET, POP; EWL 3; MTCW 2

**Gibran, Khalil**
See Gibran, Kahlil

**Gibson, William** 1914- ...................... **CLC 23**
See also CA 9-12R; CAD 2; CANR 9, 42, 75, 125; CD 5; DA; DAB; DAC; DAM DRAM, MST; DFS 2; DLB 7; LAIT 2; MTCW 2; SATA 66; YAW

**Gibson, William (Ford)** 1948- ... **CLC 39, 63, 186, 192; SSC 52**
See also AAYA 12, 59; BPFB 2; CA 126; 133; CANR 52, 90, 106; CN 7; CPW; DA3; DAM POP; DLB 251; MTCW 2; SCFW 2; SFW 4

**Gide, Andre (Paul Guillaume)**
1869-1951 ..... **SSC 13; TCLC 5, 12, 36; WLC**
See also CA 104; 124; DA; DA3; DAB; DAC; DAM MST, NOV; DLB 65; EW 8; EWL 3; GFL 1789 to the Present; MTCW 1, 2; RGSF 2; RGWL 2, 3; TWA

**Gifford, Barry (Colby)** 1946- ........... **CLC 34**
See also CA 65-68; CANR 9, 30, 40, 90

**Gilbert, Frank**
See De Voto, Bernard (Augustine)

**Gilbert, W(illiam) S(chwenck)**
1836-1911 ................................... **TCLC 3**
See also CA 104; 173; DAM DRAM, POET; RGEL 2; SATA 36

**Gilbreth, Frank B(unker), Jr.**
1911-2001 ................................. **CLC 17**
See also CA 9-12R; SATA 2

**Gilchrist, Ellen (Louise)** 1935- .. **CLC 34, 48, 143; SSC 14, 63**
See also BPFB 2; CA 113; 116; CANR 41, 61, 104; CN 7; CPW; CSW; DAM POP; DLB 130; EWL 3; EXPS; MTCW 1, 2; RGAL 4; RGSF 2; SSFS 9

**Giles, Molly** 1942- ............................ **CLC 39**
See also CA 126; CANR 98

**Gill, Eric** 1882-1940 ....................... **TCLC 85**
See Gill, (Arthur) Eric (Rowton Peter Joseph)

**Gill, (Arthur) Eric (Rowton Peter Joseph)**
1882-1940
See Gill, Eric
See also CA 120; DLB 98

**Gill, Patrick**
See Creasey, John

**Gillette, Douglas** .............................. **CLC 70**

**Gilliam, Terry (Vance)** 1940- .... **CLC 21, 141**
See Monty Python
See also AAYA 19, 59; CA 108; 113; CANR 35; INT CA-113

**Gillian, Jerry**
See Gilliam, Terry (Vance)

**Gombrowicz, Witold** 1904-1969 .... **CLC 4, 7, 11, 49**
See also CA 19-20; 25-28R; CANR 105; CAP 2; CDWLB 4; DAM DRAM; DLB 215; EW 12; EWL 3; RGWL 2, 3; TWA

**Gomez de Avellaneda, Gertrudis**
1814-1873 .............................. **NCLC 111**
See also LAW

**Gomez de la Serna, Ramon**
1888-1963 ...................................... **CLC 9**
See also CA 153; 116; CANR 79; EWL 3; HW 1, 2

**Goncharov, Ivan Alexandrovich**
1812-1891 ........................... **NCLC 1, 63**
See also DLB 238; EW 6; RGWL 2, 3

**Goncourt, Edmond (Louis Antoine Huot) de**
1822-1896 ...................................... **NCLC 7**
See also DLB 123; EW 7; GFL 1789 to the Present; RGWL 2, 3

**Goncourt, Jules (Alfred Huot) de**
1830-1870 ...................................... **NCLC 7**
See also DLB 123; EW 7; GFL 1789 to the Present; RGWL 2, 3

**Gongora (y Argote), Luis de**
1561-1627 ...................................... **LC 72**
See also RGWL 2, 3

**Gontier, Fernande** 19(?)- .................. **CLC 50**

**Gonzalez Martinez, Enrique**
See Gonzalez Martinez, Enrique
See also DLB 290

**Gonzalez Martinez, Enrique**
1871-1952 ................................... **TCLC 72**
See Gonzalez Martinez, Enrique
See also CA 166; CANR 81; EWL 3; HW 1, 2

**Goodison, Lorna** 1947- ......................... **PC 36**
See also CA 142; CANR 88; CP 7; CWP; DLB 157; EWL 3

**Goodman, Paul** 1911-1972 ..... **CLC 1, 2, 4, 7**
See also CA 19-20; 37-40R; CAD; CANR 34; CAP 2; DLB 130, 246; MTCW 1; RGAL 4

**GoodWeather, Harley**
See King, Thomas

**Googe, Barnabe** 1540-1594 .................. **LC 94**
See also DLB 132; RGEL 2

**Gordimer, Nadine** 1923- ...... **CLC 3, 5, 7, 10, 18, 33, 51, 70, 123, 160, 161; SSC 17, 80; WLCS**
See also AAYA 39; AFW; BRWS 2; CA 5-8R; CANR 3, 28, 56, 88, 131; CN 7; DA; DA3; DAB; DAC; DAM MST, NOV; DLB 225; EWL 3; EXPS; INT CANR-28; LATS 1:2; MTCW 1, 2; NFS 4; RGEL 2; RGSF 2; SSFS 2, 14, 19; TWA; WLIT 2; YAW

**Gordon, Adam Lindsay**
1833-1870 ................................... **NCLC 21**
See also DLB 230

**Gordon, Caroline** 1895-1981 . **CLC 6, 13, 29, 83; SSC 15**
See also AMW; CA 11-12; 103; CANR 36; CAP 1; DLB 4, 9, 102; DLBD 17; DLBY 1981; EWL 3; MTCW 1, 2; RGAL 4; RGSF 2

**Gordon, Charles William** 1860-1937
See Connor, Ralph
See also CA 109

**Gordon, Mary (Catherine)** 1949- .... **CLC 13, 22, 128; SSC 59**
See also AMWS 4; BPFB 2; CA 102; CANR 44, 92; CN 7; DLB 6; DLBY 1981; FW; INT CA-102; MTCW 1

**Gordon, N. J.**
See Bosman, Herman Charles

**Gordon, Sol** 1923- .............................. **CLC 26**
See also CA 53-56; CANR 4; SATA 11

**Gordone, Charles** 1925-1995 .. **CLC 1, 4; DC 8**
See also BW 1, 3; CA 93-96; 180; 150; CAAE 180; CAD; CANR 55; DAM DRAM; DLB 7; INT CA-93-96; MTCW 1

**Gore, Catherine** 1800-1861 ............. **NCLC 65**
See also DLB 116; RGEL 2

**Gorenko, Anna Andreevna**
See Akhmatova, Anna

**Gorky, Maxim** ....... **SSC 28; TCLC 8; WLC**
See Peshkov, Alexei Maximovich
See also DAB; DFS 9; DLB 295; EW 8; EWL 3; MTCW 2; TWA

**Goryan, Sirak**
See Saroyan, William

**Gosse, Edmund (William)**
1849-1928 ................................... **TCLC 28**
See also CA 117; DLB 57, 144, 184; RGEL 2

**Gotlieb, Phyllis (Fay Bloom)** 1926- .. **CLC 18**
See also CA 13-16R; CANR 7, 135; DLB 88, 251; SFW 4

**Gottesman, S. D.**
See Kornbluth, C(yril) M.; Pohl, Frederik

**Gottfried von Strassburg** fl. c.
1170-1215 ................................... **CMLC 10**
See also CDWLB 2; DLB 138; EW 1; RGWL 2, 3

**Gotthelf, Jeremias** 1797-1854 ....... **NCLC 117**
See also DLB 133; RGWL 2, 3

**Gottschalk, Laura Riding**
See Jackson, Laura (Riding)

**Gould, Lois** 1932(?)-2002 .............. **CLC 4, 10**
See also CA 77-80; 208; CANR 29; MTCW 1

**Gould, Stephen Jay** 1941-2002 ....... **CLC 163**
See also AAYA 26; BEST 90:2; CA 77-80; 205; CANR 10, 27, 56, 75, 125; CPW; INT CANR-27; MTCW 1, 2

**Gourmont, Remy(-Marie-Charles) de**
1858-1915 ................................... **TCLC 17**
See also CA 109; 150; GFL 1789 to the Present; MTCW 2

**Gournay, Marie le Jars de**
See de Gournay, Marie le Jars

**Govier, Katherine** 1948- .................... **CLC 51**
See also CA 101; CANR 18, 40, 128; CCA 1

**Gower, John** c. 1330-1408 ....... **LC 76; PC 59**
See also BRW 1; DLB 146; RGEL 2

**Goyen, (Charles) William**
1915-1983 ................... **CLC 5, 8, 14, 40**
See also AITN 2; CA 5-8R; 110; CANR 6, 71; DLB 2, 218; DLBY 1983; EWL 3; INT CANR-6

**Goytisolo, Juan** 1931- .... **CLC 5, 10, 23, 133; HLC 1**
See also CA 85-88; CANR 32, 61, 131; CWW 2; DAM MULT; EWL 3; GLL 2; HW 1, 2; MTCW 1, 2

**Gozzano, Guido** 1883-1916 ................. **PC 10**
See also CA 154; DLB 114; EWL 3

**Gozzi, (Conte) Carlo** 1720-1806 .... **NCLC 23**

**Grabbe, Christian Dietrich**
1801-1836 ................................... **NCLC 2**
See also DLB 133; RGWL 2, 3

**Grace, Patricia Frances** 1937- .......... **CLC 56**
See also CA 176; CANR 118; CN 7; EWL 3; RGSF 2

**Gracian y Morales, Baltasar**
1601-1658 ................................... **LC 15**

**Gracq, Julien** .............................. **CLC 11, 48**
See Poirier, Louis
See also CWW 2; DLB 83; GFL 1789 to the Present

**Grade, Chaim** 1910-1982 ................. **CLC 10**
See also CA 93-96; 107; EWL 3

**Graduate of Oxford, A**
See Ruskin, John

**Grafton, Garth**
See Duncan, Sara Jeannette

**Grafton, Sue** 1940- ......................... **CLC 163**
See also AAYA 11, 49; BEST 90:3; CA 108; CANR 31, 55, 111, 134; CMW 4; CPW; CSW; DA3; DAM POP; DLB 226; FW; MSW

**Graham, John**
See Phillips, David Graham

**Graham, Jorie** 1951- .... **CLC 48, 118; PC 59**
See also CA 111; CANR 63, 118; CP 7; CWP; DLB 120; EWL 3; PFS 10, 17

**Graham, R(obert) B(ontine) Cunninghame**
See Cunninghame Graham, Robert (Gallnigad) Bontine
See also DLB 98, 135, 174; RGEL 2; RGSF 2

**Graham, Robert**
See Haldeman, Joe (William)

**Graham, Tom**
See Lewis, (Harry) Sinclair

**Graham, W(illiam) S(idney)**
1918-1986 ................................... **CLC 29**
See also BRWS 7; CA 73-76; 118; DLB 20; RGEL 2

**Graham, Winston (Mawdsley)**
1910-2003 ................................... **CLC 23**
See also CA 49-52; 218; CANR 2, 22, 45, 66; CMW 4; CN 7; DLB 77; RHW

**Grahame, Kenneth** 1859-1932 ...... **TCLC 64, 136**
See also BYA 5; CA 108; 136; CANR 80; CLR 5; CWRI 5; DA3; DLB 34, 141, 178; FANT; MAICYA 1, 2; MTCW 2; NFS 20; RGEL 2; SATA 100; TEA; WCH; YABC 1

**Granger, Darius John**
See Marlowe, Stephen

**Granin, Daniil** 1918- ......................... **CLC 59**
See also DLB 302

**Granovsky, Timofei Nikolaevich**
1813-1855 ................................... **NCLC 75**
See also DLB 198

**Grant, Skeeter**
See Spiegelman, Art

**Granville-Barker, Harley**
1877-1946 ................................... **TCLC 2**
See Barker, Harley Granville
See also CA 104; 204; DAM DRAM; RGEL 2

**Granzotto, Gianni**
See Granzotto, Giovanni Battista

**Granzotto, Giovanni Battista**
1914-1985 ................................... **CLC 70**
See also CA 166

**Grass, Günter (Wilhelm)** 1927- .... **CLC 1, 2, 4, 6, 11, 15, 22, 32, 49, 88, 207; WLC**
See Grass, Guenter (Wilhelm)
See also BPFB 2; CA 13-16R; CANR 20, 75, 93, 133; CDWLB 2; CWW 2; DA; DA3; DAB; DAC; DAM MST, NOV; DLB 75, 124; EW 13; EWL 3; MTCW 1, 2; RGWL 2, 3; TWA

**Gratton, Thomas**
See Hulme, T(homas) E(rnest)

**Grau, Shirley Ann** 1929- ....... **CLC 4, 9, 146; SSC 15**
See also CA 89-92; CANR 22, 69; CN 7; CSW; DLB 2, 218; INT CA-89-92, CANR-22; MTCW 1

**Gravel, Fern**
See Hall, James Norman

**Graver, Elizabeth** 1964- .................... **CLC 70**
See also CA 135; CANR 71, 129

**Graves, Richard Perceval**
1895-1985 ................................ **CLC 44**
See also CA 65-68; CANR 9, 26, 51

**Graves, Robert (von Ranke)**
1895-1985 .. **CLC 1, 2, 6, 11, 39, 44, 45; PC 6**
See also BPFB 2; BRW 7; BYA 4; CA 5-8R; 117; CANR 5, 36; CDBLB 1914-1945; DA3; DAB; DAC; DAM MST, POET; DLB 20, 100, 191; DLBD 18; DLBY 1985; EWL 3; LATS 1:1; MTCW 1, 2; NCFS 2; RGEL 2; RHW; SATA 45; TEA

**Graves, Valerie**
See Bradley, Marion Zimmer

**Gray, Alasdair (James)** 1934- .......... **CLC 41**
See also BRWS 9; CA 126; CANR 47, 69, 106; CN 7; DLB 194, 261; HGG; INT CA-126; MTCW 1, 2; RGSF 2; SUFW 2

**Gray, Amlin** 1946- .......................... **CLC 29**
See also CA 138

**Gray, Francine du Plessix** 1930- ..... **CLC 22, 153**
See also BEST 90:3; CA 61-64; CAAS 2; CANR 11, 33, 75, 81; DAM NOV; INT CANR-11; MTCW 1, 2

**Gray, John (Henry)** 1866-1934 ...... **TCLC 19**
See also CA 119; 162; RGEL 2

**Gray, Simon (James Holliday)**
1936- ............................... **CLC 9, 14, 36**
See also AITN 1; CA 21-24R; CAAS 3; CANR 32, 69; CD 5; DLB 13; EWL 3; MTCW 1; RGEL 2

**Gray, Spalding** 1941-2004 ........ **CLC 49, 112; DC 7**
See also CA 128; 225; CAD; CANR 74; CD 5; CPW; DAM POP; MTCW 2

**Gray, Thomas** 1716-1771 .... **LC 4, 40; PC 2; WLC**
See also BRW 3; CDBLB 1660-1789; DA; DA3; DAB; DAC; DAM MST; DLB 109; EXPP; PAB; PFS 9; RGEL 2; TEA; WP

**Grayson, David**
See Baker, Ray Stannard

**Grayson, Richard (A.)** 1951- ........... **CLC 38**
See also CA 85-88; 210; CAAE 210; CANR 14, 31, 57; DLB 234

**Greeley, Andrew M(oran)** 1928- ...... **CLC 28**
See also BPFB 2; CA 5-8R; CAAS 7; CANR 7, 43, 69, 104; CMW 4; CPW; DA3; DAM POP; MTCW 1, 2

**Green, Anna Katharine**
1846-1935 ............................... **TCLC 63**
See also CA 112; 159; CMW 4; DLB 202, 221; MSW

**Green, Brian**
See Card, Orson Scott

**Green, Hannah**
See Greenberg, Joanne (Goldenberg)

**Green, Hannah** 1927(?)-1996 ............. **CLC 3**
See also CA 73-76; CANR 59, 93; NFS 10

**Green, Henry** ......................... **CLC 2, 13, 97**
See Yorke, Henry Vincent
See also BRWS 2; CA 175; DLB 15; EWL 3; RGEL 2

**Green, Julien (Hartridge)** 1900-1998
See Green, Julian
See also CA 21-24R; 169; CANR 33, 87; CWW 2; DLB 4, 72; MTCW 1

**Green, Julian** .......................... **CLC 3, 11, 77**
See Green, Julien (Hartridge)
See also EWL 3; GFL 1789 to the Present; MTCW 2

**Green, Paul (Eliot)** 1894-1981 .......... **CLC 25**
See also AITN 1; CA 5-8R; 103; CANR 3; DAM DRAM; DLB 7, 9, 249; DLBY 1981; RGAL 4

**Greenaway, Peter** 1942- ................. **CLC 159**
See also CA 127

**Greenberg, Ivan** 1908-1973
See Rahv, Philip
See also CA 85-88

**Greenberg, Joanne (Goldenberg)**
1932- ............................... **CLC 7, 30**
See also AAYA 12; CA 5-8R; CANR 14, 32, 69; CN 7; SATA 25; YAW

**Greenberg, Richard** 1959(?)- ........... **CLC 57**
See also CA 138; CAD; CD 5

**Greenblatt, Stephen J(ay)** 1943- ...... **CLC 70**
See also CA 49-52; CANR 115

**Greene, Bette** 1934- ..................... **CLC 30**
See also AAYA 7; BYA 3; CA 53-56; CANR 4; CLR 2; CWRI 5; JRDA; LAIT 4; MAICYA 1, 2; NFS 10; SAAS 16; SATA 8, 102; WYA; YAW

**Greene, Gael** ................................. **CLC 8**
See also CA 13-16R; CANR 10

**Greene, Graham (Henry)**
1904-1991 .... **CLC 1, 3, 6, 9, 14, 18, 27, 37, 70, 72, 125; SSC 29; WLC**
See also AITN 2; BPFB 2; BRWR 2; BRWS 1; BYA 3; CA 13-16R; 133; CANR 35, 61, 131; CBD; CDBLB 1945-1960; CMW 4; DA; DA3; DAB; DAC; DAM MST, NOV; DLB 13, 15, 77, 100, 162, 201, 204; DLBY 1991; EWL 3; MSW; MTCW 1, 2; NFS 16; RGEL 2; SATA 20; SSFS 14; TEA; WLIT 4

**Greene, Robert** 1558-1592 ................... **LC 41**
See also BRWS 8; DLB 62, 167; IDTP; RGEL 2; TEA

**Greer, Germaine** 1939- .................... **CLC 131**
See also AITN 1; CA 81-84; CANR 33, 70, 115, 133; FW; MTCW 1, 2

**Greer, Richard**
See Silverberg, Robert

**Gregor, Arthur** 1923- ......................... **CLC 9**
See also CA 25-28R; CAAS 10; CANR 11; CP 7; SATA 36

**Gregor, Lee**
See Pohl, Frederik

**Gregory, Lady Isabella Augusta (Persse)**
1852-1932 ................................... **TCLC 1**
See also BRW 6; CA 104; 184; DLB 10; IDTP; RGEL 2

**Gregory, J. Dennis**
See Williams, John A(lfred)

**Grekova, I.** ......................................... **CLC 59**
See Ventsel, Elena Sergeevna
See also CWW 2

**Grendon, Stephen**
See Derleth, August (William)

**Grenville, Kate** 1950- ........................ **CLC 61**
See also CA 118; CANR 53, 93

**Grenville, Pelham**
See Wodehouse, P(elham) G(renville)

**Greve, Felix Paul (Berthold Friedrich)**
1879-1948
See Grove, Frederick Philip
See also CA 104; 141, 175; CANR 79; DAC; DAM MST

**Greville, Fulke** 1554-1628 .................... **LC 79**
See also DLB 62, 172; RGEL 2

**Grey, Lady Jane** 1537-1554 ................. **LC 93**
See also DLB 132

**Grey, Zane** 1872-1939 ........................ **TCLC 6**
See also BPFB 2; CA 104; 132; DA3; DAM POP; DLB 9, 212; MTCW 1, 2; RGAL 4; TCWW 2; TUS

**Griboedov, Aleksandr Sergeevich**
1795(?)-1829 ............................ **NCLC 129**
See also DLB 205; RGWL 2, 3

**Grieg, (Johan) Nordahl (Brun)**
1902-1943 ................................... **TCLC 10**
See also CA 107; 189; EWL 3

**Grieve, C(hristopher) M(urray)**
1892-1978 ............................. **CLC 11, 19**
See MacDiarmid, Hugh; Pteleon
See also CA 5-8R; 85-88; CANR 33, 107; DAM POET; MTCW 1; RGEL 2

**Griffin, Gerald** 1803-1840 ................ **NCLC 7**
See also DLB 159; RGEL 2

**Griffin, John Howard** 1920-1980 ..... **CLC 68**
See also AITN 1; CA 1-4R; 101; CANR 2

**Griffin, Peter** 1942- ......................... **CLC 39**
See also CA 136

**Griffith, D(avid Lewelyn) W(ark)**
1875(?)-1948 ......................... **TCLC 68**
See also CA 119; 150; CANR 80

**Griffith, Lawrence**
See Griffith, D(avid Lewelyn) W(ark)

**Griffiths, Trevor** 1935- ................. **CLC 13, 52**
See also CA 97-100; CANR 45; CBD; CD 5; DLB 13, 245

**Griggs, Sutton (Elbert)**
1872-1930 ................................ **TCLC 77**
See also CA 123; DLB 50

**Grigson, Geoffrey (Edward Harvey)**
1905-1985 .............................. **CLC 7, 39**
See also CA 25-28R; 118; CANR 20, 33; DLB 27; MTCW 1, 2

**Grile, Dod**
See Bierce, Ambrose (Gwinett)

**Grillparzer, Franz** 1791-1872 ............. **DC 14; NCLC 1, 102; SSC 37**
See also CDWLB 2; DLB 133; EW 5; RGWL 2, 3; TWA

**Grimble, Reverend Charles James**
See Eliot, T(homas) S(tearns)

**Grimke, Angelina (Emily) Weld**
1880-1958 ....................................... **HR 2**
See Weld, Angelina (Emily) Grimke
See also BW 1; CA 124; DAM POET; DLB 50, 54

**Grimke, Charlotte L(ottie) Forten**
1837(?)-1914
See Forten, Charlotte L.
See also BW 1; CA 117; 124; DAM MULT, POET

**Grimm, Jacob Ludwig Karl**
1785-1863 .............. **NCLC 3, 77; SSC 36**
See also DLB 90; MAICYA 1, 2; RGSF 2; RGWL 2, 3; SATA 22; WCH

**Grimm, Wilhelm Karl** 1786-1859 .. **NCLC 3, 77; SSC 36**
See also CDWLB 2; DLB 90; MAICYA 1, 2; RGSF 2; RGWL 2, 3; SATA 22; WCH

**Grimmelshausen, Hans Jakob Christoffel von**
See Grimmelshausen, Johann Jakob Christoffel von
See also RGWL 2, 3

**Grimmelshausen, Johann Jakob Christoffel von** 1621-1676 ................. **LC 6**
See Grimmelshausen, Hans Jakob Christoffel von
See also CDWLB 2; DLB 168

**Grindel, Eugene** 1895-1952
See Eluard, Paul
See also CA 104; 193; LMFS 2

**Grisham, John** 1955- ......................... **CLC 84**
See also AAYA 14, 47; BPFB 2; CA 138; CANR 47, 69, 114, 133; CMW 4; CN 7; CPW; CSW; DA3; DAM POP; MSW; MTCW 2

**Grosseteste, Robert** 1175(?)-1253 . **CMLC 62**
See also DLB 115

**Grossman, David** 1954- ..................... **CLC 67**
See also CA 138; CANR 114; CWW 2; DLB 299; EWL 3

**Grossman, Vasilii Semenovich**
See Grossman, Vasily (Semenovich)
See also DLB 272

**Grossman, Vasily (Semenovich)**
1905-1964 ..................................... **CLC 41**
See Grossman, Vasilii Semenovich
See also CA 124; 130; MTCW 1

**Grove, Frederick Philip** .................. **TCLC 4**
  See Greve, Felix Paul (Berthold Friedrich)
  See also DLB 92; RGEL 2
**Grubb**
  See Crumb, R(obert)
**Grumbach, Doris (Isaac)** 1918- . **CLC 13, 22, 64**
  See also CA 5-8R; CAAS 2; CANR 9, 42, 70, 127; CN 7; INT CANR-9; MTCW 2
**Grundtvig, Nikolai Frederik Severin** 1783-1872 ........................ **NCLC 1, 158**
  See also DLB 300
**Grunge**
  See Crumb, R(obert)
**Grunwald, Lisa** 1959- ........................ **CLC 44**
  See also CA 120
**Gryphius, Andreas** 1616-1664 ............. **LC 89**
  See also CDWLB 2; DLB 164; RGWL 2, 3
**Guare, John** 1938- .... **CLC 8, 14, 29, 67; DC 20**
  See also CA 73-76; CAD; CANR 21, 69, 118; CD 5; DAM DRAM; DFS 8, 13; DLB 7, 249; EWL 3; MTCW 1, 2; RGAL 4
**Guarini, Battista** 1537-1612 ............... **LC 102**
**Gubar, Susan (David)** 1944- ........... **CLC 145**
  See also CA 108; CANR 45, 70; FW; MTCW 1; RGAL 4
**Gudjonsson, Halldor Kiljan** 1902-1998
  See Halldor Laxness
  See also CA 103; 164
**Guenter, Erich**
  See Eich, Gunter
**Guest, Barbara** 1920- ........... **CLC 34; PC 55**
  See also BG 2; CA 25-28R; CANR 11, 44, 84; CP 7; CWP; DLB 5, 193
**Guest, Edgar A(lbert)** 1881-1959 ... **TCLC 95**
  See also CA 112; 168
**Guest, Judith (Ann)** 1936- ........... **CLC 8, 30**
  See also AAYA 7; CA 77-80; CANR 15, 75; DA3; DAM NOV, POP; EXPN; INT CANR-15; LAIT 5; MTCW 1, 2; NFS 1
**Guevara, Che** ........................ **CLC 87; HLC 1**
  See Guevara (Serna), Ernesto
**Guevara (Serna), Ernesto** 1928-1967 ..................... **CLC 87; HLC 1**
  See Guevara, Che
  See also CA 127; 111; CANR 56; DAM MULT; HW 1
**Guicciardini, Francesco** 1483-1540 ..... **LC 49**
**Guild, Nicholas M.** 1944- .................. **CLC 33**
  See also CA 93-96
**Guillemin, Jacques**
  See Sartre, Jean-Paul
**Guillen, Jorge** 1893-1984 . **CLC 11; HLCS 1; PC 35**
  See also CA 89-92; 112; DAM MULT, POET; DLB 108; EWL 3; HW 1; RGWL 2, 3
**Guillen, Nicolas (Cristobal)** 1902-1989 .... **BLC 2; CLC 48, 79; HLC 1; PC 23**
  See also BW 2; CA 116; 125; 129; CANR 84; DAM MST, MULT, POET; DLB 283; EWL 3; HW 1; LAW; RGWL 2, 3; WP
**Guillen y Alvarez, Jorge**
  See Guillen, Jorge
**Guillevic, (Eugene)** 1907-1997 ......... **CLC 33**
  See also CA 93-96; CWW 2
**Guillois**
  See Desnos, Robert
**Guillois, Valentin**
  See Desnos, Robert
**Guimaraes Rosa, Joao** 1908-1967 .... **HLCS 2**
  See Rosa, Joao Guimaraes
  See also CA 175; LAW; RGSF 2; RGWL 2, 3

**Guiney, Louise Imogen** 1861-1920 ................................. **TCLC 41**
  See also CA 160; DLB 54; RGAL 4
**Guinizelli, Guido** c. 1230-1276 ...... **CMLC 49**
**Guiraldes, Ricardo (Guillermo)** 1886-1927 ................................. **TCLC 39**
  See also CA 131; EWL 3; HW 1; LAW; MTCW 1
**Gumilev, Nikolai (Stepanovich)** 1886-1921 ................................. **TCLC 60**
  See Gumilyov, Nikolay Stepanovich
  See also CA 165; DLB 295
**Gumilyov, Nikolay Stepanovich**
  See Gumilev, Nikolai (Stepanovich)
  See also EWL 3
**Gump, P. Q.**
  See Card, Orson Scott
**Gunesekera, Romesh** 1954- ............... **CLC 91**
  See also BRWS 10; CA 159; CN 7; DLB 267
**Gunn, Bill** ................................... **CLC 5**
  See Gunn, William Harrison
  See also DLB 38
**Gunn, Thom(son William)** 1929-2004 . **CLC 3, 6, 18, 32, 81; PC 26**
  See also BRWS 4; CA 17-20R; 227; CANR 9, 33, 116; CDBLB 1960 to Present; CP 7; DAM POET; DLB 27; INT CANR-33; MTCW 1; PFS 9; RGEL 2
**Gunn, William Harrison** 1934(?)-1989
  See Gunn, Bill
  See also AITN 1; BW 1, 3; CA 13-16R; 128; CANR 12, 25, 76
**Gunn Allen, Paula**
  See Allen, Paula Gunn
**Gunnars, Kristjana** 1948- ................. **CLC 69**
  See also CA 113; CCA 1; CP 7; CWP; DLB 60
**Gunter, Erich**
  See Eich, Gunter
**Gurdjieff, G(eorgei) I(vanovich)** 1877(?)-1949 ................. **TCLC 71**
  See also CA 157
**Gurganus, Allan** 1947- ..................... **CLC 70**
  See also BEST 90:1; CA 135; CANR 114; CN 7; CPW; CSW; DAM POP; GLL 1
**Gurney, A. R.**
  See Gurney, A(lbert) R(amsdell), Jr.
  See also DLB 266
**Gurney, A(lbert) R(amsdell), Jr.** 1930- ................................. **CLC 32, 50, 54**
  See Gurney, A. R.
  See also AMWS 5; CA 77-80; CAD; CANR 32, 64, 121; CD 5; DAM DRAM; EWL 3
**Gurney, Ivor (Bertie)** 1890-1937 ... **TCLC 33**
  See also BRW 6; CA 167; DLBY 2002; PAB; RGEL 2
**Gurney, Peter**
  See Gurney, A(lbert) R(amsdell), Jr.
**Guro, Elena (Genrikhovna)** 1877-1913 ................................. **TCLC 56**
  See also DLB 295
**Gustafson, James M(oody)** 1925- ... **CLC 100**
  See also CA 25-28R; CANR 37
**Gustafson, Ralph (Barker)** 1909-1995 ................................. **CLC 36**
  See also CA 21-24R; CANR 8, 45, 84; CP 7; DLB 88; RGEL 2
**Gut, Gom**
  See Simenon, Georges (Jacques Christian)
**Guterson, David** 1956- ..................... **CLC 91**
  See also CA 132; CANR 73, 126; DLB 292; MTCW 2; NFS 13
**Guthrie, A(lfred) B(ertram), Jr.** 1901-1991 ................................. **CLC 23**
  See also CA 57-60; 134; CANR 24; DLB 6, 212; SATA 62; SATA-Obit 67
**Guthrie, Isobel**
  See Grieve, C(hristopher) M(urray)

**Guthrie, Woodrow Wilson** 1912-1967
  See Guthrie, Woody
  See also CA 113; 93-96
**Guthrie, Woody** ................................. **CLC 35**
  See Guthrie, Woodrow Wilson
  See also DLB 303; LAIT 3
**Gutierrez Najera, Manuel** 1859-1895 ................. **HLCS 2; NCLC 133**
  See also DLB 290; LAW
**Guy, Rosa (Cuthbert)** 1925- ............. **CLC 26**
  See also AAYA 4, 37; BW 2; CA 17-20R; CANR 14, 34, 83; CLR 13; DLB 33; DNFS 1; JRDA; MAICYA 1, 2; SATA 14, 62, 122; YAW
**Gwendolyn**
  See Bennett, (Enoch) Arnold
**H. D.** ........... **CLC 3, 8, 14, 31, 34, 73; PC 5**
  See Doolittle, Hilda
**H. de V.**
  See Buchan, John
**Haavikko, Paavo Juhani** 1931- .. **CLC 18, 34**
  See also CA 106; CWW 2; EWL 3
**Habbema, Koos**
  See Heijermans, Herman
**Habermas, Juergen** 1929- ............... **CLC 104**
  See also CA 109; CANR 85; DLB 242
**Habermas, Jurgen**
  See Habermas, Juergen
**Hacker, Marilyn** 1942- ...... **CLC 5, 9, 23, 72, 91; PC 47**
  See also CA 77-80; CANR 68, 129; CP 7; CWP; DAM POET; DLB 120, 282; FW; GLL 2; PFS 19
**Hadewijch of Antwerp** fl. 1250- ... **CMLC 61**
  See also RGWL 3
**Hadrian** 76-138 ............................. **CMLC 52**
**Haeckel, Ernst Heinrich (Philipp August)** 1834-1919 ................................. **TCLC 83**
  See also CA 157
**Hafiz** c. 1326-1389(?) ...................... **CMLC 34**
  See also RGWL 2, 3
**Hagedorn, Jessica T(arahata)** 1949- ................................. **CLC 185**
  See also CA 139; CANR 69; CWP; RGAL 4
**Haggard, H(enry) Rider** 1856-1925 ................................. **TCLC 11**
  See also BRWS 3; BYA 4, 5; CA 108; 148; CANR 112; DLB 70, 156, 174, 178; FANT; LMFS 1; MTCW 2; RGEL 2; RHW; SATA 16; SCFW; SFW 4; SUFW 1; WLIT 4
**Hagiosy, L.**
  See Larbaud, Valery (Nicolas)
**Hagiwara, Sakutaro** 1886-1942 .......... **PC 18; TCLC 60**
  See Hagiwara Sakutaro
  See also CA 154; RGWL 3
**Hagiwara Sakutaro**
  See Hagiwara, Sakutaro
  See also EWL 3
**Haig, Fenil**
  See Ford, Ford Madox
**Haig-Brown, Roderick (Langmere)** 1908-1976 ................................. **CLC 21**
  See also CA 5-8R; 69-72; CANR 4, 38, 83; CLR 31; CWRI 5; DLB 88; MAICYA 1, 2; SATA 12
**Haight, Rip**
  See Carpenter, John (Howard)
**Hailey, Arthur** 1920- ........................ **CLC 5**
  See also AITN 2; BEST 90:3; BPFB 2; CA 1-4R; CANR 2, 36, 75; CCA 1; CN 7; CPW; DAM NOV, POP; DLB 88; DLBY 1982; MTCW 1, 2
**Hailey, Elizabeth Forsythe** 1938- ..... **CLC 40**
  See also CA 93-96; 188; CAAE 188; CAAS 1; CANR 15, 48; INT CANR-15

**Harris, George Washington**
1814-1869 ................................. **NCLC 23**
See also DLB 3, 11, 248; RGAL 4

**Harris, Joel Chandler** 1848-1908 ..... **SSC 19;
TCLC 2**
See also CA 104; 137; CANR 80; CLR 49;
DLB 11, 23, 42, 78, 91; LAIT 2; MAI-
CYA 1, 2; RGSF 2; SATA 100; WCH;
YABC 1

**Harris, John (Wyndham Parkes Lucas)
Beynon** 1903-1969
See Wyndham, John
See also CA 102; 89-92; CANR 84; SATA
118; SFW 4

**Harris, MacDonald** ..................... **CLC 9**
See Heiney, Donald (William)

**Harris, Mark** 1922- ........................... **CLC 19**
See also CA 5-8R; CAAS 3; CANR 2, 55,
83; CN 7; DLB 2; DLBY 1980

**Harris, Norman** ....................... **CLC 65**

**Harris, (Theodore) Wilson** 1921- .... **CLC 25,
159**
See also BRWS 5; BW 2, 3; CA 65-68;
CAAS 16; CANR 11, 27, 69, 114; CD-
WLB 3; CN 7; CP 7; DLB 117; EWL 3;
MTCW 1; RGEL 2

**Harrison, Barbara Grizzuti**
1934-2002 ................................. **CLC 144**
See also CA 77-80; 205; CANR 15, 48; INT
CANR-15

**Harrison, Elizabeth (Allen) Cavanna**
1909-2001
See Cavanna, Betty
See also CA 9-12R; 200; CANR 6, 27, 85,
104, 121; MAICYA 2; SATA 142; YAW

**Harrison, Harry (Max)** 1925- .......... **CLC 42**
See also CA 1-4R; CANR 5, 21, 84; DLB
8; SATA 4; SCFW 2; SFW 4

**Harrison, James (Thomas)** 1937- ...... **CLC 6,
14, 33, 66, 143; SSC 19**
See Harrison, Jim
See also CA 13-16R; CANR 8, 51, 79; CN
7; CP 7; DLBY 1982; INT CANR-8

**Harrison, Jim**
See Harrison, James (Thomas)
See also AMWS 8; RGAL 4; TCWW 2;
TUS

**Harrison, Kathryn** 1961- .......... **CLC 70, 151**
See also CA 144; CANR 68, 122

**Harrison, Tony** 1937- ................ **CLC 43, 129**
See also BRWS 5; CA 65-68; CANR 44,
98; CBD; CD 5; CP 7; DLB 40, 245;
MTCW 1; RGEL 2

**Harriss, Will(ard Irvin)** 1922- .......... **CLC 34**
See also CA 111

**Hart, Ellis**
See Ellison, Harlan (Jay)

**Hart, Josephine** 1942(?)- ................... **CLC 70**
See also CA 138; CANR 70; CPW; DAM
POP

**Hart, Moss** 1904-1961 ........................ **CLC 66**
See also CA 109; 89-92; CANR 84; DAM
DRAM; DFS 1; DLB 7, 266; RGAL 4

**Harte, (Francis) Bret(t)**
1836(?)-1902 ... **SSC 8, 59; TCLC 1, 25;
WLC**
See also AMWS 2; CA 104; 140; CANR
80; CDALB 1865-1917; DA; DA3; DAC;
DAM MST; DLB 12, 64, 74, 79, 186;
EXPS; LAIT 2; RGAL 4; RGSF 2; SATA
26; SSFS 3; TUS

**Hartley, L(eslie) P(oles)** 1895-1972 ... **CLC 2,
22**
See also BRWS 7; CA 45-48; 37-40R;
CANR 33; DLB 15, 139; EWL 3; HGG;
MTCW 1, 2; RGEL 2; RGSF 2; SUFW 1

**Hartman, Geoffrey H.** 1929- ............. **CLC 27**
See also CA 117; 125; CANR 79; DLB 67

**Hartmann, Sadakichi** 1869-1944 ... **TCLC 73**
See also CA 157; DLB 54

**Hartmann von Aue** c. 1170-c.
1210 ........................................ **CMLC 15**
See also CDWLB 2; DLB 138; RGWL 2, 3

**Hartog, Jan de**
See de Hartog, Jan

**Haruf, Kent** 1943- ........................... **CLC 34**
See also AAYA 44; CA 149; CANR 91, 131

**Harvey, Caroline**
See Trollope, Joanna

**Harvey, Gabriel** 1550(?)-1631 .............. **LC 88**
See also DLB 167, 213, 281

**Harwood, Ronald** 1934- ................... **CLC 32**
See also CA 1-4R; CANR 4, 55; CBD; CD
5; DAM DRAM, MST; DLB 13

**Hasegawa Tatsunosuke**
See Futabatei, Shimei

**Hasek, Jaroslav (Matej Frantisek)**
1883-1923 ................... **SSC 69; TCLC 4**
See also CA 104; 129; CDWLB 4; DLB
215; EW 9; EWL 3; MTCW 1, 2; RGSF
2; RGWL 2, 3

**Hass, Robert** 1941- ... **CLC 18, 39, 99; PC 16**
See also AMWS 6; CA 111; CANR 30, 50,
71; CP 7; DLB 105, 206; EWL 3; RGAL
4; SATA 94

**Hastings, Hudson**
See Kuttner, Henry

**Hastings, Selina** ................... **CLC 44**

**Hathorne, John** 1641-1717 .................. **LC 38**

**Hatteras, Amelia**
See Mencken, H(enry) L(ouis)

**Hatteras, Owen** ........................... **TCLC 18**
See Mencken, H(enry) L(ouis); Nathan,
George Jean

**Hauptmann, Gerhart (Johann Robert)**
1862-1946 ................... **SSC 37; TCLC 4**
See also CA 104; 153; CDWLB 2; DAM
DRAM; DLB 66, 118; EW 8; EWL 3;
RGSF 2; RGWL 2, 3; TWA

**Havel, Vaclav** 1936- ..... **CLC 25, 58, 65, 123;
DC 6**
See also CA 104; CANR 36, 63, 124; CD-
WLB 4; CWW 2; DA3; DAM DRAM;
DFS 10; DLB 232; EWL 3; LMFS 2;
MTCW 1, 2; RGWL 3

**Haviaras, Stratis** ........................... **CLC 33**
See Chaviaras, Strates

**Hawes, Stephen** 1475(?)-1529(?) .......... **LC 17**
See also DLB 132; RGEL 2

**Hawkes, John (Clendennin Burne, Jr.)**
1925-1998 .. **CLC 1, 2, 3, 4, 7, 9, 14, 15,
27, 49**
See also BPFB 2; CA 1-4R; 167; CANR 2,
47, 64; CN 7; DLB 2, 7, 227; DLBY
1980, 1998; EWL 3; MTCW 1, 2; RGAL
4

**Hawking, S. W.**
See Hawking, Stephen W(illiam)

**Hawking, Stephen W(illiam)** 1942- . **CLC 63,
105**
See also AAYA 13; BEST 89:1; CA 126;
129; CANR 48, 115; CPW; DA3; MTCW
2

**Hawkins, Anthony Hope**
See Hope, Anthony

**Hawthorne, Julian** 1846-1934 ........ **TCLC 25**
See also CA 165; HGG

**Hawthorne, Nathaniel** 1804-1864 ... **NCLC 2,
10, 17, 23, 39, 79, 95, 158; SSC 3, 29,
39; WLC**
See also AAYA 18; AMW; AMWC 1;
AMWR 1; BPFB 2; BYA 3; CDALB
1640-1865; DA; DA3; DAB; DAC; DAM
MST, NOV; DLB 1, 74, 183, 223, 269;
EXPN; EXPS; HGG; LAIT 1; NFS 1, 20;
RGAL 4; RGSF 2; SSFS 1, 7, 11, 15;
SUFW 1; TUS; WCH; YABC 2

**Hawthorne, Sophia Peabody**
1809-1871 ............................. **NCLC 150**
See also DLB 183, 239

**Haxton, Josephine Ayres** 1921-
See Douglas, Ellen
See also CA 115; CANR 41, 83

**Hayaseca y Eizaguirre, Jorge**
See Echegaray (y Eizaguirre), Jose (Maria
Waldo)

**Hayashi, Fumiko** 1904-1951 .......... **TCLC 27**
See Hayashi Fumiko
See also CA 161

**Hayashi Fumiko**
See Hayashi, Fumiko
See also DLB 180; EWL 3

**Haycraft, Anna (Margaret)** 1932-
See Ellis, Alice Thomas
See also CA 122; CANR 85, 90; MTCW 2

**Hayden, Robert E(arl)** 1913-1980 ..... **BLC 2;
CLC 5, 9, 14, 37; PC 6**
See also AFAW 1, 2; AMWS 2; BW 1, 3;
CA 69-72; 97-100; CABS 2; CANR 24,
75, 82; CDALB 1941-1968; DA; DAC;
DAM MST, MULT, POET; DLB 5, 76;
EWL 3; EXPP; MTCW 1, 2; PFS 1;
RGAL 4; SATA 19; SATA-Obit 26; WP

**Haydon, Benjamin Robert**
1786-1846 ............................. **NCLC 146**
See also DLB 110

**Hayek, F(riedrich) A(ugust von)**
1899-1992 ............................. **TCLC 109**
See also CA 93-96; 137; CANR 20; MTCW
1, 2

**Hayford, J(oseph) E(phraim) Casely**
See Casely-Hayford, J(oseph) E(phraim)

**Hayman, Ronald** 1932- ..................... **CLC 44**
See also CA 25-28R; CANR 18, 50, 88; CD
5; DLB 155

**Hayne, Paul Hamilton** 1830-1886 . **NCLC 94**
See also DLB 3, 64, 79, 248; RGAL 4

**Hays, Mary** 1760-1843 .................. **NCLC 114**
See also DLB 142, 158; RGEL 2

**Haywood, Eliza (Fowler)**
1693(?)-1756 ............................. **LC 1, 44**
See also DLB 39; RGEL 2

**Hazlitt, William** 1778-1830 ...... **NCLC 29, 82**
See also BRW 4; DLB 110, 158; RGEL 2;
TEA

**Hazzard, Shirley** 1931- ..................... **CLC 18**
See also CA 9-12R; CANR 4, 70, 127; CN
7; DLB 289; DLBY 1982; MTCW 1

**Head, Bessie** 1937-1986 ...... **BLC 2; CLC 25,
67; SSC 52**
See also AFW; BW 2, 3; CA 29-32R; 119;
CANR 25, 82; CDWLB 3; DA3; DAM
MULT; DLB 117, 225; EWL 3; EXPS;
FW; MTCW 1, 2; RGSF 2; SSFS 5, 13;
WLIT 2; WWE 1

**Headon, (Nicky) Topper** 1956(?)- ..... **CLC 30**

**Heaney, Seamus (Justin)** 1939- ..... **CLC 5, 7,
14, 25, 37, 74, 91, 171; PC 18; WLCS**
See also BRWR 1; BRWS 2; CA 85-88;
CANR 25, 48, 75, 91, 128; CDBLB 1960
to Present; CP 7; DA3; DAB; DAM
POET; DLB 40; DLBY 1995; EWL 3;
EXPP; MTCW 1, 2; PAB; PFS 2, 5, 8,
17; RGEL 2; TEA; WLIT 4

**Hearn, (Patricio) Lafcadio (Tessima Carlos)**
1850-1904 ................................. **TCLC 9**
See also CA 105; 166; DLB 12, 78, 189;
HGG; RGAL 4

**Hearne, Samuel** 1745-1792 ................. **LC 95**
See also DLB 99

**Hearne, Vicki** 1946-2001 .................. **CLC 56**
See also CA 139; 201

**Hearon, Shelby** 1931- ...................... **CLC 63**
See also AITN 2; AMWS 8; CA 25-28R;
CANR 18, 48, 103; CSW

**Hesse, Hermann** 1877-1962 ... **CLC 1, 2, 3, 6, 11, 17, 25, 69; SSC 9, 49; TCLC 148; WLC**
See also AAYA 43; BPFB 2; CA 17-18; CAP 2; CDWLB 2; DA; DA3; DAB; DAC; DAM MST, NOV; DLB 66; EW 9; EWL 3; EXPN; LAIT 1; MTCW 1, 2; NFS 6, 15; RGWL 2, 3; SATA 50; TWA

**Hewes, Cady**
See De Voto, Bernard (Augustine)

**Heyen, William** 1940- ................. **CLC 13, 18**
See also CA 33-36R, 220; CAAE 220; CAAS 9; CANR 98; CP 7; DLB 5

**Heyerdahl, Thor** 1914-2002 ............. **CLC 26**
See also CA 5-8R; 207; CANR 5, 22, 66, 73; LAIT 4; MTCW 1, 2; SATA 2, 52

**Heym, Georg (Theodor Franz Arthur)**
1887-1912 ........................... **TCLC 9**
See also CA 106; 181

**Heym, Stefan** 1913-2001 .................. **CLC 41**
See also CA 9-12R; 203; CANR 4; CWW 2; DLB 69; EWL 3

**Heyse, Paul (Johann Ludwig von)**
1830-1914 ............................ **TCLC 8**
See also CA 104; 209; DLB 129

**Heyward, (Edwin) DuBose**
1885-1940 .................... **HR 2; TCLC 59**
See also CA 108; 157; DLB 7, 9, 45, 249; SATA 21

**Heywood, John** 1497(?)-1580(?) ......... **LC 65**
See also DLB 136; RGEL 2

**Heywood, Thomas** 1573(?)-1641 ........ **LC 111**
See also DLB 62; DAM DRAM; LMFS 1; RGEL 2; TWA

**Hibbert, Eleanor Alice Burford**
1906-1993 .................................. **CLC 7**
See Holt, Victoria
See also BEST 90:4; CA 17-20R; 140; CANR 9, 28, 59; CMW 4; CPW; DAM POP; MTCW 2; RHW; SATA 2; SATA-Obit 74

**Hichens, Robert (Smythe)**
1864-1950 ............................... **TCLC 64**
See also CA 162; DLB 153; HGG; RHW; SUFW

**Higgins, Aidan** 1927- ............................. **SSC 68**
See also CA 9-12R; CANR 70, 115; CN 7; DLB 14

**Higgins, George V(incent)**
1939-1999 ................. **CLC 4, 7, 10, 18**
See also BPFB 2; CA 77-80; 186; CAAS 5; CANR 17, 51, 89, 96; CMW 4; CN 7; DLB 2; DLBY 1981, 1998; INT CANR-17; MSW; MTCW 1

**Higginson, Thomas Wentworth**
1823-1911 ................................ **TCLC 36**
See also CA 162; DLB 1, 64, 243

**Higgonet, Margaret** ed. ..................... **CLC 65**

**Highet, Helen**
See MacInnes, Helen (Clark)

**Highsmith, (Mary) Patricia**
1921-1995 ............ **CLC 2, 4, 14, 42, 102**
See Morgan, Claire
See also AAYA 48; BRWS 5; CA 1-4R; 147; CANR 1, 20, 48, 62, 108; CMW 4; CPW; DA3; DAM NOV, POP; DLB 306; MSW; MTCW 1, 2

**Highwater, Jamake (Mamake)**
1942(?)-2001 .............................. **CLC 12**
See also AAYA 7; BPFB 2; BYA 4; CA 65-68; 199; CAAS 7; CANR 10, 34, 84; CLR 17; CWRI 5; DLB 52; DLBY 1985; JRDA; MAICYA 1, 2; SATA 32, 69; SATA-Brief 30

**Highway, Tomson** 1951- ...... **CLC 92; NNAL**
See also CA 151; CANR 75; CCA 1; CD 5; DAC; DAM MULT; DFS 2; MTCW 2

**Hijuelos, Oscar** 1951- .......... **CLC 65; HLC 1**
See also AAYA 25; AMWS 8; BEST 90:1; CA 123; CANR 50, 75, 125; CPW; DA3; DAM MULT, POP; DLB 145; HW 1, 2; LLW 1; MTCW 2; NFS 17; RGAL 4; WLIT 1

**Hikmet, Nazim** 1902(?)-1963 ............ **CLC 40**
See also CA 141; 93-96; EWL 3

**Hildegard von Bingen** 1098-1179 . **CMLC 20**
See also DLB 148

**Hildesheimer, Wolfgang** 1916-1991 .. **CLC 49**
See also CA 101; 135; DLB 69, 124; EWL 3

**Hill, Geoffrey (William)** 1932- ...... **CLC 5, 8, 18, 45**
See also BRWS 5; CA 81-84; CANR 21, 89; CDBLB 1960 to Present; CP 7; DAM POET; DLB 40; EWL 3; MTCW 1; RGEL 2

**Hill, George Roy** 1921-2002 ............. **CLC 26**
See also CA 110; 122; 213

**Hill, John**
See Koontz, Dean R(ay)

**Hill, Susan (Elizabeth)** 1942- ...... **CLC 4, 113**
See also CA 33-36R; CANR 29, 69, 129; CN 7; DAB; DAM MST, NOV; DLB 14, 139; HGG; MTCW 1; RHW

**Hillard, Asa G. III** ........................... **CLC 70**

**Hillerman, Tony** 1925- ............. **CLC 62, 170**
See also AAYA 40; BEST 89:1; BPFB 2; CA 29-32R; CANR 21, 42, 65, 97, 134; CMW 4; CPW; DA3; DAM POP; DLB 206, 306; MSW; RGAL 4; SATA 6; TCWW 2; YAW

**Hillesum, Etty** 1914-1943 ............... **TCLC 49**
See also CA 137

**Hilliard, Noel (Harvey)** 1929-1996 ... **CLC 15**
See also CA 9-12R; CANR 7, 69; CN 7

**Hillis, Rick** 1956- ............................... **CLC 66**
See also CA 134

**Hilton, James** 1900-1954 ................. **TCLC 21**
See also CA 108; 169; DLB 34, 77; FANT; SATA 34

**Hilton, Walter** (?)-1396 ................. **CMLC 58**
See also DLB 146; RGEL 2

**Himes, Chester (Bomar)** 1909-1984 .. **BLC 2; CLC 2, 4, 7, 18, 58, 108; TCLC 139**
See also AFAW 2; BPFB 2; BW 2; CA 25-28R; 114; CANR 22, 89; CMW 4; DAM MULT; DLB 2, 76, 143, 226; EWL 3; MSW; MTCW 1, 2; RGAL 4

**Himmelfarb, Gertrude** 1922- .......... **CLC 202**
See also CA 49-52; CANR 28, 66, 102;

**Hinde, Thomas** ..................... **CLC 6, 11**
See Chitty, Thomas Willes
See also EWL 3

**Hine, (William) Daryl** 1936- ............. **CLC 15**
See also CA 1-4R; CAAS 15; CANR 1, 20; CP 7; DLB 60

**Hinkson, Katharine Tynan**
See Tynan, Katharine

**Hinojosa(-Smith), Rolando (R.)**
1929- ............................................. **HLC 1**
See Hinojosa-Smith, Rolando
See also CA 131; CAAS 16; CANR 62; DAM MULT; DLB 82; HW 1, 2; LLW 1; MTCW 2; RGAL 4

**Hinton, S(usan) E(loise)** 1950- .. **CLC 30, 111**
See also AAYA 2, 33; BPFB 2; BYA 2, 3; CA 81-84; CANR 32, 62, 92, 133; CDALBS; CLR 3, 23; CPW; DA; DA3; DAB; DAC; DAM MST, NOV; JRDA; LAIT 5; MAICYA 1, 2; MTCW 1, 2; NFS 5, 9, 15, 16; SATA 19, 58, 115; WYA; YAW

**Hippius, Zinaida (Nikolaevna)** ....... **TCLC 9**
See Gippius, Zinaida (Nikolaevna)
See also DLB 295; EWL 3

**Hiraoka, Kimitake** 1925-1970
See Mishima, Yukio
See also CA 97-100; 29-32R; DA3; DAM DRAM; GLL 1; MTCW 1, 2

**Hirsch, E(ric) D(onald), Jr.** 1928- .... **CLC 79**
See also CA 25-28R; CANR 27, 51; DLB 67; INT CANR-27; MTCW 1

**Hirsch, Edward** 1950- ................ **CLC 31, 50**
See also CA 104; CANR 20, 42, 102; CP 7; DLB 120

**Hitchcock, Alfred (Joseph)**
1899-1980 ................................ **CLC 16**
See also AAYA 22; CA 159; 97-100; SATA 27; SATA-Obit 24

**Hitchens, Christopher (Eric)**
1949- .................................... **CLC 157**
See also CA 152; CANR 89

**Hitler, Adolf** 1889-1945 ................... **TCLC 53**
See also CA 117; 147

**Hoagland, Edward** 1932- ................. **CLC 28**
See also ANW; CA 1-4R; CANR 2, 31, 57, 107; CN 7; DLB 6; SATA 51; TCWW 2

**Hoban, Russell (Conwell)** 1925- ... **CLC 7, 25**
See also BPFB 2; CA 5-8R; CANR 23, 37, 66, 114; CLR 3, 69; CN 7; CWRI 5; DAM NOV; DLB 52; FANT; MAICYA 1, 2; MTCW 1, 2; SATA 1, 40, 78, 136; SFW 4; SUFW 2

**Hobbes, Thomas** 1588-1679 ................. **LC 36**
See also DLB 151, 252, 281; RGEL 2

**Hobbs, Perry**
See Blackmur, R(ichard) P(almer)

**Hobson, Laura Z(ametkin)**
1900-1986 ............................. **CLC 7, 25**
See Field, Peter
See also BPFB 2; CA 17-20R; 118; CANR 55; DLB 28; SATA 52

**Hoccleve, Thomas** c. 1368-c. 1437 ...... **LC 75**
See also DLB 146; RGEL 2

**Hoch, Edward D(entinger)** 1930-
See Queen, Ellery
See also CA 29-32R; CANR 11, 27, 51, 97; CMW 4; DLB 306; SFW 4

**Hochhuth, Rolf** 1931- ............. **CLC 4, 11, 18**
See also CA 5-8R; CANR 33, 75; CWW 2; DAM DRAM; DLB 124; EWL 3; MTCW 1, 2

**Hochman, Sandra** 1936- ................. **CLC 3, 8**
See also CA 5-8R; DLB 5

**Hochwaelder, Fritz** 1911-1986 .......... **CLC 36**
See Hochwalder, Fritz
See also CA 29-32R; 120; CANR 42; DAM DRAM; MTCW 1; RGWL 3

**Hochwalder, Fritz**
See Hochwaelder, Fritz
See also EWL 3; RGWL 2

**Hocking, Mary (Eunice)** 1921- ......... **CLC 13**
See also CA 101; CANR 18, 40

**Hodgins, Jack** 1938- ...................... **CLC 23**
See also CA 93-96; CN 7; DLB 60

**Hodgson, William Hope**
1877(?)-1918 ........................... **TCLC 13**
See also CA 111; 164; CMW 4; DLB 70, 153, 156, 178; HGG; MTCW 2; SFW 4; SUFW 1

**Hoeg, Peter** 1957- ...................... **CLC 95, 156**
See also CA 151; CANR 75; CMW 4; DA3; DLB 214; EWL 3; MTCW 2; NFS 17; RGWL 3; SSFS 18

**Hoffman, Alice** 1952- ..................... **CLC 51**
See also AAYA 37; AMWS 10; CA 77-80; CANR 34, 66, 100; CN 7; CPW; DAM NOV; DLB 292; MTCW 1, 2

**Hoffman, Daniel (Gerard)** 1923- . **CLC 6, 13, 23**
See also CA 1-4R; CANR 4; CP 7; DLB 5

**Hoffman, Eva** 1945- ...................... **CLC 182**
See also CA 132

**Hoffman, Stanley** 1944- ....................... **CLC 5**
See also CA 77-80
**Hoffman, William** 1925- .................. **CLC 141**
See also CA 21-24R; CANR 9, 103; CSW;
DLB 234
**Hoffman, William M(oses)** 1939- ..... **CLC 40**
See Hoffman, William M.
See also CA 57-60; CANR 11, 71
**Hoffmann, E(rnst) T(heodor) A(madeus)**
1776-1822 ................................ **NCLC 2; SSC 13**
See also CDWLB 2; DLB 90; EW 5; RGSF
2; RGWL 2, 3; SATA 27; SUFW 1; WCH
**Hofmann, Gert** 1931- ........................ **CLC 54**
See also CA 128; EWL 3
**Hofmannsthal, Hugo von** 1874-1929 ... **DC 4;**
**TCLC 11**
See also CA 106; 153; CDWLB 2; DAM
DRAM; DFS 17; DLB 81, 118; EW 9;
EWL 3; RGWL 2, 3
**Hogan, Linda** 1947- ..... **CLC 73; NNAL; PC**
**35**
See also AMWS 4; ANW; BYA 12; CA 120,
226; CAAE 226; CANR 45, 73, 129;
CWP; DAM MULT; DLB 175; SATA
132; TCWW 2
**Hogarth, Charles**
See Creasey, John
**Hogarth, Emmett**
See Polonsky, Abraham (Lincoln)
**Hogarth, William** 1697-1764 ............. **LC 112**
See also AAYA 56
**Hogg, James** 1770-1835 ............ **NCLC 4, 109**
See also BRWS 10; DLB 93, 116, 159;
HGG; RGEL 2; SUFW 1
**Holbach, Paul Henri Thiry Baron**
1723-1789 ..................................... **LC 14**
**Holberg, Ludvig** 1684-1754 ................... **LC 6**
See also DLB 300; RGWL 2, 3
**Holcroft, Thomas** 1745-1809 .............. **NCLC 85**
See also DLB 39, 89, 158; RGEL 2
**Holden, Ursula** 1921- ......................... **CLC 18**
See also CA 101; CAAS 8; CANR 22
**Holderlin, (Johann Christian) Friedrich**
1770-1843 ..................... **NCLC 16; PC 4**
See also CDWLB 2; DLB 90; EW 5; RGWL
2, 3
**Holdstock, Robert**
See Holdstock, Robert P.
**Holdstock, Robert P.** 1948- .............. **CLC 39**
See also CA 131; CANR 81; DLB 261;
FANT; HGG; SFW 4; SUFW 2
**Holinshed, Raphael** fl. 1580- ............... **LC 69**
See also DLB 167; RGEL 2
**Holland, Isabelle (Christian)**
1920-2002 .................................... **CLC 21**
See also AAYA 11; CA 21-24R; 205; CAAE
181; CANR 10, 25, 47; CLR 57; CWRI
5; JRDA; LAIT 4; MAICYA 1, 2; SATA
8, 70; SATA-Essay 103; SATA-Obit 132;
WYA
**Holland, Marcus**
See Caldwell, (Janet Miriam) Taylor
(Holland)
**Hollander, John** 1929- .......... **CLC 2, 5, 8, 14**
See also CA 1-4R; CANR 1, 52; CP 7; DLB
5; SATA 13
**Hollander, Paul**
See Silverberg, Robert
**Holleran, Andrew** 1943(?)- ................ **CLC 38**
See Garber, Eric
See also CA 144; GLL 1
**Holley, Marietta** 1836(?)-1926 ........ **TCLC 99**
See also CA 118; DLB 11
**Hollinghurst, Alan** 1954- ............. **CLC 55, 91**
See also BRWS 10; CA 114; CN 7; DLB
207; GLL 1
**Hollis, Jim**
See Summers, Hollis (Spurgeon, Jr.)

**Holly, Buddy** 1936-1959 .................. **TCLC 65**
See also CA 213
**Holmes, Gordon**
See Shiel, M(atthew) P(hipps)
**Holmes, John**
See Souster, (Holmes) Raymond
**Holmes, John Clellon** 1926-1988 ...... **CLC 56**
See also BG 2; CA 9-12R; 125; CANR 4;
DLB 16, 237
**Holmes, Oliver Wendell, Jr.**
1841-1935 ................................ **TCLC 77**
See also CA 114; 186
**Holmes, Oliver Wendell**
1809-1894 ............................ **NCLC 14, 81**
See also AMWS 1; CDALB 1640-1865;
DLB 1, 189, 235; EXPP; RGAL 4; SATA
34
**Holmes, Raymond**
See Souster, (Holmes) Raymond
**Holt, Victoria**
See Hibbert, Eleanor Alice Burford
See also BPFB 2
**Holub, Miroslav** 1923-1998 .................. **CLC 4**
See also CA 21-24R; 169; CANR 10; CD-
WLB 4; CWW 2; DLB 232; EWL 3;
RGWL 3
**Holz, Detlev**
See Benjamin, Walter
**Homer** c. 8th cent. B.C.- .... **CMLC 1, 16, 61;**
**PC 23; WLCS**
See also AW 1; CDWLB 1; DA; DA3;
DAB; DAC; DAM MST, POET; DLB
176; EFS 1; LAIT 1; LMFS 1; RGWL 2,
3; TWA; WP
**Hongo, Garrett Kaoru** 1951- ............... **PC 23**
See also CA 133; CAAS 22; CP 7; DLB
120; EWL 3; EXPP; RGAL 4
**Honig, Edwin** 1919- ........................... **CLC 33**
See also CA 5-8R; CAAS 8; CANR 4, 45;
CP 7; DLB 5
**Hood, Hugh (John Blagdon)** 1928- . **CLC 15,**
**28; SSC 42**
See also CA 49-52; CAAS 17; CANR 1,
33, 87; CN 7; DLB 53; RGSF 2
**Hood, Thomas** 1799-1845 ............... **NCLC 16**
See also BRW 4; DLB 96; RGEL 2
**Hooker, (Peter) Jeremy** 1941- ........... **CLC 43**
See also CA 77-80; CANR 22; CP 7; DLB
40
**Hooker, Richard** 1554-1600 ................. **LC 95**
See also BRW 1; DLB 132; RGEL 2
**hooks, bell**
See Watkins, Gloria Jean
**Hope, A(lec) D(erwent)** 1907-2000 .... **CLC 3,**
**51; PC 56**
See also BRWS 7; CA 21-24R; 188; CANR
33, 74; DLB 289; EWL 3; MTCW 1, 2;
PFS 8; RGEL 2
**Hope, Anthony** 1863-1933 .............. **TCLC 83**
See also CA 157; DLB 153, 156; RGEL 2;
RHW
**Hope, Brian**
See Creasey, John
**Hope, Christopher (David Tully)**
1944- ......................................... **CLC 52**
See also AFW; CA 106; CANR 47, 101;
CN 7; DLB 225; SATA 62
**Hopkins, Gerard Manley**
1844-1889 ....... **NCLC 17; PC 15; WLC**
See also BRW 5; BRWR 2; CDBLB 1890-
1914; DA; DA3; DAB; DAC; DAM MST,
POET; DLB 35, 57; EXPP; PAB; RGEL
2; TEA; WP
**Hopkins, John (Richard)** 1931-1998 .. **CLC 4**
See also CA 85-88; 169; CBD; CD 5
**Hopkins, Pauline Elizabeth**
1859-1930 .................. **BLC 2; TCLC 28**
See also AFAW 2; BW 2, 3; CA 141; CANR
82; DAM MULT; DLB 50

**Hopkinson, Francis** 1737-1791 ............ **LC 25**
See also DLB 31; RGAL 4
**Hopley-Woolrich, Cornell George** 1903-1968
See Woolrich, Cornell
See also CA 13-14; CANR 58; CAP 1;
CMW 4; DLB 226; MTCW 2
**Horace** 65B.C.-8B.C. ......... **CMLC 39; PC 46**
See also AW 2; CDWLB 1; DLB 211;
RGWL 2, 3
**Horatio**
See Proust, (Valentin-Louis-George-Eugene)
Marcel
**Horgan, Paul (George Vincent**
**O'Shaughnessy)** 1903-1995 .. **CLC 9, 53**
See also BPFB 2; CA 13-16R; 147; CANR
9, 35; DAM NOV; DLB 102, 212; DLBY
1985; INT CANR-9; MTCW 1, 2; SATA
13; SATA-Obit 84; TCWW 2
**Horkheimer, Max** 1895-1973 ........ **TCLC 132**
See also CA 216; 41-44R; DLB 296
**Horn, Peter**
See Kuttner, Henry
**Horne, Frank (Smith)** 1899-1974 ......... **HR 2**
See also BW 1; CA 125; 53-56; DLB 51;
WP
**Horne, Richard Henry Hengist**
1802(?)-1884 ......................... **NCLC 127**
See also DLB 32; SATA 29
**Hornem, Horace Esq.**
See Byron, George Gordon (Noel)
**Horney, Karen (Clementine Theodore**
**Danielsen)** 1885-1952 ............ **TCLC 71**
See also CA 114; 165; DLB 246; FW
**Hornung, E(rnest) W(illiam)**
1866-1921 ................................ **TCLC 59**
See also CA 108; 160; CMW 4; DLB 70
**Horovitz, Israel (Arthur)** 1939- ........ **CLC 56**
See also CA 33-36R; CAD; CANR 46, 59;
CD 5; DAM DRAM; DLB 7
**Horton, George Moses**
1797(?)-1883(?) ...................... **NCLC 87**
See also DLB 50
**Horvath, odon von** 1901-1938
See von Horvath, Odon
See also EWL 3
**Horvath, Oedoen von** -1938
See von Horvath, Odon
**Horwitz, Julius** 1920-1986 .................. **CLC 14**
See also CA 9-12R; 119; CANR 12
**Hospital, Janette Turner** 1942- ........ **CLC 42,**
**145**
See also CA 108; CANR 48; CN 7; DLBY
2002; RGSF 2
**Hostos, E. M. de**
See Hostos (y Bonilla), Eugenio Maria de
**Hostos, Eugenio M. de**
See Hostos (y Bonilla), Eugenio Maria de
**Hostos, Eugenio Maria**
See Hostos (y Bonilla), Eugenio Maria de
**Hostos (y Bonilla), Eugenio Maria de**
1839-1903 ................................ **TCLC 24**
See also CA 123; 131; HW 1
**Houdini**
See Lovecraft, H(oward) P(hillips)
**Houellebecq, Michel** 1958- ............. **CLC 179**
See also CA 185
**Hougan, Carolyn** 1943- .................... **CLC 34**
See also CA 139
**Household, Geoffrey (Edward West)**
1900-1988 ................................... **CLC 11**
See also CA 77-80; 126; CANR 58; CMW
4; DLB 87; SATA 14; SATA-Obit 59
**Housman, A(lfred) E(dward)**
1859-1936 ......... **PC 2, 43; TCLC 1, 10;**
**WLCS**
See also BRW 6; CA 104; 125; DA; DA3;
DAB; DAC; DAM MST, POET; DLB 19,
284; EWL 3; EXPP; MTCW 1, 2; PAB;
PFS 4, 7; RGEL 2; TEA; WP

**Housman, Laurence** 1865-1959 ....... **TCLC 7**
See also CA 106; 155; DLB 10; FANT;
RGEL 2; SATA 25

**Houston, Jeanne (Toyo) Wakatsuki**
1934- ................................................ **AAL**
See also AAYA 49; CA 103; CAAS 16;
CANR 29, 123; LAIT 4; SATA 78

**Howard, Elizabeth Jane** 1923- ..... **CLC 7, 29**
See also CA 5-8R; CANR 8, 62; CN 7

**Howard, Maureen** 1930- ........ **CLC 5, 14, 46,**
**151**
See also CA 53-56; CANR 31, 75; CN 7;
DLBY 1983; INT CANR-31; MTCW 1, 2

**Howard, Richard** 1929- .......... **CLC 7, 10, 47**
See also AITN 1; CA 85-88; CANR 25, 80;
CP 7; DLB 5; INT CANR-25

**Howard, Robert E(rvin)**
1906-1936 .................................. **TCLC 8**
See also BPFB 2; BYA 5; CA 105; 157;
FANT; SUFW 1

**Howard, Warren F.**
See Pohl, Frederik

**Howe, Fanny (Quincy)** 1940- ........... **CLC 47**
See also CA 117, 187; CAAE 187; CAAS
27; CANR 70, 116; CP 7; CWP; SATA-
Brief 52

**Howe, Irving** 1920-1993 .................... **CLC 85**
See also AMWS 6; CA 9-12R; 141; CANR
21, 50; DLB 67; EWL 3; MTCW 1, 2

**Howe, Julia Ward** 1819-1910 ......... **TCLC 21**
See also CA 117; 191; DLB 1, 189, 235;
FW

**Howe, Susan** 1937- ....... **CLC 72, 152; PC 54**
See also AMWS 4; CA 160; CP 7; CWP;
DLB 120; FW; RGAL 4

**Howe, Tina** 1937- ................................. **CLC 48**
See also CA 109; CAD; CANR 125; CD 5;
CWD

**Howell, James** 1594(?)-1666 ................. **LC 13**
See also DLB 151

**Howells, W. D.**
See Howells, William Dean

**Howells, William D.**
See Howells, William Dean

**Howells, William Dean** 1837-1920 ... **SSC 36;**
**TCLC 7, 17, 41**
See also AMW; CA 104; 134; CDALB
1865-1917; DLB 12, 64, 74, 79, 189;
LMFS 1; MTCW 2; RGAL 4; TUS

**Howes, Barbara** 1914-1996 .................. **CLC 15**
See also CA 9-12R; 151; CAAS 3; CANR
53; CP 7; SATA 5

**Hrabal, Bohumil** 1914-1997 ...... **CLC 13, 67;**
**TCLC 155**
See also CA 106; 156; CAAS 12; CANR
57; CWW 2; DLB 232; EWL 3; RGSF 2

**Hrabanus Maurus** c. 776-856 ....... **CMLC 78**
See also DLB 148

**Hrotsvit of Gandersheim** c. 935-c.
1000 ........................................... **CMLC 29**
See also DLB 148

**Hsi, Chu** 1130-1200 ....................... **CMLC 42**

**Hsun, Lu**
See Lu Hsun

**Hubbard, L(afayette) Ron(ald)**
1911-1986 .................................... **CLC 43**
See also CA 77-80; 118; CANR 52; CPW;
DA3; DAM POP; FANT; MTCW 2; SFW
4

**Huch, Ricarda (Octavia)**
1864-1947 .................................... **TCLC 13**
See also CA 111; 189; DLB 66; EWL 3

**Huddle, David** 1942- .......................... **CLC 49**
See also CA 57-60; CAAS 20; CANR 89;
DLB 130

**Hudson, Jeffrey**
See Crichton, (John) Michael

**Hudson, W(illiam) H(enry)**
1841-1922 ................................... **TCLC 29**
See also CA 115; 190; DLB 98, 153, 174;
RGEL 2; SATA 35

**Hueffer, Ford Madox**
See Ford, Ford Madox

**Hughart, Barry** 1934- ....................... **CLC 39**
See also CA 137; FANT; SFW 4; SUFW 2

**Hughes, Colin**
See Creasey, John

**Hughes, David (John)** 1930- ............. **CLC 48**
See also CA 116; 129; CN 7; DLB 14

**Hughes, Edward James**
See Hughes, Ted
See also DA3; DAM MST, POET

**Hughes, (James Mercer) Langston**
1902-1967 ..... **BLC 2; CLC 1, 5, 10, 15,**
**35, 44, 108; DC 3; HR 2; PC 1, 53;**
**SSC 6; WLC**
See also AAYA 12; AFAW 1, 2; AMWR 1;
AMWS 1; BW 1, 3; CA 1-4R; 25-28R;
CANR 1, 34, 82; CDALB 1929-1941;
CLR 17; DA; DA3; DAB; DAC; DAM
DRAM, MST, MULT, POET; DFS 6, 18;
DLB 4, 7, 48, 51, 86, 228; EWL 3; EXPP;
EXPS; JRDA; LAIT 3; LMFS 2; MAI-
CYA 1, 2; MTCW 1, 2; PAB; PFS 1, 3, 6,
10, 15; RGAL 4; RGSF 2; SATA 4, 33;
SSFS 4, 7; TUS; WCH; WP; YAW

**Hughes, Richard (Arthur Warren)**
1900-1976 .......................... **CLC 1, 11**
See also CA 5-8R; 65-68; CANR 4; DAM
NOV; DLB 15, 161; EWL 3; MTCW 1;
RGEL 2; SATA 8; SATA-Obit 25

**Hughes, Ted** 1930-1998 . **CLC 2, 4, 9, 14, 37,**
**119; PC 7**
See Hughes, Edward James
See also BRWC 2; BRWR 2; BRWS 1; CA
1-4R; 171; CANR 1, 33, 66, 108; CLR 3;
CP 7; DAB; DAC; DLB 40, 161; EWL 3;
EXPP; MAICYA 1, 2; MTCW 1, 2; PAB;
PFS 4, 19; RGEL 2; SATA 49; SATA-
Brief 27; SATA-Obit 107; TEA; YAW

**Hugo, Richard**
See Huch, Ricarda (Octavia)

**Hugo, Richard F(ranklin)**
1923-1982 ........................ **CLC 6, 18, 32**
See also AMWS 6; CA 49-52; 108; CANR
3; DAM POET; DLB 5, 206; EWL 3; PFS
17; RGAL 4

**Hugo, Victor (Marie)** 1802-1885 .... **NCLC 3,**
**10, 21; PC 17; WLC**
See also AAYA 28; DA; DA3; DAB; DAC;
DAM DRAM, MST, NOV, POET; DLB
119, 192, 217; EFS 2; EW 6; EXPN; GFL
1789 to the Present; LAIT 1, 2; NFS 5,
20; RGWL 2, 3; SATA 47; TWA

**Huidobro, Vicente**
See Huidobro Fernandez, Vicente Garcia
See also DLB 283; EWL 3; LAW

**Huidobro Fernandez, Vicente Garcia**
1893-1948 ................................... **TCLC 31**
See Huidobro, Vicente
See also CA 131; HW 1

**Hulme, Keri** 1947- ..................... **CLC 39, 130**
See also CA 125; CANR 69; CN 7; CP 7;
CWP; EWL 3; FW; INT CA-125

**Hulme, T(homas) E(rnest)**
1883-1917 ................................... **TCLC 21**
See also BRWS 6; CA 117; 203; DLB 19

**Humboldt, Wilhelm von**
1767-1835 ................................. **NCLC 134**
See also DLB 90

**Hume, David** 1711-1776 ................. **LC 7, 56**
See also BRWS 3; DLB 104, 252; LMFS 1;
TEA

**Humphrey, William** 1924-1997 ......... **CLC 45**
See also AMWS 9; CA 77-80; 160; CANR
68; CN 7; CSW; DLB 6, 212, 234, 278;
TCWW 2

**Humphreys, Emyr Owen** 1919- ........ **CLC 47**
See also CA 5-8R; CANR 3, 24; CN 7;
DLB 15

**Humphreys, Josephine** 1945- ..... **CLC 34, 57**
See also CA 121; 127; CANR 97; CSW;
DLB 292; INT CA-127

**Huneker, James Gibbons**
1860-1921 ................................... **TCLC 65**
See also CA 193; DLB 71; RGAL 4

**Hungerford, Hesba Fay**
See Brinsmead, H(esba) F(ay)

**Hungerford, Pixie**
See Brinsmead, H(esba) F(ay)

**Hunt, E(verette) Howard, (Jr.)**
1918- ............................................ **CLC 3**
See also AITN 1; CA 45-48; CANR 2, 47,
103; CMW 4

**Hunt, Francesca**
See Holland, Isabelle (Christian)

**Hunt, Howard**
See Hunt, E(verette) Howard, (Jr.)

**Hunt, Kyle**
See Creasey, John

**Hunt, (James Henry) Leigh**
1784-1859 ............................ **NCLC 1, 70**
See also DAM POET; DLB 96, 110, 144;
RGEL 2; TEA

**Hunt, Marsha** 1946- ........................... **CLC 70**
See also BW 2, 3; CA 143; CANR 79

**Hunt, Violet** 1866(?)-1942 ............... **TCLC 53**
See also CA 184; DLB 162, 197

**Hunter, E. Waldo**
See Sturgeon, Theodore (Hamilton)

**Hunter, Evan** 1926- ...................... **CLC 11, 31**
See McBain, Ed
See also AAYA 39; BPFB 2; CA 5-8R;
CANR 5, 38, 62, 97; CMW 4; CN 7;
CPW; DAM POP; DLB 306; DLBY 1982;
INT CANR-5; MSW; MTCW 1; SATA
25; SFW 4

**Hunter, Kristin**
See Lattany, Kristin (Elaine Eggleston)
Hunter

**Hunter, Mary**
See Austin, Mary (Hunter)

**Hunter, Mollie** 1922- ........................... **CLC 21**
See McIlwraith, Maureen Mollie Hunter
See also AAYA 13; BYA 6; CANR 37, 78;
CLR 25; DLB 161; JRDA; MAICYA 1,
2; SAAS 7; SATA 54, 106, 139; SATA-
Essay 139; WYA; YAW

**Hunter, Robert** (?)-1734 ........................ **LC 7**

**Hurston, Zora Neale** 1891-1960 ........ **BLC 2;**
**CLC 7, 30, 61; DC 12; HR 2; SSC 4,**
**80; TCLC 121, 131; WLCS**
See also AAYA 15; AFAW 1, 2; AMWS 6;
BW 1, 3; BYA 12; CA 85-88; CANR 61;
CDALBS; DA; DA3; DAC; DAM MST,
MULT, NOV; DFS 6; DLB 51, 86; EWL
3; EXPN; EXPS; FW; LAIT 3; LATS 1:1;
LMFS 2; MAWW; MTCW 1, 2; NFS 3;
RGAL 4; RGSF 2; SSFS 1, 6, 11, 19;
TUS; YAW

**Husserl, E. G.**
See Husserl, Edmund (Gustav Albrecht)

**Husserl, Edmund (Gustav Albrecht)**
1859-1938 .............................. **TCLC 100**
See also CA 116; 133; DLB 296

**Huston, John (Marcellus)**
1906-1987 .................................... **CLC 20**
See also CA 73-76; 123; CANR 34; DLB
26

**Hustvedt, Siri** 1955- .......................... **CLC 76**
See also CA 137

**Hutten, Ulrich von** 1488-1523 ............. **LC 16**
See also DLB 179

Author Index

**Kingman, Lee** ................................ **CLC 17**
See Natti, (Mary) Lee
See also CWRI 5; SAAS 3; SATA 1, 67

**Kingsley, Charles** 1819-1875 ......... **NCLC 35**
See also CLR 77; DLB 21, 32, 163, 178, 190; FANT; MAICYA 2; MAICYAS 1; RGEL 2; WCH; YABC 2

**Kingsley, Henry** 1830-1876 .......... **NCLC 107**
See also DLB 21, 230; RGEL 2

**Kingsley, Sidney** 1906-1995 ............... **CLC 44**
See also CA 85-88; 147; CAD; DFS 14, 19; DLB 7; RGAL 4

**Kingsolver, Barbara** 1955- . **CLC 55, 81, 130**
See also AAYA 15; AMWS 7; CA 129; 134; CANR 60, 96, 133; CDALBS; CPW; CSW; DA3; DAM POP; DLB 206; INT CA-134; LAIT 5; MTCW 2; NFS 5, 10, 12; RGAL 4

**Kingston, Maxine (Ting Ting) Hong**
1940- .......... **AAL; CLC 12, 19, 58, 121; WLCS**
See also AAYA 8, 55; AMWS 5; BPFB 2; CA 69-72; CANR 13, 38, 74, 87, 128; CDALBS; CN 7; DA3; DAM MULT, NOV; DLB 173, 212; DLBY 1980; EWL 3; FW; INT CANR-13; LAIT 5; MAWW; MTCW 1, 2; NFS 6; RGAL 4; SATA 53; SSFS 3

**Kinnell, Galway** 1927- ..... **CLC 1, 2, 3, 5, 13, 29, 129; PC 26**
See also AMWS 3; CA 9-12R; CANR 10, 34, 66, 116; CP 7; DLB 5; DLBY 1987; EWL 3; INT CANR-34; MTCW 1, 2; PAB; PFS 9; RGAL 4; WP

**Kinsella, Thomas** 1928- ........ **CLC 4, 19, 138**
See also BRWS 5; CA 17-20R; CANR 15, 122; CP 7; DLB 27; EWL 3; MTCW 1, 2; RGEL 2; TEA

**Kinsella, W(illiam) P(atrick)** 1935- . **CLC 27, 43, 166**
See also AAYA 7, 60; BPFB 2; CA 97-100, 222; CAAE 222; CAAS 7; CANR 21, 35, 66, 75, 129; CN 7; CPW; DAC; DAM NOV, POP; FANT; INT CANR-21; LAIT 5; MTCW 1, 2; NFS 15; RGSF 2

**Kinsey, Alfred C(harles)**
1894-1956 ................................ **TCLC 91**
See also CA 115; 170; MTCW 2

**Kipling, (Joseph) Rudyard** 1865-1936 . **PC 3; SSC 5, 54; TCLC 8, 17, 167; WLC**
See also AAYA 32; BRW 6; BRWC 1, 2; BYA 4; CA 105; 120; CANR 33; CDBLB 1890-1914; CLR 39, 65; CWRI 5; DA; DA3; DAB; DAC; DAM MST, POET; DLB 19, 34, 141, 156; EWL 3; EXPS; FANT; LAIT 3; LMFS 1; MAICYA 1, 2; MTCW 1, 2; RGEL 2; RGSF 2; SATA 100; SFW 4; SSFS 8; SUFW 1; TEA; WCH; WLIT 4; YABC 2

**Kirk, Russell (Amos)** 1918-1994 .. **TCLC 119**
See also AITN 1; CA 1-4R; 145; CAAS 9; CANR 1, 20, 60; HGG; INT CANR-20; MTCW 1, 2

**Kirkham, Dinah**
See Card, Orson Scott

**Kirkland, Caroline M.** 1801-1864 . **NCLC 85**
See also DLB 3, 73, 74, 250, 254; DLBD 13

**Kirkup, James** 1918- ......................... **CLC 1**
See also CA 1-4R; CAAS 4; CANR 2; CP 7; DLB 27; SATA 12

**Kirkwood, James** 1930(?)-1989 .......... **CLC 9**
See also AITN 2; CA 1-4R; 128; CANR 6, 40; GLL 2

**Kirsch, Sarah** 1935- ......................... **CLC 176**
See also CA 178; CWW 2; DLB 75; EWL 3

**Kirshner, Sidney**
See Kingsley, Sidney

**Kis, Danilo** 1935-1989 ....................... **CLC 57**
See also CA 109; 118; 129; CANR 61; CDWLB 4; DLB 181; EWL 3; MTCW 1; RGSF 2; RGWL 2, 3

**Kissinger, Henry A(lfred)** 1923- ..... **CLC 137**
See also CA 1-4R; CANR 2, 33, 66, 109; MTCW 1

**Kivi, Aleksis** 1834-1872 ................... **NCLC 30**

**Kizer, Carolyn (Ashley)** 1925- ... **CLC 15, 39, 80; PC 66**
See also CA 65-68; CAAS 5; CANR 24, 70, 134; CP 7; CWP; DAM POET; DLB 5, 169; EWL 3; MTCW 2; PFS 18

**Klabund** 1890-1928 ........................ **TCLC 44**
See also CA 162; DLB 66

**Klappert, Peter** 1942- ........................ **CLC 57**
See also CA 33-36R; CSW; DLB 5

**Klein, A(braham) M(oses)**
1909-1972 ................................ **CLC 19**
See also CA 101; 37-40R; DAB; DAC; DAM MST; DLB 68; EWL 3; RGEL 2

**Klein, Joe**
See Klein, Joseph

**Klein, Joseph** 1946- ........................ **CLC 154**
See also CA 85-88; CANR 55

**Klein, Norma** 1938-1989 ................... **CLC 30**
See also AAYA 2, 35; BPFB 2; BYA 6, 7, 8; CA 41-44R; 128; CANR 15, 37; CLR 2, 19; INT CANR-15; JRDA; MAICYA 1, 2; SAAS 1; SATA 7, 57; WYA; YAW

**Klein, T(heodore) E(ibon) D(onald)**
1947- ................................ **CLC 34**
See also CA 119; CANR 44, 75; HGG

**Kleist, Heinrich von** 1777-1811 ...... **NCLC 2, 37; SSC 22**
See also CDWLB 2; DAM DRAM; DLB 90; EW 5; RGSF 2; RGWL 2, 3

**Klima, Ivan** 1931- ...................... **CLC 56, 172**
See also CA 25-28R; CANR 17, 50, 91; CDWLB 4; CWW 2; DAM NOV; DLB 232; EWL 3; RGWL 3

**Klimentev, Andrei Platonovich**
See Klimentov, Andrei Platonovich

**Klimentov, Andrei Platonovich**
1899-1951 ................. **SSC 42; TCLC 14**
See Platonov, Andrei Platonovich; Platonov, Andrey Platonovich
See also CA 108

**Klinger, Friedrich Maximilian von**
1752-1831 ................................ **NCLC 1**
See also DLB 94

**Klingsor the Magician**
See Hartmann, Sadakichi

**Klopstock, Friedrich Gottlieb**
1724-1803 ................................ **NCLC 11**
See also DLB 97; EW 4; RGWL 2, 3

**Kluge, Alexander** 1932- ..................... **SSC 61**
See also CA 81-84; DLB 75

**Knapp, Caroline** 1959-2002 ............. **CLC 99**
See also CA 154; 207

**Knebel, Fletcher** 1911-1993 ............... **CLC 14**
See also AITN 1; CA 1-4R; 140; CAAS 3; CANR 1, 36; SATA 36; SATA-Obit 75

**Knickerbocker, Diedrich**
See Irving, Washington

**Knight, Etheridge** 1931-1991 ... **BLC 2; CLC 40; PC 14**
See also BW 1, 3; CA 21-24R; 133; CANR 23, 82; DAM POET; DLB 41; MTCW 2; RGAL 4

**Knight, Sarah Kemble** 1666-1727 ......... **LC 7**
See also DLB 24, 200

**Knister, Raymond** 1899-1932 ......... **TCLC 56**
See also CA 186; DLB 68; RGEL 2

**Knowles, John** 1926-2001 ... **CLC 1, 4, 10, 26**
See also AAYA 10; AMWS 12; BPFB 2; BYA 3; CA 17-20R; 203; CANR 40, 74, 76, 132; CDALB 1968-1988; CLR 98; CN

7; DA; DAC; DAM MST, NOV; DLB 6; EXPN; MTCW 1, 2; NFS 2; RGAL 4; SATA 8, 89; SATA-Obit 134; YAW

**Knox, Calvin M.**
See Silverberg, Robert

**Knox, John** c. 1505-1572 ....................... **LC 37**
See also DLB 132

**Knye, Cassandra**
See Disch, Thomas M(ichael)

**Koch, C(hristopher) J(ohn)** 1932- .... **CLC 42**
See also CA 127; CANR 84; CN 7; DLB 289

**Koch, Christopher**
See Koch, C(hristopher) J(ohn)

**Koch, Kenneth (Jay)** 1925-2002 .... **CLC 5, 8, 44**
See also CA 1-4R; 207; CAD; CANR 6, 36, 57, 97, 131; CD 5; CP 7; DAM POET; DLB 5; INT CANR-36; MTCW 2; PFS 20; SATA 65; WP

**Kochanowski, Jan** 1530-1584 ............. **LC 10**
See also RGWL 2, 3

**Kock, Charles Paul de** 1794-1871 . **NCLC 16**

**Koda Rohan**
See Koda Shigeyuki

**Koda Rohan**
See Koda Shigeyuki
See also DLB 180

**Koda Shigeyuki** 1867-1947 ............. **TCLC 22**
See Koda Rohan
See also CA 121; 183

**Koestler, Arthur** 1905-1983 ... **CLC 1, 3, 6, 8, 15, 33**
See also BRWS 1; CA 1-4R; 109; CANR 1, 33; CDBLB 1945-1960; DLBY 1983; EWL 3; MTCW 1, 2; NFS 19; RGEL 2

**Kogawa, Joy Nozomi** 1935- ...... **CLC 78, 129**
See also AAYA 47; CA 101; CANR 19, 62, 126; CN 7; CWP; DAC; DAM MST, MULT; FW; MTCW 2; NFS 3; SATA 99

**Kohout, Pavel** 1928- ......................... **CLC 13**
See also CA 45-48; CANR 3

**Koizumi, Yakumo**
See Hearn, (Patricio) Lafcadio (Tessima Carlos)

**Kolmar, Gertrud** 1894-1943 .......... **TCLC 40**
See also CA 167; EWL 3

**Komunyakaa, Yusef** 1947- .. **BLCS; CLC 86, 94, 207; PC 51**
See also AFAW 2; AMWS 13; CA 147; CANR 83; CP 7; CSW; DLB 120; EWL 3; PFS 5, 20; RGAL 4

**Konrad, George**
See Konrad, Gyorgy

**Konrad, Gyorgy** 1933- ............. **CLC 4, 10, 73**
See also CA 85-88; CANR 97; CDWLB 4; CWW 2; DLB 232; EWL 3

**Konwicki, Tadeusz** 1926- ....... **CLC 8, 28, 54, 117**
See also CA 101; CAAS 9; CANR 39, 59; CWW 2; DLB 232; EWL 3; IDFW 3; MTCW 1

**Koontz, Dean R(ay)** 1945- ........ **CLC 78, 206**
See also AAYA 9, 31; BEST 89:3, 90:2; CA 108; CANR 19, 36, 52, 95; CMW 4; CPW; DA3; DAM NOV, POP; DLB 292; HGG; MTCW 1; SATA 92; SFW 4; SUFW 2; YAW

**Kopernik, Mikolaj**
See Copernicus, Nicolaus

**Kopit, Arthur (Lee)** 1937- ...... **CLC 1, 18, 33**
See also AITN 1; CA 81-84; CABS 3; CD 5; DAM DRAM; DFS 7, 14; DLB 7; MTCW 1; RGAL 4

**Kopitar, Jernej (Bartholomaus)**
1780-1844 ................................ **NCLC 117**

**Kops, Bernard** 1926- ......................... **CLC 4**
See also CA 5-8R; CANR 84; CBD; CN 7; CP 7; DLB 13

Leiber, Fritz (Reuter, Jr.)
1910-1992 .................................. **CLC 25**
See also BPFB 2; CA 45-48; 139; CANR 2, 40, 86; DLB 8; FANT; HGG; MTCW 1, 2; SATA 45; SATA-Obit 73; SCFW 2; SFW 4; SUFW 1, 2

Leibniz, Gottfried Wilhelm von
1646-1716 .................................... **LC 35**
See also DLB 168

Leimbach, Martha 1963-
See Leimbach, Marti
See also CA 130

Leimbach, Marti ............................. **CLC 65**
See Leimbach, Martha

Leino, Eino ..................................... **TCLC 24**
See Lonnbohm, Armas Eino Leopold
See also EWL 3

Leiris, Michel (Julien) 1901-1990 ..... **CLC 61**
See also CA 119; 128; 132; EWL 3; GFL 1789 to the Present

Leithauser, Brad 1953- ..................... **CLC 27**
See also CA 107; CANR 27, 81; CP 7; DLB 120, 282

le Jars de Gournay, Marie
See de Gournay, Marie le Jars

Lelchuk, Alan 1938- ......................... **CLC 5**
See also CA 45-48; CAAS 20; CANR 1, 70; CN 7

Lem, Stanislaw 1921- ...... **CLC 8, 15, 40, 149**
See also CA 105; CAAS 1; CANR 32; CWW 2; MTCW 1; SCFW 2; SFW 4

Lemann, Nancy (Elise) 1956- ........... **CLC 39**
See also CA 118; 136; CANR 121

Lemonnier, (Antoine Louis) Camille
1844-1913 .................................. **TCLC 22**
See also CA 121

Lenau, Nikolaus 1802-1850 ............ **NCLC 16**

L'Engle, Madeleine (Camp Franklin)
1918- ........................................ **CLC 12**
See also AAYA 28; AITN 2; BPFB 2; BYA 2, 4, 5, 7; CA 1-4R; CANR 3, 21, 39, 66, 107; CLR 1, 14, 57; CPW; CWRI 5; DA3; DAM POP; DLB 52; JRDA; MAICYA 1, 2; MTCW 1, 2; SAAS 15; SATA 1, 27, 75, 128; SFW 4; WYA; YAW

Lengyel, Jozsef 1896-1975 ................. **CLC 7**
See also CA 85-88; 57-60; CANR 71; RGSF 2

Lenin 1870-1924
See Lenin, V. I.
See also CA 121; 168

Lenin, V. I. ................................... **TCLC 67**
See Lenin

Lennon, John (Ono) 1940-1980 .. **CLC 12, 35**
See also CA 102; SATA 114

Lennox, Charlotte Ramsay
1729(?)-1804 .................... **NCLC 23, 134**
See also DLB 39; RGEL 2

Lentricchia, Frank, (Jr.) 1940- ......... **CLC 34**
See also CA 25-28R; CANR 19, 106; DLB 246

Lenz, Gunter .................................. **CLC 65**

Lenz, Jakob Michael Reinhold
1751-1792 .................................. **LC 100**
See also DLB 94; RGWL 2, 3

Lenz, Siegfried 1926- .......... **CLC 27; SSC 33**
See also CA 89-92; CANR 80; CWW 2; DLB 75; EWL 3; RGSF 2; RGWL 2, 3

Leon, David
See Jacob, (Cyprien-)Max

Leonard, Elmore (John, Jr.) 1925- . **CLC 28, 34, 71, 120**
See also AAYA 22, 59; AITN 1; BEST 89:1, 90:4; BPFB 2; CA 81-84; CANR 12, 28, 53, 76, 96, 133; CMW 4; CN 7; CPW; DA3; DAM POP; DLB 173, 226; INT CANR-28; MSW; MTCW 1, 2; RGAL 4; TCWW 2

Leonard, Hugh ................................ **CLC 19**
See Byrne, John Keyes
See also CBD; CD 5; DFS 13; DLB 13

Leonov, Leonid (Maximovich)
1899-1994 .................................. **CLC 92**
See Leonov, Leonid Maksimovich
See also CA 129; CANR 74, 76; DAM NOV; EWL 3; MTCW 1, 2

Leonov, Leonid Maksimovich
See Leonov, Leonid (Maximovich)
See also DLB 272

Leopardi, (Conte) Giacomo
1798-1837 ........... **NCLC 22, 129; PC 37**
See also EW 5; RGWL 2, 3; WP

Le Reveler
See Artaud, Antonin (Marie Joseph)

Lerman, Eleanor 1952- ...................... **CLC 9**
See also CA 85-88; CANR 69, 124

Lerman, Rhoda 1936- ...................... **CLC 56**
See also CA 49-52; CANR 70

Lermontov, Mikhail Iur'evich
See Lermontov, Mikhail Yuryevich
See also DLB 205

Lermontov, Mikhail Yuryevich
1814-1841 ....... **NCLC 5, 47, 126; PC 18**
See Lermontov, Mikhail Iur'evich
See also EW 6; RGWL 2, 3; TWA

Leroux, Gaston 1868-1927 ............... **TCLC 25**
See also CA 108; 136; CANR 69; CMW 4; NFS 20; SATA 65

Lesage, Alain-Rene 1668-1747 ........ **LC 2, 28**
See also EW 3; GFL Beginnings to 1789; RGWL 2, 3

Leskov, N(ikolai) S(emenovich) 1831-1895
See Leskov, Nikolai (Semyonovich)

Leskov, Nikolai (Semyonovich)
1831-1895 ................. **NCLC 25; SSC 34**
See Leskov, Nikolai Semenovich

Leskov, Nikolai Semenovich
See Leskov, Nikolai (Semyonovich)
See also DLB 238

Lesser, Milton
See Marlowe, Stephen

Lessing, Doris (May) 1919- ... **CLC 1, 2, 3, 6, 10, 15, 22, 40, 94, 170; SSC 6, 61; WLCS**
See also AAYA 57; AFW; BRWS 1; CA 9-12R; CAAS 14; CANR 33, 54, 76, 122; CD 5; CDBLB 1960 to Present; CN 7; DA; DA3; DAB; DAC; DAM MST, NOV; DFS 20; DLB 15, 139; DLBY 1985; EWL 3; EXPS; FW; LAIT 4; MTCW 1, 2; RGEL 2; RGSF 2; SFW 4; SSFS 1, 12, 20; TEA; WLIT 2, 4

Lessing, Gotthold Ephraim
1729-1781 ........................... **DC 26; LC 8**
See also CDWLB 2; DLB 97; EW 4; RGWL 2, 3

Lester, Richard 1932- ...................... **CLC 20**

Levenson, Jay ................................. **CLC 70**

Lever, Charles (James)
1806-1872 .................................. **NCLC 23**
See also DLB 21; RGEL 2

Leverson, Ada Esther
1862(?)-1933(?) ........................ **TCLC 18**
See Elaine
See also CA 117; 202; DLB 153; RGEL 2

Levertov, Denise 1923-1997 .. **CLC 1, 2, 3, 5, 8, 15, 28, 66; PC 11**
See also AMWS 3; CA 1-4R, 178; 163; CAAE 178; CAAS 19; CANR 3, 29, 50, 108; CDALBS; CP 7; CWP; DAM POET; DLB 5, 165; EWL 3; EXPP; FW; INT CANR-29; MTCW 1, 2; PAB; PFS 7, 17; RGAL 4; TUS; WP

Levi, Carlo 1902-1975 ................... **TCLC 125**
See also CA 65-68; 53-56; CANR 10; EWL 3; RGWL 2, 3

Levi, Jonathan ................................ **CLC 76**
See also CA 197

Levi, Peter (Chad Tigar)
1931-2000 .................................. **CLC 41**
See also CA 5-8R; 187; CANR 34, 80; CP 7; DLB 40

Levi, Primo 1919-1987 ...... **CLC 37, 50; SSC 12; TCLC 109**
See also CA 13-16R; 122; CANR 12, 33, 61, 70, 132; DLB 177, 299; EWL 3; MTCW 1, 2; RGWL 2, 3

Levin, Ira 1929- ............................ **CLC 3, 6**
See also CA 21-24R; CANR 17, 44, 74; CMW 4; CN 7; CPW; DA3; DAM POP; HGG; MTCW 1, 2; SATA 66; SFW 4

Levin, Meyer 1905-1981 ..................... **CLC 7**
See also AITN 1; CA 9-12R; 104; CANR 15; DAM POP; DLB 9, 28; DLBY 1981; SATA 21; SATA-Obit 27

Levine, Norman 1924- ...................... **CLC 54**
See also CA 73-76; CAAS 23; CANR 14, 70; DLB 88

Levine, Philip 1928- .. **CLC 2, 4, 5, 9, 14, 33, 118; PC 22**
See also AMWS 5; CA 9-12R; CANR 9, 37, 52, 116; CP 7; DAM POET; DLB 5; EWL 3; PFS 8

Levinson, Deirdre 1931- ................... **CLC 49**
See also CA 73-76; CANR 70

Levi-Strauss, Claude 1908- ............... **CLC 38**
See also CA 1-4R; CANR 6, 32, 57; DLB 242; EWL 3; GFL 1789 to the Present; MTCW 1, 2; TWA

Levitin, Sonia (Wolff) 1934- ............. **CLC 17**
See also AAYA 13, 48; CA 29-32R; CANR 14, 32, 79; CLR 53; JRDA; MAICYA 1, 2; SAAS 2; SATA 4, 68, 119, 131; SATA-Essay 131; YAW

Levon, O. U.
See Kesey, Ken (Elton)

Levy, Amy 1861-1889 ..................... **NCLC 59**
See also DLB 156, 240

Lewes, George Henry 1817-1878 ... **NCLC 25**
See also DLB 55, 144

Lewis, Alun 1915-1944 ....... **SSC 40; TCLC 3**
See also BRW 7; CA 104; 188; DLB 20, 162; PAB; RGEL 2

Lewis, C. Day
See Day Lewis, C(ecil)

Lewis, C(live) S(taples) 1898-1963 .... **CLC 1, 3, 6, 14, 27, 124; WLC**
See also AAYA 3, 39; BPFB 2; BRWS 3; BYA 15, 16; CA 81-84; CANR 33, 71, 132; CDBLB 1945-1960; CLR 3, 27; CWRI 5; DA; DA3; DAB; DAC; DAM MST, NOV, POP; DLB 15, 100, 160, 255; EWL 3; FANT; JRDA; LMFS 2; MAICYA 1, 2; MTCW 1, 2; RGEL 2; SATA 13, 100; SCFW; SFW 4; SUFW 1; TEA; WCH; WYA; YAW

Lewis, Cecil Day
See Day Lewis, C(ecil)

Lewis, Janet 1899-1998 ................... **CLC 41**
See Winters, Janet Lewis
See also CA 9-12R; 172; CANR 29, 63; CAP 1; CN 7; DLBY 1987; RHW; TCWW 2

Lewis, Matthew Gregory
1775-1818 ........................ **NCLC 11, 62**
See also DLB 39, 158, 178; HGG; LMFS 1; RGEL 2; SUFW

Lewis, (Harry) Sinclair 1885-1951 . **TCLC 4, 13, 23, 39; WLC**
See also AMW; AMWC 1; BPFB 2; CA 104; 133; CANR 132; CDALB 1917-1929; DA; DA3; DAB; DAC; DAM MST, NOV; DLB 9, 102, 284; DLBD 1; EWL 3; LAIT 3; MTCW 1, 2; NFS 15, 19; RGAL 4; TUS

DAC; DAM MST, NOV, POP; DLB 2,
16, 28, 185, 278; DLBD 3; DLBY 1980,
1983; EWL 3; MTCW 1, 2; NFS 10;
RGAL 4; TUS

**Maillet, Antonine** 1929- ............. **CLC 54, 118**
See also CA 115; 120; CANR 46, 74, 77,
134; CCA 1; CWW 2; DAC; DLB 60;
INT CA-120; MTCW 2

**Maimonides** 1135-1204 .................. **CMLC 76**
See also DLB 115

**Mais, Roger** 1905-1955 ..................... **TCLC 8**
See also BW 1, 3; CA 105; 124; CANR 82;
CDWLB 3; DLB 125; EWL 3; MTCW 1;
RGEL 2

**Maistre, Joseph** 1753-1821 ............. **NCLC 37**
See also GFL 1789 to the Present

**Maitland, Frederic William**
1850-1906 ....................... **TCLC 65**

**Maitland, Sara (Louise)** 1950- ......... **CLC 49**
See also CA 69-72; CANR 13, 59; DLB
271; FW

**Major, Clarence** 1936- ... **BLC 2; CLC 3, 19,
48**
See also AFAW 2; BW 2, 3; CA 21-24R;
CAAS 6; CANR 13, 25, 53, 82; CN 7;
CP 7; CSW; DAM MULT; DLB 33; EWL
3; MSW

**Major, Kevin (Gerald)** 1949- ............ **CLC 26**
See also AAYA 16; CA 97-100; CANR 21,
38, 112; CLR 11; DAC; DLB 60; INT
CANR-21; JRDA; MAICYA 1, 2; MAIC-
YAS 1; SATA 32, 82, 134; WYA; YAW

**Maki, James**
See Ozu, Yasujiro

**Makine, Andrei** 1957- ...................... **CLC 198**
See also CA 176; CANR 103

**Malabaila, Damiano**
See Levi, Primo

**Malamud, Bernard** 1914-1986 .. **CLC 1, 2, 3,
5, 8, 9, 11, 18, 27, 44, 78, 85; SSC 15;
TCLC 129; WLC**
See also AAYA 16; AMWS 1; BPFB 2;
BYA 15; CA 5-8R; 118; CABS 1; CANR
28, 62, 114; CDALB 1941-1968; CPW;
DA; DA3; DAB; DAC; DAM MST, NOV,
POP; DLB 2, 28, 152; DLBY 1980, 1986;
EWL 3; EXPS; LAIT 4; LATS 1:1;
MTCW 1, 2; NFS 4, 9; RGAL 4; RGSF
2; SSFS 8, 13, 16; TUS

**Malan, Herman**
See Bosman, Herman Charles; Bosman,
Herman Charles

**Malaparte, Curzio** 1898-1957 ........ **TCLC 52**
See also DLB 264

**Malcolm, Dan**
See Silverberg, Robert

**Malcolm, Janet** 1934- ...................... **CLC 201**
See also CA 123; CANR 89; NCFS 1

**Malcolm X** .... **BLC 2; CLC 82, 117; WLCS**
See Little, Malcolm
See also LAIT 5; NCFS 3

**Malherbe, Francois de** 1555-1628 ......... **LC 5**
See also GFL Beginnings to 1789

**Mallarme, Stephane** 1842-1898 ...... **NCLC 4,
41; PC 4**
See also DAM POET; DLB 217; EW 7;
GFL 1789 to the Present; LMFS 2; RGWL
2, 3; TWA

**Mallet-Joris, Francoise** 1930- ........... **CLC 11**
See also CA 65-68; CANR 17; CWW 2;
DLB 83; EWL 3; GFL 1789 to the Present

**Malley, Ern**
See McAuley, James Phillip

**Mallon, Thomas** 1951- ..................... **CLC 172**
See also CA 110; CANR 29, 57, 92

**Mallowan, Agatha Christie**
See Christie, Agatha (Mary Clarissa)

**Maloff, Saul** 1922- ................................ **CLC 5**
See also CA 33-36R

**Malone, Louis**
See MacNeice, (Frederick) Louis

**Malone, Michael (Christopher)**
1942- ..................................... **CLC 43**
See also CA 77-80; CANR 14, 32, 57, 114

**Malory, Sir Thomas** 1410(?)-1471(?) . **LC 11,
88; WLCS**
See also BRW 1; BRWR 2; CDBLB Before
1660; DA; DAB; DAC; DAM MST; DLB
146; EFS 2; RGEL 2; SATA 59; SATA-
Brief 33; TEA; WLIT 3

**Malouf, (George Joseph) David**
1934- ................................... **CLC 28, 86**
See also CA 124; CANR 50, 76; CN 7; CP
7; DLB 289; EWL 3; MTCW 2

**Malraux, (Georges-)Andre**
1901-1976 .......... **CLC 1, 4, 9, 13, 15, 57**
See also BPFB 2; CA 21-22; 69-72; CANR
34, 58; CAP 2; DA3; DAM NOV; DLB
72; EW 12; EWL 3; GFL 1789 to the
Present; MTCW 1, 2; RGWL 2, 3; TWA

**Malthus, Thomas Robert**
1766-1834 .............................. **NCLC 145**
See also DLB 107, 158; RGEL 2

**Malzberg, Barry N(athaniel)** 1939- ... **CLC 7**
See also CA 61-64; CAAS 4; CANR 16;
CMW 4; DLB 8; SFW 4

**Mamet, David (Alan)** 1947- .. **CLC 9, 15, 34,
46, 91, 166; DC 4, 24**
See also AAYA 3, 60; AMWS 14; CA 81-
84; CABS 3; CANR 15, 41, 67, 72, 129;
CD 5; DA3; DAM DRAM; DFS 2, 3, 6,
12, 15; DLB 7; EWL 3; IDFW 4; MTCW
1, 2; RGAL 4

**Mamoulian, Rouben (Zachary)**
1897-1987 ................................. **CLC 16**
See also CA 25-28R; 124; CANR 85

**Mandelshtam, Osip**
See Mandelstam, Osip (Emilievich)
See also EW 10; EWL 3; RGWL 2, 3

**Mandelstam, Osip (Emilievich)**
1891(?)-1943(?) ........ **PC 14; TCLC 2, 6**
See Mandelshtam, Osip
See also CA 104; 150; MTCW 2; TWA

**Mander, (Mary) Jane** 1877-1949 ... **TCLC 31**
See also CA 162; RGEL 2

**Mandeville, Bernard** 1670-1733 .......... **LC 82**
See also DLB 101

**Mandeville, Sir John** fl. 1350- ...... **CMLC 19**
See also DLB 146

**Mandiargues, Andre Pieyre de** ....... **CLC 41**
See Pieyre de Mandiargues, Andre
See also DLB 83

**Mandrake, Ethel Belle**
See Thurman, Wallace (Henry)

**Mangan, James Clarence**
1803-1849 ................................. **NCLC 27**
See also RGEL 2

**Maniere, J.-E.**
See Giraudoux, Jean(-Hippolyte)

**Mankiewicz, Herman (Jacob)**
1897-1953 ............................... **TCLC 85**
See also CA 120; 169; DLB 26; IDFW 3, 4

**Manley, (Mary) Delariviere**
1672(?)-1724 ......................... **LC 1, 42**
See also DLB 39, 80; RGEL 2

**Mann, Abel**
See Creasey, John

**Mann, Emily** 1952- .............................. **DC 7**
See also CA 130; CAD; CANR 55; CD 5;
CWD; DLB 266

**Mann, (Luiz) Heinrich** 1871-1950 ... **TCLC 9**
See also CA 106; 164, 181; DLB 66, 118;
EW 8; EWL 3; RGWL 2, 3

**Mann, (Paul) Thomas** 1875-1955 . **SSC 5, 80,
82; TCLC 2, 8, 14, 21, 35, 44, 60, 168;
WLC**
See also BPFB 2; CA 104; 128; CANR 133;
CDWLB 2; DA; DA3; DAB; DAC; DAM
MST, NOV; DLB 66; EW 9; EWL 3; GLL
1; LATS 1:1; LMFS 1; MTCW 1, 2; NFS
17; RGSF 2; RGWL 2, 3; SSFS 4, 9;
TWA

**Mannheim, Karl** 1893-1947 .......... **TCLC 65**
See also CA 204

**Manning, David**
See Faust, Frederick (Schiller)
See also TCWW 2

**Manning, Frederic** 1882-1935 ........ **TCLC 25**
See also CA 124; 216; DLB 260

**Manning, Olivia** 1915-1980 ......... **CLC 5, 19**
See also CA 5-8R; 101; CANR 29; EWL 3;
FW; MTCW 1; RGEL 2

**Mano, D. Keith** 1942- ...................... **CLC 2, 10**
See also CA 25-28R; CAAS 6; CANR 26,
57; DLB 6

**Mansfield, Katherine** ....... **SSC 9, 23, 38, 81;
TCLC 2, 8, 39, 164; WLC**
See Beauchamp, Kathleen Mansfield
See also BPFB 2; BRW 7; DAB; DLB 162;
EWL 3; EXPS; FW; GLL 1; RGEL 2;
RGSF 2; SSFS 2, 8, 10, 11; WWE 1

**Manso, Peter** 1940- ........................... **CLC 39**
See also CA 29-32R; CANR 44

**Mantecon, Juan Jimenez**
See Jimenez (Mantecon), Juan Ramon

**Mantel, Hilary (Mary)** 1952- .......... **CLC 144**
See also CA 125; CANR 54, 101; CN 7;
DLB 271; RHW

**Manton, Peter**
See Creasey, John

**Man Without a Spleen, A**
See Chekhov, Anton (Pavlovich)

**Manzano, Juan Francisco**
1797(?)-1854 ........................ **NCLC 155**

**Manzoni, Alessandro** 1785-1873 ... **NCLC 29,
98**
See also EW 5; RGWL 2, 3; TWA

**Map, Walter** 1140-1209 ................. **CMLC 32**

**Mapu, Abraham (ben Jekutiel)**
1808-1867 ............................ **NCLC 18**

**Mara, Sally**
See Queneau, Raymond

**Maracle, Lee** 1950- ............................. **NNAL**
See also CA 149

**Marat, Jean Paul** 1743-1793 ............... **LC 10**

**Marcel, Gabriel Honore** 1889-1973 . **CLC 15**
See also CA 102; 45-48; EWL 3; MTCW 1,
2

**March, William** 1893-1954 ............. **TCLC 96**
See also CA 216

**Marchbanks, Samuel**
See Davies, (William) Robertson
See also CCA 1

**Marchi, Giacomo**
See Bassani, Giorgio

**Marcus Aurelius**
See Aurelius, Marcus
See also AW 2

**Marguerite**
See de Navarre, Marguerite

**Marguerite d'Angouleme**
See de Navarre, Marguerite
See also GFL Beginnings to 1789

**Marguerite de Navarre**
See de Navarre, Marguerite
See also RGWL 2, 3

**Margulies, Donald** 1954- .................. **CLC 76**
See also AAYA 57; CA 200; DFS 13; DLB
228

**Marie de France** c. 12th cent. - ..... **CMLC 8;
PC 22**
See also DLB 208; FW; RGWL 2, 3

Author Index

**McEwan, Ian (Russell)** 1948- .... **CLC 13, 66, 169**
See also BEST 90:4; BRWS 4; CA 61-64; CANR 14, 41, 69, 87, 132; CN 7; DAM NOV; DLB 14, 194; HGG; MTCW 1, 2; RGSF 2; SUFW; TEA

**McFadden, David** 1940- .................... **CLC 48**
See also CA 104; CP 7; DLB 60; INT CA-104

**McFarland, Dennis** 1950- ................. **CLC 65**
See also CA 165; CANR 110

**McGahern, John** 1934- ... **CLC 5, 9, 48, 156; SSC 17**
See also CA 17-20R; CANR 29, 68, 113; CN 7; DLB 14, 231; MTCW 1

**McGinley, Patrick (Anthony)** 1937- . **CLC 41**
See also CA 120; 127; CANR 56; INT CA-127

**McGinley, Phyllis** 1905-1978 ............ **CLC 14**
See also CA 9-12R; 77-80; CANR 19; CWRI 5; DLB 11, 48; PFS 9, 13; SATA 2, 44; SATA-Obit 24

**McGinniss, Joe** 1942- ........................ **CLC 32**
See also AITN 2; BEST 89:2; CA 25-28R; CANR 26, 70; CPW; DLB 185; INT CANR-26

**McGivern, Maureen Daly**
See Daly, Maureen

**McGrath, Patrick** 1950- .................... **CLC 55**
See also CA 136; CANR 65; CN 7; DLB 231; HGG; SUFW 2

**McGrath, Thomas (Matthew)**
1916-1990 ........................ **CLC 28, 59**
See also AMWS 10; CA 9-12R; 132; CANR 6, 33, 95; DAM POET; MTCW 1; SATA 41; SATA-Obit 66

**McGuane, Thomas (Francis III)**
1939- ............ **CLC 3, 7, 18, 45, 127**
See also AITN 2; BPFB 2; CA 49-52; CANR 5, 24, 49, 94; CN 7; DLB 2, 212; DLBY 1980; EWL 3; INT CANR-24; MTCW 1; TCWW 2

**McGuckian, Medbh** 1950- ....... **CLC 48, 174; PC 27**
See also BRWS 5; CA 143; CP 7; CWP; DAM POET; DLB 40

**McHale, Tom** 1942(?)-1982 ............. **CLC 3, 5**
See also AITN 1; CA 77-80; 106

**McHugh, Heather** 1948- ....................... **PC 61**
See also CA 69-72; CANR 11, 28, 55, 92; CP 7; CWP

**McIlvanney, William** 1936- ............... **CLC 42**
See also CA 25-28R; CANR 61; CMW 4; DLB 14, 207

**McIlwraith, Maureen Mollie Hunter**
See Hunter, Mollie
See also SATA 2

**McInerney, Jay** 1955- ................ **CLC 34, 112**
See also AAYA 18; BPFB 2; CA 116; 123; CANR 45, 68, 116; CN 7; CPW; DA3; DAM POP; DLB 292; INT CA-123; MTCW 2

**McIntyre, Vonda N(eel)** 1948- .......... **CLC 18**
See also CA 81-84; CANR 17, 34, 69; MTCW 1; SFW 4; YAW

**McKay, Claude** .......... **BLC 3; HR 3; PC 2; TCLC 7, 41; WLC**
See McKay, Festus Claudius
See also AFAW 1, 2; AMWS 10; DAB; DLB 4, 45, 51, 117; EWL 3; EXPP; GLL 2; LAIT 3; LMFS 2; PAB; PFS 4; RGAL 4; WP

**McKay, Festus Claudius** 1889-1948
See McKay, Claude
See also BW 1, 3; CA 104; 124; CANR 73; DA; DAC; DAM MST, MULT, NOV, POET; MTCW 1, 2; TUS

**McKuen, Rod** 1933- ........................ **CLC 1, 3**
See also AITN 1; CA 41-44R; CANR 40

**McLoughlin, R. B.**
See Mencken, H(enry) L(ouis)

**McLuhan, (Herbert) Marshall**
1911-1980 .......................... **CLC 37, 83**
See also CA 9-12R; 102; CANR 12, 34, 61; DLB 88; INT CANR-12; MTCW 1, 2

**McManus, Declan Patrick Aloysius**
See Costello, Elvis

**McMillan, Terry (L.)** 1951- . **BLCS; CLC 50, 61, 112**
See also AAYA 21; AMWS 13; BPFB 2; BW 2, 3; CA 140; CANR 60, 104, 131; CPW; DA3; DAM MULT, NOV, POP; MTCW 2; RGAL 4; YAW

**McMurtry, Larry (Jeff)** 1936- .. **CLC 2, 3, 7, 11, 27, 44, 127**
See also AAYA 15; AITN 2; AMWS 5; BEST 89:2; BPFB 2; CA 5-8R; CANR 19, 43, 64, 103; CDALB 1968-1988; CN 7; CPW; CSW; DA3; DAM NOV, POP; DLB 2, 143, 256; DLBY 1980, 1987; EWL 3; MTCW 1, 2; RGAL 4; TCWW 2

**McNally, T. M.** 1961- ........................ **CLC 82**

**McNally, Terrence** 1939- .... **CLC 4, 7, 41, 91**
See also AMWS 13; CA 45-48; CAD; CANR 2, 56, 116; CD 5; DA3; DAM DRAM; DFS 16, 19; DLB 7, 249; EWL 3; GLL 1; MTCW 2

**McNamer, Deirdre** 1950- .................. **CLC 70**

**McNeal, Tom** ................................ **CLC 119**

**McNeile, Herman Cyril** 1888-1937
See Sapper
See also CA 184; CMW 4; DLB 77

**McNickle, (William) D'Arcy**
1904-1977 ...................... **CLC 89; NNAL**
See also CA 9-12R; 85-88; CANR 5, 45; DAM MULT; DLB 175, 212; RGAL 4; SATA-Obit 22

**McPhee, John (Angus)** 1931- ........... **CLC 36**
See also AMWS 3; ANW; BEST 90:1; CA 65-68; CANR 20, 46, 64, 69, 121; CPW; DLB 185, 275; MTCW 1, 2; TUS

**McPherson, James Alan** 1943- . **BLCS; CLC 19, 77**
See also BW 1, 3; CA 25-28R; CAAS 17; CANR 24, 74; CN 7; CSW; DLB 38, 244; EWL 3; MTCW 1, 2; RGAL 4; RGSF 2

**McPherson, William (Alexander)**
1933- .......................................... **CLC 34**
See also CA 69-72; CANR 28; INT CANR-28

**McTaggart, J. McT. Ellis**
See McTaggart, John McTaggart Ellis

**McTaggart, John McTaggart Ellis**
1866-1925 ............................. **TCLC 105**
See also CA 120; DLB 262

**Mead, George Herbert** 1863-1931 . **TCLC 89**
See also CA 212; DLB 270

**Mead, Margaret** 1901-1978 .............. **CLC 37**
See also AITN 1; CA 1-4R; 81-84; CANR 4; DA3; FW; MTCW 1, 2; SATA-Obit 20

**Meaker, Marijane (Agnes)** 1927-
See Kerr, M. E.
See also CA 107; CANR 37, 63; INT CA-107; JRDA; MAICYA 1, 2; MAICYAS 1; MTCW 1; SATA 20, 61, 99; SATA-Essay 111; YAW

**Medoff, Mark (Howard)** 1940- .... **CLC 6, 23**
See also AITN 1; CA 53-56; CAD; CANR 5; CD 5; DAM DRAM; DFS 4; DLB 7; INT CANR-5

**Medvedev, P. N.**
See Bakhtin, Mikhail Mikhailovich

**Meged, Aharon**
See Megged, Aharon

**Meged, Aron**
See Megged, Aharon

**Megged, Aharon**
See Megged, Aharon

**Megged, Aharon** 1920- ....................... **CLC 9**
See also CA 49-52; CAAS 13; CANR 1; EWL 3

**Mehta, Deepa** 1950- ........................ **CLC 208**

**Mehta, Gita** 1943- ........................... **CLC 179**
See also CA 225; DNFS 2

**Mehta, Ved (Parkash)** 1934- ............ **CLC 37**
See also CA 1-4R; 212; CAAE 212; CANR 2, 23, 69; MTCW 1

**Melanchthon, Philipp** 1497-1560 ......... **LC 90**
See also DLB 179

**Melanter**
See Blackmore, R(ichard) D(oddridge)

**Meleager** c. 140B.C.-c. 70B.C. ...... **CMLC 53**

**Melies, Georges** 1861-1938 ............. **TCLC 81**

**Melikow, Loris**
See Hofmannsthal, Hugo von

**Melmoth, Sebastian**
See Wilde, Oscar (Fingal O'Flahertie Wills)

**Melo Neto, Joao Cabral de**
See Cabral de Melo Neto, Joao
See also CWW 2; EWL 3

**Meltzer, Milton** 1915- ...................... **CLC 26**
See also AAYA 8, 45; BYA 2, 6; CA 13-16R; CANR 38, 92, 107; CLR 13; DLB 61; JRDA; MAICYA 1, 2; SAAS 1; SATA 1, 50, 80, 128; SATA-Essay 124; WYA; YAW

**Melville, Herman** 1819-1891 ..... **NCLC 3, 12, 29, 45, 49, 91, 93, 123, 157; SSC 1, 17, 46; WLC**
See also AAYA 25; AMW; AMWR 1; CDALB 1640-1865; DA; DA3; DAB; DAC; DAM MST, NOV; DLB 3, 74, 250, 254; EXPN; EXPS; LAIT 1, 2; NFS 7, 9; RGAL 4; RGSF 2; SATA 59; SSFS 3; TUS

**Members, Mark**
See Powell, Anthony (Dymoke)

**Membreno, Alejandro** ..................... **CLC 59**

**Menand, Louis** 1952- ....................... **CLC 208**
See also CA 200

**Menander** c. 342B.C.-c. 293B.C. .... **CMLC 9, 51; DC 3**
See also AW 1; CDWLB 1; DAM DRAM; DLB 176; LMFS 1; RGWL 2, 3

**Menchu, Rigoberta** 1959- .. **CLC 160; HLCS 2**
See also CA 175; DNFS 1; WLIT 1

**Mencken, H(enry) L(ouis)**
1880-1956 ................................. **TCLC 13**
See also AMW; CA 105; 125; CDALB 1917-1929; DLB 11, 29, 63, 137, 222; EWL 3; MTCW 1, 2; NCFS 4; RGAL 4; TUS

**Mendelsohn, Jane** 1965- ................... **CLC 99**
See also CA 154; CANR 94

**Menton, Francisco de**
See Chin, Frank (Chew, Jr.)

**Mercer, David** 1928-1980 ................... **CLC 5**
See also CA 9-12R; 102; CANR 23; CBD; DAM DRAM; DLB 13; MTCW 1; RGEL 2

**Merchant, Paul**
See Ellison, Harlan (Jay)

**Meredith, George** 1828-1909 .. **PC 60; TCLC 17, 43**
See also CA 117; 153; CANR 80; CDBLB 1832-1890; DAM POET; DLB 18, 35, 57, 159; RGEL 2; TEA

**Meredith, William (Morris)** 1919- .... **CLC 4, 13, 22, 55; PC 28**
See also CA 9-12R; CAAS 14; CANR 6, 40, 129; CP 7; DAM POET; DLB 5

**Merezhkovsky, Dmitrii Sergeevich**
See Merezhkovsky, Dmitry Sergeyevich
See also DLB 295

**Merezhkovsky, Dmitry Sergeevich**
See Merezhkovsky, Dmitry Sergeyevich
See also EWL 3

**Merezhkovsky, Dmitry Sergeyevich**
1865-1941 ................................. **TCLC 29**
See also Merezhkovsky, Dmitrii Sergeevich;
Merezhkovsky, Dmitry Sergeyevich
See also CA 169

**Merimee, Prosper** 1803-1870 ... **NCLC 6, 65;
SSC 7, 77**
See also DLB 119, 192; EW 6; EXPS; GFL
1789 to the Present; RGSF 2; RGWL 2,
3; SSFS 8; SUFW

**Merkin, Daphne** 1954- ...................... **CLC 44**
See also CA 123

**Merleau-Ponty, Maurice**
1908-1961 ................................. **TCLC 156**
See also CA 114; 89-92; DLB 296; GFL
1789 to the Present

**Merlin, Arthur**
See Blish, James (Benjamin)

**Mernissi, Fatima** 1940- .................... **CLC 171**
See also CA 152; FW

**Merrill, James (Ingram)** 1926-1995 .. **CLC 2,
3, 6, 8, 13, 18, 34, 91; PC 28**
See also AMWS 3; CA 13-16R; 147; CANR
10, 49, 63, 108; DA3; DAM POET; DLB
5, 165; DLBY 1985; EWL 3; INT CANR-
10; MTCW 1, 2; PAB; RGAL 4

**Merriman, Alex**
See Silverberg, Robert

**Merriman, Brian** 1747-1805 .......... **NCLC 70**

**Merritt, E. B.**
See Waddington, Miriam

**Merton, Thomas**
1915-1968 . **CLC 1, 3, 11, 34, 83; PC 10**
See also AMWS 8; CA 5-8R; 25-28R;
CANR 22, 53, 111, 131; DA3; DLB 48;
DLBY 1981; MTCW 1, 2

**Merwin, W(illiam) S(tanley)** 1927- ... **CLC 1,
2, 3, 5, 8, 13, 18, 45, 88; PC 45**
See also AMWS 3; CA 13-16R; CANR 15,
51, 112; CP 7; DA3; DAM POET; DLB
5, 169; EWL 3; INT CANR-15; MTCW
1, 2; PAB; PFS 5, 15; RGAL 4

**Metastasio, Pietro** 1698-1782 ............. **LC 115**
See also RGWL 2, 3

**Metcalf, John** 1938- ............ **CLC 37; SSC 43**
See also CA 113; CN 7; DLB 60; RGSF 2;
TWA

**Metcalf, Suzanne**
See Baum, L(yman) Frank

**Mew, Charlotte (Mary)** 1870-1928 .. **TCLC 8**
See also CA 105; 189; DLB 19, 135; RGEL
2

**Mewshaw, Michael** 1943- ................... **CLC 9**
See also CA 53-56; CANR 7, 47; DLBY
1980

**Meyer, Conrad Ferdinand**
1825-1898 ................. **NCLC 81; SSC 30**
See also DLB 129; EW; RGWL 2, 3

**Meyer, Gustav** 1868-1932
See Meyrink, Gustav
See also CA 117; 190

**Meyer, June**
See Jordan, June (Meyer)

**Meyer, Lynn**
See Slavitt, David R(ytman)

**Meyers, Jeffrey** 1939- ........................ **CLC 39**
See also CA 73-76, 186; CAAE 186; CANR
54, 102; DLB 111

**Meynell, Alice (Christina Gertrude
Thompson)** 1847-1922 ............. **TCLC 6**
See also CA 104; 177; DLB 19, 98; RGEL
2

**Meyrink, Gustav** ........................... **TCLC 21**
See Meyer, Gustav
See also DLB 81; EWL 3

**Michaels, Leonard** 1933-2003 ..... **CLC 6, 25;
SSC 16**
See also CA 61-64; 216; CANR 21, 62, 119;
CN 7; DLB 130; MTCW 1

**Michaux, Henri** 1899-1984 .......... **CLC 8, 19**
See also CA 85-88; 114; DLB 258; EWL 3;
GFL 1789 to the Present; RGWL 2, 3

**Micheaux, Oscar (Devereaux)**
1884-1951 ................................. **TCLC 76**
See also BW 3; CA 174; DLB 50; TCWW
2

**Michelangelo** 1475-1564 ...................... **LC 12**
See also AAYA 43

**Michelet, Jules** 1798-1874 .............. **NCLC 31**
See also EW 5; GFL 1789 to the Present

**Michels, Robert** 1876-1936 ............ **TCLC 88**
See also CA 212

**Michener, James A(lbert)**
1907(?)-1997 .... **CLC 1, 5, 11, 29, 60, 109**
See also AAYA 27; AITN 1; BEST 90:1;
BPFB 2; CA 5-8R; 161; CANR 21, 45,
68; CN 7; CPW; DA3; DAM NOV, POP;
DLB 6; MTCW 1, 2; RHW

**Mickiewicz, Adam** 1798-1855 . **NCLC 3, 101;
PC 38**
See also EW 5; RGWL 2, 3

**Middleton, (John) Christopher**
1926- ......................................... **CLC 13**
See also CA 13-16R; CANR 29, 54, 117;
CP 7; DLB 40

**Middleton, Richard (Barham)**
1882-1911 ................................. **TCLC 56**
See also CA 187; DLB 156; HGG

**Middleton, Stanley** 1919- .............. **CLC 7, 38**
See also CA 25-28R; CAAS 23; CANR 21,
46, 81; CN 7; DLB 14

**Middleton, Thomas** 1580-1627 ...... **DC 5; LC
33**
See also BRW 2; DAM DRAM, MST; DFS
18; DLB 58; RGEL 2

**Migueis, Jose Rodrigues** 1901-1980 . **CLC 10**
See also DLB 287

**Mikszath, Kalman** 1847-1910 ........ **TCLC 31**
See also CA 170

**Miles, Jack** ...................................... **CLC 100**
See also CA 200

**Miles, John Russiano**
See Miles, Jack

**Miles, Josephine (Louise)**
1911-1985 .............. **CLC 1, 2, 14, 34, 39**
See also CA 1-4R; 116; CANR 2, 55; DAM
POET; DLB 48

**Militant**
See Sandburg, Carl (August)

**Mill, Harriet (Hardy) Taylor**
1807-1858 ............................... **NCLC 102**
See also FW

**Mill, John Stuart** 1806-1873 .... **NCLC 11, 58**
See also CDBLB 1832-1890; DLB 55, 190,
262; FW 1; RGEL 2; TEA

**Millar, Kenneth** 1915-1983 ................ **CLC 14**
See Macdonald, Ross
See also CA 9-12R; 110; CANR 16, 63,
107; CMW 4; CPW; DA3; DAM POP;
DLB 2, 226; DLBD 6; DLBY 1983;
MTCW 1, 2

**Millay, E. Vincent**
See Millay, Edna St. Vincent

**Millay, Edna St. Vincent** 1892-1950 ..... **PC 6,
61; TCLC 4, 49; WLCS**
See Boyd, Nancy
See also AMW; CA 104; 130; CDALB
1917-1929; DA; DA3; DAB; DAC; DAM
MST, POET; DLB 45, 249; EWL 3;
EXPP; MAWW; MTCW 1, 2; PAB; PFS
3, 17; RGAL 4; TUS; WP

**Miller, Arthur** 1915- ...... **CLC 1, 2, 6, 10, 15,
26, 47, 78, 179; DC 1; WLC**
See also AAYA 15; AITN 1; AMW; AMWC
1; CA 1-4R; CABS 3; CAD; CANR 2,
30, 54, 76, 132; CD 5; CDALB 1941-
1968; DA; DA3; DAB; DAC; DAM
DRAM, MST; DFS 1, 3, 8; DLB 7, 266;
EWL 3; LAIT 1, 4; LATS 1:2; MTCW 1,
2; RGAL 4; TUS; WYAS 1

**Miller, Henry (Valentine)**
1891-1980 .... **CLC 1, 2, 4, 9, 14, 43, 84;
WLC**
See also AMW; BPFB 2; CA 9-12R; 97-
100; CANR 33, 64; CDALB 1929-1941;
DA; DA3; DAB; DAC; DAM MST, NOV;
DLB 4, 9; DLBY 1980; EWL 3; MTCW
1, 2; RGAL 4; TUS

**Miller, Hugh** 1802-1856 ................ **NCLC 143**
See also DLB 190

**Miller, Jason** 1939(?)-2001 ................... **CLC 2**
See also AITN 1; CA 73-76; 197; CAD;
CANR 130; DFS 12; DLB 7

**Miller, Sue** 1943- .............................. **CLC 44**
See also AMWS 12; BEST 90:3; CA 139;
CANR 59, 91, 128; DA3; DAM POP;
DLB 143

**Miller, Walter M(ichael, Jr.)**
1923-1996 ................................. **CLC 4, 30**
See also BPFB 2; CA 85-88; CANR 108;
DLB 8; SCFW; SFW 4

**Millett, Kate** 1934- ............................ **CLC 67**
See also AITN 1; CA 73-76; CANR 32, 53,
76, 110; DA3; DLB 246; FW; GLL 1;
MTCW 1, 2

**Millhauser, Steven (Lewis)** 1943- .... **CLC 21,
54, 109; SSC 57**
See also CA 110; 111; CANR 63, 114, 133;
CN 7; DA3; DLB 2; FANT; INT CA-111;
MTCW 2

**Millin, Sarah Gertrude** 1889-1968 ... **CLC 49**
See also CA 102; 93-96; DLB 225; EWL 3

**Milne, A(lan) A(lexander)**
1882-1956 ......................... **TCLC 6, 88**
See also BRWS 5; CA 104; 133; CLR 1,
26; CMW 4; CWRI 5; DA3; DAB; DAC;
DAM MST; DLB 10, 77, 100, 160; FANT;
MAICYA 1, 2; MTCW 1, 2; RGEL 2;
SATA 100; WCH; YABC 1

**Milner, Ron(ald)** 1938-2004 ..... **BLC 3; CLC
56**
See also AITN 1; BW 1; CA 73-76; CAD;
CANR 24, 81; CD 5; DAM MULT; DLB
38; MTCW 1

**Milnes, Richard Monckton**
1809-1885 ............................... **NCLC 61**
See also DLB 32, 184

**Milosz, Czeslaw** 1911- .... **CLC 5, 11, 22, 31,
56, 82; PC 8; WLCS**
See also CA 81-84; CANR 23, 51, 91, 126;
CDWLB 4; CWW 2; DA3; DAM MST,
POET; DLB 215; EW 13; EWL 3; MTCW
1, 2; PFS 16; RGWL 2, 3

**Milton, John** 1608-1674 ..... **LC 9, 43, 92; PC
19, 29; WLC**
See also BRW 2; BRWR 2; CDBLB 1660-
1789; DA; DA3; DAB; DAC; DAM MST,
POET; DLB 131, 151, 281; EFS 1; EXPP;
LAIT 1; PAB; PFS 3, 17; RGEL 2; TEA;
WLIT 3; WP

**Min, Anchee** 1957- ............................ **CLC 86**
See also CA 146; CANR 94

**Minehaha, Cornelius**
See Wedekind, (Benjamin) Frank(lin)

**Miner, Valerie** 1947- ......................... **CLC 40**
See also CA 97-100; CANR 59; FW; GLL
2

**Minimo, Duca**
See D'Annunzio, Gabriele

**Moore, George Augustus**
1852-1933 .................... **SSC 19; TCLC 7**
See also BRW 6; CA 104; 177; DLB 10,
18, 57, 135; EWL 3; RGEL 2; RGSF 2

**Moore, Lorrie** ........................ **CLC 39, 45, 68**
See Moore, Marie Lorena
See also AMWS 10; DLB 234; SSFS 19

**Moore, Marianne (Craig)**
1887-1972 .... **CLC 1, 2, 4, 8, 10, 13, 19,
47; PC 4, 49; WLCS**
See also AMW; CA 1-4R; 33-36R; CANR
3, 61; CDALB 1929-1941; DA; DA3;
DAB; DAC; DAM MST, POET; DLB 45;
DLBD 7; EWL 3; EXPP; MAWW;
MTCW 1, 2; PAB; PFS 14, 17; RGAL 4;
SATA 20; TUS; WP

**Moore, Marie Lorena** 1957- .......... **CLC 165**
See Moore, Lorrie
See also CA 116; CANR 39, 83; CN 7; DLB
234

**Moore, Thomas** 1779-1852 ....... **NCLC 6, 110**
See also DLB 96, 144; RGEL 2

**Moorhouse, Frank** 1938- ..................... **SSC 40**
See also CA 118; CANR 92; CN 7; DLB
289; RGSF 2

**Mora, Pat(ricia)** 1942- ....................... **HLC 2**
See also AMWS 13; CA 129; CANR 57,
81, 112; CLR 58; DAM MULT; DLB 209;
HW 1, 2; LLW 1; MAICYA 2; SATA 92,
134

**Moraga, Cherríe** 1952- ...... **CLC 126; DC 22**
See also CA 131; CANR 66; DAM MULT;
DLB 82, 249; FW; GLL 1; HW 1, 2; LLW
1

**Morand, Paul** 1888-1976 .... **CLC 41; SSC 22**
See also CA 184; 69-72; DLB 65; EWL 3

**Morante, Elsa** 1918-1985 .............. **CLC 8, 47**
See also CA 85-88; 117; CANR 35; DLB
177; EWL 3; MTCW 1, 2; RGWL 2, 3

**Moravia, Alberto** ........ **CLC 2, 7, 11, 27, 46;
SSC 26**
See Pincherle, Alberto
See also DLB 177; EW 12; EWL 3; MTCW
2; RGSF 2; RGWL 2, 3

**More, Hannah** 1745-1833 ...... **NCLC 27, 141**
See also DLB 107, 109, 116, 158; RGEL 2

**More, Henry** 1614-1687 ......................... **LC 9**
See also DLB 126, 252

**More, Sir Thomas** 1478(?)-1535 .... **LC 10, 32**
See also BRWC 1; BRWS 7; DLB 136, 281;
LMFS 1; RGEL 2; TEA

**Moreas, Jean** ................................... **TCLC 18**
See Papadiamantopoulos, Johannes
See also GFL 1789 to the Present

**Moreton, Andrew Esq.**
See Defoe, Daniel

**Morgan, Berry** 1919-2002 ................... **CLC 6**
See also CA 49-52; 208; DLB 6

**Morgan, Claire**
See Highsmith, (Mary) Patricia
See also GLL 1

**Morgan, Edwin (George)** 1920- ....... **CLC 31**
See also BRWS 9; CA 5-8R; CANR 3, 43,
90; CP 7; DLB 27

**Morgan, (George) Frederick**
1922-2004 ................................... **CLC 23**
See also CA 17-20R; 224; CANR 21; CP 7

**Morgan, Harriet**
See Mencken, H(enry) L(ouis)

**Morgan, Jane**
See Cooper, James Fenimore

**Morgan, Janet** 1945- ......................... **CLC 39**
See also CA 65-68

**Morgan, Lady** 1776(?)-1859 .......... **NCLC 29**
See also DLB 116, 158; RGEL 2

**Morgan, Robin (Evonne)** 1941- .......... **CLC 2**
See also CA 69-72; CANR 29, 68; FW;
GLL 2; MTCW 1; SATA 80

**Morgan, Scott**
See Kuttner, Henry

**Morgan, Seth** 1949(?)-1990 ............... **CLC 65**
See also CA 185; 132

**Morgenstern, Christian (Otto Josef
Wolfgang)** 1871-1914 ................ **TCLC 8**
See also CA 105; 191; EWL 3

**Morgenstern, S.**
See Goldman, William (W.)

**Mori, Rintaro**
See Mori Ogai
See also CA 110

**Mori, Toshio** 1910-1980 ..................... **SSC 83**
See also AAL; CA 116; DLB 312; RGSF 2

**Moricz, Zsigmond** 1879-1942 ......... **TCLC 33**
See also CA 165; DLB 215; EWL 3

**Morike, Eduard (Friedrich)**
1804-1875 ............................... **NCLC 10**
See also DLB 133; RGWL 2, 3

**Mori Ogai** 1862-1922 ...................... **TCLC 14**
See Ogai
See also CA 164; DLB 180; EWL 3; RGWL
3; TWA

**Moritz, Karl Philipp** 1756-1793 ........ **LC 2**
See also DLB 94

**Morland, Peter Henry**
See Faust, Frederick (Schiller)

**Morley, Christopher (Darlington)**
1890-1957 ................................ **TCLC 87**
See also CA 112; 213; DLB 9; RGAL 4

**Morren, Theophil**
See Hofmannsthal, Hugo von

**Morris, Bill** 1952- ................................ **CLC 76**
See also CA 225

**Morris, Julian**
See West, Morris L(anglo)

**Morris, Steveland Judkins** 1950(?)-
See Wonder, Stevie
See also CA 111

**Morris, William** 1834-1896 . **NCLC 4; PC 55**
See also BRW 5; CDBLB 1832-1890; DLB
18, 35, 57, 156, 178, 184; FANT; RGEL
2; SFW 4; SUFW

**Morris, Wright** 1910-1998 .. **CLC 1, 3, 7, 18,
37; TCLC 107**
See also AMW; CA 9-12R; 167; CANR 21,
81; CN 7; DLB 2, 206, 218; DLBY 1981;
EWL 3; MTCW 1, 2; RGAL 4; TCWW 2

**Morrison, Arthur** 1863-1945 ........... **SSC 40;
TCLC 72**
See also CA 120; 157; CMW 4; DLB 70,
135, 197; RGEL 2

**Morrison, Chloe Anthony Wofford**
See Morrison, Toni

**Morrison, James Douglas** 1943-1971
See Morrison, Jim
See also CA 73-76; CANR 40

**Morrison, Jim** ................................... **CLC 17**
See Morrison, James Douglas

**Morrison, Toni** 1931- ..... **BLC 3; CLC 4, 10,
22, 55, 81, 87, 173, 194**
See also AAYA 1, 22; AFAW 1, 2; AMWC
1; AMWS 3; BPFB 2; BW 2, 3; CA 29-
32R; CANR 27, 42, 67, 113, 124; CDALB
1968-1988; CLR 99; CN 7; CPW; DA;
DA3; DAB; DAC; DAM MST, MULT,
NOV, POP; DLB 6, 33, 143; DLBY 1981;
EWL 3; EXPN; FW; LAIT 2, 4; LATS
1:2; LMFS 2; MAWW; MTCW 1, 2; NFS
1, 6, 8, 14; RGAL 4; RHW; SATA 57,
144; SSFS 5; TUS; YAW

**Morrison, Van** 1945- ......................... **CLC 21**
See also CA 116; 168

**Morrissy, Mary** 1957- ....................... **CLC 99**
See also CA 205; DLB 267

**Mortimer, John (Clifford)** 1923- ..... **CLC 28,
43**
See also CA 13-16R; CANR 21, 69, 109;
CD 5; CDBLB 1960 to Present; CMW 4;
CN 7; CPW; DA3; DAM DRAM, POP;
DLB 13, 245, 271; INT CANR-21; MSW;
MTCW 1, 2; RGEL 2

**Mortimer, Penelope (Ruth)**
1918-1999 ................................... **CLC 5**
See also CA 57-60; 187; CANR 45, 88; CN
7

**Mortimer, Sir John**
See Mortimer, John (Clifford)

**Morton, Anthony**
See Creasey, John

**Morton, Thomas** 1579(?)-1647(?) ........ **LC 72**
See also DLB 24; RGEL 2

**Mosca, Gaetano** 1858-1941 ............. **TCLC 75**

**Moses, Daniel David** 1952- ................. **NNAL**
See also CA 186

**Mosher, Howard Frank** 1943- ......... **CLC 62**
See also CA 139; CANR 65, 115

**Mosley, Nicholas** 1923- ............... **CLC 43, 70**
See also CA 69-72; CANR 41, 60, 108; CN
7; DLB 14, 207

**Mosley, Walter** 1952- .... **BLCS; CLC 97, 184**
See also AAYA 57; AMWS 13; BPFB 2;
BW 2; CA 142; CANR 57, 92; CMW 4;
CPW; DA3; DAM MULT, POP; DLB
306; MSW; MTCW 2

**Moss, Howard** 1922-1987 . **CLC 7, 14, 45, 50**
See also CA 1-4R; 123; CANR 1, 44; DAM
POET; DLB 5

**Mossgiel, Rab**
See Burns, Robert

**Motion, Andrew (Peter)** 1952- .......... **CLC 47**
See also BRWS 7; CA 146; CANR 90; CP
7; DLB 40

**Motley, Willard (Francis)**
1909-1965 ................................... **CLC 18**
See also BW 1; CA 117; 106; CANR 88;
DLB 76, 143

**Motoori, Norinaga** 1730-1801 ........ **NCLC 45**

**Mott, Michael (Charles Alston)**
1930- ................................... **CLC 15, 34**
See also CA 5-8R; CAAS 7; CANR 7, 29

**Mountain Wolf Woman** 1884-1960 . **CLC 92;
NNAL**
See also CA 144; CANR 90

**Moure, Erin** 1955- ............................... **CLC 88**
See also CA 113; CP 7; CWP; DLB 60

**Mourning Dove** 1885(?)-1936 ............. **NNAL**
See also CA 144; CANR 90; DAM MULT;
DLB 175, 221

**Mowat, Farley (McGill)** 1921- .......... **CLC 26**
See also AAYA 1, 50; BYA 2; CA 1-4R;
CANR 4, 24, 42, 68, 108; CLR 20; CPW;
DAC; DAM MST; DLB 68; INT CANR-
24; JRDA; MAICYA 1, 2; MTCW 1, 2;
SATA 3, 55; YAW

**Mowatt, Anna Cora** 1819-1870 ..... **NCLC 74**
See also RGAL 4

**Moyers, Bill** 1934- ............................. **CLC 74**
See also AITN 2; CA 61-64; CANR 31, 52

**Mphahlele, Es'kia**
See Mphahlele, Ezekiel
See also AFW; CDWLB 3; DLB 125, 225;
RGSF 2; SSFS 11

**Mphahlele, Ezekiel** 1919- ... **BLC 3; CLC 25,
133**
See Mphahlele, Es'kia
See also BW 2, 3; CA 81-84; CANR 26,
76; CN 7; DA3; DAM MULT; EWL 3;
MTCW 2; SATA 119

**Mqhayi, S(amuel) E(dward) K(rune Loliwe)**
1875-1945 ....................... **BLC 3; TCLC 25**
See also CA 153; CANR 87; DAM MULT

**Natti, (Mary) Lee** 1919-
   See Kingman, Lee
   See also CA 5-8R; CANR 2
**Navarre, Marguerite de**
   See de Navarre, Marguerite
**Naylor, Gloria** 1950- ..... **BLC 3; CLC 28, 52, 156; WLCS**
   See also AAYA 6, 39; AFAW 1, 2; AMWS 8; BW 2, 3; CA 107; CANR 27, 51, 74, 130; CN 7; CPW; DA; DA3; DAC; DAM MST, MULT, NOV, POP; DLB 173; EWL 3; FW; MTCW 1, 2; NFS 4, 7; RGAL 4; TUS
**Neff, Debra** ........................... **CLC 59**
**Neihardt, John Gneisenau**
   1881-1973 ........................... **CLC 32**
   See also CA 13-14; CANR 65; CAP 1; DLB 9, 54, 256; LAIT 2
**Nekrasov, Nikolai Alekseevich**
   1821-1878 ............................ **NCLC 11**
   See also DLB 277
**Nelligan, Emile** 1879-1941 ............. **TCLC 14**
   See also CA 114; 204; DLB 92; EWL 3
**Nelson, Willie** 1933- .......................... **CLC 17**
   See also CA 107; CANR 114
**Nemerov, Howard (Stanley)**
   1920-1991 ........ **CLC 2, 6, 9, 36; PC 24; TCLC 124**
   See also AMW; CA 1-4R; 134; CABS 2; CANR 1, 27, 53; DAM POET; DLB 5, 6; DLBY 1983; EWL 3; INT CANR-27; MTCW 1, 2; PFS 10, 14; RGAL 4
**Neruda, Pablo** 1904-1973 .. **CLC 1, 2, 5, 7, 9, 28, 62; HLC 2; PC 4, 64; WLC**
   See also CA 19-20; 45-48; CANR 131; CAP 2; DA; DA3; DAB; DAC; DAM MST, MULT, POET; DLB 283; DNFS 2; EWL 3; HW 1; LAW; MTCW 1, 2; PFS 11; RGWL 2, 3; TWA; WLIT 1; WP
**Nerval, Gerard de** 1808-1855 ... **NCLC 1, 67; PC 13; SSC 18**
   See also DLB 217; EW 6; GFL 1789 to the Present; RGSF 2; RGWL 2, 3
**Nervo, (Jose) Amado (Ruiz de)**
   1870-1919 ................ **HLCS 2; TCLC 11**
   See also CA 109; 131; DLB 290; EWL 3; HW 1; LAW
**Nesbit, Malcolm**
   See Chester, Alfred
**Nessi, Pio Baroja y**
   See Baroja (y Nessi), Pio
**Nestroy, Johann** 1801-1862 ........... **NCLC 42**
   See also DLB 133; RGWL 2, 3
**Netterville, Luke**
   See O'Grady, Standish (James)
**Neufeld, John (Arthur)** 1938- .......... **CLC 17**
   See also AAYA 11; CA 25-28R; CANR 11, 37, 56; CLR 52; MAICYA 1, 2; SAAS 3; SATA 6, 81, 131; SATA-Essay 131; YAW
**Neumann, Alfred** 1895-1952 ........ **TCLC 100**
   See also CA 183; DLB 56
**Neumann, Ferenc**
   See Molnar, Ferenc
**Neville, Emily Cheney** 1919- ............ **CLC 12**
   See also BYA 2; CA 5-8R; CANR 3, 37, 85; JRDA; MAICYA 1, 2; SAAS 2; SATA 1; YAW
**Newbound, Bernard Slade** 1930-
   See Slade, Bernard
   See also CA 81-84; CANR 49; CD 5; DAM DRAM
**Newby, P(ercy) H(oward)**
   1918-1997 ........................... **CLC 2, 13**
   See also CA 5-8R; 161; CANR 32, 67; CN 7; DAM NOV; DLB 15; MTCW 1; RGEL 2
**Newcastle**
   See Cavendish, Margaret Lucas

**Newlove, Donald** 1928- ...................... **CLC 6**
   See also CA 29-32R; CANR 25
**Newlove, John (Herbert)** 1938- ........ **CLC 14**
   See also CA 21-24R; CANR 9, 25; CP 7
**Newman, Charles** 1938- ................. **CLC 2, 8**
   See also CA 21-24R; CANR 84; CN 7
**Newman, Edwin (Harold)** 1919- ...... **CLC 14**
   See also AITN 1; CA 69-72; CANR 5
**Newman, John Henry** 1801-1890 . **NCLC 38, 99**
   See also BRWS 7; DLB 18, 32, 55; RGEL 2
**Newton, (Sir) Isaac** 1642-1727 ...... **LC 35, 53**
   See also DLB 252
**Newton, Suzanne** 1936- .................... **CLC 35**
   See also BYA 7; CA 41-44R; CANR 14; JRDA; SATA 5, 77
**New York Dept. of Ed.** ..................... **CLC 70**
**Nexo, Martin Andersen**
   1869-1954 ............................ **TCLC 43**
   See also CA 202; DLB 214; EWL 3
**Nezval, Vitezslav** 1900-1958 .......... **TCLC 44**
   See also CA 123; CDWLB 4; DLB 215; EWL 3
**Ng, Fae Myenne** 1957(?)- ................. **CLC 81**
   See also BYA 11; CA 146
**Ngema, Mbongeni** 1955- .................. **CLC 57**
   See also BW 2; CA 143; CANR 84; CD 5
**Ngugi, James T(hiong'o)** . **CLC 3, 7, 13, 182**
   See Ngugi wa Thiong'o
**Ngugi wa Thiong'o**
   See Ngugi wa Thiong'o
   See also DLB 125; EWL 3
**Ngugi wa Thiong'o** 1938- ... **BLC 3; CLC 36, 182**
   See Ngugi, James T(hiong'o); Ngugi wa Thiong'o
   See also AFW; BRWS 8; BW 2; CA 81-84; CANR 27, 58; CDWLB 3; DAM MULT, NOV; DNFS 2; MTCW 1, 2; RGEL 2; WWE 1
**Niatum, Duane** 1938- .......................... **NNAL**
   See also CA 41-44R; CANR 21, 45, 83; DLB 175
**Nichol, B(arrie) P(hillip)** 1944-1988 . **CLC 18**
   See also CA 53-56; DLB 53; SATA 66
**Nicholas of Cusa** 1401-1464 ................. **LC 80**
   See also DLB 115
**Nichols, John (Treadwell)** 1940- ....... **CLC 38**
   See also AMWS 13; CA 9-12R, 190; CAAE 190; CAAS 2; CANR 6, 70, 121; DLBY 1982; LATS 1:2; TCWW 2
**Nichols, Leigh**
   See Koontz, Dean R(ay)
**Nichols, Peter (Richard)** 1927- .... **CLC 5, 36, 65**
   See also CA 104; CANR 33, 86; CBD; CD 5; DLB 13, 245; MTCW 1
**Nicholson, Linda ed.** ........................ **CLC 65**
**Ni Chuilleanain, Eilean** 1942- ............. **PC 34**
   See also CA 126; CANR 53, 83; CP 7; CWP; DLB 40
**Nicolas, F. R. E.**
   See Freeling, Nicolas
**Niedecker, Lorine** 1903-1970 ..... **CLC 10, 42; PC 42**
   See also CA 25-28; CAP 2; DAM POET; DLB 48
**Nietzsche, Friedrich (Wilhelm)**
   1844-1900 .................... **TCLC 10, 18, 55**
   See also CA 107; 121; CDWLB 2; DLB 129; EW 7; RGWL 2, 3; TWA
**Nievo, Ippolito** 1831-1861 ............... **NCLC 22**
**Nightingale, Anne Redmon** 1943-
   See Redmon, Anne
   See also CA 103
**Nightingale, Florence** 1820-1910 ... **TCLC 85**
   See also CA 188; DLB 166

**Nijo Yoshimoto** 1320-1388 ............. **CMLC 49**
   See also DLB 203
**Nik. T. O.**
   See Annensky, Innokenty (Fyodorovich)
**Nin, Anais** 1903-1977 ..... **CLC 1, 4, 8, 11, 14, 60, 127; SSC 10**
   See also AITN 2; AMWS 10; BPFB 2; CA 13-16R; 69-72; CANR 22, 53; DAM NOV, POP; DLB 2, 4, 152; EWL 3; GLL 2; MAWW; MTCW 1, 2; RGAL 4; RGSF 2
**Nisbet, Robert A(lexander)**
   1913-1996 ........................... **TCLC 117**
   See also CA 25-28R; 153; CANR 17; INT CANR-17
**Nishida, Kitaro** 1870-1945 .............. **TCLC 83**
**Nishiwaki, Junzaburo**
   See Nishiwaki, Junzaburo
   See also CA 194
**Nishiwaki, Junzaburo** 1894-1982 ........ **PC 15**
   See Nishiwaki, Junzaburo; Nishiwaki Junzaburo
   See also CA 194; 107; MJW; RGWL 3
**Nishiwaki Junzaburo**
   See Nishiwaki, Junzaburo
   See also EWL 3
**Nissenson, Hugh** 1933- ................... **CLC 4, 9**
   See also CA 17-20R; CANR 27, 108; CN 7; DLB 28
**Nister, Der**
   See Der Nister
   See also EWL 3
**Niven, Larry** ........................... **CLC 8**
   See Niven, Laurence Van Cott
   See also AAYA 27; BPFB 2; BYA 10; DLB 8; SCFW 2
**Niven, Laurence Van Cott** 1938-
   See Niven, Larry
   See also CA 21-24R, 207; CAAE 207; CAAS 12; CANR 14, 44, 66, 113; CPW; DAM POP; MTCW 1, 2; SATA 95; SFW 4
**Nixon, Agnes Eckhardt** 1927- .......... **CLC 21**
   See also CA 110
**Nizan, Paul** 1905-1940 ................... **TCLC 40**
   See also CA 161; DLB 72; EWL 3; GFL 1789 to the Present
**Nkosi, Lewis** 1936- .............. **BLC 3; CLC 45**
   See also BW 1, 3; CA 65-68; CANR 27, 81; CBD; CD 5; DAM MULT; DLB 157, 225; WWE 1
**Nodier, (Jean) Charles (Emmanuel)**
   1780-1844 ........................... **NCLC 19**
   See also DLB 119; GFL 1789 to the Present
**Noguchi, Yone** 1875-1947 ............. **TCLC 80**
**Nolan, Christopher** 1965- ................. **CLC 58**
   See also CA 111; CANR 88
**Noon, Jeff** 1957- ............................... **CLC 91**
   See also CA 148; CANR 83; DLB 267; SFW 4
**Norden, Charles**
   See Durrell, Lawrence (George)
**Nordhoff, Charles Bernard**
   1887-1947 ............................... **TCLC 23**
   See also CA 108; 211; DLB 9; LAIT 1; RHW 1; SATA 23
**Norfolk, Lawrence** 1963- .................. **CLC 76**
   See also CA 144; CANR 85; CN 7; DLB 267
**Norman, Marsha** 1947- . **CLC 28, 186; DC 8**
   See also CA 105; CABS 3; CAD; CANR 41, 131; CD 5; CSW; CWD; DAM DRAM; DFS 2; DLB 266; DLBY 1984; FW
**Normyx**
   See Douglas, (George) Norman

**Norris, (Benjamin) Frank(lin, Jr.)**
1870-1902 ......... **SSC 28; TCLC 24, 155**
See also AAYA 57; AMW; AMWC 2; BPFB
2; CA 110; 160; CDALB 1865-1917; DLB
12, 71, 186; LMFS 2; NFS 12; RGAL 4;
TCWW 2; TUS

**Norris, Leslie** 1921- ........................... **CLC 14**
See also CA 11-12; CANR 14, 117; CAP 1;
CP 7; DLB 27, 256

**North, Andrew**
See Norton, Andre

**North, Anthony**
See Koontz, Dean R(ay)

**North, Captain George**
See Stevenson, Robert Louis (Balfour)

**North, Captain George**
See Stevenson, Robert Louis (Balfour)

**North, Milou**
See Erdrich, Louise

**Northrup, B. A.**
See Hubbard, L(afayette) Ron(ald)

**North Staffs**
See Hulme, T(homas) E(rnest)

**Northup, Solomon** 1808-1863 ...... **NCLC 105**

**Norton, Alice Mary**
See Norton, Andre
See also MAICYA 1; SATA 1, 43

**Norton, Andre** 1912- ........................... **CLC 12**
See Norton, Alice Mary
See also AAYA 14; BPFB 2; BYA 4, 10,
12; CA 1-4R; CANR 68; CLR 50; DLB
8, 52; JRDA; MAICYA 2; MTCW 1;
SATA 91; SUFW 1, 2; YAW

**Norton, Caroline** 1808-1877 ........... **NCLC 47**
See also DLB 21, 159, 199

**Norway, Nevil Shute** 1899-1960
See Shute, Nevil
See also CA 102; 93-96; CANR 85; MTCW
2

**Norwid, Cyprian Kamil**
1821-1883 ................................. **NCLC 17**
See also RGWL 3

**Nosille, Nabrah**
See Ellison, Harlan (Jay)

**Nossack, Hans Erich** 1901-1978 ......... **CLC 6**
See also CA 93-96; 85-88; DLB 69; EWL 3

**Nostradamus** 1503-1566 ....................... **LC 27**

**Nosu, Chuji**
See Ozu, Yasujiro

**Notenburg, Eleanora (Genrikhovna) von**
See Guro, Elena (Genrikhovna)

**Nova, Craig** 1945- .......................... **CLC 7, 31**
See also CA 45-48; CANR 2, 53, 127

**Novak, Joseph**
See Kosinski, Jerzy (Nikodem)

**Novalis** 1772-1801 ........................... **NCLC 13**
See also CDWLB 2; DLB 90; EW 5; RGWL
2, 3

**Novick, Peter** 1934- .......................... **CLC 164**
See also CA 188

**Novis, Emile**
See Weil, Simone (Adolphine)

**Nowlan, Alden (Albert)** 1933-1983 ... **CLC 15**
See also CA 9-12R; CANR 5; DAC; DAM
MST; DLB 53; PFS 12

**Noyes, Alfred** 1880-1958 ...... **PC 27; TCLC 7**
See also CA 104; 188; DLB 20; EXPP;
FANT; PFS 4; RGEL 2

**Nugent, Richard Bruce** 1906(?)-1987 ... **HR 3**
See also BW 1; CA 125; DLB 51; GLL 2

**Nunn, Kem** .......................... **CLC 34**
See also CA 159

**Nussbaum, Martha** 1947- ............... **CLC 203**
See also CA 134; CANR 102

**Nwapa, Flora (Nwanzuruaha)**
1931-1993 .................... **BLCS; CLC 133**
See also BW 2; CA 143; CANR 83; CD-
WLB 3; CWRI 5; DLB 125; EWL 3;
WLIT 2

**Nye, Robert** 1939- ......................... **CLC 13, 42**
See also BRWS 10; CA 33-36R; CANR 29,
67, 107; CN 7; CP 7; CWRI 5; DAM
NOV; DLB 14, 271; FANT; HGG; MTCW
1; RHW; SATA 6

**Nyro, Laura** 1947-1997 .................... **CLC 17**
See also CA 194

**Oates, Joyce Carol** 1938- .. **CLC 1, 2, 3, 6, 9,
11, 15, 19, 33, 52, 108, 134; SSC 6, 70;
WLC**
See also AAYA 15, 52; AITN 1; AMWS 2;
BEST 89:2; BPFB 2; BYA 11; CA 5-8R;
CANR 25, 45, 74, 113, 129; CDALB
1968-1988; CN 7; CP 7; CPW; CWP; DA;
DA3; DAB; DAC; DAM MST, NOV,
POP; DLB 2, 5, 130; DLBY 1981; EWL
3; EXPS; FW; HGG; INT CANR-25;
LAIT 4; MAWW; MTCW 1, 2; NFS 8;
RGAL 4; RGSF 2; SSFS 17; SUFW 2;
TUS

**O'Brian, E. G.**
See Clarke, Arthur C(harles)

**O'Brian, Patrick** 1914-2000 ........... **CLC 152**
See also AAYA 55; CA 144; 187; CANR
74; CPW; MTCW 2; RHW

**O'Brien, Darcy** 1939-1998 ................ **CLC 11**
See also CA 21-24R; 167; CANR 8, 59

**O'Brien, Edna** 1932- ..... **CLC 3, 5, 8, 13, 36,
65, 116; SSC 10, 77**
See also BRWS 5; CA 1-4R; CANR 6, 41,
65, 102; CDBLB 1960 to Present; CN 7;
DA3; DAM NOV; DLB 14, 231; EWL 3;
FW; MTCW 1, 2; RGSF 2; WLIT 4

**O'Brien, Fitz-James** 1828-1862 ...... **NCLC 21**
See also DLB 74; RGAL 4; SUFW

**O'Brien, Flann** .......... **CLC 1, 4, 5, 7, 10, 47**
See O Nuallain, Brian
See also BRWS 2; DLB 231; EWL 3;
RGEL 2

**O'Brien, Richard** 1942- .................... **CLC 17**
See also CA 124

**O'Brien, (William) Tim(othy)** 1946- . **CLC 7,
19, 40, 103, 211; SSC 74**
See also AAYA 16; AMWS 5; CA 85-88;
CANR 40, 58, 133; CDALBS; CN 7;
CPW; DA3; DAM POP; DLB 152; DLBD
9; DLBY 1980; LATS 1:2; MTCW 2;
RGAL 4; SSFS 5, 15

**Obstfelder, Sigbjoern** 1866-1900 .... **TCLC 23**
See also CA 123

**O'Casey, Sean** 1880-1964 .... **CLC 1, 5, 9, 11,
15, 88; DC 12; WLCS**
See also BRW 7; CA 89-92; CANR 62;
CBD; CDBLB 1914-1945; DA3; DAB;
DAC; DAM DRAM, MST; DFS 19; DLB
10; EWL 3; MTCW 1, 2; RGEL 2; TEA;
WLIT 4

**O'Cathasaigh, Sean**
See O'Casey, Sean

**Occom, Samson** 1723-1792 .... **LC 60; NNAL**
See also DLB 175

**Ochs, Phil(ip David)** 1940-1976 ........ **CLC 17**
See also CA 185; 65-68

**O'Connor, Edwin (Greene)**
1918-1968 .................................. **CLC 14**
See also CA 93-96; 25-28R

**O'Connor, (Mary) Flannery**
1925-1964 .... **CLC 1, 2, 3, 6, 10, 13, 15,
21, 66, 104; SSC 1, 23, 61, 82; TCLC
132; WLC**
See also AAYA 7; AMW; AMWR 2; BPFB
3; BYA 16; CA 1-4R; CANR 3, 41;
CDALB 1941-1968; DA; DA3; DAB;
DAC; DAM MST, NOV; DLB 2, 152;

DLBD 12; DLBY 1980; EWL 3; EXPS;
LAIT 5; MAWW; MTCW 1, 2; NFS 3;
RGAL 4; RGSF 2; SSFS 2, 7, 10, 19;
TUS

**O'Connor, Frank** ................. **CLC 23; SSC 5**
See O'Donovan, Michael Francis
See also DLB 162; EWL 3; RGSF 2; SSFS
5

**O'Dell, Scott** 1898-1989 .................... **CLC 30**
See also AAYA 3, 44; BPFB 3; BYA 1, 2,
3, 5; CA 61-64; 129; CANR 12, 30, 112;
CLR 1, 16; DLB 52; JRDA; MAICYA 1,
2; SATA 12, 60, 134; WYA; YAW

**Odets, Clifford** 1906-1963 ..... **CLC 2, 28, 98;
DC 6**
See also AMWS 2; CA 85-88; CAD; CANR
62; DAM DRAM; DFS 3, 17, 20; DLB 7,
26; EWL 3; MTCW 1, 2; RGAL 4; TUS

**O'Doherty, Brian** 1928- .................... **CLC 76**
See also CA 105; CANR 108

**O'Donnell, K. M.**
See Malzberg, Barry N(athaniel)

**O'Donnell, Lawrence**
See Kuttner, Henry

**O'Donovan, Michael Francis**
1903-1966 ................................. **CLC 14**
See O'Connor, Frank
See also CA 93-96; CANR 84

**Oe, Kenzaburo** 1935- .. **CLC 10, 36, 86, 187;
SSC 20**
See also Oe Kenzaburo
See also CA 97-100; CANR 36, 50, 74, 126;
DA3; DAM NOV; DLB 182; DLBY 1994;
LATS 1:2; MJW; MTCW 1, 2; RGSF 2;
RGWL 2, 3

**Oe Kenzaburo**
See Oe, Kenzaburo
See also CWW 2; EWL 3

**O'Faolain, Julia** 1932- .... **CLC 6, 19, 47, 108**
See also CA 81-84; CAAS 2; CANR 12,
61; CN 7; DLB 14, 231; FW; MTCW 1;
RHW

**O'Faolain, Sean** 1900-1991 ...... **CLC 1, 7, 14,
32, 70; SSC 13; TCLC 143**
See also CA 61-64; 134; CANR 12, 66;
DLB 15, 162; MTCW 1, 2; RGEL 2;
RGSF 2

**O'Flaherty, Liam** 1896-1984 ....... **CLC 5, 34;
SSC 6**
See also CA 101; 113; CANR 35; DLB 36,
162; DLBY 1984; MTCW 1, 2; RGEL 2;
RGSF 2; SSFS 5, 20

**Ogai**
See Mori Ogai
See also MJW

**Ogilvy, Gavin**
See Barrie, J(ames) M(atthew)

**O'Grady, Standish (James)**
1846-1928 .................................. **TCLC 5**
See also CA 104; 157

**O'Grady, Timothy** 1951- .................... **CLC 59**
See also CA 138

**O'Hara, Frank** 1926-1966 ....... **CLC 2, 5, 13,
78; PC 45**
See also CA 9-12R; 25-28R; CANR 33;
DA3; DAM POET; DLB 5, 16, 193; EWL
3; MTCW 1, 2; PFS 8; 12; RGAL 4; WP

**O'Hara, John (Henry)** 1905-1970 . **CLC 1, 2,
3, 6, 11, 42; SSC 15**
See also AMW; BPFB 3; CA 5-8R; 25-28R;
CANR 31, 60; CDALB 1929-1941; DAM
NOV; DLB 9, 86; DLBD 2; EWL 3;
MTCW 1, 2; NFS 11; RGAL 4; RGSF 2

**O Hehir, Diana** 1922- ........................ **CLC 41**
See also CA 93-96

**Ohiyesa**
See Eastman, Charles A(lexander)

**Okada, John** 1923-1971 ........................ **AAL**
See also BYA 14; CA 212

**Okigbo, Christopher (Ifenayichukwu)**
1932-1967 .... **BLC 3; CLC 25, 84; PC 7**
See also AFW; BW 1, 3; CA 77-80; CANR
74; CDWLB 3; DAM MULT, POET; DLB
125; EWL 3; MTCW 1, 2; RGEL 2

**Okri, Ben** 1959- ........................... **CLC 87**
See also AFW; BRWS 5; BW 2, 3; CA 130;
138; CANR 65, 128; CN 7; DLB 157,
231; EWL 3; INT CA-138; MTCW 2;
RGSF 2; SSFS 20; WLIT 2; WWE 1

**Olds, Sharon** 1942- .. **CLC 32, 39, 85; PC 22**
See also AMWS 10; CA 101; CANR 18,
41, 66, 98, 135; CP 7; CPW; CWP; DAM
POET; DLB 120; MTCW 2; PFS 17

**Oldstyle, Jonathan**
See Irving, Washington

**Olesha, Iurii**
See Olesha, Yuri (Karlovich)
See also RGWL 2

**Olesha, Iurii Karlovich**
See Olesha, Yuri (Karlovich)
See also DLB 272

**Olesha, Yuri (Karlovich)** 1899-1960 . **CLC 8;
SSC 69; TCLC 136**
See also Olesha, Iurii; Olesha, Iurii Karlovich;
Olesha, Yury Karlovich
See also CA 85-88; EW 11; RGWL 3

**Olesha, Yury Karlovich**
See Olesha, Yuri (Karlovich)
See also EWL 3

**Oliphant, Mrs.**
See Oliphant, Margaret (Oliphant Wilson)
See also SUFW

**Oliphant, Laurence** 1829(?)-1888 .. **NCLC 47**
See also DLB 18, 166

**Oliphant, Margaret (Oliphant Wilson)**
1828-1897 .......... **NCLC 11, 61; SSC 25**
See Oliphant, Mrs.
See also BRWS 10; DLB 18, 159, 190;
HGG; RGEL 2; RGSF 2

**Oliver, Mary** 1935- ............... **CLC 19, 34, 98**
See also AMWS 7; CA 21-24R; CANR 9,
43, 84, 92; CP 7; CWP; DLB 5, 193;
EWL 3; PFS 15

**Olivier, Laurence (Kerr)** 1907-1989 . **CLC 20**
See also CA 111; 150; 129

**Olsen, Tillie** 1912- ... **CLC 4, 13, 114; SSC 11**
See also AAYA 51; AMWS 13; BYA 11;
CA 1-4R; CANR 1, 43, 74, 132;
CDALBS; CN 7; DA; DA3; DAB; DAC;
DAM MST; DLB 28, 206; DLBY 1980;
EWL 3; EXPS; FW; MTCW 1, 2; RGAL
4; RGSF 2; SSFS 1; TUS

**Olson, Charles (John)** 1910-1970 .. **CLC 1, 2,
5, 6, 9, 11, 29; PC 19**
See also AMWS 2; CA 13-16; 25-28R;
CABS 2; CANR 35, 61; CAP 1; DAM
POET; DLB 5, 16, 193; EWL 3; MTCW
1, 2; RGAL 4; WP

**Olson, Toby** 1937- ............................. **CLC 28**
See also CA 65-68; CANR 9, 31, 84; CP 7

**Olyesha, Yuri**
See Olesha, Yuri (Karlovich)

**Olympiodorus of Thebes** c. 375-c.
430 ......................................... **CMLC 59**

**Omar Khayyam**
See Khayyam, Omar
See also RGWL 2, 3

**Ondaatje, (Philip) Michael** 1943- .... **CLC 14,
29, 51, 76, 180; PC 28**
See also CA 77-80; CANR 42, 74, 109, 133;
CN 7; CP 7; DA3; DAB; DAC; DAM
MST; DLB 60; EWL 3; LATS 1:2; LMFS
2; MTCW 2; PFS 8, 19; TWA; WWE 1

**Oneal, Elizabeth** 1934-
See Oneal, Zibby
See also CA 106; CANR 28, 84; MAICYA
1, 2; SATA 30, 82; YAW

**Oneal, Zibby** ..................................... **CLC 30**
See Oneal, Elizabeth
See also AAYA 5, 41; BYA 13; CLR 13;
JRDA; WYA

**O'Neill, Eugene (Gladstone)**
1888-1953 ... **DC 20; TCLC 1, 6, 27, 49;
WLC**
See also AAYA 54; AITN 1; AMW; AMWC
1; CA 110; 132; CAD; CANR 131;
CDALB 1929-1941; DA; DA3; DAB;
DAC; DAM DRAM, MST; DFS 2, 4, 5,
6, 9, 11, 12, 16, 20; DLB 7; EWL 3; LAIT
3; LMFS 2; MTCW 1, 2; RGAL 4; TUS

**Onetti, Juan Carlos** 1909-1994 ... **CLC 7, 10;
HLCS 2; SSC 23; TCLC 131**
See also CA 85-88; 145; CANR 32, 63; CD-
WLB 3; CWW 2; DAM MULT, NOV;
DLB 113; EWL 3; HW 1, 2; LAW;
MTCW 1, 2; RGSF 2

**O Nuallain, Brian** 1911-1966
See O'Brien, Flann
See also CA 21-22; 25-28R; CAP 2; DLB
231; FANT; TEA

**Ophuls, Max** 1902-1957 ................. **TCLC 79**
See also CA 113

**Opie, Amelia** 1769-1853 ................. **NCLC 65**
See also DLB 116, 159; RGEL 2

**Oppen, George** 1908-1984 ..... **CLC 7, 13, 34;
PC 35; TCLC 107**
See also CA 13-16R; 113; CANR 8, 82;
DLB 5, 165

**Oppenheim, E(dward) Phillips**
1866-1946 ................................. **TCLC 45**
See also CA 111; 202; CMW 4; DLB 70

**Opuls, Max**
See Ophuls, Max

**Orage, A(lfred) R(ichard)**
1873-1934 ................................. **TCLC 157**
See also CA 122

**Origen** c. 185-c. 254 ....................... **CMLC 19**

**Orlovitz, Gil** 1918-1973 ................... **CLC 22**
See also CA 77-80; 45-48; DLB 2, 5

**O'Rourke, P(atrick) J(ake)** 1947- .. **CLC 209**
See also CA 77-80; CANR 13, 41, 67, 111;
CPW; DLB 185; DAM POP

**Orris**
See Ingelow, Jean

**Ortega y Gasset, Jose** 1883-1955 ...... **HLC 2;
TCLC 9**
See also CA 106; 130; DAM MULT; EW 9;
EWL 3; HW 1, 2; MTCW 1, 2

**Ortese, Anna Maria** 1914-1998 ........ **CLC 89**
See also DLB 177; EWL 3

**Ortiz, Simon J(oseph)** 1941- ... **CLC 45, 208;
NNAL; PC 17**
See also AMWS 4; CA 134; CANR 69, 118;
CP 7; DAM MULT, POET; DLB 120,
175, 256; EXPP; PFS 4, 16; RGAL 4

**Orton, Joe** ...... **CLC 4, 13, 43; DC 3; TCLC
157**
See Orton, John Kingsley
See also BRWS 5; CBD; CDBLB 1960 to
Present; DFS 3, 6; DLB 13; GLL 1;
MTCW 2; RGEL 2; TEA; WLIT 4

**Orton, John Kingsley** 1933-1967
See Orton, Joe
See also CA 85-88; CANR 35, 66; DAM
DRAM; MTCW 1, 2

**Orwell, George** ...... **SSC 68; TCLC 2, 6, 15,
31, 51, 128, 129; WLC**
See Blair, Eric (Arthur)
See also BPFB 3; BRW 7; BYA 5; CDBLB
1945-1960; CLR 68; DAB; DLB 15, 98,
195, 255; EWL 3; EXPN; LAIT 4, 5;
LATS 1:1; NFS 3, 7; RGEL 2; SCFW 2;
SFW 4; SSFS 4; TEA; WLIT 4; YAW

**Osborne, David**
See Silverberg, Robert

**Osborne, George**
See Silverberg, Robert

**Osborne, John (James)** 1929-1994 .... **CLC 1,
2, 5, 11, 45; TCLC 153; WLC**
See also BRWS 1; CA 13-16R; 147; CANR
21, 56; CDBLB 1945-1960; DA; DAB;
DAC; DAM DRAM, MST; DFS 4, 19;
DLB 13; EWL 3; MTCW 1, 2; RGEL 2

**Osborne, Lawrence** 1958- ................. **CLC 50**
See also CA 189

**Osbourne, Lloyd** 1868-1947 .......... **TCLC 93**

**Osgood, Frances Sargent**
1811-1850 ............................... **NCLC 141**
See also DLB 250

**Oshima, Nagisa** 1932- ...................... **CLC 20**
See also CA 116; 121; CANR 78

**Oskison, John Milton**
1874-1947 ............... **NNAL; TCLC 35**
See also CA 144; CANR 84; DAM MULT;
DLB 175

**Ossian** c. 3rd cent. - ....................... **CMLC 28**
See Macpherson, James

**Ossoli, Sarah Margaret (Fuller)**
1810-1850 ......................... **NCLC 5, 50**
See Fuller, Margaret; Fuller, Sarah Margaret
See also CDALB 1640-1865; FW; LMFS 1;
SATA 25

**Ostriker, Alicia (Suskin)** 1937- ....... **CLC 132**
See also CA 25-28R; CAAS 24; CANR 10,
30, 62, 99; CWP; DLB 120; EXPP; PFS
19

**Ostrovsky, Aleksandr Nikolaevich**
See Ostrovsky, Alexander
See also DLB 277

**Ostrovsky, Alexander** 1823-1886 .. **NCLC 30,
57**
See Ostrovsky, Aleksandr Nikolaevich

**Otero, Blas de** 1916-1979 ................ **CLC 11**
See also CA 89-92; DLB 134; EWL 3

**O'Trigger, Sir Lucius**
See Horne, Richard Henry Hengist

**Otto, Rudolf** 1869-1937 ................... **TCLC 85**

**Otto, Whitney** 1955- ........................ **CLC 70**
See also CA 140; CANR 120

**Otway, Thomas** 1652-1685 ... **DC 24; LC 106**
See also DAM DRAM; DLB 80; RGEL 2

**Ouida** ................................................ **TCLC 43**
See De la Ramee, Marie Louise (Ouida)
See also DLB 18, 156; RGEL 2

**Ouologuem, Yambo** 1940- ............... **CLC 146**
See also CA 111; 176

**Ousmane, Sembene** 1923- ... **BLC 3; CLC 66**
See Sembene, Ousmane
See also BW 1, 3; CA 117; 125; CANR 81;
CWW 2; MTCW 1

**Ovid** 43B.C.-17 ...................... **CMLC 7; PC 2**
See also AW 2; CDWLB 1; DA3; DAM
POET; DLB 211; RGWL 2, 3; WP

**Owen, Hugh**
See Faust, Frederick (Schiller)

**Owen, Wilfred (Edward Salter)**
1893-1918 ... **PC 19; TCLC 5, 27; WLC**
See also BRW 6; CA 104; 141; CDBLB
1914-1945; DA; DAB; DAC; DAM MST,
POET; DLB 20; EWL 3; EXPP; MTCW
2; PFS 10; RGEL 2; WLIT 4

**Owens, Louis (Dean)** 1948-2002 ........ **NNAL**
See also CA 137; 179; 207; CAAE 179;
CAAS 24; CANR 71

**Owens, Rochelle** 1936- ...................... **CLC 8**
See also CA 17-20R; CAAS 2; CAD;
CANR 39; CD 5; CP 7; CWD; CWP

**Oz, Amos** 1939- ...... **CLC 5, 8, 11, 27, 33, 54;
SSC 66**
See also CA 53-56; CANR 27, 47, 65, 113;
CWW 2; DAM NOV; EWL 3; MTCW 1,
2; RGSF 2; RGWL 3

**Paterson, A(ndrew) B(arton)**
    1864-1941 ............................... **TCLC 32**
    See also CA 155; DLB 230; RGEL 2; SATA 97

**Paterson, Banjo**
    See Paterson, A(ndrew) B(arton)

**Paterson, Katherine (Womeldorf)**
    1932- ..................................... **CLC 12, 30**
    See also AAYA 1, 31; BYA 1, 2, 7; CA 21-24R; CANR 28, 59, 111; CLR 7, 50; CWRI 5; DLB 52; JRDA; LAIT 4; MAI-CYA 1, 2; MAICYAS 1; MTCW 1; SATA 13, 53, 92, 133; WYA; YAW

**Patmore, Coventry Kersey Dighton**
    1823-1896 ..................... **NCLC 9; PC 59**
    See also DLB 35, 98; RGEL 2; TEA

**Paton, Alan (Stewart)** 1903-1988 ...... **CLC 4, 10, 25, 55, 106; TCLC 165; WLC**
    See also AAYA 26; AFW; BPFB 3; BRWS 2; BYA 1; CA 13-16; 125; CANR 22; CAP 1; DA; DA3; DAB; DAC; DAM MST, NOV; DLB 225; DLBD 17; EWL 3; EXPN; LAIT 4; MTCW 1, 2; NFS 3, 12; RGEL 2; SATA 11; SATA-Obit 56; TWA; WLIT 2; WWE 1

**Paton Walsh, Gillian** 1937- .............. **CLC 35**
    See Paton Walsh, Jill; Walsh, Jill Paton
    See also AAYA 11; CANR 38, 83; CLR 2, 65; DLB 161; JRDA; MAICYA 1, 2; SAAS 3; SATA 4, 72, 109; YAW

**Paton Walsh, Jill**
    See Paton Walsh, Gillian
    See also AAYA 47; BYA 1, 8

**Patterson, (Horace) Orlando (Lloyd)**
    1940- ......................................... **BLCS**
    See also BW 1; CA 65-68; CANR 27, 84; CN 7

**Patton, George S(mith), Jr.**
    1885-1945 ............................... **TCLC 79**
    See also CA 189

**Paulding, James Kirke** 1778-1860 ... **NCLC 2**
    See also DLB 3, 59, 74, 250; RGAL 4

**Paulin, Thomas Neilson** 1949-
    See Paulin, Tom
    See also CA 123; 128; CANR 98; CP 7

**Paulin, Tom** ............................. **CLC 37, 177**
    See Paulin, Thomas Neilson
    See also DLB 40

**Pausanias** c. 1st cent. - ................... **CMLC 36**

**Paustovsky, Konstantin (Georgievich)**
    1892-1968 ................................. **CLC 40**
    See also CA 93-96; 25-28R; DLB 272; EWL 3

**Pavese, Cesare** 1908-1950 .... **PC 13; SSC 19; TCLC 3**
    See also CA 104; 169; DLB 128, 177; EW 12; EWL 3; PFS 20; RGSF 2; RGWL 2, 3; TWA

**Pavic, Milorad** 1929- ...................... **CLC 60**
    See also CA 136; CDWLB 4; CWW 2; DLB 181; EWL 3; RGWL 3

**Pavlov, Ivan Petrovich** 1849-1936 . **TCLC 91**
    See also CA 118; 180

**Pavlova, Karolina Karlovna**
    1807-1893 ................................ **NCLC 138**
    See also DLB 205

**Payne, Alan**
    See Jakes, John (William)

**Paz, Gil**
    See Lugones, Leopoldo

**Paz, Octavio** 1914-1998 . **CLC 3, 4, 6, 10, 19, 51, 65, 119; HLC 2; PC 1, 48; WLC**
    See also AAYA 50; CA 73-76; 165; CANR 32, 65, 104; CWW 2; DA; DA3; DAB; DAC; DAM MST, MULT, POET; DLB 290; DLBY 1990, 1998; DNFS 1; EWL 3; HW 1, 2; LAW; LAWS 1; MTCW 1, 2; PFS 18; RGWL 2, 3; SSFS 13; TWA; WLIT 1

**p'Bitek, Okot** 1931-1982 .... **BLC 3; CLC 96; TCLC 149**
    See also AFW; BW 2, 3; CA 124; 107; CANR 82; DAM MULT; DLB 125; EWL 3; MTCW 1, 2; RGEL 2; WLIT 2

**Peacock, Molly** 1947- ........................ **CLC 60**
    See also CA 103; CAAS 21; CANR 52, 84; CP 7; CWP; DLB 120, 282

**Peacock, Thomas Love**
    1785-1866 ............................... **NCLC 22**
    See also BRW 4; DLB 96, 116; RGEL 2; RGSF 2

**Peake, Mervyn** 1911-1968 ............. **CLC 7, 54**
    See also CA 5-8R; 25-28R; CANR 3; DLB 15, 160, 255; FANT; MTCW 1; RGEL 2; SATA 23; SFW 4

**Pearce, Philippa**
    See Christie, Philippa
    See also CA 5-8R; CANR 4, 109; CWRI 5; FANT; MAICYA 2

**Pearl, Eric**
    See Elman, Richard (Martin)

**Pearson, T(homas) R(eid)** 1956- ....... **CLC 39**
    See also CA 120; 130; CANR 97; CSW; INT CA-130

**Peck, Dale** 1967- ............................ **CLC 81**
    See also CA 146; CANR 72, 127; GLL 2

**Peck, John (Frederick)** 1941- ............. **CLC 3**
    See also CA 49-52; CANR 3, 100; CP 7

**Peck, Richard (Wayne)** 1934- ........... **CLC 21**
    See also AAYA 1, 24; BYA 1, 6, 8, 11; CA 85-88; CANR 19, 38, 129; CLR 15; INT CANR-19; JRDA; MAICYA 1, 2; SAAS 2; SATA 18, 55, 97; SATA-Essay 110; WYA; YAW

**Peck, Robert Newton** 1928- .............. **CLC 17**
    See also AAYA 3, 43; BYA 1, 6; CA 81-84, 182; CAAE 182; CANR 31, 63, 127; CLR 45; DA; DAC; DAM MST; JRDA; LAIT 3; MAICYA 1, 2; SAAS 1; SATA 21, 62, 111; SATA-Essay 108; WYA; YAW

**Peckinpah, (David) Sam(uel)**
    1925-1984 ................................. **CLC 20**
    See also CA 109; 114; CANR 82

**Pedersen, Knut** 1859-1952
    See Hamsun, Knut
    See also CA 104; 119; CANR 63; MTCW 1, 2

**Peele, George** ...................................... **LC 115**
    See also BW 1; DLB 62, 167; RGEL 2

**Peeslake, Gaffer**
    See Durrell, Lawrence (George)

**Peguy, Charles (Pierre)**
    1873-1914 ............................... **TCLC 10**
    See also CA 107; 193; DLB 258; EWL 3; GFL 1789 to the Present

**Peirce, Charles Sanders**
    1839-1914 ............................... **TCLC 81**
    See also CA 194; DLB 270

**Pellicer, Carlos** 1897(?)-1977 ............ **HLCS 2**
    See also CA 153; 69-72; DLB 290; EWL 3; HW 1

**Pena, Ramon del Valle y**
    See Valle-Inclan, Ramon (Maria) del

**Pendennis, Arthur Esquir**
    See Thackeray, William Makepeace

**Penn, Arthur**
    See Matthews, (James) Brander

**Penn, William** 1644-1718 .................... **LC 25**
    See also DLB 24

**PEPECE**
    See Prado (Calvo), Pedro

**Pepys, Samuel** 1633-1703 ... **LC 11, 58; WLC**
    See also BRW 2; CDBLB 1660-1789; DA; DA3; DAB; DAC; DAM MST; DLB 101, 213; NCFS 4; RGEL 2; TEA; WLIT 3

**Percy, Thomas** 1729-1811 ............... **NCLC 95**
    See also DLB 104

**Percy, Walker** 1916-1990 ....... **CLC 2, 3, 6, 8, 14, 18, 47, 65**
    See also AMWS 3; BPFB 3; CA 1-4R; 131; CANR 1, 23, 64; CPW; CSW; DA3; DAM NOV, POP; DLB 2; DLBY 1980, 1990; EWL 3; MTCW 1, 2; RGAL 4; TUS

**Percy, William Alexander**
    1885-1942 ............................... **TCLC 84**
    See also CA 163; MTCW 2

**Perec, Georges** 1936-1982 ......... **CLC 56, 116**
    See also CA 141; DLB 83, 299; EWL 3; GFL 1789 to the Present; RGWL 3

**Pereda (y Sanchez de Porrua), Jose Maria de** 1833-1906 ......................... **TCLC 16**
    See also CA 117

**Pereda y Porrua, Jose Maria de**
    See Pereda (y Sanchez de Porrua), Jose Maria de

**Peregoy, George Weems**
    See Mencken, H(enry) L(ouis)

**Perelman, S(idney) J(oseph)**
    1904-1979 .. **CLC 3, 5, 9, 15, 23, 44, 49; SSC 32**
    See also AITN 1, 2; BPFB 3; CA 73-76; 89-92; CANR 18; DAM DRAM; DLB 11, 44; MTCW 1, 2; RGAL 4

**Peret, Benjamin** 1899-1959 .... **PC 33; TCLC 20**
    See also CA 117; 186; GFL 1789 to the Present

**Peretz, Isaac Leib**
    See Peretz, Isaac Loeb
    See also CA 201

**Peretz, Isaac Loeb** 1851(?)-1915 ...... **SSC 26; TCLC 16**
    See Peretz, Isaac Leib
    See also CA 109

**Peretz, Yitzkhok Leibush**
    See Peretz, Isaac Loeb

**Perez Galdos, Benito** 1843-1920 ..... **HLCS 2; TCLC 27**
    See Galdos, Benito Perez
    See also CA 125; 153; EWL 3; HW 1; RGWL 2, 3

**Peri Rossi, Cristina** 1941- .. **CLC 156; HLCS 2**
    See also CA 131; CANR 59, 81; CWW 2; DLB 145, 290; EWL 3; HW 1, 2

**Perlata**
    See Peret, Benjamin

**Perloff, Marjorie G(abrielle)**
    1931- ..................................... **CLC 137**
    See also CA 57-60; CANR 7, 22, 49, 104

**Perrault, Charles** 1628-1703 ........... **LC 2, 56**
    See also BYA 4; CLR 79; DLB 268; GFL Beginnings to 1789; MAICYA 1, 2; RGWL 2, 3; SATA 25; WCH

**Perry, Anne** 1938- .......................... **CLC 126**
    See also CA 101; CANR 22, 50, 84; CMW 4; CN 7; CPW; DLB 276

**Perry, Brighton**
    See Sherwood, Robert E(mmet)

**Perse, St.-John**
    See Leger, (Marie-Rene Auguste) Alexis Saint-Leger

**Perse, Saint-John**
    See Leger, (Marie-Rene Auguste) Alexis Saint-Leger
    See also DLB 258; RGWL 3

**Persius** 34-62 ................................... **CMLC 74**
    See also AW 2; DLB 211; RGWL 2, 3

**Perutz, Leo(pold)** 1882-1957 ......... **TCLC 60**
    See also CA 147; DLB 81

**Peseenz, Tulio F.**
    See Lopez y Fuentes, Gregorio

**Pesetsky, Bette** 1932- ........................ **CLC 28**
    See also CA 133; DLB 130

**Peshkov, Alexei Maximovich** 1868-1936
See Gorky, Maxim
See also CA 105; 141; CANR 83; DA; DAC; DAM DRAM, MST, NOV; MTCW 2

**Pessoa, Fernando (Antonio Nogueira)** 1888-1935 ..... **HLC 2; PC 20; TCLC 27**
See also CA 125; 183; DAM MULT; DLB 287; EW 10; EWL 3; RGWL 2, 3; WP

**Peterkin, Julia Mood** 1880-1961 ...... **CLC 31**
See also CA 102; DLB 9

**Peters, Joan K(aren)** 1945- ............... **CLC 39**
See also CA 158; CANR 109

**Peters, Robert L(ouis)** 1924- ............... **CLC 7**
See also CA 13-16R; CAAS 8; CP 7; DLB 105

**Petofi, Sandor** 1823-1849 ............... **NCLC 21**
See also RGWL 2, 3

**Petrakis, Harry Mark** 1923- .............. **CLC 3**
See also CA 9-12R; CANR 4, 30, 85; CN 7

**Petrarch** 1304-1374 ............. **CMLC 20; PC 8**
See also DA3; DAM POET; EW 2; LMFS 1; RGWL 2. 3

**Petronius** c. 20-66 ........................... **CMLC 34**
See also AW 2; CDWLB 1; DLB 211; RGWL 2, 3

**Petrov, Evgeny** ............................... **TCLC 21**
See Kataev, Evgeny Petrovich

**Petry, Ann (Lane)** 1908-1997 .. **CLC 1, 7, 18; TCLC 112**
See also AFAW 1, 2; BPFB 3; BW 1, 3; BYA 2; CA 5-8R; 157; CAAS 6; CANR 4, 46; CLR 12; CN 7; DLB 76; EWL 3; JRDA; LAIT 1; MAICYA 1, 2; MAICYAS 1; MTCW 1; RGAL 4; SATA 5; SATA-Obit 94; TUS

**Petursson, Halligrimur** 1614-1674 ........ **LC 8**
**Peychinovich**
See Vazov, Ivan (Minchov)

**Phaedrus** c. 15B.C.-c. 50 ............... **CMLC 25**
See also DLB 211

**Phelps (Ward), Elizabeth Stuart**
See Phelps, Elizabeth Stuart
See also FW

**Phelps, Elizabeth Stuart**
1844-1911 .................... **TCLC 113**
See Phelps (Ward), Elizabeth Stuart
See also DLB 74

**Philips, Katherine** 1632-1664 . **LC 30; PC 40**
See also DLB 131; RGEL 2

**Philipson, Morris H.** 1926- .............. **CLC 53**
See also CA 1-4R; CANR 4

**Phillips, Caryl** 1958- ............... **BLCS; CLC 96**
See also BRWS 5; BW 2; CA 141; CANR 63, 104; CBD; CD 5; CN 7; DA3; DAM MULT; DLB 157; EWL 3; MTCW 2; WLIT 4; WWE 1

**Phillips, David Graham**
1867-1911 ...................... **TCLC 44**
See also CA 108; 176; DLB 9, 12, 303; RGAL 4

**Phillips, Jack**
See Sandburg, Carl (August)

**Phillips, Jayne Anne** 1952- ........ **CLC 15, 33, 139; SSC 16**
See also AAYA 57; BPFB 3; CA 101; CANR 24, 50, 96; CN 7; CSW; DLBY 1980; INT CANR-24; MTCW 1, 2; RGAL 4; RGSF 2; SSFS 4

**Phillips, Richard**
See Dick, Philip K(indred)

**Phillips, Robert (Schaeffer)** 1938- .... **CLC 28**
See also CA 17-20R; CAAS 13; CANR 8; DLB 105

**Phillips, Ward**
See Lovecraft, H(oward) P(hillips)

**Philostratus, Flavius** c. 179-c.
244 .......................... **CMLC 62**

**Piccolo, Lucio** 1901-1969 .................. **CLC 13**
See also CA 97-100; DLB 114; EWL 3

**Pickthall, Marjorie L(owry) C(hristie)**
1883-1922 ...................... **TCLC 21**
See also CA 107; DLB 92

**Pico della Mirandola, Giovanni**
1463-1494 ...................... **LC 15**
See also LMFS 1

**Piercy, Marge** 1936- .... **CLC 3, 6, 14, 18, 27, 62, 128; PC 29**
See also BPFB 3; CA 21-24R; 187; CAAE 187; CAAS 1; CANR 13, 43, 66, 111; CN 7; CP 7; CWP; DLB 120, 227; EXPP; FW; MTCW 1, 2; PFS 9; SFW 4

**Piers, Robert**
See Anthony, Piers

**Pieyre de Mandiargues, Andre** 1909-1991
See Mandiargues, Andre Pieyre de
See also CA 103; 136; CANR 22, 82; EWL 3; GFL 1789 to the Present

**Pilnyak, Boris** 1894-1938 . **SSC 48; TCLC 23**
See Vogau, Boris Andreyevich
See also EWL 3

**Pinchback, Eugene**
See Toomer, Jean

**Pincherle, Alberto** 1907-1990 ...... **CLC 11, 18**
See Moravia, Alberto
See also CA 25-28R; 132; CANR 33, 63; DAM NOV; MTCW 1

**Pinckney, Darryl** 1953- .................... **CLC 76**
See also BW 2, 3; CA 143; CANR 79

**Pindar** 518(?)B.C.-438(?)B.C. ....... **CMLC 12; PC 19**
See also AW 1; CDWLB 1; DLB 176; RGWL 2

**Pineda, Cecile** 1942- .......................... **CLC 39**
See also CA 118; DLB 209

**Pinero, Arthur Wing** 1855-1934 .... **TCLC 32**
See also CA 110; 153; DAM DRAM; DLB 10; RGEL 2

**Pinero, Miguel (Antonio Gomez)**
1946-1988 .............................. **CLC 4, 55**
See also CA 61-64; 125; CAD; CANR 29, 90; DLB 266; HW 1; LLW 1

**Pinget, Robert** 1919-1997 ....... **CLC 7, 13, 37**
See also CA 85-88; 160; CWW 2; DLB 83; EWL 3; GFL 1789 to the Present

**Pink Floyd**
See Barrett, (Roger) Syd; Gilmour, David; Mason, Nick; Waters, Roger; Wright, Rick

**Pinkney, Edward** 1802-1828 .......... **NCLC 31**
See also DLB 248

**Pinkwater, Daniel**
See Pinkwater, Daniel Manus

**Pinkwater, Daniel Manus** 1941- ....... **CLC 35**
See also AAYA 1, 46; BYA 9; CA 29-32R; CANR 12, 38, 89; CLR 4; CSW; FANT; JRDA; MAICYA 1, 2; SAAS 3; SATA 8, 46, 76, 114; SFW 4; YAW

**Pinkwater, Manus**
See Pinkwater, Daniel Manus

**Pinsky, Robert** 1940- ....... **CLC 9, 19, 38, 94, 121; PC 27**
See also AMWS 6; CA 29-32R; CAAS 4; CANR 58, 97; CP 7; DA3; DAM POET; DLBY 1982, 1998; MTCW 2; PFS 18; RGAL 4

**Pinta, Harold**
See Pinter, Harold

**Pinter, Harold** 1930- .. **CLC 1, 3, 6, 9, 11, 15, 27, 58, 73, 199; DC 15; WLC**
See also BRWR 1; BRWS 1; CA 5-8R; CANR 33, 65, 112; CBD; CD 5; CDBLB 1960 to Present; DA; DA3; DAB; DAC; DAM DRAM, MST; DFS 3, 5, 7, 14; DLB 13; EWL 3; IDFW 3, 4; LMFS 2; MTCW 1, 2; RGEL 2; TEA

**Piozzi, Hester Lynch (Thrale)**
1741-1821 ................................ **NCLC 57**
See also DLB 104, 142

**Pirandello, Luigi** 1867-1936 .. **DC 5; SSC 22; TCLC 4, 29; WLC**
See also CA 104; 153; CANR 103; DA; DA3; DAB; DAC; DAM DRAM, MST; DFS 4, 9; DLB 264; EW 8; EWL 3; MTCW 2; RGSF 2; RGWL 2, 3

**Pirsig, Robert M(aynard)** 1928- ... **CLC 4, 6, 73**
See also CA 53-56; CANR 42, 74; CPW 1; DA3; DAM POP; MTCW 1, 2; SATA 39

**Pisarev, Dmitrii Ivanovich**
See Pisarev, Dmitry Ivanovich
See also DLB 277

**Pisarev, Dmitry Ivanovich**
1840-1868 ................................ **NCLC 25**
See Pisarev, Dmitrii Ivanovich

**Pix, Mary (Griffith)** 1666-1709 .............. **LC 8**
See also DLB 80

**Pixerecourt, (Rene Charles) Guilbert de**
1773-1844 ................................ **NCLC 39**
See also DLB 192; GFL 1789 to the Present

**Plaatje, Sol(omon) T(shekisho)**
1878-1932 .................... **BLCS; TCLC 73**
See also BW 2, 3; CA 141; CANR 79; DLB 125, 225

**Plaidy, Jean**
See Hibbert, Eleanor Alice Burford

**Planche, James Robinson**
1796-1880 .............................. **NCLC 42**
See also RGEL 2

**Plant, Robert** 1948- ........................... **CLC 12**

**Plante, David (Robert)** 1940- . **CLC 7, 23, 38**
See also CA 37-40R; CANR 12, 36, 58, 82; CN 7; DAM NOV; DLBY 1983; INT CANR-12; MTCW 1

**Plath, Sylvia** 1932-1963 ..... **CLC 1, 2, 3, 5, 9, 11, 14, 17, 50, 51, 62, 111; PC 1, 37; WLC**
See also AAYA 13; AMWR 2; AMWS 1; BPFB 3; CA 19-20; CANR 34, 101; CAP 2; CDALB 1941-1968; DA; DA3; DAB; DAC; DAM MST, POET; DLB 5, 6, 152; EWL 3; EXPN; EXPP; FW; LAIT 4; MAWW; MTCW 1, 2; NFS 1; PAB; PFS 1, 15; RGAL 4; SATA 96; TUS; WP; YAW

**Plato** c. 428B.C.-347B.C. .......... **CMLC 8, 75; WLCS**
See also AW 1; CDWLB 1; DA; DA3; DAB; DAC; DAM MST; DLB 176; LAIT 1; LATS 1:1; RGWL 2, 3

**Platonov, Andrei**
See Klimentov, Andrei Platonovich

**Platonov, Andrei Platonovich**
See Klimentov, Andrei Platonovich
See also DLB 272

**Platonov, Andrey Platonovich**
See Klimentov, Andrei Platonovich
See also EWL 3

**Platt, Kin** 1911- ................................ **CLC 26**
See also AAYA 11; CA 17-20R; CANR 11; JRDA; SAAS 17; SATA 21, 86; WYA

**Plautus** c. 254B.C.-c. 184B.C. ...... **CMLC 24; DC 6**
See also AW 1; CDWLB 1; DLB 211; RGWL 2, 3

**Plick et Plock**
See Simenon, Georges (Jacques Christian)

**Plieksans, Janis**
See Rainis, Janis

**Plimpton, George (Ames)**
1927-2003 ................................ **CLC 36**
See also AITN 1; CA 21-24R; 224; CANR 32, 70, 103, 133; DLB 185, 241; MTCW 1, 2; SATA 10; SATA-Obit 150

**Pliny the Elder** c. 23-79 ................. **CMLC 23**
See also DLB 211

**Pliny the Younger** c. 61-c. 112 ...... **CMLC 62**
See also AW 2; DLB 211

**Plomer, William Charles Franklin**
1903-1973 ............................. **CLC 4, 8**
See also AFW; CA 21-22; CANR 34; CAP
2; DLB 20, 162, 191, 225; EWL 3;
MTCW 1; RGEL 2; RGSF 2; SATA 24

**Plotinus** 204-270 ........................... **CMLC 46**
See also CDWLB 1; DLB 176

**Plowman, Piers**
See Kavanagh, Patrick (Joseph)

**Plum, J.**
See Wodehouse, P(elham) G(renville)

**Plumly, Stanley (Ross)** 1939- ........... **CLC 33**
See also CA 108; 110; CANR 97; CP 7;
DLB 5, 193; INT CA-110

**Plumpe, Friedrich Wilhelm**
1888-1931 ............................. **TCLC 53**
See also CA 112

**Plutarch** c. 46-c. 120 ..................... **CMLC 60**
See also AW 2; CDWLB 1; DLB 176;
RGWL 2, 3; TWA

**Po Chu-i** 772-846 ........................... **CMLC 24**

**Podhoretz, Norman** 1930- ................ **CLC 189**
See also AMWS 8; CA 9-12R; CANR 7,
78, 135

**Poe, Edgar Allan** 1809-1849 ..... **NCLC 1, 16,
55, 78, 94, 97, 117; PC 1, 54; SSC 1,
22, 34, 35, 54; WLC**
See also AAYA 14; AMW; AMWC 1;
AMWR 2; BPFB 3; BYA 5, 11; CDALB
1640-1865; CMW 4; DA; DA3; DAB;
DAC; DAM MST, POET; DLB 3, 59, 73,
74, 248, 254; EXPP; EXPS; HGG; LAIT
2; LATS 1:1; LMFS 1; MSW; PAB; PFS
1, 3, 9; RGAL 4; RGSF 2; SATA 23;
SCFW 2; SFW 4; SSFS 2, 4, 7, 8, 16;
SUFW; TUS; WP; WYA

**Poet of Titchfield Street, The**
See Pound, Ezra (Weston Loomis)

**Pohl, Frederik** 1919- ........... **CLC 18; SSC 25**
See also AAYA 24; CA 61-64, 188; CAAE
188; CAAS 1; CANR 11, 37, 81; CN 7;
DLB 8; INT CANR-11; MTCW 1, 2;
SATA 24; SCFW 2; SFW 4

**Poirier, Louis** 1910-
See Gracq, Julien
See also CA 122; 126

**Poitier, Sidney** 1927- .......................... **CLC 26**
See also AAYA 60; BW 1; CA 117; CANR
94

**Pokagon, Simon** 1830-1899 ............... **NNAL**
See also DAM MULT

**Polanski, Roman** 1933- ............ **CLC 16, 178**
See also CA 77-80

**Poliakoff, Stephen** 1952- ................... **CLC 38**
See also CA 106; CANR 116; CBD; CD 5;
DLB 13

**Police, The**
See Copeland, Stewart (Armstrong); Summers, Andrew James

**Polidori, John William** 1795-1821 . **NCLC 51**
See also DLB 116; HGG

**Pollitt, Katha** 1949- ................. **CLC 28, 122**
See also CA 120; 122; CANR 66, 108;
MTCW 1, 2

**Pollock, (Mary) Sharon** 1936- ......... **CLC 50**
See also CA 141; CANR 132; CD 5; CWD;
DAC; DAM DRAM, MST; DFS 3; DLB
60; FW

**Pollock, Sharon** 1936- ......................... **DC 20**

**Polo, Marco** 1254-1324 ................. **CMLC 15**

**Polonsky, Abraham (Lincoln)**
1910-1999 ............................. **CLC 92**
See also CA 104; 187; DLB 26; INT CA-
104

**Polybius** c. 200B.C.-c. 118B.C. ...... **CMLC 17**
See also AW 1; DLB 176; RGWL 2, 3

**Pomerance, Bernard** 1940- ................ **CLC 13**
See also CA 101; CAD; CANR 49, 134;
CD 5; DAM DRAM; DFS 9; LAIT 2

**Ponge, Francis** 1899-1988 ............. **CLC 6, 18**
See also CA 85-85; 126; CANR 40, 86;
DAM POET; DLBY 2002; EWL 3; GFL
1789 to the Present; RGWL 2, 3

**Poniatowska, Elena** 1933- . **CLC 140; HLC 2**
See also CA 101; CANR 32, 66, 107; CD-
WLB 3; CWW 2; DAM MULT; DLB 113;
EWL 3; HW 1, 2; LAWS 1; WLIT 1

**Pontoppidan, Henrik** 1857-1943 .... **TCLC 29**
See also CA 170; DLB 300

**Ponty, Maurice Merleau**
See Merleau-Ponty, Maurice

**Poole, Josephine** ................................. **CLC 17**
See Helyar, Jane Penelope Josephine
See also SAAS 2; SATA 5

**Popa, Vasko** 1922-1991 . **CLC 19; TCLC 167**
See also CA 112; 148; CDWLB 4; DLB
181; EWL 3; RGWL 2, 3

**Pope, Alexander** 1688-1744 ...... **LC 3, 58, 60,
64; PC 26; WLC**
See also BRW 3; BRWC 1; BRWR 1; CD-
BLB 1660-1789; DA; DA3; DAB; DAC;
DAM MST, POET; DLB 95, 101, 213;
EXPP; PAB; PFS 12; RGEL 2; WLIT 3;
WP

**Popov, Evgenii Anatol'evich**
See Popov, Yevgeny
See also DLB 285

**Popov, Yevgeny** ................................. **CLC 59**
See Popov, Evgenii Anatol'evich

**Poquelin, Jean-Baptiste**
See Moliere

**Porete, Marguerite** c. 1250-1310 .. **CMLC 73**
See also DLB 208

**Porphyry** c. 233-c. 305 ................... **CMLC 71**

**Porter, Connie (Rose)** 1959(?)- ........ **CLC 70**
See also BW 2, 3; CA 142; CANR 90, 109;
SATA 81, 129

**Porter, Gene(va Grace) Stratton** .. **TCLC 21**
See Stratton-Porter, Gene(va Grace)
See also BPFB 3; CA 112; CWRI 5; RHW

**Porter, Katherine Anne** 1890-1980 ... **CLC 1,
3, 7, 10, 13, 15, 27, 101; SSC 4, 31, 43**
See also AAYA 42; AITN 2; AMW; BPFB
3; CA 1-4R; 101; CANR 1, 65; CDALBS;
DA; DA3; DAB; DAC; DAM MST, NOV;
DLB 4, 9, 102; DLBD 12; DLBY 1980;
EWL 3; EXPS; LAIT 3; MAWW; MTCW
1, 2; NFS 14; RGAL 4; RGSF 2; SATA
39; SATA-Obit 23; SSFS 1, 8, 11, 16;
TUS

**Porter, Peter (Neville Frederick)**
1929- ................................. **CLC 5, 13, 33**
See also CA 85-88; CP 7; DLB 40, 289;
WWE 1

**Porter, William Sydney** 1862-1910
See Henry, O.
See also CA 104; 131; CDALB 1865-1917;
DA; DA3; DAB; DAC; DAM MST; DLB
12, 78, 79; MTCW 1, 2; TUS; YABC 2

**Portillo (y Pacheco), Jose Lopez**
See Lopez Portillo (y Pacheco), Jose

**Portillo Trambley, Estela**
1927-1998 ................ **HLC 2; TCLC 163**
See Trambley, Estela Portillo
See also CANR 32; DAM MULT; DLB
209; HW 1

**Posey, Alexander (Lawrence)**
1873-1908 ................................. **NNAL**
See also CA 144; CANR 80; DAM MULT;
DLB 175

**Posse, Abel** ................................. **CLC 70**

**Post, Melville Davisson**
1869-1930 ............................. **TCLC 39**
See also CA 110; 202; CMW 4

**Potok, Chaim** 1929-2002 ... **CLC 2, 7, 14, 26,
112**
See also AAYA 15, 50; AITN 1, 2; BPFB 3;
BYA 1; CA 17-20R; 208; CANR 19, 35,
64, 98; CLR 92; CN 7; DA3; DAM NOV;
DLB 28, 152; EXPN; INT CANR-19;
LAIT 4; MTCW 1, 2; NFS 4; SATA 33,
106; SATA-Obit 134; TUS; YAW

**Potok, Herbert Harold** -2002
See Potok, Chaim

**Potok, Herman Harold**
See Potok, Chaim

**Potter, Dennis (Christopher George)**
1935-1994 .................. **CLC 58, 86, 123**
See also BRWS 10; CA 107; 145; CANR
33, 61; CBD; DLB 233; MTCW 1

**Pound, Ezra (Weston Loomis)**
1885-1972 .. **CLC 1, 2, 3, 4, 5, 7, 10, 13,
18, 34, 48, 50, 112; PC 4; WLC**
See also AAYA 47; AMW; AMWR 1; CA
5-8R; 37-40R; CANR 40; CDALB 1917-
1929; DA; DA3; DAB; DAC; DAM MST,
POET; DLB 4, 45, 63; DLBD 15; EFS 2;
EWL 3; EXPP; LMFS 2; MTCW 1, 2;
PAB; PFS 2, 8, 16; RGAL 4; TUS; WP

**Povod, Reinaldo** 1959-1994 .............. **CLC 44**
See also CA 136; 146; CANR 83

**Powell, Adam Clayton, Jr.**
1908-1972 ..................... **BLC 3; CLC 89**
See also BW 1, 3; CA 102; 33-36R; CANR
86; DAM MULT

**Powell, Anthony (Dymoke)**
1905-2000 ..... **CLC 1, 3, 7, 9, 10, 31**
See also BRW 7; CA 1-4R; 189; CANR 1,
32, 62, 107; CDBLB 1945-1960; CN 7;
DLB 15; EWL 3; MTCW 1, 2; RGEL 2;
TEA

**Powell, Dawn** 1896(?)-1965 .............. **CLC 66**
See also CA 5-8R; CANR 121; DLBY 1997

**Powell, Padgett** 1952- ......................... **CLC 34**
See also CA 126; CANR 63, 101; CSW;
DLB 234; DLBY 01

**Powell, (Oval) Talmage** 1920-2000
See Queen, Ellery
See also CA 5-8R; CANR 2, 80

**Power, Susan** 1961- .......................... **CLC 91**
See also BYA 14; CA 160; CANR 135; NFS
11

**Powers, J(ames) F(arl)** 1917-1999 ..... **CLC 1,
4, 8, 57; SSC 4**
See also CA 1-4R; 181; CANR 2, 61; CN
7; DLB 130; MTCW 1; RGAL 4; RGSF
2

**Powers, John J(ames)** 1945-
See Powers, John R.
See also CA 69-72

**Powers, John R.** ............................. **CLC 66**
See Powers, John J(ames)

**Powers, Richard (S.)** 1957- ............... **CLC 93**
See also AMWS 9; BPFB 3; CA 148;
CANR 80; CN 7

**Pownall, David** 1938- ......................... **CLC 10**
See also CA 89-92, 180; CAAS 18; CANR
49, 101; CBD; CD 5; CN 7; DLB 14

**Powys, John Cowper** 1872-1963 ... **CLC 7, 9,
15, 46, 125**
See also CA 85-88; CANR 106; DLB 15,
255; EWL 3; FANT; MTCW 1, 2; RGEL
2; SUFW

**Powys, T(heodore) F(rancis)**
1875-1953 ............................. **TCLC 9**
See also BRWS 8; CA 106; 189; DLB 36,
162; EWL 3; FANT; RGEL 2; SUFW

**Prado (Calvo), Pedro** 1886-1952 ... **TCLC 75**
See also CA 131; DLB 283; HW 1; LAW

(Oval) Talmage; Sheldon, Walter J(ames); Sturgeon, Theodore (Hamilton); Tracy, Don(ald Fiske); Vance, John Holbrook
See also BPFB 3; CMW 4; MSW; RGAL 4

**Queen, Ellery, Jr.**
See Dannay, Frederic; Lee, Manfred B(ennington)

**Queneau, Raymond** 1903-1976 ..... **CLC 2, 5, 10, 42**
See also CA 77-80; 69-72; CANR 32; DLB 72, 258; EW 12; EWL 3; GFL 1789 to the Present; MTCW 1, 2; RGWL 2, 3

**Quevedo, Francisco de** 1580-1645 ....... **LC 23**

**Quiller-Couch, Sir Arthur (Thomas)**
1863-1944 ................................. **TCLC 53**
See also CA 118; 166; DLB 135, 153, 190; HGG; RGEL 2; SUFW 1

**Quin, Ann (Marie)** 1936-1973 ............. **CLC 6**
See also CA 9-12R; 45-48; DLB 14, 231

**Quincey, Thomas de**
See De Quincey, Thomas

**Quindlen, Anna** 1953- ...................... **CLC 191**
See also AAYA 35; CA 138; CANR 73, 126; DA3; DLB 292; MTCW 2

**Quinn, Martin**
See Smith, Martin Cruz

**Quinn, Peter** 1947- ............................. **CLC 91**
See also CA 197

**Quinn, Simon**
See Smith, Martin Cruz

**Quintana, Leroy V.** 1944- ...... **HLC 2; PC 36**
See also CA 131; CANR 65; DAM MULT; DLB 82; HW 1, 2

**Quintilian** c. 35-40-c. 96. ............... **CMLC 77**
See also AW 2; DLB 211; RGWL 2, 3

**Quiroga, Horacio (Sylvestre)**
1878-1937 ................. **HLC 2; TCLC 20**
See also CA 117; 131; DAM MULT; EWL 3; HW 1; LAW; MTCW 1; RGSF 2; WLIT 1

**Quoirez, Francoise** 1935- .................... **CLC 9**
See Sagan, Francoise
See also CA 49-52; CANR 6, 39, 73; MTCW 1, 2; TWA

**Raabe, Wilhelm (Karl)** 1831-1910 . **TCLC 45**
See also CA 167; DLB 129

**Rabe, David (William)** 1940- .. **CLC 4, 8, 33, 200; DC 16**
See also CA 85-88; CABS 3; CAD; CANR 59, 129; CD 5; DAM DRAM; DFS 3, 8, 13; DLB 7, 228; EWL 3

**Rabelais, Francois** 1494-1553 ........ **LC 5, 60; WLC**
See also DA; DAB; DAC; DAM MST; EW 2; GFL Beginnings to 1789; LMFS 1; RGWL 2, 3; TWA

**Rabinovitch, Sholem** 1859-1916
See Aleichem, Sholom
See also CA 104

**Rabinyan, Dorit** 1972- ..................... **CLC 119**
See also CA 170

**Rachilde**
See Vallette, Marguerite Eymery; Vallette, Marguerite Eymery
See also EWL 3

**Racine, Jean** 1639-1699 ............... **LC 28, 113**
See also DA3; DAB; DAM MST; DLB 268; EW 3; GFL Beginnings to 1789; LMFS 1; RGWL 2, 3; TWA

**Radcliffe, Ann (Ward)** 1764-1823 ... **NCLC 6, 55, 106**
See also DLB 39, 178; HGG; LMFS 1; RGEL 2; SUFW; WLIT 3

**Radclyffe-Hall, Marguerite**
See Hall, (Marguerite) Radclyffe

**Radiguet, Raymond** 1903-1923 ...... **TCLC 29**
See also CA 162; DLB 65; EWL 3; GFL 1789 to the Present; RGWL 2, 3

**Radnoti, Miklos** 1909-1944 ............. **TCLC 16**
See also CA 118; 212; CDWLB 4; DLB 215; EWL 3; RGWL 2, 3

**Rado, James** 1939- .............................. **CLC 17**
See also CA 105

**Radvanyi, Netty** 1900-1983
See Seghers, Anna
See also CA 85-88; 110; CANR 82

**Rae, Ben**
See Griffiths, Trevor

**Raeburn, John (Hay)** 1941- .............. **CLC 34**
See also CA 57-60

**Ragni, Gerome** 1942-1991 ................ **CLC 17**
See also CA 105; 134

**Rahv, Philip** ................................... **CLC 24**
See Greenberg, Ivan
See also DLB 137

**Raimund, Ferdinand Jakob**
1790-1836 ........................... **NCLC 69**
See also DLB 90

**Raine, Craig (Anthony)** 1944- .. **CLC 32, 103**
See also CA 108; CANR 29, 51, 103; CP 7; DLB 40; PFS 7

**Raine, Kathleen (Jessie)** 1908-2003 .. **CLC 7, 45**
See also CA 85-88; 218; CANR 46, 109; CP 7; DLB 20; EWL 3; MTCW 1; RGEL 2

**Rainis, Janis** 1865-1929 ................. **TCLC 29**
See also CA 170; CDWLB 4; DLB 220; EWL 3

**Rakosi, Carl** ................................... **CLC 47**
See Rawley, Callman
See also CA 228; CAAS 5; CP 7; DLB 193

**Ralegh, Sir Walter**
See Raleigh, Sir Walter
See also BRW 1; RGEL 2; WP

**Raleigh, Richard**
See Lovecraft, H(oward) P(hillips)

**Raleigh, Sir Walter** 1554(?)-1618 ....... **LC 31, 39; PC 31**
See Ralegh, Sir Walter
See also CDBLB Before 1660; DLB 172; EXPP; PFS 14; TEA

**Rallentando, H. P.**
See Sayers, Dorothy L(eigh)

**Ramal, Walter**
See de la Mare, Walter (John)

**Ramana Maharshi** 1879-1950 ........ **TCLC 84**

**Ramoacn y Cajal, Santiago**
1852-1934 ................................. **TCLC 93**

**Ramon, Juan**
See Jimenez (Mantecon), Juan Ramon

**Ramos, Graciliano** 1892-1953 ........ **TCLC 32**
See also CA 167; DLB 307; EWL 3; HW 2; LAW; WLIT 1

**Rampersad, Arnold** 1941- ................ **CLC 44**
See also BW 2, 3; CA 127; 133; CANR 81; DLB 111; INT CA-133

**Rampling, Anne**
See Rice, Anne
See also GLL 2

**Ramsay, Allan** 1686(?)-1758 ................ **LC 29**
See also DLB 95; RGEL 2

**Ramsay, Jay**
See Campbell, (John) Ramsey

**Ramuz, Charles-Ferdinand**
1878-1947 ................................. **TCLC 33**
See also CA 165; EWL 3

**Rand, Ayn** 1905-1982 ...... **CLC 3, 30, 44, 79; WLC**
See also AAYA 10; AMWS 4; BPFB 3; BYA 12; CA 13-16R; 105; CANR 27, 73; CDALBS; CPW; DA; DA3; DAC; DAM MST, NOV, POP; DLB 227, 279; MTCW 1, 2; NFS 10, 16; RGAL 4; SFW 4; TUS; YAW

**Randall, Dudley (Felker)** 1914-2000 . **BLC 3; CLC 1, 135**
See also BW 1, 3; CA 25-28R; 189; CANR 23, 82; DAM MULT; DLB 41; PFS 5

**Randall, Robert**
See Silverberg, Robert

**Ranger, Ken**
See Creasey, John

**Rank, Otto** 1884-1939 ................... **TCLC 115**

**Ransom, John Crowe** 1888-1974 .. **CLC 2, 4, 5, 11, 24; PC 61**
See also AMW; CA 5-8R; 49-52; CANR 6, 34; CDALBS; DA3; DAM POET; DLB 45, 63; EWL 3; EXPP; MTCW 1, 2; RGAL 4; TUS

**Rao, Raja** 1909- ........................... **CLC 25, 56**
See also CA 73-76; CANR 51; CN 7; DAM NOV; EWL 3; MTCW 1, 2; RGEL 2; RGSF 2

**Raphael, Frederic (Michael)** 1931- ... **CLC 2, 14**
See also CA 1-4R; CANR 1, 86; CN 7; DLB 14

**Ratcliffe, James P.**
See Mencken, H(enry) L(ouis)

**Rathbone, Julian** 1935- ..................... **CLC 41**
See also CA 101; CANR 34, 73

**Rattigan, Terence (Mervyn)**
1911-1977 ........................ **CLC 7; DC 18**
See also BRWS 7; CA 85-88; 73-76; CBD; CDBLB 1945-1960; DAM DRAM; DFS 8; DLB 13; IDFW 3, 4; MTCW 1, 2; RGEL 2

**Ratushinskaya, Irina** 1954- ............... **CLC 54**
See also CA 129; CANR 68; CWW 2

**Raven, Simon (Arthur Noel)**
1927-2001 ................................. **CLC 14**
See also CA 81-84; 197; CANR 86; CN 7; DLB 271

**Ravenna, Michael**
See Welty, Eudora (Alice)

**Rawley, Callman** 1903-2004
See Rakosi, Carl
See also CA 21-24R; CANR 12, 32, 91

**Rawlings, Marjorie Kinnan**
1896-1953 ................................. **TCLC 4**
See also AAYA 20; AMWS 10; ANW; BPFB 3; BYA 3; CA 104; 137; CANR 74; CLR 63; DLB 9, 22, 102; DLBD 17; JRDA; MAICYA 1, 2; MTCW 2; RGAL 4; SATA 100; WCH; YABC 1; YAW

**Ray, Satyajit** 1921-1992 ............. **CLC 16, 76**
See also CA 114; 137; DAM MULT

**Read, Herbert Edward** 1893-1968 ..... **CLC 4**
See also BRW 6; CA 85-88; 25-28R; DLB 20, 149; EWL 3; PAB; RGEL 2

**Read, Piers Paul** 1941- ........... **CLC 4, 10, 25**
See also CA 21-24R; CANR 38, 86; CN 7; DLB 14; SATA 21

**Reade, Charles** 1814-1884 ......... **NCLC 2, 74**
See also DLB 21; RGEL 2

**Reade, Hamish**
See Gray, Simon (James Holliday)

**Reading, Peter** 1946- ........................ **CLC 47**
See also BRWS 8; CA 103; CANR 46, 96; CP 7; DLB 40

**Reaney, James** 1926- ........................ **CLC 13**
See also CA 41-44R; CAAS 15; CANR 42; CD 5; CP 7; DAC; DAM MST; DLB 68; RGEL 2; SATA 43

**Rebreanu, Liviu** 1885-1944 ............ **TCLC 28**
See also CA 165; DLB 220; EWL 3

**Rechy, John (Francisco)** 1934- ...... **CLC 1, 7, 14, 18, 107; HLC 2**
See also CA 5-8R, 195; CAAE 195; CAAS 4; CANR 6, 32, 64; CN 7; DAM MULT; DLB 122, 278; DLBY 1982; HW 1, 2; INT CANR-6; LLW 1; RGAL 4

**Redcam, Tom** 1870-1933 ................. **TCLC 25**

**Riddell, Charlotte** 1832-1906 ......... **TCLC 40**
See Riddell, Mrs. J. H.
See also CA 165; DLB 156
**Riddell, Mrs. J. H.**
See Riddell, Charlotte
See also HGG; SUFW
**Ridge, John Rollin** 1827-1867 ...... **NCLC 82;
NNAL**
See also CA 144; DAM MULT; DLB 175
**Ridgeway, Jason**
See Marlowe, Stephen
**Ridgway, Keith** 1965- ..................... **CLC 119**
See also CA 172
**Riding, Laura** ......................... **CLC 3, 7**
See Jackson, Laura (Riding)
See also RGAL 4
**Riefenstahl, Berta Helene Amalia** 1902-2003
See Riefenstahl, Leni
See also CA 108; 220
**Riefenstahl, Leni** ........................ **CLC 16, 190**
See Riefenstahl, Berta Helene Amalia
**Riffe, Ernest**
See Bergman, (Ernst) Ingmar
**Riggs, (Rolla) Lynn**
1899-1954 ................... **NNAL; TCLC 56**
See also CA 144; DAM MULT; DLB 175
**Riis, Jacob A(ugust)** 1849-1914 ..... **TCLC 80**
See also CA 113; 168; DLB 23
**Riley, James Whitcomb** 1849-1916 .... **PC 48;
TCLC 51**
See also CA 118; 137; DAM POET; MAI-
CYA 1, 2; RGAL 4; SATA 17
**Riley, Tex**
See Creasey, John
**Rilke, Rainer Maria** 1875-1926 ........... **PC 2;
TCLC 1, 6, 19**
See also CA 104; 132; CANR 62, 99; CD-
WLB 2; DA3; DAM POET; DLB 81; EW
9; EWL 3; MTCW 1, 2; PFS 19; RGWL
2, 3; TWA; WP
**Rimbaud, (Jean Nicolas) Arthur**
1854-1891 ... **NCLC 4, 35, 82; PC 3, 57;
WLC**
See also DA; DA3; DAB; DAC; DAM
MST, POET; DLB 217; EW 7; GFL 1789
to the Present; LMFS 2; RGWL 2, 3;
TWA; WP
**Rinehart, Mary Roberts**
1876-1958 ................................ **TCLC 52**
See also BPFB 3; CA 108; 166; RGAL 4;
RHW
**Ringmaster, The**
See Mencken, H(enry) L(ouis)
**Ringwood, Gwen(dolyn Margaret) Pharis**
1910-1984 ............................... **CLC 48**
See also CA 148; 112; DLB 88
**Rio, Michel** 1945(?)- ............................. **CLC 43**
See also CA 201
**Rios, Alberto (Alvaro)** 1952- ............... **PC 57**
See also AMWS 4; CA 113; CANR 34, 79;
CP 7; DLB 122; HW 2; PFS 11
**Ritsos, Giannes**
See Ritsos, Yannis
**Ritsos, Yannis** 1909-1990 ........ **CLC 6, 13, 31**
See also CA 77-80; 133; CANR 39, 61; EW
12; EWL 3; MTCW 1; RGWL 2, 3
**Ritter, Erika** 1948(?)- ........................... **CLC 52**
See also CD 5; CWD
**Rivera, Jose Eustasio** 1889-1928 ... **TCLC 35**
See also CA 162; EWL 3; HW 1, 2; LAW
**Rivera, Tomas** 1935-1984 ................. **HLCS 2**
See also CA 49-52; CANR 32; DLB 82;
HW 1; LLW 1; RGAL 4; SSFS 15;
TCWW 2; WLIT 1
**Rivers, Conrad Kent** 1933-1968 ........ **CLC 1**
See also BW 1; CA 85-88; DLB 41
**Rivers, Elfrida**
See Bradley, Marion Zimmer
See also GLL 1

**Riverside, John**
See Heinlein, Robert A(nson)
**Rizal, Jose** 1861-1896 ..................... **NCLC 27**
**Roa Bastos, Augusto (Antonio)**
1917- ............................. **CLC 45; HLC 2**
See also CA 131; CWW 2; DAM MULT;
DLB 113; EWL 3; HW 1; LAW; RGSF 2;
WLIT 1
**Robbe-Grillet, Alain** 1922- .... **CLC 1, 2, 4, 6,
8, 10, 14, 43, 128**
See also BPFB 3; CA 9-12R; CANR 33,
65, 115; CWW 2; DLB 83; EW 13; EWL
3; GFL 1789 to the Present; IDFW 3, 4;
MTCW 1, 2; RGWL 2, 3; SSFS 15
**Robbins, Harold** 1916-1997 ............... **CLC 5**
See also BPFB 3; CA 73-76; 162; CANR
26, 54, 112; DA3; DAM NOV; MTCW 1,
2
**Robbins, Thomas Eugene** 1936-
See Robbins, Tom
See also CA 81-84; CANR 29, 59, 95; CN
7; CPW; CSW; DA3; DAM NOV, POP;
MTCW 1, 2
**Robbins, Tom** ........................ **CLC 9, 32, 64**
See Robbins, Thomas Eugene
See also AAYA 32; AMWS 10; BEST 90:3;
BPFB 3; DLBY 1980; MTCW 2
**Robbins, Trina** 1938- ......................... **CLC 21**
See also CA 128
**Roberts, Charles G(eorge) D(ouglas)**
1860-1943 ............................. **TCLC 8**
See also CA 105; 188; CLR 33; CWRI 5;
DLB 92; RGEL 2; RGSF 2; SATA 88;
SATA-Brief 29
**Roberts, Elizabeth Madox**
1886-1941 ............................. **TCLC 68**
See also CA 111; 166; CLR 100; CWRI 5;
DLB 9, 54, 102; RGAL 4; RHW; SATA
33; SATA-Brief 27; WCH
**Roberts, Kate** 1891-1985 .................. **CLC 15**
See also CA 107; 116
**Roberts, Keith (John Kingston)**
1935-2000 ............................. **CLC 14**
See also BRWS 10; CA 25-28R; CANR 46;
DLB 261; SFW 4
**Roberts, Kenneth (Lewis)**
1885-1957 ............................. **TCLC 23**
See also CA 109; 199; DLB 9; RGAL 4;
RHW
**Roberts, Michele (Brigitte)** 1949- .... **CLC 48,
178**
See also CA 115; CANR 58, 120; CN 7;
DLB 231; FW
**Robertson, Ellis**
See Ellison, Harlan (Jay); Silverberg, Rob-
ert
**Robertson, Thomas William**
1829-1871 ............................. **NCLC 35**
See Robertson, Tom
See also DAM DRAM
**Robertson, Tom**
See Robertson, Thomas William
See also RGEL 2
**Robeson, Kenneth**
See Dent, Lester
**Robinson, Edwin Arlington**
1869-1935 ......... **PC 1, 35; TCLC 5, 101**
See also AMW; CA 104; 133; CDALB
1865-1917; DA; DAC; DAM MST,
POET; DLB 54; EWL 3; EXPP; MTCW
1, 2; PAB; PFS 4; RGAL 4; WP
**Robinson, Henry Crabb**
1775-1867 ............................. **NCLC 15**
See also DLB 107
**Robinson, Jill** 1936- ........................... **CLC 10**
See also CA 102; CANR 120; INT CA-102
**Robinson, Kim Stanley** 1952- ............... **CLC 34**
See also AAYA 26; CA 126; CANR 113;
CN 7; SATA 109; SCFW 2; SFW 4

**Robinson, Lloyd**
See Silverberg, Robert
**Robinson, Marilynne** 1944- ...... **CLC 25, 180**
See also CA 116; CANR 80; CN 7; DLB
206
**Robinson, Mary** 1758-1800 .......... **NCLC 142**
See also DLB 158; FW
**Robinson, Smokey** ........................... **CLC 21**
See Robinson, William, Jr.
**Robinson, William, Jr.** 1940-
See Robinson, Smokey
See also CA 116
**Robison, Mary** 1949- ................... **CLC 42, 98**
See also CA 113; 116; CANR 87; CN 7;
DLB 130; INT CA-116; RGSF 2
**Rochester**
See Wilmot, John
See also RGEL 2
**Rod, Edouard** 1857-1910 ............... **TCLC 52**
**Roddenberry, Eugene Wesley** 1921-1991
See Roddenberry, Gene
See also CA 110; 135; CANR 37; SATA 45;
SATA-Obit 69
**Roddenberry, Gene** ........................... **CLC 17**
See Roddenberry, Eugene Wesley
See also AAYA 5; SATA-Obit 69
**Rodgers, Mary** 1931- ......................... **CLC 12**
See also BYA 5; CA 49-52; CANR 8, 55,
90; CLR 20; CWRI 5; INT CANR-8;
JRDA; MAICYA 1, 2; SATA 8, 130
**Rodgers, W(illiam) R(obert)**
1909-1969 ................................ **CLC 7**
See also CA 85-88; DLB 20; RGEL 2
**Rodman, Eric**
See Silverberg, Robert
**Rodman, Howard** 1920(?)-1985 ........ **CLC 65**
See also CA 118
**Rodman, Maia**
See Wojciechowska, Maia (Teresa)
**Rodo, Jose Enrique** 1871(?)-1917 .... **HLCS 2**
See also CA 178; EWL 3; HW 2; LAW
**Rodolph, Utto**
See Ouologuem, Yambo
**Rodriguez, Claudio** 1934-1999 ......... **CLC 10**
See also CA 188; DLB 134
**Rodriguez, Richard** 1944- .... **CLC 155; HLC
2**
See also AMWS 14; CA 110; CANR 66,
116; DAM MULT; DLB 82, 256; HW 1,
2; LAIT 5; LLW 1; NCFS 3; WLIT 1
**Roelvaag, O(le) E(dvart)** 1876-1931
See Rolvaag, O(le) E(dvart)
See also CA 117; 171
**Roethke, Theodore (Huebner)**
1908-1963 ......... **CLC 1, 3, 8, 11, 19, 46,
101; PC 15**
See also AMW; CA 81-84; CABS 2;
CDALB 1941-1968; DA3; DAM POET;
DLB 5, 206; EWL 3; EXPP; MTCW 1, 2;
PAB; PFS 3; RGAL 4; WP
**Rogers, Carl R(ansom)**
1902-1987 ............................. **TCLC 125**
See also CA 1-4R; 121; CANR 1, 18;
MTCW 1
**Rogers, Samuel** 1763-1855 ............. **NCLC 69**
See also DLB 93; RGEL 2
**Rogers, Thomas Hunton** 1927- ......... **CLC 57**
See also CA 89-92; INT CA-89-92
**Rogers, Will(iam Penn Adair)**
1879-1935 .............. **NNAL; TCLC 8, 71**
See also CA 105; 144; DA3; DAM MULT;
DLB 11; MTCW 2
**Rogin, Gilbert** 1929- ......................... **CLC 18**
See also CA 65-68; CANR 15
**Rohan, Koda**
See Koda Shigeyuki
**Rohlfs, Anna Katharine Green**
See Green, Anna Katharine

Author Index

**Sheldon, Alice Hastings Bradley**
1915(?)-1987
See Tiptree, James, Jr.
See also CA 108; 122; CANR 34; INT CA-108; MTCW 1
**Sheldon, John**
See Bloch, Robert (Albert)
**Sheldon, Walter J(ames)** 1917-1996
See Queen, Ellery
See also AITN 1; CA 25-28R; CANR 10
**Shelley, Mary Wollstonecraft (Godwin)**
1797-1851 ...... **NCLC 14, 59, 103; WLC**
See also AAYA 20; BPFB 3; BRW 3; BRWC 2; BRWS 3; BYA 5; CDBLB 1789-1832; DA; DA3; DAB; DAC; DAM MST, NOV; DLB 110, 116, 159, 178; EXPN; HGG; LAIT 1; LMFS 1, 2; NFS 1; RGEL 2; SATA 29; SCFW; SFW 4; TEA; WLIT 3
**Shelley, Percy Bysshe** 1792-1822 .. **NCLC 18, 93, 143; PC 14; WLC**
See also BRW 4; BRWR 1; CDBLB 1789-1832; DA; DA3; DAB; DAC; DAM MST, POET; DLB 96, 110, 158; EXPP; LMFS 1; PAB; PFS 2; RGEL 2; TEA; WLIT 3; WP
**Shepard, Jim** 1956- ......................... **CLC 36**
See also CA 137; CANR 59, 104; SATA 90
**Shepard, Lucius** 1947- ...................... **CLC 34**
See also CA 128; 141; CANR 81, 124; HGG; SCFW 2; SFW 4; SUFW 2
**Shepard, Sam** 1943- .... **CLC 4, 6, 17, 34, 41, 44, 169; DC 5**
See also AAYA 1, 58; AMWS 3; CA 69-72; CABS 3; CAD; CANR 22, 120; CD 5; DA3; DAM DRAM; DFS 3, 6, 7, 14; DLB 7, 212; EWL 3; IDFW 3, 4; MTCW 1, 2; RGAL 4
**Shepherd, Michael**
See Ludlum, Robert
**Sherburne, Zoa (Lillian Morin)**
1912-1995 ................................. **CLC 30**
See also AAYA 13; CA 1-4R; 176; CANR 3, 37; MAICYA 1, 2; SAAS 18; SATA 3; YAW
**Sheridan, Frances** 1724-1766 ................. **LC 7**
See also DLB 39, 84
**Sheridan, Richard Brinsley**
1751-1816 .... **DC 1; NCLC 5, 91; WLC**
See also BRW 3; CDBLB 1660-1789; DA; DAB; DAC; DAM DRAM, MST; DFS 15; DLB 89; WLIT 3
**Sherman, Jonathan Marc** ............... **CLC 55**
**Sherman, Martin** 1941(?)- ................. **CLC 19**
See also CA 116; 123; CAD; CANR 86; CD 5; DLB 228; GLL 1; IDTP
**Sherwin, Judith Johnson**
See Johnson, Judith (Emlyn)
See also CANR 85; CP 7; CWP
**Sherwood, Frances** 1940- .................. **CLC 81**
See also CA 146, 220; CAAE 220
**Sherwood, Robert E(mmet)**
1896-1955 ................................. **TCLC 3**
See also CA 104; 153; CANR 86; DAM DRAM; DFS 11, 15, 17; DLB 7, 26, 249; IDFW 3, 4; RGAL 4
**Shestov, Lev** 1866-1938 ................... **TCLC 56**
**Shevchenko, Taras** 1814-1861 ........ **NCLC 54**
**Shiel, M(atthew) P(hipps)**
1865-1947 ................................. **TCLC 8**
See Holmes, Gordon
See also CA 106; 160; DLB 153; HGG; MTCW 2; SFW 4; SUFW
**Shields, Carol (Ann)** 1935-2003 ...... **CLC 91, 113, 193**
See also AMWS 7; CA 81-84; 218; CANR 51, 74, 98, 133; CCA 1; CN 7; CPW; DA3; DAC; MTCW 2

**Shields, David (Jonathan)** 1956- ...... **CLC 97**
See also CA 124; CANR 48, 99, 112
**Shiga, Naoya** 1883-1971 ..... **CLC 33; SSC 23**
See Shiga Naoya
See also CA 101; 33-36R; MJW; RGWL 3
**Shiga Naoya**
See Shiga, Naoya
See also DLB 180; EWL 3; RGWL 3
**Shilts, Randy** 1951-1994 .................... **CLC 85**
See also AAYA 19; CA 115; 127; 144; CANR 45; DA3; GLL 1; INT CA-127; MTCW 2
**Shimazaki, Haruki** 1872-1943
See Shimazaki Toson
See also CA 105; 134; CANR 84; RGWL 3
**Shimazaki Toson** ........................... **TCLC 5**
See Shimazaki, Haruki
See also DLB 180; EWL 3
**Shirley, James** 1596-1666 ....... **DC 25; LC 96**
See also DLB 58; RGEL 2
**Sholokhov, Mikhail (Aleksandrovich)**
1905-1984 ........................... **CLC 7, 15**
See also CA 101; 112; DLB 272; EWL 3; MTCW 1, 2; RGWL 2, 3; SATA-Obit 36
**Shone, Patric**
See Hanley, James
**Showalter, Elaine** 1941- ................. **CLC 169**
See also CA 57-60; CANR 58, 106; DLB 67; FW; GLL 2
**Shreve, Susan**
See Shreve, Susan Richards
**Shreve, Susan Richards** 1939- .......... **CLC 23**
See also CA 49-52; CAAS 5; CANR 5, 38, 69, 100; MAICYA 1, 2; SATA 46, 95, 152; SATA-Brief 41
**Shue, Larry** 1946-1985 ..................... **CLC 52**
See also CA 145; 117; DAM DRAM; DFS 7
**Shu-Jen, Chou** 1881-1936
See Lu Hsun
See also CA 104
**Shulman, Alix Kates** 1932- ........... **CLC 2, 10**
See also CA 29-32R; CANR 43; FW; SATA 7
**Shuster, Joe** 1914-1992 ..................... **CLC 21**
See also AAYA 50
**Shute, Nevil** ..................................... **CLC 30**
See Norway, Nevil Shute
See also BPFB 3; DLB 255; NFS 9; RHW; SFW 4
**Shuttle, Penelope (Diane)** 1947- ......... **CLC 7**
See also CA 93-96; CANR 39, 84, 92, 108; CP 7; CWP; DLB 14, 40
**Shvarts, Elena** 1948- ......................... **PC 50**
See also CA 147
**Sidhwa, Bapsy (N.)** 1938- ............... **CLC 168**
See also CA 108; CANR 25, 57; CN 7; FW
**Sidney, Mary** 1561-1621 ............... **LC 19, 39**
See Sidney Herbert, Mary
**Sidney, Sir Philip** 1554-1586 . **LC 19, 39; PC 32**
See also BRW 1; BRWR 2; CDBLB Before 1660; DA; DA3; DAB; DAC; DAM MST, POET; DLB 167; EXPP; PAB; RGEL 2; TEA; WP
**Sidney Herbert, Mary**
See Sidney, Mary
See also DLB 167
**Siegel, Jerome** 1914-1996 .................. **CLC 21**
See Siegel, Jerry
See also CA 116; 169; 151
**Siegel, Jerry**
See Siegel, Jerome
See also AAYA 50
**Sienkiewicz, Henryk (Adam Alexander Pius)**
1846-1916 ................................. **TCLC 3**
See also CA 104; 134; CANR 84; EWL 3; RGSF 2; RGWL 2, 3

**Sierra, Gregorio Martinez**
See Martinez Sierra, Gregorio
**Sierra, Maria (de la O'LeJarraga) Martinez**
See Martinez Sierra, Maria (de la O'LeJarraga)
**Sigal, Clancy** 1926- ........................... **CLC 7**
See also CA 1-4R; CANR 85; CN 7
**Siger of Brabant** 1240(?)-1284(?) . **CMLC 69**
See also DLB 115
**Sigourney, Lydia H.**
See Sigourney, Lydia Howard (Huntley)
See also DLB 73, 183
**Sigourney, Lydia Howard (Huntley)**
1791-1865 ........................... **NCLC 21, 87**
See Sigourney, Lydia H.; Sigourney, Lydia Huntley
See also DLB 1
**Sigourney, Lydia Huntley**
See Sigourney, Lydia Howard (Huntley)
See also DLB 42, 239, 243
**Siguenza y Gongora, Carlos de**
1645-1700 ....................... **HLCS 2; LC 8**
See also LAW
**Sigurjonsson, Johann**
See Sigurjonsson, Johann
**Sigurjonsson, Johann** 1880-1919 ... **TCLC 27**
See also CA 170; DLB 293; EWL 3
**Sikelianos, Angelos** 1884-1951 ............ **PC 29; TCLC 39**
See also EWL 3; RGWL 2, 3
**Silkin, Jon** 1930-1997 ............... **CLC 2, 6, 43**
See also CA 5-8R; CAAS 5; CANR 89; CP 7; DLB 27
**Silko, Leslie (Marmon)** 1948- .... **CLC 23, 74, 114, 211; NNAL; SSC 37, 66; WLCS**
See also AAYA 14; AMWS 4; ANW; BYA 12; CA 115; 122; CANR 45, 65, 118; CN 7; CP 7; CPW 1; CWP; DA; DA3; DAC; DAM MST, MULT, POP; DLB 143, 175, 256, 275; EWL 3; EXPP; EXPS; LAIT 4; MTCW 2; NFS 4; PFS 9, 16; RGAL 4; RGSF 2; SSFS 4, 8, 10, 11
**Sillanpaa, Frans Eemil** 1888-1964 ... **CLC 19**
See also CA 129; 93-96; EWL 3; MTCW 1
**Sillitoe, Alan** 1928- .. **CLC 1, 3, 6, 10, 19, 57, 148**
See also AITN 1; BRWS 5; CA 9-12R, 191; CAAE 191; CAAS 2; CANR 8, 26, 55; CDBLB 1960 to Present; CN 7; DLB 14, 139; EWL 3; MTCW 1, 2; RGEL 2; RGSF 2; SATA 61
**Silone, Ignazio** 1900-1978 ..................... **CLC 4**
See also CA 25-28; 81-84; CANR 34; CAP 2; DLB 264; EW 12; EWL 3; MTCW 1; RGSF 2; RGWL 2, 3
**Silone, Ignazione**
See Silone, Ignazio
**Silver, Joan Micklin** 1935- ............... **CLC 20**
See also CA 114; 121; INT CA-121
**Silver, Nicholas**
See Faust, Frederick (Schiller)
See also TCWW 2
**Silverberg, Robert** 1935- ............ **CLC 7, 140**
See also AAYA 24; BPFB 3; BYA 7, 9; CA 1-4R, 186; CAAE 186; CAAS 3; CANR 1, 20, 36, 85; CLR 59; CN 7; CPW; DAM POP; DLB 8; INT CANR-20; MAICYA 1, 2; MTCW 1, 2; SATA 13, 91; SATA-Essay 104; SCFW 2; SFW 4; SUFW 2
**Silverstein, Alvin** 1933- ..................... **CLC 17**
See also CA 49-52; CANR 2; CLR 25; JRDA; MAICYA 1, 2; SATA 8, 69, 124
**Silverstein, Shel(don Allan)**
1932-1999 ....................................... **PC 49**
See also AAYA 40; BW 3; CA 107; 179; CANR 47, 74, 81; CLR 5, 96; CWRI 5; JRDA; MAICYA 1, 2; MTCW 2; SATA 33, 92; SATA-Brief 27; SATA-Obit 116

**Silverstein, Virginia B(arbara Opshelor)**
1937- ................................... **CLC 17**
See also CA 49-52; CANR 2; CLR 25;
JRDA; MAICYA 1, 2; SATA 8, 69, 124

**Sim, Georges**
See Simenon, Georges (Jacques Christian)

**Simak, Clifford D(onald)** 1904-1988 . **CLC 1,
55**
See also CA 1-4R; 125; CANR 1, 35; DLB
8; MTCW 1; SATA-Obit 56; SFW 4

**Simenon, Georges (Jacques Christian)**
1903-1989 ........... **CLC 1, 2, 3, 8, 18, 47**
See also BPFB 3; CA 85-88; 129; CANR
35; CMW 4; DA3; DAM POP; DLB 72;
DLBY 1989; EW 12; EWL 3; GFL 1789
to the Present; MSW; MTCW 1, 2; RGWL
2, 3

**Simic, Charles** 1938- .... **CLC 6, 9, 22, 49, 68,
130**
See also AMWS 8; CA 29-32R; CAAS 4;
CANR 12, 33, 52, 61, 96; CP 7; DA3;
DAM POET; DLB 105; MTCW 2; PFS 7;
RGAL 4; WP

**Simmel, Georg** 1858-1918 ............... **TCLC 64**
See also CA 157; DLB 296

**Simmons, Charles (Paul)** 1924- ........ **CLC 57**
See also CA 89-92; INT CA-89-92

**Simmons, Dan** 1948- .......................... **CLC 44**
See also AAYA 16, 54; CA 138; CANR 53,
81, 126; CPW; DAM POP; HGG; SUFW
2

**Simmons, James (Stewart Alexander)**
1933- ............................................ **CLC 43**
See also CA 105; CAAS 21; CP 7; DLB 40

**Simms, William Gilmore**
1806-1870 ...................................... **NCLC 3**
See also DLB 3, 30, 59, 73, 248, 254;
RGAL 4

**Simon, Carly** 1945- ........................... **CLC 26**
See also CA 105

**Simon, Claude (Eugene Henri)**
1913-1984 .................... **CLC 4, 9, 15, 39**
See also CA 89-92; CANR 33, 117; CWW
2; DAM NOV; DLB 83; EW 13; EWL 3;
GFL 1789 to the Present; MTCW 1

**Simon, Myles**
See Follett, Ken(neth Martin)

**Simon, (Marvin) Neil** 1927- ... **CLC 6, 11, 31,
39, 70; DC 14**
See also AAYA 32; AITN 1; AMWS 4; CA
21-24R; CANR 26, 54, 87, 126; CD 5;
DA3; DAM DRAM; DFS 2, 6, 12, 18;
DLB 7, 266; LAIT 4; MTCW 1, 2; RGAL
4; TUS

**Simon, Paul (Frederick)** 1941(?)- ..... **CLC 17**
See also CA 116; 153

**Simonon, Paul** 1956(?)- ..................... **CLC 30**

**Simonson, Rick ed.** ........................... **CLC 70**

**Simpson, Harriette**
See Arnow, Harriette (Louisa) Simpson

**Simpson, Louis (Aston Marantz)**
1923- ....................... **CLC 4, 7, 9, 32, 149**
See also AMWS 9; CA 1-4R; CAAS 4;
CANR 1, 61; CP 7; DAM POET; DLB 5;
MTCW 1, 2; PFS 7, 11, 14; RGAL 4

**Simpson, Mona (Elizabeth)** 1957- ... **CLC 44,
146**
See also CA 122; 135; CANR 68, 103; CN
7; EWL 3

**Simpson, N(orman) F(rederick)**
1919- ............................................ **CLC 29**
See also CA 13-16R; CBD; DLB 13; RGEL
2

**Sinclair, Andrew (Annandale)** 1935- . **CLC 2,
14**
See also CA 9-12R; CAAS 5; CANR 14,
38, 91; CN 7; DLB 14; FANT; MTCW 1

**Sinclair, Emil**
See Hesse, Hermann

**Sinclair, Iain** 1943- .......................... **CLC 76**
See also CA 132; CANR 81; CP 7; HGG

**Sinclair, Iain MacGregor**
See Sinclair, Iain

**Sinclair, Irene**
See Griffith, D(avid Lewelyn) W(ark)

**Sinclair, Mary Amelia St. Clair** 1865(?)-1946
See Sinclair, May
See also CA 104; HGG; RHW

**Sinclair, May** ........................... **TCLC 3, 11**
See Sinclair, Mary Amelia St. Clair
See also CA 166; DLB 36, 135; EWL 3;
RGEL 2; SUFW

**Sinclair, Roy**
See Griffith, D(avid Lewelyn) W(ark)

**Sinclair, Upton (Beall)** 1878-1968 ..... **CLC 1,
11, 15, 63; TCLC 160; WLC**
See also AMWS 5; BPFB 3; BYA 2; CA
5-8R; 25-28R; CANR 7; CDALB 1929-
1941; DA; DA3; DAB; DAC; DAM MST,
NOV; DLB 9; EWL 3; INT CANR-7;
LAIT 3; MTCW 1, 2; NFS 6; RGAL 4;
SATA 9; TUS; YAW

**Singe, (Edmund) J(ohn) M(illington)**
1871-1909 ...................................... **WLC**

**Singer, Isaac**
See Singer, Isaac Bashevis

**Singer, Isaac Bashevis** 1904-1991 .. **CLC 1, 3,
6, 9, 11, 15, 23, 38, 69, 111; SSC 3, 53,
80; WLC**
See also AAYA 32; AITN 1, 2; AMW;
AMWR 2; BPFB 3; BYA 1, 4; CA 1-4R;
134; CANR 1, 39, 106; CDALB 1941-
1968; CLR 1; CWRI 5; DA; DA3; DAB;
DAC; DAM MST, NOV; DLB 6, 28, 52,
278; DLBY 1991; EWL 3; EXPS; HGG;
JRDA; LAIT 3; MAICYA 1, 2; MTCW 1,
2; RGAL 4; RGSF 2; SATA 3, 27; SATA-
Obit 68; SSFS 2, 12, 16; TUS; TWA

**Singer, Israel Joshua** 1893-1944 .... **TCLC 33**
See also CA 169; EWL 3

**Singh, Khushwant** 1915- .................. **CLC 11**
See also CA 9-12R; CAAS 9; CANR 6, 84;
CN 7; EWL 3; RGEL 2

**Singleton, Ann**
See Benedict, Ruth (Fulton)

**Singleton, John** 1968(?)- .................. **CLC 156**
See also AAYA 50; BW 2, 3; CA 138;
CANR 67, 82; DAM MULT

**Siniavskii, Andrei**
See Sinyavsky, Andrei (Donatevich)
See also CWW 2

**Sinjohn, John**
See Galsworthy, John

**Sinyavsky, Andrei (Donatevich)**
1925-1997 ...................................... **CLC 8**
See Siniavskii, Andrei; Sinyavsky, Andrey
Donatovich; Tertz, Abram
See also CA 85-88; 159

**Sinyavsky, Andrey Donatovich**
See Sinyavsky, Andrei (Donatevich)
See also EWL 3

**Sirin, V.**
See Nabokov, Vladimir (Vladimirovich)

**Sissman, L(ouis) E(dward)**
1928-1976 .............................. **CLC 9, 18**
See also CA 21-24R; 65-68; CANR 13;
DLB 5

**Sisson, C(harles) H(ubert)**
1914-2003 ...................................... **CLC 8**
See also CA 1-4R; 220; CAAS 3; CANR 3,
48, 84; CP 7; DLB 27

**Sitting Bull** 1831(?)-1890 .................. **NNAL**
See also DA3; DAM MULT

**Sitwell, Dame Edith** 1887-1964 ..... **CLC 2, 9,
67; PC 3**
See also BRW 7; CA 9-12R; CANR 35;
CDBLB 1945-1960; DAM POET; DLB
20; EWL 3; MTCW 1, 2; RGEL 2; TEA

**Siwaarmill, H. P.**
See Sharp, William

**Sjoewall, Maj** 1935- ........................... **CLC 7**
See Sjowall, Maj
See also CA 65-68; CANR 73

**Sjowall, Maj**
See Sjoewall, Maj
See also BPFB 3; CMW 4; MSW

**Skelton, John** 1460(?)-1529 ..... **LC 71; PC 25**
See also BRW 1; DLB 136; RGEL 2

**Skelton, Robin** 1925-1997 ................ **CLC 13**
See Zuk, Georges
See also AITN 2; CA 5-8R; 160; CAAS 5;
CANR 28, 89; CCA 1; CP 7; DLB 27, 53

**Skolimowski, Jerzy** 1938- .................. **CLC 20**
See also CA 128

**Skram, Amalie (Bertha)**
1847-1905 ...................................... **TCLC 25**
See also CA 165

**Skvorecky, Josef (Vaclav)** 1924- ...... **CLC 15,
39, 69, 152**
See also CA 61-64; CAAS 1; CANR 10,
34, 63, 108; CDWLB 4; CWW 2; DA3;
DAC; DAM NOV; DLB 232; EWL 3;
MTCW 1, 2

**Slade, Bernard** ........................... **CLC 11, 46**
See Newbound, Bernard Slade
See also CAAS 9; CCA 1; DLB 53

**Slaughter, Carolyn** 1946- .................. **CLC 56**
See also CA 85-88; CANR 85; CN 7

**Slaughter, Frank G(ill)** 1908-2001 .... **CLC 29**
See also AITN 2; CA 5-8R; 197; CANR 5,
85; INT CANR-5; RHW

**Slavitt, David R(ytman)** 1935- ..... **CLC 5, 14**
See also CA 21-24R; CAAS 3; CANR 41,
83; CP 7; DLB 5, 6

**Slesinger, Tess** 1905-1945 ............... **TCLC 10**
See also CA 107; 199; DLB 102

**Slessor, Kenneth** 1901-1971 ............. **CLC 14**
See also CA 102; 89-92; DLB 260; RGEL
2

**Slowacki, Juliusz** 1809-1849 ........... **NCLC 15**
See also RGWL 3

**Smart, Christopher** 1722-1771 . **LC 3; PC 13**
See also DAM POET; DLB 109; RGEL 2

**Smart, Elizabeth** 1913-1986 ............. **CLC 54**
See also CA 81-84; 118; DLB 88

**Smiley, Jane (Graves)** 1949- ...... **CLC 53, 76,
144**
See also AMWS 6; BPFB 3; CA 104;
CANR 30, 50, 74, 96; CN 7; CPW 1;
DA3; DAM POP; DLB 227, 234; EWL 3;
INT CANR-30; SSFS 19

**Smith, A(rthur) J(ames) M(arshall)**
1902-1980 ...................................... **CLC 15**
See also CA 1-4R; 102; CANR 4; DAC;
DLB 88; RGEL 2

**Smith, Adam** 1723(?)-1790 .................. **LC 36**
See also DLB 104, 252; RGEL 2

**Smith, Alexander** 1829-1867 ......... **NCLC 59**
See also DLB 32, 55

**Smith, Anna Deavere** 1950- ............. **CLC 86**
See also CA 133; CANR 103; CD 5; DFS 2

**Smith, Betty (Wehner)** 1904-1972 ... **CLC 19**
See also BPFB 3; BYA 3; CA 5-8R; 33-
36R; DLBY 1982; LAIT 3; RGAL 4;
SATA 6

**Smith, Charlotte (Turner)**
1749-1806 ............................. **NCLC 23, 115**
See also DLB 39, 109; RGEL 2; TEA

**Smith, Clark Ashton** 1893-1961 ....... **CLC 43**
See also CA 143; CANR 81; FANT; HGG;
MTCW 2; SCFW 2; SFW 4; SUFW

**Smith, Dave** ........................... **CLC 22, 42**
See Smith, David (Jeddie)
See also CAAS 7; DLB 5

**Smith, David (Jeddie)** 1942-
See Smith, Dave
See also CA 49-52; CANR 1, 59, 120; CP
7; CSW; DAM POET
**Smith, Florence Margaret** 1902-1971
See Smith, Stevie
See also CA 17-18; 29-32R; CANR 35;
CAP 2; DAM POET; MTCW 1, 2; TEA
**Smith, Iain Crichton** 1928-1998 ....... **CLC 64**
See also BRWS 9; CA 21-24R; 171; CN 7;
CP 7; DLB 40, 139; RGSF 2
**Smith, John** 1580(?)-1631 ...................... **LC 9**
See also DLB 24, 30; TUS
**Smith, Johnston**
See Crane, Stephen (Townley)
**Smith, Joseph, Jr.** 1805-1844 ......... **NCLC 53**
**Smith, Lee** 1944- .......................... **CLC 25, 73**
See also CA 114; 119; CANR 46, 118;
CSW; DLB 143; DLBY 1983; EWL 3;
INT CA-119; RGAL 4
**Smith, Martin**
See Smith, Martin Cruz
**Smith, Martin Cruz** 1942- .... **CLC 25; NNAL**
See also BEST 89:4; BPFB 3; CA 85-88;
CANR 6, 23, 43, 65, 119; CMW 4; CPW;
DAM MULT, POP; HGG; INT CANR-
23; MTCW 2; RGAL 4
**Smith, Patti** 1946- .......................... **CLC 12**
See also CA 93-96; CANR 63
**Smith, Pauline (Urmson)**
1882-1959 ............................... **TCLC 25**
See also DLB 225; EWL 3
**Smith, Rosamond**
See Oates, Joyce Carol
**Smith, Sheila Kaye**
See Kaye-Smith, Sheila
**Smith, Stevie** ......... **CLC 3, 8, 25, 44; PC 12**
See Smith, Florence Margaret
See also BRWS 2; DLB 20; EWL 3; MTCW
2; PAB; PFS 3; RGEL 2
**Smith, Wilbur (Addison)** 1933- ........ **CLC 33**
See also CA 13-16R; CANR 7, 46, 66, 134;
CPW; MTCW 1, 2
**Smith, William Jay** 1918- .................... **CLC 6**
See also AMWS 13; CA 5-8R; CANR 44,
106; CP 7; CSW; CWRI 5; DLB 5; MAI-
CYA 1, 2; SAAS 22; SATA 2, 68, 154;
SATA-Essay 154
**Smith, Woodrow Wilson**
See Kuttner, Henry
**Smith, Zadie** 1976- ......................... **CLC 158**
See also AAYA 50; CA 193
**Smolenskin, Peretz** 1842-1885 ....... **NCLC 30**
**Smollett, Tobias (George)** 1721-1771 ... **LC 2, 46**
See also BRW 3; CDBLB 1660-1789; DLB
39, 104; RGEL 2; TEA
**Snodgrass, W(illiam) D(e Witt)**
1926- ..................... **CLC 2, 6, 10, 18, 68**
See also AMWS 6; CA 1-4R; CANR 6, 36,
65, 85; CP 7; DAM POET; DLB 5;
MTCW 1, 2; RGAL 4
**Snorri Sturluson** 1179-1241 ......... **CMLC 56**
See also RGWL 2, 3
**Snow, C(harles) P(ercy)** 1905-1980 ... **CLC 1, 4, 6, 9, 13, 19**
See also BRW 7; CA 5-8R; 101; CANR 28;
CDBLB 1945-1960; DAM NOV; DLB 15,
77; DLBD 17; EWL 3; MTCW 1, 2;
RGEL 2; TEA
**Snow, Frances Compton**
See Adams, Henry (Brooks)
**Snyder, Gary (Sherman)** 1930- . **CLC 1, 2, 5, 9, 32, 120; PC 21**
See also AMWS 8; ANW; BG 3; CA 17-
20R; CANR 30, 60, 125; CP 7; DA3;
DAM POET; DLB 5, 16, 165, 212, 237,
275; EWL 3; MTCW 2; PFS 9, 19; RGAL
4; WP

**Snyder, Zilpha Keatley** 1927- ........... **CLC 17**
See also AAYA 15; BYA 1; CA 9-12R;
CANR 38; CLR 31; JRDA; MAICYA 1,
2; SAAS 2; SATA 1, 28, 75, 110; SATA-
Essay 112; YAW
**Soares, Bernardo**
See Pessoa, Fernando (Antonio Nogueira)
**Sobh, A.**
See Shamlu, Ahmad
**Sobh, Alef**
See Shamlu, Ahmad
**Sobol, Joshua** 1939- ......................... **CLC 60**
See Sobol, Yehoshua
See also CA 200
**Sobol, Yehoshua** 1939-
See Sobol, Joshua
See also CWW 2
**Socrates** 470B.C.-399B.C. .............. **CMLC 27**
**Soderberg, Hjalmar** 1869-1941 ....... **TCLC 39**
See also DLB 259; EWL 3; RGSF 2
**Soderbergh, Steven** 1963- ............... **CLC 154**
See also AAYA 43
**Sodergran, Edith (Irene)** 1892-1923
See Soedergran, Edith (Irene)
See also CA 202; DLB 259; EW 11; EWL
3; RGWL 2, 3
**Soedergran, Edith (Irene)**
1892-1923 ............................... **TCLC 31**
See Sodergran, Edith (Irene)
**Softly, Edgar**
See Lovecraft, H(oward) P(hillips)
**Softly, Edward**
See Lovecraft, H(oward) P(hillips)
**Sokolov, Alexander V(sevolodovich)** 1943-
See Sokolov, Sasha
See also CA 73-76
**Sokolov, Raymond** 1941- .................... **CLC 7**
See also CA 85-88
**Sokolov, Sasha** ................................... **CLC 59**
See Sokolov, Alexander V(sevolodovich)
See also CWW 2; DLB 285; EWL 3; RGWL
2, 3
**Solo, Jay**
See Ellison, Harlan (Jay)
**Sologub, Fyodor** ............................... **TCLC 9**
See Teternikov, Fyodor Kuzmich
See also EWL 3
**Solomons, Ikey Esquir**
See Thackeray, William Makepeace
**Solomos, Dionysios** 1798-1857 ....... **NCLC 15**
**Solwoska, Mara**
See French, Marilyn
**Solzhenitsyn, Aleksandr I(sayevich)**
1918- .. **CLC 1, 2, 4, 7, 9, 10, 18, 26, 34, 78, 134; SSC 32; WLC**
See Solzhenitsyn, Aleksandr Isaevich
See also AAYA 49; AITN 1; BPFB 3; CA
69-72; CANR 40, 65, 116; DA; DA3;
DAB; DAC; DAM MST, NOV; DLB 302;
EW 13; EXPS; LAIT 4; MTCW 1, 2; NFS
6; RGSF 2; RGWL 2, 3; SSFS 9; TWA
**Solzhenitsyn, Aleksandr Isaevich**
See Solzhenitsyn, Aleksandr I(sayevich)
See also CWW 2; EWL 3
**Somers, Jane**
See Lessing, Doris (May)
**Somerville, Edith Oenone**
1858-1949 ................. **SSC 56; TCLC 51**
See also CA 196; DLB 135; RGEL 2; RGSF
2
**Somerville & Ross**
See Martin, Violet Florence; Somerville,
Edith Oenone
**Sommer, Scott** 1951- ......................... **CLC 25**
See also CA 106
**Sommers, Christina Hoff** 1950- ...... **CLC 197**
See also CA 153; CANR 95

**Sondheim, Stephen (Joshua)** 1930- . **CLC 30, 39, 147; DC 22**
See also AAYA 11; CA 103; CANR 47, 67,
125; DAM DRAM; LAIT 4
**Sone, Monica** 1919- ............................... **AAL**
**Song, Cathy** 1955- ..................... **AAL; PC 21**
See also CA 154; CANR 118; CWP; DLB
169; EXPP; FW; PFS 5
**Sontag, Susan** 1933- .... **CLC 1, 2, 10, 13, 31, 105, 195**
See also AMWS 3; CA 17-20R; CANR 25,
51, 74, 97; CN 7; CPW; DA3; DAM POP;
DLB 2, 67; EWL 3; MAWW; MTCW 1,
2; RGAL 4; RHW; SSFS 10
**Sophocles** 496(?)B.C.-406(?)B.C. .... **CMLC 2, 47, 51; DC 1; WLCS**
See also AW 1; CDWLB 1; DA; DA3;
DAB; DAC; DAM DRAM, MST; DFS 1,
4, 8; DLB 176; LAIT 1; LATS 1:1; LMFS
1; RGWL 2, 3; TWA
**Sordello** 1189-1269 ......................... **CMLC 15**
**Sorel, Georges** 1847-1922 ............... **TCLC 91**
See also CA 118; 188
**Sorel, Julia**
See Drexler, Rosalyn
**Sorokin, Vladimir** ............................ **CLC 59**
See Sorokin, Vladimir Georgievich
**Sorokin, Vladimir Georgievich**
See Sorokin, Vladimir
See also DLB 285
**Sorrentino, Gilbert** 1929- .. **CLC 3, 7, 14, 22, 40**
See also CA 77-80; CANR 14, 33, 115; CN
7; CP 7; DLB 5, 173; DLBY 1980; INT
CANR-14
**Soseki**
See Natsume, Soseki
See also MJW
**Soto, Gary** 1952- ... **CLC 32, 80; HLC 2; PC 28**
See also AAYA 10, 37; BYA 11; CA 119;
125; CANR 50, 74, 107; CLR 38; CP 7;
DAM MULT; DLB 82; EWL 3; EXPP;
HW 1, 2; INT CA-125; JRDA; LLW 1;
MAICYA 2; MAICYAS 1; MTCW 2; PFS
7; RGAL 4; SATA 80, 120; WYA; YAW
**Soupault, Philippe** 1897-1990 ........... **CLC 68**
See also CA 116; 147; 131; EWL 3; GFL
1789 to the Present; LMFS 2
**Souster, (Holmes) Raymond** 1921- .... **CLC 5, 14**
See also CA 13-16R; CAAS 14; CANR 13,
29, 53; CP 7; DA3; DAC; DAM POET;
DLB 88; RGEL 2; SATA 63
**Southern, Terry** 1924(?)-1995 ............. **CLC 7**
See also AMWS 11; BPFB 3; CA 1-4R;
150; CANR 1, 55, 107; CN 7; DLB 2;
IDFW 3, 4
**Southerne, Thomas** 1660-1746 ........... **LC 99**
See also DLB 80; RGEL 2
**Southey, Robert** 1774-1843 ........ **NCLC 8, 97**
See also BRW 4; DLB 93, 107, 142; RGEL
2; SATA 54
**Southwell, Robert** 1561(?)-1595 ........ **LC 108**
See also DLB 167; RGEL 2; TEA
**Southworth, Emma Dorothy Eliza Nevitte**
1819-1899 ............................... **NCLC 26**
See also DLB 239
**Souza, Ernest**
See Scott, Evelyn
**Soyinka, Wole** 1934- .. **BLC 3; CLC 3, 5, 14, 36, 44, 179; DC 2; WLC**
See also AFW; BW 2, 3; CA 13-16R;
CANR 27, 39, 82; CD 5; CDWLB 3; CN
7; CP 7; DA; DA3; DAB; DAC; DAM
DRAM, MST, MULT; DFS 10; DLB 125;
EWL 3; MTCW 1, 2; RGEL 2; TWA;
WLIT 2; WWE 1

**Spackman, W(illiam) M(ode)**
1905-1990 ................................... **CLC 46**
See also CA 81-84; 132

**Spacks, Barry (Bernard)** 1931- ........ **CLC 14**
See also CA 154; CANR 33, 109; CP 7;
DLB 105

**Spanidou, Irini** 1946- ........................ **CLC 44**
See also CA 185

**Spark, Muriel (Sarah)** 1918- ..... **CLC 2, 3, 5, 8, 13, 18, 40, 94; SSC 10**
See also BRWS 1; CA 5-8R; CANR 12, 36,
76, 89, 131; CDBLB 1945-1960; CN 7;
CP 7; DA3; DAB; DAC; DAM MST,
NOV; DLB 15, 139; EWL 3; FW; INT
CANR-12; LAIT 4; MTCW 1, 2; RGEL
2; TEA; WLIT 4; YAW

**Spaulding, Douglas**
See Bradbury, Ray (Douglas)

**Spaulding, Leonard**
See Bradbury, Ray (Douglas)

**Speght, Rachel** 1597-c. 1630 ............... **LC 97**
See also DLB 126

**Spelman, Elizabeth** ........................... **CLC 65**

**Spence, J. A. D.**
See Eliot, T(homas) S(tearns)

**Spencer, Anne** 1882-1975 ...................... **HR 3**
See also BW 2; CA 161; DLB 51, 54

**Spencer, Elizabeth** 1921- .... **CLC 22; SSC 57**
See also CA 13-16R; CANR 32, 65, 87; CN
7; CSW; DLB 6, 218; EWL 3; MTCW 1;
RGAL 4; SATA 14

**Spencer, Leonard G.**
See Silverberg, Robert

**Spencer, Scott** 1945- ......................... **CLC 30**
See also CA 113; CANR 51; DLBY 1986

**Spender, Stephen (Harold)**
1909-1995 .......... **CLC 1, 2, 5, 10, 41, 91**
See also BRWS 2; CA 9-12R; 149; CANR
31, 54; CDBLB 1945-1960; CP 7; DA3;
DAM POET; DLB 20; EWL 3; MTCW 1,
2; PAB; RGEL 2; TEA

**Spengler, Oswald (Arnold Gottfried)**
1880-1936 ......................................... **TCLC 25**
See also CA 118; 189

**Spenser, Edmund** 1552(?)-1599 ...... **LC 5, 39, 117; PC 8, 42; WLC**
See also AAYA 60; BRW 1; CDBLB Be-
fore 1660; DA; DA3; DAB; DAC; DAM
MST, POET; DLB 167; EFS 2; EXPP;
PAB; RGEL 2; TEA; WLIT 3; WP

**Spicer, Jack** 1925-1965 ........... **CLC 8, 18, 72**
See also BG 3; CA 85-88; DAM POET;
DLB 5, 16, 193; GLL 1; WP

**Spiegelman, Art** 1948- ................. **CLC 76, 178**
See also AAYA 10, 46; CA 125; CANR 41,
55, 74, 124; DLB 299; MTCW 2; SATA
109; YAW

**Spielberg, Peter** 1929- ......................... **CLC 6**
See also CA 5-8R; CANR 4, 48; DLBY
1981

**Spielberg, Steven** 1947- ............. **CLC 20, 188**
See also AAYA 8, 24; CA 77-80; CANR
32; SATA 32

**Spillane, Frank Morrison** 1918-
See Spillane, Mickey
See also CA 25-28R; CANR 28, 63, 125;
DA3; MTCW 1, 2; SATA 66

**Spillane, Mickey** .......................... **CLC 3, 13**
See Spillane, Frank Morrison
See also BPFB 3; CMW 4; DLB 226;
MSW; MTCW 2

**Spinoza, Benedictus de** 1632-1677 .. **LC 9, 58**

**Spinrad, Norman (Richard)** 1940- ... **CLC 46**
See also BPFB 3; CA 37-40R; CAAS 19;
CANR 20, 91; DLB 8; INT CANR-20;
SFW 4

**Spitteler, Carl (Friedrich Georg)**
1845-1924 ......................................... **TCLC 12**
See also CA 109; DLB 129; EWL 3

**Spivack, Kathleen (Romola Drucker)**
1938- ................................................... **CLC 6**
See also CA 49-52

**Spoto, Donald** 1941- ........................... **CLC 39**
See also CA 65-68; CANR 11, 57, 93

**Springsteen, Bruce (F.)** 1949- ........... **CLC 17**
See also CA 111

**Spurling, (Susan) Hilary** 1940- ......... **CLC 34**
See also CA 104; CANR 25, 52, 94

**Spyker, John Howland**
See Elman, Richard (Martin)

**Squared, A.**
See Abbott, Edwin A.

**Squires, (James) Radcliffe**
1917-1993 ........................................... **CLC 51**
See also CA 1-4R; 140; CANR 6, 21

**Srivastava, Dhanpat Rai** 1880(?)-1936
See Premchand
See also CA 118; 197

**Stacy, Donald**
See Pohl, Frederik

**Stael**
See Stael-Holstein, Anne Louise Germaine
Necker
See also EW 5; RGWL 2, 3

**Stael, Germaine de**
See Stael-Holstein, Anne Louise Germaine
Necker
See also DLB 119, 192; FW; GFL 1789 to
the Present; TWA

**Stael-Holstein, Anne Louise Germaine
Necker** 1766-1817 ............... **NCLC 3, 91**
See Stael; Stael, Germaine de

**Stafford, Jean** 1915-1979 .. **CLC 4, 7, 19, 68; SSC 26**
See also CA 1-4R; 85-88; CANR 3, 65;
DLB 2, 173; MTCW 1, 2; RGAL 4; RGSF
2; SATA-Obit 22; TCWW 2; TUS

**Stafford, William (Edgar)**
1914-1993 ........................... **CLC 4, 7, 29**
See also AMWS 11; CA 5-8R; 142; CAAS
3; CANR 5, 22; DAM POET; DLB 5,
206; EXPP; INT CANR-22; PFS 2, 8, 16;
RGAL 4; WP

**Stagnelius, Eric Johan** 1793-1823 . **NCLC 61**

**Staines, Trevor**
See Brunner, John (Kilian Houston)

**Stairs, Gordon**
See Austin, Mary (Hunter)
See also TCWW 2

**Stalin, Joseph** 1879-1953 ................ **TCLC 92**

**Stampa, Gaspara** c. 1524-1554 .... **PC 43; LC 114**
See also RGWL 2, 3

**Stampflinger, K. A.**
See Benjamin, Walter

**Stancykowna**
See Szymborska, Wislawa

**Standing Bear, Luther**
1868(?)-1939(?) ............................ **NNAL**
See also CA 113; 144; DAM MULT

**Stanislavsky, Konstantin**
1863-1938 ................................ **TCLC 167**
See also CA 118

**Stannard, Martin** 1947- ...................... **CLC 44**
See also CA 142; DLB 155

**Stanton, Elizabeth Cady**
1815-1902 ................................. **TCLC 73**
See also CA 171; DLB 79; FW

**Stanton, Maura** 1946- ......................... **CLC 9**
See also CA 89-92; CANR 15, 123; DLB
120

**Stanton, Schuyler**
See Baum, L(yman) Frank

**Stapledon, (William) Olaf**
1886-1950 ................................. **TCLC 22**
See also CA 111; 162; DLB 15, 255; SFW
4

**Starbuck, George (Edwin)**
1931-1996 ................................. **CLC 53**
See also CA 21-24R; 153; CANR 23; DAM
POET

**Stark, Richard**
See Westlake, Donald E(dwin)

**Staunton, Schuyler**
See Baum, L(yman) Frank

**Stead, Christina (Ellen)** 1902-1983 ... **CLC 2, 5, 8, 32, 80**
See also BRWS 4; CA 13-16R; 109; CANR
33, 40; DLB 260; EWL 3; FW; MTCW 1,
2; RGEL 2; RGSF 2; WWE 1

**Stead, William Thomas**
1849-1912 ................................. **TCLC 48**
See also CA 167

**Stebnitsky, M.**
See Leskov, Nikolai (Semyonovich)

**Steele, Sir Richard** 1672-1729 ............. **LC 18**
See also BRW 3; CDBLB 1660-1789; DLB
84, 101; RGEL 2; WLIT 3

**Steele, Timothy (Reid)** 1948- ........... **CLC 45**
See also CA 93-96; CANR 16, 50, 92; CP
7; DLB 120, 282

**Steffens, (Joseph) Lincoln**
1866-1936 ................................. **TCLC 20**
See also CA 117; 198; DLB 303

**Stegner, Wallace (Earle)** 1909-1993 .. **CLC 9, 49, 81; SSC 27**
See also AITN 1; AMWS 4; ANW; BEST
90:3; BPFB 3; CA 1-4R; 141; CAAS 9;
CANR 1, 21, 46; DAM NOV; DLB 9,
206, 275; DLBY 1993; EWL 3; MTCW
1, 2; RGAL 4; TCWW 2; TUS

**Stein, Gertrude** 1874-1946 .... **DC 19; PC 18; SSC 42; TCLC 1, 6, 28, 48; WLC**
See also AMW; AMWC 2; CA 104; 132;
CANR 108; CDALB 1917-1929; DA;
DA3; DAB; DAC; DAM MST, NOV,
POET; DLB 4, 54, 86, 228; DLBD 15;
EWL 3; EXPS; GLL 1; MAWW; MTCW
1, 2; NCFS 4; RGAL 4; RGSF 2; SSFS 5;
TUS; WP

**Steinbeck, John (Ernst)** 1902-1968 ... **CLC 1, 5, 9, 13, 21, 34, 45, 75, 124; SSC 11, 37, 77; TCLC 135; WLC**
See also AAYA 12; AMW; BPFB 3; BYA 2,
3, 13; CA 1-4R; 25-28R; CANR 1, 35;
CDALB 1929-1941; DA; DA3; DAB;
DAC; DAM DRAM, MST, NOV; DLB 7,
9, 212, 275, 309; DLBD 2; EWL 3;
EXPS; LAIT 3; MTCW 1, 2; NFS 1, 5, 7,
17, 19; RGAL 4; RGSF 2; RHW; SATA
9; SSFS 3, 6; TCWW 2; TUS; WYA;
YAW

**Steinem, Gloria** 1934- ........................ **CLC 63**
See also CA 53-56; CANR 28, 51; DLB
246; FW; MTCW 1, 2

**Steiner, George** 1929- ......................... **CLC 24**
See also CA 73-76; CANR 31, 67, 108;
DAM NOV; DLB 67, 299; EWL 3;
MTCW 1, 2; SATA 62

**Steiner, K. Leslie**
See Delany, Samuel R(ay), Jr.

**Steiner, Rudolf** 1861-1925 ............. **TCLC 13**
See also CA 107

**Stendhal** 1783-1842 .. **NCLC 23, 46; SSC 27; WLC**
See also DA; DA3; DAB; DAC; DAM
MST, NOV; DLB 119; EW 5; GFL 1789
to the Present; RGWL 2, 3; TWA

**Stephen, Adeline Virginia**
See Woolf, (Adeline) Virginia

**Stephen, Sir Leslie** 1832-1904 ........ **TCLC 23**
See also BRW 5; CA 123; DLB 57, 144,
190

**Stephen, Sir Leslie**
See Stephen, Sir Leslie

**Stephen, Virginia**
See Woolf, (Adeline) Virginia

**Taine, Hippolyte Adolphe**
1828-1893 .............................. **NCLC 15**
See also EW 7; GFL 1789 to the Present

**Talayesva, Don C.** 1890-(?) ................ **NNAL**

**Talese, Gay** 1932- ............................... **CLC 37**
See also AITN 1; CA 1-4R; CANR 9, 58;
DLB 185; INT CANR-9; MTCW 1, 2

**Tallent, Elizabeth (Ann)** 1954- ......... **CLC 45**
See also CA 117; CANR 72; DLB 130

**Tallmountain, Mary** 1918-1997 .......... **NNAL**
See also CA 146; 161; DLB 193

**Tally, Ted** 1952- ................................ **CLC 42**
See also CA 120; 124; CAD; CANR 125;
CD 5; INT CA-124

**Talvik, Heiti** 1904-1947 ................... **TCLC 87**
See also EWL 3

**Tamayo y Baus, Manuel**
1829-1898 ................................. **NCLC 1**

**Tammsaare, A(nton) H(ansen)**
1878-1940 ................................ **TCLC 27**
See also CA 164; CDWLB 4; DLB 220;
EWL 3

**Tam'si, Tchicaya U**
See Tchicaya, Gerald Felix

**Tan, Amy (Ruth)** 1952- . **AAL; CLC 59, 120,
151**
See also AAYA 9, 48; AMWS 10; BEST
89:3; BPFB 3; CA 136; CANR 54, 105,
132; CDALBS; CN 7; CPW 1; DA3;
DAM MULT, NOV, POP; DLB 173;
EXPN; FW; LAIT 3, 5; MTCW 2; NFS
1, 13, 16; RGAL 4; SATA 75; SSFS 9;
YAW

**Tandem, Felix**
See Spitteler, Carl (Friedrich Georg)

**Tanizaki, Jun'ichiro** 1886-1965 ... **CLC 8, 14,
28; SSC 21**
See Tanizaki Jun'ichiro
See also CA 93-96; 25-28R; MJW; MTCW
2; RGSF 2; RGWL 2

**Tanizaki Jun'ichiro**
See Tanizaki, Jun'ichiro
See also DLB 180; EWL 3

**Tannen, Deborah F.** 1945- ............... **CLC 206**
See also CA 118; CANR 95

**Tanner, William**
See Amis, Kingsley (William)

**Tao Lao**
See Storni, Alfonsina

**Tapahonso, Luci** 1953- ............ **NNAL; PC 65**
See also CA 145; CANR 72, 127; DLB 175

**Tarantino, Quentin (Jerome)**
1963- ..................................... **CLC 125**
See also AAYA 58; CA 171; CANR 125

**Tarassoff, Lev**
See Troyat, Henri

**Tarbell, Ida M(inerva)** 1857-1944 . **TCLC 40**
See also CA 122; 181; DLB 47

**Tarkington, (Newton) Booth**
1869-1946 ................................. **TCLC 9**
See also BPFB 3; BYA 3; CA 110; 143;
CWRI 5; DLB 9, 102; MTCW 2; RGAL
4; SATA 17

**Tarkovskii, Andrei Arsen'evich**
See Tarkovsky, Andrei (Arsenyevich)

**Tarkovsky, Andrei (Arsenyevich)**
1932-1986 ................................ **CLC 75**
See also CA 127

**Tartt, Donna** 1963- ........................... **CLC 76**
See also AAYA 56; CA 142

**Tasso, Torquato** 1544-1595 ............. **LC 5, 94**
See also EFS 2; EW 2; RGWL 2, 3

**Tate, (John Orley) Allen** 1899-1979 .. **CLC 2,
4, 6, 9, 11, 14, 24; PC 50**
See also AMW; CA 5-8R; 85-88; CANR
32, 108; DLB 4, 45, 63; DLBD 17; EWL
3; MTCW 1, 2; RGAL 4; RHW

**Tate, Ellalice**
See Hibbert, Eleanor Alice Burford

**Tate, James (Vincent)** 1943- ..... **CLC 2, 6, 25**
See also CA 21-24R; CANR 29, 57, 114;
CP 7; DLB 5, 169; EWL 3; PFS 10, 15;
RGAL 4; WP

**Tate, Nahum** 1652(?)-1715 ................ **LC 109**
See also DLB 80; RGEL 2

**Tauler, Johannes** c. 1300-1361 ...... **CMLC 37**
See also DLB 179; LMFS 1

**Tavel, Ronald** 1940- ............................ **CLC 6**
See also CA 21-24R; CAD; CANR 33; CD
5

**Taviani, Paolo** 1931- ......................... **CLC 70**
See also CA 153

**Taylor, Bayard** 1825-1878 .............. **NCLC 89**
See also DLB 3, 189, 250, 254; RGAL 4

**Taylor, C(ecil) P(hilip)** 1929-1981 .... **CLC 27**
See also CA 25-28R; 105; CANR 47; CBD

**Taylor, Edward** 1642(?)-1729 . **LC 11; PC 63**
See also AMW; DA; DAB; DAC; DAM
MST, POET; DLB 24; EXPP; RGAL 4;
TUS

**Taylor, Eleanor Ross** 1920- ................ **CLC 5**
See also CA 81-84; CANR 70

**Taylor, Elizabeth** 1932-1975 ..... **CLC 2, 4, 29**
See also CA 13-16R; CANR 9, 70; DLB
139; MTCW 1; RGEL 2; SATA 13

**Taylor, Frederick Winslow**
1856-1915 ................................ **TCLC 76**
See also CA 188

**Taylor, Henry (Splawn)** 1942- .......... **CLC 44**
See also CA 33-36R; CAAS 7; CANR 31;
CP 7; DLB 5; PFS 10

**Taylor, Kamala (Purnaiya)** 1924-2004
See Markandaya, Kamala
See also CA 77-80; 227; NFS 13

**Taylor, Mildred D(elois)** 1943- .......... **CLC 21**
See also AAYA 10, 47; BW 1; BYA 3, 8;
CA 85-88; CANR 25, 115; CLR 9, 59,
90; CSW; DLB 52; JRDA; LAIT 3; MAI-
CYA 1, 2; SAAS 5; SATA 135; WYA;
YAW

**Taylor, Peter (Hillsman)** 1917-1994 .. **CLC 1,
4, 18, 37, 44, 50, 71; SSC 10, 84**
See also AMWS 5; BPFB 3; CA 13-16R;
147; CANR 9, 50; CSW; DLB 218, 278;
DLBY 1981, 1994; EWL 3; EXPS; INT
CANR-9; MTCW 1, 2; RGSF 2; SSFS 9;
TUS

**Taylor, Robert Lewis** 1912-1998 ....... **CLC 14**
See also CA 1-4R; 170; CANR 3, 64; SATA
10

**Tchekhov, Anton**
See Chekhov, Anton (Pavlovich)

**Tchicaya, Gerald Felix** 1931-1988 .. **CLC 101**
See Tchicaya U Tam'si
See also CA 129; 125; CANR 81

**Tchicaya U Tam'si**
See Tchicaya, Gerald Felix
See also EWL 3

**Teasdale, Sara** 1884-1933 .... **PC 31; TCLC 4**
See also CA 104; 163; DLB 45; GLL 1;
PFS 14; RGAL 4; SATA 32; TUS

**Tecumseh** 1768-1813 ........................... **NNAL**
See also DAM MULT

**Tegner, Esaias** 1782-1846 ................. **NCLC 2**

**Fujiwara no Teika** 1162-1241 ....... **CMLC 73**
See also DLB 203

**Teilhard de Chardin, (Marie Joseph) Pierre**
1881-1955 ................................. **TCLC 9**
See also CA 105; 210; GFL 1789 to the
Present

**Temple, Ann**
See Mortimer, Penelope (Ruth)

**Tennant, Emma (Christina)** 1937- .. **CLC 13,
52**
See also BRWS 9; CA 65-68; CAAS 9;
CANR 10, 38, 59, 88; CN 7; DLB 14;
EWL 3; SFW 4

**Tenneshaw, S. M.**
See Silverberg, Robert

**Tenney, Tabitha Gilman**
1762-1837 .............................. **NCLC 122**
See also DLB 37, 200

**Tennyson, Alfred** 1809-1892 ... **NCLC 30, 65,
115; PC 6; WLC**
See also AAYA 50; BRW 4; CDBLB 1832-
1890; DA; DA3; DAB; DAC; DAM MST,
POET; DLB 32; EXPP; PAB; PFS 1, 2, 4,
11, 15, 19; RGEL 2; TEA; WLIT 4; WP

**Teran, Lisa St. Aubin de** ................. **CLC 36**
See St. Aubin de Teran, Lisa

**Terence** c. 184B.C.-c. 159B.C. ...... **CMLC 14;
DC 7**
See also AW 1; CDWLB 1; DLB 211;
RGWL 2, 3; TWA

**Teresa de Jesus, St.** 1515-1582 ............ **LC 18**

**Terkel, Louis** 1912-
See Terkel, Studs
See also CA 57-60; CANR 18, 45, 67, 132;
DA3; MTCW 1, 2

**Terkel, Studs** ................................... **CLC 38**
See Terkel, Louis
See also AAYA 32; AITN 1; MTCW 2; TUS

**Terry, C. V.**
See Slaughter, Frank G(ill)

**Terry, Megan** 1932- .............. **CLC 19; DC 13**
See also CA 77-80; CABS 3; CAD; CANR
43; CD 5; CWD; DFS 18; DLB 7, 249;
GLL 2

**Tertullian** c. 155-c. 245 ................... **CMLC 29**

**Tertz, Abram**
See Sinyavsky, Andrei (Donatevich)
See also RGSF 2

**Tesich, Steve** 1943(?)-1996 .......... **CLC 40, 69**
See also CA 105; 152; CAD; DLBY 1983

**Tesla, Nikola** 1856-1943 ................. **TCLC 88**

**Teternikov, Fyodor Kuzmich** 1863-1927
See Sologub, Fyodor
See also CA 104

**Tevis, Walter** 1928-1984 .................... **CLC 42**
See also CA 113; SFW 4

**Tey, Josephine** ................................ **TCLC 14**
See Mackintosh, Elizabeth
See also DLB 77; MSW

**Thackeray, William Makepeace**
1811-1863 .... **NCLC 5, 14, 22, 43; WLC**
See also BRW 5; BRWC 2; CDBLB 1832-
1890; DA; DA3; DAB; DAC; DAM MST,
NOV; DLB 21, 55, 159, 163; NFS 13;
RGEL 2; SATA 23; TEA; WLIT 3

**Thakura, Ravindranatha**
See Tagore, Rabindranath

**Thames, C. H.**
See Marlowe, Stephen

**Tharoor, Shashi** 1956- ...................... **CLC 70**
See also CA 141; CANR 91; CN 7

**Thelwell, Michael Miles** 1939- ......... **CLC 22**
See also BW 2; CA 101

**Theobald, Lewis, Jr.**
See Lovecraft, H(oward) P(hillips)

**Theocritus** c. 310B.C.- ................... **CMLC 45**
See also AW 1; DLB 176; RGWL 2, 3

**Theodorescu, Ion N.** 1880-1967
See Arghezi, Tudor
See also CA 116

**Theriault, Yves** 1915-1983 ................ **CLC 79**
See also CA 102; CCA 1; DAC; DAM
MST; DLB 88; EWL 3

**Theroux, Alexander (Louis)** 1939- .... **CLC 2,
25**
See also CA 85-88; CANR 20, 63; CN 7

**Tolstoy, Count Leo**
See Tolstoy, Leo (Nikolaevich)

**Tomalin, Claire** 1933- ..................... **CLC 166**
See also CA 89-92; CANR 52, 88; DLB 155

**Tomasi di Lampedusa, Giuseppe** 1896-1957
See Lampedusa, Giuseppe (Tomasi) di
See also CA 111; DLB 177; EWL 3

**Tomlin, Lily** ...................................... **CLC 17**
See Tomlin, Mary Jean

**Tomlin, Mary Jean** 1939(?)-
See Tomlin, Lily
See also CA 117

**Tomline, F. Latour**
See Gilbert, W(illiam) S(chwenck)

**Tomlinson, (Alfred) Charles** 1927- .... **CLC 2, 4, 6, 13, 45; PC 17**
See also CA 5-8R; CANR 33; CP 7; DAM POET; DLB 40

**Tomlinson, H(enry) M(ajor)**
1873-1958 ................................. **TCLC 71**
See also CA 118; 161; DLB 36, 100, 195

**Tonna, Charlotte Elizabeth**
1790-1846 ................................ **NCLC 135**
See also DLB 163

**Tonson, Jacob** fl. 1655(?)-1736 ........... **LC 86**
See also DLB 170

**Toole, John Kennedy** 1937-1969 ..... **CLC 19, 64**
See also BPFB 3; CA 104; DLBY 1981; MTCW 2

**Toomer, Eugene**
See Toomer, Jean

**Toomer, Eugene Pinchback**
See Toomer, Jean

**Toomer, Jean** 1894-1967 .. **BLC 3; CLC 1, 4, 13, 22; HR 3; PC 7; SSC 1, 45; WLCS**
See also AFAW 1, 2; AMWS 3, 9; BW 1; CA 85-88; CDALB 1917-1929; DA3; DAM MULT; DLB 45, 51; EWL 3; EXPP; EXPS; LMFS 2; MTCW 1, 2; NFS 11; RGAL 4; RGSF 2; SSFS 5

**Toomer, Nathan Jean**
See Toomer, Jean

**Toomer, Nathan Pinchback**
See Toomer, Jean

**Torley, Luke**
See Blish, James (Benjamin)

**Tornimparte, Alessandra**
See Ginzburg, Natalia

**Torre, Raoul della**
See Mencken, H(enry) L(ouis)

**Torrence, Ridgely** 1874-1950 .......... **TCLC 97**
See also DLB 54, 249

**Torrey, E(dwin) Fuller** 1937- ............ **CLC 34**
See also CA 119; CANR 71

**Torsvan, Ben Traven**
See Traven, B.

**Torsvan, Benno Traven**
See Traven, B.

**Torsvan, Berick Traven**
See Traven, B.

**Torsvan, Berwick Traven**
See Traven, B.

**Torsvan, Bruno Traven**
See Traven, B.

**Torsvan, Traven**
See Traven, B.

**Tourneur, Cyril** 1575(?)-1626 ............. **LC 66**
See also BRW 2; DAM DRAM; DLB 58; RGEL 2

**Tournier, Michel (Edouard)** 1924- .... **CLC 6, 23, 36, 95**
See also CA 49-52; CANR 3, 36, 74; CWW 2; DLB 83; EWL 3; GFL 1789 to the Present; MTCW 1, 2; SATA 23

**Tournimparte, Alessandra**
See Ginzburg, Natalia

**Towers, Ivar**
See Kornbluth, C(yril) M.

**Towne, Robert (Burton)** 1936(?)- ..... **CLC 87**
See also CA 108; DLB 44; IDFW 3, 4

**Townsend, Sue** ............................... **CLC 61**
See Townsend, Susan Lilian
See also AAYA 28; CA 119; 127; CANR 65, 107; CBD; CD 5; CPW; CWD; DAB; DAC; DAM MST; DLB 271; INT CA-127; SATA 55, 93; SATA-Brief 48; YAW

**Townsend, Susan Lilian** 1946-
See Townsend, Sue

**Townshend, Pete**
See Townshend, Peter (Dennis Blandford)

**Townshend, Peter (Dennis Blandford)**
1945- ....................................... **CLC 17, 42**
See also CA 107

**Tozzi, Federigo** 1883-1920 .............. **TCLC 31**
See also CA 160; CANR 110; DLB 264; EWL 3

**Tracy, Don(ald Fiske)** 1905-1970(?)
See Queen, Ellery
See also CA 1-4R; 176; CANR 2

**Trafford, F. G.**
See Riddell, Charlotte

**Traherne, Thomas** 1637(?)-1674 .......... **LC 99**
See also BRW 2; DLB 131; PAB; RGEL 2

**Traill, Catharine Parr** 1802-1899 .. **NCLC 31**
See also DLB 99

**Trakl, Georg** 1887-1914 ....... **PC 20; TCLC 5**
See also CA 104; 165; EW 10; EWL 3; LMFS 2; MTCW 2; RGWL 2, 3

**Tranquilli, Secondino**
See Silone, Ignazio

**Transtroemer, Tomas Gosta**
See Transtromer, Tomas (Goesta)

**Transtromer, Tomas (Gosta)**
See Transtromer, Tomas (Goesta)
See also CWW 2

**Transtromer, Tomas (Goesta)**
1931- ...................................... **CLC 52, 65**
See Transtromer, Tomas (Gosta)
See also CA 117; 129; CAAS 17; CANR 115; DAM POET; DLB 257; EWL 3; PFS 21

**Transtromer, Tomas Gosta**
See Transtromer, Tomas (Goesta)

**Traven, B.** 1882(?)-1969 ................. **CLC 8, 11**
See also CA 19-20; 25-28R; CAP 2; DLB 9, 56; EWL 3; MTCW 1; RGAL 4

**Trediakovsky, Vasilii Kirillovich**
1703-1769 ................................... **LC 68**
See also DLB 150

**Treitel, Jonathan** 1959- ..................... **CLC 70**
See also CA 210; DLB 267

**Trelawny, Edward John**
1792-1881 ................................. **NCLC 85**
See also DLB 110, 116, 144

**Tremain, Rose** 1943- ........................ **CLC 42**
See also CA 97-100; CANR 44, 95; CN 7; DLB 14, 271; RGSF 2; RHW

**Tremblay, Michel** 1942- ........... **CLC 29, 102**
See also CA 116; 128; CCA 1; CWW 2; DAC; DAM MST; DLB 60; EWL 3; GLL 1; MTCW 1, 2

**Trevanian** ......................................... **CLC 29**
See Whitaker, Rod(ney)

**Trevor, Glen**
See Hilton, James

**Trevor, William** .. **CLC 7, 9, 14, 25, 71, 116; SSC 21, 58**
See Cox, William Trevor
See also BRWS 4; CBD; CD 5; CN 7; DLB 14, 139; EWL 3; LATS 1:2; MTCW 2; RGEL 2; RGSF 2; SSFS 10

**Trifonov, Iurii (Valentinovich)**
See Trifonov, Yuri (Valentinovich)
See also DLB 302; RGWL 2, 3

**Trifonov, Yuri (Valentinovich)**
1925-1981 ............................... **CLC 45**
See Trifonov, Iurii (Valentinovich); Trifonov, Yury Valentinovich
See also CA 126; 103; MTCW 1

**Trifonov, Yury Valentinovich**
See Trifonov, Yuri (Valentinovich)
See also EWL 3

**Trilling, Diana (Rubin)** 1905-1996 . **CLC 129**
See also CA 5-8R; 154; CANR 10, 46; INT CANR-10; MTCW 1, 2

**Trilling, Lionel** 1905-1975 ..... **CLC 9, 11, 24; SSC 75**
See also AMWS 3; CA 9-12R; 61-64; CANR 10, 105; DLB 28, 63; EWL 3; INT CANR-10; MTCW 1, 2; RGAL 4; TUS

**Trimball, W. H.**
See Mencken, H(enry) L(ouis)

**Tristan**
See Gomez de la Serna, Ramon

**Tristram**
See Housman, A(lfred) E(dward)

**Trogdon, William (Lewis)** 1939-
See Heat-Moon, William Least
See also CA 115; 119; CANR 47, 89; CPW; INT CA-119

**Trollope, Anthony** 1815-1882 .... **NCLC 6, 33, 101; SSC 28; WLC**
See also BRW 5; CDBLB 1832-1890; DA; DA3; DAB; DAC; DAM MST, NOV; DLB 21, 57, 159; RGEL 2; RGSF 2; SATA 22

**Trollope, Frances** 1779-1863 .......... **NCLC 30**
See also DLB 21, 166

**Trollope, Joanna** 1943- .................... **CLC 186**
See also CA 101; CANR 58, 95; CPW; DLB 207; RHW

**Trotsky, Leon** 1879-1940 ............... **TCLC 22**
See also CA 118; 167

**Trotter (Cockburn), Catharine**
1679-1749 ..................................... **LC 8**
See also DLB 84, 252

**Trotter, Wilfred** 1872-1939 ............ **TCLC 97**

**Trout, Kilgore**
See Farmer, Philip Jose

**Trow, George W. S.** 1943- ................ **CLC 52**
See also CA 126; CANR 91

**Troyat, Henri** 1911- .......................... **CLC 23**
See also CA 45-48; CANR 2, 33, 67, 117; GFL 1789 to the Present; MTCW 1

**Trudeau, G(arretson) B(eekman)** 1948-
See Trudeau, Garry B.
See also AAYA 60; CA 81-84; CANR 31; SATA 35

**Trudeau, Garry B.** ........................... **CLC 12**
See Trudeau, G(arretson) B(eekman)
See also AAYA 10; AITN 2

**Truffaut, Francois** 1932-1984 ... **CLC 20, 101**
See also CA 81-84; 113; CANR 34

**Trumbo, Dalton** 1905-1976 .............. **CLC 19**
See also CA 21-24R; 69-72; CANR 10; DLB 26; IDFW 3, 4; YAW

**Trumbull, John** 1750-1831 ............. **NCLC 30**
See also DLB 31; RGAL 4

**Trundlett, Helen B.**
See Eliot, T(homas) S(tearns)

**Truth, Sojourner** 1797(?)-1883 ...... **NCLC 94**
See also DLB 239; FW; LAIT 2

**Tryon, Thomas** 1926-1991 ......... **CLC 3, 11**
See also AITN 1; BPFB 3; CA 29-32R; 135; CANR 32, 77; CPW; DA3; DAM POP; HGG; MTCW 1

**Tryon, Tom**
See Tryon, Thomas

**Ts'ao Hsueh-ch'in** 1715(?)-1763 ........... **LC 1**

**Tsushima, Shuji** 1909-1948
See Dazai Osamu
See also CA 107

**Vanbrugh, Sir John** 1664-1726 ............ **LC 21**
See also BRW 2; DAM DRAM; DLB 80; IDTP; RGEL 2

**Van Campen, Karl**
See Campbell, John W(ood, Jr.)

**Vance, Gerald**
See Silverberg, Robert

**Vance, Jack** ........................................ **CLC 35**
See Vance, John Holbrook
See also DLB 8; FANT; SCFW 2; SFW 4; SUFW 1, 2

**Vance, John Holbrook** 1916-
See Queen, Ellery; Vance, Jack
See also CA 29-32R; CANR 17, 65; CMW 4; MTCW 1

**Van Den Bogarde, Derek Jules Gaspard Ulric Niven** 1921-1999 .............. **CLC 14**
See Bogarde, Dirk
See also CA 77-80; 179

**Vandenburgh, Jane** .......................... **CLC 59**
See also CA 168

**Vanderhaeghe, Guy** 1951- ................ **CLC 41**
See also BPFB 3; CA 113; CANR 72

**van der Post, Laurens (Jan)**
1906-1996 ...................................... **CLC 5**
See also AFW; CA 5-8R; 155; CANR 35; CN 7; DLB 204; RGEL 2

**van de Wetering, Janwillem** 1931- ... **CLC 47**
See also CA 49-52; CANR 4, 62, 90; CMW 4

**Van Dine, S. S.** ................................ **TCLC 23**
See Wright, Willard Huntington
See also DLB 306; MSW

**Van Doren, Carl (Clinton)**
1885-1950 .................................... **TCLC 18**
See also CA 111; 168

**Van Doren, Mark** 1894-1972 ........ **CLC 6, 10**
See also CA 1-4R; 37-40R; CANR 3; DLB 45, 284; MTCW 1, 2; RGAL 4

**Van Druten, John (William)**
1901-1957 ...................................... **TCLC 2**
See also CA 104; 161; DLB 10; RGAL 4

**Van Duyn, Mona (Jane)** 1921- ...... **CLC 3, 7, 63, 116**
See also CA 9-12R; CANR 7, 38, 60, 116; CP 7; CWP; DAM POET; DLB 5; PFS 20

**Van Dyne, Edith**
See Baum, L(yman) Frank

**van Itallie, Jean-Claude** 1936- ............ **CLC 3**
See also CA 45-48; CAAS 2; CAD; CANR 1, 48; CD 5; DLB 7

**Van Loot, Cornelius Obenchain**
See Roberts, Kenneth (Lewis)

**van Ostaijen, Paul** 1896-1928 ........ **TCLC 33**
See also CA 163

**Van Peebles, Melvin** 1932- ............ **CLC 2, 20**
See also BW 2, 3; CA 85-88; CANR 27, 67, 82; DAM MULT

**van Schendel, Arthur(-Francois-Emile)**
1874-1946 .................................... **TCLC 56**
See also EWL 3

**Vansittart, Peter** 1920- ...................... **CLC 42**
See also CA 1-4R; CANR 3, 49, 90; CN 7; RHW

**Van Vechten, Carl** 1880-1964 ... **CLC 33; HR 3**
See also AMWS 2; CA 183; 89-92; DLB 4, 9, 51; RGAL 4

**van Vogt, A(lfred) E(lton)** 1912-2000 . **CLC 1**
See also BPFB 3; BYA 13, 14; CA 21-24R; 190; CANR 28; DLB 8, 251; SATA 14; SATA-Obit 124; SCFW; SFW 4

**Vara, Madeleine**
See Jackson, Laura (Riding)

**Varda, Agnes** 1928- .......................... **CLC 16**
See also CA 116; 122

**Vargas Llosa, (Jorge) Mario (Pedro)**
1939- .... **CLC 3, 6, 9, 10, 15, 31, 42, 85, 181; HLC 2**
See Llosa, (Jorge) Mario (Pedro) Vargas
See also BPFB 3; CA 73-76; CANR 18, 32, 42, 67, 116; CDWLB 3; CWW 2; DA; DA3; DAB; DAC; DAM MST, MULT, NOV; DLB 145; DNFS 2; EWL 3; HW 1, 2; LAIT 5; LATS 1:2; LAW; LAWS 1; MTCW 1, 2; RGWL 2; SSFS 14; TWA; WLIT 1

**Varnhagen von Ense, Rahel**
1771-1833 .............................. **NCLC 130**
See also DLB 90

**Vasari, Giorgio** 1511-1574 ................. **LC 114**

**Vasiliu, George**
See Bacovia, George

**Vasiliu, Gheorghe**
See Bacovia, George
See also CA 123; 189

**Vassa, Gustavus**
See Equiano, Olaudah

**Vassilikos, Vassilis** 1933- ................ **CLC 4, 8**
See also CA 81-84; CANR 75; EWL 3

**Vaughan, Henry** 1621-1695 ................ **LC 27**
See also BRW 2; DLB 131; PAB; RGEL 2

**Vaughn, Stephanie** ........................... **CLC 62**

**Vazov, Ivan (Minchov)** 1850-1921 . **TCLC 25**
See also CA 121; 167; CDWLB 4; DLB 147

**Veblen, Thorstein B(unde)**
1857-1929 .................................... **TCLC 31**
See also AMWS 1; CA 115; 165; DLB 246

**Vega, Lope de** 1562-1635 .... **HLCS 2; LC 23**
See also EW 2; RGWL 2, 3

**Vendler, Helen (Hennessy)** 1933- ... **CLC 138**
See also CA 41-44R; CANR 25, 72; MTCW 1, 2

**Venison, Alfred**
See Pound, Ezra (Weston Loomis)

**Ventsel, Elena Sergeevna** 1907-2002
See Grekova, I.
See also CA 154

**Verdi, Marie de**
See Mencken, H(enry) L(ouis)

**Verdu, Matilde**
See Cela, Camilo Jose

**Verga, Giovanni (Carmelo)**
1840-1922 ................... **SSC 21; TCLC 3**
See also CA 104; 123; CANR 101; EW 7; EWL 3; RGSF 2; RGWL 2, 3

**Vergil** 70B.C.-19B.C. ... **CMLC 9, 40; PC 12; WLCS**
See Virgil
See also AW 2; DA; DA3; DAB; DAC; DAM MST, POET; EFS 1; LMFS 1

**Vergil, Polydore** c. 1470-1555 ........... **LC 108**
See also DLB 132

**Verhaeren, Emile (Adolphe Gustave)**
1855-1916 .................................... **TCLC 12**
See also CA 109; EWL 3; GFL 1789 to the Present

**Verlaine, Paul (Marie)** 1844-1896 .. **NCLC 2, 51; PC 2, 32**
See also DAM POET; DLB 217; EW 7; GFL 1789 to the Present; LMFS 2; RGWL 2, 3; TWA

**Verne, Jules (Gabriel)** 1828-1905 ... **TCLC 6, 52**
See also AAYA 16; BYA 4; CA 110; 131; CLR 88; DA3; DLB 123; GFL 1789 to the Present; JRDA; LAIT 2; LMFS 2; MAICYA 1, 2; RGWL 2, 3; SATA 21; SCFW; SFW 4; TWA; WCH

**Verus, Marcus Annius**
See Aurelius, Marcus

**Very, Jones** 1813-1880 ...................... **NCLC 9**
See also DLB 1, 243; RGAL 4

**Vesaas, Tarjei** 1897-1970 .................. **CLC 48**
See also CA 190; 29-32R; DLB 297; EW 11; EWL 3; RGWL 3

**Vialis, Gaston**
See Simenon, Georges (Jacques Christian)

**Vian, Boris** 1920-1959(?) ................. **TCLC 9**
See also CA 106; 164; CANR 111; DLB 72; EWL 3; GFL 1789 to the Present; MTCW 2; RGWL 2, 3

**Viaud, (Louis Marie) Julien** 1850-1923
See Loti, Pierre
See also CA 107

**Vicar, Henry**
See Felsen, Henry Gregor

**Vicente, Gil** 1465-c. 1536 .................... **LC 99**
See also DLB 287; RGWL 2, 3

**Vicker, Angus**
See Felsen, Henry Gregor

**Vidal, (Eugene Luther) Gore** 1925- .. **CLC 2, 4, 6, 8, 10, 22, 33, 72, 142**
See Box, Edgar
See also AITN 1; AMWS 4; BEST 90:2; BPFB 3; CA 5-8R; CAD; CANR 13, 45, 65, 100, 132; CD 5; CDALBS; CN 7; CPW; DA3; DAM NOV, POP; DFS 2; DLB 6, 152; EWL 3; INT CANR-13; MTCW 1, 2; RGAL 4; RHW; TUS

**Viereck, Peter (Robert Edwin)**
1916- .................................... **CLC 4; PC 27**
See also CA 1-4R; CANR 1, 47; CP 7; DLB 5; PFS 9, 14

**Vigny, Alfred (Victor) de**
1797-1863 ............. **NCLC 7, 102; PC 26**
See also DAM POET; DLB 119, 192, 217; EW 5; GFL 1789 to the Present; RGWL 2, 3

**Vilakazi, Benedict Wallet**
1906-1947 ................................... **TCLC 37**
See also CA 168

**Villa, Jose Garcia** 1914-1997 .... **AAL; PC 22**
See also CA 25-28R; CANR 12, 118; EWL 3; EXPP

**Villa, Jose Garcia** 1914-1997
See Villa, Jose Garcia

**Villa, Jose Garcia** 1914-1997 .... **AAL; PC 22**
See also CA 25-28R; CANR 12, 118; EWL 3; EXPP

**Villard, Oswald Garrison**
1872-1949 ................................... **TCLC 160**
See also CA 113, 162; DLB 25, 91

**Villaurrutia, Xavier** 1903-1950 ...... **TCLC 80**
See also CA 192; EWL 3; HW 1; LAW

**Villaverde, Cirilo** 1812-1894 ........ **NCLC 121**
See also LAW

**Villehardouin, Geoffroi de**
1150(?)-1218(?) ...................... **CMLC 38**

**Villiers, George** 1628-1687 ................ **LC 107**
See also DLB 80; RGEL 2

**Villiers de l'Isle Adam, Jean Marie Mathias Philippe Auguste** 1838-1889 ... **NCLC 3; SSC 14**
See also DLB 123, 192; GFL 1789 to the Present; RGSF 2

**Villon, Francois** 1431-1463(?) . **LC 62; PC 13**
See also DLB 208; EW 2; RGWL 2, 3; TWA

**Vine, Barbara** .................................. **CLC 50**
See Rendell, Ruth (Barbara)
See also BEST 90:4

**Vinge, Joan (Carol) D(ennison)**
1948- ......................... **CLC 30; SSC 24**
See also AAYA 32; BPFB 3; CA 93-96; CANR 72; SATA 36, 113; SFW 4; YAW

**Viola, Herman J(oseph)** 1938- ......... **CLC 70**
See also CA 61-64; CANR 8, 23, 48, 91; SATA 126

**Violis, G.**
See Simenon, Georges (Jacques Christian)

**Wallant, Edward Lewis** 1926-1962 ... **CLC 5, 10**
See also CA 1-4R; CANR 22; DLB 2, 28, 143, 299; EWL 3; MTCW 1, 2; RGAL 4

**Wallas, Graham** 1858-1932 ........... **TCLC 91**

**Waller, Edmund** 1606-1687 ................. **LC 86**
See also BRW 2; DAM POET; DLB 126; PAB; RGEL 2

**Walley, Byron**
See Card, Orson Scott

**Walpole, Horace** 1717-1797 ............. **LC 2, 49**
See also BRW 3; DLB 39, 104, 213; HGG; LMFS 1; RGEL 2; SUFW 1; TEA

**Walpole, Hugh (Seymour)**
1884-1941 ........................ **TCLC 5**
See also CA 104; 165; DLB 34; HGG; MTCW 2; RGEL 2; RHW

**Walrond, Eric (Derwent)** 1898-1966 .... **HR 3**
See also BW 1; CA 125; DLB 51

**Walser, Martin** 1927- ................. **CLC 27, 183**
See also CA 57-60; CANR 8, 46; CWW 2; DLB 75, 124; EWL 3

**Walser, Robert** 1878-1956 ..... **SSC 20; TCLC 18**
See also CA 118; 165; CANR 100; DLB 66; EWL 3

**Walsh, Gillian Paton**
See Paton Walsh, Gillian

**Walsh, Jill Paton** ............................ **CLC 35**
See Paton Walsh, Gillian
See also CLR 2, 65; WYA

**Walter, Villiam Christian**
See Andersen, Hans Christian

**Walters, Anna L(ee)** 1946- ................. **NNAL**
See also CA 73-76

**Walther von der Vogelweide** c.
1170-1228 ........................ **CMLC 56**

**Walton, Izaak** 1593-1683 ..................... **LC 72**
See also BRW 2; CDBLB Before 1660; DLB 151, 213; RGEL 2

**Wambaugh, Joseph (Aloysius), Jr.**
1937- ........................................ **CLC 3, 18**
See also AITN 1; BEST 89:3; BPFB 3; CA 33-36R; CANR 42, 65, 115; CMW 4; CPW 1; DA3; DAM NOV, POP; DLB 6; DLBY 1983; MSW; MTCW 1, 2

**Wang Wei** 699(?)-761(?) ...................... **PC 18**
See also TWA

**Warburton, William** 1698-1779 .......... **LC 97**
See also DLB 104

**Ward, Arthur Henry Sarsfield** 1883-1959
See Rohmer, Sax
See also CA 108; 173; CMW 4; HGG

**Ward, Douglas Turner** 1930- ........... **CLC 19**
See also BW 1; CA 81-84; CAD; CANR 27; CD 5; DLB 7, 38

**Ward, E. D.**
See Lucas, E(dward) V(errall)

**Ward, Mrs. Humphry** 1851-1920
See Ward, Mary Augusta
See also RGEL 2

**Ward, Mary Augusta** 1851-1920 ... **TCLC 55**
See Ward, Mrs. Humphry
See also DLB 18

**Ward, Nathaniel** 1578(?)-1652 .......... **LC 114**
See also DLB 24

**Ward, Peter**
See Faust, Frederick (Schiller)

**Warhol, Andy** 1928(?)-1987 ............. **CLC 20**
See also AAYA 12; BEST 89:4; CA 89-92; 121; CANR 34

**Warner, Francis (Robert le Plastrier)**
1937- ........................................ **CLC 14**
See also CA 53-56; CANR 11

**Warner, Marina** 1946- ...................... **CLC 59**
See also CA 65-68; CANR 21, 55, 118; CN 7; DLB 194

**Warner, Rex (Ernest)** 1905-1986 ...... **CLC 45**
See also CA 89-92; 119; DLB 15; RGEL 2; RHW

**Warner, Susan (Bogert)**
1819-1885 ........................ **NCLC 31, 146**
See also DLB 3, 42, 239, 250, 254

**Warner, Sylvia (Constance) Ashton**
See Ashton-Warner, Sylvia (Constance)

**Warner, Sylvia Townsend**
1893-1978 .. **CLC 7, 19; SSC 23; TCLC 131**
See also BRWS 7; CA 61-64; 77-80; CANR 16, 60, 104; DLB 34, 139; EWL 3; FANT; FW; MTCW 1, 2; RGEL 2; RGSF 2; RHW

**Warren, Mercy Otis** 1728-1814 ..... **NCLC 13**
See also DLB 31, 200; RGAL 4; TUS

**Warren, Robert Penn** 1905-1989 .. **CLC 1, 4, 6, 8, 10, 13, 18, 39, 53, 59; PC 37; SSC 4, 58; WLC**
See also AITN 1; AMW; AMWC 2; BPFB 3; BYA 1; CA 13-16R; 129; CANR 10, 47; CDALB 1968-1988; DA; DA3; DAB; DAC; DAM MST, NOV, POET; DLB 2, 48, 152; DLBY 1980, 1989; EWL 3; INT CANR-10; MTCW 1, 2; NFS 13; RGAL 4; RGSF 2; RHW; SATA 46; SATA-Obit 63; SSFS 8; TUS

**Warrigal, Jack**
See Furphy, Joseph

**Warshofsky, Isaac**
See Singer, Isaac Bashevis

**Warton, Joseph** 1722-1800 ........... **NCLC 118**
See also DLB 104, 109; RGEL 2

**Warton, Thomas** 1728-1790 ......... **LC 15, 82**
See also DAM POET; DLB 104, 109; RGEL 2

**Waruk, Kona**
See Harris, (Theodore) Wilson

**Warung, Price** ................................ **TCLC 45**
See Astley, William
See also DLB 230; RGEL 2

**Warwick, Jarvis**
See Garner, Hugh
See also CCA 1

**Washington, Alex**
See Harris, Mark

**Washington, Booker T(aliaferro)**
1856-1915 ................... **BLC 3; TCLC 10**
See also BW 1; CA 114; 125; DA3; DAM MULT; LAIT 2; RGAL 4; SATA 28

**Washington, George** 1732-1799 .......... **LC 25**
See also DLB 31

**Wassermann, (Karl) Jakob**
1873-1934 ................................ **TCLC 6**
See also CA 104; 163; DLB 66; EWL 3

**Wasserstein, Wendy** 1950- ... **CLC 32, 59, 90, 183; DC 4**
See also CA 121; 129; CABS 3; CAD; CANR 53, 75, 128; CD 5; CWD; DA3; DAM DRAM; DFS 5, 17; DLB 228; EWL 3; FW; INT CA-129; MTCW 2; SATA 94

**Waterhouse, Keith (Spencer)** 1929- . **CLC 47**
See also CA 5-8R; CANR 38, 67, 109; CBD; CN 7; DLB 13, 15; MTCW 1, 2

**Waters, Frank (Joseph)** 1902-1995 .. **CLC 88**
See also CA 5-8R; 149; CAAS 13; CANR 3, 18, 63, 121; DLB 212; DLBY 1986; RGAL 4; TCWW 2

**Waters, Mary C.** ............................ **CLC 70**

**Waters, Roger** 1944- ......................... **CLC 35**

**Watkins, Frances Ellen**
See Harper, Frances Ellen Watkins

**Watkins, Gerrold**
See Malzberg, Barry N(athaniel)

**Watkins, Gloria Jean** 1952(?)- .......... **CLC 94**
See also BW 2; CA 143; CANR 87, 126; DLB 246; MTCW 2; SATA 115

**Watkins, Paul** 1964- .......................... **CLC 55**
See also CA 132; CANR 62, 98

**Watkins, Vernon Phillips**
1906-1967 ........................ **CLC 43**
See also CA 9-10; 25-28R; CAP 1; DLB 20; EWL 3; RGEL 2

**Watson, Irving S.**
See Mencken, H(enry) L(ouis)

**Watson, John H.**
See Farmer, Philip Jose

**Watson, Richard F.**
See Silverberg, Robert

**Watts, Ephraim**
See Horne, Richard Henry Hengist

**Watts, Isaac** 1674-1748 ...................... **LC 98**
See also DLB 95; RGEL 2; SATA 52

**Waugh, Auberon (Alexander)**
1939-2001 ........................ **CLC 7**
See also CA 45-48; 192; CANR 6, 22, 92; DLB 14, 194

**Waugh, Evelyn (Arthur St. John)**
1903-1966 .. **CLC 1, 3, 8, 13, 19, 27, 44, 107; SSC 41; WLC**
See also BPFB 3; BRW 7; CA 85-88; 25-28R; CANR 22; CDBLB 1914-1945; DA; DA3; DAB; DAC; DAM MST, NOV, POP; DLB 15, 162, 195; EWL 3; MTCW 1, 2; NFS 13, 17; RGEL 2; RGSF 2; TEA; WLIT 4

**Waugh, Harriet** 1944- ......................... **CLC 6**
See also CA 85-88; CANR 22

**Ways, C. R.**
See Blount, Roy (Alton), Jr.

**Waystaff, Simon**
See Swift, Jonathan

**Webb, Beatrice (Martha Potter)**
1858-1943 ........................ **TCLC 22**
See also CA 117; 162; DLB 190; FW

**Webb, Charles (Richard)** 1939- ....... **CLC 7**
See also CA 25-28R; CANR 114

**Webb, Frank J.** ............................ **NCLC 143**
See also DLB 50

**Webb, James H(enry), Jr.** 1946- ...... **CLC 22**
See also CA 81-84

**Webb, Mary Gladys (Meredith)**
1881-1927 ........................ **TCLC 24**
See also CA 182; 123; DLB 34; FW

**Webb, Mrs. Sidney**
See Webb, Beatrice (Martha Potter)

**Webb, Phyllis** 1927- .......................... **CLC 18**
See also CA 104; CANR 23; CCA 1; CP 7; CWP; DLB 53

**Webb, Sidney (James)** 1859-1947 .. **TCLC 22**
See also CA 117; 163; DLB 190

**Webber, Andrew Lloyd** ................... **CLC 21**
See Lloyd Webber, Andrew
See also DFS 7

**Weber, Lenora Mattingly**
1895-1971 ........................ **CLC 12**
See also CA 19-20; 29-32R; CAP 1; SATA 2; SATA-Obit 26

**Weber, Max** 1864-1920 ................... **TCLC 69**
See also CA 109; 189; DLB 296

**Webster, John** 1580(?)-1634(?) ...... **DC 2; LC 33, 84; WLC**
See also BRW 2; CDBLB Before 1660; DA; DAB; DAC; DAM DRAM, MST; DFS 17, 19; DLB 58; IDTP; RGEL 2; WLIT 3

**Webster, Noah** 1758-1843 ............... **NCLC 30**
See also DLB 1, 37, 42, 43, 73, 243

**Wedekind, (Benjamin) Frank(lin)**
1864-1918 ........................ **TCLC 7**
See also CA 104; 153; CANR 121, 122; CDWLB 2; DAM DRAM; DLB 118; EW 8; EWL 3; LMFS 2; RGWL 2, 3

**Wehr, Demaris** ............................... **CLC 65**

**Weidman, Jerome** 1913-1998 ............. **CLC 7**
See also AITN 2; CA 1-4R; 171; CAD; CANR 1; DLB 28

**Weil, Simone (Adolphine)**
1909-1943 ................. **TCLC 23**
See also CA 117; 159; EW 12; EWL 3; FW;
GFL 1789 to the Present; MTCW 2
**Weininger, Otto** 1880-1903 ............. **TCLC 84**
**Weinstein, Nathan**
See West, Nathanael
**Weinstein, Nathan von Wallenstein**
See West, Nathanael
**Weir, Peter (Lindsay)** 1944- ............... **CLC 20**
See also CA 113; 123
**Weiss, Peter (Ulrich)** 1916-1982 .. **CLC 3, 15,
51; TCLC 152**
See also CA 45-48; 106; CANR 3; DAM
DRAM; DFS 3; DLB 69, 124; EWL 3;
RGWL 2, 3
**Weiss, Theodore (Russell)**
1916-2003 ........................... **CLC 3, 8, 14**
See also CA 9-12R; 189; 216; CAAE 189;
CAAS 2; CANR 46, 94; CP 7; DLB 5
**Welch, (Maurice) Denton**
1915-1948 ................................ **TCLC 22**
See also BRWS 8, 9; CA 121; 148; RGEL
2
**Welch, James (Phillip)** 1940-2003 ..... **CLC 6,
14, 52; NNAL; PC 62**
See also CA 85-88; 219; CANR 42, 66, 107;
CN 7; CP 7; CPW; DAM MULT, POP;
DLB 175, 256; LATS 1:1; RGAL 4;
TCWW 2
**Weldon, Fay** 1931- . **CLC 6, 9, 11, 19, 36, 59,
122**
See also BRWS 4; CA 21-24R; CANR 16,
46, 63, 97; CDBLB 1960 to Present; CN
7; CPW; DAM POP; DLB 14, 194; EWL
3; FW; HGG; INT CANR-16; MTCW 1,
2; RGEL 2; RGSF 2
**Wellek, Rene** 1903-1995 ..................... **CLC 28**
See also CA 5-8R; 150; CAAS 7; CANR 8;
DLB 63; EWL 3; INT CANR-8
**Weller, Michael** 1942- .................. **CLC 10, 53**
See also CA 85-88; CAD; CD 5
**Weller, Paul** 1958- ............................. **CLC 26**
**Wellershoff, Dieter** 1925- .................. **CLC 46**
See also CA 89-92; CANR 16, 37
**Welles, (George) Orson** 1915-1985 .. **CLC 20,
80**
See also AAYA 40; CA 93-96; 117
**Wellman, John McDowell** 1945-
See Wellman, Mac
See also CA 166; CD 5
**Wellman, Mac** ................................... **CLC 65**
See Wellman, John McDowell; Wellman,
John McDowell
See also CAD; RGAL 4
**Wellman, Manly Wade** 1903-1986 ... **CLC 49**
See also CA 1-4R; 118; CANR 6, 16, 44;
FANT; SATA 6; SATA-Obit 47; SFW 4;
SUFW
**Wells, Carolyn** 1869(?)-1942 .......... **TCLC 35**
See also CA 113; 185; CMW 4; DLB 11
**Wells, H(erbert) G(eorge)** 1866-1946 . **SSC 6,
70; TCLC 6, 12, 19, 133; WLC**
See also AAYA 18; BPFB 3; BRW 6; CA
110; 121; CDBLB 1914-1945; CLR 64;
DA; DA3; DAB; DAC; DAM MST, NOV;
DLB 34, 70, 156, 178; EWL 3; EXPS;
HGG; LAIT 3; LMFS 2; MTCW 1, 2;
NFS 17, 20; RGEL 2; RGSF 2; SATA 20;
SCFW; SFW 4; SSFS 3; SUFW; TEA;
WCH; WLIT 4; YAW
**Wells, Rosemary** 1943- ...................... **CLC 12**
See also AAYA 13; BYA 7, 8; CA 85-88;
CANR 48, 120; CLR 16, 69; CWRI 5;
MAICYA 1, 2; SAAS 1; SATA 18, 69,
114; YAW
**Wells-Barnett, Ida B(ell)**
1862-1931 ............................... **TCLC 125**
See also CA 182; DLB 23, 221

**Welsh, Irvine** 1958- ......................... **CLC 144**
See also CA 173; DLB 271
**Welty, Eudora (Alice)** 1909-2001 .. **CLC 1, 2,
5, 14, 22, 33, 105; SSC 1, 27, 51; WLC**
See also AAYA 48; AMW; AMWR 1; BPFB
3; CA 9-12R; 199; CABS 1; CANR 32,
65, 128; CDALB 1941-1968; CN 7; CSW;
DA; DA3; DAB; DAC; DAM MST, NOV;
DLB 2, 102, 143; DLBD 12; DLBY 1987,
2001; EWL 3; EXPS; HGG; LAIT 3;
MAWW; MTCW 1, 2; NFS 13, 15; RGAL
4; RGSF 2; RHW; SSFS 2, 10; TUS
**Wen I-to** 1899-1946 ......................... **TCLC 28**
See also EWL 3
**Wentworth, Robert**
See Hamilton, Edmond
**Werfel, Franz (Viktor)** 1890-1945 ... **TCLC 8**
See also CA 104; 161; DLB 81, 124; EWL
3; RGWL 2, 3
**Wergeland, Henrik Arnold**
1808-1845 .................................. **NCLC 5**
**Wersba, Barbara** 1932- ...................... **CLC 30**
See also AAYA 2, 30; BYA 6, 12, 13; CA
29-32R, 182; CAAE 182; CANR 16, 38;
CLR 3, 78; DLB 52; JRDA; MAICYA 1,
2; SAAS 2; SATA 1, 58; SATA-Essay 103;
WYA; YAW
**Wertmueller, Lina** 1928- .................... **CLC 16**
See also CA 97-100; CANR 39, 78
**Wescott, Glenway** 1901-1987 .. **CLC 13; SSC
35**
See also CA 13-16R; 121; CANR 23, 70;
DLB 4, 9, 102; RGAL 4
**Wesker, Arnold** 1932- ................. **CLC 3, 5, 42**
See also CA 1-4R; CAAS 7; CANR 1, 33;
CBD; CD 5; CDBLB 1960 to Present;
DAB; DAM DRAM; DLB 13; EWL 3;
MTCW 1; RGEL 2; TEA
**Wesley, John** 1703-1791 ...................... **LC 88**
See also DLB 104
**Wesley, Richard (Errol)** 1945- ........... **CLC 7**
See also BW 1; CA 57-60; CAD; CANR
27; CD 5; DLB 38
**Wessel, Johan Herman** 1742-1785 ........ **LC 7**
See also DLB 300
**West, Anthony (Panther)**
1914-1987 ................................. **CLC 50**
See also CA 45-48; 124; CANR 3, 19; DLB
15
**West, C. P.**
See Wodehouse, P(elham) G(renville)
**West, Cornel (Ronald)** 1953- .... **BLCS; CLC
134**
See also CA 144; CANR 91; DLB 246
**West, Delno C(loyde), Jr.** 1936- ........ **CLC 70**
See also CA 57-60
**West, Dorothy** 1907-1998 .. **HR 3; TCLC 108**
See also BW 2; CA 143; 169; DLB 76
**West, (Mary) Jessamyn** 1902-1984 ... **CLC 7,
17**
See also CA 9-12R; 112; CANR 27; DLB
6; DLBY 1984; MTCW 1, 2; RGAL 4;
RHW; SATA-Obit 37; TCWW 2; TUS;
YAW
**West, Morris**
See West, Morris L(anglo)
See also DLB 289
**West, Morris L(anglo)** 1916-1999 ..... **CLC 6,
33**
See West, Morris
See also BPFB 3; CA 5-8R; 187; CANR
24, 49, 64; CN 7; CPW; MTCW 1, 2
**West, Nathanael** 1903-1940 .. **SSC 16; TCLC
1, 14, 44**
See also AMW; AMWR 2; BPFB 3; CA
104; 125; CDALB 1929-1941; DA3; DLB
4, 9, 28; EWL 3; MTCW 1, 2; NFS 16;
RGAL 4; TUS

**West, Owen**
See Koontz, Dean R(ay)
**West, Paul** 1930- ....................... **CLC 7, 14, 96**
See also CA 13-16R; CAAS 7; CANR 22,
53, 76, 89; CN 7; DLB 14; INT CANR-
22; MTCW 2
**West, Rebecca** 1892-1983 ... **CLC 7, 9, 31, 50**
See also BPFB 3; BRWS 3; CA 5-8R; 109;
CANR 19; DLB 36; DLBY 1983; EWL
3; FW; MTCW 1, 2; NCFS 4; RGEL 2;
TEA
**Westall, Robert (Atkinson)**
1929-1993 .................................. **CLC 17**
See also AAYA 12; BYA 2, 6, 7, 8, 9, 15;
CA 69-72; 141; CANR 18, 68; CLR 13;
FANT; JRDA; MAICYA 1, 2; MAICYAS
1; SAAS 2; SATA 23, 69; SATA-Obit 75;
WYA; YAW
**Westermarck, Edward** 1862-1939 . **TCLC 87**
**Westlake, Donald E(dwin)** 1933- . **CLC 7, 33**
See also BPFB 3; CA 17-20R; CAAS 13;
CANR 16, 44, 65, 94; CMW 4; CPW;
DAM POP; INT CANR-16; MSW;
MTCW 2
**Westmacott, Mary**
See Christie, Agatha (Mary Clarissa)
**Weston, Allen**
See Norton, Andre
**Wetcheek, J. L.**
See Feuchtwanger, Lion
**Wetering, Janwillem van de**
See van de Wetering, Janwillem
**Wetherald, Agnes Ethelwyn**
1857-1940 ................................. **TCLC 81**
See also CA 202; DLB 99
**Wetherell, Elizabeth**
See Warner, Susan (Bogert)
**Whale, James** 1889-1957 ................. **TCLC 63**
**Whalen, Philip (Glenn)** 1923-2002 .... **CLC 6,
29**
See also BG 3; CA 9-12R; 209; CANR 5,
39; CP 7; DLB 16; WP
**Wharton, Edith (Newbold Jones)**
1862-1937 ... **SSC 6, 84; TCLC 3, 9, 27,
53, 129, 149; WLC**
See also AAYA 25; AMW; AMWC 2;
AMWR 1; BPFB 3; CA 104; 132; CDALB
1865-1917; DA; DA3; DAB; DAC; DAM
MST, NOV; DLB 4, 9, 12, 78, 189; DLBD
13; EWL 3; EXPS; HGG; LAIT 2, 3;
LATS 1:1; MAWW; MTCW 1, 2; NFS 5,
11, 15, 20; RGAL 4; RGSF 2; RHW;
SSFS 6, 7; SUFW; TUS
**Wharton, James**
See Mencken, H(enry) L(ouis)
**Wharton, William (a pseudonym)** . **CLC 18,
37**
See also CA 93-96; DLBY 1980; INT CA-
93-96
**Wheatley (Peters), Phillis**
1753(?)-1784 ... **BLC 3; LC 3, 50; PC 3;
WLC**
See also AFAW 1, 2; CDALB 1640-1865;
DA; DA3; DAC; DAM MST, MULT,
POET; DLB 31, 50; EXPP; PFS 13;
RGAL 4
**Wheelock, John Hall** 1886-1978 ....... **CLC 14**
See also CA 13-16R; 77-80; CANR 14;
DLB 45
**Whim-Wham**
See Curnow, (Thomas) Allen (Monro)
**White, Babington**
See Braddon, Mary Elizabeth
**White, E(lwyn) B(rooks)**
1899-1985 ..................... **CLC 10, 34, 39**
See also AITN 2; AMWS 1; CA 13-16R;
116; CANR 16, 37; CDALBS; CLR 1, 21;
CPW; DA3; DAM POP; DLB 11, 22;
EWL 3; FANT; MAICYA 1, 2; MTCW 1,
2; NCFS 5; RGAL 4; SATA 2, 29, 100;
SATA-Obit 44; TUS

Author Index

**White, Edmund (Valentine III)**
1940- ...................... **CLC 27, 110**
See also AAYA 7; CA 45-48; CANR 3, 19, 36, 62, 107, 133; CN 7; DA3; DAM POP; DLB 227; MTCW 1, 2

**White, Hayden V.** 1928- .................. **CLC 148**
See also CA 128; CANR 135; DLB 246

**White, Patrick (Victor Martindale)**
1912-1990 ...... **CLC 3, 4, 5, 7, 9, 18, 65, 69; SSC 39**
See also BRWS 1; CA 81-84; 132; CANR 43; DLB 260; EWL 3; MTCW 1; RGEL 2; RGSF 2; RHW; TWA; WWE 1

**White, Phyllis Dorothy James** 1920-
See James, P. D.
See also CA 21-24R; CANR 17, 43, 65, 112; CMW 4; CN 7; CPW; DA3; DAM POP; MTCW 1, 2; TEA

**White, T(erence) H(anbury)**
1906-1964 .................... **CLC 30**
See also AAYA 22; BPFB 3; BYA 4, 5; CA 73-76; CANR 37; DLB 160; FANT; JRDA; LAIT 1; MAICYA 1, 2; RGEL 2; SATA 12; SUFW 1; YAW

**White, Terence de Vere** 1912-1994 ... **CLC 49**
See also CA 49-52; 145; CANR 3

**White, Walter**
See White, Walter F(rancis)

**White, Walter F(rancis)** 1893-1955 ... **BLC 3; HR 3; TCLC 15**
See also BW 1; CA 115; 124; DAM MULT; DLB 51

**White, William Hale** 1831-1913
See Rutherford, Mark
See also CA 121; 189

**Whitehead, Alfred North**
1861-1947 ................................ **TCLC 97**
See also CA 117; 165; DLB 100, 262

**Whitehead, E(dward) A(nthony)**
1933- ................................ **CLC 5**
See also CA 65-68; CANR 58, 118; CBD; CD 5

**Whitehead, Ted**
See Whitehead, E(dward) A(nthony)

**Whiteman, Roberta J. Hill** 1947- ...... **NNAL**
See also CA 146

**Whitemore, Hugh (John)** 1936- ....... **CLC 37**
See also CA 132; CANR 77; CBD; CD 5; INT CA-132

**Whitman, Sarah Helen (Power)**
1803-1878 ................................ **NCLC 19**
See also DLB 1, 243

**Whitman, Walt(er)** 1819-1892 .. **NCLC 4, 31, 81; PC 3; WLC**
See also AAYA 42; AMW; AMWR 1; CDALB 1640-1865; DA; DA3; DAB; DAC; DAM MST, POET; DLB 3, 64, 224, 250; EXPP; LAIT 2; LMFS 1; PAB; PFS 2, 3, 13; RGAL 4; SATA 20; TUS; WP; WYAS 1

**Whitney, Phyllis A(yame)** 1903- ....... **CLC 42**
See also AAYA 36; AITN 2; BEST 90:3; CA 1-4R; CANR 3, 25, 38, 60; CLR 59; CMW 4; CPW; DA3; DAM POP; JRDA; MAICYA 1, 2; MTCW 2; RHW; SATA 1, 30; YAW

**Whittemore, (Edward) Reed, Jr.**
1919- ................................ **CLC 4**
See also CA 9-12R, 219; CAAE 219; CAAS 8; CANR 4, 119; CP 7; DLB 5

**Whittier, John Greenleaf**
1807-1892 ................................ **NCLC 8, 59**
See also AMWS 1; DLB 1, 243; RGAL 4

**Whittlebot, Hernia**
See Coward, Noel (Peirce)

**Wicker, Thomas Grey** 1926-
See Wicker, Tom
See also CA 65-68; CANR 21, 46

**Wicker, Tom** ........................ **CLC 7**
See Wicker, Thomas Grey

**Wideman, John Edgar** 1941- ... **BLC 3; CLC 5, 34, 36, 67, 122; SSC 62**
See also AFAW 1, 2; AMWS 10; BPFB 4; BW 2, 3; CA 85-88; CANR 14, 42, 67, 109; CN 7; DAM MULT; DLB 33, 143; MTCW 2; RGAL 4; RGSF 2; SSFS 6, 12

**Wiebe, Rudy (Henry)** 1934- .. **CLC 6, 11, 14, 138**
See also CA 37-40R; CANR 42, 67, 123; CN 7; DAC; DAM MST; DLB 60; RHW

**Wieland, Christoph Martin**
1733-1813 ................................ **NCLC 17**
See also DLB 97; EW 4; LMFS 1; RGWL 2, 3

**Wiene, Robert** 1881-1938 ............... **TCLC 56**

**Wieners, John** 1934- ........................ **CLC 7**
See also BG 3; CA 13-16R; CP 7; DLB 16; WP

**Wiesel, Elie(zer)** 1928- ....... **CLC 3, 5, 11, 37, 165; WLCS**
See also AAYA 7, 54; AITN 1; CA 5-8R; CAAS 4; CANR 8, 40, 65, 125; CDALBS; CWW 2; DA; DA3; DAB; DAC; DAM MST, NOV; DLB 83, 299; DLBY 1987; EWL 3; INT CANR-8; LAIT 4; MTCW 1, 2; NCFS 4; NFS 4; RGWL 3; SATA 56; YAW

**Wiggins, Marianne** 1947- .................. **CLC 57**
See also BEST 89:3; CA 130; CANR 60

**Wigglesworth, Michael** 1631-1705 .... **LC 106**
See also DLB 24; RGAL 4

**Wiggs, Susan** ........................ **CLC 70**
See also CA 201

**Wight, James Alfred** 1916-1995
See Herriot, James
See also CA 77-80; SATA 55; SATA-Brief 44

**Wilbur, Richard (Purdy)** 1921- ..... **CLC 3, 6, 9, 14, 53, 110; PC 51**
See also AMWS 3; CA 1-4R; CABS 2; CANR 2, 29, 76, 93; CDALBS; CP 7; DA; DAB; DAC; DAM MST, POET; DLB 5, 169; EWL 3; EXPP; INT CANR-29; MTCW 1, 2; PAB; PFS 11, 12, 16; RGAL 4; SATA 9, 108; WP

**Wild, Peter** 1940- ................................ **CLC 14**
See also CA 37-40R; CP 7; DLB 5

**Wilde, Oscar (Fingal O'Flahertie Wills)**
1854(?)-1900 ........... **DC 17; SSC 11, 77; TCLC 1, 8, 23, 41; WLC**
See also AAYA 49; BRW 5; BRWC 1, 2; BRWR 2; BYA 15; CA 104; 119; CANR 112; CDBLB 1890-1914; DA; DA3; DAB; DAC; DAM DRAM, MST, NOV; DFS 4, 8, 9; DLB 10, 19, 34, 57, 141, 156, 190; EXPS; FANT; LATS 1:1; NFS 20; RGEL 2; RGSF 2; SATA 24; SSFS 7; SUFW; TEA; WCH; WLIT 4

**Wilder, Billy** ........................ **CLC 20**
See Wilder, Samuel
See also DLB 26

**Wilder, Samuel** 1906-2002
See Wilder, Billy
See also CA 89-92; 205

**Wilder, Stephen**
See Marlowe, Stephen

**Wilder, Thornton (Niven)**
1897-1975 .. **CLC 1, 5, 6, 10, 15, 35, 82; DC 1, 24; WLC**
See also AAYA 29; AITN 2; AMW; CA 13-16R; 61-64; CAD; CANR 40, 132; CDALBS; DA; DA3; DAB; DAC; DAM DRAM, MST, NOV; DFS 1, 4, 16; DLB 4, 7, 9, 228; DLBY 1997; EWL 3; LAIT 3; MTCW 1, 2; RGAL 4; RHW; WYAS 1

**Wilding, Michael** 1942- ...... **CLC 73; SSC 50**
See also CA 104; CANR 24, 49, 106; CN 7; RGSF 2

**Wiley, Richard** 1944- ...................... **CLC 44**
See also CA 121; 129; CANR 71

**Wilhelm, Kate** ........................ **CLC 7**
See Wilhelm, Katie (Gertrude)
See also AAYA 20; BYA 16; CAAS 5; DLB 8; INT CANR-17; SCFW 2

**Wilhelm, Katie (Gertrude)** 1928-
See Wilhelm, Kate
See also CA 37-40R; CANR 17, 36, 60, 94; MTCW 1; SFW 4

**Wilkins, Mary**
See Freeman, Mary E(leanor) Wilkins

**Willard, Nancy** 1936- .................... **CLC 7, 37**
See also BYA 5; CA 89-92; CANR 10, 39, 68, 107; CLR 5; CWP; CWRI 5; DLB 5, 52; FANT; MAICYA 1, 2; MTCW 1; SATA 37, 71, 127; SATA-Brief 30; SUFW 2

**William of Malmesbury** c. 1090B.C.-c. 1140B.C. ................................ **CMLC 57**

**William of Ockham** 1290-1349 ..... **CMLC 32**

**Williams, Ben Ames** 1889-1953 ..... **TCLC 89**
See also CA 183; DLB 102

**Williams, C(harles) K(enneth)**
1936- ................................ **CLC 33, 56, 148**
See also CA 37-40R; CAAS 26; CANR 57, 106; CP 7; DAM POET; DLB 5

**Williams, Charles**
See Collier, James Lincoln

**Williams, Charles (Walter Stansby)**
1886-1945 ................................ **TCLC 1, 11**
See also BRWS 9; CA 104; 163; DLB 100, 153, 255; FANT; RGEL 2; SUFW 1

**Williams, Ella Gwendolen Rees**
See Rhys, Jean

**Williams, (George) Emlyn**
1905-1987 ................................ **CLC 15**
See also CA 104; 123; CANR 36; DAM DRAM; DLB 10, 77; IDTP; MTCW 1

**Williams, Hank** 1923-1953 ............. **TCLC 81**
See Williams, Hiram King

**Williams, Helen Maria**
1761-1827 ................................ **NCLC 135**
See also DLB 158

**Williams, Hiram Hank**
See Williams, Hank

**Williams, Hiram King**
See Williams, Hank
See also CA 188

**Williams, Hugo (Mordaunt)** 1942- ... **CLC 42**
See also CA 17-20R; CANR 45, 119; CP 7; DLB 40

**Williams, J. Walker**
See Wodehouse, P(elham) G(renville)

**Williams, John A(lfred)** 1925- . **BLC 3; CLC 5, 13**
See also AFAW 2; BW 2, 3; CA 53-56, 195; CAAE 195; CAAS 3; CANR 6, 26, 51, 118; CN 7; CSW; DAM MULT; DLB 2, 33; EWL 3; INT CANR-6; RGAL 4; SFW 4

**Williams, Jonathan (Chamberlain)**
1929- ................................ **CLC 13**
See also CA 9-12R; CAAS 12; CANR 8, 108; CP 7; DLB 5

**Williams, Joy** 1944- .......................... **CLC 31**
See also CA 41-44R; CANR 22, 48, 97

**Williams, Norman** 1952- .................. **CLC 39**
See also CA 118

**Williams, Sherley Anne** 1944-1999 ... **BLC 3; CLC 89**
See also AFAW 2; BW 2, 3; CA 73-76; 185; CANR 25, 82; DAM MULT, POET; DLB 41; INT CANR-25; SATA 78; SATA-Obit 116

**Williams, Shirley**
See Williams, Sherley Anne

**Wolfram von Eschenbach** c. 1170-c.
1220 ......................................... **CMLC 5**
See Eschenbach, Wolfram von
See also CDWLB 2; DLB 138; EW 1;
RGWL 2

**Wolitzer, Hilma** 1930- ...................... **CLC 17**
See also CA 65-68; CANR 18, 40; INT
CANR-18; SATA 31; YAW

**Wollstonecraft, Mary** 1759-1797 .... **LC 5, 50,
90**
See also BRWS 3; CDBLB 1789-1832;
DLB 39, 104, 158, 252; FW; LAIT 1;
RGEL 2; TEA; WLIT 3

**Wonder, Stevie** ............................... **CLC 12**
See Morris, Steveland Judkins

**Wong, Jade Snow** 1922- ................... **CLC 17**
See also CA 109; CANR 91; SATA 112

**Woodberry, George Edward**
1855-1930 ............................... **TCLC 73**
See also CA 165; DLB 71, 103

**Woodcott, Keith**
See Brunner, John (Kilian Houston)

**Woodruff, Robert W.**
See Mencken, H(enry) L(ouis)

**Woolf, (Adeline) Virginia** 1882-1941 .. **SSC 7,
79; TCLC 1, 5, 20, 43, 56, 101, 123,
128; WLC**
See also AAYA 44; BPFB 3; BRW 7;
BRWC 2; BRWR 1; CA 104; 130; CANR
64, 132; CDBLB 1914-1945; DA; DA3;
DAB; DAC; DAM MST, NOV; DLB 36,
100, 162; DLBD 10; EWL 3; EXPS; FW;
LAIT 3; LATS 1:1; LMFS 1; MTCW 1,
2; NCFS 2; NFS 8, 12; RGEL 2; RGSF 2;
SSFS 4, 12; TEA; WLIT 4

**Woollcott, Alexander (Humphreys)**
1887-1943 ................................. **TCLC 5**
See also CA 105; 161; DLB 29

**Woolrich, Cornell** .......................... **CLC 77**
See Hopley-Woolrich, Cornell George
See also MSW

**Woolson, Constance Fenimore**
1840-1894 ................................. **NCLC 82**
See also DLB 12, 74, 189, 221; RGAL 4

**Wordsworth, Dorothy** 1771-1855 . **NCLC 25,
138**
See also DLB 107

**Wordsworth, William** 1770-1850 .. **NCLC 12,
38, 111; PC 4; WLC**
See also BRW 4; BRWC 1; CDBLB 1789-
1832; DA; DA3; DAB; DAC; DAM MST,
POET; DLB 93, 107; EXPP; LATS 1:1;
LMFS 1; PAB; PFS 2; RGEL 2; TEA;
WLIT 3; WP

**Wotton, Sir Henry** 1568-1639 ............. **LC 68**
See also DLB 121; RGEL 2

**Wouk, Herman** 1915- ................ **CLC 1, 9, 38**
See also BPFB 2, 3; CA 5-8R; CANR 6,
33, 67; CDALBS; CN 7; CPW; DA3;
DAM NOV, POP; DLBY 1982; INT
CANR-6; LAIT 4; MTCW 1, 2; NFS 7;
TUS

**Wright, Charles (Penzel, Jr.)** 1935- .. **CLC 6,
13, 28, 119, 146**
See also AMWS 5; CA 29-32R; CAAS 7;
CANR 23, 36, 62, 88, 135; CP 7; DLB
165; DLBY 1982; EWL 3; MTCW 1, 2;
PFS 10

**Wright, Charles Stevenson** 1932- ..... **BLC 3;
CLC 49**
See also BW 1; CA 9-12R; CANR 26; CN
7; DAM MULT, POET; DLB 33

**Wright, Frances** 1795-1852 ........... **NCLC 74**
See also DLB 73

**Wright, Frank Lloyd** 1867-1959 .... **TCLC 95**
See also AAYA 33; CA 174

**Wright, Jack R.**
See Harris, Mark

**Wright, James (Arlington)**
1927-1980 ....... **CLC 3, 5, 10, 28; PC 36**
See also AITN 2; AMWS 3; CA 49-52; 97-
100; CANR 4, 34, 64; CDALBS; DAM
POET; DLB 5, 169; EWL 3; EXPP;
MTCW 1, 2; PFS 7, 8; RGAL 4; TUS;
WP

**Wright, Judith (Arundell)**
1915-2000 ................ **CLC 11, 53; PC 14**
See also CA 13-16R; 188; CANR 31, 76,
93; CP 7; CWP; DLB 260; EWL 3;
MTCW 1, 2; PFS 8; RGEL 2; SATA 14;
SATA-Obit 121

**Wright, L(aurali) R.** 1939- ................ **CLC 44**
See also CA 138; CMW 4

**Wright, Richard (Nathaniel)**
1908-1960 ... **BLC 3; CLC 1, 3, 4, 9, 14,
21, 48, 74; SSC 2; TCLC 136; WLC**
See also AAYA 5, 42; AFAW 1, 2; AMW;
BPFB 3; BW 1; BYA 2; CA 108; CANR
64; CDALB 1929-1941; DA; DA3; DAB;
DAC; DAM MST, MULT, NOV; DLB 76,
102; DLBD 2; EWL 3; EXPN; LAIT 3,
4; MTCW 1, 2; NCFS 1; NFS 1, 7; RGAL
4; RGSF 2; SSFS 3, 9, 15, 20; TUS; YAW

**Wright, Richard B(ruce)** 1937- .......... **CLC 6**
See also CA 85-88; CANR 120; DLB 53

**Wright, Rick** 1945- ............................ **CLC 35**

**Wright, Rowland**
See Wells, Carolyn

**Wright, Stephen** 1946- ...................... **CLC 33**

**Wright, Willard Huntington** 1888-1939
See Van Dine, S. S.
See also CA 115; 189; CMW 4; DLBD 16

**Wright, William** 1930- ...................... **CLC 44**
See also CA 53-56; CANR 7, 23

**Wroth, Lady Mary** 1587-1653(?) ....... **LC 30;
PC 38**
See also DLB 121

**Wu Ch'eng-en** 1500(?)-1582(?) .............. **LC 7**

**Wu Ching-tzu** 1701-1754 ...................... **LC 2**

**Wulfstan** c. 10th cent. -1023 ......... **CMLC 59**

**Wurlitzer, Rudolph** 1938(?)- ... **CLC 2, 4, 15**
See also CA 85-88; CN 7; DLB 173

**Wyatt, Sir Thomas** c. 1503-1542 . **LC 70; PC
27**
See also BRW 1; DLB 132; EXPP; RGEL
2; TEA

**Wycherley, William** 1640-1716 ....... **LC 8, 21,
102**
See also BRW 2; CDBLB 1660-1789; DAM
DRAM; DLB 80; RGEL 2

**Wyclif, John** c. 1330-1384 ............ **CMLC 70**
See also DLB 146

**Wylie, Elinor (Morton Hoyt)**
1885-1928 .................... **PC 23; TCLC 8**
See also AMWS 1; CA 105; 162; DLB 9,
45; EXPP; RGAL 4

**Wylie, Philip (Gordon)** 1902-1971 ... **CLC 43**
See also CA 21-22; 33-36R; CAP 2; DLB
9; SFW 4

**Wyndham, John** ............................. **CLC 19**
See Harris, John (Wyndham Parkes Lucas)
Beynon
See also DLB 255; SCFW 2

**Wyss, Johann David Von**
1743-1818 ............................... **NCLC 10**
See also CLR 92; JRDA; MAICYA 1, 2;
SATA 29; SATA-Brief 27

**Xenophon** c. 430B.C.-c. 354B.C. ... **CMLC 17**
See also AW 1; DLB 176; RGWL 2, 3

**Xingjian, Gao** 1940-
See Gao Xingjian
See also CA 193; RGWL 3

**Yakamochi** 718-785 .......... **CMLC 45; PC 48**

**Yakumo Koizumi**
See Hearn, (Patricio) Lafcadio (Tessima
Carlos)

**Yamada, Mitsuye (May)** 1923- ........... **PC 44**
See also CA 77-80

**Yamamoto, Hisaye** 1921- ......... **AAL; SSC 34**
See also CA 214; DAM MULT; LAIT 4;
SSFS 14

**Yamauchi, Wakako** 1924- ..................... **AAL**
See also CA 214

**Yanez, Jose Donoso**
See Donoso (Yanez), Jose

**Yanovsky, Basile S.**
See Yanovsky, V(assily) S(emenovich)

**Yanovsky, V(assily) S(emenovich)**
1906-1989 ............................... **CLC 2, 18**
See also CA 97-100; 129

**Yates, Richard** 1926-1992 ......... **CLC 7, 8, 23**
See also AMWS 11; CA 5-8R; 139; CANR
10, 43; DLB 2, 234; DLBY 1981, 1992;
INT CANR-10

**Yau, John** 1950- ............................... **PC 61**
See also CA 154; CANR 89; CP 7; DLB
234

**Yeats, W. B.**
See Yeats, William Butler

**Yeats, William Butler** 1865-1939 . **PC 20, 51;
TCLC 1, 11, 18, 31, 93, 116; WLC**
See also AAYA 48; BRW 6; BRWR 1; CA
104; 127; CANR 45; CDBLB 1890-1914;
DA; DA3; DAB; DAC; DAM DRAM,
MST, POET; DLB 10, 19, 98, 156; EWL
3; EXPP; MTCW 1, 2; NCFS 3; PAB;
PFS 1, 2, 5, 7, 13, 15; RGEL 2; TEA;
WLIT 4; WP

**Yehoshua, A(braham) B.** 1936- .. **CLC 13, 31**
See also CA 33-36R; CANR 43, 90; CWW
2; EWL 3; RGSF 2; RGWL 3

**Yellow Bird**
See Ridge, John Rollin

**Yep, Laurence Michael** 1948- .......... **CLC 35**
See also AAYA 5, 31; BYA 7; CA 49-52;
CANR 1, 46, 92; CLR 3, 17, 54; DLB 52;
FANT; JRDA; MAICYA 1, 2; MAICYAS
1; SATA 7, 69, 123; WYA; YAW

**Yerby, Frank G(arvin)** 1916-1991 ..... **BLC 3;
CLC 1, 7, 22**
See also BPFB 3; BW 1, 3; CA 9-12R; 136;
CANR 16, 52; DAM MULT; DLB 76;
INT CANR-16; MTCW 1; RGAL 4; RHW

**Yesenin, Sergei Alexandrovich**
See Esenin, Sergei (Alexandrovich)

**Yesenin, Sergey**
See Esenin, Sergei (Alexandrovich)
See also EWL 3

**Yevtushenko, Yevgeny (Alexandrovich)**
1933- ...... **CLC 1, 3, 13, 26, 51, 126; PC
40**
See Evtushenko, Evgenii Aleksandrovich
See also CA 81-84; CANR 33, 54; DAM
POET; EWL 3; MTCW 1

**Yezierska, Anzia** 1885(?)-1970 .......... **CLC 46**
See also CA 126; 89-92; DLB 28, 221; FW;
MTCW 1; RGAL 4; SSFS 15

**Yglesias, Helen** 1915- .................... **CLC 7, 22**
See also CA 37-40R; CAAS 20; CANR 15,
65, 95; CN 7; INT CANR-15; MTCW 1

**Yokomitsu, Riichi** 1898-1947 ......... **TCLC 47**
See also CA 170; EWL 3

**Yonge, Charlotte (Mary)**
1823-1901 ............................... **TCLC 48**
See also CA 109; 163; DLB 18, 163; RGEL
2; SATA 17; WCH

**York, Jeremy**
See Creasey, John

**York, Simon**
See Heinlein, Robert A(nson)

**Yorke, Henry Vincent** 1905-1974 ..... **CLC 13**
See Green, Henry
See also CA 85-88; 49-52

**Yosano Akiko** 1878-1942 .... **PC 11; TCLC 59**
See also CA 161; EWL 3; RGWL 3

# Literary Criticism Series
# Cumulative Topic Index

# *NCLC* Cumulative Nationality Index

Kotzebue, August (Friedrich Ferdinand) von **25**
La Roche, Sophie von **121**
Ludwig, Otto **4**
Marx, Karl (Heinrich) **17, 114**
Mörike, Eduard (Friedrich) **10**
Novalis **13**
Schelling, Friedrich Wilhelm Joseph von **30**
Schiller, Friedrich von **39, 69**
Schlegel, August Wilhelm von **15, 142**
Schlegel, Friedrich **45**
Schleiermacher, Friedrich **107**
Schopenhauer, Arthur **51, 157**
Schumann, Robert **143**
Storm, (Hans) Theodor (Woldsen) **1**
Tieck, (Johann) Ludwig **5, 46**
Varnhagen, Rahel **130**
Wagner, Richard **9, 119**
Wieland, Christoph Martin **17**

**GREEK**

Foscolo, Ugo **8, 97**
Solomos, Dionysios **15**

**HUNGARIAN**

Arany, Janos **34**
Madach, Imre **19**
Petofi, Sándor **21**

**INDIAN**

Chatterji, Bankim Chandra **19**
Dutt, Michael Madhusudan **118**
Dutt, Toru **29**

**IRISH**

Allingham, William **25**
Banim, John **13**
Banim, Michael **13**
Boucicault, Dion **41**
Carleton, William **3**
Croker, John Wilson **10**
Darley, George **2**
Edgeworth, Maria **1, 51, 158**
Ferguson, Samuel **33**
Griffin, Gerald **7**
Jameson, Anna **43**
Le Fanu, Joseph Sheridan **9, 58**
Lever, Charles (James) **23**
Maginn, William **8**
Mangan, James Clarence **27**
Maturin, Charles Robert **6**
Merriman, Brian **70**
Moore, Thomas **6, 110**
Morgan, Lady **29**
O'Brien, Fitz-James **21**
Sheridan, Richard Brinsley **5, 91**

**ITALIAN**

Alfieri, Vittorio **101**
Collodi, Carlo **54**
Foscolo, Ugo **8, 97**
Gozzi, (Conte) Carlo **23**

Leopardi, Giacomo **22, 129**
Manzoni, Alessandro **29, 98**
Mazzini, Guiseppe **34**
Nievo, Ippolito **22**

**JAMAICAN**

Seacole, Mary Jane Grant **147**

**JAPANESE**

Akinari, Ueda **131**
Ichiyō, Higuchi **49**
Motoori, Norinaga **45**

**LITHUANIAN**

Mapu, Abraham (ben Jekutiel) **18**

**MEXICAN**

Lizardi, Jose Joaquin Fernandez de **30**
Najera, Manuel Gutierrez **133**

**NORWEGIAN**

Collett, (Jacobine) Camilla (Wergeland) **22**
Wergeland, Henrik Arnold **5**

**POLISH**

Fredro, Aleksander **8**
Krasicki, Ignacy **8**
Krasiński, Zygmunt **4**
Mickiewicz, Adam **3, 101**
Norwid, Cyprian Kamil **17**
Slowacki, Juliusz **15**

**ROMANIAN**

Eminescu, Mihail **33, 131**

**RUSSIAN**

Aksakov, Sergei Timofeyvich **2**
Bakunin, Mikhail (Alexandrovich) **25, 58**
Baratynsky, Evgenii Abramovich **103**
Bashkirtseff, Marie **27**
Belinski, Vissarion Grigoryevich **5**
Bestuzhev, Aleksandr Aleksandrovich **131**
Chernyshevsky, Nikolay Gavrilovich **1**
Dobrolyubov, Nikolai Alexandrovich **5**
Dostoevsky, Fedor Mikhailovich **2, 7, 21, 33, 43, 119**
Gogol, Nikolai (Vasilyevich) **5, 15, 31**
Goncharov, Ivan Alexandrovich **1, 63**
Granovsky, Timofei Nikolaevich **75**
Griboedov, Aleksandr Sergeevich **129**
Herzen, Aleksandr Ivanovich **10, 61**
Karamzin, Nikolai Mikhailovich **3**
Krylov, Ivan Andreevich **1**
Lermontov, Mikhail Yuryevich **5, 47, 126**
Leskov, Nikolai (Semyonovich) **25**
Nekrasov, Nikolai Alekseevich **11**
Ostrovsky, Alexander **30, 57**
Pavlova, Karolina Karlovna **138**
Pisarev, Dmitry Ivanovich **25**
Pushkin, Alexander (Sergeyevich) **3, 27, 83**
Saltykov, Mikhail Evgrafovich **16**

Smolenskin, Peretz **30**
Turgenev, Ivan **21, 37, 122**
Tyutchev, Fyodor **34**
Zhukovsky, Vasily (Andreevich) **35**

**SCOTTISH**

Baillie, Joanna **2, 151**
Beattie, James **25**
Blair, Hugh **75**
Campbell, Thomas **19**
Carlyle, Thomas **22, 70**
Ferrier, Susan (Edmonstone) **8**
Galt, John **1, 110**
Hogg, James **4, 109**
Jeffrey, Francis **33**
Lockhart, John Gibson **6**
Mackenzie, Henry **41**
Miller, Hugh **143**
Oliphant, Margaret (Oliphant Wilson) **11, 61**
Scott, Walter **15, 69, 110**
Stevenson, Robert Louis (Balfour) **5, 14, 63**
Thomson, James **18**
Wilson, John **5**
Wright, Frances **74**

**SERBIAN**

Karadžić, Vuk Stefanović **115**

**SLOVENIAN**

Kopitar, Jernej **117**
Prešeren, Francè **127**

**SPANISH**

Alarcon, Pedro Antonio de **1**
Bécquer, Gustavo Adolfo **106**
Caballero, Fernan **10**
Castro, Rosalia de **3, 78**
Espronceda, Jose de **39**
Larra (y Sanchez de Castro), Mariano Jose de **17, 130**
Martínez de la Rosa, Francisco de Paula **102**
Tamayo y Baus, Manuel **1**
Zorrilla y Moral, Jose **6**

**SWEDISH**

Almqvist, Carl Jonas Love **42**
Bremer, Fredrika **11**
Stagnelius, Eric Johan **61**
Tegner, Esaias **2**

**SWISS**

Amiel, Henri Frederic **4**
Burckhardt, Jacob (Christoph) **49**
Charriere, Isabelle de **66**
Gotthelf, Jeremias **117**
Keller, Gottfried **2**
Lavater, Johann Kaspar **142**
Meyer, Conrad Ferdinand **81**
Wyss, Johann David Von **10**

**UKRAINIAN**

Shevchenko, Taras **54**

**VENEZUELAN**

Bello, Andrés **131**

Nationality Index

# *NCLC*-159 Title Index

ISBN 0-7876-8643-3

90000